ISC Exams 2026

AF819710

All in One®

Mathematics

Class 11

- Simplified Theory
- Topic & Chapter Exercises
- Exam Pattern Questions
- Sample Question Papers

Authors
Laxman Prasad,
Brijesh Dwivedi

arihant
SUCCESS AND NOTHING LESS

ARIHANT PRAKASHAN
(School Division Series)

卐 *ADMINISTRATIVE & PRODUCTION OFFICES*

Regd. Office

'Ramchhaya' 4577/15, Agarwal Road, Darya Ganj, New Delhi -110002
Tele: 011- 47630600, 43518550; Fax: 011- 23280316

卐 *Head Office*

Kalindi, TP Nagar, Meerut (UP) - 250002, Tel: 0121-7156203, 7156204

卐 *SALES & SUPPORT OFFICES*

Agra, Ahmedabad, Bengaluru, Bareilly, Chennai, Delhi, Guwahati, Hyderabad, Jaipur, Jhansi, Kolkata, Lucknow, Nagpur & Pune.

PO No : TXT-XX-XXXXXXX-X-XX

Published By Arihant Publications (India) Ltd.

For further information about the books published by Arihant, log on to www.arihantbooks.com or e-mail at info@arihantbooks.com

Follow us on

卐 *PRICE* ₹630.00

PRODUCTION TEAM

Publishing Managers
Mahendra Singh Rawat & Keshav Mohan

Cover Designer
Salman Shaikh

Inner Designer
Ankit Tyagi

Project Head
Ashwani

Page Layouting
Shivam Prajapati

Proof Reader
Mukul Kaushik

Index *cum* Study Planner

Latest Course Structure

The syllabus is divided into **three** sections A, B and C.

Section A is compulsory for all candidates. Candidates will have a choice of attempting questions from **EITHER** Section B **OR** Section C.

There will be one paper of **three** hours duration of 100 marks.

Section A (65 Marks) : Candidates will be required to attempt all questions. Internal choice will be provided in Two question of two marks, two questions of four marks each and two questions of six marks each.

Section B/Section C (15 Marks) : Candidates will be required to attempt all questions EITHER from Section B or Section C. Internal choice will be provided in one question of two marks and one question of four marks each.

S.No.	UNIT	TOTAL WEIGHTAGE
	SECTION A: 65 Marks	
1.	Sets and Functions	20 Marks
2.	Algebra	24 Marks
3.	Coordinate Geometry	8 Marks
4.	Calculus	6 Marks
5.	Statistics & Probability	7 Marks
	SECTION B: 15 Marks	
6.	Conic Section	7 Marks
7.	Introduction to Three Dimensional Geometry	5 Marks
8.	Mathematical Reasoning	3 Marks
	Or	
	SECTION C: 15 Marks	
9.	Statistics	5 Marks
10.	Correlation Analysis	4 Marks
11.	Index Numbers & Moving Averages	6 Marks
	TOTAL	**80 Marks**

SECTION A

1. SETS AND FUNCTIONS

(i) **Sets** Sets and their representations, Empty set, Finite and Infinite sets, Equal sets, Subsets. Subsets of a set of real numbers especially intervals (with notations). Power set. Universal set. Venn diagrams. Union and Intersection of sets. Difference of sets. Complement of a set. Properties of Complement of Sets.

(ii) **Relations and Functions** Ordered pairs, Cartesian product of sets. Number of elements in the cartesian product of two finite sets. Cartesian product of the set of reals with itself (upto R×R×R). Definition of relation, pictorial diagrams, domain, co–domain and range of a relation. Function as a special type of relation. Function as a type of mapping, domain, co–domain and range of a function. Real valued functions, domain and range of these functions, constant, identity, polynomial, rational, modulus, signum, exponential, logarithmic and greatest integer functions, Sum, difference, product and quotient of functions.

- ***Sets*** *Self–explanatory.*
- ***Basic concepts of Relations and Functions***
  - *Ordered pairs, sets of ordered pairs.*
  - *Cartesian Product (Cross) of two sets, cardinal number of a cross product.*

  Relations as
  - *an association between two sets.*
  - *a subset of a Cross Product.*
  - *Domain, Range and Co–domain of a Relation.*

  Functions:
  - *As special relations, concept of writing "y is a function of x" as $y = f(x)$.*
  - *Domain and range of a function.*

(iii) **Trigonometry** Positive and negative angles. Measuring angles in radians and in degrees and conversion from one measure to another. Definition of trigonometric functions with the help of unit circle. Truth of the identity $\sin^2 x + \cos^2 x = 1$, for all x. Signs of trigonometric functions. Domain and range of trignometric functions and their graphs. Expressing $\sin(x \pm y)$ and $\cos(x \pm y)$ in terms of $\sin x, \sin y, \cos x$ & $\cos y$ and their simple applications.

Deducing the identities like the following:

$$\tan(x \pm y) = \frac{\tan x \pm \tan y}{1 \mp \tan x \tan y}$$

$$\cot(x \pm y) = \frac{\cot x \cot y \mp 1}{\cot y \pm \cot x}$$

$$\sin\alpha \pm \sin\beta = 2\sin\frac{1}{2}(\alpha \pm \beta)\cos\frac{1}{2}(\alpha \mp \beta)$$

$$\cos\alpha + \cos\beta = 2\cos\frac{1}{2}(\alpha + \beta)\cos\frac{1}{2}(\alpha - \beta)$$

$$\cos\alpha - \cos\beta = -2\sin\frac{1}{2}(\alpha + \beta)\sin\frac{1}{2}(\alpha - \beta)$$

Identities related to $\sin 2x$, $\cos 2x$, $\tan 2x$, $\sin 3x$, $\cos 3x$ and $\tan 3x$.

- ***Angles and Arc lengths***
  - *Angles: Convention of sign of angles.*
  - *Magnitude of an angle: Measures of Angles; Circular measure.*
  - *The relation $S = r\theta$ where θ is in radians. Relation between radians and degree.*
  - *Definition of trigonometric functions with the help of unit circle.*
  - *Truth of the identity $\sin^2 x + \cos^2 x = 1$*

Note Questions on the area of a sector of a circle are required to be covered.

- ***Trigonometric Functions***
  - *Relationship between trigonometric functions.*
  - *Proving simple identities.*
  - *Signs of trigonometric functions.*
  - *Domain and range of the trigonometric functions.*
  - *Trigonometric functions of all angles.*
  - *Periods of trigonometric functions.*
  - *Graphs of simple trigonometric functions (only sketches).*

Note Graphs of $\sin x$, $\cos x$, $\tan x$, $\sec x$, $\operatorname{cosec} x$ and $\cot x$ are to be included.

- ***Compound and multiple angles***
  - *Addition and subtraction formula:* $\sin(A \pm B); \cos(A \pm B); \tan(A \pm B); \tan(A + B + C)$ *etc. Double angle, triple angle, half angle and one-third angle formula as special cases.*
  - *Sum and differences as products* $\sin C + \sin D = 2\sin\left(\frac{C+D}{2}\right)\cos\left(\frac{C-D}{2}\right)$, *etc.*
  - *Product to sum or difference i.e.* $2\sin A\cos B = \sin(A+B) + \sin(A-B)$ *etc.*

2. ALGEBRA

(i) **Complex Numbers** Introduction of complex numbers and their representation, Algebraic properties of complex numbers. Argand plane and polar representation of complex numbers. Square root of a complex number. Cube root of unity.

- *Conjugate, modulus and argument of complex numbers and their properties.*
- *Sum, difference, product and quotient of two complex numbers additive and multiplicative inverse of a complex number.*
- *Square root of a complex number.*
- *Cube roots of unity and their properties.*

(ii) **Quadratic Equations** Statement of Fundamental Theorem of Algebra, solution of quadratic equations (with real coefficients).

- *Use of the formula :* $x = \frac{-b \pm \sqrt{b^2 - 4ac}}{2a}$ *In solving quadratic equations.*
- *Equations reducible to quadratic form.*
- *Nature of roots*
  - *Product and sum of roots.*
  - *Roots are rational, irrational, equal, reciprocal, one square of the other.*
  - *Complex roots.*
  - *Framing quadratic equations with given roots.*

Note Questions on equations having common roots are to be covered.

- ***Quadratic Functions.***

  Given α, β as roots then find the equation whose roots are of the form α^3, β^3, etc.

  Case I : $a > 0$ → Real roots / Complex roots / Equal roots

  Case II : $a < 0$ → Real roots / Complex roots / Equal roots

  Where 'a' is the coefficient of x^2 in the equations of the form $ax^2 + bx + c = 0$.

- ***Sign of quadratic***

  Sign when the roots are real and when they are complex.

- ***Inequalities***
  - ***Linear Inequalities*** *Algebraic solutions of linear inequalities in one variable and their representation on the number line.*
  - ***Quadratic Inequalities*** *Using method of intervals for solving problems of the type:*

    $x^2 + x - 6 \geq 0$

    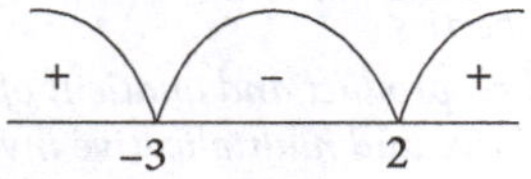

    A perfect square e.g. $x^2 - 6x + 9 \geq 0$.
  - *Inequalities involving rational expression of type $\frac{f(x)}{g(x)} \leq a$ etc, to be covered.*

(iv) **Permutations and Combinations** Fundamental principle of counting. Factorial *n*. (*n*!) Permutations and combinations, derivation of formulae for ^nP_r and ^nC_r and their connections, simple application.

- *Factorial notation $n!, n! = n(n-1)!$*
- *Fundamental principle of counting.*
- *Permutations*
  - ^nP_r.
  - *Restricted permutation.*
  - *Certain things always occur together.*
  - *Certain things never occur.*
  - *Formation of numbers with digits.*
  - *Word building - repeated letters - No letters repeated.*
  - *Permutation of alike things.*
  - *Permutation of Repeated things.*
  - *Circular permutation - clockwise counterclockwise - Distinguishable / not distinguishable.*
- *Combinations*
  - $^nC_r, {}^nC_n = 1, {}^nC_0 = 1, {}^nC_r = {}^nC_{n-r}, {}^nC_x = {}^nC_y$, *then* $x + y = n$ *or* $x = y$, $^{n+1}C_r = {}^nC_{r-1} + {}^nC_r$.
  - *When all things are different.*
  - *When all things are not different.*
  - *Mixed problems on permutation and combinations.*

(v) **Binomial Theorem** History, statement and proof of the binomial theorem for positive integral indices. Pascal's triangle, General and middle term in binomial expansion, simple applications.

- *Significance of Pascal's triangle.*
- *Binomial theorem (proof using induction) for positive integral powers*
  i.e. $(x + y)^n = {}^nC_0x^n + {}^nC_1x^{n-1}y + ... + {}^nC_ny^n$
  Questions based on the above.

(vi) **Sequence and Series** Sequence and Series. Arithmetic Progression (AP). Arithmetic Mean (AM) Geometric Progression (GP), general term of a GP, sum of first *n* terms of a GP, infinite GP and its sum, geometric mean (GM), relation between AM and GM Formulae for the following special sums $\Sigma n, \Sigma n^2, \Sigma n^3$.

- *Arithmetic Progression* (AP)
  - $T_n = a + (n-1)d$
  - $S_n = \frac{n}{2}\{2a + (n-1)d\}$
  - *Arithmetic mean:* $2b = a + c$
  - *Inserting two or more arithmetic means between any two numbers.*
  - *Three terms in* AP: $a - d, a, a + d$
  - *Four terms in* AP: $a - 3d, a - d, a + d, a + 3d$
- *Geometric Progression* (GP)
  - $T_n = ar^{n-1}, S_n = \frac{a(r^n - 1)}{r - 1}$, $S_\infty = \frac{a}{1-r}; |r| < 1$

    Geometric Mean, $b = \sqrt{ac}$
  - *Inserting two or more Geometric Means between any two numbers.*
  - *Three terms are in* GP ar, a, ar^{-1}
  - *Four terms are in* GP $ar^3, ar, ar^{-1}, ar^{-3}$
- *Special sums* $\Sigma n, \Sigma n^2, \Sigma n^3$.

  Using these summations to sum up other related expression.

3. COORDINATE GEOMETRY

(i) **Straight Lines** Brief recall of two dimensional geometry from earlier classes. Shifting of origin. Slope of a line and angle between two lines. Various forms of equations of a line: parallel to axis, point–slope form, slope– intercept form, two-point form, intercept form and normal form. General equation of a line. Equation of family of lines passing through the point of intersection of two lines. Distance of a point from a line.

- *Basic concepts of Points and their coordinates.*
- *The straight line*
  - *Slope or gradient of a line.*
  - *Angle between two lines.*
  - *Condition of perpendicularity and parallelism.*
  - *Various forms of equation of lines.*
  - *Slope intercept form.*
  - *Two-point slope form.*
  - *Intercept form.*
  - *Perpendicular /normal form.*
  - *General equation of a line.*
  - *Distance of a point from a line.*
  - *Distance between parallel lines.*
  - *Equation of lines bisecting the angle between two lines.*
  - *Equation of family of lines*
  - *Definition of a locus.*
  - *Equation of a locus.*

(ii) **Circles**

- *Equations of a circle in:*
  - *Standard form.*
  - *Diameter form.*
  - *General form.*
  - *Parametric form.*
- *Given the equation of a circle, to find the centre and the radius.*
- *Finding the equation of a circle.*
  - *Given three non-collinear points.*
  - *Given other sufficient data e.g. centre is (h, k) and it lies on a line and two points on the circle are given, etc.*

4. CALCULUS

(i) **Limits and Derivatives** Derivative introduced as rate of change both as that of distance function and geometrically.

Intuitive idea of limit. Limits of polynomials and rational functions trigonometric, exponential and logarithmic functions. Definition of derivative relate it to scope of tangent of the curve, Derivative of sum, difference, product and quotient of functions. Derivatives of polynomial and trigonometric functions.

- *Limits*
  - *Nation and meaning of limits.*
  - *Fundamental theorems on limits (statement only).*
  - *Limits of algebraic and trigonometric functions.*

Note Indeterminate forms are to be introduced while calculating limits.

- *Differentiation*
  - *Meaning and geometrical interpretation of derivative.*
  - *Derivatives of simple algebraic and trigonometric functions and their formulae.*
  - *Differentiation using first principles.*
  - *Derivatives of sum/difference.*
  - *Derivatives of product of functions. Derivatives of quotients of functions.*

5. STATISTICS AND PROBABILITY

(i) **Statistics** Measures of dispersion: range, mean deviation, variance and standard deviation of ungrouped/grouped data.

- *Mean deviation about mean and median.*
- *Standard deviation – by direct method, shortcut method and step deviation method.*

Note Mean, Median and Mode of grouped and ungrouped data are required to be covered.

(ii) **Probability** Random experiments; outcomes, sample spaces (set representation). Events; occurrence of events, 'not', 'and' and 'or' events, exhaustive events, mutually exclusive events, Axiomatic (set theoretic) probability, connections with other theories studied in earlier classes. Probability of an event, probability of 'not', 'and' and 'or' events.

- *Random experiments and their outcomes.*
- *Events: sure events, impossible events, mutually exclusive and exhaustive events.*
  - *Definition of probability of an event*
  - *Laws of probability addition theorem.*

SECTION B

6. CONIC SECTION

Sections of a cone, ellipse, parabola, hyperbola, a point, a straight line and a pair of intersecting lines as a degenerated case of a conic section. Standard equations and simple properties of parabola, ellipse and hyperbola.

- *Conics as a section of a cone.*
  - *Definition of Foci, Directrix, Latus Rectum.*
  - *PS = ePL where P is a point on the conics, S is the focus, PL is the perpendicular distance of the point from the directrix.*

(i) Parabola

- $e=1, y^2=\pm 4ax, x^2=4ay, y^2=-4ax,$ $x^2=-4ay, (y-\beta)^2=\pm 4a(x-\alpha)$ $(x-a)^2=\pm 4a(y-\beta)$
- *Rough sketch of the above.*
- *The latus rectum; quadrants they lie in; coordinates of focus and vertex; and equations of directrix and the axis.*
- *Finding equation of Parabola when Foci and directrix are given, etc.*
- *Application questions based on the above.*

(ii) *Ellipse*

- $\frac{x^2}{a^2}+\frac{y^2}{b^2}=1, e<1, b^2=a^2(1-e^2)$
- *Cases when $a>b$ and $a<b$.*
- *Rough sketch of the above.*
- *Major axis, minor axis; latus rectum; coordinates of vertices, focus and centre; and equations of directrices and the axes.*
- *Finding equation of ellipse when focus and directrix are given.*
- *Simple and direct questions based on the above.*
- *Focal property i.e. $SP + SP' = 2a$*

(iii) *Hyperbola*

- $\frac{x^2}{a^2}-\frac{y^2}{b^2}=1, e>1, b^2=a^2(e^2-1)$
- *Cases when coefficient y^2 is negative and coefficient of x^2 is negative.*
- *Rough sketch of the above.*
- *Focal property i.e. $SP - S'P = 2a$*
- *Transverse and Conjugate axes; Latus rectum; coordinates of vertices, foci and centre; and equations of the directrices and the axes.*

7. INTRODUCTION TO THREE-DIMENSIONAL GEOMETRY

Coordinate axes and coordinate planes in three dimensions. Coordinates of a point. Distance between two points and section formula.

- *As an extension of 2–D*
- *Distance formula.*
- *Section and mid-point form*

8. MATHEMATICAL REASONING

Mathematically acceptable statements. Connecting words/phrases – consolidating the understanding of "if and only if (necessary and sufficient) condition", "implies", "and/or", "implied by", "and", "or", "there exists" and their use through variety of examples related to the Mathematics and real life. Validating the statements involving the connecting words, Difference between contradiction, converse and contrapositive.

Self–explanatory.

SECTION C

9. STATISTICS

- *Combined mean and standard deviation.*
- *The Median, Quartiles and Mode of grouped and ungrouped data.*

10. CORRELATION ANALYSIS

- *Definition and meaning of covariance.*
- *Coefficient of Correlation by Karl Pearson.*

If $x-\bar{x}$, $y-\bar{y}$ are small non-fractional numbers, we use $r=\frac{\Sigma(x-\bar{x})(y-\bar{y})}{\sqrt{\Sigma(x-\bar{x})^2}\sqrt{\Sigma(y-\bar{y})^2}}$

If x and y are small numbers, we use

$$r=\frac{\Sigma xy-\frac{1}{N}\Sigma x\Sigma y}{\sqrt{\Sigma x^2-\frac{1}{N}(\Sigma x)^2}\sqrt{\Sigma y^2-\frac{1}{N}(\Sigma y)^2}}$$

Otherwise, we use assumed means A and B, where $u=x-A$, $v=y-B$

$$r=\frac{\Sigma uv-\frac{1}{N}(\Sigma u)(\Sigma v)}{\sqrt{\Sigma u^2-\frac{1}{N}(\Sigma u)^2}\sqrt{\Sigma v^2-\frac{1}{N}(\Sigma v)^2}}$$

11. INDEX NUMBERS AND MOVING AVERAGES

(i) **Index Numbers**

- *Price index or price relative.*
- *Simple aggregate method.*
- *Weighted aggregate method.*
- *Simple average of price relatives.*
- *Weighted average of price relatives (cost of living index, consumer price index).*

(ii) **Moving Averages**

- *Meaning and purpose of the moving averages.*
- *Calculation of moving averages with the given periodicity and plotting them on a graph.*
- *If the period is even, then the centered moving average is to be found out and plotted.*

CHAPTER

01

Sets

The set theory was developed by German mathematician **Georg Cantor** (1845-1918). He first encountered sets while working on 'problems on trigonometric series'. The concept of sets is used in almost every branch of Mathematics like Geometry, Algebra, etc. Further, sets are also used to define the concept of relations and functions.

- Sets, Representation of Sets and Their Types
- Subset, Power Set and Universal Set
- Venn Diagrams and Operations on Sets

TOPIC 01 Sets, Representation of Sets and Their Types

If any given collection of objects is defined in such a way that it is possible to tell without any doubt whether a given particular object belongs to this collection or not, then such a collection of objects is called a **well-defined collection of objects.**

e.g. 'The rivers of India' is a well-defined collection. Because we can definitely decide whether a given particular object belong to this collection or not, e.g. we can easily say that the river Nile does not belong to this collection, while the river Ganga belongs to this collection.

Definition of Set

A **well-defined** collection of objects, is called a set. Sets are usually denoted by the capital letters A, B, C, X, Y, Z etc. The elements of a set are represented by small letters a, b, c, x, y, z etc.

If a is an element of a set A, then we say that a belongs to A. The word *'belongs to'* is denoted by the Greek symbol $\in$ (epsilon).

Thus, in notation form, a belongs to set A is written as $a \in A$ and a does not belong to set A is written as $a \notin A$.

e.g. (i) If $A = \{1, 2, 3, 4, 5\}$, then $3 \in A$ but $6 \notin A$.

(ii) If P being the set of perfect square numbers, then $36 \in P$ but $5 \notin P$.

Note Objects, elements and members of a set are synonymous terms.

Example 1 Which of the following are sets? Justify your answer. **[NCERT]**

(i) The collection of all the months of a year beginning with the letter J.

(ii) The collection of ten most talented writers of India.

(iii) A collection of most dangerous animals of the world.

Sol. (i) We are sure that members of this collection are January, June and July.

So, this collection is well-defined. Hence, it is a set.

(ii) The criterion for determining a writer as most talented may vary from person to person. Therefore, we cannot definitely decide which writer will be there in the collection.

So, this collection is not well-defined. Hence, it is not a set.

(iii) The term most dangerous is vague term. An animal may be most dangerous for one person and may not be for the other.

So, it is not well-defined. Hence, it is not a set.

Example 2 If $A = \{0, 1, 2, 3, 4, 5, 6, 7, 8, 9, 10\}$, then insert appropriate symbol $\in$ or $\notin$ in each of the following blank spaces.

(i) 4 ... A (ii) -4 ... A

(iii) 12 ... A (iv) 0 ... A

Sol. Given, $A = \{0, 1, 2, 3, 4, 5, 6, 7, 8, 9, 10\}$

(i) Since, 4 is an element of A, therefore $4 \in A$.

(ii) Since, -4 is not an element of A, therefore $-4 \notin A$.

(iii) Since, 12 is not an element of A, therefore $12 \notin A$.

(iv) Since, 0 is an element of A, therefore $0 \in A$.

Some examples of sets used particularly in Mathematics

$N \rightarrow$ The set of natural numbers.

$Z \rightarrow$ The set of integers.

$Q \rightarrow$ The set of rational numbers.

$R \rightarrow$ The set of real numbers (both rational and irrational numbers).

$Z^+ \rightarrow$ The set of positive integers.

$Q^+ \rightarrow$ The set of positive rational numbers.

$R^+ \rightarrow$ The set of positive real numbers (positive rational and irrational numbers)

Note From now onwards, we use the symbols $N, Z, Q, R, Z^+, Q^+, R^+$ for the above sets only.

Representation of a Set

Sets are generally represented by following two ways

1. Roster Form or Tabular Form
2. Set-Builder Form or Rule Method

Roster Form or Tabular Form

In th is form, all the elements of a set are listed, the elements are being separated by commas and are enclosed within curly braces { }.

e.g.

(i) The set of all natural numbers less than 10 is represented in roster form as {1, 2, 3, 4, 5, 6, 7, 8, 9}.

(ii) The set of prime numbers is {2, 3, 5, 7, ...}. Here, three dots tell us that the list of prime numbers continue indefinitely.

Note

(i) In roster form, order in which the elements are listed is not important. i.e. the set of natural numbers less than 10 can also be written as {2, 4, 1, 3, 5, 6, 8, 7, 9} instead of {1, 2, 3, 4, 5, 6, 7, 8, 9}.

(ii) In roster form, an element is not repeated, i.e. all the elements are taken as distinct. e.g. The set of letters forming the word 'MISCELLANEOUS' is {M, I, S, C, E, L, A, N, O, U}.

(iii) If one or more elements of a set are repeated, then the set remains the same. Thus, the set $\{x, y, z, y, y, x\}$ is the same as $\{x, y, z\}$.

Example 3 Write the set of all vowels in English alphabet which precedes 's'.

Sol. The vowels which precedes 's' are a, e, i and o.

So, the required set is A = {a, e, i, o}.

Example 4 Write the set of all natural numbers x such that $4x + 9 < 50$ in roster form.

Firstly, simplify the inequality and then list all the natural numbers satisfying given condition.

Sol. We have, $4x + 9 < 50$

$\Rightarrow 4x + 9 - 9 < 50 - 9$ [subtracting 9 from both sides]

$\Rightarrow 4x < 41$

$\Rightarrow x < \frac{41}{4}$

$\Rightarrow x < 10.25$

Since, x is a natural number, so x can take values 1, 2, 3, 4, 5, 6, 7, 8, 9, 10.

$\therefore$ Required set = {1, 2, 3, 4, 5, 6, 7, 8, 9, 10}

Set-Builder Form or Rule Method

In this form, all the elements of set possess a single common property $p(x)$, which is not possessed by any other element outside the set.

In such a case, the set is described by $\{x : p(x) \text{ holds}\}$.

e.g. In the set $\{a, e, i, o, u\}$, all the elements possess a common property, namely, each of them is a vowel of English alphabet. Note that no other letter possesses this property.

If we denote the set of vowels by V, then we write

$$V = \{x : x \text{ is a vowel in English alphabet}\}$$

The above description of the set V is read as 'The set of all x such that x is a vowel in English alphabet'.

Some examples are given below

(i) Set of all natural numbers less than 10,

$$A = \{x : x \in N \text{ and } x < 10\}$$

(ii) Set of all real numbers, $B = \{x : x \in R\}$

Working Rule to Write the Set in the Set-builder Form

To convert the given set in set-builder form, we use the following steps

Step I Describe the elements of the set by using a symbol x or any other symbol y, z etc.

Step II Write the symbol of colon ':'.

Step III After the sign of colon, write the characteristic property possessed by the elements of the set.

Step IV Enclose the whole description within curly braces i.e. { }.

Example 5 Write the set $A = \{14, 21, 28, 35, 42, \ldots, 98\}$ in set-builder form.

Firstly, find the characteristic property possessed by the elements of the set, then write in set-builder form.

Sol. Let x represents the elements of given set.

Given numbers are natural numbers greater than 13, less than 99 and multiples of 7.

Thus, $A = \{x : x$ is a natural number greater than 13, less than 99 and a multiple of 7$\}$, which is the required set-builder form of given set.

This can also be written as

$$A = \{x : x \text{ is a natural number, a multiple of 7 and } 13 < x < 99\}$$

or $\quad A = \{x : x = 7n, n \in N \text{ and } 2 \le n \le 14\}$

Example 6 Write the set of all real numbers which cannot be written as the quotient of two integers in the set-builder form.

Sol. We know that all rational numbers are expressible as the quotient of two integers. Therefore, the required set is the set of those real numbers which are irrational.

$\therefore$ Required set is $\{x : x \in R \text{ but } x \notin Q\}$.

Representation of a Statement in Both Form

Statement	Roster Form	Set-builder Form
The set of all natural numbers between 10 and 14.	{11, 12, 13}	$\{x : x \in N \text{ and } 10 < x < 14\}$
The set of all prime numbers less than 11.	{2, 3, 5, 7}	$\{x : x$ is a prime number and $x < 11\}$
The set of all distinct letters used in the word 'Friend'.	{F, r, i, e, n, d}	$\{x : x$ is a letter used in the word 'Friend'$\}$

Example 7 Describe the following.

(i) "The set of all vowels in the word EQUATION" in roster form.

(ii) "The set of reciprocals of natural numbers" in set-builder form.

Sol. (i) The word "EQUATION" has following vowels, i.e. A, E, I, O and U.

Now, the given statement can be described in roster form as {A, E, I, O, U}.

(ii) Given statement can be described in set-builder form as $\{x : x$ is a reciprocal of a natural number$\}$

or $\quad \left\{x : x = \dfrac{1}{n}, n \in N\right\}$

Example 8 List the elements of the following sets.

(i) $\{x : x \in Z \text{ and } |x| \le 2\}$

(ii) $\left\{x : x = \dfrac{n}{1+n^2} \text{ and } 1 \le n \le 3, \text{ where } n \in N\right\}$

Sol. (i) Given, $\{x : x \in Z \text{ and } |x| \le 2\}$

Since, $|x| \le 2$

$\therefore \quad -2 \le x \le 2$

Also, as $x \in Z$, therefore $x = -2, -1, 0, 1, 2$

Hence, $\{x : x \in Z \text{ and } |x| \le 2\} = \{-2, -1, 0, 1, 2\}$

(ii) Given, $\left\{x : x = \dfrac{n}{1+n^2} \text{ and } 1 \le n \le 3, \text{ where } n \in N\right\}$

Here, $x = \dfrac{n}{1+n^2}, 1 \le n \le 3, n \in N$

$\Rightarrow \quad x = \dfrac{n}{1+n^2}, n = 1, 2, 3$

$\Rightarrow \quad x = \dfrac{1}{1+1^2}, \dfrac{2}{1+2^2}, \dfrac{3}{1+3^2} = \dfrac{1}{2}, \dfrac{2}{5}, \dfrac{3}{10}$

$\therefore$ Required set is $\left\{\dfrac{1}{2}, \dfrac{2}{5}, \dfrac{3}{10}\right\}$.

Example 9 Describe the following sets in roster form.

(i) $A = \{a_n : n \in N, a_{n+1} = 3a_n \text{ and } a_1 = 1\}$

(ii) $B = \{a_n : n \in N, a_{n+2} = a_{n+1} + a_n \text{ and } a_1 = a_2 = 1\}$

Sol. (i) We have, $a_1 = 1$ and $a_{n+1} = 3a_n, \forall n \in N$

On putting $n = 1, 2, 3, 4, \ldots$ in $a_{n+1} = 3a_n$, we get

$$a_2 = 3a_1 = 3 \times 1 = 3$$
$$a_3 = 3a_2 = 3 \times 3 = 3^2$$
$$a_4 = 3a_3 = 3 \times 3^2 = 3^3$$
$$a_5 = 3a_4 = 3 \times 3^3 = 3^4$$
$$a_6 = 3a_5 = 3 \times 3^4 = 3^5 \text{ and so on.}$$
$$\therefore \quad A = \{1, 3, 3^2, 3^3, 3^4, 3^5, \ldots\}$$

(ii) We have, $a_1 = 1, a_2 = 1; a_{n+2} = a_{n+1} + a_n, \forall n \in N.$

On putting $n = 1, 2, 3, \ldots$ in $a_{n+2} = a_{n+1} + a_n$, we get

$$a_3 = a_2 + a_1 = 1 + 1 = 2$$
$$a_4 = a_3 + a_2 = 2 + 1 = 3$$
$$a_5 = a_4 + a_3 = 3 + 2 = 5$$
$$a_6 = a_5 + a_4 = 5 + 3 = 8 \text{ and so on.}$$
$$\therefore \quad B = \{1, 1, 2, 3, 5, 8, \ldots\}$$

Types of Sets

In this section, we will study about different types of sets and cardinal number of a set.

1. Empty Set

A set which does not contain any element, is called an empty set or null set or void set. It is denoted by ϕ or $\{\ \}$.

e.g. $A = \{x : x \text{ is a natural number less than } 1\}$.

Since, there is no natural number less than one. Therefore, set A contains no element and hence it is an empty set.

Note $\{0\}$ and $\{\phi\}$ are not empty sets because each of these sets contains one elements.

Example 10 Which of the following sets are empty sets?

(i) Set of all even natural numbers divisible by 5.

(ii) Set of all even prime numbers. **[NCERT]**

(iii) $\{x : x^2 - 2 = 0 \text{ and } x \text{ is rational}\}$

(iv) $\{x : x \text{ is a point common to any two parallel lines}\}$ **[NCERT]**

Sol. (i) There are infinite even natural numbers which are divisible by 5. e.g. 10, 20, 30, 40, 50, etc.

Therefore, it is not an empty set.

(ii) We know that 2 is only even prime.

Therefore, it is not an empty set.

(iii) Given, $\{x : x^2 - 2 = 0 \text{ and } x \text{ is rational}\}$

Here, $x^2 - 2 = 0 \Rightarrow x^2 = 2 \Rightarrow x = \pm\sqrt{2} \notin Q$

Therefore, it is an empty set.

(iv) Given,

$\{x : x \text{ is a point common to any two parallel lines}\}$

We know that no point is common to any two parallel lines. Therefore, it is an empty set.

2. Singleton Set

A set consisting of a single element, is called a singleton set. e.g.

(i) The sets $\{0\}, \{5\}, \{-7\}$ are singleton sets.

(ii) $A = \{x : x + 8 = 0, x \in Z\}$ is a singleton set, because this set contains only one integer, namely -8.

Example 11 Let $T = \left\{x : \dfrac{x+5}{x-7} - 5 = \dfrac{4x-40}{13-x}\right\}$.

Is T a singleton set? Justify your answer

Sol. We have, $T = \left\{x : \dfrac{x+5}{x-7} - 5 = \dfrac{4x-40}{13-x}\right\}$

Consider, $\dfrac{x+5}{x-7} - 5 = \dfrac{4x-40}{13-x} \Rightarrow \dfrac{x+5}{x-7} - \dfrac{5}{1} = \dfrac{4x-40}{13-x}$

$$\Rightarrow \frac{x+5-5x+35}{x-7} = \frac{4x-40}{13-x} \Rightarrow \frac{40-4x}{x-7} = \frac{4x-40}{13-x}$$

$$\Rightarrow \frac{-(4x-40)}{x-7} - \frac{4x-40}{13-x} = 0$$

$$\Rightarrow \quad -(4x-40)\left[\frac{1}{(13-x)} + \frac{1}{(x-7)}\right] = 0$$

$$\Rightarrow \quad (4x-40)\left[\frac{6}{(13-x)(x-7)}\right] = 0$$

$$\Rightarrow \quad 4x - 40 = 0 \Rightarrow x = 10$$

$$\therefore \quad T = \{10\}$$

Hence, T is a singleton set.

3. Finite Set

A set which is empty or consists of a definite number of elements, is called a finite set. e.g.

(i) The set $\{1, 2, 3, 4\}$ is a finite set, because it contains a definite number of elements, i.e. only 4 elements.

(ii) The set of solutions of $x^2 = 25$ is a finite set, because it contains a definite number of elements, namely 5 and -5.

Note As the empty set has no elements, ϕ is a finite set.

Cardinal Number (or Order) of a Finite Set

The number of distinct elements in a finite set A is called **cardinal number** of set A and it is denoted by $n(A)$ or $O(A)$.

e.g. If $A = \{-3, -1, 8, 10, 13\}$, then $n(A) = 5$.

Note The cardinal number of an empty set is zero and the cardinal number of a singleton set is 1.

4. Infinite Set

A set which consists of infinite number of elements is called an infinite set. When a set is infinite set, it is not possible to write all the elements within braces { } because the number of elements of such a set is not finite. In such cases, we write few elements which clearly indicate the structure of the set followed by three dots.

e.g. Set of squares of natural numbers is an infinite set, because such numbers are infinite and it can be represented in roster form as $\{1, 4, 9, 16, 25, \ldots\}$.

Note (i) All infinite sets cannot be described in the roster form. e.g. The set of real numbers cannot be described in this form, because the elements of this set does not follow any particular pattern.
(ii) The cardinal number of an infinite set is not defined.

Example 12 Which of the following sets are finite and which are infinite?

(i) The set of lines which are parallel to the X-axis.
(ii) The set of animals living on the Earth. **[NCERT]**
(iii) The set of circles passing through the origin (0, 0). **[NCERT]**

Sol. (i) We can draw infinite lines parallel to X-axis.
$\therefore$ It is an infinite set.
(ii) There are finite number of animals living on Earth.
$\therefore$ It is a finite set.
(iii) We can draw infinite number of circles, passing through origin.
$\therefore$ It is an infinite set.

Example 13 Which of the following sets are finite and which are infinite?

(i) $\{x \in R : 0 < x < 1\}$
(ii) $\{x \in Z : x < 5\}$
(iii) The set of positive integers greater than 100. **[NCERT]**
(iv) The set of prime numbers less than 99.

Sol. (i) Given, $\{x \in R : 0 < x < 1\}$. Here, $0 < x < 1$
We know that between any two real numbers, there are infinite real numbers.
$\therefore$ The set $\{x \in R : 0 < x < 1\}$ is an infinite set.
(ii) Given, $\{x \in Z : x < 5\}$. Here, $x < 5$
We know that, there are infinite integers less than 5. e.g. 4, 3, 2, 1, 0, −1, etc.
$\therefore$ The set $\{x \in Z : x < 5\}$ is an infinite set.
(iii) It is an infinite set because there are infinite positive integers greater than 100, e.g. 101, 102, 103, 104, etc.
(iv) It is a finite set because there are only 25 prime numbers less than 99, namely 2, 3, 5, 7, 11, ..., 97.

5. Equivalent Sets

Two finite sets A and B are said to be equivalent, if their **cardinal numbers** are same i.e. if $n(A) = n(B)$.

e.g. Let $A = \{a, b, c, d\}$ and $B = \{1, 2, 3, 4\}$, then $n(A) = 4$ and $n(B) = 4$. Therefore, A and B are equivalent sets.

Example 14 From the sets given below, select pair of equivalent sets.
$A = \{1, 2, 3\}$, $B = \{t, p, q, r, s\}$, $C = \{\alpha, \beta, \gamma\}$ and $D = \{a, e, i, o, u\}$

Sol. Given, $A = \{1, 2, 3\} \Rightarrow n(A) = 3$
$B = \{t, p, q, r, s\} \Rightarrow n(B) = 5$
$C = \{\alpha, \beta, \gamma\} \Rightarrow n(C) = 3$
and $D = \{a, e, i, o, u\} \Rightarrow n(D) = 5$
Here $n(A) = n(C) = 3$ and $n(B) = n(D) = 5$
$\therefore$ The sets A, C and B, D are equivalent sets.

6. Equal Sets

Two sets A and B are said to be **equal**, if they have exactly the same elements and we write it as $A = B$. Otherwise, two sets are called **unequal** and we write $A \neq B$.

e.g. Let $A = \{a, b, c, d\}$ and $B = \{c, d, b, a\}$, then $A = B$, because each element of A is in B and *vice-versa*.

Note Two (finite) equal sets are always equivalent, but two equivalent sets may not be equal.

Example 15 Are the following pair of sets equal? Give reason. **[NCERT]**

(i) $A = \{2, 3\}$ and $B = \{x : x$ is a solution of $x^2 + 5x + 6 = 0\}$
(ii) $A = \{x : x$ is a letter of the word 'FOLLOW'$\}$ and $B = \{y : y$ is a letter of the word 'WOLF'$\}$

Sol. (i) Here, $A = \{2, 3\}$
and $B = \{x : x$ is a solution of $x^2 + 5x + 6 = 0\}$
Firstly, we find the solution of $x^2 + 5x + 6 = 0$.
By splitting the middle term, we get
$$x^2 + 3x + 2x + 6 = 0 \Rightarrow x(x + 3) + 2(x + 3) = 0$$
$$\Rightarrow (x + 2)(x + 3) = 0 \Rightarrow x = -2, -3$$
$$\therefore B = \{-2, -3\}$$
Since, the elements of sets A and B are not same, therefore $A \neq B$.
(ii) Here, $A = \{x : x$ is a letter of the word 'FOLLOW'$\}$ $= \{F, O, L, W\}$
and $B = \{y : y$ is a letter of the word 'WOLF'$\}$ $= \{W, O, L, F\}$
Since, every element of A is in B and every element of B is in A, i.e. both have exactly same elements.
$$\therefore A = B$$

Example 16 Which of the following pairs of sets are equal? Justify your answer.

(i) $A = \{x : x$ is a letter of the word 'LOYAL'$\}$,
$B = \{x : x$ is a letter of the word 'ALLOY'$\}$

(ii) $A = \{x : x \in Z$ and $x^2 \le 8\}$,
$B = \{x : x \in R$ and $x^2 - 4x + 3 = 0\}$

Sol. (i) Given, $A = \{x : x$ is a letter of the word 'LOYAL'$\}$
$= \{L, O, Y, A\}$
and $B = \{x : x$ is a letter of the word 'ALLOY'$\}$
$= \{A, L, O, Y\}$
Since, both sets have exactly the same elements.
$\therefore \quad A = B$

(ii) Given, $A = \{x : x \in Z$ and $x^2 \le 8\} = \{-2, -1, 0, 1, 2\}$
[$\because$ the squares of integers $0, \pm 1, \pm 2$ are less than 8]
and $B = \{x : x \in R$ and $x^2 - 4x + 3 = 0\} = \{1, 3\}$
[$\because x^2 - 4x + 3 = 0 \Rightarrow (x-1)(x-3) = 0 \Rightarrow x = 1, 3$]
Since, A has 5 distinct elements and set B has 2 distinct elements, i.e. they do not have same elements.
$\therefore \quad A \ne B$

Example 17 Identify which of the following sets is an empty set, singleton set, infinite set or equal sets.

(i) $A = \{x : x$ is a girl being living on the Jupiter$\}$
(ii) $B = \{x : x$ is a letter in the word 'MARS'$\}$
(iii) $C = \{y : y$ is a letter in the word 'ARMS'$\}$
(iv) $D = \{x : 3x - 2 = 0, x \in Q\}$
(v) $E = \{x : x \in N$ and x is an odd number$\}$

Sol. (i) $A = \{x : x$ is a girl being living on the Jupiter$\}$
We know that, there is no human being or any girl living on the Jupiter. Therefore, A is an empty set.

(ii) $B = \{x : x$ is a letter in the word 'MARS'$\}$
$\Rightarrow \quad B = \{M, A, R, S\}$

(iii) $C = \{y : y$ is a letter in the word 'ARMS'$\}$
$\Rightarrow \quad C = \{A, R, M, S\}$
Here, we observe that the elements of sets B and C are exactly same.
Therefore, these sets are equal,
i.e. $B = C$.

(iv) $D = \{x : 3x - 2 = 0, x \in Q\}$
$\Rightarrow \quad D = \left\{\frac{2}{3}\right\} \quad \left[\because 3x - 2 = 0 \Rightarrow x = \frac{2}{3} \in Q\right]$
$\therefore D$ is a singleton set.

(v) $E = \{x : x \in N$ and x is an odd number$\}$
Clearly, it is an infinite set because there are infinite natural numbers which are odd.

Topic Practice 1

Very Short Answer Type Questions

2 Marks

Directions (Q. Nos. 1-2) *Which of the following are sets? Justify your answer.*

1 A team of eleven best cricket batsman of the world. **[NCERT]**

2 The collection of all boys in your class. **[NCERT]**

3 If $A = \{1, 3, 5, 7, 9, 11, 13, 15\}$, then insert the appropriate symbol $\in$ or $\notin$ in each of the following blank spaces.
(i) 1 ... A (ii) 6 ... A (iii) 14 ... A

4 Write the set $A = \{x : x \in Z, x^2 < 20\}$ in the roster form.

5 Write the set $X = \left\{1, \frac{1}{4}, \frac{1}{9}, \frac{1}{16}, \frac{1}{25}, \ldots\right\}$ in set-builder form.

6 Write the set of all vowels in the English alphabet which precedes 'q'.

7 Write $\{x : x$ is an integer and $-3 \le x < 7\}$ in roster form. **[NCERT]**

8 Write set $A = \{3, 6, 9, 12, 15\}$ in set-builder form.

9 Write set $A = \{1, 4, 9, \ldots, 100\}$ in set-builder form. **[NCERT]**

10 Write set $D = \left\{\frac{1}{2}, \frac{2}{5}, \frac{3}{10}, \frac{4}{17}, \frac{5}{26}, \frac{6}{37}, \frac{7}{50}\right\}$ in set-builder form.

11 List the elements of the set
$A = \left\{x : x \text{ is an integer, where } -\frac{1}{2} < x < \frac{9}{2}\right\}$. **[NCERT]**

12 Express the set
$D = \left\{x : x = \frac{n^2 - 1}{n^2 + 1}, n \in N \text{ and } n < 4\right\}$ in roster form.

13 Describe the following.
(i) "The set of vowels in word MATHEMATICS" in roster form.
(ii) "The set of all odd natural numbers" in set-builder form.

Short Answer Type Questions

(4 Marks)

14 Let $A = \{1, 2, 3, 4\}$, $B = \{5, 6, 7\}$ and $C = \{7, 8, 9, 10\}$. Insert the correct symbol $\in$ or $\notin$ in each of the following blanks.

(i) $2 \ldots A$ (ii) $5 \ldots C$
(iii) $6 \ldots B$ (iv) $7 \ldots A$
(v) $5 \ldots B$ (vi) $10 \ldots C$

15 Describe the following sets in roster form.
(i) The set of all letters in the word 'ALGEBRA'.
(ii) The set of all natural numbers less than 7.
(iii) The set of squares of integers.
(iv) The set of all letters in the word "TRIGONOMETRY".

16 Describe the following sets in set-builder form.
(i) The set of all letters in the word PROBABILITY.
(ii) The set of all even natural numbers.
(iii) $\{5, 25, 125, 625\}$

17 Which of the following sets are empty sets? **[NCERT]**
(i) $A = \{x : x$ is a human being living on the Mars$\}$
(ii) $B = \{x : x$ is an even natural number divisible by 3$\}$
(iii) $C = \{x : x$ is a point common to opposite sides of parallelogram$\}$
(iv) $D = \{x : x$ is a natural number, $x < 5$ and simultaneously $x > 7\}$

18 Which of the following sets are singleton/non-singleton?
(i) $A = \{x : |x| = 7, x \in N\}$
(ii) $B = \{x : x^2 + 2x + 1 = 0, x \in N\}$
(iii) $C = \{x : x^2 = 9, |x| \leq 3, x \in N\}$

19 State which of the following sets are finite and which are infinite?
(i) $A = \{x : x \in Z$ and $x^2 - 5x + 6 = 0\}$
(ii) $B = \{x : x \in Z$ and x^2 is even$\}$
(iii) $C = \{x : x \in Z$ and $x^2 = 36\}$
(iv) $D = \{x : x \in Z$ and $x > -10\}$

20 Which of the following pairs of sets are equal?
(i) $A = \{1, 3, 3, 1\}$, $B = \{1, 4\}$
(ii) $A = \{x : x + 2 = 2\}$, $B = \{0\}$
(iii) $A = \left\{1, \frac{1}{2}, \frac{1}{3}, \ldots\right\}$, $B = \left\{\frac{1}{n}, n \in N\right\}$
(iv) $A = \{x : x \in W\}$, $B = \{x : x \in N\}$

21 Find the pairs of equal sets, from the following sets, if any, giving reasons.
$A = \{0\}$, $B = \{x : x > 15$ and $x < 5\}$, $C = \{x : x - 5 = 0\}$, $D = \{x : x^2 = 25\}$,
$E = \{x : x$ is a positive integral root of the equation $x^2 - 2x - 15 = 0\}$ **[NCERT]**

22 From the sets given below, select equal sets and equivalent sets.
$A = \{0, a\}$, $B = \{1, 2, 3, 4\}$, $C = \{4, 8, 12\}$,
$D = \{3, 1, 2, 4\}$, $E = \{1, 0\}$, $F = \{8, 4, 12\}$, $G = \{1, 5, 7, 11\}$,
$H = \{a, b\}$

23 Which of the following sets are equal?
$A = \{x : x \in N, x < 3\}$, $B = \{1, 2\}$, $C = \{3, 1\}$,
$D = \{x : x \in N, x < 5, x$ is odd$\}$, $E = \{1, 2, 1, 1\}$
$F = \{1, 1, 3\}$

24 From the sets given below, select empty set, singleton set, infinite set and equal sets.
(i) $A = \{x : x < 1$ and $x > 3\}$
(ii) $B = \{x : x^3 - 1 = 0, x \in R\}$
(iii) $C = \{x : x \in N$ and x is a prime number$\}$
(iv) $D = \{2, 4, 6, 8, 10\}$
(v) $E = \{x : x$ is a positive even integers and $x \leq 10\}$

Hints & Answers

1. Not a set **2.** Set

3. (i) $1 \in A$ (ii) $6 \notin A$ (iii) $14 \notin A$

4. It can be seen that the square of integers $0, \pm 1, \pm 2, \pm 3, \pm 4$ are less than 20.
Ans. $A = \{-4, -3, -2, -1, 0, 1, 2, 3, 4\}$

5. It can be seen that the elements of set X are the reciprocal of the squares of all natural numbers.
Ans. $X = \left\{x : x = \frac{1}{n^2}, \text{ where } n \in N\right\}$ or $X = \left\{\frac{1}{n^2} : n \in N\right\}$

6. $\{a, e, i, o\}$ **7.** $\{-3, -2, -1, 0, 1, 2, 3, 4, 5, 6\}$

8. $A = \{x : x$ is a natural number multiple of 3 and $x < 18\}$

9. $A = \{x : x = n^2, n \in N$ and $n < 11\}$

10. $D = \left\{x : x = \frac{n}{n^2 + 1}, n \in N \text{ and } n \leq 7\right\}$

11. $A = \{0, 1, 2, 3, 4\}$ **12.** $D = \left\{0, \frac{3}{5}, \frac{4}{5}\right\}$

13. (i) The word 'MATHEMATICS' has only 3 vowels namely A, E and I.
Ans. $\{A, E, I\}$.
(ii) An odd natural number can be written in the form $2n - 1$.
Ans. $\{x : x = 2n - 1, n \in N\}$

14. (i) $2 \in A$ (ii) $5 \notin C$
(iii) $6 \in B$ (iv) $7 \notin A$
(v) $5 \in B$ (vi) $10 \in C$

15. (i) {A, L, G, E, B, R}
(ii) {1, 2, 3, 4, 5, 6}
(iii) {0, 1, 4, 9, 16, ...}
(iv) {T, R, I, G, O, N, M, E, Y}

16. (i) {x: x is a letter of the word PROBABILITY}
(ii) $\{x : x = 2n, n \in N\}$ or $\{2n : n \in N\}$
(iii) $\{x : x = 5^n, n \in N \text{ and } n < 5\}$
or $\{5^n : n \in N \text{ and } n < 5\}$

17. (i) There is no human being living on the Mars.
(ii) There is no even number, which is divisible by 3.
(iii) There is no common point between opposite sides of the parallelogram.
(iv) A natural number cannot be less than 5 and greater than 7, simultaneously.
Ans. A, B, C and D

18. (i) $|x| = 7 \Rightarrow x = \pm 7$. But $x \in N$, therefore $A = \{7\}$
(ii) $x^2 + 2x + 1 = 0 \Rightarrow (x+1)^2 = 0 \Rightarrow x = -1$,
which is not a natural number.
$\therefore \quad B = \{\} = \phi$
(iii) $x^2 = 9 \Rightarrow x = \pm 3$
and $|x| \le 3 \Rightarrow x = -3, -2, -1, 0, 1, 2, 3$
But out of $-3, 3$ only $3 \in N$.
$\therefore \quad C = \{3\}$
Ans. A and C are singleton sets and B is non-singleton.

19. (i) $A = \{2, 3\}$
(ii) $B = \{\ldots, -6, -4, -2, 0, 2, 4, 6, \ldots\}$
(iii) $C = \{6, -6\}$
(iv) $D = \{-9, -8, -7, \ldots\}$
Ans. A, C are finite sets and B, D are infinite sets.

20. (i) $A = \{1, 3, 3, 1\} = \{1, 3\}$, $B = \{1, 4\}$
(ii) $A = \{x : x + 2 = 2\} = \{0\}$, $B = \{0\}$
(iii) $A = \left\{1, \frac{1}{2}, \frac{1}{3}, \ldots\right\} = \left\{\frac{1}{1}, \frac{1}{2}, \frac{1}{3}, \ldots\right\}$
and $B = \left\{\frac{1}{n} : n \in N\right\} = \left\{\frac{1}{1}, \frac{1}{2}, \frac{1}{3}, \ldots\right\}$
(iv) $A = \{0, 1, 2, 3, \ldots\}$ and $B = \{1, 2, 3, \ldots\}$
Ans. (ii) and (iii)

21. $A = \{0\}$, $B = \{\}$
$C = \{5\}$, $D = \{5, -5\}$ and $E = \{5\}$
Ans. Sets C and E are equal set.

22. Equal sets : $B = D$, $C = F$
Equivalent sets : A, E, H; B, D, G; C, F

23. $A = B = E$, $C = D = F$

24. (i) $A = \{\} = \phi$
(ii) $B = \{1\}$
(iii) $C = \{2, 3, 5, \ldots\}$
(v) $E = \{2, 4, 6, 8, 10\}$
Ans. Empty set : A; singleton set : B; Infinite set : C; Equal sets : D and E

TOPIC 02 Subset, Power Set and Universal Set

Subset

Let A and B be two sets. If every element of A is an element of B, then A is called a **subset** of B.

If A is a subset of B, then we write it as $A \subseteq B$, which is read as "A is a subset of B" or "A is contained in B".

In other words, $A \subseteq B$, if whenever $a \in A$, then $a \in B$. It is often convenient to use the symbol "$\Rightarrow$" which means **implies.** Using this symbol, we can write the definition of subset as follows

$$A \subseteq B, \text{ if } x \in A$$
$$\Rightarrow \quad x \in B$$

The above statement is read as "*A is subset of B, if x is an element of A, then it implies that x is also an element of B.*"

If A is not a subset of B, then we write $A \not\subseteq B$.

e.g. Consider the sets A and B, where set A denotes the set of all students in your class and B denotes the set of all students in your school. We observe that every element of A is also an element of B. Therefore, we can say that A is subset of B i.e. $A \subseteq B$.

If it happens for both sets A and B, i.e. every element of A is in B and every element of B is in A, then in this case, A and B are same sets.

Thus, $A \subseteq B$ **and** $B \subseteq A \Leftrightarrow A = B$, where "$\Leftrightarrow$" is a symbol for two ways implications and is usually read as if and only if (iff).

Note (i) $\{1\} \subseteq \{1, 2, 3\}$ (ii) $2 \not\subseteq \{1, 2, 3\}$

Proper Subset

If $A \subseteq B$ and $A \neq B$, then A is called a proper subset of B, written as $A \subset B$ and B is called the **superset** of A.

e.g. Let $A = \{x : x$ is an even natural number$\}$

and $B = \{x : x$ is a natural number$\}$.

Then, $A = \{2, 4, 6, 8, \ldots\}$ and $B = \{1, 2, 3, 4, 5, \ldots\}$

$\therefore \quad A \subset B$

If A is not a proper subset of B, then we write $A \not\subset B$.

Note (i) A subset, which is not a proper subset, is called **an improper subset.**

(ii) In some books, A is a subset of B is denoted by $A \subset B$ and A is a proper subset of B is denoted by '$A \subset B$ and $A \neq B$'.

Some Important Results

(i) Every set is a subset of itself but not a proper subset.

Proof Let A be any set. Then, each element of A is clearly in A. Hence, $A \subseteq A$.

(ii) Every set has two improper subset, namely itself and ϕ.

(iii) The empty set ϕ is a subset of all sets.

Proof Let A be any set and ϕ be the empty set. To show that $\phi \subseteq A$, we have to show that every element of ϕ is an element of A also. But we know that empty set ϕ contains no element. So, there is no element of ϕ which does not belong to A. Thus, we can say that every element of ϕ is in A.
Hence, $\phi \subseteq A$.

(iv) If $A \subseteq B$ and $B \subseteq C$, then $A \subseteq C$.

(v) The total number of subsets and proper subsets of a finite set containing n elements is 2^n and $2^n - 1$, respectively.

Example 1 Let $A = \{1, 2, \{3, 4\}, 5\}$. Which of the following statements are incorrect and why? **[NCERT]**

(i) $\{3, 4\} \subseteq A$ (ii) $\{3, 4\} \in A$
(iii) $\{\{3, 4\}\} \subseteq A$ (iv) $1 \in A$
(v) $1 \subseteq A$ (vi) $\{1, 2, 5\} \subseteq A$
(vii) $\{1, 2, 5\} \in A$ (viii) $\phi \subseteq A$
(ix) $\phi \in A$ (x) $\{\phi\} \subseteq A$

Sol. We have, $A = \{1, 2, \{3, 4\}, 5\}$

(i) Since, $\{3, 4\}$ is a member of set A.
$\therefore \{3, 4\} \in A$
Hence, $\{3, 4\} \subseteq A$ is incorrect.

(ii) Since, $\{3, 4\}$ is a member of set A.
$\therefore \{3, 4\} \in A$ is correct.

(iii) Since, $\{3, 4\}$ is a member of set A.
So, $\{\{3, 4\}\}$ is a subset of A.
Hence, $\{\{3, 4\}\} \subseteq A$ is correct.

(iv) Since, 1 is a member of A.
$\therefore 1 \in A$ is correct.

(v) Since, 1 is a member of set A.
$\therefore 1 \subseteq A$ is incorrect.

(vi) Since, 1, 2, 5 are members of set A.
So, $\{1, 2, 5\}$ is a subset of set A.
Hence, $\{1, 2, 5\} \subseteq A$ is correct.

(vii) Since, 1, 2 and 5 are members of set A.
So, $\{1, 2, 5\}$ is a subset of A.
Hence, $\{1, 2, 5\} \in A$ is incorrect.

(viii) Since, ϕ is subset of every set.
$\therefore \phi \subseteq A$ is correct.

(ix) Since, ϕ is not a member of set A.
$\therefore \phi \in A$ is incorrect.

(x) Since, ϕ is not a member of set A.
$\therefore \{\phi\} \subseteq A$ is incorrect.

Example 2 Insert the correct symbol $\subset$ or $\not\subset$ between each of the following pair of sets.

(i) $\{x : x$ is a student of class XI of your school$\}$ ...... $\{x : x$ is a student of your school$\}$ **[NCERT]**

(ii) $\{x : x$ is a triangle in the plane$\}$ ...... $\{x : x$ is a rectangle in the plane$\}$

(iii) $\{x : x$ is an equilateral triangle in the plane$\}$ ...... $\{x : x$ is a triangle in the plane$\}$ **[NCERT]**

(iv) $\{x : x$ is an even natural number$\}$ ...... $\{x : x$ is an integer$\}$

(v) $\{1, 4, 8\}$ ...... $\{1, 2, 4, 6, 8\}$

Sol. (i) $\{x : x$ is a student of class XI of your school$\}$ $\subset \{x : x$ is a student of your school$\}$

(ii) $\{x : x$ is a triangle in the plane$\} \not\subset \{x : x$ is a rectangle in the plane$\}$
[$\because$ all elements of Ist set are not there in the IInd set]

(iii) $\{x : x$ is an equilateral triangle in the plane$\} \subset \{x : x$ is a triangle in the plane$\}$
[$\because$ elements of IInd set are triangles, so there will also be equilateral triangles, thus all elements of Ist set will be in the IInd set]

(iv) $\{x : x$ is an even natural number$\} \subset \{x : x$ is an integer$\}$
[$\because$ integers have both even and odd natural numbers, so all elements of Ist set will be in the IInd set]

(v) $\{1, 4, 8\} \subset \{1, 2, 4, 6, 8\}$

Example 3 Prove that if $A \subseteq \phi$, then $A = \phi$.

Sol. Given, $A \subseteq \phi$ ...(i)

We know that ϕ is subset of every set.

$\therefore \quad \phi \subseteq A$ ...(ii)

From Eqs. (i) and (ii), we get

$A = \phi$ **Hence proved.**

Example 4 Two finite sets have m and n elements. The number of subsets of the first set is 112 more than that of the second set. Find the values of m and n. **[NCERT Exemplar]**

Sol. Let the two sets be A and B such that $n(A) = m$ and $n(B) = n$.

Then, number of subsets of set $A = 2^m$

and number of subsets of set $B = 2^n$.

According to the given condition, we have

$$2^m = 112 + 2^n$$

$$\Rightarrow \quad 2^m - 2^n = 2^7 - 2^4$$

On comparing both sides, we get

$$2^m = 2^7 \text{ and } 2^n = 2^4$$

$$\Rightarrow \quad m = 7 \text{ and } n = 4$$

Subsets of a Set of Real Numbers

We know that every real number is either a **rational** or an **irrational** number and the set of real numbers is denoted by R. Also, there are many important subsets of R, some of these are given below.

1. Natural Numbers

The numbers being used in counting 1, 2, 3, 4,..., called natural numbers.

The set of natural numbers is denoted by N. Thus,

$$N = \{1, 2, 3, 4, \ldots\}$$

2. Whole Numbers

The collection of natural numbers along with number 0 (zero) form the set of whole numbers i.e. 0, 1, 2, 3, ... , are whole numbers. The set of whole numbers is denoted by W. Thus,

$$W = \{0, 1, 2, 3, \ldots\}$$

Note The set of natural numbers is the proper subset of the set of whole numbers, i.e. $N \subset W$.

3. Integers

The collection of natural numbers, their negatives and zero make the set of integers and it is denoted by Z.

$$Z = \{\ldots, -5, -4, -3, -2, -1, 0, 1, 2, 3, 4, \ldots\}$$

Note The set of whole numbers is the proper subset of integers, i.e. $W \subset Z$.

4. Rational Numbers

A number of the form $\frac{p}{q}$, where p and q both are integers and $q \neq 0$ (division by 0 is not permissible), is called a rational number and the set of rational numbers is generally denoted by Q.

Thus, $Q = \left\{\frac{p}{q} : p, q \in Z \text{ and } q \neq 0\right\}$

Note (i) All integers are also rational numbers, since any integer, say n, can be represented as the ratio $\frac{n}{1}$.

(ii) The set of integers is the proper subset of the set of rational numbers i.e. $Z \subset Q$ and hence $N \subset W \subset Z \subset Q$.

5. Irrational Numbers

A number which cannot be written in the form p/q, where p and q both are integers and $q \neq 0$, is called an irrational number.

The set of irrational numbers is denoted by Q'. Thus,

$$Q' = \{x : x \in R \text{ and } x \notin Q\}$$

Note A non-terminating, non-repeating decimal number is a irrational number.

Diagrammatical Representation

Above subsets can be represented diagrammatically as given below

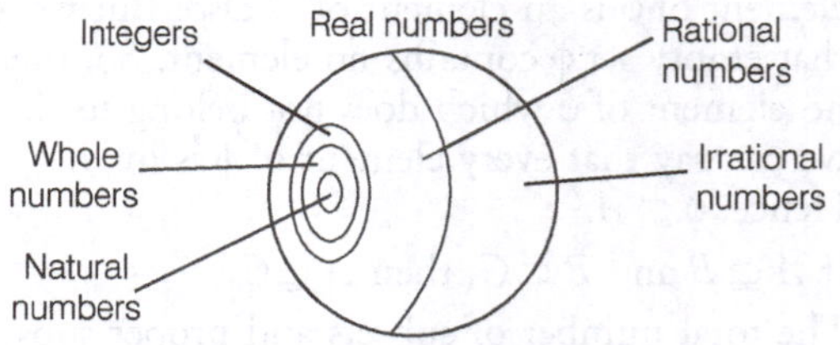

Intervals as Subsets of R

Let a, b belongs to R and $a < b$. Then, the set of real numbers $\{x : a < x < b\}$ is called an **open interval** and is denoted by (a, b). All the real numbers between a and b belongs to the open interval (a, b) but a and b do not belong to this set (interval).

The interval which contains the end points (a and b) also, is called **closed interval** and it is denoted by $[a, b]$.

Hence, $[a, b] = \{x : a \leq x \leq b\}$.

Semi-closed or Semi-open Interval

Some intervals are closed at one end and open at the other, such intervals are called **semi-closed** or **semi-open interval**.

Here, $[a, b) = \{x : a \leq x < b\}$ is a semi-open interval from a to b which includes a but excludes b.

and $(a, b] = \{x : a < x \leq b\}$ is a semi-open interval from a to b which excludes a but includes b.

e.g. (i) (2, 8) is a subset of R.

(ii) [4, 6) is a subset of R.

On real line, we can draw the interval, which is shown by the dark portion on the number line

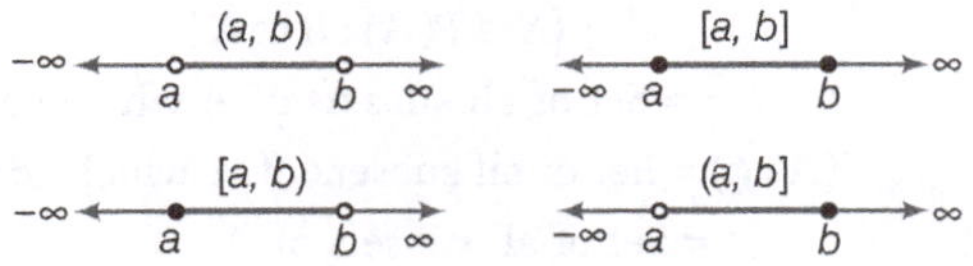

Note (i) The set $[0, \infty)$ defines the set of non-negative real numbers, where the symbol '∞' (real as infinity) represents a huge number which cannot be defined.

(ii) The set $(-\infty, 0)$ defines the set of negative real numbers, where the symbol '$-\infty$' represents a smallest number which cannot be defined.

(iii) The set $(-\infty, \infty)$ defined the set of real numbers.

Length of an Interval

The number $(b - a)$ is called the **length** of the intervals (a, b), $[a, b]$, $[a, b)$ or $(a, b]$.

Example 5 Write the following as intervals and also represent on the number line.

(i) $\{x : x \in R, -5 < x \leq 6\}$ (ii) $\{x : x \in R, -11 < x < -9\}$

(iii) $\{x : x \in R, 2 \leq x < 8\}$ (iv) $\{x : x \in R, 5 \leq x \leq 6\}$

Sol. (i) $\{x : x \in R, -5 < x \leq 6\}$ is the set that does not contain -5 but contains 6. So, it can be written as a semi-closed interval whose first end is open and last end is closed i.e. $(-5, 6]$.

On the real line, $(-5, 6]$ can be graphed as shown in figure given below

The dark portion on the number line represent $(-5, 6]$.

(ii) $\{x : x \in R, -11 < x < -9\}$ is the set that neither contains -11 nor -9, so it can be represented as open interval $(-11, -9)$.

On the real line, $(-11, -9)$ can be graphed as shown in the figure given below

The dark portion on the number line represent $(-11, -9)$.

(iii) $\{x : x \in R, 2 \leq x < 8\}$ is the set that contains 2 but not contain 8.So, it can be represented as a semi-open interval whose first end is closed and the other end is open i.e. $[2, 8)$.

On the real line, $[2, 8)$ can be graphed as shown in the figure given below

The dark portion on the number line represent $[2, 8)$.

(iv) $\{x : x \in R, 5 \leq x \leq 6\}$ is the set which contains 5 and 6 both. So, it is equivalent to a closed interval i.e. $[5, 6]$.

On the real line, $[5, 6]$ can be graphed as shown in the figure given below

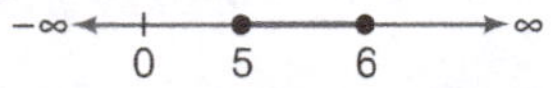

The dark portion on the number line represent $[5, 6]$.

Example 6 Write the following intervals in set-builder form.

(i) $(-3, 0)$ (ii) $[6, 12]$ (iii) $(6, 12]$ (iv) $[-23, 5)$

Sol. We know that closed interval contains end points while open interval does not contain end points.

(i) $(-3, 0) = \{x : x \in R, -3 < x < 0\}$

(ii) $[6, 12] = \{x : x \in R, 6 \leq x \leq 12\}$

(iii) $(6, 12] = \{x : x \in R, 6 < x \leq 12\}$

(iv) $[-23, 5) = \{x : x \in R, -23 \leq x < 5\}$

Power Set

The collection of all subsets of a set, say A, is called the power set of A and it is denoted by $P(A)$. In $P(A)$, every element is a set. e.g. Let $A = \{3, 4, 5\}$.

Then, $P(A) = \{\phi, \{3\}, \{4\}, \{5\}, \{3, 4\}, \{3, 5\}, \{4, 5\}, \{3, 4, 5\}\}$

Note (i) If set A has n elements, then the total number of elements in its power set is 2^n.

(ii) If A is an empty set ϕ, then $P(A)$ has just one element namely ϕ. Thus, $P(A) = \{\phi\}$.

Method to Write the Power Set of a Given Set

Let a set having n elements be given, then for writing its power set, we use the following steps

Step I Write all the possible subsets having single element of given set.

Step II Write all the possible subsets having two elements at a time of given set.

Step III Write all the possible subsets having three elements at a time of given set. Repeat this process for writing all possible subsets having n elements at a time, as the given set has n elements.

Step IV Write a set using the subsets obtained in steps I, II and III alongwith ϕ as its elements.

This gives the required power set of the given set.

Example 7 If $A = \{1, 2, 3\}$, then find the power set of A.

Sol. All possible subsets of A having single element are $\{1\}, \{2\}, \{3\}$.

All possible subsets of A having two elements at a time are $\{1, 2\}, \{2, 3\}, \{3, 1\}$.

All possible subsets of A having three elements at a time is $\{1, 2, 3\}$.

Thus, the required power set is

$\{\{1\}, \{2\}, \{3\}, \{1, 2\}, \{2, 3\}, \{3, 1\}, \{1, 2, 3\}, \phi\}$.

Example 8 Show that $n\{P[P(P(\phi))]\} = 4$.

Sol. We know, $P(\phi) = \{\phi\}$

$\therefore \quad P(P(\phi)) = \{\phi, \{\phi\}\}$

$\Rightarrow P[P(P\,\phi))] = \{\phi, \{\phi\}, \{\{\phi\}\}, \{\phi, \{\phi\}\}\}$

Hence, number of elements in $P[P(P(\phi))]$ is 4.

i.e. $n\{P[P(P(\phi))]\} = 4$ **Hence proved.**

Example 9 For any two sets A and B, prove that $P(A) = P(B)$ implies $A = B$.

Sol. Let $P(A) = P(B)$

Now, as $A \subseteq A$, therefore $A \in P(A)$

$\Rightarrow \quad A \in P(B) \quad [\because P(A) = P(B)]$

$\Rightarrow \quad A \subseteq B$ ...(i)

Again, $B \subseteq B \Rightarrow B \in P(B)$

$\Rightarrow \quad B \in P(A) \quad [\because P(A) = P(B)]$

$\Rightarrow \quad B \subseteq A$ ...(ii)

From Eqs. (i) and (ii), we get $A = B$ **Hence proved.**

Example 10 Let $A = \{1, 2, 3, 4\}$, $B = \{1, 2, 3\}$ and $C = \{2, 4\}$. Find all sets X satisfying each pair of conditions.

(i) $X \subseteq B$ and $X \not\subseteq C$ (ii) $X \subseteq B$, $X \neq B$ and $X \not\subseteq C$

(iii) $X \subset A$, $X \subset B$ and $X \subset C$

Sol. Given, $A = \{1, 2, 3, 4\}$, $B = \{1, 2, 3\}$ and $C = \{2, 4\}$.

Now, $P(A) = \{\phi, \{1\}, \{2\}, \{3\}, \{4\}, \{1, 2\}, \{1, 3\}, \{1, 4\}, \{2, 3\}, \{2, 4\}, \{3, 4\}, \{1, 2, 3\}, \{1, 2, 4\}, \{1, 3, 4\}, \{2, 3, 4\}, \{1, 2, 3, 4\}\}$ ...(i)

$P(B) = \{\phi, \{1\}, \{2\}, \{3\}, \{1, 2\}, \{1, 3\}, \{2, 3\}, \{1, 2, 3\}\}$ ...(ii)

and $P(C) = \{\phi, \{2\}, \{4\}, \{2, 4\}\}$ ...(iii)

(i) Given condition is $X \subseteq B$ and $X \not\subseteq C$.

$\Rightarrow X \in P(B)$ and $X \notin P(C)$

$\therefore \quad X = \{1\}, \{3\}, \{1, 2\}, \{1, 3\}, \{2, 3\}, \{1, 2, 3\}$

[using Eqs. (ii) and (iii)]

(ii) Given condition is $X \subseteq B$, $X \neq B$ and $X \not\subseteq C$.

$\Rightarrow X \in P(B)$, $X \neq B$ and $X \notin P(C)$

$\therefore \quad X = \{1\}, \{3\}, \{1, 2\}, \{1, 3\}, \{2, 3\}$

[using Eqs. (ii) and (iii)]

(iii) Given condition is $X \subset A$, $X \subset B$ and $X \subset C$.

$\Rightarrow X \in P(A)$, $X \in P(B)$, $X \in P(C)$ and $X \neq A, B, C$

$\Rightarrow X$ is proper subset of A, B and C

$\Rightarrow \quad X = \phi, \{2\}$

Example 11 Let B be a subset of a set A and let $P(A : B) = \{X \in P(A) : X \supset B\}$.

(i) Show that $P(A : \phi) = P(A)$.

(ii) If $A = \{1, 2, 3, 4\}$ and $B = \{1, 2\}$. List all the members of the set $P(A : B)$.

Sol. (i) Given, $P(A : B) = \{X \in P(A) : X \supset B\}$

$= \{X \in P(A) : B \subset X\}$

= Set of all subsets of A which contain B

$\therefore P(A : \phi)$ = Set of all subsets of A which contain ϕ

= Set of all subsets of A

$= P(A)$ **Hence proved.**

(ii) Here, $A = \{1, 2, 3, 4\}$, $B = \{1, 2\}$

Now, $P(A : B)$ = Set of all subsets of A which contain B

$= \{\{1, 2\}, \{1, 2, 3\}, \{1, 2, 4\}, \{1, 2, 3, 4\}\}$

Universal Set

If there are some sets under consideration, then a set can be chosen arbitrarily which is a **superset** of each one of the given sets. Such a set is known as the universal set and it is denoted by U.

e.g. (i) Let $A = \{2, 4, 6\}$, $B = \{1, 3, 5\}$ and $C = \{0, 7\}$

Then, $U = \{0, 1, 2, 3, 4, 5, 6, 7\}$ is an universal set.

(ii) For the set of all integers, the universal set can be the set of rational numbers or the set of real numbers.

Example 12 What universal sets would you propose for each of the following? **[NCERT]**

(i) The set of right triangles.

(ii) The set of equilateral triangles.

Sol. (i) The universal set for the set of right triangles is set of triangles.

(ii) The universal set for the set of equilateral triangle is set of isosceles triangles or set of triangles.

Topic Practice 2

Very Short Answer Type Questions

2 Marks

1 Consider the following sets

ϕ, $A = \{2, 5\}$, $B = \{1, 2, 3, 4\}$ and $C = \{1, 2, 3, 4, 5\}$

Insert the correct symbol $\subset$ or $\not\subset$ between each pair of sets

(i) $\phi \ldots B$ (ii) $A \ldots B$

(iii) $A \ldots C$ (iv) $B \ldots C$

2 If $A = \{3, \{4, 5\}, 6\}$, then find which of the following statements are true?
(i) $\{4, 5\} \subset A$ (ii) $\{4, 5\} \in A$
(iii) $\phi \subset A$ (iv) $\{3, 6\} \subset A$

3 Let $A = \{1, 3, 5\}$ and $B = \{x : x$ is an odd natural number $< 6\}$.
(i) Is $A \subseteq B$? (ii) Is $A = B$?

4 Write down the subsets of the following sets.
(i) $\{1, 2, 3\}$ (ii) $\{\phi\}$ **[NCERT]**

5 If $A = \{x : x = n^2, n = 1, 2, 3\}$, then find the number of proper subsets.

6 Write the following as intervals. **[NCERT]**
(i) $\{x : x \in R, -4 < x \le 6\}$
(ii) $\{x : x \in R, -12 < x < -10\}$
(iii) $\{x : x \in R, 0 \le x < 7\}$
(iv) $\{x : x \in R, 3 \le x \le 4\}$

7 Write the following subset of R as interval. Also find the length of interval and represent on number line.
$$\{x : x \in R, -12 \le x \le -10\}$$

8 If set $A = \{1, 3, 5\}$, then find the number of elements in $P\{P(A)\}$.

9 Given, the sets $A = \{1, 3, 5\}$, $B = \{2, 4, 6\}$ and $C = \{0, 2, 4, 6, 8\}$. Which of the following may be considered as universal set(s) for all three sets A, B and C?
(i) ϕ (ii) $\{0, 1, 2, 3, 4, 5, 6, 7, 8, 9, 10\}$ **[NCERT]**

Short Answer Type Questions

4 Marks

10 Write the following intervals in set-builder form.
(i) $(-6, 0)$ (ii) $[3, 21)$
(iii) $[2, 21]$ (iv) $(-20, 5]$

11 Write the following as intervals and also represent on real line.
(i) $\{x : x \in R, -3 < x \le 7\}$
(ii) $\{x : x \in R, -11 < x < -7\}$
(iii) $\{x : x \in R, 0 \le x < 11\}$
(iv) $\{x : x \in R, 2 \le x \le 9\}$

12 Write down the power set of the following sets.
(i) $B = \{0, 1, 3\}$ (ii) $C = \{1, \{2\}\}$

13 Let $A = \{a, b, c, d\}$, $B = \{a, b, c\}$ and $C = \{b, d\}$. Find all set X such that
(i) $X \subset B$ and $X \subset C$ (ii) $X \subset A$ and $X \not\subset B$

Hints & Answers

1. (i) ϕ is a proper subset of every non-empty set.
Ans. $\phi \subset B$
(ii) $5 \in A$, but $5 \notin B$.
Ans. $A \not\subset B$
(iii) $A \subset C$
(iv) $B \subset C$

2. (ii), (iii) and (iv)

3. (i) Yes (ii) Yes

4. (i) ϕ, $\{1\}$, $\{2\}$, $\{3\}$, $\{1, 2\}$, $\{2, 3\}$, $\{1, 3\}$, $\{1, 2, 3\}$
(ii) ϕ and $\{\phi\}$.

5. Number of proper subsets $= 2^n - 1$
Ans. 7

6. (i) $(-4, 6]$ (ii) $(-12, -10)$
(iii) $[0, 7)$ (iv) $[3, 4]$

7. $[-12, -10]$, 2

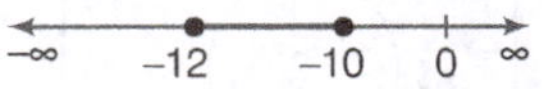

8. If $n(A) = m$, number of elements in $P(A) = 2^m$
and number of elements in $P(P(A)) = 2^{2^m}$
Ans. 256

9. Universal set for sets A, B and C is the superset of A, B and C i.e. universal set contains all elements of A, B and C.
Ans. $\{0, 1, 2, 3, 4, 5, 6, 7, 8, 9, 10\}$

10. (i) $\{x : x \in R, -6 < x < 0\}$
(ii) $\{x : x \in R, 3 \le x < 21\}$
(iii) $\{x : x \in R, 2 \le x \le 21\}$
(iv) $\{x : x \in R, -20 < x \le 5\}$

11. (i) $(-3, 7]$

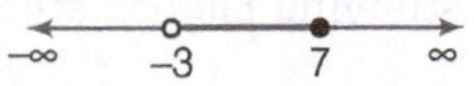

(ii) $(-11, -7)$

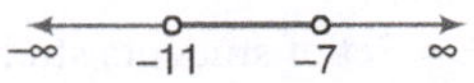

(iii) $[0, 11)$

(iv) $[2, 9]$

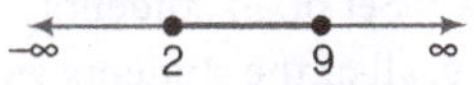

12. (i) $P(B) = \{\phi, \{0\}, \{1\}, \{3\}, \{0, 1\}, \{0, 3\}, \{1, 3\}, \{0, 1, 3\}\}$
(ii) $P(C) = \{\phi, \{1\}, \{\{2\}\}, \{1, \{2\}\}\}$

13. (i) $X \subset B$ and $X \subset C$
$\Rightarrow$ $X \in P(B)$ and $X \in P(C)$
Ans. $X = \phi, \{b\}$
(ii) $X \subset A$ and $X \not\subset B$
$\Rightarrow$ $X \in P(A)$ but $X \notin P(B)$
Ans. $X = \{d\}, \{a, b, d\}, \{b, c, d\}, \{a, c, d\}, \{a, d\}, \{b, d\}, \{c, d\}, \{a, b, c, d\}$

TOPIC 03 Venn Diagrams and Operations on Sets

Venn Diagrams

Most of the relationships between sets can be represented by means of diagrams which are known as Venn diagrams. These diagrams consist of rectangles and closed curves usually circles.

In Venn diagrams, the universal set is represented by a **rectangular region** and its subset are represented by **circle** or a **closed figure** inside the universal set. Also, an element of a set is represented by a **point** within the circle of set.

e.g. If $U = \{1, 2, 3, 4, \ldots, 10\}$ and $A = \{1, 2, 3\}$, then its Venn diagram is as shown in the figure

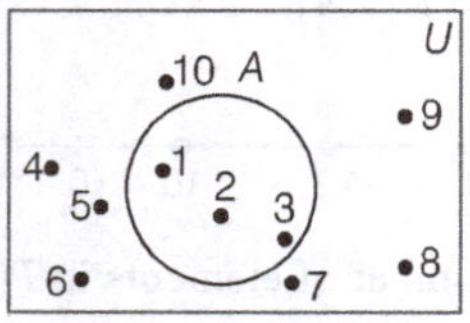

Example 1 Draw the Venn diagrams to illustrate the following relationship among sets E, M and U, where E is the set of students studying English in a school, M is the set of students studying Mathematics in the same school and U is the set of all students in that school.

(i) All the students who study Mathematics also study English, but some students who study English do not study Mathematics.

(ii) Not all students study Mathematics, but every student studying English studies Mathematics.

[NCERT Exemplar]

Sol. Given, E = Set of students studying English

M = Set of students studying Mathematics

and U = Set of all students

(i) Since, all of the students who study Mathematics also study English, but some students who study English do not study Mathematics.

$\therefore \quad M \subset E \subset U$

Through Venn diagram, we represent it as

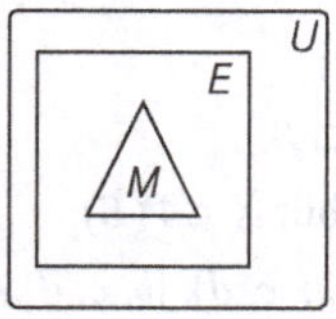

(ii) Since, every student studying English studies Mathematics.

$\therefore \quad E \subset M \subset U$

Through Venn diagram, we represent it as

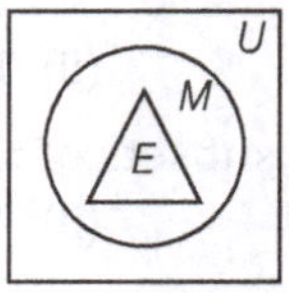

Operations on Sets

There are some operations which when performed on two sets give rise to another set. Here, we will define certain operations on sets and examine their properties.

Union of Sets

Let A and B be any two sets. Then, the union of A and B is the set of all those elements which belong to either A or B or both. It is denoted by $A \cup B$ and read as **A union B**. The symbol '$\cup$' is used to denote the union.

$\therefore \quad A \cup B = \{x : x \in A \text{ or } x \in B\}$

e.g. Let $A = \{2, 3\}$ and $B = \{3, 4, 5\}$.

Then, $A \cup B = \{2, 3, 4, 5\}$

The union of sets A and B is represented by the following Venn diagram

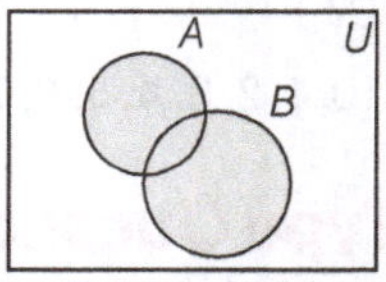

Here, shaded portion represents $A \cup B$.

Example 2 Find the union of each of the following pairs of sets.

(i) $A = \{a, e, i, o, u\}$, $B = \{a, c, d\}$

(ii) $A = \{1, 3, 5\}$, $B = \{2, 4, 6\}$

(iii) $A = \{x : x$ is a natural number and $1 < x \le 5\}$ and $B = \{x : x$ is a natural number and $5 < x \le 10\}$

Sol. (i) Given, $A = \{a, e, i, o, u\}$, $B = \{a, c, d\}$

$\therefore A \cup B = \{a, c, d, e, i, o, u\}$

(ii) Given, $A = \{1, 3, 5\}$, $B = \{2, 4, 6\}$

$\therefore A \cup B = \{1, 2, 3, 4, 5, 6\}$

(iii) Given, $A = \{x : x$ is a natural number and $1 < x \le 5\}$

$\Rightarrow \quad A = \{2, 3, 4, 5\}$

and $B = \{x : x$ is a natural number and $5 < x \le 10\}$

$\Rightarrow \quad B = \{6, 7, 8, 9, 10\}$

Now, $A \cup B = \{2, 3, 4, 5\} \cup \{6, 7, 8, 9, 10\}$

$= \{2, 3, 4, 5, 6, 7, 8, 9, 10\}$

Example 3 Is it true that for any sets A and B, $P(A) \cup P(B) = P(A \cup B)$? Justify your answer. **[NCERT]**

Sol. Let $A = \{1, 2\}$ and $B = \{2, 3\}$.

Then, $A \cup B = \{1, 2, 3\}$

Now, $P(A) = \{\phi, \{1\}, \{2\}, \{1, 2\}\}$

and $P(B) = \{\phi, \{2\}, \{3\}, \{2, 3\}\}$

$\therefore \quad P(A) \cup P(B) = \{\phi, \{1\}, \{2\}, \{3\}, \{1, 2\}, \{2, 3\}\}$ ...(i)

Now, $P(A \cup B) = \{\phi, \{1\}, \{2\}, \{3\}, \{1, 2\}, \{1, 3\}, \{2, 3\}, \{1, 2, 3\}\}$ ...(ii)

From Eqs. (i) and (ii), we observe that

$$P(A \cup B) \neq P(A) \cup P(B)$$

Hence, the given statement is not true.

Example 4 Suppose $A_1, A_2, \ldots, A_{30}$ are thirty sets each having 5 elements and $B_1, B_2, \ldots, B_n$ are n sets each with 3 elements, let $\bigcup_{i=1}^{30} A_i = \bigcup_{i=1}^{n} B_j = S$ and each element of 'S' belongs to exactly 10 of the A_i's and exactly 9 of the B_j. Find 'n'. **[NCERT Exemplar]**

Sol. If elements are not repeated, then number of elements in $A_1 \cup A_2 \cup A_3 \cup \ldots \cup A_{30}$ is 30×5.

But each element is used 10 times.

$$\therefore \quad n(S) = \frac{30 \times 5}{10} = 15$$

If elements in $B_1, B_2, \ldots, B_n$ are not repeated, then total number of elements is $3n$ but each element is repeated 9 times, so $n(S) = \frac{3n}{9}$

$$\Rightarrow \quad 15 = \frac{3n}{9} \Rightarrow n = 45$$

Example 5 Let $S =$ Set of points inside the square, $T =$ Set of points inside the triangle and $C =$ Set of points inside the circle. If the triangle and circle intersect each other and are contained in a square. Then, prove that $S \cup T \cup C = S$, by Venn diagram. **[NCERT Exemplar]**

Sol. Given, $S =$ Set of points inside the square

$T =$ Set of points inside the triangle

and $C =$ Set of points inside the circle.

According to the given condition, the Venn diagram is given below

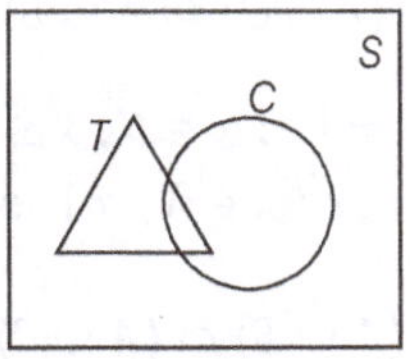

It is clear from the Venn diagram that $S \cup T \cup C = S$.

Laws of Union of Sets

For any three sets A, B and C, we have

(i) $A \cup \phi = A$ [Identity law]

(ii) $U \cup A = U$ [Universal law]

(iii) $A \cup A = A$ [Idempotent law]

(iv) $A \cup B = B \cup A$ [Commutative law]

(v) $(A \cup B) \cup C = A \cup (B \cup C)$ [Associative law]

(vi) $A \subseteq A \cup B$ and $B \subseteq A \cup B$

(vii) If $A \subseteq B$, then $A \cup B = B$

Example 6 If $A = \{1, 2, 3, 4\}$, $B = \{3, 4, 5, 6\}$, $C = \{5, 6, 7, 8\}$ and $D = \{7, 8, 9, 10\}$, then find

(i) $A \cup B \cup C$ (ii) $B \cup C \cup D$ **[NCERT]**

Sol. Given, $A = \{1, 2, 3, 4\}$, $B = \{3, 4, 5, 6\}$, $C = \{5, 6, 7, 8\}$

and $D = \{7, 8, 9, 10\}$

(i) $A \cup B \cup C = (A \cup B) \cup C$
$= (\{1, 2, 3, 4\} \cup \{3, 4, 5, 6\}) \cup \{5, 6, 7, 8\}$
$= \{1, 2, 3, 4, 5, 6\} \cup \{5, 6, 7, 8\}$
$= \{1, 2, 3, 4, 5, 6, 7, 8\}$

(ii) $B \cup C \cup D = (B \cup C) \cup D$
$= (\{3, 4, 5, 6\} \cup \{5, 6, 7, 8\}) \cup \{7, 8, 9, 10\}$
$= \{3, 4, 5, 6, 7, 8\} \cup \{7, 8, 9, 10\}$
$= \{3, 4, 5, 6, 7, 8, 9, 10\}$

Intersection of Sets

Let A and B be any two sets. The intersection of A and B is the set of all those elements which belong to both A and B. It is denoted by $A \cap B$ and read as **A intersection B**. The symbol '$\cap$' is used to denote the intersection.

$$\therefore \quad A \cap B = \{x : x \in A \text{ and } x \in B\}$$

The intersection of sets A and B is represented by the following Venn diagram

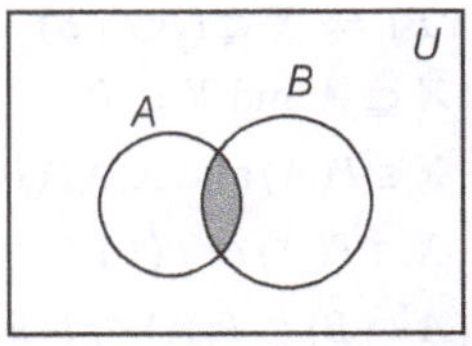

Here, shaded portion represents $A \cap B$.

Overlapping and Disjoint Sets

Two sets are called **overlapping (or joint) sets**, if they have atleast one element in common. e.g. The sets $A = \{1, 2, 5, 7\}$ and $B = \{2, 3, 9, 11\}$ are overlapping sets, since the elements 2 is common in them.

Example 7 Find the intersection of each of the following pairs of sets.

(i) $A = \{1, 3, 5, 7, 9\}, B = \{2, 3, 6, 8, 9\}$
(ii) $A = \{e, f, g\}, B = \phi$
(iii) $A = \{x : x = 3n, n \in Z\}, B = \{x : x = 4n, n \in Z\}$,

Sol. (i) Given, $A = \{1, 3, 5, 7, 9\}$ and $B = \{2, 3, 6, 8, 9\}$

$\therefore \quad A \cap B = \{3, 9\}$

[$\because$ 3 and 9 are only elements which are common]

(ii) Given, $A = \{e, f, g\}$ and $B = \phi$

$\therefore \quad A \cap B = \phi$ [since, there is no common element]

(iii) Let $x \in A \cap B$

$\Rightarrow x \in A$ and $x \in B$

$\Rightarrow x$ is a multiple of 3 and x is a multiple of 4.

$\Rightarrow x$ is a multiple of 3 and 4 both.

$\Rightarrow x$ is a multiple of 12.

$\Rightarrow x = 12n, n \in Z$

$\therefore A \cap B = \{x : x = 12n, n \in Z\}$

Example 8 For any natural number a, we define $aN = \{an : n \in N\}$. If $b, c, d \in N$ such that $bN \cap cN = dN$, then prove that d is the LCM of b and c.

Sol. Given, $aN = \{an : n \in N\}$

= Set of positive integral multiple of a.

Similarly, $bN = \{bn : n \in N\}$

= Set of positive integral multiple of b

and $cN = \{cn : n \in N\}$

= Set of positive integral multiple of c

$\therefore$ $bN \cap cN$ = Set of positive integral multiple of both b and c.

$\Rightarrow bN \cap cN = \{\lambda n : n \in N\}$, where λ is LCM of b and c.

Hence, d is the LCM of b and c. **Hence proved.**

Example 9 For any two sets A and B, prove that $P(A \cap B) = P(A) \cap P(B)$.

Sol. Let $X \in P(A \cap B) \Rightarrow X \subseteq (A \cap B)$

$\Rightarrow \quad X \subseteq A$ and $X \subseteq B$

$\Rightarrow \quad X \in P(A)$ and $X \in P(B)$

$\Rightarrow \quad X \in P(A) \cap P(B)$

$\therefore \quad P(A \cap B) \subseteq P(A) \cap P(B)$ ...(i)

Again, let $Y \in P(A) \cap P(B)$

$\Rightarrow \quad Y \in P(A)$ and $Y \in P(B)$

$\Rightarrow \quad Y \subseteq A$ and $Y \subseteq B$

$\Rightarrow \quad Y \subseteq A \cap B$

$\Rightarrow \quad Y \in P(A \cap B)$

$\therefore \quad P(A) \cap P(B) \subseteq P(A \cap B)$ ...(ii)

From Eqs. (i) and (ii), we get

$P(A \cap B) = P(A) \cap P(B)$ **Hence proved.**

Laws of Intersection of Sets

For any three sets, A, B and C, we have

(i) $A \cap \phi = \phi$ [Law of ϕ]
(ii) $U \cap A = A$ [Identity law]
(iii) $A \cap A = A$ [Idempotent law]
(iv) $A \cap B = B \cap A$ [Commutative law]
(v) $(A \cap B) \cap C = A \cap (B \cap C)$ [Associative law]
(vi) If $A \subseteq B$, then $A \cap B = A$
(vii) $A \cap B \subseteq A$ and $A \cap B \subseteq B$
(viii) **Distributive Law**
 (a) $A \cap (B \cup C) = (A \cap B) \cup (A \cap C)$
 (b) $A \cup (B \cap C) = (A \cup B) \cap (A \cup C)$

Example 10 If $A = \{4, 5, 7, 8, 10\}$, $B = \{4, 5, 9\}$ and $C = \{1, 4, 6, 9\}$, then verify that

(i) $(A \cap B) \cap C = A \cap (B \cap C)$
(ii) $A \cup (B \cap C) = (A \cup B) \cap (A \cup C)$

Sol. Given, $A = \{4, 5, 7, 8, 10\}$,

$B = \{4, 5, 9\}$ and $C = \{1, 4, 6, 9\}$

(i) Clearly, $A \cap B = \{4, 5, 7, 8, 10\} \cap \{4, 5, 9\} = \{4, 5\}$

$\therefore \quad$ LHS $= (A \cap B) \cap C$

$= \{4, 5\} \cap \{1, 4, 6, 9\} = \{4\}$ ...(i)

Now, $B \cap C = \{4, 5, 9\} \cap \{1, 4, 6, 9\} = \{4, 9\}$

$\therefore \quad$ RHS $= A \cap (B \cap C)$

$= \{4, 5, 7, 8, 10\} \cap \{4, 9\} = \{4\}$ ...(ii)

From Eqs. (i) and (ii), we get

LHS = RHS = $\{4\}$

Hence, $(A \cap B) \cap C = A \cap (B \cap C)$

(ii) Here, $B \cap C = \{4, 9\}$

$\therefore \quad$ LHS $= A \cup (B \cap C) = \{4, 5, 7, 8, 10\} \cup \{4, 9\}$

$\Rightarrow \quad$ LHS $= \{4, 5, 7, 8, 9, 10\}$ ...(iii)

Now, $A \cup B = \{4, 5, 7, 8, 10\} \cup \{4, 5, 9\}$

$= \{4, 5, 7, 8, 9, 10\}$

and $A \cup C = \{4, 5, 7, 8, 10\} \cup \{1, 4, 6, 9\}$

$= \{1, 4, 5, 6, 7, 8, 9, 10\}$

$\therefore \quad$ RHS $= (A \cup B) \cap (A \cup C)$

$= \{4, 5, 7, 8, 9, 10\} \cap \{1, 4, 5, 6, 7, 8, 9, 10\}$

$= \{4, 5, 7, 8, 9, 10\}$ ...(iv)

From Eqs. (iii) and (iv), we get

LHS = RHS = $\{4, 5, 7, 8, 9, 10\}$

Hence, $A \cup (B \cap C) = (A \cup B) \cap (A \cup C)$

Example 11 If $A = \{x : x \in N, x \le 7\}$, $B = \{x : x$ is prime, $x < 8\}$ and $C = \{x : x \in N, x$ is odd and $x < 10\}$, verify that

(i) $A \cup (B \cap C) = (A \cup B) \cap (A \cup C)$
(ii) $A \cap (B \cup C) = (A \cap B) \cup (A \cap C)$

Sol. Given, $A = \{x : x \in N, x \leq 7\} = \{1, 2, 3, 4, 5, 6, 7\}$

$B = \{x : x \text{ is prime}, x < 8\} = \{2, 3, 5, 7\}$

and $C = \{x: x \in N, x \text{ is odd and } x < 10\} = \{1, 3, 5, 7, 9\}$

(i) Clearly, $A \cup B = \{1, 2, 3, 4, 5, 6, 7\} = A$,

$A \cup C = \{1, 2, 3, 4, 5, 6, 7, 9\}$, $B \cap C = \{3, 5, 7\}$

Now, $A \cup (B \cap C) = \{1, 2, 3, 4, 5, 6, 7\} = A$ ...(i)

and $(A \cup B) \cap (A \cup C) = \{1, 2, 3, 4, 5, 6, 7\} = A$ ...(ii)

From Eqs. (i) and (ii), we get

$A \cup (B \cap C) = (A \cup B) \cap (A \cup C)$

(ii) Clearly, $A \cap B = \{2, 3, 5, 7\} = B$

$A \cap C = \{1, 3, 5, 7\}$, $B \cup C = \{1, 2, 3, 5, 7, 9\}$

Now, $A \cap (B \cup C) = \{1, 2, 3, 5, 7\}$ ...(i)

and $(A \cap B) \cup (A \cap C) = \{1, 2, 3, 5, 7\}$ ...(ii)

From Eqs. (i) and (ii), we get

$A \cap (B \cup C) = (A \cap B) \cup (A \cap C)$

Example 12 For any two sets A and B, prove that

(i) $A \cup (A \cap B) = A$ (ii) $A \cap (A \cup B) = A$

Sol. (i) $A \cup (A \cap B) = (A \cup A) \cap (A \cup B)$

[by distributive law]

$= A \cap (A \cup B) = A$ $[\because A \subseteq A \cup B]$

(ii) $A \cap (A \cup B) = (A \cap A) \cup (A \cap B)$

[by distributive law]

$= A \cup (A \cap B) = A$ $[\because A \cap B \subseteq A]$

Hence proved.

Example 13 Let A and B be two sets. If $A \cap X = B \cap X = \phi$ and $A \cup X = B \cup X$ for some set X, then prove that $A = B$.

Sol. Given, $A \cup X = B \cup X$

$\Rightarrow A \cap (A \cup X) = A \cap (B \cup X)$

$\Rightarrow$ $A = (A \cap B) \cup (A \cap X)$

$[\because A \subseteq A \cup X \Rightarrow A \cap (A \cup X) = A]$

$\Rightarrow$ $A = (A \cap B) \cup \phi \Rightarrow A = A \cap B$

$\Rightarrow$ $A \subseteq B$ $[\because A \cap B \subseteq B]$ ...(i)

Again, $A \cup X = B \cup X$

$\Rightarrow$ $B \cap (A \cup X) = B \cap (B \cup X)$

$\Rightarrow$ $(B \cap A) \cup (B \cap X) = B$

$[\because B \subseteq B \cup X \Rightarrow B \cap (B \cup X) = B]$

$\Rightarrow$ $(B \cap A) \cup \phi = B$ $[\because B \cap X = \phi]$

$\Rightarrow$ $B \cap A = B$

$\Rightarrow$ $B \subseteq A$ $[\because B \cap A \subseteq A]$ ...(ii)

From Eqs. (i) and (ii), we get

$A = B$ **Hence proved.**

Example 14 For any two sets A and B, prove that $A \cup B = A \cap B \Leftrightarrow A = B$.

Sol. Let $A = B$, then $A \cup B = A$ and $A \cap B = A$

$\Rightarrow$ $A \cup B = A \cap B$

Thus, $A = B$

$\Rightarrow$ $A \cup B = A \cap B$ ...(i)

Conversely, let $A \cup B = A \cap B$

Now, let $x \in A \Rightarrow x \in A \cup B$

$\Rightarrow$ $x \in A \cap B$ $[\because A \cup B = A \cap B]$

$\Rightarrow$ $x \in A$ and $x \in B$

$\Rightarrow$ $x \in B$

$\therefore$ $A \subseteq B$ ...(ii)

Now, let $y \in B \Rightarrow y \in A \cup B$

$\Rightarrow$ $y \in A \cap B$ $[\because A \cup B = A \cap B]$

$\Rightarrow$ $y \in A$ and $y \in B$

$\Rightarrow$ $y \in A$

$\therefore$ $B \subseteq A$ ...(iii)

From Eqs. (ii) and (iii), we get $A = B$

Thus, $(A \cup B) = (A \cap B)$

$\Rightarrow$ $A = B$ ...(iv)

From Eqs. (i) and (iv), we get

$A \cup B = A \cap B \Leftrightarrow A = B$ **Hence proved.**

Difference of Sets

Let A and B be any two sets. Then, the difference of sets A and B in this order is the set of all those elements of A which do not belong to B. It is denoted by $\boldsymbol{A - B}$ and read as ***A* minus *B***. The symbol '–' is used to denote the difference of sets.

$\therefore$ $A - B = \{x : x \in A \text{ and } x \notin B\}$

Similarly, $B - A = \{x : x \in B \text{ and } x \notin A\}$

The difference of two sets A and B can be represented by the following Venn diagram

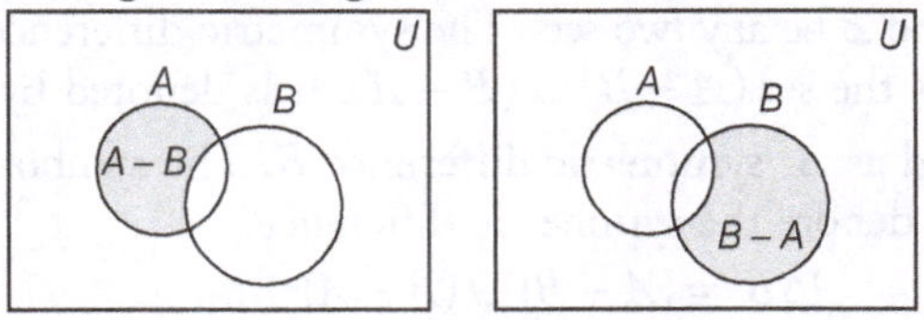

Here, shaded portion represents the difference of two sets A and B.

Example 15

(i) If $X = \{a, b, c, d, e, f\}$ and $Y = \{f, b, d, g, h, k\}$, then find $X - Y$ and $Y - X$.

(ii) If $A = \{1, 2, 3, 4, 5\}$ and $B = \{2, 4, 6\}$, then find $A - B$ and $B - A$.

Also, represent each of these by Venn Diagram.

Sol. (i) Given, $X = \{a, b, c, d, e, f\}$

and $Y = \{f, b, d, g, h, k\}$

$\therefore$ $X - Y = \{a, b, c, d, e, f\} - \{f, b, d, g, h, k\}$

$= \{a, c, e\}$

[only those elements of X which do not belong to Y]

and $Y - X = \{f, b, d, g, h, k\} - \{a, b, c, d, e, f\}$

$= \{g, h, k\}$

[only those elements of Y which do not belong to X]

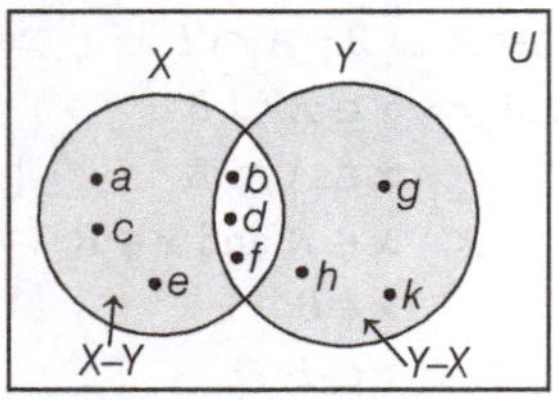

(ii) Given, $A = \{1, 2, 3, 4, 5\}$ and $B = \{2, 4, 6\}$

$\therefore \quad A - B = \{1, 2, 3, 4, 5\} - \{2, 4, 6\}$

$\Rightarrow \quad A - B = \{1, 3, 5\}$

[only those elements of A which do not belong to B]

and $B - A = \{2, 4, 6\} - \{1, 2, 3, 4, 5\} = \{6\}$

[only those elements of B which do not belongs to A]

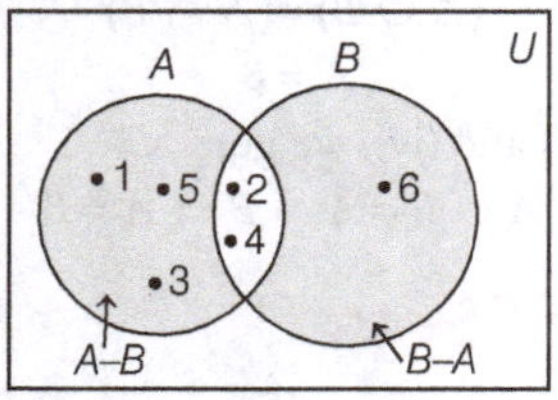

Example 16 If A, B and C are three sets such that $A \subset B$, then prove that $C - B \subset C - A$.

Sol. Let $\quad x \in C - B \Rightarrow x \in C$ and $x \notin B$

$\Rightarrow \quad x \in C$ and $x \notin A \quad [\because A \subset B]$

$\Rightarrow \quad x \in C - A$

$\therefore \quad C - B \subset C - A$ **Hence proved.**

Symmetric Difference of Two Sets

Let A and B be any two sets. The symmetric difference of A and B is the set $(A - B) \cup (B - A)$. It is denoted by $A \Delta B$ and read as A **symmetric difference** B. The symbol 'Δ' is used to denote the symmetric difference.

$$\therefore \quad A \Delta B = (A - B) \cup (B - A)$$

$$= \{x : x \in A \text{ or } x \in B \text{ but } x \notin A \cap B\}$$

The symmetric difference of sets A and B can be represented by the following Venn diagram

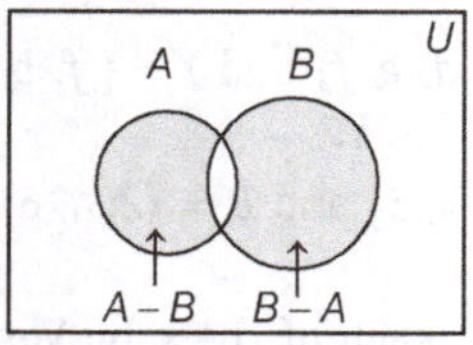

Here, shaded portion represents the symmetric difference of sets A and B.

e.g. Let $A = \{1, 2, 3, 4\}$ and $B = \{3, 4, 5, 6\}$.

Then, $A - B = \{1, 2\}$, $B - A = \{5, 6\}$

Now, $A \Delta B = (A - B) \cup (B - A) = \{1, 2, 5, 6\}$

Two sets A and B are said to be **disjoint sets** or **mutually exclusive,** if they have **no common element** i.e. $A \cap B = \phi$.

The disjoint of two sets A and B can be represented by the following Venn diagram e.g. Let $A = \{2, 4, 6\}$ and $B = \{1, 3, 5\}$.

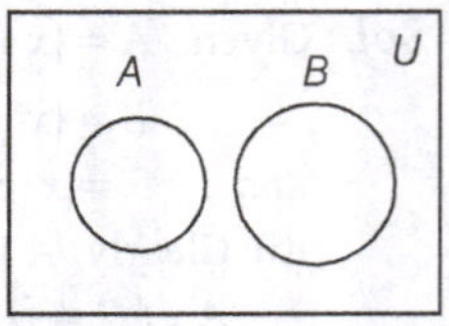

Then, $A \cap B = \phi$. Hence, A and B are disjoint sets.

Note The sets $A - B$, $A \cap B$ and $B - A$ are mutually disjoint sets i.e. the intersection of any of these two sets is an empty set.

Example 17 Find the symmetric difference of sets $A = \{1, 3, 5, 6, 7\}$ and $B = \{3, 7, 8, 9\}$.

Sol. Given sets are $A = \{1, 3, 5, 6, 7\}$ and $B = \{3, 7, 8, 9\}$.

Now, $A - B = \{1, 3, 5, 6, 7\} - \{3, 7, 8, 9\} = \{1, 5, 6\}$

[set of those elements of A, which are not present in B]

and, $B - A = \{3, 7, 8, 9\} - \{1, 3, 5, 6, 7\} = \{8, 9\}$

[set of those elements of B, which are not present in A]

$\therefore$ Required symmetric difference,

$A \Delta B = (A - B) \cup (B - A) = \{1, 5, 6\} \cup \{8, 9\} = \{1, 5, 6, 8, 9\}$

Example 18 Let $A = \{1, 2, 4, 5\}$, $B = \{2, 3, 5, 6\}$, $C = \{4, 5, 6, 7\}$, verify that $A \cap (B \Delta C) = (A \cap B) \Delta (A \cap C)$.

Sol. Given, $A = \{1, 2, 4, 5\}$, $B = \{2, 3, 5, 6\}$ and $C = \{4, 5, 6, 7\}$

Now, $A \cap B = \{2, 5\}$ and $A \cap C = \{4, 5\}$

and $\quad B \Delta C = (B - C) \cup (C - B)$

$= (B \cup C) - (B \cap C) = \{2, 3, 4, 7\}$

$\therefore \quad A \cap (B \Delta C) = \{2, 4\}$ ...(i)

and $(A \cap B) \Delta (A \cap C) = \{2, 4\}$ ...(ii)

From Eqs. (i) and (ii), we get

$A \cap (B \Delta C) = (A \cap B) \Delta (A \cap C)$ **Hence proved.**

Example 19 Which of the following pairs of sets are disjoint?

(i) $A = \{1, 2, 3, 4, 5, 6\}$ and $B = \{x : x$ is a natural number and $4 \le x \le 6\}$

(ii) $A = \{x : x$ is the boys of your school$\}$ and $B = \{x : x$ is the girls of your school$\}$

Sol. (i) Given, $A = \{1, 2, 3, 4, 5, 6\}$ and $B = \{4, 5, 6\}$

$\therefore \quad A \cap B = \{1, 2, 3, 4, 5, 6\} \cap \{4, 5, 6\} = \{4, 5, 6\} \ne \phi$

Hence, this pair of sets is not disjoint.

(ii) Let $A = \{b_1, b_2, \ldots, b_n\}$ and $B = \{g_1, g_2, \ldots, g_m\}$

where, $b_1, b_2, \ldots, b_n$ are the boys and $g_1, g_2, \ldots, g_m$ are the girls of school.

Clearly, $\quad A \cap B = \phi$

Hence, this pair of sets is disjoint set.

Law of Difference of Sets

(a) For any two sets A and B, we have

(i) If $A \subset B$, then $A - B = \phi$ and $B - A \neq \phi$

(ii) If $A = \phi$, then $A - B = \phi$ and $B - A = B$

(iii) $A - B \subseteq A$

(iv) $B - A \subseteq B$

(v) $A - B = A \Leftrightarrow A \cap B = \phi$

(vi) $(A - B) \cup B = A \cup B$

(vii) $(A - B) \cap B = \phi$

(viii) $(A - B) \cup (B - A) = (A \cup B) - (A \cap B)$

(b) If A, B and C are any three sets, then

(i) $A - (B \cap C) = (A - B) \cup (A - C)$

(ii) $A - (B \cup C) = (A - B) \cap (A - C)$

(iii) $A \cap (B - C) = (A \cap B) - (A \cap C)$

(iv) $A \cap (B \Delta C) = (A \cap B) \Delta (A \cap C)$

Example 20 Show that

(i) $A \cap (B - C) = (A \cap B) - (A \cap C)$.

(ii) $A \cap (B \Delta C) = (A \cap B) \Delta (A \cap C)$.

Sol. (i) Let x be any arbitrary element of $A \cap (B - C)$.

i.e., $x \in A \cap (B - C)$

$\Rightarrow$ $x \in A$ and $x \in B - C$

$\Rightarrow$ $x \in A$ and ($x \in B$ and $x \notin C$)

$\Rightarrow$ ($x \in A$ and $x \in B$) and ($x \in A$ and $x \notin C$)

$\Rightarrow$ $x \in (A \cap B)$ and $x \notin (A \cap C)$

$\Rightarrow$ $x \in (A \cap B) - (A \cap C)$

$\Rightarrow$ $A \cap (B - C) \subseteq (A \cap B) - (A \cap C)$ ...(i)

Now, let y be any arbitrary element of $(A \cap B) - (A \cap C)$

Then, $y \in (A \cap B) - (A \cap C)$

$\Rightarrow$ $y \in (A \cap B)$ and $y \notin (A \cap C)$

$\Rightarrow$ ($y \in A$ and $y \in B$) and ($y \in A$ and $y \notin C$)

$\Rightarrow$ $y \in A$ and ($y \in B$ and $y \notin C$)

$\Rightarrow$ $y \in A$ and $y \in B - C$

$\Rightarrow$ $y \in A \cap (B - C)$

$\Rightarrow$ $(A \cap B) - (A \cap C) \subseteq A \cap (B - C)$ ...(ii)

From Eqs. (i) and (ii), we get

$A \cap (B - C) = (A \cap B) - (A \cap C)$

(ii) LHS $= A \cap (B \Delta C) = A \cap [(B - C) \cup (C - B)]$

$[\because A \Delta B = (A - B) \cup (B - A)]$

$= [A \cap (B - C)] \cup [A \cap (C - B)]$

$[\because \cap$ distribute over $\cup]$

$= [(A \cap B) - (A \cap C)] \cup [(A \cap C) - (A \cap B)]$

$= (A \cap B) \Delta (A \cap C) =$ RHS **Hence proved.**

Complement of a Set

Let U be the universal set and A be any subset of U, then complement of A with respect to U is the set of all those elements of U which are not in A. It is denoted by $\overline{A}$ or A' and read as, '**A complement**'.

Thus, $\overline{A} = \{x : x \in U$ and $x \notin A\}$ or $A' = U - A$

The complement of set A is represented by the following Venn diagram

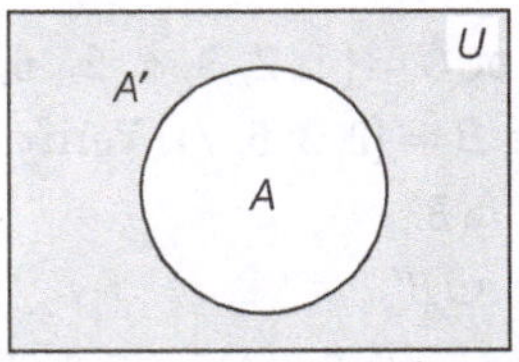

Here, the shaded portion represents the complement of set A.

e.g. Let $U = \{1, 2, 3, 4, 5, 6\}$ and $A = \{2, 4\}$.

Then, $A' = U - A = \{1, 2, 3, 4, 5, 6\} - \{2, 4\} = \{1, 3, 5, 6\}$

Note If A is a subset of the universal set U, then its complement A' is also a subset of U.

Properties of Complement of Sets

(i) $(A')' = A = U - A'$ [Law of double complementation]

(ii) (a) $A \cup A' = U$

(b) $A \cap A' = \phi$ [Complement laws]

(iii) (a) $\phi' = U$

(b) $U' = \phi$ [Laws of empty set and universal set]

(iv) $(A \cup B)' = U - (A \cup B)$

(v) **De Morgan's Law** If A and B are any two sets, then

(a) $(A \cup B)' = A' \cap B'$ (b) $(A \cap B)' = A' \cup B'$

(vi) (a) $A - B = A \cap B'$ (b) $B - A = B \cap A'$

Example 21 Let $U = \{1, 2, 3, 4, 5, 6, 7, 8, 9\}$, $A = \{1, 2, 3, 4\}$, $B = \{2, 4, 6, 8\}$ and $C = \{3, 4, 5, 6\}$. Find

(i) A' (ii) B' (iii) $(A \cap C)'$

(iv) $(A \cup B)'$ (v) $(A')'$ (vi) $(B - C)'$

Sol. Given, $U = \{1, 2, 3, 4, 5, 6, 7, 8, 9\}$, $A = \{1, 2, 3, 4\}$

$B = \{2, 4, 6, 8\}$ and $C = \{3, 4, 5, 6\}$

(i) $A' = U - A = \{1, 2, 3, 4, 5, 6, 7, 8, 9\} - \{1, 2, 3, 4\}$
$= \{5, 6, 7, 8, 9\}$

(ii) $B' = U - B = \{1, 2, 3, 4, 5, 6, 7, 8, 9\} - \{2, 4, 6, 8\}$
$= \{1, 3, 5, 7, 9\}$

(iii) $A \cap C = \{3, 4\}$

$\therefore$ $(A \cap C)' = U - (A \cap C)$
$= \{1, 2, 3, 4, 5, 6, 7, 8, 9\} - \{3, 4\}$
$= \{1, 2, 5, 6, 7, 8, 9\}$

(iv) $A \cup B = \{1, 2, 3, 4, 6, 8\}$

$(A \cup B)' = U - (A \cup B) = \{1, 2, 3, 4, 5, 6, 7, 8, 9\}$
$- \{1, 2, 3, 4, 6, 8\} = \{5, 7, 9\}$

(v) $(A')' = U - A' = \{1, 2, 3, 4, 5, 6, 7, 8, 9\} - \{5, 6, 7, 8, 9\}$
$= \{1, 2, 3, 4\}$ [using part (i)]

(vi) Now, $B - C = \{2, 8\}$

$\therefore \quad (B - C)' = U - (B - C)$
$= \{1, 2, 3, 4, 5, 6, 7, 8, 9\} - \{2, 8\}$
$= \{1, 3, 4, 5, 6, 7, 9\}$

Example 22 Let $U = \{1, 2, 3, 4, 5, 6, 7, 8, 9\}$, $A = \{2, 4, 6, 8\}$ and $B = \{2, 3, 5, 7\}$. Verify that **[NCERT]**

(i) $(A \cup B)' = A' \cap B'$

(ii) $(A \cap B)' = A' \cup B'$

Sol. (i) We have, $U = \{1, 2, 3, 4, 5, 6, 7, 8, 9\}$

$A = \{2, 4, 6, 8\}$ and $B = \{2, 3, 5, 7\}$

$\therefore \quad A \cup B = \{2, 4, 6, 8\} \cup \{2, 3, 5, 7\}$
$= \{2, 3, 4, 5, 6, 7, 8\}$

and $(A \cup B)' = U - (A \cup B)$
$= \{1, 2, 3, 4, 5, 6, 7, 8, 9\} - \{2, 3, 4, 5, 6, 7, 8\}$
$= \{1, 9\}$ ...(i)

Now, $A' = U - A$
$= \{1, 2, 3, 4, 5, 6, 7, 8, 9\} - \{2, 4, 6, 8\}$
$= \{1, 3, 5, 7, 9\}$

and $B' = U - B = \{1, 2, 3, 4, 5, 6, 7, 8, 9\} - \{2, 3, 5, 7\}$
$= \{1, 4, 6, 8, 9\}$

$\therefore A' \cap B' = \{1, 3, 5, 7, 9\} \cap \{1, 4, 6, 8, 9\} = \{1, 9\}$ ...(ii)

From Eqs. (i) and (ii), we get

$(A \cup B)' = A' \cap B'$

(ii) Here, $A \cap B = \{2, 4, 6, 8\} \cap \{2, 3, 5, 7\} = \{2\}$

$\therefore \quad (A \cap B)' = U - (A \cap B)$
$= \{1, 2, 3, 4, 5, 6, 7, 8, 9\} - \{2\}$

$\Rightarrow (A \cap B)' = \{1, 3, 4, 5, 6, 7, 8, 9\}$ ...(i)

Now, $A' \cup B' = \{1, 3, 5, 7, 9\} \cup \{1, 4, 6, 8, 9\}$
$= \{1, 3, 4, 5, 6, 7, 8, 9\}$ ...(ii)

From Eqs. (i) and (ii), we get

$(A \cap B)' = A' \cup B'$

Example 23 Prove that

$(A \cap B')' \cup (B \cap C) = A' \cup B.$ **[NCERT Exemplar]**

Sol. LHS $= (A \cap B')' \cup (B \cap C)$

$= \{A' \cup (B')'\} \cup (B \cap C)$ [by De Morgan's law]

$= (A' \cup B) \cup (B \cap C)$ $[\because (B')' = B]$

$= ((A' \cup B) \cup B) \cap ((A' \cup B) \cup C)$

$= (A' \cup (B \cup B)) \cap (A' \cup B \cup C)$

$= (A' \cup B) \cap (A' \cup B \cup C)$ $[\because B \cup B = B]$

$= (A' \cup B) =$ RHS $[\because A' \cup B \subset A' \cup B \cup C]$

Hence proved.

Example 24 Let A and B be two sets. Prove that $(A - B) \cup B = A$ if and only if $B \subset A$.

Sol. Let $(A - B) \cup B = A$

$\Rightarrow \quad (A \cap B') \cup B = A$ $[\because A - B = A \cap B']$

$\Rightarrow \quad (A \cup B) \cap (B' \cup B) = A$ [by distributive law]

$\Rightarrow \quad (A \cup B) \cap U = A$ $[\because B' \cup B = U]$

$\Rightarrow \quad A \cup B = A \Rightarrow B \subset A$

Conversely, let $B \subset A$

$\therefore (A - B) \cup B = (A \cap B') \cup B$
$= (A \cup B) \cap (B' \cup B)$ [by distributive law]
$= (A \cup B) \cap U$ $[\because B' \cup B = U]$
$= A \cup B = A$ $[\because B \subset A]$ **Hence proved.**

Example 25 Let A, B and C be three sets such that $A \cup B = C$ and $A \cap B = \phi$. Then, prove that $A = C - B$.

Sol. We have, $A \cup B = C$

$\therefore \quad C - B = (A \cup B) - B = (A \cup B) \cap B'$ $[\because X - Y = X \cap Y']$

$= (A \cap B') \cup (B \cap B')$ [by distributive law]

$= (A \cap B') \cup \phi = A \cap B' = A - B$

$= A$ $[\because A \cap B = \phi]$ **Hence proved.**

Topic Practice 3

Very Short Answer Type Questions

2 Marks

1 Let $A = \{a, e, i, o, u\}$ and $B = \{a, i, u\}$, then show that $A \cup B = A$.

2 Find the smallest set A such that $A \cup \{1, 2\} = \{1, 2, 3, 5, 9\}$.

3 If A and B are two sets such that $A \subset B$, then show that $A \cup B = B$. **[NCERT]**

4 If $A = \{3, 5, 7, 9, 11\}$, $B = \{7, 9, 11, 13\}$ and $C = \{11, 13, 15\}$, then find

(i) $A \cap B$ (ii) $B \cap C$

5 Let $A = \{x : x$ is a natural number$\}$ and $B = \{x : x$ is an even natural number$\}$. Find $A \cap B$.

6 Find $A \cap B$, if $A = \{3, 5, 7, 9, 11\}$ and $B = \{7, 9, 11, 13\}$. Also, represent it by Venn diagram. **[NCERT]**

7 For three sets A, B and C, show that $A \cap B = A \cap C$ need not imply $B = C$.

8 If $A = \{1, 3, 5, 7, 9\}$ and $B = \{2, 3, 5, 7, 11\}$, then find $A - B$.

9 Find $A-B$ and $B-A$, when $A=\{1, 2, 3, 4, 5, 6\}$ and $B=\{2, 4, 6, 8, 10\}$.

10 If $A=\{x: x \text{ is an even natural number}\}$ and $U=\{x: x \text{ is a natural number}\}$, then find A'.

11 If $X=\{x: x \text{ is a prime number}\}$ and $U=\{x: x \text{ is a natural number}\}$, then find X'.

12 Represent the following sets in Venn diagram.
(i) $A' \cap (B \cup C)$ (ii) $A' \cap (C-B)$

13 If $B' \subseteq A'$, then show that $A \subseteq B$.

14 Let $U=\{1, 2, 3, 4, 5, 6, 7, 8, 9, 10\}$, $A=\{1, 2, 3\}$, $B=\{2, 4, 6, 7\}$ and $C=\{2, 3, 4, 8\}$, then find $(B \cup C)'$, $(A \cup B)'$. **[NCERT Exemplar]**

Short Answer Type Questions

4 Marks

15 Let $A=\{x: x \in N\}$, $B=\{x: x=2n, n \in N\}$, $C=\{x: x=2n-1, n \in N\}$ and $D=\{x: x \text{ is a prime natural number}\}$. Find
(i) $A \cap B$ (ii) $A \cap C$ (iii) $B \cap C$ (iv) $B \cap D$

16 Let A, B and C be the sets such that $A \cup B = A \cup C$ and $A \cap B = A \cap C$. Show that $B = C$. **[NCERT]**

17 Which of the following pairs of sets are disjoint?
(i) $\{1, 2, 3, 4\}$ and $\{x: x \text{ is a natural number and } 4 \le x \le 6\}$
(ii) $\{a, e, i, o, u\}$ and $\{c, d, e, f\}$
(iii) $\{x: x \text{ is an even integer}\}$ and $\{x: x \text{ is an odd integer}\}$ **[NCERT]**

18 If $X=\{a, b, c, d\}$ and $Y=\{f, b, d, g\}$, then find **[NCERT]**
(i) $X \cup Y$ (ii) $X \cap Y$ (iii) $X-Y$ (iv) $Y-X$
Also, represent each of these by Venn diagram.

19 If $U=\{2, 3, 4, 5, 6, 7, 8, 9, 10, 11\}$, $A=\{2, 4, 7\}$, $B=\{3, 5, 7, 9, 11\}$ and $C=\{7, 8, 9, 10, 11\}$, then compute
(i) $(A \cap U) \cap (B \cup C)$ (ii) $C-B$ (iii) $B-C$

20 Let $A=\{3, 6, 12, 15, 18, 21\}$, $B=\{4, 8, 12, 16, 20\}$, $C=\{2, 4, 6, 8, 10, 12, 14, 16\}$ and $D=\{5, 10, 15, 20\}$. Find
(i) $A-B$ (ii) $A-C$ (iii) $B-C$ (iv) $B-D$

21 For any two sets A and B, show that the following statements are equivalent.
(i) $A \subset B$ (ii) $A-B=\phi$
(iii) $A \cup B = B$ (iv) $A \cap B = A$ **[NCERT]**

22 Find $A \Delta B$, if
(i) $A=\{1, 3, 4\}$ and $B=\{2, 5, 9, 11\}$.
(ii) $A=\{1, 3, 6, 11, 12\}$ and $B=\{1, 6\}$.

23 If $A=\{a, b, c, d, e\}$, $B=\{a, c, e, g\}$ and $C=\{b, e, f, g\}$, then verify that
(i) $A \cap (B-C) = (A \cap B) - (A \cap C)$
(ii) $A - (B \cap C) = (A-B) \cup (A-C)$

24 Taking the set of a natural numbers as the universal set, write down the complements of the following sets. **[NCERT]**
(i) $\{x: x \text{ is a natural number divisible by 3 and 5}\}$
(ii) $\{x: x \text{ is a perfect square}\}$
(iii) $\{x: x \text{ is a perfect cube}\}$
(iv) $\{x: x+5=8\}$ (v) $\{x: 2x+5=9\}$
(vi) $\{x: x \ge 7\}$ (vii) $\{x: x \in N, 2x+1>10\}$

25 If $U=\{1, 2, 3, 4, 5, 6, 7, 8, 9, 10\}$, $A=\{1, 3, 4\}$ and $B=\{5, 6\}$, verify that $A-B=A \cap B'=B'-A'$.

26 If $A=\{1, 3, 5, 7, 9, 11, 13, 15, 17\}$, $B=\{2, 4, \ldots, 18\}$ and N, the set of natural numbers is the universal set, then prove that $A' \cup \{(A \cup B) \cap B'\} = N$.

27 Let A and B be two sets. Using properties of set, prove that
(i) $A \cap B' = \phi \Rightarrow A \subseteq B$ (ii) $A' \cup B = U \Rightarrow A \subseteq B$

Hints & Answers

1. $A \cup B$ = set of those elements which belong to either A or B or both.
2. $A=\{3, 5, 9\}$
3. $A \subset B$ means that, all the elements of set A are in set B and there are some other elements in B. Also, we know that, $A \cup B$ contains all the elements which are either in A or in B or in both A and B.
4. Solve as Example 7 (i).
Ans. (i) $A \cap B=\{7, 9, 11\}$ (ii) $B \cap C=\{11, 13\}$
5. Given, $A=\{x: x \text{ is a natural number}\}=\{1, 2, 3, 4, \ldots\}$
and $B=\{x: x \text{ is an even natural number}\}=\{2, 4, 6, \ldots\}$
We observe that 2, 4, 6, ... are the elements which are common to both the sets A and B.
Ans. $A \cap B=\{2, 4, 6, \ldots\}=B$
6. $\therefore A \cap B=\{7, 9, 11\}$

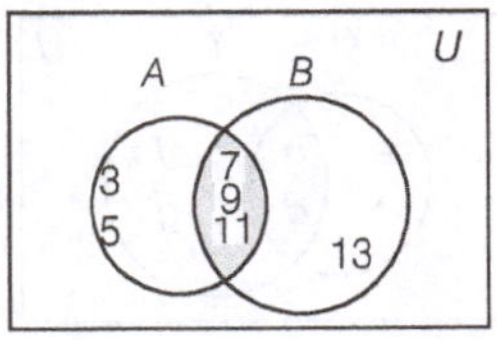

7. Let $A=\{1, 2, 3, 4\}$, $B=\{3, 4, 5, 6\}$ and $C=\{1, 3, 4, 7, 8\}$

8. Solve as Example 15 (ii). **Ans.** $A-B=\{1, 9\}$

9. $A-B=\{1, 3, 5\}$, $B-A=\{8, 10\}$

10. $\{x : x$ is an odd natural number$\}$

11. $\{x : x\in N$ and x is not a prime number$\}$

12.

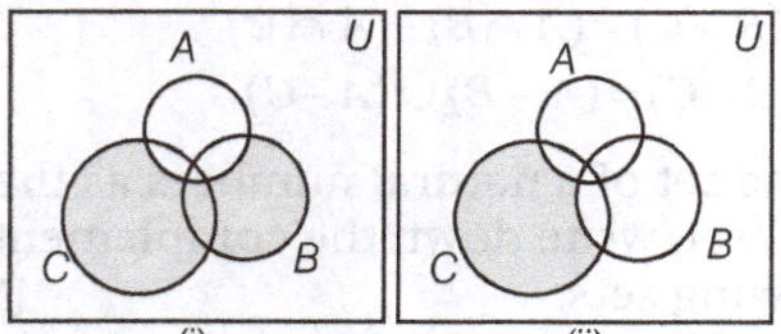

(i) (ii)

13. Let $x\in A \Rightarrow x\notin A'$

$\Rightarrow x\notin B'$ $[\because B'\subseteq A']$

$\Rightarrow x\in B$

14. $(B\cup C)'=\{1, 5, 9, 10\}$ and $(A\cup B)'=\{5, 8, 9, 10\}$

15. (i) $A\cap B=\{x : x=2n, n\in N\}=B$

(ii) $A\cap C=\{x : x=2n-1, n\in N\}=C$

(iii) $B\cap C=\{\}=\phi$

(iv) $B\cap D=\{2\}$

16. $A\cup B=A\cup C$

$\Rightarrow (A\cup B)\cap C=(A\cup C)\cap C$

$\Rightarrow (A\cap C)\cup(B\cap C)=C$

$\Rightarrow (A\cap B)\cup(B\cap C)=C$

Again, $A\cup B=A\cup C$

$\Rightarrow (A\cup B)\cap B=(A\cup C)\cap B$

$\Rightarrow B=(A\cap B)\cup(C\cap B)$

$\Rightarrow B=(A\cap B)\cup(B\cap C)$

From Eqs. (i) and (ii), we get

$B=C$

17. (i) $\{x : x$ is a natural number and $4\le x\le 6\}=\{4, 5, 6\}$

(ii) $A=\{a, e, i, o, u\}$, $B=\{c, d, e, f\}$

$\Rightarrow A\cap B=\{e\}$

(iii) $E=\{x: x$ is an even integer$\}=\{..., -4, -2, 0, 2, 4, 6, ...\}$

and $O=\{x : x$ is an odd integer$\}$

$=\{..., -5, -3, -1, 1, 3, 5, ...\}$

Ans. (iii)

18. (i) $X\cup Y=\{a, b, c, d, f, g\}$

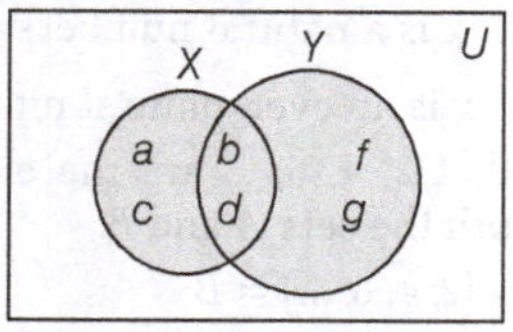

(ii) $X\cap Y=\{b, d\}$

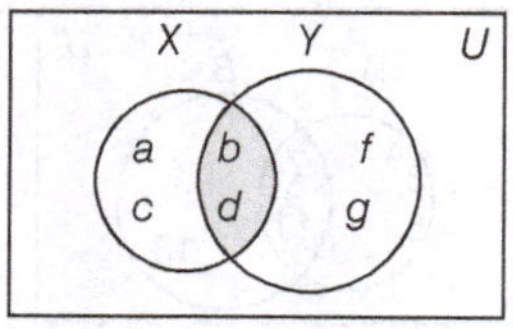

(iii) $X-Y=\{a, c\}$

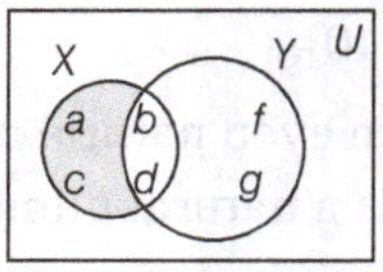

(iv) $Y-X=\{f, g\}$

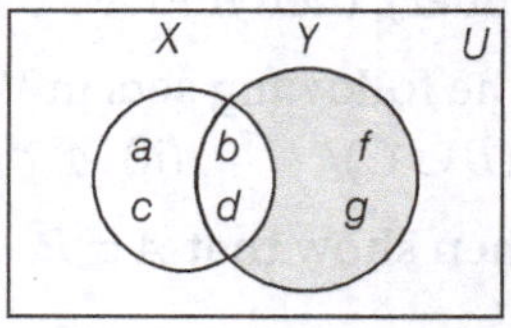

19. (i) $\{7\}$ (ii) $\{8, 10\}$ (iii) $\{3, 5\}$

20. (i) $\{3, 6, 15, 18, 21\}$ (ii) $\{3, 15, 18, 21\}$

(iii) $\{20\}$ (iv) $\{4, 8, 12, 16\}$

21. (ii) $\Rightarrow$ (iii) Let $A\subset B$.

$\because A\subset B$, therefore there is no element in A which does not belong to B.

$\therefore A-B=\phi$

(ii) $\Rightarrow$ (iii) We have, $A-B=\phi \Rightarrow A\subset B\Rightarrow A\cup B=B$

(iii) $\Rightarrow$ (iv) We have, $A\cup B=B\Rightarrow A\subset B\Rightarrow A\cap B=A$

(iv) $\Rightarrow$ (i) We have, $A\cap B=A\Rightarrow A\subset B$

22. Similar as Example 18. (i) $\{1, 2, 3, 4, 5, 9, 11\}$ (ii) $\{3, 11, 12\}$

23. Find LHS and RHS, separately, to verify the result.

24. (i) $\{x : x\in N$ and x is not divisible by $15\}$

(ii) $\{x : x\in N$ and x is not a perfect square$\}$

(iii) $\{x : x\in N$ and x is not a perfect cube$\}$

(iv) $\{x : x\in N$ and $x\ne 3\}$

(v) $\{x : x\in N$ and $x\ne 2\}$

(vi) $\{x : x\in N$ and $x<7\}$

(vii) $\left\{x : x\in N \text{ and } x\le \frac{9}{2}\right\}$

25. $A'=\{2, 5, 6, 7, 8, 9, 10\}$

$B'=\{1, 2, 3, 4, 7, 8, 9, 10\}$

$A\cap B'=\{1, 3, 4\}$

and $B'-A'=\{1, 3, 4\}$

26. $A\cup B=\{1, 2, 3, 4, 5, ..., 16, 17, 18\}$

$A'=\{2, 4, 6, 8, 10, ..., 18, 19, 20\ 21, 22, ...\}$

$B'=\{1, 3, 5, 7, 9, ..., 17, 19, 20, 21, 22, ...\}$

$\therefore (A\cup B)\cap B'=\{1, 3, 5, 7, 9, ...17\}$

27. (i) $A=A\cap U=A\cap(B\cup B')$

$=(A\cap B)\cup(A\cap B')=(A\cap B)\cup\phi$

$\Rightarrow A=A\cap B \Rightarrow A\subseteq B$

(ii) $A'\cup B=U\Rightarrow(A'\cup B)'=U'$

$\Rightarrow (A')'\cap B'=\phi$

$\Rightarrow A\cap B'=\phi$

Now, from part (i), we get

$A\subseteq B$

Chapter Practice

Multiple Choice Type Questions

1 Mark

1. Let $B = \left\{x : x = \frac{1}{2n-1}, 1 \le n \le 5, \text{ where } n \in N\right\}$, then B equals

(a) $\left\{1, \frac{1}{3}, \frac{1}{5}, \frac{1}{9}, \frac{1}{11}\right\}$ (b) $\left\{1, \frac{1}{3}, \frac{1}{7}, \frac{1}{9}, \frac{1}{11}\right\}$

(c) $\left\{1, \frac{1}{3}, \frac{1}{5}, \frac{1}{7}, \frac{1}{9}\right\}$ (d) None of these

2. The set $(A \cap B')' \cup (B \cap C)$ is equal to **[NCERT Exemplar]**

(a) $A' \cup B \cup C$ (b) $A' \cup B$

(c) $A' \cup C'$ (d) $A' \cap B$

3. If A and B are two sets, then $A \cap (A \cup B)$ equals to **[NCERT Exemplar]**

(a) A (b) B (c) ϕ (d) $A \cap B$

4. Two finite sets have m and n elements. The number of subsets of the first set is 112 more than of the second. The values of m and n are respectively

(a) 4, 7 (b) 7, 4 (c) 4, 4 (d) 7, 7

5. The intersection of all the intervals having the form $\left[1 + \frac{1}{n}, 6 - \frac{2}{n}\right]$, where n is a positive integer, is

(a) [1, 6] (b) (1, 6) (c) [2, 4] (d) $\left[\frac{3}{2}, 5\right]$

Assertion-Reason Type Questions

1 Mark

Directions (Q. Nos. 6-9) *In the questions given below are two statements labelled as Assertion (A) and Reason (R). In the context of the two statements, which one of the following is correct?*

(a) Both A and R are correct; R is the correct explanation of A
(b) Both A and R are correct; R is not the correct explanation of A
(c) A is correct; R is incorrect
(d) R is correct; A is incorrect

6. **Assertion (A)** If $A = \{1, 3, 5, 7, 9\}$ and $B = \{2, 3, 5, 7, 11\}$. Then, A and B are intersecting sets.

Reason (R) Sets A and B are intersecting if $A \cap B \ne \phi$.

7. **Assertion (A)** If $A = \{x : x \in N, x \text{ is a factor of } 6\}$ and $B = \{x \in N : x \text{ is a factor of } 8\}$, then $A - B$ is $\{4, 6\}$.

Reason (R) For any sets A and B, their difference $(A - B)$ is defined as $(A - B) = \{x : x \in A \text{ and } x \notin B\}$.

8. **Assertion (A)** If $A = \{x : x \in N, x \text{ is a factor of } 12\}$ and $B = \{x : x \in N, x \text{ is a factor of } 18\}$, then $A \cap B$ is $\{1, 3, 4, 6\}$.

Reason (R) If two sets are A and B, then $A \cap B = \{x: x \in A \text{ and } x \in B\}$.

9. **Assertion (A)** If $A = \{2, 4, 6\}$ and $B = \{1, 3, 5\}$. Then, A and B are disjoint sets.

Reason (R) Sets A and B are disjoint of $A \cap B = \phi$.

Very Short Answer Type Questions

2 Marks

10. What is the difference between a collection and a set? Give reason to support your answer.

11. Match each of the sets on the left described in the roster form with the same set on the right described in the set-builder form.

(i) {H, R, A, Y, N}	(a) $\{x : x$ is a natural number and a divisor of 18$\}$
(ii) {L, I, T, E}	(b) $\{x : x$ is a letter of the word HARYANA$\}$
(iii) {1, 2, 3,4, 6, 12}	(c) $\{x : x$ is a letter of the word LITTLE$\}$
(iv) {1, 2, 3, 6, 9, 18}	(d) $\{x : x$ is a natural number and a divisor of 12$\}$

12. Find the number of subsets of the set $A = \{1, 4, 5\}$.

13. List all the proper subsets of the set $A = \{a, b\}$.

14. Which of the following sets are empty set, singleton set and equal sets.

$A = \{x : 2x = 10 \text{ and } x^2 - 7x + 10 = 0\}$
$B = \{x : x^2 - 16x + 55 = 0 \text{ and } x^2 = 25\}$
$C = \left\{x : -\frac{1}{2} \leq x \leq \frac{1}{2}\right\}, D = \{x : 0 \leq 4x^2 \leq 1\}$

15. Let A and B be two sets. Then, prove that $A = B \Leftrightarrow A \subseteq B$ and $B \subseteq A$.

16. If $A = \{1, 2, 3, 4, 5\}$, $B = \{1, 3, 5, 8\}$, $C = \{2, 5, 7, 8\}$, verify that $A - (B \cup C) = (A - B) \cap (A - C)$.

17. Express the shaded region of the following Venn diagram in terms of union and difference of sets A, B and C.

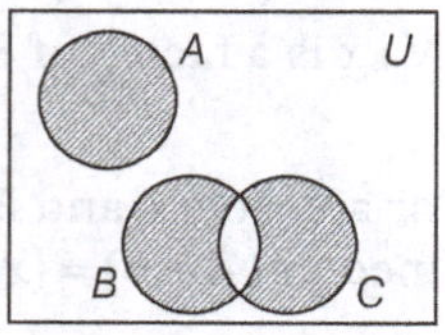

18. If $U = \{a, b, c, d, e, f\}$, $A = \{a, b, c\}$, $B = \{c, d, e, f\}$, $C = \{c, d, e\}$ and $D = \{d, e, f\}$, then calculate the following sets.

(i) $A \cap D$ (ii) $A \cap C$ (iii) $U \cap D$
(iv) $A \cup \phi$ (v) $(U \cap \phi)'$ (vi) $(U \cup A)'$.

Short Answer Type Questions

4 Marks

19. Let A, B and C be three sets.

If $A \in B$ and $B \subseteq C$, is it true that $A \subseteq C$? If not given an example.

20. Two finite sets have m and n elements. The total number of subsets of the first set is 56 more than the total number of subsets of the second set. Find the values of m and n.

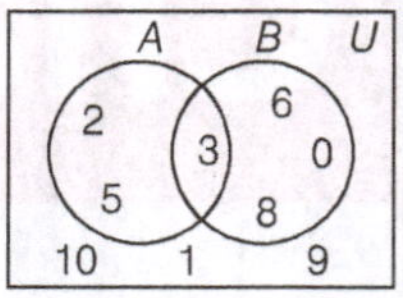

21. A is the set of all integers from 20 to 70, both inclusive.

$B = \{x : x \in A, x \text{ is a perfect square}\}$
$C = \{x : x \in A, x \text{ is a prime number}\}$
$D = \{x : x \in A, x \text{ is the first digit of } x > \text{its second digit}\}$

then, find the following sets.

(i) $B \cap C$ (ii) $B \cap D$ (iii) $B \cap C \cap D$

22. From the adjoining Venn diagram, determine the following sets.

(i) $A \cup B$ (ii) $A \cap B$
(iii) $A - B$ (iv) $(A \cap B)'$

Case-Based Type Questions

6 Marks

23. A class teacher Mamta Sharma of class XI write three sets A, B and C are such that

$A = \{1, 3, 5, 7, 9\}$, $B = \{2, 4, 6, 8\}$ and $C = \{2, 3, 5, 7, 11\}$,

then answer the following question which are based on above sets.

(i) Find $A \cap B$. (ii) Find $A \cap C$.
(iii) Find $A \cup (B \cap C)$. (iv) Find $A \cup B \cup C$.
(v) Find $(A \cup B) \cap (A \cup C)$.

Hints & Answers

1. (c) **2.** (b) **3.** (a) **4.** (b) **5.** (c)
6. (a) **7.** (d) **8.** (d) **9.** (a)

10. Every set is a collection but a collection is not necessarily a set. Only well-defined collection are sets e.g. Collection of most talented writers of India is a collection but it is not a set.

11. (i) → (b); (ii) → (c), (iii) → (d); (iv) → (a)

12. Numbr of subsets of $A = 2^3$ **Ans.** 8

13. ϕ, $\{a\}$, $\{b\}$

14. $A = \{x : x = 5 \text{ and } (x - 2)(x - 5) = 0\} = \{5\}$

$B = \{x : (x - 11)(x - 5) = 0 \text{ and } x = \pm 5\} = \{5\}$

$C = \left\{x : -\frac{1}{2} \leq x \leq \frac{1}{2}\right\}$ and $D = \{x : 0 \leq 4x^2 \leq 1\}$

$= \left\{x : 0 \leq x^2 \leq \frac{1}{4}\right\} = \left\{x : -\frac{1}{2} \leq x \leq \frac{1}{2}\right\}$

Ans. A and B are singleton sets, C and D are equal sets.

15. See the theory of subset at page 8.

16. $A - (B \cup C) = \{4\}$

and $(A - B) \cup (A - C) = \{2, 4\} \cup \{1, 3, 4\} = \{4\}$

17. $A \cup (B \,\Delta\, C)$ or $A \cup \{(B - C) \cup (C - B)\}$

18. (i) ϕ (ii) $\{c\}$ (iii) $\{d, e, f\}$ (iv) $\{a, b, c\}$ (v) U (vi) ϕ

19. Let $A = \{a\}$, $B = \{\{a\}, b\}$ and $C = \{\{a\}, b, c\}$.

20. $2^m = 56 + 2^n \Rightarrow 2^m - 2^n = 56$

Ans. $m = 6, n = 3$

21. (i) ϕ (ii) $\{64\}$ (iii) ϕ

22. (i) $\{0, 2, 3, 5, 6, 8\}$ (ii) $\{3\}$
(iii) $\{2, 5\}$ (iv) $\{0, 1, 2, 5, 6, 8, 9, 10\}$

23. (i) ϕ (ii) $\{3, 5, 7\}$
(iii) $\{1, 2, 3, 5, 7, 9\}$ (iv) $\{1, 2, 3, 4, 5, 6, 7, 8, 9, 11\}$
(v) $\{1, 2, 3, 5, 7, 9, 11\}$

CHAPTER

02

Relations and Functions

- Cartesian Product
- Relations
- Functions
- Some Standard Real Functions
- Operations on Real Functions

In our daily life, we come across many patterns that characterise relations such as brother and sister, father and son, husband and wife. In this chapter, we will learn how to link pairs of objects from two sets and then introduce relations between the two objects in pairs.

TOPIC 01 Cartesian Product

Ordered Pairs

If a pair of elements written in circular bracket and grouped together in a particular order, then such a pair, is called an **ordered pair**. Ordered pair is written by listing two objects in the specific order, separated by **comma** (,) and enclosing the pair in **parentheses**.

e.g. The ordered pair of two elements a and b is denoted by (a, b) : a is first element (or first component) and b is second element (or second component).

Equality of Ordered Pairs

Two ordered pairs are equal, if their corresponding elements are equal.

i.e. $(a, b) = (c, d) \Rightarrow a = c$ and $b = d$

Graphically, ordered pair (a, b) represents a point in cartesian plane. So, ordered pair (2, 3) implies that **abscissa** $x = 2$ and **ordinate** $y = 3$.

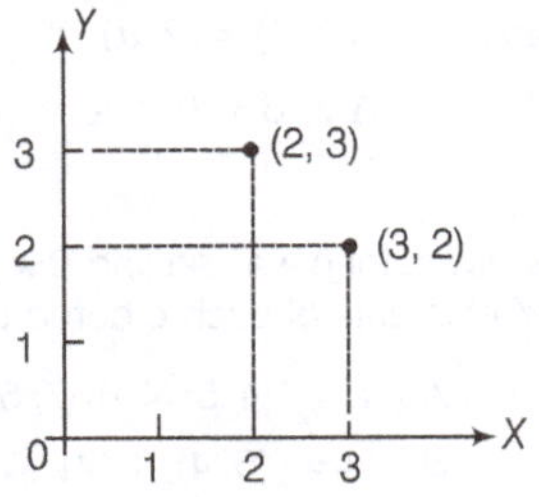

It is clear from the above graph that ordered pairs (2, 3) and (3, 2) represent two different points and hence they are not equal.

Note

(i) An ordered pair is not a set consisting of two elements. The order of two elements in an ordered pair is important and the two elements need not to be distinct.

(ii) $(a, b) \neq (b, a)$

(iii) (a, b) and $\{a, b\}$ are different to each other since, (a, b) is an ordered pair and $\{a, b\}$ is a set.

Example 1 Find the values of a and b, if

(i) $(2a-5, 4) = (5, b+6)$ (ii) $(a-3, b+7) = (3, 7)$

Sol. We know that, two ordered pairs are equal, if their corresponding elements are equal.

(i) $(2a-5, 4) = (5, b+6) \Rightarrow 2a-5 = 5$ and $4 = b+6$ [equating corresponding elements]

$\Rightarrow$ $2a = 5+5$ and $4-6 = b$

$\Rightarrow$ $2a = 10$ and $-2 = b$

$\Rightarrow$ $a = 5$ and $b = -2$

(ii) $(a-3, b+7) = (3, 7)$

$\Rightarrow a-3 = 3$ and $b+7 = 7$ [equating corresponding elements]

$\Rightarrow$ $a = 3+3$ and $b = 7-7$

$\Rightarrow$ $a = 6$ and $b = 0$

Example 2 Express $\{(x, y) : x + y = 10$, where $x, y \in N\}$ as a set of ordered pairs.

Sol. We have, $x + y = 10$ and $x, y \in N$

$\therefore$ When $x = 1$, $y = 10 - 1 = 9$

$x = 2$, $y = 10 - 2 = 8$

$x = 3$, $y = 10 - 3 = 7$

$x = 4$, $y = 10 - 4 = 6$

$x = 5$, $y = 10 - 5 = 5$

$x = 6$, $y = 10 - 6 = 4$

$x = 7$, $y = 10 - 7 = 3$

$x = 8$, $y = 10 - 8 = 2$

$x = 9$, $y = 10 - 9 = 1$

Hence, the required set of ordered pairs is

$\{(1, 9), (2, 8), (3, 7), (4, 6), (5, 5), (6, 4), (7, 3), (8, 2), (9, 1)\}$.

Cartesian (or Cross) Product of Two Sets

The set of all ordered pairs (a, b) such that $a \in A$ and $b \in B$, is called the cartesian product of sets A and B and is denoted by $A \times B$.

Or

For two non-empty sets A and B, the cartesian product $A \times B$ is the set of all ordered pairs of elements from sets A and B.

In symbolic form, it can be written as

$$A \times B = \{(a, b) : a \in A, b \in B\}$$

Note

(i) $A \times B \neq B \times A$.

(ii) $A \times B = \phi$, when either A or B is empty set.

(iii) $A \times B \neq \phi$ if and only if $A \neq \phi$ and $B \neq \phi$

Method to Write the Cartesian Product of Two Sets

If two sets say A and B are given, then we can write the cartesian product $A \times B$ with the help of following steps

***Step* I** First, write the given sets in tabular form (if not given in tabular form).

***Step* II** Now, take an element from first set say A and form all ordered pairs with this element as first element and elements of set B as second element.

***Step* III** Now, choose another element from first set A and form all ordered pairs with this element as first element and elements of set B as second element.

***Step* IV** Repeat above steps for all elements of first set A and get all ordered pairs.

Now, the set of all ordered pairs, obtained in steps II, III and IV, represent the cartesian product $A \times B$.

Example 3 Let $A = \{a, b, c\}$ and $B = \{x : x \in N, x$ is a prime number less than $5\}$. Find $A \times B$ and $B \times A$. Show that $A \times B \neq B \times A$.

Sol. Given sets are $A = \{a, b, c\}$

and $B = \{x : x \in N, x$ is a prime number less than $5\} = \{2, 3\}$

For element a of set A, all ordered pairs are $(a, 2), (a, 3)$.

For element b of set A, all ordered pairs are $(b, 2), (b, 3)$.

For element c of set A, all ordered pairs are $(c, 2), (c, 3)$.

$\therefore$ $A \times B = \{(a, 2) (a, 3), (b, 2) (b, 3) (c, 2) (c, 3)\}$

For element 2 of set B, all ordered pairs are $(2, a), (2, b), (2, c)$.

For element 3 of set B, all ordered pairs are $(3, a), (3, b), (3, c)$.

$B \times A = \{(2, a), (2, b), (2, c), (3, a), (3, b), (3, c)\}$

Since, $(a, 2) \neq (2, a)$

$\therefore$ $A \times B \neq B \times A$

Note

If $A \times B$ is given, then we can find $B \times A$ from it, just by reversing the position of elements of each ordered pair.

e.g. If $A \times B = \{(4, 5) (4, 6) (7, 5) (7, 6)\}$, then

$B \times A = \{(5, 4), (6, 4), (5, 7), (6, 7)\}$

Method to Find the Sets when Cartesian Product is Given

Sometimes the cartesian product of two sets or some elements of cartesian product of two sets are given and we have to find the sets.

For finding these two sets, we write first element of each ordered pair in first set say A and corresponding second element in second set B (say).

Example 4 If $A \times B = \{(a, 1), (b, 3), (a, 3), (b, 1), (a, 2), (b, 2)\}$. Then, find A and B.

Sol. Here, first element of each ordered pair of $A \times B$ gives the elements of set A and corresponding second element gives the elements of set B.

$\therefore \quad A = \{a, b\}$ and $B = \{1, 3, 2\}$

Note We write each element only one time in set, if it occurs more than one time.

Number of Elements in Cartesian Product of Two Sets

(i) If there are p elements in set A and q elements in set B, then there will be pq elements in $A \times B$ i.e. if $n(A) = p$ and $n(B) = q$, then $n(A \times B) = pq$.

(ii) If A and B are non-empty sets and either A or B is an infinite set, then $A \times B$ will also be an infinite set.

(iii) If A or B is the null set or an empty set, then $A \times B$ will also be an empty set, i.e. $A \times B = \phi$.

Note If there are p elements in set A and q elements in set B, then the number of subsets of $A \times B$ is 2^{pq}.

Example 5 If the set A has 3 elements and set B has 4 elements, then find the number of elements in $A \times B$.

Sol. Given, $n(A) = 3$ and $n(B) = 4$.

$\therefore$ The number of elements in $A \times B$ is

$$n(A \times B) = n(A) \times n(B) = 3 \times 4 = 12$$

Example 6 A and B are two sets given in such a way that $A \times B$ contains 6 elements. If three elements of $A \times B$ are (1, 3), (2, 5) and (3, 3), find A, B and remaining elements of $A \times B$.

Sol. It is given that $A \times B$ contains 6 elements and (1, 3), (2, 5) and (3, 3) are in $A \times B$. It follows that 1, 2, 3 are elements of A and 3, 5 are elements of B.

$\therefore \quad A = \{1, 2, 3\}$ and $B = \{3, 5\}$

$\therefore \quad A \times B = \{1, 2, 3\} \times \{3, 5\}$

$\Rightarrow \quad = \{(1, 3), (1, 5), (2, 3), (2, 5), (3, 3), (3, 5)\}$

Hence, the remaining elements of $(A \times B)$ are (1, 5), (2, 3), (3, 5).

Example 7 The cartesian product $P \times P$ has 16 elements among which are found $(a, 1)$ and $(b, 2)$. Find the set P and the remaining elements of $P \times P$.

Sol. Given, $\quad n(P \times P) = 16$

$\Rightarrow \quad n(P) \cdot n(P) = 16$

$\Rightarrow \quad n(P) = 4 \quad$ ... (i)

Now, as $\quad (a, 1) \in P \times P$

$\therefore \quad a \in P$ and $1 \in P$

Again, $\quad (b, 2) \in P \times P$

$\therefore \quad b \in P$ and $2 \in P$

$\Rightarrow \quad a, b, 1, 2 \in P$

From Eq. (i), it is clear that P has exactly four elements.

$\therefore \quad P = \{a, b, 1, 2\}$

Now, $P \times P = \{a, b, 1, 2\} \times \{a, b, 1, 2\}$

$= \{(a, a), (a, b), (a, 1), (a, 2), (b, a), (b, b), (b, 1), (b, 2)$
$(1, a), (1, b), (1, 1), (1, 2), (2, a), (2, b), (2, 1), (2, 2)\}$

Hence, the remaining elements of $P \times P$ are $(a, a), (a, b), (a, 2), (b, a), (b, b), (b, 1), (1, a), (1, b), (1, 1), (1, 2), (2, a), (2, b), (2, 1)$ and $(2, 2)$.

Example 8 Let P and Q be two sets such that $n(P) = 3$ and $n(Q) = 4$. If $(r, 4), (g, 1), (w, 3)$ and $(r, 9)$ are in $P \times Q$, then find P and Q, where r, g, w are where distinct elements. Also, write the remaining elements of $P \times Q$.

Sol. Since, r, g, w are distinct elements and $(r, 4), (g, 1), (w, 3), (r, 9)$ are elements of $P \times Q$.

$\therefore r, g, w \in P$ and $1, 3, 4, 9 \in Q$

$\because \quad n(P) = 3$ and $n(Q) = 4$

$\therefore \quad P = \{r, g, w\}$

and $\quad Q = \{1, 3, 4, 9\}$

Now, $P \times Q = \{r, g, w\} \times \{1, 3, 4, 9\}$

$= \{(r, 1), (r, 3), (r, 4), (r, 9), (g, 1), (g, 3), (g, 4), (g, 9), (w, 1), (w, 3), (w, 4)$ and $(w, 9)\}$

Hence, the remaining elements of $P \times Q$ are $(r, 1), (r, 3), (g, 3), (g, 4), (g, 9), (w, 1), (w, 4)$ and $(w, 9)$.

Example 9 Let $A = \{1, 2\}$ and $B = \{3, 4\}$. How many subsets will $A \times B$ have? List them.

Sol. Given, $A = \{1, 2\}$ and $B = \{3, 4\}$

$\Rightarrow \quad n(A) = 2$ and $n(B) = 2$

$\therefore$ Total subsets of $A \times B = 2^{2 \times 2} = 2^4 = 16$

[$\because$ number of subsets $= 2^{pq}$]

Hence, the subsets of $A \times B$ are

$\{(1, 3)\}, \{(1, 4)\}, \{(2, 3)\}, \{(2, 4)\}, \{(1, 3), (1, 4)\}, \{(1, 3), (2, 3)\}, \{(1, 3), (2, 4)\}, \{(1, 4), (2, 3)\}, \{(1, 4), (2, 4)\}, \{(2, 3), (2, 4)\}, \{(1, 3), (1, 4), (2, 3)\}, \{(1, 3), (1, 4), (2, 4)\}, \{(1, 3), (2, 3), (2, 4)\}, \{(1, 4), (2, 3), (2, 4)\}, \{(1, 3), (1, 4), (2, 3), (2, 4)\}$ and ϕ.

Graphical Representation of Cartesian Product of Two Sets

Let A and B be two non-empty sets and let (a, b) be an ordered pair, where $a \in A$ and $b \in B$. To represent it graphically, we draw two mutually perpendicular lines OX and OY intersecting each other at O and then we represent the elements of set A on horizontal line OX and elements of set B on vertical line OY by taking a suitable scale on OX and OY.

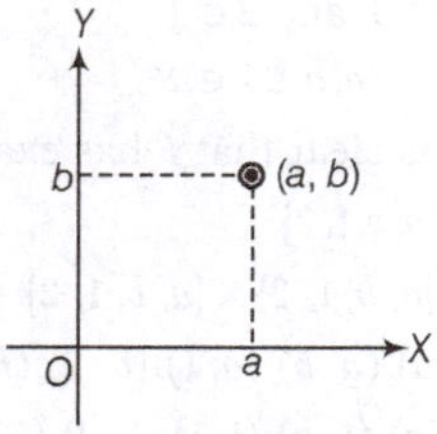

The point of intersection of a vertical line through a and horizontal line through b represent the ordered pair (a, b).

In this manner, we mark the points corresponding to each ordered pair in $A \times B$. The set of points so obtained represents $A \times B$ graphically.

Method to Represent Cartesian Product of Two Sets on Graph

We can represent the cartesian product of two sets on graph by representing each ordered pair on graph. For this, we use the following steps

***Step* I** Write the given sets in tabular form (if not given in tabular form).

***Step* II** Find the cartesian product of these two sets.

***Step* III** Draw two perpendicular lines OX and OY (say) intersecting at O and represent the elements of set A on OX and elements of set B on OY by taking a suitable scale on OX and OY.

***Step* IV** Draw vertical dotted lines through the points representing elements of set A on OX and draw horizontal dotted lines through the points representing elements of set B on OY

***Step* V** The point of intersections of these line (draw in step IV) represent the ordered pairs of cartesian product i.e. elements of cartesian product of given sets.

Example 10 Let $A = \{-1, 3, 4\}$ and $B = \{2, 3\}$. Represent the product $A \times B$ graphically.

Sol. Given sets are $A = \{-1, 3, 4\}$ and $B = \{2, 3\}$, which are in tabular form.

Now, $A \times B = \{(-1, 2), (-1, 3), (3, 2), (3, 3), (4, 2), (4, 3)\}$

Let us draw two perpendicular lines OX and OY intersecting at O. Represent the elements of set A i.e. $-1, 3, 4$ on horizontal line OX and elements of set B i.e. 2, 3 on vertical line OY, by taking 1cm = 1unit.

Draw vertical dotted lines through the points -1, 3 and 4 of OX and horizontal dotted lines through the points 2 and 3 of OY. Points of intersection of these lines are $(-1, 2), (-1, 3), (3, 3), (3, 2), (4, 3)$ and $(4, 2)$.

The points so obtained represent the cartesian product of sets A and B on graph.

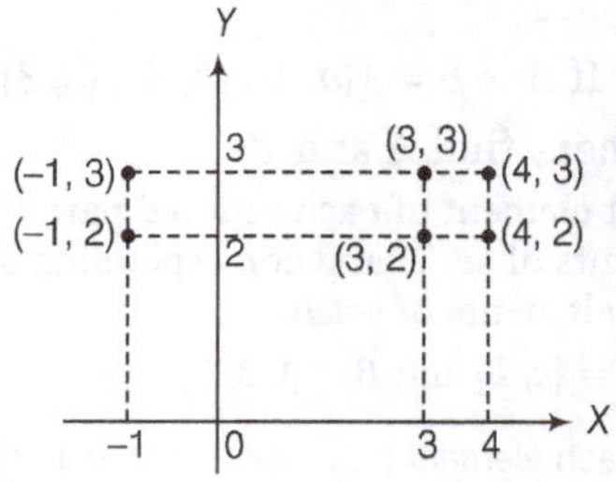

Example 11 If $A = \{2, 4, 6\}$ and $B = \{1, 4\}$, then show that $A \times B \neq B \times A$. Also, show it graphically.

Sol. We have, $A = \{2, 4, 6\}$ and $B = \{1, 4\}$

Then, $A \times B = \{(2, 1), (2, 4), (4, 1), (4, 4), (6, 1), (6, 4)\}$ ...(i)

and $B \times A = \{(1, 2), (1, 4), (1, 6), (4, 2), (4, 4), (4, 6)\}$ ...(ii)

From Eqs. (i) and (ii), we have $A \times B \neq B \times A$

Graphical Representation Firstly, draw two perpendicular lines, say OX and OY, intersecting at O.

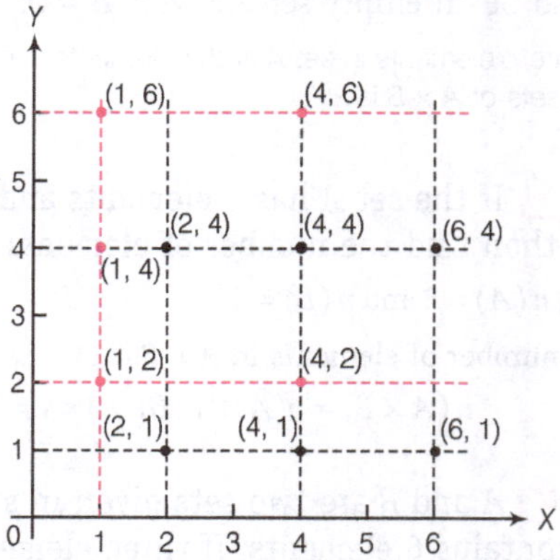

$A \times B$ To show $A \times B$ graphically, we draw three dotted vertical lines through 2, 4 and 6 of OX. Also, draw two dotted horizontal lines through 1 and 4 of OY. The point of intersection of these lines represents the ordered pairs of $A \times B$.

$B \times A$ Now, to show $B \times A$ graphically, we draw two dotted vertical lines through 1 and 4 of OX. Also, draw three dotted horizontal lines through 2, 4 and 6 of OY. The points of intersections of these lines represents the ordered pairs of $B \times A$.

Thus, from the graph, we can see that ordered pairs of $A \times B$ (**denoted by black dots**) have different position from the ordered pairs of $B \times A$ (**denoted by coloured dots**).

So, ordered pairs of both cartesian product represent different points on graph.

Hence, $A \times B \neq B \times A$.

Diagramatic Representation of Cartesian Product of Two Sets

In order to represent $A \times B$ by an **arrow diagram,** we first draw two circles representing sets A and B one opposite to the other as shown in the given figure and write the elements of sets in the corresponding circles.

Now, we draw line segments starting from each element of set A and terminating to each element of set B.

e.g. If $A = \{1, 2, 3\}$ and $B = \{f, g\}$, then following figure gives the arrow diagram of $A \times B$.

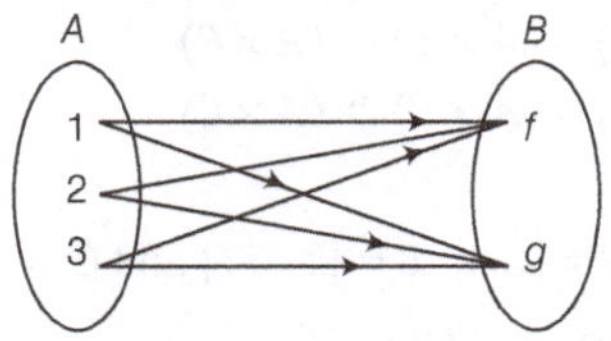

Example 12 If $A = \{1, 3, 6\}$ and $B = \{x, y\}$, then represent the following cartesian products by an arrow diagrams

(i) $A \times B$ (ii) $B \times A$
(iii) $A \times A$ (iv) $B \times B$

Sol. We have,

$$A = \{1, 3, 6\}, B = \{x, y\}$$

(i) $A \times B = \{1, 3, 6\} \times \{x\ y\}$
$= \{(1, x), (1, y), (3, x), (3, y), (6, x), (6, y)\}$

Required arrow diagram is

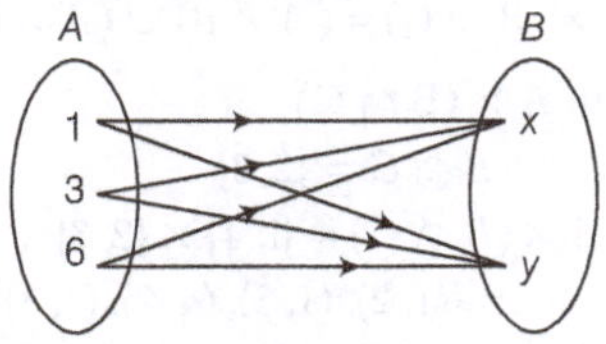

(ii) $B \times A = \{x, y\} \times \{1, 3, 6\}$
$= \{(x, 1), (x, 3), (x, 6), (y, 1), (y, 3), (y, 6)\}$

Required arrow diagram is

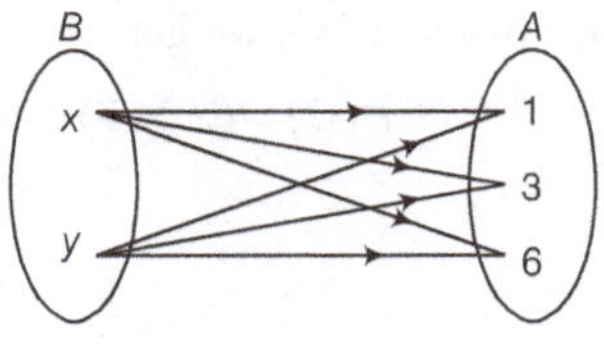

(iii) $A \times A = \{1, 3, 6\} \times \{1, 3, 6\}$
$= \{(1, 1), (1, 3), (1, 6), (3, 1), (3, 3), (3, 6), (6, 1), (6, 3) (6, 6)\}$

Required arrow diagram is

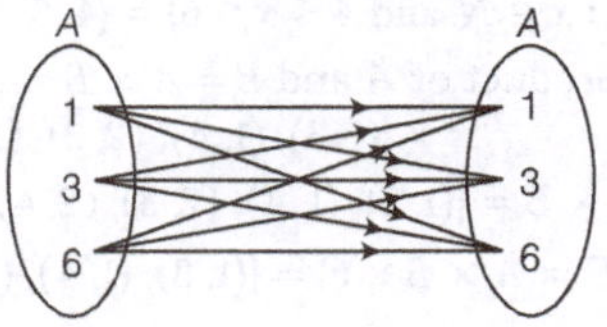

(iv) $B \times B = \{x, y\} \times \{x, y\}$
$= \{(x, x), (x, y), (y, x), (y, y)\}$

Required arrow diagram is

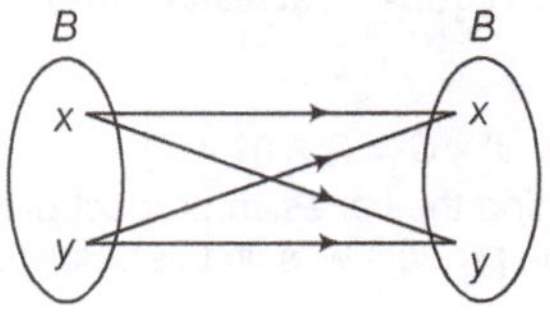

Ordered Triplet

An ordered triplet is a list of 3 elements written in a particular order and enclosed within the circular bracket. e.g. (1, 2, 3) is an ordered triplet. Ordered triplet is also called **3-tuple.**

Cartesian (or Cross) Product of Three Sets

If A, B and C are three sets, then

$$A \times B \times C = \{(a, b, c) : a \in A, b \in B, c \in C\}$$

Note In general, if $A_1, A_2, \ldots, A_n$ are n sets, then $(a_1, a_2, \ldots, a_n)$ is called a ***n*-tuple**, where $a_i \in A_i$, $i = 1, 2, \ldots, n$ and the set of all such n-tuples is called the cartesian product of $A_1, A_2, \ldots, A_n$ and is denoted by $A_1 \times A_2 \times \ldots \times A_n$.
In symbolic form, $A_1 \times A_2 \times \ldots \times A_n = \{(a_1, a_2, \ldots, a_n) : a_i \in A_i, 1 \leq i \leq n\}$.

Method to Write the Cartesian Product of Three Sets

Let three sets A, B and C be given, then to write the cartesian product $A \times B \times C$. We may use the following steps

***Step* I** First, write the given three sets A, B and C in tabular form (if not given in tabular form).

***Step* II** Take first two sets A and B and write the cartesian product of these two sets i.e. $A \times B$.

***Step* III** Now, consider the cartesian product obtained in step II as a set, say D, and then assume each ordered pair of $D (= A \times B)$ as element and write cartesian product of two sets D and C.

Now, the set of all ordered triplet, obtained in step III respresent the cartesian product $A \times B \times C$.

Example 13 Find the cartesian product of three sets $A = \{1, 2\}$, $B = \{3, 4\}$ and $C = \{x : x \in N \text{ and } 4 \le x \le 6\}$.

Sol. We have, $A = \{1, 2\}$, $B = \{3, 4\}$

and $C = \{x : x \in N \text{ and } 4 \le x \le 6\} = \{4, 5, 6\}$

Cartesian product of A and $B = A \times B = \{1, 2\} \times \{3, 4\}$
$= \{(1, 3), (1, 4), (2, 3), (2, 4)\}$

Let $D = A \times B = \{(1, 3), (1, 4), (2, 3), (2, 4)\}$

Now, $D \times C = A \times B \times C = \{(1, 3), (1, 4), (2, 3), (2, 4)\} \times \{4, 5, 6\}$
$= \{(1, 3, 4), (1, 3, 5), (1, 3, 6), (1, 4, 4) (1, 4, 5), (1, 4, 6)$
$(2, 3, 4), (2, 3, 5), (2, 3, 6), (2, 4, 4), (2, 4, 5), (2, 4, 6)\}$

It is the required cartesian product of three sets.

Note

(i) $A \times B \times C = (A \times B) \times C = A \times (B \times C)$
So, we can also find the cartesian product of last two sets and then the cartesian product with first set. But position of sets will not change.

(ii) If A, B and C are non-empty sets, then
$n(A \times B \times C) = n(A) \times n(B) \times n(C)$

Example 14 If $A = \{1, 2\}$, then find $A \times A \times A$.

Sol. We have,
$A \times A = \{1, 2\} \times \{1, 2\} = \{(1, 1), (1, 2), (2, 1), (2, 2)\}$
Now, $(A \times A) \times A = A \times A \times A$
$= \{(1, 1), (1, 2), (2, 1), (2, 2)\} \times \{1, 2\}$
$= \{(1, 1, 1), (1, 1, 2), (1, 2, 1), (1, 2, 2),$
$(2, 1, 1), (2, 1, 2), (2, 2, 1), (2, 2, 2)\}$

Theorems Based on Cartesian Product of Sets

In this section, we intend to study some results on cartesian product of sets which are given as theorems.

1. For any three non-empty sets A, B and C, we have
   (i) $A \times (B \cup C) = (A \times B) \cup (A \times C)$
   (ii) $A \times (B \cap C) = (A \times B) \cap (A \times C)$
2. For any three non-empty sets A, B and C, we have
   $A \times (B - C) = (A \times B) - (A \times C)$
3. If A and B are any two non-empty sets, then
   $A \times B = B \times A \Leftrightarrow A = B$
4. If $A \subseteq B$, then $A \times A \subseteq (A \times B) \cap (B \times A)$
5. If $A \subseteq B$, then $A \times C \subseteq B \times C$ for any non-empty set C.
6. If $A \subseteq B$ and $C \subseteq D$, then $A \times C \subseteq B \times D$
7. For any non-empty sets A, B, C and D, we have
   $(A \times B) \cap (C \times D) = (A \cap C) \times (B \cap D)$
   Corollary For any non-empty sets A and B,
   $(A \times B) \cap (B \times A) = (A \cap B) \times (B \cap A)$
   $= (A \cap B) \times (A \cap B)$
8. For any three sets A, B and C, we have
   (i) $A \times (B' \cup C')' = (A \times B) \cap (A \times C)$
   (ii) $A \times (B' \cap C')' = (A \times B) \cup (A \times C)$
9. Let A and B be two non-empty sets having n elements in common, then $A \times B$ and $B \times A$ have n^2 elements in common.
10. Let A be a non-empty set such that $A \times B = A \times C$. Then, $B = C$

Example 15 If $A = \{1, 4\}$, $B = \{2, 3, 6\}$ and $C = \{2, 3, 7\}$, then verify that

(i) $A \times (B \cup C) = (A \times B) \cup (A \times C)$
(ii) $A \times (B \cap C) = (A \times B) \cap (A \times C)$

Sol. We have,
$A = \{1, 4\}$, $B = \{2, 3, 6\}$ and $C = \{2, 3, 7\}$

(i) **To find** $A \times (B \cup C)$
$B \cup C = \{2, 3, 6\} \cup \{2, 3, 7\}$
$\Rightarrow B \cup C = \{2, 3, 6, 7\}$
$\therefore A \times (B \cup C) = \{1, 4\} \times \{2, 3, 6, 7\}$
$= \{(1, 2), (1, 3), (1, 6), (1, 7), (4, 2), (4, 3), (4, 6), (4, 7)\}$ ...(i)

To find $(A \times B) \cup (A \times C)$
$A \times B = \{(1, 2), (1, 3), (1, 6), (4, 2), (4, 3), (4, 6)\}$
and $A \times C = \{(1, 2), (1, 3), (1, 7), (4, 2), (4, 3), (4, 7)\}$
$\therefore (A \times B) \cup (A \times C) = \{(1, 2), (1, 3), (1, 6), (1, 7), (4, 2), (4, 3), (4, 6), (4, 7)\}$ ...(ii)

From Eqs. (i) and (ii), we get
$A \times (B \cup C) = (A \times B) \cup (A \times C)$

(ii) **To find** $A \times (B \cap C)$
$B \cap C = \{2, 3\}$
$\therefore A \times (B \cap C) = \{1, 4\} \times \{2, 3\}$
$= \{(1, 2), (1, 3), (4, 2), (4, 3)\}$ ...(iii)

To find $(A \times B) \cap (A \times C)$
$A \times B = \{(1, 2), (1, 3), (1, 6), (4, 2), (4, 3), (4, 6)\}$
$A \times C = \{(1, 2), (1, 3), (1, 7), (4, 2), (4, 3), (4, 7)\}$
$\therefore (A \times B) \cap (A \times C) = \{(1, 2), (1, 3), (4, 2), (4, 3)\}$ ...(iv)

From Eqs. (iii) and (iv), we get
$A \times (B \cap C) = (A \times B) \cap (A \times C)$

Topic Practice 1

Very Short Answer Type Questions

(2 Marks)

1 Find x and y, if $(x+6, y-2) = (0, 6)$.

2 Find x and y, if $(x+2, 4) = (5, 2x+y)$.

3 If $A = \{a, b, c\}$ and $B = \{r, s\}$, then find

(i) $A \times B$ (ii) $B \times A$

4 If $A \times B = \{(a, x), (a, y), (b, x), (b, y)\}$, then find A and B.

5 If $A = \{1, 3, 5\}$ and $B = \{2, 3\}$, then show that $A \times B \neq B \times A$.

6 If $A = \{1, 2, 3\}$ and $B = \{5, 6\}$, then show that $A \times B \neq B \times A$.

7 If $A = \{a, b\}$, $B = \{c, d\}$ and $C = \{d, c, e\}$, then find $A \times \{B \cup C\}$.

8 The cartesian product $A \times A$ has 9 elements among which are found $(-1, 0)$ and $(0, 1)$. Find the set A and the remaining element of $A \times A$.

9 If $P = \{1, 4\}$, then find $P \times P \times P$.

10 If $A = \{1, 2, 3\}$, $B = \{1, 2, 3, 4\}$, $C = \{5, 6\}$ and $D = \{5, 6, 7, 8\}$, then verify that $(A \times C) \subset (B \times D)$.

11 Let A and B be two sets such that $n(A) = 5$ and $n(B) = 2$. If a, b, c, d, e are distinct and $(a, 2), (b, 3), (c, 2), (d, 3), (e, 2)$ are elements of $A \times B$, find A and B.

Short Answer Type Questions

(4 Marks)

12 Let $A = \{1, 2, 3\}$ and $B = \{3, 4\}$. Represent following product graphically.

(i) $A \times B$ (ii) $B \times A$ (iii) $A \times A$

13 If $A = \{a, b, c\}$ and $B = \{x, y\}$, then represent the following cartesian product by an arrow diagram.

(i) $A \times B$ (ii) $B \times A$ (iii) $A \times A$ (iv) $B \times B$

14 If $A = \{1, 2, 3\}$, $B = \{3, 4\}$ and $C = \{4, 5, 6\}$, then find

(i) $A \times (B \cap C)$ (ii) $(A \times B) \cap (A \times C)$

15 If $A = \{a, d\}$, $B = \{b, c, e\}$ and $C = \{b, c, f\}$, then verify that

(i) $A \times (B \cup C) = (A \times B) \cup (A \times C)$

(ii) $A \times (B \cap C) = (A \times B) \cap (A \times C)$

Hints & Answers

1. Given, $(x+6, y-2) = (0, 6)$

On equating the corresponding elements,

$x + 6 = 0$ and $y - 2 = 6$ **Ans.** $x = -6$, $y = 8$

2. Solve as Question 1. **Ans.** $x = 3$, $y = -2$

3. (i) $A \times B = \{(a, r), (a, s), (b, r), (b, s), (c, r), (c, s)\}$

(ii) $B \times A = \{(r, a), (r, b), (r, c), (s, a), (s, b), (s, c)\}$

4. Solve as Example 4. **Ans.** $A = \{a, b\}$, $B = \{x, y\}$

5. Solve as Example 3.

6. Solve as Example 3.

7. $B \cup C = \{c, d, e\}$

Ans. $A \times (B \cup C) = \{(a, c), (a, d), (a, e), (b, c), (b, d), (b, e)\}$

8. $(-1, 0) \in A \times A$, therefore

$-1, 0 \in A$ and $(0, 1) \in A \times A \therefore 0, 1 \in A$

$\Rightarrow$ $-1, 0, 1 \in A \Rightarrow A = \{-1, 0, 1\}$

Ans. Remaining elements of $A \times A$ are

$(-1, -1), (-1, 1), (0, -1), (0, 0), (1, -1), (1, 0), (1, 1)$.

9. $P \times P \times P = \{(1, 1, 1), (1, 1, 4), (1, 4, 1), (1, 4, 4), (4, 1, 1)$
$(4, 1, 4), (4, 4, 1), (4, 4, 4)\}$

10. $A \times C = \{(1, 5), (1, 6), (2, 5), (2, 6), (3, 5), (3, 6)\}$

$B \times D = \{(1, 5), (1, 6), (1, 7), (1, 8), (2, 5), (2, 6),$
$(2, 7), (2, 8), (3, 5), (3, 6), (3, 7), (3, 8), (4, 5), (4, 6),$
$(4, 7), (4, 8)\}$

Here, elements $(1, 5), (1, 6), (2, 5), (2, 6), (3, 5), (3, 6)$ $\in A \times C$ are also belongs to $B \times D$, therefore $(A \times C) \subset (B \times D)$.

11. $\because (a, 2), (b, 3), (c, 2), (d, 3), (e, 2) \in A \times B$

$\therefore$ $a, b, c, d, e \in A$ and $2, 3 \in B$

Also, it is given that $n(A) = 5$, $n(B) = 2$

Ans. $A = \{a, b, c, d, e\}$, $B = \{2, 3\}$

12. (i)

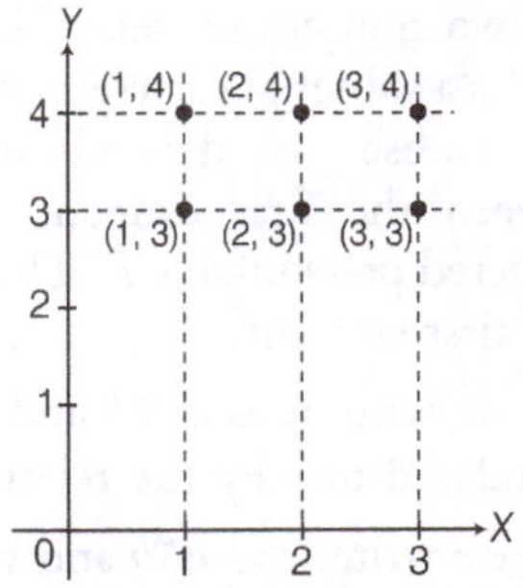

(ii)

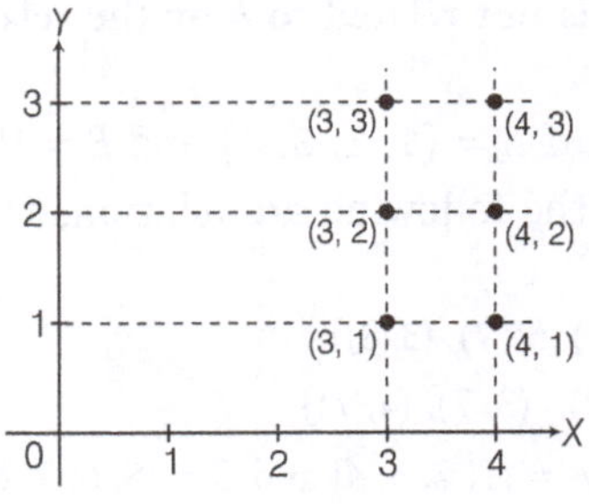

(iii)

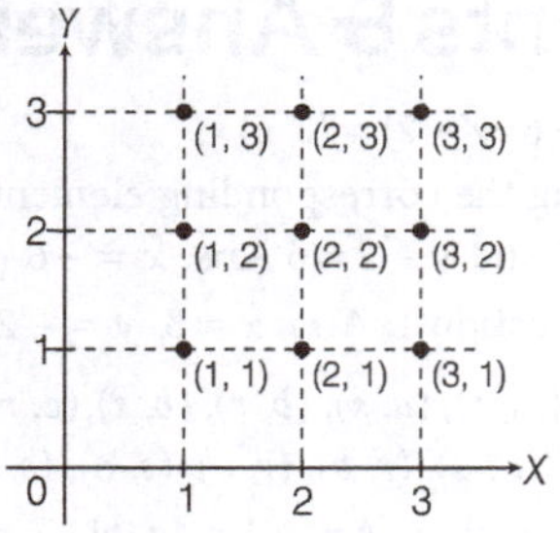

13. (i)

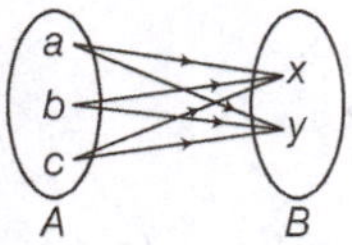

(ii)

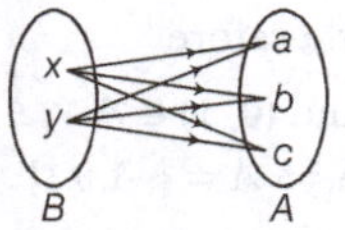

(iii)

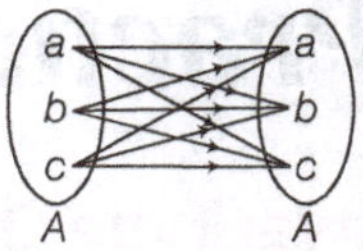

(iv)

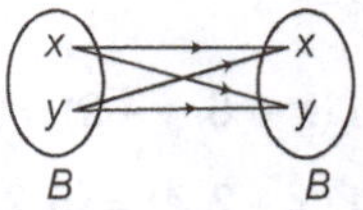

14. (i) $(B \cap C) = \{4\}$

$\therefore A \times (B \cap C) = \{1, 2, 3\} \times \{4\}$

Ans. $\{(1,4), (2,4), (3,4)\}$

(ii) $A \times B = \{(1, 3), (1, 4), (2, 3), (2, 4), (3, 3), (3, 4)\}$

$A \times C = \{(1, 4), (1, 5), (1, 6), (2, 4), (2, 5), (2, 6), (3, 4), (3, 5), (3, 6)\}$

Ans. $(A \times B) \cap (A \times C) = \{(1, 4), (2, 4), (3, 4)\}$

15. Solve as Example 15.

TOPIC 02 Relations

Relation as an Association between Two Sets

A relation is a set of all the ordered pairs of any two sets which are associated with each other.

Relation as a Subset of the Cartesian (or Cross) Product

Let A and B be two non-empty sets. Then, a relation R from set A to set B is a subset of cartesian product $A \times B$ i.e. $R \subseteq A \times B$. The subset is derived by describing a relationship between the first element and the second element of the ordered pairs in $A \times B$. The second element is called **image** of first element.

If $(a, b) \in R$, then we write it as $a\,R\,b$ and we say that

a is related to b by the relation R.

If $(a, b) \notin R$, then we write it as $a \not R b$ and we say that

a is not related to b by the relation R.

Example 1 If $A = \{1, 2, 3, 4\}$ and $B = \{5, 6, 7, 8\}$, then which of the following are relations from A to B? Give answer.

(i) $R_1 = \{(1, 5), (2, 7), (3, 8)\}$

(ii) $R_2 = \{(6, 2), (3, 7), (4, 7)\}$

Sol. We have, $A = \{1, 2, 3, 4\}$ and $B = \{5, 6, 7, 8\}$

$A \times B = \{(1, 5), (1, 6), (1, 7), (1, 8), (2, 5), (2, 6), (2, 7), (2, 8), (3, 5), (3, 6), (3, 7), (3, 8), (4, 5), (4, 6), (4, 7), (4, 8)\}$

(i) Since, $R_1 \subseteq A \times B$, therefore R_1 is a relation from A to B.

(ii) Since, $(6, 2) \in R_2$ but $(6, 2) \notin A \times B$, therefore $R_2 \not\subseteq A \times B$. Thus, R_2 is not a relation from A to B.

Representation of a Relation

A relation can be represented algebraically by roster form or by set-builder form and visually it can be represented by an arrow diagram, which are given below

(i) **Roster form** In this form, we represent the relation by the set of all ordered pairs belongs to R.

e.g. Let R is a relation from set $A = \{-3, -2, -1, 1, 2, 3\}$ to set $B = \{1, 4, 9, 10\}$, defined by $aRb \Leftrightarrow a^2 = b$,

Then, $(-3)^2 = 9, (-2)^2 = 4, (-1)^2 = 1, (1)^2 = 1, (2)^2 = 4, (3)^2 = 9$.

Then, in roster form, R can be written as

$R = \{(-1, 1), (-2, 4), (1, 1), (2, 4), (-3, 9), (3, 9)\}$

(ii) **Set-builder form** In this form, we represent the relation R from set A to set B as

$R = \{(a, b) : a \in A, b \in B$ and the rule which relate the elements of A and $B\}$.

e.g. Let R is a relation from set $A=\{1,2,4,5\}$ to set $B=\left\{1,\frac{1}{2},\frac{1}{4},\frac{1}{5}\right\}$ such that

$$R=\left\{(1,1),\left(2,\frac{1}{2}\right)\left(4,\frac{1}{4}\right)\left(5,\frac{1}{5}\right)\right\}$$

Then, in set-builder form, R can be written as

$$R=\left\{(a,b):a\in A,b\in B \text{ and } b=\frac{1}{a}\right\}.$$

Note We cannot write every relation from set A to set B in set-builder form.

(iii) **Arrow (or Pictorial) diagram** To represent a relation by an arrow diagram, we draw arrows from first element to second element of all ordered pairs belonging to relation R.

e.g. Let $R=\{(1,3)(2,5)(3,6)(2,6)(2,3)\}$ be a relation from set $A=\{1,2,3,4\}$ to set $B=\{3,4,5,6\}$.

Then, by an arrow diagram, it can be represented as

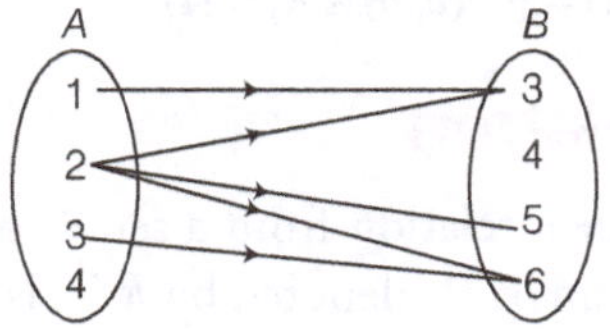

Note

(i) If $R=\phi$, then R is called an **empty relation.**

(ii) If $R=A\times B$, then R is called the **universal relation.**

(iii) If R_1 and R_2 are two relations from A to B, then $R_1\cup R_2$, $R_1\cap R_2$ and R_1-R_2 are also relations from A to B.

Example 2 Express $R=\{(a,b):2a+b=5;a,b\in W\}$ as the set of ordered pairs (in roster form).

Sol. Given, $R=\{(a,b):2a+b=5;a,b\in W\}$

Here, W represent set of whole numbers.

When $a=0$, then $b=5$

When $a=1$, then $b=3$

When $a=2$, then $b=1$

For $a\geq 3$, the value of b given by the above relation are not whole numbers.

$\therefore \quad R=\{(0,5),(1,3),(2,1)\}$

Example 3 Write the relation between sets P and Q given by an arrow diagram in

(i) roster form (ii) set-builder form

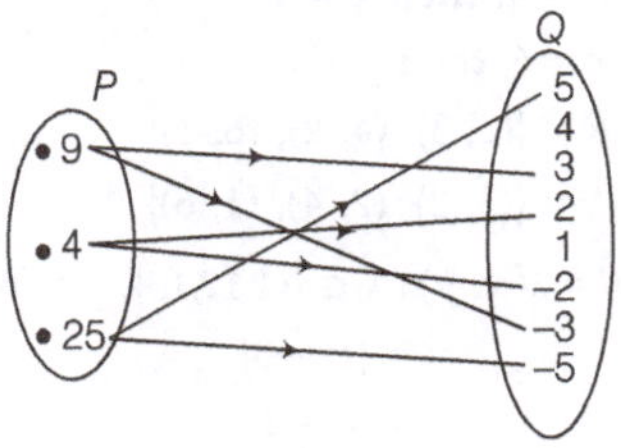

Sol. From arrow diagram, we have

$$P=\{9,4,25\} \text{ and } Q=\{5,4,3,2,1,-2,-3,-5\}$$

Here, the relation R is 'x is the square of y', where $x\in P$ and $y\in Q$.

In roster form, it can be written as

$$R=\{(9,3)(9,-3)(4,2)(4,-2)(25,5)(25,-5)\}$$

In set-builder form, R can be written as

$$R=\{(x,y):x\in P, y\in Q \text{ and } x \text{ is the square of } y\}$$

Example 4 A relation R is defined, from a set $A=\{2,3,4,5\}$ to a set $B=\{3,6,7,10\}$, as $(x,y)\in R\Leftrightarrow x$ is relatively prime to y. Express R as a set of ordered pairs and depict this relations by arrow diagram.

Sol. Given, $R=\{(x,y): x\in A, y\in B, x \text{ is relatively prime to } y\}$

Here, x is relatively prime to y means $\gcd(x,y)=1$.

$\therefore \; R=\{(2,3),(2,7),(3,7),(3,10),(4,3),(4,7),(5,3),(5,6),(5,7)\}$

Visual representation is shown below:

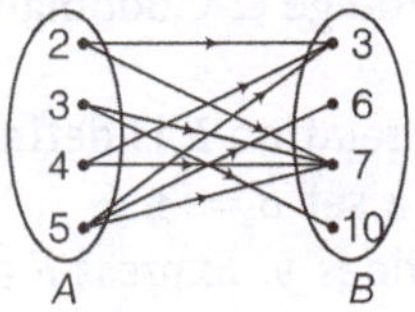

Number of Relations

Let A and B be any two non-empty finite sets containing m and n elements, respectively. Then, the number of ordered pairs in $A\times B$ is mn.

$\therefore$ Total number of subsets of $A\times B$ is 2^{mn}.

Hence, the total number of relations from set A to B is 2^{mn}, because each relation from A to B is a subset of $A\times B$.

Among these 2^{mn} relation, the void relation ϕ and the universal relation $A\times B$ are **trivial relations** from A to B.

Example 5 If $A=\{a,b\}$ and $B=\{2,3\}$, then find the number of relations from A to B.

Sol. We have, $A=\{a,b\}$ and $B=\{2,3\}$,

$\therefore \; n(A\times B)=n(A)\times n(B)=2\times 2=4$

Now, number of subsets of $A\times B$

$$=2^{n(A\times B)}=2^4=16$$

Thus, the number of relations from A to B is 16.

Example 6 If $n(A)=3$ and $B=\{2,3,4,6,7,8\}$, then find the number of relations from A to B.

Sol. Given, $n(A)=3$ and $B=\{2,3,4,6,7,8\}$

$\Rightarrow \quad n(B)=6$

$\therefore$ Number of relations from A to B

$$=2^{n(A)\times n(B)}=2^{3\times 6}=2^{18}$$

Domain, Codomain and Range of a Relation

Let us consider the relation R from A to B. Then, the set of first elements of all the ordered pairs present in R is called the **domain** of relation and the set of second elements of all the ordered pairs present in R is called **range** of the relation. The set B is called the **codomain** of relation R

i.e. **Domain** $(R) = \{a : (a, b) \in R\}$

and **Range** $(R) = \{b : (a, b) \in R\}$

Note that the domain of a relation from set A to B is a subset of set A and range is a subset of set B i.e. range is a subset of codomain. (Range $\subseteq$ Codomain)

e.g. Let $R = \{(1, 2), (1, 5), (3, 4), (6, 7)\}$ be a relation from set $A = \{1, 3, 6, 7\}$ to set $B = \{2, 4, 5, 6, 7\}$.

Then, domain $= \{1, 3, 6\}$, range $= \{2, 4, 5, 7\}$

and codomain = set $B = \{2, 4, 5, 6, 7\}$

Clearly, Range $\subseteq$ Codomain

Example 7 A relation R is defined from a set $A = \{2, 3, 4, 5\}$ to a set $B = \{3, 6, 7, 10\}$ as follows $(x, y) \in R \Leftrightarrow x$ divides y. Express R as a set of ordered pairs and determine the domain and range of R.

Sol. We have, $A = \{2, 3, 4, 5\}$ and $B = \{3, 6, 7, 10\}$

Relation R is defined as $(x, y) \in R \Leftrightarrow x$ divides y.

$\therefore$ 2 divides 6, 2 divides 10, 3 divides 3, 3 divides 6, 5 divides 10.

$\therefore \quad R = \{(2, 6) (2, 10) (3, 3) (3, 6) (5, 10)\}$

$\because$ Domain (R) = Set of first elements of the ordered pairs present in R

$\therefore$ Domain of $R = \{2, 3, 5\}$

$\because$ Range (R) = Set of second elements of the ordered pairs present in R

$\therefore$ Range of $R = \{3, 6, 10\}$

Example 8 Determine the domain and range of the relation $R = \{(x, y) : x \in N, y \in N$ and $x + y = 10\}$.

Sol. We have, $R = \{(x, y) : x \in N, y \in N$ and $x + y = 10\}$

$\Rightarrow \quad R = \{(1, 9), (2, 8), (3, 7), (4, 6), (5, 5), (6, 4), (7, 3), (8, 2), (9, 1)\}$

$\therefore$ Domain (R) = Set of first elements of the ordered pairs present in R

$= \{1, 2, 3, 4, 5, 6, 7, 8, 9\}$

Range (R) = Set of second elements of the ordered pairs present in $R = \{9, 8, 7, 6, 5, 4, 3, 2, 1\}$

Example 9 Let $A = \{1, 2, 3, 4, 5\}$. Define a relation R from A to A by $R = \{(x, y) : y = x - 1, x, y \in A\}$

(i) Depict this relation using an arrow diagram.

(ii) Write down the domain, codomain and range of R.

Sol. (i) Given, $R = \{(x, y) : y = x - 1, x, y \in A\}$

$\therefore \quad R = \{(2, 1), (3, 2), (4, 3), (5, 4)\}$

The corresponding arrow diagram is shown in following figure.

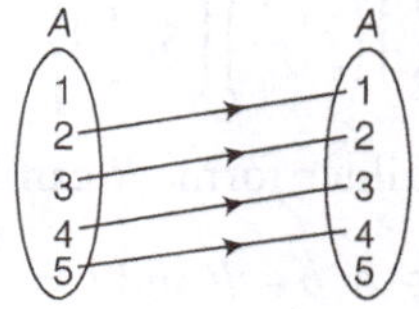

(ii) It is clear from the arrow diagram, that

domain $= \{2, 3, 4, 5\}$, codomain $= \{1, 2, 3, 4, 5\}$ and range $= \{1, 2, 3, 4\}$.

Example 10 Determine the domain and range of the relation $R = \{(a, b) : a \in N, a < 5, b = 4\}$

Sol. Given, $R = \{(a, b) : a \in N, a < 5, b = 4\}$

$\Rightarrow \quad R = \{(1, 4), (2, 4), (3, 4), (4, 4)\}$

Domain $(R) = \{a : (a, b) \in R\} = \{1, 2, 3, 4\}$

Range $(R) = \{b : (a, b) \in R\} = \{4\}$

Inverse Relation

Let $R \subseteq A \times B$ be a relation from a set A to a set B. Then, the inverse relation of R, denoted by R^{-1}, is a relation from B to A and is defined by $R^{-1} = \{(b, a) : (a, b) \in R\}$.

Thus, $(a, b) \in R \Leftrightarrow (b, a) \in R^{-1}, \forall a \in A, b \in B$

Clearly, **domain** (R^{-1}) = **range** (R)

and **range** (R^{-1}) = **domain** (R)

Example 11 Find the inverse relation (R^{-1}) in each of the following cases

(i) $R = \{(1, 2), (1, 3), (2, 3), (3, 2), (5, 6)\}$

(ii) $R = \{(x, y) : x, y \in N, x + 2y = 8\}$

(iii) R is a relation from $\{11, 12, 13\}$ to $\{8, 10, 12\}$ defined by $y = x - 3$

Sol. (i) Given, $R = \{(1, 2), (1, 3), (2, 3), (3, 2), (5, 6)\}$

$\Rightarrow R^{-1} = \{(2, 1), (3, 1), (3, 2), (2, 3), (6, 5)\}$

(ii) $R = \{(x, y) : x, y \in N, x + 2y = 8\}$

$\because x + 2y = 8$

When $x = 2$, then $y = 3$

When $x = 4$, then $y = 2$

When $x = 6$, then $y = 1$

$\Rightarrow \quad R = \{(2, 3), (4, 2), (6, 1)\}$

$\Rightarrow \quad R^{-1} = \{(3, 2), (2, 4), (1, 6)\}$

(iii) Here, $R = \{(x, y) : x \in \{11, 12, 13\}, y \in \{8, 10, 12\}$

and $\quad y = \{x - 3\}$

$\because \quad y = x - 3$

When $x = 11$, then $y = 8$

When $x = 13$, then $y = 10$

$\therefore \quad R = \{(11, 8), (13, 10)\}$

$\Rightarrow \quad R^{-1} = \{(8, 11), (10, 13)\}$

Example 12 Let A be the set of first 10 natural numbers and let R be a relation on A defined by

$$(x, y) \in R \Leftrightarrow x + 2y = 10,$$

i.e $R = \{(x, y) : x \in A, y \in A \text{ and } x + 2y = 10\}$.
Express R and R^{-1} as sets of ordered pair. Also, determine

(i) domain of R and R^{-1}

(ii) Range of R and R^{-1}.

Sol. Given, $R = \{(x, y) : x \in A, y \in A \text{ and } x + 2y = 10\}$

Here, $x + 2y = 10$

$$\Rightarrow \quad y = \frac{10 - x}{2} \forall\, x, y \in A \quad \text{...(i)}$$

and $A = \{1, 2, 3, 4, 5, 6, 7, 8, 9, 10\}$

From Eq. (i),

When $x = 2$, $y = 4$; When $x = 4$, $y = 3$

When $x = 6$, $y = 2$; When $x = 8$, $y = 1$

$\therefore \quad R = \{(2, 4), (4, 3), (6, 2), (8, 1)\}$

$\Rightarrow \quad R^{-1} = \{(4, 2), (3, 4), (2, 6), (1, 8)\}$

Clearly, domain $(R) = \{2, 4, 6, 8\} =$ Range (R^{-1})

and range $(R) = \{4, 3, 2, 1\} =$ Domain (R^{-1})

Topic Practice 2

Very Short Answer Type Questions

2 Marks

1. If $A = \{x, y, z\}$ and $B = \{1, 2\}$, then find the number of relation from A to B. [NCERT]

2. Determine the domain and range of the relation R, defined by $R = \{(x, x + 5) : x \in \{0, 1, 2, 3, 4, 5\}\}$. [NCERT]

3. If $R = \{(x, y) : x, y \in N, x < 5 \text{ and } y = 3\}$ is a relation, then find domain and range of R.

4. Let $A = \{1, 2, 3, 5\}$ and $B = \{4, 6, 9\}$. If a relation R from A to B is defined by $R = \{(x, y)$: the difference between x and y is odd, $x \in A$, $y \in B\}$, then write R in roster form. [NCERT]

5. If $A = \{1, 2, 3, 4, 6\}$ and R be the relation defined on A by $R = \{(a, b) : a \in A, b \in A$ and a divides $b\}$, then find domain and range of R.

6. Let $A = \{1, 2, 3\}$; $B = \{a, b, c, d\}$ be two sets and $R = \{(1, a), (1, c), (2, d), (2, c)\}$ be a relation from A to B, then find R^{-1}, range of R and domain of R.

7. Determine the domain and range of the relations R, where $R = (x, x^3) : x$ is a prime number less than 10$\}$ [NCERT]

8. Express $R = \{(x, y) : x^2 + y^2 = 25$, where $x, y \in W\}$ as a set of ordered pairs

9. Determine the domain and range of the relation R, where
   (i) $R = \{(-3, 1), (-1, 1), (1, 0), (3, 0)\}$
   (ii) $R = \{(x - 2, x^2) : x$ is a prime number less than 15$\}$

10. Let $A = \{2, 4, 6, 9\}$ and $B = \{4, 6, 18, 27, 54\}$, then find the set of ordered pair (a, b) such that $a \in A$, $b \in B$, a is factor of b, and $a < b$.

11. The given figure shows a relationship between the sets P and Q.

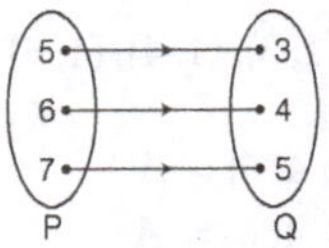

Write this relation
(i) in setbuilder form (ii) in roster form
What is its domain and range?

12. Suppose a relation $R = \{(1, 4), (2, 5), (4, 4), (6, 5)\}$ is defined from A to B. Find the inverse of R. Also, find the domain and range of R^{-1}?

Short Answer Type Questions

4 Marks

13. Let $A = \{1, 2, 3, 4\}$ and $B = \{1, 4, 9, 16, 25\}$ and R be a relation defined from A to B, as $R = \{(x, y) : x \in A, y \in B \text{ and } y = x^2\}$
   (i) Depict this relation using arrow diagram
   (ii) Find domain of R.
   (iii) Find range of R.
   (iv) Write codomain of R

14 If $A = \{1, 2, 3, 4, 5, 6\}$, then define a relation R from A to A by $R = \{(x, y) : y = x + 1\}$
(i) Depict this relation using an arrow diagram.
(ii) Write down the domain, codomain and range of R.

15 Suppose a set $A = \{$January, February, August$\}$ and set $B = \{28, 15, 30\}$. Write a relation R given by $R = \{(a, b) \in A \times B$, where a is month and b is date$\}$. Also, find R^{-1}.

Hints & Answers

1. Solve as Example 5. **Ans.** 64
2. $R = \{(0, 5), (1, 6), (2, 7), (3, 8), (4, 9), (5, 10)\}$
Ans. Domain $(R) = \{0, 1, 2, 3, 4, 5\}$;
Range $(R) = \{5, 6, 7, 8, 9, 10\}$
3. $R = \{(1, 3), (2, 3), (3, 3), (4, 3)\}$
Ans. Domain $(R) = \{1, 2, 3, 4\}$ and range $(R) = \{3\}$
4. $R = \{(x, y)$: the difference between x and y is odd, $x \in A,\ y \in B\}$
Ans. In roster form
$R = \{(1, 4), (1, 6), (2, 9), (3, 4), (3, 6), (5, 4), (5, 6)\}$
5. Let $R = \{(a, b) : a \in A,\ b \in A$, and a divides $b\}$
$R = \{(1, 1), (1, 2), (1, 3), (1, 4), (1, 6), (2, 2), (2, 4), (2, 6), (3, 3), (3, 6), (4, 4), (6, 6)\}$
Domain $= \{1, 2, 3, 4, 6\} = A$
Range $= \{1, 2, 3, 4, 6\} = A$
6. $R = \{(1, a), (1, c), (2, d)(2, c)\}$
Ans. $R^{-1} = \{(a, 1), (c, 1), (d, 2), (c, 2)\}$
Domain $(R) = \{1, 2\}$; Range $(R) = \{a, c, d\}$
7. $R = (x, x^3) : x$ is a prime number less than $10\}$
$R = \{(2, 8), (3, 27), (5, 125), (7, 343)\}$
[$\because$ 2, 3, 5, 7 are primes less than 10]
Ans. Domain $(R) = \{2, 3, 5, 7\}$
Range $(R) = \{8, 27, 125, 343\}$
8. Here, W is the set of whole number
$\because \quad x^2 + y^2 = 25 \quad$ ...(i)
Put $x = 0, 1, 2, 3, 4, 5$ in Eq. (i) and obtain the value of y.
Ans. $R = \{(0, 5), (3, 4), (4, 3), (5, 0)\}$
9. (i) Given, $R = \{(-3, 1), (-1, 1), (1, 0), (3, 0)\}$
Ans. Domain $(R) = \{-3, -1, 1, 3\}$; Range $(R) = \{0, 1\}$
(ii) Given, $R = \{(x - 2, x^2) : x$ is a prime number less than $15\}$
$\therefore R = \{(0, 4), (1, 9), (3, 25), (5, 49), (9, 121), (11, 169)\}$
Ans. Domain $(R) = \{0, 1, 3, 5, 9, 11\}$
and range $(R) = \{4, 9, 25, 49, 121, 169\}$
10. Here, $A = \{2, 4, 6, 9\}$; $B = \{4, 6, 18, 27, 54\}$
Let $R = \{(a, b) : a \in A, b \in B, a$ is factor of b and $a < b\}$
Ans. $R = \{(2, 4), (2, 6), (2, 18), (2, 54), (6, 18), (6, 54), (9, 18), (9, 27), (9, 54)\}$
11. (i) $\{(x, y) : x \in P, y \in Q, x = y + 2\}$
(ii) $\{(5, 3), (6, 4), (7, 5)\}$
(iii) Domain $(R) = \{5, 6, 7\}$ and range $(R) = \{3, 4, 5\}$
12. Given, $R = \{(1, 4), (2, 5), (4, 4), (6, 5)\}$
Ans. $R^{-1} = \{(4, 1), (5, 2), (4, 4), (5, 6)\}$
Domain $(R^{-1}) = \{4, 5\}$ and Range $(R^{-1}) = \{1, 2, 4, 6\}$
13. (i) The relation $R = \{(1, 1), (2, 4), (3, 9), (4, 16)\}$

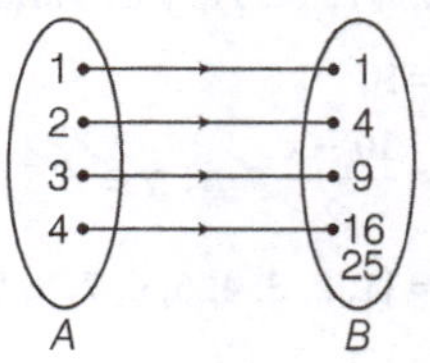

(ii) Domain $(R) = \{1, 2, 3, 4\}$
(iii) Range $(R) = \{1, 4, 9, 16\}$
(iv) Codomain $(R) = \{1, 4, 9, 16, 25\}$
14. Given, $A = \{1, 2, 3, 4, 5, 6\}$
$R = \{(x, y) : y = x + 1\} = \{(1, 2), (2, 3), (3, 4), (4, 5), (5, 6)\}$
(i) The arrow diagram is shown below

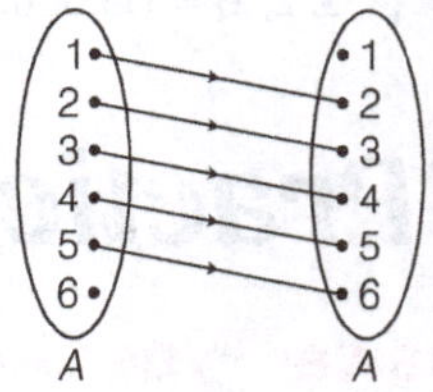

(ii) **Ans.** domain $(R) = \{1, 2, 3, 4, 5\}$
Range $(R) = \{2, 3, 4, 5, 6\}$;
Codomain $= \{1, 2, 3, 4, 5, 6\}$
15. Given, $R = \{(a, b) \in A \times B$, where a is month and b is date$\}$
Ans. $R = \{$(January, 28), (January, 15), (January, 30), (February, 28), (February, 15), (August, 28), (August, 15), (August, 30)$\}$
and $R^{-1} = \{$(28, January), (15, January), (30, January), (28, February), (15, February), (28, August), (15, August), (30, August)$\}$

TOPIC 03 **Functions**

A special type of relation is called **function.** The word 'function' is derived from a Latin word meaning **operation.** Function is a very important concept in Mathematics and it shows the correspondence between two sets. A function is also known as **mapping** or **map.**

Function as a Special Relation

A **function** from A to B is a rule (or correspondence) which associates to each element a of A, a unique element b of B. In other words, if A and B are two non-empty sets, then a subset f of $A \times B$ is called the function (or mapping) from A to B if and only if for each $a \in A$, there exists a unique $b \in B$ such that $(a, b) \in f$. It is written as $f : A \to B$ or $A \xrightarrow{f} B$ and it is read as f is a function from A to B or f maps from A to B.

Thus, a subset f of $A \times B$ is called a function from A to B if and only if

(i) for each $a \in A$, there exists, $b \in B$ such that $(a, b) \in f$ and

(ii) no two different ordered pairs have the same first component.

If $(a, b) \in f$, then we can also write it as $f(a) = b$.
Here, b is called the **image** of a under f and a is called the **pre-image** of b under f.

e.g. Let $A = \{2, 3, 4\}$, $B = \{3, 4, 5\}$ and f_1, f_2 and f_3 be three subsets of $A \times B$ defined as

$f_1 = \{(2,3)\ (3,4)\ (4,5)\}$; $f_2 = \{(2,3)\ (2,4)\ (3,4), (4,5)\}$ and $f_3 = \{(2,4)\ (3,5)\}$.

Then, f_1 is a function from A to B, since every element of A has one and only one image in set B. f_2 is not a function from A to B, since $2 \in A$ has two images 3 and 4 in B. Also, f_3 is not a function from A to B, since $4 \in A$ has no image in B.

Example 1 Which of the following relations are functions?

(i) {(3, 3), (4, 2), (5, 1), (6, 0), (7, 7)}

(ii) {(2,0), (4, 8), (2, 1), (3, 6)}

Sol. (i) {(3, 3), (4, 2), (5, 1), (6, 0), (7, 7)}

It is a function, because first element of each ordered pair is different.

(ii) {(2, 0), (4, 8), (2, 1), (3, 6)}

It is not a function, because first elements of (2, 0) and (2, 1) are same.

Function as a Correspondence

A function f from a non-empty set A to a non-empty set B is a **rule or method or correspondence** which associates elements of set A to elements of set B such that

(i) All elements of set A are associated to elements in set B.

(ii) An element of set A is associated with one and only one element of set B.

In other words, a function 'f' from a non-empty set A to a non-empty set B, associate each element of set A to a unique element of set B.

Characteristics of a Function $f: A \to B$

(i) For each element $x \in A$, there is unique element $y \in B$.

(ii) The element $y \in B$ is called the **image** of x under the function f. Also, y is called the **value of function f at x** i.e. $f(x) = y$.

(iii) $f : A \to B$ is not a function if there is an element in A which has more than one image in B. But more than one element of A may be associated to the same element of B.

(iv) $f : A \to B$ is not a function, if an element in A does not have an image in B.

Example 2 Let A be the set of persons and B be the set of their heights and let f_1, f_2 be rules associating elements of A to elements of B as shown in following figures.

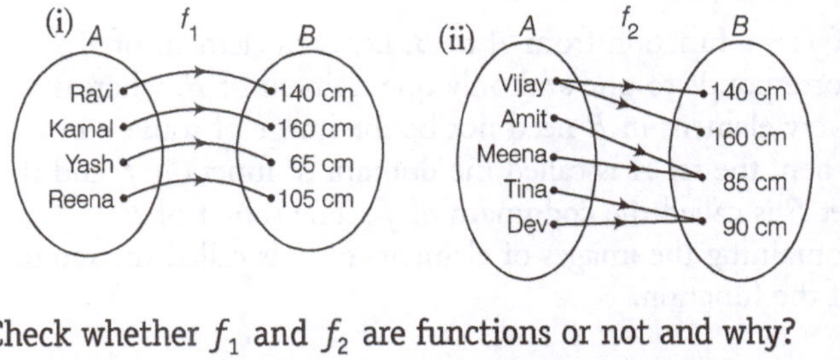

Check whether f_1 and f_2 are functions or not and why?

Sol. In f_1 [arrow diagram (i)], we observe that each element of A is associated with exactly one element of B, Therefore, f_1 is a function from A to B.

In f_2 [arrow diagram (ii)], we observe that Vijay is associated with 140 cm and 160 cm. Any person can have only one unique height, so the height of Vijay cannot be 140 cm and 160 cm together.

Hence, $f_2 : A \to B$ is not a function.

Note Every function is a relation but its converse is not true. e.g. Let us consider

$$R_1 = \{(1, 3), (1, 5), (2, 5)\}$$

and $$R_2 = \{(2, 5), (3, 4)\}.$$

Here, set R_1 and R_2 both are relations but R_1 is not a function because element 1 has two images and set R_2 is a function because no two elements has same image.

Example 3 If $x, y \in \{1, 2, 3, 4\}$, then check whether f_1, f_2 and f_3 are functions or not where

$$f_1 = \{(x, y) : y = x + 1\},$$

$$f_2 = \{(x, y) : x + y = 5\}$$

and $$f_3 = \{(x, y) : x + y > 4\}.$$

Also find the the range in case of a function.

Sol. Let $A = \{1, 2, 3, 4\}$, then f_1, f_2 and f_3 are defined from A to A.

First express f_1, f_2 and f_3 as sets of ordered pairs, i.e. write $f_1 = \{(1, 2), (2, 3), (3, 4)\}$

$$f_2 = \{(1, 4), (2, 3), (3, 2), (4, 1)\}$$

and $$f_3 = \{(1, 4), (2, 3), (2, 4), (3,3), (3,2), (3,4)$$
$$(4, 1), (4, 2), (4, 3), (4, 4)\}$$

Now in f_1, we observe that an element $4 \in A$ is not appeared at first place of any ordered pair of f_1.

So, f_1 is not a function from A to A.

In f_2, we observe that each element of set A is appeared at first place in one and only one ordered pair of f_2.

So, f_2 is a function from A to A and Range of $f_2 = \{1, 2, 3, 4\}$. In f_3, we observe that $2, 3, 4 \in A$ have appeared at first place of ordered pair more than one time. So, f_3 is not a function.

Domain, Codomain and Range of a Function

If f is a function from A to B, i.e. each element of A corresponds to one and only one element of B, whereas every element in B need not be the image of some x in A. Then, the set A is called the **domain** of function f and the set B is called the **codomain** of f. The subset of B containing the images of elements of A is called the **range** of the function.

Thus, if a function f is expressed as the set of ordered pairs, then the domain of f is the **set of first elements** of all ordered pairs of f and the range of f is **the set of second elements** of all ordered pairs of f, i.e.

$$\textbf{Domain of } f = \{a : (a, b) \in f\}$$

and $$\textbf{range of } f = \{b : (a, b) \in f\}$$

Example 4 Which of the following relations are functions? Give reasons. If it is a function, determine its domain and range. **[NCERT]**

(i) $\{(2, 1), (5, 1), (8, 1), (11, 1), (14, 1), (17, 1)\}$

(ii) $\{(2, 1), (4, 2), (6, 3), (8, 4), (10, 5), (12, 6), (14, 7)\}$

(iii) $\{(1, 3), (1, 5), (2, 5)\}$

Sol. Here, (i) $\{(2, 1), (5, 1), (8, 1), (11, 1), (14, 1), (17, 1)\}$

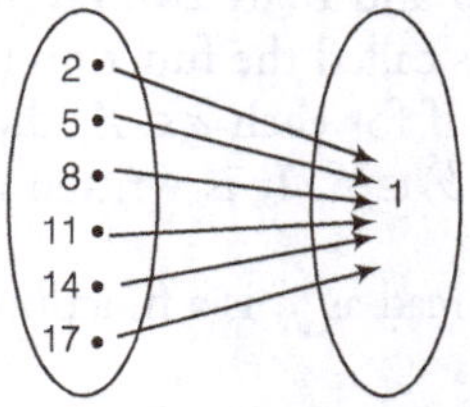

It is clear from arrow diagram that

(a) it is a function, as each element have a unique image.

(b) its domain is $\{2, 5, 8, 11, 14, 17\}$.

(c) its range is $\{1\}$.

(ii) $\{(2, 1), (4, 2), (6, 3), (8, 4), (10, 5), (12, 6), (14, 7)\}$.

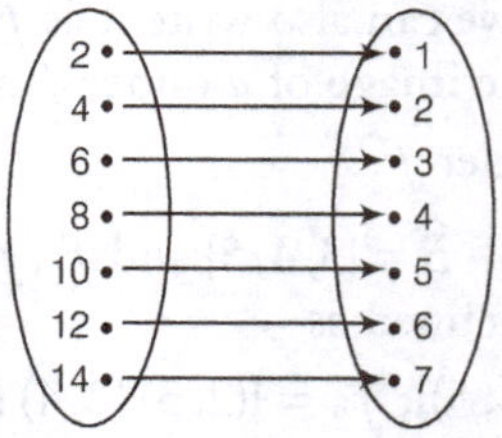

It is clear from arrow diagram that

(a) it is a function, as each element have a unique image.

(b) its domain is $\{2, 4, 6, 8, 10, 12, 14\}$.

(c) its range is $\{1, 2, 3, 4, 5, 6, 7\}$.

(iii) $\{(1, 3), (1, 5), (2, 5)\}$

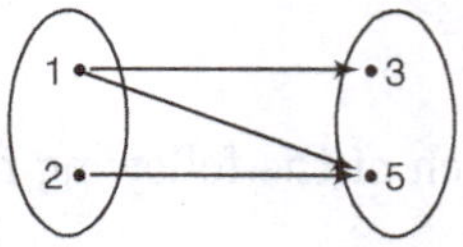

It is clear from the arrow diagram that it is not a function because 1 has two images 3 and 5.

Identification of a Function with its Graph

We draw a vertical line i.e. *any line parallel to Y-axis*. If this line intersect the graph of the curve in more than one point, then the curve is a relation and if it intersect at only one point, then the curve is a function.

In figure (i), the vertical line intersects the curve at two points, therefore the curve is a relation whereas in figure (ii), the vertical line intersects the curve at only one point, therefore the curve is a function.

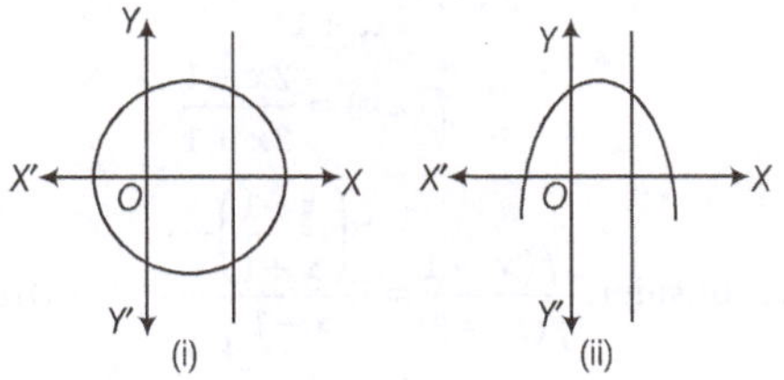

(i) (ii)

Example 5 Identify the curve, which is a relation or function.

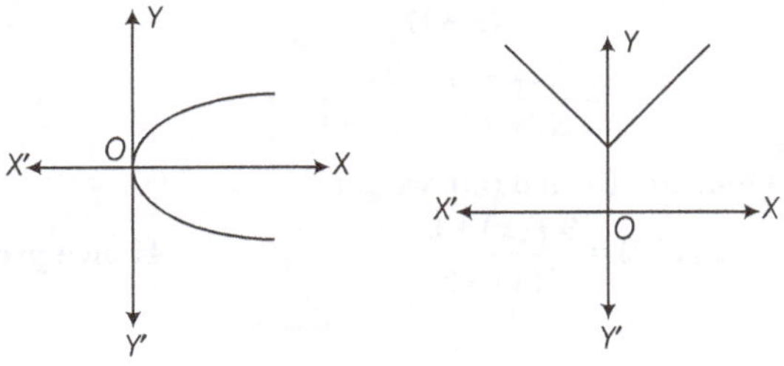

(i) (ii)

Sol. (i) If we draw a vertical line, then it will intersect the curve at two points. It shows that given curve is a relation.

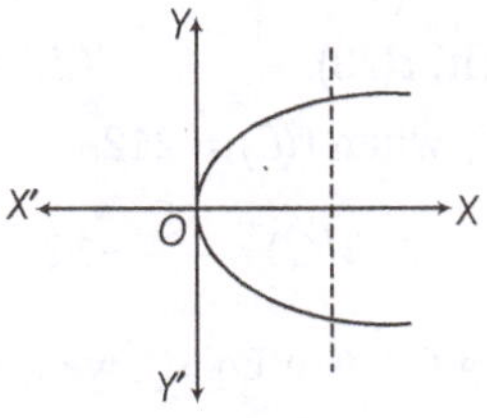

(i)

(ii) If we draw a vertical line, then it will intersect the curve at only one point. It shows that given curve is a function.

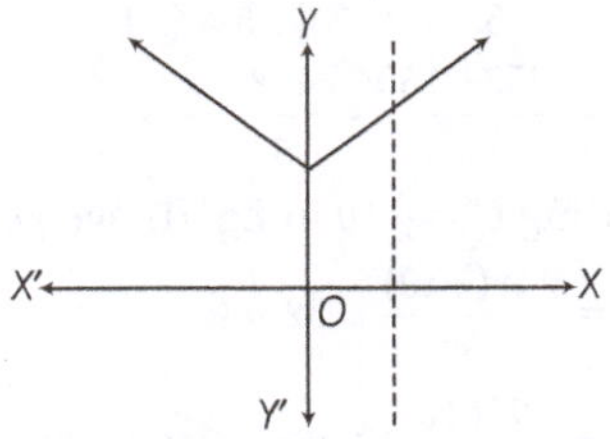

(ii)

Equal Functions

Two functions f and g are said to be equal iff

(i) domain of f = domain of g

(ii) codomain of f = codomain of g

(iii) $f(x) = g(x)$ for every x belonging to their common domain and then we write $f = g$.

e.g. Let $A = \{1, 2\}$, $B = \{3, 6\}$ and $f : A \to B$ is given by $f(x) = x^2 + 2$ and $g : A \to B$ given by $g(x) = 3x$. Here, we observe that f and g have the same domain and codomain.

Also, $\quad f(1) = 3 = g(1)$

and $\quad f(2) = 6 = g(2)$

Hence, $\quad f = g$

Example 6 Let $A = \left\{-2, \frac{1}{2}\right\}$ and $B = \left\{7, \frac{-1}{2}\right\}$, $f : A \to B$ defined by $f(x) = 2x^2 - 1$ and $g : A \to B$ defined by $g(x) = 1 - 3x$. Find whether $f = g$ or not.

Sol. We observe that f and g both have same domain and codomain. Also, we have

$$f(-2) = 7 = g(-2) \text{ and } f\left(\frac{1}{2}\right) = \frac{-1}{2} = g\left(\frac{1}{2}\right)$$

Hence, $f = g$

Example 7 $f : R - \{3\} \to R$ be defined by $f(x) = \dfrac{x^2 - 9}{x - 3}$ and $g : R \to R$ be defined by $g(x) = x + 3$. Find whether $f = g$ or not.

Sol. Here, $f(x) = \dfrac{x^2 - 9}{x - 3} = \dfrac{(x-3)(x+3)}{x-3} = (x + 3)$

and $\quad g(x) = x + 3 \Rightarrow f(x) = g(x) = x + 3$

But $f(x) \neq g(x)$ as domain of $f(x)$ is $R - \{3\}$ and domain of $g(x)$ is R.

$\Rightarrow$ Domain of $f(x) \neq$ Domain of $g(x) \Rightarrow f \neq g$

Example 8 Find the values of x for which the functions $f(x) = 3x^2 - 1$ and $g(x) = 3 + x$ are equal.

Sol. Given, $f(x) = 3x^2 - 1$ and $g(x) = 3 + x$

Let $\quad f(x) = g(x)$

Then, $\quad 3x^2 - 1 = 3 + x$

$\Rightarrow \quad 3x^2 - x - 4 = 0$

$\Rightarrow \quad 3x^2 - 4x + 3x - 4 = 0$

$\Rightarrow \quad x(3x - 4) + 1(3x - 4) = 0$

$\Rightarrow \quad (3x - 4)(x + 1) = 0$

$\Rightarrow \quad x = -1, \frac{4}{3}$

Real Functions

A function which has either R (set of real numbers) or one of its subsets as its range is called a **real valued function** and if its domain is also either R or a subset of R i.e. range and domain both are either R or a subset of R, then the function is called **real function.**

For real functions, generally domain and codomain both are infinite subsets of R. Therefore, a real function is generally described by some general formula. In other words we can say that, images of various elements of the domain of a real function are provided by some general formula. e.g. Let f be a function define by $f(x) = 2x + 1$ from N to N. Then,

x	1	2	3	4	5
$f(x) = y$	$f(1) = 3$	$f(2) = 5$	$f(3) = 7$	$f(4) = 9$	$f(5) = 11$

Thus, range $= \{3, 5, 7, 9, 11, \ldots\} \subseteq R$, codomain $= N$ and domain $= N \subseteq R$.

Example 9 If $f(x) = x^2 + 2x + 3$, then find $f(1)$, $f(2)$ and $f(3)$.

Sol. We have, $f(x) = x^2 + 2x + 3$ ...(i)

$f(1) = (1)^2 + 2(1) + 3$ [putting $x = 1$ in Eq. (i)]

$= 1 + 2 + 3 = 6$

$f(2) = (2)^2 + 2(2) + 3$ [putting $x = 2$ in Eq. (i)]

$= 4 + 4 + 3 = 11$

$f(3) = (3)^2 + 2(3) + 3$ [putting $x = 3$ in Eq. (i)]

$= 9 + 6 + 3 = 18$

Example 10 If $f(1 + x) = x^2 + 1$, then find $f(2 - h)$.

Sol. We have, $f(1 + x) = x^2 + 1$ ...(i)

On substituting $x = (1 - h)$ in Eq. (i), we get

$f(1 + 1 - h) = (1 - h)^2 + 1$

$f(2 - h) = 1 + h^2 - 2h + 1 = h^2 - 2h + 2$

Example 11 If $y = f(x) = \dfrac{1 - x}{1 + x}$, then show that $x = f(y)$.

Sol. We have, $y = f(x) = \dfrac{1 - x}{1 + x}$ ...(i)

Then, $f(y) = \dfrac{1 - y}{1 + y} = \dfrac{1 - \left(\dfrac{1 - x}{1 + x}\right)}{1 + \left(\dfrac{1 - x}{1 + x}\right)}$ [from Eq. (i)]

$= \dfrac{\dfrac{1 + x - (1 - x)}{1 + x}}{\dfrac{1 + x + 1 - x}{1 + x}} = \dfrac{2x}{2}$

$\Rightarrow \quad f(y) = x$

$\therefore \quad x = f(y)$, when $y = f(x) = \dfrac{1 - x}{1 + x}$

Example 12 If f is a real function defined by $f(x) = \dfrac{x - 1}{x + 1}$, then prove that $f(2x) = \dfrac{3f(x) + 1}{f(x) + 3}$.

Sol. Given, $f(x) = \dfrac{x - 1}{x + 1}$ ...(i)

$\Rightarrow \quad f(2x) = \dfrac{2x - 1}{2x + 1}$ ...(ii)

Now, consider $\dfrac{3f(x) + 1}{f(x) + 3} = \dfrac{3\left(\dfrac{x - 1}{x + 1}\right) + 1}{\dfrac{x - 1}{x + 1} + 3}$ [from Eq. (i)]

$= \dfrac{\dfrac{3(x - 1) + (x + 1)}{(x + 1)}}{\dfrac{(x - 1) + 3(x + 1)}{(x + 1)}} = \dfrac{3x - 3 + x + 1}{x - 1 + 3x + 3} = \dfrac{4x - 2}{4x + 2}$

$= \dfrac{2(2x - 1)}{2(2x + 1)} = \dfrac{2x - 1}{2x + 1}$ ...(iii)

From Eqs. (ii) and (iii), we get

$f(2x) = \dfrac{3f(x) + 1}{f(x) + 3}$ **Hence proved.**

Example 13 If the function t which maps temperature in degree Celcius into temperature in degree Fahrenheit is defined by $t(C) = \dfrac{9C}{5} + 32$, then find

(i) $t(0)$ (ii) $t(28)$ (iii) $t(-10)$ **[NCERT]**

(iv) the value of C, when $t(C) = 212$

Sol. Given, $t(C) = \dfrac{9C}{5} + 32$ ...(i)

(i) On putting $C = 0$ in Eq. (i), we get

$t(0) = \dfrac{9 \times 0}{5} + 32 = 0 + 32 = 32$

(ii) On putting $C = 28$ in Eq. (i), we get

$t(28) = \dfrac{9 \times 28}{5} + 32 = \dfrac{252}{5} + \dfrac{32}{1}$

$= \dfrac{252 + 160}{5} = \dfrac{412}{5}$

(iii) On putting $C = -10$ in Eq. (i), we get

$t(-10) = \dfrac{9 \times (-10)}{5} + 32$

$= \dfrac{-9 \times 10}{5} + 32 = -9 \times 2 + 32$

$= -18 + 32 = 14$

(iv) Now, on putting $t(C) = 212$ in Eq. (i), we get

$$212 = \frac{9C}{5} + 32$$

$$\Rightarrow \quad \frac{9C}{5} = 212 - 32$$

$$\Rightarrow \quad \frac{9C}{5} = 180$$

$$\because \quad C = \frac{5 \times 180}{9}$$

$$\therefore \quad C = 5 \times 20 = 100$$

Example 14 Given $A = \{-1, 0, 2, 5, 6, 11\}$, $B = \{-2, -1, 0, 18, 28, 108\}$ and $f(x) = x^2 - x - 2$. Is $f(A) = B$? Find $f(A)$. [NCERT]

Sol. Given, $f(x) = x^2 - x - 2$,

$A = \{-1, 0, 2, 5, 6, 11\}$

and $B = \{-2, -1, 0, 18, 28, 108\}$

Clearly, $f(-1) = (-1)^2 - (-1) - 2 = 0$

$f(0) = (0)^2 - 0 - 2 = -2$

$f(2) = (2)^2 - 2 - 2 = 0$

$f(5) = (5)^2 - 5 - 2 = 18$

$f(6) = (6)^2 - 6 - 2 = 28$

and $f(11) = (11)^2 - 11 - 2 = 108$

Now, $f(A) = \{f(x) : x \in A\} = \{0, -2, 18, 28, 108\}$

Here, we see that $-1 \in B$ but $-1 \notin f(A)$

$\therefore$ $f(A) \neq B$.

Example 15 $f = (1, 1), (2, 3), (0, -1), (-1, -3)\}$ be a function describe by the formula $f(x) = ax + b$ for some integers a, b. Determine a, b. [NCERT]

Sol. Given, $f = \{(1, 1), (2, 3), (0, -1), (-1, -3)\}$

Here, $f(1) = 1$, $f(2) = 3$, $f(0) = -1$, $f(-1) = -3$

It is given that $f(x) = ax + b$

$\therefore$ $f(1) = 1$ and $f(2) = 3$

$\Rightarrow$ $a + b = 1$ and $2a + b = 3$

On solving both equations, we get

$a = 2, b = -1$

Thus, $f(x) = 2x - 1$

This also satisfy $f(0) = -1$ and $f(-1) = -3$

Hence, $a = 2, b = -1$

Domain of Real Functions

As we know that real functions are generally described by providing the general formula for finding the images of elements of its domain.

In such cases, the domain of the real function $f(x)$ is the set of all those real numbers for which the expression for $f(x)$ or the formula for $f(x)$ assumes real values only.

In other words, we can say that the domain of $f(x)$ is the set of all those real numbers for which $f(x)$ is meaningful.

Note A function does not exist, if its domain is empty set.

Working Rule for Finding the Domain of Real Functions

The domain of a real function depends on the nature of function. e.g. Polynomial function is always define for all real numbers, so its domain is R. Depending upon function, we may use the following steps to determine their domain.

For Rational Functions

***Step* I** First put the denominator equal to zero and find the values of variable.

***Step* II** The value of variable obtained in step I are the values at which rational function is not defined. Then, omit the set of these values from R to get required domain.

Example 16 Find the domain of real function

$$f(x) = \frac{x^2 + 3x + 5}{x^2 - 5x + 4}$$

Sol. Here, denominator $= x^2 - 5x + 4$

On putting it equal to zero, we get

$$x^2 - 5x + 4 = 0$$

$$\Rightarrow \quad x^2 - 4x - x + 4 = 0$$

$$\Rightarrow \quad x(x-4) - 1(x-4) = 0$$

$$\Rightarrow \quad (x-4)(x-1) = 0$$

$\Rightarrow$ $x = 4$ or $x = 1$

Clearly, at $x = 1$ and $x = 4$ denominator becomes zero and thus given function will not be define for these value.

So, required domain of given function $= R - \{1, 4\}$

For Square Root Function

We know that expression under the square root should not be negative. So, for finding the domain of square root function, put the expression without root greater than or equal to zero and then find the value of variable.

Example 17 Find the domain of each of the following function.

(i) $\frac{1}{\sqrt{x-2}}$ (ii) $\sqrt{4 - x^2}$

Sol. (i) Let $f(x) = \frac{1}{\sqrt{x-2}}$

$f(x)$ assumes real values if $x - 2 > 0$

[here, we take only greater than sign, because it is in rational form and so denominator should not be equal to zero]

$\Rightarrow \quad x > 2 \Rightarrow x \in (2, \infty)$.

Hence, domain of f is $(2, \infty)$.

(ii) Given, $f(x) = \sqrt{4 - x^2}$

Clearly, $f(x)$ assumes real values, if $4 - x^2 \geq 0$

$\Rightarrow \quad -(x^2 - 4) \geq 0 \Rightarrow x^2 - 4 \leq 0$

[multiplying by -1 on both sides]

$\Rightarrow (x - 2)(x + 2) \leq 0$

$[\because a^2 - b^2 = (a - b)(a + b)]$

$\Rightarrow \quad x \in [-2, 2]$

Hence, domain of $f = [-2, 2]$

Example 18 Find the domain for which the functions $f(x) = 2x^2 - 1$ and $g(x) = 1 - 3x$ are equal. **[NCERT Exemplar]**

Sol. Given, $f(x) = 2x^2 - 1$ and $g(x) = 1 - 3x$

Since, $f(x) = g(x)$

$\therefore \quad 2x^2 - 1 = 1 - 3x$

$\Rightarrow \quad 2x^2 + 3x - 2 = 0$

$\Rightarrow \quad 2x^2 + 4x - x - 2 = 0$

$\Rightarrow \quad 2x(x + 2) - 1(x + 2) = 0$

$\Rightarrow \quad (2x - 1)(x + 2) = 0$

$\Rightarrow \quad 2x - 1 = 0$ or $x + 2 = 0$

$\Rightarrow \quad x = \frac{1}{2}$ or $x = -2$

Thus, domain for which the function

$f(x) = g(x)$ is $\left\{\frac{1}{2}, -2\right\}$

Example 19 Find the domain of $f(x) = \dfrac{1}{\sqrt{x + |x|}}$.

Sol. We have, $f(x) = \dfrac{1}{\sqrt{x + |x|}}$

We know that, $|x| = \begin{cases} x, & \text{if } x \geq 0 \\ -x, & \text{if } x < 0 \end{cases}$

$\therefore \quad x + |x| = \begin{cases} x + x, & \text{if } x \geq 0 \\ x - x, & \text{if } x < 0 \end{cases}$

$\Rightarrow \quad x + |x| = \begin{cases} 2x, & \text{if } x \geq 0 \\ 0, & \text{if } x < 0 \end{cases}$ ...(i)

Here, the function $f(x) = \dfrac{1}{\sqrt{x + |x|}}$ assumes real values, if $x + |x| > 0$.

$\Rightarrow \quad 2x > 0 \Rightarrow x > 0$ [using Eq. (i)]

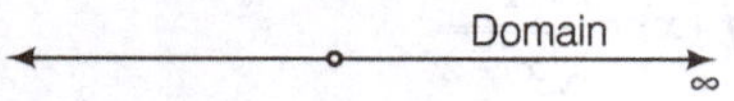

$\therefore \quad x \in (0, \infty)$

Hence, domain of $f = (0, \infty)$.

Note Domain of modulus function is always R i.e. $(-\infty, \infty)$.

Range of Real Functions

The range of a real function of a real variable is the set of all real values taken by $f(x)$ at points of its domain.

Working Rule for Finding Range of Real Functions

Let $y = f(x)$ be a real function, then for finding the range we may use the following steps

***Step* I** Find the domain of the function $y = f(x)$.

***Step* II** Transform the equation $y = f(x)$ as $x = g(y)$. i.e. convert x in terms of y.

***Step* III** Find the values of y from $x = g(y)$ such that the values of x are real and lying in the domain of f.

***Step* IV** The set of values of y obtained in step III be the range of function f.

Example 20 Find the range of $f(x) = \dfrac{x - 2}{3 - x}$.

Sol. Given, $f(x) = \dfrac{x - 2}{3 - x} = y$ (say)

Here, denominator $= 3 - x$

Put denominator $= 0$, we get

$3 - x = 0$

$\Rightarrow \quad x = 3$

$\therefore \quad$ Domain of $y = f(x)$ is $R - \{3\}$.

Now, consider $y = \dfrac{x - 2}{3 - x}$

$\Rightarrow \quad y(3 - x) = (x - 2)$

$\Rightarrow \quad 3y - xy = x - 2$

$\Rightarrow \quad x + xy = 3y + 2$

$\Rightarrow \quad x(1 + y) = 3y + 2$

$\Rightarrow \quad x = \dfrac{3y + 2}{1 + y}$

It will define, if $1 + y \neq 0 \Rightarrow y \neq -1$.

So, $x = g(y)$ takes real values, if $y \in R - \{-1\}$.

Also, $\dfrac{3y + 2}{1 + y} \neq 3$ for all $y \in R - \{-1\}$

$\left[\because \text{if } \dfrac{3y + 2}{1 + y} = 3, \text{ then } 3y + 2 = 3 + 3y \Rightarrow 2 = 3, \text{ which is absurd}\right]$

$\Rightarrow \quad x = \dfrac{3y + 2}{1 + y} \neq 3$ for all $y \in R - \{-1\}$

Thus, $\quad x = \dfrac{3y + 2}{1 + y} \in$ Domain (f), $\forall\ y \in R - \{-1\}$

Hence, the range of $f(x)$ is $R - \{-1\}$.

Example 21 Find the domian and range of the function $f(x) = \left\{\left(x, \frac{1}{1-x^2}\right) : x \in R\ x \neq \pm 1\right\}$.

Sol. Given, $f(x) = \left\{\left(x, \frac{1}{1-x^2}\right) : x \in R,\ x \neq \pm 1\right\}$

Clearly, $f(x) = \frac{1}{1-x^2}$ is not defined, when $(1-x^2) = 0$

i.e. when $x = \pm 1$.

$\therefore$ Domain of $f(x) = R - \{-1, 1\}$

Further, let $\qquad y = \frac{1}{1-x^2}$

$\Rightarrow \qquad (1-x^2) = \frac{1}{y} \Rightarrow x^2 = 1 - \frac{1}{y}$

$\Rightarrow \qquad x = \pm\sqrt{\left(1 - \frac{1}{y}\right)} = \pm\sqrt{\frac{y-1}{y}}$

Clearly, x is define, if $\frac{y-1}{y} \geq 0$ and $y \neq 0$

$(y-1)\,y \geq 0$ and $y \neq 0$

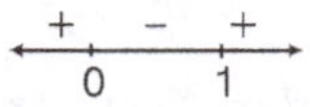

$\Rightarrow \qquad -\infty < y < 0$ or $1 \leq y < \infty$

Also, $\sqrt{\frac{y-1}{y}} \neq 1$ for all $y \in (-\infty, 0) \cup [1, \infty)$

$\Rightarrow \qquad x = \pm\sqrt{\frac{y-1}{y}} \neq \pm 1$ for all $y \in (-\infty, 0) \cup [1, \infty)$

$\left[\because \text{ if } \sqrt{\frac{y-1}{y}} = 1,\ y - 1 = y \Rightarrow -1 = 0, \text{ which is absured}\right]$

Thus, $x = \pm\sqrt{\frac{y-1}{y}} \in$ domain (f), $\forall\ y \in (-\infty, 0) \cup [1, \infty)$

Hence, range $(f) = (-\infty, 0) \cup [1, \infty)$.

Example 22 Find the domain and range of the function $f(x) = \left\{\left(x, \frac{x^2-1}{x-1}\right) : x \in R,\ x \neq 1\right\}$.

Sol. Let $f(x) = \left\{\left(x, \frac{x^2-1}{x-1}\right) : x \in R,\ x \neq 1\right\}$

Clearly, f is not defined, when $x = 1$

So, f is defined for all real values of x, except $x = 1$.

$\therefore \qquad$ Domain $(f) = R - \{1\}$

Let $\qquad y = \frac{x^2-1}{x-1}$

$= \frac{(x-1)(x+1)}{(x-1)} = x + 1 \qquad [\text{as } x \neq 1]$

$\Rightarrow \qquad x = y - 1$

Clearly, x is not defined, when $y = 2$ as $x \neq 1$.

Range $(f) = R - \{2\}$

Example 23 Find the domain and the range of the function $f(x) = \sqrt{16 - x^2}$.

Sol. Given, $f(x) = \sqrt{16 - x^2}$

Domain of f We observe that $f(x)$ is defined for all x satisfying $16 - x^2 \geq 0$

$\Rightarrow \qquad x^2 - 16 \leq 0$

$\Rightarrow \quad (x-4)(x+4) \leq 0 \qquad [\because a^2 - b^2 = (a-b)(a+b)]$

$\Rightarrow \qquad -4 \leq x \leq 4$

$\Rightarrow \qquad x \in [-4, 4]$

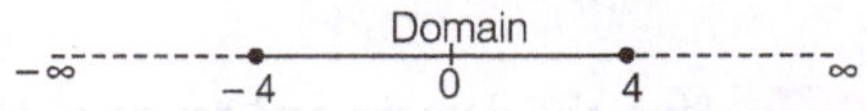

Range of f Let $y = f(x)$.

Then, $\qquad y = \sqrt{16 - x^2} \Rightarrow y^2 = 16 - x^2$

$\Rightarrow \qquad x^2 = 16 - y^2$

$\Rightarrow \qquad x = \pm\sqrt{16 - y^2}$

Clearly, x will take real values, if

$16 - y^2 \geq 0 \Rightarrow y^2 - 16 \leq 0$

$\Rightarrow \quad (y-4)(y+4) \leq 0 \Rightarrow -4 \leq y \leq 4$

$\Rightarrow \qquad y \in [-4, 4]$

Also, $\quad y = \sqrt{16 - x^2} \geq 0$ for all $x \in [-4, 4]$

$\therefore \qquad y \in [0, 4]$ for $x \in [-4, 4]$

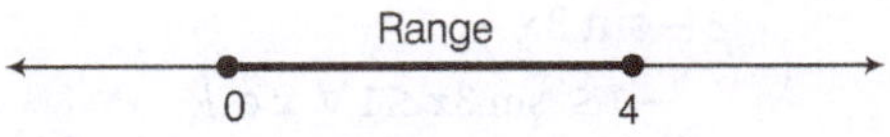

Hence, the range of f is $[0, 4]$.

Example 24 Find the domain and range of the function $f(x) = \frac{1}{\sqrt{x-5}}$.

Sol. We have, $f(x) = \frac{1}{\sqrt{x-5}}$

Domain of f Clearly, $f(x)$ takes real values, if

$x - 5 > 0 \Rightarrow x > 5 \Rightarrow x \in (5, \infty)$

Domain of $f = (5, \infty)$

Range of f For $x > 5$, we have $x - 5 > 0$

$\Rightarrow \quad \sqrt{x-5} > 0 \Rightarrow \dfrac{1}{\sqrt{x-5}} > 0 \Rightarrow f(x) > 0$

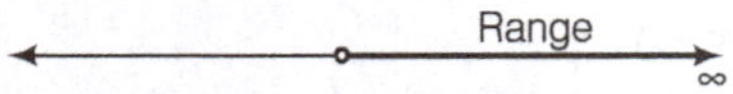

Thus, $f(x)$ takes all real values greater than zero.
Hence, range of $f = (0, \infty)$.

Example 25 Find the domain and range of the real valued function $f(x)$ given by $f(x) = \dfrac{4-x}{x-4}$

Sol. Given, $f(x) = \dfrac{4-x}{x-4}$

Domain of f Here, we see that $f(x)$ is defined for all x except $= 4$

$\therefore \quad \text{Domain}(f) = R - \{4\}$

$\because \quad f(x) = \dfrac{4-x}{x-4} = \dfrac{-(x-4)}{x-4} = -1$

$\therefore \quad \text{Range}(f) = \{-1\}$

Example 26 Find the domain and range of the function $f(x) = 1 - |x-2|$.

Sol. Given function is $f(x) = 1 - |x-2|$.

We know that, $|x|$ is defined for $x \in (-\infty, \infty)$.

$\therefore$ Domain of $|x-2|$ is $(-\infty, \infty)$.

Hence, domain of $f(x) = 1 - |x-2|$ is $(-\infty, \infty)$.

Also we know that, range of $|x|$ is $[0, \infty)$.

$\therefore$ Range of $|x-2|$ is $[0, \infty)$.

$\therefore \quad 0 \le |x-2| < \infty \Rightarrow -\infty < -|x-2| \le 0$

$\Rightarrow -\infty + 1 < 1 - |x-2| \le 1 \Rightarrow \quad -\infty < f(x) \le 1$

$\therefore$ Range of $f(x)$ is $(-\infty, 1]$.

Example 27 Find the domain and range of the function $f(x) = \dfrac{1}{2 - \sin 3x}$.

Sol $\because \quad -1 \le \sin 3x \le 1 \; \forall \; x \in R$

$\Rightarrow \quad -1 \le -\sin 3x \le 1, \forall x \in R$

$\Rightarrow \quad 1 \le 2 - \sin 3x \le 3, \forall x \in R$

$\Rightarrow \quad 2 - \sin 3x \ne 0$ for any $x \in R$

$\Rightarrow \quad f(x) = \dfrac{1}{2 - \sin 3x}$ is defined, $\forall \; x \in R$.

$\therefore \quad \text{Domain}(f) = R$

From the above discussion, $1 \le 2 - \sin 3x \le 3, \forall \; x \in R$

$\Rightarrow \quad \dfrac{1}{3} \le \dfrac{1}{2 - \sin 3x} \le 1, \forall x \in R$

$\Rightarrow \dfrac{1}{3} \le f(x) \le 1, \forall \; x \in R \Rightarrow f(x) \in \left[\dfrac{1}{3}, 1\right]$

$\therefore \quad \text{Range}(f) = \left[\dfrac{1}{3}, 1\right]$

Topic Practice 3

Very Short Answer Type Questions

(2 Marks)

1 Which of the relations are functions?
(i) $f_1 = \{(2,1), (3,1), (4,1), (3,2), (4,2), (4,3)\}$
(ii) $f_2 = \{(1,4), (2,3), (3,2), (4,1)\}$

2 Let f be a relation on the set N of natural numbers defined by $f = \{(n, 3n) : n \in N\}$. Is f a function from N to N. If so, find the range of f.

3 Let $f : Z \to Z$, $g : Z \to Z$ be functions defined by $f = \{(x, x^2) : x \in Z\}$ and $g = \{(x, |x|^2) : x \in Z\}$, show that $f = g$.

4 Let $f : R \to R$ be given by $f(x) = x^2 + 3$. Find $\{x : f(x) = 28\}$

5 In question 4, find the pre-images of 39 and 2 under f.

6 Let f be defined by $f(x) = (x - 4)$ and g be defined by $g(x) = \begin{cases} \dfrac{x^2 - 16}{x + 4}, & x \ne -4 \\ \lambda, & x = -4 \end{cases}$

Find λ such that $f(x) = g(x)$ for all x.

7 If $f(x) = 3x^4 - 5x^2 + 9$, then find $f(x-1)$.

8 If $f : R \to R$ be defined as follows
$$f(x) = \begin{cases} 1, & x \in Q \\ -1, & x \notin Q \end{cases}$$
Find (i) $f\left(\dfrac{1}{2}\right)$, $f(\pi)$ (ii) pre-image of 1 and -1.

9 A function $f : R \to R$ is defined by $f(x) = x^2$. Determine
(i) Range of f (ii) $\{x : f(x) = 4\}$

10 If $A = \{1, 2, 3, 4\}$, $B = \{1, 2, \ldots, 10\}$ and $f : A \to B$ is a function defined by $f(x) = 2x + 1$, $x \in A$, then find the range of f.

11 Find the domain of the function
$$f(x) = \frac{x}{x^2 + 3x + 2}.$$

12 If $f(x) = x + \dfrac{1}{x}$, prove that $[f(x)]^3 = f(x^3) + 3f\left(\dfrac{1}{x}\right)$

13 Is $g = \{(1, 1), (2, 3), (3, 5), (4, 7),\}$ a function, justify? If this is described by the relation, $g(x) = \alpha x + \beta$, then what values should be assigned to α and β? **[NCERT Exemplar]**

Short Answer Type Questions

4 Marks

14 If $f(x) = \dfrac{1}{2x+1}, x \neq -\dfrac{1}{2}$, then show that $f(f(x)) = \dfrac{2x+1}{2x+3}$, provided that $x \neq -\dfrac{3}{2}$.

15 Find the range of the following function.

$$f(x) = \frac{x}{1+x^2}$$

16 Let f and g be real functions defined by $f(x) = 2x + 1$ and $g(x) = 4x - 7$.

(i) For what real numbers x, $f(x) = g(x)$?

(ii) For what real numbers x, $f(x) < g(x)$?

[NCERT Exemplar]

17 Let $f = \left\{\left(x, \dfrac{x^2}{1+x^2}\right) : x \in R\right\}$ be a functions R into R determine the range of R. **[NCERT]**

Hints & Answers

1. (i) It is not a function because the first elements 3 and 4 of ordered pairs have more than one images.

(ii) It is a function bacause first element of each ordered pair has one and only one image.

2. Since, for each $n \in N$. There exist a unique $3n \in N$ such $(n, 3n) \in f$. Therefore f is a function from N to N

Ans. Now, range $(f) = \{3n : n \in N\}$

3. Here, domain (f) = domain (g)

codomain f = codomain g

Now, $f(x) = x^2$ and $g(x) = |x|^2 = x^2 \quad (\because |x|^2 = x^2)$

Ans. $f(x) = g(x), \forall x \in Z$

4. Given, $f(x) = x^2 + 3$ and $f(x) = 28$

$\therefore \quad x^2 + 3 = 28 \Rightarrow x^2 = 28 - 3$

$\Rightarrow \quad x^2 = 25 \Rightarrow x = \pm 5$

Ans. $x \in \{-5, 5\}$

5. Let x be the pre-image of 39

$\Rightarrow \quad f(x) = 39 \Rightarrow x^2 + 3 = 39$

$\Rightarrow \quad x^2 = 36 \Rightarrow x = \pm 6$

Ans. ±6

Again, let pre-image of 2 be x.

$\Rightarrow \quad f(x) = 2 \Rightarrow x^2 + 3 = 2$

$\Rightarrow \quad x^2 = -1$ [which is not possible]

Ans. 2 does not have any pre-image.

6. Given, $f(x) = g(x), \forall x \in R$

$\Rightarrow \quad f(-4) = g(-4)$

$\Rightarrow \quad -4 - 4 = \lambda \Rightarrow \lambda = -8$ **Ans.** –8

7. Here, $f(x) = 3x^4 - 5x^2 + 9$

$\therefore \quad f(x-1) = 3(x-1)^4 - 5(x-1)^2 + 9$

Ans. $3x^4 - 12x^3 + 13x^2 - 2x + 7$

8. (i) The value of the function for every rational number is 1 and for every irrational number is –1.

$\therefore \quad \dfrac{1}{2} \in Q \Rightarrow f\left(\dfrac{1}{2}\right) = 1$

and $\quad \pi \notin Q \Rightarrow f(\pi) = -1$

(ii) $\because \quad f(x) = 1 \,\forall\, x \in Q$

$\therefore$ pre-image of 1 is rational numbers

$\because \quad f(x) = -1 \,\forall\, x \notin Q$

$\therefore$ Pre-image of –1 is all real number except rational number i.e. $R - Q$ = Set of irrational numbers.

Ans. (i) 1, –1 (ii) Set of rational number, set of irrational number.

9. (i) $f(x) = x^2$, clearly $\forall\, x \in R, f(x) = x^2 \geq 0$

Ans. Range = $[0, \infty)$

(ii) $f(x) = 4 \Rightarrow x^2 = 4 \Rightarrow x = \pm 2$

Ans. $x \in \{-2, 2\}$

10. Given, $f(x) = 2x + 1$

$\therefore \quad f(1) = 2 \times 1 + 1 = 2 + 1 = 3 \in B$

$\Rightarrow \quad f(2) = 2 \times 2 + 1 = 4 + 1 = 5 \in B$

$\Rightarrow \quad f(3) = 2 \times 3 + 1 = 6 + 1 = 7 \in B$

$\Rightarrow \quad f(4) = 2 \times 4 + 1 = 8 + 1 = 9 \in B$

$\therefore \quad$ Range $f = \{3, 5, 7, 9\}$

11. Here, $f(x) = \dfrac{x}{x^2 + 3x + 2} = \dfrac{x}{(x+1)(x+2)}$

Clearly, $f(x)$ is not defined at $x = -1, -2$.

Ans. Domain $(f) = R - \{-1, -2\}$.

12. $\because \quad f(x) = x + \dfrac{1}{x}$

$\Rightarrow \quad f(x^3) = x^3 + \dfrac{1}{x^3}$

Now, $[f(x)]^3 = \left(x + \dfrac{1}{x}\right)^3 = x^3 + \dfrac{1}{x^3} + 3\left(x + \dfrac{1}{x}\right)$

$[\because (a+b)^3 = a^3 + b^3 + 3ab(a+b)]$

$= f(x^3) + 3f(x)$

$= f(x^3) + 3f\left(\dfrac{1}{x}\right) \quad \left[\because f(x) = f\left(\dfrac{1}{x}\right)\right]$

13. We have, $g = \{(1, 1), (2, 3), (3, 5), (4, 7)\}$

Since, every element has unique image under g. So, g is a function. Solve as Example 22.

Ans. $\alpha = 2, \beta = -1$

14. $f(f(x)) = f\left(\frac{1}{2x+1}\right) = \frac{1}{2\left(\frac{1}{2x+1}\right)+1} = \frac{2x+1}{2x+3}$

Clearly, it is not defined at $x \neq -\frac{3}{2}$.

15. Let $y = f(x) = \frac{x}{1+x^2}$; $yx^2 - x + y = 0$

$\Rightarrow \quad x = \frac{1 \pm \sqrt{1-4y^2}}{2y}$

Clearly, x will assume real values, if

$1 - 4y^2 \geq 0$ and $y \neq 0$

$\Rightarrow \quad -\frac{1}{2} \leq y \leq \frac{1}{2}$ and $y \neq 0$

$\Rightarrow \quad y \in \left[\frac{-1}{2}, \frac{1}{2}\right] - \{0\}$

Also, $\quad y = 0$ for $x = 0$

Ans. Range $(f) = \left[-\frac{1}{2}, \frac{1}{2}\right]$

16. We have, $f(x) = 2x+1$ and $g(x) = 4x-7$

(i) $\because \quad f(x) = g(x)$

$\therefore \quad 2x+1 = 4x-7 \Rightarrow 2x = 8 \Rightarrow x = 4$

(ii) $\because \quad f(x) < g(x)$

$\therefore \quad 2x+1 < 4x-7 \quad -2x+1 < -7$

$\Rightarrow \quad -2x < -8 \Rightarrow x > 4$

Ans. (i) 4 (ii) $x > 4$

17. $f(x)$ is defined for all $x \in R$. As $x^2 + 1 \neq 0$ for any $x \in R$.

Now, let $y = f(x) = \frac{x^2}{x^2+1}$

$\Rightarrow \quad x^2 = \frac{y}{1-y} \Rightarrow x = \pm\sqrt{\frac{y}{1-y}}$

Clearly, x will be real, if

$\frac{y}{1-y} \geq 0$ and $y \neq 1 \Rightarrow \frac{y}{y-1} \leq 0$ and $y \neq 1 \Rightarrow 0 \leq y < 1$

Ans. Range $(f) = [0, 1)$.

TOPIC 04 Some Standard Real Functions

Here, we shall study some important real functions, which are frequently used in the study of calculus.

Constant Function

A function $f : R \rightarrow R$ is said to be a **constant function**, if there exists a **real number** k, such that

$f(x) = k$ for all $x \in R$.

Here, domain of $f = R$ and its range $= \{k\}$

e.g. $\quad f(x) = 5, \forall x \in R$ (symbol '$\forall$' means for all)

Here, $f(x)$ is a constant function whose

domain $= \{x : x \in R\}$ and range $= \{5\}$

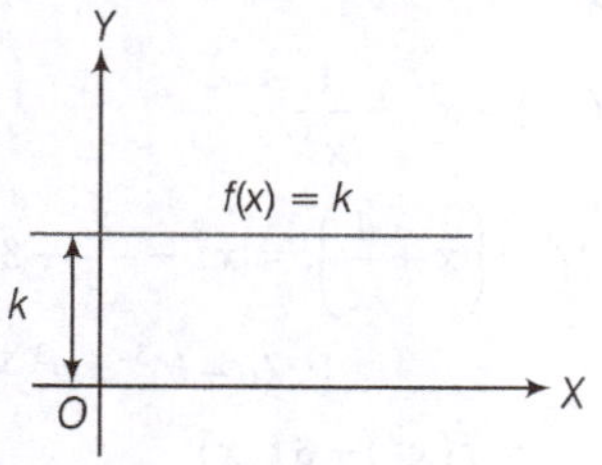

It may be observed that

(i) The graph of a constant function is a line parallel to X-axis.

(ii) If $k > 0$, then the line will be above X-axis.

(iii) If $k = 0$, then graph coincides with the X-axis.

(iv) If $k < 0$, then the line will be below X-axis.

Identity Function

The real function $f : R \rightarrow R$ defined by $f(x) = x, \forall x \in R$ is called an **identity function.** Its domain is R and range is also R.

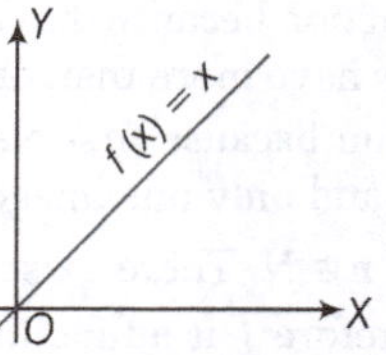

It may be observed that

(i) The graph of identity function is a straight line.

(ii) it passes through origin.

Example 1 Draw the graph of each the following function.

(i) $f(x) = 5$ (ii) $f(x) = -5$ (iii) $f(x) = 0$

Sol. (i) Given, $f(x) = 5 \; \forall \; x \in R$

Clearly, domain of f is R.

Range of f is $\{5\}$.

Now, we prepare a table for different value of x as shown below

x	−3	−2	−1	0	1	2	3
$f(x)$	5	5	5	5	5	5	5

Locate the points (–3, 5), (–2, 5), (–1, 5), (0, 5), (1, 5), (2, 5) and (3, 5) on the graph paper and joint them, we obtained the required graph as shown below.

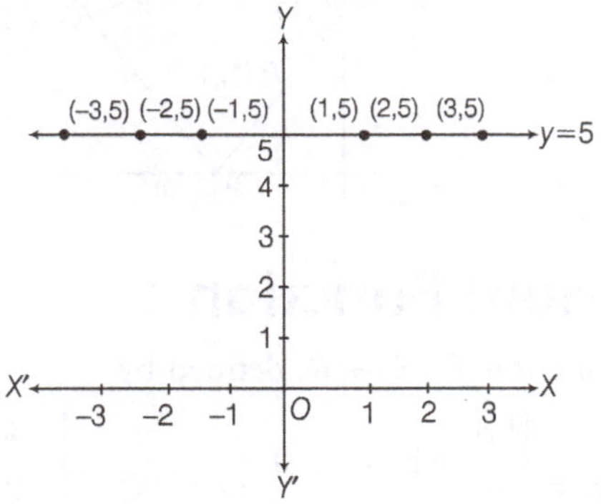

Clearly the graph of $f(x)=5$ represents a straight line parallel to X-axis and at a distance of 5 unit above the X-axis and symmetric with respect to Y-axis.

(ii) Given, $f(x)=-5$

Clearly, domain of $f(x)$ is R.

Range of $f(x)$ is $\{-5\}$.

Now, we prepare a table for different values of x as shown below

x	–3	–2	–1	0	1	2	3
f(x)	–5	–5	–5	–5	–5	–5	–5

Locate the points $(-3,-5)$, $(-2,-5)$, $(-1,-5)$, $(0,-5)$, $(1,-5)$, $(2,-5)$, $(3,-5)$ on the graph paper and join them we obtained the graph of the function as shown below.

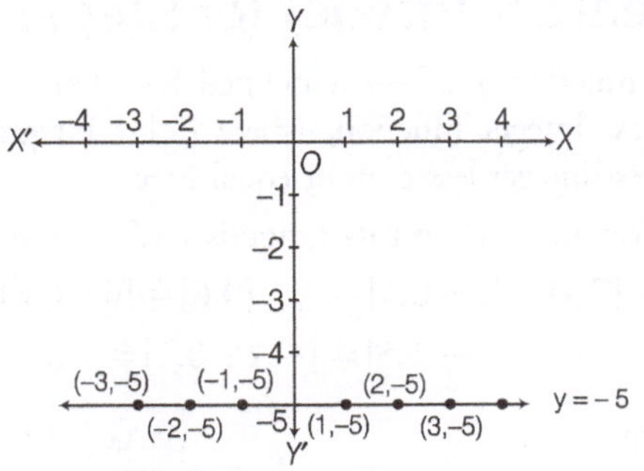

Clearly, the graph of $f(x)=-5$ represent a straight line parallel to X-axis and at a distance of 5 unit below the X-axis and symmetric with respect to Y-axis.

(iii) Given, $f(x)=0$

Clearly, domain of f is R.

Range f is $\{0\}$,

We have the following table for different value of x.

x	–2	–1	0	1	2
f(x)	0	0	0	0	0

Now, locate the point $(-2,0),(-1,0),(0,0),(1,0),(2,0)$ on the graph paper, we get the required graph of the function.

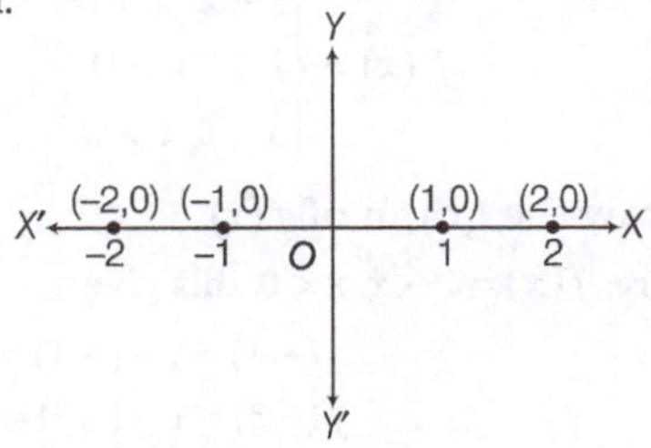

Clearly, the graph of $f(x)=0$ represent X-axis and symmetric with respect to Y-axis.

Modulus or Absolute Value Function

The function $f: R \to R$ defined by

$$f(x)=|x|=\begin{cases} x, \text{if } x \geq 0 \\ -x, \text{if } x < 0 \end{cases}$$

is called the modulus function. It is also called **absolute value function.** Its domain is R and its range is $[0, \infty)$.

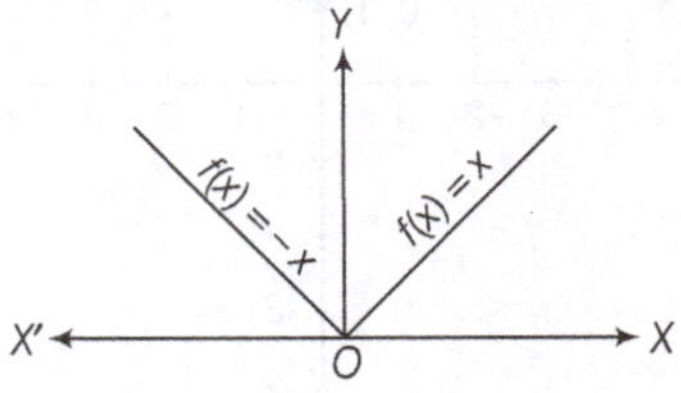

It may be observed that

(i) The graph is symmetrical with respect to Y-axis.
(ii) The graph lies above the X-axis.
(iii) It passes through the origin.
(iv) In the first quadrant, it coincides with the graph of the identity function.

Properties of Modulus Function

(i) For any real number x, we have $\sqrt{x^2}=|x|$

(ii) If a and b are positive real numbers, then

(a) $x^2 \leq a^2 \Leftrightarrow |x| \leq a \Leftrightarrow -a \leq x \leq a$

(b) $x^2 \geq a^2 \Leftrightarrow |x| \geq a \Leftrightarrow x \leq -a$ or $x \geq a$

(c) $x^2 < a^2 \Leftrightarrow |x| < a \Leftrightarrow -a < x < a$

(d) $x^2 > a^2 \Leftrightarrow |x| > a \Leftrightarrow x < -a$ or $x > a$

(e) $a^2 \leq x^2 \leq b^2 \Leftrightarrow a \leq |x| \leq b$
$\Leftrightarrow x \in [-b,-a] \cup [a,b]$

(f) $a^2 < x^2 < b^2 \Leftrightarrow a < |x| < b$
$\Leftrightarrow x \in (-b,-a) \cup (a,b)$

Example 2 The function f is defined by

$$f(x)=\begin{cases}1-x, & x<0\\ 1, & x=0\\ x+1, & x>0\end{cases}$$

Draw the graph of $f(x)$. **[NCERT]**

Sol. Here, $f(x)=1-x, x<0$, this gives

$$f(-4)=1-(-4)=5$$
$$f(-3)=1-(-3)=4$$
$$f(-2)=1-(-2)=3$$
$$f(-1)=1-(-1)=2$$

and $\quad f(x)=x+1, x>0$

$$f(1)=2, f(2)=3,\ f(3)=4$$
$$f(4)=5 \text{ and so on.}$$

Now, the graph of f is as shown in following figure.

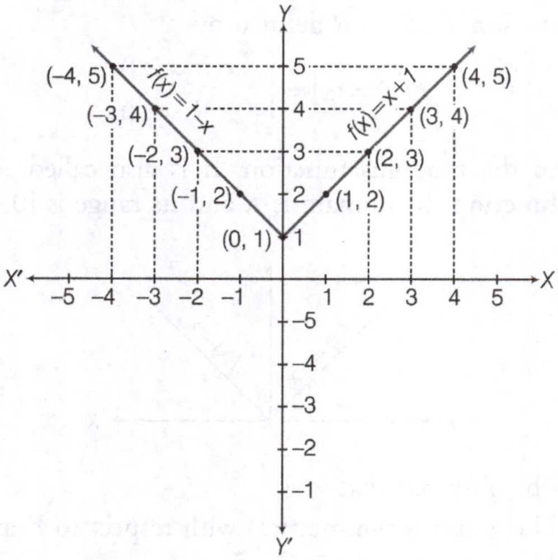

Example 3 Draw the graph of the function $f: R \to R$ such that $f(x)=|x-2|$.

Sol. Clearly,

$$y=|x-2|=\begin{cases}x-2, & \text{if } x-2\ge 0\\ -(x-2), & \text{if } x-2<0\end{cases}=\begin{cases}x-2, & \text{if } x\ge 2\\ 2-x, & \text{if } x<2\end{cases}$$

We know that, a linear equation in x and y represents a line. For drawing a line, we need only two points.

For $y=x-2$,

x	2	4
y	0	2

So, plot the points $P(2, 0)$, $Q(4, 2)$ and join PQ to get the graph of $y=x-2$. For $y=2-x$

x	1	0
y	1	2

Plot the points $R(1, 1)$, $S(0, 2)$ and join RS to get the graph of $y=2-x$.

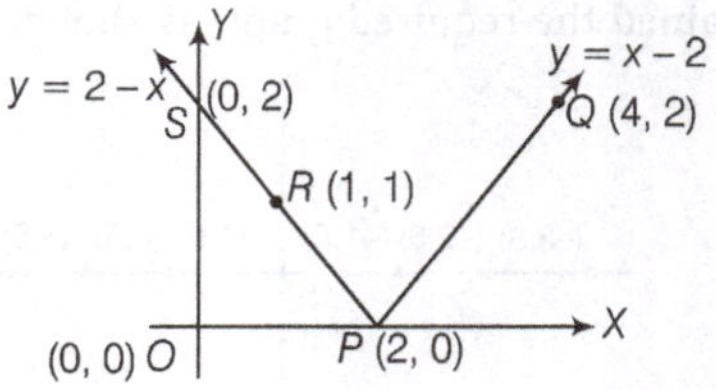

Signum Function

The function $f: R \to R$ defined by

$$f(x)=\begin{cases}\dfrac{|x|}{x}, & \text{when } x\ne 0\\ 0, & \text{when } x=0\end{cases} \quad \text{or} \quad f(x)=\begin{cases}1, & \text{when } x>0\\ 0, & \text{when } x=0\\ -1, & \text{when } x<0\end{cases}$$

is called the **signum function.**

Therefore, its domain is R, range is $\{-1, 0, 1\}$ and its graph is given below

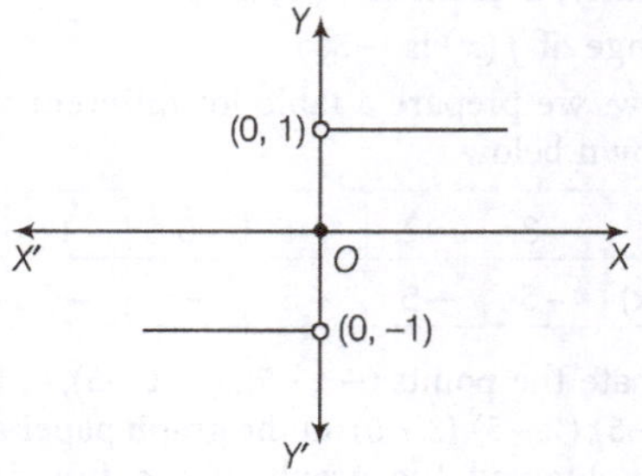

Greatest Integer (or Step) Function

The function $f: R \to R$ defined by $f(x)=[x]$ is called the greatest integer function, where $[x]$ = **integral** part of x or greatest integer less than or equal to x.

Its domain is R and its range is I (I = set of integer).

e.g. $[7.4]=[7+0.4]=7$; $\quad [0.6]=[0+0.6]=0$

and $\quad [-1.5]=[-2+0.5]=-2$

Graph	Values of x	$f(x)=[x]$
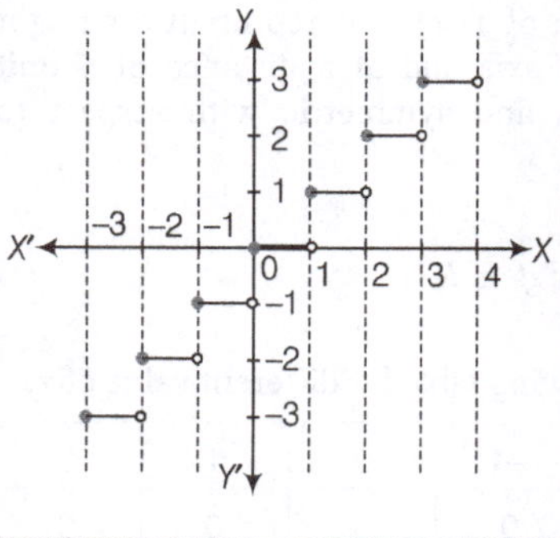	⋮	⋮
	$-3\le x<-2$	-3
	$-2\le x<-1$	-2
	$-1\le x<0$	-1
	$0\le x<1$	0
	$1\le x<2$	1
	$2\le x<3$	2
	$3\le x<4$	3
	⋮	⋮

It may be observed that

(i) $[x]$ = [Integer + Proper positive fraction] = Integer

(ii) It passes through origin.

(iii) It is symmetrical in the opposite quadrant.

Properties of Greatest Integer Function

If n is an integer and x is a real number between n and $n+1$, then

(i) $[-n]=-n$

(ii) $[x+k]=[x]+k$ for any integer k.

(iii) $[-x]=-[x]-1$

(iv) $[x]+[-x]=\begin{cases}-1, & \text{if } x\notin Z\\ 0, & \text{if } x\in Z\end{cases}$

(v) $[x]-[-x]=\begin{cases}2[x]+1, & \text{if } x\notin Z\\ 2[x], & \text{if } x\in Z\end{cases}$

(vi) $[x]\ge k \Rightarrow x\ge k$, where $k\in Z$.

(vii) $[x]\le k \Rightarrow x<k+1$, where $k\in Z$.

(viii) $[x]>k \Rightarrow x\ge k+1$, where $k\in Z$.

(ix) $[x]<k \Rightarrow x<k$, where $k\in Z$.

Least (or Smallest) Integer Function (or Ceiling Function)

The function $f:R\to R$ defined by $f(x)=\lceil x\rceil$ for all $x\in R$ is called the smallest integer function or the ceiling function. It is also a **step function.** Its domain is R and range is I.

For any real number x, we use the symbol $\lceil x\rceil$ or (x) to denote the smallest integer greater than or equal to x.

e.g. $\lceil 5.9\rceil=6, \lceil -7.2\rceil=-7$, etc.

Graph	Values of x	$f(x)=\lceil x\rceil$
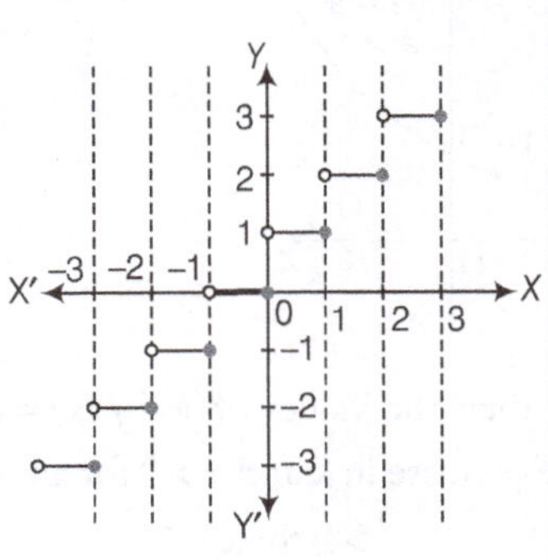	⋮	⋮
	$-3<x\le -2$	-2
	$-2<x\le -1$	-1
	$-1<x\le 0$	0
	$0<x\le 1$	1
	$1<x\le 2$	2
	$2<x\le 3$	3
	⋮	⋮

It may be observed that

(i) It passes through origin.

(ii) It is symmetrical in the opposite quadrants.

Properties of Smallest Integer Function

Following are some properties of smallest integer function

(i) $\lceil -n\rceil=-\lceil n\rceil$, where $n\in Z$

(ii) $\lceil -x\rceil=-\lceil x\rceil+1$, where $x\in R-Z$

(iii) $\lceil x+n\rceil=\lceil x\rceil+n$, where $x\in R-Z$ and $n\in Z$

(iv) $\lceil x\rceil+\lceil -x\rceil=\begin{cases}1, & \text{if } x\notin Z\\ 0, & \text{if } x\in Z\end{cases}$

(v) $\lceil x\rceil-\lceil -x\rceil=\begin{cases}2\lceil x\rceil-1, & \text{if } x\notin Z\\ 2\lceil x\rceil, & \text{if } x\in Z\end{cases}$

Polynomial Function

A function $f:R\to R$, defined by $f(x)=a_0+a_1x+a_2x^2+\ldots+a_nx^n$, where n is a non-negative integer and $a_0, a_1, a_2, \ldots, a_n\in R$, is called a polynomial function.

If $a_n\ne 0$, then n is called the **degree of the polynomial.**

If $n=1$, then it is called a **linear function** and if $n=2$, then it is called a **quadratic function.**

The domain of a polynomial function is R and range depends on the polynomial representing the function. e.g.

(i) $f(x)=x^3-x^2+9$ is polynomial function in x.

(ii) $h(x)=x^5+\sqrt{3}x$ is polynomial function in x.

(iii) $g(x)=x^{3/2}+3x$ is not a polynomial function. Since, power $\frac{3}{2}$ is not an integer.

Example 4 Let R be the set of real numbers. Define the real function $f:R\to R$ by $f(x)=x+10$. Sketch the graph of this function.

Sol. Given, $f:R\to R$ define by $f(x)=x+10$.

Here, at $x=0$, $f(0)=10$

At $x=1$, $f(1)=11$

At $x=2$, $f(2)=12$

… …

At $x=10$, $f(10)=20$ and so on

Also, at $x=-1$, $f(-1)=9$

At $x=-2$, $f(-2)=8$

At $x=-10$, $f(-10)=0$ and so on

On plotting the points (0, 10), (1, 11), (2, 12)... (10, 20), (−1, 9), (−2, 8) and (−10, 0) on graph paper, we get the following graph

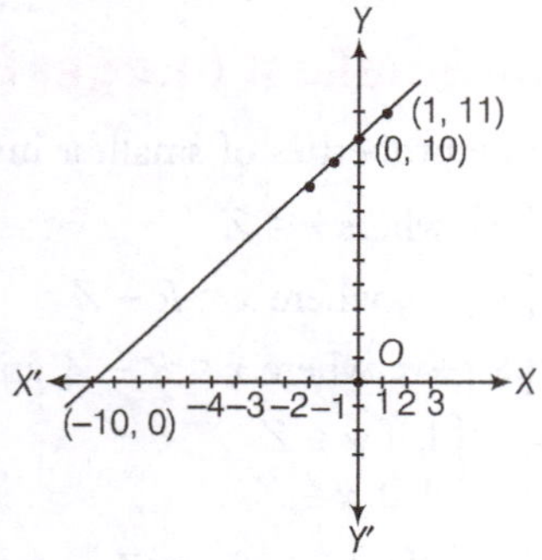

This is an example of linear function.

Note The function f defined by $f(x) = mx + c$, $x \in R$ is called the **linear function**, where m and c are constants.

Square Root Function

The square root of a function is defined as $f(x) = \sqrt{x}$, whose domain is $[0, \infty)$ and range is R^+ i.e. $[0, \infty)$.

We observe that the values of $f(x) = \sqrt{x}$ increase with the increase in x.

So, its graph is given below

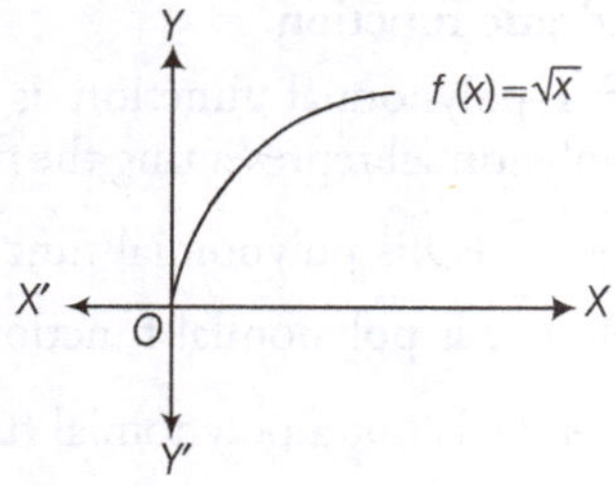

It may be observe that it is passing through origin.

Rational Function

A function of the form $f(x) = \dfrac{P(x)}{Q(x)}$, where $P(x)$ and $Q(x)$ are polynomial functions of x defined in a domain and $Q(x) \neq 0$, is called a rational function.

The domain of a rational function is $R - \{x : Q(x) = 0\}$ and range depends on the expression representing the function.

Thus, $f(x) = \left(\dfrac{x^2 + 4}{x^3 - 6x + 4}\right)$ is called a rational function, where $x^3 - 6x + 4 \neq 0$.

Its domain is $R - \{x : x^3 - 6x + 4 = 0\}$.

Reciprocal Function

The function $f : R - \{0\} \to R$ defined by $f(x) = \dfrac{1}{x}$ is called the reciprocal function. Its domain as well as range is $R - \{0\}$.

We observe that the sign of $\dfrac{1}{x}$ is same as that of x and $\dfrac{1}{x}$ decreases with the increase in x.

So, its graph is given below

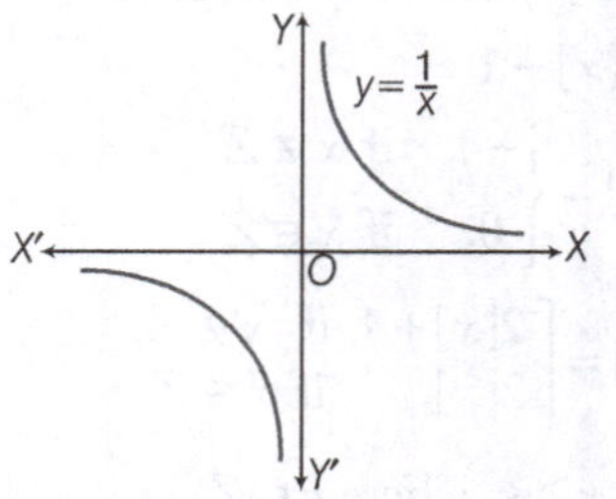

It is also a rational function.

Exponential Function

Let $a (\neq 1)$ be a positive real number. Then, the function $f : R \to R$, defined by $f(x) = a^x$, is called the exponential function. Its domain is R and range is $(0, \infty)$ as it attains only positive values. As, $a > 0$ and $a \neq 1$.

So, there are following two cases arise

Case I When $a > 1$, then the values of $y = f(x) = a^x$ increase as the values of x increase.

Thus, $f(x) = a^x = \begin{cases} < 1, & \text{for } x < 0 \\ 1, & \text{for } x = 0 \\ > 1, & \text{for } x > 0 \end{cases}$

Its graph is given below

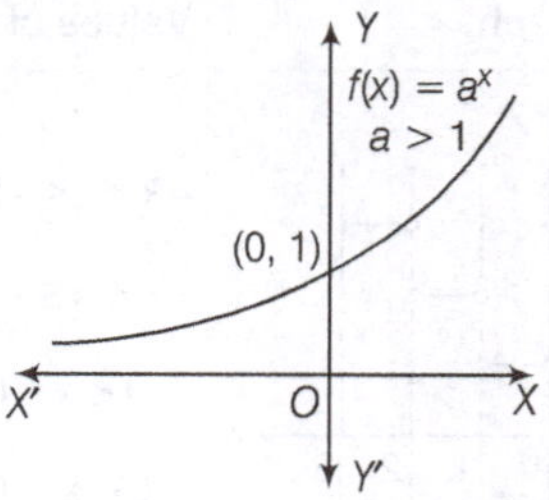

Case II When $0 < a < 1$, then the values of $y = f(x) = a^x$ decrease with the increase in x and $y > 0$ for all $x \in R$. Thus, $f(x) = a^x = \begin{cases} > 1, & \text{for } x < 0 \\ 1, & \text{for } x = 0 \\ < 1, & \text{for } x > 0 \end{cases}$

Its graph is given below

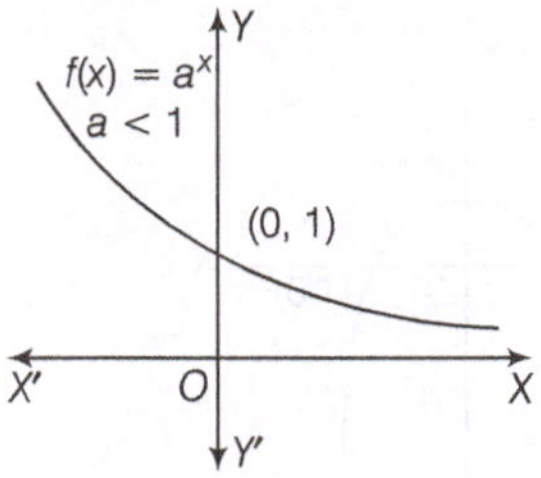

Example 5 Draw the graphs of $y = e^x + 1, e^x - 1,$ with the help of $y = e^x$.

Sol. $y = e^x$ (exponential function) could be plotted as

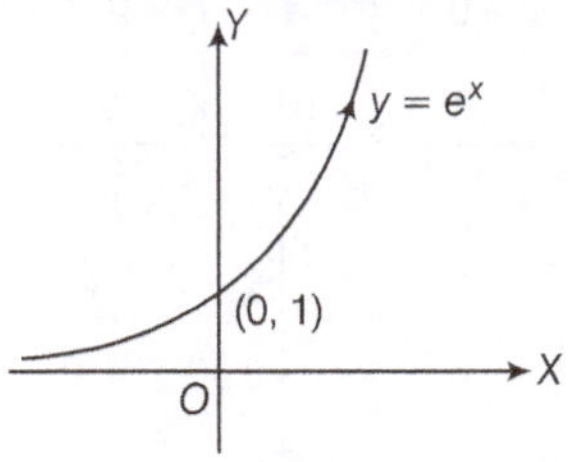

Now, $y = e^x + 1$ is shifted upwards by 1 unit, shown as

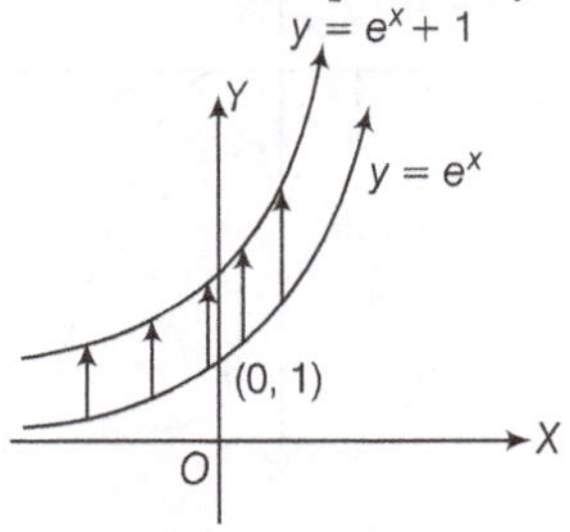

Also, $y = e^x - 1$ is shifted downwards by 1 unit, shown as

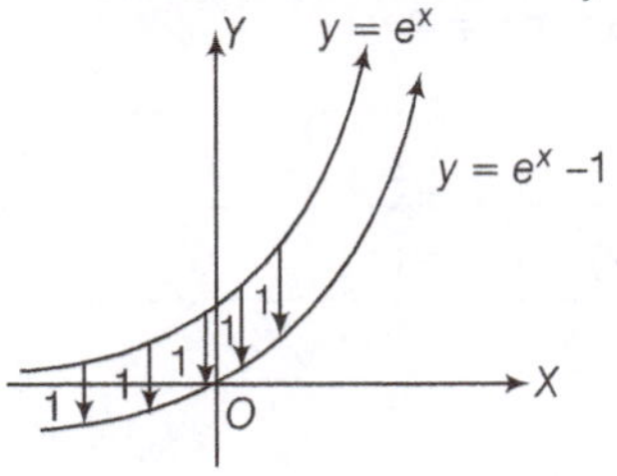

Logarithmic Function

Let $a (\neq 1)$ be a positive real number. Then, the function $f: (0, \infty) \to R$, defined by $f(x) = \log_a x$, is called the logarithmic function. Its domain is $(0, \infty)$ and range is R.

As, $a > 0$ and $a \neq 1$. So, there are following two cases arise

Case I When $a > 1$, then values of y increases with the increase in x. So, $y = \log_a x = \begin{cases} < 0, & \text{for } x < 1 \\ 0, & \text{for } x = 1 \\ > 0, & \text{for } x > 1 \end{cases}$

Its graph is given below

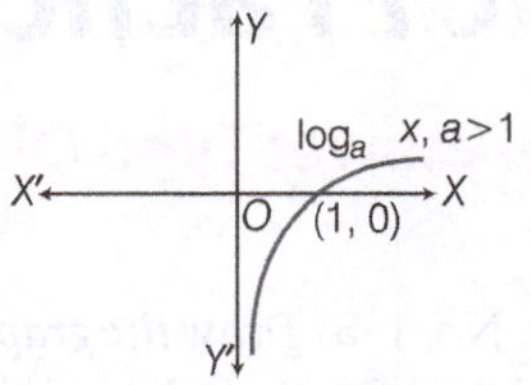

Case II When $0 < a < 1$, then values of y decreases with the increase in x.

So, $y = \log_a x = \begin{cases} > 0, & \text{for } 0 < x < 1 \\ 0, & \text{for } x = 1 \\ < 0, & \text{for } x > 1 \end{cases}$

Its graph is given below

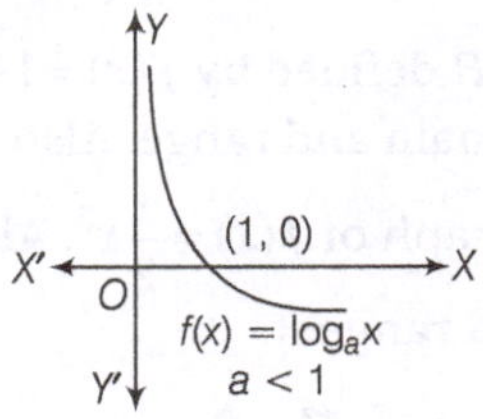

Properties of Logarithmic Function

(i) $\log_a 1 = 0$, where $a > 0, a \neq 1$

(ii) $\log_a a = 1$, where $a > 0, a \neq 1$

(iii) $\log_a (xy) = \log_a (x) + \log_a (y)$, where $a > 0, a \neq 1$ and $x / y > 0$.

(iv) $\log_a (x / y) = \log_a (x) - \log_a (y)$, where $a > 0, a \neq 1$, and $xy > 0$.

(v) $\log_a x^m = m \log_a x$, where $a > 0, a \neq 1$ and $x > 0$

(vi) $\log_{a^n} x^m = \frac{m}{n} \log_a (x)$, where $a > 0, a \neq 1$ and $x > 0$

Note Functions $\log_a x$ and a^x are inverse of each other. So, their graphs are mirror images of each other in the line $y = x$.

Example 6 Draw the graph of $y = \log_x \sqrt{x}$.

Sol. Given $y = \log_x \sqrt{x}$

$$= \log_x (x)^{1/2} = \frac{1}{2} \log_x x = \frac{1}{2}, x \in (0, \infty) - \{1\}$$

Now, the graph of given curve is the line $y = \frac{1}{2}$, for $x \in (0, \infty) - \{1\}$ as shown below

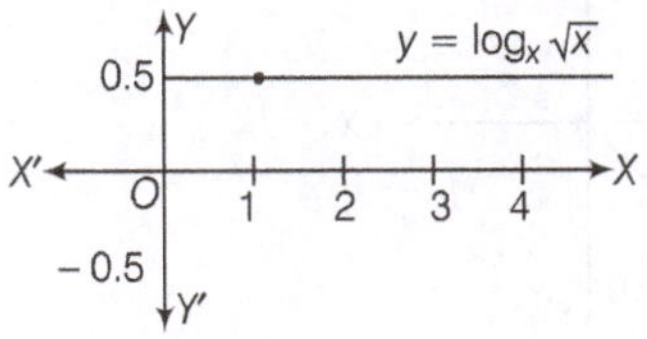

Topic Practice 4

Very Short Answer Type Questions

(2 Marks)

Directions (Q. No. 1-5) *Draw the graph of the following function. Also, determine their domain and range.*

1 $f(x) = 2$ 2 $f(x) = -2$ 3 $f(x) = |x - 3|$

4 $f(x) = \begin{cases} x^2, & x \geq 0 \\ x, & x < 0 \end{cases}$ 5 $f(x) = 1 - x^2$

Short Answer Type Questions

(4 Marks)

6 Let $f: R \to R$ defined by $f(x) = 1 - x^2$ for all $x \in R^+$. Find its domain and range. Also, draw its graph.

7 Draw the graph of $f(x) = \frac{1}{2}x^3$. Also, find the domain and range it.

Hints & Answers

1.

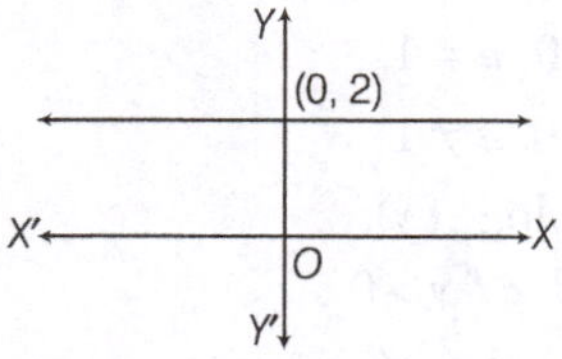

Ans. Domain $(f) = R$; Range $(f) = \{2\}$

2.

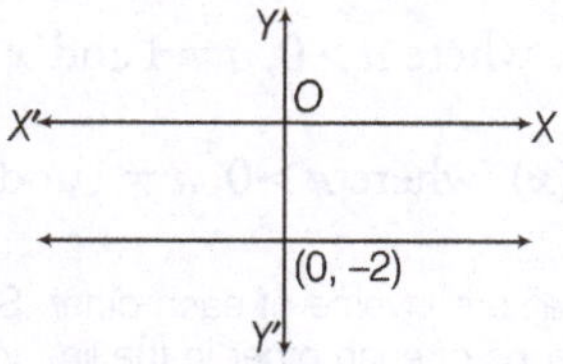

Ans. Domain $(f) = R$; Range $(f) = \{-2\}$

3.

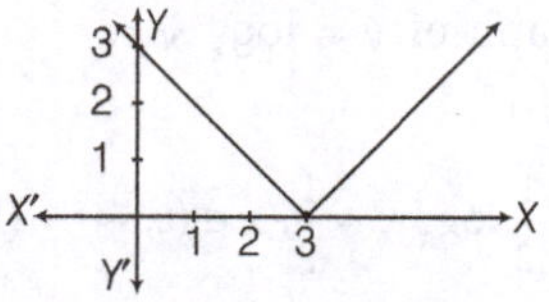

Ans. Domain $(f) = R$; Range $(f) = [0, \infty)$

4.

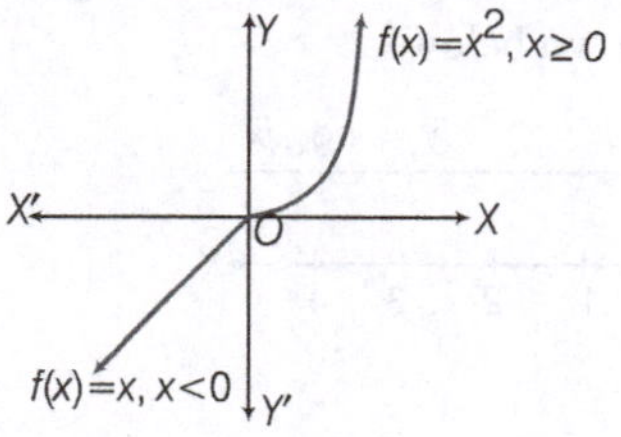

Ans. Domain $(f) = R$; Range $(f) = R$

5.

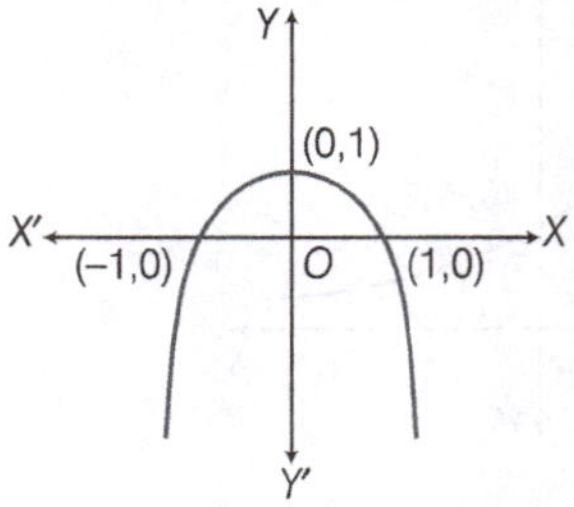

Ans. Domain $(f) = R$; Range $(f) = (-\infty, 1]$

6. $\because f(x) = 1 - x^2$, so $\forall x \in R^+$

x	0	1	2	3
f(x)	1	0	–3	–8

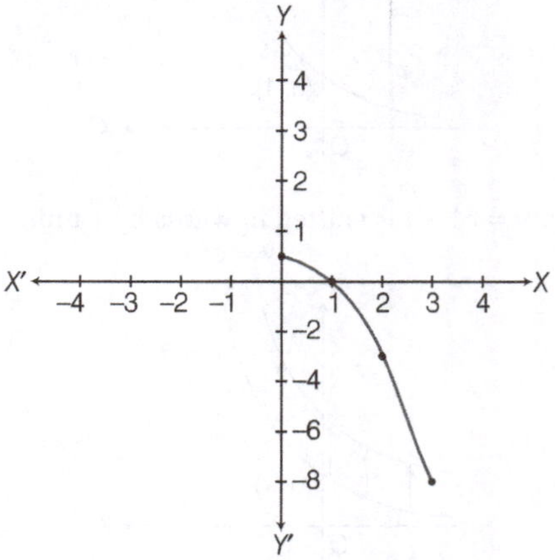

Ans. Domain of $f = (0, \infty)$ and Range of $f = (-\infty, 1)$

7. $f(x) = \frac{1}{2}x^3, \forall x \in R$

x	–2	0	2
f(x)	–4	0	4

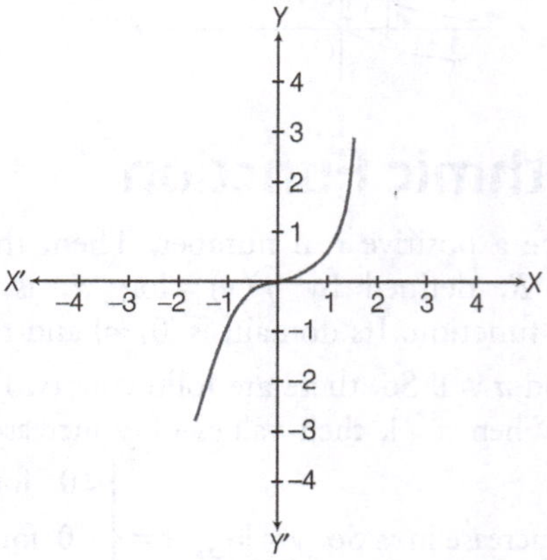

Ans. Domain of $f = (-\infty, \infty)$; Range of $f = (-\infty, \infty)$

TOPIC 05 Operations on Real Functions

Let $f: D_1 \to R$ and $g: D_2 \to R$ be two real functions with domain D_1 and D_2, respectively. Then, algebraic operations such as addition, subtraction, multiplication, division and scalar multiplication on two real functions are given below

(i) **Addition of Two Real Functions**

The sum function $(f+g)$ is defined by

$$(f+g)(x) = f(x) + g(x), \forall x \in D_1 \cap D_2$$

The domain of $(f+g)$ is $D_1 \cap D_2$.

(ii) **Subtraction of Two Real Functions**

The difference function $(f-g)$ is defined by

$$(f-g)(x) = f(x) - g(x), \forall x \in D_1 \cap D_2$$

The domain of $(f-g)$ is $D_1 \cap D_2$.

(iii) **Multiplication of Two Real Functions**

The product function (fg) is defined by

$$(fg)(x) = f(x) \cdot g(x), \forall x \in D_1 \cap D_2$$

The domain of (fg) is $D_1 \cap D_2$.

(iv) **Quotient of Two Real Functions**

The quotient function is defined by

$$\frac{f}{g}(x) = \frac{f(x)}{g(x)}, \forall x \in D_1 \cap D_2 - \{x : g(x) = 0\}$$

The domain of $\left(\frac{f}{g}\right)$ is $D_1 \cap D_2 - \{x : g(x) = 0\}$.

(v) **Multiplication of a Real Function by a Scalar**

The scalar multiple function cf is defined by

$$(cf)(x) = c \cdot f(x), \forall x \in D_1$$

where, c is a scalar (or real number).

The domain of cf is D_1.

(vi) $(f+k)x = f(x) + k$, where k is a constant.

Note For any real function $f: D \to R$ and $n \in N$, we define

$$(\underbrace{fff \ldots f}_{n \text{ times}})(x) = \underbrace{f(x)\, f(x) \ldots f(x)}_{n \text{ times}} = \{f(x)\}^n, \forall x \in D$$

Example 1 If two functions are defined as $f(x) = \frac{1}{(x-2)}$, $x \neq 2$ and $g(x) = (x-2)^2$, then find

(i) $f+g$ (ii) $f-g$ (iii) fg (iv) $\frac{f}{g}$

Sol. Given functions are

$$f(x) = \frac{1}{x-2}, x \neq 2 \text{ and } g(x) = (x-2)^2$$

(i) $(f+g)(x) = f(x) + g(x) = \frac{1}{x-2} + (x-2)^2, x \neq 2$

$$= \frac{1+(x-2)^3}{x-2}, x \neq 2$$

(ii) $(f-g)(x) = f(x) - g(x)$

$$= \frac{1}{(x-2)} - (x-2)^2, x \neq 2$$

$$= \frac{1-(x-2)^3}{(x-2)}, x \neq 2$$

(iii) $(fg)(x) = f(x) \cdot g(x)$

$$= \frac{1}{(x-2)} \times (x-2)^2, x \neq 2$$

$$= (x-2), x \neq 2$$

(iv) $\left(\frac{f}{g}\right)(x) = \frac{f(x)}{g(x)} = \frac{\left(\frac{1}{x-2}\right)}{(x-2)^2}, x \neq 2$

$$= \frac{1}{(x-2)^3}, x \neq 2$$

Example 2 Find the sum and difference of the identity function and the modulus function.

Sol. We know that,

$f: R \to R$ defined by $f(x) = x$ is the identity function.

$g: R \to R$ defined by $g(x) = |x|$ is the modulus function.

$\therefore$ Sum, $(f+g): R \to R$ defined by

$$(f+g)(x) = f(x) + g(x) = x + |x|$$

$$= \begin{cases} x+x, & \text{if } x \geq 0 \\ x-x, & \text{if } x < 0 \end{cases} = \begin{cases} 2x, & \text{if } x \geq 0 \\ 0, & \text{if } x < 0 \end{cases}$$

Difference, $(f-g): R \to R$ defined by

$$(f-g)(x) = f(x) - g(x) = x - |x|$$

$$= \begin{cases} x-x, & \text{if } x \geq 0 \\ x-(-x), & \text{if } x < 0 \end{cases} = \begin{cases} 0, & \text{if } x \geq 0 \\ 2x, & \text{if } x < 0 \end{cases}$$

Example 3 Find the quotient of the identity function by the modulus function.

Sol. Let f and g denote respectively the identity function and the modulus function. Then,

$f: R \rightarrow R$ is defined as $f(x) = x$

and $g: R \rightarrow R$ is defined as $g(x) = |x|$.

Clearly, f and g have the same domain.

Also, $g(x) = 0 \Rightarrow |x| = 0$

$\Rightarrow x = 0.$

Therefore, the quotient of f by g i.e. $\frac{f}{g}$ is a function from $R - \{0\} \rightarrow R$ and it is defined as

$$\left(\frac{f}{g}\right)(x) = \frac{f(x)}{g(x)}$$

$$= \frac{x}{|x|} = \begin{cases} \frac{x}{x} = 1, & x > 0 \\ \frac{x}{-x} = -1, & x < 0 \end{cases}$$

Example 4 Find the product of the identity function and the reciprocal function.

Sol. Let f and g denote respectively the identity function and the reciprocal function. Then,

$f: R \rightarrow R$ is defined as $f(x) = x$ for all $x \in R$ and

$g: R - \{0\} \rightarrow R$ and is defined as $g(x) = \frac{1}{x}$ for all $x \in R - \{0\}$

We have, domain $(f) \cap$ domain (g)

$= R \cap R - \{0\} = R - \{0\}$

Therefore, the product fg is a function from $R - \{0\}$ to R and is defined as

$$(fg)(x) = f(x)g(x) = x \times \frac{1}{x} = 1 \text{ for all } x \in R - \{0\}$$

Example 5 Let λ be a non-zero number and $f: R \rightarrow R$ be a function defined by $f(x) = \frac{x}{\lambda}\ \forall\ x \in R$.

Find

(i) λf (ii) $\lambda^2 f$ (iii) $\left(\frac{1}{\lambda}\right)f$

Sol. Clearly, λf, $\lambda^2 f$ and $\left(\frac{1}{\lambda}\right)f$ are functions from R to itself

(i) $(\lambda f)(x) = \lambda \cdot f(x) = \lambda \times \frac{x}{\lambda} = x, \forall\ x \in R$

(ii) $(\lambda^2 f)(x) = \lambda^2 \cdot f(x) = \lambda^2 \times \frac{x}{\lambda} = \lambda x, \forall\ x \in R$

(iii) $\left(\frac{1}{\lambda} f\right)(x) = \frac{1}{\lambda} \cdot f(x) = \frac{1}{\lambda} \times \frac{x}{\lambda} = \frac{x}{\lambda^2}, \forall\ x \in R$

Example 6 Let f be the exponential function and g be the logarithmic function. Find

(i) $(f + g)(1)$ (ii) $(f \cdot g)(1)$

(iii) $(3f)(1)$ (iv) $(5g)(1)$

Sol. We have, $f: R \rightarrow R$ given by $f(x) = e^x$

and $g: R \rightarrow R$ given by $g(x) = \log_e x$

(i) Since, domain $(f) \cap$ domain $(g) = R \cap R^+ = R^+$

$\therefore f + g: R^+ \rightarrow R$ is defined as

$(f + g)(x) = f(x) + g(x) = e^x + \log_e x \forall\ x \in R^+$

Clearly, $1 \in R^+$

$\therefore\ (f + g)(1) = f(1) + g(1) = e^1 + \log_e 1 = e + 0 = e$

$[\because \log 1 = 0]$

(ii) $f \cdot g: R^+ \rightarrow R$ and is defined as

$(f.g)(x) = f(x)\, g(x) = e^x \log_e x$

$(f.g)(1) = f(1)\, g(1) = e^1 \log_e 1 = 0$

(iii) $(3f)(x) = 3 \cdot (f(x)) = 3e^x$; $(3f)(1) = 3 \cdot e^1 = 3e$

(iv) $(5g)(x) = 5(g(x)) = 5\log_e x$; $(5g)(1) = 5\log_e 1 = 0$

Topic Practice 5

Very Short Answer Type Questions

2 Marks

1 Let f and g be real functions defined by $f(x) = \sqrt{x+2}$ and $g(x) = \sqrt{4 - x^2}$, then find each of the following functions

(i) $f + g$ (i) $f - g$ (iii) $f \cdot g$ (iv) $\frac{f}{g}$

2 Let $f: [2, \infty) \rightarrow R$ and $g: [-2, \infty) \rightarrow R$ be two real functions defined by $f(x) = \sqrt{x-2}$ and $g(x) = \sqrt{x+2}$. Find $f + g$ and $f - g$.

3 What are the sum and difference of identity function and the reciprocal function? **[NCERT]**

4 Let $f(x) = x^2$ and $g(x) = 2x + 1$ be two real functions. Find **[NCERT]**

(i) $f + g$ (ii) $f - g$ (iii) $f \cdot g$ (iv) $\frac{f}{g}$

5 Let $f: R \rightarrow R$ and $g: R \rightarrow R$ defined by $f(x) = x + 1$, $g(x) = 2x - 3$ **[NCERT]**

Find $f + g$, $f - g$, and $\frac{f}{g}$.

Short Answer Type Questions

(4 Marks)

6 If f and g be two real function defined by $f(x)=\sqrt{x+1}$ and $g(x)=\sqrt{9-x^2}$.

Then, describe each of the following functions.

(i) $f+g$ (ii) $g-f$

(iii) $f\cdot g$ (iv) $\frac{f}{g}$

(v) $\frac{g}{f}$ (vi) $2f-\sqrt{5}g$

(vii) f^2+7f (viii) $\frac{5}{g}$

7 If $f(x)=\log(1-x)$ and $g(x)=[x]$, then determine each of the following functions.

(i) $f+g$ (ii) $f.g$

(iii) $\frac{f}{g}$ (iv) $\frac{g}{f}$

Also, find :$(f+g)(-1)$, $(f\cdot g)(0)$, $\left(\frac{f}{g}\right)\left(\frac{1}{2}\right)$, $\left(\frac{g}{f}\right)\left(\frac{1}{2}\right)$.

Hints & Answers

1. $f(x)=\sqrt{x+2},\ g(x)=\sqrt{4-x^2}$

$f(x)$ is defined for $x+2\ge 0 \Rightarrow x\ge -2$

$\therefore$ Domain $(f)=[-2,\infty)$

$g(x)$ is defined for $4-x^2 \ge= 0 \Rightarrow x^2-4\le 0$

$\Rightarrow (x-2)(x+2)\le 0 \Rightarrow x\in[-2,2]$; Domain $(g)=[-2,2]$

Domain $(f)\cap$ domain $(g)=[-2,2]$

Ans. (i) $(\sqrt{x+2})[1+\sqrt{2-x}]$ (ii) $\sqrt{x+2}\ [1-\sqrt{2-x}]$

(iii) $(x+2)\sqrt{2-x}$ (iv) $1/\sqrt{2-x}$

2. Domain $(f)=[2,\infty)=D_1$ [say]

Domain $g=[-2,\infty)=D_2$ [say]; $D_1\cap D_2=[2,\infty)$

Ans. $(\sqrt{x-2}+\sqrt{x+2})$ and $(\sqrt{x-2}-\sqrt{x+2})$

3. Let $f(x)=x,\ g(x)=\frac{1}{x}$; Domain $(f)=R=D_1$

Domain $(g)=R-\{0\}=D_2$; $D_1\cap D_2=R-\{0\}$

Ans. Sum $=x+\frac{1}{x}$ and difference $=x-\frac{1}{x}$

4. (i) $f+g=(x+1)^2$ (ii) $f-g=x^2-2x-1$,

(iii) $f\cdot g=2x^3+x^2$ (iv) $\frac{f}{g}=\frac{x^2}{2x+1}$

5. $f+g=3x-2$; $f-g=-x+4$

$\frac{f}{g}:R-\left\{\frac{3}{2}\right\}\to R,\ \frac{f}{g}=\frac{x+1}{2x-3}$

6. Domain $(f)\cap$ Domain $(g)=[-1,3]$

Ans.

(i) $(f+g)(x)=\sqrt{x+1}+\sqrt{9-x^2}$

(ii) $(g-f)(x)=\sqrt{9-x^2}-\sqrt{x+1}$

(iii) $(fg)(x)=\sqrt{9+9x-x^2-x^3}$

(iv) $\left(\frac{f}{g}\right)(x)=\sqrt{\frac{x+1}{9-x^2}}$

(v) $\left(\frac{g}{f}\right)(x)=\sqrt{\frac{9-x^2}{x+1}},\ x\ne -1$

(vi) $(2f-\sqrt{5}g)(x)=2\sqrt{x+1}-\sqrt{45-5x^2}$

(vii) $(f^2+7f)(x)=x+1+7\sqrt{x+1}$

(viii) $\left(\frac{5}{g}\right)(x)=\frac{5}{\sqrt{9-x^2}},\ x\ne -3,3$

7. (i) $f+g:(-\infty,1)\to R$ defined by

$(f+g)(x)=\log(1-x)+[x]$

(ii) $fg:(-\infty,1)\to R,\ (f.g)(x)=[x].\log(1-x)$

(iii) $\frac{f}{g}:(-\infty,0)\to R,\ \frac{f}{g}(x)=\frac{\log(1-x)}{[x]}$

(iv) $\frac{g}{f}:(-\infty,0)\cup(0,1)\to R,\ \left(\frac{g}{f}\right)(x)=\frac{[x]}{\log(1-x)}$

$(f+g)(-1)=\log_e 2-1$

$(f\cdot g)(0)=0,\ \left(\frac{f}{g}\right)\left(\frac{1}{2}\right)=$ does not exist, $\left(\frac{g}{f}\right)\left(\frac{1}{2}\right)=0$

Chapter Practice

Multiple Choice Type Questions

1 Mark

1. If two sets A and B are having 99 elements in common, then the number of elements common to each of the sets $A\times B$ and $B\times A$ are
(a) 2^{99} (b) 99^2
(c) 100 (d) 18

2. If $A=\{1, 2, 5, 6\}$ and $B=\{1, 2, 3\}$, then what is $(A\times B)\cap(B\times A)$ equal to?
(a) $\{(1,1),(2,1),(6,1),(3,2)\}$
(b) $\{(1,1),(1,2),(2,1),(2,2)\}$
(c) $\{(1,1),(2,2)\}$
(d) $\{(1,1),(1,2),(2,5),(2,6)\}$

3. Let $R=\{x \mid x\in N, x$ is a multiple of 3 and $x\le 100\}$
$S=\{x \mid x\in N, x$ is a multiple of 5 and $x\le 100\}$.
What is the number of elements in $(R\times S)\cap(S\times R)$?
(a) 36 (b) 33
(c) 20 (d) 6

4. If A is a finite set having n elements, then the number of relations which can be defined in A is
(a) 2^n
(b) n^2
(c) 2^{n^2}
(d) n^n

5. Let R be a relation in N defined by
$$R=\{(1+x, 1+x^2): x\le 5, x\in N\}.$$
Which of the following is false?
(a) $R=\{(2,2),(3,5),(4,10),(5,17),(6,25)\}$
(b) Domain of $R=\{2, 3, 4, 5, 6\}$
(c) Range of $R=\{2,5,10,17,26\}$
(d) None of the above

6. If $f(x)=\dfrac{1+x}{1-x}$, then $\dfrac{f(x)\cdot f(x^2)}{1+[f(x)]^2}$ is equal to
(a) $\frac{1}{4}$
(b) $\frac{1}{6}$
(c) $\frac{1}{8}$
(d) $\frac{1}{2}$

Assertion-Reason Type Questions

1 Mark

Directions (Q. Nos. 7-10) *In the questions given below are two statements labelled as Assertion (A) and Reason (R). In the context of the two statements, which one of the following is correct?*

(a) Both A and R are correct; R is the correct explanation of A
(b) Both A and R are correct; R is not the correct explanation of A
(c) A is correct; R is incorrect
(d) R is correct; A is incorrect

7. **Assertion (A)** If $n(A)=4$ and $B=\{3, 4, 5, 6, 8, 9\}$, then the number of relations from A to B is 2^{20}.
Reason (R) If A and B be any two non-empty finite sets containing m and n elements respectively, then total number of relations from set A to B is 2^{mn}.

8. **Assertion (A)** If $f: R-\{4\}\to R$ be defined by $f(x)=\dfrac{x^2-16}{x-4}$ and $g: R\to R$ be defined by $g(x)=x+4$, then $f=g$.
Reason (R) Two function f and g are said to be equal iff
(i) domain of f = domain of g
(ii) Codomain of f = Codomain of g and
(iii) $f(x)=g(x)$ for every x belonging to their common domain.

9. **Assertion (A)** If f and g be two real functions defined by $f(x)=\dfrac{1}{x+5}$ and $g(x)=(x+5)^3$, then $(f+g)$ is $\dfrac{(x+5)^4+1}{x+5}$.
Reason (R) The composite function $(f+g)$ is defined by $(f+g)x=f(x)\cdot g(x), \forall x\in D_1\cap D_2$.

10. **Assertion (A)** The domain of the function
$$f(x)=\frac{x^2+3x+5}{x^2-5x+4} \text{ is } R-\{1, 4\}.$$
Reason (R) The set which contains all the first elements of all the ordered pairs of relation R is known as the domain of the function.

Very Short Answer Type Questions

2 Marks

11. If $\left(\frac{x}{3}+1, y-\frac{2}{3}\right)=\left(\frac{5}{3}, \frac{1}{3}\right)$, then find the values of x and y. **[NCERT]**

12. If $n(A)=m$ and $n(B)=n$, then find the total number of non-empty relations that can be defined from A to B. **[NCERT Exemplar]**

13. If $A \times B=\{(1, x),(1, y),(1, z),(1, w)\}$, then find A and B. **[NCERT]**

14. If $A \times B=\{(a, 1),(a, 5),(a, 2),(b, 2),(b, 5),(b, 1)\}$, then find A, B and $B \times A$.

15. If the set A has 3 elements and set $B=\{3, 4, 5\}$, then find the number of elements in $A \times B$.

16. If $A=\{a, b\}, B=\{2, 3, 5, 6, 7\}$ and $C=\{5,6,7,8,9\}$, then find $A \times(B \cap C)$.

17. If $A=\{-1, 1\}$, then find $A \times A \times A$.

18. If $A=\{1, 2\}$ and $B=\{3,4,5\}$. Then, write down
    (i) cartesian product $A \times B$.
    (ii) the relation $R: A \rightarrow B$ such that $(a+b)$ is an even number.

19. If $A=\{0, 1, 2\}$ and $B=\{1,2,3,4,5\}$, then represent the rule $f: A \rightarrow B$ given by $f(x)=x+2$ by an arrow diagram.

20. If $X=\{0, \pm 2, 4\}$ and $Y=\{0,4,5,16\}$, then represent the rule $f: X \rightarrow Y$ given by $f(x)=x^2$ by an arrow diagram.

21. If $A=\{9,10,11,12,13\}$ and $f: A \rightarrow N$ be defined by $f(n)=$ the highest prime factor of n, then find the range of f. **[NCERT Exemplar]**

22. If $f(x)=[x]$, then find $(3f)(x)$.

23. Find the range of each of the following function. $f(x)=x$, x is a real number. **[NCERT]**

24. If $U=\{1, 2, 3, 4\}$ and $R=\{(x, y): y>x$ for all, $x, y \in U\}$, then find domain and range of R.

25. Find the domain and range of the relation $R=\{(x, y): x+y=8 ; x, y \in N\}$

26. If $N=\{1, 2, 3, \ldots\}$, then find the relation $R=\{(x, y): x \in N, y \in N$ and $2x+y=10\}$ in $N \times N$. Also, find its domain and range.

27. Which of the following are functions, if $X=\{a, b, c, d\}$ and $Y=\{1, 2, 3, 4, 5\}$?
    (i) $f_1=\{(a, 1),(b, 1),(c, 3),(d, 4)\}$
    (ii) $f_2=\{(a, 1),(b, 2),(c, 4),(a, 2),(d, 5)\}$

28. Write the range of $y=\frac{|x-1|}{x-1}$.

29. Find the range of $f(x)=2-3x, x \in R, x>0$. **[NCERT]**

30. Find the range of $f(x)=x^2+2, x \in R$. **[NCERT]**

31. If $f(x)=\frac{x^2-x+1}{x^2+x+1}$, then find $f(1+h)$.

32. If $f(x)=\frac{x+1}{x-1}$, then find $f(x^2)$ and $[f(x)]^2$.

Short Answer Type Questions

4 Marks

33. Let A and B be two sets, such that $A \times B$ consists of 6 elements. If 3 elements of $A \times B$ are (1, 4), (2, 6) and (3, 6), then find $A \times B$ and $B \times A$.

34. If A and B be two sets, such that $n(A)=3$ and $n(B)=2$. If $(x, 1)$, $(y, 2)$ and $(z, 1)$ are in $A \times B$, then find A, B and $A \times B$, where x, y and z are distinct elements. **[NCERT]**

35. Determine the domain and range of the relation R, where $R=\{(2x+3, x^3): x$ is a prime number less than $10\}$.

36. If $X=\{1,2,3,4,5\}$,
    $Y=\{1,2,5,6,7,9,10,11,12,13,14\}$
    and $f: X \rightarrow Y$ be defined by $f(x)=2x+3$, then find the domain and range of f.

37. Is $g=\{(2, 3),(4, 5),(6, 7)\}$ a function? If this is described by the formula $g(x)=\alpha x+2\beta$, then what values would be assigned to α and β ?

38. Find the domain of the function f defined by $f(x)=\sqrt{4-x}+\frac{1}{\sqrt{x^2-1}}$. **[NCERT Exemplar]**

39. If a function $f: R \rightarrow R$ be defined by
$$f(x)=\begin{cases}3x-2, & x<0 \\ 1, & x=0 \\ 4x+1, & x>0\end{cases}$$
Then, find $f(1)$, $f(-1)$, $f(0)$, $f(2)$.

40. If $f(x)=\begin{cases}x^2, & x<0 \\ x, & 0 \leq x<1 \\ \frac{1}{x}, & x \geq 1\end{cases}$ Then, find

    (i) $f\left(\frac{1}{2}\right)$ (ii) $f(-2)$ (iii) $f(1)$ (iv) $f(\sqrt{3})$.

41. If $f(x)=x^2$, then find $\dfrac{f(1.1)-f(1)}{1.1-1}$ **[NCERT]**

42. If $f(x)=x^3-\dfrac{1}{x^3}$, show that $f(x)+f\left(\dfrac{1}{x}\right)=0$.

43. If $A=\{1, 2\}, B=\{1, 2, 3, 4\}, C=\{5, 6\}$ and $D=\{5, 6, 7, 8\}$, then verify that **[NCERT]**

(i) $A\times(B\cap C)=(A\times B)\cap(A\times C)$.

(ii) $A\times C$ is a subset of $B\times D$.

44. If $A=\{1, 2, 3\}, B=\{2, 3, 4\}, C=\{1, 3, 4\}$ and $D=\{2, 4, 5\}$, then verify that

$(A\times B)\cap(C\times D)=(A\cap C)\times(B\cap D)$.

45. Let $A=\{1, 2, 3,\ldots, 14\}$. Define a relation R from A to A by $R=\{(x, y): 3x-y=0$, where $x, y\in A\}$. Depict this relationship using an arrow diagram. Write down its domain, codomain and range. **[NCERT]**

Long Answer Type Questions

6 Marks

46. Find the domain and range of the following relations.

(i) $R=\{(x,y): x,y\in N,\ y=x^2+3$ and $0<x<5\}$

(ii) $R=\{(x,y): x,y\in N,\ y=\dfrac{1}{1+x}$ and x is odd natural number$\}$

47. Determine the domain and range of the following relations.

(i) $R_1=\left\{\left(x,\dfrac{1}{x}\right): 0<x<6, x\in N\right\}$

(ii) $R_2=\{(x,x^2): x$ is prime number less than $10\}$

48. If $f(x)=\begin{cases}1+x, & -1\le x<0\\ x^2-1, & 0<x<2\\ 2x, & 2\le x\end{cases}$. Then, find

$f(3), f(-2), f(0), f\left(\dfrac{1}{2}\right), f(2-h)$ and $f(-1+h)$, where $h>0$ is very small.

49. Write the following after removing the modulus $f(x)=|2x-1|, -1\le x\le 1$. Also, sketch the graph of $f(x)$.

50. Let $A=\{-3,-2,-1,4\}$ and $f: A\to Z$ given by $f(x)=x^2+x+2$. Find

(i) the range of f. (ii) pre-images of 6 and 4.

51. Find the domain and range of the following real functions.

(i) $f(x)=-|2x|$

(ii) $f(x)=\sqrt{9-x^2}$ **[NCERT]**

52. Find the range of the function $f(x)=\dfrac{|x+4|}{x+4}$.

53. (i) Let $A=\{8,11,12,15,18,23\}$ and f is a function from $A\to N$ such that $f(x)=$ highest prime factor of x, find f and its range.

(ii) Find the domain of the function $f(x)=\dfrac{x^2+2x+1}{x^2-8x+12}$.

54. (i) If $f(x)=\sqrt{x^2+1}$ and $g(x)=2x^2+3$, then find $(f+g)(x)$.

(ii) Find the product of the identity function and the modulus function.

55. The relation f is defined by $f(x)=\begin{cases}x^2, 0\le x\le 3\\ 3x, 3\le x\le 10\end{cases}$ and the relation g is defined by $g(x)=\begin{cases}x^2, 0\le x\le 2\\ 3x, 2\le x\le 10\end{cases}$.

Show that f is a function and g is not a function. **[NCERT]**

56. Find the simplified form of $f(x)=|x-2|+|2+x|$, if $-3\le x\le 3$. **[NCERT Exemplar]**

57. Everyone wants to be a perfect ideal human being. Let us assume that dishonesty is one of the factors that affects our perfectness and perfectness has an inverse relation with dishonesty. For any value x of level of dishonesty, we have a unique value y of perfection.

(i) Write down the equation that relates y with x.

(ii) Does this relationship from $x\in(0,\infty)$ to $y\in(0,\infty)$, form a function?

(iii) For what level of dishonesty one can achieve $\left(\dfrac{1}{4}\right)$th level of perfection?

(iv) What will be the change in level of perfection when the level of dishonesty changes from 4 to 2?

58. (i) Find the domain and range of the function $f(x)=\dfrac{x^2-9}{x-3}$.

(ii) Find the domain of the function $f(x)=\dfrac{x^2+3x+5}{x^2+x-6}$.

59. Find domain and range of the real function f(x) defined by

$f(x)=\begin{cases}1-x, & x<0\\ 1, & x=0\\ x-1, & x>0\end{cases}$ and draw its graph.

60. State whether each of the following statements are true or false. If the statement is false, then rewrite the given statement correctly.

(i) If $P = \{m, n\}$ and $Q = \{n, m\}$, then $P \times Q = \{(m, n), (n, m)\}$. **[NCERT]**

(ii) If A and B are non-empty sets, then $A \times B$ is a non-empty set of ordered pairs (x, y) such that $x \in B$ and $y \in A$.

(iii) If $A = \{1, 2\}$ and $B = \{3, 4\}$, then $A \times (B \cap \phi) = \phi$.

Case-Based Type Questions

(6 Marks)

61. Hanuman Pareek and Pawan Saini are two students of class XIth in a school.

The ages of both students is represented by f and g be real functions defined by $f(x) = \sqrt{x+4}$ and $g(x) = \sqrt{16 - x^2}$.

Then, answer the some questions which are based on above ages.

(i) Find the domain of sum of both ages i.e. $(f + g)$.

(ii) Find the product of both ages i.e. (fg).

(iii) Find the domain of $\left(\frac{f}{g}\right)$.

(iv) Find the difference of both ages i.e. $(f - g)$.

(v) Find the $\left(\frac{f}{g}\right)$.

Hints & Answers

1. (b) **2.** (b) **3.** (a) **4.** (c) **5.** (a)

6. (d) **7.** (d) **8.** (d) **9.** (c) **10.** (a)

11. $x = 2, y = 1$

12. $2^{mn} - 1$

13. $A = \{1\}, B = \{x, y, z, w\}$

14. $A = \{a, b\}, B = \{1, 5, 2\}$
$B \times A = \{(1, a), (1, b), (5, a), (5, b)(2, a)(2, b)\}$

15. 9

16. $\{(a, 5), (a, 6), (a, 7), (b, 5), (b, 6), (b, 7)\}$

17. $\{(-1, -1, -1), (-1, -1, 1), (-1, 1, -1), (-1, 1, 1), (1, -1, -1), (1, -1, 1), (1, 1, -1)(1, 1, 1)\}$

18. (i) $A \times B = \{(1, 3), (1, 4), (1, 5), (2, 3), (2, 4), (2, 5)\}$
(ii) $R : A \to B$ is $R = \{(1, 3), (1, 5), (2, 4)\}$

19.

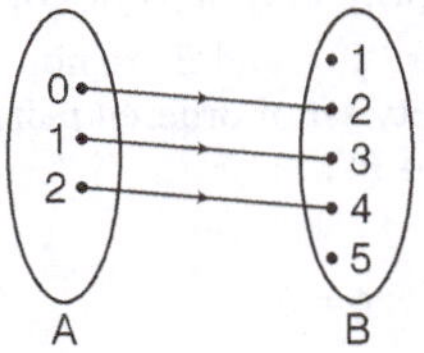

20.

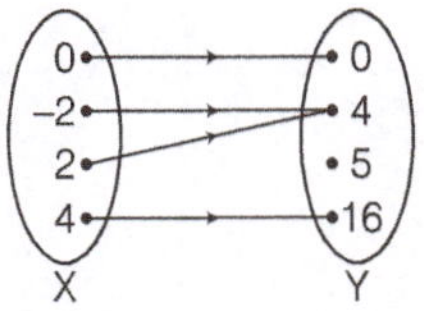

21. $\{3, 5, 11, 13\}$ **22.** $3[x]$ **23.** Range $= R$

24. Domain $(R) = \{1, 2, 3, 4\}$, Range $(R) = \{2, 3, 4\}$

25. Domain $(R) = \{1, 2, 3, 4, 5, 6, 7\}$
Range $(R) = \{7, 6, 5, 4, 3, 2, 1\}$

26. Since, $2x + y = 10$, $x, y \in N \Rightarrow y = 10 - 2x$
$\therefore \quad R = \{(1, 8), (2, 6), (3, 4), (4, 2)\}$
Ans. Domain $(R) = \{1, 2, 3, 4\}$ and Range $(R) = \{2, 4, 6, 8\}$

27. (i) f_1 is a function.
(ii) $\because f(a) = 1$ and $f(a) = 2$, f_2 is not a function.

28. $\{-1, 1\}$ **29.** $(-\infty, 2)$ **30.** $[2, \infty)$ **31.** $\frac{h^2 + h + 1}{h^2 + 3h + 3}$

32. $f(x^2) = \frac{x^2 + 1}{x^2 - 1}, (f(x))^2 = \left(\frac{x + 1}{x - 1}\right)^2$

33. $A \times B = \{(1, 4), (1, 6), (2, 4), (2, 6), (3, 4), (3, 6)\}$
$B \times A = \{(4, 1), (4, 2), (4, 3), (6, 1), (6, 2), (6, 3)\}$

34. $A = \{x, y, z\}, B = \{1, 2\}$
$A \times B = \{(x, 1), (x, 2), (y, 1), (y, 2), (z, 1), (z, 2)\}$

35. Domain $= \{7, 9, 13, 17\}$ Range $= \{8, 27, 125, 343\}$

36. Domain $= \{1, 2, 3, 4, 5\}$ Range $= \{5, 7, 9, 11, 13\}$

37. g is a function; $\alpha = 1, \beta = 1/2$

38. Domain $= (-\infty, -1) \cup (1, 4]$

39. $f(1) = 5, f(-1) = -5, f(0) = 1, f(2) = 9$

40. (i) $\frac{1}{2}$ (ii) 4 (iii) 1 (iv) $\frac{1}{\sqrt{3}}$

41. $f(1.1) = (1.1)^2 = 1.21, f(1) = 1^2 = 1$
$\therefore \frac{f(1.1) - f(1)}{1.1 - 1} = \frac{1.21 - 1}{0.1}$
Ans. 2.1

42. Solve as Example 12 of Topic 3.

43. Solve as Example 15 of Topic 1.

44. Solve as Example 15 of Topic 1.

45. 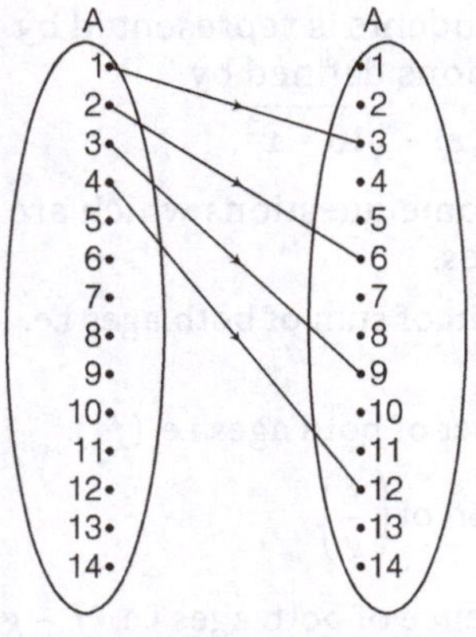

Domain = {1, 2, 3, 4}, Codomain = A, Range = {3, 6, 9, 12}

46. (i) Domain = {1, 2, 3, 4}, Range = {4, 7, 12, 19}

(ii) Domain = {1, 3, 5, ...}, Range = $\left\{\frac{1}{2}, \frac{1}{4}, \frac{1}{6}, \ldots\right\}$

47. (i) Domain = {1, 2, 3, 4, 5}, Range = $\left\{1, \frac{1}{2}, \frac{1}{3}, \frac{1}{4}, \frac{1}{5}\right\}$

(ii) Domain = {2, 3, 5, 7}, Range = {4, 9, 25, 49}

48. $f(3) = 6$, $f(-2) =$ Not defined, $f(0) =$ Not defined,

$f\left(\frac{1}{2}\right) = \frac{-3}{4}$; $f(2-h) = h^2 - 4h + 3$, $f(-1+h) = h$

49. $f(x) = \begin{cases} 1 - 2x, & -1 \le x < \frac{1}{2} \\ 2x - 1, & \frac{1}{2} \le x \le 1 \end{cases}$

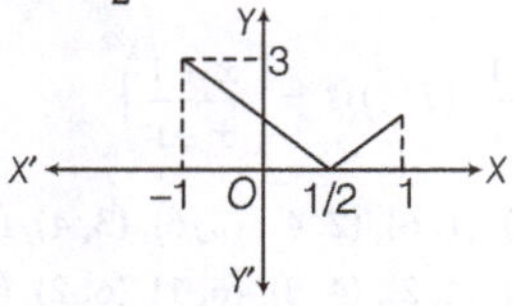

50. (i) Range (f) = {8, 4, 2, 22}

(ii) There is no pre-image of 6, pre-image of 4 is -2.

51. (i) Domain = R Range = $(-\infty, 0]$

(ii) $f(x)$ to be defined, $9 - x^2 \ge 0$

$\Rightarrow \quad x^2 - 9 \le 0 \Rightarrow -3 \le x \le 3$

and for range, let $y = f(x) = \sqrt{9 - x^2} \Rightarrow x = \sqrt{9 - y^2}$

$\Rightarrow \quad 9 - y^2 \ge 0$

Ans. Domain $= [-3, 3]$ Range $= [0, 3]$

52. $\{-1, 1\}$

53. (i) $f = \{(8, 2), (11, 11), (12, 3), (15, 5), (18, 3), (23, 23)\}$

Range = {2, 3, 5, 11, 23}

(ii) Domain = $R - \{2, 6\}$

54. (i) $(f + g)(x) = \sqrt{x^2 + 1} + 2x^2 + 3$

(ii) $(f \cdot g)(x) = \begin{cases} x^2, & \text{if } x \ge 0 \\ -x^2, & \text{if } x < 0 \end{cases}$

56. We have, $|x - 2| = \begin{cases} x - 2, & x \ge 2 \\ -(x - 2), & x < 2 \end{cases}$

$|x + 2| = \begin{cases} x + 2, & x \ge -2 \\ -(x + 2), & x < -2 \end{cases}$

$\Rightarrow f(x) = \begin{cases} (x-2) + (2+x), & 2 \le x \le 3 \\ -(x-2) + (x+2), & -2 \le x < 2 \\ -(x-2) - (x+2), & -3 \le x < -2 \end{cases}$

Ans. $f(x) = \begin{cases} 2x, & \text{if } 2 \le x \le 3 \\ 4, & \text{if } -2 \le x < 2 \\ -2x, & \text{if } -3 \le x < -2 \end{cases}$

57. (i) $y = \frac{k}{x}$, k is constant (ii) Yes

(iii) 4th level (iv) $\frac{1}{4}$ to $\frac{1}{2}$

58. (i) Domain = $R - \{3\}$, Range = $R - \{6\}$

(ii) Here, $f(x)$ is not defined, when

$x^2 + x - 6 = 0 \Rightarrow (x - 2)(x + 3) = 0$

Ans. Domain = $R - \{-3, 2\}$

59. Domain = R, Range = $(-1, \infty)$

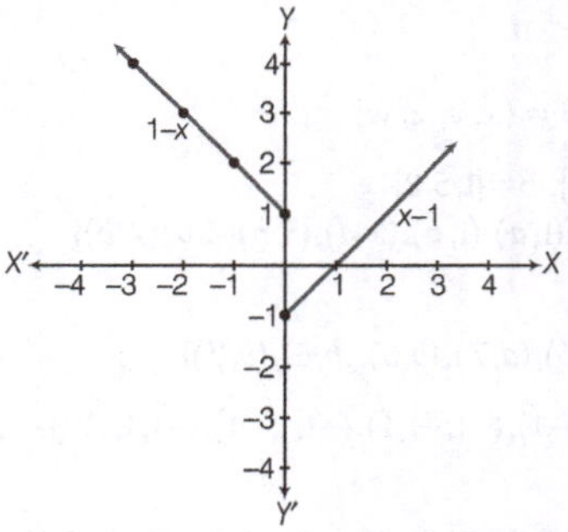

60. (i) It is false, because if $P = \{m, n\}$ and $Q = \{n, m\}$, then $P \times Q = \{m, n\} \times \{n, m\} = \{(m, n), (m, m), (n, n), (n, m)\}$

(ii) It is false, correct statement is "If A and B are non-empty sets, then $A \times B$ is a non-empty set of ordered pairs (x, y), such that $x \in A$ and $y \in B$".

(iii) It is true, because $B \cap \phi = \phi$

$\therefore \quad A \times (B \cap \phi) = A \times \phi = \phi$

61. (i) $[-4, 4]$

(ii) $(x + 4)\sqrt{4 - x}$

(iii) $(-4, 4)$

(iv) $\sqrt{x + 4} - \sqrt{16 - x^2}$

(v) $\frac{1}{\sqrt{4 - x}}$

CHAPTER

03

Trigonometry

The word 'Trigonometry' is derived from the Greek words '*Trigon*' and '*Metron*' and it means **Measuring the sides of a triangle.** It is developed to solve geometric problems involving triangles. Currently it is used in many areas such as designing electric circuits, analysing a musical tone and in many other areas.

In earlier classes, we have studied the trigonometric ratios of acute angle, trigonometric identities and its application in solving problems related to heights and distances. In this chapter, we will extend the concept of trigonometric ratios to trigonometric functions and study their properties.

TOPIC 01 Angles and Its Measures

Angles

When a ray OA starting from its initial position OA rotates about its initial point O and takes the final position OB, we say that $\angle AOB$ has been formed.

Here, initial position OA and final position OB are respectively known as the **initial side** and the **terminal side** of $\angle AOB$ and the point O, is called its **vertex.**

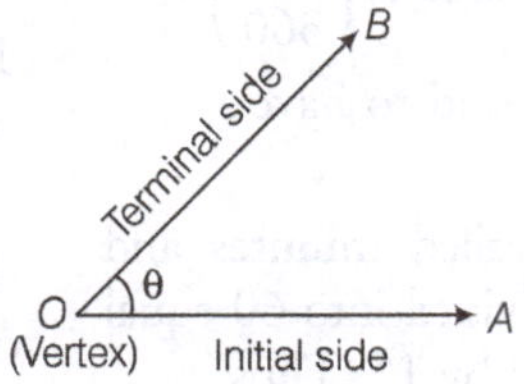

Note Two angles are called the **coterminal**, if they have the same position of initial side and terminal side.

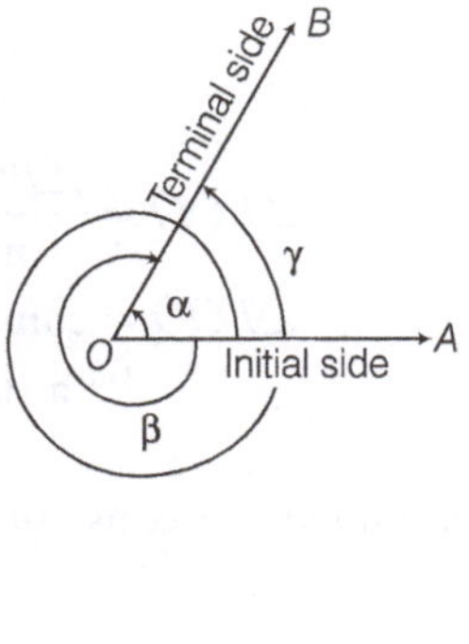

Convention of Sign of Angles (Positive and Negative Angles)

If the direction of rotation is **anti-clockwise**, then the angle is said to be positive and if the direction of rotation is **clockwise**, then the angle is said to be negative.

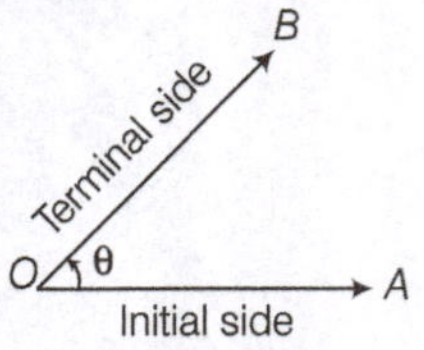

(Positive angle)

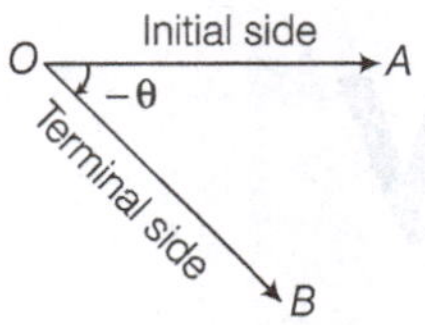

(Negative angle)

Note In general, the amount of rotation of an angle is denoted by following Greek letters.

(i) θ (theta) (ii) ϕ (phi) (iii) α (alpha)
(iv) β (beta) (v) γ (gamma) (vi) δ (delta)
(vii) λ (lambda) (viii) ω (omega), etc.

Magnitude of an Angle

The amount of rotation from the initial side to the terminal side, is called the **magnitude of an angle.**

Measures of an Angle

There are several units for measuring angles, but the most commonly used units are degree and radian, two systems for measuring an angle, which are defined below

1. Sexagesimal System (Degree Measure)

If the rotation from initial side to terminal side is $\left(\frac{1}{360}\right)$th of a complete revolution, then the angle is said to have a measure of one degree (1°).

A degree is divided into 60 equal parts, called **minutes** and 1 minute is denoted by **1′**. One minute is divided into 60 equal parts, called **second** and 1 seconds is denoted by **1″**. Thus,

$$1° = 60' \text{ and } 1' = 60''$$

Some of the angles, whose measures are 360°, 180°, 270°, 430°, – 40°, – 430°, are shown below

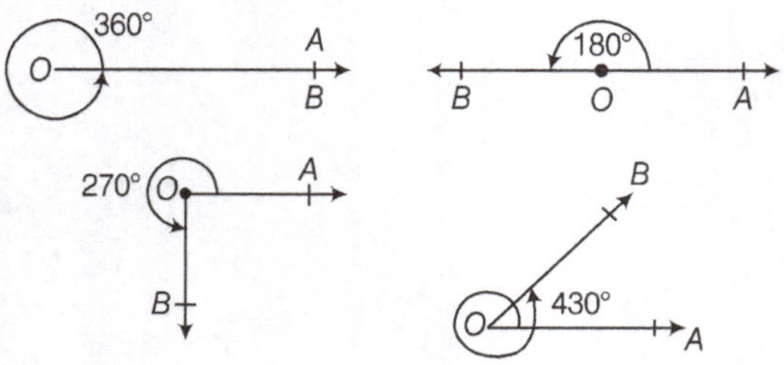

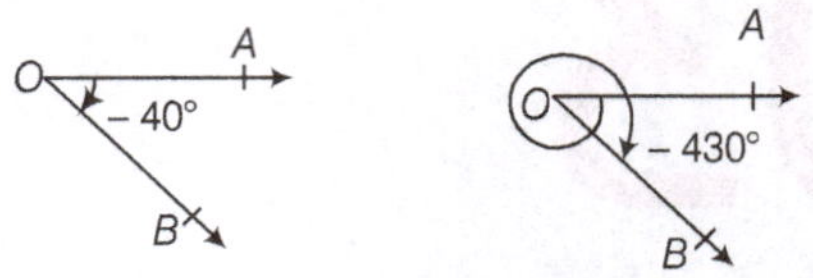

2. Circular System (Radian Measure)

Angle subtended at the centre by an arc of length one unit in a circle of radius 1 unit is said to have a measure of 1 radian.

More generally, in a circle of radius r, an arc of length r will subtend an angle of 1 radian at the centre. 1 radian is written as 1^c. The following figures show the angles, whose measures are 1 radian (1^c) and -1 radian (-1^c).

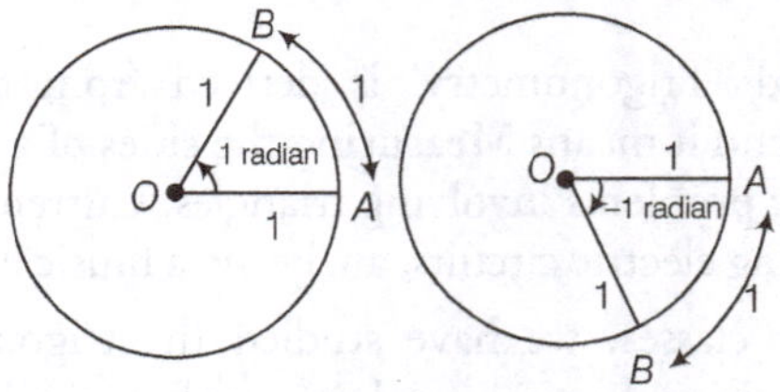

Note (i) In the sexagesimal system, we measure angles in degree, minutes and seconds.

1 right angle = 90°, 1° = 60′ and 1′ = 60″

(ii) In the circular measure, we measure angles in radians.

(iii) The circumference of a circle bears a constant ratio to its diameter. This constant ratio is denoted by the Greek letter π.

Thus, $\pi = \frac{\text{Circumference of a circle}}{\text{Diameter of the circle}}$

Theorem *A radian is a constant angle.*

Proof Let $C(O, r)$ be a circle.

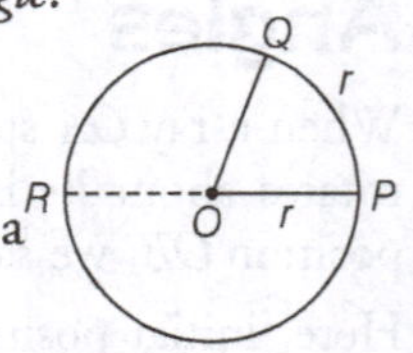

Let $\widehat{PQ} = r$, join OP and OQ.

Now, produce PO towards O in such a way that it intersect circle at R.

Then, $\angle POR = 2$ right angles

We know that the angles at the centre of a circle are proportional to the length of arcs subtending them

$$\therefore \quad \frac{\angle POQ}{\angle POR} = \frac{\widehat{PQ}}{\widehat{PR}} \Rightarrow \frac{\angle POQ}{\angle POR} = \frac{r}{\pi r} = \frac{1}{\pi}$$

$$\left[\because \widehat{PR} = \frac{1}{2}(2\pi r) = \pi r\right]$$

$$\Rightarrow \quad \angle POQ = \frac{\angle POR}{\pi} = \frac{\text{Straight angle}}{\pi}$$

$$\Rightarrow \quad \angle POQ = \text{constant}$$

[∵ a straight angle and π both are constants]

Hence, radian is a constant angle.

Relation between Degree and Radian

A circle subtends at its centre an angle whose radian measure is 2π and its degree measure is 360°. It follows that

$$\boxed{2\pi \text{ radian} = 360^\circ} \quad \text{or} \quad \pi \text{ radian} = 180^\circ$$

We can express a radian measure in terms of degree measure and a degree measure in terms of radian measure by using this relation.

Using approximate value of π as $\frac{22}{7}$, we have

$$1 \text{ rad} = \frac{180^\circ}{\pi} = \left(\frac{180 \times 7}{22}\right)^\circ$$
$$= \left(\frac{630}{11}\right)^\circ = \left(57 + \frac{3}{11}\right)^\circ$$
$$= 57^\circ + \frac{1}{11} \times 60' \quad [\because 1^\circ = 60']$$
$$= 57^\circ + \left(16 + \frac{4}{11}\right)'$$
$$= 57^\circ + 16' + \frac{4}{11} \times 60'' \quad [1' = 60'']$$
$$= 57^\circ 16' 22'' \text{ (approx.)}$$

Also, $$\boxed{1^\circ = \frac{\pi}{180} \text{ rad} = 0.01746 \text{ rad (approx.)}}$$

If D denotes degree measure and 'R' denotes radian measure then relation between degree and radian is given by $\frac{D}{180} = \frac{R}{\pi}$. Thus,

$$\boxed{\begin{aligned} \text{Radian measure} &= \frac{\pi}{180} \times \text{Degree measure} \\ \text{Degree measure} &= \frac{180}{\pi} \times \text{Radian measure} \end{aligned}}$$

Note (i) Generally, when an angle is expressed in radians, the word 'radian' is frequently omitted, e.g., $45^\circ = \pi/4$, is written with the understanding that $\pi/4$ is radian measure.

(ii) π is always a number whose approximate value is $\frac{22}{7} = 3.1428$. When we say that $\pi = 180^\circ$, then we mean that π radians (i.e. 3.1428 times one radian)

The relation between degree measure and radian measure of some common angles are given in the following table

Degree	30°	45°	60°	90°	180°	270°	360°
Radian	$\frac{\pi}{6}$	$\frac{\pi}{4}$	$\frac{\pi}{3}$	$\frac{\pi}{2}$	π	$\frac{3\pi}{2}$	2π

Method to Convert Degree Measure into Radians

To convert degree measure into radians, we use the following steps

***Step* I** First, convert the seconds (if given) into minutes by using the relation

$$1 \text{ second} = \frac{1}{60} \text{ minutes or } 1'' = \left(\frac{1}{60}\right)'$$

***Step* II** Convert the total minutes (given minutes + minutes obtained in step I) into degrees by using the relation

$$1 \text{ minute} = \frac{1}{60} \text{ degree or } 1' = \left(\frac{1}{60}\right)^\circ$$

***Step* III** Now, convert the total degrees (given degree + degree obtained in step II) into radians by using the relation

$$\text{Radian measure} = \frac{\pi}{180} \times \text{Degree measure}$$

Thus, we convert given degree measure into radians.

Example 1 Convert the following into radians.

(i) 240° (ii) 520° (iii) 25° (iv) $-47^\circ 30'$ **[NCERT]**

Sol. (i) We know that,

$$\text{Radian measure} = \frac{\pi}{180} \times \text{Degree measure}$$

$\therefore$ Required radian measure

$$= \left(\frac{\pi}{180} \times 240\right) \text{rad} = \frac{4\pi}{3} \text{ rad}$$

(ii) Required radian measure $= \frac{\pi}{180} \times$ Degree measure

$$= \left(\frac{\pi}{180} \times 520\right) \text{rad} = \frac{26}{9}\pi \text{ rad}$$

(iii) Required radian measure

$$= \left(\frac{\pi}{180} \times 25\right) \text{rad} = \frac{5\pi}{36} \text{ rad}$$

(iv) We have,

$$-47^\circ 30' = -\left[47^\circ + \left(\frac{30}{60}\right)^\circ\right] \quad \left[\because 1' = \left(\frac{1}{60}\right)^\circ\right]$$
$$= -\left[47^\circ + \left(\frac{1}{2}\right)^\circ\right] = -\left(\frac{95}{2}\right)^\circ$$

Now, required radian measure

$$= \frac{\pi}{180} \times \text{Degree measure}$$
$$= -\left(\frac{\pi}{180} \times \frac{95}{2}\right) \text{rad} = \frac{-19\pi}{72} \text{ rad}$$

Hence, radian measure of $-47^\circ 30'$ is $-\frac{19\pi}{72}$ rad.

Example 2 Express the following in radians.

(i) 40° 20′ (ii) 48° 37′ 30″

Sol. (i) Here, given degree measure have minutes. Firstly, convert minutes into degree.

$$\because \quad 1' = \left(\frac{1}{60}\right)^\circ$$

$$\therefore \quad 20' = \left(\frac{20}{60}\right)^\circ = \left(\frac{1}{3}\right)^\circ$$

Now, total degree to convert $= 40° + \dfrac{1}{3}^\circ$

$$= \left(\frac{120+1}{3}\right)^\circ = \left(\frac{121}{3}\right)^\circ$$

$\because$ Radian measure $= \dfrac{\pi}{180} \times$ Degree measure

$\therefore$ Required radian measure $= \dfrac{\pi}{180} \times \dfrac{121}{3}$

$$= \frac{121\pi}{540} \text{ radian}$$

(ii) Here, given degree measure have seconds and minutes. So, firstly convert seconds into minutes.

$$\because \quad 1'' = \left(\frac{1}{60}\right)'$$

$$\therefore \quad 30'' = \left(\frac{30}{60}\right)' = \left(\frac{1}{2}\right)'$$

$\therefore$ Total minutes to convert

$$= 37' + \frac{1}{2}' = \left(\frac{74+1}{2}\right)' = \left(\frac{75}{2}\right)'$$

$$\because \quad 1' = \left(\frac{1}{60}\right)^\circ$$

$$\therefore \quad \left(\frac{75}{2}\right)' = \left(\frac{75}{2 \times 60}\right)^\circ = \left(\frac{5}{8}\right)^\circ$$

$\therefore$ Total degree to convert

$$= 48° + \left(\frac{5}{8}\right)^\circ$$

$$= \left(\frac{384+5}{8}\right)^\circ = \left(\frac{389}{8}\right)^\circ$$

$\because$ Radian measure $= \dfrac{\pi}{180} \times$ Degree measure

$$\therefore \quad \left(\frac{389}{8}\right)^\circ = \frac{\pi}{180} \times \frac{389}{8}$$

$$= \frac{389\pi}{1440} \text{ rad}$$

Hence, 48° 37′ 30″ is $\dfrac{389\pi}{1440}$ rad.

Method to Convert Radian Measure into Degree

To convert given radian into degree, we use the following steps

***Step* I** First, convert given radian into degree by using the relation,

$$\text{Degree measure} = \frac{180}{\pi} \times \text{Radian measure}$$

$[\text{use } \pi = 22/7]$

***Step* II** Convert the fraction part obtained in step I into minutes by using the relation

$$1° = 60' \text{ or } 1 \text{ degree } = 60 \text{ min}$$

***Step* III** If we again get a fraction part in step II, then we convert it into second by using the relation

$$1' = 60'' \text{ or } 1 \text{ min } = 60 \text{ seconds}$$

Thus, we convert given radian measure into degree which have minutes and seconds also.

Example 3 Find the degree measure corresponding to following radians.

(i) $\dfrac{\pi}{64}$ rad (ii) 6 rad

Sol. (i) We know that, Degree measure $= \dfrac{180}{\pi} \times$ Radian measure

$$\therefore \quad \frac{\pi}{64} \text{ rad} = \left(\frac{\pi}{64} \times \frac{180}{\pi}\right)^\circ = \left(\frac{45}{16}\right)^\circ = \left(2\frac{13}{16}\right)^\circ$$

Here, we see that fraction part is $\left(\dfrac{13}{16}\right)^\circ$. So, convert it into minutes.

$$\because \quad 1° = 60'$$

$$\therefore \quad \left(2\frac{13}{16}\right)^\circ = 2° + \left(\frac{13}{16} \times 60\right)' = 2° + \left(\frac{195}{4}\right)' = 2° + \left(48\frac{3}{4}\right)'$$

Here, fraction part is $\dfrac{3}{4}$. So, we convert it into seconds.

$$\because \quad 1' = 60''$$

$$\therefore \quad \left(2\frac{13}{16}\right)^\circ = 2° + 48' + \left(\frac{3}{4} \times 60\right)'' = 2° \, 48' \, 45''$$

Hence, the degree measure of $\dfrac{\pi}{64}$ rad is 2°48′45″.

(ii) We know that, Degree measure $= \dfrac{180}{\pi} \times$ Radian measure

$\therefore$ Required degree measure $= \left(\dfrac{180}{\frac{22}{7}} \times 6\right)^\circ \quad \left[\because \pi = \dfrac{22}{7}\right]$

$$= \left(\frac{1080 \times 7}{22}\right)^\circ = \left(343\frac{7}{11}\right)^\circ$$

$$= 343^\circ + \frac{7}{11} \times 60 \text{ min} \quad [\because 1^\circ = 60']$$

$$= 343^\circ + 38\frac{2}{11}\text{min} = 343^\circ + 38' + \frac{2}{11}\text{min}$$

$$= 343^\circ + 38' + \frac{2}{11} \times 60'' \quad [\because 1' = 60'']$$

$$= 343^\circ + 38' + 10.9'' = 343^\circ 38' 11'' \text{ (approx.)}$$

Hence, the degree measure of 6 rad is $343^\circ\, 38'\, 11''$ (approx.).

Length of an Arc of a Circle

If in a circle of radius r, an arc of length s subtend an angle θ radian at the centre, then

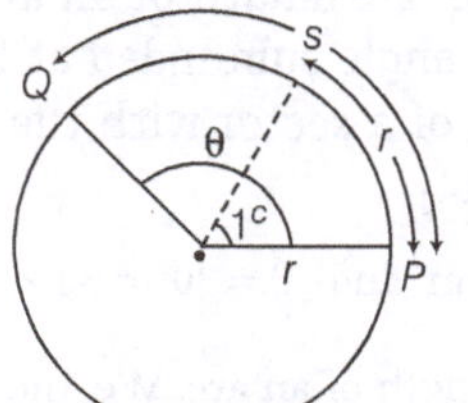

$$\theta = \frac{s}{r} = \frac{\textbf{Length of arc}}{\textbf{Radius}} \quad \textbf{or } s = r\theta$$

Example 4 Find the degree measure of the angle subtended at the centre of a circle of radius 100 cm by an arc of length 22 cm as shown in the figure.

[use $\pi = 22/7$]

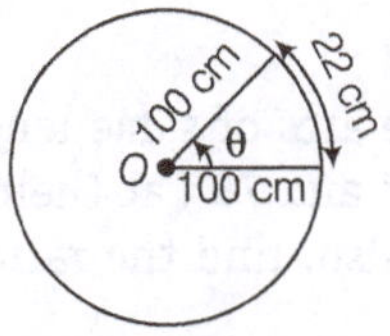

Sol. Given, radius, $r = 100$ cm and arc length, $s = 22$ cm

We know that, $s = r\theta$

$$\therefore \quad \theta = \frac{s}{r} = \frac{\text{Arc length}}{\text{Radius}} = \frac{22}{100} = 0.22 \text{ rad}$$

$$= \left(0.22 \times \frac{180}{\pi}\right) \text{degree}$$

$$= \left(0.22 \times \frac{180 \times 7}{22}\right)^\circ$$

$$= \left(\frac{22}{100} \times \frac{180 \times 7}{22}\right)^\circ$$

$$= \left(\frac{126}{10}\right)^\circ = \left(12\frac{6}{10}\right)^\circ$$

$$= 12^\circ + \frac{6}{10} \times 60' \quad [\because 1^\circ = 60']$$

$$= 12^\circ + 36' = 12^\circ\, 36'$$

Hence, the degree measure of the required angle is $12^\circ 36'$.

Example 5 In a circle of diameter 44 cm, the length of chord is 22 cm. Find the length of minor arc of the chord. **[NCERT]**

Sol. Given, diameter = 44 cm

$$\therefore \quad \text{Radius, } r = \frac{44}{2} = 22 \text{ cm}$$

Let a chord $AB = 22$ cm [given]

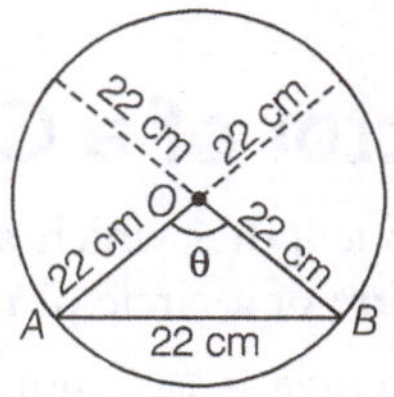

Since, $OA = OB = AB = 22$ cm

$\therefore$ ΔOAB is equilateral.

$$\Rightarrow \quad \theta = \angle AOB = 60^\circ$$

Now, we convert 60° into radian measure.

Clearly, $60^\circ = \left(60 \times \frac{\pi}{180}\right)$ rad

$$\left[\because \text{radian measure} = \frac{\pi}{180} \times \text{degree measure}\right]$$

$$\Rightarrow \quad 60^\circ = \frac{\pi}{3} \text{ radian}$$

$\therefore$ Length of minor arc $AB = r\theta$ $[\because \text{arc length } (s) = r\theta]$

$$= 22 \times \frac{\pi}{3}$$

$$= \frac{22}{3} \times \frac{22}{7} \quad \left[\because \pi = \frac{22}{7}\right]$$

$$= \frac{484}{21} \text{ cm}$$

Note Always remember that in formula $\theta = \frac{s}{r}$, θ is measured in radian. So, first convert the degree in radian whenever use this formula.

Example 6 The perimeter of a certain sector of a circle is equal to the length of the arc of a semi-circle having the same radius. Express the angle of the sector in degrees, minute and seconds.

Sol. Let 'r' be the radius of the circle and θ be the sector angle.

Then, perimeter of the sector $= 2r + r\theta$ $\left[\because \theta = \frac{s}{r}\right]$

and length of arc of semi-circle $= \pi r$

[$\because$ it is a semi-circle]

$$2r + r\theta = \pi r$$

$$\Rightarrow \quad (2 + \theta) = \pi$$

$$\Rightarrow \quad \theta = (\pi - 2) \text{ rad}$$

$$= (\pi - 2) \times \frac{180^\circ}{\pi} \quad \left[\because 1 \text{ rad} = \frac{180^\circ}{\pi}\right]$$

$$= \pi \times \frac{180^\circ}{\pi} - \frac{2 \times 180^\circ}{\pi} = 180^\circ - \frac{360^\circ}{\pi}$$
$$= 180^\circ - 114^\circ\, 32'\, 44''$$
$$= (179^\circ + 1^\circ) - 114^\circ 32' 44''$$
$$= (179^\circ + 60') - 114^\circ 32' 44''$$
$$= (179^\circ + 59' + 1') - 114^\circ 32' 44''$$
$$= (179^\circ + 59' + 60'') - 114^\circ 32' 44''$$
$$= 65^\circ\, 27'\, 16''$$

Area of Sector of a Circle

Let AB be an arc of length s which subtends an angle θ (in radian) at the centre of a circle of radius r.

Then, area of whole circle is πr^2 and angle subtended by the entire circumference at the centre $= 2\pi$ radians.

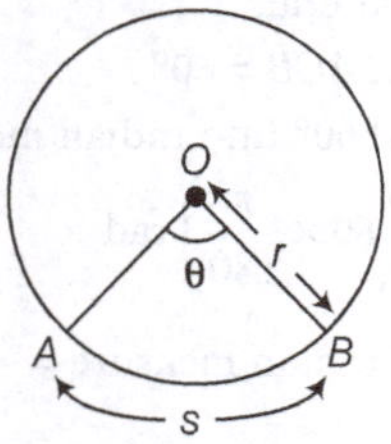

$\therefore$ $\dfrac{\text{Area of sector } AOB}{\text{Area of whole circle}} = \dfrac{\theta}{2\pi}$

$\Rightarrow$ $\dfrac{\text{Area of sector } AOB}{\pi r^2} = \dfrac{\theta}{2\pi}$

$\Rightarrow$ $\boxed{\text{Area of sector } AOB = \frac{1}{2} r^2 \theta}$

or $\boxed{\text{Area of sector } AOB = \frac{1}{2} sr}$ $[\because s = r\theta]$

Example 7 What is the area of the sector of the following figure? Also, find the length of an arc. [use $\pi = 3.14$]

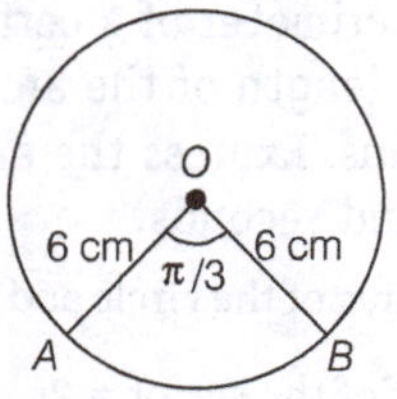

Sol. Given, $r = 6$ cm and $\theta = \dfrac{\pi}{3}$

We know that, area of sector $= \dfrac{1}{2} r^2 \theta$

$$= \frac{1}{2}(6)^2 \times \frac{\pi}{3} = 6 \times 3.14 = 18.84 \text{ cm}^2$$

Now, length of an arc $(s) = r\theta = 6 \times \dfrac{\pi}{3} = 2\pi$ cm $= 6.28$ cm

Problems Based on Applications

Some Useful Points

(i) The angle between two consecutive digits in a clock is $30^\circ (= \pi/6 \text{ radian})$.

(ii) The hour hand rotates through an angle of 30° in one hour i.e. $\left(\dfrac{1}{2}\right)^\circ$ in one minute.

(iii) The minute hand rotates through an angle of 6° in one minute.

Example 8 Find the length of an arc of a circle of radius 3 cm, if the angle subtended at the centre is 30°. Also, find the area of a sector with the help of length of an arc. [use $\pi = 3.14$]

Sol. Given, $r = 3$ cm and $\theta = 30^\circ = 30 \times \dfrac{\pi}{180} = \dfrac{\pi}{6}$ rad

Let s be the length of an arc. We know that,

Angle $\theta = \dfrac{s}{r}$, where θ is in radian. ...(i)

On putting the values of r and θ in Eq. (i), we get

$$\frac{\pi}{6} = \frac{s}{3} \Rightarrow s = \frac{\pi}{2} = \frac{3.14}{2} = 1.57 \text{ cm}$$

We know that, area of a sector $= \dfrac{1}{2} sr$

$$= \frac{1}{2}(1.57) \times 3 = 2.355 \approx 2.36 \text{ cm}^2$$

Example 9 If the arcs of same length in two circles subtend angle of 60° and 75° at their centres. Find the ratio of their radii. Also, find the ratio of their areas of the sectors.

Sol. Let r_1 and r_2 be the radii of the given circles and let their arcs of same length s subtend angles of 60° and 75° at their centres.

Now, $60^\circ = \left(60 \times \dfrac{\pi}{180}\right) = \left(\dfrac{\pi}{3}\right)$ rad

$75^\circ = \left(75 \times \dfrac{\pi}{180}\right) = \left(\dfrac{5\pi}{12}\right)$ rad

$\Rightarrow$ $\dfrac{\pi}{3} = \dfrac{s}{r_1}$ and $\dfrac{5\pi}{12} = \dfrac{s}{r_2}$ $\left[\because \theta = \dfrac{s}{r}\right]$

$\Rightarrow$ $s = \dfrac{\pi}{3} r_1$ and $s = \dfrac{5\pi}{12} r_2$

$\Rightarrow$ $\dfrac{\pi}{3} r_1 = \dfrac{5\pi}{12} r_2$

$\Rightarrow$ $4r_1 = 5r_2 \Rightarrow \dfrac{r_1}{r_2} = \dfrac{5}{4}$

$\Rightarrow \quad r_1 : r_2 = 5 : 4$

Let A_1 and A_2 be the areas of the sectors of the given circles.

$\therefore$ Ratios of areas of sectors $= \dfrac{A_1}{A_2}$

$$= \frac{\frac{1}{2}sr_1}{\frac{1}{2}sr_2} \quad \left[\because \text{area of a sector} = \frac{1}{2}sr\right]$$

$$= \frac{r_1}{r_2} = \frac{5}{4}$$

Hence, the required ratios of areas of the sectors of a given circles is 5 : 4.

Example 10 Find the angle in radian through which a pendulum swings, if its length is 75 cm and tip describes an arc of length 21 cm. **[NCERT]**

Sol. Given, length of pendulum = 75 cm

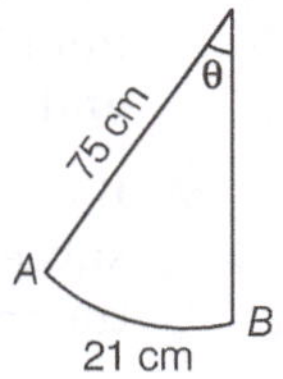

Radius (r) = length of the pendulum

= 75 cm

Also, length of arc (s) = 21 cm

Now, $\theta = \dfrac{s}{r} = \dfrac{21}{75} = \dfrac{7}{25}$ rad

Example 11 A horse is tied to a post by a rope. If the horse moves along a circular path always keeping the rope tight and describes 88 m when it has traced out 54° at the centre. Find the length of the rope.

Sol. Let the post be at point P and PA be the length of the rope in tight position.

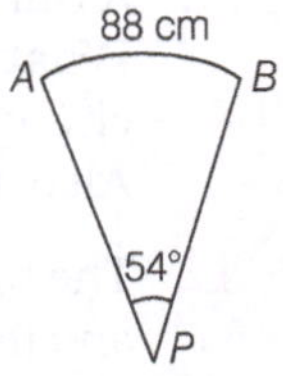

Suppose the horse moves along the arc AB, such that $\angle APB = 54°$. So, length of arc AB, $s = 88$ m.

Let r be the length of the rope i.e. $PA = r$ m.

Now, $\theta = 54° = \left(54 \times \dfrac{\pi}{180}\right) = \left(\dfrac{3\pi}{10}\right) \quad \left[\because 1° = \dfrac{\pi}{180} \text{ rad}\right]$

$\because \quad \theta = \dfrac{s}{r}$

$\therefore \quad \dfrac{3\pi}{10} = \dfrac{88}{r}$

$\Rightarrow \quad r = \dfrac{88 \times 10}{3\pi}$

$\Rightarrow \quad r = \dfrac{880}{9.42} = 93.41$ m $\quad [\because \pi = 3.14]$

Example 12 Assuming that a person of normal sight can read print at such a distance that the letters subtend an angle of 5′ at his eye. What is the height of the letters that he can read at a distance of 12 m?

Sol. Let 'h' be the required height in meters. Here, h metre can be considered as the length of arc of a circle of radius 12 m, which subtends an angle of 5′ at its centre.

Clearly, $5' = \left(\dfrac{5}{60}\right)^\circ = \left(\dfrac{1}{12} \times \dfrac{\pi}{180}\right)^c$

Now, $\quad \theta = \dfrac{s}{r} \Rightarrow \dfrac{\pi}{12 \times 180} = \dfrac{h}{12}$

$\Rightarrow \quad h = \left(\dfrac{\pi}{180}\right)$ m $= 1.7$ cm

Example 13 The minute hand of a watch is 1.5 cm long. How far does its tip move in 40 min? [use $\pi = 3.14$]

Sol. We know that, the minute hand of a watch rotates through 360° in 60 min.

$\therefore$ Angle traced out by minute hand in 1 min

$$= \left(\frac{360°}{60}\right) = 6°$$

$\therefore$ Angle traced by the minute hand in 40 min

$= (40 \times 6)° = 240° = 240 \times \dfrac{\pi}{180} = \left(\dfrac{4\pi}{3}\right)$ rad

We know that, $\theta = \dfrac{s}{r} \Rightarrow \dfrac{4\pi}{3} = \dfrac{s}{1.5}$

$\Rightarrow \quad s = \dfrac{4\pi}{3} \times 1.5 = 2\pi = 2 \times 3.14 = 6.28$ cm

Hence, tip of the minute hand travels 6.28 cm in 40 min.

Example 14 Find in degrees and radians, the angle between the hour hand and the minute hand of a clock at half past three.

Sol. The angle traced by the hour hand in 12 h = 360°

$\therefore$ The angle traced by the hour hand in 3 h 30 min

i.e. $\quad \dfrac{7}{2}\text{h} = \left(\dfrac{360}{12} \times \dfrac{7}{2}\right)^\circ = 105°$

The angle traced by the minute hand in 60 min = 360°

$\therefore$ The angle traced by the minute hand in 30 min

$$= \left(\frac{360}{60} \times 30\right)^\circ = 180°$$

Hence, required angle between two hands

$= 180° - 105° = 75°$ or $\left(75 \times \dfrac{\pi}{180}\right) = \dfrac{5\pi}{12}$ rad

Example 15 The angles of a triangle are in AP. The number of degrees in the least is to the number of radians in the greatest is as 60 : π. Find the angles in degree.

Sol. Let the three angles in AP be $(a-d)°$, a, $(a+d)°$.

$\therefore \quad (a-d)°+a+(a+d)°=180°$

[$\because$ sum of all the angles of a triangle is 180°]

$\Rightarrow \quad 3a=180 \Rightarrow a=60$

So, the angles are $(60-d)°$, $60°$, $(60+d)°$.

Number of degrees in least angle $=(60-d)°$

Number of degrees in greatest angle $=(60+d)°$

$\therefore$ Number of radians in greatest angle

$$=\frac{\pi}{180}\times(60+d)\text{ rad}$$

According to the given condition,

$$\frac{(60-d)}{\frac{\pi}{180}\times(60+d)}=\frac{60}{\pi}$$

$$\Rightarrow \quad \frac{60-d}{60+d}\times\frac{180}{\pi}=\frac{60}{\pi}$$

$$\Rightarrow \quad \frac{60-d}{60+d}=\frac{1}{3}$$

$$\Rightarrow \quad 180-3d=60+d$$

$$\Rightarrow \quad 4d=120$$

$$\Rightarrow \quad d=30$$

Hence, angles are $(60-30)°$, $60°$ and $(60+30)°$

i.e. 30°, 60° and 90°.

Topic Practice 1

Very Short Answer Type Questions

2 Marks

1 Find the radian measure corresponding to the following degree measures.

(i) 75° (ii) 135°

(iii) $-22°\ 30'$ (iv) $-300°$

2 Find the radian measures corresponding to following degree measures.

(i) $5°37'\ 30''$ (ii) $-125°\ 30'$

3 Find the degree measure corresponding to the following radian measures. [use $\pi=22/7$]

(i) $\frac{\pi}{9}$ rad (ii) $\frac{9\pi}{5}$

(iii) $-\frac{\pi}{3}$ rad (iv) $-\frac{5\pi}{6}$

4 Find the degree measure corresponding to following radian measures.

(i) $(-3)^c$

(ii) 11^c

5 Find the length of arc of a circle of radius 5 cm, subtending a central angle measuring 15°.

6 Find the angle in degree subtends at the centre of a circle by an arc whose length is 2.2 times the radius.

7 A wheel makes 360° revolutions in a minute. Through how many radians does it turn in one second? [NCERT]

Short Answer Type Questions

4 Marks

8 In a circle of diameter 40 cm, a chord is 20 cm. Find the length of the minor arc of the chord and area of the minor sector.

9 If the arc of the same length in two circles subtend angles 65° and 110° at the centre, find the ratio of their radii.

10 A horse is tied to a post by a rope. If the horse moves along a circular path always keeping the rope tight and describe 70 m when it has traced out 80° at the centre, find the length of the rope and area of sector when it has traced out 120°.

11 A rail road curve is to be laid out on a circle. What radius should be used if the track is to change direction by 25° in a distance of 40 m? Also, find area of its sector.

12 The Moon's distance from the Earth is 360000 km and its diameter subtend an angle of 31′ at the eye of observer. Find the diameter of the Moon and find the area swept of an observer.

13 The minute hand of a watch is 2.2 cm long. How far does its tip move in 50 min. Also, find the area swept by minute hand.

14 Find the angle in radians between the hands of a clock at 7:20 pm.

15 The number of sides of two regular polygons are in the ratio 5 : 4 and the difference between their angles is 9°. Find the number of sides of the polygons.

Hints & Answers

1. (i) $\frac{5\pi}{12}$ rad

(ii) $\frac{3\pi}{4}$ rad

(iii) Let $\theta = -(22°30') = -\left[22° + \left(\frac{1}{2}\right)^\circ\right] = -\left(\frac{45}{2}\right)^\circ$

Ans. $-\frac{\pi}{8}$ rad

(iv) $-\frac{5\pi}{3}$ rad

2. (i) $(30)'' = \left(\frac{1}{2}\right)' \Rightarrow 37'\,30'' = \left(37\frac{1}{2}\right)' = \left(\frac{75}{2} \times \frac{1}{60}\right)^\circ = \left(\frac{5}{8}\right)^\circ$

$\therefore\ 5°37'\,30'' = \left(5 + \frac{5}{8}\right)^\circ = \left(\frac{45}{8}\right)^\circ$ **Ans.** $\frac{\pi}{32}$ rad

(ii) $-\frac{251\pi}{360}$

3. (i) 20°

(ii) 324°

(iii) − 60°

(iv) −150°

4. (i) $(-3)^c = -\left(3 \times \frac{180}{\pi}\right)^\circ = -\left(3 \times \frac{180}{22} \times 7\right)^\circ$

$= -\left(\frac{1890}{11}\right)^\circ$

Ans. $-171°49'5''$

(ii) **Ans.** 630°

5. $s = r\theta = 5 \times \frac{\pi}{12}$ **Ans.** 1.30 cm

6. $\theta = \frac{l}{r} = \left(\frac{2.2 \times r}{r}\right)$ rad $= \left(2.2 \times \frac{180}{22/7}\right)^\circ$ **Ans.** 126°

7. In 1 minute wheel makes 360 revolutions.

$\therefore$ In 1 second wheel makes 6 revolutions.

Also, in one revolution wheel turn by 2π radians.

Ans. 12π

8. (i) Similar as Example 5. **Ans.** $\frac{20}{3}\pi$ cm.

(ii) Area of the minor sector $= \frac{1}{2}r^2\theta$ **Ans.** $\frac{200\,\pi}{3}$ cm^2

9. Solve as Example 9. **Ans.** 22 : 13

10. Here, $\theta = 80° = \left(80 \times \frac{\pi}{180}\right)^c = \frac{4\pi}{9}$ and $s = 70$ m

$\therefore\quad \theta = \frac{s}{r} \Rightarrow \frac{4\pi}{9} = \frac{70}{r}$

$\Rightarrow\quad r = 50.11$ m

and area of the sector when it has traced out 120° is given by

$\frac{1}{2}r^2\theta_1$, where $\theta_1 = 120° = \frac{2\pi}{3}$ rad.

Ans. 50.11 m; 2630.57 m^2

11. Here, $\theta = 25° = \left(25 \times \frac{\pi}{180}\right)^c$ and $s = 40$ m

Ans. 91.64; 1832.8 m^2

12. $\theta = 31' = \left(\frac{31}{60} \times \frac{\pi}{180}\right)$ rad and $r = 360000$ km

$\because\quad \theta = \frac{s}{r}$

$s = r\theta$

Also, area swept by an observer $= \frac{1}{2}sr$

Ans. 3247.62 km; 584571600 km^2

13. Angle traced by minute hand in 50 min

$= (50 \times 6)°$

$= 50 \times 6 \times \frac{\pi}{180} = \frac{5\pi}{3}$

Now, $s = \theta r$

and area swept by minute hand $= \frac{1}{2}sr$

Ans. 11.52 cm; 12.67 cm^2

14. Solve as Example 14. Ans. $\frac{5\pi}{9}$ rad.

15. Let $\frac{n_1}{n_2} = \frac{5}{4} \Rightarrow n_1 = 5k,\ n_2 = 4k$ for some $k \in N$.

Also, let $\theta_2 - \theta_1 = 9°$ [given]

$\Rightarrow\quad \frac{360°}{n_2} - \frac{360°}{n_1} = 9°$ [as $n_1 > n_2 \Rightarrow \theta_1 < \theta_2$]

$\Rightarrow\quad \frac{1}{n_2} - \frac{1}{n_1} = \frac{9}{360}$

$\Rightarrow\quad \frac{1}{4k} - \frac{1}{5k} = \frac{1}{40}$

$\Rightarrow\quad k = 2$

Ans. $n_1 = 10$ and $n_2 = 8$

TOPIC 02 Trigonometric Functions

We have already studied trigonometric ratios for acute angles in earlier classes. In this topic, we will study trigonometric ratios for any angle which are termed as **trigonometric functions**.

Trigonometric Functions for Quick Review

In a right angled triangle, there are actually six trigonometric ratios, which are given below.

In right angled ΔABC,

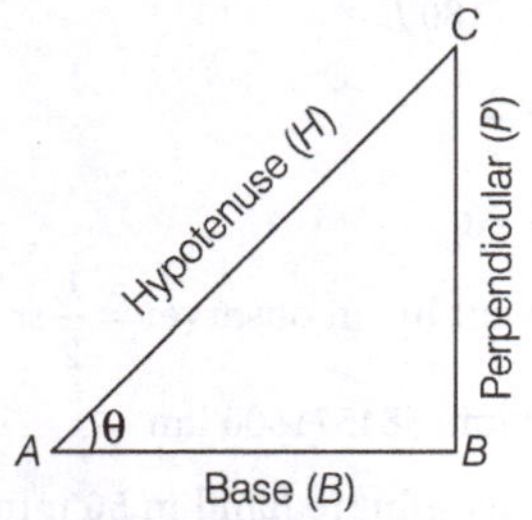

(i) $\sin\theta = \dfrac{\text{Perpendicular}}{\text{Hypotenuse}}\left(\text{or } \dfrac{P}{H}\right) = \dfrac{BC}{AC}$

(ii) $\cos\theta = \dfrac{\text{Base}}{\text{Hypotenuse}}\left(\text{or } \dfrac{B}{H}\right) = \dfrac{AB}{AC}$

(iii) $\tan\theta = \dfrac{\text{Perpendicular}}{\text{Base}}\left(\text{or } \dfrac{P}{B}\right) = \dfrac{BC}{AB}$

(iv) $\cot\theta = \dfrac{\text{Base}}{\text{Perpendicular}}\left(\text{or } \dfrac{B}{P}\right) = \dfrac{AB}{BC}$

(v) $\sec\theta = \dfrac{\text{Hypotenuse}}{\text{Base}}\left(\text{or } \dfrac{H}{B}\right) = \dfrac{AC}{AB}$

(vi) $\text{cosec}\,\theta = \dfrac{\text{Hypotenuse}}{\text{Perpendicular}}\left(\text{or } \dfrac{H}{P}\right) = \dfrac{AC}{BC}$

Note Here, $\sin\theta$ does not mean the product of sin and θ. The $\sin\theta$ is correctly read as sine of angle θ.

Example 1 In ΔABC, $\angle B$ is right angled triangle. If $\tan A = 1$, then show that $2\sin A\cos A = 1$.

Sol. Given, $\angle B$ is right angled in ΔABC and $\tan A = 1$

$\therefore \tan A = \dfrac{BC}{AB} = 1 \Rightarrow BC = AB$

Let $AB = BC = k$, where k is a positive real number. In right angled ΔABC,

$$AC^2 = AB^2 + BC^2$$

$$\Rightarrow AC = \sqrt{AB^2 + BC^2}$$

$$\Rightarrow AC = \sqrt{k^2 + k^2}$$

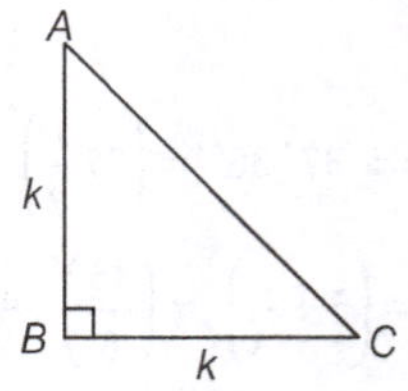

$\Rightarrow AC = \sqrt{2k^2} \Rightarrow AC = k\sqrt{2}$

Now, $\sin A = \dfrac{BC}{AC} = \dfrac{k}{k\sqrt{2}} = \dfrac{1}{\sqrt{2}}$

and $\cos A = \dfrac{AB}{AC} = \dfrac{k}{k\sqrt{2}} = \dfrac{1}{\sqrt{2}}$

$\therefore$ LHS $= 2\sin A\cos A$

$= 2\left(\dfrac{1}{\sqrt{2}}\right)\left(\dfrac{1}{\sqrt{2}}\right) = 2 \times \dfrac{1}{2} = 1 =$ RHS

Definition of Trigonometric Functions with the Help of Unit Circle

Let a circle be drawn with centre O and unit radius which cut the $X'OX$ and $Y'OY$ axes at A, A' and B, B' respectively as shown in the following figure

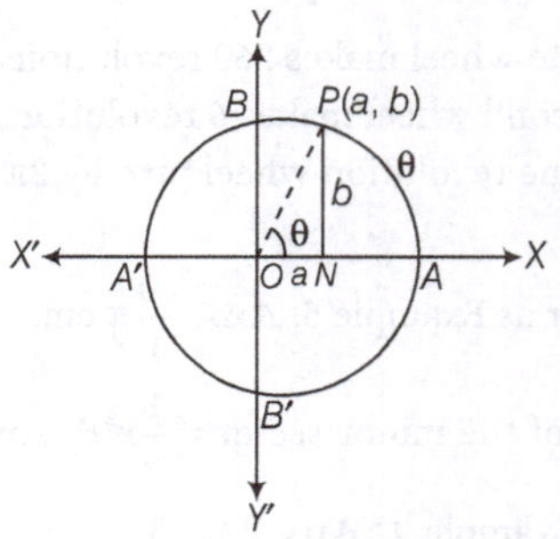

Let a moving point P start from A and move along the circumference of the circle. Let it cover an arc length θ.

Then, the circular measure of $\angle AOP = \dfrac{\text{arc } AP}{\text{Radius}} = \dfrac{\theta}{1} = \theta$

Let the coordinates of P be (a, b) and let PN be perpendicular on the X-axis. Then, $ON = a$ and $PN = b$. Now, the trigonometric functions of x are defined as

$\sin\theta = b$, $\cos\theta = a$, $\tan\theta = \frac{b}{a}$, $\operatorname{cosec}\theta = \frac{1}{b}$, $\sec\theta = \frac{1}{a}$ and $\cot\theta = \frac{a}{b}$.

It can be seen that the trigonometric functions of a real number θ and trigonometric ratios of $\angle AOP$ are same. But value of trigonometric fucntions may by negative, because can be lies in any quadrant.

Note

(i) Here, the angle θ can be any magnitude.

(ii) P is a point, where the terminal side of the angle meets the unit circle.

(iii) $P(a, b) \equiv P(\cos\theta, \sin\theta)$

(iv) As $-1 \le a \le 1$ and $-1 \le b \le 1$ in unit circle, therefore $-1 \le \cos\theta \le 1$ and $-1 \le \sin\theta \le 1$.

Quadrantal Angles and Related Trigonometric Functions

All angles which are integral multiples of $\frac{\pi}{2}$ are called **quadrantal angles.** e.g. $0, \pm\pi, \pm\frac{3\pi}{2}$, etc.

If θ is an **integral multiples** of π i.e. $\theta = 0, \pm\pi, \pm 2\pi, \pm 3\pi, \ldots$, then $\sin\theta = 0$

and if θ is an **odd multiples** of $\frac{\pi}{2}$,

i.e. $\theta = \pm\frac{\pi}{2}, \pm\frac{3\pi}{2}, \pm\frac{5\pi}{2}, \ldots$, then $\cos\theta = 0$.

Thus, we can say that

$\sin\theta = 0 \Rightarrow \theta = n\pi$, where n is any integer.

and $\cos\theta = 0 \Rightarrow \theta = (2n+1)\frac{\pi}{2}$, where n is any integer.

Trigonometric Functions of Standard Angles

Angle	0°	30° $\left(\frac{\pi}{6}\right)$	45° $\left(\frac{\pi}{4}\right)$	60° $\left(\frac{\pi}{3}\right)$	90° $\left(\frac{\pi}{2}\right)$	120° $\left(\frac{2\pi}{3}\right)$	135° $\left(\frac{3\pi}{4}\right)$	150° $\left(\frac{5\pi}{6}\right)$	180° (π)	270° $\left(\frac{3\pi}{2}\right)$	360° (2π)
$\sin\theta$	0	$\frac{1}{2}$	$\frac{1}{\sqrt{2}}$	$\frac{\sqrt{3}}{2}$	1	$\frac{\sqrt{3}}{2}$	$\frac{1}{\sqrt{2}}$	$\frac{1}{2}$	0	-1	0
$\cos\theta$	1	$\frac{\sqrt{3}}{2}$	$\frac{1}{\sqrt{2}}$	$\frac{1}{2}$	0	$-\frac{1}{2}$	$-\frac{1}{\sqrt{2}}$	$-\frac{\sqrt{3}}{2}$	-1	0	1
$\tan\theta$	0	$\frac{1}{\sqrt{3}}$	1	$\sqrt{3}$	∞	$-\sqrt{3}$	-1	$-\frac{1}{\sqrt{3}}$	0	∞	0
$\cot\theta$	∞	$\sqrt{3}$	1	$\frac{1}{\sqrt{3}}$	0	$-\frac{1}{\sqrt{3}}$	-1	$-\sqrt{3}$	∞	0	∞
$\sec\theta$	1	$\frac{2}{\sqrt{3}}$	$\sqrt{2}$	2	∞	-2	$-\sqrt{2}$	$-\frac{2}{\sqrt{3}}$	-1	∞	1
$\operatorname{cosec}\theta$	∞	2	$\sqrt{2}$	$\frac{2}{\sqrt{3}}$	1	$\frac{2}{\sqrt{3}}$	$\sqrt{2}$	2	∞	-1	∞

Note Here, the symbol '∞' is used for not defined.

Example 2 Find the value of

$$\sin^2\frac{\pi}{6} + \cos^2\frac{\pi}{6} + \sin^2\frac{\pi}{4}.$$

Sol. $\sin^2\frac{\pi}{6} + \cos^2\frac{\pi}{6} + \sin^2\frac{\pi}{4}$

$$= \left(\frac{1}{2}\right)^2 + \left(\frac{\sqrt{3}}{2}\right)^2 + \left(\frac{1}{\sqrt{2}}\right)^2$$

$$= \frac{1}{4} + \frac{3}{4} + \frac{1}{2}$$

$$= \frac{1+3+2}{4} = \frac{6}{4} = \frac{3}{2}$$

Note $(\sin\theta)^2$ is written as $\sin^2\theta$ and $(\cos\theta)^2$ is written as $\cos^2\theta$.

Relationship between Trigonometric Functions

The folloiwng relations are the immediate consequences of the above definitions of trigonometric fucntions.

Reciprocal Relations

(i) $\sin\theta = \frac{1}{\operatorname{cosec}\theta}$ and $\operatorname{cosec}\theta = \frac{1}{\sin\theta}$

(ii) $\cos\theta = \frac{1}{\sec\theta}$ and $\sec\theta = \frac{1}{\cos\theta}$

(iii) $\tan\theta = \frac{1}{\cot\theta}$ and $\cot\theta = \frac{1}{\tan\theta}$

Quotient Relations

(i) $\tan\theta = \frac{\sin\theta}{\cos\theta}$ (ii) $\cot\theta = \frac{\cos\theta}{\sin\theta}$

Trigonometric Identities

The relations involving trigonometric functions, which are true for all values of the angle involved, are called trigonometric identities.

Fundamental Identities

$$\cos^2\theta + \sin^2\theta = 1;$$
$$1 + \tan^2\theta = \sec^2\theta;$$
$$1 + \cot^2\theta = \text{cosec}^2\theta$$

With the help of these identities, we can write one trigonometric function in terms of all other trigonometric function, which are given in the table

Transformation of One Trigonometric Function to Another Trigonometric Function

Trigonometric function	$\sin\theta$	$\cos\theta$	$\tan\theta$	$\cot\theta$	$\sec\theta$	$\text{cosec}\,\theta$
$\sin\theta$	$\sin\theta$	$\pm\sqrt{(1-\cos^2\theta)}$	$\pm\frac{\tan\theta}{\sqrt{(1+\tan^2\theta)}}$	$\pm\frac{1}{\sqrt{(1+\cot^2\theta)}}$	$\pm\frac{\sqrt{(\sec^2\theta-1)}}{\sec\theta}$	$\frac{1}{\text{cosec}\,\theta}$
$\cos\theta$	$\pm\sqrt{(1-\sin^2\theta)}$	$\cos\theta$	$\pm\frac{1}{\sqrt{(1+\tan^2\theta)}}$	$\pm\frac{\cot\theta}{\sqrt{(1+\cot^2\theta)}}$	$\frac{1}{\sec\theta}$	$\pm\frac{\sqrt{(\text{cosec}^2\theta-1)}}{\text{cosec}\,\theta}$
$\tan\theta$	$\pm\frac{\sin\theta}{\sqrt{(1-\sin^2\theta)}}$	$\pm\frac{\sqrt{(1-\cos^2\theta)}}{\cos\theta}$	$\tan\theta$	$\frac{1}{\cot\theta}$	$\pm\sqrt{(\sec^2\theta-1)}$	$\pm\frac{1}{\sqrt{(\text{cosec}^2\theta-1)}}$
$\cot\theta$	$\pm\frac{\sqrt{(1-\sin^2\theta)}}{\sin\theta}$	$\pm\frac{\cos\theta}{\sqrt{(1-\cos^2\theta)}}$	$\frac{1}{\tan\theta}$	$\cot\theta$	$\pm\frac{1}{\sqrt{(\sec^2\theta-1)}}$	$\pm\sqrt{(\text{cosec}^2\theta-1)}$
$\sec\theta$	$\pm\frac{1}{\sqrt{(1-\sin^2\theta)}}$	$\frac{1}{\cos\theta}$	$\pm\sqrt{(1+\tan^2\theta)}$	$\pm\frac{\sqrt{(1+\cot^2\theta)}}{\cot\theta}$	$\sec\theta$	$\pm\frac{\text{cosec}\,\theta}{\sqrt{(\text{cosec}^2\theta-1)}}$
$\text{cosec}\,\theta$	$\frac{1}{\sin\theta}$	$\pm\frac{1}{\sqrt{(1-\cos^2\theta)}}$	$\pm\frac{\sqrt{(1+\tan^2\theta)}}{\tan\theta}$	$\pm\sqrt{(1+\cot^2\theta)}$	$\pm\frac{\sec\theta}{\sqrt{(\sec^2\theta-1)}}$	$\text{cosec}\,\theta$

Example 3 If $\text{cosec}\, A = \frac{x}{y}$, then find the value of $\cot A$.

Sol. Given, $\text{cosec}\, A = \frac{x}{y}$

We know that, $\cot^2 A = \text{cosec}^2 A - 1$

$$\cot^2 A = \left(\frac{x}{y}\right)^2 - 1 = \frac{x^2}{y^2} - 1 = \frac{x^2 - y^2}{y^2}$$

$$\Rightarrow \quad \cot A = \pm\frac{\sqrt{x^2 - y^2}}{y}$$

Proving Simple Identities

Example 4 Prove that

$$\tan^2\theta - \sin^2\theta = \tan^2\theta\sin^2\theta.$$

Sol. LHS $= \tan^2\theta - \sin^2\theta = \frac{\sin^2\theta}{\cos^2\theta} - \sin^2\theta \quad \left[\because \tan\theta = \frac{\sin\theta}{\cos\theta}\right]$

$$= \frac{\sin^2\theta - \sin^2\theta\cos^2\theta}{\cos^2\theta} = \frac{\sin^2\theta(1-\cos^2\theta)}{\cos^2\theta}$$

$[\because 1 - \cos^2\theta = \sin^2\theta]$

$$= \frac{\sin^2\theta \cdot \sin^2\theta}{\cos^2\theta} = \tan^2\theta \cdot \sin^2\theta \quad \left[\because \frac{\sin\theta}{\cos\theta} = \tan\theta\right]$$

= LHS **Hence proved.**

Example 5 Prove that

$$\frac{1 + \tan^2 A}{1 + \cot^2 A} = \left(\frac{1 - \tan A}{1 - \cot A}\right)^2 = \tan^2 A.$$

Sol. LHS $= \frac{1 + \tan^2 A}{1 + \cot^2 A}$

$$= \frac{1 + \frac{\sin^2 A}{\cos^2 A}}{1 + \frac{\cos^2 A}{\sin^2 A}} \quad \left[\because \tan\theta = \frac{\sin\theta}{\cos\theta} \text{ and } \cot\theta \ \frac{\cos\theta}{\sin\theta}\right]$$

$$= \frac{\frac{\cos^2 A + \sin^2 A}{\cos^2 A}}{\frac{\sin^2 A + \cos^2 A}{\sin^2 A}} = \frac{\frac{1}{\cos^2 A}}{\frac{1}{\sin^2 A}} \quad [\because \sin^2\theta + \cos^2\theta = 1]$$

$$= \frac{1}{\cos^2 A} \times \frac{\sin^2 A}{1} = \frac{\sin^2 A}{\cos^2 A} = \tan^2 A = \text{RHS}$$

$\left[\because \tan\theta = \frac{\sin\theta}{\cos\theta}\right]$

$$\text{Mid-term} = \left(\frac{1-\tan A}{1-\cot A}\right)^2 = \left(\frac{1-\dfrac{\sin A}{\cos A}}{1-\dfrac{\cos A}{\sin A}}\right)^2$$

$$\left[\because \tan\theta = \frac{\sin\theta}{\cos\theta} \text{ and } \cot\theta = \frac{\cos\theta}{\sin\theta}\right]$$

$$= \frac{\dfrac{(\cos A - \sin A)^2}{\cos^2 A}}{\dfrac{(\sin A - \cos A)^2}{\sin^2 A}} = \frac{(\cos A - \sin A)^2 \times \sin^2 A}{(\sin A - \cos A)^2 \times \cos^2 A}$$

$$= \frac{\sin^2 A}{\cos^2 A} = \tan^2 A = \text{RHS}$$

$\therefore$ LHS = Mid-term = RHS **Hence proved.**

Example 6 Prove the following identities.

(i) $(1+\cot\theta - \operatorname{cosec}\theta)(1+\tan\theta+\sec\theta) = 2$

(ii) $\dfrac{\tan\theta+\sec\theta-1}{\tan\theta-\sec\theta+1} = \dfrac{1+\sin\theta}{\cos\theta}$

Sol. (i) LHS $= (1+\cot\theta - \operatorname{cosec}\theta)(1+\tan\theta+\sec\theta)$

$$= \left(1+\frac{\cos\theta}{\sin\theta} - \frac{1}{\sin\theta}\right)\left(1+\frac{\sin\theta}{\cos\theta}+\frac{1}{\cos\theta}\right)$$

$$= \left(\frac{\sin\theta+\cos\theta-1}{\sin\theta}\right)\left(\frac{\sin\theta+\cos\theta+1}{\cos\theta}\right)$$

$$= \frac{(\sin\theta+\cos\theta)^2-1}{\sin\theta\cos\theta}$$

$$= \frac{\sin^2\theta+\cos^2\theta+2\sin\theta\cos\theta-1}{\sin\theta\cos\theta}$$

$$= \frac{1+2\sin\theta\cos\theta-1}{\sin\theta\cos\theta} \quad [\because \sin^2\theta+\cos^2\theta=1]$$

$$= \frac{2\sin\theta\cos\theta}{\sin\theta\cos\theta} = 2 = \text{RHS}$$ **Hence proved.**

(ii) LHS $= \dfrac{\tan\theta+\sec\theta-1}{\tan\theta-\sec\theta+1}$

$$= \frac{(\tan\theta+\sec\theta)-(\sec^2\theta-\tan^2\theta)}{\tan\theta-\sec\theta+1}$$

$$[\because \sec^2\theta - \tan^2\theta = 1]$$

$$= \frac{(\tan\theta+\sec\theta)\,\{1-(\sec\theta-\tan\theta)\}}{\tan\theta-\sec\theta+1}$$

$$[\because a^2-b^2=(a-b)(a+b)]$$

$$= \frac{(\tan\theta+\sec\theta)(\tan\theta-\sec\theta+1)}{\tan\theta-\sec\theta+1}$$

$$= \tan\theta+\sec\theta$$

$$= \frac{\sin\theta}{\cos\theta}+\frac{1}{\cos\theta}$$

$$= \frac{\sin\theta+1}{\cos\theta} = \text{RHS}$$ **Hence proved.**

Sign of Trigonometric Functions in Different Quadrants

If we draw two mutually perpendicular (intersecting) lines in the plane of paper, then these lines divide the plane of paper into four parts, known as quadrants.

In anti-clockwise order, these quadrants are numbered as I, II, III and IV. All angles from 0° to 90° are taken in I quardant, 90° to 180° in II quardant, 180° to 270° in III quadrant and 270° to 360° in IV quadrant.

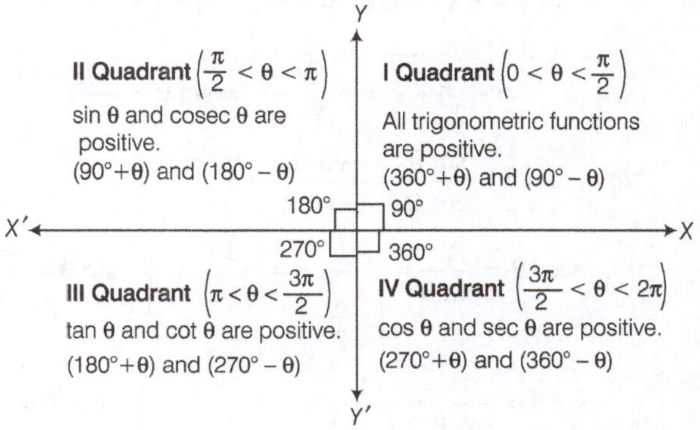

To remember the signs of trigonometrical functions in different quadrants, we use the following four word phrase 'After School To College'.

After
Indicate that **all trigonometric functions** are positive in I quadrant.

School
Indicate that **sine and its reciprocal** are positive in II quadrant.

To
Indicate that **tan and its reciprocal** are positive in III quadrant.

College
Indicate that **cosine and its reciprocal** are positive in IV quadrant.

Example 7 Find the value of $\cos\theta$ and $\tan\theta$, if $\sin\theta = -\dfrac{3}{5}$ and $\pi < \theta < \dfrac{3\pi}{2}$.

Sol. We know that,

$$\cos^2\theta+\sin^2\theta = 1 \Rightarrow \cos\theta = \pm\sqrt{1-\sin^2\theta}$$

Given that, $\pi < \theta < \dfrac{3\pi}{2} \Rightarrow \theta$ lies in third quadrant.

In third quadrant, $\cos\theta$ is negative.

$$\therefore \quad \cos\theta = -\sqrt{1-\sin^2\theta} \Rightarrow \theta = -\sqrt{1-\frac{9}{25}} = -\frac{4}{5}$$

Now, $\quad \tan\theta = \dfrac{\sin\theta}{\cos\theta} = -\left(\dfrac{3}{5}\right)\times\left(-\dfrac{5}{4}\right) = \dfrac{3}{4}$

Example 8 If $\cos\theta = -\frac{1}{2}$, θ lies in third quadrant, then find other five trigonometric functions. **[NCERT]**

Sol. We have, $\cos\theta = -\frac{1}{2}$ and θ lies in third quadrant.

We know that, $\sin^2\theta + \cos^2\theta = 1$

$$\Rightarrow \quad \sin\theta = \pm\sqrt{1-\cos^2\theta}$$

In third quadrant, $\sin\theta$ is negative, therefore

$$\sin\theta = -\sqrt{1-\cos^2\theta} = -\sqrt{1-\left(-\frac{1}{2}\right)^2}$$

$$= -\sqrt{1-\frac{1}{4}} = -\sqrt{\frac{4-1}{4}} \Rightarrow \sin\theta = \frac{-\sqrt{3}}{2}$$

Now, $\tan\theta = \frac{\sin\theta}{\cos\theta} = \frac{-\sqrt{3}/2}{-1/2} = \sqrt{3}$

$$\operatorname{cosec}\theta = \frac{1}{\sin\theta} = \frac{1}{\left(\frac{-\sqrt{3}}{2}\right)} = \frac{-2}{\sqrt{3}} \qquad \left[\because \sin\theta = \frac{-\sqrt{3}}{2}\right]$$

$$\sec\theta = \frac{1}{\cos\theta} = \frac{1}{\left(-\frac{1}{2}\right)} = -2 \qquad \left[\because \cos\theta = -\frac{1}{2}\right]$$

and $\cot\theta = \frac{1}{\tan\theta} = \frac{1}{\sqrt{3}}$ $\qquad [\because \tan\theta = \sqrt{3}]$

Hence, other five trigonometric functions are

$\sin\theta = \frac{-\sqrt{3}}{2}$, $\operatorname{cosec}\theta = \frac{-2}{\sqrt{3}}$,

$\sec\theta = -2$, $\tan\theta = \sqrt{3}$ and $\cot\theta = \frac{1}{\sqrt{3}}$.

Example 9 If $\sec x = \frac{13}{5}$, where x lies in fourth quadrant, then find the values of other five trigonometric functions. **[NCERT]**

Sol. Given, $\sec x = \frac{13}{5}$ and x lies in fourth quadrant.

i.e. $\frac{3\pi}{2} < x < 2\pi$

Now, $\cos x = \frac{1}{\sec x} = \frac{1}{13/5} = \frac{5}{13}$

We know that, $\sin^2 x + \cos^2 x = 1$

$$\therefore \quad \sin^2 x = 1 - \cos^2 x = 1 - \left(\frac{5}{13}\right)^2 = 1 - \frac{25}{169}$$

$$= \frac{169-25}{169} = \frac{144}{169} = \left(\frac{12}{13}\right)^2$$

$$\Rightarrow \quad \sin x = \pm\frac{12}{13}$$

Since, x lies in fourth quadrant and $\sin x$ is negative in fourth quadrant.

$$\therefore \quad \sin x = -\frac{12}{13}$$

Now, $\operatorname{cosec} x = \frac{1}{\sin x} = \frac{-13}{12}$,

$$\tan x = \frac{\sin x}{\cos x} = \frac{-\left(\frac{12}{13}\right)}{\left(\frac{5}{13}\right)} = -\frac{12}{5}$$

and $\cot x = \frac{1}{\tan x} = -\frac{5}{12}$

Example 10 If $\sin\theta = -\frac{3}{5}$ and $\pi < \theta < \frac{3\pi}{2}$, then find the value of $\frac{\sec\theta - \cot\theta}{\tan\theta - \operatorname{cosec}\theta}$.

Sol. Here, $\pi < \theta < \frac{3\pi}{2}$, it means θ lies in third quadrant.

We have, $\sin\theta = -\frac{3}{5}$, then

$$\operatorname{cosec}\theta = \frac{1}{\sin\theta} = \frac{1}{-3/5} = -\frac{5}{3}$$

Now, $\sin^2\theta + \cos^2\theta = 1$

$$\Rightarrow \quad \left(-\frac{3}{5}\right)^2 + \cos^2\theta = 1$$

$$\Rightarrow \quad \cos^2\theta = 1 - \frac{9}{25} = \frac{16}{25}$$

$$\Rightarrow \quad \cos\theta = \pm\sqrt{\frac{16}{25}}$$

$$\Rightarrow \quad \cos\theta = \pm\frac{4}{5}$$

Since, θ lies in third quadrant. So, $\cos\theta$ is negative.

$$\therefore \quad \cos\theta = -\frac{4}{5}$$

Now, $\sec\theta = \frac{1}{\cos\theta} = -\frac{5}{4}$

$$\tan\theta = \frac{\sin\theta}{\cos\theta} = \frac{-3/5}{-4/5} = \frac{3}{5} \times \frac{5}{4} = \frac{3}{4}$$

and $\cot\theta = \frac{1}{\tan\theta} = \frac{1}{3/4} = \frac{4}{3}$

On putting these values in given expression, we get

$$\frac{\sec\theta - \cot\theta}{\tan\theta - \operatorname{cosec}\theta} = \frac{\left(-\frac{5}{4} - \frac{4}{3}\right)}{\left(\frac{3}{4} + \frac{5}{3}\right)} = \frac{\left(\frac{-15-16}{12}\right)}{\left(\frac{9+20}{12}\right)} = -\frac{31}{29}$$

Domain and Range of Trigonometric Functions

The domain of a trigonometric function consists of all the values that you can use as input into the angles i.e. the values for which trigonometric function is defined. The range of trigonometric functions consists of all its output value i.e. the values which are obtained by trigonometric functions. e.g. sin x is defined for all real values of x, so its domain is R and obtained value lies between 1 and -1, so its range is the interval $[-1, 1]$.

The domain, range and graph of each one of the six trigonometric functions are given below

T-function	Domain	Range	Graph of Trigonometric Functions
$\sin\theta$	R	$[-1, 1]$	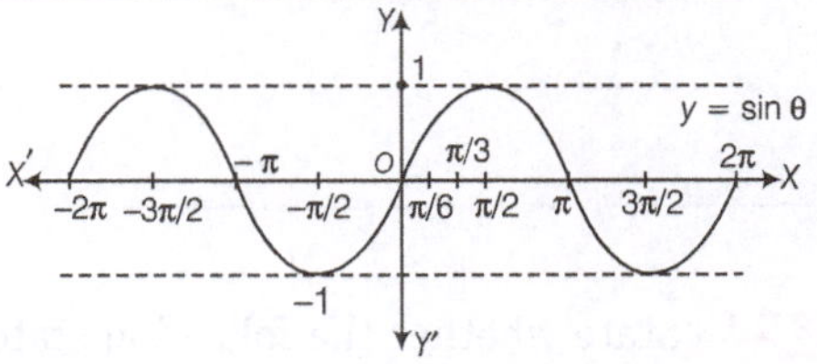
$\cos\theta$	R	$[-1, 1]$	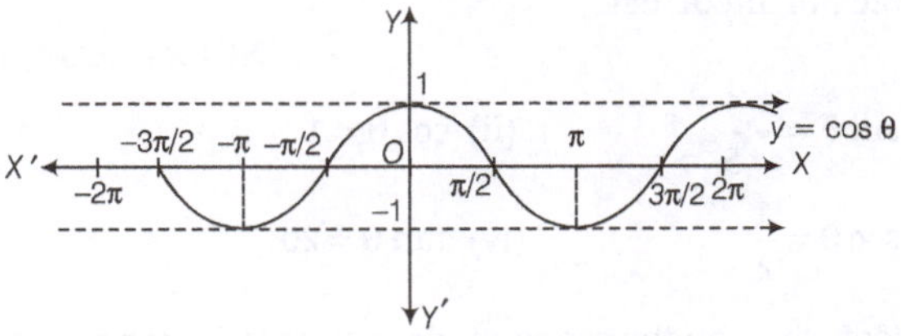
$\tan\theta$	$\{x : x \in R \text{ and } x \neq (2n+1)\pi/2, n \in I\}$	R	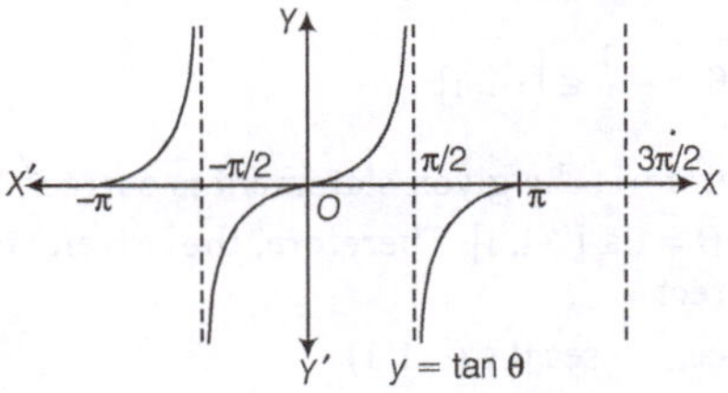
$\cot\theta$	$\{x : x \in R \text{ and } x \neq n\pi, n \in I\}$	R	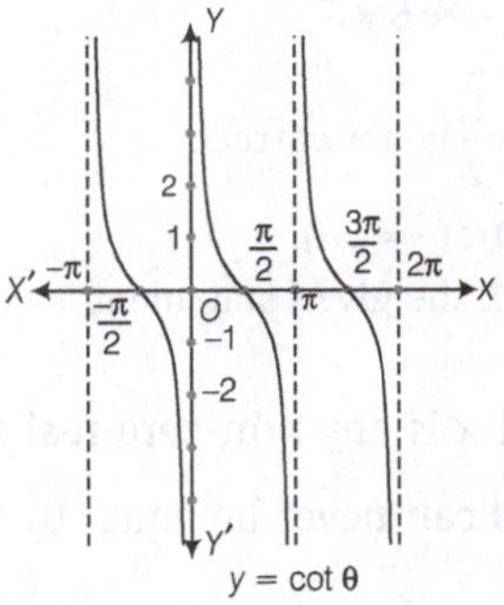
cosec θ	$\{x : x \in R \text{ and } x \neq n\pi, n \in I\}$	$R - (-1, 1)$	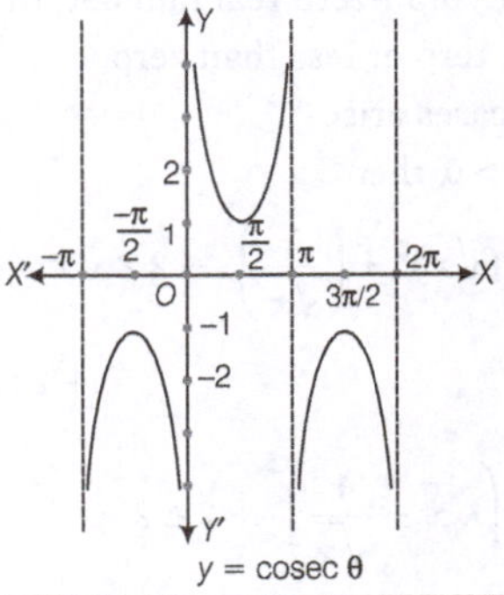

T-function	Domain	Range	Graph of Trigonometric Functions
$\sec\theta$	$\{x : x \in R \text{ and } x \neq (2n+1)\pi/2, n \in I\}$	$R-(-1, 1)$	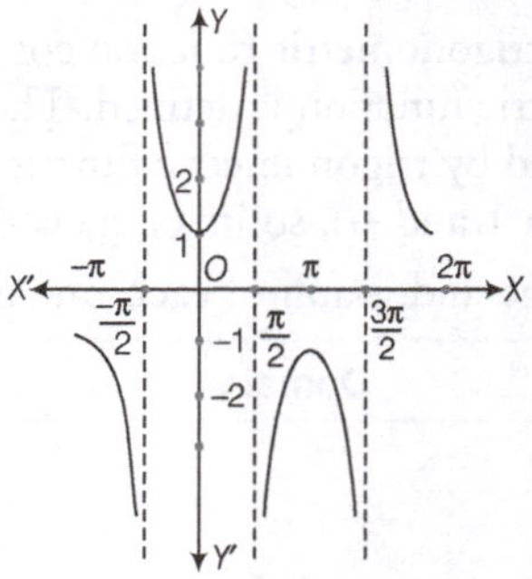 $y = \sec\theta$

Example 11 State whether the following statement is correct or incorrect. **[NCERT Exemplar]**

(i) $\sin\theta = -\frac{1}{5}$ (ii) $\cos\theta = 1$

(iii) $\sec\theta = \frac{1}{2}$ (iv) $\tan\theta = 20$

Verify through the range of trigonometric function.

Sol. (i) $\sin\theta = -\frac{1}{5} \in [-1, 1]$.

Therefore, the given statement is correct.

(ii) $\cos\theta = 1 \in [-1, 1]$. Therefore, the given statement is correct.

(iii) Since, $\sec\theta \notin (-1, 1)$

$\therefore \quad \sec\theta \neq \frac{1}{2}$,

$\Rightarrow \sec\theta = \frac{1}{2}$ is not correct.

(iv) $\tan\theta = 20 \in (-\infty, \infty)$.

Therefore, the given statement is correct.

Example 12 If x is any non-zero real number, show that $\cos\theta$ and $\sin\theta$ can never be equal to $x + \frac{1}{x}$.

Sol. Given x is any non-zero real number, then x may be greater than zero or less than zero.

Hence, two cases arise

(i) When $x > 0$, then

$$x + \frac{1}{x} = (\sqrt{x})^2 + \left(\frac{1}{\sqrt{x}}\right)^2 - 2 \times \sqrt{x} \times \frac{1}{\sqrt{x}} + 2 \times \sqrt{x} \times \frac{1}{\sqrt{x}}$$

$$x + \frac{1}{x} = \left(\sqrt{x} - \frac{1}{\sqrt{x}}\right)^2 + 2 \geq 2$$

(ii) When $x < 0$, then let

$$x = -y, \text{ where } y > 0$$

$$\therefore \quad -y - \frac{1}{y} = -\left(y + \frac{1}{y}\right)$$

$$\Rightarrow \quad -\left(y + \frac{1}{y}\right) \leq -2 \Rightarrow x + \frac{1}{x} \leq -2$$

$\therefore$ $x + \frac{1}{x} \geq 2$ for $x > 0$ and $x + \frac{1}{x} \leq -2$ for $x < 0$.

But $-1 \leq \sin\theta \leq 1$ and $-1 \leq \cos\theta \leq 1$ for all θ.

$\therefore$ $x + \frac{1}{x}$ can not be equal to $\sin\theta$ or $\cos\theta$.

Behaviour of Trigonometric Functions in Different Quadrants

Behaviour of trigonometric functions in different quadrants i.e. the variation in the value of trigonometric ratios in different quadrants, can be understood from the table given below

	I quadrant	II quadrant	III quadrant	IV quadrant
sin	Increases from 0 to 1	Decreases from 1 to 0	Decreases from 0 to −1	Increases from −1 to 0
cos	Decreases from 1 to 0	Decreases from 0 to −1	Increases from −1 to 0	Increases from 0 to 1
tan	Increases from 0 to ∞	Increases from −∞ to 0	Increases from 0 to ∞	Increases from −∞ to 0
cot	Decreases from ∞ to 0	Decreases from 0 to −∞	Decreases from ∞ to 0	Decreases from 0 to −∞
sec	Increases from 1 to ∞	Increases from −∞ to −1	Decreases from −1 to −∞	Decreases from ∞ to 1
cosec	Decreases from ∞ to 1	Increases from 1 to ∞	Increases from −∞ to −1	Decreases from −1 to −∞

Trigonometric Functions of Allied Angles

Two angles are said to be **allied** when their sum or difference is either zero or a multiple of $\pi/2$. The angles $-\theta, \frac{\pi}{2}\pm\theta, \pi\pm\theta, 2\pi\pm\theta$ etc., are allied to the angle θ, if θ is measured in radians.

Note If θ is measured in degrees, then the angles allied to θ are $-\theta, 90°\pm\theta, 180°\pm\theta, 270°\pm\theta$, etc.

The trigonometric functions changes at allied angles which are given in the following table

Allied angle /Trigonometric functions	sin	cosec	cos	sec	tan	cot
$-\theta$	$-\sin\theta$	$-\text{cosec}\,\theta$	$\cos\theta$	$\sec\theta$	$-\tan\theta$	$-\cot\theta$
$\frac{\pi}{2}-\theta$	$\cos\theta$	$\sec\theta$	$\sin\theta$	$\text{cosec}\,\theta$	$\cot\theta$	$\tan\theta$
$\frac{\pi}{2}+\theta$	$\cos\theta$	$\sec\theta$	$-\sin\theta$	$-\text{cosec}\,\theta$	$-\cot\theta$	$-\tan\theta$
$\pi-\theta$	$\sin\theta$	$\text{cosec}\,\theta$	$-\cos\theta$	$-\sec\theta$	$-\tan\theta$	$-\cot\theta$
$\pi+\theta$	$-\sin\theta$	$-\text{cosec}\,\theta$	$-\cos\theta$	$-\sec\theta$	$\tan\theta$	$\cot\theta$
$\frac{3\pi}{2}-\theta$	$-\cos\theta$	$-\sec\theta$	$-\sin\theta$	$-\text{cosec}\,\theta$	$\cot\theta$	$\tan\theta$
$\frac{3\pi}{2}+\theta$	$-\cos\theta$	$-\sec\theta$	$\sin\theta$	$\text{cosec}\,\theta$	$-\cot\theta$	$-\tan\theta$
$2\pi-\theta$	$-\sin\theta$	$-\text{cosec}\,\theta$	$\cos\theta$	$\sec\theta$	$-\tan\theta$	$-\cot\theta$
$2\pi+\theta$	$\sin\theta$	$\text{cosec}\,\theta$	$\cos\theta$	$\sec\theta$	$\tan\theta$	$\cot\theta$

Periodic of Trigonometric Functions

A real function f is said to be periodic iff there exists a constant real number m such that $f(x+m)=f(x)$ for all $x\in D_f$ and the least positive value m is called **period** of f.

The t-functions $\sin\theta, \cos\theta, \text{cosec}\,\theta$ and $\sec\theta$ are periodic with period 2π. Because $\sin(2\pi+\theta)=\sin\theta$ and $\cos(2\pi+\theta)=\cos\theta$.

Also, $\tan\theta$ and $\cot\theta$ are periodic functions with period π. Because $\tan(\pi+\theta)=\tan\theta$ and $\cot(\pi+\theta)=\cot\theta$.

Note (i) Trigonometric functions for $(2\pi-\theta)$ and $(2n\pi-\theta)$ are same $(-\theta)$, where $n\in Z$.

(ii) Trigonometric functions for $(2\pi+\theta)$ and $(2n\pi+\theta)$ are same, where $n\in Z$.

Knowledge Plus

Even Function A function $f(x)$ is said to be an even function, if $f(-x)=f(x)$ for all x in its domain.

e.g. $\cos x$ is an even function, as $\cos(-x)=\cos x$.

Odd Function A function $f(x)$ is said to be an odd function, if $f(-x)=-f(x)$ for all x in its domain.

e.g. $\sin x$ is an odd function, as $\sin(-x)=-\sin x$.

Method to Find the Values of Trigonometrical Functions for any Angle

(i) Check whether the given angle is positive or negative. If it is negative, then make it positive by using the following formulae

$\sin(-\theta)=-\sin\theta, \cos(-\theta)=\cos\theta, \tan(-\theta)=-\tan\theta$, etc.

(ii) If the given angle is greater than $360°$ (or 2π), then split it as $360°n\pm\theta$ (or $2n\pi\pm\theta$), $n\in Z$ and then use the results mention in the above note.

(iii) If the given angle is less than $360°$ (or 2π), then split it as $90°\pm\theta, 180°\pm\theta, 270°\pm\theta, 360°-\theta$ $\left(\text{or } \frac{\pi}{2}\pm\theta, \pi\pm\theta, \frac{3\pi}{2}\pm\theta, 2\pi-\theta\right)$, where θ is an acute angle.

Example 13 Evaluate

(i) $\sin(-1125°)$ (ii) $\sin 930°$

(iii) $\cos(-870°)$ (iv) $\tan(-2025°)$

(i) First, use the following formulae $\cos(-\theta)=\cos\theta$, $\sin(-\theta)=-\sin\theta$ and $\tan(-\theta)=-\tan\theta$

(ii) Split the given angle as $360°n\pm\theta$ (or $2n\pi\pm\theta$), $n\in Z$

Sol. (i) $\sin(-1125°)=-\sin(1125°)$ $[\because \sin(-\theta)=-\sin\theta]$

$=-\sin(1080°+45°)$

$=-\sin(3\times360°+45°)$

$=-\sin45°$ $[\because \sin(n\times360°+\theta)=\sin\theta]$

$=-\frac{1}{\sqrt{2}}$

(ii) $\sin(930°)=\sin(3\times360°-150°)$

$=-\sin150°$ $[\because \sin(n\times360°-\theta)=-\sin\theta, n\in Z]$

$=-\sin(180°-30°)$

$=-\sin30°$ $[\because \sin(180°-\theta)=\sin\theta]$

$=-\frac{1}{2}$

(iii) $\cos(-870°)=\cos870°$ $[\because \cos(-\theta)=\cos\theta]$

$=\cos(720°+150°)$

$=\cos(2\times360°+150°)$

$=\cos150°$ $[\because \cos(n\times360°+\theta)=\cos\theta, n\in Z]$

$=\cos(180°-30°)=-\cos30°$ $[\because \cos(180°-\theta)=-\cos\theta]$

$=-\frac{\sqrt{3}}{2}$

(iv) $\tan(-2025°)=-\tan(2025°)$ $[\because \tan(-\theta)=-\tan\theta]$

$=-\tan(6\times360°-135°)$

$=\tan135°$ $[\because \tan(n\times360°-\theta)=-\tan\theta, n\in Z]$

$=\tan(90°+45°)=-\cot45°$ $[\because \tan(90°+\theta)=-\cot\theta]$

$=-1$

Example 14 Find the value of

(i) $\sin\left(\frac{25\pi}{3}\right)$ (ii) $\cos\left(\frac{41\pi}{4}\right)$

Sol. (i) $\sin\left(\frac{25\pi}{3}\right) = \sin\left(8\pi + \frac{\pi}{3}\right) = \sin\left(2\pi \times 4 + \frac{\pi}{3}\right) = \sin\frac{\pi}{3}$

$[\because \sin(2n\pi + \theta) = \sin\theta, n \in Z]$

$= \frac{\sqrt{3}}{2}$

(ii) $\cos\left(\frac{41\pi}{4}\right) = \cos\left(10\pi + \frac{\pi}{4}\right)$

$= \cos\left(2\pi \times 5 + \frac{\pi}{4}\right) = \cos\frac{\pi}{4}$

$[\because \cos(2n\pi + \theta) = \cos\theta, n \in Z]$

$= \frac{1}{\sqrt{2}}$

Example 15 Prove that

$$\cos\frac{\pi}{8} + \cos\frac{3\pi}{8} + \cos\frac{5\pi}{8} + \cos\frac{7\pi}{8} = 0.$$

Sol. LHS $= \cos\frac{\pi}{8} + \cos\frac{3\pi}{8} + \cos\frac{5\pi}{8} + \cos\frac{7\pi}{8}$

$= \cos\frac{\pi}{8} + \cos\frac{3\pi}{8} + \cos\left(\pi - \frac{3\pi}{8}\right) + \cos\left(\pi - \frac{\pi}{8}\right)$

$= \cos\frac{\pi}{8} + \cos\frac{3\pi}{8} - \cos\frac{3\pi}{8} - \cos\frac{\pi}{8}$

$[\because \cos(\pi - \theta) = -\cos\theta]$

$= 0 =$ RHS **Hence proved.**

Topic Practice 2

Very Short Answer Type Questions

(2 Marks)

1 If $\cos\theta + \sin\theta = \sqrt{2}\cos\theta$, then prove that $\cos\theta - \sin\theta = \sqrt{2}\sin\theta$.

2 Prove that

$$\frac{\cos(90° + \theta)\sec(-\theta)\tan(180° - \theta)}{\sec(360° - \theta)\sin(180° + \theta)\cot(90° - \theta)} = -1$$

3 Prove that $2\sin^2\frac{\pi}{6} + \quad {}^2\frac{7\pi}{6}\cos^2\frac{\pi}{3} = \frac{3}{2}$.

Short Answer Type Questions

(4 Marks)

4 Prove the following identities.

(i) $\cot^4\theta + \cot^2\theta = \text{cosec}^4\theta - \text{cosec}^2\theta$

(ii) $2\sec^2\theta - \sec^4\theta - 2\text{cosec}^2\theta + \text{cosec}^4\theta = \cot^4\theta - \tan^4\theta$

5 If $\tan\theta + \sin\theta = m$ and $\tan\theta - \sin\theta = n$, show that $m^2 - n^2 = 4\sqrt{mn}$.

6 If $10\sin^4\alpha + 15\cos^4\alpha = 6$, then find the value of $27\,\text{cosec}^6\alpha + 8\sec^6\alpha$.

7 If $\cot x = -\frac{5}{12}$, x lies in II quadrant, then find the value of other five trigonometric functions. **[NCERT]**

8 If $\sec x = -2$ and $\pi < x < \frac{3\pi}{2}$, then find the values of all other five trigonometric functions.

9 If $\cos\theta = \frac{-3}{5}$ and $\pi < \theta < \frac{3\pi}{2}$, then find the values of remaining trigonometric functions and hence evaluate $\frac{\text{cosec}\,\theta + \cot\theta}{\sec\theta - \tan\theta}$.

10 Prove that

$$\tan 315° \cot(-405°) + \cot 495° \tan(-585°) = 2$$

11 Prove that

$$\cos 510° \cos 330° + \sin 390° \cos 120° = -1$$

12 Prove that $\sin(-420°)\cos(390°) + \cos(-660°)\sin(330°) = -1$.

13 Prove that

$$\sin 150° \cos 120° + \cos 330° \sin 660° = -1$$

Hints & Answers

1. $\because (\cos\theta + \sin\theta)^2 = (\sqrt{2}\cos\theta)^2$

$\Rightarrow 1 + 2\sin\theta\cos\theta = 2\cos^2\theta$

$\Rightarrow 1 + 2\sin\theta\cos\theta = 2 - 2\sin^2\theta$

$\Rightarrow 2\sin^2\theta = 1 - 2\sin\theta\cos\theta$

$\Rightarrow 2\sin^2\theta = \sin^2\theta + \cos^2\theta - 2\sin\theta\cos\theta$

2. LHS $= \frac{\cos(90° + \theta)\sec(-\theta)\tan(180° - \theta)}{\sec(360° - \theta)\sin(180° + \theta)\cot(90° - \theta)}$

$= \frac{(-\sin\theta)(\sec\theta)(-\tan\theta)}{(\sec\theta)(-\sin\theta)(\tan\theta)}$

3. LHS $= 2\sin^2\frac{\pi}{6} + \text{cosec}^2\frac{7\pi}{6}\cos^2\frac{\pi}{3}$

$= 2\left(\sin\frac{\pi}{6}\right)^2 + \left(\text{cosec}\frac{7\pi}{6}\right)^2\left(\cos\frac{\pi}{3}\right)^2$

$= 2\left(\sin\frac{\pi}{6}\right)^2 + \left\{\text{cosec}\left(\pi + \frac{\pi}{6}\right)\right\}^2\left(\cos\frac{\pi}{3}\right)^2$

$= 2\left(\sin\frac{\pi}{6}\right)^2 + \left\{-\text{cosec}\frac{\pi}{6}\right\}^2\left(\cos\frac{\pi}{3}\right)^2$

4. (i) LHS $= \cot^4\theta + \cot^2\theta$

$= (\cot^2\theta)^2 + (\cot^2\theta) = (\text{cosec}^2\theta - 1)^2 + \cot^2\theta$

$[\because 1 + \cot^2\theta = \text{cosec}^2\theta]$

$= \text{cosec}^4\theta + 1 - 2\,\text{cosec}^2\theta + \text{cosec}^2\theta - 1$

(ii) LHS $= 2\sec^2\theta - \sec^4\theta - 2\text{cosec}^2\theta + \text{cosec}^4\theta$

$= 2\sec^2\theta - (\sec^2\theta)^2 - 2\text{cosec}^2\theta + (\text{cosec}^2\theta)^2$

$= 2(1+\tan^2\theta) - (1+\tan^2\theta)^2 - 2(1+\cot^2\theta) + (\cot^2\theta + 1)^2$

$= 2 + 2\tan^2\theta - (1 + \tan^4\theta + 2\tan^2\theta) - 2 - 2\cot^2\theta + (\cot^4\theta + 1 + 2\cot^2\theta)$

5. LHS $= m^2 - n^2$

$= (\tan\theta + \sin\theta)^2 - (\tan\theta - \sin\theta)^2$

$= (\tan\theta + \sin\theta + \tan\theta - \sin\theta)(\tan\theta + \sin\theta - \tan\theta + \sin\theta)$

$[\because a^2 - b^2 = (a+b)(a-b)]$

$= (2\tan\theta)(2\sin\theta)$

$\Rightarrow m^2 - n^2 = 4\tan\theta\sin\theta$ ... (i)

RHS $= 4\sqrt{mn}$

$= 4\sqrt{(\tan\theta + \sin\theta)(\tan\theta - \sin\theta)}$

$= 4\sqrt{\tan^2\theta - \sin^2\theta}$ $[\because (a+b)(a-b) = (a^2 - b^2)]$

$= 4\sqrt{\sin^2\theta\left(\dfrac{1}{\cos^2\theta} - 1\right)}$

$= 4\sqrt{\sin^2\theta(\sec^2\theta - 1)} = 4\sqrt{\sin^2\theta\tan^2\theta}$

$\Rightarrow 4\sqrt{mn} = 4\sin\theta\tan\theta$ ...(ii)

6. Given, $10\sin^4\alpha + 15\cos^4\alpha = 6$

$\Rightarrow 10\sin^4\alpha + 15\cos^4\alpha = 6(\sin^2\alpha + \cos^2\alpha)^2$

$[\because \sin^2\alpha + \cos^2\alpha = 1]$

$\Rightarrow 4\tan^4\alpha + 9 - 12\tan^2\alpha = 0$

$\Rightarrow (2\tan^2\alpha)^2 + (3)^2 - 2\times 3\times 2\tan^2\alpha = 0$

$\Rightarrow (2\tan^2\alpha - 3)^2 = 0 \Rightarrow \tan^2\alpha = \dfrac{3}{2}$

$\therefore 27\,\text{cosec}^6\alpha + 8\sec^6\alpha = \text{cosec}^6\alpha(27 + 8\tan^6\alpha)$

$= (1+\cot^2\alpha)^3\left(27 + 8\times\dfrac{27}{8}\right) = \left(1+\dfrac{2}{3}\right)^3 (54)$ **Ans.** 250

7. $\tan x = \dfrac{-12}{5}$, $\sec x = \dfrac{-13}{5}$, $\cos x = \dfrac{-5}{13}$, $\sin x = \dfrac{12}{13}$, $\text{cosec}\,x = \dfrac{13}{12}$

8. $\sin x = -\dfrac{\sqrt{3}}{2}$, $\cos x = -\dfrac{1}{2}$, $\tan x = \sqrt{3}$, $\cot x = \dfrac{1}{\sqrt{3}}$

and $\text{cosec}\,x = \dfrac{-2}{\sqrt{3}}$

9. Similar as Example 10. **Ans.** $\dfrac{1}{6}$

10. LHS $= \tan(360° - 45°)[(-\cot(360° + 45°)] + \cot(360° + 135°)[-\tan(360° + 225°)]$

$= -\tan 45°(-\cot 45°) + \cot(135°)(-\tan 225°)$

$= 1 - \cot(90° + 45°)\tan(180° + 45°)$

11. LHS $= \cos 510° \cos 330° + \sin 390° \cos 120°$

$= \cos(90° \times 5 + 60°)\cos(90° \times 3 + 60°) + \sin(90° \times 4 + 30°)\cos(90° \times 1 + 30°)$

$= (-\sin 60°)(\sin 60°) + (\sin 30°)(-\sin 30°)$

12. Solve as Q. 11.

13. LHS $= \sin 150° \cos 120° + \cos 330° \sin 660°$

$= \sin(90° + 60°)\cos(180° - 60°) + \cos(360° - 30°)\sin(2\times 360° - 60°)$

$= \cos 60°(-\cos 60°) + (\cos 30°)(-\sin 60°)$

TOPIC 03 Trigonometric Functions of Compound Angles

The algebraic sum of two or more angles are generally called **compound angles** and the angles are known as the **constituent angles.**

e.g. If A, B and C are three angles, then $A \pm B$, $A + B + C$, $A - B + C$ etc., are **compound angles.**

Now, some formulae or identities which will express the trigonometric ratios of compound angles in terms of trigonometric ratios of constituent angles are given below.

***Formula* 1.** $\cos(A+B) = \cos A\cos B - \sin A\sin B$

***Formula* 2.** $\cos(A-B) = \cos A\cos B + \sin A\sin B$

***Formula* 3.** $\sin(A+B) = \sin A\cos B + \cos A\sin B$

***Formula* 4.** $\sin(A-B) = \sin A\cos B - \cos A\sin B$

***Formula* 5.** $\tan(A+B) = \dfrac{\tan A + \tan B}{1 - \tan A\tan B}$, where A, B and $(A+B)$ are not odd multiples of $\dfrac{\pi}{2}$.

***Formula* 6.** $\tan(A-B) = \dfrac{\tan A - \tan B}{1 + \tan A\tan B}$, where A, B and $(A-B)$ are not odd multiples of $\dfrac{\pi}{2}$.

***Formula* 7.** $\cot(A+B) = \dfrac{\cot A\cot B - 1}{\cot B + \cot A}$, where A, B and $(A+B)$ are not multiples of π

Formula 8. $\cot(A-B)=\dfrac{\cot A\cot B+1}{\cot B-\cot A}$, where A, B and $(A-B)$ are not multiples of π

Some Important Results

(i) $\sin(A+B)\sin(A-B)=\sin^2 A-\sin^2 B=\cos^2 B-\cos^2 A$

(ii) $\cos(A+B)\cos(A-B)=\cos^2 A-\sin^2 B=\cos^2 B-\sin^2 A$

(iii) $\tan(A+B)\tan(A-B)=\dfrac{\tan^2 A-\tan^2 B}{1-\tan^2 A\cdot\tan^2 B}$

(iv) $\sin(A+B+C)=\sin A\cos B\cos C+\cos A\sin B\cos C$
$+\cos A\cos B\sin C-\sin A\sin B\sin C$

(v) $\cos(A+B+C)=\cos A\cos B\cos C-\cos A\sin B\sin C$
$-\sin A\cos B\sin C-\sin A\sin B\cos C$

(vi) $\tan(A+B+C)=\dfrac{\tan A+\tan B+\tan C-\tan A\tan B\tan C}{1-\tan A\tan B-\tan B\tan C-\tan C\tan A}$

Example 1 Evaluate $\cos 47^\circ\cos 13^\circ-\sin 47^\circ\sin 13^\circ$

Sol. $\cos 47^\circ\cos 13^\circ-\sin 47^\circ\sin 13^\circ=\cos(47^\circ+13^\circ)$

$[\because \cos A\cos B-\sin A\sin B=\cos(A+B)]$

$=\cos 60^\circ=\dfrac{1}{2}$

Example 2 Find the value of $\sin 75^\circ$.

Sol. $\sin 75^\circ=\sin(45^\circ+30^\circ)$

$=\sin 45^\circ\cos 30^\circ+\cos 45^\circ\sin 30^\circ$

$[\because \sin(A+B)=\sin A\cos B+\cos A\sin B]$

$=\dfrac{1}{\sqrt2}\cdot\dfrac{\sqrt3}{2}+\dfrac{1}{\sqrt2}\cdot\dfrac{1}{2}$

$\left[\because \sin 30^\circ=\dfrac{1}{2},\ \cos 30^\circ=\dfrac{\sqrt3}{2}\text{ and }\sin 45^\circ=\cos 45^\circ=\dfrac{1}{\sqrt2}\right]$

$=\dfrac{\sqrt3}{2\sqrt2}+\dfrac{1}{2\sqrt2}=\dfrac{\sqrt3+1}{2\sqrt2}$

Example 3 Find the value of $\sin 23^\circ\cos 67^\circ+\cos 23^\circ\sin 67^\circ$.

Sol. $\sin 23^\circ\cos 67^\circ+\cos 23^\circ\sin 67^\circ$

$=\sin(23^\circ+67^\circ)$

$[\because \sin(A+B)=\sin A\cos B+\cos A\sin B]$

$=\sin 90^\circ=1$

Example 4 Evaluate $\sin 78^\circ\cos 18^\circ-\cos 78^\circ\sin 18^\circ$.

Sol. $\sin 78^\circ\cos 18^\circ-\cos 78^\circ\sin 18^\circ=\sin(78^\circ-18^\circ)$

$[\because \sin A\cos B-\cos A\sin B=\sin(A-B)]$

$=\sin 60^\circ=\dfrac{\sqrt3}{2}$

Example 5 Prove that

$$\frac{\sin(A-B)}{\cos A\cos B}+\frac{\sin(B-C)}{\cos B\cos C}+\frac{\sin(C-A)}{\cos C\cos A}=0.$$

Sol. LHS $=\dfrac{\sin(A-B)}{\cos A\cos B}+\dfrac{\sin(B-C)}{\cos B\cos C}+\dfrac{\sin(C-A)}{\cos C\cos A}$

$=\dfrac{\cos C\sin(A-B)+\cos A\sin(B-C)+\cos B\sin(C-A)}{\cos A\cos B\cos C}$

$=\dfrac{\left[\begin{array}{l}\cos C(\sin A\cos B-\cos A\sin B)+\cos A(\sin B\cos C\\-\cos B\sin C)+\cos B(\sin C\cos A-\cos C\sin A)\end{array}\right]}{\cos A\cos B\cos C}$

$=\dfrac{\left[\begin{array}{l}\sin A\cos B\cos C-\cos A\cos C\sin B+\cos A\\\cos C\sin B-\cos A\cos B\sin C+\cos B\cos A\\\sin C-\cos B\cos C\sin A\end{array}\right]}{\cos A\cos B\cos C}$

$=\dfrac{0}{\cos A\cos B\cos C}$

$=0=$ RHS **Hence proved.**

Example 6 Find the value of $\tan 105^\circ$.

Sol. $\tan 105^\circ=\tan(60^\circ+45^\circ)$

$=\dfrac{\tan 60^\circ+\tan 45^\circ}{1-\tan 60^\circ\tan 45^\circ}$ $\left[\because \tan(A+B)=\dfrac{\tan A+\tan B}{1-\tan A\tan B}\right]$

$=\dfrac{\sqrt3+1}{1-\sqrt3\cdot1}$ $[\because \tan 45^\circ=1\text{ and }\tan 60^\circ=\sqrt3]$

$=\dfrac{\sqrt3+1}{1-\sqrt3}=\dfrac{(1+\sqrt3)}{(1-\sqrt3)}\times\dfrac{(1+\sqrt3)}{(1+\sqrt3)}$ [on rationalisation]

$=\dfrac{(\sqrt3+1)^2}{1-3}$ $[\because (a-b)(a+b)=a^2-b^2]$

$=\dfrac{3+1+2\sqrt3}{1-3}=\dfrac{4+2\sqrt3}{-2}=\dfrac{2(2+\sqrt3)}{-2}=-(2+\sqrt3)$

Example 7 If $\tan A=\dfrac{1}{4}$ and $\tan B=\dfrac{1}{5}$, then find the value of $\tan(A+B)$.

Sol. Given, $\tan A=\dfrac{1}{4}$ and $\tan B=\dfrac{1}{5}$

We know that,

$\tan(A+B)=\dfrac{\tan A+\tan B}{1-\tan A\tan B}$

$=\dfrac{\frac{1}{4}+\frac{1}{5}}{1-\frac{1}{4}\times\frac{1}{5}}=\dfrac{\frac{5+4}{20}}{\frac{20-1}{20}}=\dfrac{\frac{9}{20}}{\frac{19}{20}}=\dfrac{9}{19}$

Example 8 Prove that $\dfrac{\cos 15° + \sin 15°}{\cos 15° - \sin 15°} = \sqrt{3}$.

Sol. $\text{LHS} = \dfrac{\cos 15° + \sin 15°}{\cos 15° - \sin 15°} = \dfrac{\dfrac{\cos 15°}{\cos 15°} + \dfrac{\sin 15°}{\cos 15°}}{\dfrac{\cos 15°}{\cos 15°} - \dfrac{\sin 15°}{\cos 15°}}$

$= \dfrac{1 + \tan 15°}{1 - \tan 15°}$ $\left[\because \tan\theta = \dfrac{\sin\theta}{\cos\theta}\right]$

$= \dfrac{\tan 45° + \tan 15°}{1 - \tan 45° \tan 15°}$ $[\because \tan 45° = 1]$

$= \tan(45° + 15°)$ $\left[\because \tan(A + B) = \dfrac{\tan A + \tan B}{1 - \tan A \tan B}\right]$

$= \tan 60° = \sqrt{3} = \text{RHS}$ **Hence proved.**

Example 9 Find the value of tan 15°.

Sol. $\tan 15° = \tan(60° - 45°)$

$= \dfrac{\tan 60° - \tan 45°}{1 + \tan 60° \tan 45°}$ $\left[\because \tan(A - B) = \dfrac{\tan A - \tan B}{1 + \tan A \tan B}\right]$

$= \dfrac{\sqrt{3} - 1}{1 + \sqrt{3} \cdot 1}$ $[\because \tan 45° = 1 \text{ and } \tan 60° = \sqrt{3}]$

$= \dfrac{\sqrt{3} - 1}{1 + \sqrt{3}} = \dfrac{\sqrt{3} - 1}{\sqrt{3} + 1} = \dfrac{\sqrt{3} - 1}{\sqrt{3} + 1} \times \dfrac{\sqrt{3} - 1}{\sqrt{3} - 1}$ [on rationalisation]

$= \dfrac{(\sqrt{3} - 1)^2}{(\sqrt{3})^2 - (1)^2}$ $[\because (a - b)(a + b) = a^2 - b^2]$

$= \dfrac{(\sqrt{3})^2 + (1)^2 - 2\sqrt{3}}{3 - 1}$ $[\because (a - b)^2 = a^2 + b^2 - 2ab]$

$= \dfrac{3 + 1 - 2\sqrt{3}}{3 - 1} = \dfrac{4 - 2\sqrt{3}}{2} = \dfrac{2(2 - \sqrt{3})}{2} = (2 - \sqrt{3})$

Example 10 Find the value of $\dfrac{\cot 47° \cot 43° - 1}{\cot 47° + \cot 43°}$.

Sol. $\dfrac{\cot 47° \cot 43° - 1}{\cot 47° + \cot 43°} = \cot(47° + 43°)$

$\left[\because \cot(A + B) = \dfrac{\cot A \cot B - 1}{\cot A + \cot B}\right]$

$= \cot 90° = 0$ $[\because \cot 90° = 0]$

Example 11 Show that

$\sin(40° + \theta)\cos(10° + \theta) - \cos(40° + \theta)\sin(10° + \theta) = \dfrac{1}{2}$.

[NCERT]

Use the formula, $\sin A \cos B - \cos A \sin B = \sin(A - B)$ and then simplify it.

Sol. LHS

$= \sin(40° + \theta)\cos(10° + \theta) - \cos(40° + \theta) \cdot \sin(10° + \theta)$

$= \sin\{(40° + \theta) - (10° + \theta)\}$

$[\because \sin(x - y) = \sin x \cdot \cos y - \cos x \cdot \sin y]$

$= \sin 30° = 1/2$ $[\because \sin 30° = 1/2]$

$= \text{RHS}$ **Hence proved.**

Example 12 Prove that

$$\frac{\tan\left(\dfrac{\pi}{4} + x\right)}{\tan\left(\dfrac{\pi}{4} - x\right)} = \left(\frac{1 + \tan x}{1 - \tan x}\right)^2.$$

[NCERT]

Sol. $\text{LHS} = \dfrac{\tan\left(\dfrac{\pi}{4} + x\right)}{\tan\left(\dfrac{\pi}{4} - x\right)} = \dfrac{\left(\dfrac{\tan\dfrac{\pi}{4} + \tan x}{1 - \tan\dfrac{\pi}{4} \cdot \tan x}\right)}{\left(\dfrac{\tan\dfrac{\pi}{4} - \tan x}{1 + \tan\dfrac{\pi}{4} \cdot \tan x}\right)}$

$\left[\because \tan(x + y) = \dfrac{\tan x + \tan y}{1 - \tan x \cdot \tan y} \text{ and } \tan(x - y) = \dfrac{\tan x - \tan y}{1 + \tan x \cdot \tan y}\right]$

$= \dfrac{\left(\dfrac{1 + \tan x}{1 - \tan x}\right)}{\left(\dfrac{1 - \tan x}{1 + \tan x}\right)} = \left(\dfrac{1 + \tan x}{1 - \tan x}\right)^2 = \text{RHS}$

$\therefore \text{LHS} = \text{RHS}$ **Hence proved.**

Example 13 If $A + B = \dfrac{\pi}{4}$, then prove that

(i) $(1 + \tan A)(1 + \tan B) = 2$

(ii) $(\cot A - 1)(\cot B - 1) = 2$.

Sol. (i) We have, $A + B = \dfrac{\pi}{4}$

$\Rightarrow \tan(A + B) = \tan\dfrac{\pi}{4}$

$\Rightarrow \dfrac{\tan A + \tan B}{1 - \tan A \tan B} = 1$

$\Rightarrow \tan A + \tan B = 1 - \tan A \tan B$

$\Rightarrow \tan A + \tan B + \tan A \tan B = 1$ ...(i)

On adding 1 both sides of Eq. (i), we get

$1 + \tan A + \tan B + \tan A \tan B = 2$

$\Rightarrow (1 + \tan A) + \tan B(1 + \tan A) = 2$

$\Rightarrow (1 + \tan A)(1 + \tan B) = 2$

Hence proved.

(ii) On dividing both sides of Eq. (i) by $\tan A \tan B$, we get

$\dfrac{\tan A + \tan B + \tan A \tan B}{\tan A \tan B} = \dfrac{1}{\tan A \tan B}$

$\Rightarrow \cot B + \cot A + 1 = \cot A \cot B$

$\Rightarrow \cot A \cot B - \cot A - \cot B = 1$

$\Rightarrow \cot A \cot B - \cot A - \cot B + 1 = 2$

$\Rightarrow \cot A(\cot B - 1) - (\cot B - 1) = 2$

$\Rightarrow (\cot B - 1)(\cot A - 1) = 2$ **Hence proved.**

Example 14 If $3 \tan A \tan B = 1$, then prove that $2\cos(A+B) = \cos(A-B)$.

Sol. Given, $3\tan A \tan B = 1$

$$\Rightarrow \frac{3\sin A \sin B}{\cos A \cos B} = 1 \Rightarrow \frac{\cos A \cos B}{\sin A \sin B} = \frac{3}{1}$$

$$\Rightarrow \frac{\cos A \cos B + \sin A \sin B}{\cos A \cos B - \sin A \sin B} = \frac{3+1}{3-1}$$

[applying componendo and dividendo rule]

$$\Rightarrow \frac{\cos(A-B)}{\cos(A+B)} = \frac{4}{2}$$

$\left[\because \cos(A-B) = \cos A \cos B + \sin A \sin B \text{ and } \cos(A+B) = \cos A \cos B - \sin A \sin B\right]$

$$\Rightarrow \frac{\cos(A-B)}{\cos(A+B)} = 2$$

$$\Rightarrow \cos(A-B) = 2\cos(A+B)$$ **Hence proved.**

Example 15 Prove that $\dfrac{\sin(x+y)}{\sin(x-y)} = \dfrac{\tan x + \tan y}{\tan x - \tan y}$. **[NCERT]**

Sol. $$\text{LHS} = \frac{\sin(x+y)}{\sin(x-y)} = \frac{\sin x \cos y + \cos x \sin y}{\sin x \cos y - \cos x \sin y}$$

$$= \frac{\dfrac{\sin x \cos y + \cos x \sin y}{\cos x \cos y}}{\dfrac{\sin x \cos y - \cos x \sin y}{\cos x \cos y}}$$

[dividing numerator and denominator by $\cos x \cos y$]

$$= \frac{\dfrac{\sin x}{\cos x} + \dfrac{\sin y}{\cos y}}{\dfrac{\sin x}{\cos x} - \dfrac{\sin y}{\cos y}} = \frac{\tan x + \tan y}{\tan x - \tan y} = \text{RHS}$$

Hence proved.

Example 16 If $\tan A - \tan B = x$ and $\cot B - \cot A = y$, then prove that $\cot(A-B) = \dfrac{1}{x} + \dfrac{1}{y}$.

Sol. Given, $\tan A - \tan B = x$ and $\cot B - \cot A = y$

$$\Rightarrow \frac{\tan A - \tan B}{\tan A \tan B} = y$$

$$\Rightarrow \frac{x}{\tan A \tan B} = y \Rightarrow \tan A \tan B = \frac{x}{y}$$

$$\therefore \cot(A-B) = \frac{1}{\tan(A-B)} = \frac{1 + \tan A \tan B}{\tan A - \tan B}$$

$$= \frac{1 + \dfrac{x}{y}}{x} = \frac{x+y}{xy} = \frac{1}{x} + \frac{1}{y}$$ **Hence proved.**

Example 17 If $\sin A = \dfrac{4}{5}$ and $\cos B = \dfrac{5}{13}$, where $0 < A, B < \dfrac{\pi}{2}$, then find the values of the following.

(i) $\sin(A+B)$ (ii) $\cos(A+B)$

(iii) $\sin(A-B)$ (iv) $\cos(A-B)$

Sol. Given, $\sin A = \dfrac{4}{5}, 0 < A < \dfrac{\pi}{2}$

$$\therefore \cos A = \sqrt{1 - \sin^2 A}$$ [$\because$ A lies in Ist quadrant]

$$= \sqrt{1 - \left(\frac{4}{5}\right)^2} = \sqrt{1 - \frac{16}{25}}$$

$$\Rightarrow \cos A = \sqrt{\frac{9}{25}} = \frac{3}{5}$$

Also, we have $\cos B = \dfrac{5}{13}, 0 < B < \dfrac{\pi}{2}$

$$\therefore \sin B = \sqrt{1 - \cos^2 B}$$ [$\because$ B lies in Ist quadrant]

$$= \sqrt{1 - \left(\frac{5}{13}\right)^2} = \sqrt{1 - \frac{25}{169}}$$

$$\Rightarrow \sin B = \sqrt{\frac{144}{169}} = \frac{12}{13}$$

(i) $\sin(A+B) = \sin A \cos B + \cos A \sin B$

$$= \frac{4}{5} \times \frac{5}{13} + \frac{3}{5} \times \frac{12}{13} = \frac{20}{65} + \frac{36}{65} = \frac{56}{65}$$

(ii) $\cos(A+B) = \cos A \cos B - \sin A \sin B$

$$= \frac{3}{5} \times \frac{5}{13} - \frac{4}{5} \times \frac{12}{13} = \frac{15-48}{65} = \frac{-33}{65}$$

(iii) $\sin(A-B) = \sin A \cos B - \cos A \sin B$

$$= \frac{4}{5} \times \frac{5}{13} - \frac{3}{5} \times \frac{12}{13} = \frac{20-36}{65} = \frac{-16}{65}$$

(iv) $\cos(A-B) = \cos A \cos B + \sin A \sin B$

$$= \frac{3}{5} \times \frac{5}{13} + \frac{4}{5} \times \frac{12}{13} = \frac{15+48}{65} = \frac{63}{65}$$

Example 18 If x and y are acute angles such that $\cos x = \dfrac{13}{14}$ and $\cos y = \dfrac{1}{7}$, then prove that $x - y = -\dfrac{\pi}{3}$.

Sol. Given, $0 < x, y < \dfrac{\pi}{2}, \cos x = \dfrac{13}{14}$ and $\cos y = \dfrac{1}{7}$

$$\because 0 < x < \frac{\pi}{2}$$

$$\therefore \sin x = \sqrt{1 - \cos^2 x}$$ [$\because$ sine is +ve in first quadrant]

$$= \sqrt{1 - \frac{169}{196}} = \sqrt{\frac{196-169}{196}} = \sqrt{\frac{27}{196}} = \frac{3\sqrt{3}}{14}$$

Similarly, $\sin y = \sqrt{1 - \cos^2 y}$

[$\because 0 < y < \pi/2$ and sine is +ve in first quadrant]

$$= \sqrt{1 - \frac{1}{49}} = \sqrt{\frac{48}{49}} = \frac{4\sqrt{3}}{7}$$

Now, consider $\cos(x - y) = \cos x \cos y + \sin x \sin y$

$$= \frac{13}{14} \times \frac{1}{7} + \frac{3\sqrt{3}}{14} \times \frac{4\sqrt{3}}{7}$$

$$= \frac{13 + 36}{14 \times 7} = \frac{49}{14 \times 7} = \frac{1}{2} \quad \text{...(i)}$$

Since, $\cos x > \cos y$, therefore $y > x$

[∵ $\cos x$ is a decreasing function]

$\Rightarrow \quad x - y < 0$

Now, as $\cos\left(\frac{-\pi}{3}\right) = \cos\frac{\pi}{3} = \frac{1}{2}$

$\therefore \quad x - y = \frac{-\pi}{3}$ **Hence proved.**

Example 19 Find the value of $\tan(\alpha + \beta)$, if $\cot\alpha = \frac{1}{2}, \alpha \in \left(\pi, \frac{3\pi}{2}\right)$ and $\sec\beta = \frac{-5}{3}, \beta \in \left(\frac{\pi}{2}, \pi\right)$.

Sol. We have, $\tan(\alpha + \beta) = \frac{\tan\alpha + \tan\beta}{1 - \tan\alpha \cdot \tan\beta}$

$\left[\because \tan(x + y) = \frac{\tan x + \tan y}{1 - \tan x \cdot \tan y}\right]$

Given, $\cot\alpha = \frac{1}{2} \Rightarrow \tan\alpha = 2$ $\left[\because \tan\alpha = \frac{1}{\cot\alpha}\right]$

Also, $\sec\beta = \frac{-5}{3}$

Then, $\tan\beta = \pm\sqrt{\sec^2\beta - 1}$

$\Rightarrow \quad \tan\beta = \pm\sqrt{\frac{25}{9} - 1} = \pm\sqrt{\frac{16}{9}}$ $\left[\because \sec\beta = \frac{-5}{3}\right]$

$\therefore \quad \tan\beta = \pm\frac{4}{3}$

But $\quad \tan\beta \neq \frac{4}{3}$

$\left[\because \beta \in \left(\frac{\pi}{2}, \pi\right) \text{and } \tan\beta \text{ is –ve in II quadrant}\right]$

$\therefore \quad \tan\beta = -\frac{4}{3}$

$$\therefore \quad \tan(\alpha + \beta) = \frac{\tan\alpha + \tan\beta}{1 - \tan\alpha \cdot \tan\beta} = \frac{2 + \left(-\frac{4}{3}\right)}{1 - (2)\left(\frac{-4}{3}\right)}$$

$\left[\because \tan\alpha = 2 \text{ and } \tan\beta = \frac{-4}{3}\right]$

$$= \frac{\left(2 - \frac{4}{3}\right)}{\left(1 + \frac{8}{3}\right)} = \frac{\left(\frac{2}{3}\right)}{\left(\frac{11}{3}\right)} = \frac{2}{11}$$

Example 20 If $\cos(\alpha - \beta) + \cos(\beta - \gamma) + \cos(\gamma - \alpha) = -\frac{3}{2}$, then prove that

$$\cos\alpha + \cos\beta + \cos\gamma = \sin\alpha + \sin\beta + \sin\gamma = 0.$$

Sol. Given, $\cos(\alpha - \beta) + \cos(\beta - \gamma) + \cos(\gamma - \alpha) = -\frac{3}{2}$

$\Rightarrow \quad 2\cos(\alpha - \beta) + 2\cos(\beta - \gamma) + 2\cos(\gamma - \alpha) = -3$

$\Rightarrow (2\cos\alpha\cos\beta + 2\cos\beta\cos\gamma + 2\cos\gamma\cos\alpha) + (2\sin\alpha\sin\beta + 2\sin\beta\sin\gamma + 2\sin\gamma\sin\alpha) + 1 + 1 + 1 = 0$

$\Rightarrow (2\cos\alpha\cos\beta + 2\cos\beta\cos\gamma + 2\cos\gamma\cos\alpha) + (2\sin\alpha\sin\beta + 2\sin\beta\sin\gamma) + 2\sin\gamma\sin\alpha) + (\cos^2\alpha + \sin^2\alpha) + (\cos^2\beta + \sin^2\beta) + (\cos^2\gamma + \sin^2\gamma) = 0$

$\Rightarrow (\cos^2\alpha + \cos^2\beta + \cos^2\gamma + 2\cos\alpha\cos\beta + 2\cos\beta\cos\gamma + 2\cos\gamma\cos\alpha) + (\sin^2\alpha + \sin^2\beta + \sin^2\gamma + 2\sin\alpha\sin\beta + 2\sin\beta\sin\gamma + 2\sin\gamma\sin\alpha) = 0$

$\Rightarrow (\cos\alpha + \cos\beta + \cos\gamma)^2 + (\sin\alpha + \sin\beta + \sin\gamma)^2 = 0$

$\Rightarrow \quad \cos\alpha + \cos\beta + \cos\gamma = 0$

and $\quad \sin\alpha + \sin\beta + \sin\gamma = 0$ **Hence proved.**

Example 21 If $a\tan\alpha + b\tan\beta = (a + b)\tan\left(\frac{\alpha + \beta}{2}\right)$, where $\alpha \neq \beta$. Prove that $\quad a\cos\beta = b\cos\alpha$.

Sol. Given, $a\tan\alpha + b\tan\beta = (a + b)\tan\left(\frac{\alpha + \beta}{2}\right)$, where $\alpha \neq \beta$

$$\Rightarrow a\left\{\tan\alpha - \tan\left(\frac{\alpha + \beta}{2}\right)\right\} = b\left\{\tan\left(\frac{\alpha + \beta}{2}\right) - \tan\beta\right\}$$

$$\Rightarrow \quad \frac{a\sin\left(\alpha - \frac{\alpha + \beta}{2}\right)}{\cos\alpha\cos\left(\frac{\alpha + \beta}{2}\right)} = \frac{b\sin\left(\frac{\alpha + \beta}{2} - \beta\right)}{\cos\left(\frac{\alpha + \beta}{2}\right) \cdot \cos\beta}$$

$$\left[\because \tan A - \tan B = \frac{\sin A}{\cos A} - \frac{\sin B}{\cos B} = \frac{\sin A\cos B - \cos A\sin B}{\cos A\cos B} = \frac{\sin(A - B)}{\cos A\cos B}\right]$$

$$\Rightarrow \quad \frac{a\sin\left(\frac{\alpha - \beta}{2}\right)}{\cos\alpha} = \frac{b\sin\left(\frac{\alpha - \beta}{2}\right)}{\cos\beta}$$

$\Rightarrow \quad a\cos\beta = b\cos\alpha$

$\left[\because \alpha \neq \beta, \text{ so } \sin\left(\frac{\alpha - \beta}{2}\right) \neq 0\right]$

Hence proved.

Example 22 If $\tan\alpha = \frac{1}{\sqrt{x(x^2+x+1)}}$,

$\tan\beta = \frac{\sqrt{x}}{\sqrt{x^2+x+1}}$ and $\tan\gamma = \sqrt{x^{-3}+x^{-2}+x^{-1}}$,

then prove that $\alpha+\beta=\gamma$.

Sol. We know that,

$$\tan(\alpha+\beta) = \frac{\tan\alpha+\tan\beta}{1-\tan\alpha\tan\beta}$$

$$\Rightarrow \quad \tan(\alpha+\beta) = \frac{\frac{1}{\sqrt{x(x^2+x+1)}}+\frac{\sqrt{x}}{\sqrt{x^2+x+1}}}{1-\frac{\sqrt{x}}{\sqrt{x(x^2+x+1)}\sqrt{x^2+x+1}}}$$

$$\Rightarrow \quad \tan(\alpha+\beta) = \frac{\frac{1+x}{\sqrt{x(x^2+x+1)}}}{1-\frac{1}{x^2+x+1}}$$

$$\Rightarrow \quad \tan(\alpha+\beta) = \frac{1+x}{\sqrt{x(x^2+x+1)}} \times \frac{x^2+x+1}{x^2+x+1-1}$$

$$\Rightarrow \quad \tan(\alpha+\beta) = \frac{(1+x)(x^2+x+1)}{x(x+1)\sqrt{x(x^2+x+1)}}$$

$$\Rightarrow \quad \tan(\alpha+\beta) = \frac{\sqrt{x(x^2+x+1)}}{x^2}$$

$$= \sqrt{\frac{x^3+x^2+x}{x^4}}$$

$$= \sqrt{x^{-1}+x^{-2}+x^{-3}}$$

$$\Rightarrow \quad \tan(\alpha+\beta) = \tan\gamma$$

$$\therefore \quad \alpha+\beta=\gamma$$

Hence proved.

Example 23 Prove that

$\sin^2 A = \cos^2(A-B)+\cos^2 B - 2\cos(A-B)\cos A\cos B$.

Sol. RHS $= \cos^2(A-B)+\cos^2 B - 2\cos(A-B)\cos A\cos B$

$= \cos^2 B + \cos^2(A-B) - 2\cos(A-B)\cos A\cos B$

$= \cos^2 B + \cos(A-B)\{\cos(A-B) - 2\cos A\cos B\}$

$= \cos^2 B + \cos(A-B)\{\cos A\cos B + \sin A\sin B - 2\cos A\cos B\}$

$= \cos^2 B + \cos(A-B)[\sin A\sin B - \cos A\cos B]$

$= \cos^2 B + \cos(A-B)[-(\cos A\cos B - \sin A\sin B)]$

$= \cos^2 B - \cos(A-B)\cos(A+B)$

$= \cos^2 B - (\cos^2 A - \sin^2 B)$

$= \cos^2 B + \sin^2 B - \cos^2 A$

$= 1 - \cos^2 A = \sin^2 A = $ LHS **Hence proved.**

Topic Practice 3

Very Short Answer Type Questions

2 Marks

1 Find the value of the following trigonometric functions. (Each part carries 1 Mark)

(i) $\sin(105°)$ and $\cos(-75°)$

(ii) $\tan(435°)$ and $\sec(105°)$

2 Evaluate the following.

(i) $\sin\frac{\pi}{4}\cos\frac{\pi}{12}+\cos\frac{\pi}{4}\sin\frac{\pi}{12}$

(ii) $\sin\frac{7\pi}{12}\cos\frac{\pi}{4}-\cos\frac{7\pi}{12}\sin\frac{\pi}{4}$

3 Find the value of $\sin(45°+\theta)-\cos(45°-\theta)$. **[NCERT Exemplar]**

4 If $\tan\alpha = \frac{m}{m+1}$ and $\tan\beta = \frac{1}{2m+1}$, then find the value of $\alpha+\beta$. **[NCERT Exemplar]**

5 Find the value of $\tan 3A - \tan 2A - \tan A$. **[NCERT Exemplar]**

6 Prove that $\frac{\cos 17° + \sin 17°}{\cos 17° - \sin 17°} = \tan 62°$.

7 Find the values of the following.

(i) $\tan 75°$ (ii) $\tan\frac{13\pi}{12}$

8 Prove that $\frac{\sqrt{3}\cos 23° - \sin 23°}{2} = \cos 53°$.

9 Prove that $\sin(n+1)x\sin(n+2)x + \cos(n+1)x\cdot\cos(n+2)x = \cos x$. **[NCERT]**

10 Show that

$$\cos\left(\frac{\pi}{4}-\theta\right)\cos\left(\frac{\pi}{4}-\phi\right)-\sin\left(\frac{\pi}{4}-\theta\right)\sin\left(\frac{\pi}{4}-\phi\right) = \sin(\theta+\phi).$$ **[NCERT]**

11 Prove that $\tan 15° + \cot 15° = 4$.

12 Prove that

$$\cos\left(\frac{3\pi}{4}+x\right)-\cos\left(\frac{3\pi}{4}-x\right) = -\sqrt{2}\sin x.$$

13 Prove that $\sin^2\left(\frac{\pi}{8}+\frac{A}{2}\right)-\sin^2\left(\frac{\pi}{8}-\frac{A}{2}\right) = \frac{1}{\sqrt{2}}\sin A$.

14 Prove that

$$\cos 2\alpha \cos 2\beta + \sin^2(\alpha - \beta) - \sin^2(\alpha + \beta) = \cos 2(\alpha + \beta).$$

Short Answer Type Questions

4 Marks

15 If $\cos A = \frac{4}{5}$ and $\cos B = \frac{12}{13}$; $\frac{3\pi}{2} < A, B < 2\pi$, then find the values of the following.

(i) $\cos(A + B)$ (ii) $\sin(A - B)$

16 If $\sin A = \frac{3}{5}, 0 < A < \frac{\pi}{2}$ and $\cos B = -\frac{12}{13}, \pi < B < \frac{3\pi}{2}$, then find the following.

(i) $\sin(A - B)$ (ii) $\cos(A + B)$

(iii) $\tan(A - B)$

17 If x and y are acute angles such that $\sin x = \frac{1}{\sqrt{5}}$ and $\sin y = \frac{1}{\sqrt{10}}$, then prove that $x + y = \frac{\pi}{4}$.

18 If $\tan \beta = \frac{n \sin \alpha \cos \alpha}{1 - n \sin^2 \alpha}$, then show that

$$\tan(\alpha - \beta) = (1 - n) \tan \alpha.$$

19 If $\cos(\alpha + \beta) = \frac{4}{5}$, $\sin(\alpha - \beta) = \frac{5}{13}$ and α, β lie between 0 and $\frac{\pi}{4}$, then prove that $\tan 2\alpha = \frac{56}{33}$.

20 If $\theta + \phi = \alpha$ and $\tan\theta = k \tan\phi$, then prove that $\sin(\theta - \phi) = \frac{k-1}{k+1} \sin\alpha$.

21 If $\tan(\pi \cos \theta) = \cot(\pi \sin \theta)$, then prove that $\cos\left(\theta - \frac{\pi}{4}\right) = \pm \frac{1}{2\sqrt{2}}$.

Hints & Answers

1. (i) $\sin(105°) = \sin(60° + 45°)$

Ans. $\frac{\sqrt{3}+1}{2\sqrt{2}}$

and $\cos(-75°) = \cos 75° = \cos(45° + 30°)$

Ans. $\frac{\sqrt{3}-1}{2\sqrt{2}}$

(ii) $\tan(435°) = \tan(360° + 75°) = \tan 75°$

$= \tan(45° + 30°)$

Ans. $\frac{\sqrt{3}+1}{\sqrt{3}-1}$

and $\cos(105°) = \cos(60° + 45°)$

$= \cos 60° \cos 45° - \sin 60° \sin 45°$

$= \frac{1-\sqrt{3}}{2\sqrt{2}}$

Ans. $\frac{2\sqrt{2}}{1-\sqrt{3}}$

2. (i) Use the formula of $\sin(A + B)$. **Ans.** $\frac{\sqrt{3}}{2}$

(ii) Use the formula of $\sin(A - B)$. **Ans.** $\frac{\sqrt{3}}{2}$

3. Use the formula of $\sin(A + B)$ and $\cos(A - B)$

Ans. 0

4. Consider, $\tan(\alpha + \beta) = \frac{\tan\alpha + \tan\beta}{1 - \tan\alpha \tan\beta}$

$$= \frac{\frac{m}{m+1} + \frac{1}{2m+1}}{1 - \frac{m}{m+1} \times \frac{1}{2m+1}}$$

$\Rightarrow \tan(\alpha + \beta) = 1$

Ans. $\frac{\pi}{4}$

5. $\tan 3A = \tan(2A + A)$

$\Rightarrow \tan 3A = \frac{\tan 2A + \tan A}{1 - \tan 2A \tan A}$

Ans. $\tan 3A \tan 2A \tan A$

6. Solve as Example 8.

7. (i) $\frac{\sqrt{3}+1}{\sqrt{3}-1}$

(ii) $\tan \frac{13\pi}{12} = \tan\left(\pi + \frac{\pi}{12}\right)$

$= \tan \frac{\pi}{12} = \tan 15°$

$= \tan(45° - 30°)$

$= \frac{\tan 45° - \tan 30°}{1 + \tan 45° \tan 30°}$

Ans. $\frac{\sqrt{3}-1}{\sqrt{3}+1}$

8. LHS $= \frac{\sqrt{3} \cos 23° - \sin 23°}{2}$

$= \frac{\sqrt{3}}{2} \cdot \cos 23° - \frac{1}{2} \cdot \sin 23°$

$= \cos 30° \cdot \cos 23° - \sin 30° \cdot \sin 23°$

9. LHS $= \sin(n+1)x \cdot \sin(n+2)x + \cos(n+1)x \cdot \cos(n+2)x$

$= \cos(n+1)x \cdot \cos(n+2)x + \sin(n+1)x \cdot \sin(n+2)x$

$= \cos[(n+1)x - (n+2)x]$

10. Use the formula of $\cos(A+B)$.

11. $\tan 15° = \tan(45° - 30°)$

$$= \frac{\tan 45° - \tan 30°}{1 + \tan 45° \tan 30°} = \frac{\sqrt{3}-1}{\sqrt{3}+1}$$

$$\Rightarrow \cot 15° = \frac{\sqrt{3}+1}{\sqrt{3}-1}$$

12. $\cos\left(\frac{3\pi}{4}+x\right) - \cos\left(\frac{3\pi}{4}-x\right)$

$$= \left(-\frac{1}{\sqrt{2}}\cos x - \frac{1}{\sqrt{2}}\sin x\right) - \left(-\frac{1}{\sqrt{2}}\cos x + \frac{1}{\sqrt{2}}\sin x\right)$$

13. Use the formula, $\sin^2 A - \sin^2 B = \sin(A+B)\sin(A-B)$ and then simplify it.

14. $\cos 2\alpha \cos 2\beta + \sin(\alpha - \beta + \alpha + \beta)\sin[\alpha - \beta - (\alpha+\beta)]$

$= \cos 2\alpha \cos 2\beta + \sin 2\alpha \sin(-2\beta)$

$= \cos 2\alpha \cos 2\beta - \sin 2\alpha \sin 2\beta$

15. Given, $\cos A = \frac{4}{5}, \frac{3\pi}{2} < A < 2\pi$

$\therefore \quad \sin A = -\sqrt{1-\cos^2 A} = -\frac{3}{5}$

[$\because$ *A* lies in IVth quadrant]

Also, $\quad \cos B = \frac{12}{13}, \frac{3\pi}{2} < B < 2\pi$

$\Rightarrow \quad \sin B = -\sqrt{1-\cos^2 B} = -\frac{5}{13}$

[$\because$ *B* lies in IVth quadrant]

(i) $\cos(A+B) = \frac{4}{5} \times \frac{12}{13} - \left(-\frac{3}{5}\right)\left(-\frac{5}{13}\right)$

Ans. $\frac{33}{65}$

(ii) $\sin(A-B) = \left(-\frac{3}{5}\right) \times \frac{12}{13} - \frac{4}{5} \times \left(-\frac{5}{13}\right)$

Ans. $-\frac{16}{65}$

16. $\cos A = \sqrt{1-\frac{9}{25}} = \frac{4}{5},$

$\sin B = -\sqrt{1-\frac{144}{169}} = -\frac{5}{13}$

(i) $-\frac{16}{65}$ (ii) $-\frac{33}{65}$ (iii) $\frac{16}{63}$

17. Solve as Example 18.

18. $\tan(\alpha - \beta) = \frac{\tan\alpha - \tan\beta}{1 + \tan\alpha \tan\beta}$

$$\Rightarrow \tan(\alpha-\beta) = \frac{\frac{\sin\alpha}{\cos\alpha} - \frac{n\sin\alpha\cos\alpha}{1-n\sin^2\alpha}}{1 + \frac{\sin\alpha}{\cos\alpha}\cdot\frac{n\sin\alpha\cos\alpha}{1-n\sin^2\alpha}}$$

$$\Rightarrow \tan(\alpha-\beta) = \frac{\sin\alpha - n\sin^3\alpha - n\sin\alpha(1-\sin^2\alpha)}{\cos\alpha - n\sin^2\alpha\cos\alpha + n\sin^2\alpha\cos\alpha}$$

$$\Rightarrow \tan(\alpha-\beta) = \frac{\sin\alpha - n\sin\alpha}{\cos\alpha}$$

19. Since, α and β lie between 0 and $\frac{\pi}{4}$.

$\therefore \quad -\frac{\pi}{4} < \alpha - \beta < \frac{\pi}{4}$ and $0 < \alpha + \beta < \frac{\pi}{2}$

$\Rightarrow \cos(\alpha-\beta)$ and $\sin(\alpha+\beta)$ are positive.

Now, $\sin(\alpha+\beta) = \sqrt{1-\cos^2(\alpha+\beta)} = \frac{3}{5}$

and $\quad \cos(\alpha-\beta) = \sqrt{1-\sin^2(\alpha-\beta)} = \frac{12}{13}$

$\therefore \quad \tan(\alpha+\beta) = \frac{\sin(\alpha+\beta)}{\cos(\alpha+\beta)} = \frac{3/5}{4/5} = \frac{3}{4}$

and $\quad \tan(\alpha-\beta) = \frac{\sin(\alpha-\beta)}{\cos(\alpha-\beta)} = \frac{5/13}{12/13} = \frac{5}{12}$

Now, $\tan 2\alpha = \tan[(\alpha+\beta)+(\alpha-\beta)]$

$$= \frac{\tan(\alpha+\beta) + \tan(\alpha-\beta)}{1 - \tan(\alpha+\beta)\tan(\alpha-\beta)}$$

20. Given, $\quad \tan\theta = k\tan\phi$

$$\Rightarrow \frac{\tan\theta}{\tan\phi} = \frac{k}{1} \Rightarrow \frac{\tan\theta + \tan\phi}{\tan\theta - \tan\phi} = \frac{k+1}{k-1}$$

[applying componendo and dividendo]

$$\Rightarrow \frac{\frac{\sin\theta}{\cos\theta} + \frac{\sin\phi}{\cos\phi}}{\frac{\sin\theta}{\cos\theta} - \frac{\sin\phi}{\cos\phi}} = \frac{k+1}{k-1}$$

$$\Rightarrow \frac{\sin\theta\cdot\cos\phi + \cos\theta\cdot\sin\phi}{\sin\theta\cdot\cos\phi - \cos\theta\cdot\sin\phi} = \frac{k+1}{k-1}$$

$$\Rightarrow \frac{\sin(\theta+\phi)}{\sin(\theta-\phi)} = \frac{k+1}{k-1} \Rightarrow \frac{\sin(\theta-\phi)}{\sin(\theta+\phi)} = \frac{k-1}{k+1}$$

21. $\frac{\sin(\pi\cos\theta)}{\cos(\pi\cos\theta)} = \frac{\cos(\pi\sin\theta)}{\sin(\pi\sin\theta)}$

$\Rightarrow \quad \cos(\pi\cos\theta + \pi\sin\theta) = 0$

$\Rightarrow \quad \cos\theta + \sin\theta = \pm\frac{1}{2}$

$\Rightarrow \cos\theta\cos\frac{\pi}{4} + \sin\theta\sin\frac{\pi}{4} = \pm\frac{1}{2\sqrt{2}}$

TOPIC 04 Transformation Formulae

In this topic, we will deal with mainly two types of transformation

(i) Transformation of product into sum or difference.

(ii) Transformation of sum or difference into product.

Transformation of Product into Sum or Difference

Here, we transform the products of two sines or two cosines or one sine and one cosine of constituent angles into the sum or difference of two sines or two cosines of compound angles.

(i) $2\cos A\cos B = \cos(A+B)+\cos(A-B)$

(ii) $2\sin A\sin B = \cos(A-B)-\cos(A+B)$

(iii) $2\sin A\cos B = \sin(A+B)+\sin(A-B)$

(iv) $2\cos A\sin B = \sin(A+B)-\sin(A-B)$

Example 1 Find the value of the following functions.

(i) $2\cos 45^\circ\sin 15^\circ$ (ii) $2\sin 15^\circ\cos 75^\circ$

(iii) $\cos 315^\circ\cos 75^\circ$

Sol. (i) $2\cos 45^\circ\sin 15^\circ$

$= \sin(45^\circ+15^\circ)-\sin(45^\circ-15^\circ)$

$[\because 2\cos A\sin B = \sin(A+B)-\sin(A-B)]$

$= \sin 60^\circ - \sin 30^\circ$

$= \frac{\sqrt{3}}{2}-\frac{1}{2}=\frac{\sqrt{3}-1}{2}$ $\left[\because \sin 60^\circ = \frac{\sqrt{3}}{2} \text{ and } \sin 30^\circ = \frac{1}{2}\right]$

(ii) $2\sin 15^\circ\cos 75^\circ = \sin(15^\circ+75^\circ)+\sin(15^\circ-75^\circ)$

$[\because 2\sin A\cdot\cos B = \sin(A+B)+\sin(A-B)]$

$= \sin 90^\circ + \sin(-60^\circ)$

$= \sin 90^\circ - \sin 60^\circ$ $[\because \sin(-\theta) = -\sin\theta]$

$= 1-\frac{\sqrt{3}}{2}=\frac{2-\sqrt{3}}{2}$

(iii) $\cos 315^\circ\cos 75^\circ = \frac{1}{2}(2\cos 315^\circ\cos 75^\circ)$

$= \frac{1}{2}\{\cos(315^\circ+75^\circ)+\cos(315^\circ-75^\circ)\}$

$[\because 2\cos A\cos B = \cos(A+B)+\cos(A-B)]$

$= \frac{1}{2}\{\cos 390^\circ + \cos 240^\circ\}$

$= \frac{1}{2}\{\cos(360^\circ+30^\circ)+\cos(180^\circ+60^\circ)\}$

$= \frac{1}{2}\{\cos 30^\circ + (-\cos 60^\circ)\}$

$[\because \cos(360^\circ+\theta) = \cos\theta \text{ and } \cos(180^\circ+\theta) = -\cos\theta]$

$= \frac{1}{2}\left(\frac{\sqrt{3}}{2}-\frac{1}{2}\right)$ $\left[\because \cos 30^\circ = \frac{\sqrt{3}}{2} \text{ and } \cos 60^\circ = \frac{1}{2}\right]$

$= \frac{1}{2}\left(\frac{\sqrt{3}-1}{2}\right)=\frac{\sqrt{3}-1}{4}$

Example 2 Prove that

$$\sin 7A\cos 3A = \frac{1}{2}(\sin 10A + \sin 4A).$$

Sol. LHS $= \sin 7A\cos 3A = \frac{1}{2}(2\sin 7A\cos 3A)$

$= \frac{1}{2}[\sin(7A+3A)+\sin(7A-3A)]$

$[\because 2\sin A\cos B = \sin(A+B)+\sin(A-B)]$

$= \frac{1}{2}(\sin 10A + \sin 4A) =$ RHS **Hence proved.**

Example 3 Find the value of $2\sin 52\frac{1^\circ}{2}\sin 7\frac{1^\circ}{2}$.

Sol. $2\sin 52\frac{1^\circ}{2}\sin 7\frac{1^\circ}{2} = 2\sin\frac{105^\circ}{2}\sin\frac{15^\circ}{2}$

$= \cos\left(\frac{105^\circ}{2}-\frac{15^\circ}{2}\right)-\cos\left(\frac{105^\circ}{2}+\frac{15^\circ}{2}\right)$

$[\because 2\sin A\sin B = \cos(A-B)-\cos(A+B)]$

$= \cos\left(\frac{90^\circ}{2}\right)-\cos\left(\frac{120^\circ}{2}\right)=\cos 45^\circ-\cos 60^\circ$

$= \frac{1}{\sqrt{2}}-\frac{1}{2}$ $\left[\because \cos 45^\circ = \frac{1}{\sqrt{2}} \text{ and } \cos 60^\circ = \frac{1}{2}\right]$

$= \frac{2-\sqrt{2}}{2\sqrt{2}}=\frac{\sqrt{2}(\sqrt{2}-1)}{2\sqrt{2}}=\frac{\sqrt{2}-1}{2}$ $[\because \sqrt{2}\times\sqrt{2}=2]$

Example 4 Find the value of

$$\cos 33^\circ\cos 27^\circ - \cos 57^\circ\cos 63^\circ.$$

Sol. $\cos 33^\circ\cos 27^\circ - \cos 57^\circ\cos 63^\circ$

$= \frac{1}{2}(2\cos 33^\circ\cos 27^\circ - 2\cos 57^\circ\cos 63^\circ)$

$= \frac{1}{2}[\{\cos(33^\circ+27^\circ)+\cos(33^\circ-27^\circ)\}$
$-\{\cos(63^\circ+57^\circ)+\cos(63^\circ-57^\circ)\}]$

$[\because 2\cos A\cos B = \cos(A+B)+\cos(A-B)]$

$= \frac{1}{2}[(\cos 60^\circ+\cos 6^\circ)-(\cos 120^\circ+\cos 6^\circ)]$

$= \frac{1}{2}(\cos 60^\circ-\cos 120^\circ)=\frac{1}{2}[\cos 60^\circ-\cos(180^\circ-60^\circ)]$

$= \frac{1}{2}(\cos 60^\circ+\cos 60^\circ)$ $[\because \cos(180^\circ-\theta) = -\cos\theta]$

$= \frac{1}{2}\left(\frac{1}{2}+\frac{1}{2}\right)=\frac{1}{2}$ $\left[\because \cos 60^\circ = \frac{1}{2}\right]$

Example 5 Find the value of
$$\cos\left(\frac{\pi}{6}-x\right)\cos\left(\frac{\pi}{6}+x\right).$$

Sol. $\cos\left(\frac{\pi}{6}-x\right)\cos\left(\frac{\pi}{6}+x\right)$

$$=\frac{1}{2}\left[2\cos\left(\frac{\pi}{6}+x\right)\cos\left(\frac{\pi}{6}-x\right)\right]$$

$$=\frac{1}{2}\left[\cos\left\{\left(\frac{\pi}{6}+x\right)+\left(\frac{\pi}{6}-x\right)\right\}+\cos\left\{\left(\frac{\pi}{6}+x\right)-\left(\frac{\pi}{6}-x\right)\right\}\right]$$

$[\because 2\cos A\cos B=\cos(A+B)+\cos(A-B)]$

$$=\frac{1}{2}\left(\cos\frac{\pi}{3}+\cos 2x\right)=\frac{1}{2}\left(\frac{1}{2}+\cos 2x\right)\left[\because \cos\frac{\pi}{3}=\frac{1}{2}\right]$$

$$=\frac{1}{4}+\frac{1}{2}\cos 2x$$

Example 6 Prove that
$$\cos 2A\cos\frac{A}{2}-\cos 3A\cos\frac{9A}{2}=\sin 5A\sin\frac{5A}{2}.$$

Sol. $\text{LHS}=\cos 2A\cos\frac{A}{2}-\cos 3A\cos\frac{9A}{2}$

$$=\frac{1}{2}\left[2\cos 2A\cos\frac{A}{2}\right]-\frac{1}{2}\left[2\cos\frac{9A}{2}\cos 3A\right]$$

$$=\frac{1}{2}\left[\cos\left(2A+\frac{A}{2}\right)+\cos\left(2A-\frac{A}{2}\right)\right]-\frac{1}{2}\left[\cos\left(\frac{9A}{2}+3A\right)+\cos\left(\frac{9A}{2}-3A\right)\right]$$

$[\because 2\cos A\cos B=\cos(A+B)+\cos(A-B)]$

$$=\frac{1}{2}\left[\cos\left(\frac{4A+A}{2}\right)+\cos\left(\frac{4A-A}{2}\right)\right]-\frac{1}{2}\left[\cos\left(\frac{9A+6A}{2}\right)+\cos\left(\frac{9A-6A}{2}\right)\right]$$

$$=\frac{1}{2}\left(\cos\frac{5A}{2}+\cos\frac{3A}{2}\right)-\frac{1}{2}\left(\cos\frac{15A}{2}+\cos\frac{3A}{2}\right)$$

$$=\frac{1}{2}\cos\frac{5A}{2}+\frac{1}{2}\cos\frac{3A}{2}-\frac{1}{2}\cos\frac{15A}{2}-\frac{1}{2}\cos\frac{3A}{2}$$

$$=\frac{1}{2}\cos\frac{5A}{2}-\frac{1}{2}\cos\frac{15A}{2}=\frac{1}{2}\left(\cos\frac{5A}{2}-\cos\frac{15A}{2}\right)$$

$$\text{RHS}=\sin 5A\sin\frac{5A}{2}=\frac{1}{2}\left(2\sin 5A\sin\frac{5A}{2}\right)$$

$$=\frac{1}{2}\left[\cos\left(5A-\frac{5A}{2}\right)-\cos\left(5A+\frac{5A}{2}\right)\right]$$

$[\because 2\sin A\sin B=\cos(A-B)-\cos(A+B)]$

$$=\frac{1}{2}\left[\cos\left(\frac{10A-5A}{2}\right)-\cos\left(\frac{10A+5A}{2}\right)\right]$$

$$=\frac{1}{2}\left(\cos\frac{5A}{2}-\cos\frac{15A}{2}\right)$$

$\therefore$ LHS = RHS **Hence proved.**

Example 7 Prove that
$$4\cos 12^\circ\cos 48^\circ\cos 72^\circ=\cos 36^\circ.$$

Sol. $\text{LHS}=4\cos 12^\circ\cos 48^\circ\cos 72^\circ$

$=2(2\cos 12^\circ\cos 48^\circ)\cos 72^\circ$

$=2[\cos(12^\circ+48^\circ)+\cos(12^\circ-48^\circ)]\cos 72^\circ$

$[\because 2\cos A\cos B=\cos(A+B)+\cos(A-B)]$

$=2[\cos 60^\circ+\cos(-36^\circ)]\cos 72^\circ$

$=2[\cos 60^\circ+\cos 36^\circ]\cos 72^\circ$ $[\because \cos(-\theta)=\cos\theta]$

$=2\left[\frac{1}{2}\cos 72^\circ+\cos 36^\circ\cos 72^\circ\right]$

$=\cos 72^\circ+2\cos 36^\circ\cos 72^\circ$

$=\cos 72^\circ+\cos(36^\circ+72^\circ)+\cos(36^\circ-72^\circ)$

$=\cos 72^\circ+\cos 108^\circ+\cos 36^\circ$

$=\cos 72^\circ+\cos(180^\circ-72^\circ)+\cos 36^\circ$

$=\cos 72^\circ-\cos 72^\circ+\cos 36^\circ$

$=\cos 36^\circ$

= RHS **Hence proved.**

Example 8 Prove that
$$\sin 10^\circ\sin 30^\circ\sin 50^\circ\sin 70^\circ=\frac{1}{16}.$$

Sol. $\text{LHS}=\sin 10^\circ\sin 30^\circ\sin 50^\circ\sin 70^\circ$

$=\sin 30^\circ(\sin 50^\circ\sin 10^\circ)\sin 70^\circ$

$=\frac{1}{2}\times\frac{1}{2}(2\sin 50^\circ\sin 10^\circ)\sin 70^\circ$

$=\frac{1}{4}[\cos(50^\circ-10^\circ)-\cos(50^\circ+10^\circ)]\sin 70^\circ$

$[\because 2\sin A\sin B=\cos(A-B)-\cos(A+B)]$

$=\frac{1}{4}[\cos 40^\circ-\cos 60^\circ]\sin 70^\circ$

$=\frac{1}{4}[\sin 70^\circ\cos 40^\circ-\sin 70^\circ\cos 60^\circ]$

$=\frac{1}{4}\left[\sin 70^\circ\cos 40^\circ-\frac{1}{2}\sin 70^\circ\right]$

$=\frac{1}{8}[2\sin 70^\circ\cos 40^\circ-\sin 70^\circ]$

$=\frac{1}{8}[\sin(70^\circ+40^\circ)+\sin(70^\circ-40^\circ)-\sin 70^\circ]$

$[\because 2\sin A\cos B=\sin(A+B)+\sin(A-B)]$

$=\frac{1}{8}[\sin 110^\circ+\sin 30^\circ-\sin 70^\circ]$

$=\frac{1}{8}\left[\sin(180^\circ-70^\circ)+\frac{1}{2}-\sin 70^\circ\right]$

$=\frac{1}{8}\left[\sin 70^\circ+\frac{1}{2}-\sin 70^\circ\right]=\frac{1}{8}\times\frac{1}{2}=\frac{1}{16}$

= RHS **Hence proved.**

Example 9 Prove that

$$\tan\theta\tan(60^\circ-\theta)\tan(60^\circ+\theta)=\tan 3\theta.$$

Sol. LHS $=\tan\theta\tan(60^\circ-\theta)\tan(60^\circ+\theta)$

$$=\frac{\sin\theta}{\cos\theta}\cdot\frac{\sin(60^\circ-\theta)}{\cos(60^\circ-\theta)}\cdot\frac{\sin(60^\circ+\theta)}{\cos(60^\circ+\theta)}$$

$$=\frac{\sin\theta[2\sin(60^\circ-\theta)\sin(60^\circ+\theta)]}{\cos\theta[2\cos(60^\circ-\theta)\cos(60^\circ+\theta)]}$$

$$=\frac{\sin\theta(\cos 2\theta-\cos 120^\circ)}{\cos\theta(\cos 120^\circ+\cos 2\theta)}$$

$$\left[\because 2\sin A\sin B=\cos(A-B)-\cos(A+B) \text{ and } 2\cos A\cos B=\cos(A+B)+\cos(A-B)\right]$$

$$=\frac{\sin\theta\left(\cos 2\theta+\frac{1}{2}\right)}{\cos\theta\left(\cos 2\theta-\frac{1}{2}\right)}\quad\left[\because \cos 120^\circ=\cos(180^\circ-60^\circ)=-\cos 60^\circ=-\frac{1}{2}\right]$$

$$=\frac{\sin\theta\cos 2\theta+\frac{1}{2}\sin\theta}{\cos\theta\cos 2\theta-\frac{1}{2}\cos\theta}=\frac{2\sin\theta\cos 2\theta+\sin\theta}{2\cos\theta\cos 2\theta-\cos\theta}$$

$$=\frac{\sin(\theta+2\theta)+\sin(-\theta)+\sin\theta}{\cos(\theta+2\theta)+\cos(-\theta)-\cos\theta}$$

$$\left[\because 2\sin A\cos B=\sin(A+B)+\sin(A-B) \text{ and } 2\cos A\cos B=\cos(A+B)+\cos(A-B)\right]$$

$$=\frac{\sin 3\theta-\sin\theta+\sin\theta}{\cos 3\theta+\cos\theta-\cos\theta}\quad\left[\because \sin(-\theta)=-\sin\theta \text{ and } \cos(-\theta)=\cos\theta\right]$$

$$=\frac{\sin 3\theta}{\cos 3\theta}=\tan 3\theta=\text{RHS}$$

Hence proved.

Example 10 If $\frac{\tan(\theta+\alpha)}{a}=\frac{\tan(\theta+\beta)}{b}=\frac{\tan(\theta+\gamma)}{c}$, then prove that $\frac{a+b}{a-b}\sin^2(\alpha-\beta)+\frac{b+c}{b-c}\sin^2(\beta-\gamma)+\frac{c+a}{c-a}\sin^2(\gamma-\alpha)=0.$

[HOTS]

Sol. Given, $\frac{\tan(\theta+\alpha)}{a}=\frac{\tan(\theta+\beta)}{b}$

$$\Rightarrow\quad \frac{a}{b}=\frac{\tan(\theta+\alpha)}{\tan(\theta+\beta)}$$

$$\Rightarrow\quad \frac{a+b}{a-b}=\frac{\tan(\theta+\alpha)+\tan(\theta+\beta)}{\tan(\theta+\alpha)-\tan(\theta+\beta)}$$

[applying componendo and dividendo rule]

$$\Rightarrow\quad \frac{a+b}{a-b}=\frac{\sin(\theta+\alpha+\theta+\beta)}{\sin(\theta+\alpha-\theta-\beta)}$$

$$\left[\because \frac{\tan A+\tan B}{\tan A-\tan B}=\frac{\frac{\sin A\cos B+\cos A\sin B}{\cos A\cos B}}{\frac{\sin A\cos B-\cos A\sin B}{\cos A\cos B}}=\frac{\sin(A+B)}{\sin(A-B)}\right]$$

$$\Rightarrow\quad \frac{a+b}{a-b}=\frac{\sin(2\theta+\alpha+\beta)}{\sin(\alpha-\beta)}$$

$$\Rightarrow\quad \left(\frac{a+b}{a-b}\right)\sin(\alpha-\beta)=\sin(2\theta+\alpha+\beta)$$

$$\Rightarrow\quad \left(\frac{a+b}{a-b}\right)\sin^2(\alpha-\beta)=\sin(2\theta+\alpha+\beta)\sin(\alpha-\beta)$$

$$\Rightarrow\quad \left(\frac{a+b}{a-b}\right)\sin^2(\alpha-\beta)=\frac{1}{2}[2\sin(2\theta+\alpha+\beta)\sin(\alpha-\beta)]$$

$$\Rightarrow\quad \left(\frac{a+b}{a-b}\right)\sin^2(\alpha-\beta)=\frac{1}{2}[\cos(2\theta+2\beta)-\cos(2\theta+2\alpha)]$$

$$[\because 2\sin A\sin B=\cos(A-B)-\cos(A+B)]$$

Similarly, $\frac{b+c}{b-c}\sin^2(\beta-\gamma)=\frac{1}{2}[\cos(2\theta+2\gamma)-\cos(2\theta+2\beta)]$

and $\frac{c+a}{c-a}\sin^2(\gamma-\alpha)=\frac{1}{2}[\cos(2\theta+2\alpha)-\cos(2\theta+2\gamma)]$

Now, $\left(\frac{a+b}{a-b}\right)\sin^2(\alpha-\beta)+\left(\frac{b+c}{b-c}\right)\sin^2(\beta-\gamma)+\left(\frac{c+a}{c-a}\right)\sin^2(\gamma-\alpha)$

$$=\frac{1}{2}[\cos(2\theta+2\beta)-\cos(2\theta+2\alpha)+\cos(2\theta+2\gamma)-\cos(2\theta+2\beta)+\cos(2\theta+2\alpha)-\cos(2\theta+2\gamma)]$$

$$=\frac{1}{2}\times 0=0$$

$\therefore$ LHS = RHS **Hence proved.**

Transformation of Sum or Difference into Product

Here, we transform the sum and difference of two sines or cosines of two constituent angles into product of sine and cosine of compound angles.

(i) $\cos C+\cos D=2\cos\left(\frac{C+D}{2}\right)\cdot\cos\left(\frac{C-D}{2}\right)$

(ii) $\cos C-\cos D=-2\sin\left(\frac{C+D}{2}\right)\cdot\sin\left(\frac{C-D}{2}\right)$

(iii) $\sin C+\sin D=2\sin\left(\frac{C+D}{2}\right)\cdot\cos\left(\frac{C-D}{2}\right)$

(iv) $\sin C-\sin D=2\cos\left(\frac{C+D}{2}\right)\cdot\sin\left(\frac{C-D}{2}\right)$

Example 11 Find the value of $\sin 75^\circ+\sin 15^\circ$.

Sol. $\sin 75^\circ+\sin 15^\circ=2\sin\left(\frac{75^\circ+15^\circ}{2}\right)\cos\left(\frac{75^\circ-15^\circ}{2}\right)$

$$\left[\because \sin C+\sin D=2\sin\left(\frac{C+D}{2}\right)\cos\left(\frac{C-D}{2}\right)\right]$$

$= 2\sin\frac{90^\circ}{2}\cos\frac{60^\circ}{2} = 2\sin 45^\circ \cos 30^\circ$

$= 2\cdot\frac{1}{\sqrt{2}}\cdot\frac{\sqrt{3}}{2}$ $\left[\because \sin 45^\circ = \frac{1}{\sqrt{2}} \text{ and } \cos 30^\circ = \frac{\sqrt{3}}{2}\right]$

$= \frac{\sqrt{3}}{\sqrt{2}} \times \frac{\sqrt{2}}{\sqrt{2}} = \frac{\sqrt{6}}{2}$

Example 12 Find the value of $\sin 10^\circ + \sin 50^\circ - \sin 70^\circ$.

Sol. $\sin 10^\circ + \sin 50^\circ - \sin 70^\circ$

$= \sin 10^\circ - (\sin 70^\circ - \sin 50^\circ)$

$= \sin 10^\circ - \left[2\cos\left(\frac{70^\circ + 50^\circ}{2}\right)\sin\left(\frac{70^\circ - 50^\circ}{2}\right)\right]$

$\left[\because \sin C - \sin D = 2\cos\left(\frac{C+D}{2}\right)\sin\left(\frac{C-D}{2}\right)\right]$

$= \sin 10^\circ - \left[2\cos\left(\frac{120^\circ}{2}\right)\sin\left(\frac{20^\circ}{2}\right)\right]$

$= \sin 10^\circ - (2\cos 60^\circ \sin 10^\circ)$

$= \sin 10^\circ - \left(2\cdot\frac{1}{2}\cdot\sin 10^\circ\right)$ $\left[\because \cos 60^\circ = \frac{1}{2}\right]$

$= \sin 10^\circ - \sin 10^\circ = 0$

Example 13 Prove

$$(\cos A - \cos B)^2 + (\sin A - \sin B)^2 = 4\sin^2\frac{A-B}{2}.$$

Sol. LHS $= (\cos A - \cos B)^2 + (\sin A - \sin B)^2$

$= \left(-2\sin\frac{A+B}{2}\sin\frac{A-B}{2}\right)^2 + \left(2\cos\frac{A+B}{2}\sin\frac{A-B}{2}\right)^2$

$\left[\because \cos C - \cos D = -2\sin\left(\frac{C+D}{2}\right)\sin\left(\frac{C-D}{2}\right) \text{ and } \sin C - \sin D = 2\cos\left(\frac{C+D}{2}\right)\sin\left(\frac{C-D}{2}\right)\right]$

$= 4\sin^2\frac{A+B}{2}\sin^2\frac{A-B}{2} + 4\cos^2\frac{A+B}{2}\sin^2\frac{A-B}{2}$

$= 4\sin^2\frac{A-B}{2}\left(\sin^2\frac{A+B}{2} + \cos^2\frac{A+B}{2}\right)$

$= 4\sin^2\frac{A-B}{2} \times 1$ $[\because \sin^2\theta + \cos^2\theta = 1]$

$= 4\sin^2\frac{A-B}{2} =$ RHS **Hence proved.**

Example 14 Prove that

$$\frac{\sin 5x + \sin 3x}{\cos 5x + \cos 3x} = \tan 4x.$$ **[NCERT]**

Sol. LHS $= \frac{\sin 5x + \sin 3x}{\cos 5x + \cos 3x}$

$= \frac{2\sin\left(\frac{5x+3x}{2}\right)\cos\left(\frac{5x-3x}{2}\right)}{2\cos\left(\frac{5x+3x}{2}\right)\cos\left(\frac{5x-3x}{2}\right)}$ [by formulae]

$= \frac{\sin 4x \cos x}{\cos 4x \cos x} = \tan 4x =$ RHS **Hence proved.**

Example 15 If $m\sin\theta = n\sin(\theta + 2\alpha)$, then prove that $\tan(\theta + \alpha)\cot\alpha = \frac{m+n}{m-n}$. **[NCERT Exemplar]**

Sol. Given, $m\sin\theta = n\sin(\theta + 2\alpha)$

$\Rightarrow \frac{m}{n} = \frac{\sin(\theta + 2\alpha)}{\sin\theta}$

Applying componendo and dividendo rule, we get

$\frac{m+n}{m-n} = \frac{\sin(\theta + 2\alpha) + \sin\theta}{\sin(\theta + 2\alpha) - \sin\theta}$

$= \frac{2\sin\left(\frac{\theta + 2\alpha + \theta}{2}\right)\cos\left(\frac{\theta + 2\alpha - \theta}{2}\right)}{2\cos\left(\frac{\theta + 2\alpha + \theta}{2}\right)\sin\left(\frac{\theta + 2\alpha - \theta}{2}\right)}$

$\left[\because \sin C + \sin D = 2\sin\left(\frac{C+D}{2}\right)\cos\left(\frac{C-D}{2}\right) \text{ and } \sin C - \sin D = 2\cos\left(\frac{C+D}{2}\right)\sin\left(\frac{C-D}{2}\right)\right]$

$= \frac{2\sin(\theta + \alpha)\cos\alpha}{2\cos(\theta + \alpha)\sin\alpha}$

$= \tan(\theta + \alpha)\cot\alpha$ **Hence proved.**

Example 16 If

$$\cos(\alpha + \beta)\sin(\gamma + \delta) = \cos(\alpha - \beta)\sin(\gamma - \delta),$$

then prove that $\cot\alpha\cot\beta\cot\gamma = \cot\delta$.

Sol. Given, $\cos(\alpha + \beta)\sin(\gamma + \delta) = \cos(\alpha - \beta)\sin(\gamma - \delta)$

$\Rightarrow \frac{\cos(\alpha - \beta)}{\cos(\alpha + \beta)} = \frac{\sin(\gamma + \delta)}{\sin(\gamma - \delta)}$

$\Rightarrow \frac{\cos(\alpha - \beta) + \cos(\alpha + \beta)}{\cos(\alpha - \beta) - \cos(\alpha + \beta)} = \frac{\sin(\gamma + \delta) + \sin(\gamma - \delta)}{\sin(\gamma + \delta) - \sin(\gamma - \delta)}$

[applying componendo and dividendo rule]

$\Rightarrow \frac{2\cos\alpha\cos(-\beta)}{-2\sin\alpha\sin(-\beta)} = \frac{2\sin\gamma\cos\delta}{2\cos\gamma\sin\delta}$

$\Rightarrow \frac{2\cos\alpha\cos\beta}{2\sin\alpha\sin\beta} = \frac{2\sin\gamma\cos\delta}{2\cos\gamma\sin\delta}$

$[\because \cos(-\theta) = \cos\theta \text{ and } \sin(-\theta) = -\sin\theta]$

$\Rightarrow \cot\alpha\cot\beta = \tan\gamma\cot\delta$

$\Rightarrow \cot\alpha\cot\beta\cot\gamma = \cot\delta$ **Hence proved.**

Example 17 Prove that

$$\sin x + \sin y + \sin z - \sin(x+y+z) = 4\sin\left(\frac{x+y}{2}\right)\cdot\sin\left(\frac{y+z}{2}\right)\cdot\sin\left(\frac{z+x}{2}\right)$$

Sol. LHS $= (\sin x + \sin y) + [\sin z - \sin(x+y+z)]$

$$= 2\sin\left(\frac{x+y}{2}\right)\cdot\cos\left(\frac{x-y}{2}\right) + 2\cos\left(\frac{z+x+y+z}{2}\right)\cdot\sin\left(\frac{z-x-y-z}{2}\right)$$

$$\left[\because \sin C + \sin D = 2\sin\left(\frac{C+D}{2}\right)\cdot\cos\left(\frac{C-D}{2}\right) \text{ and } \sin C - \sin D = 2\cos\left(\frac{C+D}{2}\right)\cdot\sin\left(\frac{C-D}{2}\right)\right]$$

$$= 2\sin\left(\frac{x+y}{2}\right).\cos\left(\frac{x-y}{2}\right) + 2\cos\left(\frac{x+y+2z}{2}\right)\cdot\sin\left[-\left(\frac{x+y}{2}\right)\right]$$

$$= 2\sin\left(\frac{x+y}{2}\right)\cdot\cos\left(\frac{x-y}{2}\right) - 2\cos\left(\frac{x+y+2z}{2}\right)\cdot\sin\left(\frac{x+y}{2}\right) \quad [\because \sin(-\theta) = -\sin\theta]$$

$$= 2\sin\left(\frac{x+y}{2}\right)\left[\cos\left(\frac{x-y}{2}\right) - \cos\left(\frac{x+y+2z}{2}\right)\right]$$

$$= 2\sin\left(\frac{x+y}{2}\right)\left[-2\sin\frac{\left(\frac{x-y}{2}+\frac{x+y+2z}{2}\right)}{2}\sin\frac{\left(\frac{x-y}{2}-\frac{x+y+2z}{2}\right)}{2}\right]$$

$$\left[\because \cos x - \cos y = -2\sin\left(\frac{x+y}{2}\right)\sin\left(\frac{x-y}{2}\right)\right]$$

$$= -4\sin\left(\frac{x+y}{2}\right)\cdot\sin\left(\frac{x+z}{2}\right)\cdot\sin\left(\frac{-y-z}{2}\right)$$

$$= -4\sin\left(\frac{x+y}{2}\right)\cdot\sin\left(\frac{x+z}{2}\right)\left[-\sin\left(\frac{y+z}{2}\right)\right] \quad [\because \sin(-\theta) = -\sin\theta]$$

$$= 4\sin\left(\frac{x+y}{2}\right)\cdot\sin\left(\frac{x+z}{2}\right)\cdot\sin\left(\frac{y+z}{2}\right)$$

= RHS **Hence proved.**

Example 18 If $\dfrac{\sin(x+y)}{\sin(x-y)} = \dfrac{a+b}{a-b}$, then show that $\dfrac{\tan x}{\tan y} = \dfrac{a}{b}$. **[NCERT Exemplar]**

Sol. Given, $\dfrac{\sin(x+y)}{\sin(x-y)} = \dfrac{a+b}{a-b}$

Using componendo and dividendo rule, we get

$$\frac{\sin(x+y)+\sin(x-y)}{\sin(x+y)-\sin(x-y)} = \frac{a+b+a-b}{a+b-a+b}$$

$$\Rightarrow \frac{2\sin\left(\frac{x+y+x-y}{2}\right)\cdot\cos\left(\frac{x+y-x+y}{2}\right)}{2\cos\left(\frac{x+y+x-y}{2}\right)\cdot\sin\left(\frac{x+y-x+y}{2}\right)} = \frac{2a}{2b}$$

$$\left[\because \sin C + \sin D = 2\sin\frac{C+D}{2}\cdot\cos\frac{C-D}{2} \text{ and } \sin C - \sin D = 2\cos\frac{C+D}{2}\cdot\sin\frac{C-D}{2}\right]$$

$$\Rightarrow \frac{\sin x\cdot\cos y}{\cos x\cdot\sin y} = \frac{a}{b} \Rightarrow \frac{\tan x}{\tan y} = \frac{a}{b}$$

Hence proved.

Example 19 Prove that

$$\frac{\cos 4x + \cos 3x + \cos 2x}{\sin 4x + \sin 3x + \sin 2x} = \cot 3x.$$ **[NCERT]**

Sol. LHS $= \dfrac{\cos 4x + \cos 3x + \cos 2x}{\sin 4x + \sin 3x + \sin 2x}$

$$= \frac{(\cos 4x + \cos 2x) + \cos 3x}{(\sin 4x + \sin 2x) + \sin 3x}$$

$$= \frac{2\cos\left(\frac{4x+2x}{2}\right)\cos\left(\frac{4x-2x}{2}\right) + \cos 3x}{2\sin\left(\frac{4x+2x}{2}\right)\cos\left(\frac{4x-2x}{2}\right) + \sin 3x}$$

$$= \frac{2\cos 3x\cos x + \cos 3x}{2\sin 3x\cos x + \sin 3x} = \frac{\cos 3x(2\cos x + 1)}{\sin 3x(2\cos x + 1)}$$

$= \cot 3x$

= RHS **Hence proved.**

Example 20 Prove that

$$\frac{\cos 2A\cos 3A - \cos 2A\cos 7A + \cos A\cos 10A}{\sin 4A\sin 3A - \sin 2A\sin 5A + \sin 4A\sin 7A} = \cot 6A\cdot\cot 5A.$$

Sol. LHS $= \dfrac{\cos 2A\cos 3A - \cos 2A\cos 7A + \cos A\cdot\cos 10A}{\sin 4A\sin 3A - \sin 2A\cdot\sin 5A + \sin 4A\sin 7A}$

$$= \frac{2\cos 2A\cos 3A - 2\cos 7A\cos 2A + 2\cos 10A\cos A}{2\sin 4A\sin 3A - 2\sin 5A\sin 2A + 2\sin 7A\sin 4A}$$

$$= \frac{[\cos(3A+2A) + \cos(3A-2A) - [\cos(7A+2A) + \cos(7A-2A)] + [\cos(10A+A) + \cos(10A-A)]]}{[\cos(4A-3A) - \cos(4A+3A) - [\cos(5A-2A) - \cos(5A+2A)] + [\cos(7A-4A) - \cos(7A+4A)]]}$$

$$= \frac{\cos 5A + \cos A - \cos 9A - \cos 5A + \cos 11A + \cos 9A}{\cos A - \cos 7A - \cos 3A + \cos 7A + \cos 3A - \cos 11A}$$

$$= \frac{\cos A + \cos 11A}{\cos A - \cos 11A}$$

$$= \frac{2\cos\left(\frac{A+11A}{2}\right)\cos\left(\frac{A-11A}{2}\right)}{2\sin\left(\frac{A+11A}{2}\right)\sin\left(\frac{11A-A}{2}\right)}$$

$$\left[\begin{array}{l} \because \cos C + \cos D = 2\cos\left(\frac{C+D}{2}\right)\cos\left(\frac{C-D}{2}\right) \\ \text{and} \cos C - \cos D = -2\sin\left(\frac{C+D}{2}\right)\cdot\sin\left(\frac{C-D}{2}\right) \\ \qquad = 2\sin\left(\frac{C+D}{2}\right)\sin\left(\frac{D-C}{2}\right) \end{array}\right]$$

$$= \frac{\cos 6A \cdot \cos 5A}{\sin 6A \cdot \sin 5A} \qquad [\because \cos(-\theta) = \cos\theta]$$

$= \cot 6A \cdot \cot 5A = \text{RHS}$ **Hence proved.**

Example 21 Prove that

$$\left(\frac{\cos A + \cos B}{\sin A - \sin B}\right)^n + \left(\frac{\sin A + \sin B}{\cos A - \cos B}\right)^n = \begin{cases} 2\cot^n\left(\frac{A-B}{2}\right), & n \text{ is even} \\ 0, & n \text{ is odd.} \end{cases}$$

Sol. $\text{LHS} = \left(\frac{\cos A + \cos B}{\sin A - \sin B}\right)^n + \left(\frac{\sin A + \sin B}{\cos A - \cos B}\right)^n$

$$= \left[\frac{2\cos\left(\frac{A+B}{2}\right)\cos\left(\frac{A-B}{2}\right)}{2\cos\left(\frac{A+B}{2}\right)\sin\left(\frac{A-B}{2}\right)}\right]^n + \left[\frac{2\sin\left(\frac{A+B}{2}\right)\cos\left(\frac{A-B}{2}\right)}{-2\sin\left(\frac{A+B}{2}\right)\sin\left(\frac{A-B}{2}\right)}\right]^n$$

$$= \left[\frac{\cos\left(\frac{A-B}{2}\right)}{\sin\left(\frac{A-B}{2}\right)}\right]^n + \left[-\frac{\cos\left(\frac{A-B}{2}\right)}{\sin\left(\frac{A-B}{2}\right)}\right]^n$$

$$\Rightarrow \text{LHS} = \cot^n\left(\frac{A-B}{2}\right) + (-1)^n\cot^n\left(\frac{A-B}{2}\right)$$

Now, there are two cases arise.

Case **I** When n is even, then

$$\cot^n\left(\frac{A-B}{2}\right) + \cot^n\left(\frac{A-B}{2}\right) \qquad [\because (-1)^n = 1, \text{ if } n \text{ is even}]$$

$$= 2\cot^n\left(\frac{A-B}{2}\right)$$

Case **II** When n is odd, then

$$\cot^n\left(\frac{A-B}{2}\right) - \cot^n\left(\frac{A-B}{2}\right) \qquad [\because (-1)^n = -1, \text{ if } n \text{ is odd}]$$

$$= 0$$

$$\text{Hence, LHS} = \begin{cases} 2\cot^n\left(\frac{A-B}{2}\right), & n \\ & n \end{cases}$$

Example 22 If $\sin\theta + \sin\phi = \sqrt{3}(\cos\phi - \cos\theta)$, prove that $\sin 3\theta + \sin 3\phi = 0$.

Sol. Given, $\sin\theta + \sin\phi = \sqrt{3}(\cos\phi - \cos\theta)$

$$\Rightarrow 2\sin\left(\frac{\theta+\phi}{2}\right)\cos\left(\frac{\theta-\phi}{2}\right) = 2\sqrt{3}\sin\left(\frac{\theta+\phi}{2}\right)\sin\left(\frac{\theta-\phi}{2}\right)$$

$$\Rightarrow 2\sin\left(\frac{\theta+\phi}{2}\right)\left[\cos\left(\frac{\theta-\phi}{2}\right) - \sqrt{3}\sin\left(\frac{\theta-\phi}{2}\right)\right] = 0$$

$$\Rightarrow \sin\left(\frac{\theta+\phi}{2}\right) = 0 \text{ or } \cos\left(\frac{\theta-\phi}{2}\right) - \sqrt{3}\sin\left(\frac{\theta-\phi}{2}\right) = 0$$

$$\Rightarrow \sin\left(\frac{\theta+\phi}{2}\right) = 0$$

$$\text{or} \quad \tan\left(\frac{\theta-\phi}{2}\right) = \frac{1}{\sqrt{3}}$$

$$\Rightarrow \left(\frac{\theta+\phi}{2}\right) = 0 \quad \text{or} \quad \left(\frac{\theta-\phi}{2}\right) = \frac{\pi}{6}$$

$$\left[\because \sin 0 = 0 \text{ and } \tan\frac{\pi}{6} = \frac{1}{\sqrt{3}}\right]$$

$$\Rightarrow \theta = -\phi \text{ or } \theta - \phi = \frac{\pi}{3}$$

Now, there are two cases.

Case **I** When $\theta = -\phi$, then

$$\sin 3\theta + \sin 3\phi = \sin 3(-\phi) + \sin 3\phi$$
$$= -\sin 3\phi + \sin 3\phi = 0$$

Case **II** When $\theta - \phi = \frac{\pi}{3}$, then $3\theta - 3\phi = \pi$

$$\Rightarrow 3\theta = \pi + 3\phi$$

$$\therefore \sin 3\theta + \sin 3\phi = \sin(\pi + 3\phi) + \sin 3\phi$$
$$= -\sin 3\phi + \sin 3\phi \qquad [\because \sin(\pi + \theta) = -\sin\theta]$$
$$= 0$$

Topic Practice 4

Very Short Answer Type Questions

(2 Marks)

1 Convert each of the following products into the sum or difference of sines and cosines and hence, find the value.

(i) $2\cos 22\frac{1^\circ}{2}\cdot\cos 67\frac{1^\circ}{2}$

(ii) $\sin\frac{5\pi}{12}\sin\frac{\pi}{12}$

(iii) $\sin 75^\circ\cos 15^\circ$

2 Show that

$$\tan(60^\circ+\theta)\tan(60^\circ-\theta)=\frac{2\cos 2\theta+1}{2\cos 2\theta-1}.$$

3 Prove that $\sin 50^\circ\cos 85^\circ=\frac{1-\sqrt{2}\sin 35^\circ}{2\sqrt{2}}$.

4 Express each of the following as a product.

(i) $\sin 4\theta+\sin 2\theta$ (ii) $\sin 6\theta-\sin 2\theta$

(iii) $\cos 4\theta+\cos 8\theta$ (iv) $\cos 6\theta-\cos 8\theta$

5 Prove that

$$2\cos\frac{\pi}{13}\cos\frac{9\pi}{13}+\cos\frac{3\pi}{13}+\cos\frac{5\pi}{13}=0.$$

[NCERT]

6 Prove that

$$\cos 55^\circ+\cos 65^\circ+\cos 75^\circ=2\cos 40^\circ\cos 35^\circ.$$

7 Prove that $\sin 65^\circ+\cos 65^\circ=\sqrt{2}\cos 20^\circ$.

8 Prove that $\sin 47^\circ+\cos 77^\circ=\cos 17^\circ$.

9 Prove that

(i) $\frac{\sin A+\sin B}{\sin A-\sin B}=\tan\left(\frac{A+B}{2}\right)\cot\left(\frac{A-B}{2}\right)$

(ii) $\frac{\sin A+\sin 3A}{\cos A-\cos 3A}=\cot A.$

10 Prove that

(i) $\frac{\sin 9A-\sin 7A}{\cos 7A-\cos 9A}=\cot 8A$

(ii) $\frac{\cos A+\cos B}{\cos B-\cos A}=\cot\left(\frac{A+B}{2}\right)\cot\left(\frac{A-B}{2}\right).$

Short Answer Type Questions

(4 Marks)

11 Prove that $\cos 20^\circ\cos 40^\circ\cos 60^\circ\cos 80^\circ=\frac{1}{16}$.

12 Prove that $\sin 20^\circ\sin 40^\circ\sin 60^\circ\sin 80^\circ=\frac{3}{16}$.

13 If $\alpha+\beta=90^\circ$, find the maximum and minimum values of $\sin\alpha\sin\beta$.

14 If $\alpha+\beta=90^\circ$, then show that maximum value of $\cos\alpha\cos\beta$ is $\frac{1}{2}$.

Directions (Q. Nos. 15-19) *Prove each of the following.*

15 $\frac{\cos 3A+2\cos 5A+\cos 7A}{\cos A+2\cos 3A+\cos 5A}=\frac{\cos 5A}{\cos 3A}$

16 $\frac{\sin 3A+\sin 5A+\sin 7A+\sin 9A}{\cos 3A+\cos 5A+\cos 7A+\cos 9A}=\tan 6A$

17 $\frac{\sin 5A\cos 2A-\sin 6A\cos A}{\sin A\sin 2A-\cos 2A\cos 3A}=\tan A$

18 $\frac{\sin A\sin 2A+\sin 3A\cdot\sin 6A}{\sin A\cdot\cos 2A+\sin 3A\cdot\cos 6A}=\tan 5A$

19 $\frac{\sin(\theta+\phi)-2\sin\theta+\sin(\theta-\phi)}{\cos(\theta+\phi)-2\cos\theta+\cos(\theta-\phi)}=\tan\theta$

20 If $\cos x+\cos y=\frac{1}{3}$ and $\sin x+\sin y=\frac{1}{4}$, then prove that $\tan\left(\frac{x+y}{2}\right)=\frac{3}{4}$.

Long Answer Type Questions

(6 Marks)

21 If $\frac{\cos(A-B)}{\cos(A+B)}+\frac{\cos(C+D)}{\cos(C-D)}=0$, then prove that $\tan A\tan B\tan C\tan D=-1$.

22 Prove that
$4\sin A\cdot\sin(60^\circ-A)\cdot\sin(60^\circ+A)=\sin 3A.$
Hence, deduce that
$\sin 20^\circ\sin 40^\circ\sin 60^\circ\sin 80^\circ=\frac{3}{16}$.

23 If $\sin B=3\sin(2A+B)$, then prove that $2\tan A+\tan(A+B)=0$.

24 If $\cos(\theta+\phi)=m\cos(\theta-\phi)$, then prove that $\tan\theta=\frac{1-m}{1+m}\cot\phi$.

[NCERT Exemplar]

25 If $a\sin\theta = b\sin\left(\theta+\frac{2\pi}{3}\right) = c\sin\left(\theta+\frac{4\pi}{3}\right)$, then prove that $ab+bc+ca=0$.

26 If $x\cos\theta = y\cos\left(\theta+\frac{2\pi}{3}\right) = z\cos\left(\theta+\frac{4\pi}{3}\right)$, then show that $xy+yz+zx=0$.

Hints & Answers

1. (i) $2\cos 22\frac{1°}{2}\cdot\cos 67\frac{1°}{2}$

$= \cos\left(22\frac{1}{2}+67\frac{1}{2}\right)^\circ + \cos\left(22\frac{1}{2}-67\frac{1}{2}\right)^\circ$

Ans. $\frac{1}{\sqrt{2}}$

(ii) $\sin\frac{5\pi}{12}\cdot\sin\frac{\pi}{12} = \frac{1}{2}\left[2\sin\frac{5\pi}{12}\cdot\sin\frac{\pi}{12}\right]$

$= \frac{1}{2}\left[\cos\left(\frac{5\pi}{12}-\frac{\pi}{12}\right)-\cos\left(\frac{5\pi}{12}+\frac{\pi}{12}\right)\right]$

Ans. $\frac{1}{4}$

(iii) $\frac{2+\sqrt{3}}{4}$

2. $\text{LHS} = \frac{\sin(60°+\theta)\sin(60°-\theta)}{\cos(60°+\theta)\cos(60°-\theta)}\times\frac{2}{2}$

$= \frac{\cos(2\theta)-\cos(120°)}{\cos 120°+\cos 2\theta} = \frac{\cos 2\theta+\frac{1}{2}}{\left(-\frac{1}{2}\right)+\cos 2\theta}$

3. $\text{LHS} = \frac{1}{2}[2\sin 50°\cos 85°] = \frac{1}{2}[\sin 135° - \sin 35°]$

$= \frac{1}{2}[\sin(90°+45°)-\sin 35°] = \frac{1}{2}[\cos 45° - \sin 35°]$

4. (i) $2\sin 3\theta\cos\theta$

(ii) $2\cos 4\theta\sin 2\theta$

(iii) $2\cos 6\theta\cos 2\theta$

(iv) $2\sin 7\theta\sin\theta$

5. $\text{LHS} = 2\cos\frac{\pi}{13}\cos\frac{9\pi}{13}+2\cos\frac{4\pi}{13}\cos\left(\frac{-\pi}{13}\right)$

$= 2\cos\left(\frac{\pi}{13}\right)\left[\cos\frac{9\pi}{13}+\cos\frac{4\pi}{13}\right]$

$= 2\cos\left(\frac{\pi}{13}\right)\times 2\cos\frac{\pi}{2}\cos\frac{5\pi}{26}$

$= 4\cos\frac{\pi}{13}\times 0\times\cos\frac{5\pi}{26}$

6. $(\cos 55°+\cos 65°)+\cos 75°$

$= 2\cos 60°\cos 5°+\cos 75°$

$= \cos 5° + \cos 75°$

7. $\sin 65°+\cos 65° = \sin 65° + \cos(90°-25°)$

$= \sin 65°+\sin 25° = 2\sin 45°\cos 20°$

8. Solve as Q. 7.

9. (i) $\text{LHS} = \dfrac{2\sin\left(\frac{A+B}{2}\right)\cos\left(\frac{A-B}{2}\right)}{2\cos\left(\frac{A+B}{2}\right)\sin\left(\frac{A-B}{2}\right)}$

(ii) $\text{LHS} = \dfrac{2\sin 2A\cos A}{2\sin 2A\sin A}$

10. Solve as Q. 9.

11. Solve as Example 8.

12. Solve as Example 8.

13. Let $x = \sin\alpha\cdot\sin\beta$

$\Rightarrow\quad x = \frac{1}{2}(2\sin\alpha\sin\beta) = \frac{1}{2}[\cos(\alpha-\beta)-\cos(\alpha+\beta)]$

$= \frac{1}{2}[\cos(\alpha-\beta)-\cos 90°]\quad [\because \alpha+\beta=90°]$

$= \frac{1}{2}[\cos(\alpha-\beta)-0] = \frac{1}{2}\cos(\alpha-\beta)$

Now, as $-1\le\cos(\alpha-\beta)\le 1$

$\therefore\quad -\frac{1}{2}\le\frac{1}{2}\cos(\alpha-\beta)\le\frac{1}{2}$

$\Rightarrow\quad -\frac{1}{2}\le x\le\frac{1}{2} \Rightarrow -\frac{1}{2}\le\sin\alpha\sin\beta\le\frac{1}{2}$

Ans. $\frac{1}{2}$ and $-\frac{1}{2}$

14. Let $x = \cos\alpha\cos\beta = \frac{1}{2}[2\cos\alpha\cos\beta]$

$= \frac{1}{2}[\cos(\alpha+\beta)+\cos(\alpha-\beta)]$

$= \frac{1}{2}[\cos 90°+\cos(\alpha-\beta)] = \frac{1}{2}[\cos(\alpha-\beta)]$

since $-1\le\cos(\alpha-\beta)\le 1$

$\therefore\quad -\frac{1}{2}\le\frac{1}{2}\cos(\alpha-\beta)\le\frac{1}{2}\ \Rightarrow -\frac{1}{2}\le x\le\frac{1}{2}$

15. $\text{LHS} = \dfrac{\cos 3A+\cos 7A+2\cos 5A}{\cos A+\cos 5A+2\cos 3A}$

$= \dfrac{2\cos 5A\cos 2A+2\cos 5A}{2\cos 3A\cos 2A+2\cos 3A} = \dfrac{2\cos 5A}{2\cos 3A}$

16. $\text{LHS} = \dfrac{(\sin 3A+\sin 9A)+(\sin 5A+\sin 7A)}{(\cos 3A+\cos 9A)+(\cos 5A+\cos 7A)}$

$= \dfrac{2\sin 6A\cos 3A+2\sin 6A\cos A}{2\cos 6A\cos 3A+2\cos 6A\cos A} = \dfrac{2\sin 6A}{2\cos 6A}$

17. $\text{LHS} = \dfrac{2\sin 5A\cos 2A-2\sin 6A\cos A}{2\sin A\sin 2A-2\cos 2A\cos 3A}$

$= \dfrac{(\sin 7A+\sin 3A)-(\sin 7A+\sin 5A)}{\cos(A)-\cos 3A-(\cos 5A+\cos A)}$

$= \dfrac{\sin 3A-\sin 5A}{-(\cos 3A+\cos 5A)} = \dfrac{2\cos 4A\sin(-A)}{-2\cos 4A\cos A}$

18. Solve as Q.17.

19. LHS $= \dfrac{\sin(\theta+\phi)+\sin(\theta-\phi)-2\sin\theta}{\cos(\theta+\phi)+\cos(\theta-\phi)-2\cos\theta}$

$= \dfrac{2\sin\theta\cos\phi-2\sin\theta}{2\cos\theta\cos\phi-2\cos\phi} = \dfrac{2\sin\theta(\cos\phi-1)}{2\cos\theta(\cos\phi-1)}$

20. $\because \cos x+\cos y=\dfrac{1}{3} \Rightarrow 2\cos\left(\dfrac{x+y}{2}\right)\cos\left(\dfrac{x-y}{2}\right)=\dfrac{1}{3}$

and $\sin x+\sin y=\dfrac{1}{4} \Rightarrow 2\sin\left(\dfrac{x+y}{2}\right)\cos\left(\dfrac{x-y}{2}\right)=\dfrac{1}{4}$

21. $\dfrac{\cos(A-B)}{\cos(A+B)}+\dfrac{\cos(C+D)}{\cos(C-D)}=0$

$\Rightarrow \dfrac{\cos(A-B)}{\cos(A+B)}=\dfrac{-\cos(C+D)}{\cos(C-D)}$

$\Rightarrow \dfrac{\cos(A-B)+\cos(A+B)}{\cos(A-B)-\cos(A+B)}$

$= \dfrac{-\cos(C+D)+\cos(C-D)}{-\cos(C+D)-\cos(C-D)}$

[applying componendo and dividendo rule]

$\Rightarrow \dfrac{\cos(A+B)+\cos(A-B)}{\cos(A-B)-\cos(A+B)}$

$= \dfrac{\cos(C-D)-\cos(C+D)}{-[\cos(C+D)+\cos(C-D)]}$

$\Rightarrow \dfrac{2\cos A\cos B}{2\sin A\sin B}=-\dfrac{2\sin C\sin D}{2\cos C\cos D}$

$\Rightarrow \dfrac{1}{\tan A\tan B}=-\tan C\tan D$

22. LHS $=\sin A\sin(60°-A)\sin(60°+A)$

$=\dfrac{1}{2}\sin A[2\sin(60°-A)\sin(60°+A)]$

$=\dfrac{1}{2}\sin A\,[\cos\{(60°-A)-(60°+A)\}$

$-\cos\{(60°-A)+(60°+A)\}]$

$=\dfrac{1}{2}\sin A[\cos(-2A)-\cos 120°]$

$=\dfrac{1}{2}\sin A\left\{\cos 2A+\dfrac{1}{2}\right\}=\dfrac{1}{2}\sin A\cos 2A+\dfrac{1}{4}\sin A$

$=\dfrac{1}{4}[\sin(A+2A)+\sin(A-2A)]+\dfrac{1}{4}\sin A$

$=\dfrac{1}{4}[\sin 3A+\sin(-A)]+\dfrac{1}{4}\sin A$

23. Given, $\sin B=3\sin(2A+B)$

$\Rightarrow \dfrac{\sin(2A+B)}{\sin B}=\dfrac{1}{3} \Rightarrow \dfrac{\sin\{(A+B)+A\}}{\sin\{(A+B)-A\}}=\dfrac{1}{3}$

$\Rightarrow \dfrac{\sin\{(A+B)+A\}+\sin\{(A+B)-A\}}{\sin\{(A+B)+A\}-\sin\{(A+B)-A\}}=\dfrac{4}{-2}$

[applying componendo and dividendo rule]

$\Rightarrow \dfrac{2\sin(A+B)\cos A}{2\cos(A+B)\sin A}=-2$

24. Given, $\cos(\theta+\phi)=m\cos(\theta-\phi)$

$\Rightarrow \dfrac{\cos(\theta+\phi)}{\cos(\theta-\phi)}=\dfrac{m}{1} \Rightarrow \dfrac{\cos(\theta-\phi)}{\cos(\theta+\phi)}=\dfrac{1}{m}$

Using componendo and dividendo rule, we get

$\dfrac{\cos(\theta-\phi)-\cos(\theta+\phi)}{\cos(\theta-\phi)+\cos(\theta+\phi)}=\dfrac{1-m}{1+m}$

$\Rightarrow \dfrac{-2\sin\left(\dfrac{\theta-\phi+\theta+\phi}{2}\right)\cdot\sin\left(\dfrac{\theta-\phi-\theta-\phi}{2}\right)}{2\cos\left(\dfrac{\theta-\phi+\theta+\phi}{2}\right)\cdot\cos\left(\dfrac{\theta-\phi-\theta-\phi}{2}\right)}=\dfrac{1-m}{1+m}$

$\Rightarrow \dfrac{\sin\theta\cdot\sin\phi}{\cos\theta\cdot\cos\phi}=\dfrac{1-m}{1+m}$ $\left[\because \sin(-\theta)=-\sin\theta \text{ and } \cos(-\theta)=\cos\theta\right]$

$\Rightarrow \tan\theta\cdot\tan\phi=\dfrac{1-m}{1+m}$

25. Let $a\sin\theta=b\sin\left(\theta+\dfrac{2\pi}{3}\right)=c\sin\left(\theta+\dfrac{4\pi}{3}\right)=k$ (say)

$\Rightarrow \sin\theta=\dfrac{k}{a}$, $\sin\left(\theta+\dfrac{2\pi}{3}\right)=\dfrac{k}{b}$ and $\sin\left(\theta+\dfrac{4\pi}{3}\right)=\dfrac{k}{c}$

On adding these, we get

$\dfrac{k}{a}+\dfrac{k}{b}+\dfrac{k}{c}=\sin\theta+\sin\left(\theta+\dfrac{2\pi}{3}\right)+\sin\left(\theta+\dfrac{4\pi}{3}\right)$

$\Rightarrow \dfrac{k}{a}+\dfrac{k}{b}+\dfrac{k}{c}=\left[\sin\left(\theta+\dfrac{4\pi}{3}\right)+\sin\theta\right]+\sin\left(\theta+\dfrac{2\pi}{3}\right)$

$\Rightarrow \dfrac{k}{a}+\dfrac{k}{b}+\dfrac{k}{c}=-\sin\left(\theta+\dfrac{2\pi}{3}\right)+\sin\left(\theta+\dfrac{2\pi}{3}\right)$

$\Rightarrow \dfrac{1}{a}+\dfrac{1}{b}+\dfrac{1}{c}=0$ $[\because k\neq 0]$

$\Rightarrow \dfrac{bc+ca+ab}{abc}=0$

26. Solve as Q. 25.

TOPIC 05 Trigonometric Functions of Multiple and Sub-multiple Angles

Trigonometric Functions of Multiple Angles (Double and Triple)

Some important trigonometric functions of angles $2x$ and $3x$, in terms of the trigonometric functions of angle x are given below

Formula 1. $\sin 2x = 2\sin x \cos x = \dfrac{2\tan x}{1+\tan^2 x}$

Formula 2. $\cos 2x = \cos^2 x - \sin^2 x = 2\cos^2 x - 1$

$$= 1 - 2\sin^2 x = \frac{1-\tan^2 x}{1+\tan^2 x}$$

Formula 3. $\tan 2x = \dfrac{2\tan x}{1-\tan^2 x}$

Formula 4. $\cos 3x = 4\cos^3 x - 3\cos x$

Formula 5. $\sin 3x = 3\sin x - 4\sin^3 x$

Formula 6. $\tan 3x = \dfrac{3\tan x - \tan^3 x}{1 - 3\tan^2 x}$

Note $\cos x = \pm\sqrt{\dfrac{1+\cos 2x}{2}}$; $\sin x = \pm\sqrt{\dfrac{1-\cos 2x}{2}}$;

$\tan x = \pm\sqrt{\dfrac{1-\cos 2x}{1+\cos 2x}}$

Example 1 If $\cos A = \dfrac{2}{3}$, then find the value of $\cos 2A$.

Sol. Given, $\cos A = \dfrac{2}{3}$

$$\therefore \quad \cos 2A = 2\cos^2 A - 1 = 2\left(\frac{2}{3}\right)^2 - 1$$

$$= 2 \times \frac{4}{9} - 1 = \frac{8}{9} - 1 = -\frac{1}{9}$$

Example 2 Find the value of $\tan 2A$, if $\tan A = \dfrac{5}{12}$.

Sol. Given, $\tan A = \dfrac{5}{12}$

$$\therefore \quad \tan 2A = \frac{2\tan A}{1-\tan^2 A} = \frac{2 \times \frac{5}{12}}{1 - \left(\frac{5}{12}\right)^2} = \frac{\frac{5}{6}}{1 - \frac{25}{144}}$$

$$= \frac{\frac{5}{6}}{\frac{144-25}{144}} = \frac{5}{6} \times \frac{144}{119} = \frac{5 \times 24}{119} = \frac{120}{119}$$

Example 3 Find the value of $2\sin A \cos A$, if $A = 15°$.

Sol. Given, $A = 15°$

$$\therefore \quad 2\sin A \cos A = \sin 2A \qquad [\because \sin 2A = 2\sin A \cos A]$$

$$= \sin 2 \times 15°$$

$$= \sin 30° = \frac{1}{2} \qquad \left[\because \sin 30° = \frac{1}{2}\right]$$

Example 4 If $a\sin\theta = b\cos\theta$, then find the value of $\sin 2\theta$.

Sol. Given, $a\sin\theta = b\cos\theta$

$$\Rightarrow \quad \frac{\sin\theta}{\cos\theta} = \frac{b}{a} \Rightarrow \tan\theta = \frac{b}{a} \qquad \left[\because \tan\theta = \frac{\sin\theta}{\cos\theta}\right]$$

$$\therefore \quad \sin 2\theta = \frac{2\tan\theta}{1+\tan^2\theta} = \frac{2 \times \frac{b}{a}}{1 + \left(\frac{b}{a}\right)^2}$$

$$= \frac{\frac{2b}{a}}{1 + \frac{b^2}{a^2}} = \frac{\frac{2b}{a}}{\frac{a^2+b^2}{a^2}}$$

$$= \frac{2b}{a} \times \frac{a^2}{a^2+b^2} = \frac{2ab}{a^2+b^2}$$

Example 5 If $x = a\tan\theta$, then find the value of $\cos 2\theta$.

Sol. Given, $x = a\tan\theta \Rightarrow \tan\theta = \dfrac{x}{a}$ ...(i)

$$\therefore \quad \cos 2\theta = \frac{1-\tan^2\theta}{1+\tan^2\theta} = \frac{1 - \left(\frac{x}{a}\right)^2}{1 + \left(\frac{x}{a}\right)^2} = \frac{1 - \frac{x^2}{a^2}}{1 + \frac{x^2}{a^2}} = \frac{\frac{a^2-x^2}{a^2}}{\frac{a^2+x^2}{a^2}}$$

$$= \frac{a^2-x^2}{a^2} \times \frac{a^2}{a^2+x^2} = \frac{a^2-x^2}{a^2+x^2}$$

Example 6 Prove that $\cos 4x = 1 - 8\sin^2 x \cos^2 x$. **[NCERT]**

Sol. LHS $= \cos 4x = \cos 2(2x) = 1 - 2\sin^2 2x$

$$[\because \cos 2\theta = 1 - 2\sin^2\theta]$$

$$= 1 - 2(\sin 2x)^2$$

$$= 1 - 2(2\sin x \cdot \cos x)^2 \qquad [\because \sin 2\theta = 2\sin\theta\cos\theta]$$

$$= 1 - 8\sin^2 x \cdot \cos^2 x = \text{RHS}$$

Hence proved.

Example 7 Prove that

$$\sin A \sin (60° - A) \sin (60° + A) = \frac{1}{4} \sin 3A.$$

Sol. LHS $= \sin A \sin (60° - A) \sin (60° + A)$

$= \sin A (\sin^2 60° - \sin^2 A)$ $\quad [\because \sin (A+B) \sin (A-B) = \sin^2 A - \sin^2 B]$

$= \sin A \left(\frac{3}{4} - \sin^2 A\right)$ $\quad \left[\because \sin 60° = \frac{\sqrt{3}}{2}\right]$

$= \frac{1}{4} \sin A (3 - 4\sin^2 A)$

$= \frac{1}{4}(3\sin A - 4\sin^3 A) = \frac{1}{4} \sin 3A =$ RHS **Hence proved.**

Example 8 Prove that

$$\cot A + \cot (60° + A) - \cot (60° - A) = 3 \cot 3A.$$

Sol. LHS $= \cot A + \cot (60° + A) - \cot (60° - A)$

$$= \frac{1}{\tan A} + \frac{1}{\tan (60° + A)} - \frac{1}{\tan (60° - A)}$$

$$= \frac{1}{\tan A} + \frac{1}{\frac{\tan 60° + \tan A}{1 - \tan 60° \tan A}} - \frac{1}{\frac{\tan 60° - \tan A}{1 + \tan 60° \tan A}}$$

$$= \frac{1}{\tan A} + \frac{1 - \sqrt{3}\tan A}{\sqrt{3} + \tan A} - \frac{1 + \sqrt{3}\tan A}{\sqrt{3} - \tan A}$$

$$\left[\because \tan (A \pm B) = \frac{\tan A \pm \tan B}{1 \mp \tan A \tan B} \text{ and } \tan 60° = \sqrt{3}\right]$$

$$= \frac{1}{\tan A} - \frac{8\tan A}{3 - \tan^2 A} = \frac{3 - 9\tan^2 A}{3\tan A - \tan^3 A}$$

$$= 3\left(\frac{1 - 3\tan^2 A}{3\tan A - \tan^3 A}\right) = \frac{3}{\tan 3A} = 3\cot 3A = \text{RHS}$$

Hence proved.

Example 9 If $\sin A = \frac{3}{5}$ and A is in I quadrant, then find the values of $\sin 2A$, $\cos 2A$ and $\tan 2A$.

Sol. We have, $\sin A = \frac{3}{5} \Rightarrow \cos A = +\sqrt{1 - \sin^2 A}$

$[\because \sin^2 A + \cos^2 A = 1 \Rightarrow \cos^2 A = 1 - \sin^2 A]$

$$= \sqrt{1 - \frac{9}{25}} = \sqrt{\frac{16}{25}} = \frac{4}{5}$$

and $\quad \tan A = \frac{\sin A}{\cos A} = \frac{3/5}{4/5} = \frac{3}{4}$

Now, $\sin 2A = 2\sin A \cdot \cos A = 2 \times \frac{3}{5} \times \frac{4}{5} = \frac{24}{25}$

$$\cos 2A = 1 - 2\sin^2 A = 1 - 2 \times \frac{9}{25} = 1 - \frac{18}{25} = \frac{7}{25}$$

and $\quad \tan 2A = \frac{2\tan A}{1 - \tan^2 A} = \frac{2 \times \frac{3}{4}}{1 - \frac{9}{16}} = \frac{24}{7}$

Example 10 If $\cos\alpha + \cos\beta = 0 = \sin\alpha + \sin\beta$, then find the value of $\cos 2\alpha + \cos 2\beta$. **[NCERT Exemplar]**

Sol. Given, $\cos\alpha + \cos\beta = 0$ and $\sin\alpha + \sin\beta = 0$

On squaring both equations, we get

$$(\cos\alpha + \cos\beta)^2 = 0 \quad \text{...(i)}$$

and $\quad (\sin\alpha + \sin\beta)^2 = 0 \quad$ ...(ii)

On subtracting Eq. (ii) from Eq. (i), we get

$$(\cos\alpha + \cos\beta)^2 - (\sin\alpha + \sin\beta)^2 = 0$$

$\Rightarrow \quad (\cos^2\alpha + \cos^2\beta + 2\cos\alpha\cos\beta) - (\sin^2\alpha + \sin^2\beta + 2\sin\alpha\sin\beta) = 0$

$[\because (a+b)^2 = a^2 + b^2 + 2ab]$

$\Rightarrow \cos^2\alpha + \cos^2\beta + 2\cos\alpha\cos\beta - \sin^2\alpha - \sin^2\beta - 2\sin\alpha\sin\beta = 0$

$\Rightarrow \quad (\cos^2\alpha - \sin^2\alpha) + (\cos^2\beta - \sin^2\beta) + 2[\cos\alpha\cos\beta - \sin\alpha\sin\beta] = 0$

$\Rightarrow \quad \cos 2\alpha + \cos 2\beta + 2\cos(\alpha + \beta) = 0$

$\left[\begin{array}{l}\because \cos 2x = \cos^2 x - \sin^2 x \text{ and} \\ \cos A\cos B - \sin A\sin B = \cos(A+B)\end{array}\right]$

$\therefore \quad \cos 2\alpha + \cos 2\beta = -2\cos(\alpha + \beta)$

Example 11 Prove that

$$\cos 5A = 16\cos^5 A - 20\cos^3 A + 5\cos A.$$

Sol. LHS $= \cos 5A = \cos (3A + 2A)$

$= \cos 3A \cdot \cos 2A - \sin 3A \cdot \sin 2A$

$[\because \cos (A+B) = \cos A \cdot \cos B - \sin A \cdot \sin B]$

$= (4\cos^3 A - 3\cos A)(2\cos^2 A - 1) - (3\sin A - 4\sin^3 A)(2\sin A \cdot \cos A)$

$[\because \cos 3x = 4\cos^3 x - 3\cos x,$
$\sin 3x = 3\sin x - 4\sin^3 x,$
$\cos 2x = 2\cos^2 x - 1$ and $\sin 2x = 2\sin x \cdot \cos x]$

$= (4\cos^3 A - 3\cos A)(2\cos^2 A - 1) - (3 - 4\sin^2 A)(2\sin^2 A \cdot \cos A)$

$= (4\cos^3 A - 3\cos A)(2\cos^2 A - 1) - [3 - 4(1 - \cos^2 A)] \times [2(1 - \cos^2 A) \cdot \cos A]$

$[\because \sin^2 x + \cos^2 x = 1 \Rightarrow \sin^2 x = 1 - \cos^2 x]$

$= (8\cos^5 A - 4\cos^3 A - 6\cos^3 A + 3\cos A) - (3 - 4 + 4\cos^2 A) \times 2\cos A(1 - \cos^2 A)$

$= (8\cos^5 A - 10\cos^3 A + 3\cos A) - 2\cos A(1 - \cos^2 A) \times (4\cos^2 A - 1)$

$= (8\cos^5 A - 10\cos^3 A + 3\cos A) - 2\cos A(4\cos^2 A - 1 - 4\cos^4 A + \cos^2 A)$

$= (8\cos^5 A - 10\cos^3 A + 3\cos A) - 2\cos A(5\cos^2 A - 4\cos^4 A - 1)$

$= 8\cos^5 A - 10\cos^3 A + 3\cos A - 10\cos^3 A + 8\cos^5 A + 2\cos A$

$= 16\cos^5 A - 20\cos^3 A + 5\cos A = \text{RHS}$

Hence proved.

Example 12 Prove that

$\cos 6x = 32\cos^6 x - 48\cos^4 x + 18\cos^2 x - 1$. [NCERT]

Sol. We know that, $\cos 3x = 4\cos^3 x - 3\cos x$

On replacing x by $2x$, we get

$\cos 3(2x) = 4\cos^3(2x) - 3\cos 2x$

$\Rightarrow \cos 6x = 4(2\cos^2 x - 1)^3 - 3(2\cos^2 x - 1)$ $[\because \cos 2x = 2\cos^2 x - 1]$

$= 4[8\cos^6 x - 12\cos^4 x + 6\cos^2 x - 1] - 6\cos^2 x + 3$ $[\because (a-b)^3 = a^3 - 3a^2b + 3ab^2 - b^3]$

$= 32\cos^6 x - 48\cos^4 x + 24\cos^2 x - 4 - 6\cos^2 x + 3$

$\Rightarrow \cos 6x = 32\cos^6 x - 48\cos^4 x + 18\cos^2 x - 1$

Hence proved.

Example 13 Show that

$$\sqrt{2+\sqrt{2+\sqrt{2+2\cos 8\theta}}} = 2\cos\theta.$$

Sol. LHS $= \sqrt{2+\sqrt{2+\sqrt{2+2\cos 8\theta}}}$

$= \sqrt{2+\sqrt{2+\sqrt{2(1+\cos 8\theta)}}}$

$= \sqrt{2+\sqrt{2+\sqrt{2(1+2\cos^2 4\theta - 1)}}}$

$= \sqrt{2+\sqrt{2+\sqrt{4\cos^2 4\theta}}} = \sqrt{2+\sqrt{2+2\cos 4\theta}}$

$= \sqrt{2+\sqrt{2(1+\cos 4\theta)}} = \sqrt{2+\sqrt{2(1+2\cos^2 2\theta - 1)}}$

$= \sqrt{2+\sqrt{4\cos^2 2\theta}} = \sqrt{2+2\cos 2\theta}$

$= \sqrt{2(1+\cos 2\theta)} = \sqrt{2(1+2\cos^2\theta - 1)}$

$= \sqrt{4\cos^2\theta} = 2\cos\theta$ **Hence proved.**

Example 14 Prove that

$\sin 2x + 2\sin 4x + \sin 6x = 4\cos^2 x \cdot \sin 4x$. [NCERT]

Sol. LHS $= \sin 2x + 2\sin 4x + \sin 6x$

$= \sin 2x + \sin 6x + 2\sin 4x$

$= 2\sin\left(\frac{2x+6x}{2}\right)\cos\left(\frac{2x-6x}{2}\right) + 2\sin 4x$

$\left[\because \sin A + \sin B = 2\sin\left(\frac{A+B}{2}\right)\cdot\cos\left(\frac{A-B}{2}\right)\right]$

$= 2\sin 4x \cdot \cos(-2x) + 2\sin 4x$

$= 2\sin 4x \cdot \cos 2x + 2\sin 4x$ $[\because \cos(-\theta) = \cos\theta]$

$= 2\sin 4x(\cos 2x + 1)$

$= 2\sin 4x(2\cos^2 x) = 4\sin 4x \cdot \cos^2 x$

$[\because \cos 2x = 2\cos^2 x - 1]$

$\therefore$ LHS = RHS **Hence proved.**

Example 15 Prove that

$$\frac{\sin x}{\cos 3x} + \frac{\sin 3x}{\cos 9x} + \frac{\sin 9x}{\cos 27x} = \frac{1}{2}(\tan 27x - \tan x).$$

Sol. LHS $= \frac{\sin x}{\cos 3x} + \frac{\sin 3x}{\cos 9x} + \frac{\sin 9x}{\cos 27x}$

$= \frac{1}{2}\left[\frac{2\sin x\cos x}{\cos 3x\cos x} + \frac{2\sin 3x\cos 3x}{\cos 9x\cos 3x} + \frac{2\sin 9x\cos 9x}{\cos 27x\cos 9x}\right]$

$= \frac{1}{2}\left[\frac{\sin 2x}{\cos 3x\cos x} + \frac{\sin 6x}{\cos 9x\cos 3x} + \frac{\sin 18x}{\cos 27x\cos 9x}\right]$

$= \frac{1}{2}\left[\frac{\sin(3x-x)}{\cos 3x\cos x} + \frac{\sin(9x-3x)}{\cos 9x\cos 3x} + \frac{\sin(27x-9x)}{\cos 27x\cos 9x}\right]$

$= \frac{1}{2}\left[\frac{\sin 3x\cos x - \cos 3x\sin x}{\cos 3x\cos x} + \frac{\sin 9x\cos 3x - \cos 9x\sin 3x}{\cos 9x\cos 3x} + \frac{\sin 27x\cos 9x - \cos 27x\sin 9x}{\cos 27x\cos 9x}\right]$

$= \frac{1}{2}(\tan 3x - \tan x + \tan 9x - \tan 3x + \tan 27x - \tan 9x)$

$= \frac{1}{2}(\tan 27x - \tan x)$ **Hence proved.**

Example 16 If $\tan\alpha = \frac{1}{7}$, $\sin\beta = \frac{1}{\sqrt{10}}$. Prove that $\alpha + 2\beta = \frac{\pi}{4}$, where $0 < \alpha < \frac{\pi}{2}$ and $0 < \beta < \frac{\pi}{2}$.

Sol. Given, $\sin\beta = \frac{1}{\sqrt{10}}, 0 < \beta < \frac{\pi}{2}$

$\Rightarrow \cos\beta = +\sqrt{1-\sin^2\beta}$ $[\because \beta$ lies in I quadrant$]$

$\Rightarrow \cos\beta = \sqrt{1-\sin^2\beta}$

$\Rightarrow \cos\beta = \sqrt{1-\frac{1}{10}} \Rightarrow \cos\beta = \frac{3}{\sqrt{10}}$

$\tan\beta = \frac{\sin\beta}{\cos\beta} = \frac{\frac{1}{\sqrt{10}}}{\frac{3}{\sqrt{10}}} = \frac{1}{3}$

Now, $\tan 2\beta = \frac{2\tan\beta}{1-\tan^2\beta}$

$\tan 2\beta = \frac{2\times\frac{1}{3}}{1-\frac{1}{9}} = \frac{2/3}{8/9} = \frac{2}{3}\times\frac{9}{8} = \frac{3}{4}$

$\therefore \tan(\alpha+2\beta) = \frac{\tan\alpha + \tan 2\beta}{1-\tan\alpha\tan 2\beta} = \frac{\frac{1}{7}+\frac{3}{4}}{1-\frac{1}{7}\times\frac{3}{4}} = \frac{25}{25} = 1$

$\Rightarrow \tan(\alpha+2\beta) = 1 \Rightarrow \tan(\alpha+2\beta) = \tan\frac{\pi}{4}$

$\therefore (\alpha+2\beta) = \frac{\pi}{4}$ **Hence proved.**

Example 17 Prove that

$$\cos A\cdot\cos 2A\cdot\cos 2^2A\cdot\cos 2^3A\ldots\cos 2^{n-1}A=\frac{\sin 2^nA}{2^n\sin A}.$$

Sol. LHS $=\cos A\cdot\cos 2A\cdot\cos 2^2A\cdot\cos 2^3A\ldots\cos 2^{n-1}A$

$$=\frac{1}{2\sin A}[(2\sin A\cos A)\cos 2A\cos 2^2A\cdot\cos 2^3A\ldots\cos 2^{n-1}A]$$

$$=\frac{1}{2\sin A}[(\sin 2A\cos 2A)\cdot\cos 2^2A\cos 2^3A\ldots\cos 2^{n-1}A]$$

$$=\frac{1}{2^2\sin A}[(2\sin 2A\cos 2A)\cos 2^2A\cdot\cos 2^3A\ldots\cos 2^{n-1}A]$$

$$=\frac{1}{2^2\sin A}[(\sin 2^2A\cos 2^2A)\cos 2^3A\ldots\cos 2^{n-1}A]$$

$$=\frac{1}{2^3\sin A}[(2\sin 2^2A\cos 2^2A)\cos 2^3A\ldots\cos 2^{n-1}A]$$

$$=\frac{1}{2^3\sin A}[\sin 2^3A\cos 2^3A\ldots\cos 2^{n-1}A]$$

On proceeding in this manner, we get

$$\text{LHS}=\frac{1}{2^{n-1}\sin A}[\sin 2^{n-1}A\cdot\cos 2^{n-1}A]$$

$$=\frac{1}{2^n\sin A}[2\sin 2^{n-1}A\cos 2^{n-1}A]$$

$$=\frac{1}{2^n\sin A}\sin 2^nA=\text{RHS}$$

Hence proved.

Example 18 Prove that

$$\cos\frac{2\pi}{15}\cos\frac{4\pi}{15}\cos\frac{8\pi}{15}\cos\frac{16\pi}{15}=\frac{1}{16}$$

[NCERT Exemplar]

Sol. LHS $=\cos\frac{2\pi}{15}\cos\frac{4\pi}{15}\cos\frac{8\pi}{15}\cos\frac{16\pi}{15}$

$$=\cos 24^\circ\cos 48^\circ\cos 96^\circ\cos 192^\circ$$

$$=\frac{1}{16\sin 24^\circ}[(2\sin 24^\circ\cos 24^\circ)(2\cos 48^\circ)(2\cos 96^\circ)(2\cos 192^\circ)]$$

$$=\frac{1}{16\sin 24^\circ}[2\sin 48^\circ\cos 48^\circ(2\cos 96^\circ)(2\cos 192^\circ)]$$

$[\because 2\sin\theta\cos\theta=\sin 2\theta]$

$$=\frac{1}{16\sin 24^\circ}[(2\sin 96^\circ\cos 96^\circ)(2\cos 192^\circ)]$$

$$=\frac{1}{16\sin 24^\circ}(2\sin 192^\circ\cos 192^\circ)=\frac{1}{16\sin 24^\circ}\sin 384^\circ$$

$$=\frac{\sin(360^\circ+24^\circ)}{16\sin 24^\circ}=\frac{1}{16}=\text{RHS}$$

Hence proved.

Example 19 If $\tan\beta=\frac{\tan\alpha+\tan\gamma}{1+\tan\alpha\tan\gamma}$, then prove that $\sin 2\beta=\frac{\sin 2\alpha+\sin 2\gamma}{1+\sin 2\alpha\sin 2\gamma}$.

Sol. Given, $\tan\beta=\frac{\tan\alpha+\tan\gamma}{1+\tan\alpha\cdot\tan\gamma}=\frac{\frac{\sin\alpha}{\cos\alpha}+\frac{\sin\gamma}{\cos\gamma}}{1+\frac{\sin\alpha}{\cos\alpha}\cdot\frac{\sin\gamma}{\cos\gamma}}$

$$=\frac{\sin\alpha\cos\gamma+\cos\alpha\sin\gamma}{\cos\alpha\cos\gamma+\sin\alpha\sin\gamma}$$

$$\Rightarrow\quad\tan\beta=\frac{\sin(\alpha+\gamma)}{\cos(\alpha-\gamma)}$$

Now, $\sin 2\beta=\frac{2\tan\beta}{1+\tan^2\beta}=\frac{2\times\frac{\sin(\alpha+\gamma)}{\cos(\alpha-\gamma)}}{1+\frac{\sin^2(\alpha+\gamma)}{\cos^2(\alpha-\gamma)}}$

$$=\frac{2\sin(\alpha+\gamma)\cos(\alpha-\gamma)}{\cos^2(\alpha-\gamma)+\sin^2(\alpha+\gamma)}$$

$$=\frac{\sin 2\alpha+\sin 2\gamma}{\cos^2(\alpha-\gamma)+\sin^2(\alpha+\gamma)}$$

$[\because 2\sin A\cos B=\sin(A+B)+\sin(A-B)]$

$$=\frac{2(\sin 2\alpha+\sin 2\gamma)}{2\cos^2(\alpha-\gamma)+2\sin^2(\alpha+\gamma)}$$

$$=\frac{2(\sin 2\alpha+\sin 2\gamma)}{1+\cos 2(\alpha-\gamma)+1-\cos 2(\alpha+\gamma)}$$

$\left[\begin{array}{l}\because 2\cos^2A=1+\cos 2A\\ \text{and } 2\sin^2A=1-\cos 2A\end{array}\right]$

$$=\frac{2(\sin 2\alpha+\sin 2\gamma)}{2+\cos 2(\alpha-\gamma)-\cos 2(\alpha+\gamma)}$$

$$=\frac{2(\sin 2\alpha+\sin 2\gamma)}{2+2\sin 2\alpha\sin 2\gamma}=\frac{\sin 2\alpha+\sin 2\gamma}{1+\sin 2\alpha\sin 2\gamma}$$

Example 20 Prove that

$$\tan 4x=\frac{4\tan x(1-\tan^2x)}{1-6\tan^2x+\tan^4x}.$$

[NCERT]

Sol. LHS $=\tan 4x=\tan 2(2x)$

$$=\frac{2\tan 2x}{1-\tan^2 2x}=\frac{2\frac{2\tan x}{1-\tan^2x}}{1-\left(\frac{2\tan x}{1-\tan^2x}\right)^2}$$

$$=\frac{4\tan x}{1-\tan^2x}\times\frac{(1-\tan^2x)^2}{(1-\tan^2x)^2-4\tan^2x}$$

$$=\frac{4\tan x(1-\tan^2x)}{1+\tan^4x-2\tan^2x-4\tan^2x}$$

$$=\frac{4\tan x(1-\tan^2x)}{1-6\tan^2x+\tan^4x}=\text{RHS}$$

$\therefore$ LHS = RHS

Hence proved.

Example 21 Prove that $\dfrac{\tan 3x}{\tan x}$ never lies between $\dfrac{1}{3}$ and 3.

Sol. Let $y = \dfrac{\tan 3x}{\tan x}$

$\Rightarrow \quad y = \dfrac{3\tan x - \tan^3 x}{\tan x(1 - 3\tan^2 x)} \Rightarrow y = \dfrac{3 - \tan^2 x}{1 - 3\tan^2 x}$

$\Rightarrow \quad y - 3y\tan^2 x = 3 - \tan^2 x$

$\Rightarrow \quad (1 - 3y)\tan^2 x = 3 - y$

$\Rightarrow \quad \tan^2 x = \dfrac{3 - y}{1 - 3y}$

$\Rightarrow \quad \dfrac{3 - y}{1 - 3y} \geq 0 \Rightarrow \dfrac{y - 3}{3y - 1} \geq 0 \quad [\because \tan^2 x \geq 0 \text{ for all } x]$

Case I When $y - 3 \geq 0$ and $3y - 1 > 0$

$\Rightarrow \quad y \geq 3$ and $y > \dfrac{1}{3}$

$\therefore \quad y \geq 3$

Case II When $y - 3 \leq 0$ and $3y - 1 < 0$

$\Rightarrow \quad y \leq 3$ and $y < \dfrac{1}{3}$

$\therefore \quad y < \dfrac{1}{3}$

$\Rightarrow \quad y \in \left(-\infty, \dfrac{1}{3}\right) \cup [3, \infty)$

Hence, y does not lie between $\dfrac{1}{3}$ and 3.

Trigonometric Functions of Sub-Multiple Angles (Half and One-third)

Some important trigonometric functions of angle x in terms of trigonometric function of sub-multiple angles $\dfrac{x}{2}$ and $\dfrac{x}{3}$ are given below

Trigonometric Functions of Angle x in Terms of $\dfrac{x}{2}$

(i) $\sin x = 2\sin\dfrac{x}{2}\cos\dfrac{x}{2} = \dfrac{2\tan\dfrac{x}{2}}{1 + \tan^2\dfrac{x}{2}}$

(ii) $\cos x = \cos^2\left(\dfrac{x}{2}\right) - \sin^2\left(\dfrac{x}{2}\right) = 2\cos^2\left(\dfrac{x}{2}\right) - 1$

$= 1 - 2\sin^2\left(\dfrac{x}{2}\right) = \dfrac{1 - \tan^2\left(\dfrac{x}{2}\right)}{1 + \tan^2\left(\dfrac{x}{2}\right)}$

(iii) $\tan x = \dfrac{2\tan\left(\dfrac{x}{2}\right)}{1 - \tan^2\left(\dfrac{x}{2}\right)}$

Note (i) $\cos\left(\dfrac{x}{2}\right) = \pm\sqrt{\dfrac{1 + \cos x}{2}}$

(ii) $\sin\left(\dfrac{x}{2}\right) = \pm\sqrt{\dfrac{1 - \cos x}{2}}$

(iii) $\tan\dfrac{x}{2} = \pm\sqrt{\dfrac{1 - \cos x}{1 + \cos x}}$

Trigonometric Functions of Angle x in Terms of $\dfrac{x}{3}$

(i) $\sin x = 3\sin\left(\dfrac{x}{3}\right) - 4\sin^3\left(\dfrac{x}{3}\right)$

(ii) $\cos x = 4\cos^3\left(\dfrac{x}{3}\right) - 3\cos\left(\dfrac{x}{3}\right)$

(iii) $\tan x = \dfrac{3\tan\left(\dfrac{x}{3}\right) - \tan^3\left(\dfrac{x}{3}\right)}{1 - 3\tan^2\left(\dfrac{x}{3}\right)}$

Example 22 Find the value of $\sin 22\dfrac{1^\circ}{2}$.

Sol. We know that,

$\cos A = 1 - 2\sin^2\dfrac{A}{2}$

$\Rightarrow \quad 2\sin^2\dfrac{A}{2} = 1 - \cos A$

$\Rightarrow \quad \sin^2\dfrac{A}{2} = \dfrac{1 - \cos A}{2}$

$\Rightarrow \quad \sin\dfrac{A}{2} = \pm\sqrt{\dfrac{1 - \cos A}{2}}$

$\therefore \quad \sin 22\dfrac{1^\circ}{2} = \sin\dfrac{45^\circ}{2} = \sqrt{\dfrac{1 - \cos 45^\circ}{2}}$

$\left[\because \dfrac{45^\circ}{2} \text{ lies in I quadrant}\right]$

$= \sqrt{\dfrac{1 - \dfrac{1}{\sqrt{2}}}{2}} = \sqrt{\dfrac{\dfrac{\sqrt{2} - 1}{\sqrt{2}}}{2}} \quad \left[\because \cos 45^\circ = \dfrac{1}{\sqrt{2}}\right]$

$\Rightarrow \quad \sin\dfrac{45^\circ}{2} = \sqrt{\dfrac{\sqrt{2} - 1}{2\sqrt{2}}}$

$= \sqrt{\dfrac{\sqrt{2} - 1}{2\sqrt{2}} \times \dfrac{\sqrt{2}}{\sqrt{2}}}$

$= \sqrt{\dfrac{2 - \sqrt{2}}{4}}$

$\therefore \quad \sin 22\dfrac{1^\circ}{2} = \dfrac{\sqrt{2 - \sqrt{2}}}{2}$

Example 23 Prove that $\dfrac{1+\sin A-\cos A}{1+\sin A+\cos A}=\tan\dfrac{A}{2}$.

Sol. LHS $=\dfrac{1+\sin A-\cos A}{1+\sin A+\cos A}=\dfrac{1-\cos A+\sin A}{1+\cos A+\sin A}$

$$=\frac{1-\left(1-2\sin^2\dfrac{A}{2}\right)+\sin A}{1+\left(2\cos^2\dfrac{A}{2}-1\right)+\sin A}$$

$$\left[\because \cos A=1-2\sin^2\frac{A}{2}=2\cos^2\frac{A}{2}-1\right]$$

$$=\frac{1-1+2\sin^2\dfrac{A}{2}+\sin A}{1+2\cos^2\dfrac{A}{2}-1+\sin A}=\frac{2\sin^2\dfrac{A}{2}+\sin A}{2\cos^2\dfrac{A}{2}+\sin A}$$

$$=\frac{2\sin^2\dfrac{A}{2}+2\sin\dfrac{A}{2}\cos\dfrac{A}{2}}{2\cos^2\dfrac{A}{2}+2\sin\dfrac{A}{2}\cos\dfrac{A}{2}}$$

$$\left[\because \sin A=2\sin\frac{A}{2}\cos\frac{A}{2}\right]$$

$$=\frac{2\sin\dfrac{A}{2}\left(\sin\dfrac{A}{2}+\cos\dfrac{A}{2}\right)}{2\cos\dfrac{A}{2}\left(\sin\dfrac{A}{2}+\cos\dfrac{A}{2}\right)}$$

$$=\frac{\sin\dfrac{A}{2}}{\cos\dfrac{A}{2}}=\tan\frac{A}{2}\qquad\left[\because \frac{\sin\theta}{\cos\theta}=\tan\theta\right]$$

= RHS **Hence proved.**

Example 24 If $\tan\dfrac{\theta}{2}=\sqrt{\dfrac{1-e}{1+e}}\tan\dfrac{\phi}{2}$, then prove that $\cos\phi=\dfrac{\cos\theta-e}{1-e\cos\theta}$.

Sol. Given, $\tan\dfrac{\theta}{2}=\sqrt{\dfrac{1-e}{1+e}}\tan\dfrac{\phi}{2}\Rightarrow\tan\dfrac{\phi}{2}=\sqrt{\dfrac{1+e}{1-e}}\tan\dfrac{\theta}{2}$

We know that, $\cos\phi=\dfrac{1-\tan^2\dfrac{\phi}{2}}{1+\tan^2\dfrac{\phi}{2}}$

$$\Rightarrow\quad \cos\phi=\frac{1-\dfrac{1+e}{1-e}\tan^2\dfrac{\theta}{2}}{1+\dfrac{1+e}{1-e}\tan^2\dfrac{\theta}{2}}$$

$$\Rightarrow\quad \cos\phi=\frac{(1-e)-(1+e)\tan^2\dfrac{\theta}{2}}{(1-e)+(1+e)\tan^2\dfrac{\theta}{2}}$$

$$\Rightarrow\quad \cos\phi=\frac{(1-e)\cos^2\dfrac{\theta}{2}-(1+e)\sin^2\dfrac{\theta}{2}}{(1-e)\cos^2\dfrac{\theta}{2}+(1+e)\sin^2\dfrac{\theta}{2}}$$

$$=\frac{\cos^2\dfrac{\theta}{2}-\sin^2\dfrac{\theta}{2}-e\left(\cos^2\dfrac{\theta}{2}+\sin^2\dfrac{\theta}{2}\right)}{\left(\cos^2\dfrac{\theta}{2}+\sin^2\dfrac{\theta}{2}\right)-e\left(\cos^2\dfrac{\theta}{2}-\sin^2\dfrac{\theta}{2}\right)}$$

$$=\frac{\cos\theta-e}{1-e\cos\theta}$$

Hence proved.

Example 25 If $\tan x=\dfrac{3}{4}$, where $\pi<x<\dfrac{3\pi}{2}$, then find the values of $\sin\dfrac{x}{2}$, $\cos\dfrac{x}{2}$ and $\tan\dfrac{x}{2}$. **[NCERT]**

Sol. Given, $\tan x=\dfrac{3}{4}$, $\pi<x<\dfrac{3\pi}{2}$

$$\because\quad \cos x=\pm\frac{1}{\sqrt{1+\tan^2 x}}$$

$$\therefore\quad \cos x=-\frac{1}{\sqrt{1+\tan^2 x}}\qquad[\because x \text{ lies in III quadrant}]$$

$$\Rightarrow\quad \cos x=-\frac{1}{\sqrt{1+\dfrac{9}{16}}}=-\frac{4}{\sqrt{25}}$$

$$\Rightarrow\quad \cos x=-\frac{4}{5}$$

Now, $\cos\dfrac{x}{2}=-\sqrt{\dfrac{1+\cos x}{2}}=-\sqrt{\dfrac{1-\dfrac{4}{5}}{2}}=-\dfrac{1}{\sqrt{10}}$

$$\left[\begin{array}{l}\because \cos A=2\cos^2\dfrac{A}{2}-1\Rightarrow\cos\dfrac{A}{2}=\pm\sqrt{\dfrac{1+\cos A}{2}}\\ \text{and } \cos A=1-2\sin^2\dfrac{A}{2}\Rightarrow\sin\dfrac{A}{2}=\pm\sqrt{\dfrac{1-\cos A}{2}}\\ \text{Also, } \pi<x<\dfrac{3\pi}{2}\Rightarrow\dfrac{\pi}{2}<\dfrac{x}{2}<\dfrac{3\pi}{4}\Rightarrow\cos\dfrac{x}{2}<0,\ \sin\dfrac{x}{2}>0\end{array}\right]$$

$$\sin\frac{x}{2}=\sqrt{\frac{1-\cos x}{2}}=\sqrt{\frac{1+4/5}{2}}=\sqrt{\frac{9}{10}}=\frac{3}{\sqrt{10}}$$

and $\tan\dfrac{x}{2}=\dfrac{\sin x/2}{\cos x/2}=\dfrac{3/\sqrt{10}}{-1/\sqrt{10}}=-3$

Example 26 If $\cos\theta=\dfrac{\cos\alpha-\cos\beta}{1-\cos\alpha\cos\beta}$, then prove that $\tan\dfrac{\theta}{2}=\pm\tan\dfrac{\alpha}{2}\cot\dfrac{\beta}{2}$.

Sol. Given, $\cos\theta=\dfrac{\cos\alpha-\cos\beta}{1-\cos\alpha\cos\beta}$

$$\Rightarrow \frac{1-\tan^2\frac{\theta}{2}}{1+\tan^2\frac{\theta}{2}} = \frac{\cos\alpha - \cos\beta}{1-\cos\alpha\cos\beta} \quad \left[\because \cos x = \frac{1-\tan^2\frac{x}{2}}{1+\tan^2\frac{x}{2}}\right]$$

$$\Rightarrow \frac{1-\tan^2\frac{\theta}{2}+1+\tan^2\frac{\theta}{2}}{1-\tan^2\frac{\theta}{2}-1-\tan^2\frac{\theta}{2}} = \frac{\cos\alpha-\cos\beta+1-\cos\alpha\cos\beta}{\cos\alpha-\cos\beta-1+\cos\alpha\cos\beta}$$

[applying componendo and dividendo rule]

$$\Rightarrow -\frac{2}{2\tan^2\frac{\theta}{2}} = \frac{(\cos\alpha+1)(1-\cos\beta)}{(\cos\alpha-1)(\cos\beta+1)}$$

$$\Rightarrow \frac{1}{\tan^2\frac{\theta}{2}} = \frac{(1+\cos\alpha)(1-\cos\beta)}{(1-\cos\alpha)(1+\cos\beta)}$$

$$\Rightarrow \frac{1}{\tan^2\frac{\theta}{2}} = \frac{\left(1+2\cos^2\frac{\alpha}{2}-1\right)\left(1-1+2\sin^2\frac{\beta}{2}\right)}{\left(1-1+2\sin^2\frac{\alpha}{2}\right)\left(1+2\cos^2\frac{\beta}{2}-1\right)}$$

$$\Rightarrow \frac{1}{\tan^2\frac{\theta}{2}} = \frac{4\cos^2\frac{\alpha}{2}\sin^2\frac{\beta}{2}}{4\sin^2\frac{\alpha}{2}\cos^2\frac{\beta}{2}} \Rightarrow \tan^2\frac{\theta}{2} = \frac{\sin^2\frac{\alpha}{2}\cos^2\frac{\beta}{2}}{\cos^2\frac{\alpha}{2}\sin^2\frac{\beta}{2}}$$

$$\Rightarrow \tan^2\frac{\theta}{2} = \tan^2\frac{\alpha}{2}\cot^2\frac{\beta}{2}$$

$$\therefore \tan\frac{\theta}{2} = \pm\tan\frac{\alpha}{2}\cot\frac{\beta}{2}$$

Hence proved.

Example 27 If $\cos\theta = \cos\alpha\cos\beta$, then prove that $\tan\frac{\theta+\alpha}{2}\tan\frac{\theta-\alpha}{2} = \tan^2\frac{\beta}{2}$.

Sol. Given, $\cos\theta = \cos\alpha\cos\beta$

$$\Rightarrow \cos\beta = \frac{\cos\theta}{\cos\alpha} \Rightarrow \frac{1-\tan^2\frac{\beta}{2}}{1+\tan^2\frac{\beta}{2}} = \frac{\cos\theta}{\cos\alpha}$$

$$\Rightarrow \frac{1-\tan^2\frac{\beta}{2}+1+\tan^2\frac{\beta}{2}}{1-\tan^2\frac{\beta}{2}-1-\tan^2\frac{\beta}{2}} = \frac{\cos\theta+\cos\alpha}{\cos\theta-\cos\alpha}$$

[applying componendo and dividendo]

$$\Rightarrow \frac{2}{-2\tan^2\frac{\beta}{2}} = \frac{2\cos\left(\frac{\theta+\alpha}{2}\right)\cos\left(\frac{\theta-\alpha}{2}\right)}{-2\sin\left(\frac{\theta+\alpha}{2}\right)\sin\left(\frac{\theta-\alpha}{2}\right)}$$

$$\Rightarrow \frac{1}{\tan^2\frac{\beta}{2}} = \cot\left(\frac{\theta+\alpha}{2}\right)\cot\left(\frac{\theta-\alpha}{2}\right)$$

$$\Rightarrow \tan^2\frac{\beta}{2} = \tan\left(\frac{\theta+\alpha}{2}\right)\tan\left(\frac{\theta-\alpha}{2}\right)$$

Hence proved.

Trigonometric Ratios of Some More Angles

(i) $\sin 18° = \cos 72° = \frac{\sqrt{5}-1}{4}$

(ii) $\cos 18° = \sin 72° = \frac{\sqrt{10+2\sqrt{5}}}{4}$

(iii) $\cos 36° = \sin 54° = \frac{\sqrt{5}+1}{4}$

(iv) $\sin 36° = \cos 54° = \frac{\sqrt{10-2\sqrt{5}}}{4}$

Example 28 Prove that $\tan 6°\tan 42°\tan 66°\tan 78° = 1$.

Sol. LHS $= \tan 6°\cdot\tan 42°\cdot\tan 66°\cdot\tan 78°$

$$= \frac{\sin 6°}{\cos 6°}\cdot\frac{\sin 42°}{\cos 42°}\cdot\frac{\sin 66°}{\cos 66°}\cdot\frac{\sin 78°}{\cos 78°}$$

$$= \frac{(2\sin 66°\sin 6°)}{(2\cos 66°\cos 6°)}\times\frac{(2\sin 78°\sin 42°)}{(2\cos 78°\cos 42°)}$$

$$= \frac{\cos 60° - \cos 72°}{\cos 60° + \cos 72°}\times\frac{\cos 36° - \cos 120°}{\cos 36° + \cos 120°}$$

$$= \frac{\cos 60° - \cos(90°-18°)}{\cos 60° + \cos(90°-18°)}\times\frac{\cos 36° - \cos(90°+30°)}{\cos 36° + \cos(90°+30°)}$$

$$= \frac{\cos 60° - \sin 18°}{\cos 60° + \sin 18°}\times\frac{\cos 36° + \sin 30°}{\cos 36° - \sin 30°}$$

$$= \frac{\left(\frac{1}{2}-\frac{\sqrt{5}-1}{4}\right)}{\left(\frac{1}{2}+\frac{\sqrt{5}-1}{4}\right)}\times\frac{\left(\frac{\sqrt{5}+1}{4}+\frac{1}{2}\right)}{\left(\frac{\sqrt{5}+1}{4}-\frac{1}{2}\right)}$$

$$= \frac{(3-\sqrt{5})(3+\sqrt{5})}{(\sqrt{5}+1)(\sqrt{5}-1)} = \frac{9-5}{5-1} = 1 = \text{RHS}$$

Hence proved.

Example 29 Prove that $16\cos\frac{2\pi}{15}\cdot\cos\frac{4\pi}{15}\cdot\cos\frac{8\pi}{15}\cdot\cos\frac{14\pi}{15} = 1$.

Sol. LHS $= 16\cos\frac{2\pi}{15}\cdot\cos\frac{4\pi}{15}\cdot\cos\frac{8\pi}{15}\cdot\cos\frac{14\pi}{15}$

$= 4(2\cos 24°\cos 96°)(2\cos 48°\cdot\cos 168°)$

$= 4(\cos 120° + \cos 72°)(\cos 216° + \cos 120°)$

$= 4(-\sin 30° + \sin 18°)(-\cos 36° - \sin 30°)$

$$= 4\left(-\frac{1}{2}+\frac{\sqrt{5}-1}{4}\right)\left(-\frac{\sqrt{5}+1}{4}-\frac{1}{2}\right)$$

$$= 4\left(\frac{\sqrt{5}-3}{4}\right)\left(\frac{-\sqrt{5}-3}{4}\right)$$

$$= 4\left(\frac{3-\sqrt{5}}{4}\right)\left(\frac{3+\sqrt{5}}{4}\right) = \frac{9-5}{4} = 1$$

Hence proved.

Example 30 Find the value of
$\cos 12° + \cos 84° + \cos 156° + \cos 132°$.
[NCERT Exemplar]

Sol. We have, $\cos 12° + \cos 84° + \cos 156° + \cos 132°$

$$= \cos 12° + \cos 156° + \cos 84° + \cos 132°$$
$$= 2\cos\left(\frac{12° + 156°}{2}\right)\cdot\cos\left(\frac{12° - 156°}{2}\right) + 2\cos\left(\frac{84° + 132°}{2}\right)\cdot\cos\left(\frac{84° - 132°}{2}\right)$$
$$= 2\cos 84° \cos 72° + 2\cos 108° \cdot \cos 24°$$
$$[\because \cos(-72°) = \cos 72° \text{ and } \cos(-24°) = \cos 24°]$$
$$= 2\cos 84° \cos(90° - 18°) + 2\cos(90° + 18°)\cdot \cos 24°$$
$$= 2\cos 84° \sin 18° - 2\sin 18° \cdot \cos 24°$$
$$= 2\sin 18°(\cos 84° - \cos 24°)$$
$$= 2\sin 18°\left[-2\sin\left(\frac{84° + 24°}{2}\right)\cdot\sin\left(\frac{84° - 24°}{2}\right)\right]$$
$$= -4\sin 18° \cdot \sin 54° \sin 30°$$
$$= -4\left(\frac{\sqrt{5} - 1}{4}\right)\cdot \cos 36° \cdot \frac{1}{2} \qquad [\because \sin(90° - 36°) = \cos 36°]$$
$$= -(\sqrt{5} - 1)\left(\frac{\sqrt{5} + 1}{4}\right)\cdot\frac{1}{2} = -\left(\frac{5 - 1}{8}\right) = \frac{-4}{8} = \frac{-1}{2}$$

Topic Practice 5

Very Short Answer Type Questions
2 Marks

1. Find the value of $2\sin A \cos A$, if $A = 22\frac{1}{2}°$.
2. If $\cos A = \frac{1}{3}$, then find the value of $\cos 2A$.
3. If $\tan A = \frac{2}{5}$, then find the value of $\tan 2A$.
4. If $3\sin\theta = 2\cos\theta$, then find the value of $\sin 2\theta$.
5. Prove that $\frac{\sin x - \sin 3x}{\sin^2 x - \cos^2 x} = 2\sin x$.
6. Prove that $\frac{\sin 2\theta}{1 + \cos 2\theta} = \tan\theta$.
7. Prove that $\frac{\sin 2\theta}{1 - \cos 2\theta} = \cot\theta$.
8. Prove that $\frac{1 + \sin 2\theta + \cos 2\theta}{1 + \sin 2\theta - \cos 2\theta} = \cot\theta$.
9. Prove that $\frac{1 - \cos 2A + \sin 2A}{1 + \cos 2A + \sin 2A} = \tan A$.
10. Prove that $\frac{\sec 8\theta - 1}{\sec 4\theta - 1} = \frac{\tan 8\theta}{\tan 2\theta}$.
11. Find the value of trigonometric ratio $\cos 22\frac{1}{2}°$.
12. Find the value of trigonometric ratio $\tan 22\frac{1}{2}°$.

Or Find the value of $\tan\frac{\pi}{8}$.

13. Find the value of $\sin 7\frac{1}{2}°$.
14. Prove that $\frac{\cos 2\theta}{1 + \sin 2\theta} = \tan\left(\frac{\pi}{4} - \theta\right)$
15. Prove the following results.
    (i) $\frac{\cos\theta}{1 + \sin\theta} = \tan\left(\frac{\pi}{4} - \frac{\theta}{2}\right)$
    (ii) $\frac{\cos A}{1 - \sin A} = \tan\left(\frac{\pi}{4} + \frac{A}{2}\right)$

Short Answer Type Questions
4 Marks

16. Show that $\sqrt{\frac{1 + \sin\theta}{1 - \sin\theta}} = \tan\left(\frac{\pi}{4} + \frac{\theta}{2}\right)$.
17. Prove that $4\cos\theta\cos\left(\frac{\pi}{3} + \theta\right)\cos\left(\frac{\pi}{3} - \theta\right) = \cos 3\theta$.
18. Prove that $4\sin\theta\sin\left(\frac{\pi}{3} + \theta\right)\sin\left(\frac{2\pi}{3} + \theta\right) = \sin 3\theta$.
19. If $\tan x = \frac{b}{a}$, then find the value of $\sqrt{\frac{a + b}{a - b}} + \sqrt{\frac{a - b}{a + b}}$. **[NCERT Exemplar]**

Long answer Type Questions
6 Marks

20. Find the value of the expression
$$\cos^4\frac{\pi}{8} + \cos^4\frac{3\pi}{8} + \cos^4\frac{5\pi}{8} + \cos^4\frac{7\pi}{8}.$$
[NCERT Exemplar]
21. Prove that $\cos^3 A + \cos^3(120° + A) + \cos^3(240° + A) = \frac{3}{4}\cos 3A$.

22 Prove that
$\cot\theta\cot 2\theta+\cot 2\theta\cot 3\theta+2=\cot\theta(\cot\theta-\cot 3\theta)$.

23 Prove that $\cot 7\frac{1^\circ}{2}=\tan 82\frac{1^\circ}{2}=(\sqrt{3}+\sqrt{2})(\sqrt{2}+1)$.

24 If $A+B+C=180^\circ$, then prove that

$$\cos A+\cos B+\cos C=1+4\sin\frac{A}{2}\sin\frac{B}{2}\sin\frac{C}{2}.$$

Hints & Answers

1. Use the formula, $\sin 2A=2\sin A\cos A$ **Ans.** $\frac{1}{\sqrt{2}}$

2. Use formula, $\cos 2A=2\cos^2 A-1$. **Ans.** $-\frac{7}{9}$

3. Use formula, $\tan 2A=\frac{2\tan A}{1-\tan^2 A}$. **Ans.** $\frac{20}{21}$

4. $\tan\theta=\frac{2}{3}$; Use $\sin 2\theta=\frac{2\tan\theta}{1+\tan^2\theta}$ **Ans.** $\frac{12}{13}$

5. $\text{LHS}=\frac{2\cos 2x\sin(-x)}{-\cos 2x}$

6. Use the formulae, $\sin 2\theta=2\sin\theta\cos\theta$ and $\cos 2\theta=2\cos^2\theta-1$.

7. Use the formulae, $\sin 2\theta=2\sin\theta\cos\theta$ and $\cos 2\theta=1-2\sin^2\theta$.

8. $\text{LHS}=\frac{1+\cos 2\theta+\sin 2\theta}{1-\cos 2\theta+\sin 2\theta}$

$$=\frac{2\cos^2\theta+2\sin\theta\cos\theta}{2\sin^2\theta+2\sin\theta\cos\theta}=\frac{2\cos\theta(\cos\theta+\sin\theta)}{2\sin\theta(\sin\theta+\cos\theta)}$$

9. Solve as Q. 8.

10. $\text{LHS}=\frac{\frac{1}{\cos 8\theta}-1}{\frac{1}{\cos 4\theta}-1}=\frac{(1-\cos 8\theta)\cos 4\theta}{(1-\cos 4\theta)\cos 8\theta}=\frac{2\sin^2 4\theta\cos 4\theta}{2\sin^2 2\theta\cos 8\theta}$

$$=\frac{\sin 4\theta(2\sin 4\theta\cos 4\theta)}{2\sin^2 2\theta\cos 8\theta}=\frac{2\sin 2\theta\cos 2\theta\cdot\sin 8\theta}{2\sin^2 2\theta\cos 8\theta}$$

11. $\cos 22\frac{1}{2}^\circ=\sqrt{\frac{\cos 45^\circ+1}{2}}$ **Ans.** $\sqrt{\frac{1+\sqrt{2}}{2\sqrt{2}}}$

12. $\tan 2\theta=\frac{2\tan\theta}{1-\tan^2\theta}$

$$\therefore\quad \tan 45^\circ=\frac{2\tan\frac{45^\circ}{2}}{1-\tan^2\frac{45^\circ}{2}}$$

$$\Rightarrow\quad 1-\tan^2\frac{45^\circ}{2}=2\tan\left(\frac{45^\circ}{2}\right)$$

$$\Rightarrow\quad \tan^2\frac{45^\circ}{2}+2\tan\left(\frac{45^\circ}{2}\right)-1=0$$

$$\Rightarrow\quad \tan\frac{45^\circ}{2}=\frac{-2\pm\sqrt{(2)^2-4\times(-1)}}{2\times 1}$$

$$=\frac{-2\pm\sqrt{8}}{2}=-1\pm\sqrt{2}$$

Since, $\left(\frac{45^\circ}{2}\right)$ is in I quadrant, so we take '+ve' sign.

Ans. $-1+\sqrt{2}$

13. $\sin 7\frac{1^\circ}{2}=\sin\frac{15^\circ}{2}=\sqrt{\frac{1-\cos 15^\circ}{2}}=\sqrt{\frac{1-\frac{\sqrt{3}+1}{2\sqrt{2}}}{2}}$

Ans. $\frac{\sqrt{4-\sqrt{6}-\sqrt{2}}}{2\sqrt{2}}$

14. $\text{LHS}=\frac{\sin\left(\frac{\pi}{2}-2\theta\right)}{1+\cos\left(\frac{\pi}{2}-2\theta\right)}=\frac{2\sin\left(\frac{\pi}{4}-\theta\right)\cdot\cos\left(\frac{\pi}{4}-\theta\right)}{2\cos^2\left(\frac{\pi}{4}-2\theta\right)}$

15. (i) Similar as Q. 14.

(ii) $\frac{\cos A}{1-\sin A}=\cot\left(\frac{\pi}{4}-\frac{A}{2}\right)=\tan\left[\frac{\pi}{2}-\left(\frac{\pi}{4}-\frac{A}{2}\right)\right]$

16. $\text{LHS}=\sqrt{\frac{1+\sin\theta}{1-\sin\theta}}=\sqrt{\frac{\cos^2\frac{\theta}{2}+\sin^2\frac{\theta}{2}+2\sin\frac{\theta}{2}\cos\frac{\theta}{2}}{\cos^2\frac{\theta}{2}+\sin^2\frac{\theta}{2}-2\sin\frac{\theta}{2}\cos\frac{\theta}{2}}}$

$$=\sqrt{\frac{\left(\cos\frac{\theta}{2}+\sin\frac{\theta}{2}\right)^2}{\left(\cos\frac{\theta}{2}-\sin\frac{\theta}{2}\right)^2}}=\frac{\cos\frac{\theta}{2}+\sin\frac{\theta}{2}}{\cos\frac{\theta}{2}-\sin\frac{\theta}{2}}$$

$$=\frac{1+\tan\frac{\theta}{2}}{1-\tan\frac{\theta}{2}}=\frac{\tan\frac{\pi}{4}+\tan\frac{\theta}{2}}{1-\tan\frac{\pi}{4}\tan\frac{\theta}{2}}$$

17. $\text{LHS}=2\cos\theta\left[2\cos\left(\frac{\pi}{3}+\theta\right)\cos\left(\frac{\pi}{3}-\theta\right)\right]$

$$=2\cos\theta\left[\cos\left(\frac{2\pi}{3}\right)+\cos(2\theta)\right]$$

$$=2\cos\theta\left(-\frac{1}{2}+\cos 2\theta\right)=2\cos\theta\left(\frac{-1}{2}+2\cos^2\theta-1\right)$$

$$=2\cos\theta\left(\frac{-3+4\cos^2\theta}{2}\right)$$

$$=4\cos^3\theta-3\cos\theta$$

18. Solve as Q.17.

19. $\sqrt{\frac{a+b}{a-b}}+\sqrt{\frac{a-b}{a+b}}=\frac{2a}{\sqrt{a^2-b^2}}=\frac{2}{\sqrt{1-\tan^2 x}}$

Ans. $\frac{2\cos x}{\sqrt{\cos 2x}}$

20. $\cos^4\frac{\pi}{8}+\cos^4\frac{3\pi}{8}+\cos^4\frac{5\pi}{8}+\cos^4\frac{7\pi}{8}$

$$=\cos^4\frac{\pi}{8}+\cos^4\frac{3\pi}{8}+\cos^4\left(\pi-\frac{3\pi}{8}\right)+\cos^4\left(\pi-\frac{\pi}{8}\right)$$

$$=\cos^4\frac{\pi}{8}+\cos^4\frac{3\pi}{8}+\cos^4\frac{3\pi}{8}+\cos^4\frac{\pi}{8}$$

$$=2\left[\cos^4\frac{\pi}{8}+\cos^4\frac{3\pi}{8}\right]=2\left[\cos^4\frac{\pi}{8}+\cos^4\left(\frac{\pi}{2}-\frac{\pi}{8}\right)\right]$$

$$=2\left[\cos^4\frac{\pi}{8}+\sin^4\frac{\pi}{8}\right]$$

Ans. $\frac{3}{2}$

21. LHS $=\cos^3 A+\cos^3(120°+A)+\cos^3(240°+A)$

$$=\left[\frac{3}{4}\cos A+\frac{1}{4}\cos 3A\right]+\left[\frac{3}{4}\cos(120°+A)+\frac{1}{4}\cos 3(120°+A)\right]+\left[\frac{3}{4}\cos(240°+A)+\frac{1}{4}\cos 3(240°+A)\right]$$

$$=\left[\frac{3}{4}\cos A+\frac{1}{4}\cos 3A\right]+\left[\frac{3}{4}\cos(120°+A)+\frac{1}{4}\cos(360°+3A)\right]+\left[\frac{3}{4}\cos(240°+A)+\frac{1}{4}\cos(720°+3A)\right]$$

$$=\frac{3}{4}[\cos A+\cos(120°+A)+\cos(240°+A)]+\frac{1}{4}[\cos 3A+\cos(360°+3A)+\cos(360°\times 2+3A)]$$

22. RHS $=\cot\theta\left(\cot\theta-\left(\frac{\cot^3\theta-3\cot\theta}{3\cot^2\theta-1}\right)\right)$

$$=\cot^2\theta\left(\frac{2\cot^2\theta+2}{3\cot^2\theta-1}\right)=\frac{2\cot^2\theta(\cot^2\theta+1)}{3\cot^2\theta-1}$$

LHS $=\cot\theta\left(\frac{\cot^2\theta-1}{2\cot\theta}\right)+\left(\frac{\cot^2\theta-1}{2\cot\theta}\right)\left(\frac{\cot^3\theta-3\cot\theta}{3\cot^2\theta-1}\right)+2$

$$=\frac{\cot^2\theta-1}{2}+\left(\frac{\cot^2\theta-1}{2}\right)\left(\frac{\cot^2\theta-3}{3\cot^2\theta-1}\right)+2$$

$$=\frac{(\cot^2\theta-1)(3\cot^2\theta-1)+(\cot^2\theta-1)(\cot^2\theta-3)+4(3\cot^2\theta-1)}{2(3\cot^2\theta-1)}$$

$$=\frac{4\cot^4\theta+4\cot^2\theta}{2(3\cot^2\theta-1)}=\frac{2\cot^2\theta(\cot^2\theta+1)}{3\cot^2\theta-1}$$

23. LHS $=\tan 82\frac{1°}{2}=\tan\left(90°-7\frac{1°}{2}\right)$

$$=\cot 7\frac{1°}{2}=\cot A\ \text{(say)}$$

where, $A=7\frac{1°}{2}$

Now, $\cot A=\frac{\cos A}{\sin A}=\frac{\cos A(2\cos A)}{\sin A(2\cos A)}=\frac{1+\cos 2A}{\sin 2A}$

$$\therefore\ \cot 7\frac{1°}{2}=\frac{1+\cos 2\left(\frac{15}{2}\right)^\circ}{\sin 2\left(\frac{15}{2}\right)^\circ}=\frac{1+\cos 15°}{\sin 15°}$$

24. LHS $=(\cos A+\cos B)+\cos C$

$$=2\cos\left(\frac{A+B}{2}\right)\cos\left(\frac{A-B}{2}\right)+1-2\sin^2\frac{C}{2}$$

$$=2\cos\left(\frac{\pi}{2}-\frac{C}{2}\right)\cos\left(\frac{A-B}{2}\right)-2\sin^2\frac{C}{2}+1$$

$$=2\sin\frac{C}{2}\cos\left(\frac{A-B}{2}\right)-2\sin^2\frac{C}{2}+1$$

$$=2\sin\frac{C}{2}\left[\cos\left(\frac{A-B}{2}\right)-\sin\frac{C}{2}\right]+1$$

Chapter Practice

Multiple Choice Type Questions

1 Mark

1. The value of $\cos 1° \cos 2° \cos 3° \ldots \cos 179°$ is **[NCERT Exemplar]**

(a) $\frac{1}{\sqrt{2}}$ (b) 0 (c) 1 (d) –1

2. If $\tan x = \frac{a}{b}$, then $b\cos 2x + a\sin 2x$ is equal to

(a) a (b) b (c) ab (d) $\frac{a}{b}$

3. If $\frac{\pi}{2} < \alpha < \pi$ and $0 < \beta < \frac{\pi}{2}$ and $\sin\alpha = \frac{4}{5}$ and $\cos\beta = \frac{5}{13}$, then value of $\tan\left(\frac{\alpha - \beta}{2}\right)$ is

(a) $\frac{1}{8}$ (b) $\frac{4}{7}$ (c) $\frac{-2}{7}$ (d) $\frac{1}{4}$

4. If $\tan\alpha = \frac{m}{m+1}$ and $\tan\beta = \frac{1}{2m+1}$, then $\alpha + \beta$ is equal to **[NCERT Exemplar]**

(a) $\frac{\pi}{2}$ (b) $\frac{\pi}{3}$ (c) $\frac{\pi}{6}$ (d) $\frac{\pi}{4}$

5. $\frac{(\sin 7x + \sin 5x) + (\sin 9x + \sin 3x)}{(\cos 7x + \cos 5x) + (\cos 9x + \cos 3x)}$ is equal to

(a) $\tan 3x$ (b) $\cot 3x$ (c) $\tan 6x$ (d) $\cot 6x$

Assertion-Reason Type Questions

1 Mark

Directions (Q. Nos. 6-9) *In the questions given below are two statements labelled as Assertion (A) and Reason (R). In the context of the two statements, which one of the following is correct?*

(a) Both A and R are correct; R is the correct explanation of A
(b) Both A and R are correct; R is not the correct explanation of A
(c) A is correct; R is incorrect
(d) R is correct; A is incorrect

6. **Assertion (A)** The degree measure corresponding to (–2) radian is – 114° 19 min.

Reason (R) The degree measure of a given radian measure $= \frac{180}{\pi} \times$ Radian measure.

7. **Assertion (A)** If $A = \cos^2\theta + \sin^4\theta$ for all values of θ, then $\frac{3}{4} \le A \le 1$.

Reason (R) $\sin^2\theta + \cos^4\theta = 1$.

8. **Assertion (A)** If $3\tan(\theta - 15°) = \tan(\theta + 15°)$ $0° < \theta < 90°$, then $\theta = \frac{\pi}{4}$.

Reason (R) $\tan 3\theta = \frac{3\tan\theta - \tan^3\theta}{1 - 3\tan^2\theta}$.

9. **Assertion (A)** If $\sin = \frac{2}{5}$, $0 < A < \frac{\pi}{2}$ and $\cos B = -\frac{12}{13}$ $\pi < B < \frac{3\pi}{2}$, then the value of $\tan(A - B)$ is $\frac{16}{63}$.

Reason (R) $\tan(A - B) = \frac{\tan A - \tan B}{1 + \tan A \tan B}$.

Very Short Answer Type Questions

2 Marks

10. Find the radian measure corresponding the degree measure 125° 30′.

11. Find the degree measure corresponding the radian measure -2^c.

12. The minute hand of a watch is 1.8 cm long. How far does its tip move in 30 min?

13. A rail road curve is to be laid out on a circle. What radius should be used, if the track is to change direction by 30° is a distance of 50 m?

14. Find the degree measure of the angle subtended at the centre of a circle of radius 100 cm by an arc of length 22 cm. Also, find the area of a sector. **[NCERT]**

15. Find the value of the following trigonomitric ratios.

(i) $\sin\left(\frac{-11\pi}{3}\right)$ **[NCERT]**

(ii) $\cot\left(\frac{-15\pi}{4}\right)$ **[NCERT]**

16. Find $\sin\theta$ and $\tan\theta$, if $\cos\theta = -\frac{3}{5}$ and θ lies in the third quadrant.

17. Prove the following result.
(Each part carries 2 Marks) **[NCERT]**

(i) $\cot^2\frac{\pi}{6}+\text{cosec}\frac{5\pi}{6}+3\tan^2\frac{\pi}{6}=6$

(ii) $\tan 720°-\cos 70°-\sin 150°\cos 120°=\frac{1}{4}$

18. In any quadilateral $ABCD$, prove that
$\cos(A+B)=\cos(C+D)$.

19. If θ is an acute angle and $\tan\theta=\frac{1}{\sqrt{7}}$, then find the value of $\frac{\text{cosec}^2\theta-\sec^2\theta}{\text{cosec}^2\theta+\sec^2\theta}$.

20. If $a\cos\theta-b\sin\theta=c$, then show that
$a\sin\theta+b\cos\theta=\pm\sqrt{a^2+b^2-c^2}$.

21. If $\sec\theta+\tan\theta=p$, obtain the values of $\sec\theta$, $\tan\theta$ and $\sin\theta$ in terms of p.

22. If $\text{cosec}\theta+\cot\theta=\frac{11}{2}$, then find the value of $\tan\theta$.

23. Prove that

$$2\sec^2\theta-\sec^4\theta-2\,\text{cosec}^2\theta+\text{cosec}^4\theta=\frac{1-\tan^8\theta}{\tan^4\theta}.$$

24. Prove the following identities.

(i) $\frac{\sin^3x+\cos^3x}{\sin x+\cos x}+\frac{\sin^3x-\cos^3x}{\sin x-\cos x}=2$

(ii) $\text{cosec}\,\theta(\sec\theta-1)-\cot\theta(1-\cos\theta)=\tan\theta-\sin\theta$

(iii) $\frac{\tan^3\theta}{1+\tan^2\theta}+\frac{\cot^3\theta}{1+\cot^2\theta}=\frac{1-2\sin^2\theta\cos^2\theta}{\sin\theta\cos\theta}$

(iv) $1-\frac{\sin^2\theta}{1+\cot\theta}-\frac{\cos^2\theta}{1+\tan\theta}=\sin\theta\cos\theta$

25. Prove that

$$\sqrt{\frac{1-\sin\theta}{1+\sin\theta}}=\begin{cases}\sec\theta-\tan\theta, & \text{if } -\frac{\pi}{2}<\theta<\frac{\pi}{2}\\ -\sec\theta+\tan\theta, & \text{if } \frac{\pi}{2}<\theta<\frac{3\pi}{2}\end{cases}.$$

26. Prove that
$$\frac{\sin(x+\theta)}{\sin(x+\phi)}=\cos(\theta-\phi)+\cot(x+\phi)\sin(\theta-\phi).$$

27. If $\tan(\alpha+\theta)=n\tan(\alpha-\theta)$ show that
$(n+1)\sin 2\theta=(n-1)\sin 2\alpha$.

28. Prove that (Each part carries 2 Marks)

(i) $8\cos^3\frac{\pi}{9}-6\cos\frac{\pi}{9}=1$

(ii) $108\sin\frac{\pi}{18}-144\sin^3\frac{\pi}{18}=18$

Short Answer Type Questions
(4 Marks)

29. If x lies in the IInd quadrant such that $\sin x=\frac{1}{4}$.
Find the value of $\cos\frac{x}{2}$, $\sin\frac{x}{2}$ and $\tan\frac{x}{2}$.

30. Express $3\cos\theta-4\sin\theta$ as sine and cosine of a single expression.

31. Prove that

(i) $\cos^2A+\cos^2B-2\cos A\cos B\cos(A+B)=\sin^2(A+B)$

(ii) $4\cos 12°\cos 48°\cos 72°=\cos 36°$

32. If $2\alpha+2\beta=90°$, then find the maximum and minimum values of $\sin 2\alpha\sin 2\beta$.

Long Answer Type Questions
(6 Marks)

33. Prove that

(i) $\cos 3A+\cos 5A+\cos 7A+\cos 15A=4\cos 4A\cos 5A\cos 6A$.

(ii) $\sin\frac{\theta}{2}\sin\frac{7\theta}{2}+\sin\frac{3\theta}{2}\sin\frac{11\theta}{2}=\sin 2\theta\sin 5\theta$

34. Prove that

$$\cos^2A+\cos^2\left(A+\frac{2\pi}{3}\right)+\cos^2\left(A-\frac{2\pi}{3}\right)=\frac{3}{2}.$$

35. Prove that $\tan\frac{11\pi}{24}=\sqrt{2}+\sqrt{3}+\sqrt{4}+\sqrt{6}$.

Case-Based Type Questions
(6 Marks)

36. In the figure, it is given that $\angle C=90°$, $AD=DB$, ED is perpendicular to AB, $AB=20$ cm and $AC=12$ cm.

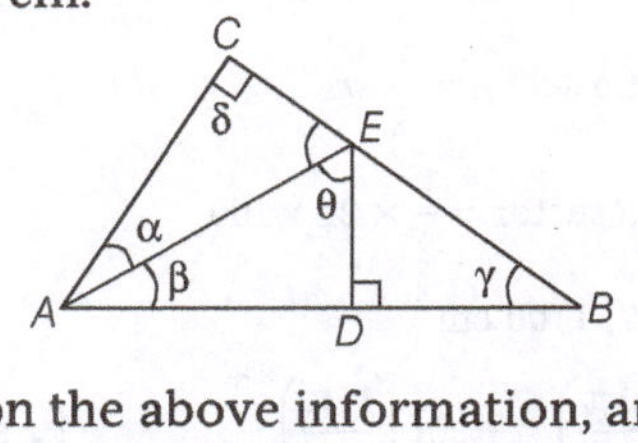

Based on the above information, answer the following questions.

(i) Find the value of $\cos(\alpha+\theta)$.

(ii) Find the value of $\tan 2\alpha$.

(iii) Find the value of
$\sin\left(\frac{\alpha+\theta+\gamma+\delta}{2}\right)\sin\left(\frac{\alpha+\theta-\gamma-\delta}{2}\right)$.

(iv) Find the value of $\tan\beta+\tan\theta$.

Hints & Answers

1. (b) **2.** (b) **3.** (b) **4.** (d) **5.** (c)
6. (d) **7.** (c) **8.** (b) **9.** (c)

10. Let $\theta = 125°30'$

$$= 125° + \left(\frac{30}{60}\right)^{\circ} \qquad \left[\because 1° = 60' \Rightarrow 1' = \left(\frac{1}{60}\right)^{\circ}\right]$$

$$= 125° + \left(\frac{1}{2}\right)^{\circ} = \left(\frac{251}{2}\right)^{\circ}$$

Ans. $\frac{251\pi}{360}$

11. Let $\theta = (-2)^c = \left[\frac{180}{\pi} \times (-2)\right]^{\circ}$

$$= \left(\frac{180}{22} \times 7 \times -2\right)^{\circ}$$

$$= \left(-114\frac{6}{11}\right)^{\circ} = \left[-114°\left(\frac{6}{11} \times 60\right)'\right]$$

Ans. $-[114° 32' 44'']$

12. $\because$ Angle traced by the minute hand in 1 min $= \left(\frac{360}{60}\right)^{\circ} = 6°$

$\therefore$ Angle traced by the minute hand in 30 min

$$= (30 \times 6)° = 180° = \left(180 \times \frac{\pi}{180}\right)^c = \pi^c$$

$\because \quad \theta = \frac{\text{Arc}}{\text{Radius}} \Rightarrow \pi = \frac{\text{Arc}}{1.8}$

$\therefore \quad \text{Arc} = \frac{22}{7} \times 1.8$ **Ans.** 5.66 cm

13. Here, $\theta = 30° = \left(30 \times \frac{\pi}{180}\right)^c = \left(\frac{\pi}{6}\right)^c$ and arc $= 50$ m

$\because \quad \theta = \frac{\text{Arc}}{\text{Radius}} \Rightarrow \frac{\pi}{6} = \frac{50}{\text{Radius}}$

$\therefore$ Radius $= \frac{50 \times 6 \times 7}{22}$ **Ans.** 95.45 m

14. If a circle of radius r and an arc of length l subtends an angle θ radian at the centre, we use the formula, $\theta = \frac{s}{r}$.

Use area of a sector $= \frac{1}{2} sr$

$\therefore$ Area of a sector $= \frac{1}{2} \times 22 \times 100$

Ans. $12°36'$, 1100 cm^2

15. (i) $\sin\left(\frac{-11\pi}{3}\right) = -\sin\left(\frac{11\pi}{3}\right) \qquad [\because \sin(-\theta) = -\sin\theta]$

$$= -\sin\left(4\pi - \frac{\pi}{3}\right) = -\left(-\sin\frac{\pi}{3}\right)$$

$$[\because \sin(2n\pi - \theta) = -\sin\theta]$$

Ans. $\frac{\sqrt{3}}{2}$

(ii) Solve as part (i). **Ans.** 1

16. $\sin\theta = \frac{-4}{5}$ and $\tan\theta = \frac{4}{3}$

17. (i) $\cot^2\frac{\pi}{6} + \operatorname{cosec}\frac{5\pi}{6} + 3\tan^2\frac{\pi}{6}$

$$= \left(\cot\frac{\pi}{6}\right)^2 + \operatorname{cosec}\left(\pi - \frac{\pi}{6}\right) + 3\left(\tan\frac{\pi}{6}\right)^2$$

$$= (\sqrt{3})^2 + 2 + 3\left(\frac{1}{\sqrt{3}}\right)^2$$

(ii) Solve as part (i).

18. It is given that $ABCD$ is a quadrilateral.

$\therefore A + B + C + D = 360°$

[$\because$ sum of all angles of a quadrilateral is 360°]

$\Rightarrow \quad A + B = 360° - (C + D)$

On taking cosine both sides, we get

$$\cos(A + B) = \cos[360° - (C + D)]$$

19. $\frac{3}{4}$

20. Given, $a\cos\theta - b\sin\theta = c$

$\Rightarrow a^2\cos^2\theta + b^2\sin^2\theta - 2ab\cos\theta\sin\theta = c^2$

[squaring both sides]

$\Rightarrow a^2(1 - \sin^2\theta) + b^2(1 - \cos^2\theta) - 2ab\sin\theta\cos\theta = c^2$

$\Rightarrow a^2 - a^2\sin^2\theta + b^2 - b^2\cos^2\theta - 2ab\sin\theta\cos\theta = c^2$

$\Rightarrow \quad a^2\sin^2\theta + b^2\cos^2\theta + 2ab\sin\theta\cos\theta = a^2 + b^2 - c^2$

$\Rightarrow (a\sin\theta + b\cos\theta)^2 = a^2 + b^2 - c^2$

21. We know that, $\sec^2\theta - \tan^2\theta = 1$

$\Rightarrow (\sec\theta - \tan\theta)(\sec\theta + \tan\theta) = 1$

$\Rightarrow \quad (\sec\theta - \tan\theta)p = 1 \quad [\because \sec\theta + \tan\theta = p, \text{given}]$

$\Rightarrow \quad \sec\theta - \tan\theta = \frac{1}{p}$

Now, $(\sec\theta + \tan\theta) + (\sec\theta - \tan\theta) = p + \frac{1}{p}$

$\Rightarrow \quad 2\sec\theta = \frac{p^2 + 1}{p}$

and $\quad (\sec\theta + \tan\theta) - (\sec\theta - \tan\theta) = p - \frac{1}{p}$

$\Rightarrow \quad 2\tan\theta = \frac{p^2 - 1}{p}$

Ans. $\sec\theta = \frac{p^2 + 1}{2p}$; $\tan\theta = \frac{p^2 - 1}{2p}$ and $\sin\theta = \frac{p^2 - 1}{p^2 + 1}$

22. $\frac{44}{117}$

23. LHS $= 2\sec^2\theta - \sec^4\theta - 2\operatorname{cosec}^2\theta + \operatorname{cosec}^4\theta$

$= 2(1 + \tan^2\theta) - (1 + \tan^2\theta)^2 - 2(1 + \cot^2\theta) + (1 + \cot^2\theta)^2$

$= 2(1 + \tan^2\theta - 1 - \cot^2\theta) + (1 + 2\cot^2\theta + \cot^4\theta)$
$\qquad - (1 + 2\tan^2\theta + \tan^4\theta)$

$= 2(\tan^2\theta - \cot^2\theta) + (2\cot^2\theta - 2\tan^2\theta) + (\cot^4\theta - \tan^4\theta)$

$= \frac{1}{\tan^4\theta} - \tan^4\theta$

24. (i) $\text{LHS} = \dfrac{\sin^3 x + \cos^3 x}{\sin x + \cos x} + \dfrac{\sin^3 x - \cos^3 x}{\sin x - \cos x}$

$= \dfrac{(\sin x + \cos x)(\sin^2 x + \cos^2 x - \sin x \cos x)}{(\sin x + \cos x)}$

$+ \dfrac{(\sin x - \cos x)(\sin^2 x + \cos^2 x + \sin x \cos x)}{(\sin x - \cos x)}$

$\left[\begin{array}{l} \because a^3 + b^3 = (a+b)(a^2 + b^2 - ab) \\ \text{and } a^3 - b^3 = (a-b)(a^2 + b^2 + ab) \end{array}\right]$

$= 1 - \sin x \cos x + 1 + \sin x \cos x \quad [\because \sin^2\theta + \cos^2\theta = 1]$

(ii) $\text{LHS} = \operatorname{cosec}\theta(\sec\theta - 1) - \cot\theta(1 - \cos\theta)$

$= \dfrac{1}{\sin\theta}\left(\dfrac{1}{\cos\theta} - 1\right) - \dfrac{\cos\theta}{\sin\theta}(1 - \cos\theta)$

$= \dfrac{1}{\sin\theta}\left(\dfrac{1 - \cos\theta}{\cos\theta}\right) - \dfrac{\cos\theta}{\sin\theta}(1 - \cos\theta)$

$= (1 - \cos\theta)\left(\dfrac{1}{\sin\theta\cos\theta} - \dfrac{\cos\theta}{\sin\theta}\right)$

$= (1 - \cos\theta)\left(\dfrac{1 - \cos^2\theta}{\sin\theta\cos\theta}\right) = (1 - \cos\theta)\left(\dfrac{\sin^2\theta}{\sin\theta\cos\theta}\right)$

$= (1 - \cos\theta)\left(\dfrac{\sin\theta}{\cos\theta}\right)$

(iii) $\text{LHS} = \dfrac{\tan^3\theta}{1 + \tan^2\theta} + \dfrac{\cot^3\theta}{1 + \cot^2\theta}$

$= \dfrac{\dfrac{\sin^3\theta}{\cos^3\theta}}{1 + \dfrac{\sin^2\theta}{\cos^2\theta}} + \dfrac{\dfrac{\cos^3\theta}{\sin^3\theta}}{1 + \dfrac{\cos^2\theta}{\sin^2\theta}}$

$= \dfrac{\sin^3\theta}{\cos^3\theta\left(\dfrac{\cos^2\theta + \sin^2\theta}{\cos^2\theta}\right)} + \dfrac{\cos^3\theta}{\sin^3\theta\left(\dfrac{\sin^2\theta + \cos^2\theta}{\sin^2\theta}\right)}$

$= \dfrac{\sin^3\theta}{\cos\theta} + \dfrac{\cos^3\theta}{\sin\theta} \quad [\because \sin^2\theta + \cos^2\theta = 1]$

$= \dfrac{\sin^4\theta + \cos^4\theta}{\sin\theta\cos\theta} = \dfrac{(\sin^2\theta + \cos^2\theta)^2 - 2\sin^2\cos^2\theta}{\sin\theta\cos\theta}$

(iv) $\text{LHS} = 1 - \dfrac{\sin^2\theta}{1 + \cot\theta} - \dfrac{\cos^2\theta}{1 + \tan\theta}$

$= 1 - \dfrac{\sin^2\theta}{1 + \dfrac{\cos\theta}{\sin\theta}} - \dfrac{\cos^2\theta}{1 + \dfrac{\sin\theta}{\cos\theta}}$

$= 1 - \dfrac{\sin^3\theta}{(\sin\theta + \cos\theta)} - \dfrac{\cos^3\theta}{(\sin\theta + \cos\theta)}$

$= 1 - \left[\dfrac{\sin^3\theta + \cos^3\theta}{\sin\theta + \cos\theta}\right]$

$= 1 - \dfrac{(\sin\theta + \cos\theta)(\sin^2\theta + \cos^2\theta - \sin\theta\cos\theta)}{(\sin\theta + \cos\theta)}$

$= 1 - (1 - \sin\theta\cos\theta)$

25. $\sqrt{\dfrac{1 - \sin\theta}{1 + \sin\theta}} = \sqrt{\dfrac{(1 - \sin\theta)(1 - \sin\theta)}{(1 + \sin\theta)(1 - \sin\theta)}}$

$= \sqrt{\dfrac{(1 - \sin\theta)^2}{1 - \sin^2\theta}} = \dfrac{1 - \sin\theta}{\sqrt{\cos^2\theta}}$

$[\because -1 \le \sin\theta \le 1, \text{ therefore } 1 - \sin\theta \ge 0]$

$= \dfrac{1 - \sin\theta}{|\cos\theta|}$

$= \begin{cases} \dfrac{1 - \sin\theta}{\cos\theta}, \text{ if } -\dfrac{\pi}{2} < \theta < \dfrac{\pi}{2} \\ \dfrac{1 - \sin\theta}{-\cos\theta}, \text{ if } \dfrac{\pi}{2} < \theta < \dfrac{3\pi}{2} \end{cases} \quad \left[\because |x| = \begin{cases} x, \text{ if } x \ge 0 \\ -x, \text{ if } x < 0 \end{cases}\right]$

Note $\sqrt{x^2} = |x|$. Do not write $\sqrt{x^2} = x$ unless it is given that $x \ge 0$.

26. $\text{RHS} = \cos(\theta - \phi) + \dfrac{\cos(x + \phi)}{\sin(x + \phi)}\sin(\theta - \phi)$

$= \dfrac{\cos(\theta - \phi)\sin(x + \phi) + \cos(x + \phi)\sin(\theta - \phi)}{\sin(x + \phi)}$

$= \dfrac{\sin(x + \phi + \theta - \phi)}{\sin(x + \phi)}$

27. We have, $\dfrac{\tan(\alpha + \theta)}{\tan(\alpha - \theta)} = \dfrac{n}{1}$

$\Rightarrow \dfrac{\tan(\alpha + \theta) + \tan(\alpha - \theta)}{\tan(\alpha + \theta) - \tan(\alpha - \theta)} = \dfrac{n+1}{n-1}$

[by componendo and dividendo rule]

$\Rightarrow \dfrac{\dfrac{\sin(\alpha + \theta)}{\cos(\alpha + \theta)} + \dfrac{\sin(\alpha - \theta)}{\cos(\alpha - \theta)}}{\dfrac{\sin(\alpha + \theta)}{\cos(\alpha + \theta)} - \dfrac{\sin(\alpha - \theta)}{\cos(\alpha - \theta)}} = \dfrac{n+1}{n-1}$

$\Rightarrow \dfrac{\sin(\alpha + \theta)\cos(\alpha - \theta) + \sin(\alpha - \theta)\cos(\alpha + \theta)}{\sin(\alpha + \theta)\cos(\alpha - \theta) - \cos(\alpha + \theta)\sin(\alpha - \theta)} = \dfrac{n+1}{n-1}$

$\Rightarrow \dfrac{\sin(\alpha + \theta + \alpha - \theta)}{\sin(\alpha + \theta - \alpha + \theta)} = \dfrac{n+1}{n-1}$

$\Rightarrow \dfrac{\sin 2\alpha}{\sin 2\theta} = \dfrac{n+1}{n-1}$

28. (i) Use the formula, $\cos 3A = 4\cos^3 A - 3\cos A$

(ii) Use the formula, $\sin 3A = 3\sin A - 4\sin^3 A$

29. $\sqrt{\dfrac{4 - \sqrt{15}}{8}}, \sqrt{\dfrac{4 + \sqrt{15}}{8}}$ and $4 + \sqrt{15}$

30. Let $f(\theta) = 3\cos\theta - 4\sin\theta$

On multiplying and dividing by $\sqrt{3^2 + (-4)^2} = 5$, we get

$f(\theta) = 5\left(\dfrac{3}{5}\cos\theta - \dfrac{4}{5}\sin\theta\right)$

$= 5[\sin\alpha\cos\theta - \cos\alpha\sin\theta]$ where, $\sin\alpha = \dfrac{3}{5}$

and $\cos\alpha = \dfrac{4}{5}$

Again, $f(\theta) = 5\left(\dfrac{3}{5}\cos\theta - \dfrac{4}{5}\sin\theta\right)$

$= 5(\cos\alpha\cos\theta - \sin\alpha\sin\theta)$

$\left[\text{where, } \cos\alpha = \dfrac{3}{5} \text{ and } \sin\alpha = \dfrac{4}{5}\right]$

Ans. $5\sin(\alpha-\theta)$, where α is given by $\tan\alpha=\frac{3}{4}$

and $5\cos(\alpha+\theta)$, where α is given by $\tan\alpha=\frac{4}{3}$

31. (i) LHS

$= \cos^2 A+\cos^2 B-[\cos(A+B)+\cos(A-B)]\cos(A+B)$

$= \cos^2 A+\cos^2 B-\cos^2(A+B)-\cos(A-B)\cos(A+B)$

$= \cos^2 A+\cos^2 B-\cos^2(A+B)-\cos^2 A+\sin^2 B$

$=1-\sin^2 B-\cos^2(A+B)+\sin^2 B$

$=1-\cos^2(A+B)$

(ii) LHS $=4\cos12°\cos48°\cos72°$

$=2\cos12°(2\cos48°\cos72°)$

$=2\cos12°(\cos120°+\cos24°)$

$=2\cos12°\left(-\frac{1}{2}+\cos24°\right)=-\cos12°+2\cos12°\cos24°$

$=-\cos12°+\cos36°+\cos12°$

32. $\sin2\alpha\sin2\beta=\frac{1}{2}(2\sin2\alpha\sin2\beta)$

$=\frac{1}{2}[\cos(2\alpha-2\beta)-\cos(2\alpha+2\beta)]$

$=\frac{1}{2}[\cos2(\alpha-\beta)-\cos90°]=\frac{1}{2}\cos2(\alpha-\beta)$

Ans. $\frac{1}{2}$ and $-\frac{1}{2}$

33. (i) LHS $=(\cos3A+\cos7A)+(\cos5A+\cos15A)$

$=2\cos5A\cos2A+2\cos10A\cos5A$

$=2\cos5A(\cos2A+\cos10A)$

$=2\cos5A(2\cos6A\cos4A)$

(ii) LHS $=\frac{1}{2}\left(2\sin\frac{\theta}{2}\sin\frac{7\theta}{2}+2\sin\frac{3\theta}{2}\sin\frac{11\theta}{2}\right)$

$=\frac{1}{2}(\cos3\theta-\cos4\theta+\cos4\theta-\cos7\theta)$

$=\frac{1}{2}(\cos3\theta-\cos7\theta)$

34. LHS $=\frac{1}{2}\left[2\cos^2 A+2\cos^2\left(A+\frac{2\pi}{3}\right)+2\cos^2\left(A-\frac{2\pi}{3}\right)\right]$

$=\frac{1}{2}\left[1+\cos2A+\left\{1+\cos2\left(A+\frac{2\pi}{3}\right)\right\}\right.$

$\left.+\left\{1+\cos2\left(A-\frac{2\pi}{3}\right)\right\}\right]$

$=\frac{1}{2}\left[1+\cos2A+1+\cos\left(2A+\frac{4\pi}{3}\right)+1+\cos\left(2A-\frac{4\pi}{3}\right)\right]$

$=\frac{1}{2}\left[3+\cos2A+\cos\left(2A+\frac{4\pi}{3}\right)+\cos\left(2A-\frac{4\pi}{3}\right)\right]$

$=\frac{1}{2}\left[3+\cos2A+2\cos2A\cos\frac{4\pi}{3}\right]$

$[\because \cos(A+B)+\cos(A-B)=2\cos A\cos B]$

$=\frac{1}{2}\left[3+\cos2A+2\cos2A\left(\frac{-1}{2}\right)\right]$

35. LHS $=\tan\frac{11\pi}{24}$

$=\tan\left(\frac{\pi}{2}-\frac{\pi}{24}\right)=\cot\frac{\pi}{24}$

$=\frac{\cos\pi/24}{\sin\pi/24}=\frac{2\cos^2\pi/24}{2\sin\frac{\pi}{24}\cos\frac{\pi}{24}}$

$=\frac{1+\cos\frac{\pi}{12}}{\sin\frac{\pi}{12}}=\frac{1+\cos\left(\frac{\pi}{3}-\frac{\pi}{4}\right)}{\sin\left(\frac{\pi}{3}-\frac{\pi}{4}\right)}$

36. (i) $\frac{44}{125}$ (ii) $\frac{336}{527}$ (iii) $\frac{-119}{250}$ (iv) $\frac{25}{12}$

CHAPTER 04

Complex Numbers

When we come across equations like $x^2+1=0$, $x^2+9=0$, we found ourselves unable to solve these equations, because $x^2+1=0$ gives $x^2=-1$ or $x=\pm\sqrt{-1}$, as there is no number in the real number system, whose square is a negative number. Thus, to solve such type of problems, there is another number system called complex number system.

- Introduction to Complex Numbers
- Algebra of Complex Numbers
- Conjugate and Modulus of a Complex Number
- Geometrical and Polar Representation of Complex Number
- Square Root of a Complex Number and Cube Roots of Unity

TOPIC 01 Introduction to Complex Numbers

A **complex number** can be defined as a number of the form $a+ib$, where a and b are real numbers. The form $a+ib$, where $a, b \in R$ and $i=\sqrt{-1}$ is also known as **standard form** of a complex number. e.g. $6+9i$, $-3+4i$ etc., are complex numbers.

Here, the symbol i is used to denote $\sqrt{-1}$ and it is called **iota.**

The complex number is generally denoted by z i.e. $z=a+ib$. Complex number z can be represented in the form of order pair, i.e. z can be represented as (a, b).

Euler (1707-43) was the first mathematician, who introduced the symbol i (read as **iota**) for $\sqrt{-1}$ with property $i^2+1=0$, i.e. $i^2=-1$. He also called this symbol as **the imaginary unit.**

Integral Powers of a Complex Number

If z is any complex number, then positive integral powers of z are defined as $z^1=z, z^2=z\cdot z$, $z^3=z^2\cdot z, z^4=z^3\cdot z$ and so on.

Note If $z\neq 0$, then $z^0=1$.

Power of i (Iota)

I. Positive Integral Powers of i

As we have seen, $i=\sqrt{-1}$. So, we can write the higher powers of i as follows

(i) $i^2=-1$ (ii) $i^3=i^2\cdot i=(-1)\cdot i=-i$

(iii) $i^4=(i^2)^2=(-1)^2=1$

(iv) $i^5=i^{4+1}=i^4\cdot i=1\cdot i=i$

(v) $i^6=i^{4+2}=i^4\cdot i^2=1\cdot i^2=-1$

⋮ ⋮ ⋮ ⋮

While evaluating i^n for $n>4$, we are writing n as $4q+r$ for some $q, r\in N$ and $0\le r\le 3$. So, in order to compute i^n for $n>4$, write $i^n=i^{4q+r}$ for some $q, r\in N$ and $0\le r\le 3$. Then, $i^n=i^{4q}\cdot i^r=(i^4)^q\cdot i^r=(1)^q\cdot i^r=i^r$

e.g. $i^{17}=i^{4\times 4+1}=i^{4\times 4}\cdot i=(i^4)^4\cdot i=1\cdot i=i$

i^4 is defined as 1.

Note In general for any integer k, $i^{4k}=1$, $i^{4k+1}=i$, $i^{4k+2}=-1$ and $i^{4k+3}=-i$

II. Negative Integral Powers of i

Negative integral powers of i can be evaluated as follows

(i) $i^{-1}=\frac{1}{i}=\frac{1}{i}\times\frac{i}{i}$

[multiply numerator and denominator by i]

$=\frac{i}{i^2}=\frac{i}{(-1)}=-i$ $[\because i^2=-1]$

(ii) $i^{-2}=\frac{1}{i^2}=\frac{1}{(-1)}=-1$

(iii) $i^{-3}=\frac{1}{i^3}=\frac{1}{i^3}\times\frac{i}{i}$

[multiplying numerator and denominator by i]

$=\frac{i}{(i^4)}=\frac{i}{(1)}=i$

(iv) $i^{-4}=\frac{1}{i^4}=\frac{1}{1}=1$

In order to compute i^{-n} for $n>4$, first write

$i^{-n}=\frac{1}{i^n}=\frac{1}{i^{4q+r}}$ for some $q, r\in N$ and $0\le r\le 3$. Then, evaluate i^{4q+r}. Further, use above four negative integral powers of i.

e.g. $i^{-15}=\frac{1}{i^{15}}=\frac{1}{i^{4\times 3+3}}=\frac{1}{i^3}$ $[\because i^{4q+3}=i^3]$

$=\frac{1}{i^3}\times\frac{i}{i}=\frac{i}{i^4}=\frac{i}{1}=i$ $[\because i^4=1]$

Example 1 Find the value of

(i) i^{37} (ii) i^{-30} (iii) $\frac{1}{i^7}$

Sol. (i) We have, $i^{37}=(i)^{36+1}=(i)^{4\times 9}i$

$=(i^4)^9\cdot i=(1)^9\cdot i=i$ $[\because i^4=1]$

(ii) We have, $i^{-30}=\frac{1}{i^{30}}$

Now, $i^{30}=(i)^{4\times 7+2}=(i^{4\times 7})\,i^2=(i^4)^7\,(-1)$ $[\because i^2=-1]$

$=(1)^7\,(-1)=-1$ $[\because i^4=1]$

$\Rightarrow$ $i^{-30}=\frac{1}{(-1)}=-1$

(iii) We have, $\frac{1}{i^7}=\frac{1}{(i)^{4+3}}=\frac{1}{i^4\cdot i^3}$

$=\frac{1}{1\cdot(-i)}$ $[\because i^4=1$ and $i^3=-i]$

$=\frac{1}{-i}\times\frac{i}{i}=\frac{i}{-i^2}=\frac{i}{-(-1)}=i$ $[\because i^2=-1]$

Example 2 Express the following in the form of $a+ib$, where $a, b\in R$.

(i) i^{103} (ii) $(-\sqrt{-1})^{4x+3}$ (iii) $\left(i^{29}+\frac{1}{i^{29}}\right)$

Sol. (i) $i^{103}=i^{25\times 4+3}=(i^4)^{25}\cdot i^3=(1)^{25}\cdot(-i)$

$[\because i^4=1$ and $i^3=-i]$

$=-i=0-i$

(ii) $(-\sqrt{-1})^{4x+3}=(-i)^{4x+3}=(-i)^{4x}\cdot(-i)^3$

$=i^{4x}(-i^3)=(i^4)^x(-(-i))$ $[\because i^3=-i]$

$=(1)^x(i)$ $[\because i^4=1]$

$=i=0+i$

(iii) $i^{29}+\frac{1}{i^{29}}=\frac{i^{29}\cdot i^{29}+1}{i^{29}}=\frac{(i^2)^{29}+1}{i^{29}}$

$=\frac{(-1)^{29}+1}{i^{29}}=\frac{-1+1}{i^{29}}=0=0+0i$

Example 3 Evaluate $\frac{i^{592}+i^{590}+i^{588}+i^{586}+i^{584}}{i^{582}+i^{580}+i^{578}+i^{576}+i^{574}}$.

Sol. Given expression

$=\frac{i^{592}+i^{590}+i^{588}+i^{586}+i^{584}}{i^{582}+i^{580}+i^{578}+i^{576}+i^{574}}$

$$= \frac{i^{584+8} + i^{584+6} + i^{584+4} + i^{584+2} + i^{584}}{i^{574+8} + i^{574+6} + i^{574+4} + i^{574+2} + i^{574}}$$

$$= \frac{i^{584}(i^8 + i^6 + i^4 + i^2 + 1)}{i^{574}(i^8 + i^6 + i^4 + i^2 + 1)}$$

$$= \frac{i^{584}}{i^{574}} = i^{584-574} = i^{10}$$

$$= i^{4\times 2+2} = (i^4)^2 \cdot i^2$$

$$= (1)^2 \cdot i^2 = -1 \qquad [\because i^4 = 1 \text{ and } i^2 = -1]$$

Example 4 What is the value of $\dfrac{i^{4x+1} - i^{4x-1}}{2}$? **[NCERT Exemplar]**

Sol. Consider, $\dfrac{i^{4x+1} - i^{4x-1}}{2} = \dfrac{i^{4x} \cdot i - i^{4x} \cdot i^{-1}}{2} = \dfrac{i - \dfrac{1}{i}}{2}$ $\quad [\because i^{4x} = 1]$

$$= \frac{i^2 - 1}{2i} = \frac{-2}{2i} \qquad [\because i^2 = -1]$$

$$= \frac{-1}{i} = \frac{-i}{i^2} = \frac{-i}{-1} = i \qquad [\because i^2 = -1]$$

Real and Imaginary Parts of a Complex Number

Let $z = a + ib$ be a complex number, then a is called the **real part** and b is called the **imaginary part** of z and it may be denoted as **Re** (z) and **Im** (z), respectively.

e.g. If $z = 2 + 3i$, then Re $(z) = 2$ and Im $(z) = 3$.

Purely Real and Purely Imaginary Complex Numbers

A complex number $z = a + ib$, is called **purely real**, if $b = 0$ i.e. Im $(z) = 0$ and is called **purely imaginary**, if $a = 0$ i.e. Re $(z) = 0$.

e.g. $z = 6$ is purely real and $z = 6i$ is purely imaginary.

Zero Complex Number

A complex number is said to be zero, if its both real and imaginary parts are zero.

In other words, $z = a + ib = 0$ if and only if $a = 0$ and $b = 0$.

Set of Complex numbers

The product set $R \times R$ consisting of the ordered pair of real number called the **set of real numbers.** The set of complex numbers is denoted by C and it is defined as

$$C = \{a + ib;\ a, b \in R\}.$$

Note A real number cannot be equal to a imaginary number.

Example 5 Find the real and imaginary parts of the following complex numbers.

(i) 7 (ii) $3i$

Sol. (i) Let $z = 7 = 7 + 0i$

Here, Re $(z) = 7$ and Im $(z) = 0$

(ii) Let $z = 3i = 0 + 3i$

Here, Re $(z) = 0$ and Im $(z) = 3$

Example 6 Find the real value of 'a' for which $3i^3 - 2ai^2 + (1 - a)i + 5$ is real. **[NCERT Exemplar]**

Sol. $3i^3 - 2ai^2 + (1 - a)i + 5$

$$= 3(-i) + 2a + (1 - a)i + 5 \qquad [\because i^3 = -i \text{ and } i^2 = -1]$$

$$= (2a + 5) + i(1 - a - 3)$$

which will be real, if $1 - a - 3 = 0$, i.e. $a = -2$.

Equality of Complex Numbers

Two complex numbers $z_1 = a + ib$ and $z_2 = c + id$ are said to be **equal**, if $a = c$ and $b = d$. e.g. If two complex numbers $z_1 = a + ib$ and $z_2 = -1 + 3i$ are equal, then $a = -1$ and $b = 3$.

Note Two complex numbers are equal, if their real and imaginary parts are equal, i.e. $a + ib = x + iy$ if and only if $a = x$ and $b = y$.

Example 7 Find the real values of a and b, if

(i) $(3a - 6) + 2ib = -6b + (6 + a)i$

(ii) $(2a + 2b) + i(b - a) = -4i$

Sol. (i) We have, $(3a - 6) + 2ib = -6b + (6 + a)i$

On equating real and imaginary parts, we get

$$3a - 6 = -6b$$

$\Rightarrow$ $a - 2 = -2b$ [dividing both sides by 3]

and $2b = 6 + a$

Above equations can be rewritten as

$$a + 2b = 2 \qquad \text{...(i)}$$

and $a - 2b = -6$ ...(ii)

On adding Eqs. (i) and (ii), we get

$$a + 2b + a - 2b = 2 - 6$$

$\Rightarrow$ $2a = -4$

$\Rightarrow$ $a = -2$

On substituting $a = -2$ in Eq. (ii), we get

$$-2 - 2b = -6$$

$\Rightarrow$ $-2b = -6 + 2$

$\Rightarrow$ $b = \dfrac{-4}{-2} = 2$

Hence, $a = -2$ and $b = 2$.

(ii) We have,
$(2a + 2b) + i(b - a) = -4i$, which can be rewritten as

$$(2a + 2b) + i(b - a) = 0 - 4i$$

On equating real and imaginary parts, we get

$$2a + 2b = 0$$

$\Rightarrow \quad a + b = 0 \quad [\because 2 \neq 0]$ ...(i)

and $\quad b - a = -4$ ...(ii)

On adding Eqs. (i) and (ii), we get

$$a + b + b - a = 0 - 4$$

$\Rightarrow \quad 2b = -4 \Rightarrow b = -2$

On substituting $b = -2$ in Eq. (i), we get

$$a - 2 = 0$$

$\Rightarrow \quad a = 2$

Hence, $a = 2$ and $b = -2$.

Some Important Result

We already know that, $\sqrt{a} \times \sqrt{b} = \sqrt{ab}$ for all positive real numbers a and b. This result also holds true when either $a > 0, b < 0$ or $a < 0, b > 0$. But above result is not true for $a < 0, b < 0$, which can be explained as follows.

Let us consider, $i^2 = \sqrt{-1}\sqrt{-1} = \sqrt{(-1)(-1)}$

[by assuming $\sqrt{a} \times \sqrt{b} = \sqrt{ab}$ for all real numbers]

$$= \sqrt{1} = 1$$

which is a contradiction to the fact that $i^2 = -1$.

Therefore, $\sqrt{a} \times \sqrt{b} \neq \sqrt{ab}$, if both a and b are negative real numbers.

Note

(i) If a is positive real number, then
$\sqrt{-a} = \sqrt{a \times (-1)} = \sqrt{a} \times \sqrt{-1} = (\sqrt{a})i$.

(ii) If any of a and b is zero, then $\sqrt{a} \times \sqrt{b} = \sqrt{ab} = 0$.

Example 8 Find the value of $\sqrt{-25} + 3\sqrt{-4} + 2\sqrt{-9}$.

Sol. We have, $\sqrt{-25} + 3\sqrt{-4} + 2\sqrt{-9}$

$= \sqrt{25}\sqrt{-1} + 3\sqrt{4}\sqrt{-1} + 2\sqrt{9}\sqrt{-1}$

$= 5 \times i + 3 \times 2 \times i + 2 \times 3 \times i \quad [\because \sqrt{-1} = i]$

$= 5i + 6i + 6i = 17i$

Example 9 Write the real and imaginary parts of the complex number $\sqrt{37} + \sqrt{-19}$.

Sol. Let $z = \sqrt{37} + \sqrt{-19} = \sqrt{37} + \sqrt{19}\sqrt{-1}$

$\Rightarrow \quad z = \sqrt{37} + \sqrt{19}\,i \quad [\because \sqrt{-1} = i]$

$\therefore$ Re $(z) = \sqrt{37}$ and Im $(z) = \sqrt{19}$

Topic Practice 1

Very Short Answer Type Questions

(2 Marks)

1 Evaluate the following.

(i) (a) i^{80} (b) $\frac{1}{i}$

(ii) (a) $(-\sqrt{-1})^{31}$ (b) $\frac{i^2 + i^4 + i^6 + i^7}{1 + i^2 + i^3}$

2 Write the following as complex numbers.

(i) (a) $\sqrt{-27}$ (b) $\sqrt{-16}$

(ii) (a) $4 - \sqrt{-5}$ (b) $-1 - \sqrt{-5}$

3 Write the real and imaginary parts of the complex number.

(i) $\sqrt{37} + \sqrt{-19}$ (ii) $z = \frac{\sqrt{17}}{2} + \frac{2}{\sqrt{70}}i$

4 Write the real and imaginary parts of the following complex numbers.

(i) (a) $2 - i\sqrt{2}$ (b) $-\frac{1}{5} + \frac{i}{5}$

(ii) (a) $\frac{\sqrt{5}}{7}i$ (b) $\sqrt{41} + \sqrt{-29}$

5 Write the following as complex numbers.

(i) $\frac{\sqrt{3}}{2} - \frac{\sqrt{-2}}{\sqrt{7}}$ (ii) $\sqrt{x}\,; x > 0$

6 Express the following in the form of $a + ib$.

(i) (a) i^{-35} (b) i^{998}

(ii) (a) $(\sqrt{-1})^{90}$ (b) $\left(i^{37} \times \frac{1}{i^{67}}\right)$

Short Answer Type Questions

(4 Marks)

7 Simplify the following.

(i) (a) $2i^2 + 6i^3 + 3i^{16} - 6i^{19} + 4i^{25}$
(b) $1 + i^{10} + i^{110} + i^{1000}$

(ii) (a) $i^n + i^{n+1} + i^{n+2} + i^{n+3}$ (b) $\left\{i^{17} - \left(\frac{1}{i}\right)^{34}\right\}^2$

(iii) (a) $(-i)^{4n+3}$, where n is a positive integer. (b) $(2i)^3$

(iv) (a) i^{-35} (b) i^{-39}

(v) (a) $i^9 + i^{19}$ (b) $\left[i^{18} + \left(\frac{1}{i}\right)^{25}\right]^3$

(vi) (a) $i^6 + i^8$ (b) $i + i^2 + i^3 + i^4$

(vii) (a) $i^{12} + i^{13} + i^{14} + i^{15}$ (b) $i^4 + i^8 + i^{12} + i^{16}$

8 Prove that $i^{107}+i^{112}+i^{117}+i^{122}=0$.

9 Simplify $i^{n+100}+i^{n+50}+i^{n+48}+i^{n+46}$.

10 Explain the fallacy in the following.
$$-1=i\cdot i=\sqrt{-1}\cdot\sqrt{-1}=\sqrt{(-1)(-1)}=\sqrt{1}=1$$

11 Find the values of x and y, if $4x+i(3x-y)=3-6i$.

12 Evaluate $\sqrt{-16}+3\sqrt{-25}+\sqrt{-36}-\sqrt{-625}$.

13 If $i=\sqrt{-1}$, then prove that
$$(x+1+i)(x+1-i)(x-1+i)(x-1-i)=x^4+4.$$

Hints & Answers

1. (i) (a) $i^{80}=(i^4)^{20}=1^{20}$ **Ans.** 1(b) $-i$

(ii) (a) i

(b) $\dfrac{i^2+i^4+i^6+i^7}{1+i^2+i^3}=\dfrac{(-1)+(1)+(-1)+(-i)}{1+(-1)+(-i)}$

$=\dfrac{-1-i}{-i}=\dfrac{1}{i}+1$ **Ans.** $1-i$

2. (i) (a) $\sqrt{-27}=3\sqrt{3}\sqrt{-1}$ **Ans.** $0+i3\sqrt{3}$

(b) $0+4i$

(ii) (a) $4-\sqrt{-5}=4-\sqrt{5}\sqrt{-1}$ **Ans.** $4-i\sqrt{5}$

(b) $-1-i\sqrt{5}$

3. (i) Let $z=\sqrt{37}+\sqrt{-19}$

Then, $z=\sqrt{37}+\sqrt{19(-1)}=\sqrt{37}+i\sqrt{19}$

Ans. Re $(z)=37$ and Im $(z)=\sqrt{19}$

(ii) $\text{Re}(z)=\dfrac{\sqrt{17}}{2}$, $\text{Im}(z)=\dfrac{2}{\sqrt{70}}$

4. (i) (a) $2; -\sqrt{2}$ (b) $-\dfrac{1}{5};\dfrac{1}{5}$

(ii) (a) $0, \dfrac{\sqrt{5}}{7}$ (b) $\sqrt{41}, \sqrt{29}$

5. (i) $\dfrac{\sqrt{3}}{2}-i\dfrac{\sqrt{2}}{7}$ (ii) $\sqrt{x}+0i$

6. (i) (a) $i^{-35}=\dfrac{1}{i^{35}}=\dfrac{1}{i^{4\times 8+3}}$ **Ans.** $(0+i)$

(b) $i^{998}=i^{4\times 249+2}$ **Ans.** $-1+0\,i$

(ii) (a) $-1+0i$ (b) $-1+0i$

7. (i) (a) $2i^2+6i^3+3i^{16}-6i^{19}+4i^{25}$
$=2(-1)+6(-i)+3(1)-6(-i)+4(i)$ **Ans.** $1+4i$

(b) 0

(ii) (a) 0 (b) $2i$ (iii) (a) i (b) $-8i$

(iv) (a) i (b) i (v) (a) 0 (b) $2-2i$

(vi) (a) 0 (b) 0 (vii) (a) 0 (b) 4

8. $i^{4\times 26+3}+i^{4\times 28+0}+i^{4\times 29+1}+i^{4\times 30+2}$
$=(i^4)^{26}\cdot i^3+(i^4)^{28}\cdot i^0+(i^4)^{29}\cdot i+(i^4)^{30}\cdot i^2$

Ans. 0

9. Given expression $=i^{n+100}+i^{n+50}+i^{n+48}+i^{n+46})$
$=i^n\,(i^{100}+i^{50}+i^{48}+i^{46})$

Ans. 0

10. We know, $\sqrt{a}\,\sqrt{b}=\sqrt{ab}$ holds, if and only if atleast one of a and b is non-negative.

11. Solve as Example 7. **Ans.** $x=\dfrac{3}{4}$ and $y=\dfrac{33}{4}$

12. Solve as Example 8. **Ans.** 0

13. $(x+1+i)(x+1-i)(x-1+i)(x-1-i)$
$$=((x+1)^2-i^2)((x-1)^2-i^2)$$
$$=((x+1)^2+1)((x-1)^2+1)$$
$$=(x^2+2x+1+1)(x^2-2x+1+1)$$
$$=(x^2+2+2x)(x^2+2-2x)$$
$$=(x^2+2)^2-4x^2$$
$$=x^4+4x^2+4-4x^2$$
$$=x^4+4$$

TOPIC 02 Algebra of Complex Numbers

In this section, we shall study how to add, subtract, multiply and divide the complex numbers.

Addition of Complex Numbers

Let $z_1=a_1+i\,b_1$ and $z_2=a_2+i\,b_2$ be two complex numbers, then their addition is defined as
$$z=z_1+z_2=(a_1+a_2)+i\,(b_1+b_2)$$

e.g. (i) $(5+3i)+(-4-i)=(5-4)+i(3-1)=1+2i$

(ii) $(2+3i)+(-6+7i)=(2-6)+i(3+7)=-4+10i$

Note It can be observed that

(i) Real part of $(z_1+z_2)=\text{Re}(z_1+z_2)=\text{Re}(z_1)+\text{Re}(z_2)$.

(ii) Imaginary part of $(z_1+z_2)=\text{Im}(z_1+z_2)=\text{Im}(z_1)+\text{Im}(z_2)$.

Properties of Addition of Complex Numbers

The addition of complex numbers satisfy the following properties

(i) **Closure Property** If z_1 and z_2 are any two complex numbers, then $z_1 + z_2$ is also a complex number.

(ii) **Commutative Property** If z_1 and z_2 are two complex numbers, then $z_1 + z_2 = z_2 + z_1$.

(iii) **Associative Property** If z_1, z_2 and z_3 are any three complex numbers, then

$$(z_1 + z_2) + z_3 = z_1 + (z_2 + z_3)$$

(iv) **Existence of Additive Identity** There exists the complex number $0 = 0 + 0\,i$ called the identity element for addition (or simply additive identity) i.e. $z + 0 = z = 0 + z$ for all $z \in C$.

(v) **Existence of Additive Inverse** For every complex number $z = a + ib$, there exists $-z = (-a) + i(-b)$ such that $z + (-z) = 0 = (-z) + z$. Here, complex number $(-z)$, is called the additive inverse of z.

e.g. Additive inverse of $z = (-4 + 3i)$ is

$$-z = -(-4 + 3i) = (4 - 3i)$$

Subtraction of Complex Numbers

Let $z_1 = a_1 + ib_1$ and $z_2 = a_2 + ib_2$ be two complex numbers. Then, their subtraction $z_1 - z_2$ is defined as the addition of z_1 and $(-z_2)$.

Thus, $z_1 - z_2 = z_1 + (-z_2) = (a_1 + ib_1) + (-a_2 - ib_2)$

$$z_1 - z_2 = (a_1 - a_2) + i(b_1 - b_2)$$

e.g. (i) $(-4 + 7i) - (-11 - 23i) = (-4 + 7i) + (11 + 23i)$

$$= (-4 + 11) + (7 + 23)i = 7 + 30i$$

(ii) $(6 + 5i) - (3 + 2i) = (6 + 5i) + (-3 - 2i)$

$$= (6 - 3) + (5 - 2)\,i = 3 + 3i$$

Note It can be observed that

(i) Real part of $(z_1 - z_2) = \text{Re}\,(z_1 - z_2) = \text{Re}\,(z_1) - \text{Re}\,(z_2)$

(ii) Imaginary part of $(z_1 - z_2) = \text{Im}(z_1 - z_2) = \text{Im}(z_1) - \text{Im}(z_2)$

Example 1 Express the following in the form of $a + ib$.

(i) $\left[\left(\frac{1}{3} + \frac{7}{3}i\right) + \left(4 + \frac{1}{3}i\right)\right] - \left(-\frac{4}{3} + i\right)$ **[NCERT]**

(ii) $\left(\frac{1}{2} + \frac{5}{2}i\right) - \frac{3}{2}i + \left(-\frac{5}{2} - i\right)$

Sol. (i) Consider the given expression,

$$\left[\left(\frac{1}{3} + \frac{7}{3}i\right) + \left(4 + \frac{1}{3}i\right)\right] - \left(-\frac{4}{3} + i\right)$$

$$= \left[\left(\frac{1}{3} + 4\right) + i\left(\frac{7}{3} + \frac{1}{3}\right)\right] - \left(-\frac{4}{3} + i\right)$$

$$= \left(\frac{13}{3} + \frac{8}{3}i\right) + \left(\frac{4}{3} - i\right) = \left(\frac{13}{3} + \frac{4}{3}\right) + i\left(\frac{8}{3} - 1\right)$$

$= \frac{17}{3} + \frac{5}{3}i$, which is in the form of $a + ib$.

(ii) $\left(\frac{1}{2} + \frac{5}{2}i\right) - \frac{3}{2}i + \left(-\frac{5}{2} - i\right)$

$$= \left(\frac{1}{2} - \frac{5}{2}\right) + i\left(\frac{5}{2} - \frac{3}{2} - 1\right)$$

$= -2 + i0$, which is in the form of $a + ib$.

Note For expressing the given expression in standard form i.e. in the form of $a + ib$, just simplify the expression according to the rules of algebra.

Example 2 Find the real values of x and y, if

$$(x^4 + 2xi) - (3x^2 + iy) = (3 - 5\,i) + (1 + 2\,iy).$$

Sol. We have, $(x^4 + 2xi) - (3x^2 + iy) = (3 - 5\,i) + (1 + 2\,iy)$

$\Rightarrow \quad (x^4 - 3x^2) + (2x - y)\,i = 4 + (-5 + 2y)\,i$

On equating real and imaginary parts both sides, we get

$$x^4 - 3x^2 = 4 \quad \text{... (i)}$$

and $\quad 2x - y = -5 + 2y$

$\Rightarrow \quad 2x - 3y = -5 \quad \text{...(ii)}$

On solving Eq. (i), we get

$$x^4 - 3x^2 = 4 \Rightarrow x^4 - 3x^2 - 4 = 0$$

$\Rightarrow \quad x^4 - 4x^2 + x^2 - 4 = 0$

$\Rightarrow (x^2 - 4)(x^2 + 1) = 0 \Rightarrow x^2 - 4 = 0$

$[\because x^2 + 1 \neq 0$, for any real value of $x]$

$\therefore \quad x = \pm 2$

On putting $x = \pm 2$ in Eq. (ii), we get

$y = 3$, when $x = 2$ and $y = \frac{1}{3}$, when $x = -2$

Thus, $x = -2$, $y = \frac{1}{3}$ or $x = 2$, $y = 3$.

Multiplication of Complex Numbers

The product of two complex numbers $z_1 = a + ib$ and $z_2 = c + id$ can be as follow

$$z_1 z_2 = (a + ib)\,(c + id) = ac + iad + ibc + i^2 bd$$

$$= ac + i(ad + bc) + (-1)bd \quad [\because i^2 = -1]$$

$\therefore \quad z_1 z_2 = (ac - bd) + i(ad + bc)$

e.g. (i) $(2 + 9i)\,(11 + 3i)$

$$= 2 \times 11 + 2 \times 3i + 11 \times 9i + 9 \times 3i^2$$

$$= 22 + 6i + 99i - 27 = -5 + 105i \quad [\because i^2 = -1]$$

(ii) $(-5+7i)(-13-3i)$

$=(-5)(-13)+(-5)(-3i)+(7i)(-13)+(7i)(-3i)$

$=65+15i-91i-21i^2=65-76i+21$ $[\because i^2=-1]$

$=86-76i$

(iii) $(5i)\left(\frac{-3}{5}i\right)=\left[5\times\left(\frac{-3}{5}\right)\right](i\times i)$

$=(-3)(i^2)=-3\times(-1)=3$

Multiplication of a Complex Number and a Rational Number

(i) Let $z=x+iy$ be a complex number and p/q be a rational number, then the multiplication of p/q and z is $\frac{p}{q}(x+iy)=\frac{p}{q}x+i\frac{p}{q}y$.

(ii) Let a be a real number, then $a(x+iy)=ax+iay$.

Properties of Multiplication of Complex Numbers

(i) **Closure Property** If z_1 and z_2 are any two complex numbers, then $z_1 z_2$ is also a complex number.

(ii) **Commutative Property** If z_1 and z_2 are any two complex numbers, then $z_1 z_2 = z_2 z_1$.

(iii) **Associative Property** If z_1, z_2 and z_3 are any three complex numbers, then $(z_1 z_2)z_3 = z_1(z_2 z_3)$.

(iv) **Existence of Multiplicative Identity** There exists the complex number $1=1+0\cdot i$ is the **identity** element for multiplication i.e. for every complex number z, we have $z\cdot 1=1\cdot z=z$.

(v) **Existence of Multiplicative Inverse** Corresponding to every non-zero complex number $z=a+ib$, there exists a complex number $z_1=x+iy$ such that $z\cdot z_1=1=z_1\cdot z$, where

$$x=\frac{a}{a^2+b^2} \text{ and } y=\frac{-b}{a^2+b^2}.$$

Then, z_1 is called multiplicative inverse of z and it is denoted by $\frac{1}{z}$ or z^{-1}. We also called z_1, the **reciprocal** of z.

e.g. Let $z=3-7i$. Then, $a=3$ and $b=-7$.

Its multiplicative inverse,

$$z^{-1}=\left[\frac{3}{(3)^2+(-7)^2}\right]+i\left[\frac{-(-7)}{(3)^2+(-7)^2}\right]$$

$$=\left(\frac{3}{9+49}\right)+i\left(\frac{7}{9+49}\right)=\frac{3}{58}+\frac{7i}{58}$$

(vi) **Distributive Law** If z_1, z_2 and z_3 are any three complex numbers.

Then, $z_1(z_2+z_3)=z_1z_2+z_1z_3$ [left distributive law]

and $(z_1+z_2)z_3=z_1z_3+z_2z_3$ [right distributive law]

Example 3 If z_1 and z_2 are complex numbers, then prove that $\text{Re}(z_1 z_2)=\text{Re}(z_1)\,\text{Re}(z_2)-\text{Im}(z_1)\,\text{Im}(z_2)$. **[NCERT]**

Sol. Let $z_1=x_1+iy_1$ and $z_2=x_2+iy_2$

Then, $z_1z_2=(x_1x_2-y_1y_2)+i(x_1y_2+y_1x_2)$

$\therefore$ $\text{Re}(z_1z_2)=x_1x_2-y_1y_2$

$=\text{Re}(z_1)\,\text{Re}(z_2)-\text{Im}(z_1)\,\text{Im}(z_2)$

Hence proved.

Example 4 Express the following in the form $a+ib$

(i) $(-i)(3i)\left(-\frac{1}{6}i\right)^3$ (ii) $(-\sqrt{3}+\sqrt{-2})(-2+\sqrt{-3})$

Sol. (i) $(-i)(3i)\left(-\frac{1}{6}i\right)^3=(-3i^2)\left(-\frac{1}{216}i^3\right)$

$=(-3\times(-1))\left(-\frac{1}{216}(-i)\right)$ $[\because i^2=-1 \text{ and } i^3=-i]$

$=3\times\frac{1}{216}\times i=\frac{i}{72}=0+\frac{1}{72}i$

which is in the form of $a+ib$.

(ii) $(-\sqrt{3}+\sqrt{-2})(-2+\sqrt{-3})$

$=(-\sqrt{3}+i\sqrt{2})(-2+i\sqrt{3})$

$[\because \sqrt{-2}=\sqrt{2}\times\sqrt{-1}=\sqrt{2}i, \text{ similarly } \sqrt{-3}=\sqrt{3}i]$

$=2\sqrt{3}-3i-2\sqrt{2}\,i+i^2\sqrt{6}$

$=2\sqrt{3}-i(3+2\sqrt{2})-\sqrt{6}$ $[\because i^2=-1]$

$=(2\sqrt{3}-\sqrt{6})-i(3+2\sqrt{2})$

which is in the form of $a+ib$.

Example 5 Find the values of x and y, given that $(x+iy)(2-3i)=4+i$. **[ISC 2008]**

Sol. Given, $(x+iy)(2-3i)=4+i$

$\Rightarrow$ $x(2-3i)+iy(2-3i)=4+i$

$\Rightarrow$ $2x-3xi+2yi-3yi^2=4+i$

$\Rightarrow$ $2x-3x\,i+2yi+3y=4+i$ $[\because i^2=-1]$

$\Rightarrow$ $2x+3y+i(2y-3x)=4+i$

On comparing real and imaginary parts both sides, we get

$2x+3y=-4$ ...(i)

and $2y-3x=1$ ...(ii)

On multiplying Eq. (i) by 3 and Eq. (ii) by 2, we get

$$6x + 9y = 12 \quad \text{...(iii)}$$

and $$4y - 6x = 2 \quad \text{...(iv)}$$

On adding Eqs. (iii) and (iv), we get

$$13y = 14 \Rightarrow y = \frac{14}{13}$$

On putting $y = \frac{14}{13}$ in Eq. (i), we get

$$2x + 3 \times \frac{14}{13} = 4$$

$$\Rightarrow \quad 2x = 4 - \frac{42}{3}$$

$$\Rightarrow \quad 2x = \frac{10}{13} \Rightarrow x = \frac{5}{13}$$

Some Important Identities

Identity is an equation which is true for all values of the variable (complex number) involved in it. Here, we have the following identities.

(i) $(z_1 + z_2)^2 = z_1^2 + z_2^2 + 2z_1z_2$, for all complex numbers z_1 and z_2.

(ii) $(z_1 - z_2)^2 = z_1^2 - 2z_1z_2 + z_2^2$

(iii) $(z_1 + z_2)^3 = z_1^3 + 3z_1^2z_2 + 3z_1z_2^2 + z_2^3$

(iv) $(z_1 - z_2)^3 = z_1^3 - 3z_1^2z_2 + 3z_1z_2^2 - z_2^3$

(v) $z_1^2 - z_2^2 = (z_1 + z_2)(z_1 - z_2)$

(vi) $(z_1 + z_2)(z_1 - z_2) = z_1^2 - z_2^2$

Proof (i) We have, $(z_1 + z_2)^2 = (z_1 + z_2)(z_1 + z_2)$

$= (z_1 + z_2)z_1 + (z_1 + z_2)z_2$

[assume first bracket as one term and then apply distributive law]

$= z_1^2 + z_2z_1 + z_1z_2 + z_2^2$ [by distributive law]

$= z_1^2 + z_1z_2 + z_1z_2 + z_2^2$

[by commutative law of multiplication]

$= z_1^2 + 2z_1z_2 + z_2^2$

Similarly, we can prove the other parts.

Note Many other identities which are true for all real numbers, can be true for all complex numbers.

Example 6 Simplify each of the following and put it in the form $a + ib$.

(i) $(2 + \sqrt{-3})^2$ (ii) $\left(\frac{1}{3} + 3i\right)^3$ **[NCERT]**

(iii) $(3 + \sqrt{-5})(3 - \sqrt{-5})$

Sol. (i) $(2 + \sqrt{-3})^2 = (2 + \sqrt{3}i)^2$

$= 2^2 + 2\cdot(2)(\sqrt{3}i) + (\sqrt{3}i)^2$

$[\because (z_1 + z_2)^2 = z_1^2 + 2z_1z_2 + z_2^2]$

$= 4 + 4\sqrt{3}i + 3i^2 = 4 + 4\sqrt{3}i - 3$

$= 1 + 4\sqrt{3}i$ $[\because i = -1]$

(ii) $\left(\frac{1}{3} + 3i\right)^3 = \left(\frac{1}{3}\right)^3 + 3\left(\frac{1}{3}\right)^2(3i) + 3\left(\frac{1}{3}\right)(3i)^2 + (3i)^3$

$[\because (z_1 + z_2)^3 = z_1^3 + 3z_1^2z_2 + 3z_1z_2^2 + z_2^3]$

$= \frac{1}{27} + 3\left(\frac{1}{9}\right)(3i) + 3\left(\frac{1}{3}\right)(9i^2) + 27i^3$

$= \frac{1}{27} + i + 9(-1) + 27(-i)$ $[\because i^2 = -1 \text{and } i^3 = -i]$

$= \frac{1}{27} - 9 - 26i = \frac{1 - 243}{27} - 26i = \frac{-242}{27} - 26i$

(iii) $(3 + \sqrt{-5})(3 - \sqrt{-5}) = (3 + \sqrt{5}i)(3 - \sqrt{5}i)$

$= (3)^2 - (\sqrt{5}i)^2$ $[\because (z_1 - z_2)(z_1 + z_2) = z_1^2 - z_2^2]$

$= 9 - 5i^2 = 9 + 5 = 14$ $[\because i^2 = -1]$

Example 7 Express $\frac{1 - 2i}{2 + i} + \frac{3 + i}{2 - i}$ in the form $a + ib$. **[ISC 2006]**

Sol. Given, $\frac{1 - 2i}{2 + i} + \frac{3 + i}{2 - i}$

$= \frac{(1 - 2i)(2 - i) + (3 + i)(2 + i)}{(2 + i)(2 - i)}$

$= \frac{(2 - i - 4i - 2) + (6 + 3i + 2i - 1)}{(2)^2 + (1)^2}$

$[\because i^2 = -1 \text{ and } (a + ib)(a - ib) = a^2 + b^2]$

$= \frac{-5i + 5 + 5i}{5} = \frac{5}{5} \Rightarrow a + ib = 1 + 0i$

Example 8 Evaluate $(1 + i)^6 + (1 - i)^3$. **[NCERT Exemplar]**

Sol. We have, $(1 + i)^6 = ((1 + i)^2)^3$

$= (1 + i^2 + 2i)^3$

$[\because (z_1 + z_2)^2 = z_1^2 + z_2^2 + 2z_1z_2]$

$= (1 - 1 + 2i)^3$ $[\because i^2 = -1]$

$\Rightarrow (1 + i)^6 = (2i)^3 = 8i^3 = -8i$ $[\because i^3 = -1]$ ...(i)

and $(1 - i)^3 = 1^3 - i^3 - 3(1)^2i + 3(1)(i)^2$

$[\because (z_1 - z_2)^3 = z_1^3 - 3z_1^2z_2 + 3z_1z_2^2 - z_2^3]$

$= 1 - (-i) - 3i - 3$ $[\because i^3 = -i \text{ and } i^2 = -1]$

$\Rightarrow (1 - i)^3 = -2 - 2i$ ...(ii)

On adding Eqs. (i) and (ii), we get

$(1 + i)^6 + (1 - i)^3 = -8i - 2 - 2i = -2 - 10i$

Example 9 Find the values of x and y, if $(3x-2iy)(2+i)^2=10(1+i)$.

Sol. We have, $(3x-2iy)(2+i)^2=10(1+i)$

$\Rightarrow \quad (3x-2iy)(4+i^2+4i)=10+10i$

$[\because (z_1+z_2)^2=z_1^2+z_2^2+2z_1z_2]$

$\Rightarrow \quad (3x-2iy)(4-1+4i)=10+10i \qquad [\because i^2=-1]$

$\Rightarrow \quad (3x-2iy)(3+4i)=10+10i$

$\Rightarrow \quad (9x+8y)+i(12x-6y)=10+10i$

On equating real and imaginary parts of both sides, we get

$$9x+8y=10 \qquad \dots \text{(i)}$$

and

$$12x-6y=10 \qquad \dots \text{(ii)}$$

On multiplying Eq. (i) by 6 and Eq. (ii) by 8, then adding the result, we get

$54x+48y+96x-48y=60+80$

$\Rightarrow \quad 150x=140 \Rightarrow x=\frac{14}{15}$

On substituting $x=\frac{14}{15}$ in Eq. (i), we get

$$9\times\frac{14}{15}+8y=10 \Rightarrow \frac{42}{5}+8y=10$$

$\Rightarrow \quad 8y=10-\frac{42}{5} \Rightarrow 8y=\frac{8}{5}$

$\Rightarrow \quad y=\frac{1}{5}$

$\therefore \quad x=\frac{14}{15}$ and $y=\frac{1}{5}$

Example 10 If $(x+iy)^{1/3}=a+ib$, where $x, y, a, b \in R$, then show that $\frac{x}{a}-\frac{y}{b}=-2(a^2+b^2)$.

[NCERT Exemplar]

Sol. We have, $(x+iy)^{1/3}=a+ib$

$\Rightarrow \quad x+iy=(a+ib)^3 \qquad$ [cubing both sides]

$\Rightarrow \quad x+iy=a^3+i^3b^3+3a^2bi+3ab^2i^2$

$[\because (z_1+z_2)^3=z_1^3+z_2^3+3z_1^2z_2+3z_1z_2^2]$

$\Rightarrow \quad x+iy=a^3-ib^3+i3a^2b-3ab^2$

$[\because i^3=-i \text{ and } i^2=-1]$

$\Rightarrow \quad x+iy=a^3-3ab^2+i(3a^2b-b^3)$

On equating real and imaginary parts from both sides, we get

$$x=a^3-3ab^2 \text{ and } y=3a^2b-b^3$$

$\Rightarrow \quad \frac{x}{a}=a^2-3b^2$ and $\frac{y}{b}=3a^2-b^2$

Now, $\frac{x}{a}-\frac{y}{b}=a^2-3b^2-3a^2+b^2$

$=-2a^2-2b^2=-2(a^2+b^2)$

Example 11 Find the value of $2x^4+5x^3+7x^2-x+41$, when $x=-2-\sqrt{3}i$.

[NCERT Exemplar]

Sol. We have, $x=-2-\sqrt{3}i \Rightarrow x+2=-\sqrt{3}i$

On squaring both sides, we get

$(x+2)^2=(-\sqrt{3}i)^2 \Rightarrow x^2+4+4x=3i^2$

$[\because (z_1+z_2)^2=z_1^2+z_2^2+2z_1z_2]$

$\Rightarrow \quad x^2+4x+4=-3 \qquad [\because i^2=-1]$

$\Rightarrow \quad x^2+4x+7=0$

Now, divide $2x^4+5x^3+7x^2-x+41$ by x^2+4x+7.

$$\begin{array}{r|l} & 2x^2-3x+5 \\ x^2+4x+7 & 2x^4+5x^3+7x^2-x+41 \\ & 2x^4+8x^3+14x^2 \\ & -\quad -\quad - \\ \hline & -3x^3-7x^2-x+41 \\ & -3x^3-12x^2-21x \\ & +\quad +\quad + \\ \hline & 5x^2+20x+41 \\ & 5x^2+20x+35 \\ & -\quad -\quad - \\ \hline & 6 \end{array}$$

Thus, $2x^4+5x^3+7x^2-x+41$

$=(x^2+4x+7)(2x^2-3x+5)+6$

[$\because$ dividend = quotient × divisor + remainder]

$=0\times(2x^2-3x+5)+6=6 \qquad [\because x^2+4x+7=0]$

Division of Complex Numbers

The division of a complex number z_1 by a non-zero complex number z_2 is defined as the multiplication of z_1 by the multiplicative inverse of z_2 and is denoted by $\frac{z_1}{z_2}$.

Therefore, $\frac{z_1}{z_2}=z_1\cdot z_2^{-1}=z_1\cdot\left(\frac{1}{z_2}\right)$

Multiplication and Division of a Complex Number by an Integer

Let $z=x+iy$ be a complex number and m be an integer, then $m(x+iy)=mx+imy$

and $\quad \frac{1}{m}(x+iy)=\frac{x}{m}+i\frac{y}{m}$

e.g. $\quad -7(2+3i)=-14-2i$

and $\quad \frac{1}{4}(6+9i)=\frac{6}{4}+\frac{9}{4}i=\frac{3}{2}+\frac{9}{4}i$

Note Order relations i.e. greater than and less than are not defined for complex numbers.

Method for Expressing the Division of Complex Numbers in Standard Form

In this method, we use the following steps

Step I Simplify the numerator and denominator separately and convert it in the form of $\frac{a+ib}{c+id}$.

Step II On rationalising the denominator of the result obtained in step I, i.e. multiply the numerator and denominator by $c-id$.

Step III Simplify and write it in the $x+iy$ form.

Example 12 Express $\frac{(3+\sqrt{5}i)(3-\sqrt{5}i)}{(\sqrt{3}+\sqrt{2}i)-(\sqrt{3}-\sqrt{2}i)}$ in the form of $a+ib$. **[NCERT]**

Sol. $\frac{(3+\sqrt{5}i)(3-\sqrt{5}i)}{(\sqrt{3}+\sqrt{2}i)-(\sqrt{3}-\sqrt{2}i)} = \frac{(3)^2-(\sqrt{5}i)^2}{\sqrt{3}+\sqrt{2}i-\sqrt{3}+\sqrt{2}i}$

$[\because (z_1+z_2)(z_1-z_2)=z_1^2-z_2^2]$

$$=\frac{9+5}{2\sqrt{2}i}=\frac{14}{2\sqrt{2}i}=\frac{7}{\sqrt{2}i}\times\frac{\sqrt{2}i}{\sqrt{2}i}$$

[by rationalising the denominator]

$$=\frac{7\sqrt{2}i}{2i^2}=\frac{7\sqrt{2}i}{-2}=0-i\frac{7\sqrt{2}}{2}$$

$=0+i\left(\frac{-7\sqrt{2}}{2}\right)$, which is in the form of $(a+ib)$.

Example 13 Reduce $\left(\frac{1}{1-4i}-\frac{2}{1+i}\right)\left(\frac{3-4i}{5+i}\right)$ to the standard form. **[NCERT]**

Sol. $\left(\frac{1}{1-4i}-\frac{2}{1+i}\right)\left(\frac{3-4i}{5+i}\right)$

$$=\left[\frac{1+i-2(1-4i)}{(1-4i)(1+i)}\right]\left(\frac{3-4i}{5+i}\right)$$

$$=\left(\frac{1+i-2+8i}{1+i-4i-4i^2}\right)\left(\frac{3-4i}{5+i}\right)$$

$$=\left(\frac{-1+9i}{1-3i+4}\right)\left(\frac{3-4i}{5+i}\right) \quad [\because i^2=-1]$$

$$=\left(\frac{-1+9i}{5-3i}\right)\left(\frac{3-4i}{5+i}\right)$$

$$=\frac{-3+4i+27i-36i^2}{25+5i-15i-3i^2}$$

$$=\frac{-3+31i+36}{25-10i+3}=\frac{33+31i}{28-10i} \quad [\because i^2=-1]$$

$$=\frac{(33+31i)}{(28-10i)}\times\frac{(28+10i)}{(28+10i)}$$

[by rationalising the denominator]

$$=\frac{924+868i+330i+310i^2}{784-100i^2}$$

$$=\frac{924+1198i-310}{784+100}$$

$$=\frac{614+1198i}{884}=\frac{307}{442}+\frac{599}{442}i$$

Example 14 Express $\left(\frac{4i^3-1}{2i+1}\right)^2$ in the form of $a+ib$, where $a, b \in R$.

Sol. $\left(\frac{4i^3-1}{2i+1}\right)^2=\left[\frac{4\cdot(-i)-1}{2i+1}\right]^2 \quad [\because i^3=-i]$

$$=\left(\frac{-4i-1}{2i+1}\right)^2=\frac{(1+4i)^2}{(1+2i)^2}=\frac{1+16i^2+8i}{1+4i^2+4i}$$

$[\because (z_1+z_2)^2=z_1^2+z_2^2+2z_1z_2]$

$$=\frac{1-16+8i}{1-4+4i}=\frac{-15+8i}{-3+4i} \quad [\because i^2=-1]$$

$$=\frac{15-8i}{3-4i}=\frac{15-8i}{3-4i}\times\frac{3+4i}{3+4i}$$

[by rationalising the denominator]

$$=\frac{(15-8i)(3+4i)}{9^2-16i^2}$$

$[\because (z_1-z_2)(z_1+z_2)=z_1^2-z_2^2]$

$$=\frac{(15-8i)(3+4i)}{9-16i^2}$$

$$=\frac{45+60i-24i-32i^2}{9+16}$$

$$=\frac{45+36i+32}{25}=\frac{77+36i}{25}$$

$$=\frac{77}{25}+\frac{36}{25}i$$

which is in the form of $(a+ib)$.

Example 15 If $a+ib=\frac{x+i}{x-i}$, where x is real, then prove that $a^2+b^2=1$ and $\frac{b}{a}=\frac{2x}{x^2-1}$. **[NCERT]**

Sol. We have, $a+ib=\frac{x+i}{x-i}=\frac{x+i}{x-i}\times\frac{x+i}{x+i}$

[by rationalising the denominator]

$$=\frac{x^2+2xi+i^2}{x^2-i^2}=\frac{x^2-1+2xi}{x^2+1} \quad [\because i^2=-1]$$

$$\Rightarrow \quad a+ib=\frac{x^2-1}{x^2+1}+\frac{2x}{x^2+1}i$$

On comparing real and imaginary parts both sides, we get

$$a = \frac{x^2 - 1}{x^2 + 1} \text{ and } b = \frac{2x}{x^2 + 1} \quad ...(i)$$

Now, $a^2 + b^2 = \left(\frac{x^2 - 1}{x^2 + 1}\right)^2 + \left(\frac{2x}{x^2 + 1}\right)^2$ [from Eq. (i)]

$$= \frac{(x^2 - 1)^2 + 4x^2}{(x^2 + 1)^2}$$

$$= \frac{x^4 + 1 - 2x^2 + 4x^2}{(x^2 + 1)^2}$$

$$= \frac{x^4 + 1 + 2x^2}{(x^2 + 1)^2} = \frac{(x^2 + 1)^2}{(x^2 + 1)^2} = 1$$

Also, $\frac{b}{a} = \frac{\frac{2x}{x^2 + 1}}{\frac{x^2 - 1}{x^2 + 1}} = \frac{2x}{x^2 - 1}$ [from Eq. (i)]

Hence proved.

Example 16 If $\left(\frac{1+i}{1-i}\right)^3 - \left(\frac{1-i}{1+i}\right)^3 = x + iy$, then find (x, y). **[NCERT Exemplar]**

Sol. Consider, $\frac{1+i}{1-i} = \frac{1+i}{1-i} \times \frac{1+i}{1+i}$

[by rationalising the denominator]

$$= \frac{(1+i)^2}{1-i^2} = \frac{1 + i^2 + 2i}{1+1}$$

$\Rightarrow \quad \frac{1+i}{1-i} = \frac{1 - 1 + 2i}{2} = i \quad [\because i^2 = -1] ...(i)$

Now, $\frac{1-i}{1+i} = \frac{1}{\left(\frac{1+i}{1-i}\right)} = \frac{1}{i}$ [from Eq. (i)]

$$= \frac{1}{i} \times \frac{i}{i} = \frac{i}{i^2}$$

$$= \frac{i}{(-1)} = -i \quad [\because i^2 = -1] ...(ii)$$

Hence, $\left(\frac{1+i}{1-i}\right)^3 - \left(\frac{1-i}{1+i}\right)^3 = i^3 - (-i)^3$

$$= i^3 + i^3 = 2i^3$$

$$= 2(-i) = 0 - 2i \quad [\because i^3 = -i]$$

$\therefore \quad x + iy = 0 - 2i$

On comparing real and imaginary parts both sides, we get $x = 0$ and $y = -2$

$\therefore \quad (x, y) = (0, -2)$

Topic Practice 2

Very Short Answer Type Questions

(2 Marks)

1. Express the following in the form $a + ib$.
   (i) $\left(\frac{1}{5} + \frac{2}{5}i\right) - \left(4 + i\frac{5}{2}\right)$ **[NCERT]**
   (ii) $3(1 - 2i) - (-4 - 5i) + (-8 + 3i)$
2. Find the real values of x and y for which $(1 + i)y^2 + (6 + i) = (2 + i)x$.
3. Find the real values of x and y for which $(x + iy)(2 - 3i) = 4 + i$.
4. Express $(7 + 5i)(7 - 5i)$ in the form of $a + ib$ and also find its additive inverse.
5. Express $\frac{5 + \sqrt{2}i}{1 - \sqrt{2}i}$ in the form $a + ib$ and also find its additive inverse.
6. Express the following in the form of $a + ib$.
   (i) (a) $(7 - i2) - (4 + i) + (-3 + i5)$
   (b) $\left[\left(\frac{1}{3} + i\frac{7}{3}\right) + \left(4 + i\frac{1}{3}\right)\right] - \left(-\frac{4}{3} + i\right)$
   (ii) (a) $i^3 + (6 + 3i) - (20 + 5i) + (14 + 3i)$
   (b) $3i^3(15i^6)$
7. Evaluate $\frac{(1 - i)^3}{1 - i^3}$ and also find its multiplicative inverse. **[NCERT Exemplar]**
8. If $\left(\frac{1-i}{1+i}\right)^{100} = a + ib$, then find (a, b).
9. If $\frac{(1+i)^2}{2-i} = x + iy$, then find the value of $x + y$.
10. Express $\left[\left(\sqrt{5} + \frac{i}{2}\right)(\sqrt{5} - 2i)\right] \div (6 + 5i)$ in the form $a + ib$.
11. If $x + iy = \frac{a + i}{a - i}$, then prove that $ay - 1 = x$.
12. Express $(5 - 3i)^3$ in the form $a + ib$. **[NCERT]**

13 Express the following in the form $a+ib$.

(i) $(1+i)^4$ (ii) $\left(\frac{1}{2}+i2\right)^3$

(iii) $\left(-2-i\frac{1}{3}\right)^3$ (iv) $\left(\frac{1}{3}+3i\right)^3$

(v) $(5-3i)^3$ (vi) $(1-i)^4$

14 What is the smallest positive integer n, for which $(1+i)^{2n}=(1-i)^{2n}$?

15 If $z_1, z_2 \in C$, prove that $\text{Im}(z_1 \cdot z_2)=\text{Re}(z_1)\cdot\text{Im}(z_2)+\text{Im}(z_1)\cdot\text{Re}(z_2)$.

16 Find x and y, if $(3x-2iy)(2+i)^2=10(1+i)$.

17 Find the real values of x and y, if $\frac{x-1}{3+i}+\frac{y-1}{3-i}=i$.

18 Find the following as a single complex number $x+iy$.

(i) $\frac{(3+i\sqrt{5})(3-i\sqrt{5})}{(\sqrt{3}+i\sqrt{2})-(\sqrt{3}-i\sqrt{2})}$

(ii) $\left(\frac{1}{1-4i}-\frac{2}{1+i}\right)\left(\frac{3-4i}{5+i}\right)$

Short Answer Type Questions

4 Marks

19 Find the values of x and y, if

$$\frac{(1+i)x-2i}{3+i}+\frac{(2-3i)y+i}{3-i}=i.$$

20 If $x=\sqrt{-2}-1$, then find the value of $x^4+4x^3+6x^2+4x+9$.

21 If $x=3+4i$, then find the value of $x^4-12x^3+70x^2-204x+225$.

22 If $x=3+2i$, then find the value of $x^4-4x^3+4x^2+8x+39$.

23 If $x=-5+2\sqrt{-4}$, then find the value of $x^4+9x^3+35x^2-x+4$.

24 Evaluate $2x^3+2x^2-7x+72$, when $x=\frac{3-5i}{2}$.

Hints & Answers

1. (i) $-\frac{19}{5}-\frac{21}{10}i$ (ii) $-1+2i$

2. $y^2+iy^2+6+i=2x+ix$

$\Rightarrow \quad y^2+6=2x$ and $y^2+1=x$

Ans. $(x=5,\ y=2)$ or $(x=5,\ y=-2)$

3. $x=\frac{5}{13}$ and $y=\frac{14}{13}$

4. Use the identity, $(z_1+z_2)(z_1-z_2)=z_1^2-z_2^2$.

Ans. $74+0i$ and $-74-0i$

5. Multiply numerator and denominator by $1+\sqrt{2i}$, we get

$$\frac{5+\sqrt{2i}}{1-\sqrt{2i}}\times\frac{1+\sqrt{2i}}{1+\sqrt{2i}}=\frac{3+6\sqrt{2i}}{1+2}$$

Ans. $1+2\sqrt{2}\,i$ and $-1-2\sqrt{2}i$

6. (i) (a) $0+2i$ (b) $\frac{17}{3}+\frac{5}{3}i$

(ii) (a) $0+0i$ (b) $0+45i$

7. $\frac{(1-i)^3}{1-i^3}=\frac{1^3-i^3-3i+3i^2}{1+i}$

Ans. -2 and $\frac{-1}{2}$

8. $\left(\frac{1-i}{1+i}\right)^{100}=\left(\frac{1-i}{1+i}\times\frac{1-i}{1-i}\right)^{100}$

$$=\left(\frac{1^2+i^2-2i}{1+1}\right)^{100}=\left(\frac{1-1-2i}{2}\right)^{100}$$

Ans. $(1, 0)$

9. $\frac{(1+i)^2}{2-i}=\frac{1+i^2+2i}{2-i}=\frac{2i}{2-i}\times\frac{2+i}{2+i}$

Ans. $\frac{2}{5}$

10. $$\frac{\left(\sqrt{5}+\frac{i}{2}\right)(\sqrt{5}-2i)}{6+5i}=\frac{5+1+\left(\frac{\sqrt{5}}{2}-2\sqrt{5}\right)i}{6+5i}$$

$$=\frac{6-\frac{3\sqrt{5}i}{2}}{(6+5i)}\times\frac{6-5i}{6-5i}$$

Ans. $\frac{72-15\sqrt{5}}{122}-i\left(\frac{30+9\sqrt{5}}{61}\right)$

11. $\frac{a+i}{a-i}\times\frac{a+i}{a+i}=\frac{a^2-1+2ai}{a^2+1}$

12. $(5-3i)^3=5^3-(3i)^3-3\times5^2\times3i+3\times5\times(3i)^2$

$$=125+27i-225i-135$$

Ans. $-10-198i$

13. (i) $(1+i)^4 = (1+i)^2(1+i)^2$
$= (1-1+2i)(1-1+2i) = (2i)(2i)$

Ans. $-4+0i$

(ii) $\left(\frac{1}{2}+2i\right)^3 = \left(\frac{1}{2}\right)^3 + (2i)^3 + 3\left(\frac{1}{2}\right)^2(2i) + 3\left(\frac{1}{2}\right)(2i)^2$
$= \frac{1}{8} - 8i + \frac{3i}{2} - 6$

Ans. $-\frac{47}{8} - \frac{13}{2}i$

(iii) $-\frac{22}{3} - \frac{107}{27}i$ (iv) $-\frac{242}{27} - 26i$

(v) $-10-198\,i$ (vi) $-4+0i$

14. Write the given expression as $\left(\frac{1+i}{1-i}\right)^{2n} = 1$

Ans. $n = 2$

15. Now, $z_1z_2 = (a_1+ib_1)(a_2+ib_2)$

$\Rightarrow$ $z_1z_2 = a_1a_2 - b_1b_2 + (b_1a_2 + a_1b_2)i$

$\therefore$ $\text{Im}(z_1z_2) = a_1b_2 + b_1a_2$
$= \text{Re}(z_1)\,\text{Im}(z_2) + \text{Re}(z_2)\,\text{Im}(z_1)$

16. Given, $(3x-2iy)(2+i)^2 = 10(1+i)$

$\Rightarrow$ $(3x-2iy)(4+4i+i^2) = 10+10i$

$\Rightarrow$ $(9x-6yi+12xi-8i^2y) = 10+10i$

$\therefore$ $9x+8y=10$ and $12x-6y=10$

Ans. $x = \frac{14}{15}$, $y = \frac{1}{5}$

17. $\frac{(x-1)(3-i)+(y-1)(3+i)}{(3+i)(3-i)} = i$

$\Rightarrow$ $\frac{(3x+3y-6)+i(y-x)}{9-i^2} = i$

Ans. $x = -4$, $y = 6$

18. (i) $\frac{(3+i\sqrt{5})(3-i\sqrt{5})}{(\sqrt{3}+i\sqrt{2})-(\sqrt{3}-i\sqrt{2})} = \frac{9+5}{2i\sqrt{2}}$ **Ans.** $-\frac{7\sqrt{2}}{2}i$

(ii) $\left(\frac{1}{1-4i} - \frac{2}{1+i}\right)\left(\frac{3-4i}{5+i}\right)$
$= \frac{(-1+9i)(3-4i)}{(5-3i)(5+i)} = \frac{33+31i}{28-10i} \times \frac{28+10i}{28+10i}$

Ans. $\frac{307}{442} + \frac{599}{442}i$

19. Given, $\frac{(1+i)x-2i}{3+i} + \frac{(2-3i)\,y+i}{3-i} = i$

$\Rightarrow$ $\frac{x+(x-2)i}{3+i} + \frac{2y+(1-3y)i}{3-i} = i$

$\Rightarrow$ $\frac{[x+(x-2)i](3-i)+[2y+(1-3y)i](3+i)}{(3+i)(3-i)} = i$

$\Rightarrow$ $(4x+9y-3)+i\,(2x-7y-3) = 10i$

$\Rightarrow$ $4x+9y-3 = 0$

and $2x-7y-3 = 10.$

Ans. $x = 3$ and $y = -1$

20. $x+1 = \sqrt{2i} \Rightarrow x^2+1+2x = -2$

$\Rightarrow x^2+2x+3 = 0$

Further, solve as Example 11. **Ans.** 12

21. $x-3 = 4i \Rightarrow x^2+9-6x = -16$

$\Rightarrow$ $x^2-6x+25 = 0$

Further, solve as Example 11. **Ans.** 0

22. Solve as Example 11. **Ans.** 0

23. Solve as Example 11. **Ans.** -160

24. Solve as Example 11. **Ans.** 4

TOPIC 03 Conjugate and Modulus of a Complex Number

Conjugate of a Complex Number

A pair of complex numbers z_1 and z_2 is said to be **conjugate** of each other, if the sum and product of z_1 and z_2 both are real.

Let $z_1 = a+ib$ and $z_2 = a-ib$.

Then, sum of z_1 and $z_2 = (a+ib)+(a-ib) = 2a$ (real)

and product of z_1 and $z_2 = (a+ib)\,(a-ib)$

$= a^2 - i^2b^2$ $[\because (x+y)(x-y) = x^2-y^2]$

$= a^2+b^2$ (real) $[\because i^2 = -1]$

Hence, z_1 and z_2 are conjugate to each other.

The conjugate of a complex number z, is the complex number, obtained by changing the sign of imaginary part of z and it is denoted by $\bar{z}$.

e.g. If $z = 2+3i$, then $\bar{z} = 2-3i$

and if $z = -4-3i$, then $\bar{z} = -4+3i$.

Note

(i) The conjugate of a complex number $z = a + ib$ is $\bar{z} = \overline{a + ib} = a - ib$.

(ii) A pair of complex numbers z_1 and z_2 is said to be **conjugate** of each other, if $\bar{z}_1 = z_2$ and $\bar{z}_2 = z_1$.

(iii) The conjugate of purely real complex number is same, i.e. if $z = 3$, then $\bar{z} = 3$.

Example 1 Find the conjugate of complex number $3 + i$.

Sol. Let $z = 3 + i$

$\therefore \bar{z} = 3 - i$

[$\because$ conjugate of complex number z, is the complex number, obtained by changing the sign of imaginary part of z]

Example 2 Simplify the following complex number.

$$\overline{9 - i} + \overline{6 + i^3} - \overline{9 + i^2}$$

Sol. $\overline{9 - i} + \overline{6 + i^3} - \overline{9 + i^2}$

$= (9 + i) + \overline{6 - i} - \overline{9 - 1}$ $\quad [\because i^3 = -i \text{ and } i^2 = -1]$

$= (9 + i) + (6 + i) - \bar{8}$

$= 15 + 2i - 8 = 7 + 2i$

Example 3 Find the real and imaginary parts of the conjugate of the complex number $-5i^{-15} - 6i^{-8}$.

Sol. Let $z = -5i^{-15} - 6i^{-8}$

$$= \frac{-5}{i^{15}} - \frac{6}{i^8} = \frac{-5}{(i^4)^3 \cdot i^3} - \frac{6}{(i^4)^2} \quad [\because i^{15} = i^{4\times3+3}]$$

$$= \frac{-5}{(1)^3 \cdot (-i)} - \frac{6}{(1)^2} \quad [\because i^4 = 1 \text{ and } i^3 = -i]$$

$$= \frac{-5}{-i} - 6 = \frac{5}{i} - 6 = \frac{5 - 6i}{i} = \frac{(5 - 6i)i}{i \cdot i}$$

[by rationalising the denominator]

$$= \frac{5i - 6i^2}{i^2} = \frac{5i + 6}{-1} = -6 - 5i \quad [\because i^2 = -1]$$

$\therefore \quad \bar{z} = -6 + 5i$

Hence, $\text{Re}(\bar{z}) = -6$ and $\text{Im}(\bar{z}) = 5$

Example 4 Find the real numbers x and y, if $(x - iy)(3 + 5i)$ is the conjugate of $-6 - 24i$.

Sol. We have, $(x - iy)(3 + 5i)$ is the conjugate of $-6 - 24i$.

$\Rightarrow \quad (x - iy)(3 + 5i) = -6 + 24i$

[$\because$ conjugate of $-6 - 24i = -6 + 24i$]

$\Rightarrow \quad 3x - 3iy + 5ix - 5i^2y = -6 + 24i$

$\Rightarrow \quad (3x + 5y) + i(5x - 3y) = -6 + 24i \quad [\because i^2 = -1]$ ...(i)

On equating real and imaginary parts both sides of Eq. (i), we get

$3x + 5y = -6$ ...(ii)

and $\quad 5x - 3y = 24$ ...(iii)

On multiplying Eq. (i) by 3 and Eq. (ii) by 5, then adding the result, we get

$9x + 15y + 25x - 15y = -18 + 120$

$\Rightarrow \quad 34x = 102 \Rightarrow x = 3$

On substituting $x = 3$ in Eq. (i), we get

$9 + 5y = -6 \Rightarrow 5y = -15 \Rightarrow y = -3$

Hence, the required values of x and y are respectively 3 and -3.

Example 5 Let $z_1 = 2 - i$ and $z_2 = -2 + i$, then find $\text{Re}\left(\frac{z_1 z_2}{\bar{z}_1}\right)$. **[NCERT]**

Sol. We have, $z_1 = 2 - i$ and $z_2 = -2 + i$

Now, $\frac{z_1 z_2}{\bar{z}_1} = \frac{(2 - i)(-2 + i)}{\overline{(2 - i)}} = \frac{-(2 - i)(2 - i)}{2 + i}$

$$= -\frac{(4 + i^2 - 4i)}{2 + i} = -\frac{(4 - 1 - 4i)}{2 + i} = -\frac{(3 - 4i)}{2 + i} \times \frac{2 - i}{2 - i}$$

[by rationalising the denominator]

$$= -\frac{(6 - 3i - 8i + 4i^2)}{4 - i^2} \quad [\because (z_1 + z_2)(z_1 - z_2) = z_1^2 - z_2^2]$$

$$= -\frac{(6 - 11i - 4)}{5} \quad [\because i^2 = -1]$$

$$= -\frac{2 - 11i}{5} = \frac{-2}{5} + \frac{11}{5}i \therefore \text{Re}\left(\frac{z_1 z_2}{\bar{z}_1}\right) = \text{Re}\left(\frac{-2}{5} + \frac{11i}{5}\right) = \frac{-2}{5}$$

Example 6 What is the conjugate of $\frac{2 - i}{(1 - 2i)^2}$? **[NCERT Exemplar]**

Sol. Let $z = \frac{2 - i}{(1 - 2i)^2} = \frac{2 - i}{(1^2 - 2(1)(2i) + (2i)^2)}$

$[\because (z_1 - z_2)^2 = z_1^2 - 2z_1 z_2 + z_2^2]$

$$\Rightarrow z = \frac{2 - i}{(1 - 4i - 4)} \quad [\because i^2 = -1]$$

$$\Rightarrow z = \frac{2 - i}{-3 - 4i} \Rightarrow z = \frac{2 - i}{-3 - 4i} \times \frac{-3 + 4i}{-3 + 4i}$$

[by rationalising the denominator]

$$\Rightarrow z = \frac{(2 - i)(-3 + 4i)}{(-3)^2 - (4i)^2}$$

$[\because (z_1 + z_2)(z_1 - z_2) = z_1^2 - z_2^2]$

$$\Rightarrow z = \frac{-6 + 8i + 3i - 4i^2}{9 - 16i^2} \Rightarrow z = \frac{-6 + 11i + 4}{9 + 16} \quad [\because i^2 = -1]$$

$$\Rightarrow z = \frac{-2 + 11i}{25} \Rightarrow z = -\frac{2}{25} + \frac{11}{25}i$$

Hence, $\quad \bar{z} = -\frac{2}{25} - \frac{11}{25}i$

Example 7 Solve the equation $z^2 = \bar{z}$, where $z = x + iy$. **[NCERT Exemplar]**

Sol. We have, $z^2 = \bar{z} \Rightarrow (x+iy)^2 = x - iy$

$$\Rightarrow \quad x^2 + (iy)^2 + 2xyi = x - iy \quad [\because (z_1+z_2)^2 = z_1^2 + z_2^2 + 2z_1z_2]$$

$$\Rightarrow \quad x^2 - y^2 + 2xyi = x - iy \quad [\because i^2 = -1]$$

On equating real and imaginary parts, we get

$$x^2 - y^2 = x \quad \text{...(i)}$$

and $$2xy = -y \quad \text{...(ii)}$$

From Eq. (ii), we have

$$2xy + y = 0$$

$$\Rightarrow \quad y(2x+1) = 0$$

$$\Rightarrow \quad y = 0 \text{ or } x = -\frac{1}{2}$$

Case **I** When $y = 0$.

In this case, we have $x^2 = x$ [from Eq. (i)]

$$\Rightarrow \quad x^2 - x = 0 \Rightarrow x(x-1) = 0 \Rightarrow x = 0 \text{ or } x = 1$$

$$\therefore \quad z = 0 + 0i \text{ or } z = 1 + 0i$$

Case **II** When $x = -\frac{1}{2}$.

In this case, we have

$$\frac{1}{4} - y^2 = -\frac{1}{2} \quad \text{[from Eq. (i)]}$$

$$\Rightarrow \quad y^2 = \frac{1}{4} + \frac{1}{2} = \frac{3}{4} \Rightarrow y = \pm\frac{\sqrt{3}}{2}$$

$$\therefore \quad z = -\frac{1}{2} \pm i\frac{\sqrt{3}}{2}$$

Hence, the solutions of given equation are $0 + 0i, 1 + 0i, -\frac{1}{2} + i\frac{\sqrt{3}}{2}$ and $-\frac{1}{2} - i\frac{\sqrt{3}}{2}$.

Properties of Conjugate of a Complex Number

Property 1. The conjugate of the conjugate of a complex number is the complex number itself, i.e. if z is a complex number. Then, $\overline{(\bar{z})} = z$.

Property 2. $z = \bar{z} \Leftrightarrow z$ is purely real, i.e. a complex number is equal to its conjugate, if it is a purely real number.

Property 3. The conjugate of the sum of two complex numbers is the sum of their conjugates, i.e. if z_1 and z_2 are two complex numbers, then $\overline{z_1 + z_2} = \overline{z_1} + \overline{z_2}$.

Property 4. The conjugate of the difference of two complex numbers is equal to the difference of their conjugates, i.e. if z_1 and z_2 are two complex numbers, then $\overline{z_1 - z_2} = \overline{z_1} - \overline{z_2}$.

Property 5. The conjugate of the product of two complex numbers is the product of their conjugates, i.e. $\overline{z_1 z_2} = \overline{z_1} \cdot \overline{z_2}$ where, z_1 and z_2 are two complex numbers.

Property 6. The conjugate of the quotient of two complex numbers (non-zero denominator) is the quotient of their conjugates, i.e. $\overline{\left(\frac{z_1}{z_2}\right)} = \frac{\overline{z_1}}{\overline{z_2}}$.

Property 7. The square of the conjugate of a complex number is equal to the conjugate of the square of that complex number, i.e. $(\bar{z})^2 = \overline{(z^2)}$.

Example 8 If $z_1 = 3 + 2i$ and $z_2 = 2 - i$, then verify that

(i) $\overline{z_1 + z_2} = \bar{z}_1 + \bar{z}_2$ (ii) $\overline{z_1 z_2} = \bar{z}_1 \, \bar{z}_2$

Sol. Given that, $z_1 = 3 + 2i$ and $z_2 = 2 - i$

(i) Now, $z_1 + z_2 = (3+2i) + (2-i) = 5 + i$

$$\Rightarrow \quad \overline{z_1 + z_2} = \overline{5+i} = 5 - i \quad \text{...(i)}$$

Now, consider $\bar{z}_1 + \bar{z}_2 = \overline{(3+2i)} + \overline{(2-i)}$

$$= 3 - 2i + 2 + i = 5 - i \quad \text{...(ii)}$$

From Eqs. (i) and (ii), we get

$$\overline{z_1 + z_2} = \bar{z}_1 + \bar{z}_2$$

(ii) Now, $z_1 z_2 = (3+2i)(2-i) = 6 - 3i + 4i - 2i^2$

$$= 6 + i - 2(-1) = 8 + i \quad [\because i^2 = -1]$$

$$\Rightarrow \quad \overline{z_1 z_2} = \overline{8+i} = 8 - i \quad \text{...(i)}$$

Now, consider $\bar{z}_1 \, \bar{z}_2 = (3-2i)(2+i)$

$$= 6 + 3i - 4i - 2i^2$$

$$= 6 - i - 2(-1) = 8 - i \quad [\because i^2 = -1] \text{...(ii)}$$

From Eqs. (i) and (ii), we get

$$\overline{z_1 z_2} = \bar{z}_1 \, \bar{z}_2$$

Example 9 If $z_1 = 3 + 5i$ and $z_2 = 2 - 3i$, then verify that $\overline{\left(\frac{z_1}{z_2}\right)} = \frac{\bar{z}_1}{\bar{z}_2}$.

Sol. Given, $z_1 = 3 + 5i$ and $z_2 = 2 - 3i$

Now, $$\frac{z_1}{z_2} = \frac{3+5i}{2-3i} = \frac{3+5i}{2-3i} \times \frac{2+3i}{2+3i}$$

[by rationalising the denominator]

$$= \frac{6 + 9i + 10i + 15i^2}{4 - 9i^2}$$

$$= \frac{6 + 19i - 15}{4 + 9} \quad [\because i^2 = -1]$$

$$= \frac{-9+19i}{13} = \frac{-9}{13} + \frac{19}{13}i \quad ...(i)$$

$$\therefore \quad \text{LHS} = \overline{\left(\frac{z_1}{z_2}\right)} = \overline{\left(\frac{-9}{13} + \frac{19}{13}i\right)} = \frac{-9}{13} - \frac{19}{13}i$$

Now, consider RHS $= \dfrac{\overline{z_1}}{\overline{z_2}} = \dfrac{3+5i}{2-3i} = \dfrac{3-5i}{2+3i}$

$$= \frac{3-5i}{2+3i} \times \frac{2-3i}{2-3i}$$

[by rationalising the denominator]

$$= \frac{6-9i-10i+15i^2}{4-9i^2}$$

$$= \frac{6-19i-15}{4+9} \quad [\because i^2 = -1]$$

$$= \frac{-9-19i}{13} = \frac{-9}{13} - \frac{19}{13}i \quad ...(ii)$$

From Eqs. (i) and (ii), we get

$$\overline{\left(\frac{z_1}{z_2}\right)} = \frac{\overline{z_1}}{\overline{z_2}}$$

Example 10 If $x + iy = \dfrac{(a^2+1)^2}{2a-i}$, what is the value of $x^2 + y^2$?

Sol. We have, $\quad x + iy = \dfrac{(a^2+1)^2}{2a-i} \quad ...(i)$

$$\therefore \quad \overline{x+iy} = \overline{\left\{\frac{(a^2+1)^2}{2a-i}\right\}}$$

$$\Rightarrow \quad x - iy = \frac{\overline{(a^2+1)^2}}{\overline{2a-i}} \quad \left[\because \overline{\left(\frac{z_1}{z_2}\right)} = \frac{\overline{z_1}}{\overline{z_2}}\right]$$

$$\Rightarrow \quad x - iy = \frac{(a^2+1)^2}{2a+i} \quad ...(ii)$$

On multiplying Eqs. (i) and (ii), we get

$$(x+iy)(x-iy) = \frac{(a^2+1)^2(a^2+1)^2}{(2a-i)(2a+i)}$$

$$\Rightarrow \quad x^2 - (iy)^2 = \frac{(a^2+1)^4}{(2a)^2 - i^2}$$

$$[\because (z_1+z_2)(z_1-z_2) = z_1^2 - z_2^2]$$

$$\Rightarrow \quad x^2 - i^2y^2 = \frac{(a^2+1)^4}{4a^2+1} \quad [\because i^2 = -1]$$

$$\therefore \quad x^2 + y^2 = \frac{(a^2+1)^4}{4a^2+1}$$

Example 11 If $x + iy = \sqrt{\dfrac{1+i}{1-i}}$, then prove that $x^2 + y^2 = 1$.

Sol. We have, $x + iy = \sqrt{\dfrac{1+i}{1-i}} \Rightarrow x + iy = \sqrt{\dfrac{1+i}{1-i} \times \dfrac{1+i}{1+i}}$

[by rationalising the denominator]

$$\Rightarrow \quad x + iy = \sqrt{\frac{(1+i)^2}{1-i^2}} \quad [\because (z_1 - z_2)(z_1 + z_2) = z_1^2 - z_2^2]$$

$$\Rightarrow \quad x + iy = \frac{1+i}{\sqrt{1+1}} = \frac{1+i}{\sqrt{2}} \quad [\because i^2 = -1]$$

$$= \frac{1}{\sqrt{2}} + \frac{i}{\sqrt{2}} \quad ...(i)$$

Now, taking conjugate on both sides, we get

$$\overline{x+iy} = \overline{\left(\frac{1}{\sqrt{2}} + \frac{i}{\sqrt{2}}\right)} \Rightarrow x - iy = \frac{1}{\sqrt{2}} - \frac{i}{\sqrt{2}} \quad ...(ii)$$

On multiplying Eqs. (i) and (ii), we get

$$(x+iy)(x-iy) = \left(\frac{1}{\sqrt{2}} + \frac{i}{\sqrt{2}}\right)\left(\frac{1}{\sqrt{2}} - \frac{i}{\sqrt{2}}\right)$$

$$\Rightarrow \quad x^2 - (iy)^2 = \left(\frac{1}{\sqrt{2}}\right)^2 - \left(\frac{i}{\sqrt{2}}\right)^2$$

$$[\because (z_1+z_2)(z_1-z_2) = z_1^2 - z_2^2]$$

$$\Rightarrow x^2 - i^2y^2 = \frac{1}{2} - \frac{i^2}{2} \Rightarrow x^2 + y^2 = \frac{1}{2} + \frac{1}{2} = 1 \quad [\because i^2 = -1]$$

Hence proved.

Modulus (or Absolute Value) of a Complex Number

The **modulus** (or absolute value) of a complex number, $z = a + ib$ is defined as non-negative real number $\sqrt{a^2 + b^2}$ and it is denoted by $|z|$. i.e. $|z| = \sqrt{a^2 + b^2}$.

e.g. If $z = 2 + 3i$, then $|z| = \sqrt{2^2 + 3^2} = \sqrt{4+9} = \sqrt{13}$

and if $z = 1 - i$, then $|z| = \sqrt{(1)^2 + (-1)^2} = \sqrt{1+1} = \sqrt{2}$.

Note

(i) The multiplicative inverse of z is $\dfrac{\bar{z}}{|z|^2}$ and it is also called the **reciprocal** of z.

(ii) $z\bar{z} = |z|^2$

Example 12 Find the modulus of the complex number $\dfrac{\sqrt{3} - i\sqrt{2}}{2\sqrt{3} - i\sqrt{2}}$.

Sol. Let $z = \dfrac{\sqrt{3} - i\sqrt{2}}{2\sqrt{3} - i\sqrt{2}} = \dfrac{\sqrt{3} - i\sqrt{2}}{2\sqrt{3} - i\sqrt{2}} \times \dfrac{2\sqrt{3} + i\sqrt{2}}{2\sqrt{3} + i\sqrt{2}}$

[by rationalising the denominator]

$$= \frac{6 + i\sqrt{6} - 2\sqrt{6}\,i - 2\,i^2}{(2\sqrt{3})^2 - (\sqrt{2}\,i)^2}$$

$$[\because (z_1 - z_2)(z_1 + z_2) = z_1^2 - z_2^2]$$

$$= \frac{6-\sqrt{6}\,i+2}{12+2} \qquad [\because i^2=-1]$$

$$= \frac{8-\sqrt{6}\,i}{14} = \frac{8}{14} - \frac{\sqrt{6}}{14}i \Rightarrow z = \frac{4}{7} - \frac{\sqrt{6}}{14}i$$

Now, modulus of z, $|z| = \sqrt{\left(\frac{4}{7}\right)^2 + \left(\frac{-\sqrt{6}}{14}\right)^2}$

$$= \sqrt{\frac{16}{49}+\frac{6}{196}} = \sqrt{\frac{64+6}{196}} = \sqrt{\frac{70}{196}} = \sqrt{\frac{5}{14}}$$

Example 13 If $|z|=1$, then find the value of $\frac{1+z}{1+\bar{z}}$.

Sol. Given, $|z|=1 \Rightarrow |z|^2=1$

$$\Rightarrow \quad z\bar{z}=1 \qquad [\because |z|^2 = z\bar{z}]$$

Now, $\frac{1+z}{1+\bar{z}} = \frac{z\bar{z}+z}{1+\bar{z}} = \frac{z(\bar{z}+1)}{(\bar{z}+1)} = z \qquad [\because 1 = z\bar{z}]$

Example 14 Find the modulus and argument of the complex number $\frac{2+i}{4i+(1+i)^2}$. **[ISC 2011]**

Sol. Suppose $z = \frac{2+i}{4i+(1+i)^2} = \frac{2+i}{4i+1+i^2+2i}$

$$= \frac{2+i}{1-1+6i} = \frac{2+i}{6i}\times\frac{i}{i}$$

[multiplying numerator and denominator by i]

$$= \frac{[2+i]\,i}{6\times(-1)} = -\left(\frac{2i-1}{6}\right) = \frac{1}{6} - \frac{1}{3}i \qquad [\because i^2=-1]$$

Now, modulus of z is

$$|z| = \sqrt{\left(\frac{1}{6}\right)^2 + \left(\frac{-1}{3}\right)^2} = \sqrt{\frac{1}{36}+\frac{1}{9}}$$

$$[\because x = x+iy = |z| = \sqrt{z^2+y^2}]$$

$$= \sqrt{\frac{1+4}{36}} = \sqrt{\frac{5}{36}} = \frac{\sqrt{5}}{6}$$

Argument of $z = -\tan^{-1}\left|\frac{(-1/3)}{1/6}\right|$

[$\because$ z lies in fourth quadrant as imaginary part is negative]

$$= -\tan^{-1}|-2| = -\tan^{-1} 2$$

$$= -63^\circ 20' \text{ (approx.)}$$

Example 15 If $|z|=1$, then prove that $\frac{z-1}{z+1}$; $(z \neq 1)$ is a purely imaginary number. What will you conclude, if $z=1$?

Sol. Let $z = a+ib$, such that $|z| = \sqrt{a^2+b^2} = 1$

$$\Rightarrow \quad a^2+b^2=1$$

Now, consider $\left(\frac{z-1}{z+1}\right) = \left(\frac{a+ib-1}{a+ib+1}\right)$

$$= \frac{(a-1+ib)}{(a+1+ib)} \times \frac{(a+1-ib)}{(a+1-ib)}$$

[by rationalising the denominator]

$$= \frac{[(a-1)+ib][(a+1)-ib]}{(a+1)^2-(ib)^2}$$

$$[\because (z_1+z_2)(z_1-z_2) = z_1^2 - z_2^2]$$

$$= \frac{a^2-1-iab+ib+iab+ib-i^2b^2}{(a+1)^2-i^2b^2}$$

$$= \frac{(a^2+b^2-1)+2bi}{(a+1)^2+b^2} \qquad [\because i^2=-1]$$

$$= \frac{(1-1)+2bi}{a^2+1+2a+b^2}$$

$$[\because a^2+b^2=1 \text{ and } (z_1+z_2)^2 = z_1^2+z_2^2+2z_1z_2]$$

$$= \frac{0+2bi}{(a^2+b^2)+1+2a} = \frac{2bi}{2+2a} \qquad [\because a^2+b^2=1]$$

$$= 0 + \frac{bi}{1+a}$$

Clearly, real part of $\left(\frac{z-1}{z+1}\right)$ is zero and imaginary part of $\left(\frac{z-1}{z+1}\right)$ is $\frac{b}{1+a}$.

$\therefore$ $\left(\frac{z-1}{z+1}\right) = \frac{ib}{1+a}$ is purely imaginary.

Again, when $z=1$, then

$\left(\frac{z-1}{z+1}\right) = \frac{1-1}{1+1} = 0$, which is purely real.

Example 16 If $(-2+\sqrt{-3})(-3+2\sqrt{-3}) = a+ib$, then find the real numbers a and b. With these values of a and b, also find the modulus of $a+ib$. **[ISC 2014]**

Sol. Given, $(-2+\sqrt{-3})(-3+2\sqrt{-3}) = a+ib$

$$\Rightarrow \quad (-2+\sqrt{3}i)(-3+2\sqrt{3}i) = a+ib \qquad [\because \sqrt{-1}=i]$$

$$\Rightarrow \quad -2\times(-3)+(-2)(2\sqrt{3})\,i - 3\sqrt{3}i - 6 = a+ib$$

$$[\because i^2 = -1]$$

$$\Rightarrow \quad 6-4\sqrt{3}i-3\sqrt{3}i-6 = a+ib$$

$$\Rightarrow \quad -7\sqrt{3}i = a+ib \Rightarrow 0-7\sqrt{3}i = a+ib$$

On comparing real and imaginary parts both sides, we get

$a=0$ and $b=-7\sqrt{3}$

Now, modulus of $a+ib = \sqrt{a^2+b^2}$

$$= \sqrt{0^2+(-7\sqrt{3})^2} = 7\sqrt{3}$$

[put $a=0$ and $b=-7\sqrt{3}$]

Properties of Modulus of a Complex Number

If z, z_1 and z_2 are complex numbers, then

Property 1. The modulus of a complex number is zero if and only if the complex number is zero, i.e.

$$|z| = 0 \Leftrightarrow z = \theta, \text{ i.e. } \operatorname{Re}(z) = \operatorname{Im}(z) = 0.$$

Property 2. $z\bar{z} = |z|^2$.

Property 3. The modulus of a complex number and that of its conjugate are equal, i.e. $|z| = |\bar{z}|$

Property 4. (i) $-|z| \le \operatorname{Re}(z) \le |z|$ (ii) $-|z| \le \operatorname{Im}(z) \le |z|$

Property 5. $z^{-1} = \dfrac{\bar{z}}{|z|^2}$.

Property 6. The modulus of the product of two complex numbers is equal to the product of their moduli, i.e. $|z_1 z_2| = |z_1| \cdot |z_2|$.

Property 7. The moduli of the quotient of two complex numbers is the quotient of their moduli, i.e. $\left|\dfrac{z_1}{z_2}\right| = \dfrac{|z_1|}{|z_2|}$.

Example 17 If $z_1 = 3 + 2i$ and $z_2 = 1 - 3i$, then find the modulus of z_1 and z_2. Also, verify that $|z_1 z_2| = |z_1||z_2|$.

Sol. Given, $z_1 = 3 + 2i$ and $z_2 = 1 - 3i$

Clearly, $|z_1| = \sqrt{(3)^2 + (2)^2} = \sqrt{9+4} = \sqrt{13}$

and $|z_2| = \sqrt{1^2 + (-3)^2} = \sqrt{1+9} = \sqrt{10}$

$\therefore$ $|z_1||z_2| = \sqrt{13}\sqrt{10} = \sqrt{130}$ ...(i)

Now, consider $z_1 z_2 = (3+2i)(1-3i)$

$= 3 - 9i + 2i - 6(i^2)$

$= 3 - 7i + 6 = 9 - 7i$ $[\because i^2 = -1]$

$\therefore$ $|z_1 z_2| = \sqrt{9^2 + (-7)^2}$

$= \sqrt{81 + 49} = \sqrt{130}$ ...(ii)

From Eqs. (i) and (ii), we get $|z_1 z_2| = |z_1||z_2|$

Example 18 If $z_1 = 3 + 2i$ and $z_2 = 2 - 4i$, then verify that $|z_1 + z_2|^2 + |z_1 - z_2|^2 = 2(|z_1|^2 + |z_2|^2)$.

Sol. We have, $z_1 = 3 + 2i$ and $z_2 = 2 - 4i$

Now, LHS $= |z_1 + z_2|^2 + |z_1 - z_2|^2$

On substituting the values of z_1 and z_2, we get

LHS $= |3 + 2i + 2 - 4i|^2 + |3 + 2i - 2 + 4i|$

$= |5 - 2i|^2 + |1 + 6i|^2 = (5)^2 + (-2)^2 + (1)^2 + (6)^2$

[if $z = a + ib$, then $|z|^2 = a^2 + b^2$]

$= 25 + 4 + 1 + 36$

$\therefore$ LHS $= 66$ ...(i)

and RHS $= 2(|z_1|^2 + |z_2|^2) = 2(|3 + 2i|^2 + |2 - 4i|^2)$

$= 2[(3)^2 + (2)^2 + (2)^2 + (-4)^2]$

$= 2(9 + 4 + 4 + 16) = 2 \times 33$

$\therefore$ RHS $= 66$ ...(ii)

From Eq. (i) and (ii), we get

LHS = RHS **Hence proved.**

Example 19 If $z_1 = 2 - i$ and $z_2 = 1 + i$, then find $\left|\dfrac{z_1 + z_2 + 1}{z_1 - z_2 + 1}\right|$. **[NCERT]**

Sol. We have, $z_1 = 2 - i$ and $z_2 = 1 + i$

$\therefore$ $\left|\dfrac{z_1 + z_2 + 1}{z_1 - z_2 + 1}\right| = \left|\dfrac{2 - i + 1 + i + 1}{2 - i - 1 - i + 1}\right|$

$= \left|\dfrac{4}{2 - 2i}\right| = \left|\dfrac{2}{1 - i}\right| = \dfrac{2}{|1 - i|}$ $\left[\because \left|\dfrac{z_1}{z_2}\right| = \dfrac{|z_1|}{|z_2|}\right]$

$= \dfrac{2}{\sqrt{(1)^2 + (-1)^2}} = \dfrac{2}{\sqrt{1+1}} = \dfrac{2}{\sqrt{2}} \times \dfrac{\sqrt{2}}{\sqrt{2}} = \sqrt{2}$

Example 20 Find $\left|(1 + i)\dfrac{(2 + i)}{(3 + i)}\right|$. **[NCERT Exemplar]**

Sol. Let $z = \dfrac{(1 + i)(2 + i)}{(3 + i)} = \dfrac{2 + i + 2i + i^2}{3 + i} = \dfrac{2 + 3i - 1}{3 + i}$

$\Rightarrow$ $z = \dfrac{1 + 3i}{3 + i}$ $[\because i^2 = -1]$

Now, $|z| = \left|\dfrac{1 + 3i}{3 + i}\right| = \dfrac{|1 + 3i|}{|3 + i|}$ $\left[\because \left|\dfrac{z_1}{z_2}\right| = \dfrac{|z_1|}{|z_2|}\right]$

$= \dfrac{\sqrt{1^2 + 3^2}}{\sqrt{3^2 + 1^2}} = 1$

Hence, $\left|(1 + i)\dfrac{(2 + i)}{(3 + i)}\right| = 1$

Example 21 If $(2 + i)(2 + 2i)(2 + 3i)\ldots(2 + ni) = x + iy$, then prove that $5 \cdot 8 \cdot 13 \ldots (4 + n^2) = x^2 + y^2$. **[NCERT Exemplar]**

Sol. We have, $(2 + i)(2 + 2i)(2 + 3i)\ldots(2 + ni) = x + iy$

On taking modulus both sides, we get

$|(2 + i)(2 + 2i)(2 + 3i)\ldots(2 + ni)| = |x + iy|$

$\Rightarrow$ $|2 + i||2 + 2i|\ldots|2 + ni| = |x + iy|$

$[\because |z_1 z_2 \ldots z_n| = |z_1||z_2|\ldots|z_n|]$

$\Rightarrow$ $(\sqrt{4 + 1})(\sqrt{4 + 4})\ldots(\sqrt{4 + n^2}) = \sqrt{x^2 + y^2}$

On squaring both sides, we get

$5 \cdot 8 \ldots (4 + n^2) = x^2 + y^2$ **Hence proved.**

Topic Practice 3

Very Short Answer Type Questions

(2 Marks)

1 Find the conjugate of the complex numbers.
(i) $-i\sqrt{5}$ (ii) $\sqrt{3}$

2 Find the complex conjugates of
(i) $2+i5$ (ii) $-6-i7$ (iii) $\sqrt{3}$

3 Find the conjugate of the complex number $\dfrac{1-i}{1+i}$.
[NCERT Exemplar]

4 Find the conjugate of $(6+5i)^2$.

5 Find the real numbers x and y, if $(x-iy)(3+5i)$ is the conjugate of $(-1-3i)$.

6 If $(1+i)z=(1-i)\bar{z}$, then show that $z=-i\bar{z}$.
[NCERT Exemplar]

7 Find the modulus of the conjugate of the complex number $-3i$.

8 Find the number of non-zero integral solutions of the equation $|1-i|^x=2^x$.

9 Find the conjugate and modulus of the complex number $(3-2i)(3+2i)(1+i)$.

10 If $z=12+5i$, then verify that
(i) $\overline{(\bar{z})}=z$ (ii) $z+\bar{z}=2\text{Re}(z)$

11 Find the conjugate and modulus of the complex number $\dfrac{2+3i}{3+2i}$.
[ISC 2007]

12 Find the modulus of the complex number $4+3i^7$.

13 If $(a+ib)(c+id)(e+if)(g+ih)=A+iB$, then show that $(a^2+b^2)(c^2+d^2)(e^2+f^2)(g^2+h^2)=A^2+B^2$.
[NCERT]

Short Answer Type Questions

(4 Marks)

14 Find the conjugate of $\dfrac{(3-2i)(2+3i)}{(1+2i)(2-i)}$.
[NCERT]

15 Find real values of x and y for which the complex numbers $-3+ix^2y$ and x^2+y+4i are conjugate of each other.

16 Find all non-zero complex numbers z satisfying $\bar{z}=iz^2$.

17 If $x+iy=\dfrac{a+ib}{a-ib}$, then prove that $x^2+y^2=1$.
[NCERT]

18 If $a+ib=\dfrac{(x^2+1)}{2x^2+1}$, then prove that
$$a^2+b^2=\frac{(x^2+1)^2}{(2x^2+1)^2}.$$
[NCERT]

19 Find the modulus of $\dfrac{1+i}{1-i}-\dfrac{1-i}{1+i}$.

20 If $z=12-5i$, then verify that
(i) $-|z|\le\text{Re}(z)\le|z|$ (ii) $-|z|\le\text{Im}(z)\le|z|$

21 If $z_1=3+i$ and $z_2=1+4i$, then verify that $|z_1-z_2|\ge|z_2|-|z_1|$.

22 If $f(z)=\dfrac{7-z}{1-z^2}$, where $z=1+2i$, then find $|f(z)|$.
[NCERT Exemplar]

23 If $\dfrac{z-1}{z+1}$ is a purely imaginary number $(z\ne-1)$, then find the value of $|z|$.
[NCERT Exemplar]

24 If $|z+1|=z+2(1+i)$, then find z.

25 If $z=x+iy$, $w=\dfrac{1-iz}{z-i}$ and $|w|=1$, then show that z is purely real.

26 If z is a complex number such that $|z-1|=|z+1|$, then show that $\text{Re}(z)=0$.

Hints & Answers

1. (i) $z=0-i\sqrt{5}\Rightarrow\bar{z}=0+i\sqrt{5}$ **Ans.** $i\sqrt{5}$ (ii) $\sqrt{3}$

2. (i) $\overline{2+i5}=2-i5$ **Ans.** $2-5i$
(ii) $\overline{-6-i7}=-6+i7$ **Ans.** $-6+7i$
(iii) $\overline{\sqrt{3}}=\overline{\sqrt{3}+0i}=\sqrt{3}-0i$ **Ans.** $\sqrt{3}$

3. $z=\dfrac{1-i}{1+i}\times\dfrac{1-i}{1-i}=\dfrac{1-1-2i}{1+1}=-i$ **Ans.** i

4. $\because z=(6+5i)^2=36-25+60i=11+60i$ **Ans.** $11-60i$

5. Solve as Example 4. **Ans.** $x=\dfrac{6}{17}$ and $y=-\dfrac{7}{17}$

6. We have, $(1+i)z=(1-i)\bar{z}\Rightarrow\dfrac{z}{\bar{z}}=\dfrac{1-i}{1+i}\times\dfrac{1-i}{1-i}=\dfrac{1-1-2i}{1+1}$

7. $\because z=3i$ **Ans.** 3

8. We have, $(\sqrt{1^2+(-1)^2})^x=2^x\Rightarrow2^{x/2}=2^x\Rightarrow\dfrac{x}{2}=x$
$x=0$ **Ans.** No solution

9. Let $z=(3-2i)(3+2i)(1+i)$
$\therefore z=(9+6i-6i-4i^2)(1+i)=(9+4)(1+i)=13+13i$
Ans. $\bar{z}=13-13i$ and $|z|=13\sqrt{2}$

10. $z=12+5i\Rightarrow\bar{z}=12-5i$
(i) $\overline{(\bar{z})}=\overline{12-5i}=12+5i=z$
(ii) $z+\bar{z}=(12+5i)+(12-5i)=24=2\times12=2\,\text{Re}(z)$

11. $\because\ z=\dfrac{2+3i}{3+2i}\times\dfrac{3-2i}{3-2i}=\dfrac{12+5i}{13}$ **Ans.** $\bar{z}=\dfrac{12}{13}-\dfrac{5}{13}i$ and $|z|=1$

12. $\because\ z=4+3i^4i^3=4-3i$ **Ans.** 5

13. Solve as Example 21.

14. $\because\ z=\dfrac{12+5i}{4+3i}\times\dfrac{4-3i}{4-3i}=\dfrac{63-16i}{16+9}$ **Ans.** $\dfrac{63}{25}+\dfrac{16}{25}i$

15. Since, $-3+ix^2y$ and x^2+y+4i are conjugate of each other

$$\therefore\quad -3+ix^2y=\overline{x^2+y+4i}$$

After this, equate real and imaginary parts, to get the values of x and y.

Ans. $(x=1,\ y=-4)$ or $(x=-1,\ y=-4)$

16. Solve as Example 7. **Ans.** $0+0i,\ 0+i,\ \dfrac{\sqrt{3}}{2}-\dfrac{1}{2}i,-\dfrac{\sqrt{3}}{2}-\dfrac{1}{2}i$

17. We have, $x+iy=\dfrac{a+ib}{a-ib}$ ...(i)

Take modulus both sides of Eq. (i) and then solve it.

18. We have, $a+ib=\dfrac{x^2+1}{2x^2+1}$ ...(i)

Take modulus both sides of Eq. (i) and then solve it.

19. $\dfrac{(1+i)^2-(1-i)^2}{1^2-i^2}=\dfrac{4i}{2}=2i$ **Ans.** 2

20. $z=12-5i$

$\therefore\ |z|=\sqrt{(12)^2+(-5)^2}=13$

(i) $\text{Re}(z)=12;\quad \therefore\ -13\le 12\le 13\Rightarrow -|z|\le \text{Re}(z)\le |z|$

(ii) $\text{Im}(z)=-5;\quad \therefore\ -13\le -5\le 13\Rightarrow -|z|\le \text{Im}(z)\le |z|$

21. $\because\ |z_1-z_2|=|2-3i|=\sqrt{4+9}=\sqrt{13}$

$\therefore\ |z_1|=\sqrt{9+1}=\sqrt{10}$ and $|z_2|=\sqrt{1+16}=\sqrt{17}$

22. $f(z)=\dfrac{2+i}{2}$

23. Let $z=x+iy$, then

$$\frac{z-1}{z+1}=\frac{(x^2-1)+y^2+i[y(x+1)-y(x-1)]}{(x^2+1)^2+y^2}$$

$\because\ \dfrac{z-1}{z+1}$ is purely imaginary.

$\therefore\quad \text{Re}\left(\dfrac{z-1}{z+1}\right)=0$, i.e. $\dfrac{(x^2-1)+y^2}{(x+1)^2+y^2}=0$ **Ans.** $|z|=1$

24. Let $z=x+iy$, then $|x+iy+1|=x+iy+2(1+i)$

$\Rightarrow\ \sqrt{(x+1)^2+y^2}=x+2+i(y+2)$ **Ans.** $z=\dfrac{1}{2}-2i$

25. We have, $|w|=1\ \Rightarrow\ \dfrac{|1-iz|}{|z-i|}=1\Rightarrow |1-iz|=|z-i|$

$\Rightarrow\quad |1+y-ix|=|x+i(y-1)|$

26. Let $z=x+iy$, then $|z-1|=|z+1|$

$\Rightarrow\quad |x+iy-1|=|x+iy+1|$

$\Rightarrow\quad |(x-1)+iy|=|(x+1)+iy|$

$\Rightarrow\quad \sqrt{(x-1)^2+y^2}=\sqrt{(x+1)^2+y^2}$

TOPIC 04 Geometrical and Polar Representation of Complex Number

Argand Plane

A complex number $z=a+ib$ can be represented by a unique point $P(a,b)$ in the cartesian plane referred to a pair of rectangular axes. A purely real number a, i.e. $(a+0i)$ is represented by the point $(a,0)$ on X-axis. Therefore, X-axis is called the **real axis.**

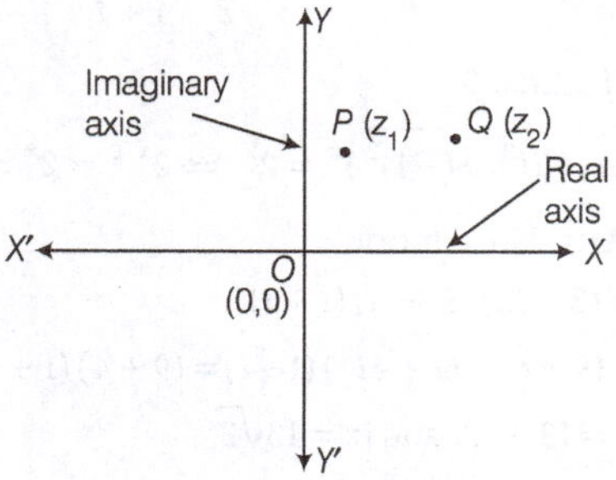

A purely imaginary number ib i.e. $(0+ib)$ is represented by the point $(0,b)$ on Y-axis. Therefore, Y-axis is called the **imaginary axis.** The intersection (common) of two axes is called zero complex number i.e. $z=0+0i$.

Similarly, the representation of complex numbers as points in the plane is known as **Argand diagram.** The plane representing complex numbers as points, is called **complex plane or Argand plane or Gaussian plane.**

If two complex numbers z_1 and z_2 are represented by the points P and Q in the complex plane, then $|z_1-z_2|=PQ$, = Distance between the points P and Q e.g. The complex numbers such as $2+3i$, $-2+3i$, $-1+0i$, $0+4i$ and $-4-2i$ which correspond to the ordered pairs $(2,3)$, $(-2,3)$, $(-1,0)$, $(0,4)$ and $(-4,-2)$ respectively, can be represented geometrically by the points A, B, C, D and E respectively, in the cartesian plane, as shown in the figure below.

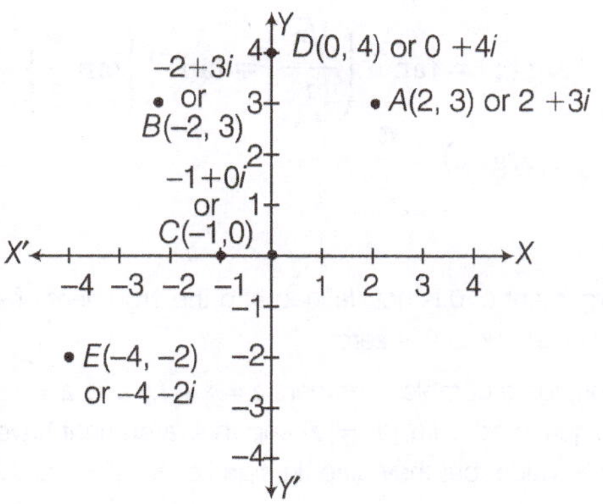

Example 1 If $z_1 = \sqrt{3} + i\sqrt{3}$ and $z_2 = \sqrt{3} + i$, then find the quadrant in which $\left(\frac{z_1}{z_2}\right)$ lies. **[NCERT Exemplar]**

Sol. We have, $z_1 = \sqrt{3} + i\sqrt{3}$ and $z_2 = \sqrt{3} + i$.

$$\therefore \quad \frac{z_1}{z_2} = \frac{\sqrt{3}(1+i)}{\sqrt{3}+i} = \frac{\sqrt{3}(1+i)}{(\sqrt{3}+i)} \times \frac{\sqrt{3}-i}{\sqrt{3}-i}$$

[by rationalising the denominator]

$$= \frac{\sqrt{3}(1+i)(\sqrt{3}-i)}{(\sqrt{3})^2-(i)^2}$$

$[\because (z_1+z_2)(z_1-z_2) = z_1^2 - z_2^2]$

$$= \frac{\sqrt{3}(\sqrt{3}-i+i\sqrt{3}-i^2)}{3-i^2}$$

$$= \frac{\sqrt{3}(\sqrt{3}+i(\sqrt{3}-1)+1)}{3+1} \quad [\because i^2 = -1]$$

$$= \frac{\sqrt{3}}{4}((\sqrt{3}+1)+i(\sqrt{3}-1))$$

$$= \frac{\sqrt{3}(\sqrt{3}+1)}{4} + \frac{i\sqrt{3}(\sqrt{3}-1)}{4}$$

which is represented by a point in first quadrant.

Representation of Conjugate of z on Argand Plane

Geometrically, the mirror image of the complex number $z = a + ib$ (represented by the ordered pair (a, b) about the X-axis is called **conjugate of** z which is represented by the ordered pair $(a, -b)$.

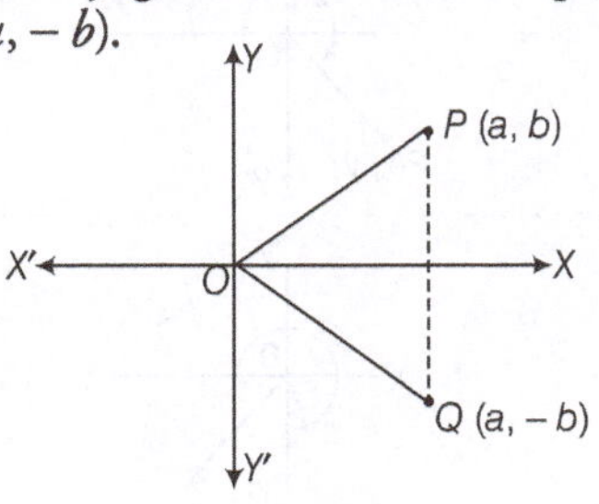

If $z = a + ib$, then $\bar{z} = a - ib$.

Representation of Modulus of z on Argand Plane

Geometrically, the distance of the complex number $z = a + ib$ [represented by the ordered pair (a, b)] from origin, is called the **modulus** of z.

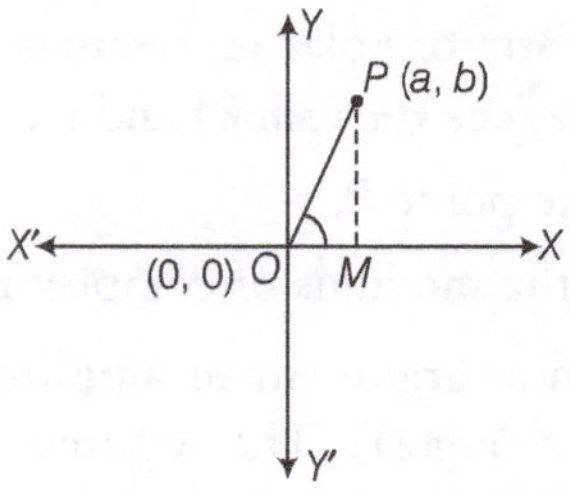

$$\therefore \quad OP = \sqrt{(a-0)^2 + (b-0)^2}$$

$$= \sqrt{a^2+b^2} = \sqrt{\{\text{Re}(z)\}^2 + \{\text{Im}(z)\}^2} = |a+ib|$$

Polar Form of a Complex Number

Let O be the origin and OX and OY be the real axis and imaginary axis, respectively.

Let $z = x + iy$ be represented by a point $P(x, y)$.

Draw $PQ \perp OX$.

Then, $OQ = x$ and $PQ = y$.

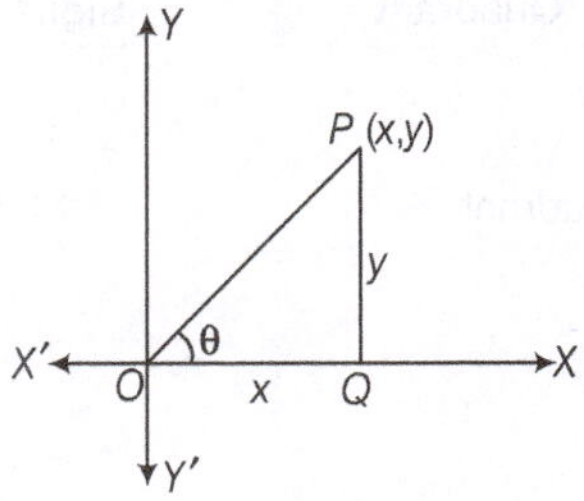

Now, join OP.

Let $OP = r$ and $\angle POX = \theta$

Then, in ΔPQO, $\cos\theta = \frac{x}{r} \Rightarrow x = r\cos\theta$ ...(i)

and $\sin\theta = \frac{y}{r} \Rightarrow y = r\sin\theta$ ...(ii)

On squaring Eqs. (i) and (ii) and then adding, we get

$$r^2\cos^2\theta + r^2\sin^2\theta = x^2 + y^2$$

$$\Rightarrow \quad r^2(\cos^2\theta + \sin^2\theta) = x^2 + y^2$$

$$\Rightarrow \quad r^2 = x^2 + y^2 \quad [\because \cos^2\theta + \sin^2\theta = 1]$$

$$\Rightarrow \quad r = \sqrt{x^2+y^2} = |z|$$

On dividing Eq. (ii) by Eq. (i), we get

$$\tan\theta = \frac{y}{x}$$

$$\Rightarrow \quad \theta = \tan^{-1}\left(\frac{y}{x}\right) = \arg(z)$$

Thus, the **polar form** or **polar representation** of a complex number z is $z = r(\cos\theta + i\sin\theta)$ and (r, θ) is called **polar coordinates** of the point P.

Here, r is called the modulus of complex number z.

Angle θ is known as **argument** or **amplitude** of $z = x + iy$ and is written as 'arg(z)'. The **argument** of a complex number is not defined **uniquely**.

$$\text{Thus,} \quad \theta = \tan^{-1}\left(\frac{y}{x}\right) = \tan^{-1}\left(\frac{\text{Im}(z)}{\text{Re}(z)}\right)$$

This angle θ has infinitely many values differing by multiples of 2π.

e.g. Let $z = 1 + i\sqrt{3}$.

Here, $x = 1$ and $y = \sqrt{3}$

$$\therefore \quad \arg(z) = \tan^{-1}\left(\frac{\sqrt{3}}{1}\right) = \tan^{-1}\left\{\tan\frac{\pi}{3}\right\}$$

$$\Rightarrow \quad \arg(z) = \frac{\pi}{3}$$

Note

(i) The argument of 0 is not defined and the argument of a positive real number is zero.

(ii) The conjugate complex numbers $z = x + iy$ and $\bar{z} = x - iy$ have equal moduli i.e. $|z| = |\bar{z}|$ and their argument have same absolute value, but they differ in sign i.e. $\arg z = -\arg \bar{z}$.

Principal Argument

The unique value of θ such that $-\pi < \theta \le \pi$ is called the **principal value of the argument or amplitude or argument** or **principal argument.**

The argument of a complex number depends upon the quadrant in which the point P lies.

In different quadrant, the signs of real and imaginary parts of a complex number $z = x + iy$, its argument and graph are given in the tables

I. General Argument, when $0 \le \theta \le 2\pi$

Quadrant	Signs of x and y	Argument	Graph
In I quadrant	$x > 0, y > 0$	$0 < \theta < \frac{\pi}{2}$	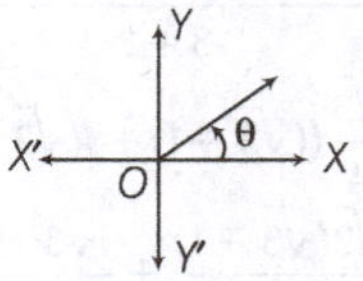
In II quadrant	$x < 0, y > 0$	$\frac{\pi}{2} < \theta < \pi$	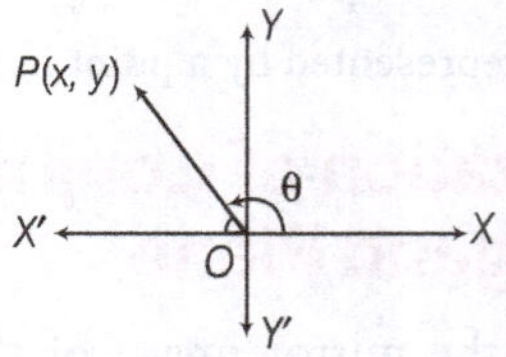
In III quadrant	$x < 0, y < 0$	$\pi < \theta < \frac{3\pi}{2}$	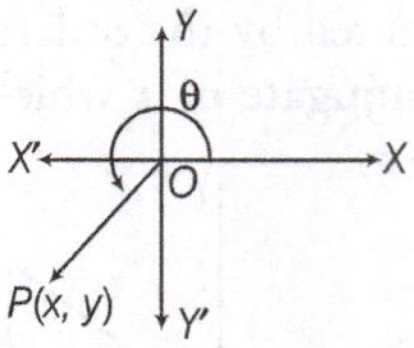
In IV quadrant	$x > 0, y < 0$	$\frac{3\pi}{2} < \theta < 2\pi$	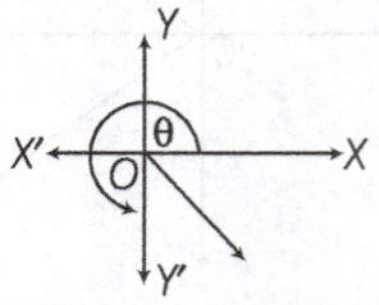

II. Principal Argument, when $-\pi < \theta \leq \pi$

Quadrant	Signs of x and y	Argument	Graph
In I quadrant	$x > 0, y > 0$	$\theta = \alpha$ and $0 < \theta < \frac{\pi}{2}$	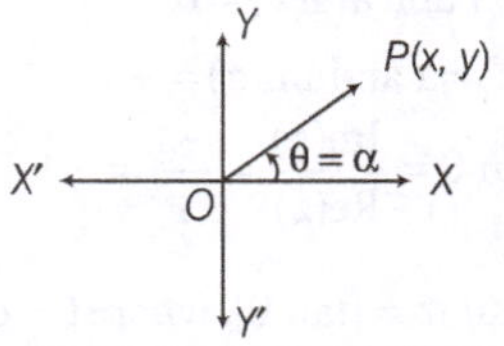
In II quadrant	$x < 0, y > 0$	$\theta = \pi - \alpha$ and $\frac{\pi}{2} < \theta < \pi$	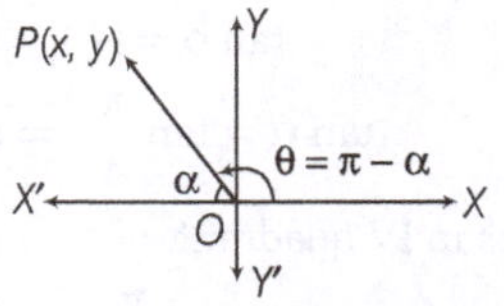
In III quadrant	$x < 0, y < 0$	$\theta = -(\pi - \alpha) = \alpha - \pi$ and $-\pi < \theta < -\frac{\pi}{2}$	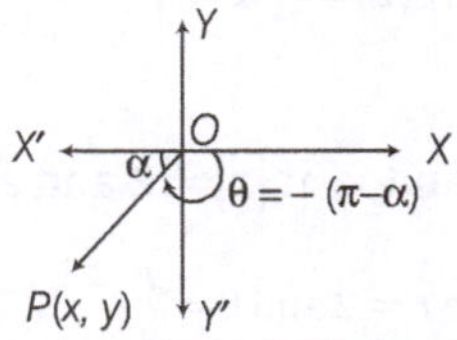
In IV quadrant	$x > 0, y < 0$	$\theta = -\alpha$ and $-\frac{\pi}{2} < \theta < 0$	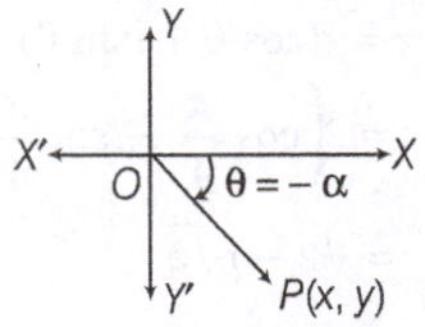

Properties of Argument of a Complex Number

If z_1, z_2 and z_3 are three complex numbers, then

(i) $\arg(z_1 z_2) = \arg(z_1) + \arg(z_2)$

In general, $\arg(z_1 z_2 z_3 \ldots z_n) = \arg(z_1) + \arg(z_2) + \arg(z_3) + \ldots + \arg(z_n)$

(ii) $\arg\left(\frac{z_1}{z_2}\right) = \arg(z_1) - \arg(z_2)$

(iii) $\arg\left(\frac{z}{\bar{z}}\right) = 2\arg(z)$

(iv) $\arg(z^n) = n\arg(z)$

(v) If $\arg\left(\frac{z_2}{z_1}\right) = \theta$, then $\arg\left(\frac{z_1}{z_2}\right) = -\theta$

(vi) $\arg(\bar{z}) = -\arg(z)$

(vii) If $\arg(z) = 0 \Rightarrow z$ is real.

(viii) $\arg(z_1 \bar{z}_2) = \arg(z_1) - \arg(z_2)$

(ix) $|z_1 + z_2| = |z_1 - z_2| \Rightarrow \arg(z_1) - \arg(z_2) = \frac{\pi}{2}$

(x) $|z_1 + z_2| = |z_1| + |z_2| \Rightarrow \arg(z_1) = \arg(z_2)$

(xi) $|z_1 + z_2|^2 = |z_1|^2 + |z_2|^2 \Rightarrow \frac{z_1}{z_2}$ is purely imaginary.

Method for Finding Argument

For finding argument of given complex number, we use the following working steps

***Step* I** First, simplify the given complex number to write in standard form $a + ib$ (if not given in standard form).

***Step* II** Now, check in which quadrant complex number $a + ib$ lies.

***Step* III** Find the value of $\tan\alpha$, using the formula

$$\tan\alpha = \left|\frac{\text{Im}(z)}{\text{Re}(z)}\right|.$$

***Step* IV** Find the value of θ with the help of step II and step III.

Example 2 Find the argument of the complex number $1-i$.

Sol. Let $z = 1 - i$ and $\arg(z) = \theta$.

Here, $\text{Re}(z) = 1$ and $\text{Im}(z) = -1$

Then, $\tan\theta = \dfrac{\text{Im}(z)}{\text{Re}(z)} = \dfrac{-1}{1} = -1$

Now, let $\tan\alpha = |\tan\theta|$, where $0 < \alpha < \dfrac{\pi}{2}$.

Then, $\tan\alpha = |-1| = 1$

$\Rightarrow \quad \tan\alpha = \tan\dfrac{\pi}{4} \Rightarrow \alpha = \dfrac{\pi}{4}$

Since, z lies in IV quadrant.

$\therefore \quad \arg(z) = -\alpha = -\dfrac{\pi}{4}$

Example 3 Find z, if $|r| = 2$ and $\arg(z) = \dfrac{\pi}{4}$.

Sol. Here, we have $r = 2$ and $\theta = \dfrac{\pi}{4}$

$\therefore \quad z = r(\cos\theta + i\sin\theta)$

$= 2\left(\cos\dfrac{\pi}{4} + i\sin\dfrac{\pi}{4}\right) = 2\left(\dfrac{1}{\sqrt{2}} + i\dfrac{1}{\sqrt{2}}\right)$

$= \sqrt{2} + i\sqrt{2}$

Example 4 Find the modulus and argument of the complex number $\dfrac{1+2i}{1-3i}$. **[NCERT]**

Sol. Let $z = \dfrac{1+2i}{1-3i}$, then $z = \dfrac{1+2i}{1-3i} \times \dfrac{1+3i}{1+3i}$

[by rationalising the denominator]

$= \dfrac{(1+2i)(1+3i)}{1^2 - (3i)^2}$ $[\because (z_1+z_2)(z_1-z_2) = z_1^2 - z_2^2]$

$= \dfrac{1+3i+2i+6i^2}{1-9i^2}$

$= \dfrac{1+5i-6}{1+9} = \dfrac{-5+5i}{10} = -\dfrac{1}{2} + \dfrac{i}{2}$ $[\because i^2 = -1]$

$\Rightarrow \quad z = -\dfrac{1}{2} + \dfrac{i}{2}$

$\therefore \quad |z| = \sqrt{\left(-\dfrac{1}{2}\right)^2 + \left(\dfrac{1}{2}\right)^2} = \sqrt{\left(\dfrac{1}{2}\right)^2 + \left(\dfrac{1}{2}\right)^2}$

$= \sqrt{2\cdot\left(\dfrac{1}{2}\right)^2} = \dfrac{1}{2} \times \sqrt{2}$

$= \dfrac{1}{\sqrt{2}}$

Let $\arg(z) = \theta$, then, $\tan\theta = \dfrac{\frac{1}{2}}{\left(-\frac{1}{2}\right)} = -1$

Now, let $\tan\alpha = |\tan\theta|$, where $0 < \alpha < \dfrac{\pi}{2}$

$\Rightarrow \quad \tan\alpha = |-1| = 1 = \tan\dfrac{\pi}{4} \Rightarrow \alpha = \dfrac{\pi}{4}$

Since, z lies is II quadrant, therefore

$\theta = \pi - \alpha = \pi - \dfrac{\pi}{4} = \dfrac{3\pi}{4}$

Hence, $|z| = \dfrac{1}{\sqrt{2}}$ and $\arg(z) = \dfrac{3\pi}{4}$

Method for Writing Polar Form of a Complex Number

For writing polar form of a complex number, we use the following steps

***Step* I** First, write the given complex in standard form $z = a + ib$ (if not given in standard form).

***Step* II** Put the standard form $z = a + ib$ equal to $r(\cos\theta + i\sin\theta)$ and equate the real and imaginary part from both sides.

***Step* III** Find the value of r and θ by using suitable method.

***Step* IV** Put the values of r and θ in $z = r[\cos\theta + i\sin\theta]$ which gives the required polar form of given complex number.

Example 5 Convert the complex number i in the polar form. **[NCERT]**

Sol. Let $z = i = r(\cos\theta + i\sin\theta)$.

On equating real and imaginary part, we get

$r\cos\theta = 0$ ...(i)

and $r\sin\theta = 1$ ...(ii)

On squaring and adding Eqs. (i) and (ii), we get

$r^2\cos^2\theta + r^2\sin^2\theta = 0^2 + 1^2$

$\Rightarrow \quad r^2(\cos^2\theta + \sin^2\theta) = 1$

$\Rightarrow \quad r^2 = 1$ $[\because \cos^2\theta + \sin^2\theta = 1]$

$\Rightarrow \quad r = 1$ $[\because r > 0]$

Now, from Eqs. (i) and (ii), we get

$\cos\theta = 0$ and $\sin\theta = 1$

$\therefore \quad \theta = \dfrac{\pi}{2}$

[$\because z$ is purely imaginary and lies on positive Y-axis]

Hence, polar form of z is

$1\cdot\left(\cos\dfrac{\pi}{2} + i\sin\dfrac{\pi}{2}\right)$.

Example 6 Change the complex number $2-2i$ into polar form.

Sol. Let $z = 2-2i = r(\cos\theta + i\sin\theta)$

On equating real and imaginary parts, we get

$$r\cos\theta = 2 \quad \text{...(i)}$$

and $$r\sin\theta = -2 \quad \text{...(ii)}$$

On squaring and adding Eqs. (i) and (ii), we get

$$r^2\cos^2\theta + r^2\sin^2\theta = 2^2 + (-2)^2$$

$$\Rightarrow r^2(\cos^2\theta + \sin^2\theta) = 4+4 \quad [\because \cos^2\theta + \sin^2\theta = 1]$$

$$\Rightarrow r^2 = 8$$

$$\Rightarrow r = 2\sqrt{2} \quad [\because r > 0]$$

Now, from Eqs. (i) and (ii), we get

$$r\cos\theta = 2 \text{ and } r\sin\theta = -2$$

$$\Rightarrow \tan\theta = -1 \quad \left[\because \tan\theta = \frac{\sin\theta}{\cos\theta}\right]$$

Now, let $\tan\alpha = |\tan\theta|$, where $0 < \alpha < \frac{\pi}{2}$

$$\Rightarrow \tan\alpha = 1 = \tan\frac{\pi}{4}$$

$$\Rightarrow \alpha = \frac{\pi}{4}$$

Since, z lies in IV quadrant.

$$\therefore \arg(z) = -\alpha = -\frac{\pi}{4}$$

Hence, polar form of z is $2\sqrt{2}\left[\cos\left(-\frac{\pi}{4}\right) + \sin\left(-\frac{\pi}{4}\right)\right]$.

Example 7 Convert the complex number $-\sqrt{3}-i$ into polar form and determine the modulus and the principal value of the argument of given complex number.

Sol. Let $z = -\sqrt{3} - i = r(\cos\theta + i\sin\theta)$

On equating real and imaginary parts, we get

$$r\cos\theta = -\sqrt{3} \quad \text{...(i)}$$

and $$r\sin\theta = -1 \quad \text{...(ii)}$$

On squaring and adding Eqs. (i) and (ii), we get

$$r^2\cos^2\theta + r^2\sin^2\theta = (-\sqrt{3})^2 + (-1)^2$$

$$\Rightarrow r^2(\cos^2\theta + \sin^2\theta) = 3+1$$

$$\Rightarrow r^2 = 4 \quad [\because \cos^2\theta + \sin^2\theta = 1]$$

$$\Rightarrow r = 2 \quad [\because r > 0]$$

Now, from Eqs. (i) and (ii), we get

$$\cos\theta = -\frac{\sqrt{3}}{2} \text{ and } \sin\theta = -\frac{1}{2}$$

$$\Rightarrow \tan\theta = \frac{1}{\sqrt{3}} \quad \left[\because \tan\theta = \frac{\sin\theta}{\cos\theta}\right]$$

Now, let $\tan\alpha = |\tan\theta|$, where $0 < \alpha < \frac{\pi}{2}$

$$\Rightarrow \tan\alpha = \frac{1}{\sqrt{3}} = \tan\frac{\pi}{6}$$

$$\Rightarrow \alpha = \frac{\pi}{6}$$

Since, z lies in III quadrant.

$$\therefore \theta = -\pi + \alpha = -\pi + \frac{\pi}{6} = -\frac{5\pi}{6}$$

So, polar form of z is $2\left(\cos\left(\frac{-5\pi}{6}\right) + i\sin\left(\frac{-5\pi}{6}\right)\right)$.

Hence, modulus of z is 2 and argument of z is $-\frac{5\pi}{6}$.

Example 8 Write the complex number $z = \dfrac{1-i}{\cos\frac{\pi}{3} + i\sin\frac{\pi}{3}}$ in polar form. **[NCERT Exemplar]**

Sol. We have, $z = \dfrac{1-i}{\cos\frac{\pi}{3} + i\sin\frac{\pi}{3}}$

$$= \frac{1-i}{\frac{1}{2} + i\frac{\sqrt{3}}{2}}$$

$$= \frac{1-i}{\frac{1}{2} + i\frac{\sqrt{3}}{2}} \times \frac{\frac{1}{2} - i\frac{\sqrt{3}}{2}}{\frac{1}{2} - i\frac{\sqrt{3}}{2}}$$

[multiplying numerator and denominator by conjugate of $\frac{1}{2} + i\frac{\sqrt{3}}{2}$]

$$= \frac{(1-i)\left(\frac{1}{2} - i\frac{\sqrt{3}}{2}\right)}{\left(\frac{1}{2}\right)^2 - \left(\frac{i\sqrt{3}}{2}\right)^2} \quad [\because (z_1+z_2)(z_1-z_2) = z_1^2 - z_2^2]$$

$$= \frac{\frac{1}{2} - i\frac{\sqrt{3}}{2} - \frac{i}{2} + i^2\frac{\sqrt{3}}{2}}{\frac{1}{4} - i^2\frac{3}{4}}$$

$$= \frac{\frac{1}{2} - i\frac{(\sqrt{3}+1)}{2} - \frac{\sqrt{3}}{2}}{\frac{1}{4} + \frac{3}{4}} \quad [\because i^2 = -1]$$

$$\Rightarrow z = \left(\frac{1-\sqrt{3}}{2}\right) - i\left(\frac{1+\sqrt{3}}{2}\right)$$

Now, let $\left(\frac{1-\sqrt{3}}{2}\right)-i\left(\frac{1+\sqrt{3}}{2}\right)=r(\cos\theta+i\sin\theta)$

On equating real and imaginary parts, we get

$$r\cos\theta=\frac{1-\sqrt{3}}{2} \quad \text{...(i)}$$

and $$r\sin\theta=-\frac{(1+\sqrt{3})}{2} \quad \text{...(ii)}$$

On squaring and adding Eqs. (i) and (ii), we get

$$r^2\cos^2\theta+r^2\sin^2\theta=\left(\frac{1-\sqrt{3}}{2}\right)^2+\left(-\frac{(1+\sqrt{3})}{2}\right)^2$$

$$\Rightarrow \quad r^2(\cos^2\theta+\sin^2\theta)=\frac{(1-\sqrt{3})^2+(1+\sqrt{3})^2}{4}$$

$$\Rightarrow \quad r^2=\frac{1+3-2\sqrt{3}+1+3+2\sqrt{3}}{4}$$

$$[\because \cos^2\theta+\sin^2\theta=1]$$

$$\Rightarrow \quad r^2=\frac{8}{4}=2$$

$$\Rightarrow \quad r=\sqrt{2} \quad [\because r>0]$$

Now, from Eqs. (i) and (ii), we get

$$\cos\theta=\frac{1-\sqrt{3}}{2\sqrt{2}} \text{ and } \sin\theta=\frac{-(1+\sqrt{3})}{2\sqrt{2}}$$

$$\Rightarrow \quad \tan\theta=-\frac{(1+\sqrt{3})}{1-\sqrt{3}} \quad \left[\because \tan\theta=\frac{\sin\theta}{\cos\theta}\right]$$

Now, let $\tan\alpha=|\tan\theta|$, where $0<\alpha<\frac{\pi}{2}$

$$\Rightarrow \quad \tan\alpha=\frac{1+\sqrt{3}}{1-\sqrt{3}}$$

$$=\tan\left(\frac{\pi}{4}+\frac{\pi}{3}\right)$$

$$\left[\because \tan\left(\frac{\pi}{4}+\frac{\pi}{3}\right)=\frac{\tan\frac{\pi}{4}+\tan\frac{\pi}{3}}{1-\tan\frac{\pi}{4}\tan\frac{\pi}{3}}=\frac{1+\sqrt{3}}{1-\sqrt{3}}\right]$$

$$\Rightarrow \quad \alpha=\frac{\pi}{4}+\frac{\pi}{3}$$

$$=\frac{3\pi+4\pi}{12}=\frac{7\pi}{12}$$

$$\therefore \quad \alpha=\frac{7\pi}{12}$$

Since, $\text{Re}(z)<0$ and $\text{Im}(z)<0$, therefore z lies in III quadrant.

$$\therefore \quad \theta=-\pi+\alpha=-\pi+\frac{7\pi}{12}=\frac{-12\pi+7\pi}{12}=\frac{-5\pi}{12}$$

Hence, required polar form of z is

$$\sqrt{2}\left[\cos\left(\frac{-5\pi}{12}\right)+i\sin\left(\frac{-5\pi}{12}\right)\right].$$

Topic Practice 4

Very Short Answer Type Questions

(2 Marks)

1 Find the principal argument of the following complex numbers.

(i) (a) $1+i\sqrt{3}$ (b) $-1-i\sqrt{3}$

(ii) (a) $-\sqrt{3}+i$ (b) $\frac{1}{1+i}$

2 Find z, if $|r|=4$ and $\arg(z)=\frac{5\pi}{6}$.

3 If $z_1=\sqrt{2}-3i$ and $z_2=5-i\sqrt{2}$, then find the quadrant in which $\frac{z_1}{z_2}$ lies.

4 Find the modulus and principal argument of $-\sqrt{3}+i$.

5 Find the modulus and argument of complex number $\frac{1+i}{1-i}$. **[NCERT]**

6 Find the argument of the complex number $\frac{1+3i}{1-2i}$.

Short Answer Type Questions

(4 Marks)

7 Convert each of the following complex numbers in polar form.

(i) $1-i$ (ii) $-1+i$

(iii) -3 (iv) $\frac{1-i}{1+i}$

8 Write the complex number $\sqrt{3}+i$ into polar form and determine the modulus and the principal value of the argument.

9 Change the complex number $-4+i4\sqrt{3}$ in polar form.

10 Convert the complex number $\frac{-16}{1+i\sqrt{3}}$ into polar form. **[NCERT]**

11 Express the complex number $\frac{2+6\sqrt{3}i}{5+\sqrt{3}i}$ into polar form.

12 Convert the complex number $z=\frac{i-1}{\cos\frac{\pi}{3}+i\sin\frac{\pi}{3}}$ into polar form.

Hints & Answers

1. (i) (a) $\because\ \tan\theta = \left|\frac{\sqrt{3}}{1}\right| = \tan\frac{\pi}{3} \Rightarrow \theta = \frac{\pi}{3}$

Since, complex number lies in Ist quadrant.

Ans. $\arg(z) = \frac{\pi}{3}$

(b) $\frac{-2\pi}{3}$

(ii) (a) $\frac{5\pi}{3}$

(b) $\because\ z = \frac{1}{1+i} \times \frac{1-i}{1-i} = \frac{1-i}{1+1} = \frac{1-i}{2}$

$\Rightarrow\ \tan\theta = \left|\frac{-\frac{1}{2}}{\frac{1}{2}}\right| = 1 \Rightarrow \theta = \frac{\pi}{4}$

Since, z lies in IV quadrant.

Ans. $\arg(z) = \frac{-\pi}{4}$

2. $\cos\frac{5\pi}{6} = \cos\left(\pi - \frac{\pi}{6}\right) = -\cos\frac{\pi}{6}$

and $\sin\frac{5\pi}{6} = \sin\left(\pi - \frac{\pi}{6}\right) = \sin\frac{\pi}{6}$

$$z = 4\left[-\cos\frac{\pi}{6} + i\sin\frac{\pi}{6}\right]$$

Ans. $z = -2\sqrt{3} + 2i$

3. Solve as Example 1.
Ans. IV quadrant

4. Solve as Example 4.
Ans. $2, \frac{5\pi}{6}$

5. $\because\ z = \frac{1+i}{1-i} \times \frac{1+i}{1+i} = \frac{1-1+2i}{2} = i$

Futher, solve as Example 4. **Ans.** $1, \frac{\pi}{2}$

6. $\frac{3\pi}{4}$

7. (i) $\because\ z = 1 - i$

Here, $r\cos\theta = 1$ and $r\sin\theta = -1$

$\therefore\quad r^2 = 1^2 + (-1)^2$

$\Rightarrow\quad r = \sqrt{2}$ and $\tan\theta = \left|\frac{-1}{1}\right| = \frac{\pi}{4}$

$\therefore\ \arg(z) = \frac{-\pi}{4}$ [$\because$ z lies in IVth quadrant]

Ans. $z = \sqrt{2}\left[\cos\left(\frac{-\pi}{4}\right) + i\sin\left(\frac{-\pi}{4}\right)\right]$

(ii) $z = \sqrt{2}\left[\cos\frac{3\pi}{4} + i\sin\frac{3\pi}{4}\right]$

(iii) $\because\ z = -3$

Here, $r\cos\theta = -3$ and $r\sin\theta = 0$

$\Rightarrow \tan\theta = 0 \Rightarrow \theta = 0$

$\therefore\ \arg(z) = \pi$ [$\because$ z lies in IInd quadrant]

(iv) $\because\ z = \frac{1-i}{1+i} = \frac{(1-i)^2}{1^2 - i^2} = \frac{1-1-2i}{2} = -i$

Now, $\tan\theta = \left|\frac{-1}{0}\right| = \tan\frac{\pi}{2} \Rightarrow \theta = \frac{\pi}{2}$

$\therefore\quad \arg(z) = \frac{-\pi}{2}$

Ans. $z = 1\left[\cos\left(\frac{-\pi}{2}\right) + i\sin\left(\frac{-\pi}{2}\right)\right]$

8. Let $z = \sqrt{3} + i = r(\cos\theta + i\sin\theta)$

Now, equate real and imaginary parts of this equation and solve it for r and θ.

Ans. $2\left(\cos\frac{\pi}{6} + i\sin\frac{\pi}{6}\right);\ 2, \frac{\pi}{6}$

9. Let $z = -4 + i\,4\sqrt{3} = r(\cos\theta + i\sin\theta)$.

Now, equate the real and imaginary parts of this equation and then solve it for r and θ.

Ans. $8\left(\cos\frac{2\pi}{3} + i\sin\frac{2\pi}{3}\right)$

10. $8\left(\cos\frac{2\pi}{3} + i\sin\frac{2\pi}{3}\right)$

11. First, convert the given complex in the standard form and then find its polar form.

Ans. $2\left(\cos\frac{\pi}{3} + i\sin\frac{\pi}{3}\right)$

12. Solve as Example 8.

Ans. $\sqrt{2}\left(\cos\frac{5\pi}{12} + i\sin\frac{5\pi}{12}\right)$

TOPIC 05 Square Root of a Complex Number and Cube Roots of Unity

Square Root of a Complex Number

Let $z = a + ib$ be a complex number such that $\sqrt{a+ib} = x + iy$, where x and y are real numbers.

Now, we have $\quad \sqrt{a+ib} = x+iy$

On squaring both sides, we get

$$(x+iy)^2 = a+ib$$

$$\Rightarrow \quad (x^2 - y^2) + 2ixy = a + ib \quad [\because i^2 = -1]$$

On equating real and imaginary parts of both sides, we get

$$x^2 - y^2 = a \quad \text{...(i)}$$

and $$2xy = b \quad \text{...(ii)}$$

Now, consider the identity

$$(x^2+y^2)^2 = (x^2-y^2)^2 + 4x^2y^2$$

$$\Rightarrow \quad (x^2+y^2)^2 = a^2 + b^2 \quad \text{[from Eqs. (i) and (ii)]}$$

$$\Rightarrow \quad (x^2+y^2) = \sqrt{a^2+b^2} \quad \text{[taking square root] ...(iii)}$$

On solving Eqs. (i) and (iii), we get

$$x^2 = \left(\frac{1}{2}\right)(\sqrt{a^2+b^2} + a)$$

and $$y^2 = \left(\frac{1}{2}\right)(\sqrt{a^2+b^2} - a)$$

$$\Rightarrow \quad x = \pm\sqrt{\left(\frac{1}{2}\right)[\sqrt{a^2+b^2} + a]}$$

and $$y = \pm\sqrt{\left(\frac{1}{2}\right)[\sqrt{a^2+b^2} - a]}$$

[taking square root]

If b is positive, then the sign of x and y from Eq. (ii) will be same.

Hence, $$\sqrt{a+ib} = \pm\left[\sqrt{\left(\frac{1}{2}\right)(\sqrt{a^2+b^2}+a)} + i\sqrt{\left(\frac{1}{2}\right)(\sqrt{a^2+b^2}-a)}\right]$$

or $$\sqrt{z} = \pm\left[\sqrt{\frac{|z| + \text{Re}(z)}{2}} + i\sqrt{\frac{|z| - \text{Re}(z)}{2}}\right]$$

If b is negative, then the sign of x and y will be opposite.

Hence, $$\sqrt{a+ib} = \pm\left[\sqrt{\left(\frac{1}{2}\right)(\sqrt{a^2+b^2}+a)} - i\sqrt{\left(\frac{1}{2}\right)(\sqrt{a^2+b^2}-a)}\right]$$

or $$\sqrt{z} = \pm\left[\sqrt{\frac{|z| + \text{Re}(z)}{2}} - i\sqrt{\frac{|z| - \text{Re}(z)}{2}}\right]$$

Example 1 Find the square root of i.

Sol. Let $z = x + iy = \sqrt{i}$ ...(i)

On squaring both sides of Eq. (i), we get

$$(x+iy)^2 = i$$

$$\Rightarrow \quad x^2 + i^2y^2 + 2ixy = i$$

$$\Rightarrow \quad x^2 - y^2 + 2ixy = i \quad [\because i^2 = -1]$$

On equating the real and imaginary parts of both sides, we get

$$x^2 - y^2 = 0 \quad \text{...(ii)}$$

and $$2xy = 1 \quad \text{...(iii)}$$

Now, consider the identity

$$(x^2+y^2)^2 = (x^2-y^2)^2 + (2xy)^2$$

$$\Rightarrow \quad (x^2+y^2)^2 = 0 + 1 \quad \text{[from Eqs. (ii) and (iii)]}$$

$$\Rightarrow \quad (x^2+y^2) = \pm 1$$

$$\Rightarrow \quad x^2 + y^2 = 1 \quad [\because x^2+y^2 \ge 0] \text{ ...(iv)}$$

On adding Eqs. (ii) and (iv), we get

$$2x^2 = 1 \Rightarrow x^2 = \frac{1}{2} \Rightarrow x = \pm\frac{1}{\sqrt{2}}$$

On putting $x^2 = \frac{1}{2}$ in Eq. (iv), we get

$$\frac{1}{2} + y^2 = 1 \Rightarrow y^2 = \frac{1}{2} \Rightarrow y = \pm\frac{1}{2}$$

Since, the product xy is positive. So, we have

$$x = \frac{1}{\sqrt{2}} \text{ and } y = \frac{1}{\sqrt{2}} \text{ or } x = -\frac{1}{\sqrt{2}} \text{ and } y = -\frac{1}{\sqrt{2}}$$

Hence, the square roots are $\frac{1}{\sqrt{2}} + i\frac{1}{\sqrt{2}}$ and $-\frac{1}{\sqrt{2}} - i\frac{1}{\sqrt{2}}$.

Example 2 Find the square root of $1 + i$. **[NCERT]**

Sol. Let $x + iy = \sqrt{1+i}$

On squaring both sides, we get

$$(x+iy)^2 = 1 + i \Rightarrow x^2 - y^2 + 2xyi = 1 + i$$

On equating real and imaginary parts of both sides, we get

$$x^2 - y^2 = 1 \quad \text{...(i)}$$

and $$2xy = 1 \quad \text{...(ii)}$$

We know the identity,

$$(x^2+y^2)^2 = (x^2-y^2)^2 + (2xy)^2$$

$$= 1 + 1 = 2 \quad \text{[from Eqs. (i) and (ii)]}$$

Thus, $\quad x^2 + y^2 = \sqrt{2} \quad \text{...(iii)}$

On solving Eqs. (i) and (iii), we get

$$x^2 = \frac{1+\sqrt{2}}{2} \text{ and } y^2 = \frac{\sqrt{2}-1}{2}$$

$$\Rightarrow \quad x = \pm\sqrt{\frac{\sqrt{2}+1}{2}} \text{ and } y = \pm\sqrt{\frac{\sqrt{2}-1}{2}}$$

Since, the product of xy is positive. So, we have

$$x = \sqrt{\frac{\sqrt{2}+1}{2}} \text{ and } y = \sqrt{\frac{\sqrt{2}-1}{2}}$$

or

$$x = -\sqrt{\frac{\sqrt{2}+1}{2}} \text{ and } y = -\sqrt{\frac{\sqrt{2}-1}{2}}$$

Thus, the square roots of $1+i$ are

$$\sqrt{\frac{\sqrt{2}+1}{2}} + i\sqrt{\frac{\sqrt{2}-1}{2}} \text{ and } -\sqrt{\frac{\sqrt{2}+1}{2}} - i\sqrt{\frac{\sqrt{2}-1}{2}}.$$

Example 3 Find the square root of $-15-8i$. **[NCERT]**

Sol. Let $\quad x + iy = \sqrt{-15-8i}$

Then, $\quad (x+iy)^2 = -15-8i \quad$ [squaring both sides]

$\Rightarrow x^2 - y^2 + 2ixy = -15-8i$

On equating real and imaginary parts, we get

$$x^2 - y^2 = -15 \quad \text{...(i)}$$

and $\quad 2xy = -8 \quad \text{...(ii)}$

We know the identity,

$$(x^2+y^2)^2 = (x^2-y^2)^2 + 4x^2y^2 = 225 + 64 = 289$$

$$\Rightarrow \quad x^2 + y^2 = \sqrt{289} \quad [\because x^2+y^2 \geq 0]$$

$$\Rightarrow \quad x^2 + y^2 = 17 \quad \text{...(iii)}$$

On solving Eqs. (i) and (iii), we get

$$x^2 = 1 \text{ and } y^2 = 16$$

$$\Rightarrow \quad x = \pm 1 \text{ and } y = \pm 4$$

Since, the product xy is negative. So, we have

$$x = 1, y = -4$$

or $\quad x = -1, y = 4$

Hence, the square roots of $-15-8i$ are $1-4i$ and $-1+4i$.

Cube Roots of Unity

Let x be the cube root of 1.

i.e. $x = 1^{1/3} \Rightarrow x^3 = 1 \Rightarrow x^3 - 1 = 0$

$$\Rightarrow \quad (x-1)(x^2+x+1) = 0$$

After solving, we get $x = 1, x = \dfrac{-1 \pm i\sqrt{3}}{2}$

Hence, the three cube roots of unity are 1, ω and ω^2,

where $\omega = \dfrac{-1+i\sqrt{3}}{2}$ and $\omega^2 = \dfrac{-1-i\sqrt{3}}{2}$.

Properties of Cube Roots of Unity

(i) Each complex cube root of unity is the square of other.

(ii) If one of the cube roots of unity is ω, then $\omega^3 = 1$.

(iii) The product of three cube roots of unity is 1.

(iv) Each complex cube root of unity is the reciprocal of the other, i.e. $\omega = \dfrac{1}{\omega^2}$ or $\omega^2 = \dfrac{1}{\omega}$.

(v) The sum of three cube roots of unity is zero, i.e. $1 + \omega + \omega^2 = 0$.

(vi) $\omega^{3r} = 1, \omega^{3r+1} = \omega$ and $\omega^{3r+2} = \omega^2$, where $r \in Z$ (integers).

(vii) Cube roots of -1 are $-1, -\omega, -\omega^2$.

(viii) Cube roots of $(x-2)^3 - 1 = 0$ are $2+1, 2+\omega$ and $2+\omega^2$

Example 4 If 1, ω and ω^2 are the three cube roots of unity, then simplify $(3+5\omega+3\omega^2)^2(1+2\omega+\omega^2)$.

[ISC 2010]

Sol. $(3+5\omega+3\omega^2)^2(1+2\omega+\omega^2)$

$$= (3+3\omega+3\omega^2+2\omega)^2(1+\omega+\omega+\omega^2)$$

$$= [3(1+\omega+\omega^2)+2\omega]^2(1+\omega+\omega^2+\omega)$$

$$= [3\times 0+2\omega]^2(0+\omega) \quad [\because 1+\omega+\omega^2 = 0]$$

$$= 4\omega^2(0+\omega) = 4\omega^3 = 4\times 1 = 4 \quad [\because \omega^3 = 1]$$

Example 5 If 1, ω and ω^2 are the cube roots of unity, evaluate $(1-\omega^4+\omega^8)(1-\omega^8+\omega^{16})$. **[ISC 2013]**

Sol. $(1-\omega^4+\omega^8)(1-\omega^8+\omega^{16})$

$$= 1(1-\omega^8+\omega^{16}) - \omega^4(1-\omega^8+\omega^{16}) + \omega^8(1-\omega^8+\omega^{16})$$

$$= 1-\omega^8+\omega^{16}-\omega^4+\omega^{12}-\omega^{20}+\omega^8-\omega^{16}+\omega^{24}$$

$$= 1-\omega^4+\omega^{12}-\omega^{20}+\omega^{24}$$

$$= 1-\omega^3\cdot\omega+(\omega^3)^4-\omega^{18}\cdot\omega^2+(\omega^3)^8$$

$$= 1-\omega+1-(\omega^3)^6\cdot\omega^2+1 \quad [\because \omega^3 = 1]$$

$$= 1-\omega+1-\omega^2+1 = 3-(\omega+\omega^2)$$

$$= 3-(-1) \quad [\because 1+\omega+\omega^2 = 0 \text{ and } \omega^3 = 1]$$

$$= 4$$

Example 6 Find the cube roots of – 27 and show that the sum of the cube roots is equal to zero. **[ISC 2006]**

Sol. Let the cube root of – 27 be x.

i.e. $x = (-27)^{1/3} \Rightarrow x^3 = -27$

$\Rightarrow x^3 + 27 = 0 \Rightarrow x^3 + (3)^3 = 0$

$\Rightarrow (x+3)(x^2 - 3x + 9) = 0$

$[\because a^3 + b^3 = (a+b)(a^2 - ab + b^2)]$

$\Rightarrow x = -3$ or $x^2 - 3x + 9 = 0$

Now, $x^2 - 3x + 9 = 0$

On comparing with $ax^2 + bx + c = 0$, we get

$a = 1, b = -3, c = 9$

$$\because \quad x = \frac{-b \pm \sqrt{b^2 - 4ac}}{2a}$$

$$\therefore \quad x = \frac{3 \pm \sqrt{9-36}}{2} = \frac{3 \pm \sqrt{27}\, i}{2}$$

$$= \frac{3 \pm 3\sqrt{3}\, i}{2} = \frac{3}{2}(1 \pm \sqrt{3}\, i)$$

Hence, the cube roots of – 27 are

$-3, \frac{3}{2}(1 + \sqrt{3}\, i)$ and $\frac{3}{2}(1 - \sqrt{3}\, i)$.

Therefore, sum of cube roots

$$= -3 + \frac{3}{2}(1 + \sqrt{3}\, i) + \frac{3}{2}(1 - \sqrt{3}\, i)$$

$$= -3 + 2 \times \frac{3}{2} = -3 + 3 = 0$$ **Hence proved.**

Topic Practice 5

Short Answer Type Questions

(4 Marks)

Directions (Q. Nos. 1-11) Find the square roots of the following.

1. $16 - 30i$
2. $1 + 4\sqrt{-3}$
3. $-8 - 6i$
4. $7 - 24i$
5. $1 - i$
6. $-11 - 60i$
7. $-8 - 6i$
8. $-5 + 12i$
9. $4 - 6\sqrt{5}i$
10. $6\sqrt{2}i - 7$
11. $-i$
12. Simplify $(1-\omega)(1-\omega^2)(1-\omega^4)(1-\omega^8)$.
13. If ω and ω^2 are cube roots of unity, then prove that $(2 - \omega + 2\omega^2)(2 + 2\omega - \omega^2) = 9$.
14. If 1, ω and ω^2 are three cube roots of unity, then show that $(a + b\omega + \omega^2 c)(a + b\omega^2 + \omega c) = a^2 + b^2 + c^2 - ab - bc - ca$.
15. If $x = a + b$, $y = a\alpha + b\beta$ and $z = a\beta + b\alpha$, where α and β are complex cube roots of unity, then show that $xyz = a^3 + b^3$.
16. Using De-Moivre's theorem, find the value of $(1 + i\sqrt{3})^6 + (1 - i\sqrt{3})^6$.

Hints & Answers

1. Let $\sqrt{16 - 30i} = (x + iy)$ ...(i)

$\Rightarrow (16 - 30i) = (x^2 - y^2) - i(2xy)$ ...(ii)

$\Rightarrow (x^2 - y^2) = 16$ and $2xy = 30$

$\therefore (x^2 + y^2) = \sqrt{(x^2 - y^2)^2 + 4x^2y^2}$

$= \sqrt{(16)^2 + (30)^2} = 34$

Ans. $\pm(5 - 3i)$

2. Solve as Q. 1.
Also, write $1 + 4\sqrt{-3} = 1 + 4\sqrt{3}i$. **Ans.** $\pm(2 + \sqrt{3}i)$

3. Solve as Q. 1. **Ans.** $\pm(1 - 3i)$
4. Solve as Q. 1. **Ans.** $\pm(4 - 3i)$
5. Solve as Q. 1. **Ans.** $\pm\left(\sqrt{\frac{\sqrt{2}+1}{2}} - \sqrt{\frac{\sqrt{2}-1}{2}}\, i\right)$
6. Solve as Q. 1. **Ans.** $\pm(5 - 6i)$
7. Solve as Q. 1. **Ans.** $\pm(1 - 3i)$
8. Solve as Q. 1. **Ans.** $\pm(2 + 3i)$
9. Solve as Q. 1. **Ans.** $\pm(3 - \sqrt{5}i)$
10. Solve as Q. 1. **Ans.** $\pm(\sqrt{2} + 3i)$
11. Solve as Example 1. **Ans.** $\pm\frac{1}{\sqrt{2}}(1 - i)$
12. Solve as Example 4 **Ans.** 9
13. Solve as Example 5.
14. LHS $= (a + b\omega + \omega^2 c)(a + \omega^2 b + \omega c)$

$= a^2 + \omega^2 ab + \omega ac + \omega ab + \omega^3 b^2 + \omega^2 bc + \omega^2 ac + \omega^4 bc + \omega^2 c^2$

$= a^2 + \omega^2 ab + \omega ac + \omega ab + b^2 + \omega^2 bc + \omega^2 ac + \omega \cdot bc + c^2$

$[\because \omega^3 = 1, \omega^4 = \omega^3, \omega = 1 \cdot \omega = \omega]$

$= a^2 + b^2 + c^2 + (\omega^2 + \omega)ab + (\omega + \omega^2)ac + (\omega^2 + \omega)bc$

15. Solve as Q. 14.
16. Solve as Example 7. **Ans.** –16

Chapter Practice

Multiple Choice Type Questions

1 Mark

1. If $x = \sqrt{-16}$, then
   (a) $x = 4i$ (b) $x = 4$
   (c) $x = -4$ (d) All of these

2. Which of the following is true?
   (a) $1 - i < 1 + i$ (b) $2i + 1 > -2i + 1$
   (c) $2i > 1$ (d) None of these

3. If $z + 0 = z$, where $z = x + i\,y$ and $0 = 0 + i\,0$, then 0 is called
   (a) additive identity (b) additive inverse
   (c) closure (d) None of these

4. If $z_1 = 2 + 3\,i$ and $z_2 = = 3 - 2\,i$, then $z_1 - z_2$ is equal to
   (a) $-1 + 5\,i$ (b) $5 - i$
   (c) $i + 5$ (d) None of these

5. If $z = 5i\left(-\dfrac{3}{5}i\right)$, then z is equal to
   (a) $0 + 3\,i$ (b) $3 + 0i$ (c) $0 - 3i$ (d) $-3 + 0i$

6. If $z \neq 0$ is a complex number, then
   (a) $\text{Re}(z) = 0 \Rightarrow \text{Im}\,(z^2) = 0$
   (b) $\text{Re}(z^2) = 0 \Rightarrow \text{Im}\,(z^2) = 0$
   (c) $\text{Re}(z) = 0 \Rightarrow \text{Re}(z^2) = 0$
   (d) None of the above

Assertion-Reason Type Questions

1 Mark

Directions (Q. Nos. 7-10) *In the questions given below are two statements labelled as Assertion (A) and Reason (R). In the context of the two statements, which one of the following is correct?*

(a) Both A and R are correct; R is the correct explanation of A
(b) Both A and R are correct; R is not the correct explanation of A
(c) A is correct; R is incorrect
(d) R is correct; A is incorrect

7. **Assertion (A)** If x and y are real numbers and $\dfrac{(1+i)x - 2i}{3+i} + \dfrac{(2-3i)\,y + i}{3-i} = i$, then $x = 3$ and $y = -1$.

   Reason (R) If $2a + i4b$ and $2i$ represent the same complex number, then $a = 0$, $b = \dfrac{1}{2}$.

8. **Assertion (A)** If z is a complex number, then $(\bar{z}^{-1})(\bar{z})$ is equal to 4.

   Reason (R) The region of the complex plane for which $\left|\dfrac{z-a}{z+a}\right| = 1[\text{Re}(a) \neq 0]$ is Y-axis.

9. **Assertion (A)** If $\sqrt{a + ib} = x + iy$, then $\sqrt{a - ib} = x - iy$.

   Reason (R) A complex number z is said to be purely imaginary. If $\text{Re}(z) = 0$.

10. **Assertion (A)** If $(3x - 2iy)\,(2 + i)^2 = 10\,(1 + i)$, then the values of x and are $\dfrac{14}{15}$ and $\dfrac{1}{5}$.

    Reason (R) For every complex number $z = a + ib$, there exist $-z = (-a) + i\,(-b)$ such that $z + (-z) = 0 = (-z) + z$, then $(-z)$ is called the additive inverse of z.

Very Short Answer Type Questions

2 Marks

11. Find the values of x and y, if $x + 4iy = ix + y + 3$.

12. Show that $1 + i^{10} + i^{20} + i^{30}$ is a real number.

13. Find the value of $1 + i^2 + i^4 + i^6 + \ldots + i^{20}$. **[NCERT Exemplar]**

14. Find the value of i^{-1097}.

15. Prove that $\left(\dfrac{2+3i}{3+4i}\right)\left(\dfrac{2-3i}{3-4i}\right)$ is purely real.

16. Express $\left(-2 - \dfrac{1}{3}i\right)^3$ in the form $a + ib$.

17. Express $\dfrac{1}{-2 + \sqrt{-3}}$ in the form $a + ib$.

18. Express $\frac{2-\sqrt{-25}}{1-\sqrt{-16}}$ in the form $a+ib$.

19. Express $\frac{1}{1-\cos\theta+2i\sin\theta}$ in the form $a+ib$.

20. Find the smallest positive integral value of n for which $\frac{(1+i)^n}{(1-i)^{n-2}}$ is a real number.

21. Find the real value of θ for which the expression $\frac{1+i\cos\theta}{1-2i\cos\theta}$ is a real number. **[NCERT Exemplar]**

22. What is the reciprocal of $3+\sqrt{7}i$?

23. Find the multiplicative inverse of $1+i$.

24. Find the quadrant in which conjugate of $\frac{1+2i}{1-i}$ lies.

25. Change the following complex numbers in cartesian form.

(i) $2(\cos 0°+i\sin 0°)$ (ii) $3(\cos 210°+i\sin 210°)$

26. Find the modulus and argument of the complex number $z=-3-i3\sqrt{3}$.

27. If 1, ω and ω^2 are cube roots of unity, then prove that $(x+y)^2+(x\omega+y\omega^2)^2+(x\omega^2+y\omega)^2=6xy$.

Short Answer Type Questions

4 Marks

28. If $z=2-3i$, show that $z^2-4z+13=0$ and hence find the value of $4z^3-3z^2+169$.

29. If $(1+i)(1+2i)(1+3i)\dots(1+ni)=(x+iy)$, then show that $2\cdot 5\cdot 10\ \dots\ (1+n^2)=x^2+y^2$.

30. Solve the equation $|z|=z+1+2i$.

31. If $|z_1|=|z_2|=\dots=|z_n|=1$, then show that

$$|z_1+z_2+\dots+z_n|=\left|\frac{1}{z_1}+\frac{1}{z_2}+\dots+\frac{1}{z_n}\right|.$$

32. Find the principal argument of $(1+i\sqrt{3})^2$.

33. Find the modulus and argument of the complex number $\frac{1}{1+i}$.

34. What is the polar form of the complex number $(i^{25})^3$?

35. Express $-3\sqrt{2}+3\sqrt{2}i$ in the polar form.

36. Express the complex number $\frac{(1+\sqrt{3}i)^2}{\sqrt{3}-i}$ in the form of $a+ib$. Then, find the modulus and argument of the complex number. **[ISC 2014]**

37. Find the square root of $1-i$.

Case-Based Type Questions

6 Marks

38. A complex number z is purely real if and only if $\bar{z}=z$ and is purely imaginary if and only if $\bar{z}=-z$.

Based on the above information, anwer the following qustions.

(i) If $\frac{3+2i\sin\theta}{1-2i\sin\theta}$ is purely real, then find the value of θ.

(ii) If x and y are real numbers and the complex number $\frac{(2+i)x-i}{4+i}+\frac{(1-i)y+2i}{4i}$ is purely real, what is the relation between x and y?

(iii) If z be a complex number satisfying $|\text{Re}(z)|+|\text{Im}(z)|=4$, then find the value of $|z|$.

(iv) What is the smallest positive integer (n) for which $(1+i)^{2n}=(1-i)^{2n}$?

39. Consider $z=a+ib$ and $\bar{z}=a-ib$, where a and b are real numbers are conjugate of each other.

Based on the above information, answer the following questions.

(i) If the complex numbers $-3+i(x^2y)$ and x^2+y+4i, where x and y are real are conjugate to each other, then find the number of ordered pairs (x, y).

(ii) Find the conjugate of $(6+5i)^2$.

(iii) Let $z=x^2-7x-9yi$ such that $\bar{z}=y^2i+20i-12$, then the find the number of ordered pairs (x, y).

(iv) If $z_1=3+2i$ and $z_2=2-i$, then find the value of $\overline{z_1+z_2}$.

(v) What is the number of real values of x such that $\sin x+i\cos 2x$ and $\cos x-i\sin 2x$ are conjugate to each other?

Hints & Answers

1. (a) **2.** (d) **3.** (a) **4.** (a) **5.** (b)
6. (a) **7.** (b) **8.** (a) **9.** (b) **10.** (b)

11. $\because\ x + 4iy = ix + y + 3 \Rightarrow x = y + 3$ and $4y = x$

Ans. $x = 4$ and $y = 1$

12. $1 + i^{10} + i^{20} + i^{30} = 1 + (i^4)^2 i^2 + (i^4)^5 + (i^4)^7 i^2$
$= 1 - 1 + 1 - 1 = 0$

13. $1 + i^2 + i^4 + ... + i^{20} = \dfrac{1((i^2)^{11} - 1)}{(i^2) - 1} = \dfrac{1(-1-1)}{-1-1}$ **Ans.** 1

14. $i^{-1097} = \dfrac{1}{i^{4\times 274+1}} = \dfrac{1}{i} \times \dfrac{i}{i}$ **Ans.** $-i$

15. $\left(\dfrac{2+3i}{3+4i}\right)\left(\dfrac{2-3i}{3-4i}\right) = \dfrac{(2)^2 - (3i)^2}{(3)^2 - (4i)^2}$

16. $\left(-2 - \dfrac{1}{3}i\right)^3 = \left[(2)^3 + \left(\dfrac{1}{3}i\right)^3 + 3 \times 2^2 \times \left(\dfrac{i}{3}\right) + 3 \times 2 \times \left(\dfrac{i}{3}\right)^2\right]$

Ans. $-\dfrac{22}{3} - \dfrac{107}{27}i$

17. $\because\ \dfrac{1}{-2+\sqrt{3}i} \times \dfrac{-2-\sqrt{3}i}{-2-\sqrt{3}i} = \dfrac{-2-\sqrt{3}i}{(-2)^2 - (\sqrt{3}i)^2}$

Ans. $-\dfrac{2}{7} - \dfrac{\sqrt{3}}{7}i$

18. $\dfrac{2-\sqrt{25}i}{1-\sqrt{16}i} = \dfrac{2-5i}{1-4i} \times \dfrac{1+4i}{1+4i} = \dfrac{22+3i}{17}$

Ans. $\dfrac{22}{17} + \dfrac{3}{17}i$

19. $z = \dfrac{1}{(1-\cos\theta) + 2 - \sin\theta} \times \dfrac{(1-\cos\theta) - 2i\sin\theta}{(1-\cos\theta) - 2i\sin\theta}$

$= \dfrac{(1-\cos\theta) - 2i\sin\theta}{(1-\cos\theta)^2 + 4\sin^2\theta} = \dfrac{(1-\cos\theta) - 2i\sin\theta}{1 + \cos^2\theta - 2\cos\theta + 4\sin^2\theta}$

Ans. $\left(\dfrac{1-\cos\theta}{2 - 2\cos\theta + 3\sin^2\theta}\right) + i\left(\dfrac{-2\sin\theta}{2 - 2\cos\theta + 3\sin^2\theta}\right)$

20. We have,

$$z = \left(\frac{1+i}{1-i}\right)^n \times (1-i)^2 = \left[\left(\frac{(1+i)^2}{1^2 - i^2}\right)\right]^n (1^2 + i^2 - 2i)$$

$$= \left(\frac{1-1+2i}{2}\right)^n (-2i)$$

$= (i)^n(-2i)$ **Ans.** 1

21. $\because\ z = \dfrac{1 + i\cos\theta}{1 - 2i\cos\theta} \times \dfrac{1 + 2i\cos\theta}{1 + 2i\cos\theta}$

$= \dfrac{1 - 2\cos^2\theta + 3i\cos\theta}{1 + 4\cos^2\theta}$

For Re (z), put $3\cos\theta = 0 \Rightarrow \cos\theta = 0$

Ans. $2n\pi \pm \dfrac{\pi}{2}$

22. $\because\ z = 3 + \sqrt{7}i$

$\therefore\ \dfrac{1}{z} = \dfrac{1}{3+\sqrt{7}i} \times \dfrac{3-\sqrt{7}i}{3-\sqrt{7}i} = \dfrac{3-\sqrt{7}i}{9+7}$

Ans. $\dfrac{3}{16} - \dfrac{\sqrt{7}}{16}i$

23. $\because\ z = 1 + i$

$\therefore$ Multiplicative inverse $= \dfrac{1}{z} = \dfrac{1}{1+i} \times \dfrac{1-i}{1-i} = \dfrac{1-i}{2}$

Ans. $\dfrac{1}{2} - \dfrac{i}{2}$

24. $\because\ z = \dfrac{1+2i}{1-i} \times \dfrac{1+i}{1+i} = \dfrac{-1+3i}{1+1} = \dfrac{1}{2}(-1+3i)$

$\therefore\ \bar{z} = \dfrac{1}{2}(-1-3i)$

Ans. III quadrant

25. (i) Here, $r = 2$

$\therefore\ x = 2\cos 0°, y = 2\sin 0° \Rightarrow x = 2, y = 0$

Ans. $2 + 0i$

(ii) $\dfrac{-3\sqrt{3}}{2} - \dfrac{3i}{2}$

26. $\because\ |z| = \sqrt{(3)^2 + (3\sqrt{3})^2} = 3\sqrt{1+3} = 6$

Now, $\tan\theta = \left|\dfrac{3\sqrt{3}}{3}\right| = \dfrac{\pi}{3}$

$\therefore\ \arg(z) = -\left(\pi - \dfrac{\pi}{3}\right) = \dfrac{-2\pi}{3}$ **Ans.** 6, $\dfrac{-2\pi}{3}$

27. LHS $= (x+y)^2 + (x\omega + y\omega^2)^2 + (x\omega^2 + y\omega)^2$

$= (x^2 + 2xy + y^2) + (x^2\omega^2 + 2xy\omega^3 + y^2\omega^4)$
$+ (x^2\omega^4 + 2xy\omega^3 + y^2\omega^2)$

$= (x^2 + 2xy + y^2) + (x^2\omega^2 + 2xy + \omega y^2)$
$+ (x^2\omega + 2xy + y^2\omega^2)$

28. $\because\ z^2 = (2-3i)^2 = 4 - 9 - 12i = -5 - 12i$

and $z^3 = (2-3i)^3$

$= (2)^3 - (3i)^3 - 3(2)^2(3i) + 3(2)(3i)^2$

$= 8 + 27i - 36i - 54 = -46 - 9i$

Now, $z^2 - 4z + 13 = (-5 - 12i) - 4(2 - 3i) + 13 = 0$

and $4z^3 - 3z^2 + 169 = -46 - 9i - 3(-5 - 12i) + 169$

Ans. $138 + 27i$

29. $\because\ |(1+i)(1+2i)(1+3i)...(1+ni)| = |x+iy|$

$\Rightarrow\ |1+i|\,|1+2i|\,|1+3i|...|1+ni| = |x+iy|$

$\Rightarrow \sqrt{1+1}\sqrt{1+4}\sqrt{1+9}...\sqrt{1+n^2} = \sqrt{x^2+y^2}$

30. Put $z = x + iy$

$\therefore\ |x+iy| = (x+iy) + 1 + 2i$

$\Rightarrow\ \sqrt{x^2+y^2} = (x+1) + i(y+2)$

$\Rightarrow\ \sqrt{x^2+y^2} = x + 1$ and $y + 2 = 0$ **Ans.** $\dfrac{3}{2} - 2i$

31. Given, $|z_1| = |z_2| = \ldots = |z_n| = 1$

$\Rightarrow \quad |z_1|^2 = |z_2|^2 = \ldots = |z_n|^2 = 1$

$\therefore \quad z_1\bar{z}_1 = z_2\bar{z} = \ldots = z_n\bar{z}_n = 1$

$\therefore \quad z_1 = \frac{1}{\bar{z}_1}, z_2 = \frac{1}{\bar{z}_2}, \ldots, z_n = \frac{1}{\bar{z}_n}$

$\therefore |z_1 + z_2 + \ldots + z_n| = |\overline{z_1 + z_2 + \ldots + z_n}|$

32. $\because z = (1 + i\sqrt{3})^2 = 1 - 3 + 2\sqrt{3}i = -2 + 2\sqrt{3}i$

$\therefore \tan\theta = \left|\frac{2\sqrt{3}}{-2}\right| = \sqrt{3}$ **Ans.** $\frac{2\pi}{3}$

33. $\because z = \frac{1}{1+i} \times \frac{1-i}{1-i} = \frac{1-i}{2}$ **Ans.** $\frac{1}{\sqrt{2}}, -\frac{\pi}{4}$

34. $\because z = (i^{25})^3 = i^{75} = i^{4\times 18+3} = 1 \times i^3 = -i$

Ans. $\cos\left(-\frac{\pi}{2}\right) + i\sin\left(-\frac{\pi}{2}\right)\left(\cos\frac{\pi}{2} - i\sin\frac{\pi}{2}\right)$

35. Here, $r\cos\theta = -3\sqrt{2}$ and $r\sin\theta = 3\sqrt{2}$

$\therefore \quad r^2 = 18 + 18 = 36 \Rightarrow r = 6$

Now, $\tan\theta = \left|\frac{3\sqrt{2}}{-3\sqrt{2}}\right| = 1 \Rightarrow \theta = \frac{\pi}{4}$

$\therefore \quad \arg(z) = \pi - \frac{\pi}{4} = \frac{3\pi}{4}$

Ans. $6\left(\cos\frac{3\pi}{4} + i\sin\frac{3\pi}{4}\right)$

36. Modulus of $z = 2$ and argument of $z = \frac{5\pi}{6}$

37. Let $x + iy = \sqrt{1-i}$

$\Rightarrow x^2 - y^2 + 2ixy = 1 - i$

$\Rightarrow \quad x^2 - y^2 = 1$

and $\quad 2xy = -1$ ...(i)

Now, $(x^2 + y^2) = (x^2 - y^2)^2 + (2xy)^2$

$= (1)^2 + (-1)^2 = 2$

$\Rightarrow \quad x^2 + y^2 = \sqrt{2}$ ...(ii)

$\therefore \quad 2x^2 = 1 + \sqrt{2}$

and $\quad 2y^2 = \sqrt{2} - 1$

$\Rightarrow \quad x = \pm\sqrt{\frac{1+\sqrt{2}}{2}}$

and $\quad y = \pm\sqrt{\frac{\sqrt{2}-1}{2}}$

Since, the product of xy is negative.

Ans. $\pm\left\{\sqrt{\frac{\sqrt{2}+1}{2}} - \sqrt{\frac{\sqrt{2}-1}{2}}i\right\}$

38. (i) $n\pi$ (ii) $8x - 17y = 16$

(iii) $\sqrt{\frac{17}{2}}, \sqrt{10}, \sqrt{8}$ (iv) 2

39. (i) 2 (ii) $11 - 60i$ (iii) 4

(iv) $5 - i$ (v) 0

CHAPTER

05

Quadratic Equations

In this chapter, we will study quadratic equation and methods to find their roots. We will also discuss about nature of roots and quadratic function.

- Quadratic Equation and Its Solution
- Nature of Roots of a Quadratic Equation
- Quadratic Functions

TOPIC 01 Quadratic Equation and Its Solution

Quadratic Equation

An equation of the form $ax^2 + bx + c = 0$ is called **quadratic equation** in variable x, where a, b and c are real numbers and $a \neq 0$.

e.g. $2x^2 + x - 100 = 0$, $-x^2 + 1 + 300x = 0$, $4x - 3x^2 + 7 = 0$ and $4x^2 - 25 = 0$ are quadratic equations.

The form $ax^2 + bx + c = 0$ is called the **standard form of a quadratic equation.**

To express a quadratic equation in its standard form, write the terms of given equation in the decreasing order of their degrees.

e.g. $3x^2 + x + 2 = 0$ and $x^2 - 2x + 6 = 0$ are in standard form, where as $x^2 - 3 + 4x = 0$ and $x + x^2 + 8 = 0$ are not in their standard form.

Solution Set

A real or complex number α which satisfies the given quadratic equation is called root or solution of the equation. Set of these roots is called as solution set.

Fundamental Theorem of Algebra

A polynomial of degree n has atleast one root and upto n roots. A quadratic equation have atmost two roots.

Solution of a Quadratic Equation by Quadratic Formula

The method of completing the square to solve the quadratic equation is a lengthy process to solve it. To avoid such lengthy process we will introduce quadratic formula which stated as if $b^2 - 4ac \geq 0$, then the roots of the quadratic equation $ax^2 + bx + c = 0$ are as

$$x = \frac{-b \pm \sqrt{b^2 - 4ac}}{2a} \text{ or } x = \frac{-b \pm \sqrt{D}}{2a}$$

where, $D = b^2 - 4ac$ is known as **discriminant.** This result is known as **quadratic formula** or **Sridharacharya formula.**

Proof Let the quadratic equation be $ax^2 + bx + c = 0$, where $a \neq 0$; $a, b, c \in R$

$\Rightarrow \quad ax^2 + bx = -c$ [transposing the constant term]

$\Rightarrow \quad x^2 + \frac{b}{a}x = -\frac{c}{a}$ [dividing by coefficient by x^2]

$\Rightarrow \quad x^2 + \frac{b}{a}x + \frac{b^2}{4a^2} = \frac{b^2}{4a^2} - \frac{c}{a}$ [adding $\frac{b^2}{4a^2}$ on both sides to make LHS a perfect square]

$\Rightarrow \quad \left(x + \frac{b}{2a}\right)^2 = \frac{b^2 - 4ac}{4a^2}$

$\Rightarrow \quad x + \frac{b}{2a} = \pm \frac{\sqrt{b^2 - 4ac}}{2a}$

$\therefore \quad x = -\frac{b}{2a} \pm \frac{\sqrt{b^2 - 4ac}}{2a} = \frac{-b \pm \sqrt{b^2 - 4ac}}{2a}$

Hence, the roots of the equation $ax^2 + bx + c = 0$ are $\frac{-b + \sqrt{b^2 - 4ac}}{2a}$ and $\frac{-b - \sqrt{b^2 - 4ac}}{2a}$.

Example 1 Solve $12x^2 + 5x - 3 = 0$ by quadratic formula.

Sol. Given quadratic equation is $12x^2 + 5x - 3 = 0$.
On comparing the given equation with $ax^2 + bx + c = 0$, we get $a = 12$, $b = 5$ and $c = -3$
On substituting the values of $a = 12$, $b = 5$ and $c = -3$ in quadratic formula,

$$x = \frac{-b \pm \sqrt{b^2 - 4ac}}{2a}, \text{ we get}$$

$$x = \frac{-5 \pm \sqrt{(5)^2 - 4 \times 12 \times (-3)}}{2 \times 12}$$

$$\Rightarrow \quad x = \frac{-5 \pm \sqrt{25 + 144}}{24} = \frac{-5 \pm \sqrt{169}}{24} = \frac{-5 \pm 13}{24}$$

Now, $x = \frac{-5 + 13}{24} = \frac{8}{24} = \frac{1}{3}$ [taking +ve sign]

Or $x = \frac{-5 - 13}{24} = -\frac{18}{24} = -\frac{3}{4}$ [taking –ve sign]

Hence, the roots of the given equation are $\frac{1}{3}$ and $-\frac{3}{4}$.

Example 2 Using the quadratic formula, solve the quadratic equation $\sqrt{3}x^2 + 11x + 6\sqrt{3} = 0$.

Sol. The given equation is $\sqrt{3}x^2 + 11x + 6\sqrt{3} = 0$.
On comparing with $ax^2 + bx + c = 0$, we get

$$a = \sqrt{3}, b = 11 \text{ and } c = 6\sqrt{3}$$

On substituting the values of a, b and c in the quadratic formula,

$$x = \frac{-b \pm \sqrt{b^2 - 4ac}}{2a}$$

$$\Rightarrow x = \frac{-11 \pm \sqrt{(11)^2 - 4(\sqrt{3})(6\sqrt{3})}}{2(\sqrt{3})}$$

$$= \frac{-11 \pm \sqrt{121 - 72}}{2\sqrt{3}} = \frac{-11 \pm \sqrt{49}}{2\sqrt{3}} = \frac{-11 \pm 7}{2\sqrt{3}}$$

$\Rightarrow x = \frac{-11 + 7}{2\sqrt{3}} = \frac{-4}{2\sqrt{3}} = \frac{-2}{\sqrt{3}}$ [taking +ve sign]

$\Rightarrow x = \frac{-11 - 7}{2\sqrt{3}} = \frac{-18}{2\sqrt{3}} = \frac{-9}{\sqrt{3}}$ [taking –ve sign]

Hence, $\frac{-2}{\sqrt{3}}$ and $\frac{-9}{\sqrt{3}}$ (or $\frac{-2\sqrt{3}}{3}$ and $-3\sqrt{3}$) are the required solutions of the given equation.

Example 3 Find two numbers such that their sum is 10 and their product is 24.

Sol. Let the two number be x and $10 - x$.
According to the question, $x(10 - x) = 24$

$$\Rightarrow \quad 10x - x^2 = 24 \Rightarrow x^2 - 10x + 24 = 0$$

Comparing it with $ax^2 + bx + c = 0$, we get

$$a = 1,\ b = -10,\ c = 24$$

$$\therefore \quad x = \frac{-b \pm \sqrt{b^2 - 4ac}}{2a}$$

$$= \frac{-(-10) \pm \sqrt{(-10)^2 - 4(1)(24)}}{2 \times 1}$$

$$= \frac{10 \pm \sqrt{100 - 96}}{2} = \frac{10 \pm \sqrt{4}}{2} = \frac{10 \pm 2}{2}$$

$$= \frac{10 + 2}{2}, \frac{10 - 2}{2} = 6, 4$$

Hence, the two numbers are 6 and 4.

Equation Reducible to Quadratic Form

Sometimes, the given algebraic equation is not in the form of quadratic equation but can be reduced to quadratic equations by using simplification or squaring or substituting etc. Such types of equations are solved after reducing.

Example 4 Solve the equation

$$\frac{1}{x-2} + \frac{2}{x-1} = \frac{6}{x},\ x \neq 1, 2.$$

Sol. We have, $\frac{1}{x-2} + \frac{2}{x-1} = \frac{6}{x}$

$$\Rightarrow \quad \frac{(x-1) + 2(x-2)}{(x-2)(x-1)} = \frac{6}{x}$$

$$\Rightarrow \quad x(3x - 5) = 6(x^2 - 3x + 2)$$

$$\Rightarrow \quad 3x^2 - 5x = 6x^2 - 18x + 12$$

$$\Rightarrow \quad 3x^2 - 13x + 12 = 0$$

$$\Rightarrow \quad x = \frac{-(-13) \pm \sqrt{(-13)^2 - 4(3)(12)}}{2 \times 3}$$

$$= \frac{13 \pm \sqrt{169 - 144}}{6} = \frac{13 \pm 5}{6}$$

$$= \frac{13+5}{6}; \frac{13-5}{6} = 3, \frac{4}{3}$$

Hence, $x = 3$ and $\frac{4}{3}$.

Example 5 Solve $2^{2x+8} + 1 = 32 \cdot 2^x$.

Sol. We have, $2^{2x+8} + 1 = 32 \cdot 2^x$

$$\Rightarrow \quad 2^{2x} \cdot 2^8 + 1 = 32 \cdot 2^x$$

$$\Rightarrow \quad 256 \cdot 2^{2x} + 1 = 32 \cdot 2^x$$

$$\Rightarrow \quad 256 \cdot (2^x)^2 - 32 \cdot 2^x + 1 = 0$$

Let $2^x = y$, we get

$$256y^2 - 32y + 1 = 0$$

$$\Rightarrow \quad y = \frac{-(-32) \pm \sqrt{(-32)^2 - 4 \times 256 \times 1}}{2 \times 256}$$

$$\Rightarrow \quad y = \frac{32 \pm \sqrt{1045 - 1024}}{512} \Rightarrow y = \frac{1}{16}, \frac{1}{16}$$

But $y = 2^x$

$$\therefore \quad 2^x = \frac{1}{16}, \frac{1}{16}$$

$$\Rightarrow \quad 2^x = 2^{-4}, 2^{-4}$$

$$\Rightarrow \quad x = -4, -4$$

$$\therefore \quad x = -4$$

Example 6 Solve $(x + 1)(x + 2)(x + 3)(x + 4) + 1 = 0$.

Sol. If we have equation in the form of $(x + a)(x + b)(x + c)(x + d)$ and sum of two of the number a, b, c, d is equal to sum of the remaining two, then we solve it as given below

We have, $(x+1)(x+2)(x+3)(x+4) + 1 = 0$

$$\Rightarrow \quad (x+1)(x+4)(x+2)(x+3) + 1 = 0$$

$$\Rightarrow \quad (x^2 + 5x + 4)(x^2 + 5x + 6) + 1 = 0$$

Let $x^2 + 5x = y$, we get

$$(y+4)(y+6) + 1 = 0$$

$$\Rightarrow \quad y^2 + 10y + 24 + 1 = 0$$

$$\Rightarrow \quad y^2 + 10y + 25 = 0$$

$$\Rightarrow \quad y = \frac{-10 \pm \sqrt{(10)^2 - 4 \times 1 \times 25}}{2 \times 1}$$

$$\Rightarrow \quad y = -5 \Rightarrow x^2 + 5x = -5$$

$$\Rightarrow \quad x^2 + 5x + 5 = 0$$

$$\Rightarrow \quad x = \frac{-5 \pm \sqrt{(5)^2 - 4 \times 1 \times 5}}{2 \times 1}$$

$$\Rightarrow \quad x = \frac{-5 \pm \sqrt{25 - 20}}{2}$$

$$\Rightarrow \quad x = \frac{-5 \pm \sqrt{5}}{2}$$

Example 7 Solve $\sqrt{\frac{4x-1}{4x+1}} - \sqrt{\frac{4x+1}{4x-1}} = \frac{8}{3},\ x \neq \pm\frac{1}{4}.$

Sol. We have, $\sqrt{\frac{4x-1}{4x+1}} - \sqrt{\frac{4x+1}{4x-1}} = \frac{8}{3}$

Let $\sqrt{\frac{4x-1}{4x+1}} = y$, we get $y - \frac{1}{y} = \frac{8}{3}$

$$\Rightarrow \quad \frac{y^2 - 1}{y} = \frac{8}{3} \Rightarrow 3y^2 - 3 = 8y$$

$$\Rightarrow \quad 3y^2 - 8y - 3 = 0$$

$$\Rightarrow \quad y = \frac{-(-8) \pm \sqrt{(-8)^2 - 4(3)(-3)}}{2 \times 3}$$

$$\Rightarrow \quad y = \frac{8 \pm \sqrt{64 + 36}}{6}$$

$$\Rightarrow \quad y = \frac{8 \pm 10}{6} \Rightarrow y = 3, -\frac{2}{3}$$

$$\Rightarrow \quad y = 3 \quad \left[\because y \neq -\frac{2}{3} \text{ as } y = \sqrt{\frac{4x-1}{4x+1}}\right]$$

$$\Rightarrow \quad \sqrt{\frac{4x-1}{4x+1}} = 3 \Rightarrow \frac{4x-1}{4x+1} = 9$$

$$\Rightarrow \quad 4x - 1 = 36x + 9$$

$$\Rightarrow \quad -32x = 10 \Rightarrow x = -\frac{5}{16}$$

Topic Practice 1

Very Short Answer Type Questions

2 Marks

Directions (Q. Nos. 1-5) *Solve the following Equations*

1 $6x^2 + 7x - 20 = 0$

2 $x^2 + 3x - 3 = 0$

3 $25x^2 + 30x + 7 = 0$

4 $x^2 - x + 2 = 0$

5 $\sqrt{3}\, x^2 - \sqrt{2}x + 3\sqrt{3} = 0$

Short Answer Type Questions

4 Marks

6 The sum of two numbers is 9 and the sum of their squares is 41. Find the numbers.

7 The sum of the squares of two consecutive positive even integers is 340. Find the numbers.

8 Solve $\frac{2x}{x-4} + \frac{2x-5}{x-3} = 8\frac{1}{3}$.

9 Find the value of x, if $\frac{1}{x+1} - \frac{2}{x+2} = \frac{3}{x+3} - \frac{4}{x+4}$.

10 Solve $5^{x+1} + 5^{2-x} = 5^3 + 1$.

11 Solve $(x-7)(x-3)(x+1)(x+5) = 1680$.

12 Solve $\sqrt{\frac{2x^2+x+2}{x^2+3x+1}} + 2\sqrt{\frac{x^2+3x+1}{2x^2+x+2}} - 3 = 0$.

13 Solve $\sqrt{x+3} + \sqrt{x-3} = 6$.

14 Solve $\frac{x-2}{x+2} + \frac{x+2}{x-2} = 4$.

Hints & Answers

1. Solve as Example 1. **Ans.** $x = \frac{4}{3}, \frac{-5}{2}$

2. Solve as Example 1. **Ans.** $x = \frac{-3 \pm \sqrt{21}}{2}$

3. Solve as Example 1. **Ans.** $x = \frac{-3 \pm \sqrt{2}}{5}$

4. Solve as Example 1. **Ans.** $x = \frac{1 \pm \sqrt{7}\, i}{2}$

5. Solve as Example 2. **Ans.** $x = \frac{\sqrt{2} \pm i\sqrt{34}}{2\sqrt{3}}$

6. Solve as Example 3. **Ans.** 4, 5

7. Solve as Example 3. **Ans.** 12, 14

8. Reduce the given equation to the equation

$$13x^2 - 118x + 240 = 0$$

Ans. $x = 6, \frac{40}{13}$

9. Reduce the given equation to the form

$$4x^2 + 10x = 0$$

Ans. $x = 0, -\frac{5}{2}$

10. Solve as Example 5. **Ans.** $x = -1, 2$

11. Solve as Example 6. **Ans.** $x = 9, -7, 1 \pm \sqrt{-24}$

12. Solve as Example 7. **Ans.** $x = 1, \frac{-11 \pm \sqrt{105}}{4}$

13. We have, $\sqrt{x+3} + \sqrt{x-3} = 6$

$$\Rightarrow \quad x + 3 + x - 3 + 2\sqrt{x^2 - 9} = 36$$

$$\Rightarrow \quad \sqrt{x^2 - 9} = 18 - x$$

$$\Rightarrow \quad x^2 - 9 = 324 + x^2 - 36x$$ **Ans.** $x = \frac{37}{4}$

14. Put $\frac{x-2}{x+2} = y$. **Ans.** $x = \pm 2\sqrt{3}$

TOPIC 02 Nature of Roots of a Quadratic Equation

Relation between Discriminant and Nature of Roots

By quadratic formula, the roots of the quadratic equation $ax^2 + bx + c = 0$, $a \neq 0$ are given by

$$x = \frac{-b \pm \sqrt{b^2 - 4ac}}{2a} \quad \text{or} \quad x = \frac{-b \pm \sqrt{D}}{2a}$$

where, $D = b^2 - 4ac$ is called **discriminant**. The nature of roots depends upon the value of the discriminant D.

Case I When $D = 0$, i.e. $b^2 - 4ac = 0$. If $D = b^2 - 4ac = 0$, then $x = \frac{-b \pm 0}{2a} \Rightarrow x = -\frac{b}{2a}, -\frac{b}{2a}$

So, the quadratic equation has **two equal real roots** or **repeated roots** or **coincident roots.**

Case II When $D > 0$, i.e. $b^2 - 4ac > 0$. If $D = b^2 - 4ac > 0$, then $x = \frac{-b + \sqrt{D}}{2a}$ and $\frac{-b - \sqrt{D}}{2a}$

So, the quadratic equation has **two distinct real roots.**

Case III When $D < 0$, i.e. $b^2 - 4ac < 0$. If $D = b^2 - 4ac < 0$, then $\sqrt{D}$ can not be evaluated as there is no real number whose square is $b^2 - 4ac$. So, **the quadratic equation has no real roots** or **imaginary root** or we can say that roots of quadratic equation do not exist. This can be explained using the flow chart

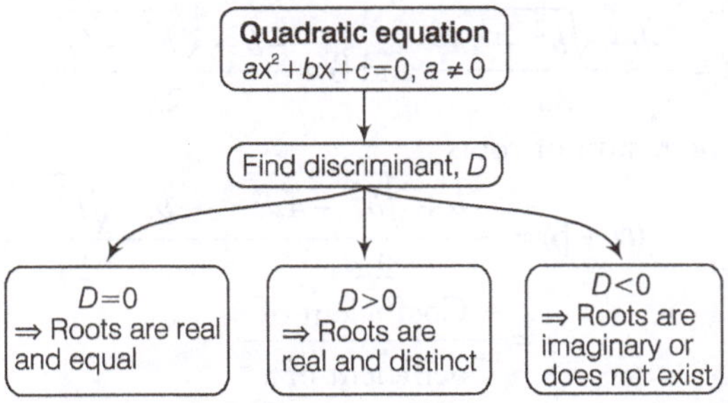

Note When a, b and c are rational numbers, $a \neq 0$

(i) If $D = b^2 - 4ac = 0$, then roots are rational and equal.

(ii) If $D = b^2 - 4ac > 0$ and D is a perfect square of a rational number, then roots are **rational** and **unequal**.

(iii) If $D = b^2 - 4ac > 0$ but D is not a perfect square of rational number, then roots are irrational and **unequal**. They form a **pair of irrational conjugates** $p + \sqrt{q}$ and $p - \sqrt{q}$, where $p, q \in Q; q > 0$.

(iv) If $D = b^2 - 4ac < 0$, then the roots are pair of complex conjugates.

Example 1 Find the discriminant of the quadratic equation $x^2 - 4x + 1 = 0$.

Sol. Given quadratic equation is $x^2 - 4x + 1 = 0$.

On comparing with $ax^2 + bx + c = 0$, we get

$$a = 1,\ b = -4 \text{ and } c = 1$$

Now, discriminant

$$(D) = \sqrt{b^2 - 4ac} = \sqrt{(-4)^2 - 4 \times 1 \times 1}$$
$$= \sqrt{16 - 4} = \sqrt{12} = \sqrt{2 \times 2 \times 3}$$
$$= 2\sqrt{3}$$

Example 2 If the discriminant of the equation $6x^2 - bx + 2 = 0$ is 1, then find the value of b.

Sol. Given, $6x^2 - bx + 2 = 0$

On comparing with $Ax^2 + Bx + C = 0$, we get

$$A = 6,\ B = -b \text{ and } C = 2$$

We know that,

Discriminant, $D = B^2 - 4AC$

$\Rightarrow \quad 1 = (-b)^2 - 4 \times 6 \times 2 \quad$ [given, $D = 1$]

$\Rightarrow \quad 1 = b^2 - 48 \Rightarrow b^2 = 49$

$\Rightarrow \quad b = \pm 7$ [taking square root on both sides]

Hence, the required value of b is -7 or 7.

Example 3 Find the nature of roots of the following quadratic equations. If the real roots exist, then also find the roots.

(i) $4x^2 + 12x + 9 = 0$ (ii) $3x^2 + 5x - 7 = 0$

(iii) $7y^2 - 4y + 5 = 0$

Sol. (i) Given quadratic equation is $4x^2 + 12x + 9 = 0$

On comparing with $ax^2 + bx + c = 0$, we get

$$a = 4,\ b = 12 \text{ and } c = 9$$

Now, $\quad D = b^2 - 4ac = (12)^2 - 4(4)(9)$

$$= 144 - 144 = 0$$

Since, $D = 0$, so given quadratic equation has two equal and real roots which are given by

$$x = \frac{-b \pm \sqrt{D}}{2a} = \frac{-12 \pm 0}{2(4)} = \frac{-12 \pm 0}{8}$$

$\Rightarrow \quad x = \frac{-12 + 0}{8}$ or $x = \frac{-12 - 0}{8}$

$\Rightarrow \quad x = -\frac{3}{2}$ or $x = -\frac{3}{2}$

Hence, the roots are $\frac{-3}{2}$ and $-\frac{3}{2}$.

(ii) Given quadratic equation is

$$3x^2 + 5x - 7 = 0$$

On comparing with $ax^2 + bx + c = 0$, we get

$$a = 3,\ b = 5 \text{ and } c = -7$$

Now, $D = b^2 - 4ac = (5)^2 - 4(3)(-7) = 25 + 84 = 109$

Since, $D > 0$, so given quadratic equation has two distinct real roots which are given by

$$x = \frac{-b \pm \sqrt{D}}{2a} = \frac{-5 \pm \sqrt{109}}{2(3)}$$

$$\Rightarrow \quad x = \frac{-5+\sqrt{109}}{6} \quad \text{[taking +ve sign]}$$

$$\text{or} \quad x = \frac{-5-\sqrt{109}}{6} \quad \text{[taking −ve sign]}$$

Hence, the roots are $\frac{-5+\sqrt{109}}{6}$ and $\frac{-5-\sqrt{109}}{6}$.

(iii) Given quadratic equation is $7y^2 - 4y + 5 = 0$

On comparing with $ay^2 + by + c = 0$, we get

$$a = 7,\ b = -4 \text{ and } c = 5$$

Now, $D = b^2 - 4ac = (-4)^2 - 4(7)(5)$

$$= 16 - 140 = -124 < 0$$

Since, $D < 0$, so given quadratic equation has no real roots.

Example 4 Find the value of k for which the given equation has equal roots.

$$(k-12)x^2 + 2(k-12)x + 2 = 0$$

Sol. Given quadratic equation is

$$(k-12)x^2 + 2(k-12)x + 2 = 0$$

On comparing with $ax^2 + bx + c = 0$, we get

$$a = k - 12,\ b = 2(k-12) \text{ and } c = 2$$

Now, $D = b^2 - 4ac$

$$= [2(k-12)]^2 - 4(k-12)(2)$$
$$= 4(k-12)^2 - 8(k-12)$$
$$= (k-12)[4(k-12) - 8]$$
$$= (k-12)(4k-48-8)$$
$$= (k-12)(4k-56)$$

Since, roots of given equation are equal.

$\therefore \quad D = 0$

$\Rightarrow \quad (k-12)(4k-56) = 0$

$\Rightarrow \quad k - 12 = 0$ or $4k - 56 = 0$

$\Rightarrow \quad k = 12$ or $k = \frac{56}{4}$

$\Rightarrow \quad k = 12$ or $k = 14$

But $k = 12$ does not satisfy the given equation because if $k = 12$, then coefficients of x^2 and x become zero.

Hence, the required value of k is 14.

Example 5 Find the values of k for which the equation $9x^2 + 3kx + 4 = 0$ has real roots.

Sol. Given quadratic equation is $9x^2 + 3kx + 4 = 0$

On comparing with $ax^2 + bx + c = 0$, we get

$$a = 9,\ b = 3k \text{ and } c = 4$$

Now, $D = b^2 - 4ac = (3k)^2 - 4(9)(4)$

$$= 9k^2 - 144$$

Since, roots of given equation are real.

$\therefore \quad D \ge 0$

$\Rightarrow \quad 9k^2 - 144 \ge 0$

$\Rightarrow \quad 9(k^2 - 16) \ge 0$

$\therefore \quad k^2 - 16 \ge 0 \quad [\because 9 \ne 0]$

$\Rightarrow \quad k^2 - (4)^2 \ge 0$

$\Rightarrow \quad (k-4)(k+4) \ge 0 \quad [\because a^2 - b^2 = (a-b)(a+b)]$

$\Rightarrow \quad k \le -4$ or $k \ge 4$

Note
- $x^2 - a^2 > 0 \Rightarrow x < -a$ or $x > a$
- $x^2 - a^2 \ge 0 \Rightarrow x \le -a$ or $x \ge a$
- $x^2 - a^2 < 0 \Rightarrow -a < x < a$
  $x^2 - a^2 \le 0 \Rightarrow -a \le x \le a$
- $(x-a)(x-b) > 0$ and $a < b \Rightarrow x < a$ or $x > b$
  $(x-a)(x-b) \ge 0$ and $a < b \Rightarrow x \le a$ or $x \ge b$
- $(x-a)(x-b) < 0$ and $a < b \Rightarrow a < x < b$
- $(x-a)(x-b) \le 0$ and $a < b \Rightarrow a \le x \le b$

Sum and Product of Roots

Let the roots of the quadratic equation $ax^2 + bx + c = 0$.

By quadratic formula, we have

$$\alpha = \frac{-b + \sqrt{b^2 - 4ac}}{2a} \text{ and } \beta = \frac{-b - \sqrt{b^2 - 4ac}}{2a}$$

Then, sum of roots

$$(\alpha + \beta) = \frac{-b + \sqrt{b^2 - 4ac}}{2a} + \frac{-b - \sqrt{b^2 - 4ac}}{2a} = -\frac{b}{a}$$

$$= \frac{-\text{Coefficient of } x}{\text{Coefficient of } x^2}$$

and product of roots

$$(\alpha\beta) = \frac{-b + \sqrt{b^2 - 4ac}}{2a} \times \frac{-b - \sqrt{b^2 - 4ac}}{2a}$$

$$= \frac{(-b)^2 - (\sqrt{b^2 - 4ac})^2}{4a^2}$$

$$= \frac{b^2 - b^2 + 4ac}{4a^2} = \frac{c}{a} = \frac{\text{Constant term}}{\text{Coefficient of } x^2}$$

Example 6 For the quadratic equation $3x^2 - 9x + 11 = 0$, find sum and product of the roots.

Sol. Let α, β be the roots of the equation

$3x^2 - 9x + 11 = 0$, then $\alpha + \beta = -\left(-\frac{9}{3}\right) = 3$ and $\alpha\beta = \frac{11}{3}$.

Example 7 Find the value of k, if the sum of the roots of the equation $(k-1)x^2 = kx - 1$, where $k \neq 0$ is 2.

Sol. We have,

$$(k-1)x^2 = kx - 1$$

$$\Rightarrow \quad (k-1)x^2 - kx + 1 = 0$$

Now, sum of the roots of the given equation is 2.

$$\therefore \quad -\frac{(-k)}{k-1} = 2$$

$$\Rightarrow \quad k = 2(k-1)$$

$$\Rightarrow \quad k = 2k - 2 \Rightarrow k = 1$$

Values of the Symmetric Expressions of the Roots

If α, β are the roots of the quadratic equation $ax^2 + bx + c = 0$, then the expressions of the form $\alpha + \beta, \alpha\beta, \alpha^2 + \beta^2, \alpha^2 - \beta^2, \frac{\alpha}{\beta} + \frac{\beta}{\alpha}$ etc. are known as the functions of the roots α and β. When there is no effect on the expression when α and β are inter change with each other then such expressions are known as symmetric. e.g.

$$\alpha^2 + \beta^2 \text{ or } \frac{\alpha}{\beta} + \frac{\beta}{\alpha} \text{ etc.}$$

Note The expressions $\alpha + \beta$ and $\alpha\beta$ are called the **elementary symmetric functions.**

Some Important Identities

(i) $\alpha^2 + \beta^2 + (\alpha + \beta)^2 - 2\alpha\beta$

(ii) $(\alpha - \beta)^2 = (\alpha + \beta)^2 - 4\alpha\beta$

(iii) $\alpha^2 - \beta^2 = (\alpha + \beta)(\alpha - \beta)$

$= (\alpha + \beta)\sqrt{(\alpha + \beta)^2 - 4\alpha\beta}$

(iv) $\alpha^3 + \beta^3 = (\alpha + \beta)^3 - 3\alpha\beta(\alpha + \beta)$

(v) $\alpha^3 - \beta^3 = (\alpha - \beta)(\alpha^2 + \alpha\beta + \beta^2)$

$= (\alpha - \beta)[(\alpha - \beta)^3 + 3\alpha\beta)]$

(vi) $\alpha^4 + \beta^4 = (\alpha^2 + \beta^2)^2 - 2\alpha^2\beta^2$

$= [(\alpha + \beta)^2 - 2\alpha\beta]^2 - 2(\alpha\beta)^2$

(vii) $\alpha^4 - \beta^4 = (\alpha^2 - \beta^2)(\alpha^2 + \beta^2)$

$= (\alpha - \beta)(\alpha + \beta)(\alpha^2 + \beta^2)$

$= \sqrt{(\alpha + \beta)^2 - 4\alpha\beta}\,(\alpha + \beta)[(\alpha + \beta)^2 - 2\alpha\beta]$

(viii) $\frac{\alpha}{\beta} + \frac{\beta}{\alpha} = \frac{\alpha^2 + \beta^2}{\alpha\beta} = \frac{(\alpha + \beta)^2 - 2\alpha\beta}{\alpha\beta}$

Example 8 If α, β are roots of the equation $x^2 - 4x + 2 = 0$, find the values of

(i) $\alpha^2 + \beta^2$ (ii) $\alpha^3 + \beta^3$

(iii) $\frac{1}{\alpha} + \frac{1}{\beta}$

Sol. We have, α and β are the roots of the equation

$x^2 - 4x + 2 = 0$, then $\alpha + \beta = \frac{-(-4)}{1} = 4$ and $\alpha\beta = \frac{2}{1} = 2$

(i) $\alpha^2 + \beta^2 = (\alpha + \beta)^2 - 2\alpha\beta$

$= (4)^2 - 2(2) = 16 - 4 = 12$

(ii) $\alpha^3 + \beta^3 = (\alpha + \beta)^3 - 3\alpha\beta(\alpha + \beta)$

$= (4)^3 - 3 \times 2 \times 4 = 64 - 24 = 40$

(iii) $\frac{1}{\alpha} + \frac{1}{\beta} = \frac{\alpha + \beta}{\alpha\beta} = \frac{4}{2} = 2$

Formation of a Quadratic Equation

If we have sum and product of the roots of a quadratic equation, then quadratic equation is given as

$$\boxed{x^2 - (\text{sum of roots})\, x + \text{product of roots} = 0}$$

Example 9 If α, β are the roots of the equation $ax^2 + bx + c = 0$, then form a equation whose roots are $\frac{\alpha}{\beta}$ and $\frac{\beta}{\alpha}$.

Sol. We have, α and β are the roots of the equation

$ax^2 + bx + c = 0$, then $\alpha + \beta = -\frac{b}{a}$ and $\alpha\beta = \frac{c}{a}$

$\therefore$ Sum of the required equation $= \frac{\alpha}{\beta} + \frac{\beta}{\alpha}$

$$= \frac{\alpha^2+\beta^2}{\alpha\beta} = \frac{(\alpha+\beta)^2-2\alpha\beta}{\alpha\beta}$$

$$= \frac{(-b/a)^2-2(c/a)}{(c/a)} = \frac{b^2-2ac}{ac}$$

and product of the required equation $= \frac{\alpha}{\beta}\cdot\frac{\beta}{\alpha} = 1$

Hence, the required equation is

x^2 – (sum of roots) x + (product of roots) = 0

$$\Rightarrow \quad x^2 - \left(\frac{b^2-2ac}{ac}\right)x + 1 = 0$$

$$\Rightarrow \quad ac\,x^2 - (b^2-2ac)x + ac = 0$$

Special Roots

If the roots of the equation, $ax^2+bx+c=0$ are α and β, then

(i) $\alpha \pm h$ and $\beta \pm h$ are the roots of the equation

$$a(x \mp h)^2 + b(x \mp h) + c = 0$$

(ii) αh and βh are the roots of the equation

$$ax^2 + bhx + h^2c = 0$$

(iii) $\frac{\alpha}{h}$ and $\frac{\beta}{h}$ are the roots of the equation

$$ah^2x^2 + bhx + c = 0$$

(iv) $-\alpha$ and $-\beta$ are the roots of the equation

$$ax^2 - bx + c = 0$$

(v) $\frac{1}{\alpha}$ and $\frac{1}{\beta}$ are the roots of the equation

$$cx^2 + bx + a = 0.$$

Common Roots

Sometimes two given quadratic equation can have one or both two common roots.

1. Condition that One Root is Common

Let the two quadratic equations are $a_1x^2+b_1x+c_1=0$ and $a_2x^2+b_2x+c_2=0$. Let α be the common root of both the equation. Then the condition that both the equation have one common root α, is

$$\frac{b_1c_2-b_2c_1}{c_1a_2-c_2a_1} = \frac{c_1a_2-c_2a_1}{a_1b_2-a_2b_1}.$$

2. Condition that Both Roots are Common

Let the two quadratic equations are $a_1x^2+b_1x+c_1=0$ and $a_2x^2+b_2x+c_2=0$. Let α and β are the roots of both the equation. Then the condition that both the equation have both common roots α and β is

$$\frac{a_1}{a_2} = \frac{b_1}{b_2} = \frac{c_1}{c_2}.$$

Example 10 Find the value of k so that the equations $x^2 - kx - 21 = 0$ and $x^2 - 3kx + 35 = 0$ have one root common.

Sol. Let the common root be α. Then, for α to be common root

$$\frac{(-k)(35)-(-3k)(-21)}{(-21)(1)-(35)(1)} = \frac{(-21)(1)-(35)(1)}{1(-3k)-(1)(-k)}$$

$$\Rightarrow \quad \frac{-35k-63k}{-21-35} = \frac{-21-35}{-3k+k}$$

$$\Rightarrow \quad \frac{-98k}{-56} = \frac{-56}{-2k}$$

$$\Rightarrow \quad 196k^2 = (56)^2$$

$$\Rightarrow \quad k = \pm 4$$

Topic Practice 2

Very Short Answer Type Questions

2 Marks

1 Find the discriminant of the equation $(4x-3)^2 + 20x = 11$.

2 If discriminant of the equation $5x^2 + ax + 4 = 0$ is 1, then find the value of a.

3 Discuss the nature of the roots of the equation $3\sqrt{3}\,x^2 + 10x + \sqrt{3} = 0$.

4 Find a so that the sum of the roots of the equation $ax^2 + 2x + 3a = 0$ may be equal to their product.

5 Formulate a quadratic equation whose roots are $2, -\frac{1}{2}$.

Short Answer Type Questions

4 Marks

6 If one of the roots of $3x^2 - 7px + 10p = 0$ be 5, find p and also the other root.

7 If α, β are the roots of the equation $ax^2 + bx + c = 0$, then evaluate $(\alpha a + b)^{-2} + (\beta a + b)^{-2}$.

8 Let p, q be the roots of the equation $3x^2 + 6x + 2 = 0$. Form an equation whose roots are $\frac{-p^2}{q}, \frac{-q^2}{p}$.

9 If the equations $x^2 + ax + b = 0$ and $x^2 + bx + a = 0$ have a common root and $a \neq b$, then prove that $a + b + 1 = 0$.

10 Find k so that one root of the equation $2kx^2 - 20x + 21 = 0$ exceeds the other by 2.

Long Answer Type Questions

6 Marks

11 The sum of roots of the equation $\frac{1}{x+a} + \frac{1}{x+b} = \frac{1}{c}$ is zero. Prove that the product of the roots is $-\frac{1}{2}(a^2 + b^2)$.

12 If α, β be the roots of the equation $3x^2 + 2x + 1 = 0$, form an equation whose roots are $\frac{1-\alpha}{1+\alpha}, \frac{1-\beta}{1+\beta}$.

13 Both the roots of equation $x^2 - (a+1)x + a + 4 = 0$ are negative. Calculate the values of a.

14 If $ax^2 + bx + c = 0$ and $bx^2 + cx + a = 0$ have a common root, then prove that $a^3 + b^3 + c^3 = 3abc$.

Hints & Answers

1. Solve as Example 1. **Ans.** 144
2. Solve as Example 2. **Ans.** – 9 or 9
3. Solve as Example 3. **Ans.** Real and distinct
4. We have, $\alpha + \beta = \alpha\beta$

$$\Rightarrow \quad -\frac{2}{a} = \frac{3a}{a} \Rightarrow a = -\frac{2}{3}$$

5. Required equation is given as

$$x^2 - \left[2 + \left(-\frac{1}{2}\right)\right]x + (2)\left(-\frac{1}{2}\right) = 0$$

Ans. $2x^2 - 3x - 2 = 0$

6. Let the roots be α, 5.

Then, $\alpha + 5 = -\left(\frac{-7p}{3}\right) = \frac{7p}{3}$ and $\alpha \times 5 = \frac{10p}{3}$

Ans. $p = 3, \alpha = 2$

7. Solve as Example 8. **Ans.** $\frac{b^2 - 2ac}{a^2c^2}$

8. Solve as Example 9. **Ans.** $3x^2 - 18x + 2 = 0$

9. Let α be the common root of $x^2 + ax + b = 0$ and $x^2 + bx + a = 0$, then

$$\alpha^2 + a\alpha + b = 0 \quad \text{...(i)}$$

and $$\alpha^2 + b\alpha + a = 0 \quad \text{...(ii)}$$

On subtracting Eq. (ii) from Eq. (i), we get

$$(a - b)\alpha + (b - a) = 0$$

$$\Rightarrow \quad \alpha = 1$$

10. Let α and β are the roots of the equation $2kx^2 - 20x + 21 = 0$.

Then, use $(\alpha + \beta)^2 - 4\alpha\beta = 4$ **Ans.** $k = 2, \frac{-25}{2}$

11. We have, $\frac{1}{x+a} + \frac{1}{x+b} = \frac{1}{c}$

$$\Rightarrow \quad \frac{x+b+x+a}{(x+a)(x+b)} = \frac{1}{c}$$

$$\Rightarrow \quad x^2 + (a + b - 2c)x + (ab - bc - ca) = 0$$

Here, sum of roots = 0

$$\Rightarrow \quad \frac{-(a+b-2c)}{1} = 0$$

$$\Rightarrow \quad c = \frac{a+b}{2}$$

$\therefore$ Product of roots $= \frac{ab - bc - ca}{1}$

$$= -\frac{1}{2}(a^2 + b^2)$$

12. Solve as Example 9. **Ans.** $x^2 - 2x + 3 = 0$

13. As both roots of equation $x^2 - (a+1)x + a + 4 = 0$ are negative.

Sum of roots is negative and product of root is positive, and discriminant ≥ 0.

Ans. $-4 < a \leq -3$

14. Solve as Example 10.

TOPIC 03 Quadratic Functions

Let $f(x) = ax^2 + bx + c$, $a \neq 0$ and a, b, c are real, then $f(x)$ is known as **quadratic polynomial** or **quadratic function.**

Sign of Expression $ax^2 + bx + c$

Let D be the discriminant of the quadratic expression $ax^2 + bx + c$, and $\alpha, \beta, (\alpha < \beta)$ are zeroes, then

(i) $ax^2 + bx + c > 0, \forall x \in R$ iff $a > 0, D < 0$

(ii) $ax^2 + bx + c < 0, \forall x \in R$ iff $a < 0, D < 0$

(iii) $ax^2 + bx + c < 0, \forall x \in R$ iff $a < 0, D = 0$

(iv) $ax^2 + bx + c > 0, \forall x \in R$ iff $a > 0, D = 0$

(v) $ax^2 + bx + c = 0$, when $x = \alpha$ and β, $D > 0$

(vi) $ax^2 + bx + c$ has sign opposite to a when $\alpha < x < \beta$ otherwise same sign as a when $x < \alpha$ and $x > \beta$.

The sign of the expression $ax^2 + bx + c$ is always the same as that of a, except when the roots of the equation $ax^2 + bx + c = 0$ are real and distinct and x lies between them.

Example 1 Discuss the sign of the quadratic function $2 + x - x^2$.

Sol. We have, $f(x) = 2 + x - x^2$

$\Rightarrow \quad f(x) = -x^2 + x + 2$

$\therefore \quad a = -1, b = 1, c = 2$

and $\quad D = b^2 - 4ac = (1)^2 - 4(-1)(2) = 9 > 0$

$\therefore \; f(x) = 0$ has two real and distinct roots.

Now, $f(x) = 0$

$\Rightarrow \quad -x^2 + x + 2 = 0$

$\Rightarrow \quad -(x+1)(x-2) = 0$

$\Rightarrow \quad x = -1, 2$

$$\text{Hence, } f(x) = \begin{cases} < 0, & \text{when } x < -1 \text{ or } x > 2 \\ > 0, & \text{when } -1 < x < 2 \\ = 0, & \text{when } x = -1, 2 \end{cases}$$

Topic Practice 3

Short Answer Type Questions

4 Marks

1 Determine the values of a, so that the expression $x^2 - 2(a+1)x + 4$ is always positive.

2 Find the sign of $6x^2 - 5x + 1$ for all real values of x.

3 Under what conditions is $2x^2 + kx + 2$ always positive?

4 Show that $f(x) = -x^2 + 3x - 3$ is always negative.

5 Explain why $3x^2 + kx - 1$ is never always positive for any value of k.

Hints & Answers

1. Given, $x^2 - 2(a+1)x + 4 > 0 \; \forall \; x \in R$

Here, $a = 1 > 0$ and $D = (-2(a+1))^2 - 4 \times 1 \times 4 = 4(a^2 + 2a - 3)$.

For the given expression to be always positive, $D < 0$ as $a > 0$

Ans. $-3 < a < 1$

2. Solve as Example 1.

Ans. Positive for all real values of x except for those $\frac{1}{3} < x < \frac{1}{2}$

3. Solve as Question 1.

Ans. $-4 < k < 4$

4. Solve as Example 1.

5. $a = 3$ which is positive and $D = k^2 + 12$ which is also always positive (as $k^2 > 0 \; \forall \; k \in R$).

$\therefore \; 3x^2 + kx - 1$ is both positive and negative.

Chapter Practice

Multiple Choice Type Questions

1 Mark

1. If $x^2 - x + 2 = 0$, then x is equal to
(a) $\frac{1 \pm i\sqrt{7}}{2}$ (b) $\frac{1 \pm i\sqrt{5}}{2}$ (c) $\frac{1 \pm i}{2}$ (d) $\frac{1 \pm i\sqrt{2}}{2}$

2. If one root of the equation $5x^2 + 2x + p = 2$ is reciprocal of another, then the value of p is
(a) 5 (b) 3 (c) 2 (d) 7

3. If α and β are the roots of the equation $x^2 - 7x + 1 = 0$, then the value of $\alpha^4 + \beta^4$ is
(a) 2127 (b) 2207 (c) 2247 (d) 2317

4. If quadratic equation $(k-12)x^2 + 2(k-12)x + 2 = 0$ has equal roots, then the value of k is
(a) 9 or 11 (b) 12 or 14 (c) 4 or 6 (d) 8 or 10

5. The quadratic equation, whose roots are $2 + \sqrt{5}$ and $2 - \sqrt{5}$ is
(a) $x^2 + 4x + 1 = 0$ (b) $x^2 - 4x + 1 = 0$
(c) $x^2 - 4x - 1 = 0$ (d) $x^2 + 4x - 1 = 0$

Assertion-Reason Type Questions

1 Mark

Directions (Q. Nos. 6-10) *In the questions given below are two statements labelled as Assertion (A) and Reason (R). In the context of the two statements, which one of the following is correct?*

(a) Both A and R are correct; R is the correct explanation of A
(b) Both A and R are correct; R is not the correct explanation of A
(c) A is correct; R is incorrect
(d) R is correct; A is incorrect

6. **Assertion (A)** The roots of quadratic equation $4x^2 + 3x + 5 = 0$ are $\frac{-3 \pm \sqrt{-61}}{8}$.

Reason (R) Roots of quadratic equation $ax^2 + bx + c = 0$ are $x = \frac{-b \pm \sqrt{D}}{2a}$, where $D = b^2 - 4ac$.

7. **Assertion (A)** If the roots of equation $(1 + m^2)x^2 + 2\,cmx + (c^2 - a^2) = 0$ are equal, then $c^2 = a^2(1 + m^2)$.

Reason (R) The nature of roots of quadratic equations $ax^2 + bx + c = 0$ depend on the value of discriminant $b^2 - 4ac$.

8. **Assertion (A)** The nature of the roots of quadratic equation $3x^2 + 2x - 1 = 0$ is real and unequal.

Reason (R) The roots of quadratic equation $ax^2 + bx + c = 0$ are real and unequal if the value of discriminant $D = b^2 - 4ac$ is greater than 0 and perfect square also.

9. **Assertion (A)** For $a > 4$, the quadratic equation $x^2 - 4x + a = 0$ has no real roots.

Reason (R) The quadratic equation $ax^2 + bx + c = 0$ has no real root if and only if $b^2 - 4ac > 0$.

10. **Assertion (A)** The quadratic equation whose roots are 3 and $\frac{1}{3}$ is $3x^2 - 10x + 3 = 0$.

Reason (R) If α and β are the roots of a quadratic equation, then quadratic equation is given by $x^2 - (\alpha + \beta)x + \alpha\beta = 0$.

Very Short Answer Type Questions

2 Marks

11. Find the root of the equation $3x^2 - 17x + 25 = 0$.

12. Find the nature of the roots of the equation $3x^2 + 7x + 2 = 0$.

13. Write the sum and product of the roots of the equation $\sqrt{2}x^2 - \sqrt{2}x + 4 = 0$.

Short Answer Type Questions

(4 Marks)

14. If $a, b, h \in R$, then show that the equation $(x-a)(x-b)=h^2$ has real roots.

15. For the quadratic equation $(k-1)x^2 - kx + 1, k \neq 1$, find the value of k, so that the roots are numerically equal but opposite in sign.

16. If α, β are the roots of the equation $3x^2 - 6x + 4 = 0$, find the value of $\alpha^2 + \beta^2$.

17. Find the condition for which the roots of the equation $ax^2 + bx + c = 0$ that one is positive and other is negative.

18. Form an equation with real coefficients one of whose roots is $-1-2i$.

19. Solve $x^2 - 2x + \frac{3}{2} = 0$

20. Solve $2^{x+1} + 4^x = 8$.

21. Find x iff $x(x+2)(x^2-1) = -1$.

22. Solve $(x^2+2)^2 + 8x^2 = 6x(x^2+2)$.

23. For what value of k, $(4-k)x^2 + 2(k+2)x + (8k+1)$, is a perfect square.

24. If the roots of the equation $a(b-c)x^2 + b(c-a)x + c(a-b) = 0$ are equal, show that $\frac{2}{b} = \frac{1}{a} + \frac{1}{c}$.

25. Prove that the equation $x^2 + px - 1 = 0$ has real and distinct roots for all real values of p.

26. Given that $a, b, c \in Q$, show that the roots of the equation $(b-c)x^2 + (c-a)x + (a-b) = 0$ are rational. Find the condition for the roots to be equal.

27. Find the equation whose roots are n times the roots of the equation $ax^2 + bx + c = 0$.

28. If the roots of the equation $ax^2 + bx + b = 0$, $b^2 - 4ab \geq 0$, are in the ratio $p:q$, then show that $\sqrt{\frac{p}{q}} + \sqrt{\frac{q}{p}} = \sqrt{\frac{b}{a}}$.

29. Solve the equation $x^2 + px + 45 = 0$, given that the square of the difference of its roots is 144.

30. If the roots of the equation

$$2x^2 + (k+1)x + (k^2 - 5k + 6) = 0$$

are of opposite sign, show that $2 < k < 3$.

Long Answer Type Questions

(6 Marks)

31. If α, β are the roots of the equation $p(x^2 - x) + x + 5 = 0$ and P_1, P_2 are the values of p for which α, β are connected by $\frac{\alpha}{\beta} + \frac{\beta}{\alpha} = \frac{4}{5}$, then find the value of $\frac{P_1}{P_2^2} + \frac{P_2}{P_1^2}$.

32. If $\alpha \quad \beta$ are roots of $a(x^2 + m^2) + a\,mx + bm^2x^2 = 0$, then show that

$$a(\alpha^2 + \beta^2) + a\,\alpha\beta + b\,\alpha^2\beta^2 = 0.$$

33. Solve $(7+4\sqrt{3})^{x^2-4x+3} + (7-4\sqrt{3})^{x^2-4x+3} = 14$.

34. If the equations $x^2 - ax + b = 0$ and $x^2 - cx + d = 0$ have one root in common and the second equation has equal roots, then prove that $ac = 2(b+d)$.

35. If one root of the quadratic equation $ax^2 + bx + c = 0$ is equal to the nth power of the other root, then show that

$$(ac^n)^{\frac{1}{n+1}} + (a^n c)^{\frac{1}{n+1}} + b = 0.$$

36. Discuss the nature of the roots of the equation $(m+6)x^2 + (m+6)x + 2 = 0$.

37. Solve $4x^4 - 16x^3 + 7x^2 + 16x + 4 = 0$.

38. Find x iff

$$\frac{\sqrt{a+x} + \sqrt{a-x}}{\sqrt{a+x} - \sqrt{a-x}} = \frac{a}{x}, x \neq 0.$$

39. A two-digit number is four times the sum and twice the product of its digits. Find the number.

Case-Based Type Question

(6 Marks)

40. Rahul and Ramdas are very close friends. Both the families decide to go to Ayodhya by their own cars. Rahul's car travels at a speed of x km/h while Ramdas's car travels 5 km/h faster than Rahul's car. Rahul took 4 h more than Ramdas to complete the journey of 400 km.

(i) What will be the distance covered by Ramdas's car in 3 h?

(ii) Find the quadratic equation that describes the speed of Rahul's car.

(iii) What is the speed of Rahul's car?

(iv) How much time took Ramdas to travel half distance of total journey?

Hints & Answers

1. (a) **2.** (d) **3.** (b) **4.** (b) **5.** (c)

6. (d) **7.** (b) **8.** (a) **9.** (c) **10.** (a)

11. $\frac{17 \pm \sqrt{11}\, i}{6}$

12. $\because D > 0$ **Ans.** Real, unequal and rational

13. Sum $= 1$, Product $= 2\sqrt{2}$

14. $D > 0$

15. $\because$ Sum $= 0$ **Ans.** $k = 0$

16. Use $\alpha^2 + \beta^2 = (\alpha + \beta)^2 - 2\alpha\beta$ **Ans.** $\frac{4}{3}$

17. $\because$ Product < 0, c and a are of opposite signs.

18. Other root is $-1 + 2i$ **Ans.** $x^2 + 2x + 5 = 0$

19. $\frac{2 \pm \sqrt{2}\, i}{2}$

20. Put $2^x = y$ **Ans.** $x = 1$

21. Solve as Example 6 of Topic 1. **Ans.** $\frac{-1 \pm \sqrt{5}}{2}$

22. Divide whole equation by x^2 and put $\frac{1}{x} = y$.

Ans. $1 + i$, $2 \pm \sqrt{2}$

23. $\because D = 0$ **Ans.** $k = 0, 3$

24. Put $D = 0$.

25. $D = P^2 + 4 > 0$.

26. $\because D = 0$ **Ans.** $b = \frac{a + c}{2}$

27. $ax^2 + hbx + n^2 c = 0$

28. Roots $= \alpha, \frac{p}{q}\alpha$.

29. Use $\alpha^2 - \beta^2 = (\alpha - \beta)(\alpha + \beta)$

Ans. $x = -3, -15$ or $x = 3, 15$

30. $\because D < 0$

31. 4048

32. Put $7 + 4\sqrt{3} = y$ and $7 - 4\sqrt{3} = \frac{1}{y}$

Ans. $2 \pm \sqrt{2}$, 2

33. $x = 2 \pm \sqrt{2}$, 2.

34. $x^2 - cx + d = 0$ has equal roots, then $c^2 = 4d$.

Then, common root is

$$x^2 - cx + \frac{c^2}{4} = 0 \Rightarrow x = \frac{c}{2}.$$

35. Roots $= \alpha, \alpha^n$.

36. (i) Equal, if $m = 2$ or -6.

(ii) Real and unequal, if $m < -6$ or $m > 2$.

(iii) Complex conjugates, if $-6 < m < 2$.

37. $x = 2, -\frac{1}{2}, \frac{5 \pm \sqrt{41}}{4}$

38. $x = a, -a$

39. 36

40. (i) $3(x + 5)$ km

(ii) $x^2 + 5x - 500 = 0$

(iii) 20 km/h

(iv) 8 h

CHAPTER

06

Linear Inequalities

We have already deal with equations in one variable and two variables. We have also solved some word problems by translating them in the form of equation. But it is not necessary that every word problems translate into equation. It may involve the sign(s) '$<$', '$>$', '$\leq$' and '$\geq$'.

In this chapter, we will study about inequalities, linear inequalities in one and two variables and various application involving these inequalities.

- Inequality and Linear Inequalities in One Variable
- Quadratic Inequalities

TOPIC 01 | Inequality and Linear Inequalities in One Variable

Inequality

Two real numbers or two algebraic expressions related by the symbols $>$, $<$, $\leq$ or $\geq$ form an inequality or inequation.

In other words, a statement involving the symbols $>$, $<$, $\leq$ or $\geq$ is called an **inequality** or **inequation.**

Here, the symbols $<$ (less than), $>$ (greater than), $\leq$ (less than or equal to) and $\geq$ (greater than or equal to) are known as symbol of **inequalities.**

e.g. $5 < 7$, $x \leq 2$, $x + y \geq 11$

Types of Inequalities

There are various types of inequalities, which are as follow

(i) **Numerical inequality** An inequality which does not involve any variable is called a numerical **inequality.** e.g. $4 > 2$, $8 < 21$

(ii) **Literal inequality** An inequality which have variables is called literal inequality. e.g. $x < 7$, $y \geq 11$, $x - y \leq 4$

(iii) **Strict inequality** An inequality which have only $<$ or $>$ is called strict inequality. e.g. $3x + y < 0$, $x > 7$

(iv) **Slack inequality** An inequality which have only $\geq$ or $\leq$ is called slack inequality. e.g. $3x + 2y \leq 0$, $y \geq 4$

Linear Inequality

An inequality is said to be linear, if the variable (s) occurs in first degree only and there is no term involving the product of the variables. e.g. $ax+b\leq 0$, $ax+by+c>0$, $ax\leq 4$.

Linear Inequality in One Variable

A linear inequality which has only one variable, is called linear inequality in one variable.

e.g. $ax+b<0$, where $a\neq 0$

Note An inequality in one variable, in which degree of variable is 2, is called quadratic inequality in one variable.

e.g. $ax^2+bx+c\geq 0,\ a\neq 0;\ 3x^2+2x+1\leq 0$

Linear Inequality in Two Variables

A linear inequality which have only two variables, is called linear inequality in two variables.

e.g. $3x+11y\leq 0$, $4t+3y>0$

Representation of Linear Inequality on Number Line

To understand the representation of linear inequality on number line, we need to understand the concept of intervals. On number line or real line, various types of infinite subsets, known as **intervals**, are defined below

Closed Interval

If a and b are real numbers, such that $a<b$, then the set of all real numbers x, such that $a\leq x\leq b$, is called a closed interval and is denoted by $[a, b]$.

$\therefore\quad [a, b]=\{x: a\leq x\leq b, x\in R\}$

On the number line, $[a, b]$ may be represented as follows

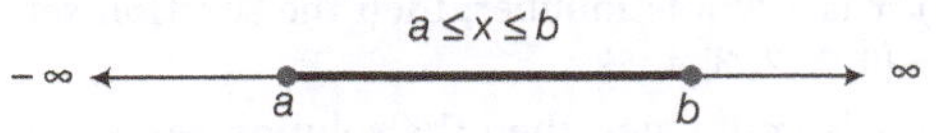

Here, end points of the interval i.e. a and b are included in the interval. So, on number line, draw filled circle (•) at a and b.

Open Interval

If a and b are real numbers, such that $a<b$, then the set of all real numbers x, such that $a<x<b$, is called an open interval and is denoted by (a, b) or $]a, b[$.

$\therefore\quad (a, b)=\{x: a<x<b, x\in R\}$

On the number line, (a, b) may be represented as follows

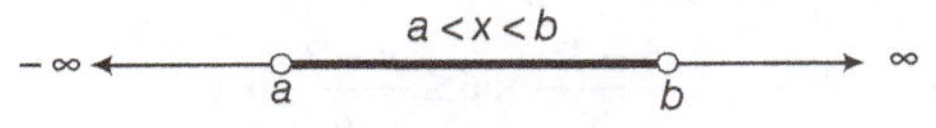

Here, end points of the interval i.e. a and b are not included in the interval. So, on number line, draw open circle (o) at a and b.

Semi-open or Semi-closed Intervals

If a and b are real numbers, such that $a<b$.

Then, $(a, b]=\{x: a<x\leq b, x\in R\}$

and $\quad [a, b)=\{x: a\leq x<b, x\in R\}$

are known as semi-open or semi-closed intervals.

On the number line, these intervals may be represented as follows

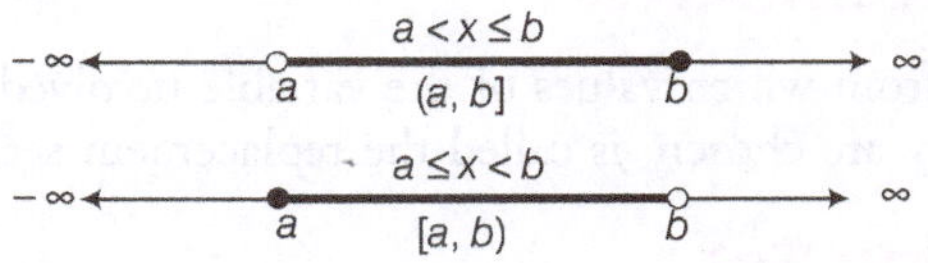

Solution of an Inequality

Any solution of an inequality is the value(s) of variable(s) which makes it a true statement.

We can find the solutions of an inequality by hit and trial method but it is not very efficient because this method is time consuming and sometimes not feasible. So, we solve inequalities with systematic technique.

Some properties or rules which are used to solve the inequalities, are given below

1. Addition or Subtraction

Addition or subtraction of same number to/from an inequality does not produce any change in it, i.e. if $a>b$, then for any number c,

$$a+c>b+c \text{ or } a-c>b-c$$

e.g. (i) $10>5\Rightarrow 10+7>5+7$ [adding 7 on both sides]

$\Rightarrow\ 17>12$, which is true.

(ii) $-8>-13\ \Rightarrow\ -8-2>-13-2$ [subtracting 2 from both sides]

$\Rightarrow -10>-15$, which is true.

2. Multiplication or Division

If both sides of an inequality are multiplied (or divided) by the same positive number, then the sign of inequality remains the same. But when both sides are multiplied (or divided) by the same negative number, then the sign of inequality is reversed.

Let a, b and c be three real numbers, such that $a>b$ and $c\neq 0$.

(i) If $c>0$, then $\frac{a}{c}>\frac{b}{c}$ and $ac>bc$.

(ii) If $a>b$ and $c<0$, then $\frac{a}{c}<\frac{b}{c}$ and $ac<bc$.

e.g.

(i) $6>4\ \Rightarrow\ 6\times 2>4\times 2$ [multiplying both sides by 2]

$\Rightarrow\ 12>8$, which is true.

(ii) $-32 < -24 \Rightarrow \frac{-32}{-8} > \frac{-24}{-8}$

[dividing both sides by -8]

$\Rightarrow 4 > 3$, which is true.

Note When we multiply or divide by the same **negative** number, then the inequality is **reversed**.

Replacement Set

The set from which values of the variable involved in the inequality are chosen, is called the replacement set.

Solution Set

The set of all solutions of an inequality is called the solution set or truth set of the inequality.

Algebraic Solution of Linear Inequalities in One Variable

Any solution of a linear inequality in one variable is a value of the variable which makes it a true statement.

e.g. $x = 1$ is the solution of the linear inequality $4x + 7 > 0$.

Method to Solve the Linear Inequality in One Variable

In this method, we use the following steps

***Step* I** Collect all terms involving the variable (x) on one side and constant terms on other side with the help of above rules and then reduce it in the form $ax < b$ or $ax \le b$ or $ax > b$ or $ax \ge b$.

***Step* II** Divide this inequality by the coefficient of variable (x), which gives the solution set of given inequality.

***Step* III** Write the solution set.

Example 1 Solve $24x < 100$, when

(i) x is a natural number. (ii) x is an integer. [NCERT]

Given inequality is of the form $ax < b$, so divide both sides by 24.

Sol. We have, $24x < 100$

On dividing both sides by 24, we get

$$= \frac{24x}{24} < \frac{100}{24} \Rightarrow x < \frac{25}{6}$$

(i) When x is a natural number, then solutions of the inequality $x < \frac{25}{6}$, are all natural numbers, which are less than $\frac{25}{6}$. In this case, the following values of x make the statement true.

$$x = 1, 2, 3, 4$$

Hence, the solution set of inequality is $\{1, 2, 3, 4\}$.

(ii) When x is an integer.

In this case, solutions of given inequality are

$$\ldots, -4, -3, -2, -1, 0, 1, 2, 3, 4$$

Hence, the solution set of inequality is

$$\{\ldots, -4, -3, -2, -1, 0, 1, 2, 3, 4\}$$

Example 2 Solve the linear inequality $-5x + 25 > 0$.

Sol. We have, $-5x + 25 > 0$

On adding $5x$ to both sides, we get

$$-5x + 25 + 5x > 0 + 5x$$

$\Rightarrow \quad 25 > 5x \Rightarrow 5x < 25$

On dividing both sides by 5, we get

$\Rightarrow \quad \frac{5x}{5} < \frac{25}{5} \Rightarrow x < 5$

Hence, the required solution set is $(-\infty, 5)$.

Example 3 Solve the linear inequality $3x - 5 < x + 7$, when [NCERT Exemplar]

(i) x is a natural number. (ii) x is a whole number.
(iii) x is an integer. (iv) x is a real number.

Sol. We have, $3x - 5 < x + 7$

$\Rightarrow \quad 3x - 5 + 5 < x + 7 + 5$ [adding 5 on both sides]

$\Rightarrow \quad 3x < x + 12$

$\Rightarrow \quad 3x - x < x + 12 - x$

[subtracting x from both sides]

$\Rightarrow \quad 2x < 12$

$\Rightarrow \quad \frac{2x}{2} < \frac{12}{2}$ [dividing both sides by 2]

$\Rightarrow \quad x < 6$

Now, if

(i) x is natural number, then the solution set is $\{1, 2, 3, 4, 5\}$.

(ii) x is a whole number, then the solution set $\{0, 1, 2, 3, 4, 5\}$.

(iii) x is an integer, then the solution set is $\{\ldots, -3, -2, -1, 0, 1, 2, 3, 4, 5\}$

(iv) x is a real number, then the solution set is $\{x : x \in R \text{ and } x < 6\}$, i.e. any real number less than 6. This can also be written as $(-\infty, 6)$.

Example 4 Solve the inequality $\frac{5-3x}{3} \le \frac{x}{6} - 5$.

Sol. We have, $\frac{5-3x}{3} \le \frac{x}{6} - 5$

$\Rightarrow \quad \frac{5-3x}{3} \le \frac{x-30}{6}$

$\Rightarrow \quad \frac{5-3x}{3} \times 6 \le \frac{x-30}{6} \times 6$

[multiplying both sides by 6]

$\Rightarrow \quad 2(5-3x) \le x - 30$

$\Rightarrow \quad 10 - 6x \leq x - 30 \Rightarrow 10 - 6x - 10 \leq x - 30 - 10$ [subtracting 10 from both sides]

$\Rightarrow \quad -6x \leq x - 40 \Rightarrow -6x - x \leq x - 40 - x$ [subtracting x from both sides]

$\Rightarrow \quad -7x \leq -40$

$\Rightarrow \quad 7x \geq 40$ [multiplying by -1 on both sides]

$\Rightarrow \quad \frac{7x}{7} \geq \frac{40}{7}$ [dividing by 7 on both sides]

$\Rightarrow \quad x \geq \frac{40}{7}$

i.e. $\quad x \in \left[\frac{40}{7}, \infty\right)$

Hence, the required solution set is $\left[\frac{40}{7}, \infty\right)$.

Representation of Solution of Linear Inequality in One Variable on Number Line

To represent the solution of a linear inequality in one variable on a number line, use the following rules

(i) To represent $x < a$ (or $x > a$) on a number line, put a circle (o) on the number a and dark the line to the left (or right) of the number a.

(ii) To represent $x \leq a$ (or $x \geq a$) on a number line, put a dark circle (•) on the number a and dark the line to the left (or right) of the number a.

Example 5 Solve the following inequality and show the graph of the solution in each case on number line.

(i) $\frac{x}{4} < \frac{5x-2}{3} - \frac{7x-3}{5}$ (ii) $x + \frac{x}{2} + \frac{x}{3} < 11$

(iii) $\frac{1}{2}\left(\frac{3}{5}x + 4\right) \geq \frac{1}{3}(x - 6)$ (iv) $\frac{(2x-1)}{3} \leq \frac{(3x-2)}{4} - \frac{(2-x)}{5}$

Sol. (i) We have, $\frac{x}{4} < \frac{5x-2}{3} - \frac{7x-3}{5}$

$\Rightarrow \quad \frac{x}{4} < \frac{5(5x-2) - 3(7x-3)}{15}$

$\Rightarrow \quad \frac{x}{4} < \frac{25x - 10 - 21x + 9}{15}$

$\Rightarrow \quad 60\left(\frac{x}{4}\right) < \frac{(4x-1)}{15} \times 60$ [multiplying both sides by LCM (4, 15) = 60]

$\Rightarrow \quad 15x < 4(4x - 1)$

$\Rightarrow \quad 15x < 16x - 4$

$\Rightarrow \quad 15x + 4 < 16x - 4 + 4$ [adding 4 on both sides]

$\Rightarrow \quad 15x + 4 < 16x$

$\Rightarrow \quad 15x + 4 - 15x < 16x - 15x$ [subtracting $15x$ from both sides]

$\Rightarrow \quad 4 < x$ or $x > 4$

$\therefore \quad x \in (4, \infty)$

On number line, it can be represented as

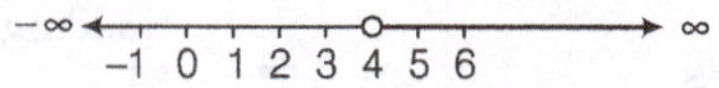

Here, the dark portion on the number line represents the solution of inequality.

(ii) We have, $x + \frac{x}{2} + \frac{x}{3} < 11$

$\Rightarrow \quad \frac{6x + 3x + 2x}{6} < 11 \Rightarrow \frac{11x}{6} < 11$

On multiplying both sides by $\frac{6}{11}$, we get

$$\frac{11x}{6} \times \frac{6}{11} < 11 \times \frac{6}{11} \Rightarrow x < 6$$

$\therefore \quad x \in (-\infty, 6)$

This can be represented on number line as

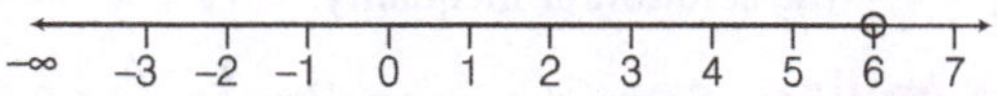

Here, the dark portion on the number line represents the solution of inequality.

(iii) We have, $\frac{1}{2}\left(\frac{3}{5}x + 4\right) \geq \frac{1}{3}(x - 6)$

$\Rightarrow \quad \frac{1}{2}\left(\frac{3x + 20}{5}\right) \geq \frac{1}{3}(x - 6)$

$\Rightarrow \quad \frac{1}{10}(3x + 20) \geq \frac{1}{3}(x - 6)$

$\Rightarrow \quad \frac{30}{10}(3x + 20) \geq \frac{30}{3}(x - 6)$ [multiplying both sides by LCM (10, 3) = 30]

$\Rightarrow \quad 3(3x + 20) \geq 10(x - 6)$

$\Rightarrow \quad 9x + 60 \geq 10x - 60$

$\Rightarrow \quad 9x + 60 - 60 \geq 10x - 60 - 60$ [subtracting 60 from both sides]

$\Rightarrow \quad 9x \geq 10x - 120$

$\Rightarrow \quad 9x - 10x \geq 10x - 120 - 10x$ [subtracting $10x$ from both sides]

$\Rightarrow \quad -x \geq -120 \Rightarrow x \leq 120$ [multiplying both sides by -1]

$\therefore \quad x \in (-\infty, 120]$

On number line, it can be represented as

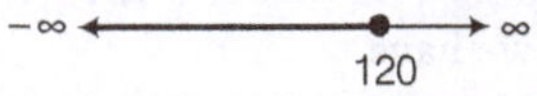

Here, the dark portion on the number line represents the solution of inequality.

(iv) We have, $\frac{2x-1}{3} \leq \frac{3x-2}{4} - \frac{2-x}{5}$

On multiplying both sides by LCM of 3, 4 and 5 i.e. 60, we get

$$\frac{2x-1}{3} \times 60 \leq \frac{3x-2}{4} \times 60 - \frac{2-x}{5} \times 60$$

$\Rightarrow \quad 20(2x - 1) \leq 15(3x - 2) - 12(2 - x)$

$\Rightarrow \quad 40x - 20 \leq 45x - 30 - 24 + 12x$

$\Rightarrow \quad 40x - 20 \leq 57x - 54$

$\Rightarrow \quad 40x - 20 + 20 \le 57x - 54 + 20$ [adding 20 on both sides]

$\Rightarrow \quad 40x \le 57x - 34$

$\Rightarrow \quad 40x - 57x \le 57x - 34 - 57x$ [subtracting $57x$ from both sides]

$\Rightarrow \quad -17x \le -34$

$\Rightarrow \quad \dfrac{-17x}{17} \le \dfrac{-34}{17}$ [dividing both sides by 17]

$\Rightarrow \quad -x \le -2 \Rightarrow x \ge 2$ [multiplying both sides by -1]

Thus, the solution set is $[2, \infty)$.

On number line, it can be represented as

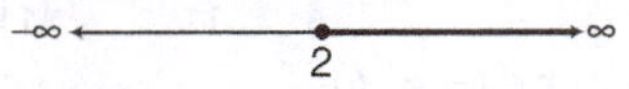

Here, the dark portion on the number line represents the solution of inequality.

Example 6 Solve the inequality $\dfrac{x-4}{x+2} \le 2$. Also, represent the solution on number line.

Sol. We have, $\dfrac{x-4}{x+2} \le 2$

$\Rightarrow \quad \dfrac{x-4}{x+2} - 2 \le 2 - 2$ [subtracting 2 from both sides]

$\Rightarrow \quad \dfrac{x-4}{x+2} - 2 \le 0$

$\Rightarrow \quad \dfrac{x-4-2(x+2)}{x+2} \le 0$

$\Rightarrow \quad \dfrac{x-4-2x-4}{x+2} \le 0$

$\Rightarrow \quad \dfrac{-x-8}{x+2} \le 0$ here $x + 2 \ne 0$; i.e. $x \ne -2$

$\Rightarrow \quad \dfrac{x+8}{x+2} \ge 0$ [multiplying both sides by -1]

$\Rightarrow \quad \dfrac{x+8}{x+2} \times (x+2)^2 \ge 0 \times (x+2)^2$ [multiplying both sides by $(x+2)^2$]

$\Rightarrow \quad (x+8)(x+2) \ge 0$

The factors $(x + 8)$ and $(x + 2)$ have the same signs.

Case **I When both are non-negative**

In this case, we have

$x + 8 \ge 0$ and $x + 2 > 0$ [$\because x + 2 \ne 0$ because for $x = -2$, denominator of given inequality becomes 0]

$\Rightarrow \quad x \ge -8$ and $x > -2$

On number line, these can be represented as

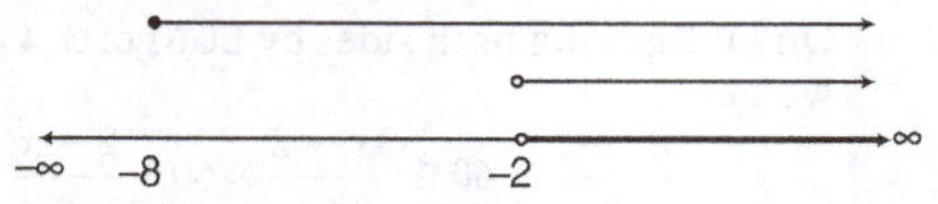

Clearly, the common values of x are lying in the interval $(-2, \infty)$.

$\therefore$ The solution set is $(-2, \infty)$.

Case **II When both are non-positive**

In this case, we have

$x + 8 \le 0$ and $x + 2 < 0 \Rightarrow x \le -8$ and $x < -2$

On number line, these can be represented as

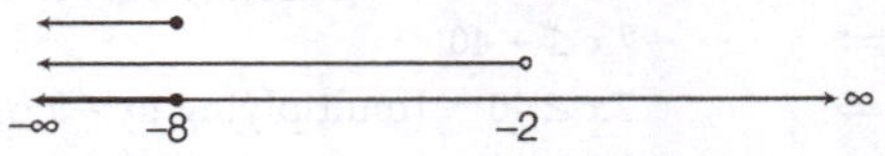

Clearly, the common values of x are lying in the interval $(-\infty, -8]$

$\therefore$ The solution set is $(-\infty, -8]$.

Hence, the required solution set is $(-\infty, -8] \cup (-2, \infty)$ and this can be represented on the number line as

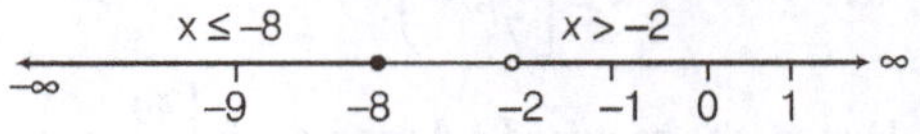

When Inequality of the Form $|ax + b| >, <, \ge, \le k$, where a, b, k are Real Numbers and $a \ne 0$, $k > 0$

If the given inequality is any of the form $|ax + b| < k$ or $|ax + b| > k$ or $|ax + b| \ge k$ or $|ax + b| \le k$, where $a \ne 0$ and $k > 0$, then we solve the inequality with the help of following results.

If $a > 0$ is any real number, then

(i) $|x| < a \Rightarrow -a < x < a$

$|x| \le a \Rightarrow -a \le x \le a$

(ii) $|x| > a \Rightarrow x > a$ or $x < -a$

$|x| \ge a \Rightarrow x \ge a$ or $x \le -a$

Note In the above results, x can be any real number or any linear expression.

Expansion of Modulus Function

$$|x - a| = \begin{cases} x - a, & \text{if } x \ge a \\ -(x - a), & \text{if } x < a \end{cases}, \text{ where } a \text{ is any real number.}$$

Example 7 Solve $|3x - 2| \le \dfrac{1}{2}$.

Sol. Given, $|3x - 2| \le \dfrac{1}{2}$

$\therefore \quad \dfrac{-1}{2} \le (3x - 2) \le \dfrac{1}{2}$ [$\because |x| \le a \Rightarrow -a \le x \le a$]

$\Rightarrow \quad -\dfrac{1}{2} + 2 \le 3x - 2 + 2 \le \dfrac{1}{2} + 2$ [adding 2 on each term]

$\Rightarrow \quad \dfrac{3}{2} \le 3x \le \dfrac{5}{2}$

$\Rightarrow \quad \dfrac{3}{2} \times \dfrac{1}{3} \le \dfrac{3x}{3} \le \dfrac{5}{2} \times \dfrac{1}{3}$ [dividing each term by 3]

$\Rightarrow \quad \dfrac{1}{2} \le x \le \dfrac{5}{6}$ i.e. $x \in \left[\dfrac{1}{2}, \dfrac{5}{6}\right]$

Hence, the required solution set is $\left[\dfrac{1}{2}, \dfrac{5}{6}\right]$.

Example 8 Solve $|x-2| \geq 6$.

Sol. We have, $|x-2| \geq 6$

$\Rightarrow x-2 \geq 6$ or $x-2 \leq -6$ $[\because |x| \geq a \Rightarrow x \geq a$ or $x \leq -a]$

$\Rightarrow x \geq 8$ or $x \leq -4$ [adding 2 on both sides in each inequality]

$\Rightarrow x \in [8, \infty)$ or $x \in (-\infty, 4]$

$\Rightarrow x \in [8, \infty) \cup (-\infty, 4]$

Hence, the required solution set is $(-\infty, 4] \cup [8, \infty)$.

Example 9 Solve graphically for x, $|x-1| \leq 5$, $|x| \geq 2$. **[NCERT Exemplar]**

Sol. We have the following inequalities

$|x-1| \leq 5$ ...(i)

and $|x| \geq 2$ ...(ii)

From inequality (i), we have

$-5 \leq x-1 \leq 5$ $[\because |x| \leq a \Rightarrow -a \leq x \leq a]$

$\Rightarrow -5+1 \leq x \leq 5+1$ [adding 1 on each term]

$\Rightarrow -4 \leq x \leq 6 \Rightarrow x \in [-4, 6]$

$\therefore$ The solution set is $[-4, 6]$.

From inequality (ii), we have

$|x| \geq 2$

$\Rightarrow x \geq 2$ or $x \leq -2$ $[\because |x| \geq a$ $x \geq a$ or $x \leq -a]$

$\Rightarrow x \in [2, \infty)$ or $(-\infty, -2]$

$\Rightarrow x \in (-\infty, -2] \cup [2, \infty)$

$\therefore$ The solution set is $(-\infty, -2] \cup [2, \infty)$.

Now, let us draw the graphs of solutions of both inequality.

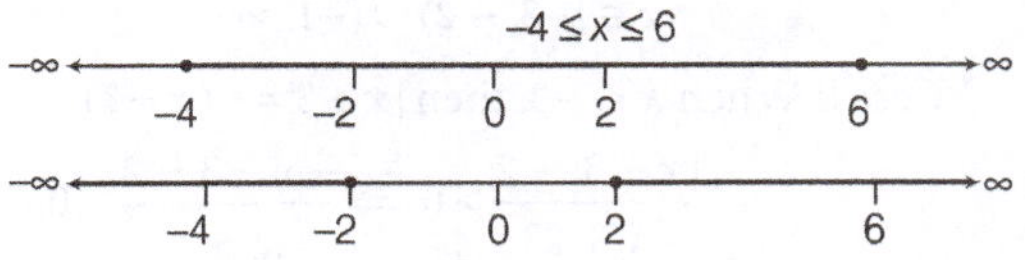

Clearly, the common values of x are lying in the interval $[-4, -2]$ or $[2, 6]$.

Hence, the required solution set is $[-4, -2] \cup [2, 6]$.

Example 10 Solve $|x-1| + |x-2| \geq 4$.

Sol. We have, $|x-1| + |x-2| \geq 4$

Put $x-1=0 \Rightarrow x=1$

and $x-2=0 \Rightarrow x=2$

Thus, $x=1$ and 2 are critical points, so we will consider three intervals $(-\infty, 1)$, $[1, 2)$ and $[2, \infty)$.

Case **I** When $-\infty < x < 1$

Then, $|x-1| = -(x-1)$ and $|x-2| = -(x-2)$

$$\left[\because |x-a| = \begin{cases} x-a, & \text{if } x \geq a \\ -(x-a), & \text{if } x < a \end{cases}\right]$$

$\therefore |x-1| + |x-2| \geq 4$

$\Rightarrow -(x-1)-(x-2) \geq 4$

$\Rightarrow -x+1-x+2 \geq 4 \Rightarrow -2x+3 \geq 4$

$\Rightarrow -2x \geq 1$ [subtracting 3 from both sides]

$\Rightarrow x \leq -\dfrac{1}{2}$ [dividing both sides by −2]

$\therefore$ Solution set of given inequality in this case is

$$-\infty < x \leq -\frac{1}{2} \quad ...(i)$$

Case **II** When $1 \leq x < 2$

Then, $|x-1| = x-1$ and $|x-2| = -(x-2)$

$\therefore |x-1| + |x-2| \geq 4$

$\Rightarrow x-1-x+2 \geq 4$

$\Rightarrow 1 \geq 4$, which is absurd.

So, in this case, given inequality has no solution.

Case **III** When $2 \leq x < \infty$

Then, $|x-1| = x-1$ and $|x-2 = x-2$

$\therefore |x-1| + |x-2| \geq 4$

$\Rightarrow x-1+x-2 \geq 4 \Rightarrow 2x-3 \geq 4$

$\Rightarrow 2x \geq 7$ [adding 3 on both sides]

$\Rightarrow x \geq \dfrac{7}{2}$ [dividing both sides by 2]

Here, $2 \leq x < \infty$.

$\therefore$ Solution set of given inequality in this case is

$$\frac{7}{2} \leq x < \infty \quad ...(ii)$$

On combining inequalities (i) and (ii), we get

$$-\infty < x \leq -\frac{1}{2} \text{ and } \frac{7}{2} \leq x < \infty$$

i.e. $x \in \left(-\infty, -\dfrac{1}{2}\right] \cup \left[\dfrac{7}{2}, \infty\right)$

Example 11 Solve the inequality $\dfrac{|x|-1}{|x|-2} \geq 0$, $x \in R$ and $x \neq \pm 2$.

Sol. We have, $\dfrac{|x|-1}{|x|-2} \geq 0$

Now, put $|x| = 0 \Rightarrow x = 0$

Thus, $x = 0$ is the critical point. So, we will consider two intervals $(-\infty, 0)$ and $[0, \infty)$.

Case **I** When $x \in (-\infty, 0)$, i.e. $-\infty < x < 0$

In this case, we have

$$\frac{-x-1}{-x-2} \geq 0 \quad \left[\because |x| = \begin{cases} x, & \text{if } x \geq 0 \\ -x, & \text{if } x < 0 \end{cases}\right]$$

$$\Rightarrow \frac{-(x+1)}{-(x+2)} \geq 0 \Rightarrow \frac{x+1}{x+2} \geq 0$$

Now, multiplying both sides by $(x+2)^2$, we get

$$(x+1)(x+2) \geq 0$$

So, the factors $(x+1)$ and $(x+2)$ have the same sign.

Then, we have

$$x+1 \geq 0 \text{ and } x+2 > 0 \quad \text{...(i)}$$

or $$x+1 \leq 0 \text{ and } x+2 < 0 \quad \text{...(ii)}$$

[$\because x+2 \neq 0$, as $x \neq -2$]

From inequality (i), we get

$$x \geq -1 \text{ and } x > -2$$

$\Rightarrow$ $x \geq -1$ [common values of x]

Thus, the common values of x are lying in the interval $[-1, 0)$.

[$\because$ we are considering the case, where $-\infty < x < 0$]

$\therefore$ The solution set is $[-1, 0)$.

From inequality (ii), we have

$$x \leq -1 \text{ and } x < -2$$

$\Rightarrow$ $x < -2$ [common values of x]

Thus, the common values of x are lying in the interval $(-\infty, -2)$

$\therefore$ The solution set is $(-\infty, -2)$.

Hence, $x \in (-\infty, -2) \cup [-1, 0)$

Case **II** When $x \in [0, \infty)$,

i.e. $0 \leq x < \infty$

In this case, we have

$$\frac{x-1}{x-2} \geq 0 \quad \left[\because |x| = \begin{cases} x, & \text{if } x \geq 0 \\ -x, & \text{if } x < 0 \end{cases}\right]$$

On multiplying both sides by $(x-2)^2$, we get

$$(x-1)(x-2) \geq 0$$

So, the factors $(x-1)$ and $(x-2)$ have the same sign.

Then, $(x-1) \geq 0$ and $(x-2) > 0$ ...(iii)

or $(x-1) \leq 0$ and $(x-2) < 0$ ...(iv)

[$\because x-2 \neq 0$ as $x \neq 2$]

From inequality (iii), we get

$$x \geq 1 \text{ and } x > 2$$

$\Rightarrow$ $x > 2$ [common values of x]

$\Rightarrow$ $x \in (2\ \infty)$

$\therefore$ The solution set is $(2, \infty)$.

From inequality (iv), we get

$$x \leq 1 \text{ and } x < 2$$

$\Rightarrow$ $x \leq 1$ [common values of x]

$\Rightarrow$ $x \in [0, 1]$

[$\because$ we are considering the case, where $0 \leq x < \infty$]

$\therefore$ The solution set is $[0, 1]$

Hence, $x \in [0, 1] \cup (2, \infty)$

Now, from cases I and II, we conclude that

$$x \in (-\infty, -2) \cup [-1, 0) \cup [0, 1] \cup (2, \infty)$$

i.e. $$x \in (-\infty, -2) \cup [-1, 1] \cup (2, \infty)$$

Hence, the required solution set is

$$(-\infty, -2) \cup [-1, 1] \cup (2, \infty)$$

Example 12 Solve for x, $\dfrac{|x+3|+x}{x+2} > 1$. **[NCERT Exemplar]**

Sol. We have, $\dfrac{|x+3|+x}{x+2} > 1 \Rightarrow \dfrac{|x+3|+x}{x+2} - 1 > 0$

$$\Rightarrow \frac{|x+3|+x-x-2}{x+2} > 0 \Rightarrow \frac{|x+3|-2}{x+2} > 0$$

Put $x+3=0 \Rightarrow x=-3$

$\therefore$ $x=-3$ is a critical point.

So, here we consider two intervals $(-\infty, -3)$ and $[-3, \infty)$.

Case **I** When $-3 \leq x < \infty$, then $|x+3| = (x+3)$

$$\therefore \quad \frac{|x+3|-2}{x+2} > 0$$

$$\Rightarrow \frac{x+3-2}{x+2} > 0 \Rightarrow \frac{x+1}{x+2} > 0$$

$$\Rightarrow \frac{(x+1)(x+2)^2}{(x+2)} > 0 \times (x+2)^2$$

[multiplying both sides by $(x+2)^2$]

$$\Rightarrow (x+1)(x+2) > 0$$

Product of $(x+1)$ and $(x+2)$ will be positive, if both are of same signs.

$\therefore$ $(x+1) > 0$ and $(x+2) > 0$

or $(x+1) < 0$ and $(x+2) < 0$

$\Rightarrow$ $(x > -1$ and $x > -2)$

or $(x < -1$ and $x < -2)$

Thus, $-1 < x < \infty$ or $-\infty < x < -2$

But, here $-3 \leq x < \infty$

$\therefore$ $-1 < x < \infty$ or $-3 \leq x < -2$

Hence, solution set in this case is

$$x \in [-3, -2) \cup (-1, \infty)$$

Case II When $x < -3$, then $|x+3| = -(x+3)$

$$\therefore \quad \frac{|x+3|-2}{x+2} > 0 \Rightarrow \frac{-x-3-2}{x+2} > 0$$

$$\Rightarrow \frac{-(x+5)}{x+2} > 0 \Rightarrow \frac{x+5}{x+2} < 0$$

$$\Rightarrow \frac{(x+5)(x+2)^2}{x+2} < 0 \times (x+2)^2$$

$$\Rightarrow (x+5)(x+2) < 0$$

Product of $(x+5)$ and $(x+2)$ will be negative, if both are of opposite sign.

$\therefore$ $(x+5) > 0$ and $(x+2) < 0$

or $(x+5) < 0$ and $(x+2) > 0$

$\Rightarrow$ $x > -5$ and $x < -2$

or $x < -5$ and $x > -2$ [not possible]

Thus, $-5 < x < -2$. i.e. solution set in the case is $(-5, -2)$.

On combining cases I and II, we get the required solution set of given inequality, which is

$$(-5, -2) \cup (-1, \infty).$$

Solution of System of Linear Inequalities in One Variable

We know that the solution set of a linear inequality in one variable is the set of all points on the number line satisfying the given inequality.

Therefore, the solution set of a system of linear inequalities in one variable is defined as the **intersection of the solution set** of the linear inequalities in the system.

e.g. If the solution sets of linear inequalities in the system are $(-\infty, 5]$ and $[5, \infty)$, then the solution of system of linear inequalities in one variable is 5 only. Because, if we represent the solution sets on the number line, we see that the value which are common to both is 5 only.

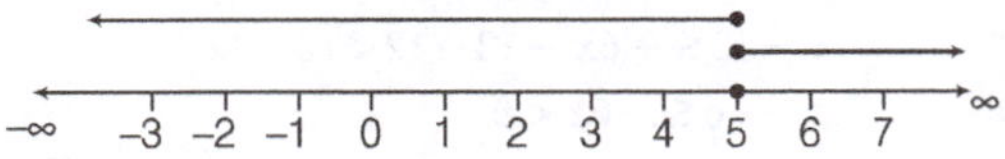

When Two Separate Linear Inequalities are Given

If the given system of inequalities comprise by two separate linear inequalities, then to solve these we use the following steps

Step I Solve each inequality separately and obtain their solution sets.

Step II Represent the solution sets on a number line and then find the values of the variable which are common to them.

Or

Find the intersection of the solution sets obtained in step I.

Example 13 Solve the following system of inequalities $2x - 3 < 7$ and $2x > -4$. Also, represent the solution graphically on the number line.

Sol. We have the following inequalities,

$$2x - 3 < 7 \quad \text{...(i)}$$

and $$2x > -4 \quad \text{...(ii)}$$

From inequality (i), we have $2x - 3 < 7$

$\Rightarrow$ $2x - 3 + 3 < 7 + 3$ [adding 3 on both sides]

$\Rightarrow$ $2x < 10$

$\Rightarrow$ $\frac{2x}{2} < \frac{10}{2}$ [dividing both sides by 2]

$\Rightarrow$ $x < 5$

$\therefore$ The solution set is $(-\infty, 5)$.

From inequality (ii), we have $2x > -4$

$\frac{2x}{2} > \frac{-4}{2}$ [dividing both sides by 2]

$\Rightarrow$ $x > -2$

$\therefore$ The solution set is $(-2, \infty)$.

Now, let us draw the graphs of the solutions of both inequalities on number line.

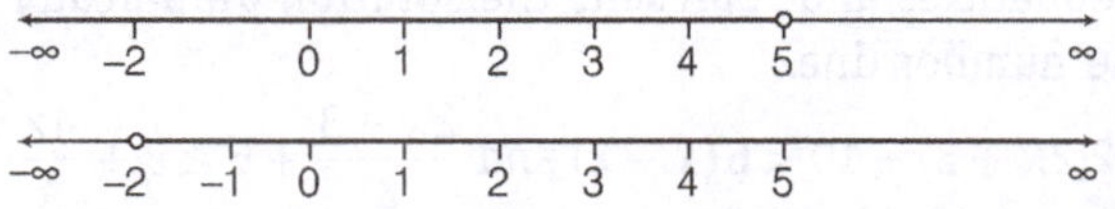

It can be seen that the values of x, which are common to both are lying in the interval $(-2, 5)$.

Hence, the solution set of given system of inequations is $(-2, 5)$ and this can be represented graphically on the number line as

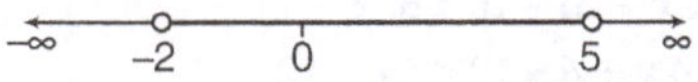

Example 14 Solve the following system of inequalities and represent the solution graphically on the number line. **[NCERT]**

$$5(2x - 7) - 3(2x + 3) \le 0,\ 2x + 19 \le 6x + 47$$

Sol. We have the following inequalities

$$5(2x - 7) - 3(2x + 3) \le 0 \quad \text{...(i)}$$

and $$2x + 19 \le 6x + 47 \quad \text{...(ii)}$$

From inequality (i), we get

$5(2x - 7) - 3(2x + 3) \le 0$

$\Rightarrow$ $10x - 35 - 6x - 9 \le 0 \Rightarrow 4x - 44 \le 0$

$\Rightarrow$ $4x - 44 + 44 \le 44$ [adding 44 on both sides]

$\Rightarrow$ $4x \le 44$

$\Rightarrow$ $x \le 11$ ...(iii)

[dividing both sides by 4]

$\therefore$ The solution set is $(-\infty, 11]$.

From inequality (ii), we get

$2x + 19 \le 6x + 47$

$\Rightarrow$ $2x + 19 - 2x \le 6x + 47 - 2x$

[subtracting $2x$ from both sides]

$\Rightarrow$ $19 \le 4x + 47$

$\Rightarrow$ $19 - 47 \le 4x + 47 - 47$

[subtracting 47 from both sides]

$\Rightarrow$ $-28 \le 4x$ or $4x \ge -28$

$\Rightarrow$ $\frac{4x}{4} \ge \frac{-28}{4}$ [dividing both sides by 4]

$\Rightarrow$ $x \ge -7$

$\therefore$ The solution set is $[-7, \infty)$.

Now, let us draw the graphs of the solutions of both inequalities on number line.

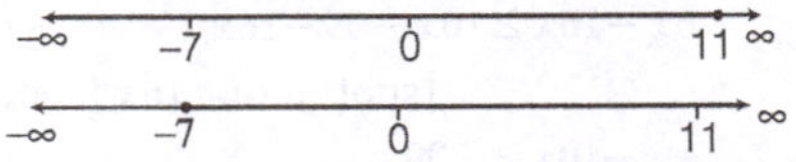

It can be seen that the values of x, which are common to both are lying in the interval $[-7, 11]$.

Hence, the solution set of given system of inequations is $[-7, 11]$ and this can be represented graphically on the number line as

Example 15 Solve the following system of linear inequalities and represent the solution graphically on the number line.

$$2(2x+3)-10<6(x-2) \text{ and } \frac{2x-3}{4}+6\geq 2+\frac{4x}{3}$$

Sol. Given system of linear inequalities is

$$2(2x+3)-10<6(x-2) \quad \ldots\text{(i)}$$

and $$\frac{2x-3}{4}+6\geq 2+\frac{4x}{3} \quad \ldots\text{(ii)}$$

From inequality (i), we get

$$2(2x+3)-10<6(x-2)$$

$\Rightarrow$ $4x+6-10<6x-12$

$\Rightarrow$ $4x-4<6x-12$

$\Rightarrow$ $4x-4+4<6x-12+4$ [adding 4 on both sides]

$\Rightarrow$ $4x<6x-8$

$\Rightarrow$ $4x-6x<6x-8-6x$ [subtracting $6x$ from both sides]

$\Rightarrow$ $-2x<-8$

$\Rightarrow$ $2x>8$ [dividing both sides by -1, then inequality sign will also change]

$\Rightarrow$ $\frac{2x}{2}>\frac{8}{2}$ [dividing both sides by 2]

$\therefore$ $x>4$ ...(iii)

Thus, any value of x greater than 4 satisfies the inequality.

$\therefore$ The solution set is $(4, \infty)$.

The representation of solution of inequality (i) is

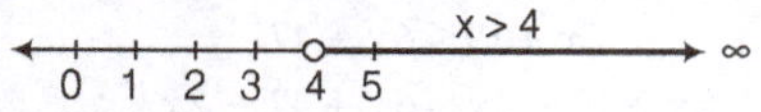

From inequality (ii), we get

$$\frac{2x-3}{4}+6\geq 2+\frac{4x}{3}$$

$\Rightarrow$ $\frac{2x-3+24}{4}\geq\frac{6+4x}{3} \Rightarrow \frac{2x+21}{4}\geq\frac{6+4x}{3}$

$\Rightarrow$ $3(2x+21)\geq 4(6+4x)$ [multiplying both sides by LCM (4, 3) = 12]

$\Rightarrow$ $6x+63\geq 24+16x$

$\Rightarrow$ $6x+63-63\geq 24+16x-63$ [subtracting 63 from both sides]

$\Rightarrow$ $6x\geq 16x-39$

$\Rightarrow$ $6x-16x\geq 16x-39-16x$ [subtracting $16x$ from both sides]

$\Rightarrow$ $-10x\geq -39$

$\Rightarrow$ $10x\leq 39$ [multiplying both sides by -1, the inequality sign will also change]

$\Rightarrow$ $\frac{10x}{10}\leq\frac{39}{10}$ [dividing both sides by 10]

$\Rightarrow$ $x\leq 3.9$ ...(iv)

Thus, any value of x less than or equal to 3.9 satisfies the inequality.

$\therefore$ The solution set is $(-\infty, 3.9]$.

Its representation on number line is

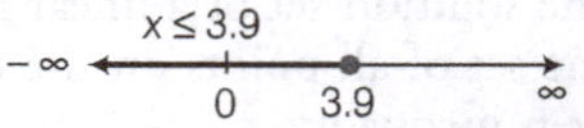

We see that there is no common value of x, which satisfies both inequalites (iii) and (iv).

Hence, the given system of inequalities has no solution set.

Example 16 Solve the inequalities

$$6\leq -3(2x-4)<12. \quad \textbf{[NCERT]}$$

Sol. We have, $6\leq -3(2x-4)<12$ or $6\leq -6x+12<12$

On subtracting 12 from each term, we get

$$6-12\leq -6x+12-12<12-12$$

$\Rightarrow$ $-6\leq -6x<0$

On dividing each term by -6, we get $\frac{-6}{-6}\geq\frac{-6x}{-6}>\frac{0}{-6}$

[while dividing each term by the same negative number, then sign of inequalities will get change]

$\Rightarrow$ $1\geq x>0$

which can be written as $0<x\leq 1$.

Hence, solution set of given system of inequations is $(0, 1]$.

Applications of Linear Inequalities in One Variable

In this topic, we will discuss with various word problems which are based on linear inequalities of one variable. Let us look at the following examples.

| TYPE I |

Based on Marks of Students

Example 17 Ram needs a minimum of 360 marks in four tests in a Mathematics course to obtain A grade. In his first three tests, he scored 88, 96 and 79 marks. What should his score be in the fourth test, so that he can make A grade?

Sol. Let Ram scores x marks in the fourth test. Then, the sum of Ram's test scores should be greater than or equal to 360.

i.e. $88+96+79+x\geq 360$

$\Rightarrow$ $263+x\geq 360$

$\Rightarrow$ $263+x-263\geq 360-263$ [subtracting 263 from both sides]

$\therefore$ $x\geq 97$

Hence, Ram should score 97 or greater than 97 marks in fourth test to obtain A grade.

Example 18 To receive grade A in a course, one must obtain an average of 90 marks or more in five examinations (each of 100 marks). If Sunita's marks in first four examinations are 87, 92, 94 and 95, then find minimum marks that Sunita must obtain in fifth examinations to get grade A in the course. **[NCERT]**

Sol. Let Sunita obtains x marks in her fifth examination.

Then, $\frac{87+92+94+95+x}{5} \geq 90$

$\Rightarrow \quad 368 + x \geq 450$ [multiplying both sides by 5]

$\Rightarrow \quad 368 + x - 368 \geq 450 - 368$ [subtracting 368 from both sides]

$\therefore \quad x \geq 82$

Thus, Sunita must obtain a minimum of 82 marks to get grade A in the course.

Example 19 In the first four examinations, each of 100 marks, Mohan got 94, 73, 72 and 84 marks. If a final average greater than or equal to 80 and less than 90 is needed to obtain a final grade B in a course, then what range of marks in the fifth (last) examination will result, if Mohan receiving grade B in the course?

Sol. Let x be the score obtained by Mohan in the last examination.

Then, $80 \leq \frac{94+73+72+84+x}{5} < 90$

$\Rightarrow \quad 80 \leq \frac{323+x}{5} < 90$

$\Rightarrow \quad 400 \leq 323 + x < 450$ [multiplying both sides by 5]

$\Rightarrow \quad 400 - 323 \leq 323 + x - 323 < 450 - 323$ [subtracting 323 from each term]

$\Rightarrow \quad 77 \leq x < 127$

Since, the upper limit is 100, therefore the required range is $77 \leq x \leq 100$.

| TYPE II |

Based on Numbers

Example 20 The sum of three consecutive integers must not be more than 12. What are the integers?

Sol. Let the three consecutive integers be x, $(x+1)$ and $(x+2)$. Since, sum of these integers must not be more than 12, i.e. $x+(x+1)+(x+2)$ cannot exceed 12, therefore, we have

$\Rightarrow \quad x+(x+1)+(x+2) \leq 12$

$\Rightarrow \quad 3x+3 \leq 12 \Rightarrow 3x+3-3 \leq 12-3$ [subtracting 3 from both sides]

$\Rightarrow \quad 3x \leq 9$

$\therefore \quad x \leq 3$ [dividing both sides by 3]

Example 21 Find all pairs of consecutive even positive integers, both of which are larger than 5, such that their sum is less than 23.

Sol. Let x be the smaller of the two positive even integers, so that the other one is $x + 2$, then we should have

$x > 5$ ...(i)

$x + 2 > 5$ ...(ii)

and their sum, $x + (x+2) < 23$ ...(iii)

From inequalities (i) and (ii), we get

$x > 5$ ...(iv)

From inequality (iii), we get $2x + 2 < 23$

$\Rightarrow \quad 2x + 2 - 2 < 23 - 2$ [subtracting 2 from both sides]

$\Rightarrow \quad 2x < 21$

$\Rightarrow \quad x < 10.5$ [dividing both sides by 2]...(v)

Now, from inequalities (iv) and (v), we get $5 < x < 10.5$

Since, x is an even number. So, x can take the values 6, 8 and 10. Hence, the required possible pairs will be (6, 8), (8, 10) and (10, 12).

Example 22 Find all the pairs of consecutive odd positive integers, both of which are smaller than 10, such that their sum is more than 11. **[NCERT]**

Sol. Let x be the smaller of two positive odd integers, so that other one is $x + 2$.

We should have $x < 10$ ...(i)

$x + 2 < 10 \Rightarrow x < 8$ ...(ii)

and $x + (x+2) > 11$ ...(iii)

From inequalities (i) and (ii), we get $x < 8$ ...(iv)

From inequality (iii), we get

$2x + 2 > 11 \Rightarrow 2x > 9 \Rightarrow x > 4.5$ ...(v)

From inequalities (iv) and (v), we get $4.5 < x < 8$

Since, x is an odd number, so x can take the values 5 and 7. Hence the required possible pairs will be (5, 7) and (7, 9).

| TYPE III |

Based on Profit, Cost and Revenue

Example 23 The cost and revenue functions of a product are given by $C(x) = 20x + 4000$ and $R(x) = 60x + 2000$ respectively, where x is the number of items produced and sold. How many items must be sold to realise some profit? **[NCERT Exemplar]**

Sol. We know that, Profit = Revenue − Cost

$\therefore$ In order to realise some profit, revenue should be greater than the cost.

Thus, we should have $R(x) > C(x)$

$\Rightarrow \quad 60x + 2000 > 20x + 4000$

$\Rightarrow \quad 60x + 2000 - 20x > 20x + 4000 - 20x$ [subtracting $20x$ from both sides]

$\Rightarrow \quad 40x + 2000 > 4000$

$\Rightarrow \quad 40x + 2000 - 2000 > 4000 - 2000$

[subtracting 2000 from both sides]

$\Rightarrow \quad 40x > 2000 \Rightarrow \dfrac{40x}{40} > \dfrac{2000}{40}$

[dividing both sides by 40]

$\Rightarrow \quad x > 50$

Hence, the manufacturer must sell more than 50 items to realise some profit.

| TYPE IV |

Based on Temperature

Example 24 A solution is to be kept between 68°F and 77°F. What is the range of temperature in degree Celsius (C), if the Celsius/Fahrenheit (F) conversion formula is given by $F = \frac{9}{5}C + 32$? **[NCERT]**

Sol. It is given that, $68 < F < 77$

On putting $F = \frac{9}{5}C + 32$, we get

$$68 < \frac{9}{5}C + 32 < 77 \Rightarrow 68 - 32 < \frac{9}{5}C < 77 - 32$$

[subtracting 32 from each term]

$\Rightarrow \quad 36 < \frac{9}{5}C < 45$

$\Rightarrow \quad 36 \times \frac{5}{9} < C < 45 \times \frac{5}{9}$ $\left[\text{multiplying } \frac{5}{9} \text{ in each term}\right]$

$\Rightarrow \quad 4 \times 5 < C < 5 \times 5 \Rightarrow 20 < C < 25$

Hence, the required range of temperature is between 20°C and 25°C.

Example 25 A solution is to be kept between 40°C and 45°C. What is the range of temperature in degree Fahrenheit, if the conversion formula is $F = \frac{9}{5}C + 32$?

Sol. We have, $40 < C < 45$

On multiplying each term by $\frac{9}{5}$, we get

$$40 \times \frac{9}{5} < \frac{9}{5}C < \frac{9}{5} \times 45$$

$\Rightarrow \quad 8 \times 9 < \frac{9}{5}C < 9 \times 9 \Rightarrow 72 < \frac{9}{5}C < 81$

On adding 32 in each term, we get

$$72 + 32 < \frac{9}{5}C + 32 < 81 + 32$$

$\Rightarrow \quad 104 < F < 113$ $\left[\because F = \frac{9}{5}C + 32\right]$

Hence, the required range of temperature is between 104°F and 113°F.

| TYPE V |

Based on Geometry

Example 26 The longest side of a triangle is twice the shortest side and the third side is 2 cm longer than the shortest side. If the perimeter of the triangle is more than 166 cm then find the minimum length of the shortest side. **[NCERT Exemplar]**

Sol. Let the length of shortest side be x cm.

Then, according to question, we have

Length of longest side = $2x$ cm

and length of third side = $(x + 2)$ cm

Since, the perimeter of the triangle is more than 166 cm.

$\therefore \quad 2x + x + (x + 2) > 166$

$\Rightarrow \quad 4x + 2 > 166$

$\Rightarrow \quad 4x > 164$ [subtracting 2 from both sides]

$\Rightarrow \quad x > 41$ [dividing both sides by 4]

Hence, the length of the shortest side should be greater than 41 cm.

Example 27 A man wants to cut three lengths from a single piece of board of length 91 cm, the second length is to be 3 cm longer than the shortest and third length is to be twice as long as the shortest. What are the possible lengths for the shortest board, if third piece is to be atleast 5 cm longer than the second? **[NCERT]**

Sol. Let the length of the shortest piece be x cm, so that the lengths of second and third piece are $(x + 3)$ cm and $2x$ cm, respectively.

Then, $\quad x + (x + 3) + 2x \le 91$ ...(i)

and $\quad 2x \ge (x + 3) + 5$ ...(ii)

From inequality (i), we get

$$4x + 3 \le 91$$

$\Rightarrow \quad 4x + 3 - 3 \le 91 - 3$

[subtracting 3 from both sides]

$\Rightarrow \quad 4x \le 88$

[dividing both sides by 4]

$\Rightarrow \quad \frac{4x}{4} \le \frac{88}{4}$

$\Rightarrow \quad x \le 22$ ...(iii)

From inequality (ii), we get

$$2x \ge x + 8$$

$\Rightarrow \quad 2x - x \ge x + 8 - x$

[subtracting x from both sides]

$\Rightarrow \quad x \ge 8$ ...(iv)

From inequalities (iii) and (iv), we get

$$8 \le x \le 22$$

Hence, the shortest piece must be atleast 8 cm long but not more than 22 cm long.

| TYPE VI |

Based on Dilution of Acid

Example 28 A solution of 8% boric acid is to be diluted by adding a 2% boric acid solution to it. The resulting mixture is to be more than 4% but less than 6% boric acid. If we have 640 litres of the 8% solution, how many litres of the 2% solution will have to be added? **[NCERT]**

Sol. Let x be the number of litres of 2% boric acid solution.

Then, total mixture = $(640 + x)$ litres

According to the question,

$$2\% \text{ of } x + 8\% \text{ of } 640 > 4\% \text{ of } (640 + x)$$

$$\Rightarrow \frac{2x}{100} + \frac{8}{100} \times 640 > \frac{4}{100}(640 + x)$$

$$\Rightarrow 2x + 5120 > 2560 + 4x$$

[multiplying both sides by 100]

$$\Rightarrow 2x + 5120 - 2x > 2560 + 4x - 2x$$

[subtracting $2x$ from both sides]

$$\Rightarrow 5120 > 2560 + 2x$$

$$\Rightarrow 5120 - 2560 > 2560 + 2x - 2560$$

[subtracting 2560 from both sides]

$$\Rightarrow 2560 > 2x \Rightarrow 2x < 2560$$

$$\Rightarrow x < 1280 \quad \text{[dividing both sides by 2]} \quad ...(i)$$

Also, 2% of x + 8% of 640 < 6% of $(640 + x)$

$$\Rightarrow \frac{2}{100} \times x + \frac{8}{100} \times 640 < \frac{6}{100} \times (640 + x)$$

$$\Rightarrow 2x + 5120 < 3840 + 6x$$

[multiplying both sides by 100]

$$\Rightarrow 2x + 5120 - 2x < 3840 + 6x - 2x$$

[subtracting $2x$ from both sides]

$$\Rightarrow 5120 < 3840 + 4x$$

$$\Rightarrow 5120 - 3840 < 3840 + 4x - 3840$$

[subtracting 3840 from both sides]

$$\Rightarrow 1280 < 4x \text{ or } 4x > 1280$$

$$\Rightarrow \frac{4x}{4} > \frac{1280}{4} \quad \text{[dividing both sides by 4]}$$

$$\Rightarrow x > 320 \quad ...(ii)$$

Now, from inequalities (i) and (ii), we get

$$320 < x < 1280$$

Thus, the number of litres of the 2% boric acid solution will have to be greater than 320 litres and less than 1280 litres.

Example 29 How many litres of water will have to be added to 1125 litres of the 45% solution of acid so that the resulting mixture will contain more than 25% but less than 30% acid content? **[NCERT]**

Sol. Let x litres of water is required to be added.

Then, total mixture = $(x + 1125)$ litres.

Clearly, the amount of acid in the resulting mixture is 45% of 1125 litres. Since, the resulting mixture contain more than 25% but less than 30% acid content.

Therefore, we have

$$45\% \text{ of } 1125 > 25\% \text{ of } (x + 1125) \quad ...(i)$$

and $$45\% \text{ of } 1125 < 30\% \text{ of } (x + 1125) \quad ...(ii)$$

From Eq. (i), we have

$$\frac{45}{100} \times 1125 > \frac{25}{100} \times (x + 1125)$$

$$\Rightarrow 45 \times 1125 > 25 \times (x + 1125)$$

[multiplying both sides by 100]

$$\Rightarrow 45 \times 1125 > 25x + (25 \times 1125)$$

$$\Rightarrow 45 \times 1125 - (25 \times 1125) > 25x$$

[subtracting 25×1125 from both sides]

$$\Rightarrow 25x < 1125(45 - 25)$$

$$\Rightarrow 25x < 1125 \times 20$$

$$\Rightarrow x < \frac{1125 \times 20}{25} = 225 \times 4 = 900$$

[dividing both sides by 25]

$$\Rightarrow x < 900 \quad ...(iii)$$

From Eq. (ii), we have

$$\frac{45}{100} \times 1125 < \frac{30}{100} \times (x + 1125)$$

$$45 \times 1125 < 30x + (30 \times 1125)$$

[multiplying both sides by 100]

$$\Rightarrow 45 \times 1125 - (30 \times 1125) < 30x$$

[subtracting 30×1125 from both sides]

$$\Rightarrow 30x > 1125(45 - 30)$$

$$\Rightarrow x > \frac{1125 \times 15}{30} = \frac{1125}{2} = 562.5$$

$$\Rightarrow x > 562.5 \quad ...(iv)$$

From Eqs. (iii) and (iv), we get

$$562.5 < x < 900$$

Thus, the required number of litres of water that is to be added will have to be more than 526.5 but less than 900 litres.

Topic Practice 1

Very Short Answer Type Questions

2 Marks

1 Solve $-12x > 30$, when
(i) x is a natural number.
(ii) x is an integer. [NCERT]

2 Solve the inequality for real x,
$4x + 3 < 6x + 7$. [NCERT]

3 Solve the inequality $5x - 3 < 3x + 1$, when x is an integer.

4 Solve the inequality $3(x - 1) \le 2(x - 3)$ for real x.

5 Solve $3x + 8 > 2$, when
(i) x is an integer.
(ii) x is a real number. [NCERT]

6 Solve the inequality $2(2x + 3) - 10 < 6(x - 2)$ for real x. [NCERT]

7 Solve the inequality $5x - 1 > 3x + 7$ and show the graph of the solution on number line.

8 Solve the inequality $2 \le 3x - 4 \le 5$.

9 Solve the inequality $\frac{1}{x-4} < 0$.

10 Solve the inequality $7 \le \frac{3x + 11}{2} \le 11$.

11 Solve the inequality $|x - 1| \le 2$.

12 A company manufactures cassettes and its cost equation for a week is $C = 300 + 1.5x$ and its revenue equation is $R = 2x$, where x is the number of cassettes sold in a week. How many cassettes must be sold for the company to realise a profit?

13 IQ (Intelligence Quotient) of a person is given by formula, $IQ = \frac{MA}{CA} \times 100$
where, MA stands for the mental age of the person and CA for the chronological age. If $80 \le IQ \le 140$ for a group of 12 yr children, then find the range of their mental age. [NCERT]

14 In drilling world's deepest hole it was found that the temperature T in degree celsius x km below the Earth's surface was given by $T(x) = 30 + 25(x - 3)$, where $3 \le x \le 15$. At what depth will the temperature be between 155°C and 205°C?. [NCERT Exemplar]

Short Answer Type Questions

4 Marks

15 Solve $37 - (3x + 5) \ge 9x - 8(x - 3)$.
Show the graph of the solution on number line. [NCERT]

16 Solve the inequality $\frac{x}{2} \ge \frac{(5x-2)}{3} - \frac{(7x-3)}{5}$ and show the graph of the solution on number line. [NCERT]

17 Solve the following system of inequalities and represent the solution graphically on number line.
$$3x - 7 > 2(x - 6)$$
and $$6 - x > 11 - 2x$$

18 Solve the inequality $\frac{x+8}{x-2} \ge 0$ and show the solution on number line.

19 Solve for x, $\frac{1}{|x| - 3} < 0$.

Long Answer Type Questions

6 Marks

20 Solve for x, $\frac{4}{x+1} \le 3 \le \frac{6}{x+1}$, $x > 0$. [NCERT Exemplar]

21 The sum of four consecutive integers must not be more than 22. What are the integers?

22 Find all pairs of consecutive odd natural numbers, both of which are larger than 10, such that their sum is less than 40. [NCERT]

23 A solution is to be kept between 86°F and 95°F. What is the range of temperature in degree Celsius, if the Celsius (C)/Fahrenheit (F) conversion formula is given by
$F = \frac{9}{5}C + 32$.

24 The longest side of a triangle is 3 times the shortest side and the third side is 2 cm shorter than the longest side. If the perimeter of the triangle is atleast 61 cm. Find the minimum length of the shortest side. [NCERT]

25 Solve the following system of inequalities.
$$\frac{x}{2x+1} \ge \frac{1}{4} \text{ and } \frac{6x}{4x-1} < \frac{1}{2}$$
[NCERT Exemplar]

Hints & Answers

1. $-12x > 30 \Rightarrow x < -\dfrac{30}{12}$

   Ans. (i) No solution (ii) $\{\ldots, -4, -3\}$

2. Subtracting $(4x+7)$ from both sides of $4x+3 < 6x+7$.

   Ans. $(-2, \infty)$

3. Subtracting $(3x-3)$ from both sides of $5x-3 < 3x+1$.

   Ans. $\{\ldots, -4, -3, -2, -1, 0, 1\}$

4. Solve as Example 4. **Ans.** $(-\infty, -3]$

5. Solve as Example 3. **Ans.** (i) $\{-1, 0, 1, 2, 3, \ldots\}$ (ii) $(-2, \infty)$

6. $(4, \infty)$

7. Subtracting $(3x-1)$ from both sides of $5x-1 > 3x+7$.

   Ans. $(4, \infty)$

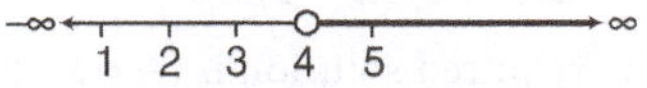

8. $2 \le 3x - 4 \le 5$

   On adding each term by 4, we get

   $\Rightarrow \quad 6 \le 3x \le 9$

   On dividing each term by 3, we get

   Ans. $x \in [2, 3]$

9. Multiplying both sides by $(x-4)^2$. **Ans.** $(-\infty, 4)$

10. Solve as Example 16. **Ans.** $\left[1, \dfrac{11}{3}\right]$

11. Use $|x| \le a \Rightarrow -a \le x \le a$. **Ans.** $[-1, 3]$

12. Profit = Revenue − Cost

    and in order to realise some profit, revenue should be greater than the cost. Now, proceed as Example 5.

    Ans. More than 600 cassettes.

13. Also, $\text{IQ} = \dfrac{\text{MA}}{\text{CA}} \times 100$

    $\therefore \quad 80 \le \dfrac{\text{MA}}{\text{CA}} \times 100 \le 140 \Rightarrow 80 \le \dfrac{\text{MA}}{12} \times 100 \le 140$

    Ans. $9.6 \le \text{MA} \le 16.8$

14. Let at x km below the Earth's surface, the temperature is between 155°C and 205°C.

    $\therefore \; 155 < T(x) < 205$

    $\Rightarrow 155 < 30 + 25(x-3) < 205$ **Ans.** $8 < x < 10$.

15. Solve as Example 5, part (iii).

    Ans. $(-\infty, 2]$

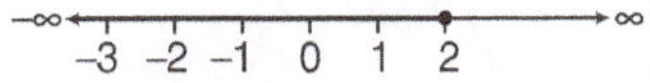

16. Solve as Example 5, part (iv).

    Ans. $\left[-\dfrac{2}{7}, \infty\right)$

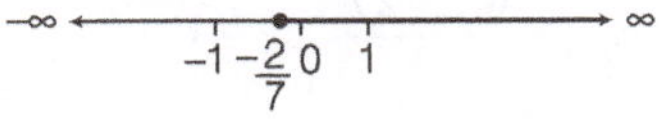

17. Solve as Example 14.

    Ans. $(5, \infty)$

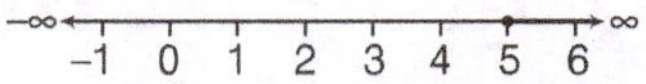

18. Multiply both sides by $(x-2)^2$

    Ans. $(-\infty, -8] \cup (2, \infty)$

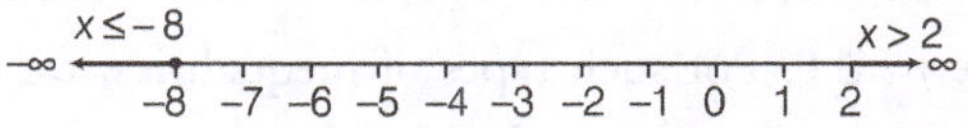

19. Let $y = |x|$. **Ans.** $(-3, 3)$

20. We have, $\dfrac{4}{x+1} \le 3 \le \dfrac{6}{x+1}$

    $\Rightarrow \quad 4 \le 3(x+1) \le 6 \qquad [\because x+1 \ne 0 \Rightarrow x \ne -1]$

    Fist dividing each term by 3 and then subtracting 1 from resultant of each term, we get

    Ans. $\left[\dfrac{1}{3}, 1\right]$

21. Solve as Example 20. **Ans.** Less than or equal to 4.

22. Solve as Example 22.

    Ans. (11, 13), (13, 15), (15, 17), (17, 19)

23. Solve as Example 24.

    Ans. Between 30°C and 35°C

24. Let the length of shortest side be x cm. Then, we have $3x + x + (3x - 2) \ge 61$ and then proceed as Example 28.

    Ans. 9 cm.

25. Now, $\dfrac{x}{2x+1} \ge \dfrac{1}{4} \Rightarrow \dfrac{x}{2x+1} - \dfrac{1}{4} \ge 0$

    $\Rightarrow \quad (2x-1)(2x+1) \ge 0$

    Case **I** When both are non-negative

    $2x - 1 \ge 0$ and $2x + 1 > 0$

    $\therefore \quad x \in \left[\dfrac{1}{2}, \infty\right) \quad \ldots \text{(i)}$

    Case **II** When both are non-positive

    $(2x-1) \le 0$ and $2x + 1 < 0$

    $\therefore \quad x \in \left(-\infty, -\dfrac{1}{2}\right) \quad \ldots \text{(ii)}$

    From Eqs. (i) and (ii), we get

    $x \in \left(-\infty, -\dfrac{1}{2}\right) \cup \left[\dfrac{1}{2}, \infty\right) \quad \ldots \text{(iii)}$

    Now, $\dfrac{6x}{4x-1} < \dfrac{1}{2} \Rightarrow \dfrac{6x}{4x-1} - \dfrac{1}{2} < 0$

    $\Rightarrow \quad (8x+1)(4x-1) < 0$

    We have, $\quad (8x+1) < 0$ and $(4x-1) > 0$

    or $\quad (8x+1) > 0$ and $(4x-1) < 0$

    $\Rightarrow \quad \dfrac{-1}{8} < x < \dfrac{1}{4} \quad \ldots \text{(iv)}$

    Ans. Solution set is a empty set.

TOPIC 02 **Quadratic Inequalities**

In this topic we solve the following quadratic inequalities: $ax^2 + bx + c > 0$, $ax^2 + bx + c < 0$, $ax^2 + bx + c \le 0$ and $ax^2 + bx + c \ge 0$. For such types of inequalities, we use method of intervals method.

Method of Intervals

Let $f(x) = (x - a_1)^{k_1} (x - a_2)^{k_2} \dots (x - a_{n-1})^{k_{n-1}}$ $(x - a_n)^{k_n}$ where $k_1, k_2, \dots, k_n \in z$ and $a_1 < a_2 < a_3 < \dots < a_{n-1} < a_n$.

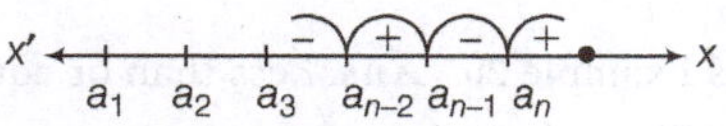

For solving $f(x) > 0$ or $f(x) < 0$, consider the following algorithm

(i) First, mark the numbers $a_1\ a_2, \dots, a_n$ on the number line and put a plus (+) sign in the interval on the right of the largest of these numbers i.e. on the right of a_n.

(ii) Now, put the plus (+) sign in the interval on the left of a_n, if k_n is an even number and a minus sign if k_n is an odd number. In the next interval, we put a sign according to the following rule.

When passing through the point a_{n-1}, the polynomial $f(x)$ changes sign if k_{n-1} is an odd number. Then, we consider the next interval and put a sign in it using the same rule.

(iii) Thus, we consider all the intervals. The solution of the inequality $f(x) > 0$ is the union of all intervals in which we have put the plus sign, and the solution of the inequality $f(x) < 0$ is the union of all intervals in which we have put the minus sign.

Example 1 Solve the quadratic inequality

$$x^2 + x - 6 \ge 0.$$

Sol. We have,

$$x^2 + x - 6 \ge 0$$

$\Rightarrow$ $(x + 3)(x - 2) \ge 0$

$\therefore$ $x = -3, 2.$

On the number line, mark $x = -3$ and $x = 2$.

Hence, the sign scheme of $x^2 + x - 6$ is

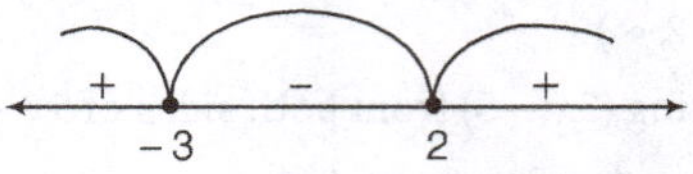

Now, when $x \ge 2$, then $x - 2 \ge 0$ and $x + 3 > 0$

$\Rightarrow$ $(x + 3)(x - 2) \ge 0$

When $-3 < x \le 2$, then $x + 3 > 0$ but $x - 2 \le 0$

$\Rightarrow$ $(x + 3)(x - 2) \le 0$

When $x \le -3$, then $x + 3 \le 0$ and $x - 2 < 0$

$\Rightarrow$ $(x + 3)(x - 2) \ge 0$

$\therefore$ Hence, the required solution is $(-\infty, -3] \cup [2, \infty)$.

Example 2 Solve the quadratic inequality

$$3 - 2x^2 > 5x.$$

Sol. We have, $3 - 2x^2 > 5x$

$\Rightarrow$ $2x^2 + 5x - 3 < 0$

$\Rightarrow$ $(2x - 1)(x + 3) < 0$

$\Rightarrow$ $2\left(x - \frac{1}{2}\right)(x + 3) < 0$

$\therefore$ $x = \frac{1}{2}, -3,$

On the number line, mark $x = -3$ and $x = \frac{1}{2}$.

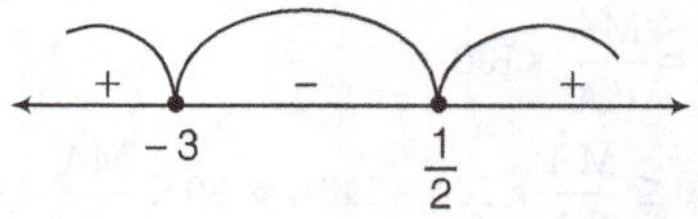

Now, when $x > \frac{1}{2}$, then

$$\left(x - \frac{1}{2}\right) > 0 \text{ and } (x + 3) > 0$$

$\Rightarrow$ $2\left(x - \frac{1}{2}\right)(x + 3) > 0$

When $-3 < x < \frac{1}{2}$, then

$$(x + 3) > 0 \text{ and } \left(x - \frac{1}{2}\right) < 0$$

$\Rightarrow$ $2\left(x - \frac{1}{2}\right)(x + 3) < 0$

When $x < -3$, then $(x+3) < 0$ and $\left(x - \frac{1}{2}\right) < 0$

$$\Rightarrow \quad (x+3)\left(x-\frac{1}{2}\right) < 0$$

$\therefore$ Hence, the required solution is $\left(-3, \frac{1}{2}\right)$.

Inequalities involving Rational Expression

To solve the inequality of the form $\frac{f(x)}{g(x)} > 0$ or $\frac{f(x)}{g(x)} < 0$ etc., we use the method of intervals.

To make it more clear, let us take the following examples.

Example 3 Solve the inequality $\frac{2x-3}{(x-2)(x-4)} \le 0$.

Sol. We have,

$$\frac{2x-3}{(x-2)(x-4)} \le 0$$

We know that, $x \ne 2, 4$

Since, $(x-2)^2(x-4)^2 > 0$

$$\Rightarrow \quad \frac{(2x-3)(x-2)^2(x-4)^2}{(x-2)(x-4)} \le 0$$

$$\Rightarrow \quad (2x-3)(x-2)(x-4) \le 0$$

$$\Rightarrow \quad 2\left(x-\frac{3}{2}\right)(x-2)(x-4) \le 0$$

$$\therefore \quad x = \frac{3}{2}, 2, 4$$

On the number line, mark $x = \frac{3}{2}$, 2, 4.

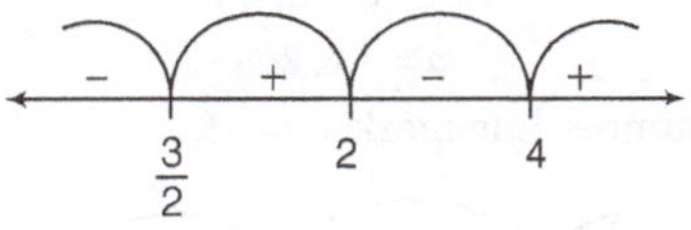

Now, when $x > 4$, $\left(x-\frac{3}{2}\right) > 0, (x-2) > 0, (x-4) > 0$

$$\Rightarrow \quad \left(x-\frac{3}{2}\right)(x-2)(x-4) > 0$$

When $2 < x < 4$, $x - \frac{3}{2} > 0$, $x - 2 > 0$, $x - 4 < 0$

$$\Rightarrow \quad \left(x-\frac{3}{2}\right)(x-2)(x-4) < 0$$

When $\frac{3}{2} < x < 2$, $x - \frac{3}{2} > 0$, $x - 2 < 0$, $x - 4 < 0$

$$\Rightarrow \quad \left(x-\frac{3}{2}\right)(x-2)(x-4) > 0$$

When $x < \frac{3}{2}$, $x - \frac{3}{2} < 0$, $x - 2 < 0$, $x - 4 < 0$

$$\Rightarrow \quad \left(x-\frac{3}{2}\right)(x-2)(x-4) < 0$$

Hence, the required solution is $\left(-\infty, \frac{3}{2}\right] \cup (2, 4)$.

Example 4 Find the solution set of the inequality $\frac{x^2-3x+24}{x^2-3x+3} < 4$.

Sol. We have,

$$\frac{x^2-3x+24}{x^2-3x+3} < 4$$

$$\Rightarrow \quad \frac{x^2-3x+24}{x^2-3x+3} - 4 < 0$$

$$\Rightarrow \quad \frac{x^2-3x+24-4x^2+12x-12}{x^2-3x+3} < 0$$

$$\Rightarrow \quad \frac{-3x^2+9x+12}{x^2-3x+3} < 0$$

$$\Rightarrow \quad \frac{-3(x^2-3x-4)}{x^2-3x+3} < 0$$

$$\Rightarrow \quad \frac{x^2-3x-4}{x^2-3x+3} > 0$$

$$\Rightarrow \quad \frac{(x+1)(x-4)}{x^2-3x+3} > 0$$

We have,

$$x^2 - 3x + 3 = \left(x - \frac{3}{2}\right)^2 + \frac{3}{4} \ge \frac{3}{4} > 0 - \forall\, x \in R.$$

Now, $(x+1)(x-4) = 0 \Rightarrow x = -1, 4$

Hence, the sign scheme is

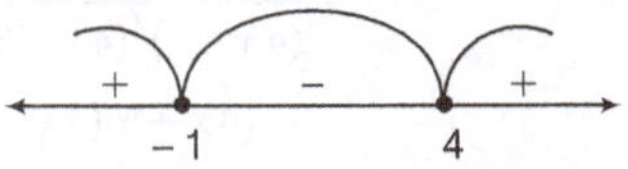

When $x > 4$, then $(x+1) > 0, (x-4) > 0$

$\Rightarrow \quad (x+1)(x-4) > 0$

When $-1 < x < 4$, then $(x+1) > 0, (x-4) < 0$

$\Rightarrow \quad (x+1)(x-4) < 0$

When $x < -1$, then $(x+1) < 0, (x-4) < 0$

$\Rightarrow \quad (x+1)(x-4) > 0$

Hence, the required solution set is $(-\infty, -1) \cup (4, \infty)$.

Example 5 Find the range of the expression $\dfrac{2x^2-2x+4}{x^2-4x+3}$.

Sol. Let $\dfrac{2x^2-2x+4}{x^2-4x+3}=y$

$$\Rightarrow \quad 2x^2-2x+4=x^2y-4xy+3y$$

$$\Rightarrow \quad (y-2)x^2+2(1-2y)x+(3y-4)=0$$

Since $x \in R$, then discriminant, $D \geq 0$

$$\Rightarrow \quad [2(1-2y)]^2-4(y-2)(3y-4)\geq 0$$

$$\Rightarrow \quad 4(1+4y^2-4y)-(4y-8)(3y-4)\geq 0$$

$$\Rightarrow 4+16y^2-16y-12y^2+16y+24y-32\geq 0$$

$$\Rightarrow \quad 4y^2+24y-28\geq 0$$

$$\Rightarrow \quad y^2+6y-7\geq 0$$

$$\Rightarrow \quad (y+7)(y-1)\geq 0$$

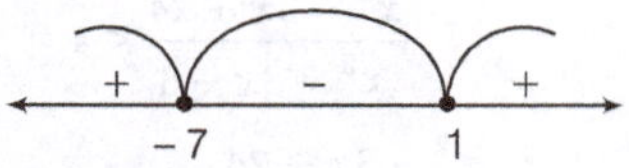

$\therefore y \in (-\infty, -7] \cup [1, \infty)$.

Example 6 Find the range of real values of x for which $\dfrac{x-1}{4x+5}<\dfrac{x-3}{4x-3}$.

Sol. We have, $\dfrac{x-1}{4x+5}<\dfrac{x-3}{4x-3}$

$$\Rightarrow \quad \frac{x-1}{4x+5}-\frac{x-3}{4x-3}<0$$

$$\Rightarrow \quad \frac{(x-1)(4x-3)-(x-3)(4x+5)}{(4x+5)(4x-3)}<0$$

$$\Rightarrow \quad \frac{4x^2-3x-4x+3-(4x^2+5x-12x-15)}{(4x+5)(4x-3)}<0$$

$$\Rightarrow \quad \frac{4x^2-7x+3-4x^2+7x+15}{(4x+5)(4x-3)}<0$$

$$\Rightarrow \quad \frac{18}{(4x+5)(4x-3)}<0$$

$$\Rightarrow \quad \frac{18(4x+5)(4x-3)}{(4x+5)^2(4x-3)^2}<0$$

$$\Rightarrow \quad (4x+5)(4x-3)<0$$

$$\Rightarrow \quad 16\left(x+\frac{5}{4}\right)\left(x-\frac{3}{4}\right)<0$$

$$\therefore \quad x=-\frac{5}{4}, \frac{3}{4}$$

On the number line mark $x=\dfrac{-5}{4}, \dfrac{3}{4}$

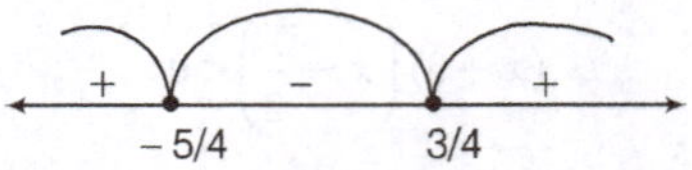

By the method of intervals, we get the required range $-\dfrac{5}{4}<x<\dfrac{3}{4}$.

Example 7 Find what value of a is the inequality $\dfrac{x^2+ax-2}{x^2-x+1}<2$ satisfied for all real values of x?

Sol. We have, $\dfrac{x^2+ax-2}{x^2-x+1}<2$

$$\Rightarrow \quad \frac{x^2+ax-2}{x^2-x+1}-2<0$$

$$\Rightarrow \quad \frac{-x^2+(a+2)x-4}{x^2-x+1}<0 \quad \text{....(i)}$$

Now, $x^2-x+1=\left[x^2-2\left(\dfrac{1}{2}\right)x+\left(\dfrac{1}{2}\right)^2\right]+1-\left(\dfrac{1}{2}\right)^2$

$$=\left(x-\frac{1}{2}\right)^2+\frac{3}{4},$$

which is positive for all real values of x.

$\therefore \; -x^2+(a+2)x-4<0$ [from Eq. (i)]

$$\Rightarrow \quad x^2-(a+2)x+4>0$$

$$\therefore \quad x^2-(a-2)x+4 \text{ is positive}$$

We know that if ax^2+bx+c and 'a' have the same sign, then $b^2-4ac<b$.

Here, $x^2-(a+2)x+4$ and coefficient of x^2(i.e. 1) are positive, i.e. have same sign, therefore discriminant <0.

$$\Rightarrow \quad (a+2)^2-4\times 4\times 1<0$$

$$\Rightarrow \quad a^2+4a-12<0$$

$$\Rightarrow \quad (a+6)(a-2)<0$$

$$\therefore \quad a=-6, 2$$

On the number line mark, $a=-6, 2$

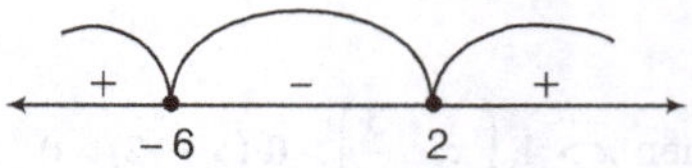

Now, by method of intervals, we get $-6<a<2$, which is the required range of a.

Topic Practice 2

Short Answer Type Questions

4 Marks

1 Solve the inequality $2x^2 + x - 15 \geq 0$.

2 Solve the inequality $-x^2 + 3x - 2 \geq 0$.

3 Solve the inequality $x^2 - 6x + 19 \geq 0$.

Long Answer Type Questions

6 Marks

4 Show that the value of $\frac{x^2 - x + 1}{x^2 + x + 1}$ always lies between $\frac{1}{3}$ to 3.

5 Solve the inequality $\frac{x^2 + 6x - 11}{x + 3} < -1$.

6 Solve the inequality $\frac{3x^2 - 2x - 5}{x^2 - 2x + 5} < 2$.

7 Fing the range of real values of x for which $\frac{x-2}{3x+4} < \frac{x-4}{3x-2}$.

8 Find the values of m for which the expression $\frac{2x^2 - 5x + 3}{4x - m}$ can take all real values for all real values of x.

Hints & Answers

1. Solve as Example 1. **Ans.** $(-\infty, -3] \cup \left[\frac{5}{2}, \infty\right)$
2. Solve as Example 1. **Ans.** $[1, 2]$
3. Solve as example 1. **Ans.** $(-\infty, \infty)$
4. Solve as Example 4.
5. Solve as Example 4 **Ans.** $(-\infty, -8) \cup (-3, 1)$
6. Solve as Example 5. **Ans.** $(-5, 3)$
7. Solve as Example 6.
   Ans. $-\frac{4}{3} < x < \frac{2}{3}$
8. Solve as Example 7.
   Ans. $m \in [4,6]$

Chapter Practice

Multiple Choice Type Questions

1 Mark

1. Two real numbers or two algebraic expressions related by the symbol '<', '>', '≤' or '≥' forms an

(a) equation (b) inequality
(c) set (d) None of these

2. The graph of the solutions of inequality $\frac{3x-4}{2} \geq \frac{x+1}{4} - 1$ on number line is

(a) 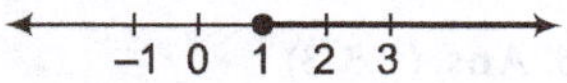

(b) 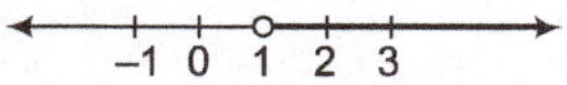

(c) 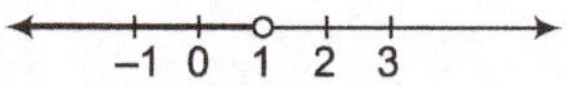

(d) 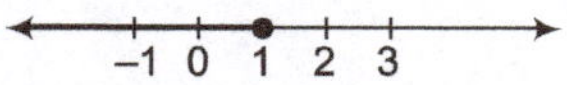

3. The solution set of $\frac{2x-1}{3} \geq \left(\frac{3x-2}{4}\right) - \left(\frac{2-x}{5}\right)$ is

(a) $(-\infty, 2)$ (b) $(-\infty, 2]$ (c) $\left(-\infty, -\frac{1}{2}\right)$ (d) $\left(-\infty, -\frac{1}{2}\right]$

4. The set of values of x satisfying $2 \leq |x-3| < 4$ is

(a) $(-1, 1] \cup [5, 7)$ (b) $-4 \leq x \leq 2$
(c) $-1 < x < 7$ or $x \geq 5$ (d) $x < 7$ or $x \geq 5$
(e) $-\infty < x \leq 1$ or $5 \leq x < \infty$

5. The solution set of the linear inequalities $-15 < \frac{3(x-2)}{5} \leq 0$, is

(a) $(-23, 2]$ (b) $(-20, 4)$
(c) $[-23, 2)$ (d) None of these

Assertion-Reason Type Questions

1 Mark

Directions (Q. Nos. 6-9) *In the questions given below are two statements labelled as Assertion (A) and Reason (R). In the context of the two statements, which one of the following is correct?*

(a) Both A and R are correct; R is the correct explanation of A
(b) Both A and R are correct; R is not the correct explanation of A
(c) A is correct; R is incorrect
(d) R is correct; A is incorrect

6. **Assertion (A)** If $-3x + 12 < 0$, then $x \in (4, \infty)$.

Reason (R) If $a < b$, then $ka > kb$, if $k < 0$.

7. **Assertion (A)** If $|4 - x| + 1 < 3$, then $x \in (2, 6)$.

Reason (R) If $|x - c| < a$, then $x \in (c - a, c + a)$.

8. **Assertion (A)** If $2x - 7 > 5 - x$ and $11 - 5x \leq 1$, then $x \in (4, \infty)$.

Reason (R) The solution set of system of linear inequations is the intersection of solution set of individual inequations.

9. **Assertion (A)** If $3x + 8 > 2$, then $x \in \{-1, 0, 1, 2, \ldots\}$, when x is an integer.

Reason (R) The solution set of the inequality $4x + 3 < 5x + 7 \forall x \in R$ is $[4, \infty)$.

Very Short Answer Type Questions

2 Marks

10. Solve $12 + 1\frac{5}{6}x \leq 5 + 3x$, when (i) $x \in N$ (ii) $x \in R$.

11. Solve the inequality $3(2 - x) \geq 2(1 - x)$ and show the graph of solution on number line. [NCERT]

12. Solve the inequality $\frac{2x-3}{4} + 9 \geq 3 + \frac{4x}{3}$ and show the graph of the solution on number line.

13. Solve for $x: 4x + 3 \geq 2x + 17, 3x - 5 < -2$.

14. Solve the following system of linear inequalities.

$$\frac{4x}{3} - \frac{9}{4} < x + \frac{3}{4} \text{ and } \frac{7x-1}{3} - \frac{7x+2}{6} > x$$

15. Solve for $x: -5 \leq \frac{2-3x}{4} \leq 9$. [NCERT Exemplar]

16. Solve $2x - 1 > x + \frac{7-x}{3} > 2, x \in R$.

17. Anshu obtained 73, 67 and 72 marks in the Mathematics test. How many marks should he get in his fourth test, so as to have an average of at least 75?

18. Solve $x^2 - 4x + 3 < 0$.

Short Answer Type Questions

(4 Marks)

19. Solve for $x : \dfrac{x-3}{x-5} > 0$.

20. Solve $\dfrac{5}{x-2} > 3$ and represent the solution set on number line.

21. Solve the inequality $\left|\dfrac{2}{x-4}\right| > 1; x \neq 4$.

22. Solve the following system of inequalities.

$$\frac{2x+1}{7x-1} > 5, \ \frac{x+7}{x-8} > 2$$

23. Solve $|x| < 4$ and represent the solution set on the number line.

24. Solve the inequality $\dfrac{|x-1|}{x+2} < 1$.

25. A company manufactures cassettes. Its cost and revenue functions are $C(x) = 26000 + 30x$ and $R(x) = 43x$, respectively, where x is the number of cassettes produced and sold in a week. How many cassettes must be sold by the company to realise some profit? **[NCERT Exemplar]**

26. The water acidity in a pool is considered normal when the average pH reading of three daily measurements is between 8.2 and 8.5. If the two pH readings are 8.48 and 8.35, find the range of pH value for the third reading that will result in the acidity level being normal. **[NCERT Exemplar]**

27. The length of rectangle is three times the breadth. If the minimum perimeter of the rectangle is 160 cm, then find the shortest value for its breadth.

28. A manufacturer has 600 L of a 12% solution of acid. How many litres of a 30% acid solution must be added to it so that acid content in the resulting mixture will be more than 15% but less than 18%? **[NCERT]**

29. Solve the inequality $\dfrac{x+3}{x-1} > x$.

30. Solve the following inequality $\dfrac{x^2-2x+3}{x^2-4x+3} > -3$.

31. Find the range of the expression $\dfrac{x^2+2x-3}{x^2+2x-8}$.

32. If x is real, then prove that the value of $\dfrac{(x-1)(x+3)}{(x-2)(x+4)}$ cannot lies between $\dfrac{4}{9}$ and 1.

Case-Based Type Questions

(6 Marks)

33. Aman questioned his maths teacher that "if he has more that one linear inequality, then what will be the solution?"

Teacher replies, "The solution set of a system of linear inequations in one variable is the intersection of the solution sets of the linear inequations in the given system."

After that teacher gave Aman some problems to solve.

On the basis of given information, answer the following questions.

(i) Find the solution of the linear inequality $2(2x+3)-10 < 6(x-2)$.

(ii) Find the solution of the linear inequality $\dfrac{2x-3}{4}+6 \geq 2+\dfrac{4x}{3}$.

(iii) Find the solution of the linear inequality $\dfrac{x}{2x+1} \geq \dfrac{1}{4}$.

(iv) Find the solution of system of linear inequality given by (i) and (ii).

(v) Find the solution of system of inequation given by $-11 \leq 4x-3 \leq 13$.

34. The water acidity in a pool is considered normal, when the average pH reading of three daily measurements is between 7.2 and 7.8. The first two pH reading are 7.48 and 7.85, and pH reading of 3rd day is x.

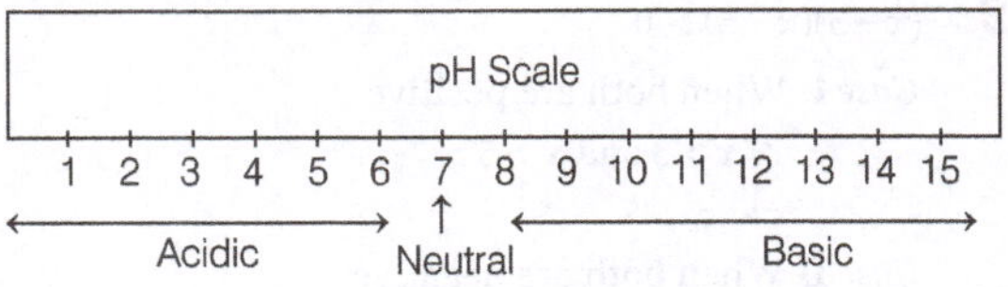

On the basis of above information, answer the following questions.

(i) Find the average pH of three days.

(ii) Find the system of linear inequality, which shows the given information.

(iii) Find the solution of linear inequality $7.2 \leq 5.11+\dfrac{x}{3}$.

(iv) Find the solution of linear inequality $5.11+\dfrac{x}{3} \leq 7.8$.

(v) Find the value of pH on third day.

Hints & Answers

1. (b) **2.** (a) **3.** (b) **4.** (a) **5.** (a)
6. (a) **7.** (a) **8.** (d) **9.** (c)

10. $12+\frac{11x}{6}\le 5+3x \Rightarrow \frac{7x}{6}\ge 7 \Rightarrow x\ge 6$

Ans. (i) {6, 7, 8, 9, ...} (ii) $[6, \infty)$

11. $3(2-x)\ge 2(1-x) \Rightarrow 6-2\ge 3x-2x \Rightarrow x\le 4$

Ans. $(-\infty, 4]$

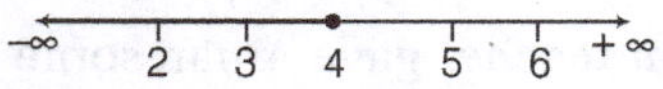

12. Solve as Question 1. **Ans.** $(-\infty, 9.9]$

13. $4x+3\ge 2x+17$ and $3x-5<-2$

$\Rightarrow 2x\ge 14$ and $3x<3 \Rightarrow x\ge 7$ and $x<1$

Ans. No solution exists.

14. Solve as Question 4. **Ans.** (4, 9)

15. $-5\le\frac{2-3x}{4}\le 9 \Rightarrow -20\le 2-3x\le 36 \Rightarrow -22\le -3x\le 34$

$\Rightarrow$ **Ans.** $\left[\frac{-34}{3}, \frac{22}{3}\right]$

16. $2x-1>\frac{2x+7}{3}>2 \Rightarrow 6x-3>2x+7<6$

$\Rightarrow 6x-3>2x+7$ and $2x+7>6$

$\Rightarrow 4x>10$ and $2x>-1$

Ans. $\left]\frac{5}{2}, \infty\right[$

17. $\frac{73+67+72+x}{4}\ge 75$ **Ans.** 88 marks

18. $1<x<3$.

19. $(x-3)(x-5)>0$

Case **I** When both are positive

$\therefore x>3$ and $x>5$

$\Rightarrow x>5$

Case **II** When both are negative

$x-3<0$ and $x-5<0$

$\Rightarrow x<3$ and $x<5 \Rightarrow x<3$

Ans. $(-\infty, 3)\cup(5, \infty)$

20. $\frac{5}{x-2}-3>0$

$\Rightarrow \left(\frac{11-3x}{x-2}\right)>0$

Further, solve as Question 8.

Ans. $\left]2, \frac{11}{3}\right[$

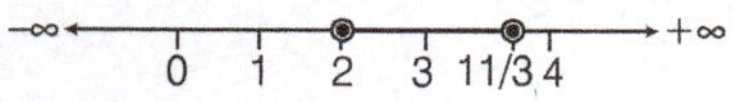

21. $\left|\frac{2}{x-4}\right|>1 \Rightarrow \frac{2}{x-4}<-1, \frac{2}{x-4}>1$

$\Rightarrow \frac{2}{x-4}+1<0, \frac{2}{x-4}-1>0 \Rightarrow \frac{-2+x}{x-4}<0, \frac{6-x}{x-4}>0$

$\Rightarrow (-2+x)(x-4)<0$ and $(6-x)(x-4)>0$

Further, solve as Question 11. **Ans.** $(2, 4)\cup(4, 6)$

22. $\frac{2x+1}{7x-1}-5>0, \frac{x+7}{x-8}-2>0 \Rightarrow \frac{-33x+6}{7x-1}>0, \frac{-x+23}{(x-8)}>0$

$\Rightarrow (-33x+6)(7x-1)>0, (-x+23)(x-8)>0$

$\Rightarrow x>7, x<23$

Ans. No solution exists

23. $|x|<4 \Rightarrow -4<x<4$

Ans. $]-4, 4[$

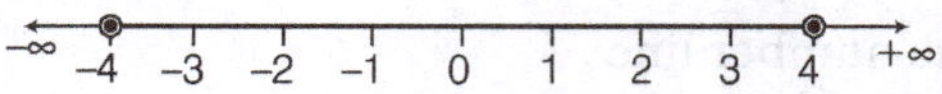

24. Solve as Question 13. **Ans.** $(-\infty, -2)\cup\left(\frac{-1}{2}, \infty\right)$

25. For profit, $R(x)>C(x)$ **Ans.** More than 2000.

26. $8.2<\frac{8.48+8.35+x}{3}<8.5$ **Ans.** Between 7.77 and 8.77.

27. Let length and breadth of a rectangle is x and y

$\because x=3y$

$\therefore 2(x+y)\ge 160 \Rightarrow 2(3y+y)\ge 160$ **Ans.** 20 cm

28. Solve as Example 28 of Topic 1.

Ans. Greater than 120 L and less than 300 L.

29. $x<-1$ or $1<x<3$

30. $x<1$ or $\frac{3}{2}<x<2$ or $x>3$

31. $\left[\frac{4}{9}, 1\right]$

32. Solve as Example 5 of Topic 4.

33. (i) $(4, \infty)$

(ii) $(-\infty, 3.9]$

(iii) $\left[\frac{1}{2}, \infty\right)$

(iv) ϕ

(v) $[-2, 4]$

34. (i) $5.11+\frac{x}{3}$

(ii) $7.2<5.11+\frac{x}{3}<7.8$

(iii) $x\ge 6.27$

(iv) $x\le 8.07$

(v) $(6.27, 8.07)$

CHAPTER

07

Permutations and Combinations

The study of permutation and combination is concerned with determining the number of different ways of arranging and selecting objects, out of a given number of objects.

In this chapter, we will learn about some basic counting techniques which will be useful in determining the number of different ways of arranging and selecting objects, without actually listing them.

- Fundamental Principles of Counting and Factorial Notation
- Permutations
- Combinations

TOPIC 01 Fundamental Principles of Counting and Factorial Notation

There are two fundamental principles of counting which are the base of permutations and combinations.

1. Fundamental Principle of Multiplication (FPM)

If an event can occur in m different ways, another event can occur in n different ways, then the total number of occurrence of the events in the given order is $m \times n$.

In other words, if there are two operations say E and F such that E can be performed in m ways and associated with each way of performing operation E, operation F can be performed in n ways. Then, the two operations in succession can be performed in $m \times n$ ways.

e.g. In a school, there are 200 boys and 150 girls. The teacher wants to select a boy and a girl to represent the school in inter school competition.

Here, the teacher can select a boy in 200 ways and a girl in 150 ways. So, by principle of multiplication, the teacher can select a boy and a girl in $200 \times 150 = 30000$ ways.

Note The above principle can be extended to any finite number of events (or operations) as stated below

If there are n events, say $E_1, E_2, \ldots, E_n$ such that E_1 can occur in m_1 ways, E_2 can occur in m_2 ways, E_3 can occur in m_3 ways and so on, then the total number of ways in which all the events can be occurred in the stated order is $m_1 \times m_2 \times m_3 \times \ldots \times m_n$.

Example 1 In a monthly test, the teacher decides that there will be three questions, one from each of the Exercises 7, 8 and 9 of textbook. If there are 11 questions in Exercise 7, 15 in Exercise 8 and 10 in Exercise 9, in how many ways can three questions be selected?

Sol. Clearly, from Exercise 7, one question can be selected in 11 ways.

From Exercise 8, one question can be selected in 15 ways.

and from Exercise 9, one question can be selected in 10 ways.

Since, each operation is performed after performing the previous operation, so we use fundamental principle of multiplication.

$\therefore$ Number of ways of selecting three questions

$$= 11 \times 15 \times 10 = 1650$$

Example 2 In how many ways can 6 letters be posted in 5 letter boxes?

Sol. Let L_1, L_2, L_3, L_4, L_5 and L_6 be six letters. Since, each letter can be posted in anyone of the five letter boxes.

So, L_1 can be posted in 5 ways. Similarly, each of L_2, L_3, L_4, L_5 and L_6 can be posted in 5 ways.

Hence, the total number of ways in which all the six letters can be posted is $5 \times 5 \times 5 \times 5 \times 5 \times 5 = 5^6 = 15625$ ways.

Example 3 In an examination, there are three multiple choice questions and each question has 4 choices. Find the number of ways in which a student can fail to get all answer correct.

Sol. Since, each question can be answered in 4 ways.

So, the total number of ways answering 3 questions is $4 \times 4 \times 4 = 64$.

Out of these possible answers, only one will be correct and hence the number of ways in which a student can fail to get all correct answer is $64 - 1 = 63$.

Example 4 The flag of a newly formed forum is in the form of three blocks ooo, each to be coloured differently. If there are six different colours on the whole to choose from, how many such designs are possible?

Sol. Here, we have six colours to colour three blocks.

So, first block can be coloured in 6 ways.

Since, each block should be coloured differently, so second block can be coloured by anyone of the remaining 5 colours.

Thus, second block can be coloured in 5 ways.

Similarly, third block can be coloured in 4 ways.

Since, each block is coloured after colouring the previous block.

$\therefore$ By FPM, required number of designs

$$= 6 \times 5 \times 4 = 120$$

Example 5 How many 3-digit numbers can be formed from the digits 1, 2, 3, 4 and 5 assuming

(i) repetition of digits allowed? **[NCERT]**

(ii) repetition of digits not allowed?

Sol. (i) There are 5 digits *viz.* 1, 2, 3, 4 and 5.

Since, every digit can be repeated any number of times and we have to form 3-digit numbers.

So, hundred's place can be fill in 5 ways, ten's place can be fill in 5 ways and unit's place can be fill in 5 ways.

Hundred's place	Ten's place	Unit's place
5 ways	5 ways	5 ways

Thus, by the fundamental principle of multiplication, the number of ways in which the 3-digit number can be formed $= 5 \times 5 \times 5 = 125$ ways.

Hence, number of 3-digit numbers is 125.

(ii) When repetition of digit is not allowed.

Hundred's place can be fill in 5 ways.

Ten's place can be fill in 4 ways.

Unit's place can be fill in 3 ways.

Hundred's place	Ten's place	Unit's place
5 ways	4 ways	3 ways

According to FPM, total number of ways

$$= 5 \times 4 \times 3$$
$$= 60 \text{ ways}$$

Hence, number of 3-digit numbers is 60.

Example 6 In a certain city, all telephone numbers have six digits, the first two digits always being 41 or 42 or 46 or 62 or 64. How many telephone numbers have all six digits distinct?

Sol. Suppose first two digit is 41. Then we left with 8 digits, namely 0, 2, 3, 5, 6, 7, 8, 9 which can be used in constructing the telephone numbers.

Clearly, third digit can be selected in 8 ways.

Fourth digit can be selected in $8-1=7$ ways.

Fifth digit can be selected in 6 ways.

and sixth digit can be selected in 5 ways.

Now, according to fundamental principle of multiplication, number of telephone starting with 41

$$=8\times7\times6\times5=1680$$

Similarly, if the telephone number start with 42 or 46 or 62 or 64, the remaining 4 digits can be selected in 1680 ways.

Hence, total number of required telephone numbers

$$=1680\times5=8400$$

Example 7 How many numbers divisible by 5 and lying between 4000 and 5000 can be formed from the digits 2, 4, 5, 7 and 9, if

(i) repetition of digits is allowed?

(ii) repetition of digits is not allowed?

Sol. There are 5 digits *viz.* 2, 4, 5, 7 and 9.

The numbers divisible by 5 and lying between 4000 and 5000 consist of 4 digits having the digit 5 at unit's place and the digit 4 at thousand's place.

(i) If the repetition of digits is allowed, then each of hundred's place and ten's place can be filled in 5 ways.

$\therefore$ Required number of numbers $=1\times5\times5\times1=25.$

(ii) If the repetition of digits is not allowed, then hundred's place can be filled in 3 ways and ten's place in 2 ways.

$\therefore$ Required number of numbers $=1\times3\times2\times1=6.$

Example 8 In how many ways can 3 prizes be distributed among 4 boys, when

(i) no boy gets more than one prize?

(ii) a boy may get any number of prizes?

(iii) no boy gets all the prizes?

Sol. (i) The first prize can be given in 4 ways. The 2nd prize can be given in 3 ways because the boy who got the first prize cannot receive the prize.

The 3rd prize can be given to anyone of the remaining 2 boys in 2 ways.

$\therefore$ Total number of ways in which all the prizes can be given $=4\times3\times2=24$

(ii) The first prize can be given in 4 ways.

The 2nd prize can also be given in 4 ways, because it may be obtained by the boy who has already received a prize.

Similarly, 3rd prize can be given in 4 ways.

Hence, the number of ways in which all the prizes can be given $=4\times4\times4=4^3=64$

(iii) If any one of the 4 boys may get all the prizes, then, the number of ways in which all the 3 prizes given to a boy $=4$

So, the number of ways in which no boy get all the prizes $=64-4=60.$

2. Fundamental Principle of Addition (FPA)

If there are two events such that they can be performed independently in m and n ways respectively, then either of the two events can be occurred in $(m+n)$ ways.

In other words, if an operation can be performed in m different ways and another operation which is independent of the first operation, can be performed in n different ways. Then, either of the two operations can be performed in $(m+n)$ ways.

e.g. In a school, there are 200 boys and 150 girls. The teacher wants to select either a boy or a girl to represent the school in inter school competition. Here, the teacher can select a boy in 200 ways and a girl in 150 ways.

So, by fundamental principle of addition, the teacher can select a boy or a girl in $(200+150)=350$ ways.

Note The above principle can be extended to any finite number of operation.

Example 9 Find the number of different signals that can be generated by arranging atleast 2 flags in order (one below the other) on a vertical staff, if five different flags are available. **[NCERT]**

Sol. Here, we have to find number of different signals that can be generated by arranging atleast 2 flags in order. So a signal can consist of either 2 flags, 3 flags, 4 flags or 5 flags. If a signal consist of 2 flags, then two vacant places are available.

$\therefore$ Number of ways of filling first vacant place $=5$

and number of ways of filling second vacant place $=4$

Thus, total number of signals consisting 2 flags $=5\times4=20$

Now, if a signal consist of 3 flags, then three vacant places are available.

$\therefore$ Number of ways of filling first vacant place $=5$

number of ways of filling second vacant place $=4$

and number of ways of filling third vacant place $=3$

Thus, total number of signals consisting 3 flags $=5\times4\times3=60$

Similarly, total number of signals consisting 4 flags $=5\times4\times3\times2=120$

and total number of signals consisting 5 flags $=5\times4\times3\times2\times1=120$

Since, different signals can be generated by arranging either 2 flags or 3 flags or 4 flags or 5 flags.

$\therefore$ Total number of signals $=20+60+120+120$
$=320$

Example 10 How many numbers are there between 100 and 1000 which have exactly one of their digits as 7?

Sol. We have to find numbers between 100 and 1000, i.e. 3-digit numbers which have exactly one of their digits as 7. Now, consider the following cases

Case I *When 7 is at unit's place*

In this case, ten's and hundred's place can be filled by the digits 0, 1, 2, 3, 4, 5, 6, 8 and 9.

Clearly, the number of ways to fill ten's place = 9

[by anyone of the digits 0, 1, 2, 3, 4, 5, 6, 8, 9]

and the number of ways to fill the hundred's place = 8

$\therefore$ Number of such numbers $= 1\times 9\times 8 = 72$

Case II *When 7 is at ten's place*

In this case, unit's and hundred's place can be filled by the digits 0, 1, 2, 3, 4, 5, 6, 8 and 9.

Clearly, the number of ways to fill unit's place = 9

[by anyone of digits 0, 1, 2, 3, 4, 5, 6, 8, 9]

and the number of ways to fill hundred's place = 8

[$\because$ hundred's place cannot be filled by zero]

$\therefore$ Number of such numbers $= 9\times 1\times 8 = 72$

Case III *When 7 is at hundred's place*

In this case, unit's and ten's place can be filled by the digits 0, 1, 2, 3, 4, 5, 6, 8 and 9.

Clearly, the number of ways to fill unit's place = 9

[by anyone of the digits 0, 1, 2, 3, 4, 5, 6, 8, 9]

and the number of ways to fill the tens place = 9

[by anyone of the digits 0, 1, 2, 3, 4, 5, 6, 8, 9]

$\therefore$ Number of such numbers $= 1\times 9\times 9 = 81$

Hence, total number of required numbers

$= 72 + 72 + 81 = 225$

n Factorial

Many times, we come across the products of the form $1\times 2, 1\times 2\times 3, 1\times 2\times 3\times 4, \ldots$. For our convenience, we use a special notation instead of writing all the factors of such a product. We write

$$1! = 1$$
$$2! = 2\times 1$$
$$3! = 3\times 2\times 1$$
$$\vdots \quad \vdots$$
$$n! = n(n-1)(n-2)\ldots 3\cdot 2\cdot 1$$

Thus, the notation $n!$ represent the product of first n natural numbers. We read this notation as 'n factorial' and it is denoted by $n!$.

Clearly, for a natural number n,

$$n! = n(n-1)!$$
$$= n(n-1)(n-2)! \quad [\text{provided } n \geq 2]$$
$$= n(n-1)(n-2)(n-3)! \quad [\text{provided } n \geq 3]$$
$$\vdots \quad \vdots$$
$$= n(n-1)(n-2)(n-3)\ldots 3\cdot 2\cdot 1$$

e.g. $5! = 5\times 4\times 3\times 2\times 1 = 120$

and $8! = 8\times (7)! = 8\times 7\times (6!)$

Zero Factorial

It does not make any sense to define 0! as product of the integers from 1 to 0. So, we define $0! = 1$.

Note Factorial of proper fractions or negative integers are not defined. $n!$ is defined only for whole numbers, i.e. for non-negative integers.

Example 11 Compute $\frac{8!}{4!}$. Is $\frac{8!}{4!} = 2!$?

Sol. We have, $\frac{8!}{4!} = \frac{8\times 7\times 6\times 5\times 4!}{4!}$

$[\because n! = n(n-1)(n-2)\ldots 3\cdot 2\cdot 1]$

$= 8\times 7\times 6\times 5 = 1680$

Also, $2! = 2\times 1 = 2 \neq 1680$

$\therefore \frac{8!}{4!} \neq 2!$

Example 12 Evaluate $\frac{n!}{(n-r)!}$ when $r = 3$.

Sol. We have, $\frac{n!}{(n-r)!} = \frac{n!}{(n-3)!}$ $[\because r = 3, \text{ given}]$

$= \frac{n(n-1)(n-2)(n-3)!}{(n-3)!}$

$[\because n! = n(n-1)(n-2)(n-3)!]$

$= n(n-1)(n-2)$

Example 13 Convert product into factorials.

(i) $6\cdot 7\cdot 8\cdot 9\cdot 10$ (ii) $2\cdot 4\cdot 6\cdot 8\cdot 10$

Sol. (i) We have, $6\cdot 7\cdot 8\cdot 9\cdot 10 = \frac{(1\cdot 2\cdot 3\cdot 4\cdot 5)\cdot 6\cdot 7\cdot 8\cdot 9\cdot 10}{(1\cdot 2\cdot 3\cdot 4\cdot 5)}$

[multiplying numerator and denominator by $1\cdot 2\cdot 3\cdot 4\cdot 5$]

$= \frac{10!}{5!}$

(ii) We have, $2\cdot 4\cdot 6\cdot 8\cdot 10$

$= (2\times 1)\cdot(2\times 2)\cdot(2\times 3)\cdot(2\times 4)\cdot(2\times 5)$

$= 2^5\cdot(1\cdot 2\cdot 3\cdot 4\cdot 5) = 2^5\cdot 5!$

Example 14 If $\frac{1}{7!} + \frac{1}{9!} = \frac{x}{10!}$, then find x.

Sol. Given, $\frac{1}{7!} + \frac{1}{9!} = \frac{x}{10!} \Rightarrow \frac{1}{7!} + \frac{1}{9\times 8\times 7!} = \frac{x}{10\times 9\times 8\times 7!}$

$\Rightarrow \frac{1}{7!}\left(1 + \frac{1}{72}\right) = \frac{1}{7!}\left(\frac{x}{10\times 9\times 8}\right) \Rightarrow \frac{73}{72} = \frac{x}{10\times 9\times 8}$

$\therefore \quad x = \frac{73}{72}\times 10\times 9\times 8 = 730$

Example 15 If $(n+3)! = 56 \times (n+1)!$, then find n.

Sol. We have, $(n+3)! = 56 \times (n+1)!$

$\Rightarrow (n+3)(n+2)(n+1)! = 56 \times (n+1)!$

$\Rightarrow (n+3)(n+2) = 56 \quad [\because (n+1)! \neq 0]$

$\Rightarrow n^2 + 5n + 6 - 56 = 0 \Rightarrow n^2 + 5n - 50 = 0$

$\Rightarrow n^2 + 10n - 5n - 50 = 0 \Rightarrow n(n+10) - 5(n+10) = 0$

$\Rightarrow (n+10)(n-5) = 0 \Rightarrow n = 5$

[$\because n$ can't be negative, as n is a natural number]

Example 16 Prove that $\dfrac{(2n)!}{n!} = \{1 \cdot 3 \cdot 5 \ldots (2n-1)\}2^n$.

Sol. LHS $= \dfrac{(2n)!}{n!} = \dfrac{1 \cdot 2 \cdot 3 \cdot 4 \cdot 5 \ldots (2n-2)(2n-1)(2n)}{n!}$

$= \dfrac{\{1 \cdot 3 \cdot 5 \ldots (2n-1)\}\{2 \cdot 4 \cdot 6 \ldots (2n-2)(2n)\}}{n!}$

$= \dfrac{\{1 \cdot 3 \cdot 5 \ldots (2n-1)\} \cdot 2^n \{1 \cdot 2 \cdot 3 \ldots (n-1)n\}}{n!}$

$= \dfrac{\{1 \cdot 3 \cdot 5 \ldots (2n-1)\} \cdot 2^n \cdot n!}{n!} \quad [\because 1 \cdot 2 \cdot 3 \ldots (n-1)\, n = n!]$

$= \{1 \cdot 3 \cdot 5 \ldots (2n-1)\}2^n$

= RHS **Hence proved.**

Example 17 If $\dfrac{n!}{2!(n-2)!}$ and $\dfrac{n!}{4!(n-4)!}$ are in the ratio 2 : 1, then find the value of n.

Sol. We have, $\dfrac{n!}{2!(n-2)!} : \dfrac{n!}{4!(n-4)!} = 2:1$

$\Rightarrow \dfrac{n!}{2!(n-2)!} \times \dfrac{4!(n-4)!}{n!} = \dfrac{2}{1}$

$\Rightarrow \dfrac{4!(n-4)!}{2!(n-2)!} = 2$

$\Rightarrow \dfrac{4 \times 3 \times 2! \times (n-4)!}{2! \times (n-2)(n-3)(n-4)!} = 2$

$\Rightarrow \dfrac{12}{(n-2)(n-3)} = 2$

$\Rightarrow 12 = 2(n-2)(n-3)$

$\Rightarrow 12 = 2(n^2 - 5n + 6)$

$\Rightarrow 6 = n^2 - 5n + 6$

$\Rightarrow n^2 - 5n = 0 \Rightarrow n(n-5) = 0$

$\Rightarrow n = 0$ or 5

When $n = 0$, then $(n-2)!$ and $(n-4)!$ are not defined, so rejecting $n = 0$.

$\therefore n = 5$

Topic Practice 1

Very Short Answer Type Questions

(2 Marks)

1. How many AP's with 10 terms are there whose first terms is in the set {1, 2, 3} and whose common difference is in the set {1, 2, 3, 4, 5}?
2. How many words (with or without meaning) of three distinct letters of the English alphabets are there?
3. How many 2-digit even numbers can be formed from the digits 1, 2, 3, 4 and 5, if the digits can be repeated? **[NCERT]**
4. In how many ways can this diagram be coloured subject to the following two conditions.
   (i) Each of the smaller triangle is to be painted with one of three colours : red, black, green.
   (ii) No two adjacent regions have the same colour. **[NCERT Exemplar]**

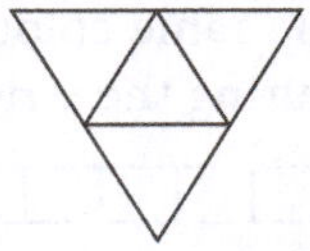

5. A gentleman has 6 friends to invite. In how many ways can he send invitation cards to them, if he has three servants to carry the cards?
6. Given 5 flags of different colours. How many different signals can be generated, if each signal requires the use of 2 flags, one below the other? **[NCERT]**
7. How many numbers are there between 100 and 1000 in which all the digits are distinct?
8. How many 4-digit numbers are there, when a digit may be repeated any number of times?
9. How many 3-digit numbers more than 600 can be formed by using the digits 2, 3, 4, 6 and 7.
10. Evaluate the following.
    (i) $4! - 3!$ (ii) $2 \times 6! - 3 \times 5!$
11. If $\dfrac{1}{8!} + \dfrac{1}{9!} = \dfrac{x}{10!}$, then find the value of x.
12. Prove that $n(n-1)(n-2)\ldots(n-r+1) = \dfrac{n!}{(n-r)!}$.
13. Convert the following products into factorials.
    $(n+1)(n+2)(n+3)\ldots(2n)$

14 Prove that $(n!) \cdot (n+2) = [n! + (n+1)!]$.

15 Find n, if $(n+2)! = 2550 \times n!$.

16 Prove that

$$\frac{n!}{(n-r)!r!} + \frac{n!}{(n-r+1)!(r-1)!} = \frac{(n+1)!}{r!(n-r+1)!}.$$

Short Answer Type Questions

4 Marks

17 Five persons entered in the lift cabin on the ground floor of an 8-floor house. Suppose each of them can leave the cabin independently at any floor beginning with the first. Find the total number of ways in which each of the five persons can leave the cabin

(i) at anyone of the 7 floor.

(ii) at different floors.

18 Each of the six squares in the strip, shown in figure, is to be coloured with anyone of 10 different colours so that no two adjacent squares have the same colour. Find the number of ways of colouring the strip.

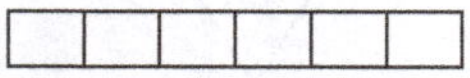

19 How many natural numbers less than 1000 can be formed with the digits 1, 2, 3, 4 and 5, if repetition of digits is allowed?

20 There are 3 candidates for Classical language, 5 for Mathematics and 4 for Natural Science scholarship.

(i) In how many ways can these scholarship be awarded?

(ii) In how many ways, one of these scholarship be awarded?

21 How many numbers greater than 1000, but not greater than 4000 can be formed with the digits 0, 1, 2, 3, 4, if

(i) repetition of digits is allowed?

(ii) repetition of digits is not allowed?

22 Prove that $\frac{(2n+1)!}{n!} = 2^n[1 \cdot 3 \cdot 5 \ldots (2n-1)(2n+1)]$.

23 If $\frac{(2n)!}{3!(2n-3)!}$ and $\frac{n!}{2!(n-2)!}$ are in the ratio 44 : 3, then find n.

Hints & Answers

1. There are 3 ways to choose the first term and corresponding to each such way, there are 5 ways of selecting the common difference. **Ans.** 15

2. There are 26 letters of English alphabet and we have to fill three places by distinct letters of English alphabet. **Ans.** 15600

3. In unit's place number, only one even number (2, 4) can be placed in 2 ways and in ten's place, anyone of the given number can be placed. **Ans.** 10

4. (i) Total ways $= 3 \times 3 \times 3 \times 3$

(ii) The given condition can be satisfied only when we paint the central triangle with any one of the three colours and remaining 3 triangles with anyone of the remaining two colours. **Ans.** (i) 81 (ii) 24

5. Since, the gentleman has 3 servants, so number of ways of sending the invitation card to the first friend $= 3$. Similarly, for each of the remaining friends, there are 3 ways each. **Ans.** $= 729$

6. First, flag can be selected in 5 ways and the second flag can be selected in 4 ways. **Ans.** 20

7. A number between 100 and 1000 has three digits. So, we need to form all possible 3-digit numbers with distinct digits. 0 cannot be placed at hundred's place, so hundred's place can be filled in 9 ways. Since, repetition of digits is not allowed, therefore each of the remaining ten's and unit's place be filled in 9 and 8 ways. **Ans.** 648

8. 0 cannot be placed at thousand's place. So, thousand's place can be filled in 9 ways. Since, repetition of digits is allowed, therefore each of the remaining 3 places can be filled in 10 ways. **Ans.** 9000

9. Digit at hundred's place will be either 6 or 7. So, hundred's place can be filled in 2 ways. Since repetition of digits is allowed, therefore each of the ten's and one's places can be filled in 5 ways. **Ans.** 50

10. (i) $4! - 3! = 4 \times 3 \times 2 \times 1 - 3 \times 2 \times 1 = 18$ (ii) 1080

11. Solve as Example 14. **Ans.** $x = 100$

12. In LHS, multiply numerator and denominator by $(n-r)!$.

13. Multiply numerator and denominator by $n!$. **Ans.** $\frac{(2n)!}{n!}$

14. Consider RHS and write it as $n! + (n+1)\,n!$.

15. Solve as Example 15.
Ans. $n = 49$

16. LHS can be written as

$$\frac{n!}{(n-r)!r\,(r-1)!} + \frac{n!}{(n-r+1)(n-r)!(r-1)!}$$

$$= \frac{n!}{(n-r)!(r-1)!}\left[\frac{1}{r} + \frac{1}{n-r+1}\right]$$

$$\left[\because (n-r+1)(n-r)! = (n-r+1)! \text{ and } (n+1)n! = (n+1)!\right]$$

17. (i) Each person can leave the cabin at anyone of the seven floors. So, each person can leave the cabin in 7 ways.

Ans. 7^5

(ii) First person can leave the cabin at anyone of the seven floors. Second person can leave the cabin at anyone of the remaining 6 floors. Similarly, we can calculate for others.

Ans. 2520

18. First square can be coloured in 10 ways (by using anyone of the given colour). Second square can be coloured in 9 ways (by using anyone of the remaining 9 colours). Third square can be coloured in 9 ways (by using anyone of the given colours except the colour used in second square). Similarly, other squares can be coloured.

Ans. 590490

19. Required numbers will be of 1-digit, 2-digit or 3-digit.

Ans. 155

20. Number of ways of awarding scholarship for Classical language = 3

Number of ways of awarding scholarship for Mathematics = 5

Number of ways of awarding scholarship for Natural Science = 4.

Ans. (i) 60 (ii) 12

21. Thousand's place can be filled either by 1 or 2 or 3, i.e. thousand's place can be filled in 3 ways.

Ans. (i) 375 (ii) 72

22. Solve as Example 16.

23. Solve as Example 17. **Ans.** $n = 6$

TOPIC 02 Permutations

A **permutation** is an arrangement of objects in a definite order. Arrangement can be made by taking some or all objects at a time.

In other words, each of the arrangements which can be made by taking some or all of a number of object is called the **permutation.**

e.g. If there are three objects say *A*, *B* and *C*, then the permutations of these three objects taking two at a time are *AB*, *BA*, *AC*, *CA BC*, *CB* and the permutations of these three objects taking all at a time are *ABC*, *ACB*, *BAC*, *BCA*, *CAB*, *CBA*.

Here, in each case, number of permutations is 6.

Note that the order of arrangement is important. Because when the order is changed, then different permutation is obtained.

Permutations When all the Objects are Distinct (Different)

When all given objects are distinct, then we can find the number of permutations with the help of following theorem

Theorem 1. The number of permutations of n different objects taken r at a time, where $0 < r \le n$ and the objects do not repeat, is $n(n-1)(n-2) \ldots (n-r+1)$, which is denoted by ^nP_r or $P(n, r)$.

i.e. $$P(n, r) = {}^nP_r = \frac{n!}{(n-r)!}, 0 \le r \le n$$

In particular,

(i) When $r = 0$, then $^nP_0 = \dfrac{n!}{(n-0)!} = \dfrac{n!}{n!} = 1$

(ii) When $r = n$, then

$$^nP_n = \frac{n!}{(n-n)!} = \frac{n!}{0!} = n! \qquad [\because 0! = 1]$$

Note The number of permutations of n different things taken all at a time = $n!$

Example 1 Find the values of the following.

(i) $^6P_4$ (ii) $P(15, 2)$

Sol. We know that, $^nP_r = P(n, r) = \dfrac{n!}{(n-r)!}$

(i) $^6P_4 = \dfrac{6!}{(6-4)!} = \dfrac{6!}{2!} = \dfrac{6 \times 5 \times 4 \times 3 \times 2!}{2!}$

$= 6 \times 5 \times 4 \times 3 = 360$

(ii) $P(15, 2) = {}^{15}P_2 = \dfrac{15!}{(15-2)!} = \dfrac{15!}{13!} = \dfrac{15 \times 14 \times 13!}{13!}$

$= 15 \times 14 = 210$

Example 2 If $P(9, r) = 3024$, then find r.

Sol. We have, $P(9, r) = 3024 \Rightarrow {}^9P_r = 3024$

$\Rightarrow \dfrac{9!}{(9-r)!} = 3024 \Rightarrow \dfrac{9!}{(9-r)!} = 9 \times 336$

$\Rightarrow \dfrac{9!}{(9-r)!} = 9 \times 8 \times 7 \times 6$

$\Rightarrow \dfrac{9!}{(9-r)!} = \dfrac{9 \times 8 \times 7 \times 6 \times 5!}{5!}$

[multiplying numerator and denominator by 5!]

$$\Rightarrow \frac{9!}{(9-r)!} = \frac{9!}{5!} \Rightarrow (9-r)! = 5!$$

On comparing, we get

$$9 - r = 5 \Rightarrow r = 4$$

Example 3 If ${}^9P_5 + 5 \cdot {}^9P_4 = {}^{10}P_r$, then find r.

Sol. We have, ${}^9P_5 + 5 \cdot {}^9P_4 = {}^{10}P_r$

$$\Rightarrow \frac{9!}{(9-5)!} + 5 \cdot \frac{9!}{(9-4)!} = \frac{10!}{(10-r)!}$$

$$\Rightarrow \frac{9!}{4!} + 5 \cdot \frac{9!}{5!} = \frac{10!}{(10-r)!}$$

$$\Rightarrow \frac{9!}{4!} + 5 \cdot \frac{9!}{5 \times 4!} = \frac{10 \times 9!}{(10-r)!}$$

[dividing both sides by 9!]

$$\Rightarrow \frac{1}{4!} + \frac{1}{4!} = \frac{10}{(10-r)!} \Rightarrow \frac{2}{4!} = \frac{10}{(10-r)!}$$

$$\Rightarrow (10-r)! = 5 \times 4! = 5! \Rightarrow (10-r)! = 5!$$

On comparing, we get $10 - r = 5 \Rightarrow r = 5$

Example 4 If $P(2n-1, n) : P(2n+1, n-1) = 22 : 7$, find n.

Sol. We have, ${}^{2n-1}P_n : {}^{2n+1}P_{n-1} = 22 : 7$

$$\Rightarrow \frac{\frac{(2n-1)!}{(2n-1-n)!}}{\frac{(2n+1)!}{(2n+1-n+1)!}} = \frac{22}{7}$$

$$\Rightarrow \frac{(2n-1)!}{(n-1)!} \times \frac{(n+2)!}{(2n+1)!} = \frac{22}{7}$$

$$\Rightarrow \frac{(2n-1)!}{(n-1)!} \times \frac{(n+2)(n+1)n(n-1)!}{(2n+1)(2n)(2n-1)!} = \frac{22}{7}$$

$$\Rightarrow \frac{(n+2)(n+1)n}{(2n+1)(2n)} = \frac{22}{7} \Rightarrow \frac{(n+1)(n+2)}{2(2n+1)} = \frac{22}{7}$$

$$\Rightarrow 7(n^2 + 3n + 2) = 44(2n+1)$$

$$\Rightarrow 7n^2 + 21n + 14 = 88n + 44$$

$$\Rightarrow 7n^2 - 67n - 30 = 0$$

$$\Rightarrow 7n^2 - 70n + 3n - 30 = 0$$

$$\Rightarrow 7n(n-10) + 3(n-10) = 0$$

$$\Rightarrow (n-10)(7n+3) = 0$$

$$\Rightarrow n = 10 \text{ or } n = \frac{-3}{7}$$

$$\therefore \quad n = 10 \quad [\because n \text{ cannot be negative}]$$

Example 5 Prove that

$$P(n, r) = P(n-1, r) + r \cdot P(n-1, r-1).$$

Sol. RHS $= P(n-1, r) + r \cdot P(n-1, r-1)$

$$= \frac{(n-1)!}{(n-1-r)!} + r \cdot \frac{(n-1)!}{(n-1-r+1)!}$$

$$= \frac{(n-1)!}{(n-r-1)!} + r \cdot \frac{(n-1)!}{(n-r)!}$$

$$= \frac{(n-1)!}{(n-r-1)!} + \frac{r \cdot (n-1)!}{(n-r)(n-r-1)!}$$

$$= \frac{(n-1)!}{(n-r-1)!}\left[1 + \frac{r}{n-r}\right] = \frac{(n-1)!}{(n-r-1)!}\left[\frac{n-r+r}{(n-r)}\right]$$

$$= \frac{n(n-1)!}{(n-r)(n-r-1)!} = \frac{n!}{(n-r)!}$$

$= P(n, r) =$ LHS **Hence proved.**

Applications on Permutations

Here, we will discuss some simple practical problems, where the formula for ${}^nP_r$ and its meaning can be applicable.

Example 6 In how many ways can 6 persons occupy 4 vacants seats?

Sol. Required number of ways is same as number of permutations of 6 different things taken 4 at a time.

Hence, required number of ways

$$= {}^6P_4 = \frac{6!}{(6-4)!} = \frac{6!}{2!}$$

$$= 6 \times 5 \times 4 \times 3 = 360$$

Example 7 How many 3-digit numbers can be formed by using the digits 1 to 9, if no digit is repeated?

Sol. Required number of 3-digit numbers is same as number of permutations of 9 different things taken 3 at a time.

Hence, total number of 3-digit numbers $= {}^9P_3$

$$= \frac{9!}{(9-3)!} = \frac{9!}{6!} = \frac{9 \times 8 \times 7 \times 6!}{6!} = 504$$

Example 8 From a committee of 8 persons, in how many ways can we choose a chairman and a vice-chairman assuming one person can not hold more than one position? **[NCERT]**

Sol. Since, a person cannot hold more than one position, therefore required number of ways is same as number of permutations of 8 different things taken 2 at a time.

Hence, required number of ways $= {}^8P_2$

$$= \frac{8!}{(8-2)!}$$

$$= \frac{8!}{6!} = \frac{8 \times 7 \times 6!}{6!} = 56$$

Example 9 How many words, with or without meaning can be made from the letters of the word 'MONDAY,' assuming that no letter is repeated, if

(i) 4 letters are used at a time?

(ii) all letters are used at a time? **[NCERT]**

Sol. Here, word 'MONDAY' contains 6 distinct letters.

(i) Required number of words = Number of permutations of 6 different things taken 4 at a time

$$= {}^6P_4 = \frac{6!}{2!} = \frac{6 \times 5 \times 4 \times 3 \times 2!}{2!} = 360$$

(ii) Required number of words = Number of permutations of 6 different things taken all at a time

$$= {}^6P_6 = 6! = 720$$

Example 10 How many different signals can be made by using any number of flags from 6 flags of different colours? **[NCERT Exemplar]**

Sol. Clearly, the signals can be made by using one or two or three or four or five or six flags.

Now, number of signals when one flag is used at a time = ${}^6P_1$.

Number of signals when two flags are used at a time = ${}^6P_2$.

Similarly, number of signals when three, four, five, six flags are used at a time are ${}^6P_3$, ${}^6P_4$, ${}^6P_5$, ${}^6P_6$, respectively.

Hence, by fundamental principle of addition, total number of signals formed from 6 flags of different colours = ${}^6P_1 + {}^6P_2 + {}^6P_3 + {}^6P_4 + {}^6P_5 + {}^6P_6$

$$= \frac{6!}{(6-1)!} + \frac{6!}{(6-2)!} + \frac{6!}{(6-3)!} + \frac{6!}{(6-4)!} + \frac{6!}{(6-5)!} + \frac{6!}{(6-6)!}$$

$$= \frac{6!}{5!} + \frac{6!}{4!} + \frac{6!}{3!} + \frac{6!}{2!} + \frac{6!}{1!} + \frac{6!}{0!}$$

$$= 6 + 6 \times 5 + 6 \times 5 \times 4 + 6 \times 5 \times 4 \times 3 + 6 \times 5 \times 4 \times 3 \times 2 + 6!$$

$$= 6 + 30 + 120 + 360 + 720 + 720 = 1956$$

Permutations of Repeated Objects

When repetition of objects is allowed, then number of permutations can be obtained with the help of following theorem.

***Theorem* 2.** The number of permutation of n different objects taken r at a time, when each may be repeated any number of times in each arrangement, is n^r (permutation with repetitions).

Note The number of permutations of n different objects, all at a time, when each may be repeated any number of times in each arrangement, is n^n.

Example 11 In how many ways, 3 prizes can be given to 7 boys when each boy is eligible for any of the prizes?

Sol. Here, three prizes can be given to the same boy but two boys cannot get the same prize. Thus, boys can be repeated. So, here we have $n = 7$ and $r = 3$.

Hence, required number of ways = $7^3 = 343$.

Example 12 How many 4-digit numbers can be formed with the digits 1, 2, 3, 4, 5, 6 when a digit may be repeated any number of times in any arrangement?

Sol. Required number of numbers is same as number of permutation of 6 different things taken 4 at a time, when a digit may be repeated any number of times.

Hence, required number of numbers = $6^4 = 1296$.

Example 13 Find the number of 5-digit telephone numbers having atleast one of their digits repeated. **[NCERT Exemplar]**

Sol. Using the digits 0, 1, 2, ..., 9, the number of 5-digits telephone numbers which can be formed is 10^5 (since, repetition is allowed).

The number of 5-digits telephone numbers, which have none of the digits repeated = ${}^{10}P_5 = \frac{10!}{5!} = 30240$

Hence, the required number of telephone numbers having atleast one of their digits repeated

$$= 10^5 - {}^{10}P_5$$

$$= 100000 - 30240$$

$$= 69760$$

Permutations When all the Objects are not Distinct

When all the objects are not distinct, i.e. some objects are of same kind, then we can find the number of permutations with the help of following theorems (without proof).

Theorem 3. The number of permutations of n objects, where p objects are of the same kind or identical and other are distinct, is given by $\frac{n!}{p!}$.

Example 14 How many permutations of the letters of the words 'INDIA' are there?

Sol. Here, we have 5 letters, two of which are of the same kind and others are different.

∴ Required number of permutations (or arrangements)

$$= \frac{5!}{2!} = 5 \times 4 \times 3 = 60$$

Permutations of alike objects

***Theorem* 4.** The number of permutations of n objects, where p_1 objects are of one kind, p_2 are of second kind, … p_k are of kth kind and the rest if any, are of different kind is $\frac{n!}{p_1!\,p_2!\ldots p_k!}$.

Example 15 Find the number of permutations of the letters of the word 'INDEPENDENCE'.

Sol. Here, we have 12 letters of which 3 are N's, 4 are E's, 2 are D's and rest are different.

$\therefore$ Required number of permutations $= \dfrac{12!}{3!4!2!}$

[here, $n = 12$, $p_1 = 3$, $p_2 = 4$ and $p_3 = 2$]

$$= \frac{12 \times 11 \times 10 \times 9 \times 8 \times 7 \times 6 \times 5 \times 4!}{6 \times 2 \times 4!}$$

$$= 11 \times 10 \times 9 \times 8 \times 7 \times 6 \times 5$$
$$= 1663200$$

Example 16 In how many ways, 5 flags in which 3 are red, 1 is white and 1 is blue, be arranged on a staff, one below the other, if flags of one colour are not distinguishable?

Sol. Since, out of 5 flags, 3 are of the same kind (red) and others are different.

$\therefore$ Required number of ways $= \dfrac{5!}{3!1!1!} = 5 \times 4 = 20$

Restricted Permutations

Here, we will discuss permutations of objects under certain conditions, e.g. permutation when certain objects occur together, when position of particular objects are fixed, when a particular object occurs in every arrangement etc.

|Type I|

When Certain Things always Occur Together

Example 17 In how many of the permutations of 9 things taken 4 at a time will one thing always occur?

Sol. Keeping aside the particular thing which will always occur, the number of permutations of 8 things taken 3 at a time is ${}^8P_3$. Now, this particular thing can take up any one of the four places and so can be arranged in 4 ways. Hence, the total number of permutations

$$= {}^8P_3 \times 4 = 8 \times 7 \times 6 \times 4 = 1344$$

Example 18 In how many of the permutations of n things taken r at a time will 5 things always occur?

Sol. Keeping a side the 5 things, the number of permutations of $(r-5)$ things taken out of $(n-5)$ things is ${}^{n-5}P_{r-5}$.

Now these 5 things can be arranged in r places in ${}^rP_5$ ways. Hence, the total number of permutations is ${}^rP_5 \times {}^{n-5}P_{r-5}$.

|Type II|

When Certain Things never Occur

Case **I.** *When the number of things not occuring together is two.*

Example 19 Find the number of ways in which n books can be placed an a shelf when two particular books are never together.

Sol. Regarding the two particular books as one book, there are $(n-1)$ books now which can be arranged in ${}^{n-1}P_{n-1}$, i.e. $(n-1)!$ ways. Now, these two books can be arranged amongst themselves in 2! ways. Hence, the total number of permutations in which these two books are placed together is $2!.(n-1)!$. The number of permutations of n books without any restriction is $n!$.

Therefore, the number of arrangements in which these two books never occur together

$$= n! - 2! \cdot (n-1)! = n \cdot (n-1)! - 2 \cdot (n-1)! = (n-2) \cdot (n-1)!$$

Case **II.** *When the number of things not occuring together is more than two.*

Example 20 In how many ways can 5 boys and 3 girls be arranged in a straight line so that no two girls are ever together?

Sol. The seating arrangement may be done as desired in two operations.

(i) First we fix the positions of 5 boys. Their positions are indicated by B_1 B_2, ..., B_5.

$$\times B_1 \times B_2 \times B_3 \times B_4 \times B_5 \times$$

This can be done in 5! ways.

(ii) Now, if the positions of girls are fixed at places (including those at the two ends) shown by the crosses, the 3 girls will never come together. In any one of these arrangements there are 6 places for 3 girls and so the girls can sit in ${}^6P_3$ ways.

Hence, the required number of ways of seating 5 boys and 3 girls under the given condition

$$= {}^5P_3 \times 5!$$
$$= 5 \times 4 \times 3 \times 5 \times 4 \times 3 \times 2 \times 1 = 7200$$

Some Important Results

(i) If r particular things out of n different things are to be together, then we count these r particular things as one things and remaining $(n-r)$ things as separate things.

Then, total number of things $= (n-r)+1 = n-r+1$.

Since, these are different things, therefore number of permutations of these things $= (n-r+1)!$.

But r particular things can also be arrange among themselves in $r!$ ways.

$\therefore$ Required number of permutations $= (n - r + 1)!\, r!$

Note If r particular things are identical, then required number of permutations $= (n - r + 1)!$

(ii) The number of permutations of n objects taken r at a time, when a particular object is taken in each arrangement, is $r \cdot {}^{n-1}P_{r-1}$.

(iii) The number of permutations of n objects taken r at a time, when a particular object is never taken in each arrangement, is ${}^{n-1}P_r$.

(iv) The number of permutations of n different objects taken r at a time in which two specific objects always occur together, is $2!\,(r-1) \cdot {}^{n-2}P_{r-2}$.

Restricted Permutation When all the Objects are Distinct

Example 21 Find the number of different words that can be formed from the letters of the word 'TRIANGLE', so that
(i) all vowels occur together.
(ii) all vowels do not occur together.

Sol. There are 8 distinct letters in the word TRIANGLE, out of which 3 are vowels, namely A, E, I and 5 are consonants, namely T, R, N, G, L.

(i) Since, the vowels have to occur together, so let us assume them as a single object (AEI).

[A E I] T, R, N, G, L

Now, this single object together with 5 remaining letters will be counted as 6 objects and these can be arrange in ${}^6P_6 = 6!$ ways.

Corresponding to each of these permutations, we have $3! = 6$ permutations of the three vowels A, E and I taken all at a time.

Hence, by fundamental principle of multiplication, the required number of words $= 6! \times 3! = 4320$

(ii) Clearly, required number of words = Number of all possible arrangements of 8 letters taken all at a time − Number of permutation in which the vowels are always together

$= {}^8P_8 - 6! \times 3! = 8! - 6! \times 3!$

$= 8 \times 7 \times 6! - 6! \times 3! = 6!\,(56 - 6)$

$= 720 \times 50 = 36000$

Example 22 How many words, with or without meaning, can be formed using all the letters of the word EQUATION at a time so that the vowels and consonant occurs together? **[NCERT]**

Sol. There are 8 distinct letters in the word EQUATION, out of which 5 are vowels, namely A, E, I, O, U and 3 are consonants namely Q, T, N.

Now, let us take all vowels together as one object and all consonants together as another object.

(A, E, I, O, U) (Q, T, N)

Clearly, these objects can be arranged in $2! = 2$ ways.

Again, all vowels taken together can be arranged in $5! = 120$ ways and all consonants taken together can be arranged in $3! = 6$ ways.

Hence, by fundamental principle of multiplication required number of words $= 2 \times 5! \times 3!$

$= 2 \times 120 \times 6$

$= 1440$

Example 23 In how many ways, can 8 Indians, 4 Americans and 4 Englishmen be seated in a row so that all persons of the same nationality sit together?

Sol. Let us take persons of same nationality as one unit. Then, there are 3 units which can be arranged in $3! = 6$ ways. Now, in each of arrangements, 8 Indians can be arranged among themselves in 8! ways, 4 Americans can be arranged among themselves in 4! ways and 4 Englishmen can be arranged among themselves in 4! ways.

Hence, by fundamental principle of multiplication, required number of ways $= 3! \times 8! \times 4! \times 4!$.

Example 24 All the letters of the word 'EAMCOT' are arranged in different possible ways. Find the number of such arrangements in which no two vowels are adjacent to each other. **[NCERT Exemplar]**

Sol. There are 3 consonants and 3 vowels.

Since, no two vowels can occur together, therefore the possible choices for vowels are the places marked as '×'.

$\times M \times C \times T \times$

Clearly, the vowels can be arranged in ${}^4P_3$ ways and the consonants can be arranged in 3! ways. Hence, by fundamental principle of multiplication, required

number of ways $= {}^4P_3 \times 3! = \dfrac{4!}{1!} \times 3! = 24 \times 6 = 144$

Example 25 The letters of the word 'TUESDAY' are arranged in a line, each arrangement ending with letter S. How many different arrangements are possible? How many of them start with letter D?

Sol. Here, the given word contains 7 letters. Since, all words must end with S, so we fix S at last place. Now, remaining 6 letters can be arranged in $P(6, 6) = 6!$ ways.

$\therefore$ Total number of words $= 6! = 6 \times 5 \times 4 \times 3 \times 2 \times 1 = 720$

If the words begin with D and end with S, we fix D at the first place and S at the last place. Now, remaining 5 letters can be arranged in $P(5, 5) = 5!$

$= 5 \times 4 \times 3 \times 2 \times 1$

$= 120$ ways

$\therefore$ Required number of words $= 120$

Example 26 Find the number of ways in which 5 boys and 5 girls be seated in a row, so that

(i) no two girls sit together.

(ii) boys and girls sit alternatively. **[NCERT Exemplar]**

Sol. We have 5 boys and 5 girls.

(i) Since, no two girls sit together, therefore the possible choices for girls are the places marked as '×'.

$$\times B_1 \times B_2 \times B_3 \times B_4 \times B_5 \times$$

Clearly, the girls can be arranged in ${}^6P_5$ ways and the boys can be arranged in 5! ways.

Hence, by fundamental principle of multiplication, required number of ways $= {}^6P_5 \times 5!$

$$= \frac{6!}{(6-5)!} \times 5! = 6! \times 5! = 86400$$

(ii) Let us first seat the 5 girls (or 5 boys). This can be done in 5! ways.

Now, for each such arrangement, the 5 boys can be seated only at the cross marked place as shown below:

(I) $\times G_1 \times G_2 \times G_3 \times G_4 \times G_5$

(II) $G_1 \times G_2 \times G_3 \times G_4 \times G_5 \times$

In case I, 5 boys can be seated in ${}^5P_5 = 5!$ ways

Thus, number of ways of seating $= 5! \times 5! = (5!)^2$

Similarly, in case II, number of ways of seating $= (5!)^2$

Hence, required number of ways $= (5!)^2 + (5!)^2$

$$= 2 \cdot (5!)^2 = 28800$$

Finding the Number of Numbers having Distinct Digits which are Formed under Certain Conditions

For solving this type of problem, we used the following steps

Step I First, decide that from how many digits the required number will be formed.

Step II Fill up the places on which restrictions are present and let the number of ways of filling up these places be k.

Step III Find the number of ways of filling the remaining places with remaining digits by using the formula ${}^nP_r$.

Step IV Required number of numbers is $k \cdot {}^nP_r$.

Example 27 How many numbers between 400 and 1000 can be made with the digits 2, 3, 4, 5, 6 and 0, when repetition of digits is not allowed?

Sol. Given digits are, 2, 3, 4, 5, 6 and 0.

Any number between 400 and 1000 will be of three digits.

Since, the number should be greater than 400.

Therefore, hundred's place can be filled up by anyone of the digits 4, 5 and 6 in 3 ways.

$$\therefore \quad k = 3$$

Now, remaining two places can be filled up by the remaining five digits in ${}^5P_2$ ways.

Hence, required numbers $= 3 \times {}^5P_2 = 3 \times \frac{5!}{3!} = 60$

Example 28 How many different 4-digit numbers can be formed from the digits 2, 3, 4 and 6, if each digit is used only once in a number? Further, how many of these numbers

(i) end at 4? (ii) end at 3? (iii) end at 3 or 4?

Sol. The number of 4-digit numbers formed by the digits 2, 3, 4 and 6

$$= P(4, 4) = \frac{4!}{(4-4)!} = \frac{4!}{0!} \quad \left[\because {}^nP_r = \frac{n!}{(n-r)!}\right]$$

$$= \frac{4!}{1} = 4 \times 3 \times 2 \times 1 = 24 \quad [\because 0! = 1]$$

(i) In this case, '4' is fixed at the unit's place. Therefore, remaining 3-digits can be 2, 3 and 6. Hence, the required number of 4-digits number $= P(3, 3)$

$$= \frac{3!}{(3-3)!} \quad \left[\because {}^nP_r = \frac{n!}{(n-r)!}\right]$$

$$= \frac{3!}{0!} = 3 \times 2 \times 1 = 6 \quad \text{...(i)}$$

(ii) In this case, '3' is fixed at unit's place. Therefore, remaining 3-digits can be 2, 4 and 6. Hence, the required number of 4-digits numbers $= P(3, 3)$

$$= \frac{3!}{0!} = 6 \quad \text{...(ii)}$$

(iii) Number of 4-digit numbers ending with either 3 or 4 $= 6 + 6 = 12$ [from Eqs. (i) and (ii)]

Restricted Permutation When all the Objects are not Distinct

Example 29 In how many different ways, the letters of the word 'ALGEBRA' can be arranged in a row, if

(i) the two A's are together?

(ii) the two A's are not together?

Sol. There are 7 letters in the word ALGEBRA. In these letters, 'A' occurs twice and rest all are different.

(i) Since, two A's are always together, so let us consider two A's as one letter.

[AA], L, G, E, B, R

Now, we have 6 letters, which can be arranged in ${}^6P_6 = 6!$ ways

Hence, required number of ways $= 6! = 720$

[$\because$ two A's can be arranged among themselves in one way only]

(ii) Required number of ways = Number of all possible arrangements of the letters of the word ALGEBRA − Number of arrangements in which two A's are together

$$= \frac{7!}{2!} - 6! = 6!\left(\frac{7}{2} - 1\right) = 720 \times \frac{5}{2}$$

$$= 360 \times 5 = 1800$$

Example 30 Find the number of different words that can be formed from the letters of the word 'INTERMEDIATE' such that two vowels never come together.

[NCERT Exemplar]

Sol. There are 12 letters in the word INTERMEDIATE.

In these letters, I occurs twice, T occurs twice, E occurs thrice and rest all are distinct. Also the word INTERMEDIATE contains 6 vowels I, I, E, E, E and A.

Since, two vowels never come together, therefore possible choices for vowels are the places marked with '×'.

$$\times N \times T \times R \times M \times D \times T \times$$

Clearly, number of ways of arranging vowels

$$= {}^7P_6 \times \frac{1}{3!} \times \frac{1}{2!}$$

[$\because$ E occurs three times and I occurs two times]

and number of ways of arranging 6 consonants of which two are alike $= \frac{6!}{2!}$

Hence, required number of words

$$= {}^7P_6 \times \frac{1}{3!} \times \frac{1}{2!} \times \frac{6!}{2!} = \frac{7! \times 6!}{3! \times 2! \times 2!} = 151200$$

Example 31 How many numbers can be formed with the digits 1, 2, 3, 4, 3, 2 and 1, so that odd digits always occupy the odd places?

Sol. The given digits are 1, 2, 3, 4, 3, 2, 1. Out of these, 1, 3, 3, 1 are odd digits.

Since, there are 4 odd places, therefore odd digits can occupy the odd places in ${}^4P_4 \times \frac{1}{2!} \times \frac{1}{2!} = \frac{4!}{2!\,2!} = 6$ ways.

Now, we left with 3 places in which remaining 3 digits (2, 2 and 1) can be arranged in ${}^3P_3 \times \frac{1}{2!} = \frac{3!}{2!} = 3$ ways

Hence, required number of numbers $= 6 \times 3 = 18$

Example 32 In how many ways can the letters of the word 'PERMUTATIONS' be arranged, if

(i) word start with P and end with S.

(ii) vowels are all together. **[NCERT]**

Sol. There are 12 letters in the word PERMUTATIONS.

In these letters, T occurs twice and rest all are different. Also, the word PERMUTATIONS contains all the five vowels, namely, A, E, I, O and U.

(i) Since, the word start with P and end with S, so let us fix P at first place and S at last place.

P	I	II	III	IV	V	VI	VII	VIII	IX	X	S

Now, we left with 10 letters (E, R, M, U, T, A, T, I, O, N) which can be arranged in $\frac{10!}{2!}$ ways.

[$\because$ T occurs twice]

Hence, required number of ways $= \frac{10!}{2!} = 1814400$

(ii) Since, the vowels are occur together, so let us take all vowels together and consider it as one letter.

$\boxed{AEIOU}$, P, R, M, T, T, N, S

Now, we have 8 letters, which can be arranged in $\frac{8!}{2!}$ ways. Corresponding to each such arrangement, all the five vowels can be arranged among themselves in ${}^5P_5 = 5!$ ways.

Hence, required number of ways $= \frac{8!}{2!} \times 5! = 2419200$

Circular Permutations

If we arrange the objects along a closed curve *viz.* a circle, the permutations are known as circular permutations. As we have seen that every linear arrangement has a beginning and an end, but there is nothing like beginning or end in a circular permutation. Thus, in a circular permutation, we consider one object as fixed and the remaining objects are arranged as in case of linear arrangements.

Theorem. *The number of circular permutations of n distinct objects is* $(n-1)!$.

Clockwise and Counter-clockwise Permutations

Consider the following circular permutations

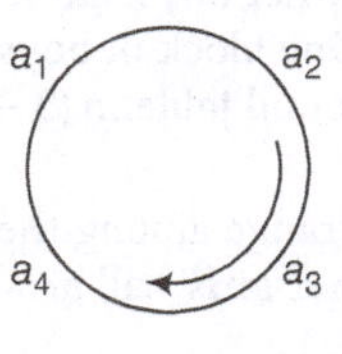

Clockwise
Fig. 1

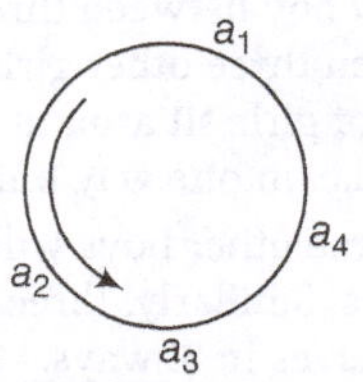

Counter-clockwise
Fig. 2

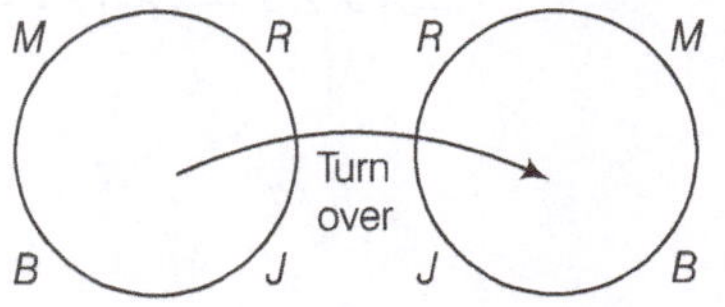

Fig. 3

We observe that in both, the order of the circular arrangement is a_1, a_2, a_3, a_4. In Fig 1. the order is clockwise where as in Fig 2. the order is counter-clockwise (or anticlockwise). Thus, the number of circular permutations of n things in which clockwise and anticlockwise arrangements give rise to different permutations is $(n-1)!$.

If anticlockwise and clockwise order of arrangements are not distinct e.g. arrangements of beads in a necklace, arrangements of flowers in a garland etc., then the number of circular permutations of n distinct items is $\frac{1}{2}(n-1)!$.

Example 33

(i) In how many ways can a party of 4 boys and 4 girls be seated at a circular table so that no 2 boys are sit together?

(ii) In how many ways can 10 boys and 5 girls sit around a circular table, so that no two girls sit together?

Sol. (i) Let the girls first take up their seats. They can sit in 3! ways. When they have been seated, then there remain 4 places for the boys each between two girls. Therefore, the boys can sit in 4! ways. Therefore, there are $3! \times 4!$, i.e. 144 ways of seating the party.

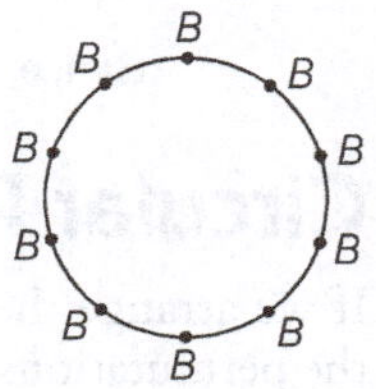

(ii) Let B denote the position of the boys around the table. 10 boys can be seated around the table in 9! ways. There are 10 spaces between the boys, which can be occupied by 5 girls in ${}^{10}P_5$ ways.

Hence, total number of ways $= 9! \times {}^{10}P_5 = \frac{9!10!}{5!}$.

Example 34 Four boys and four girls go out for dinner. A shy boy does not want to sit with any girl and a shy girl does not want any boy as a neighbour. How many seating arrangements are possible?

Sol. Fix shy boy between three other boys and fix shy girls between three other girls. One block of boys and one block of girls sit around a round table in $(3-1)! = 2!$ ways, i.e. in one way only.

But three other boys will arrange among themselves in 3! ways. Similarly, three other girls will arrange among themselves in 3! ways.

Hence, the required number of ways

$$= 2! \times 3! \times 3! = 2 \times 6 \times 6 = 72$$

Example 35

(i) In how many ways can 5 beads of different colours form a necklace?

(ii) In how many ways can a garland be formed from 5 similar marigolds and 6 roses all of different colours?

Sol. (i) Here, we are to form circular permutations of 5 things taken all at a time but there clockwise and anti-clockwise permutations are same.

Hence, the required number of ways $= \frac{1}{2}(5-1)!$

$$= \frac{1}{2}(4)! = \frac{1}{2} \times 24 = 12$$

(ii) A garland from 11 different flowers can be made in $\frac{1}{2}(11-1)! = \frac{1}{2}(10)!$ ways. However, as 5 marigolds all colours are alike, the required number of ways

$$= \frac{1}{2} \cdot \frac{10!}{5!} = \frac{10 \times 9 \times 8 \times 7 \times 6}{2} = 15120$$

Topic Practice 2

Very Short Answer Type Questions

(2 Marks)

1 Evaluate (i) ${}^{75}P_2$ (ii) ${}^{8}P_8$.

2 If ${}^{n}P_4 = 360$, then find the value of n.

3 If ${}^{n}P_4 : {}^{n}P_5 = 1:2$, then find n.

4 In how many ways can the letters of the word 'GOLDEN' be arranged so that N and E are always together.

5 In how many ways can the letters of the word 'PENCIL' be arranged so that N is always next to E?

6 Find the number of different words that can be formed with the letters of the word 'ENGLISH' so that the word begin with E and end with I?

7 How many 3-digit even numbers can be made using the digits 1, 2, 3, 4, 5, 6, 7, if no digits is repeated?

8 In how many ways 3 Mathematics books, 4 History books, 3 Chemistry books and 2 Biology books can be arranged on a shelf so that all books of the same subjects are together? **[NCERT Exemplar]**

9 Find the number of different words that can be formed from the letters of the word 'TRIANGLE' so that no vowels are together.

10 In how many ways can 5 girls and 3 boys be seated in a row so that no two boys are together? **[NCERT]**

11 Find the number of ways in which the letters of the word 'MACHINE' can be arranged so that the vowels occupy the odd places.

Short Answer Type Questions

4 Marks

12 If ${}^{10}P_r = 5040$, then find the value of r.

13 Find r, if $5 \cdot {}^4P_r = 6 \cdot {}^5P_{r-1}$.

14 If ${}^{n-1}P_3 : {}^{n+1}P_3 = 5 : 12$, then find n.

15 If ${}^{22}P_{r+1} : {}^{20}P_{r+2} = 11 : 52$, then find r.

16 Prove the following.

(i) ${}^nP_n = 2 \cdot {}^nP_{n-2}$ (ii) ${}^nP_n = {}^nP_{n-1}$

(iii) ${}^nP_r = n \cdot {}^{n-1}P_{r-1}$

17 How many numbers lying between 100 and 1000 can be formed with the digits 1, 2, 3, 4 and 5, if the repetition of digits is not allowed?

18 Find the number of 4-digit numbers that can be formed with the digits 2, 3, 4, 7 and using each digit only once.

19 In how many ways can 18 people line up at a ticket window of a cinema hall?

20 How many words, with or without meaning can be formed using all the letters of the word EQUATION, using each letter exactly once? **[NCERT]**

21 Find the number of different 4-letter words, with or without meaning that can be formed from the letters of the word 'NUMBER'.

22 How many different signals can be made by 5 flags from 8 flags of different colours?

23 From a committee of 12 persons, in how many ways can we choose a chairman and a vice-chairman assuming one person can not hold more than one position?

24 Sunil wants to arrange 3 Economics, 2 History and 4 Language books on a shelf. If the books of the same subject are different. Determine the number of all possible arrangements.

25 In how many ways can 4 red, 3 yellow and 2 green discs be arranged in a row if the discs of the same colour are indistinguishable?

26 How many 4-digit numbers are there with no digit repeated? **[NCERT]**

27 In how many ways can 7 plus (+) signs and 5 minus (–) signs be arranged in a row so that no two minus signs are together?

28 How many different words can be formed with the letters of the word SUNDAY? How many of these begin with N? How many begin N and end in Y?

29 In how many ways can the letters of the word 'MATHEMATICS' be arranged so that vowels are always together?

30 (i) In how many ways can 10 people sit around a table so that all will not have the same neighbours in any two arrangements?

(ii) In how many ways can 20 persons be seated round a table if there are 9 chairs?

Long Answer Type Questions

6 Marks

31 If x denotes the number of permutations of $(n+2)$ things taken all at a time, y denotes the number of permutations of n things taken 12 at a time and z denotes the number of permutation of $n-12$ things taken all at a time such that $x = 132yz$, find the value of n.

32 Ten different letters of English alphabet are given. Words with five letters are formed from these given letters. Find the number of words which have atleast one letter repeated.

33 Find the number of different 8 letters arrangements that can be made from the letters of the word 'DAUGHTER', so that

(i) all vowels occur together.

(ii) all vowels do not occur together.

34 How many numbers lying between 100 and 1000 can be formed with the digits 0, 1, 2, 3, 4, 5, if the repetition of the digits is not allowed? **[NCERT]**

35 How many different words can be formed with the letters of the word 'HARYANA'? How many of these
(i) have H and N together?
(ii) begin with H and end with N?
(iii) have three vowels together?

36 Three married couples are to be seated in a row having six seats in a cinema halls. If spouses are to be seated next to each other, in how many ways can they be seated? Also, find the number of ways of their seating, if all the ladies sit together. **[NCERT Exemplar]**

37 Find the number of ways in which 5 boys and 5 girls be seated in a row, so that
(i) all the girls sit together.
(ii) all the girls and all the boys sit together.
(iii) all the girls are never sit together.

Hints & Answers

1. Solve as Example 1. **Ans.** (i) 5550 (ii) 40320
2. Write the given equation as $n(n-1)(n-2)(n-3) = 6\times5\times4\times3 = 6(6-1)(6-2)(6-3)$ and then compare it. **Ans.** $n=6$
3. Solve as Example 2. **Ans.** $n=6$
4. 240
5. Here, we consider E and N together as one unit. **Ans.** 120
6. 120
7. For even numbers, even number should be placed on unit (2, 4, 6)
$\therefore$ 3-digit distinct even number of ways $= 6\times5\times3$.
Ans. 90
8. Solve as Example 22. **Ans.** 41472
9. First, fix the position of consonant on C's position is $5!\times C_1\times C_2\times C_3\times C_4\times C_5$.
Now, in any six '×' position, 3 vowels can be arrange in ${}^6P_3$ ways. **Ans.** 14400
10. 14400
11. Firstly, fix the odd position of vowels (A, I, E) 1, 2, 3, 4, 5, 6, 7 i.e. ${}^4P_3$ ways and sent of the 5 places can be arranged in 5! ways. **Ans.** 576
12. Solve as Example 2. **Ans.** $r=4$
13. Solve as Example 2. **Ans.** $r=3$
14. Solve as Example 4. **Ans.** $n=8$
15. Solve as Example 4. **Ans.** $r=7$
16. Consider RHS and use the formula ${}^nP_r = \frac{n!}{(n-r)!}$ to simplify RHS.
17. Required numbers are 3-digit numbers, formed with the given digits. Solve as Example 7. **Ans.** 60
18. Required number of numbers is same as number of permutations of 4 distinct objects taken all at a time. **Ans.** 24
19. 18!
20. Their are 8 distinct letters in a given word. So, total number of words can be formed is 8. **Ans.** 40320
21. Their are 6 distinct letters in a given word. So, number of different 4-letter words can be formed is ${}^6P_4$.
Ans. 360
22. Required number of signals is same as number of permutations of 8 different things taken 5 at a time.
Ans. 6720
23. Solve as Example 8. **Ans.** 132
24. Number of possible arrangements is same as number of permutations of 9 different things taking all at a time.
Ans. 362880
25. (i) Solve as Example 16.
(ii) Here, $n=9$, $p_1=4$, $p_2=3$ and $p_3=2$
Ans. Required number of ways $= \frac{9!}{4!\,3!\,2!} = 1260$
26. 4536
27. Solve as Example 22. **Ans.** 56
28. Solve as Example 28. **Ans.** 720, 120, 24
29. Solve as Example 31, part (ii). **Ans.** 120960
30. (i) $\frac{1}{2}(9!)$ (ii) $\frac{{}^{20}P_9}{9}$
31. We have, $(n+2)! = 132\ {}^nP_{12}(n-12)!$
On solving, we get $n=10$, which is not satisfied ${}^nP_{12}$.
Hence, no value of n exists.
32. Solve as Example 13. **Ans.** 69760
33. Solve as Example 20. **Ans.** (i) 4320 (ii) 36000
34. 100
35. 840; (i) 240 (ii) 20 (iii) 120
36. Consider each married couple as one unit, then the three units can be arranged in $3! = 6$ ways.
Again each couple can be arranged in $2! = 2$ ways.
If the ladies sit together, then consider all ladies together as one unit. Now this single unit together with 3 remaining mens will be counted as 4 objects.
Ans. 48; 144
37. (i) Take all the girls together as one unit. **Ans.** $6!\times5!$
(ii) Take all the girls together as one unit and all the boys together as another unit. **Ans.** $2!\times5!\times5!$
(iii) Required number of ways = Number of all possible arrangements of 5 boys and 5 girls − Number of arrangement in which all girls sit together
Ans. $10! - 5!\times6!$

TOPIC 03 Combinations

The word **combination** means selection.

Each of the different groups or selections, which is made by taking some or all of a number of different objects at a time, irrespective of their arrangements is called the **combination**.

e.g. The different combinations formed from three letters A, B, C taking two at a time are AB, AC, BC.

Difference between Permutations and Combinations

The process of selecting objects is called combination and that of arranging objects is called permutation.

If we have 4 objects A, B, C and D, the possible selection (or combination) and arrangement (or permutation) of 3 objects out of 4 are given below. This will help you to understand clearly the difference between permutations and combinations.

Selection ↓ Combination	Arrangement ↓ Permutation
ABC	ABC, ACB, BAC, BCA, CAB, CBA
ABD	ABD, ADB, BAD, BDA, DAB, DBA
ACD	ACD, ADC, CAD, CDA, DAC, DCA
BCD	BCD, BDC, CBD, CDB, DBC, DCB
Total 4 combinations	24 permutations

Meaning of ${}^nC_r$

The number of combinations of n different things taken r at a time is meant the number of groups of r things which can be formed from n things and generally it is denoted by symbol ${}^nC_r$ or $C(n, r)$ or $\left(\frac{n}{r}\right)$.

Combinations of n Different Things Taken r at a Time

Theorem. The number of combinations of n distinct objects taken r at a time is given by ${}^nC_r = \dfrac{n!}{r!(n-r)!}$.

Proof Let ${}^nC_r = x$ ...(i)

Each one of these x combinations contains r things and these r things can be arranged among themselves in $r!$ ways. Hence, one combination gives $r!$ permutations.

So, x combinations will give rise to $(x \cdot r!)$ permutations. But the number of permutations of n things taken r at a time is $\dfrac{n!}{(n-r)!}$.

$$\therefore \quad x \cdot r! = \frac{n!}{(n-r)!} \Rightarrow x = \frac{n!}{r!(n-r)!}$$

$$\Rightarrow \quad {}^nC_r = \frac{n!}{r!(n-r)!} \quad \text{[from Eq. (i)]}$$

$$\therefore \quad {}^nC_r = \frac{n!}{r!(n-r)!};\ 1 \le r \le n$$

In particular,

(i) When $r = 0$, then ${}^nC_0 = \dfrac{n!}{0!(n-0)!} = \dfrac{n!}{1 \times n!} = 1$

${}^nC_0 = 1$, can be interpreted as the number of combinations of n different things taken nothing at all is considered to be 1.

Selecting nothing at all is the same as leaving behind all the objects and there is only one way of doing so. In this way, we define

$${}^nC_0 = 1$$

(ii) When $r = n$, then

$${}^nC_n = \frac{n!}{n!(n-n)!} = \frac{n!}{n!0!} = \frac{1}{0!} = 1$$

$$\therefore \quad \boxed{{}^nC_0 = {}^nC_n = 1}$$

It means number of combination taking all the objects at a time is always 1.

Note ${}^nC_r = \dfrac{n(n-1)(n-2)\ldots r \text{ factors}}{r!}$

Example 1 Evaluate the following.

(i) ${}^{14}C_3$ (ii) ${}^{100}C_{99}$ (iii) ${}^{35}C_{35}$ (iv) ${}^{30}C_0$

Sol. (i) ${}^{14}C_3 = \dfrac{14!}{3!(14-3)!}$ $\left[\because {}^nC_r = \dfrac{n!}{r!(n-r)!}\right]$

$$= \frac{14!}{3! \times 11!} = \frac{14 \times 13 \times 12 \times 11!}{(3 \times 2 \times 1) \times 11!}$$

$$= \frac{14 \times 13 \times 12}{6} = 14 \times 13 \times 2 = 364$$

(ii) ${}^{100}C_{99} = \dfrac{100!}{99!(100-99)!} = \dfrac{100!}{99! \times 1!} = \dfrac{100 \times 99!}{99! \times 1} = 100$

(iii) ${}^{35}C_{35} = 1$ $[\because {}^nC_n = 1]$

(iv) ${}^{30}C_0 = 1$ $[\because {}^nC_0 = 1]$

Example 2 If $^nP_r = 840$ and $^nC_r = 35$, find r.

[NCERT Exemplar]

Sol. We know that, $^nP_r = r! \times {}^nC_r$

$\therefore \quad 840 = r! \times 35$

$\Rightarrow \quad r! = \frac{840}{35}$

$\Rightarrow \quad r! = 24 = 4!$

$\Rightarrow \quad r = 4$

Example 3 If $^{n+2}C_8 : {}^{n-2}P_4 = 57 : 16$, then find the value of n.

Sol. We have, $^{n+2}C_8 : {}^{n-2}P_4 = 57 : 16$

$$\Rightarrow \frac{^{n+2}C_8}{^{n-2}P_4} = \frac{57}{16} \Rightarrow \frac{\frac{(n+2)!}{8!(n+2-8)!}}{\frac{(n-2)!}{(n-2-4)!}} = \frac{57}{16}$$

$$\Rightarrow \frac{(n+2)!}{8!(n-6)!} \times \frac{(n-6)!}{(n-2)!} = \frac{57}{16}$$

$$\Rightarrow \frac{(n+2)(n+1)n(n-1)(n-2)!}{8!} \times \frac{1}{(n-2)!} = \frac{57}{16}$$

$$\Rightarrow (n+2)(n+1)n(n-1) = \frac{57}{16} \times 8!$$

$$= \frac{19 \times 3}{16} \times 8 \times 7 \times 6 \times 5 \times 4 \times 3 \times 2 \times 1$$

$$\Rightarrow (n-1)n(n+1)(n+2) = 19 \times 3 \times 7 \times 6 \times 5 \times 4 \times 3$$

$$\Rightarrow (n-1)n(n+1)(n+2) = 19 \times (3 \times 7) \times (6 \times 3) \times (5 \times 4)$$

$$\Rightarrow (n-1)n(n+1)(n+2) = 18 \times 19 \times 20 \times 21$$

On comparing both sides, we get

$$n - 1 = 18 \Rightarrow n = 19$$

Example 4 Prove that $r \cdot {}^nC_r = n \cdot {}^{n-1}C_{r-1}$.

Sol. LHS $= r \cdot {}^nC_r = r \cdot \frac{n!}{r!(n-r)!}$ $\quad \left[\because {}^nC_r = \frac{n!}{r!(n-r)!}\right]$

$= \frac{r \cdot n!}{r(r-1)!(n-r)!}$ $\quad [\because r! = r(r-1)!]$

$= \frac{n!}{(r-1)!(n-r)!}$ $\quad$ ...(i)

RHS $= n \cdot {}^{n-1}C_{r-1} = n \cdot \frac{(n-1)!}{(r-1)!\{(n-1)-(r-1)\}!}$

$= \frac{n \cdot (n-1)!}{(r-1)!(n-r)!} = \frac{n!}{(r-1)!(n-r)!}$

$[\because n(n-1)! = n!]$ ...(ii)

From Eqs. (i) and (ii), we get

LHS = RHS

$\Rightarrow \quad r \cdot {}^nC_r = n \cdot {}^{n-1}C_{r-1}$ **Hence proved.**

Some Important Theorems

Theorem 1. $^nP_r = {}^nC_r \cdot r!, 0 < r \le n$

Proof The number of combinations of n distinct objects taken r at a time is ^nC_r. In these combinations, r things can be arranged among themselves in $r!$ ways. So, we have $r!$ permutations.

Therefore, the total number of permutations of n different things taken r at a time is $^nC_r \times r!$, which is equal to ^nP_r.

$\therefore \quad {}^nP_r = r! \times {}^nC_r, 0 < r \le n$ **Hence proved.**

Theorem 2. $^nC_r = {}^nC_{n-r}, 0 \le r \le n$

Note This theorem is used to simplify the calculation when r is large.

Theorem 3. $^nC_r + {}^nC_{r-1} = {}^{n+1}C_r, 1 \le r \le n$

[Pascal's rule]

Proof LHS $= {}^nC_r + {}^nC_{r-1} = \frac{n!}{r!(n-r)!} + \frac{n!}{(r-1)!(n-r+1)!}$

$$= \frac{n!(n-r+1)}{r!(n-r+1)(n-r)!} + \frac{n!r}{r(r-1)!(n-r+1)!}$$

$$= \frac{n!(n-r+1)}{r!(n-r+1)!} + \frac{n!r}{r!(n-r+1)!}$$

$$= n!\left[\frac{n-r+1+r}{r!(n-r+1)!}\right]$$

$$= \frac{(n+1)n!}{r!(n+1-r)!} = \frac{(n+1)!}{r!(n+1-r)!} = {}^{n+1}C_r = \text{RHS}$$

Theorem 4. If $^nC_x = {}^nC_y$, then either $x = y$ or $x + y = n$.

Theorem 5. For non-negative integers n and r, where

$$1 \le r \le n, \ {}^nC_r = \frac{n}{r} \times {}^{n-1}C_{r-1}.$$

Theorem 6. If $1 \le r \le n$, then

$$n \cdot {}^{n-1}C_{r-1} = (n-r+1) \cdot {}^nC_{r-1}$$

Theorem 7. $\frac{^nC_r}{^nC_{r-1}} = \frac{n-r+1}{r}, 1 \le r \le n$

Example 5 Evaluate $^{13}C_6 + {}^{13}C_5$.

Sol. We have,

$^{13}C_6 + {}^{13}C_5 = {}^{14}C_6$ $\quad [\because {}^nC_r + {}^nC_{r-1} = {}^{n+1}C_r]$

$= \frac{14!}{6!(14-6)!}$ $\quad \left[\because {}^nC_r = \frac{n!}{r!(n-r)!}\right]$

$= \frac{14!}{6! \times 8!} = \frac{14 \times 13 \times 12 \times 11 \times 10 \times 9 \times 8!}{6 \times 5 \times 4 \times 3 \times 2 \times 1 \times 8!}$

$= 7 \times 13 \times 11 \times 3$

$= 3003$

Example 6 Evaluate $\sum_{r=1}^{5} {}^5C_r$.

Sol. Consider, $\sum_{r=1}^{5} {}^5C_r = {}^5C_1 + {}^5C_2 + {}^5C_3 + {}^5C_4 + {}^5C_5$

$= {}^5C_1 + {}^5C_2 + {}^5C_2 + {}^5C_1 + {}^5C_0 \quad [\because {}^nC_r = {}^nC_{n-r}]$

$= 5 + 2 \times {}^5C_2 + 5 + 1 \quad [\because {}^nC_1 = n \text{ and } {}^nC_0 = 1]$

$= 11 + 2 \times \frac{5 \times 4}{2 \times 1} = 11 + 20 = 31$

Alternate Method

Consider, $\sum_{r=1}^{5} {}^5C_r = ({}^5C_1 + {}^5C_2) + ({}^5C_3 + {}^5C_4) + {}^5C_5$

$= {}^6C_2 + {}^6C_4 + 1$

$[\because {}^nC_r + {}^nC_{r-1} = {}^{n+1}C_r \text{ and } {}^nC_n = 1]$

$= \frac{6!}{2!4!} + \frac{6!}{4!2!} + 1$

$= 2\left[\frac{6 \times 5 \times 4}{2 \times 4}\right] + 1$

$= 30 + 1 = 31$

Example 7 If ${}^nC_{10} = {}^nC_{12}$, then find the value of ${}^{23}C_n$.

Sol. We know that, ${}^nC_x = {}^nC_y$

$\Rightarrow \quad x + y = n \text{ or } x = y$

Here $x \neq y$, so $x + y = n$.

$\Rightarrow \quad n = 10 + 12 = 22$

Now, $\quad {}^{23}C_n = {}^{23}C_{22} = {}^{23}C_{23-22} = {}^{23}C_1 = 23$

$[\because {}^nC_r = {}^nC_{n-r}]$

Example 8 If ${}^{16}C_r = {}^{16}C_{r+2}$, then find ${}^rC_4$.

Sol. We know that, ${}^nC_x = {}^nC_y \Rightarrow x = y \text{ or } x + y = n$

$\therefore \quad r + (r + 2) = 16 \quad [\because r \neq r + 2]$

$\Rightarrow \quad 2r + 2 = 16$

$\Rightarrow \quad 2r = 14 \Rightarrow r = 7$

Hence, ${}^7C_4 = {}^7C_3 = \frac{7 \times 6 \times 5}{3 \times 2 \times 1} = 35$

Example 9 If ${}^8C_r - {}^7C_3 = {}^7C_2$, then find r.

Sol. We have, ${}^8C_r - {}^7C_3 = {}^7C_2$

$\Rightarrow \quad {}^8C_r = {}^7C_3 + {}^7C_2$

$\Rightarrow \quad {}^8C_r = {}^8C_3 \quad [\because {}^nC_r + {}^nC_{r-1} = {}^{n+1}C_r]$

$\Rightarrow \quad r = 3 \text{ or } r + 3 = 8$

$[\because {}^nC_x = {}^nC_y \Rightarrow x = y \text{ or } x + y = n]$

$\Rightarrow \quad r = 3 \text{ or } r = 5$

Example 10 Evaluate ${}^nC_r + 2 \cdot {}^nC_{r-1} + {}^nC_{r-2}$.

Sol. Consider, ${}^nC_r + 2 \cdot {}^nC_{r-1} + {}^nC_{r-2}$

$= {}^nC_r + {}^nC_{r-1} + {}^nC_{r-1} + {}^nC_{r-2}$

$= ({}^nC_r + {}^nC_{r-1}) + ({}^nC_{r-1} + {}^nC_{r-2})$

$= {}^{n+1}C_r + {}^{n+1}C_{r-1} = {}^{n+2}C_r$

$[\because {}^nC_r + {}^nC_{r-1} = {}^{n+1}C_r]$

Example 11 Find the value of the expression

${}^{47}C_4 + \sum_{j=1}^{5} {}^{52-j}C_3$.

Sol. We have,

${}^{47}C_4 + \sum_{j=1}^{5} {}^{52-j}C_3$

$= {}^{47}C_4 + {}^{52-1}C_3 + {}^{52-2}C_3 + {}^{52-3}C_3 + {}^{52-4}C_3 + {}^{52-5}C_3$

$= {}^{47}C_4 + {}^{51}C_3 + {}^{50}C_3 + {}^{49}C_3 + {}^{48}C_3 + {}^{47}C_3$

$= ({}^{47}C_3 + {}^{47}C_4) + {}^{48}C_3 + {}^{49}C_3 + {}^{50}C_3 + {}^{51}C_3$

$= {}^{48}C_4 + {}^{48}C_3 + {}^{49}C_3 + {}^{50}C_3 + {}^{51}C_3$

$[\because {}^nC_{r-1} + {}^nC_r = {}^{n+1}C_r]$

$= {}^{49}C_4 + {}^{49}C_3 + {}^{50}C_3 + {}^{51}C_3$

$= {}^{50}C_4 + {}^{50}C_3 + {}^{51}C_3$

$= {}^{51}C_4 + {}^{51}C_3 = {}^{52}C_4$

$= \frac{52 \times 51 \times 50 \times 49}{4 \times 3 \times 2 \times 1}$

$= 13 \times 17 \times 25 \times 49$

$= 270725$

Practical Problems on Combinations

Here, we will discuss some practical problems, where the formula for ${}^nC_r$ and its meaning can be applied.

|Type I|

Problems Based on the Formula of ${}^nC_r$

Example 12 In how many ways, can 5 sportsmen be selected from a group of 10?

Here, order of selection is immaterial. So, we use the concept of combination.

Sol. Required number of ways = ${}^{10}C_5$

$= \frac{10 \times 9 \times 8 \times 7 \times 6}{5 \times 4 \times 3 \times 2 \times 1}$

$= 2 \times 3 \times 7 \times 6 = 252$

Example 13 Everybody in a room shakes hands with everybody else. The total number of hand-shakes is 66. Find the total number of persons in the room. **[NCERT Exemplar]**

Sol. Let total number of persons be n.

Since, total number of hand-shakes = 66

$\therefore \quad {}^nC_2 = 66$

$\Rightarrow \quad \dfrac{n(n-1)}{2} = 66 \Rightarrow n^2 - n - 132 = 0$

$\Rightarrow (n-12)(n+11) = 0$

$\therefore \quad n = 12 \quad [\because n \text{ cannot be negative}]$

|Type II|

Finding the Number of Combinations When Some Particular Things are Included or Excluded

Example 14 In how many ways, can a cricket team of 11 players be selected out of 16 players,

(i) if two particular players are always be included?

(ii) if two particular players are always be excluded?

Sol. (i) Since, two particular players are always included, so we have to select 9 players out of 14 players. This can be done in ${}^{14}C_9$ ways.

Hence, required number of ways = ${}^{14}C_9 = {}^{14}C_5$

$[\because {}^nC_r = {}^nC_{n-r}]$

$= \dfrac{14 \times 13 \times 12 \times 11 \times 10}{5 \times 4 \times 3 \times 2 \times 1} = 14 \times 13 \times 11 = 2002$

(ii) Since, two particular players are always excluded, so we have to select 11 players out of 14 players. This can be done in ${}^{14}C_{11}$ ways.

Hence, required number of ways = ${}^{14}C_{11} = {}^{14}C_3$

$[\because {}^nC_r = {}^nC_{n-r}]$

$= \dfrac{14 \times 13 \times 12}{3 \times 2 \times 1} = 14 \times 13 \times 2 = 364$

Example 15 From a class of 25 students, 10 are to be chosen for an excursion party. There are 3 students who decide that either all of them will join or none of them will join. In how many ways can the excursion party be chosen? **[NCERT]**

Sol. Here, we have to choose 10 students out of a class of 25 students, such that the given condition satisfied.

Let us make the following cases and find the number of possible choices in each case.

Case **I When 3 particular students join the party** In this case, we have to choose 7 students out of 22 students. This can be done in ${}^{22}C_7$ ways.

Case **II When 3 particular students does not join the party** In this case, we have to choose 10 students out of 22 students. This can be done in ${}^{22}C_{10}$ ways.

Hence, total number of ways in which excursion party can be chosen = ${}^{22}C_7 + {}^{22}C_{10}$.

|Type III|

Finding the Number of Combination When Given Number of Things are to be Selected from Different Groups of Things

Example 16 In how many ways, can a team of 3 boys and 3 girls be selected from 5 boys and 4 girls? **[NCERT]**

Sol. There are 5 boys and 4 girls. We have to select 3 boys out of 5 boys and 3 girls out of 4 girls.

Clearly, 3 boys out of 5 boys can be selected in ${}^5C_3$ ways, and 3 girls out of 4 girls can be selected in ${}^4C_3$ ways.

Hence, by fundamental principle of multiplication, number of ways of selecting 3 boys and 3 girls

$= {}^5C_3 \times {}^4C_3$

$= {}^5C_2 \times {}^4C_1 \quad [\because {}^nC_r = {}^nC_{n-r}]$

$= \dfrac{5 \times 4}{2 \times 1} \times 4 \quad [\because {}^nC_1 = n]$

$= 10 \times 4 = 40$

Example 17 Find the number of ways of selecting 9 balls from 6 red balls, 5 white balls and 5 blue balls, if each selection consists of 3 balls of each colour. **[NCERT]**

Sol. The required number of ways

= Number of ways of selecting 3 balls from 6 red balls

× Number of ways of selecting 3 balls from 5 white balls

× Number of ways of selecting 3 balls from 5 blue balls

$= {}^6C_3 \times {}^5C_3 \times {}^5C_3 = {}^6C_3 \times {}^5C_2 \times {}^5C_2$

$= \dfrac{6 \times 5 \times 4}{3 \times 2 \times 1} \times \dfrac{5 \times 4}{2 \times 1} \times \dfrac{5 \times 4}{2 \times 1}$

$= 20 \times 10 \times 10 = 2000$

Hence, the number of ways of selecting 3 balls of each colour is 2000.

Example 18 There are 10 professors and 20 students out of whom a committee of 2 professors and 3 students is to be formed. Find the number of ways in which this can be done. Further find in how many of these committees

(i) a particular professors is included?

(ii) a particular student is included?

(iii) a particular student is excluded?

Sol. Clearly, for forming a committee of 2 professors and 3 students, we have to select 2 professors out of 10 professors and 3 students out of 20 students.

This can be done in ${}^{10}C_2 \times {}^{20}C_3$ ways.

Thus, required number of ways

$$= \frac{10 \times 9}{2 \times 1} \times \frac{20 \times 19 \times 18}{3 \times 2 \times 1} = 45 \times 60 \times 19 = 51300$$

(i) When a particular professor is included, then we have to select 1 professor out of 9 professors and 3 students out of 20 students.

This can be done in ${}^9C_1 \times {}^{20}C_3$ ways.

Thus, required number of ways

$$= 9 \times \frac{20 \times 19 \times 18}{3 \times 2 \times 1} = 9 \times 60 \times 19 = 10260$$

(ii) When a particular student is included, then we have to select 2 professors out of 10 professors and 2 students out of 19 students.

This can be done in ${}^{10}C_2 \times {}^{19}C_2$.

Thus, required number of ways

$$= \frac{10 \times 9}{2 \times 1} \times \frac{19 \times 18}{2 \times 1} = 45 \times 171 = 7695$$

(iii) When a particular student is excluded, then we have to select 2 professors out of 10 professors and 3 students out of 19 students. This can be done in ${}^{10}C_2 \times {}^{19}C_3$ ways.

Thus, required number of ways

$$= \frac{10 \times 9}{2 \times 1} \times \frac{19 \times 18 \times 17}{3 \times 2 \times 1} = 45 \times 969 = 43605$$

Example 19 **A bag contains six white marbles and five red marbles. Find the number of ways in which four marbles can be drawn from the bag, if**

(i) they can be of any colour.

(ii) two must be white and two red.

(iii) they must all be of the same colour. [NCERT Exemplar]

Sol. Total number of marbles white + 5 red = 11 marbles

(i) Since, the 4 marbles can be of any colour, therefore we have to select 4 marbles out of 11 marbles.

This can be done in ${}^{11}C_4$ ways.

Hence, required number of ways = 330 ways.

(ii) Since out of four marbles two are white and two are red, therefore we have to select 2 white marbles out of 6 white marbles and 2 red marbles out of 5 red marbles.

This can be done in ${}^6C_2 \times {}^5C_2$ ways.

Hence, required number of ways $= 15 \times 10 = 150$

(iii) Since, all the 4 marbles must be of same colour, therefore we have to select 4 marbles of white colour or red colour.

Clearly, number of ways of selecting 4 white marbles out of 6 white marbles $= {}^6C_4 = {}^6C_2 = 15$

and number of ways of selecting 4 red marbles out of 5 red marbles $= {}^5C_4 = {}^5C_1 = 5$

Hence, required number of ways $= 15 + 5 = 20$ ways.

|Type IV|

Finding the Number of Combinations When Selection of Things involves Given under Conditions

Example 20 **A committee of 7 members has to be formed from 9 boys and 4 girls. In how many ways, can this be done when the committee consists of**

(i) exactly 3 girls? (ii) atleast 3 girls?

(iii) atmost 3 girls? [NCERT]

Sol. There are 9 boys and 4 girls. We have to form a committee of 7 members.

(i) Since, the committee has exactly 3 girls. Therefore, we have to choose 3 girls out of 4 girls and the rest 4 members out of 9 boys.

This can be done in ${}^4C_3 \times {}^9C_4$ ways.

Hence, number of ways of forming a committee

$$= {}^4C_3 \times {}^9C_4 = {}^4C_1 \times \frac{9 \times 8 \times 7 \times 6}{4 \times 3 \times 2 \times 1}$$

$$= 4 \times 9 \times 7 \times 2 = 504 \text{ ways}$$

(ii) Since the committee has at least 3 girls. Therefore, we can form the committee in the following ways

(a) Selecting 3 girls and 4 boys

(b) Selecting 4 girls and 3 boys

Hence, the number of ways of forming a committee

$$= {}^4C_3 \times {}^9C_4 + {}^4C_4 \times {}^9C_3$$

$$= 504 + 1 \times \frac{9 \times 8 \times 7}{3 \times 2 \times 1} = 504 + 84 = 588 \text{ ways}$$

(iii) Since, the committee has atmost 3 girls, therefore we can form committee in the following ways

(a) Selecting 7 boys and no girl

(b) Selecting 6 boys and 1 girl

(c) Selecting 5 boys and 2 girls

(d) Selecting 4 boys and 3 girls

Hence, the number of ways of forming a committee

$$= {}^9C_7 \times {}^4C_0 + {}^9C_6 \times {}^4C_1 + {}^9C_5 \times {}^4C_2 + {}^9C_4 \times {}^4C_3$$

$$= {}^9C_2 + {}^9C_3 \times 4 + {}^9C_4 \times {}^4C_2 + {}^9C_4 \times {}^4C_1$$

$$[\because {}^nC_r = {}^nC_{n-r}, {}^nC_1 = n \text{ and } {}^nC_0 = 1]$$

$$= 36 + 84 \times 4 + 126 \times 6 + 126 \times 4$$

$$= 36 + 336 + 756 + 504 = 1632$$

Example 21 **A committee of 10 is to be formed from 8 gentlemen and 9 ladies. In how many ways this can be done if atleast five ladies have to be included in a committee? In how many of these committees**

(i) the ladies are in majority?

(ii) the gentlemen are in majority?

Sol. There are 9 ladies and 8 gentlemen. We have to form a committee of 10, consisting of atleast 5 ladies.

This can be formed by selecting

(a) 5 ladies and 5 gentlemen
(b) 6 ladies and 4 gentlemen
(c) 7 ladies and 3 gentlemen
(d) 8 ladies and 2 gentlemen
(e) 9 ladies and 1 gentleman

Now, number of ways of forming a committee

$$= {}^9C_5 \times {}^8C_5 + {}^9C_6 \times {}^8C_4 + {}^9C_7 \times {}^8C_3 + {}^9C_8 \times {}^8C_2 + {}^9C_9 \times {}^8C_1$$

$$= {}^9C_4 \times {}^8C_3 + {}^9C_3 \times {}^8C_4 + {}^9C_2 \times {}^8C_3 + {}^9C_1 \times {}^8C_2 + {}^9C_0 \times {}^8C_1 \quad [\because {}^nC_r = {}^nC_{n-r}]$$

$$= \frac{9\times8\times7\times6}{4\times3\times2\times1} \times \frac{8\times7\times6}{3\times2\times1} + \frac{9\times8\times7}{3\times2\times1} \times \frac{8\times7\times6\times5}{4\times3\times2\times1} + \frac{9\times8}{2\times1} \times \frac{8\times7\times6}{3\times2\times1} + 9 \times \frac{8\times7}{2\times1} + 1\times8$$

$$= 126 \times 56 + 84 \times 70 + 36 \times 56 + 9 \times 28 + 8$$

$$= 7056 + 5880 + 2016 + 252 + 8$$

$$= 15212$$

(i) Clearly, ladies are in majority in (b), (c), (d) and (e) cases as discussed above.

$\therefore$ Number of committees in which ladies are in majority $= 15212 - {}^9C_5 \times {}^8C_5$

$$= 15212 - 7056$$

$$= 8156$$

(ii) Clearly, gentlemen are not in majority in the cases discussed above.

Thus, there is no committee in which gentlemen are in majority. Hence, number of such committee = 0.

Example 22 A sports team of 11 students is to be constituted, choosing atleast 5 from class XI and atleast 5 from class XII. If there are 20 students in each of these classes, then how many ways can the team be constituted? **[NCERT Exemplar]**

Sol. To constitute a sports team, there are two cases

Case **I** Choose 5 students from class XI and 6 students from class XII.

$\therefore$ In this case, number of ways $= {}^{20}C_5 \times {}^{20}C_6$

Case **II** Choose 6 students from class XI and 5 students from class XII.

In this case, number of ways $= {}^{20}C_6 \times {}^{20}C_5$

$\therefore$ Required number of ways

$$= ({}^{20}C_5 \times {}^{20}C_6) + ({}^{20}C_6 \times {}^{20}C_5)$$

$$= 2({}^{20}C_5 \times {}^{20}C_6)$$

Hence, the total number of ways of constituting a sports team of 11 students is $2({}^{20}C_5 \times {}^{20}C_6)$ ways.

Example 23 In an examination, a question paper consist of 12 questions divided into two parts I and II containing 5 and 7 questions, respectively. A students is required to attempt 8 questions in all, selecting atleast 3 from each part. In how many ways, can a student select the questions? **[NCERT]**

Sol. Student may select 8 questions, according to following scheme.

	I (5 Questions)	II (7 Questions)
(i)	3	5
(ii)	4	4
(iii)	5	3

Now, the required number of ways

$$= {}^5C_3 \times {}^7C_5 + {}^5C_4 \times {}^7C_4 + {}^5C_5 \times {}^7C_3$$

$$= {}^5C_2 \times {}^7C_2 + {}^5C_1 \times {}^7C_3 + {}^5C_0 \times {}^7C_3$$

$$= 10 \times 21 + 5 \times 35 + 1 \times 35$$

$$= 210 + 175 + 35 = 420.$$

Hence, the total number of ways of selecting the questions by the student is 420 ways.

Example 24 A man has 7 friends. In how many ways, can he invite one or more of them to party?

Sol. A man may invite one of them, two of them, three of them, ... or all of them and this can be done in ${}^7C_1, {}^7C_2, {}^7C_3, \dots, {}^7C_7$ ways, respectively.

$\therefore$ Total number of ways

$$= {}^7C_1 + {}^7C_2 + {}^7C_3 + {}^7C_4 + {}^7C_5 + {}^7C_6 + {}^7C_7$$

$$= 7 + 21 + 35 + 35 + 21 + 7 + 1 = 127$$

|Type V|

Problems Based on Geometry

Example 25 How many chords can be drawn through 21 points on a circle? **[NCERT]**

We can get a chord by joining any two points. So, here for finding the number of chords, we make combination of 2 points from 21 points.

Sol. Number of chords that can be drawn from 21 points $= {}^{21}C_2 = \dfrac{21 \times 20}{2 \times 1} = 210$

Hence, total number of chords that can be drawn through 21 points on a circle is 210.

Example 26 If 20 lines are drawn in a plane such that no two of them are parallel and no three are concurrent, in how many points will they intersect each other? **[NCERT Exemplar]**

Sol. There are 20 lines in a plane.

Since, it is given that no two lines are parallel, therefore all lines are intersecting lines. Also, as no three lines are concurrent, i.e. no three lines intersect at a point, therefore only pair of lines intersect at a point.

We know that a pair of lines intersect at a unique point. Therefore, corresponding to every pair of lines, we have a unique point of intersection.

Thus, number of point of intersection

= Number of pair of lines

$$= {}^{20}C_2 = \frac{20 \times 19}{2 \times 1} = 190.$$

Example 27 Find the number of parallelograms that can be formed from a set of four parallel lines intersecting another set of three parallel lines. **[NCERT Exemplar]**

Sol. Clearly, a parallelogram is formed by choosing two parallel lines from the set of 4 parallel lines and two parallel lines from the set of 3 parallel lines.

$\therefore$ Total number of parallelogram formed

= Number of ways of selecting two lines from set I

× Number of ways of selecting two lines from set II

$$= {}^4C_2 \times {}^3C_2 = 6 \times 3 = 18$$

Example 28 Find the number of triangles that are formed by choosing the vertices from a set of 12 points, seven of which lie on the same line. **[NCERT Exemplar]**

Sol. We know that, a triangle will be formed by taking three non-collinear points at a time.

$\therefore$ Required number of triangles $= {}^{12}C_3 - {}^7C_3$

$$= \frac{12 \times 11 \times 10}{3 \times 2 \times 1} - \frac{7 \times 6 \times 5}{3 \times 2} = 220 - 35 = 185$$

Hence, total number of such triangle is 185.

Example 29 The straight lines l_1, l_2 and l_3 are parallel and lie in the same plane. A total numbers of m points are taken on l_1; n points on l_2 ; k points on l_3. Find the maximum number of triangles formed with vertices at these points. **[NCERT Exemplar]**

Sol. Total number of points $= m + n + k$

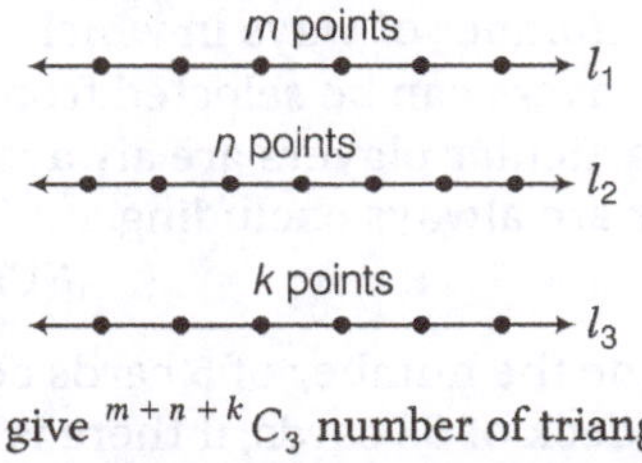

This can give ${}^{m+n+k}C_3$ number of triangles. But m points on l_1, taking 3 at a time, gives ${}^mC_3$ combinations which produce no triangle.

Similarly, ${}^nC_3$ and ${}^kC_3$ number of triangles cannot formed.

$\therefore$ Required number of triangles

$$= {}^{m+n+k}C_3 - {}^mC_3 - {}^nC_3 - {}^kC_3$$

Mixed Problems Based on Permutations and Combinations

|Type I|

Total Number of Combinations

To find the total number of combinations of n objects taking any number of them at a time.

Case I When all objects are different

Each object may be selected in two ways.

It may be either included or excluded.

The total number of ways of selecting the objects

$$= 2 \times 2 \times 2 \times \ldots n \text{ times} = 2^n$$

But this includes the case in which all the objects are excluded.

Hence, the total number of ways in which one or more objects are taken $= 2^n - 1$

Example 30 There are 4 questions in a question paper. In how many ways can a boy solve one or more questions?

Sol. The boy can dispose of each question in two ways. He may either solve it or leave it. Thus, the number of ways of disposing of all the questions $= 2^4$.

But this includes the case in which he has left all the questions unsolved.

Hence, the total number of ways of solving the paper

$= 2^4 - 1 = 15$

Case II When all objects are not different

Suppose, out of $(p + q + r + \ldots)$ things, p are alike of one kind, q are alike of a second kind, r alike of a third kind, and the rest different. Out of p objects we may take 0, 1, 2, 3 ... or p. Hence, they may be selected in $(p + 1)$ ways. Similarly, q alike objects may be selected in $(q + 1)$ and r alike objects in $(r + 1)$ ways. The t different objects may be selected in 2^t ways.

This includes that case in which all are rejected.

$\therefore$ The total number of selections

$$= (p + 1)(q + 1)(r + 1)\, 2^t - 1.$$

Example 31 Prove that from the letters of the sentence, 'Daddy did a deadly deed', one or more letters can be selected in 1919 ways.

Sol. In the given sentence, there are 9 d's ; 3 a's; 3 e's; 2y's; 1 i and 1l.

$\therefore$ The total number of selections

$= (9+1)(3+1)(3+1)(2+1)(1+1)(1+1) - 1$

$= 10 \times 4 \times 4 \times 3 \times 2 \times 2 - 1 = 1919.$

|Type III|

Permutations and Combinations occurring Simultaneously

Example 32 The English alphabet has 5 vowels and 21 consonants. How many words with 2 different vowels and 2 different consonants can be formed from the alphabet?

Sol. Here, we have 5 vowels and 21 consonants. We have to select 2 vowels out of 5 vowels and 2 consonants out of 21 consonants. Also, we have to arrange these 4 letters which can be done in 4! ways.

$\therefore$ Required number of words $= {}^5C_2 \times {}^{21}C_2 \times 4!$

$$= \frac{5 \times 4}{2} \times \frac{21 \times 20}{2} \times 24$$

$= 10 \times 210 \times 24 = 50400$

Hence, the total number of words having 2 consonants and 2 vowels is 50400.

Example 33 How many words with or without meaning, each of 2 vowels and 3 consonants can be formed from the letters of the word 'DAUGHTER'? [NCERT]

Sol. There are 8 letters in the word 'DAUGHTER' including 3 vowels and 5 consonants. We have to select 2 vowels out of 3 vowels and 3 consonants out of 5 consonants.

$\therefore$ Number of ways of selection

$= {}^3C_2 \times {}^5C_3 = 3 \times 10 = 30$

Since, each word containing 5 letters can be arranged among themselves in 5! ways.

So, total number of words

$= 5! \times 30 = 120 \times 30 = 3600$

Topic Practice 3

Very Short Answer Type Questions

(2 Marks)

1 Evaluate the following.

(i) ${}^{10}C_8$

(ii) ${}^{50}C_{50}$

2 If ${}^nP_r = 720$ and ${}^nC_r = 120$, then find r.

3 Verify that $2 \times {}^7C_4 = {}^8C_4$.

4 Evaluate (i) ${}^{10}C_4 + {}^{10}C_5$

(ii) ${}^{31}C_{26} - {}^{30}C_{26}$.

5 Evaluate ${}^{15}C_8 + {}^{15}C_9 - {}^{15}C_6 - {}^{15}C_7$.

6 If ${}^nC_r$ denotes the number of combinations of n things taken r at a time, then the expression ${}^nC_{r+1} + {}^nC_{r-1} + 2 \times {}^nC_r$ equals.

7 If ${}^nC_9 = {}^nC_8$, then find ${}^nC_{17}$.

8 If ${}^{24}C_x = {}^{24}C_{2x+3}$, then find x.

9 If $\alpha = {}^mC_2$, then find the value of ${}^\alpha C_2$.

10 Prove that ${}^nC_r \times {}^rC_s = {}^nC_s \times {}^{n-s}C_{r-s}$.

11 Determine n, if ${}^{2n}C_3 : {}^nC_3 = 12:1$. [NCERT]

12 If ${}^{28}C_{2r} : {}^{24}C_{2r-4} = 225:11$, then find r.

13 From a class of 32 students, 4 are to be chosen for a competition. In how many ways can this be done?

14 If there are 10 persons in a party and each two of them shake hands with each other, how many hand-shakes happen in the party?

15 In how many ways can a student choose a programme of 5 courses, if 9 courses are available and 2 specific courses are compulsory for every student?

16 A committee of 3 persons is to be constituted from a group of 2 men and 3 women. In how many ways can this be done?

17 In a football championship, 153 matches were played. Every two teams played one match with each other. Find the number of teams, participating in the championship. [NCERT Exemplar]

18 Find the number of ways in which a team of eleven players can be selected from 22 players, if two particular players are always including and four are always excluding. [NCERT Exemplar]

19 Determine the number of 5 cards combination out of a deck of 52 cards, if there is exactly one ace in each combination.

20 A boy has 3 library tickets and 8 books of his interest in the library. Of these 8, he does not want to borrow Mathematics Part II, unless Mathematics Part I is also borrowed. In how many ways can he choose the three books to be borrowed? **[NCERT Exemplar]**

Short Answer Type Questions

4 Marks

21 Prove that ${}^{2n}C_n = \dfrac{2^n\{1\cdot 3\cdot 5\ldots(2n-1)\}}{n!}$.

22 Evaluate ${}^{20}C_5 + \sum_{r=1}^{5} {}^{25-r}C_4$.

23 If ${}^nC_{r-1} = 36$, ${}^nC_r = 84$ and ${}^nC_{r+1} = 126$, then find ${}^rC_2$. **[NCERT Exemplar]**

24 A box contains two white, three black and four red balls. In how many ways can three balls be drawn from the box, if atleast one black ball is to be included in the draw. **[NCERT Exemplar]**

25 Find the number of ways in which we can choose a committee from 4 men and 6 women, so that the committee includes atleast 2 men and exactly twice as many women as men. **[NCERT Exemplar]**

26 A candidate is required to answer 7 questions out of 12 questions, which are divided into two groups each containing 6 questions. He is not permitted to attempt more than 5 questions from either group. Find the number of different ways of doing questions. **[NCERT Exemplar]**

Long Answer Type Questions

6 Marks

27 Find the total number of words formed by 2 vowels and 3 consonants taken from 4 vowels and 5 consonants. **[NCERT Exemplar]**

28 How many words each of 3 vowels and 2 consonants can be formed from the letters of the word 'INVOLUTE'? **[NCERT]**

29 What is the number of ways of choosing 4 cards from a pack of 52 playing cards? In how many of these

(i) four cards are of the same suit?
(ii) four cards belong to four different suits?
(iii) are face cards?
(iv) two are red and two are black cards?
(v) cards are of the same colour? **[NCERT]**

Hints & Answers

1. Solve as Example 1. **Ans.** (i) 45 (ii) 1
2. Solve as Example 2. **Ans.** $r = 3$
3. Evaluate LHS and RHS separately and verify the result.
4. (i) Solve as Example 5. **Ans.** 462

   (ii) Use ${}^nC_r + {}^nC_{r-1} = {}^{n+1}C_r$

   i.e. ${}^{x+1}C_r - {}^nC_r = {}^nC_{r-1}$

   $\therefore {}^{31}C_{26} - {}^{30}C_{26} = {}^{30}C_{26-1} = {}^{30}C_{25}$ **Ans.** 142506
5. Given expression $= {}^{16}C_9 - {}^{16}C_7$ **Ans.** 0
6. ${}^{n+2}C_{r+1}$
7. Solve as Example 7. **Ans.** 1
8. Solve as Example 7. **Ans.** 7
9. $\because \alpha = \dfrac{m(m-1)}{2}$ and ${}^{\alpha}C_2 = \dfrac{\alpha(\alpha-1)}{2}$

   $$\Rightarrow {}^{\alpha}C_2 = \frac{\dfrac{m(m-1)}{2}\left(\dfrac{m(m-1)}{2} - 1\right)}{2}$$

   Ans. $\dfrac{(m+1)m(m-1)(m-2)}{8}$
10. Simplify LHS and RHS separately and get the result.
11. 5
12. Use ${}^nC_r = \dfrac{n!}{r!(n-r)!}$ and simplify. **Ans.** 7
13. Solve as Example 12. **Ans.** 35960
14. Solve as Example 13. **Ans.** 45
15. Since, 2 specific courses are compulsory, therefore we have to select 3 courses out of rest 7 courses i.e. ${}^7C_3$ ways.

    Ans. 35
16. Required number of ways $= {}^5C_3$ **Ans.** 10
17. Let the number of team participating in championship be n.

    Since, it is given that every two teams played one match with each other.

    $\therefore$ Total number of match played $= {}^nC_2$.

    According to the question, ${}^nC_2 = 153$

    Ans. $n = 18$
18. We have to select 9 players out of 16 players **Ans.** 11440
19. 778320
20. Let us make the following cases and find the number of possible choices in each case.

    Case **I** *Boy borrows Mathematics Part II*

    In this case, boy borrows Mathematics Part I also.

    So, number of possible choices are ${}^6C_1$.

    Case **II** *Boy does not borrow Mathematics Part II.*

    In this case, possible choices are ${}^7C_3$.

    Ans. 41

21. $^{2n}C_n = \frac{(2n)!}{n!\,n!} = \frac{(2n)(2n-1)(2n-2)\ldots 4\cdot 3\cdot 2\cdot 1}{n!\,n!}$

$= \frac{\{(2n-1)(2n-3)\ldots 3\cdot 1\}\{(2n)(2n-2)\ldots 4\cdot 2\}}{n!\cdot n!}$

$= \frac{\{(2n-1)(2n-3)\ldots 3\cdot 1\}2^n\{n(n-1)\ldots 2\cdot 1\}}{n!\,n!}$

22. Solve as Example 11. **Ans.**42504

23. Solving $\frac{^nC_{r-1}}{^nC_r} = \frac{36}{84}$ and $\frac{^nC_r}{^nC_{r-1}} = \frac{84}{126}$, we get

$r = 3$

$\therefore$ $^rC_2 = {}^3C_2 = 3$ **Ans.** 3

24. Selection of three balls, consisting of atleast one black ball can be done in following ways

(i) Selecting 1 black ball and 2 non-black balls
(ii) Selecting 2 black balls and 1 non-black ball
(iii) Selecting 3 black balls and 0 non-black ball

Required number of ways

$= {}^3C_1 \times {}^6C_2 + {}^3C_2 \times {}^6C_1 + {}^3C_3$

Ans. 64

25. Committee can be choose in following ways

(i) Selecting 2 men and 4 women
(ii) Selecting 3 men and 6 women

Ans. 94

26. Total number of ways of attempting 7 questions out of 12 questions = Number of ways of

(Attempting 2 from group I and 5 from group II)
+ (Attempting 3 from group I and 4 from group II)
+ (Attempting 4 from group I and 3 from group II)
+ (Attempting 5 from group I and 2 from group II)

Now, solve as Example 23. **Ans.** 780

27. Solve as Example 32. **Ans.** 7200

28. Solve as Example 33. **Ans.** 2880

29. Number of ways of choosing 4 cards = $^{52}C_4$ **Ans.** 270725

(i) There are 4 suits and each suit have 13 cards. So, from each suit, 4 cards can be choosed in $^{13}C_4$ ways separately.

$\therefore$ Required number of ways

$= {}^{13}C_4 + {}^{13}C_4 + {}^{13}C_4 + {}^{13}C_4$

Ans. 2860

(ii) We have to select one card from each suit.

Required number of ways = $^{13}C_1 \times {}^{13}C_1 \times {}^{13}C_1 \times {}^{13}C_1$

Ans. 13^4

(iii) There are 12 face cards and we have to select 4 cards out of these.

Required number of ways = $^{12}C_4$. **Ans.** 495

(iv) There are 26 red cards and 26 black cards.

$\therefore$ Required number of ways = $^{26}C_2 \times {}^{26}C_2$

Ans. 105625

(v) Required number of ways = $2 \times {}^{26}C_4$ **Ans.** 29900

Chapter Practice

Multiple Choice Type Questions

1 Mark

1. Suppose you have a suitcase with a number lock. The number lock has 4 wheels each labelled with 10 digits from 0 to 9. The lock can be opened, if 4 specific digits are arranged in a particular sequence with no repetition. Some how, you have forgotten this specific sequence of digits. You remember only the first digit which is 7. In order to open the lock, how many sequences of 3 digits you may have to check with?
   (a) 720 (b) 504
   (c) 500 (d) None of these

2. The sum of the digits in unit place of all the numbers formed with the help of 3, 4, 5 and 6 taken all at a time is **[NCERT Exemplar]**
   (a) 432 (b) 108 (c) 36 (d) 18

3. Match the following columns and choose the correct option from the codes given below.

Column I		Column II
A. $\frac{7!}{5!}$ equals	1.	28
B. $\frac{12!}{(10!)(2!)}$ equals	2.	42
C. $\frac{8!}{6!\times 2!}$ equals	3.	66

Codes

	A	B	C		A	B	C
(a)	1	2	3	(b)	1	3	2
(c)	3	2	1	(d)	2	3	1

4. Consider the following statements
   Statement I If $5\,{}^4P_r = 6\,{}^5P_{r-1}$, then $r = 8, 3$
   Statement II If ${}^5P_r = {}^6P_{r-1}$, then $r = 5$
   Which of the above statements (s) is/are true?
   (a) Only I (b) Only II
   (c) Both I and II (d) Neither I nor II

5. Identify the correct combination of true (T) and false (F) of the given two statements.
   Statement I The number of permutations of letters of word 'ROOT' are 12.
   Statement II The number of permutations of letters of word 'INSTITUTE' are $\frac{9!}{2!\,3!}$.
   (a) F T (b) TF (c) FF (d) T T

6. A five-digit number divisible by 3 is to be formed using the numbers 0, 1, 2, 3, 4 and 5, without repetition. The total number of ways this can be done, is **[NCERT Exemplar]**
   (a) 216 (b) 240 (c) 600 (d) 3125

Assertion-Reason Type Questions

1 Mark

Directions (Q. Nos. 7-10) *In the questions given below are two statements labelled as Assertion (A) and Reason (R). In the context of the two statements, which one of the following is correct?*

(a) Both A and R are correct; R is the correct explanation of A
(b) Both A and R are correct; R is not the correct explanation of A
(c) A is correct; R is incorrect
(d) R is correct; A is incorrect

7. **Assertion (A)** If $P(n, 5) = 20\,P(n, 3)$, then value of n is 8.
   Reason (R) $P(n, r) = {}^nP_r = \frac{n!}{(n-r)!}, 0 \le r \le n.$

8. **Assertion (A)** If ${}^{n-1}C_r : {}^nC_r : {}^{n+1}C_r = 6:9:13$, then values of n and r are 12 and 4 respectively.
   Reason (R) ${}^nC_r = \frac{n!}{r!\,(n-r)!}$.

9. **Assertion (A)** If a polygon has 54 diagonals, then the number of its sides is 13.
   Reason (R) When diagonals are formed by joining any two non-adjacent vertices of a polygon. Then, the total number of diagonals is ${}^nC_2 - n$.

10. **Assertion (A)** ${}^{15}C_r : {}^{15}C_{r-1} = 11 : 5$, then $r = 5$
    Reason (R) ${}^nC_r = \frac{n!}{r!\,(n-r)!}$.

Very Short Answer Type Questions

2 Marks

11. If $\frac{1}{9!}+\frac{1}{10!}=\frac{x}{11!}$, then find the value of x.

12. Evaluate $\frac{n!}{(n-r)!}$, when $n=9$ and $r=5$.

13. Evaluate the following.
(i) ${}^5P_2$ (ii) ${}^{10}P_4$ (iii) ${}^6P_6$

14. If $P(n, 4)=12 \cdot P(n, 2)$, then find n.

15. Find the value of n such that
$P(n, 4): P(n-1, 4)=5: 3, n>4$.

16. If ${}^{56}P_{r+6}:{}^{54}P_{r+3}=30800: 1$, then find r.

17. If ${}^nC_{12}={}^nC_5$, then find the value of n.

18. If ${}^nC_8={}^nC_6$, then find ${}^nC_2$.

19. Find the number of ways in which (i) n different beads (ii) 10 different beads can be arranged to form a necklace.

20. There are 5 questions in a question paper. In how many ways can a boy solve one or more questions?

21. Find n, if $(n+1)!=12 \times(n-1)!$.

22. If ${}^{15}C_r:{}^{15}C_{r-1}=11: 5$, then find r.

23. If ${}^{2n}C_3:{}^nC_2=44: 3$, then find n.

24. In a cinema hall, there are three entrance doors and two exit doors. In how many ways can a person enter the hall and then come out?

25. 25 buses are running between Delhi and Noida. In how many ways, can a person go from Delhi to Noida and return by a different bus?

26. There are 6 multiple choice questions in an examination. How many sequences of answers are possible, if the first three questions have 4 choices each and remaining three have 3 each?

27. In how many ways, can 50 voters vote for the 4 candidates contesting the election for the post of secretary of their association?

28. How many numbers are there between 100 and 1000 such that every digit is either 2 or 9?

Short Answer Type Questions

4 Marks

29. How many 3 letter words can be made using the letters of the word 'ORIENTAL'?

30. Find how many arrangements can be made with the letters of the word 'MATHEMATICS'?

31. In how many ways can the letters of the word 'PENCIL' be arranged so that N and E are always together?

32. How many different words can be formed with the letters of the word 'TRIANGLE' so that the word begin with T and end with E.

33. From a group of 15 cricket players, a team of 11 players is to be chosen. In how many ways can this be done?

34. 7 points lie on a circle. How many chords can be drawn by joining these points?

35. How many 4 letters code can be formed using the first 10 letters of the English alphabet, if no letters can be repeated? [NCERT]

36. How many 5-digit telephone numbers can be constructed using the digits 0 to 9, if each number starts with 67 (e.g. 67125 etc.) and no digit appear more than once? [NCERT]

37. How many 3-digit numbers can be formed using the digits 0, 2, 3, 6, 8, when the digits may be repeated any number of times?

38. How many 3-digit numbers can be formed without using the digits 0, 2, 3, 4, 5 and 6?

39. A coin is tossed 6 times and the outcomes are recorded. How many possible outcomes are there?

40. In how many ways 5 rings of different types can be worn in 4 fingers?

41. Find the number of ways in which 8 distinct toys can be distributed among 5 children.

42. In how many ways can three jobs I, II and III be assigned to three persons A, B and C, if one person is assigned only one job and all are capable of doing each job?

43. From among the 35 teachers in a school, one principal and one vice-principal are to be appointed. In how many ways can this be done?

Long Answer Type Questions

6 Marks

44. How many 6-digit numbers can be formed from the digits 0, 1, 3, 5, 7 and 9, which are divisible by 10 and no digit is repeated?

45. If the different permutations of the word 'EXAMINATION' are listed as in a dictionary, then how many words are there in the list before the first word starting with E? **[NCERT]**

46. Out of 5 men and 2 women, a committee of 3 is to be formed. In how many ways can it be formed, if atleast one women is to be included?

47. There are 12 points in a plane of which 5 points are collinear. Find the number of lines obtained by joining these points in pairs.

48. Three balls are drawn from a bag containing 5 red, 4 white and 3 black balls. Find the number of ways in which this can be done, if atleast 2 balls are red. **[NCERT Exemplar]**

49. Find the number of combinations, when some or all of n objects are taken at a time. **[NCERT Exemplar]**

50. How many odd numbers less than 1000 can be formed by using the digits 0, 2, 5, 7 when the repetition of digits is allowed?

Case-Based Type Questions

6 Marks

51. Find the number of arrangements of the letters of the word 'INDEPENDENCE'. In how many of these arrangements

(i) do the words start with P?

(ii) do all the vowels always occur together?

(iii) do all the vowels never occur together?

(iv) do the words begin with I and end in P? **[NCERT]**

52. Using the digits 1, 2, 3, 4, 5, 6, 7, a number of 4 different digits is formed. Find how many numbers are formed? Further, find how many of these are

(i) exactly divisible by 2?

(ii) exactly divisible by 25?

(iii) exactly divisible by 4? **[NCERT Exemplar]**

Hints & Answers

1. (b) **2.** (b) **3.** (d) **4.** (d) **5.** (d)

6. (a) **7.** (a) **8.** (a) **9.** (d) **10.** (a)

11. $\because \frac{11\times 10}{11!}+\frac{11}{11!}=\frac{x}{11!} \Rightarrow 121 = x$

12. $\because \frac{9!}{(9-5)!}=3024$

13. (i) ${}^5P_2=\frac{5!}{3!}=20$

(ii) 5040

(iii) 720

14. $\because {}^nP_4 = 12\cdot {}^nP_2$

$\Rightarrow \frac{n!}{(n-4)!}=12\times\frac{n!}{(n-2)!}$

$\Rightarrow \quad 1 = 12\times\frac{1}{(n-2)(n-3)}$

$\Rightarrow \quad (n-2)(n-3)=12$

$\Rightarrow \quad (n-2)(n-3)=4\times 3 \Rightarrow n=6$

15. 10

16. 41

17. $\because {}^nC_{12}={}^nC_5$

$\Rightarrow {}^nC_{n-12}={}^nC_5$ **Ans.** $n=17$

18. ${}^nC_8={}^nC_6 \Rightarrow {}^nC_{n-8}={}^nC_6 \Rightarrow n-8=6 \Rightarrow n=14$

Ans. 91

19. (i) $\frac{(n-1)!}{2}$ (ii) $\frac{9!}{2}10\cdot 31$

21. Given, $(n+1)! = 12\times(n-1)!$

$\Rightarrow \quad (n+1)\,n=12$

Ans. $n=3$

22. $\frac{{}^{15}C_r}{{}^{15}C_{r-1}}=\frac{11}{5}$

$\Rightarrow \frac{15!}{(15-r)!\,r!}\times\frac{(15-r+1)!\times(r-1)!}{15!}=\frac{11}{5}$

Ans. $r=5$

23. $n=6$

24. 6

25. 600

26. Total number of sequences of answers are possible $=4\times4\times4\times3\times3\times3$

27. Each person gives a vote for any of the four persons.

28. Only three-digit number exists between 100 and 1000. But each digit only any of two numbers 2 or 9 can be place.

Ans. 8

29. All letters in a given word are distinct.
The number of ways in which 3-letter words can be formed from 8 letters $= {}^8P_3$
Ans. = 336

30. The letters in the word 'MATHEMATICS' are (MM, AA, TT, H, E, I, C, S).
Ans. $\frac{11!}{2!\,2!\,2!}$

31. We consider N and E as one letter and remaining four letters are (P, C, I, L).
Ans. $5! \times 2!$

32. In a word, 'TRIANGLE', all letters are distrinct.
When we fix the letters T and E in the beginning and end, **Ans.** 6! ways

33. Required number of ways $= {}^{15}C_{11}$

34. Required number of chords $= {}^7C_2$

35. Total number of 4 letters code $= {}^{10}C_4$

36. In 5-digit telephone number, first two digits are fixed and rest of the three place number appears 8, 7, 6 ways = 336

37. 0 do not comes in hundred's place, so only 4 numbers are possible in hundred's place. Since, the digits are repeated, so remaining two digits, 5 numbers are possible in each place. **Ans.** 100

38. 64

39. 36

40. Each ring can be worn in any four fingers. **Ans.** 4^5

41. Each toy can be ditributed to any of the children. **Ans.** 5^8

42. 3!

43. ${}^{35}P_2$

44. 5!

45. The letters of given word are A, A, E, I, I, M, N, O, T, X i.e. word starting with *A* are formed with the letters $2I's,\ 2N's,\ A, E, X, M, T, O$ (total 10 letters).
Ans. 907200

46. Required number of ways $= {}^2C_1 \times {}^5C_2 + {}^2C_2 \times {}^5C_1$

47. Required number of ways $= {}^{12}C_2 - {}^5C_2 + 1$

48. Required number of ways $= {}^5C_2 \times {}^7C_1 + {}^5C_3$

49. Required number of ways $= {}^nC_1 + {}^nC_2 + \ldots + {}^nC_n$
Ans. $2^n - 1$

50. For odd number, first place should be odd number and rest of places may any of the number.
Also, less than 1000 means, number should be one digit, two digits and three digits odd numbers.
Number of one digit odd number = 2
Number of two digits odd number $= {}^2C_1 \times 4 = 8$
Number of three digits odd number $= {}^2C_1 \times 4 \times 4 = 32$

51. The letters in the word INDEPENDENCE are (I, N, N, N, D, D, E, E, E, E, P, C).
$\therefore$ Total number of arrangement $= \frac{12!}{3! \times 2! \times 4!}$
Ans. 1663200

(i) Total number of words start with P $= \frac{11!}{3! \times 2! \times 4!}$
Ans. 138600

(ii) Total number of words, when all the vowels occur together $= \frac{8! \times 5!}{3! \times 2! \times 4!}$
[consider all vowels at one unit]
Ans. 16800

(iii) Total number of ways = Total arrangements − Number of arrangements when vowels occurs together $= \frac{12!}{3! \times 2! \times 4!} - \frac{8! \times 5!}{3! \times 2! \times 4!}$
Ans. 1646400

(iv) Total number of words $= \frac{10!}{3! \times 2! \times 4!}$
Ans. 12600

52. Number of four different digits formed $= {}^7P_4$
Ans. 840

(i) Even number should be in unit's place and remaining any three digits, any different number can be placed.
$\therefore$ Total number of ways $= {}^6P_3 \times {}^3C_1$
Ans. 360

(ii) Any four digit number is divisible by 25, if last two digits should be divisible by 25 i.e. 25, 75.
$\therefore$ Total number of ways $= {}^5P_2 \times {}^2C_1$
Ans. 40

(iii) Any number is divisible by 4, if last two digits is divisible by 4 i.e. last digits can be 12, 16, 24, 32, 36, 52, 56, 54, 72, 76.
$\therefore$ Total number of ways $= {}^5P_2 \times {}^{10}C_1$
Ans. 200

53. (i) $\frac{n!}{p_1!\,p_2!\ldots p_k!}$
(ii) 138600
(iii) 16800
(iv) 1646400
(v) 12600

54. (i) 1
(ii) $\frac{n!}{(n-r)!}$
(iii) −1
(iv) 6 yrs
(v) 3 feet

CHAPTER

08

Binomial Theorem

In earlier classes, we have already learnt how to find the squares and cubes of expression of the form $a+b$ and $a-b$. But for higher powers like $(a+b)^8$, $(a-b)^{10}$, etc. the calculation become difficult. This difficulty can be overcome by using binomial theorem. It gives an easier way to expand $(a+b)^n$, where n is a positive integer.

- Binomial Theorem for Positive Integral Power (or Index)
- General and Middle Terms in the Binomial Expansion
- Applications of Binomial Theorem

TOPIC 01 Binomial Theorem for Positive Integral Power (or Index)

Binomial Expression

An algebraic expression consisting of two terms with +ve or −ve sign between them, is called **binomial expression.**

e.g. $(a+2b)$, $\left(\frac{p}{x^2}-\frac{q}{x^4}\right)$, $\left(3x-\frac{2}{y}\right)$

Significance of Pascal's Triangle

In earlier classes, we have already studied that

(i) $(a+b)^0=1$ (ii) $(a+b)^1=a+b$

(iii) $(a+b)^2=a^2+2ab+b^2$ (iv) $(a+b)^3=a^3+3a^2b+3ab^2+b^3$

(v) $(a+b)^4=a^4+4a^3b+6a^2b^2+4ab^3+b^4$

In these expansions, we observe that

(i) The total number of terms in the expansion is one more than the index.

(ii) Powers of first quantity 'a' is decreasing by 1, whereas powers of second quantity 'b' increase by 1, in the successive terms.

(iii) In each term of the expansion, the sum of indices of a and b is the same and is equal to the index of $(a+b)$.

Also, the coefficient of variables in the above expansions follow a particular pattern, which is given below

Index	Coefficients
0	1
1	1 ∇ 1
2	1 ∇ 2 ∇ 1
3	1 ∇ 3 ∇ 3 ∇ 1
4	1 ∇ 4 ∇ 6 ∇ 4 ∇ 1
5	1 ∇ 5 ∇ 10 ∇ 10 ∇ 5 ∇ 1

It can be seen that the addition of 1's in the row for index 1 gives rise to 2 in the row for index 2. The addition of 1, 2 and 2, 1 in the row for index 2 gives rise to 3 and 3 in the row for index 3 and so on.

Also each row is bounded by 1 on both sides. The structure looks like a triangle with 1 at the top vertex and running down the two slanting sides. This structure or array of numbers, is known as Pascal's triangle.

Pascal's Triangle with the Help of Combination

To find the expansion of the binomial for any power without writing all the rows of the Pascal's triangle that come before the row of the desired index. We can use a rule which is based on combination.

We know that

$${}^nC_r = \frac{n!}{r!(n-r)!} (0 \le r \le n) \text{ and } n \text{ is non-negative integer.}$$

Here, ${}^nC_0 = {}^nC_n = 1$.

Write the Pascal triangle as given below

Index	Coefficients
0	${}^0C_0$ (=1)
1	${}^1C_0$ (=1) ${}^1C_1$ (=1)
2	${}^2C_0$ (=1) ${}^2C_1$ (=2) ${}^2C_2$ (=1)
3	${}^3C_0$ (=1) ${}^3C_1$ (=3) ${}^3C_2$ (=3) ${}^3C_3$ (=1)
4	${}^4C_0$ (=1) ${}^4C_1$ (=4) ${}^4C_2$ (=6) ${}^4C_3$ (=4) ${}^4C_4$ (=1)
5	${}^5C_0$ (=1) ${}^5C_1$ (=5) ${}^5C_2$ (=10) ${}^5C_3$ (=10) ${}^5C_4$ (=5) ${}^5C_5$ (=1)

Clearly, with the help of this pattern, row of the Pascal's triangle for any index can be written without writing the earlier rows.

e.g. For $n = 7$, the row would be

$${}^7C_0, {}^7C_1, {}^7C_2, {}^7C_3, {}^7C_4, {}^7C_5, {}^7C_6, {}^7C_7$$

Binomial Theorem for Positive Integral Power

Theorem If a and b are two real numbers, then for any positive integer n, we have

$$(a+b)^n = {}^nC_0a^nb^0 + {}^nC_1a^{n-1}b^1 + {}^nC_2a^{n-2}b^2 + \ldots + {}^nC_na^0b^n$$

$$(a+b)^n = {}^nC_0a^n + {}^nC_1a^{n-1}b + {}^nC_2a^{n-2}b^2 + \ldots + {}^nC_nb^n$$

$$\Rightarrow \quad (a+b)^n = \sum_{r=0}^{n} {}^nC_ra^{n-r}b^r$$

where, ${}^nC_0, {}^nC_1, \ldots, {}^nC_n$ are called **binomial coefficients.**

These binomial coefficients can also be written as $C_0, C_1, \ldots, C_n$.

Proof Here, we will proof this theorem with the help of mathematical induction.

Let $P(n)$ be the statement

$$P(n): (a+b)^n = {}^nC_0\,a^n + {}^nC_1\,a^{n-1}\,b + {}^nC_2\,a^{n-2}\,b^2 + \ldots + {}^nC_{n-1}\,ab^{n-1} + {}^nC_n\,b^n \quad \ldots \text{(i)}$$

On putting $n = 1$, we get

$$P(1): (a+b)^1 = {}^1C_0\,a^1 + {}^1C_1\,b^1$$

i.e. $\quad P(1): (a+b) = 1 \times a + 1 \times b$, which is true

$\therefore \quad P(1)$ is true.

Let $P(k)$ is true,

i.e. $$P(k): {}^kC_0\,a^k + {}^kC_1\,a^{k-1}\,b + {}^kC_2\,a^{k-2}\,b^2 + \ldots + {}^kC_{k-1}\,ab^{k-1} + {}^kC_k\,b^k \quad \ldots \text{(ii)}$$

Now, putting $n = k+1$ in Eq. (i), we get

$$P(k+1): (a+b)^{k+1} = (a+b)^k\,(a+b)$$

$$= ({}^kC_0\,a^k + {}^kC_1\,a^{k-1}\,b + {}^kC_2\,a^{k-2}\,b^2 + \ldots + {}^kC_{k-1}\,ab^{k-1} + {}^kC_k\,b^k)\,(a+b)$$

[from Eq. (i)]

$$= {}^kC_0\,a^{k+1} + {}^kC_1\,a^k\,b + {}^kC_2\,a^{k-1}\,b^2 + \ldots + {}^kC_{k-1}\,a^2\,b^{k-1} + {}^kC_k\,ab^k + {}^kC_0\,a^k\,b + {}^kC_1\,a^{k-1}\,b^2 + {}^kC_2\,a^{k-2}\,b^3 + \ldots + {}^kC_{k-1}\,ab^k + {}^kC_k\,b^{k+1}$$

[by actual multiplication]

$$= {}^kC_0\,a^{k+1} + ({}^kC_1 + {}^kC_0)\,a^k b + ({}^kC_2 + {}^kC_1)\,a^{k-1}\,b^2 + \ldots + ({}^kC_k + {}^kC_{k-1})\,ab^k + {}^kC_k\,b^{k+1}$$

[grouping like terms]

$$= {}^{k+1}C_0\, a^{k+1} + {}^{k+1}C_1\, a^k\, b + {}^{k+1}C_2\, a^{k-1}\, b^2 + \ldots + {}^{k+1}C_k\, ab^k + {}^{k+1}C_{k+1}\, b^{k+1}$$

We know that, ${}^kC_0 = 1 = {}^{k+1}C_0$, ${}^kC_k = 1 = {}^{k+1}C_{k+1}$

and ${}^kC_r + {}^kC_{r-1} = {}^{k+1}C_r$, $r = 1, 2, 3, \ldots, k$

$\Rightarrow$ ${}^kC_1 + {}^kC_0 = {}^{k+1}C_1$, ${}^kC_2 + {}^kC_1 = {}^{k+1}C_2$

$+ \ldots + {}^kC_k + {}^kC_{k-1} = {}^{k+1}C_k$

$\therefore$ $P(k+1)$ is true.

Hence, by principle of mathematical induction, $P(k)$ is true for all $n \in N$.

Some Important Observations

(i) The total number of terms in the expansion is one more than the index, i.e. the total number of terms in $(a+b)^n$ is $(n+1)$.

(ii) In the successive terms of the expansion, powers of the first quantity a go on decreasing by 1, i.e. it is n in the first term, $(n-1)$ in the second term and so on ending with zero in the last term whereas the powers of the second quantity b increase by 1, i.e. it is zero in first term, 1 in the second term and so on ending with n in the last term.

(iii) In each term of the expansion, the sum of the indices of a and b is the same and is equal to the index of $(a+b)^n$ i.e. n.

(iv) The binomial coefficients of terms equidistant from the beginning and end are equal.

Formulae Related to Binomial Coefficients

(i) ${}^nC_r = \dfrac{n!}{r!\,(n-r)!}$ $(0 \le r \le n)$

(ii) ${}^nC_0 = {}^nC_n = 1$, ${}^nC_1 = n$

(iii) ${}^nC_r = {}^nC_{n-r}$

(iv) ${}^nC_r + {}^nC_{r-1} = {}^{n+1}C_r$

(v) ${}^nC_x = {}^nC_y \Leftrightarrow x = y$ or $x + y = n$

(vi) $\dfrac{{}^nC_r}{{}^nC_{r-1}} = \dfrac{n-r+1}{r}$

(vii) ${}^nC_0 + {}^nC_1 + {}^nC_2 + \ldots + {}^nC_n = 2^n$

(viii) ${}^nC_0 + {}^nC_2 + {}^nC_4 + \ldots = {}^nC_1 + {}^nC_3 + {}^nC_5 + \ldots = 2^{n-1}$

Example 1 Find the number of terms in the expansions of following expressions.

(i) $(x+3y)^2$ (ii) $(1-z)^4$

Sol. (i) Given expression is $(x+3y)^2$. Here, $n = 2$

$\therefore$ The number of terms in expansion is $(n+1)$

i.e. $2+1=3$

(ii) Given expression is $(1-z)^4$.

Here, $n = 4$

$\therefore$ The number of terms in the expansion is $(n+1)$

i.e. $4+1=5$.

Example 2 Using binomial theorem, expand $(x^2+2y)^5$.

Sol. By binomial theorem, we have

$(a+b)^n = {}^nC_0\, a^n + {}^nC_1\, a^{n-1}b + {}^nC_2\, a^{n-2}b^2 + \ldots + {}^nC_n (b)^n$

Here, $a = x^2$, $b = 2y$ and $n = 5$

$$\therefore (x^2+2y)^5 = {}^5C_0\,(x^2)^5 + {}^5C_1\,(x^2)^4\,(2y) + {}^5C_2\,(x^2)^3\,(2y)^2 + {}^5C_3\,(x^2)^2\,(2y)^3 + {}^5C_4\,(x^2)(2y)^4 + {}^5C_5\,(2y)^5$$

$$= x^{10} + 5x^8(2y) + 10x^6(4y^2) + 10x^4(8y^3) + 5x^2(16y^4) + 32y^5$$

$$= x^{10} + 10x^8y + 40x^6y^2 + 80x^4y^3 + 80x^2y^4 + 32y^5$$

Example 3 Prove that $\sum_{r=0}^{n} 3^r\, {}^nC_r = 4^n$. **[NCERT]**

Use $(1+x)^n = {}^nC_0 + {}^nC_1x + {}^nC_2x^2 + {}^nC_3x^3 + \ldots + {}^nC_nx^n$ and prove the result.

Sol. We have, $\sum_{r=0}^{n} {}^nC_r \times 3^r = {}^nC_0 3^0 + {}^nC_1 3 + {}^nC_2 3^2 + {}^nC_3 3^3 + \ldots + {}^nC_n 3^n$

[on putting $r = 0, 1, 2, \ldots, n$]

$= {}^nC_0 + {}^nC_1 3 + {}^nC_2 3^2 + {}^nC_3 3^3 + \ldots + {}^nC_n 3^n$

$= (1+3)^n$ $[\because (1+x)^n = {}^nC_0 + {}^nC_1x + {}^nC_2x^2 + \ldots + {}^nC_nx^n]$

$= 4^n$ **Hence proved.**

Particular Cases of Binomial Theorem

(i) **Expansion of $(a-b)^n$** Replacing b by $(-b)$ in the expansion of $(a+b)^n$, we get

$$(a-b)^n = [a+(-b)]^n = {}^nC_0a^n - {}^nC_1a^{n-1}b + {}^nC_2a^{n-2}b^2 + \ldots + (-1)^n\, {}^nC_nb^n$$

(ii) **Expansion of $(1+x)^n$** Replacing a by 1 and b by x in the expansion of $(a+b)^n$, we get

$$(1+x)^n = {}^nC_0 1^n + {}^nC_1 1^{n-1}x + {}^nC_2 1^{n-2}x^2 + \ldots + {}^nC_nx^n$$

$$= 1 + {}^nC_1x + {}^nC_2x^2 + \ldots + {}^nC_nx^n$$

$$= 1 + nx + \frac{n(n-1)}{2!}x^2 + \ldots + x^n$$

(iii) **Expansion of $(1-x)^n$** Replacing a by 1 and b by $(-x)$ in the expansion of $(a+b)^n$, we get

$$(1-x)^n = {}^nC_0 - {}^nC_1x + {}^nC_2x^2 + \dots + (-1)^n\, {}^nC_n\, x^n$$
$$= 1 - nx + \frac{n(n-1)}{2!}x^2 - \dots + (-1)^n x^n$$

(iv) $(x+a)^n + (x-a)^n = 2[{}^nC_0x^n + {}^nC_2x^{n-2}a^2 + \dots]$
$= 2$ (sum of terms at odd places)

Note

(i) The last term will be ${}^nC_na^n$ or ${}^nC_{n-1}xa^{n-1}$ according as n is even or odd, respectively.

(ii) If n is odd, then number of terms in $[(x+a)^n + (x-a)^n]$ is $\left(\frac{n+1}{2}\right)$ and if n is even, then number of terms is $\left(\frac{n}{2}+1\right)$.

(v) $(x+a)^n - (x-a)^n = 2[{}^nC_1x^{n-1}a^1 + {}^nC_3x^{n-3}a^3 + \dots]$
$= 2$ (sum of terms at even places)

Note

(i) The last term will be ${}^nC_{n-1}xa^{n-1}$ or ${}^nC_na^n$ as n is even or odd, respectively.

(ii) If n is odd, then number of terms in $[(x+a)^n - (x-a)^n]$ is $\left(\frac{n+1}{2}\right)$ and if n is even, then number of terms is $\left(\frac{n}{2}\right)$.

Example 4 Using binomial theorem, expand the following expressions.

(i) $(2x-3)^6$

(ii) $(1-2x)^5$

Sol. (i) We have, $(2x-3)^6 = {}^6C_0(2x)^6 - {}^6C_1(2x)^5 \times 3 + {}^6C_2(2x)^4(3)^2 - {}^6C_3(2x)^3(3)^3 + {}^6C_4(2x)^2(3)^4 - {}^6C_5(2x)3^5 + {}^6C_63^6$

$$= {}^6C_0\, 64x^6 - {}^6C_1 32x^5 \times 3 + {}^6C_2 16x^4 \times 9 - {}^6C_3 8x^3 \times 27 + {}^6C_2\, 4x^2 \times 81 - {}^6C_1\, 2x \times 243 + {}^6C_0 729$$
$[\because {}^nC_r = {}^nC_{n-r}]$

$$= 64x^6 - 6 \times 32 \times 3 \times x^5 + \frac{6\times5}{2} \times 16x^4 \times 9 - \frac{6\times5\times4\times8x^3\times27}{6} + \frac{6\times5}{2}\times4x^2\times81 - 6\times2x\times243 + 729$$
$$= 64x^6 - 576x^5 + 2160x^4 - 4320x^3 + 4860x^2 - 2916x + 729$$

(ii) Consider, $(1-2x)^5 = [1+(-2x)]^5$

$$= {}^5C_0 + {}^5C_1(-2x) + {}^5C_2(-2x)^2 + {}^5C_3(-2x)^3 + {}^5C_4(-2x)^4 + {}^5C_5(-2x)^5$$
$$= 1 + 5(-2x) + 10(4x^2) + 10(-8x^3) + 5(16x^4) + 1(-32x^5)$$
$$= 1 - 10x + 40x^2 - 80x^3 + 80x^4 - 32x^5$$

which is the required expansion.

Example 5 Expand $\left(\frac{2x}{3} - \frac{3}{2x}\right)^4$.

Sol. We have, $\left(\frac{2x}{3} - \frac{3}{2x}\right)^4 = {}^4C_0\left(\frac{2x}{3}\right)^4 - {}^4C_1\left(\frac{2x}{3}\right)^3\left(\frac{3}{2x}\right) + {}^4C_2\left(\frac{2x}{3}\right)^2\left(\frac{3}{2x}\right)^2 - {}^4C_3\left(\frac{2x}{3}\right)\left(\frac{3}{2x}\right)^3 + {}^4C_4\left(\frac{3}{2x}\right)^4$

$$= 1 \times \frac{16x^4}{81} - 4 \times \frac{8x^3}{27}\left(\frac{3}{2x}\right) + 6 \cdot \frac{4x^2}{9}\left(\frac{9}{4x^2}\right) - 4\left(\frac{2x}{3}\right)\left(\frac{27}{8x^3}\right) + 1 \times \left(\frac{81}{16x^4}\right)$$

$\left[\because {}^4C_0 = {}^4C_4 = 1,\ {}^4C_3 = {}^4C_1 = 4 \text{ and } {}^4C_2 = \frac{4!}{2!2!} = \frac{4\times3\times2!}{2\times1\times2!} = 6\right]$

$$= \frac{16}{81}x^4 - \frac{16}{9}x^2 + 6 - \frac{9}{x^2} + \frac{81}{16x^4}$$

Example 6 Find the number of terms in the expansions of the following expressions.

(i) $(x+a)^{100} + (x-a)^{100}$ (ii) $(1+\sqrt{5}x)^7 + (1-\sqrt{5}x)^7$

(iii) $(y+a)^{30} - (y-a)^{30}$ **[NCERT Exemplar]**

Sol. (i) Given expression is $(x+a)^{100} + (x-a)^{100}$.

Here, $n = 100$, which is even.

$\therefore$ Total number of terms $= \frac{n}{2} + 1 = \frac{100}{2} + 1 = 51$

(ii) Given expression is $(1+\sqrt{5}x)^7 + (1-\sqrt{5}x)^7$.

Here, $n = 7$, which is odd.

$\therefore$ Total number of terms $= \frac{n+1}{2} = \frac{7+1}{2} = \frac{8}{2} = 4$

(iii) Given expression is $(y+a)^{30} - (y-a)^{30}$.

Here $n = 30$, which is even.

$\therefore$ Total number of terms $= \frac{n}{2} = \frac{30}{2} = 15$

Example 7 Find $(x+1)^6 + (x-1)^6$. Hence evaluate $(\sqrt{2}+1)^6 + (\sqrt{2}-1)^6$. Also, show that the value of $(\sqrt{2}+1)^6$ lies between 197 and 198. **[NCERT]**

Sol. We have, $(x+1)^6 = {}^6C_0x^6 + {}^6C_1x^5 \times 1 + {}^6C_2x^4 \times (1)^2 + {}^6C_3x^3 \times (1)^3 + {}^6C_4x^2 \times (1)^4 + {}^6C_5x \times (1)^5 + {}^6C_6(1)^6$

$\Rightarrow (x+1)^6 = {}^6C_0x^6 + {}^6C_1x^5 + {}^6C_2x^4 + {}^6C_3x^3 + {}^6C_2x^2 + {}^6C_1x + {}^6C_0$ $[\because {}^nC_r = {}^nC_{n-r}]$

$$\Rightarrow (x+1)^6 = x^6 + 6x^5 + \frac{6\times5}{2}x^4 + \frac{6\times5\times4}{6}x^3 + \frac{6\times5}{2}x^2 + 6x + 1$$

$$\Rightarrow (x+1)^6 = x^6 + 6x^5 + 15x^4 + 20x^3 + 15x^2 + 6x + 1 \quad \dots(i)$$

Similarly,

$$(x-1)^6 = x^6 - 6x^5 + 15x^4 - 20x^3 + 15x^2 - 6x + 1 \quad \dots(ii)$$

On adding Eqs. (i) and (ii), we get

$$(x+1)^6+(x-1)^6=2[x^6+15x^4+15x^2+1]$$

Now, putting $x=\sqrt{2}$, we get

$$(\sqrt{2}+1)^6+(\sqrt{2}-1)^6=2[(\sqrt{2})^6+15(\sqrt{2})^4+15(\sqrt{2})^2+1]$$
$$=2(2^3+15\times 2^2+15\times 2+1)=2(8+15\times 4+30+1)$$
$$=2(8+60+30+1)=2\times 99=198$$

Since, $(\sqrt{2}-1)^6=(1.42-1)^6=(0.42)^6<1$

$\therefore\ (\sqrt{2}+1)^6+(\sqrt{2}-1)^6=198$

$\Rightarrow (\sqrt{2}+1)^6=198-(\sqrt{2}-1)^6$

$=198-$ A number lies between 0 and 1

$\therefore\ (\sqrt{2}+1)^6=$ A number lies between 197 and 198

Hence, the integral part of $(\sqrt{2}+1)^6$ is 197.

Example 8 In the expansion of $(x+a)^n$, if the sum of odd terms is denoted by O and the sum of even terms by E. Then, prove that

(i) $O^2-E^2=(x^2-a^2)^n$ (ii) $4OE=(x+a)^{2n}-(x-a)^{2n}$.

Sol. (i) We know that, $(x+a)^n={}^nC_0\,x^na^0+{}^nC_1x^{n-1}a^1+{}^nC_2x^{n-2}a^2+{}^nC_3x^{n-3}a^3+\dots+{}^nC_na^n$

Now, sum of odd terms,

$$O={}^nC_0x^n+{}^nC_2x^{n-2}a^2+\dots$$

and sum of even terms,

$$E={}^nC_1x^{n-1}a+{}^nC_3x^{n-3}a^3+\dots$$

Thus $(x+a)^n=O+E$ ...(i)

Similarly, $(x-a)^n=O-E$ ...(ii)

Now, multiplying Eqs. (i) and (ii), we get

$$(O+E)(O-E)=(x+a)^n(x-a)^n$$
$$\Rightarrow O^2-E^2=(x^2-a^2)^n$$

(ii) Clearly, $4\,OE=(O+E)^2-(O-E)^2$

$$\Rightarrow 4OE=[(x+a)^n]^2-[(x-a)^n]^2$$

[from Eqs. (i) and (ii)]

$=(x+a)^{2n}-(x-a)^{2n}$ **Hence proved.**

Example 9 Evaluate $(x^2-\sqrt{1-x^2})^4+(x^2+\sqrt{1-x^2})^4$. **[NCERT Exemplar]**

Sol. Let $E=(x^2-\sqrt{1-x^2})^4+(x^2+\sqrt{1-x^2})^4$

Put $\sqrt{1-x^2}=y$, we get $E=(x^2-y)^4+(x^2+y)^4$

$$=2[{}^4C_0(x^2)^4y^0+{}^4C_2(x^2)^2y^2+{}^4C_4(x^2)^0y^4]$$

[if n is even, then $(x-a)^n+(x+a)^n=2\{{}^nC_0\,x^na^0+{}^nC_2\,x^{n-2}a^2+{}^nC_4x^{n-4}a^4+\dots\}$]

$$=2[1\times x^8\times 1+6\times x^4y^2+1\times 1\times y^4]$$
$$=2[x^8+6x^4(1-x^2)+(1-x^2)^2]\quad [\text{put } y=\sqrt{1-x^2}]$$
$$=2(x^8+6x^4-6x^6+1+x^4-2x^2)$$
$$=2x^8-12x^6+14x^4-4x^2+2$$

Example 10 Using binomial theorem, expand $(x^2-2x+1)^3$.

Sol. We have, $(x^2-2x+1)^3=[(x-1)^2]^3=(x-1)^6$

$$={}^6C_0(x)^6-{}^6C_1(x)^5(1)^1+{}^6C_2(x)^4(1)^2-{}^6C_3(x)^3(1)^3+{}^6C_4(x)^2(1)^4-{}^6C_5(x)^1(1)^5+{}^6C_6(1)^6$$
$$=x^6-6x^5+15x^4-20x^3+15x^2-6x+1$$

Example 11 Expand the following using binomial theorem.

(i) $(1-x+x^2)^4$ (ii) $\left(1+\frac{x}{2}-\frac{2}{x}\right)^4,\ x\neq 0$

Sol. (i) We have, $(1-x+x^2)^4=[(1-x)+x^2]^4$

$$={}^4C_0(1-x)^4+{}^4C_1(1-x)^3(x^2)+{}^4C_2(1-x)^2(x^2)^2+{}^4C_3(1-x)(x^2)^3+{}^4C_4(x^2)^4$$

[taking $(1-x)$ as a and x^2 as b]

$$=(1-x)^4+4x^2(1-x)^3+6x^4(1-x)^2+4x^6(1-x)+1\cdot x^8$$
$$=(1-4x+6x^2-4x^3+x^4)+4x^2(1-3x+3x^2-x^3)+6x^4(1-2x+x^2)+4(1-x)x^6+x^8$$
$$=1-4x+6x^2-4x^3+x^4+4x^2-12x^3+12x^4-4x^5+6x^4-12x^5+6x^6+4x^6-4x^7+x^8$$
$$=1-4x+10x^2-16x^3+19x^4-16x^5+10x^6-4x^7+x^8$$

(ii) We have, $\left(1+\frac{x}{2}-\frac{2}{x}\right)^4=\left[\left(1+\frac{x}{2}\right)-\frac{2}{x}\right]^4$

$$={}^4C_0\left(1+\frac{x}{2}\right)^4-{}^4C_1\left(1+\frac{x}{2}\right)^3\left(\frac{2}{x}\right)+{}^4C_2\left(1+\frac{x}{2}\right)^2\left(\frac{2}{x}\right)^2-{}^4C_3\left(1+\frac{x}{2}\right)\left(\frac{2}{x}\right)^3+{}^4C_4\left(\frac{2}{x}\right)^4$$
$$=\left(1+\frac{x}{2}\right)^4-4\left(1+\frac{x}{2}\right)^3\frac{2}{x}+\frac{4\times 3}{2}\left(1+\frac{x}{2}\right)^2\frac{4}{x^2}-4\left(1+\frac{x}{2}\right)\times\frac{8}{x^3}+\frac{16}{x^4}$$
$$=\left(1+\frac{x}{2}\right)^4-\frac{8}{x}\left(1+\frac{x}{2}\right)^3+\frac{24}{x^2}\left(1+\frac{x}{2}\right)^2-\frac{32}{x^3}\left(1+\frac{x}{2}\right)+\frac{16}{x^4}$$

Now, expanding $\left(1+\frac{x}{2}\right)^4,\left(1+\frac{x}{2}\right)^3,\left(1+\frac{x}{2}\right)^2$, we get

$$\left(1+\frac{x}{2}-\frac{2}{x}\right)^4=\left(1+4\cdot\frac{x}{2}+6\cdot\frac{x^2}{4}+4\cdot\frac{x^3}{8}+\frac{x^4}{16}\right)-8\cdot\frac{1}{x}\left(1+3\cdot\frac{x}{2}+3\cdot\frac{x^2}{4}+\frac{x^3}{8}\right)+24\cdot\frac{1}{x^2}\left(1+x+\frac{x^2}{4}\right)-32\times\frac{1}{x^3}\left(1+\frac{x}{2}\right)+\frac{16}{x^4}$$

$$= \left(1 + 2x + \frac{3x^2}{2} + \frac{x^3}{2} + \frac{x^4}{16}\right) - \left(\frac{8}{x} + 12 + 6x + x^2\right) + \left(\frac{24}{x^2} + \frac{24}{x} + 6\right) - \left(\frac{32}{x^3} + \frac{16}{x^2}\right) + \frac{16}{x^4}$$

$$= \frac{x^4}{16} + \frac{x^3}{2} + x^2\left(\frac{3}{2} - 1\right) + x(2-6) + (1 - 12 + 6) + (24-8)\frac{1}{x} + (24-16)\frac{1}{x^2} - \frac{32}{x^3} + \frac{16}{x^4}$$

$$= \frac{x^4}{16} + \frac{x^3}{2} + \frac{x^2}{2} - 4x - 5 + \frac{16}{x} + \frac{8}{x^2} - \frac{32}{x^3} + \frac{16}{x^4}$$

Note To solve such questions we consider any two terms as one term and then expand by using suitable theorem.

Topic Practice 1

Very Short Answer Type Questions

(2 Marks)

1 Find the number of terms in the expansions of the following expressions. (Each part carries 2 Marks)

(i) (a) $(1 + x^2)^4$ (b) $(1 - x)^5$

(c) $\left(x + \frac{y}{x}\right)^7$ (d) $\left(x - \frac{1}{3x}\right)^7$

(ii) (a) $(3x + 2y)^4$ (b) $[(a + 2b)^2]^4$

(c) $(4 + x^2 + 4x)^3$ (d) $(x^2 + 1 - 2x)^8$

2 Find the number of terms in the expansions of the following expressions. (Each part carries 2 Marks)

(i) (a) $(x + 2a)^{10} + (x - 2a)^{10}$

(b) $(1 + 5\sqrt{2}x)^9 + (1 - 5\sqrt{2}x)^9$

(c) $(y + b)^{20} - (y - b)^{20}$

(ii) (a) $(3x + 2y)^6 + (3x - 2y)^6$

(b) $\left(2x + \frac{1}{y}\right)^7 + \left(2x - \frac{1}{y}\right)^7$

(c) $(z + 3y)^8 - (z - 3y)^8$

3 Prove that $\sum_{r=0}^{n} 5^r \cdot {}^nC_r = 6^n$.

4 Using binomial theorem, expand the following expressions. (Each part carries 2 Marks)

(i) $(2x + 3y)^5$ (ii) $(2x - 3y)^4$

(iii) $(1 - x)^6$ (iv) $(1 - 3x)^7$

(v) $(x^2 + 2a)^4$ (vi) $(\sqrt{x} + \sqrt{y})^{10}$

(vii) $\left(x + \frac{1}{x}\right)^5$ (viii) $\left(x^2 + \frac{3}{x}\right)^4, x \neq 0.$

(ix) $\left(\frac{x}{3} + \frac{1}{x}\right)^5$ (x) $\left(ax - \frac{b}{x}\right)^6$

(xi) $\left(x - \frac{1}{2x}\right)^5$ (xii) $(1 - 2x + x^2)^3$

5 Using binomial theorem, expand the following expressions. (Each part carries 2 Marks)

(i) $(2 + \sqrt{3})^7 + (2 - \sqrt{3})^7$ (ii) $(\sqrt{2} + 1)^6 + (\sqrt{2} - 1)^6$

(iii) $(3 + \sqrt{2})^5 - (3 - \sqrt{2})^5$

6 Find the value of (Each part carries 2 Marks)

(i) $(\sqrt{y+1} + \sqrt{y-1})^6 + (\sqrt{y+1} - \sqrt{y-1})^6$

(ii) $(x + \sqrt{x^2 - 1})^6 + (x - \sqrt{x^2 - 1})^6$

7 Using binomial theorem, expand $(x + y)^6 - (x - y)^6$. Hence, find the value of $(\sqrt{2} + 1)^6 - (\sqrt{2} - 1)^6$.

8 Using binomial theorem, expand the following expansions. (Each part carries 2 Marks)

(i) $(1 + x + x^2)^3$ (ii) $(1 - x + x^2)^3$

(iii) $(x^2 + 3 + 2\sqrt{3}x)^3$

Hints & Answers

1. (i) (a) Given, $n = 4$

$\therefore$ Number of terms $= (n + 1) = 4 + 1 = 5$

(b) Solve as part (a). **Ans.** 6

(c) Solve as part (a). **Ans.** 8

(d) Solve as part (a). **Ans.** 8

(ii) (a) Solve as part (i) (a). **Ans.** 5

(b) Solve as part (i) (a). **Ans.** 9

(c) $(4 + x^2 + 4x)^3 = \{(x + 2)^2\}^3 = (x + 2)^6$

Now, solve as part (i) (a). **Ans.** 7

(d) $(x^2 + 1 - 2x)^8 = \{(x - 1)^2\}^8 = (x - 1)^{16}$

Now, solve as part (i) (a). **Ans.** 17

2. (i) (a) $(x + 2a)^{10} + (x - 2a)^{10}$

Here, $n = 10$, which is even.

$\therefore$ Total number of terms $\frac{n}{2} + 1 = \frac{10}{2} + 1 = 6$

(b) Solve as part (a). **Ans.** 5

(c) Here, $n = 20$, which is even.

$\therefore$ Total number of terms $= \frac{20}{2} = 10$

(ii) (a) Solve as part (i) (a). **Ans.** 4

(b) Solve as part (i) (a). **Ans.** 4

(c) Solve as part (i) (c). **Ans.** 4

3. $\sum_{r=0}^{n} 5^r \cdot {}^nC_r = {}^nC_0\, 5^0 + {}^nC_1\, 5^1 + {}^nC_2\, 5^2 + \ldots + {}^nC_n\, 5^n$

$= (1+5)^n = 6^n$

4. (i) Here, $a = 2x$, $b = 3y$ and $n = 5$

Given, $(2x+3y)^5$

$= {}^5C_0\,(2x)^5 + {}^5C_1(2x)^4\,(3y)^1 + {}^5C_2\,(2x)^3\,(3y)^2 + {}^5C_3\,(2x)^2 \times (3y)^3 + {}^5C_4 \times (2x)^1 \times (3y)^4 + {}^5C_5 \times (2x)^0 \times (3y)^5$

$= 32x^5 + 240x^4y + 720x^3y^2 + 1080x^2y^3 + 810xy^4 + 243y^5$

(ii) Here, $a = 2x$, $b = 3y$ and $n = 5$

$\therefore\ (2x-3y)^4 = {}^4C_0\,(2x)^4 - {}^4C_1\,(2x)^3 \times (3y)^1 + {}^4C_2\,(2x)^2 \times (3y)^2 - {}^4C_3\,(2x)^1 \times (3y)^3 + {}^4C_4\,(2x)^0\,(3y)^4$

Ans. $16x^4 - 96x^3y + 216x^2y^2 - 216xy^3 + 81y^4$

(iii) Solve as part (ii).

Ans. $1 - 6x + 15x^2 - 20x^3 + 15x^4 - 6x^5 + x^6$

(iv) Solve as part (ii).

Ans. $1 - 21x + 189\,x^2 - 945\,x^3 + 2835\,x^4 - 5103\,x^5 + 5103x^6 - 2187x^7$

(v) Solve as part (i).

Ans. $x^8 + 8x^6a + 24x^4a^2 + 32x^2a^3 + 16a^4$

(vi) Solve as part (i).

Ans. $x^5 + 10x^{9/2}y^{1/2} + 45x^4y + 120x^{7/2}y^{3/2} + 210x^3y^2 + 252x^{5/2}y^{5/2} + 210x^2y^3 + 120x^{3/2}y^{7/2} + 45xy^4 + 10x^{1/2}y^{9/2} + y^5$

(vii) Solve as part (i). **Ans.** $x^5 + 5x^3 + 10x + \frac{10}{x} + \frac{5}{x^3} + \frac{1}{x^5}$

(viii) Solve as part (i). **Ans.** $x^8 + 12x^5 + 54\,x^2 + \frac{108}{x} + \frac{81}{x^4}$

(ix) Solve as part (i). **Ans.** $\frac{x^5}{243} + \frac{5x^3}{81} + \frac{10x}{27} + \frac{10}{9x} + \frac{5}{3x^3} + \frac{1}{x^5}$

(x) Solve as part (ii).

Ans. $a^6x^6 - 6a^5x^4\,b + 15a^4x^2b^2 - 20a^3b^3 + \frac{15a^2b^4}{x^2} - \frac{6ab^5}{x^4} + \frac{b^6}{x^6}$

(xi) $x^5 - \frac{5x^3}{2} + \frac{5x}{2} - \frac{5}{4x} + \frac{5}{16x^3} - \frac{1}{32x^5}$

(xii) $(1-2x+x^2)^3 = \{(1-x)^2\}^3 = (1-x)^6$

Now, solve as part (ii). **Ans.** $1 + 4x + 6x^2 + 4x^3 + x^4$

5. (i) $(2+\sqrt{3})^7 = {}^7C_0(2)^7 \times (\sqrt{3})^0 + {}^7C_1\,(2)^6 \times (\sqrt{3})^1 + {}^7C_2\,(2)^5\,(\sqrt{3})^2 + {}^7C_2\,(2)^4\,(\sqrt{3})^3 + {}^7C_4\,(2)^3\,(\sqrt{3})^4 + {}^7C_5\,(2)^2\,(\sqrt{3})^5 + {}^7C_6\,(2)^1\,(\sqrt{3})^6 + {}^7C_7 \times 2^0 \times (\sqrt{3})^7$ ...(i)

and $(2-\sqrt{3})^7 = {}^7C_0(2)^7\,(\sqrt{3})^0 - {}^7C_1\,(2)^6\,(\sqrt{3})^1 + {}^7C_2\,(2)^5\,(\sqrt{3})^2 - {}^7C_2\,(2)^4\,(\sqrt{3})^3 + {}^7C_4\,(2)^3\,(\sqrt{3})^4 - {}^7C_5\,(2)^2\,(\sqrt{3})^5 + {}^7C_6\,(2)^1\,(\sqrt{3})^6 - {}^7C_7\,2^0(\sqrt{3})^7$ ...(ii)

Now, adding Eqs. (i) and (ii), we get

$(2+\sqrt{3})^7 + (2-\sqrt{3})^7$

$= 2\,[{}^7C_0\,(2)^7\,(\sqrt{3})^0 + {}^7C_2\,(2)^5\,(\sqrt{3})^2 + {}^7C_4\,(2)^3\,(\sqrt{3})^4 + {}^7C_6\,(2)^1\,(\sqrt{3})^6]$ **Ans.** 10084

(ii) Solve as part (i). **Ans** 198

(iii) $(3+\sqrt{2})^5 - (3-\sqrt{2})^5$

$(3+\sqrt{2})^5 = {}^5C_0\,(3)^5 \times (\sqrt{2})^0 + {}^5C_1\,(3)^4 \times (\sqrt{2}) + {}^5C_2\,(3)^3 \times (\sqrt{2})^2 + {}^5C_3\,(3)^2 \times (\sqrt{2})^3. + {}^5C_4\,(3)^1 \times (\sqrt{2})^4 + {}^5C_5\,(3)^0 \times (\sqrt{2})^5$ ...(i)

$(3-\sqrt{2})^5 = {}^5C_0\,(3)^5 \times (\sqrt{2})^0 - {}^5C_1\,(3)^4 \times (\sqrt{2})^1 + {}^5C_2\,(3)^3 \times (\sqrt{2})^2 - {}^5C_3\,(3)^2 \times (\sqrt{2})^3 + {}^5C_4\,(3)^1 \times (\sqrt{2})^4 - {}^5C_5\,(3)^0 \times (\sqrt{2})^5$

Now, subtracting Eq. (ii) from Eq. (i), we get

$(3+\sqrt{2})^5 - (3-\sqrt{2})^5 = 1178\sqrt{2}$

6. (i) Solved as Example 9. **Ans.** $16y\,(4y^2 - 3)$

(ii) Solved as Example 9. **Ans.** $64x^6 - 96x^4 + 36x^2 - 2$

7. $(x+y)^6 - (x-y)^6$

$= {}^6C_0x^6 + {}^6C_1x^5y + {}^6C_2x^4y^2 + {}^6C_3x^3y^3 + {}^6C_4x^2y^4 + {}^6C_5xy^5 + {}^6C_6y^6 - [{}^6C_0x^6 + {}^6C_1x^5(-y)^1 + {}^6C_2x^4(-y)^2 + {}^6C_3x^3\,(-y)^3 + {}^6C_4x^2(-y)^4 + {}^6C_5x\,(-y)^5 + {}^6C_6(-y)^6]$

$= 2\,(6x^5y + 20x^3y^3 + 6xy^5) = 4xy\,(3x^4 + 10x^2y^2 + 3y^4)$

On substituting $x = \sqrt{2}$ and $y = 1$, we get the answer.

Ans. $140\sqrt{2}$

8. (i) $(1+x+x^2)^3 = [(1+x)+x^2]^3$

$= {}^3C_0\,(1+x)^3 + {}^3C_1\,(1+x)^2\,(x^2)^1 + {}^3C_2\,(1+x)\,(x^2)^2 + {}^3C_3(x^2)^3$

$= x^6 + 3x^5 + 6x^4 + 7x^3 + 6x^2 + 3x + 1$

(ii) $(1-x+x^2)^3 = [(1-x)+x^2]^3$

$= {}^3C_0\,(1-x)^3 - {}^3C_1\,(1-x)^2(x^2)^1 + {}^3C_2\,(1-x)^1\,(x^2)^2 - {}^3C_3\,(x^2)^3$

$= -x^6 - 3x^5 + 5x^3 - 3x + 1$

(iii) $(x^2 + 3 + 2\sqrt{3}x)^3 = (x+\sqrt{3})^6$

$= {}^nC_0\,(x)^6 \times (\sqrt{3})^0 + {}^nC_1\,x^5\,(\sqrt{3})^1 + {}^nC_2\,x^4\,(\sqrt{3})^2 + {}^nC_3x^3\,(\sqrt{3})^3 + {}^nC_4\,x^2\,(\sqrt{3})^4 + {}^nC_5\,x^1\,(\sqrt{3})^5 + {}^nC_6\,(\sqrt{3})^6$

$= x^6 + 6\sqrt{3}x^5 + 45x^4 + 60\sqrt{3}x^3 + 135x^2 + 54\sqrt{3}x + 27$

TOPIC 02 General and Middle Terms in Binomial Expansion

General Term in a Binomial Expansion

Consider the binomial expansion of $(a+b)^n$, i.e.

$(a+b)^n = {}^nC_0 a^n + {}^nC_1 a^{n-1} b + {}^nC_2 a^{n-2} b^2 + \dots + {}^nC_n b^n$

Here, we observed that

First term $= {}^nC_0 a^n$

Second term $= {}^nC_1 a^{n-1} b^1$

Third term $= {}^nC_2 a^{n-2} b^2$

Fourth term $= {}^nC_3 a^{n-3} b^3$

$\vdots$

$(r+1)$th term $= {}^nC_r a^{n-r} b^r$

Here, $(r+1)$th term is called the **general term of the expansion** $(a+b)^n$ and it is denoted by T_{r+1}.

i.e. $$T_{r+1} = {}^nC_r a^{n-r} b^r$$

Thus, $(n+1)$th term, $T_{n+1} = {}^nC_n a^{n-n} b^n = {}^nC_n b^n$

Note **The pth term from the end** in $(a+b)^n$ is $[(n+1)-(p-1)] = (n-p+2)$th term from the beginning.

General Term of Particular Cases of Binomial Theorem

(i) In the expansion of $(a-b)^n$,
$$T_{r+1} = (-1)^r \, {}^nC_r \, x^{n-r} y^r$$

(ii) In the expansion of $(1+x)^n$,
$$T_{r+1} = {}^nC_r x^r$$

(iii) In the expansion of $(1-x)^n$,
$$T_{r+1} = (-1)^r \, {}^nC_r \, x^r$$

Note The coefficient of x^r in the expansion of $(1+x)^n$ is ${}^nC_r$.

Example 1 Evaluate the following terms.

(i) General term in the expansion of $(3x^2+4y)^{10}$.

(ii) 6th term in the expansion of $\left(y-\frac{1}{y}\right)^{20}$.

(iii) 7th term in the expansion of $\left(2x+\frac{y}{3}\right)^{15}$.

(iv) 5th term from the end in the expansion of $\left(x-\frac{1}{x^2}\right)^{12}$.

Sol. (i) The general term in the expansion of $(3x^2+4y)^{10}$ is

$$T_{r+1} = {}^{10}C_r (3x^2)^{10-r}(4y)^r \quad [\because T_{r+1} = {}^nC_r a^{n-r} b^r]$$
$$= {}^{10}C_r \times 3^{10-r} \times 4^r \times x^{20-2r} y^r$$

(ii) The general term in the expansion of $\left(y-\frac{1}{y}\right)^{20}$ is

$$T_{r+1} = {}^{20}C_r (y)^{20-r}\left(-\frac{1}{y}\right)^r \quad [\because T_{r+1} = {}^nC_r a^{n-r} b^r]$$
$$= {}^{20}C_r \, y^{20-2r}(-1)^r$$

For determining 6th term, put $r=5$, we get

$$T_{5+1} = {}^{20}C_5 \, y^{20-10}(-1)^5 = -{}^{20}C_5 \, y^{10}$$

(iii) The general term in the expansion of $\left(2x+\frac{y}{3}\right)^{15}$ is

$$T_{r+1} = {}^{15}C_r (2x)^{15-r}\left(\frac{y}{3}\right)^r \quad [\because T_{r+1} = {}^nC_r a^{n-r} b^r]$$
$$= {}^{15}C_r \, 2^{15-r} \times 3^{-r} \times x^{15-r} y^r$$

For determining 7th term, put $r=6$, we get

$$T_{6+1} = {}^{15}C_6 \, 2^{15-6} \times 3^{-6} \times x^{15-6} y^6$$
$$= {}^{15}C_6 \, 2^9 \times 3^{-6} \times x^9 y^6$$

(iv) The 5th term from the end in the expansion of $\left(x-\frac{1}{x^2}\right)^{12}$ = The $(12-5+2)$th i.e. 9th term from the beginning in the expansion of $\left(x-\frac{1}{x^2}\right)^{12}$

[$\because$ pth term from the end $= (n-p+2)$th term from the beginning]

$$\text{Now, } T_{8+1} = {}^{12}C_8 (x)^{12-8}\left(-\frac{1}{x^2}\right)^8$$
$$= {}^{12}C_4 x^4 (-1)^8 \cdot \frac{1}{x^{16}}$$
$$= \frac{12\times 11\times 10\times 9}{4\times 3\times 2\times 1} \times x^{4-16} = 495\, x^{-12} = \frac{495}{x^{12}}$$

Example 2 Find the coefficient of 5th term in the expansion of $\left(\frac{x}{3}-3y\right)^7$.

Sol. Given expression is $\left(\frac{x}{3}-3y\right)^7$.

General term, $T_{r+1} = {}^7C_r \left(\frac{x}{3}\right)^{7-r} \cdot (-3y)^r$

Put $r+1=5 \Rightarrow r=4$

Then, $T_5 = T_{4+1} = {}^7C_4\left(\frac{x}{3}\right)^3(-3y)^4$

$= \frac{7\cdot6\cdot5}{3\cdot2\cdot1}\cdot\frac{x^3}{27}\times81\cdot y^4 = 35\cdot3\,x^3y^4 = 105\,x^3y^4$

Thus, the coefficient of 5th term is 105.

Example 3 Find the sixth term in the expansion of $(y^{1/2}+x^{1/3})^n$, if the binomial coefficient of the third term from the end is 45.

Sol. Given expression is $(y^{1/2}+x^{1/3})^n$.

Then, sixth term of this expansion is

$$T_6 = T_{5+1} = {}^nC_5(y^{1/2})^{n-5}(x^{1/3})^5 \quad \text{...(i)}$$

We know that,

Binomial coefficient of third term from the end

= Binomial coefficient of third term from the beginning

$= {}^nC_2$

$\therefore \quad {}^nC_2 = 45$ [$\because$ the binomial coefficient of the third term from the end is 45]

$\Rightarrow \quad \frac{n(n-1)(n-2)!}{2!(n-2)!} = 45$

$\Rightarrow \quad n(n-1) = 90 \Rightarrow n^2 - n - 90 = 0$

$\Rightarrow \quad n^2 - 10n + 9n - 90 = 0$

$\Rightarrow \quad n(n-10) + 9(n-10) = 0$

$\Rightarrow \quad (n-10)(n+9) = 0$

$\Rightarrow \quad (n+9) = 0$ or $(n-10) = 0$

$\therefore \quad n = 10 \quad [\because n \neq -9]$

From Eq. (i), $T_6 = {}^{10}C_5\,y^{5/2}\,x^{5/3}$

$= \frac{10\times9\times8\times7\times6}{5\times4\times3\times2\times1}y^{5/2}\cdot x^{5/3}$

$= 252y^{5/2}\cdot x^{5/3}$

Example 4 If the third term in the expansion of $\left(\frac{1}{x}+x^{\log_{10}x}\right)^5$ is 1000, then find x.

Sol. Given, $T_3 = 1000$

$\Rightarrow \quad {}^5C_2\left(\frac{1}{x}\right)^{5-2}(x^{\log_{10}x})^2 = 1000$

$\Rightarrow \quad 10(x^{\log_{10}x})^2\times x^{-3} = 1000 \Rightarrow x^{2\log_{10}x}\times x^{-3} = 100$

$\Rightarrow \quad x^{2(\log_{10}x)-3} = 10^2$

$\Rightarrow \quad 2(\log_{10}x) - 3 = \log_x 10^2$

$\Rightarrow \quad 2(\log_{10}x) - 3 = \frac{2}{\log_{10}x}$

$\Rightarrow \quad 2y - 3 = \frac{2}{y}$

where, $y = \log_{10}x$

$\Rightarrow \quad 2y^2 - 3y - 2 = 0 \Rightarrow (2y+1)(y-2) = 0$

$\Rightarrow \quad y = 2$ or $y = -\frac{1}{2} \Rightarrow \log_{10}x = 2$ or $\log_{10}x = -\frac{1}{2}$

$\Rightarrow \quad x = 10^2$ or $x = 10^{-1/2}$ $\therefore x = 100$ or $x = \frac{1}{\sqrt{10}}$

Middle Terms in a Binomial Expansion

We know that the binomial expansion $(a+b)^n$ has $(n+1)$ terms. So for middle terms, there are two cases

***Case* I** If n is even, then total number of terms (i.e. $n+1$) is odd and the middle term is $\left(\frac{n}{2}+1\right)$th term.

e.g. In the expansion of $(a+b)^6$, the middle term is $\left(\frac{6}{2}+1\right)$ th term i.e. 4th term.

***Case* II** If n is odd, then total number of terms i.e. $(n+1)$ is even and there are two middle terms which are given by $\left(\frac{n+1}{2}\right)$th and $\left(\frac{n+1}{2}+1\right)$th terms i.e. by $\left(\frac{n+1}{2}\right)$th and $\left(\frac{n+3}{2}\right)$th terms.

e.g. In the expansion of $(a+b)^9$, the middle terms are $\left(\frac{9+1}{2}\right)$th and $\left(\frac{9+1}{2}+1\right)$th terms i.e. 5th and 6th terms.

Example 5 Find the middle term(s) in the expansion of $(2x+3y)^9$.

Sol. The index of binomial expansion $(2x+3y)^9$ is $n = 9$, which is an odd number. So there are two middle terms which are given by $\left(\frac{9+1}{2}\right)$th and $\left(\frac{9+1}{2}+1\right)$th terms i.e. T_5 and T_6 terms.

In the expansion of $(2x+3y)^9$, $T_5 = {}^9C_4(2x)^{9-4}(3y)^4$

$\Rightarrow \quad T_5 = \frac{9\times8\times7\times6}{4\times3\times2\times1}(2x)^5(3y)^4$

$= 126\times32\times81x^5y^4 = 326592x^5y^4$

and $\quad T_6 = {}^9C_5(2x)^{9-5}(3y)^5 = \frac{9\times8\times7\times6}{4\times3\times2\times1}(2x)^4(3y)^5$

$= 126\times16\times243x^4y^5 = 489888x^4y^5$

Hence, middle terms in the expansion of $(2x+3y)^9$ are $489888\,x^4y^5$ and $326592\,x^5y^4$.

Example 6 Find the middle term in the expansion of $\left(\frac{2x^2}{3}+\frac{3}{2x^2}\right)^{10}$.

Sol. Here, value of index n is 10 (even), therefore there is only one middle term given by $T_{\frac{10}{2}+1}$ i.e. T_6.

Now, $T_6 = T_{5+1} = {}^{10}C_5\left(\frac{2x^2}{3}\right)^{10-5}\left(\frac{3}{2x^2}\right)^5$ $[\because T_{r+1} = {}^nC_r a^{n-r} b^r]$

$$= {}^{10}C_5\left(\frac{2x^2}{3}\right)^5\left(\frac{3}{2x^2}\right)^5$$

$$= \frac{10\cdot 9\cdot 8\cdot 7\cdot 6}{5\cdot 4\cdot 3\cdot 2\cdot 1}\cdot\frac{2^5\cdot x^{10}}{3^5}\cdot\frac{3^5}{2^5\cdot x^{10}} = 252$$

which is independent of x.

Example 7 Find the middle term in the expansion of $\left(3-\frac{x^3}{6}\right)^7$. **[NCERT]**

Sol. Here, $n = 7$ (odd)

$\therefore$ Middle terms are given by $\left(\frac{n+1}{2}\right)$th and $\left(\frac{n+3}{2}\right)$th terms, i.e. $\left(\frac{7+1}{2}\right)$th term and $\left(\frac{7+3}{2}\right)$th term,

i.e. 4th and 5th terms.

Now, $T_4 = T_{3+1} = {}^7C_3(3)^{7-3}\left(-\frac{x^3}{6}\right)^3$ $[\because T_{r+1} = {}^nC_r a^{n-r} b^r]$

$$= \frac{7\times 6\times 5}{6}\times\frac{3^4(-1)^3\times x^9}{6^3} = \frac{35\times 81\times(-1)\times x^9}{6\times 6\times 6}$$

$$= -\frac{35\times 27\times x^9}{2\times 6\times 6} = -\frac{105}{8}x^9$$

and $T_5 = T_{4+1} = {}^7C_4 3^{7-4}\left(-\frac{x^3}{6}\right)^4$

$$= {}^7C_3\frac{3^3(-1)^4(x^3)^4}{6^4} \quad [\because {}^nC_r = {}^nC_{r-1}]$$

$$= \frac{7\times 6\times 5}{6}\times\frac{3\times 3\times 3\times x^{12}}{6\times 6\times 6\times 6} = \frac{35}{48}x^{12}$$

Example 8 If the middle term of $\left(\frac{1}{x}+x\sin x\right)^{10}$ is equal to $7\frac{7}{8}$, then find the value of x. **[NCERT Exemplar]**

Sol. Here, $n = 10$, which is an even number.

$\therefore$ Middle term is given by $\left(\frac{10}{2}+1\right)$th term, i.e. 6th term.

Let T_{r+1} be its general term.

Then, $T_{r+1} = {}^{10}C_r\left(\frac{1}{x}\right)^{10-r}(x\sin x)^r$

$$= {}^{10}C_r\, x^{r-10+r}\sin^r x = {}^{10}C_r x^{2r-10}\sin^r x$$

Now, $T_6 = T_{5+1} = {}^{10}C_5 x^{10-10}\sin^5 x = {}^{10}C_5\sin^5 x$

$\because$ Middle term $= 7\frac{7}{8}$

$$\therefore \quad {}^{10}C_5\sin^5 x = \frac{63}{8} \Rightarrow \sin^5 x = \frac{63}{8\times 252} = \frac{1}{8\times 4} = \frac{1}{32}$$

$$\Rightarrow \quad \sin x = \frac{1}{2} \Rightarrow \sin x = \sin\frac{\pi}{6}$$

$$\therefore \quad x = n\pi + (-1)^n\frac{\pi}{6}$$

Some More Problems Related to Binomial Theorem

There are many other types of problems related to binomial theorem along with its general term, middle term, coefficients of consecutive terms, etc.

Some of these types of problems are discussed below

|TYPE I|

Finding the Coefficient for a Given Index of the Variable

In this type of problem first find the general term, then equate the index of variable obtained in general term to the given index to find the value of r and then use the value of r to calculate required coefficient.

Note Sometimes we simply expand the given expression to get the coefficient of required term.

Example 9 Find the coefficient of x^4 in $(1+2x)^4(2-x)$.

Sol. We have, $(1+2x)^4(2-x)$

$$= [1 + {}^4C_1(2x)^1 + {}^4C_2(2x)^2 + {}^4C_3(2x)^3 + {}^4C_4(2x)^4](2-x)$$

$$= (1 + 4\times 2x + 6\times 4x^2 + 4\times 8x^3 + 1\times 16x^4)(2-x)$$

$$= (1 + 8x + 24x^2 + 32x^3 + 16x^4)(2-x)$$

$$= 2 + 16x + 48x^2 + 64x^3 + 32x^4 - x - 8x^2 - 24x^3 - 32x^4 - 16x^5$$

$$= 2 + 15x + 40x^2 + 40x^3 - 16x^5$$

Since, there is no term containing x^4, hence the coefficient of x^4 is zero.

Example 10 Find the coefficients of x^{32} and x^{-17} in the expansion of $\left(x^4 - \frac{1}{x^3}\right)^{15}$.

Sol. Let general term in the expansion of $\left(x^4 - \frac{1}{x^3}\right)^{15}$ be T_{r+1}.

Then, $T_{r+1} = {}^{15}C_r (x^4)^{15-r}\left(-\frac{1}{x^3}\right)^r$

$\Rightarrow \quad T_{r+1} = (-1)^r \times {}^{15}C_r x^{60-7r}$ ...(i)

This term will contain x^{32}, if $60 - 7r = 32$

$\Rightarrow \quad 7r = 60 - 32 = 28 \Rightarrow r = \frac{28}{7} = 4$

Thus, the term containing x^{32} is T_{4+1} i.e. T_5.

$\therefore$ Coefficient of $x^{32} = (-1)^4 \times {}^{15}C_4 = 1365$ [using Eq. (i)]

Now, for the term containing x^{-17}, put $60 - 7r = -17$

$\Rightarrow \quad 7r = 77 \Rightarrow r = 11$

Thus, the term containing x^{-17} is T_{11+1} i.e. T_{12}.

$\therefore$ Coefficient of $x^{-17} = (-1)^{11} \times {}^{15}C_{11} = -1365$

[using Eq. (i)]

Example 11 Prove that there is no term involving y^6 in the expansion of $\left(2y^2 - \frac{3}{y}\right)^{11}$, where $y \neq 0$.

Sol. Let $(r+1)$th term involve y^6.

Then, $T_{r+1} = (-1)^r \, {}^{11}C_r \, (2y^2)^{11-r}\left(\frac{3}{y}\right)^r$

$= (-1)^r \, {}^{11}C_r \, 2^{11-r} (y^2)^{11-r} \cdot 3^r \cdot y^{-r}$

$= (-1)^r \, {}^{11}C_r \, 2^{11-r} (3)^r \times y^{22-3r}$

Since, T_{r+1} involve y^6, therefore $22 - 3r = 6$

$\Rightarrow \quad 3r = 16 \Rightarrow r = \frac{16}{3}$, which is not an integer.

Hence, there is no term containing y^6. **Hence proved.**

Example 12 If x^p occurs in the expansion of $\left(x^2 + \frac{1}{x}\right)^{2n}$, then prove that its coefficient is

$$\frac{(2n)!}{\left(\frac{4n-p}{3}\right)!\left(\frac{2n+p}{3}\right)!}.$$

[NCERT Exemplar]

Sol. The general term in the expansion of $\left(x^2 + \frac{1}{x}\right)^{2n}$ is

$$T_{r+1} = {}^{2n}C_r \, (x^2)^{2n-r}\left(\frac{1}{x}\right)^r = {}^{2n}C_r x^{4n-2r} \frac{1}{x^r}$$

$\Rightarrow \quad T_{r+1} = {}^{2n}C_r \, x^{4n-3r}$

On putting $4n - 3r = p$, we get

$$3r = 4n - p \Rightarrow r = \frac{4n-p}{3}$$

Now, coefficient of x^p

$$= {}^{2n}C_{\frac{4n-p}{3}} = \frac{(2n)!}{\left(\frac{4n-p}{3}\right)!\left(2n - \frac{4n-p}{3}\right)!}$$

$$= \frac{(2n)!}{\left(\frac{2n+p}{3}\right)!\left(\frac{4n-p}{3}\right)!}$$

Hence proved.

Example 13 In the expansion of $(1+a)^{m+n}$, prove that the coefficients of a^m and a^n are equal. **[NCERT]**

Sol. In the expansion of $(1+a)^{m+n}$, the general term is given by $T_{r+1} = {}^{m+n}C_r (a)^r$. For coefficient of a^m, put $r = m$, we get

$$T_{m+1} = {}^{m+n}C_m a^m$$

$\Rightarrow \quad$ Coefficient of $a^m = {}^{m+n}C_m$ ...(i)

For coefficient of a^n, put $r = n$, we get

$$T_{n+1} = {}^{m+n}C_n a^n$$

$\Rightarrow \quad$ Coefficient of $a^n = {}^{m+n}C_n$

$= {}^{m+n}C_{m+n-n}$ $\quad [\because {}^nC_r = {}^nC_{n-r}]$

$= {}^{m+n}C_m$ ...(ii)

From Eqs. (i) and (ii), the coefficient of a^m is equal to coefficient of a^n. **Hence proved.**

Example 14 Find the coefficient of x^{50} after simplifying and collecting the like terms in the expansion of $(1+x)^{1000} + x(1+x)^{999} + x^2(1+x)^{998} + \ldots + x^{1000}$. **[NCERT Exemplar]**

Sol. Given series is

$$(1+x)^{1000} + x(1+x)^{999} + x^2(1+x)^{998} + \ldots + x^{1000}$$

Here first term, $a = (1+x)^{1000}$

and common ratio, $r = \frac{x(1+x)^{99}}{(1+x)^{1000}} = \frac{x^2(1+x)^{998}}{x(1+x)^{999}} = \frac{x}{1+x}$

Thus, the given series is a geometric series with the common ratio $\frac{x}{1+x}$.

Now, sum of geometric series $= \frac{a(1-r^n)}{1-r}$

$$= \frac{(1+x)^{1000}\left[1 - \left(\frac{x}{1+x}\right)^{1001}\right]}{\left[1 - \left(\frac{x}{1+x}\right)\right]} = \frac{(1+x)^{1000} - \frac{x^{1001}}{1+x}}{\frac{1+x-x}{1+x}}$$

$= (1+x)^{1001} - x^{1001}$

Hence, coefficient of x^{50} in $\{(1+x)^{1001} - x^{1001}\}$ is given by

$${}^{1001}C_{50} = \frac{1001!}{50!\,951!}$$

|TYPE II|

Finding the Independent Term of the Variable

Independent Term (Constant term) The term which is free from variable (say x), i.e. which have x^0 is known as independent term. e.g. The $(n+1)$th term in the expansion of $\left(x+\frac{1}{x}\right)^{2n}$, where $x \neq 0$, is

$$T_{n+1} = {}^{2n}C_n x^n \left(\frac{1}{x}\right)^n = {}^{2n}C_n$$

which is an independent term.

In this type of problem, we put the index of variable x obtained in general term, equal to zero and find the value of r to calculate the required term.

Example 15 Find the term independent of x in the expansion of $\left(2x-\frac{1}{x}\right)^{10}$.

Sol. Let $(r+1)$th term be the independent term.

Then, $T_{r+1} = {}^{10}C_r (2x)^{10-r}\left(-\frac{1}{x}\right)^r = {}^{10}C_r\, 2^{10-r}(-1)^r x^{10-2r}$

For this term to be independent of x, put $10-2r=0$

$\Rightarrow \quad 2r = 10 \Rightarrow r = 5$

So, $(5+1)$th = 6th term is independent of x.

Now, $T_6 = (-1)^5 \times {}^{10}C_5\, 2^{10-5} = -\frac{10\times9\times8\times7\times6}{5\times4\times3\times2}\times 32$

$= -8064$

Example 16 If the term free from x in the expansion of $\left(\sqrt{x}-\frac{k}{x^2}\right)^{10}$ is 405, then find the value of k. **[NCERT Exemplar]**

Sol. Given expansion is $\left(\sqrt{x}-\frac{k}{x^2}\right)^{10}$.

Let T_{r+1} be the general term.

Then, $T_{r+1} = {}^{10}C_r(\sqrt{x})^{10-r}\left(\frac{-k}{x^2}\right)^r$

$= {}^{10}C_r (x)^{\frac{1}{2}(10-r)}(-k)^r \cdot x^{-2r}$

$= {}^{10}C_r\, x^{5-\frac{r}{2}}(-k)^r \cdot x^{-2r}$

$= {}^{10}C_r\, x^{5-\frac{r}{2}-2r}(-k)^r$

$= {}^{10}C_r\, x^{\frac{10-5r}{2}}(-k)^r$

For this term to be free from x, $\frac{10-5r}{2}=0$

$\Rightarrow \quad 10-5r=0 \Rightarrow r=2$

Thus, $T_{2+1} = T_3$ is free from x.

Now, $\quad T_3 = T_{2+1} = {}^{10}C_2(-k)^2 = 405$

[$\because$ term free from $x = 405$]

$\Rightarrow \quad \frac{10\times9\times8!}{2!\times8!}(-k)^2 = 405 \Rightarrow 45k^2 = 405$

$\Rightarrow \quad k^2 = \frac{405}{45} = 9$

$\therefore \quad k = \pm 3$

|TYPE III|

Problems Based on Three Consecutive Terms

In this type of problem, relation between consecutive terms or coefficient of consecutive terms of the expansion will be given. For finding the required values, we use the given relation and the following results.

$$\frac{{}^nC_r}{{}^nC_{r-1}} = \frac{n-r+1}{r} \quad \text{and} \quad \frac{{}^nC_{r+1}}{{}^nC_r} = \frac{n-r}{r+1}$$

Example 17 If the coefficient of second, third and fourth terms in the expansion of $(1+x)^{2n}$ are in AP, then show that $2n^2-9n=-7$. **[NCERT Exemplar]**

Sol. The general term of $(1+x)^{2n}$ is $T_{r+1} = {}^{2n}C_r x^r$

Then, $\quad T_2 = {}^{2n}C_1 x^1, T_3 = {}^{2n}C_2 x^2$ and $T_4 = {}^{2n}C_3 x^3$

Given, coefficients of T_2, T_3 and T_4 are in AP.

i.e. ${}^{2n}C_1$, ${}^{2n}C_2$ and ${}^{2n}C_3$ are in AP.

$\therefore \quad 2\times{}^{2n}C_2 = {}^{2n}C_1 + {}^{2n}C_3 \Rightarrow 2 = \frac{{}^{2n}C_1}{{}^{2n}C_2} + \frac{{}^{2n}C_3}{{}^{2n}C_2}$

$\Rightarrow \quad 2 = \frac{(2n)!}{1!(2n-1)!}\times\frac{2!(2n-2)!}{(2n)!} + \frac{(2n)!}{3!(2n-3)!}\times\frac{2!(2n-2)!}{(2n)!}$

$\Rightarrow \quad 2 = \frac{2(2n-2)!}{(2n-1)(2n-2)!} + \frac{2(2n-2)(2n-3)!}{6(2n-3)!}$

$\Rightarrow \quad 2 = \frac{2}{2n-1} + \frac{2n-2}{3} \Rightarrow 2 = \frac{6+(2n-2)(2n-1)}{3(2n-1)}$

$\Rightarrow \quad 6(2n-1) = 6+4n^2-2n-4n+2$

$\Rightarrow \quad 12n-6 = 8+4n^2-6n$

$\Rightarrow \quad 4n^2-6n-12n = -6-8$

$\Rightarrow \quad 4n^2-18n = -14$

$\therefore \quad 2n^2-9n = -7$ [dividing by 2] **Hence proved.**

Example 18 The coefficients of the $(r-1)$th, rth and $(r+1)$th terms in the expansion of $(x+1)^n$ are in the ratio 1 : 3 : 5. Find n and r. **[NCERT]**

Sol. In the expansion of $(x+1)^n$, the general term is

$$T_{R+1} = {}^nC_R x^{n-R}(1)^R \text{ or } T_{R+1} = {}^nC_R x^{n-R}$$

For coefficient of $(r-1)$th term, put $R = r-2$, we get

$$T_{(r-2)+1} = {}^nC_{r-2} x^{n-(r-2)}$$

$$\Rightarrow \quad T_{(r-1)} = {}^nC_{r-2} x^{n-r+2}$$

$\therefore$ Coefficient of $(r-1)$th term $= {}^nC_{r-2}$

For coefficient of rth term, put $R = r-1$, we get

$$T_{r-1+1} = {}^nC_{r-1} x^{n-(r-1)} \Rightarrow T_r = {}^nC_{r-1} x^{n-r+1}$$

$\therefore$ Coefficient of rth term $= {}^nC_{r-1}$

For coefficient of $(r+1)$th term, put $R = r$, we get

$$T_{r+1} = {}^nC_r x^{n-r}$$

Then, coefficient of $(r+1)$th term $= {}^nC_r$

Now, according to question, it is given that

$${}^nC_{r-2} : {}^nC_{r-1} : {}^nC_r = 1:3:5$$

On taking first two parts, we get ${}^nC_{r-2} : {}^nC_{r-1} = 1:3$

$$\frac{n!}{(r-2)![n-(r-2)]!} : \frac{n!}{(r-1)![n-(r-1)]!} = 1:3$$

$$\left[\because {}^nC_r = \frac{n!}{r!(n-r)!}\right]$$

$$\Rightarrow \frac{1}{(r-2)!(n-r+2)!} : \frac{1}{(r-1)(r-2)!(n-r+1)!} = 1:3$$

$$\Rightarrow \frac{1}{(n-r+2)(n-r+1)!} : \frac{1}{(r-1)(n-r+1)!} = 1:3$$

$$\Rightarrow \frac{1}{n-r+2} : \frac{1}{r-1} = 1:3 \Rightarrow \frac{r-1}{n-r+2} = \frac{1}{3}$$

$$\Rightarrow \quad 3r-3 = n-r+2 \quad \Rightarrow n-4r+5 = 0 \quad \text{...(i)}$$

On taking last two parts, we get ${}^nC_{r-1} : {}^nC_r = 3:5$

$$\Rightarrow \frac{n!}{(r-1)![n-(r-1)]!} : \frac{n!}{r!(n-r)!} = 3:5$$

$$\left[\because {}^nC_r = \frac{n!}{r!(n-r)!}\right]$$

$$\Rightarrow \frac{1}{(r-1)!(n-(r-1))!} : \frac{1}{r(r-1)!(n-r)!} = 3:5$$

$$\Rightarrow \frac{1}{n-r+1} : \frac{1}{r} = 3:5 \Rightarrow \frac{r}{n-r+1} = \frac{3}{5}$$

$$\Rightarrow \quad 5r = 3n-3r+3$$

$$\therefore \quad 3n-8r+3 = 0 \quad \text{...(ii)}$$

On solving Eqs. (i) and (ii), we get

$$n = 7 \text{ and } r = 3$$

Note Sometimes, we need to assume the consecutive terms. In such cases, we assume that the consecutive terms are rth, $(r+1)$th and $(r+2)$th terms or $(r-1)$th, rth and $(r+1)$th terms.

Topic Practice 2

Very Short Answer Type Questions

(2 Marks)

1 Find the general term in the expansion of the following expressions. (Each part carries 2 Marks)

(i) (a) $(3y+6z)^9$ (b) $(5x-3)^{12}$

(ii) (a) $\left(x-\dfrac{4}{z}\right)^{50}$ (b) $\left(z^2-\dfrac{3}{z^2}\right)^{35}$

(iii) (a) $(x^2-y)^{12}, x \neq 0$ (b) $(x+3y)^{10}$ **[NCERT]**

(iv) (a) $(3x-4y)^8$ (b) $(y^2+6y+9)^{20}$

2 Evaluate the following terms in the given expansion. (Each part carries 2 Marks)

(i) (a) 7th term in the binomial expansion $(x+3y)^8$.

(b) 5th term in the binomial expansion $\left(2x-\dfrac{1}{x}\right)^{10}$.

(ii) (a) 6th term in the binomial expansion $\left(z^2+\dfrac{2z}{3}+\dfrac{1}{9}\right)^5$.

(b) 4th term in the expansion $(x-2y)^{12}$. **[NCERT]**

(iii) (a) 6th term in the expansion $\left(\dfrac{x^3}{2}-\dfrac{2}{x^2}\right)^9$.

(b) 5th term in the expansion $(x+3)^6$.

(iv) (a) 4th term in the expansion $\left(\dfrac{4x}{5}+\dfrac{5}{2x}\right)^8$.

(b) 7th term in the expansion $\left(3x-\dfrac{2y}{3}\right)^{10}$.

(v) (a) 13th term in the expansion $\left(9x-\dfrac{1}{3\sqrt{x}}\right)^{18}, x \neq 0$. **[NCERT]**

(b) rth term in the expansion $\left(x+\dfrac{1}{x}\right)^{2r}$.

3 Each part carries 2 Marks.

(i) (a) Find the rth term from the end in the expansion of $(x+a)^n$. **[NCERT]**

(b) Find the 5th term from the end in the expansion $\left(\dfrac{4x}{5}-\dfrac{5}{2x}\right)^9$.

(ii) (a) Find the 4th term from the end in the expansion of $\left(\dfrac{3}{x^2}-\dfrac{x^3}{6}\right)^7$.

(b) Find the 5th term from the end in the expansion of $\left(\frac{x^3}{2}-\frac{2}{x^2}\right)^6$.

4 Find the coefficient of (Each part carries 2 Marks)

(i) x^3 in the expansion of $\left(3x-\frac{1}{x}\right)^7$.

(ii) y^5 in the expansion of $\left(3y^2+\frac{1}{3y}\right)^{10}$.

(iii) x^4 in the expansion of $(2x+5)^8$.

(iv) x^{11} in the expansion of $\left(x^3-\frac{2}{x^2}\right)^{12}$.

(v) x^7 in the expansion of $\left(x^2+\frac{1}{x}\right)^{11}$.

(vi) x^{10} in the expansion of $(x^2-2)^{11}$.

(vii) x^{-15} in the expansion of $\left(3x^2-\frac{a}{3x^3}\right)^{10}$.

(viii) y^m in the expansion of $\left(y+\frac{1}{y}\right)^n$.

(ix) x^{40} in the expansion of $(1+x^2+2x)^{20}$.

5 Find the middle term(s) in the given expansion. (Each part carries 2 Marks)

(i) $\left(\frac{x}{3}+9y\right)^{10}$

(ii) $\left(3x-\frac{x^3}{6}\right)^9$ (iii) $\left(2ax-\frac{b}{x^2}\right)^{12}$

(iv) $\left(x^2-\frac{2}{x}\right)^{10}$ (v) $\left(\frac{a}{x}+bx\right)^{12}$

(vi) $(x^2+a^2)^5$ (vii) $\left(3x-\frac{2}{x^2}\right)^{15}$

(viii) $(1-2x+x^2)^n$ (ix) $(1+3x+3x^2+x^3)^{2n}$

6 Find the term independent of x (constant term) in the expansion of (Each part carries 2 Marks)

(i) $\left(\sqrt{x}+\frac{1}{3x^2}\right)^{10}$ (ii) $\left(2x-\frac{1}{x}\right)^9$

(iii) $\left(3x^2+\frac{1}{x^5}\right)^7$ (iv) $\left(x+\frac{1}{x}\right)^{10}$

(v) $\left(x^2-\frac{2}{x^3}\right)^{15}$ (vi) $\left(x-\frac{1}{x^2}\right)^{3n}$

(vii) $\left(2x^2-\frac{3}{x^3}\right)^{25}$ (viii) $\left(\frac{1}{2}x^{1/3}+x^{-1/5}\right)^8$

(ix) $\left(\sqrt[3]{x}+\frac{1}{2\cdot\sqrt[3]{x}}\right)^{18}, x>2$

7 Find the coefficient of x^6y^3 in the expansion of $(x+2y)^9$. **[NCERT]**

8 In the binomial expansion $(x+y)^n$, the coefficients of 4th and 13th terms are equal. Find the value of n.

9 If p is a real number and the middle term in the expansion of $\left(\frac{p}{2}+2\right)^8$ is 1120, then find the value of p.

10 Show that the term containing x^3 does not exist in the expansion of $\left(3x+\frac{1}{2x}\right)^8$.

11 Prove that there is no term involving x^6 in the expansion of $\left(2x^2-\frac{3}{x}\right)^{11}$, where $x\neq 0$.

12 Find the coefficient of x^4 in the expansion of $(1+x)^n(1-x)^n$.

13. Find the coefficient of x^n in the expansion of $(1+x)^n(1-x)^n$.

14 Find the coefficient of x^4 in the expansion of $(1+x+x^2+x^3)^{11}$. **[NCERT Exemplar]**

15 Find the coefficient of x in the expansion of $(1-3x+7x^2)(1-x)^{16}$.

16 If the coefficients of $(r-5)$th and $(2r-1)$th terms in the expansion $(1+x)^{34}$ are equal, then find the value of r. **[NCERT]**

Short Answer Type Questions

4 Marks

17 Find a, if the 17th and 18th terms of the expansion $(2+a)^{50}$ are equal.

18 Find the two successive terms in the expansion of $(1+x)^{24}$, whose coefficients are in the ratio 1 : 4. **[NCERT Exemplar]**

19 If the coefficients of 2nd, 3rd and 4th terms in the expansion of $(1+x)^n$ are in AP, then find the value of n.

20 Find the coefficient of a^4 in the product $(1+2a)^4(2-a)^5$ using binomial theorem. **[NCERT]**

21 The sum of the coefficients of the first three terms in the expansion of $\left(x-\frac{3}{x^2}\right)^m$, $x\neq 0, m$ being a natural number, is 559. Find the term of the expansion containing x^3. **[NCERT]**

22 Find n, if the ratio of the fifth term from the beginning to the fifth term from the end in the expansion of $\left(\sqrt[4]{2}+\frac{1}{\sqrt[4]{3}}\right)^n$ is $\sqrt{6}:1$.

23 Find the greatest value of term independent of x in the expansion of $\left(x\sin\alpha+\frac{\cos\alpha}{x}\right)^{10}$, where $\alpha\in R$.

24 Show that the ratio of the coefficient of x^{10} in $(1-x^2)^{10}$ and the term independent of x in $\left(x-\frac{2}{x}\right)^{10}$ is 1: 32.

Long Answer Type Questions

6 Marks

25 The coefficients of three consecutive terms in the expansion of $(1+a)^n$ are in the ratio 1 : 7 : 42. Find the value of n. **[NCERT]**

26 The 2nd, 3rd and 4th terms in the binomial expansion $(x+a)^n$ are 240, 720 and 1080, respectively. Find the values of x, a and n. **[NCERT]**

27 Find the term independent of x in the expansion of $(1+x+2x^3)\left(\frac{3}{2}x^2-\frac{1}{3x}\right)^9$. **[NCERT Exemplar]**

28 Show that the middle term in the expansion of $(1+x)^{2n}$ is $\frac{1\cdot 3\cdot 5\ldots(2n-1)}{n!}2^n\cdot x^n$, where n is a positive integer. **[NCERT]**

29 Show that the middle term in the expansion of $\left(x^2+\frac{1}{x^2}+2\right)^n$ is $\frac{1\cdot 3\cdot 5\ldots(2n-1)}{n!}\cdot 2^n$.

30 Prove that the coefficient of x^n in the expansion of $(1+x)^{2n}$ is twice the coefficient of x^n in the expansion of $(1+x)^{2n-1}$. **[NCERT]**

31 Find the middle terms in the expansion of $\left(x+\frac{1}{x}\right)^{2n+1}$.

32 Find numerically the greatest term in the expansion of $(2+3x)^9$, where $x=\frac{3}{2}$. **[NCERT Exemplar]**

Hints & Answers

1. (i) (a) Here, $a=3y$, $b=6z$ and $n=9$

Using formula, $T_{r+1}={}^nC_r\,a^{n-r}\,b^r$

$={}^9C_r\,(3y)^{9-r}\,(6z)^r$

(b) Here, $a=5x$, $b=(-3)$ and $n=12$

Using formula, $T_{r+1}={}^nC_r\,a^{n-r}\,b^r$

$={}^{12}C_r\,(5x)^{12-r}\,(-3)^r$

(ii) (a) Solve as part (i) (b) **Ans.** ${}^{50}C_r(x)^{50-r}\left(-\frac{4}{z}\right)^r$

(b) Solve as part (i) (b) **Ans.** ${}^{35}C_r\,z^{70-4r}\,(-3)^r$

(iii) (a) Solve as part (i) (b) **Ans.** ${}^{12}C_r\,x^{24-2r}\,y^r\,(-1)^r$

(b) Solve as part (i) (a) **Ans.** ${}^{10}C_r\,x^{10-r}\,(3y)^r$

(iv) (a) Solve as part (i) (b) **Ans.** ${}^8C_r\,(3x)^{8-r}\,(-4y)^r$

(b) $(y^2+6y+9)^{20}=(y+3)^{40}$ Now, solve as (i) part (a)

Ans. ${}^{40}C_r\,y^{40-r}\cdot 3^r$

2. (i) (a) $(x+3y)^8$

Here, $a=x$, $b=3y$ and $n=8$

$\therefore$ General term, $T_{r+1}={}^8C_r\,(x)^{8-r}\,(3r)^r$.

Put $r+1=7\Rightarrow r=6$

Then, $T_7=T_{6+1}={}^8C_6\,(x)^{8-6}\,(3y)^6=20412x^2\,y^6$

(b) $\left(2x-\frac{1}{x}\right)^{10}$

Here, $a=2x$, $b=\left(\frac{-1}{x}\right)$ and $n=10$

$\therefore$ General term, $T_{r+1}={}^{10}C_r\,(2x)^{10-r}\left(\frac{-1}{x}\right)^r$

Put $r+1=5\Rightarrow r=4$

Then, $T_5=T_{4+1}={}^{10}C_4\,(2x)^{10-4}\cdot\left(-\frac{1}{x}\right)^4=13440x^2$

(ii) (a) $\left(z^2+\frac{2z}{3}+\frac{1}{9}\right)^5=\left(z+\frac{1}{3}\right)^{10}$ and now solve as part (i). **Ans.** $\frac{252}{243}z^2$

(b) Solve as part (i) (a). **Ans.** $-1760x^9y^3$

(iii) (a) Solve as part (i) (b). **Ans.** $-252x^2$

(b) Solve as part (i) (a). **Ans.** $1215x^2$

(iv) (a) Solve as part (i) (a). **Ans.** $\frac{7168}{25}x^2$

(b) Solve as part (i) (b). **Ans.** $\frac{4480}{3}x^4y^6$

(v) (a) Solve as part (i) (b). **Ans.** 18564

(b) Solve as part (i) (a). **Ans.** $\frac{(2r)!}{(r-1)!(r+1)!}x^2$

3. (i) (a) rth term from the end in the expansion of $(x+a)^n$

$= (n-r+2)$ th term from the beginning in the expansion of $(x+a)^n$

$= {}^nC_{n-r+1}\, x^{n-(n-r+1)}\, (a)^{n-r+1}$

$= {}^nC_{n-r+1}\, x^{r-1}\, a^{n-r+1}$

(b) 5th term from the end $= (9-5+2)$th term $=$ 6th term from the beginning. Now, use the general term formula. **Ans.** $\frac{-5040}{x}$

(ii) (a) Solve as part (i) (b) **Ans.** $\frac{35}{48}x^6$

(b) Solve as part (i) (b) **Ans.** $\frac{15}{4}x^8$

4. (i) $T_{r+1} = {}^7C_r\, 3^{7-r} \times x^{7-2r}\, (-1)^r$

For coefficient of x^3, put $7-2r=3 \Rightarrow r=2$

$$T_3 = T_{2+1} = {}^7C_2\, 3^{7-2}\, x^{7-4} = 5103$$

(ii) Solve as part (i). **Ans.** 252

(iii) Solve as part (i). **Ans.** 700000

(iv) Solve as part (i). **Ans.** -25344

(v) Solve as part (i). **Ans.** 462

(vi) Solve as part (i). **Ans.** 29568

(vii) Solve as part (i). **Ans.** $\frac{-40}{27}a^7$

(viii) Solve as part (i). **Ans.** $\frac{n!}{\left(\frac{n-m}{2}\right)!\left(\frac{n+m}{2}\right)!}$

(ix) $(1+x^2+2x)^{20} = \{(1+x)^2\}^{20} = (1+x)^{40}$

Now solve as part (i) **Ans.** 1

5. (i) Here, $n=10$ (even). So, there will be one middle term i.e. $\left(\frac{10+2}{2}\right)$th term or 6th term.

$$T_6 = T_{5+1} = {}^{10}C_5\left(\frac{x}{3}\right)^{10-5}(9y)^5 = 61236\, x^5y^5$$

(ii) Here, $n=9$ (odd)

So, the binomial expansion has two middle terms *viz.* $\left(\frac{9+1}{2}\right)$th and $\left(\frac{9+1}{2}+1\right)$th terms i.e. 5th term and 6th term.

$$T_5 = T_{4+1} = {}^9C_4\,(3x)^{9-4}\left(\frac{-x^3}{6}\right)^4 = \frac{189}{8}x^{17}$$

and $T_6 = T_{5+1} = {}^9C_5\,(3x)^{9-5}\left(\frac{-x^3}{6}\right)^5 = \frac{-21}{16}x^{19}$

(iii) Solve as part (i). **Ans.** $\frac{59136\,a^6\,b^6}{x^6}$

(iv) Solve as part (i). **Ans.** $-8064\,x^5$

(v) Solve as part (i). **Ans.** $924a^6b^6$

(vi) Solve as part (ii). **Ans.** $10x^6a^4$ and $10x^4a^6$

(vii) Solve as part (ii).

Ans. $\frac{-6435\times 3^8\times 2^7}{x^6}$ and $\frac{6435\times 3^7\times 2^8}{x^9}$

(viii) $(1-2x+x^2)^n = \{(1-x)^2\}^n = (1-x)^{2n}$

Now, solve as part (i). **Ans.** $\frac{(2n)!}{(n!)^2}(-1)^n\,x^n$

(ix) $(1+3x+3x^2+x^3)^{2n} = \{(1+x)^3\}^{2n} = (1+x)^{6n}$

Now, solve at part (i). **Ans.** $\frac{(6n)!}{(3n!)^2}x^{3n}$

6. (i) $T_{r+1} = {}^{10}C_r \times 3^{-r} \times x^{5-\frac{5r}{2}}$

For term independent of x, put $5-\frac{5r}{2}=0 \Rightarrow r=2$

Ans. 5

(ii) $T_{r+1} = {}^9C_r\, 2^{9-r}\, x^{9-2r}\,(-1)^r$

For term independent of x, put $9-2r=0$

$\Rightarrow r=4.5$, which is not an integer.

$\therefore$ No independent term.

(iii) Solve as part (i). **Ans.** 5103

(iv) Solve as part (i). **Ans.** 252

(v) Solve as part (i). **Ans.** 320320

(vi) Solve as part (i). **Ans.** $(-1)^n\cdot{}^{3n}C_n$

(vii) Solve as part (i). **Ans.** ${}^{25}C_{10}\times 2^{15}\times 3^{10}$

(viii) Solve as part (i). **Ans.** 7

(ix) Solve as part (i). **Ans.** $\frac{{}^{18}C_9}{2^9}$

7. $\because T_{r+1} = {}^9C_r\cdot 2^r\cdot x^{9-r}\cdot y^r$

This will contain x^6y^3, if $9-r=6$ or $r=3$. **Ans.** 672

8. Here, $T_4 = T_{3+1} = {}^nC_3\, x^{n-3}\cdot y^3$

and $T_{13} = T_{12+1} = {}^nC_{12}\, x^{n-12}\cdot y^{12}$

$\therefore$ ${}^nC_3 = {}^nC_{12} \Rightarrow n=15$ **Ans.** 15

9. Here, $n=8$

So, middle term $=\left(\frac{8}{2}+1\right)$th term 5th term.

Now use the general term formula for finding the value of p. **Ans.** $p=\pm 2$

10. Solve as Example 11.

11. Solve as Example 11.

12. $(1+x)^n\,(1-x)^n = (1-x^2)^n$

Now solve as Example 10. **Ans.** $T_3 = {}^nC_2$

13. $(-1)^n\,(1-x^2)^n$, Now solve as Example 10. **Ans.** ${}^nC_2$

14. $(1+x+x^2+x^3)^{11} = [(1+x)+x^2(1+x)]^{11}$

$= (1+x)^{11}\cdot(1+x^2)^{11}$

$= (1 + 11x + 55x^2 + 165x^3 + 330x^4 + \ldots)$
$(1 + 11x^2 + 55x^4 + \ldots)$

$\therefore$ Coefficient of $x^4 = 55 + 605 + 330 = 990$ **Ans.** 990

15. $(1 - 3x + 7x^2)(1 - x)^{16}$

$= (1 - 3x + 7x^2)({}^{16}C_0 - {}^{16}C_1 x + {}^{16}C_2 x^2 + \ldots)$

$= ({}^{16}C_0 - {}^{16}C_1\, x + {}^{16}C_2 x^2 - \ldots) - 3x\,({}^{16}C_0 - {}^{16}C_1 x + \ldots) + 7x^2\,({}^{16}C_0 - {}^{16}C_1\, x + \ldots)$

Here, the term containing x is

$- {}^{16}C_1\, x - 3\,{}^{16}C_0 x = -16x - 3x$

$\therefore$ Coefficient of $x = -16 - 3 = -19$ **Ans.** -19

16. The coefficient of $(r - 5)$ th term in the expansion of $(1 + x)^{34}$ is ${}^{34}C_{r-6}$ and the coefficient of $(2r - 1)$th term in the expansion of $(1 + x)^{34}$ is ${}^{34}C_{2r-2}$. Also, given

${}^{34}C_{r-6} = {}^{34}C_{2r-2}$

$\Rightarrow$ Either $r - 6 = 2r - 2$ or $r - 6 = 34 - (2r - 2) \Rightarrow r = 14$

17. Here, $T_{17} = {}^{50}C_{16}(2)^{50-16}(a)^{16}$

$T_{18} = {}^{50}C_{17}(2)^{50-17}a^{17}$

Also ${}^{50}C_{16} \cdot 2^{34} a^{16} = {}^{50}C_{17} 2^{33} a^{17}$ **Ans.** $a = 1$

18. Let two successive terms be $(r + 1)$th and $(r + 2)$th terms.

Then, $T_{r+1} = {}^{24}C_r\, x^r$ and $T_{r+2} = {}^{24}C_{r+1}\, x^{r+1}$

Now, according to the given condition, we have

$\therefore \quad \dfrac{{}^{24}C_r}{{}^{24}C_{r+1}} = \dfrac{1}{4}$ **Ans.** 5th and 6th terms

19. Coefficient of 2nd, 3rd and 4th terms are ${}^nC_1$, ${}^nC_2$ and ${}^nC_3$, respectively. Given, ${}^nC_1$, ${}^nC_2$ and ${}^nC_3$ are in AP.

$\therefore \quad 2\,{}^nC_2 = {}^nC_1 + {}^nC_3$

Ans. $n = 7$.

20. Coefficient of a^4 in the product $(1 + 2a)^4\,(2 - a)^5$

= The coefficient of a^4 in $[{}^4C_0 + {}^4C_1\,(2a) + {}^4C_2\,(2a)^2 + {}^4C_3\,(2a)^3 + {}^4C_4\,(2a)^4] \times [{}^5C_0\,(2)^5 - {}^5C_1\,(2)^4\, a + {}^5C_2\,(2)^3\,(a)^2 - {}^5C_3\,(2)^2\,(a)^3 + {}^5C_4\,(2)\,(a)^4 - {}^5C_5\,(a)^5]$

= Coefficient of a^4 in $[1 + 8a + 24a^2 + 32a^3 + 16a^4] \times [32 - 80a + 80a^2 - 40a^3 + 10a^4 - a^5]$

Ans. -438

21. The coefficient of first three terms of $\left(x - \dfrac{3}{x^2}\right)^m$ are ${}^mC_0$, $(-3) \cdot {}^mC_1$ and $9 \cdot {}^mC_2$.

Then, we have ${}^mC_0 - 3 \cdot {}^mC_1 + 9 \cdot {}^mC_2 = 559$

Ans. $-5940x^3$

22. $\left(\sqrt[4]{2} + \dfrac{1}{\sqrt[4]{3}}\right) = \left(2^{1/4} + \dfrac{1}{3^{1/4}}\right)^n = (2^{1/4} + 3^{-1/4})^n$

Now, $T_5 = {}^nC_4\,(2^{1/4})^{n-4}\,(3^{-1/4})^4 = {}^nC_4\, 2^{\frac{n-4}{4}}\, 3^{-1}$

and 5th term from end $= T_{n-3} = T_{(n-4)+1}$

$= {}^nC_{n-4}\,(2^{1/4})^{n-(n-4)} \cdot (3^{-1/4})^{n-4}$

Then, $\dfrac{{}^nC_4\, 2^{\frac{n-4}{4}}\, 3^{-1}}{{}^nC_4\, 3^{-\frac{(n-4)}{4}}\, 2^1} = \dfrac{\sqrt{6}}{1}$ **Ans.** $n = 10$

23. $T_{r+1} = {}^{10}C_r\, x^{10-2r}\,(\sin\alpha)^{10-r}\,(\cos\alpha)^r$

For the term independent of x, put $10 - 2r = 0 \Rightarrow r = 5$,

$\therefore$ Term independent of $x = T_6 = {}^{10}C_5\,(\sin\alpha\,\cos\alpha)^5$

$= {}^{10}C_5 \times 2^{-5}\,(\sin 2\alpha)^5$

Clearly, it is greatest when $2\alpha = \pi/2$. **Ans.** $\dfrac{10!}{2^5(5!)^2}$

24. $T_{r+1} = {}^{10}C_r\,(-1)^r\, x^{2r}$

For coefficient of x^{10}, put $2r = 10 \Rightarrow r = 5$, then

Coefficient of $x^{10} = {}^{10}C_5\,(-1)^5$ and $T'_{r+1} = {}^{10}C_r\, x^{10-2r}\,(-2)^r$

For independent of x, put $10 - 2r = 0$, $\Rightarrow r = 5$,

Then, $T_6' = {}^{10}C_5\,(-2)^5$

Now $\dfrac{{}^{10}C_5\,(-1)^5}{{}^{10}C_5\,(-2)^5} = \dfrac{1}{32}$

25. Suppose three consecutive terms in the expansion of $(1 + a)^n$ are $(r - 1)$ th, rth and $(r + 1)$th terms.

Then, $T_{r-1} = {}^nC_{r-2}a^{r-2} \Rightarrow T_r = {}^nC_{r-1}a^{r-1}$

and $T_{r+1} = {}^nC_r a^r$

Since, coefficients are in the ratio $1 : 7 : 42$, so we have

$\dfrac{\text{Coefficient of } T_{r-1}}{\text{Coefficient of } T_r} = \dfrac{1}{7} \Rightarrow \dfrac{{}^nC_{r-2}}{{}^nC_{r-1}} = \dfrac{1}{7}$

$\Rightarrow \dfrac{\dfrac{n!}{(r-2)!(n-r+2)!}}{\dfrac{n!}{(r-1)!(n-r+1)!}} = \dfrac{1}{7} \Rightarrow 8r - n = 9 \quad \ldots(i)$

Similarly, $\dfrac{\text{Coefficient of } T_r}{\text{Coefficient of } T_{r+1}} = \dfrac{7}{42} \Rightarrow \dfrac{{}^nC_{r-1}}{{}^nC_r} = \dfrac{7}{42}$

$\Rightarrow \dfrac{\dfrac{n!}{(r-1)!\,(n-r+1)!}}{\dfrac{n!}{r!(n-r)!}} = \dfrac{1}{6} \Rightarrow 7r - n = 1 \quad \ldots(ii)$

Solve Eqs. (i) and (ii) **Ans.** $n = 55$

26. $T_2 = T_{1+1} = {}^nC_1 x^{n-1} \cdot a = 240 \quad \ldots(i)$

Similarly, $T_3 = {}^nC_2 x^{n-2} \cdot a^2 = 720 \quad \ldots(ii)$

and $T_4 = {}^nC_3 x^{n-3} a^3 = 1080 \quad \ldots(iii)$

On dividing Eq. (ii) by Eq. (i), we get

$\dfrac{{}^nC_2 \cdot x^{n-2} \cdot a^2}{{}^nC_1 \cdot x^{n-1} \cdot a} = \dfrac{720}{240} \Rightarrow \dfrac{a}{x} = \dfrac{6}{n-1}$

On dividing Eq. (iii) by Eq. (ii), we get

$\dfrac{a}{x} = \dfrac{9}{2(n-2)} \Rightarrow \dfrac{6}{n-1} = \dfrac{9}{2(n-2)} \Rightarrow n = 5$

Now $T_2 = {}^5C_1 x^{5-1} \cdot a = 240 \Rightarrow 5 \cdot x^4 \cdot a = 240$

$\because \quad \dfrac{a}{x} = \dfrac{6}{n-1} = \dfrac{6}{5-1} = \dfrac{6}{4} = \dfrac{3}{2}$

$\Rightarrow \quad a = \dfrac{3}{2}x$

$\therefore \quad 5 \cdot x^4 \cdot \dfrac{3}{2} \cdot x = 240$ **Ans.** $x = 2, a = 3$ and $n = 5$

27. General term in $\left(\dfrac{3}{2}x^2 - \dfrac{1}{3x}\right)^9$

$$T_{r+1} = {}^9C_r \left(\frac{3}{2}\right)^{9-r} \left(-\frac{1}{3}\right)^r x^{18-3r}$$

So, general form in the expansion of

$$(1 + x + 2x^3)\left(\frac{3}{2}x^2 - \frac{1}{3x}\right)^9$$

$$= {}^9C_r \left(\frac{3}{2}\right)^{9-r} \left(-\frac{1}{3}\right)^r x^{18-3r} + {}^9C_r \left(\frac{3}{2}\right)^{9-r} \left(-\frac{1}{3}\right)^r x^{19-3r} + 2\,{}^9C_r \left(\frac{3}{2}\right)^{9-r} \left(-\frac{1}{3}\right)^r x^{21-3r}$$

For the term independent of x

$18 - 3r = 0,\ 19 - 3r = 0$ and $21 - 3r = 0$

$\Rightarrow \quad r = 6, \dfrac{19}{3}$ and 7

Thus, posible value of r are 6 and 7.

$\therefore$ Term independent of x

$$= {}^9C_6 \left(\frac{3}{2}\right)^{9-6} \left(-\frac{1}{3}\right)^6 + 2 \cdot {}^9C_7 \left(\frac{3}{2}\right)^{9-7} \left(-\frac{1}{3}\right)^7$$

Ans. $\dfrac{17}{54}$

28. As $2n$ is even, the middle term in the expansion of $(1 + x)^{2n}$ is given by $\left(\dfrac{2n}{2} + 1\right)$th term i.e. $(n + 1)$th term,

Now, $T_{n+1} = {}^{2n}C_n (1)^{2n-n} (x)^n = {}^{2n}C_n x^n = \dfrac{(2n)!}{n!\,(2n-n)!} \cdot x^n$

$$= \frac{(2n)!}{n!n!} \cdot x^n = \frac{2n(2n-1)(2n-2) \ldots 4 \cdot 3 \cdot 2 \cdot 1}{n!n!} \cdot x^n$$

$$= \frac{1 \cdot 2 \cdot 3 \cdot 4 \ldots (2n-2)(2n-1)(2n)}{n!n!} \cdot x^n$$

$$= \frac{[1 \cdot 3 \cdot 5 \ldots (2n-1)][2 \cdot 4 \cdot 6 \ldots (2n)]}{n!n!} \cdot x^n$$

$$= \frac{[1 \cdot 3 \cdot 5 \ldots (2n-1)] \cdot 2^n}{n!} \cdot x^n$$

29. $\left(x^2 + \dfrac{1}{x^2} + 2\right)^n = \left(x + \dfrac{1}{x}\right)^{2n}$. Here, $2n$ is even and total number of terms is $(2n + 1)$, which is odd.

$\therefore$ Middle term $= T_{\frac{(2n+1)+1}{2}} = T_{n+1}$

$= \dfrac{(2n)!}{n!n!}$, after that do same as Q. 28.

30. In the expansion of $(1 + x)^{2n}$, the general term is

$$T_{r+1} = {}^{2n}C_r x^r$$

For coefficient of x^n, put $r = n$, we get

$$T_{n+1} = {}^{2n}C_n x^n$$

$\therefore$ Coefficient of x^n in the expansion of $(1 + x)^{2n} = {}^{2n}C_n$

Now, in the expansion of $(1 + x)^{2n-1}$, the general term is

$$T_{r+1} = {}^{2n-1}C_r \cdot x^r$$

For coefficient of x^n, put $r = n$, we get

$$T_{n+1} = {}^{2n-1}C_n x^n$$

$\therefore$ Coefficient of x^n in the expansion of $(1 + x)^{2n-1}$

$$= {}^{2n-1}C_n$$

31. Number of terms in the expansion of $\left(x + \dfrac{1}{x}\right)^{2n+1}$ is $2n + 1 + 1 = 2n + 2$ (even). Therefore, there are two middle terms $T_{\left(\frac{2n+1+1}{2}\right)}$ and $T_{\left(\frac{2n+1+1}{2}+1\right)}$ i.e. T_{n+1} and T_{n+2}.

Ans. $\dfrac{(2n+1)!}{n!(n+1)!}x$ and $\dfrac{(2n+1)!}{n!(n+1)!} \cdot \dfrac{1}{x}$

32. We have, $(2 + 3x)^9 = 2^9\left(1 + \dfrac{3x}{2}\right)^9$

Now, $\dfrac{T_{r+1}}{T_r} = \dfrac{2^9\left[{}^9C_r \left(\frac{3x}{2}\right)^r\right]}{2^9\left[{}^9C_{r-1} \left(\frac{3x}{2}\right)^{r-1}\right]}$

[$\because$ general term in the binomial expansion $(a + x)^n$ is $T_{r+1} = {}^nC_r\, a^{n-r}\, x^r$]

$$= \frac{{}^9C_r}{{}^9C_{r-1}} \cdot \left(\frac{3x}{2}\right) = \frac{9!}{r!(9-r)!} \cdot \frac{(r-1)!(10-r)!}{9!} \cdot \left(\frac{3x}{2}\right)$$

$$= \frac{10-r}{r} \cdot \left(\frac{3x}{2}\right) = \frac{10-r}{r}\left(\frac{9}{4}\right) \qquad \left[\because x = \frac{3}{2}\right]$$

But $\dfrac{T_{r+1}}{T_r} \geq 1$

$\Rightarrow \quad \dfrac{90 - 9r}{4r} \geq 1 \Rightarrow 90 - 9r \geq 4r$

$\Rightarrow \quad r \leq \dfrac{90}{13} \Rightarrow r \leq 6\dfrac{12}{13}$

Thus, the maximum value of r is 6. Therefore, the greatest term is $T_{r+1} = T_7$.

Hence, $T_7 = 2^9\left[{}^9C_6 \left(\dfrac{3x}{2}\right)^6\right] = 2^9 \cdot {}^9C_6 \left(\dfrac{9}{4}\right)^6$

$\left[\text{putting } x = \dfrac{3}{2}\right]$

$= 2^9 \cdot \dfrac{9 \times 8 \times 7}{3 \times 2 \times 1} \left(\dfrac{3^{12}}{2^{12}}\right)$ **Ans.** $\dfrac{7 \times 3^{13}}{2}$

TOPIC 03

Applications of Binomial Theorem

Sometimes, the calculations for powers of higher numbers like $(98)^5$, $(101)^6$ etc., become difficult by using repeated multiplication. Also, division of an expression, involving n (a rational number) as index by a number is difficult to calculate by division method. Such problems can be solved easily by using the binomial theorem which are given below

Problems Based on Exponent of a Number

If exponent of a number is integer and the given number without index is less than or greater than 100 then write it as difference of two numbers or sum of two numbers. Out of these two numbers by to take one number as multiple of 10. Also, if the given number without index is decimal, then write it as the difference/sum of two numbers out of which one number is 1 and then use suitable binomial expansion.

Example 1 Compute the value of $(96)^3$.

Sol. Here, given number without index is 96. Since, it is less than 100, so it can be written as $100 - 4$.

Now, $(96)^3 = (100-4)^3$

$$= {}^3C_0(100)^3 - {}^3C_1(100)^2\,4 + {}^3C_2(100)4^2 - {}^3C_3 4^3$$

[by binomial theorem]

$$= 1000000 - 3(10000)4 + 3(100)(16) - 64$$
$$= 1000000 - 120000 + 4800 - 64$$
$$= 884736$$

Note If given number without index is less than 100, then write it as difference of two numbers and if number is greater than 100, then write it as sum of two numbers.

Example 2 Expand $(102)^5$.

Sol. We have, $(102)^5 = (100+2)^5$

$$= {}^5C_0(100)^5 + {}^5C_1(100)^4(2)^1 + {}^5C_2(100)^3(2)^2 + {}^5C_3(100)^2(2)^3 + {}^5C_4(100)(2)^4 + {}^5C_5(2)^5$$

$$= {}^5C_0(10)^{10} + {}^5C_1(10)^8\,2 + {}^5C_2(10)^6 \times 4 + {}^5C_2(10)^4 \times 8 + {}^5C_1(10)^2 \times 16 + ({}^5C_0) \times 32$$

$[\because {}^nC_r = {}^nC_{n-r}]$

$$= 1 \times 10^{10} + 5 \times 10^8 \times 2 + \frac{5 \times 4}{2} \times 10^6 \times 4 + \frac{5 \times 4}{2} \times 10^4 \times 8 + 5 \times 100 \times 16 + 32$$

$$= 10000000000 + 1000000000 + 40000000 + 800000 + 8000 + 32$$

$$= 11040808032$$

Example 3 Find an approximation of $(0.99)^5$, using the first three terms of its expansion. **[NCERT]**

Sol. We have, $(0.99)^5 = (1-0.01)^5$

$$= 1 - {}^5C_1 \times (0.01) + {}^5C_2 \times (0.01)^2 - \dots$$
$$= 1 - 0.05 + 10 \times 0.0001 - \dots$$
$$= 1.001 - 0.05$$
$$= 0.951$$

Example 4 Which number is larger, $(1.1)^{10000}$ or 1000? **[NCERT]**

Sol. We have, $(1.1)^{10000} = [1 + (0.1)]^{10000}$

$$= {}^{10000}C_0 + {}^{10000}C_1(0.1) + {}^{10000}C_2(0.1)^2 + \dots$$

[expanding by binomial theorem]

$$= 1 + 10000(0.1) + \text{Other positive terms}$$
$$= 1 + 1000 + \text{Other positive terms}$$
$$= 1001 + \text{Other positive terms} > 1000$$

Hence, $(1.1)^{10000} > 1000$

Problems Based on Division

First, write the term having exponent, as the sum or difference of two terms or numbers in such a way that after expanding, terms will become a multiple of divisor. In the expansion $(1+\alpha)^n = 1 + {}^nC_1\alpha + {}^nC_2\alpha^2 + \dots + {}^nC_n\alpha^n$

We can conclude that

$$(1+\alpha)^n - 1 = {}^nC_1\alpha + {}^nC_2\alpha^2 + \dots + {}^nC_n\alpha^n$$

is divisible by α i.e. it is a multiple of α.

Note While writing the term having exponent as sum or difference of two numbers, number should be a factor of given divisor.

Example 5 If 25^{15} is divided by 13, then find the remainder. **[NCERT Exemplar]**

Sol. We have, $25^{15} = (26-1)^{15}$

$$= {}^{15}C_0(26)^{15} - {}^{15}C_1(26)^{14}(1)^1 + {}^{15}C_2(26)^{13}(1)^2 - \dots - {}^{15}C_{15}$$

$$= {}^{15}C_0(26)^{15} - {}^{15}C_1(26)^{14} + \dots - 1 - 12 + 12$$

$= ({}^{15}C_6 2\times13\times(26)^{14} - {}^{15}C_1 2\times13\times(26)^{13}+.....13)+12$

$=13({}^{15}C_0\times2\times(26)^{14} - {}^{15}C_1\times2\times(26)^{13}+...-1)+12$

It is clear that when right hand side is divided by 13, we get the remainder 12.

Example 6 Find the remainder, when 5^{99} is divided by 13.

Sol. We know that, $5^4 = 625 = 13\times48+1$

$\Rightarrow \quad 5^4 = 13\lambda + 1$, where λ is a positive integer.

$\Rightarrow \quad (5^4)^{24} = (13\lambda+1)^{24}$

$= {}^{24}C_0(13\lambda)^{24} + {}^{24}C_1(13\lambda)^{23} + {}^{24}C_2(13\lambda)^{22} + \cdots + {}^{24}C_{23}(13\lambda) + {}^{24}C_{24}$ [by binomial theorem]

$\Rightarrow 5^{96} = 13[{}^{24}C_0 13^{23}\lambda^{24} + {}^{24}C_1 13^{23}\lambda^{22}+...+{}^{24}C_{23}\lambda]+1$

$=$ (A multiple of 13) + 1

On multiplying both sides by 5^3, we get

$5^{96}\cdot5^3 = 5^3\cdot$(A multiple of 13) $+ 5^3$

$\Rightarrow 5^{99} =$ [(A multiple of 13) $+[13\times9+8]$

$[\because 5^3 = 125 = 13\times9+8]$

Hence, the required remainder is 8.

Example 7 Find the remainder when $6^n - 5n$ is divided by 25.

Sol. We have, $6^n - 5n = (1+5)^n - 5n$

$= {}^nC_0 + {}^nC_1(5) + {}^nC_2(5)^2 + \cdots + {}^nC_n5^n - 5n$

$= 1 + n5 + \dfrac{n(n-1)}{2}\times(25) + \cdots + 1(5^n) - 5n$

$= 1 + 25\left[\dfrac{n(n-1)}{2} + \cdots + 5^{n-2}\right]$

$= 25\times$ An integer $+1$

Hence, $6^n - 5n$ leaves the remainder 1, when divided by 25.

Example 8 Using binomial theorem, prove that $2^{3n} - 7n - 1$ is divisible by 49, where $n \in N$.

Sol. We have,

$(2^3)^n - 7n - 1 = (8)^n - 7n - 1$

Here, 8 can be written as $1+7$. $[\because 7$ is a factor of 49]

$\therefore \quad 2^{3n} - 7n - 1 = (1+7)^n - 7n - 1$

By using binomial theorem, we get

$2^{3n} - 7n - 1 = ({}^nC_0 + {}^nC_1 7 + {}^nC_2 7^2 + ... + {}^nC_n 7^n) - 7n - 1$

$= \left(1 + \dfrac{n!}{1!(n-1)!}\cdot7 + \dfrac{n!}{2!(n-2)!}7^2 + ... + 7^n\right) - 7n - 1$

$= 1 + 7n + \dfrac{n(n-1)}{2}7^2 + ... + 7^n - 7n - 1$

$= \dfrac{n(n-1)}{2}7^2 + ... + 7^n$

Take common number outside, we get

$2^{3n} - 7n - 1 = 7^2\left[\dfrac{n(n-1)}{2} + ... + 7^{n-2}\right]$

$= 49\left[\dfrac{n(n-1)}{2} + ... + 7^{n-2}\right]$

Here, we see that above series is a multiple of 49.

Therefore, $2^{3n} - 7n - 1$ is divisible by 49. **Hence proved.**

Example 9 Using binomial theorem, show that the expression $7^9 + 9^7$ is divisible by 64.

Sol. We have, $7^9 + 9^7 = (1+8)^7 - (1-8)^9$

$= {}^7C_0 + {}^7C_1(8) + {}^7C_2(8)^2 + {}^7C_3(8)^3 + ... + {}^7C_7(8)^7]$

$- [{}^9C_0 - {}^9C_1(8)^1 + {}^9C_2(8)^2 - ... - {}^9C_9(8)^9]$

$= [1 + 7\times(8)^1 + 21\times(8)^2 + 35(8)^3 ... + (8)^7]$

$-[1 - 9\times(8)^1 + 36(8)^2 - ... -(8)^9]$

$= (7+9)\times(8)^1 + (21-36)\times(8)^2 + ...$

$= 2\times64 - 15\times64 + ...$

$= 64(2 - 15 + ...)$

Hence, it is clear that it is divisible by 64. **Hence proved.**

Example 10 If a and b are distinct integers, then prove that $(a-b)$ is a factor of $a^n - b^n$, whenever n is a positive integer. **[NCERT]**

Sol. We can write, $a^n = (a - b + b)^n$, then using expansion of $(x+y)^n$, we get

$a^n = {}^nC_0(a-b)^n + {}^nC_1(a-b)^{n-1}b + {}^nC_2(a-b)^{n-2}b^2 + ... + {}^nC_nb^n$

[taking $(a-b)$ as x and b as y]

$\Rightarrow \quad a^n = (a-b)[{}^nC_0(a-b)^{n-1} + {}^nC_1(a-b)^{n-2}b + {}^nC_2(a-b)^{n-3}b^2 + ...] + b^n$

$\therefore \quad a^n - b^n = (a-b)[{}^nC_0(a-b)^{n-1} + ...]$

Hence, $(a-b)$ is a factor of $a^n - b^n$. **Hence proved.**

Topic Practice 3

Very Short Answer Type Questions

2 Marks

1 Using binomial theorem, evaluate each of the following. (Each part carries 2 Marks)

(i) $(96)^3$ (ii) $(101)^4$ (iii) $(90)^5$

2 Using binomial theorem, evaluate each of the following expansions. (Each part carries 2 Marks)

(i) $(100.3)^4$ (ii) $(9.97)^5$ (iii) $(0.98)^4$

Short Answer Type Questions

4 Marks

3 Which is larger $(1.01)^{10000}$ or 100?

4 Using binomial theorem, evaluate each of the following. (Each part carries 4 Marks)

(i) $(12)^5 + (8)^5$ (ii) $(53)^7 - (47)^7$

(iii) $(13)^5 + (7)^5$ (iv) $(33)^6 - (27)^6$

5 Using binomial theorem, evaluate each of the following. (Each part carries 4 Marks)

(i) $(10.3)^5 + (9.7)^5$

(ii) $(100.5)^4 - (99.5)^4$

(iii) $(10.4)^4 + (9.6)^4$

(iv) $(20.5)^5 - (19.5)^5$

6 Using binomial theorem, evaluate the following. (Each part carries 4 Marks)

(i) $(9999)^4$ (ii) $(1001)^5$

(iii) $(105)^3$ (iv) $(98)^5$

(v) $(103)^3$ (vi) $(0.998)^8$

7 Prove that $11^n - 10n$, when divided by 100, always leave a remainder 1 where $n \in +N$

8 Show that $2^{4n} - 15n - 1$ is divisible by 225.

9 Show that $9^{n+1} - 8n - 9$ or $3^{2n+2} - 8n + 9$ is divisible by 64, whenever n is a positive integer. **[NCERT]**

Hints & Answers

1. (i) $(96)^3 = (100-4)^3$

$= {}^3C_0\,(100)^3 - {}^3C_1\,(1000)^2\,(4)^1 + {}^3C_2\,(100)^1\,4^2 + {}^3C_3\,4^3$

Ans. 884736

(ii) $(101)^4 = (100+1)^4$

$= {}^4C_0\,(100)^4 + {}^4C_1\,(100)^3\,(1)^1 + {}^4C_2\,(100)^2\,(1)^2 + {}^4C_3\,(100)^1\,(1)^3 + {}^4C_4\,(1)^4$

Ans. 104060401

(iii) $(90)^5 = (100-10)^5$

Now, solve as part (i). **Ans.** 5904900000

2. (i) $(100.3)^4 = (100+0.3)^4$

$= {}^4C_0\,(100)^4 + {}^4C_1\,(100)^3\,(0.3)^1 + {}^4C_2\,(100)^2\,(0.3)^2 + {}^4C_3\,(100)^1\,(0.3)^3 + {}^4C_4\,(0.3)^4$

Ans. 101205410.8

(ii) $(9.97)^3 = (10-0.03)^3$

Now, solve as part (i).

Ans. 98508.97

(iii) $(0.98)^4 = (1-0.2)^4$ Now solve as part (i).

Ans. 0.922

3. Solve as Example 4. $(1.01)^{10000}$ is greater than 100.

4. (i) $(12)^5 + (8)^5 = (10+2)^5 + (10-2)^5$

$(10+2)^5 = {}^5C_0 \times 10^5 + {}^5C_1 \times 10^4 \times 2 + {}^5C_2 \times 10^3 \times 2^2 + \ldots$ ...(i)

$(10-2)^5 = {}^{10}C_5 \times 5 - {}^5C_1 \times 10^4 \times 2 + {}^5C_2 \times 10^3 \times 2^2$...(ii)

Now, adding Eqs. (i) and (ii)

$(12)^5 + (8)^5 = 2\,[\,{}^5C_0\,(10)^5 + {}^5C_2\,(10)^3\,(2)^2 + {}^5C_4\,(10)^1\,(2)^4]$

Ans. 281600

(ii) $(53)^7 - (47)^7 = (50+3)^7 - (50-3)^7$

$(50+3)^7 = {}^7C_0\,(50)^7 + {}^7C_1\,(5)^6\,(3)^1 + {}^7C_2\,(50)^5\,(2)^2$ ...(i)

$(50-3)^7 = {}^7C_0\,(50)^7 - {}^7C_1\,(50)^6\,(3)^1 + {}^7C_2\,(3)^2$ ...(ii)

Subtract Eq. (ii) from Eq. (i)

$(50+3)^7 - (50-3)^7$

$= 2\,[\,{}^7C_1\,(50)^6\,(3)^1 + {}^7C_3\,(50)^4\,(3)^3 + {}^7C_5\,(50)^2\,(3)^5 + {}^7C_7\,(3)^7]$

Ans. 668088019374

(iii) Solve as part (i). **Ans.** 388100

(iv) Solve as part (ii). **Ans.** 904047480

5. (i) $(10.3)^5 + (9.7)^5 = (10 + 0.3)^5 + (10 - 0.3)^5$

$$(10 + 0.3)^5 = {}^5C_0\, 10^5 + {}^5C_1\, (10)^4\, (0.3)^1 + {}^5C_2\, (10)^3\, (0.3)^2 + \dots \quad \dots\text{(i)}$$

$$(10 - 0.3)^5 = {}^5C_0\, 10^5 - {}^5C_1\, (10)^4\, (0.3)^1 + {}^5C_2\, (10)^3\, (0.3)^2 \quad \dots\text{(ii)}$$

On adding Eq. (i) and (ii)

$$(10+0.3)^5 + (10-0.3)^5 = 2\,[{}^5C_0\,(10)^5 + {}^5C_2\,(10)^3\,(0.3)^2 + {}^5C_4\,(10)^1\,(0.3)^4]$$

Ans. 201800.81

(ii) Solve as part (i). **Ans.** 4000100

(iii) Solve as part (i). **Ans.** 20192.0512

(iv) Solve as part (i). **Ans.** 801000.0625

6. (i) $(9999)^4 = (10000 - 1)^4$

Now, solve as Q. 1 (i). **Ans.** 996005996001

(ii) $(1001)^5 = (1000 + 1)^5$

Now, solve as Q. 1 (ii). **Ans.** 1005010010005001

(iii) $(105)^5 = (100 + 5)^5$

Now, solve as Q. 1 (ii). **Ans.** 1157625

(iv) $(98)^5 = (100 - 2)^5$

Now, solve as Q. 1 (i). **Ans.** 9039207968

(v) $(103)^3 = (100 + 3)^3$

Now, solve as Q. 1 (ii). **Ans.** 1092727

(vi) $(0.998)^8 = (1 - 0.002)^8$

Now, solve as Q. 2 (iii). **Ans.** 0.9841114

7. $11^n - 10^n = (1+10)^n - 10n$

$$= 1 + 10n + {}^nC_2(10)^2 + {}^nC_3(10)^3 + - 10n$$

$$= 1 + 100\,\{{}^nC_2 + {}^nC_3 10 + \dots + {}^nC_n 10^{n-2}\}$$

$$= 100 \times \text{An integer} + 1$$

$\Rightarrow 11^n - 10n$ leaves remainder 1 when divided by 100.

8. Solve as Example 8.

9. Solve as Example 8.

Chapter Practice

Multiple Choice Type Questions

1 Mark

1 In every term, the sum of indices of a and b in the expansion of $(a+b)^n$ is

(a) n (b) $n+1$ (c) $n+2$ (d) $n-1$

2 $(100)^{50}+(99)^{50}$ **[NCERT Exemplar]**

(a) $<(101)^{50}$ (b) $=101$
(c) $>(101)^{50}$ (d) >101

3 The coefficient of x^n in the expansion of $(1+x)(1-x)^n$ is

(a) $(1-n)$ (b) $(-1)^n(1-n)$
(c) $n-1$ (d) $(-1)^n(n-1)$

4 If the coefficients of 2nd, 3rd and the 4th terms in the expansion of $(1+x)^n$ are in AP, then value of n is

(a) 2 (b) 7 (c) 11 (d) 14

5 If 6^n-5n is divided by 25, then remainder is

(a) 0 (b) 2 (c) 4 (d) 1

6 The coefficient of x^{50} after simplifying and collecting the like terms in the expansion of $(1+x)^{1000}+x(1+x)^{999}+x^2(1+x)^{998}+....+x^{1000}$ is **[NCERT Exemplar]**

(a) $\frac{(1001)!}{(50)!(951)!}$ (b) $\frac{(101)!}{(50)!(49)!}$
(c) $\frac{(1001)!}{(150)!(851)!}$ (d) None of these

Assertion-Reason Type Questions

1 Mark

Directions (Q. Nos. 7-10) *In the questions given below are two statements labelled as Assertion (A) and Reason (R). In the context of the two statements, which one of the following is correct?*

(a) Both A and R are correct; R is the correct explanation of A
(b) Both A and R are correct; R is not the correct explanation of A
(c) A is correct; R is incorrect
(d) R is correct; A is incorrect

7. **Assertion (A)** The number of terms in the expansion of $(1+2x+x^2)^{20}$ is 41.

Reason (R) The number of terms in the expansion of $(a+b)^n$ is $n+1$.

8. **Assertion (A)** The number of terms in the expansions of $(x+3y)^3$ is 5.

Reason (R) The number of terms in expansion of $(a+b)^n$ is $(n+1)$.

9. **Assertion (A)** $\sum_{r=0}^{n} 4^r\,{}^nC_r$ is 5^n.

Reason (R) $(1+x)^n={}^nC_0+{}^nC_1x+{}^nC_2x^2+\ldots+{}^nC_nx^n$.

10. **Assertion (A)** The remainder when 6^n-5n is divided by 25 is 2.

Reason (R) $(a+b)^n=\sum_{r=0}^{n}{}^nC_r a^{n-r}b^r$.

Very Short Answer Type Questions

2 Marks

11. Find $(a+b)^4-(a-b)^4$.
Hence, evaluate $(\sqrt{3}+\sqrt{2})^4-(\sqrt{3}-\sqrt{2})^4$. **[NCERT]**

12. Simplify the following expression.
(Each part carries 2 Marks)

(i) $\left(y+\frac{1}{y}\right)^6-\left(y-\frac{1}{y}\right)^6$ (ii) $(2+\sqrt{y})^4+(2-\sqrt{y})^4$

13. If P and Q are the sum of odd and even terms in the expansion $(y+b)^n$, then prove that
$(y+b)^{2n}+(y-b)^{2n}=2(P^2+Q^2)$.

14. Find n in the binomial $\left(\sqrt[3]{2}+\frac{1}{\sqrt[3]{3}}\right)^n$, if the ratio of 7th term from the beginning to the 7th term from the end is $\frac{1}{6}$. **[NCERT Exemplar]**

15. Find the value of r, if the coefficients of $(2r+4)$th and $(r-2)$th terms in the expansion of $(1+x)^{18}$ are equal.

16. Find the ratio of coefficient of x^n in the expansion of $(1+x)^{2n}$ and $(1+x)^{2n-1}$. **[NCERT Exemplar]**

Short Answer Type Questions

4 Marks

17. If the integers $r\ (>1)$, $n\ (>2)$ and coefficients of $(3r)$th and $(r+2)$nd terms in the expansion of $(1+x)^{2n}$ are equal, then prove that $n = 2r$. **[NCERT Exemplar]**

18. Find the coefficient of x^5 in the expansion of $(1+x)^3\,(1-x)^6$.

19. For what value of m, the coefficients of the $(2m+1)$th and $(4m+5)$th terms in the expansion of $(1+x)^{10}$ are equal?

20. Find the value of α for which the coefficients of the middle terms in the expansions of $(1+\alpha x)^4$ and $(1-\alpha x)^6$ are equal.

21. Find the coefficient of x^7 in $\left(ax^2+\dfrac{1}{bx}\right)^{11}$ and x^{-7} in $\left(ax-\dfrac{1}{bx^2}\right)^{11}$ and find the relation between a and b so that these coefficients are equal.

22. Prove that there is no term involving x^8 in the expansion of $\left(2x^2-\dfrac{3}{x}\right)^{11}$.

Long Answer Type Questions

6 Marks

23. In the expansion of $(1+x)^n$, the binomial coefficients of three consecutive terms are respectively 220, 495 and 792. Find the value of n.

24. If in the expansion of $(1+x)^n$, the coefficients of three consecutive terms are 56, 70 and 56, then find n and the position of the terms of these coefficients.

25. The coefficients of 5th, 6th and 7th terms in the expansion of $(1+x)^n$ are in AP. Find the value of n.

26. If 3rd, 4th, 5th and 6th terms in the expansion of $(x+y)^n$ are respectively a, b, c and d, then prove that $\dfrac{b^2-ac}{c^2-bd}=\dfrac{5a}{3c}$.

27. If the 6th, 7th and 8th terms in the expansion of $(x+a)^n$ are respectively 112, 7 and 1/4, then find x, a, n.

28. The first three terms in the expansion of $(x+y)^n$ are 1, 56 and 1372 respectively. Find the values of x and y.

29. Using binomial theorem, determine which number is larger $(1.2)^{4000}$ or 800? **[NCERT Exemplar]**

30. Show that $2^{4n+4}-15n-16$, where $n \in N$, is divisible by 225. **[NCERT Exemplar]**

Case-Based Type Question

6 Marks

31. An algebraic expression containing two terms is called a binomial expression $(a+b)^n$ is a binomial expression. The number of terms in a binomial expansion is always one greater than index.

On the basis of above information answer the following questions.

(i) Find the number of terms in the expansion of $(2y-3z)^4$.

(ii) Find the number of terms in the expansion of $\left(x^2-\dfrac{1}{3x}\right)^9$.

(iii) Find the number of terms in the expansion of $(x^3-3x^2+3x+1)^4$.

(iv) Find the number of terms in the expansion of $[(4x^2+12xy+9y^2)^5]^{\frac{1}{2}}$.

(v) Find the number of terms in the expansion of $\left[\left[\left(x^2-\dfrac{1}{2x}\right)^{10}\right]^{\frac{1}{3}}\right]^9$.

Hints & Answers

1. (a) **2.** (a) **3.** (b) **4.** (b) **5.** (d)
6. (a) **7.** (a) **8.** (d) **9.** (a) **10.** (d)

11. $(a+b)^4-(a-b)^4=2[{}^4C_1\,a^3b^1+{}^4C_3\,ab^3]$
$=2\,[4\,a^3b+4ab^3]$
$=8\,(a^3b+ab^3)$

Put $a=\sqrt{3},\ b=\sqrt{2}$ to get the required answer. **Ans.** $(40\sqrt{6})$

12. (i) $\left(y+\frac{1}{y}\right)^6-\left(y-\frac{1}{y}\right)^6$

$$=2\left[{}^6C_1y^{6-1}\left(\frac{1}{y}\right)^1+{}^6C_3\,y^{6-3}\left(\frac{1}{y}\right)^3+{}^6C_5y^{6-5}\left(\frac{1}{y}\right)^5\right]$$

$$=2\left[6\,y^5\cdot\frac{1}{y}+20y^3\cdot\frac{1}{y^3}+6y\cdot\frac{1}{y^5}\right]=12\left(y^4+\frac{1}{y^4}+\frac{10}{3}\right)$$

(ii) Use
$(x+a)^n+(x-a)^n=2\,[{}^nC_0\,x^n+{}^nC_2\,x^{n-2}\,a^2+\dots]$
Here, $x=2,\ a=\sqrt{y}$ **Ans.** $(32+48y+2y^2)$

13. $(y+b)^n={}^nC_0\,y^n+{}^nC_1\,y^{n-1}\,b+{}^nC_2y^{n-2}\,b^2+\dots+{}^nC_n\,b^n$
$=P+Q$ ...(i)
$(y-b)^n={}^nC_0\,y^n-{}^nC_1y^{n-1}\,b+{}^nC_2y^{n-2}\,b^2-\dots+(-1)^n\,{}^nC_n\,b^n$
$=P-Q$ ...(ii)

On squaring Eqs. (i) and (ii) and then adding, we get
$(y+b)^{2n}+(y-b)^{2n}=(P+Q)^2+(P-Q)^2$
$=P^2+Q^2+2PQ+P^2+Q^2-2PQ=2\,(P^2+Q^2)$

14. $T_7={}^nC_6\,(\sqrt[3]{2})^{n-6}\left(\frac{1}{\sqrt[3]{3}}\right)^6={}^nC_6\,2^{\frac{n-6}{3}}\left(\frac{1}{3}\right)^2$

and 7th term from the end $=(n+1)-(7-1)$ th term from beginning $=(n-5)$th term from beginning.

$$={}^nC_{n-6}\,(\sqrt[3]{2})^{n-n+6}\left(\frac{1}{\sqrt[3]{3}}\right)^{(n-6)}={}^nC_{n-6}\,2^2\cdot\left(\frac{1}{3}\right)^{\frac{n-6}{3}}$$

Now, $$\frac{{}^nC_6\,2^{\frac{n-6}{3}}\cdot\left(\frac{1}{3}\right)^2}{{}^nC_{n-6}\,2^2\cdot\left(\frac{1}{3}\right)^{\left(\frac{n-6}{3}\right)}}=\frac{1}{6}\Rightarrow\frac{n-12}{3}=-1\Rightarrow n=9$$

Ans. 9

15. Coefficient of $(2r+4)$th term $={}^{18}C_{2r+3}$
Coefficient of $(r-2)$th term $={}^{18}C_{r-3}$
According to the question, ${}^{18}C_{2r+3}={}^{18}C_{r-3}$
$\Rightarrow\quad r=6$

16. Coefficient of x^n in the expansion of $(1+x)^{2n}={}^{2n}C_n$
Coefficient of x^n in the expansion of
$(1+x)^{2n-1}={}^{2n-1}C_{n-1}$

Required ratio $=\frac{{}^{2n}C_n}{{}^{2n-1}C_{n-1}}=\frac{(2n)!}{n!\,n!}\times\frac{(n-1)!\,n!}{(2n-1)!}=\frac{2}{1}$ or $2:1$

17. Here, $r>1,\ n>2$
$\therefore\quad T_{3r}={}^{2n}C_{3r-1}\,x^{3r-1}$
$T_{r+2}={}^{2n}C_{r+1}\,x^{r+1}$
Then, ${}^{2n}C_{3r-1}={}^{2n}C_{r+1}$
$\Rightarrow\quad 3r-1+r+1=2n$
$\Rightarrow\quad n=2r$

18. $(1+x)^3\,(1-x)^6=(1+x^3+3x+3x^2)$
$(1+{}^6C_1x+{}^6C_2\,x^2-{}^6C_3x^3+{}^6C_4\,x^4-{}^6C_5x^5+{}^6C_6\,x^6)$
Coefficient of $x^5=-{}^6C_5+{}^6C_2+3\,{}^6C_4-3\,{}^6C_3$
$=-6+15+45-60=-6$

19. Coefficient of $(2m+1)$th term $={}^{10}C_{2m}$
and coefficient of $(4m+5)$ th term $={}^{10}C_{4m+4}$
Now, ${}^{10}C_{2m}={}^{10}C_{4m+4}$
Ans. $m=1$

20. Middle term in $(1+\alpha x)^4=\left(\frac{4}{2}+1\right)$th $=3$ th term
$\therefore$ Coefficient of middle term $={}^4C_2\,(\alpha)^2$
Middle term in $(1-\alpha x)^6=\left(\frac{6}{2}+1\right)$th $=4$th term
$\therefore$ Coefficient of middle term $=(-1)^3\,{}^6C_3\,(\alpha)^3$
Now, ${}^4C_2\,(\alpha)^2=-{}^6C_3(\alpha)^3$
$\Rightarrow\quad 6\alpha^2+20\alpha^3=0$
$\Rightarrow\quad 2\alpha^2\,(3+10\alpha)=0$
$\Rightarrow\quad \alpha=0,\ \frac{-3}{10}$
Ans. $\alpha=\frac{-3}{10}$

21. General term in $\left(ax^2+\frac{1}{bx}\right)^{11}$,
$T_{r+1}={}^{11}C_r\,a^{11-r}\,b^{-r}\,x^{22-3r}$
For x^7, $22-3r=7\Rightarrow r=5$
$\therefore$ Coefficient of x^7 in $\left(ax^2+\frac{1}{bx}\right)^{11}={}^{11}C_5\,a^6b^{-5}$

General term in $\left(ax-\frac{1}{bx^2}\right)^{11}$,
$T_{r+1}={}^{11}C_r\,a^{11-r}\,(-1)^r\,b^{-r}\,x^{11-3r}$
For x^{-7}, $11-3r=-7\Rightarrow r=6$
$\therefore$ Coefficient of x^{-7} in $\left(ax-\frac{1}{bx^2}\right)^{11}={}^{11}C_6\,a^5b^{-6}\,(-1)^6$

According to the question,
${}^{11}C_5\,a^6b^{-5}={}^{11}C_6a^5b^{-6}\,(-1)^6$
$\Rightarrow\quad {}^{11}C_5\,ab={}^{11}C_6$
$\Rightarrow\quad ab=1$

22. General term in $\left(2x^2 - \frac{3}{x}\right)^{11}$,

$$T_{r+1} = {}^{11}C_r\,(2x^2)^{11-r}\left(\frac{-3}{x}\right)^r$$

$$= {}^{11}C_r\, 2^{11-r}\, x^{22-2r-r}\,(-3)^r$$

For x^8, $22 - 2r - r = 8 \Rightarrow 3r = 22 - 8 \Rightarrow r = \frac{14}{3}$

which is not an integer.

So, no term involving x^8 exist.

23. In the expansion of $(1+x)^n$, there consecutive terms are T_{r-1}, T_r and T_{r+1}.

Then, coefficient of $T_{r-1} = {}^nC_{r-2} = 220$ ...(i)

Coefficient of $T_r = {}^nC_{r-1} = 495$ ...(ii)

and coefficient of $T_{r+1} = {}^nC_r = 792$ ...(iii)

Now, solving Eqs. (i), (ii) and (iii). **Ans.** $n = 12$

24. Solve as Q. 13. **Ans.** $n = 8$

25. $T_5 = {}^nC_4\,x^4$, $T_6 = {}^nC_5\,x^5$ and $T_7 = {}^nC_6\,x^6$

$\because$ Coefficient of these terms are in AP.

$\therefore\ 2\,{}^nC_5 = {}^nC_4 + {}^nC_6$ **Ans.** $n = 7, 14$

26. $T_3 = {}^nC_2\,x^{n-2}\,y^2 = a$, $T_4 = {}^nC_3\,x^{n-3}y^3 = b$

$T_5 = {}^nC_4\,x^{n-4}\,y^4 = C$ and $T_6 = {}^nC_5\,x^{n-5}\,y^5$

27. Here, $T_6 = {}^nC_5\,x^{n-5}\,a^5 = 112$ ...(i)

$T_7 = {}^nC_6\,x^{n-6}\,a^6 = 7$ ...(ii)

and $T_8 = {}^nC_7\,x^{n-7}a^7 = \frac{1}{4}$ ...(iii)

On dividing Eq. (i) by (ii), we get,

$$\frac{{}^nC_5\,x^{n-5}\,a^5}{{}^nC_6\,x^{n-6}\,a^6} = \frac{112}{7}$$

$\Rightarrow \frac{6}{n-5}\cdot\frac{x}{a} = \frac{112}{7} \Rightarrow 42x = 112a\,(n-5)$ ...(iv)

On dividing Eq. (ii) by (iii), we get

$$\frac{{}^nC_6\,x^{n-6}a^6}{{}^nC_7 x^{n-7}a^7} = \frac{7}{1/4}$$

$\Rightarrow \frac{7}{n-6}\,\frac{x}{a} = 28 \Rightarrow 7x = 28\,a\,(n-6)$ ...(v)

On solving Eq. (iv) and (v). **Ans.** $n = 8$, $a = \frac{1}{2}$, $x = 4$

28. $(x+y)^n = {}^nC_0\,x^ny^0 + {}^nC_1\,x^{n-1}\,y + {}^nC_2\,x^{n-2}\,y^2 + {}^nC_3\,x^{n-3}\,y^3 + \ldots$

Given, ${}^nC_0\,x^ny^0 = 1 \Rightarrow x^n = 1$ ...(i)

${}^nC_1\,x^{n-1}y = 56 \Rightarrow nx^{n-1}\,y = 56$ ...(ii)

${}^nC_2\,x^{n-2}\,y^2 = 1372 \Rightarrow \frac{n\,(n-1)}{2}\cdot x^{n-2}\,y^2 = 1372$ ...(iii)

On dividing Eq. (i) by Eq. (ii), we get

$$\frac{x^n}{nx^{n-1}y} = \frac{1}{56}$$

$\Rightarrow \frac{x}{ny} = \frac{1}{56}$

$\Rightarrow 56\,x = ny$ ...(iv)

On dividing Eq. (ii) by Eq. (iii), we get

$$\frac{nx^{n-1}\,y}{\frac{n\,(n-1)}{2}\,x^{n-2}\,y^2} = \frac{56}{1372}$$

$\Rightarrow \frac{2x}{(n-1)y} = \frac{56}{1372}$

$\Rightarrow 2744\,x = 56\,(n-1)y$ ...(v)

Ans. $n = 8$, $x = 1$, $y = 7$

29. $(1.2)^{4000} = (1 + 0.2)^{4000}$

$= {}^{4000}C_0 + {}^{4000}C_1\,(0.2) +$ Sum of positive terms

$= 1 + 4000\,(0.2) +$ A positive number

$= 1 + 800 +$ Positive number

$\therefore (1.2)^{4000} > 800$

30. $2^{4n+4} - 15n - 16 = (2)^{4n+1} - 15\,(n+1) - 1$

$= 16^{n+1} - 15\,(n+1) - 1$

$= (1+15)^{n+1} - 15\,(n+1) - 1$

$= \{{}^{n+1}C_0 + {}^{n+1}C_1(15) + {}^{n+1}C_2\,(15)^2 + {}^{n+1}C_3\,(15)^3 + \ldots + {}^{n+1}C_{n+1}\,(15)^{n+1}\} - 15\,(n+1) - 1$

$= 1 + 15\,(n+1) + {}^{n+1}C_2(15)^2 + {}^{n+1}C_3\,(15)^3 + \ldots + {}^{n+1}C_{n+1}\,(15)^{n+1} - 15\,(n+1) - 1$

$= 225\,\{{}^{n+1}C_2 + {}^{n+1}C_3(15) + \ldots + {}^{n+1}C_{n+1}\,(15)^{n-1}\}$

$= 225 \times$ A natural number

31. (i) 5 (ii) 10 (iii) 13 (iv) 6 (v) 31

CHAPTER

09

Sequences and Series

- Sequences and Series
- Arithmetic Progression (AP) and Its General Terms
- Sum of n Terms of an AP and Arithmetic Mean (AM)
- Geometric Progression (GP)
- Sum of First n Terms of a GP
- Geometric Mean and Relation between AM & GM
- Some Special Sum

Sequence, generally means a collection, ordered in such a way that it has an indentified first, second and third members and so on. e.g. Amount of money deposited in bank over a number of years, population of human beings at different times etc. Sequences, following specific patterns are called **progressions.**

TOPIC 01 Sequences and Series

Sequence

A sequence is a succession of numbers or terms formed according to some rule. e.g. 3, 6, 9,... is a sequence.

The various numbers occurring in a sequence are called its **terms** and generally denoted by $a_1, a_2, a_3, \ldots, a_n$, respectively. Here, $a_1, a_2, a_3, \ldots, a_n$ are known as **first term, second term, third term, ..., nth term,** respectively of the sequence. The nth term is also called **general term** and it is denoted by 'a_n'.

e.g. 2, 6, 10, 14, ... is a sequence in which $a_1 = 2, a_2 = 6, a_3 = 10$ and $a_4 = 14$.

Types of Sequence

There are two types of sequences, which are as follow

1. Finite Sequence

A sequence containing finite number of terms, is called a finite sequence.

e.g.

(i) 1, 3, 5, 7 is a finite sequence as it contains only 4 terms.

(ii) 2, 5, 8, 11, 14 is a finite sequence as it contains only 5 terms.

2. Infinite Sequence

A sequence which is not a finite sequence, is known as infinite sequence. i.e. in an infinite sequence, **number of terms never ends.** e.g.

(i) 1, 3, 5, 7,... is an infinite sequence, as it contains infinite number of terms.

(ii) The sequence of successive quotients obtain in the division of 10 by 3 i.e. 3, 3.3, 3.33, 3.333, ...is an infinite sequence.

Representation of a Sequence

A real sequence can be represented by different ways. Some ways of reprsentation are given below

(i) A real sequence can be represented by listing its few terms till the rule for writing down other terms becomes clear.

e.g. 3, 5, 7, ... is a sequence and rule for writing down other terms is $(2n+1)$, where $n = 1, 2, 3 \ldots$.

(ii) A real sequence can be represented in terms of a rule or an algebraic formula of writing the nth term of the sequence.

e.g. The sequence 1, 3, 5, 7, ... can be written as $a_n = 2n - 1$.

(iii) Sometimes the sequence i.e. an arrangement of numbers has no visible pattern but the sequence can be represented by the **recurrence relation.**

e.g. The sequence 1, 1, 2, 3, 5, 8, ... has no visible pattern but its recurrence relation is $a_1 = a_2 = 1$ and $a_{n+1} = a_n + a_{n-1}, n \geq 2$

This sequence is called **Fibonacci sequence.**

> **Sequence as a Function**
>
> A sequence can be regarded as a function whose domain is the set of natural numbers or some subset of it of the type $(1, 2, 3, \ldots, k)$. Sometimes, we use the functional notation $a(n)$ for a_n.

Example 1 Find the 20th term a_{20} of the sequence, whose nth term is $a_n = \dfrac{n(n-2)}{n+3}$ **[NCERT]**

Sol. We have, $a_n = \dfrac{n(n-2)}{n+3}$

On putting $n = 20$, we get $a_{20} = \dfrac{20(20-2)}{20+3}$

$$\Rightarrow \quad a_{20} = \frac{20 \times 18}{23} = \frac{360}{23}$$

Example 2 Write first five terms of sequence

(i) $a_n = (-1)^{n-1} 5^{n+1}$ (ii) $a_n = 2n^2 - n + 1$ **[NCERT]**

Sol. (i) We have, $a_n = (-1)^{n-1} 5^{n+1}$

On putting $n = 1$, we get

$$a_1 = (-1)^{1-1} 5^{1+1} = (-1)^0 5^2 = 25$$

On putting $n = 2$, we get

$$a_2 = (-1)^{2-1} 5^{2+1} = (-1)^1 5^3 = -125$$

On putting $n = 3$, we get

$$a_3 = (-1)^{3-1} 5^{3+1} = (-1)^2 5^4 = 625$$

On putting $n = 4$, we get

$$a_4 = (-1)^{4-1} 5^{4+1} = (-1)^3 5^5 = -3125$$

On putting $n = 5$, we get

$$a_5 = (-1)^{5-1} 5^{5+1} = (-1)^4 5^6 = 15625$$

Hence, the first five terms of the given sequence are 25, − 125, 625, − 3125, 15625.

(ii) We have, $a_n = 2n^2 - n + 1$

On putting $n = 1$, we get

$$a_1 = 2(1)^2 - 1 + 1 = 2 - 1 + 1 = 2$$

On putting $n = 2$, we get

$$a_2 = 2(2)^2 - 2 + 1 = 8 - 2 + 1 = 7$$

On putting $n = 3$, we get

$$a_3 = 2(3)^2 - 3 + 1 = 18 - 3 + 1 = 16$$

On putting $n = 4$, we get

$$a_4 = 2(4)^2 - 4 + 1 = 32 - 4 + 1 = 29$$

On putting $n = 5$, we get

$$a_5 = 2(5)^2 - 5 + 1 = 50 - 5 + 1 = 46$$

Hence, the first five terms of the given sequence are 2, 7, 16, 29 and 46.

Example 3 Fibonacci sequence is defined by $1 = a_1 = a_2$ and $a_n = a_{n-1} + a_{n-2}, n > 2$. Find $\dfrac{a_{n+1}}{a_n}$, for $n = 1, 2, 3, 4$. **[NCERT]**

Sol. Given, $1 = a_1 = a_2$ and $a_n = a_{n-1} + a_{n-2}, n > 2$

On putting $n = 3, 4, 5, 6$ respectively, we get

For $n = 3, a_3 = a_{3-1} + a_{3-2} = a_2 + a_1 = 1 + 1 = 2$

For $n = 4, a_4 = a_{4-1} + a_{4-2} = a_3 + a_2 = 2 + 1 = 3$

For $n = 5, a_5 = a_{5-1} + a_{5-2} = a_4 + a_3 = 3 + 2 = 5$

For $n = 6, a_6 = a_{6-1} + a_{6-2} = a_5 + a_4 = 5 + 3 = 8$

Now, $\dfrac{a_{n+1}}{a_n}$, for $n = 1, 2, 3, 4, 5$.

For $n = 1$, $\dfrac{a_2}{a_1} = \dfrac{1}{1} = 1$; For $n = 2$, $\dfrac{a_3}{a_2} = \dfrac{2}{1} = 2$

For $n = 3$, $\dfrac{a_4}{a_3} = \dfrac{3}{2}$; For $n = 4$, $\dfrac{a_5}{a_4} = \dfrac{5}{3}$

Hence, the required terms are 1, 2, $\dfrac{3}{2}$ and $\dfrac{5}{3}$.

Series

Let a sequence is $a_1, a_2, a_3, \ldots, a_n, \ldots$. Then, the expression $a_1 + a_2 + a_3 + \ldots + a_n + \ldots$ is called the series associated with the given sequence. A series is **finite** or **infinite**, according as number of terms in the corresponding sequence is finite or infinite. Series can be represented in compact form, called **sigma notation.** It is denoted by the Greek letter 'Σ' **(sigma)** e.g. series $a_1 + a_2 + \ldots + a_n + \ldots$ can be represented in compact form as $\sum_{k=1}^{\infty} a_k$.

e.g. (i) $2+4+6+8+\ldots+102$ (ii) $1-\frac{1}{2}-\frac{1}{4}-\frac{1}{8}-\ldots$

Generally, the sum of first n terms is denoted by S_n.

If S_n denotes the sum of n terms of a sequence, then $S_n - S_{n-1} = (a_1 + a_2 + \ldots + a_n) - (a_1 + a_2 + \ldots + a_{n-1})$.

Thus, $\boxed{a_n = S_n - S_{n-1}}$

Note When we use the term 'Sum of series', then it means we add all these terms.

Example 4 Let the sequence a_n is defined as follows

$$a_1 = 2, a_n = a_{n-1} + 3 \text{ for } n \ge 2.$$

Find first five terms and write corresponding series.

Sol. We have, $a_1 = 2$ and $a_n = a_{n-1} + 3$

On putting $n = 2$, we get $a_2 = a_1 + 3 = 2 + 3 = 5$

On putting $n = 3$, we get $a_3 = a_2 + 3 = 5 + 3 = 8$

On putting $n = 4$, we get $a_4 = a_3 + 3 = 8 + 3 = 11$

On putting $n = 5$, we get $a_5 = a_4 + 3 = 11 + 3 = 14$

Thus, first five terms of given sequence are 2, 5, 8, 11 and 14. Also, the corresponding series is $2+5+8+11+14+\ldots$

Topic Practice 1

Very Short Answer Type Questions

(2 Marks)

1 Write the first five terms of each of the following sequence whose nth terms are **[NCERT]**

(i) $a_n = \frac{n}{n+1}$ (ii) $a_n = (-1)^{n+1} 3^{n+2}$

(iii) $b_n = \frac{n(n^2+5)}{4}$ (iv) $a_n = \frac{n^3+1}{2}$

(v) $a_1 = 1, a_n = a_{n-1} + 3$ for $n \ge 2$

2 Find the indicated terms in each of the sequence, where nth terms are given.

(i) $a_n = 5n - 3$, a_{12}, a_{15}

(ii) $b_n = (-1)^n (n^2 - 1), b_7, b_{13}$

(iii) $a_n = \frac{n^2}{2^n}, a_7$

3 Write the first five terms of each of the sequence and obtain the corresponding series.

(i) $a_1 = 3, a_n = 3a_{n-1} + 2, \forall n > 1$

(ii) $a_1 = a_2 = 2,\ a_n = a_{n-1} - 1, n > 2$

(iii) $a_n = \frac{1}{6}(2n-3)$

(iv) $a_1 = -1,\ a_n = \frac{a_{n-1}}{n}, n \ge 2$

Hints & Answers

1. (i) $\frac{1}{2}, \frac{2}{3}, \frac{3}{4}, \frac{4}{5}, \frac{5}{6}$

(ii) 27, −81, 243, −729, 2187

(iii) $\frac{3}{2}, \frac{9}{2}, \frac{21}{2}, 21, \frac{75}{2}$

(iv) $1, \frac{9}{2}, 14, \frac{65}{2}, 63$

(v) 1, 4, 7, 10, 13,

2. (i) $a_{12} = 57, a_{15} = 72$

(ii) $b_7 = -48, b_{13} = -168$

(iii) $a_7 = \frac{49}{128}$

3. (i) We have, $a_1 = 3,\ a_n = 3a_{n-1} + 2$ for all $n > 1$.

On putting $n = 2$, we get $a_2 = 3a_{2-1} + 2 = 11$

On putting $n = 3$, we get $a_3 = 3a_{3-1} + 2 = 35$

On putting $n = 4$, we get $a_4 = 3a_{4-1} + 2 = 107$

On putting $n = 5$, we get $a_5 = 3a_{5-1} + 2 = 323$

∴ Sequence is 3, 11, 35, 107, 323, ...

∴ Series is $3 + 11 + 35 + 107 + 323 + \ldots$

(ii) Sequence is 2, 2, 1, 0, −1, ...

Series is $2 + 2 + 1 + 0 + (-1) + \ldots$

(iii) Sequence is $-\frac{1}{6}, \frac{1}{6}, \frac{1}{2}, \frac{5}{6}, \frac{7}{6}, \ldots$

Series is $-\frac{1}{6} + \frac{1}{6} + \frac{1}{2} + \frac{5}{6} + \frac{7}{6} + \ldots$

(iv) Sequence is $-1, -\frac{1}{2}, -\frac{1}{6}, -\frac{1}{24}, -\frac{1}{120}, \ldots$

Series is $-1 - \frac{1}{2} - \frac{1}{6} - \frac{1}{24} - \frac{1}{120} - \ldots$

TOPIC 02 Arithmetic Progression (AP) and Its General Terms

Progressions

It is not necessary that the terms of a sequence always follow a certain pattern. Those sequence whose terms follow a certain pattern or rule, are called the **progression.**

e.g. 2, 4, 6, 8,..., 100

We observe that each term in above example is formed by adding 2 to the preceding term.

Arithmetic Progression (AP)

A sequence whose terms **increases or decreases** by a fixed number, is called an **arithmetic progression.**

In other words, we can say that, a sequence is called an arithmetic progression if the difference of a term and the previous term is always same i.e.

$$a_{n+1} - a_n = \text{constant for all } n.$$

This constant or same difference is called the **common difference** of an AP and it is denoted by d.

In an AP, we usually denote the first term by a, common difference by d and the nth term by a_n or T_n and then AP is $a, a+d, a+2d, \ldots,$ e.g., 1, 4, 7, 10, ... is an AP.

Here, first term $= 1$ and common difference $= 4 - 1 = 3$.

To check whether a given sequence is an AP or not, we use the following steps

Step I Find nth term a_n.

Step II Replace n by $n+1$ to get $(n+1)$th term i.e. a_{n+1}.

Step III Find difference between a_n and a_{n+1} *i.e.* calculate $a_{n+1} - a_n$.

Step IV If value obtained in step III is independent of n i.e. does not contain n, then given sequence is an AP otherwise not.

Example 1 Show that the sequence a_n defined by $a_n = 2n^2 + 1$, is not an AP.

Sol. We have, $a_n = 2n^2 + 1$

On replacing n by $n+1$, we get

$$a_{n+1} = 2(n+1)^2 + 1 = 2(n^2 + 1 + 2n) + 1$$
$$= 2n^2 + 2 + 4n + 1 = 2n^2 + 4n + 3$$

Here, $a_{n+1} - a_n = (2n^2 + 4n + 3) - (2n^2 + 1)$

$$= 2n^2 + 4n + 3 - 2n^2 - 1 = 4n + 2$$

It is not independent of n. So, given sequence is not an AP.

Example 2 The nth term of a sequence is $3n - 2$. Is the sequence an AP? If it is an AP, then find its 6th term.

Sol. Given, $a_n = 3n - 2$

On replacing n by $n+1$ in a_n, we get

$$a_{n+1} = 3(n+1) - 2 = 3n + 3 - 2 = 3n + 1$$

Then, $d = a_{n+1} - a_n = (3n+1) - (3n-2)$

$$= 3n + 1 - 3n + 2 = 3$$

It is independent of n, so given sequence is an AP and its 6th term, $a_6 = 3 \times 6 - 2 = 18 - 2 = 16$

Example 3 Write down the next term of the sequence $\frac{1}{6}, \frac{1}{3}, \frac{1}{2}, \ldots$.

Sol. Given sequence is $\frac{1}{6}, \frac{1}{3}, \frac{1}{2}, \ldots$

Here, $a_1 = \frac{1}{6}, a_2 = \frac{1}{3}, a_3 = \frac{1}{2}$

Then $a_2 - a_1 = \frac{1}{3} - \frac{1}{6} = \frac{2-1}{6} = \frac{1}{6}$

$$a_3 - a_2 = \frac{1}{2} - \frac{1}{3} = \frac{3-2}{6} = \frac{1}{6}$$

Since, common difference is same, so it is an AP.

Then, $d = \frac{1}{6}$

$\therefore \quad a_4 = a_3 + d = \frac{1}{2} + \frac{1}{6} = \frac{3+1}{6} = \frac{4}{6} = \frac{2}{3}$

Hence, the next term of the given sequence is $\frac{2}{3}$.

General Term of an AP

Let a be the first term and d be the common difference of an AP. Then, its nth term is denoted by a_n or T_n and defined as

$$\boxed{T_n = a_n = a + (n-1)\,d}$$

Also, $l = a + (n-1)d$, where l is the **last term** of the sequence.

Example 4 Find the indicated term of given AP.

$a = 3, d = 2; T_n, T_{10}$

Sol. Given, $a = 3$ and $d = 2$

$\because \quad T_n = a + (n-1)d$ ...(i)

On putting the values of a and d in Eq. (i) we get

$$T_n = 3 + (n-1)2 = 3 + 2n - 2$$

$\Rightarrow \quad T_n = 1 + 2n$

and $\quad T_{10} = a + (10-1)d = a + 9d$ [from Eq. (i)]

$= 3 + 9(2)$ [$\because a = 3,\ d = 2$]

$= 3 + 18 = 21$

Example 5 Is 667 a term of an AP 11, 18, 25,...?

Sol. Given AP is 11, 18, 25,...

Here, $a = 11$, $d = 18 - 11 = 7$ and $a_n = 667$ (say)

$\because \quad a + (n-1)d = a_n$

$\therefore \quad 11 + (n-1)7 = 667 \Rightarrow 11 + 7n - 7 = 667$

$\Rightarrow \quad 7n + 4 = 667 \Rightarrow 7n = 667 - 4$

$\Rightarrow \quad 7n = 663$

$\Rightarrow n = \frac{663}{7}$, which is not a whole number.

Hence, 667 is not a term of an AP.

Example 6 How many terms are there in AP 20, 25, 30,..., 100?

Sol. Given AP is 20, 25, 30,..., 100.

Here, $a = 20$, $d = 25 - 20 = 5$ and $l = 100$

$\because$ Last term, $l = 100$

$\Rightarrow \quad a + (n-1)d = 100$

$\Rightarrow \quad 20 + (n-1)5 = 100$ [$\because a = 20$ and $d = 5$]

$\Rightarrow \quad 20 + 5n - 5 = 100 \Rightarrow 15 + 5n = 100$

$\Rightarrow \quad 5n = 100 - 15 = 85 \Rightarrow n = 17$

Hence, there are 17 terms in given AP.

Example 7 Which term of the sequence 72, 70, 68, 66,... is 40?

Sol. Given seqeunce is 72, 70, 68, 66, ...

Clearly, the successive difference of the terms is same. So, the above sequence forms an AP with first term, $a = 72$ and common difference, $d = 70 - 72 = -2$.

Let nth term, $T_n = 40$ and $T_n = a + (n-1)d$

$\therefore \quad 40 = 72 + (n-1)(-2)$

$\Rightarrow \quad 40 = 72 - 2n + 2 \Rightarrow 2n = 72 - 40 + 2$

$\Rightarrow \quad 2n = 34 \Rightarrow n = 17$

Hence, 17th term of the given sequence is 40.

Example 8 The 10th term of an AP is 41 and 18th term is 73. Find AP.

Sol. Given, $\quad a_{10} = 41$ and $a_{18} = 73$

We know that, nth term, $a_n = a + (n-1)d$

$\therefore \quad a_{10} = a + (10-1)d = 41$

and $\quad a_{18} = a + (18-1)d = 73$

$\Rightarrow \quad a + 9d = 41$ and $a + 17d = 73$

On solving above two equations, we get

$a = 5$ and $d = 4$

Hence, the required AP is 5,5 + 4, 5 + 2(4), ...

i.e. 5, 9, 13, ... [$\because$ AP is $a, a+d, a+2d, \ldots$]

Example 9 Which term of the sequence $20, 19\frac{1}{4}, 18\frac{1}{2}, 17\frac{3}{4}, \ldots$ is the first negative term?

Sol. The given sequence is $20, 19\frac{1}{4}, 18\frac{1}{2}, 17\frac{3}{4}, \ldots$

Clearly, the successive difference of the terms is same. So, the above sequence forms an AP with first term, $a = 20$ and common difference, $d = 19\frac{1}{4} - 20 = -\frac{3}{4}$.

Let the n term of the given AP be the first negative term.

Then, $\quad a_n < 0 \Rightarrow a + (n-1)d < 0$

$\Rightarrow \quad 20 + (n-1) \times (-3/4) < 0$

$\Rightarrow \quad \frac{83}{4} - \frac{3n}{4} < 0 \Rightarrow \frac{3n}{4} > \frac{83}{4}$

$\Rightarrow \quad 3n > 83 \Rightarrow n > 27\frac{2}{3}$

Since 28 is just greater than $27\frac{2}{3}$. So, $n = 28$. Thus, 28th term of the given sequence will be first negative term.

Example 10 How many three-digit numbers are divisible by 7?

Sol. The series of numbers divisible by 7 having three digits is 105, 112, 119, ...,994.

Clearly, the successive difference of the terms is same. So, the above list of numbers forms an AP with first term, $a = 105$, common difference, $d = 112 - 105 = 7$ and last term, $a_n = 994$.

$\because \quad a + (n-1)d = a_n$

$\Rightarrow \quad 105 + (n-1)7 = 994$

$\Rightarrow \quad (n-1)7 = 994 - 105$

$\Rightarrow \quad 7n - 7 = 889 \Rightarrow 7n = 889 + 7$

$\Rightarrow \quad 7n = 896 \Rightarrow n = 128$

Hence, there are 128 three-digit numbers which are divisible by 7.

Example 11 In the arithmetic progressions 2, 5, 8, ... upto 50 terms and 3, 5, 7, 9, ... upto 60 terms, find how many terms are identical?

Sol. Given, first AP is 2, 5, 8, ... upto 50 terms, we have $a_1 = 2$, $d_1 = 5 - 2 = 3$ and second AP is 3, 5, 7, 9... upto 60 terms,.

Here $a_2 = 3$, $d_2 = 5 - 3 = 2$

Let the mth term of the first AP be equal to the nth term of the second AP.

Then, $\quad 2 + (m-1) \times 3 = 3 + (n-1) \times 2$

$\Rightarrow \quad 3m - 1 = 2n + 1 \quad \Rightarrow 3m = 2n + 2$

$\Rightarrow \quad \frac{m}{2} = \frac{n+1}{3} = k$ (say)

$\Rightarrow \quad m = 2k$ and $n = 3k - 1$

$\Rightarrow \quad 2k \le 50$ and $3k - 1 \le 60$ [$\because m \le 50$ and $n \le 60$]

$\Rightarrow \quad k \le 25$ and $k \le 20\frac{1}{3}$

$\Rightarrow \quad k \le 20 \quad$ [$\because k$ is a natural number]

$\therefore \quad k = 1, 2, 3, \ldots, 20$

Corresponding to each value of k, we get a pair of identical terms. Hence, there are 20 identical terms in the two AP's.

Example 12 If the mth term of a given AP is n and its nth term is m, then show that its pth term is $(n+m-p)$. **[NCERT]**

Sol. In the given AP, let the first term = a and the common difference = d.

According to the question,

mth term of a given AP $= n \Rightarrow a_m = n$

and nth term of a given AP $= m \Rightarrow a_n = m$

$$\therefore \quad a + (m-1)\,d = n \quad \ldots(i)$$

$$\text{and} \quad a + (n-1)\,d = m \quad \ldots(ii)$$

On subtracting Eq. (ii) from Eq. (i), we get

$$(m-n)\,d = (n-m) \Rightarrow d = -1$$

On putting $d = -1$ in Eq. (i), we get $a = (n+m-1)$.

$\therefore$ pth term $= a + (p-1)\,d = (n+m-1) + (p-1)(-1)$

[$\because a = (n+m-1)$ and $d = -1$]

$$= (n+m-p)$$

Hence, the pth term of the given AP is $(n+m-p)$.

Example 13 If the mth term of an AP be $1/n$ and its nth term be $1/m$, then show that its mnth term is 1.

Sol. In the given AP, let the first term = a and the common difference = d.

According to the question, $a_m = \frac{1}{n}$ and $a_n = \frac{1}{m}$

$$\therefore \quad a + (m-1)\,d = 1/n \quad \ldots(i)$$

$$\text{and} \quad a + (n-1)\,d = \frac{1}{m} \quad \ldots(ii)$$

On subtracting Eq. (ii) from Eq. (i), we get

$$(m-n)\,d = \left(\frac{1}{n} - \frac{1}{m}\right) \Rightarrow d = \frac{1}{mn}$$

On putting $d = \frac{1}{mn}$ in Eq. (i), we get

$$a + \frac{(m-1)}{mn} = \frac{1}{n} \Rightarrow a = \left\{\frac{1}{n} - \frac{(m-1)}{mn}\right\} = \frac{1}{mn}$$

Now, $\quad mn$th term $= a + (mn-1)\,d$

$$= \left\{\frac{1}{mn} + \frac{(mn-1)}{mn}\right\} = \frac{mn}{mn} = 1$$

Hence, the mnth term of the given AP is 1.

Example 14 The pth, qth and rth terms of an AP are a, b, c, respectively. Show that

$$(q-r)a + (r-p)b + (p-q)c = 0. \quad \textbf{[NCERT]}$$

Sol. In the given AP, let the first term = A and the common difference = D.

Given, pth term $= A + (p-1)D = a \quad \ldots(i)$

qth term $= A + (q-1)D = b \quad \ldots(ii)$

rth term $= A + (r-1)D = c \quad \ldots(iii)$

Now, we have to prove

$$(q-r)a + (r-p)b + (p-q)c = 0$$

On taking LHS $= (q-r)a + (r-p)b + (p-q)c \quad \ldots(iv)$

On putting the values of a, b and c from Eqs. (i), (ii) and (iii) in Eq. (iv), we get

$$\text{LHS} = (q-r)[A+(p-1)D] + (r-p)[A+(q-1)D] + (p-q)[A+(r-1)D]$$

$$= (q-r)A + (q-r)(p-1)D + (r-p)A + (r-p)(q-1)D + (p-q)A + (p-q)(r-1)D$$

$$= A(q-r+r-p+p-q) + D[(q-r)(p-1) + (r-p)(q-1) + (p-q)(r-1)]$$

$$= A(0) + D[qp - q - rp + r + rq - r - pq + p + pr - p - qr + q]$$

$$= 0 + 0 = 0 = \text{RHS}$$

Hence, $(q-r)\,a + (r-p)b + (p-q)c = 0$

mth Term of an AP from the End

Let a be the first term and d be the common difference of an AP having n terms. Then, mth term from the end is $(n-m+1)$ th term from the beginning.

$\therefore$ mth term from the end, a_{n-m+1}

$$= a + (n-m+1-1)\,d$$

$$= a + (n-m)\,d, \text{ where } n > m$$

Also, **mth term from the end**

$$= a_n + (m-1)(-d)$$

$$= a_n - (m-1)d \quad \text{or} \quad l - (m-1)d$$

where, a_n (or l) is the last term of a sequence.

Example 15 Find the 6th term from the end of the sequence 9, 12, 15, ..., 20th term.

Sol. Given sequence is 9, 12, 15, ..., 20th term.

Clearly, the successive difference of the terms is same. So, the above sequence forms an AP with first term, $a = 9$ and common difference, $d = 12 - 9 = 3$.

We know that if a sequence has n term, then mth term from end is equal to $(n-m+1)$th term from the beginning.

Here, $n = 20$, $m = 6$, $a = 9$ and $d = 3$

Now, 6th term from the end of sequence $= (20-6+1)$ i.e. 15th term from the beginning.

$$\therefore \quad T_{15} = 9 + (15-1)\,3 \quad [\because T_n = a + (n-1)\,d]$$

$$= 9 + (14)\,3 = 9 + 42 = 51$$

Hence, the 6th term from the end of the sequence is 51.

Example 16 Determine the number of terms in the AP 3, 7, 11, ..., 407. Also, find the 18th term from the end.

Sol. Given AP is 3, 7, 11, ..., 407

Here, first term, $a = 3$ and common difference, $d = 4$ and nth term, $T_n = 407$

Also, $T_n = a + (n-1)d$

$\therefore \quad 407 = 3 + (n-1)4 \Rightarrow 407 = 3 + 4n - 4$

$\Rightarrow \quad 4n = 407 - 3 + 4 \Rightarrow 4n = 408 \Rightarrow n = 102$

Hence, there are 102 terms in the given AP.

Now, 18th term from the end = $[n - m + 1]$th term from the beginning = $[102 - 18 + 1]$th term from the beginning = 85th term from the beginning = $3 + (85-1)4 = 339$

Selection of Terms in an AP

Sometimes, we have to select certain terms in an AP. The convenient ways of selecting terms are given below

Number of terms	Terms	Common difference
3	$a - d, a, a + d$	d
4	$a - 3d, a - d, a + d, a + 3d$	$2d$
5	$a - 2d, a - d, a, a + d, a + 2d$	d
6	$a - 5d, a - 3d, a - d, a + d, a + 3d, a + 5d$	$2d$

From this table, it is clear that if number of terms is odd, then middle term is a and the common difference is d and if number of terms is even, then middle terms are $a - d$, $a + d$ and the common difference is $2d$.

Note If the terms of an AP are not given, then the terms are chosen as $a, a + d, a + 2d, \ldots$

Example 17 The sum of three consecutive terms of an AP is 15 and their product is 105. Find the numbers.

Sol. Let three numbers in AP be $a - d$, a and $a + d$.

According to the question,

Sum of three consecutive terms = 15

$\therefore (a - d) + a + (a + d) = 15 \Rightarrow 3a = 15 \Rightarrow a = 5$

and the product of three consecutive terms = 105

$\therefore \quad (a-d)(a)(a+d) = 105$

$\Rightarrow \quad (5-d)(5)(5+d) = 105$ [put $a = 5$]

$\Rightarrow \quad (25 - d^2)5 = 105$ [$\because (A-B)(A+B) = A^2 - B^2$]

$\Rightarrow \quad 25 - d^2 = 21$ [dividing both sides by 5]

$\Rightarrow \quad d^2 = 4 \therefore d = \pm 2$

When $d = 2$, then terms in AP are $5 - 2$, 5 and $5 + 2$ i.e. 3, 5, 7.

When $d = -2$, then terms in AP are $5 + 2$, 5, $5 - 2$ i.e. 7, 5, 3.

Example 18 The product of three numbers in AP is 224, and the largest number is 7 times the smallest. Find the numbers.

Sol. Let the three numbers in AP be $a - d, a, a + d$. [$\because d < 0$]

According to the question,

$$(a-d)\,a(a+d) = 224$$

$$\Rightarrow \quad a(a^2 - d^2) = 224 \quad \ldots\text{(i)}$$

Also, the largest number is 7 times the smallest,

i.e. $a + d = 7(a - d) \Rightarrow 8d = 6a$

$$\Rightarrow \quad d = \frac{3a}{4}$$

On substituting this value of d in Eq. (i), we get

$$a\left(a^2 - \frac{9a^2}{16}\right) = 224$$

$$\Rightarrow \quad \frac{7a^3}{16} = 224 \Rightarrow a^3 = 512 \Rightarrow a = 8$$

Then , $d = \frac{3a}{4} = \frac{3}{4} \times 8 = 6$

Hence, the three numbers are $8 - 6$, 8, $8 + 6$ i.e. 2, 8, 14.

Properties of an Arithmetic Progression

(i) If a **constant is added** to each term of an AP, then the resulting sequence is also an AP with the same common difference.

(ii) If a **constant is subtracted** from each term of an AP, then the resulting sequence is also an AP with the same common difference.

(iii) If each term of an AP is **multiplied by a constant** say k, then the resulting sequence is also an AP with common difference kd, where d is the common difference of the given AP.

(iv) If each term of an AP is **divided by a non-zero constant** say k, then the resulting sequence is also an AP with common difference d/k, where d is the common difference of the given AP.

(v) In an AP, the sum of terms equidistant from the beginning and end is constant and equal to the sum of first and last term.

i.e. $a_1 + a_n = a_2 + a_{n-1} = a_3 + a_{n-2} = \ldots$

(vi) The resulting sequence formed by adding or subtracting the corresponding terms of two AP's is also an AP.

(vii) A sequence is an AP, iff its nth term is a linear expression in n i.e. $a_n = An + B$, where A and B are constants and coefficient of n is the common difference of the AP.

Example 19 If $a\left(\frac{1}{b} + \frac{1}{c}\right), b\left(\frac{1}{c} + \frac{1}{a}\right), c\left(\frac{1}{a} + \frac{1}{b}\right)$ are in AP, prove that a, b, c are in AP. **[NCERT]**

Sol. Given, $a\left(\frac{1}{b} + \frac{1}{c}\right), b\left(\frac{1}{c} + \frac{1}{a}\right), c\left(\frac{1}{a} + \frac{1}{b}\right)$ are in AP.

$\Rightarrow a\left(\frac{b+c}{bc}\right), b\left(\frac{a+c}{ac}\right), c\left(\frac{b+a}{ab}\right)$ are in AP.

$\Rightarrow \frac{ab+ac}{bc}, \frac{ba+bc}{ac}, \frac{cb+ca}{ab}$ are in AP.

On adding 1 to each term, we get

$\frac{ab+ac}{bc}+1, \frac{ba+bc}{ac}+1, \frac{cb+ca}{ab}+1$ are in AP.

$\Rightarrow \frac{ab+ac+bc}{bc}, \frac{ba+bc+ac}{ac}, \frac{bc+ac+ab}{ab}$ are in AP.

On dividing each term by $ab+bc+ac$, we get

$$\frac{1}{bc}, \frac{1}{ac}, \frac{1}{ab} \text{ are in AP.}$$

On multiplying each term by abc, we get

$\frac{abc}{bc}, \frac{abc}{ac}, \frac{abc}{ab}$ are in AP $\Rightarrow a, b, c$ are in AP.

Topic Practice 2

Very Short Answer Type Questions

2 Marks

1 Show that each of the following sequence is an AP. And also write three more terms in each case.

(i) $-1, \frac{1}{4}, \frac{3}{2}, \frac{11}{4}$ (ii) $\sqrt{2}, 3\sqrt{2}, 5\sqrt{2}, 7\sqrt{2}, \ldots$

2 Find the 23rd term of the sequence 7, 5, 3, 1,...

3 Find the nth term of the sequence 8, 3, −2, −7,...

4 Which term of the sequence

(i) 5, 8, 11, 14,..., is 320?

(ii) 84, 80, 76,.., is 0?

5 (i) Is 68 a term of the AP 7, 10, 13,... ?

(ii) Is 302 a term of the AP 3, 8, 13,... ?

6 How many terms are there in the AP

$$-1, -\frac{5}{6}, -\frac{2}{3}, -\frac{1}{2}, \ldots, \frac{10}{3}?$$

7 The first term of an AP is 5, the common difference is 3 and the last term is 80, find the number of terms.

8 The 6th and 17th terms of an AP are 19 and 41 respectively, find the 40th term.

9 If 9 times the 9th term of an AP is equal to 13 times the 13th term, then find the 22nd term of the AP. **[NCERT Exemplar]**

10 The nth term of a sequence is given by $a_n = 2n + 7$. Show that it is an AP. Also, find its 8th term.

11 The 5th and 13th terms of an AP are 5 and −3. respectively. Find the AP and obtain its 16th term.

12 If the 9th term of an AP is 0, prove that its 29th term is double the 19th term.

13 If 7 times the 7th term of an AP is equal to 11 times its 11th term, show that its 18th term is 0.

14 Which term of the progression $19, 18\frac{1}{5}, 17\frac{2}{5}, \ldots$ is negative term?

Short Answer Type Questions

4 Marks

15 The 2nd, 31st and last term of an AP are $7\frac{3}{4}, \frac{1}{2}$ and $-6\frac{1}{2}$, respectively. Find the first term and the number of terms.

16 Find the number of terms common to the two AP's : 3, 7, 11, ... 407 and 2, 9, 16, ... 709.

17 Find the middle terms in the AP :

20, 16, 12, ..., −176.

18 Find the 15th term from the end of the AP :

3, 5, 7, 9, ..., 201.

19 Three numbers are in AP. If their sum is 27 and the product 648, find the numbers.

20 Find four numbers in AP whose sum is 20 and the sum of whose squares is 120.

21 In an AP, the first term is 2 and the sum of the first five terms is one-fourth of the next five terms, show that 20th terms is − 112. **[NCERT]**

22 If the nth term of a progression is a linear expression in n, then show that it is an AP.

Long Answer Type Questions

6 Marks

23 If a, b, c are in AP, then prove that $(b+c)^2 - a^2$, $(c+a)^2 - b^2, (a+b)^2 - c^2$ are also in AP.

24 Let a, b, c be respectively the pth, qth, rth terms of an AP. Prove that **[NCERT]**

(i) $a(q-r) + b(r-p) + c(p-q) = 0$.

(ii) $(a-b)r + (b-c)p + (c-a)q = 0$.

25 If $a_1, a_2, a_3, \ldots, a_n$ are in AP, where $a_i > 0$ for all i, show that $\frac{1}{\sqrt{a_1}+\sqrt{a_2}} + \frac{1}{\sqrt{a_2}+\sqrt{a_3}} + \ldots + \frac{1}{a_{n-1}+\sqrt{a_n}}$

$= \frac{n-1}{\sqrt{a_1}+\sqrt{a_n}}$. **[NCERT Exemplar]**

Hints & Answers

1. (i) $4, \frac{21}{4}, \frac{13}{2}$ (ii) $9\sqrt{2}, 11\sqrt{2}, 13\sqrt{2}$
2. -37
3. $13-5n$
4. (i) $320 = 5 + (n-1)3$ **Ans.** 106
 (ii) $0 = 84 + (n-1)(-4)$ **Ans.** 22
5. (i) No (ii) No
6. $\frac{10}{3} = -1 + (n-1)\frac{1}{6}$ **Ans.** 27
7. $80 = 5 + (n-1)3$ **Ans.** 26
8. $19 = a + (6-1)d$ and $41 = a + (17-1)d$ **Ans.** 87
9. $9T_9 = 13T_{13} \Rightarrow 9(a+8d) = 13(a+12d)$
 $\Rightarrow a = -21d$ **Ans.** 0
10. 23
11. 9, 8, 7, 6, ... and $a_{16} = -6$
12. Let a and d be the first term and common difference, respectively of the given AP.
 According to the question,
 $$a_9 = 0 \Rightarrow a + 8d = 0 \Rightarrow a = -8d \quad \text{...(i)}$$
 and $$a_{29} = a + 28d = a + 28d + 8d - 8d$$
 $$= a + 36d + a \quad \text{[from Eq. (i)]}$$
 $$= 2a + 36d = 2(a + 18d)$$
13. $7(a+6d) = 11(a+10d) \Rightarrow a = -17d$
14. Let $T_n < 0 \Rightarrow \left[19 + (n-1)\left(-\frac{4}{5}\right)\right] < 0$
 $\Rightarrow n > 24\frac{3}{4} = $ 25th term **Ans.** 25th
15. $T_2 = 7\frac{3}{4} \Rightarrow a + d = \frac{31}{4}$ and $T_{31} = \frac{1}{2} \Rightarrow a + 30d = \frac{1}{2}$
 On solving, we get $d = \frac{-1}{4}$, $a = 8$
 Now, $8 + (n-1)\left(-\frac{1}{4}\right) = \frac{-13}{2}$ **Ans.** 8, 59
16. $407 = 3 + (m-1) \times 4$ and $709 = 2 + (n-1) \times 7$
 $\Rightarrow m = 102$ and $n = 102$
 Let pth term of first AP = qth term of second AP.
 $\Rightarrow 3 + (p-1) \times 4 = 2 + (q-1) \times 7$
 $\Rightarrow \frac{p+1}{7} = \frac{q}{4} = k$ (say) $\Rightarrow p = 7k - 1$ and $q = 4k$
 Since, each AP consists of 102 terms.
 $\therefore p \le 102$ and $q \le 102$
 $\Rightarrow k \le \frac{103}{7}$ and $k \le \frac{102}{4}$ **Ans.** 14 term
17. $-176 = 20 + (n-1)(-4) \Rightarrow n = 50$
 Then, middle term = T_{25} and T_{26} **Ans.** $-76, -72$
18. Solve as Example 15. **Ans.** 173
19. 6, 9, 12 or 12, 9, 6
20. $(a-3d) + (a-d) + (a+d) + (a+3d) = 20 \Rightarrow a = 5$
 and $(a-3d)^2 + (a-d)^2 + (a+d)^2 + (a-3d)^2 = 120$
 $\Rightarrow 4a^2 + 20d^2 = 120 \Rightarrow 25 + 5d^2 = 30 \Rightarrow d = \pm 1$
 Ans. 2, 4, 6, 8 or 8, 6, 4, 2
21. $a + (a+d) + (a+2d) + (a+3d) + a + 4d$
 $= \frac{1}{4}[a + 5d + a + 6d + a + 7d + a + 8d + a + 9d]$
 $\Rightarrow d = -6$
22. Let $T_n = an + b$, where a and b are constants.
 Then, $T_{n-1} = a(n-1) + b$
 $\therefore T_n - T_{n-1} = (an+b) - [a(n-1) + b]$
 $= an - an + b + a - b = a$, which is constant.
23. $(b+c)^2 - a^2, (c+a)^2 - b^2, (a+b)^2 - c^2$ are in AP,
 $\Rightarrow (b+c+a)(b+c-a), (c+a+b)(c+a-b),$
 $(a+b+c)(a+b-c)$ are in AP.
 $\Rightarrow (b+c-a), (c+a-b), (a+b-c)$ are in AP.
 $\Rightarrow (b+c-a)-(a+b+c)$
 $(c+a-b)-(a+b+c), (a+b-c)-(a+b+c)$ are in AP.
 $\Rightarrow -2a, -2b, -2c$ are in AP.
 $\Rightarrow a, b, c$ are in AP, which is true.
24. Let A be the first term and d be the common difference.
 Since, $T_p = a \Rightarrow A + (p-1)d = a$ ...(i)
 $T_q = b \Rightarrow A + (q-1)d = b$ ...(ii)
 and $T_r = c \Rightarrow A + (r-1)d = c$ ...(iii)
 (i) On multiplying Eq. (i) by $(q-r)$, Eq. (ii) by $(r-p)$ and Eq. (iii) by $(p-q)$, we get
 $(q-r)A + (p-1)(q-r)d = a(q-r)$ ...(iv)
 $(r-p)A + (q-1)(r-p)d = b(r-p)$ ...(v)
 and $(p-q)A + (r-1)(p-q)d = c(p-q)$ ...(vi)
 On adding Eqs. (iv), (v) and (vi), we get
 $$a(q-r) + b(r-p) + c(p-q) = 0$$
 (ii) On subtracting Eq. (ii) from Eq. (i), Eq. (iii) from Eq. (ii) and Eq. (i) from Eq. (iii), we get
 $a - b = (p-q)d$ ...(vii)
 $b - c = (q-r)d$ ...(viii)
 and $c - a = (r-p)d$ ...(ix)
 On multiplying Eq. (vii) by r, Eq. (viii) by p and Eq. (ix) by q and then adding, we get
 $$r(a-b) + p(b-c) + q(c-a) = 0$$
25. $a_2 - a_1 = a_3 - a_2 = \ldots = a_n - a_{n-1} = d$ (say)
 If $a_2 - a_1 = d$, then $(\sqrt{a_2})^2 - (\sqrt{a_1})^2 = d$
 $\Rightarrow (\sqrt{a_2} - \sqrt{a_1})(\sqrt{a_2} + \sqrt{a_1}) = d$
 $\Rightarrow \frac{1}{\sqrt{a_1} + \sqrt{a_2}} = \frac{\sqrt{a_2} - \sqrt{a_1}}{d}$
 On adding, we get
 $$\frac{1}{\sqrt{a_1} + \sqrt{a_2}} + \frac{1}{\sqrt{a_2} + \sqrt{a_3}} + \ldots + \frac{1}{\sqrt{a_{n-1}} + \sqrt{a_n}}$$
 $$= \frac{1}{d}[\sqrt{a_2} - \sqrt{a_1} + \sqrt{a_3} - \sqrt{a_2} + \ldots + \sqrt{a_n} - \sqrt{a_{n-1}}]$$
 $$= \frac{1}{d}[\sqrt{a_n} - \sqrt{a_1}] \quad \text{...(i)}$$
 Also, $a_n - a_1 = (n-1)d \Rightarrow (\sqrt{a_n})^2 - (\sqrt{a_1})^2 = (n-1)d$
 $\Rightarrow \sqrt{a_n} - \sqrt{a_1} = \frac{(n-1)d}{\sqrt{a_n} + \sqrt{a_1}}$

TOPIC 03 Sum of n Terms of an AP and Arithmetic Mean (AM)

Sum of n Terms of an AP

If a be the first term and d be the common difference of an AP, then the sum of n terms, S_n of this AP is given by

$$S_n = \frac{n}{2}[2a + (n-1)d]$$

Also, if a be the first term and l be the last term, then the sum of n terms of this AP is

$$S_n = \frac{n}{2}(a + l)$$

Note If sum of n terms, S_n of an AP is given, then nth term, a_n of that AP can be determined by the formula, $a_n = S_n - S_{n-1}$, where $a_1 = S_1$.

Problems Based on Sum of n Terms of an AP

There are many types of problems which can be solved directly or indirectly by using the sum of n terms.

|TYPE I|

Problems Based on Finding the Sum of Given Number of Terms

In this type of problems, an AP is given and we have to find sum of given number of terms directly.

Example 1 Find the sum of 20 terms of the progression.

$$1, 3, 5, 7, 9, \ldots$$

Sol. Here, first term $(a) = 1$

and common difference $(d) = 2$

We know that,

$$S_n = \frac{n}{2}[2a + (n-1)d]$$

$$\therefore \quad S_{20} = \frac{20}{2}[2 \times 1 + (20-1)2]$$

$$= 10[2 + (19) \times 2]$$

$$= 10[2 + 38] = 10 \times 40 = 400$$

Example 2 Find the sum of the series

$$45 + 47 + 49 + \ldots + 99.$$

Sol. Given series is $45 + 47 + 49 + \ldots + 99$.

Here, $a = 45$ and $d = 47 - 45 = 2$ and $l = a_n = 99$

$$\because \quad a_n = 99 \Rightarrow a + (n-1)d = 99$$

$$\Rightarrow \quad 45 + (n-1)2 = 99$$

$$\Rightarrow \quad 45 + 2n - 2 = 99 \Rightarrow 2n = 56$$

$$\Rightarrow \quad n = 28$$

$$\because \quad S_n = \frac{n}{2}(a + l)$$

$$\therefore \quad S_{28} = \frac{28}{2}(45 + 99) = 14(144) = 2016$$

Example 3 Find the sum of 20 terms of an AP, whose first term is 3 and last term is 57.

Sol. We have, $a = 3$, $l = 57$ and $n = 20$

$$\because \quad S_n = \frac{n}{2}[a + l]$$

$$\therefore \quad S_{20} = \frac{20}{2}[3 + 57] = 10 \times 60 = 600$$

Example 4 Find the sum of indicated number of terms in the following AP.

$$x + y, x - y, x - 3y, \ldots, 22 \text{ terms}$$

Sol. Given series is $x + y, x - y, x - 3y, \ldots, 22$ terms.

Here, $a = x + y, d = a_2 - a_1 = (x - y) - (x + y) = -2y$

and $\quad n = 22$

$$\because \quad S_n = \frac{n}{2}[2a + (n-1)d]$$

$$\therefore \quad S_{22} = \frac{22}{2}[2 \times (x + y) + (22 - 1)(-2y)]$$

$$= 11[2x + 2y + (21)(-2y)]$$

$$= 11[2x + 2y - 42y]$$

$$= 11[2x - 40y] = 22[x - 20y]$$

Example 5 If the first term of an AP is a and the sum of the first p terms is zero, then find the sum of its next q terms. **[NCERT Exemplar]**

Sol. Let the common difference be d.

Given, sum of first p terms $= 0$

$$\Rightarrow \quad S_p = 0$$

$$\Rightarrow \quad \frac{p}{2}[2a + (p-1)d] = 0$$

[given, a = first term of an AP]

$$\Rightarrow \quad 2a + (p-1)d = 0$$

$$\Rightarrow \quad d = -\frac{2a}{p-1} \quad \ldots \text{(i)}$$

∴ Required sum of next q terms

$= \text{Sum of first } (p+q) \text{ terms} - \text{Sum of first } p \text{ terms}$

$= S_{p+q} - S_p$

$= \frac{p+q}{2}[2a+(p+q-1)d] - 0$

$[\because S_p = 0]$

$= \frac{p+q}{2}\left[2a+(p+q-1)\left(\frac{-2a}{p-1}\right)\right]$ [from Eq. (i)]

$= \frac{p+q}{2} \times 2a\left[\frac{1}{1} - \frac{p+q-1}{p-1}\right]$

$= (p+q)\,a\left[\frac{p-1-p-q+1}{p-1}\right] = \frac{-a(p+q)q}{p-1}$

Example 6 Find the sum to n terms of the sequence $\log a, \log ar, \log ar^2, \ldots$

Sol. Given sequence is $\log a, \log ar, \log ar^2, \ldots$

Above sequence can be expressed as

$\log a, (\log a + \log r), (\log a + 2\log r), \ldots$

$[\because \log mn = \log m + \log n \text{ and } \log a^x = x \log a]$

which is clearly an AP with first term, $A = \log a$ and common difference, $D = \log r$.

We know that, Sum of n terms,

$$S_n = \frac{n}{2}[2A + (n-1)D]$$

$$\therefore \quad S_n = \frac{n}{2}[2\log a + (n-1)\log r]$$

$$= \frac{n}{2}[\log a^2 + \log r^{n-1}] \quad [\because x \log a = \log a^x]$$

$$= \frac{n}{2}[\log a^2 r^{n-1}] \quad [\because \log m + \log n = \log mn]$$

Example 7 Find the sum of all numbers between 200 and 400 which are divisible by 7. **[NCERT]**

Sol. The numbers which are divisible by 7 between 200 and 400 are 203, 210, 217,..., 399.

Clearly, they form an AP.

where, $a = 203$, $d = 7$ and $T_n = 399$

Now, $T_n = a + (n-1)d$

$\Rightarrow \quad 399 = 203 + (n-1)7$

$\Rightarrow (n-1)7 = 399 - 203$

$\Rightarrow (n-1)7 = 196 \Rightarrow n - 1 = \frac{196}{7}$

$\Rightarrow \quad n - 1 = 28 \Rightarrow n = 29$

Now, $S_n = \frac{n}{2}(a + T_n)$ $[\because T_n = \text{last term of given AP}]$

$\therefore \quad S_{29} = \frac{29}{2}[203 + 399] = \frac{29}{2} \times 602 = 29 \times 301 = 8729$

Note Students should remember that numbers 200 and 400 are excluded.

Example 8 If the first term of an AP is 100 and the sum of first six terms is five times the sum of the next six terms, then find the common difference.

Sol. Given, $a = 100$

Let d be the common difference.

According to the question,

$a_1 + a_2 + \ldots + a_6 = 5(a_7 + a_8 + \ldots + a_{12})$

$\Rightarrow \frac{6}{2}[2a + (6-1)d]$

$= 5[(a+6d) + (a+7d) + \ldots + (a+11d)]$

$[\because a_7 = a + 6d, \ldots, a_{12} = a + 11d]$

$\Rightarrow 3[2a + 5d] = 5[6a + (6d + 7d + \ldots + 11d)]$

$= 5\left[6a + \left\{\frac{6}{2}[2 \times 6d + (6-1)d]\right\}\right]$

$\left[\because S_n = \frac{n}{2}\{2a + (n-1)d\}\right]$

$= 5[6a + \{3(12d + 5d)\}]$

$= 5[6a + 36d + 15d] = 5[6a + 51d]$

$\Rightarrow 3(2a + 5d) = 5 \times 3(2a + 17d)$

$\Rightarrow 2a + 5d = 10a + 85d$

$\Rightarrow -80d = 8a \Rightarrow -80d = 8(100)$ $[\because a = 100]$

$\Rightarrow d = -10$

|TYPE III|

Problems Based on Finding the Number of Terms, When Sum of Its Terms is Given

In this type of problems, sum of certain number of terms is given and we have to find that certain number of terms with the help of sum.

Example 9 How many terms in the AP $-9, -6, -3, \ldots$ must be added together so that the sum may be 66?

Sol. Let 66 be the sum of n terms.

We have, $a = -9$ and $d = -6 - (-9) = -6 + 9 = 3$

$\because \quad S_n = \frac{n}{2}[2a + (n-1)d]$

$\therefore \quad 66 = \frac{n}{2}[2(-9) + (n-1)3]$

$\Rightarrow \quad 66 = \frac{n}{2}[-18 + 3n - 3] \Rightarrow 132 = n[3n - 21]$

$\Rightarrow \quad 44 = n[n-7]$ [dividing both sides by 3]

$\Rightarrow n^2 - 7n - 44 = 0$

$\Rightarrow (n-11)(n+4) = 0$

$\Rightarrow n = 11 \text{ or } -4$

Rejecting $n = -4$ because number of terms cannot be negative.

$\therefore \quad n = 11$

Example 10 Find the number of terms of the sequence 54, 51, 48, ..., when there sum is 513.

Sol. Given series is 54, 51, 48, ...

Clearly, the successive difference of the terms is same. So, the above sequence forms an AP, with first term, $a = 54$ and common difference, $d = 51 - 54 = -3$.

Let number of terms be n, then

Their sum $(S_n) = 513$

$$\therefore \quad \frac{n}{2}[2a + (n-1)d] = 513$$

$$\Rightarrow \quad \frac{n}{2}[2 \times 54 + (n-1)(-3)] = 513$$

$$\Rightarrow \quad n(108 - 3n + 3) = 513 \times 2$$

$$\Rightarrow \quad -3n^2 + 111n = 1026$$

$$\Rightarrow \quad -(3n^2 - 111n + 1026) = 0$$

$$\Rightarrow \quad n^2 - 37n + 342 = 0 \text{ [dividing both sides by } (-3)]$$

$$\Rightarrow \quad (n-18)(n-19) = 0 \Rightarrow n = 18 \text{ or } 19$$

Here, the common difference is negative.

$\therefore$ 19th term, $T_{19} = 54 + (19-1)(-3) = 0$

So, the sum of 18 terms as well as that of 19 terms is 513.

Example 11 How many terms of the AP $-6, -\frac{11}{2}, -5$ ..... are needed to give sum -25? **[NCERT]**

Sol. Given that the sequence $-6, -\frac{11}{2}, -5, \ldots$ is in AP.

Here, $a = (-6)$ and $d = -\frac{11}{2} - (-6) = -\frac{11}{2} + 6$

$$d = \frac{-11 + 12}{2} = \frac{1}{2}$$

Now, $$S_n = \frac{n}{2}[2a + (n-1)d]$$

$$\Rightarrow \quad -25 = \frac{n}{2}\left[2(-6) + (n-1)\frac{1}{2}\right]$$

$$\Rightarrow \quad -25 \times 2 = n\left[\frac{-12}{1} + \frac{(n-1)}{2}\right]$$

$$\Rightarrow \quad -50 = n\left[\frac{-24 + n - 1}{2}\right]$$

$$\Rightarrow \quad -50 \times 2 = n(n - 25)$$

$$\Rightarrow \quad -100 = n^2 - 25n$$

$$\Rightarrow \quad n^2 - 25n + 100 = 0$$

$$\Rightarrow \quad n^2 - 20n - 5n + 100 = 0$$

$$\Rightarrow \quad n(n - 20) - 5(n - 20) = 0$$

$$\Rightarrow \quad (n - 20)(n - 5) = 0$$

$$\Rightarrow \quad n = 5 \text{ or } 20$$

|TYPE III|

Proving Results Related to the Sum of *n* Terms of an AP

In this type of problems, some basic terms related to given AP as its sum of finite number of terms i.e. nth term etc are given and we have to prove result based on sum of the n terms of AP.

Example 12 If S_n denotes the sum of n terms of an AP and $S_1 = 6$ and $S_7 = 105$, then show that $S_n : S_{n-3} = (n + 3) : (n - 3)$.

Sol. Given, $S_1 = 6$ and $S_7 = 105$

We know that, $a_1 = S_1$

$\therefore \quad a_1 = 6$

Again, $S_7 = 105$

$$\Rightarrow \quad \frac{7}{2}[2(6) + (7-1)d] = 105 \quad \left[\because S_n = \frac{n}{2}\{2a + (n-1)d\}\right]$$

$$\Rightarrow \quad \frac{7}{2}[12 + 6d] = 105 \Rightarrow 7(6 + 3d) = 105$$

$$\Rightarrow \quad 6 + 3d = 15 \Rightarrow 3d = 9 \Rightarrow d = 3$$

Now, $$S_n = \frac{n}{2}[2(6) + (n-1)3] = \frac{3n}{2}[n + 3] \quad \text{...(i)}$$

On replacing n by $n - 3$ in Eq. (i), we get

$$S_{n-3} = \frac{3(n-3)(n)}{2} \quad \text{...(ii)}$$

On dividing Eq. (i) by Eq. (ii), we get

$$\frac{S_n}{S_{n-3}} = \frac{n+3}{n-3}$$

or $$S_n : S_{n-3} = (n + 3) : (n - 3)$$

Example 13 The first term of an AP is a, the second term is b and the last term is c. Show that the sum of the AP is $\frac{(b + c - 2a)(c + a)}{2(b - a)}$.

Sol. Let d be the common difference and n be the number of terms of the AP.

Since, the first term is a and the second term is b.

Therefore, $d = b - a$

Also, last term, $l = c$

$$\because \quad l = a + (n-1)d$$

$$\therefore \quad c = a + (n-1)(b - a) \quad [\because d = b - a]$$

$$\Rightarrow \quad n - 1 = \frac{c - a}{b - a}$$

$$\Rightarrow \quad n = 1 + \frac{c - a}{b - a} = \frac{b - a + c - a}{b - a} = \frac{b + c - 2a}{b - a}$$

Therefore, $$S_n = \frac{n}{2}(a + l) = \frac{(b + c - 2a)}{2(b - a)}(a + c)$$

Example 14 If the sum of p terms of an AP is q and the sum of q terms is p, then show that the sum of $p+q$ terms is $-(p+q)$. Also, find the sum of first $p-q$ terms (where, $p>q$). **[NCERT Exemplar]**

Sol. Let first term and common difference of the AP be a and d, respectively.

Then, $S_p = q$

$$\Rightarrow \frac{p}{2}[2a+(p-1)d] = q \quad \left[\because S_n = \frac{n}{2}\{2a+(n-1)d\}\right]$$

$$\Rightarrow 2a+(p-1)d = \frac{2q}{p} \quad \text{...(i)}$$

and $S_q = p \Rightarrow \frac{q}{2}[2a+(q-1)d] = p$

$$\Rightarrow 2a+(q-1)d = \frac{2p}{q} \quad \text{...(ii)}$$

On subtracting Eq. (ii) from Eq. (i), we get

$$2a+(p-1)d-2a-(q-1)d = \frac{2q}{p}-\frac{2p}{q}$$

$$\Rightarrow [(p-1)-(q-1)]\,d = \frac{2q^2-2p^2}{pq}$$

$$\Rightarrow [p-1-q+1]\,d = \frac{2(q^2-p^2)}{pq}$$

$$\Rightarrow (p-q)\,d = \frac{2(q^2-p^2)}{pq}$$

$$\therefore d = \frac{-2(p+q)}{pq} \quad \text{...(iii)}$$

On substituting the value of d in Eq. (i), we get

$$2a+(p-1)\left(\frac{-2(p+q)}{pq}\right) = \frac{2q}{p}$$

$$\Rightarrow 2a = \frac{2q}{p}+\frac{2(p+q)(p-1)}{pq}$$

$$\Rightarrow a = \left[\frac{q}{p}+\frac{(p+q)(p-1)}{pq}\right] \quad \text{...(iv)}$$

Now, $S_{p+q} = \frac{p+q}{2}[2a+(p+q-1)d]$

$$= \frac{p+q}{2}\left[\frac{2q}{p}+\frac{2(p+q)(p-1)}{pq}-\frac{(p+q-1)2(p+q)}{pq}\right]$$

$$= (p+q)\left[\frac{q}{p}+\frac{(p+q)(p-1)-(p+q-1)(p+q)}{pq}\right]$$

$$= (p+q)\left[\frac{q}{p}+\frac{(p+q)(p-1-p-q+1)}{pq}\right]$$

$$= (p+q)\left[\frac{q}{p}-\frac{p+q}{p}\right] = (p+q)\left[\frac{q-p-q}{p}\right]$$

$$\Rightarrow S_{p+q} = -(p+q)$$

Now, $S_{p-q} = \frac{p-q}{2}[2a+(p-q-1)d]$

$$= \frac{p-q}{2}\left[\frac{2q}{p}+\frac{2(p+q)(p-1)}{pq}-\frac{(p-q-1)2(p+q)}{pq}\right]$$

$$= (p-q)\left[\frac{q}{p}+\frac{(p+q)(p-1-p+q+1)}{pq}\right]$$

$$= (p-q)\left[\frac{q}{p}+\frac{(p+q)q}{pq}\right]$$

$$= (p-q)\left[\frac{q}{p}+\frac{p+q}{p}\right] = (p-q)\frac{(p+2q)}{p}$$

Example 15 The pth term of an AP is a and qth term is b. Prove that sum of its $(p+q)$th term is $\frac{p+q}{2}\left[a+b+\frac{a-b}{p-q}\right]$. **[NCERT Exemplar]**

Sol. Let A be the first term and D be the common difference of the given AP.

Then, $T_p = a \Rightarrow A+(p-1)D = a$ ...(i)

and $T_q = b \Rightarrow A+(q-1)D = b$ ...(ii)

On subtracting Eq. (ii) from Eq. (i), we get

$$(p-q)D = a-b \Rightarrow D = \frac{a-b}{p-q} \quad \text{...(iii)}$$

On adding Eqs. (i) and (ii), we get

$$2A+(p+q-2)D = a+b$$

$$\Rightarrow 2A+pD+qD-2D = a+b$$

$$\Rightarrow 2A+pD+qD-D = a+b+D$$

$$\Rightarrow 2A+(p+q-1)D = a+b+D$$

$$\Rightarrow 2A+(p+q-1)D = a+b+\left(\frac{a-b}{p-q}\right)$$

[from Eq. (iii)] ...(iv)

Now, $S_{p+q} = \frac{p+q}{2}[2A+(p+q-1)D]$

$$= \frac{p+q}{2}\left[a+b+\frac{a-b}{p-q}\right] \quad \text{[from Eq. (iv)]}$$

Hence proved.

Example 16 If the sum of m terms of an AP is equal to the sum of either the next n terms or the next p terms; then prove that

$$(m+n)\left(\frac{1}{m}-\frac{1}{p}\right) = (m+p)\left(\frac{1}{m}-\frac{1}{n}\right).$$

Sol. Let the AP be $a, a+d, a+2d, \ldots$.

We are given

$$a_1+a_2+\ldots+a_m = a_{m+1}+a_{m+2}+\ldots+a_{m+n} \quad \text{...(i)}$$

On adding $a_1+a_2+\ldots+a_m$ both sides of Eq. (i), we get

$$2[a_1+a_2+\ldots+a_m] = a_1+a_2+\ldots+a_m+a_{m+1}+\ldots+a_{m+n}$$

$$\Rightarrow \quad 2S_m = S_{m+n}$$

$$\Rightarrow 2\frac{m}{2}\{2a+(m-1)d\} = \frac{m+n}{2}\{2a+(m+n-1)d\}$$

On putting $2a+(m-1)d = x$ in the above equation, we get

$$mx = \frac{m+n}{2}(x+nd)$$

$$\Rightarrow \quad (2m-m-n)x = (m+n)nd$$

$$\Rightarrow \quad (m-n)x = (m+n)nd \quad \text{...(ii)}$$

Similarly, $a_1 + a_2 + \ldots + a_m = a_{m+1} + a_{m+2} + \ldots + a_{m+p}$

On adding $a_1 + a_2 + \ldots + a_m$ both sides, we get

$$2(a_1 + a_2 + \ldots + a_m) = a_1 + a_2 + \ldots + a_{m+1} + \ldots + a_{m+p}$$

$$\Rightarrow \quad 2S_m = S_{m+p}$$

$$\Rightarrow 2\left[\frac{m}{2}\{2a+(m-1)d\}\right] = \frac{m+p}{2}\{2a+(m+p-1)d\}$$

$$\Rightarrow \quad mx = \frac{(m+p)}{2}(x+pd)$$

$$\Rightarrow 2mx = mx + mpd + px + p^2d$$

$$\Rightarrow \quad (m-p)x = (m+p)pd \quad \text{...(iii)}$$

On dividing Eq. (ii) by Eq. (iii), we get

$$\frac{(m-n)x}{(m-p)x} = \frac{(m+n)nd}{(m+p)pd}$$

$$\Rightarrow \quad (m-n)(m+p)p = (m-p)(m+n)n$$

On dividing both sides by mnp, we get

$$(m+p)\left(\frac{1}{n}-\frac{1}{m}\right) = (m+n)\left(\frac{1}{p}-\frac{1}{m}\right)$$

or $$(m+n)\left(\frac{1}{m}-\frac{1}{p}\right) = (m+p)\left(\frac{1}{m}-\frac{1}{n}\right)$$

Example 17 If the ratio between the sums of n terms of two arithmetic progressions is $(7n+1):(4n+27)$, find the ratio of their 11th terms.

Sol. Let a_1, a_2 be the first terms and d_1, d_2 be the common differences of the first and second arithmetic progressions, respectively. Then, the sums of n terms of these progressions are given by

$$S_n = \frac{n}{2}\cdot\{2a_1+(n-1)d_1\} \quad \text{...(i)}$$

and $$S'_n = \frac{n}{2}\cdot\{2a_2+(n-1)d_2\}. \quad \text{...(ii)}$$

On dividing Eq. (i) by (ii), we get

$$\frac{\frac{n}{2}\cdot\{2a_1+(n-1)d_1\}}{\frac{n}{2}\cdot\{2a_2+(n-1)d_2\}} = \frac{S_n}{S'_n} = \frac{7n+1}{4n+27} \quad \text{[given]}$$

$$\Rightarrow \quad \frac{2a_1+(n-1)d_1}{2a_2+(n-1)d_2} = \frac{7n+1}{4n+27} \quad \text{...(iii)}$$

$$\text{Ratio of 11th terms} = \frac{a_1+10d_1}{a_2+10d_2}$$

$$= \frac{2a_1+20d_1}{2a_2+20d_2} = \frac{2a_1+(21-1)d_2}{2a_2+(21-1)d_2}$$

$$= \frac{7\times 21+1}{4\times 21+27} = \frac{148}{111}$$

[putting $n = 21$ in Eq. (iii)].

Hence, the required ratio is 148 : 111.

Applications of an AP

Sometimes we can solve the some real life problems by using the concept of AP. Some of them are given below

Example 18 In a potato race, 20 potatoes are placed in a line at intervals of 4 m with the first potato 24 m from the starting point. A contestant is required to put the potatoes back to the starting place on that time. How far would he run in bringing back all the potatoes? **[NCERT Exemplar]**

Sol. As per the given information we have the following diagram

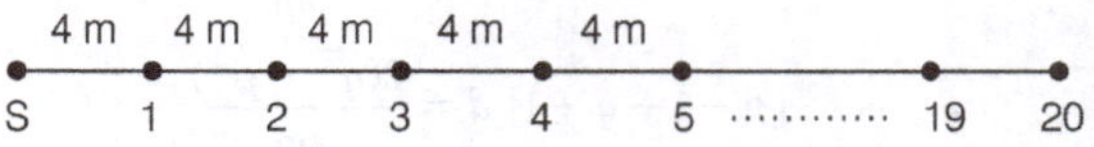

Starting point = S

Distance travelled to bring the first potato

$$= 24 + 24 = 48 \text{ m}$$

Distance travelled to bring the second potato

$$= 2(24+4) = 56 \text{ m}$$

Distance travelled to bring the third potato

$$= 2(24+4+4) = 64 \text{ m}$$

Therefore, the series will be 48, 56, 64, …

which is clearly an AP in which $a = 48$, $d = 56 - 48 = 8$

We have to find the total distance to bring all the potatoes back, so, $n = 20$

$$\because \quad S_n = \frac{n}{2}[2a+(n-1)d]$$

$$\therefore \quad S_{20} = \frac{20}{2}[2\times 48+(20-1)8] = 10[96+152]$$

$$= 10\times 248 = 2480 \text{ m}$$

Hence, the required distance is 2480 m.

Example 19 A man arranges to pay-off a debt of ₹ 3600 by 40 annual instalments, which are in AP, when 30 of the instalments are paid, he dies leaving one-third of the debt unpaid. Find the 8th instalment. **[NCERT]**

Sol. Here, total debt, $S =$ ₹ 3600

and total instalments, $n = 40$

Let a and d be the first instalment and increment in instalment, respectively.

Thus, we get an AP here.

By using sum of n terms, we get

$$3600 = \frac{40}{2}[2a + (40-1)d]$$

$\Rightarrow \quad 180 = 2a + 39d \quad$ ...(i)

Now, after 30 instalments, one-third of the debt is unpaid. i.e. $\frac{3600}{3} =$ ₹ 1200 is unpaid and then paid money $= 3600 - 1200 =$ ₹ 2400

So, again by using sum of n terms, we get

$$S_{30} = 2400 = \frac{30}{2}[2a + (30-1)d]$$

$\Rightarrow \quad 160 = 2a + 29d \quad$ ...(ii)

On solving Eqs. (i) and (ii), we get

$$a = 51, d = 2$$

We know that, nth term $(T_n) = a + (n-1)d$

$\therefore$ 8th instalment, $T_8 = a + (8-1)d = 51 + 7 \times 2$
$= 51 + 14 =$ ₹ 65

Hence, the 8th instalment is ₹ 65.

Example 20 Shamshad Ali buys a scooter for ₹22000. He pays ₹ 4000 cash and agrees to pay the balance in annual instalments of ₹ 1000 plus 10% interest on the unpaid amount. How much will scooter cost him?

Sol. Given, cost of scooter = ₹ 22000,

Down payment = ₹ 4000, balance payment = ₹ 18000

Now, interest on I instalment $= \frac{18000 \times 10 \times 1}{100} =$ ₹ 1800

$$\left[\because I = \frac{P \times R \times T}{100}\right]$$

Unpaid amount = 18000 – 1000 = ₹ 17000

Interest on II instalment $= \frac{17000 \times 10 \times 1}{100} =$ ₹ 1700

Unpaid amount = 17000 – 1000 = ₹ 16000

Interest on III instalment $= \frac{16000 \times 10 \times 1}{100} =$ ₹ 1600

....

....

$\therefore$ Total interest paid by him

$= 1800 + 1700 + 1600 + \dots + 18$ terms

which is clearly an AP with $a = 1800, d = 1700 - 1800 = -100$

Therefore, total interest $= \frac{18}{2}[2 \times 1800 + (18-1)(-100)]$

$$\left[\because \text{sum of an AP, } S_n = \frac{n}{2}\{2a + (n-1)d\}\right]$$

$= 9(3600 - 1700) = 9 \times 1900 = 17100$

Hence, total amount or actual cost = 22000 + 17100
= ₹ 39100

Example 21 A man accepts a position with an initial salary of ₹ 5200 per month. It is understood that he will receive an automatic increase of ₹ 320 in the very next month and each month thereafter.

(i) Find his salary for the tenth month. **[NCERT]**

(ii) What is his total earnings during the first year?

Sol. Here, the man get a fixed increment of ₹ 320 each month.

Therefore, this forms an AP whose first term = 5200 and common difference $(d) = 320$

(i) Salary for tenth month i.e. for $n = 10$,

$a_{10} = a + (n-1)d$

$\Rightarrow a_{10} = 5200 + (10-1) \times 320$

$\Rightarrow a_{10} = 5200 + 9 \times 320$

$\Rightarrow a_{10} = 5200 + 2880$

$\therefore a_{10} = 8080$

(ii) In a year there are 12 month i.e. $n = 12$,

Total earning during the first year.

$$S_{12} = \frac{12}{2}[2 \times 5200 + (12-1)320]$$

$= 6[10400 + 11 \times 320]$

$= 6[10400 + 3520] = 6 \times 13920 =$ ₹ 83520

Example 22 The digit of a three-digit number are in AP and their sum is 21. The number obtained by reversing the digit is 396 less than the original number. Find the number.

Sol. Let the hundred's, ten's and unit's digits be $(a + d), a, (a - d)$.

Then, $(a + d) + a + (a - d) = 21$

$\Rightarrow 3a = 21$

$\Rightarrow a = 7$

$\therefore$ Original three-digit number

$= (7 + d) \times 100 + 7 \times 10 + (7 - d)$

According to the given condition,

$(7 + d) \times 100 + 7 \times 10 + (7 - d)$
$- \{(7 - d) \times 100 + 7 \times 10 + (7 + d)\} = 396$

$\Rightarrow 693 + 99d - \{693 - 99d\} = 396$

$\Rightarrow 198d = 396 \Rightarrow d = 2$

$\therefore$ Original three-digit numbers

$= (7 + 2) \times 100 + 7 \times 10 + (7 - 2)$

$= 900 + 70 + 5 = 975$

Example 23 The interior angles of a polygon are in AP. The smallest angle is 120° and the common difference is 5°. Find the number of sides of polygon.

Sol. Let n be the number of sides of the polygon. We know that, sum of interior angles of a polygon of n sides

$= (2n - 4) \times 90 \quad$ ...(i)

Given, $a = 120°$ and $d = 5°, n = n$

$\therefore$ Sum of interior angles of polygon of n sides

$$= \frac{n}{2}[2(120) + (n-1)5] \quad \text{...(ii)}$$

Now, from Eqs. (i) and (ii), we get

$$\frac{n}{2}[2(120) + (n-1)5] = (2n-4)90$$

$$\Rightarrow n(240 + 5n - 5) = 180(2n-4)$$

$$\Rightarrow n(235 + 5n) = 360n - 720$$

$$\Rightarrow 5n^2 + 235n = 360n - 720$$

$$\Rightarrow 5n^2 - 125n + 720 = 0$$

$$\Rightarrow n^2 - 25n + 144 = 0 \text{ [divide both sides by 5]}$$

$$\Rightarrow (n-9)(n-16) = 0$$

$$\therefore n = 9 \text{ or } 16$$

But, if $n = 16$, last (greatest) angle of the polygon $= 120 + (16-1)5 = 195°$.

No, interior angle of the polygon can be greater than or equal to 180°. So, $n \neq 16$. Therefore, $n = 9$

Hence, the number of sides of polygon is 9.

Arithmetic Mean (AM)

Let a and b be any two numbers and A be a number between them so that a, A, b are in AP, then such a number A is called an **arithmetic mean.**

Thus, a, A, b are in AP.

$$\therefore \quad A - a = b - A \quad \text{[common difference]}$$

$$\Rightarrow \quad 2A = a + b \Rightarrow A = \frac{a+b}{2}$$

Thus, Arithmetic mean (or average) between two given numbers is equal to half of their sum.

i.e. $$\boxed{AM = \frac{a+b}{2}}$$

Example 24 Find AM between 16 and 20.

Sol. $AM = \frac{a+b}{2} = \frac{16+20}{2} = \frac{36}{2} = 18$

Inserting Two or More Arithmetic Means between any Two Numbers

Let a and b be any two positive numbers and $A_1, A_2, A_3, \ldots, A_n$ be the n AM's between a and b. Then, $a, A_1, A_2, \ldots, A_n, b$ are in AP and total number of terms $= n+2$.

Here, b is $(n+2)$th term.

i.e. $$b = T_{n+2} = a + (n+2-1)d$$

$$\Rightarrow b = a + (n+1)d$$

$$\Rightarrow d = \frac{b-a}{n+1}$$

Thus, the n arithmetic means between a and b are given below

$$A_1 = a + d = a + \frac{b-a}{n+1}$$

$$A_2 = a + 2d = a + \frac{2(b-a)}{n+1}$$

$$A_3 = a + 3d = a + \frac{3(b-a)}{n+1}$$

$$\cdots \quad \cdots \quad \cdots$$

$$\cdots \quad \cdots \quad \cdots$$

$$A_n = a + nd = a + \frac{n(b-a)}{n+1}$$

Note The sum of n AM's between a and b is equal to n times the single arithmetic mean between a and b,

i.e. $A_1 + A_2 + \ldots + A_n = n\left(\frac{a+b}{2}\right)$.

Example 25 Insert 6 arithmetic means between 3 and 24.

Sol. Let A_1, A_2, A_3, A_4, A_5 and A_6 be six arithmetic means between 3 and 24.

Then, $3, A_1, A_2, A_3, A_4, A_5, A_6, 24$ are in AP and number of terms is 8.

$$\therefore \quad a = 3, \text{ and } T_8 = 24$$

$$\Rightarrow a + (8-1)d = 24 \quad [\because T_n = a + (n-1)d]$$

$$\Rightarrow a + 7d = 24$$

$$\Rightarrow 3 + 7d = 24$$

$$\Rightarrow 7d = 21 \Rightarrow d = 3$$

Now,
$$A_1 = a + d = 3 + 3 = 6$$
$$A_2 = a + 2d = 3 + 2(3) = 9$$
$$A_3 = a + 3d = 3 + 3(3) = 12$$
$$A_4 = a + 4d = 3 + 4(3) = 15$$
$$A_5 = a + 5d = 3 + 5(3) = 18$$
and
$$A_6 = a + 6d = 3 + 6(3) = 21$$

Hence, 6 arithmetic means between 3 and 24 are 6, 9, 12, 15, 18 and 21.

Example 26 Prove that the sum of n arithmetic means between two numbers is n times the single AM between them.

Sol. Let $A_1, A_2, \ldots, A_n$ be n arithmetic means between a and b. Then, $a, A_1, A_2, \ldots, A_n, b$ is an AP with common difference d given by $d = \frac{b-a}{n+1}$.

Now, $$A_1 + A_2 + \ldots + A_n = \frac{n}{2}(A_1 + A_n) \left[\because S_n = \frac{n}{2}(a+l)\right]$$

$$= \frac{n}{2}(a+b)$$

$[\because a, A_1, A_2, \ldots, A_n, b$ is an AP, so $a + b = A_1 + A_n]$

$$= n\left(\frac{a+b}{2}\right) = n \times (\text{AM between } a \text{ and } b)$$

Example 27 If the AM between pth and qth terms of an AP be equal to the AM between rth and sth terms of the AP, then show that $p+q=r+s$.

Sol. Let a be the first term and d be the common difference of the given AP.

Then, $a_p = p\text{th term} = a+(p-1)d$;

$a_q = q\text{th term} = a+(q-1)d$

$a_r = r\text{th term} = a+(r-1)d$

and $a_s = s\text{th term} = a+(s-1)d$

It is given that,

AM between a_p and a_q = AM between a_r and a_s

$$\Rightarrow \frac{1}{2}(a_p+a_q)=\frac{1}{2}(a_r+a_s)$$

$$\Rightarrow a_p+a_q=a_r+a_s$$

$$\Rightarrow \{a+(p-1)d\}+\{a+(q-1)d\} = \{a+(r-1)d\}+\{a+(s-1)d\}$$

$$\Rightarrow (p+q-2)d=(r+s-2)d$$

$$\therefore p+q=r+s$$

Example 28 If $\dfrac{a^n+b^n}{a^{n-1}+b^{n-1}}$ is AM between a and b, then find the value of n. **[NCERT]**

Sol. We know that AM between a and b is $\dfrac{a+b}{2}$.

$$\therefore \frac{a^n+b^n}{a^{n-1}+b^{n-1}}=\frac{a+b}{2}$$

$$\Rightarrow 2a^n+2b^n=a^n+ab^{n-1}+ba^{n-1}+b^n$$

$$\Rightarrow 2a^n-a^n+2b^n-b^n=ab^{n-1}+ba^{n-1}$$

$$\Rightarrow a^n+b^n=ab^{n-1}+ba^{n-1}$$

$$\Rightarrow a^n-ba^{n-1}=ab^{n-1}-b^n$$

$$\Rightarrow a^{n-1}[a-b]=b^{n-1}[a-b]$$

$$\Rightarrow a^{n-1}=b^{n-1} \qquad [\because a\neq b]$$

$$\Rightarrow \left(\frac{a}{b}\right)^{n-1}=1=\left(\frac{a}{b}\right)^0 \qquad [\because x^0=1]$$

On comparing the exponential powers, we get

$$n-1=0$$

$$\Rightarrow n=1$$

Example 29 Suppose x and y are two real numbers such that the rth mean between x and $2y$ is equal to the rth mean between $2x$ and y when n arithmetic means are inserted between them in both the cases. Show that $\dfrac{n+1}{r}-\dfrac{y}{x}=1$.

Sol. Let $A_1, A_2, \ldots, A_n$ be n arithmetic means between x and $2y$. Then, $x, A_1, A_2, \ldots, A_n, 2y$ are in AP with common difference d_1 given by $d_1=\dfrac{2y-x}{n+1}$.

$$\therefore r\text{th mean} = A_r = x+rd_1 = x+r\left(\frac{2y-x}{n+1}\right)$$

$\therefore$ Let $A'_1, A'_2, \ldots, A'_n$ be n arithmetic means between $2x$ and y. Then, $2x, A_1', A_2', \ldots, A_n', y$ are in AP with common difference d_2 given by $d_2=\left(\dfrac{y-2x}{n+1}\right)$.

$$\therefore r\text{th mean}, A'_r = 2x+rd_2 = 2x+r\left(\frac{y-2x}{n+1}\right)$$

It is given that, $A_r=A_r'$

$$\Rightarrow x+r\left(\frac{2y-x}{n+1}\right)=2x+r\left(\frac{y-2x}{n+1}\right)$$

$$\Rightarrow (n+1)x+r(2y-x)=(n+1)2x+r(y-2x)$$

$$\Rightarrow (n+1)x-ry=rx$$

$$\therefore \frac{n+1}{r}-\frac{y}{x}=1$$

Topic Practice 3

Very Short Answer Type Questions

2 Marks

1. If the sum of first n terms of a progression is a quadratic expression in n, then show that it is an AP.
2. If the sum of n terms of an AP is given by $S_n=3n+2n^2$, then find the common difference of the AP. **[NCERT Exemplar]**
3. Find the sum of 24 terms of an AP 1, 3, 5, 7, ...
4. Find the sum of 10 terms of an AP $6, 5\frac{1}{3}, 4\frac{2}{3}, \ldots$
5. Find the sum of 20 terms of the sequence $\sqrt{2}, 2\sqrt{2}, 3\sqrt{2}, \ldots$
6. Find the sum of 100 terms of the series $0.7+0.71+0.72+\ldots$
7. Find the sum of $-0.5, -1.0, -1.5, \ldots$ upto 10 terms.
8. Find the value of x, when $1+6+11+\ldots+x=148$.

9 Determine the sum of first 35 terms of an AP, if its second term is 2 and seventh term is 22.

10 Find the sum of odd integers from 1 to 2001.

11 Find the arithmetic mean between
(i) $(a-b)$ and $(a+b)$ (ii) 12 and 22.

12 Insert five numbers bewteen 8 and 26 such that the resulting sequence is an AP. **[NCERT]**

13 Insert the three numbers between 3 and 19 such that the resulting sequence is an AP.

14 The sum of first 7 terms of an AP is 10 and that of next 7 terms is 17. Find the AP.

15 Find the sum of first 20 terms of an AP, in which 3rd terms is 7 and 7th term is two more than thrice of its 3rd term.

16 Find the sum of all natural numbers between 250 and 1000 which are exactly divisible by 3.

17 Find the sum of all two digit numbers which when divided by 4, yield 1 as remainder. **[NCERT]**

18 Find the sum of all natural numbers lying between 100 and 1000, which are multiples of 5.

19 If the sum of n terms of an AP is $(pn+qn^2)$, where p and q are constants, find the common difference. **[NCERT]**

20 If the sum of n terms of an AP is $3n^2+5n$ and its mth term is 164, find the value of m.

21 In an AP, the pth term is q and the $(p+q)$th term is 0. Then, find the qth term. **[NCERT Exexmplar]**

22 The income of a person is ₹ 300000, in the first year and he receives an case of ₹ 10000 his income per year for the next 19 years. Find the total amount, he received in 20 years. **[NCERT]**

23 On the first day strike of physicians in a hospital, the attendence of the OPD was 1500 patients. As the strike continued, the attendence declined by 100 patients every day. Find from which day of the strike, the OPD would have no patient?

24 The gate receipts at the show of 'Comedy Nights' amounted ₹ 9500 on the first night and showed a drop of ₹ 250 every succeeding night. If the operational expenses of the show are ₹ 2000 a day, then find on which night, the show ceases to be profitable?

25 A carpenter was hired to build 192 window frames. The first day he made five frames and each day, thereafter he made two more frames than he made the day before. How many days did it take him to finish the job? **[NCERT Exemplar]**

Short Answer Type Questions

4 Marks

26 How many terms of the AP 18, 16, 14, 12, ... are needed to give the sum 78? Explain the double answer?

27 The sum of n terms of two arithmetic progressions are in the ratio $(7n-5):(5n+17)$. Show that their 6th terms are equal.

28 If in an AP, $S_n = qn^2$ and $S_m = qm^2$, where S_r denotes the sum of r terms of the AP, then find S_q. **[NCERT Exemplar]**

29 Let S_n denote the sum of the first n terms of an AP. If $S_{2n} = 3S_n$, then find $S_{3n} : S_n$. **[NCERT Exemplar]**

30 In an AP, if the pth term is $\frac{1}{q}$ and qth term is $\frac{1}{p}$. Prove that the sum of first pq terms is $\frac{1}{2}(pq+1)$ where, $p \neq q$. **[NCERT]**

31 If the sum of first p terms of an AP is equal to the sum of first q terms, then find the sum of first $(p+q)$ terms. **[NCERT]**

32 Let the sum of n, $2n$, $3n$ terms of an AP be S_1, S_2 and S_3, respectively. Show that $S_3 = 3(S_2 - S_1)$.

33 Sum of the first p, q and r terms of an AP are a, b and c, respectively. Prove that

$$\frac{a}{p}(q-r)+\frac{b}{q}(r-p)+\frac{c}{r}(p-q)=0.$$

34 If the first term of an AP is 2 and the sum of first five terms is equal to one-fourth of the sum of the next five terms, then show that the 20th term is –112. **[NCERT]**

35 The sum of interior angles of a triangle is 180°. Show that the sum of the interior angles of polygons with 3, 4, 5, 6, ... sides form an arithmetic progression. Find the sum of the interior angles for a 21 sided polygon.

36 The sum of two numbers is $\frac{13}{6}$. An even number of AM's are being inserted between them. The sum of means inserted exceeds the number of means by 1. Find the number of AM's inserted.

37 Show that $(x^2 + xy + y^2)$, $(z^2 + xz + x^2)$ and $(y^2 + yz + z^2)$ are consecutive terms of an AP, if x, y and z are in AP.

38 Between 1 and 31, m AM's have been inserted in such a way that the ratio of the 7th and $(m-1)$th means is 5 : 9. Find the value of m. **[NCERT]**

39 If n arithmetic means are inserted between 20 and 80 such that the ratio of first mean to the last mean is 1 : 3, then find the value of n.

Long Answer Type Questions

6 Marks

40 The digits of a positive number having three digits are in AP and their sum is 15. The number obtained by reversing the digits is 594 less than the original number. Find the number.

41 A farmer buys a used tractor of ₹ 12000. He pays ₹ 6000 cash and agrees to pay the balance in annual instalment of ₹ 500 plus 12% interest on the unpaid amount. How much will the tractor cost him?

42 Find the sum of integers from 1 to 100 that are divisible by 2 or 5.

Hints & Answers

1. Let $S_n = an^2 + bn + c$ ...(i)

where a, b, c are constant and $a \neq 0$.

On replacing n by $(n-1)$ in Eq. (i) we get

$$S_{n-1} = a(n-1)^2 + b(n-1) + c$$
$$= a(n^2 + 1 - 2n) + b(n-1) + c \quad \text{...(ii)}$$

Now, $a_n = S_n - S_{n-1}$

$$= (an^2 + bn + c) - [a(n^2 + 1 - 2n) + b(n-1) + c]$$
$$= 2an + (b - a)$$

$\therefore\ a_{n-1} = 2a(n-1) + (b-a)$ [replacing n by $(n-1)$]

$\Rightarrow a_n - a_{n-1} = 2a$, which is constant.

Hence, the given progression is an AP.

2. 4

3. $S_{24} = \frac{24}{2}[2 \times 1 + (24-1) \times 2]$ **Ans.** 576

4. $S_{10} = \frac{10}{2}\left[2 \times 6 + (10-1)\left(\frac{-2}{3}\right)\right]$ **Ans.** 30

5. $S_{20} = \frac{20}{2}[2 \times \sqrt{2} + (20-1)\sqrt{2}]$ **Ans.** $210\sqrt{2}$

6. $S_{100} = \frac{100}{2}[2 \times 0.7 + (100-1)(0.01)]$ **Ans.** 119.5

7. – 27.5

8. $a = 1$, $d = 5$, $S_n = 148$ **Ans.** $x = 36$

9. 2310

10. 1002001

11. (i) a (ii) 17

12. Solve as Example 25. **Ans.** 11, 14, 17, 21, 24

13. Solve as Example 25. **Ans.** 7, 11, 15

14. $1 + 1\frac{1}{7} + 1\frac{2}{7} + \ldots$

15. 740

16. 156375

17. 1210

18. 98450

19. Common difference = $2q$

20. $m = 27$

21. $T_q = p$

22. 7900000

23. The 16th day of strike, the OPD will have no patient.

24. 31

25. 12

26. 6, 13

27. Solve as Example 17.

28. $S_q = q^3$

29. 6

30. $\because S_p = \frac{1}{q}$ and $S_q = \frac{1}{p}$

$$\Rightarrow \frac{p}{2}(2a + (p-1)d) = \frac{1}{q}$$

and $$\frac{q}{2}(2a + (q-1)d) = \frac{1}{p}$$

On solving these equations, we get $a = d = \frac{1}{pq}$

$$S_{pq} = \frac{pq}{2}(2a + (pq-1)d)$$
$$= \frac{1}{2}(pq + 1)$$

31. $S_{p+q} = 0$

32. Here, $S_1 = \frac{n}{2}(2a + (n-1)d)$ ...(i)

Also, sum of $2n$ terms $= S_2$

i.e. $\frac{2n}{2}[2a + (2n-1)d] = S_2$ ...(ii)

and sum of $3n$ terms $= S_3$

i.e. $\frac{3n}{2}[2a + (3n-1)d] = S_3$ ...(iii)

Then, show $S_3 = 3(S_2 - S_1)$

33. Here, $a = \frac{p}{2}[2A + (p-1)D]$

$$b = \frac{q}{2}[2A + (q-1)D]$$

and $$c = \frac{r}{2}[2A + (r-1)D]$$

34. $\because \; S_5 = \frac{1}{4}(S_{10} - S_5)$

$\Rightarrow \quad 5S_5 = S_{10}$

$\Rightarrow \quad 5 \times \frac{5}{2}(4+4d) = \frac{10}{2}(8+9d)$

$\Rightarrow \quad d = -6$

$\because \quad a_{20} = a + 19d$

35. We know that, sum of interior angles of a polygon of side $n = (2n-4)\times 90° = (n-2)\times 180°$

The series will be 180°, 360° 540°, 720°, 900°, ...

We have to find the sum of interior angles of a 21 sides polygon. It means, we have to find the 19th term of the above series. [since, 180° is the sum of three angle]

36. Let a and b be two numbers and $A_1, A_2, \dots A_{2n}$ be $2n$ (even numbers) AMs. Then, $a + b = \frac{13}{6}$

and $A_1 + A_2 + \dots + A_{2n} = 2n\left(\frac{a+b}{2}\right) = \left(\frac{13}{6}\right)n$

According to the question,

$A_1 + A_2 + \dots + A_{2n} = 2n + 1 \Rightarrow n = 6$ **Ans.** 12

37. $(z^2 + xz + x^2) - (x^2 + xy + y^2)$

$= (y^2 + yz + z^2) - (z^2 + xz + x^2)$

$\Rightarrow \quad z^2 + xz - xy - y^2 = y^2 + yz - xz - x^2$

$\Rightarrow \quad x + z = 2y$

38. Let $A_1, A_2, A_3, A_4, \dots, A_m$ be m AM's between 1 and 31.

Therefore, $1, A_1, A_2, A_3, \dots, A_m, 31$ are in AP.

Here, the total number of terms is $m+2$ and $T_{m+2} = 31$

$\Rightarrow \quad 1 + (m+2-1)d = 31 \Rightarrow (m+1)d = 30$

$\Rightarrow \quad d = \frac{30}{m+1}$ ...(i)

$\therefore \quad A_7 = T_8 = a + 7d$

$= 1 + 7 \times \frac{30}{m+1} = \frac{m+211}{m+1}$ [from Eq. (i)]

$A_{m-1} = T_m = 1 + (m-1)d = 1 + (m-1)\frac{30}{m+1}$

$= \frac{m+1+30m-30}{m+1}$ [from Eq. (i)]

$= \frac{31m-29}{m+1}$

$\therefore \quad \frac{A_7}{A_{m-1}} = \frac{(m+211)/(m+1)}{(31m-29)/m+1} = \frac{m+211}{31m-29}$

Ans $m = 14$

39. Let $A_1, A_2, \dots, A_n$ be n arithmetic means between 20 and 80 and d be the common difference of the AP $20, A_1, A_2, \dots, A_n, 80$. Here, $a = 20, b = 80$

Then, $d = \frac{b-a}{n+1} = \frac{60}{n+1}$

Now, $A_1 = a + d = 20 + \frac{60}{n+1} = \frac{20(n+4)}{n+1}$

and $A_n = a + nd = 20 + \frac{60n}{n+1} = \frac{20(4n+1)}{n+1}$

According to the question, $A_1 : A_n = 1:3$

$\Rightarrow \quad \frac{A_1}{A_n} = \frac{1}{3}$

$\Rightarrow \quad \frac{\frac{20(n+4)}{n+1}}{\frac{20(4n+1)}{n+1}} = \frac{1}{3} \Rightarrow \frac{n+4}{4n+1} = \frac{1}{3}$

Ans. $n = 11$

40. Here, $a - d + a + a + d = 15 \Rightarrow 3a = 15 \Rightarrow a = 5$

Original number $= 100(a+d) + 10a + (a-d)$

$= 111a + 99d$ ...(i)

Number after reversing the digits

$= 100(a-d) + 10a + a + d = 111a - 99d$ ...(ii)

According to the question, $111a + 99d - 594 = 111a - 99d$

$\Rightarrow \quad d = 3$ **Ans.** 852

41. ₹16680

42. The numbers from 1 to 100 which are divisible by 2 are 2, 4, 6, 8, ..., 100. Then, $100 = 2 + (n-1)2 \Rightarrow n = 50$

$S_{50} = \frac{50}{2}(2\times 2 + (50-1)2)$

$\Rightarrow \quad S_{50} = 2550$

The numbers from 1 to 100 which are divisible by 5 are 5, 10, 15, 20, ...,100.

$\therefore \quad 100 = 5 + (n-1)5 \Rightarrow n = 20$

and $\quad S_{20} = \frac{20}{2}[2\times 5 + (20-1)5] \Rightarrow S_{20} = 1050$

The numbers from 1 to 100 which are divisible by 10 are 10, 20, 30, ..., 100.

Then, $n = 10$ and $S_{10} = \frac{10}{2}[2\times 10 + (10-1)10] = 550$

Hence, required sum of integers from 1 to 100 which are divisible by 2 or 5 = 2550 + 1050 − 550

Ans. 3050

TOPIC 04

Geometric Progression (GP)

Geometric Progression (GP)

A sequence of non-zero numbers is said to be a geometric progression, if the ratio of each term, except the first one, by its preceding term is always constant.

In other words, we can say that a sequence $a_1, a_2, \ldots, a_n$ is called geometric progression (geometric sequence), if it follows the relation $\frac{a_{k+1}}{a_k} = r$ (constant) for all $k \in N$.

The constant ratio is called **common ratio** of the GP and it is denoted by r. In a GP, we usually denote the first term by a, the **nth** term by T_n or a_n.

Thus, a GP can be written as $a, ar, ar^2, ar^3, \ldots$ and so on.

e.g. The sequence 4, 12, 36, 108, ... is a GP.

Here, $a = 4, \quad r = \frac{12}{4} = \frac{36}{12} = \frac{108}{36} = \ldots = 3$

Geometric Series

Let $a_1, a_2, a_3, \ldots, a_n$ be a GP. Then, the expression $a_1 + a_2 + a_3 + \ldots + a_n + \ldots$ is called a **geometric series**. Geometric series is finite, if the corresponding GP is **finite**, otherwise it is an **infinite** geometric series.

Note To show that given numbers a, b, c, d and so on are in GP, we have to show that $\frac{b}{a} = \frac{c}{b}$.

Example 1 For what values of k, the numbers $-\frac{2}{7}$, $k, -\frac{7}{2}$ are in GP? **[NCERT]**

Sol. If $-\frac{2}{7}, k, -\frac{7}{2}$ are in GP.

Then, $\frac{a_2}{a_1} = \frac{a_3}{a_2}$ $\left[\because \text{common ratio } (r) = \frac{a_2}{a_1} = \frac{a_3}{a_2} = \frac{a_4}{a_3} = \ldots\right]$

$\therefore \quad \frac{k}{-2/7} = \frac{-7/2}{k} \Rightarrow \frac{7}{-2}k = \frac{-7}{2} \times \frac{1}{k}$

$\Rightarrow 7k \times 2k = -7 \times (-2) \Rightarrow 14k^2 = 14 \Rightarrow k^2 = 1 \Rightarrow k = \pm 1$

Example 2 If a, b and c are in GP, then find the value of $\frac{a-b}{b-c}$.

Sol. Given that, a, b and c are in GP.

Then, $\quad \frac{b}{a} = \frac{c}{b} = r$ (constant)

$\Rightarrow \quad b = ar, c = br$

Now, $\frac{a-b}{b-c} = \frac{a-ar}{ar-br} = \frac{a(1-r)}{r(a-b)}$

$= \frac{a(1-r)}{r(a-ar)} = \frac{a(1-r)}{ar(1-r)} = \frac{1}{r}$

$\Rightarrow \quad \frac{a-b}{b-c} = \frac{1}{r} = \frac{a}{b}$ or $\frac{b}{c}$

General Term of a GP

If a is the first term of a GP and its common ratio is r, then

General term or nth term, $T_n = ar^{n-1}$

or $\quad l = ar^{n-1}$, where l is the **last term.**

mth Term of a Finite GP from the End

Let a be the first term and r be the common ratio of a GP having n terms. Then, mth term from the end is $(n-m+1)$th term from the beginning.

$\therefore$ **mth term from the end** $= ar^{n-m+1-1} = ar^{n-m}$

where, $n > m$. Also, nth term from the end $= l\left(\frac{1}{r}\right)^{n-1}$,

where, l is the last term of the finite GP.

Problems Based on General Term of a GP

Some problems can be solved directly or indirectly with the help of general term. Some types are given below

|TYPE I|

Problems Based on Finding the Indicated Term

In this type of problems, first term and common ratio of a GP are given and we have to find the value of indicated term.

Example 3 Find the 6th term of the sequence 2, 6, 18 ... .

Sol. Here, first term $(a) = 2$ and common ratio $(r) = \frac{6}{2} = 3$

We know that, $T_n = ar^{n-1}$

$\therefore \quad T_6 = 2 \times (3)^{6-1} = 2(3)^5 = 486$

Example 4 Find the 5th term from the end of the sequence 2, 6, 18, ..., 39366.

Sol. Here, common ratio $(r) = \frac{6}{2} = 3$ and last term $(l) = 39366$

We know that, nth term from the end $= l\left(\frac{1}{r}\right)^{n-1}$

$\therefore$ 5th term from the end $= 39366\left(\frac{1}{3}\right)^{5-1}$

$$= 39366\left(\frac{1}{3}\right)^{4} = 486$$

Example 5 If the pth and qth terms of a GP are q and p respectively, then show that its $(p+q)$th term is $\left(\frac{q^p}{p^q}\right)^{\frac{1}{p-q}}$.

Sol. Let the first term and common ratio of GP be a and r, respectively.

According to the question, pth term $= q$

$$\Rightarrow \quad a \cdot r^{p-1} = q \quad \text{...(i)}$$

and qth term $= p$

$$\Rightarrow \quad ar^{q-1} = p \quad \text{...(ii)}$$

On dividing Eq. (i) by Eq. (ii), we get

$$\frac{ar^{p-1}}{ar^{q-1}} = \frac{q}{p} \Rightarrow r^{p-1-q+1} = \frac{q}{p}$$

$$\Rightarrow \quad r^{p-q} = \frac{q}{p} \Rightarrow r = \left(\frac{q}{p}\right)^{\frac{1}{p-q}}$$

On substituting the value of r in Eq. (i), we get

$$a\left(\frac{q}{p}\right)^{\frac{p-1}{p-q}} = q \Rightarrow a = \frac{q}{\left(\frac{q}{p}\right)^{\frac{p-1}{p-q}}} = q \cdot \left(\frac{p}{q}\right)^{\frac{p-1}{p-q}}$$

$\therefore$ $(p+q)$th term, $T_{p+q} = a \cdot r^{p+q-1}$

$$= q \cdot \left(\frac{p}{q}\right)^{\frac{p-1}{p-q}} \cdot (r)^{p+q-1}$$

$$= q \cdot \left(\frac{p}{q}\right)^{\frac{p-1}{p-q}} \times \left(\frac{q}{p}\right)^{\frac{p+q-1}{p-q}}$$

$$= \frac{q^{1-\frac{p-1}{p-q}+\frac{p+q-1}{p-q}}}{p^{\frac{p+q-1}{p-q}-\frac{p-1}{p-q}}} = \frac{q^{\frac{p-q-p+1+p+q-1}{p-q}}}{p^{\frac{p+q-1-p+1}{p-q}}}$$

$$= \frac{q^{\frac{p}{p-q}}}{p^{\frac{q}{p-q}}} = \left(\frac{q^p}{p^q}\right)^{\frac{1}{p-q}}$$

Example 6 The $(m+n)$th and $(m-n)$th terms of a GP are p and q respectively. Show that the mth and nth terms are $\sqrt{pq}$ and $p\left(\frac{q}{p}\right)^{m/2n}$, respectively.

Sol. Let a be the first term and r be the common ratio. then,

$$a_{m+n} = p \text{ and } a_{m-n} = q$$

$$\Rightarrow \quad ar^{m+n-1} = p \text{ and } ar^{m-n-1} = q$$

$$\Rightarrow \quad \frac{ar^{m+n-1}}{ar^{m-n-1}} = \frac{p}{q} \Rightarrow r^{2n} = \frac{p}{q}$$

$$\Rightarrow \quad r = \left(\frac{p}{q}\right)^{1/2n} \Rightarrow \frac{1}{r} = \left(\frac{q}{p}\right)^{1/2n}$$

Now, $\quad a_m = ar^{m-1}$

$$\Rightarrow \quad a_m = ar^{(m+n-1)}\left(\frac{1}{r}\right)^n$$

$$\Rightarrow \quad a_m = a_{m+n}\left(\frac{1}{r}\right)^n \quad [\because a_{m+n} = ar^{m+n-1}]$$

$$\Rightarrow \quad a_m = p\left(\frac{q}{p}\right)^{n/2n} \quad \left[\because a_{m+n} = p \text{ and } \frac{1}{r} = \left(\frac{q}{p}\right)^{1/2n}\right]$$

$$\Rightarrow \quad a_m = p\left(\frac{q}{p}\right)^{1/2} = \sqrt{pq}$$

and $\quad a_n = ar^{n-1}$

$$\Rightarrow a_n = ar^{m+n-1}\left(\frac{1}{r}\right)^m = a_{m+n}\left(\frac{1}{r}\right)^m \quad [\because a_{m+n} = ar^{m+n-1}]$$

$$\therefore \quad a_n = p\left(\frac{q}{p}\right)^{m/2n} \quad \left[\because a_{m+n} = p \text{ and } \frac{1}{r} = \left(\frac{q}{p}\right)^{1/2n}\right]$$

|TYPE III|

Problems Based on Finding the Position of a Given Term

In this type of problems, a GP is given from which we get first term and common ratio. Then, assume that the given term is nth term and find the value of n. This value of n gives its position in given GP.

Example 7 Which term of the GP : 5, 10, 20, 40, ... is 5120?

Sol. Given GP is 5, 10, 20, 40, ...

Here, $\quad a = 5$ and $r = \frac{10}{5} = 2$

Let nth term of given GP = 5120 i.e. $T_n = 5120$

Now, $\quad T_n = ar^{n-1} = 5120$

$$\Rightarrow \quad 5(2)^{n-1} = 5120 \quad [\because a = 5, r = 2]$$

$$\Rightarrow \quad 2^{n-1} = \frac{5120}{5} = 1024$$

$$\Rightarrow \quad 2^{n-1} = 1024$$

$$\Rightarrow \quad 2^{n-1} = 2^{10}$$

On equating the powers, we get

$$n - 1 = 10$$

$$\Rightarrow \quad n = 10 + 1 = 11$$

Hence, 11th term of given GP is 5120.

Note We can equate the powers from both sides only when the bases are same, i.e. if $b^n = b^m$, then we can equate the powers (here, b is base).

|TYPE III|

Problems Based on Finding the General Term from the End

In this type of problems, a finite GP is given from which we can find a and r and then we find a general term or mth term from the end of given finite GP.

Example 8 Find the 8th term from the end of the sequence 3, 6, 12, ... 25th term.

Sol. We know that if a sequence has n terms, then mth term from end is equal to $(n - m + 1)$th term from the beginning.

Here, $a = 3$, $r = \frac{6}{3} = 2$, $m = 8$ and $n = 25$.

Now, 8th term from the end of sequence is equal to the $(25 - 8 + 1)$. i.e. 18th term from the beginning.

$$\because \quad T_n = ar^{n-1}$$

$$\therefore \quad T_{18} = ar^{18-1} = 3(2)^{18-1} \quad [\because a = 3, r = 2]$$

$$= 3(2)^{17} = 3 \times 131072 = 393216$$

Hence, the 8th term from the end is 393216.

|TYPE IV|

Problems Based on Finding the GP

In this type of problem, two or more than two terms are given and we have to find the GP by using these terms. It can be understand with the help of following examples.

Example 9 If the 4th and 9th term of a GP are 54 and 13122 respectively, then find the GP.

Sol. Let a be the first term and r be the common ratio of GP.

Given, 4th term, $T_4 = 54$

$$\Rightarrow \quad ar^{4-1} = 54 \Rightarrow ar^3 = 54 \quad \text{...(i)}$$

and 9th term, $T_9 = 13122$

$$\Rightarrow \quad ar^{9-1} = 13122$$

$$\Rightarrow \quad ar^8 = 13122 \quad \text{...(ii)}$$

On dividing Eq. (ii) by Eq. (i), we get

$$\frac{ar^8}{ar^3} = \frac{13122}{54} \Rightarrow r^5 = 243 \Rightarrow r^5 = (3)^5$$

$$\therefore \quad r = 3$$

On putting the value of r in Eq. (i), we get

$$a(3)^3 = 54 \Rightarrow 27a = 54 \Rightarrow a = \frac{54}{27} = 2$$

$\therefore$ Required GP is $a, ar, ar^2, ar^3, \ldots$

i.e. 2, 6, 18, 54, ...

Example 10 Find four numbers forming a GP in which the third term is greater than the first term by 9 and the second term is greater than 4th by 18.

Sol. Let the GP is $a, ar, ar^2, ar^3, \ldots$

Given, third term = first term +9

$$\Rightarrow \quad T_3 = a + 9$$

$$\Rightarrow \quad ar^2 = a + 9$$

$$\Rightarrow \quad ar^2 - a = 9 \quad \text{...(i)}$$

Again, second term = fourth term +18

$$T_2 = T_4 + 18 \Rightarrow ar = ar^3 + 18$$

$$\Rightarrow \quad ar - ar^3 = 18 \quad \text{...(ii)}$$

On dividing Eq. (i) by Eq. (ii), we get

$$\frac{ar^2 - a}{ar - ar^3} = \frac{9}{18} \Rightarrow \frac{a(r^2 - 1)}{ar(1 - r^2)} = \frac{1}{2}$$

$$\Rightarrow \quad \frac{-1}{r}\frac{(1 - r^2)}{(1 - r^2)} = \frac{1}{2} \Rightarrow -\frac{1}{r} = \frac{1}{2} \Rightarrow r = -2$$

On putting $r = -2$ in Eq. (ii)

$$a(-2) - a(-2)^3 = 18 \Rightarrow -2a + 8a = 18$$

$$\Rightarrow \quad 6a = 18 \Rightarrow a = 3$$

$\therefore$ GP is $3, 3(-2), 3(-2)^2, 3(-2)^3, \ldots$

i.e. $\quad 3, -6, 12, -24, \ldots$

Note Here, greater than word stands for excess in term.

Selection of Terms in GP

Sometimes we have to select certain number of terms in GP.The convenient method of selecting terms is given below

Number of terms	Terms	Common ratio
3	$\frac{a}{r}, a, ar$	r
4	$\frac{a}{r^3}, \frac{a}{r}, ar, ar^3$	r^2
5	$\frac{a}{r^2}, \frac{a}{r}, a, ar, ar^2$	r

It is clear from the above table that, if number of terms is odd, then the middle term is a and common difference is r and if number of terms is even, then the middle terms are a/r, ar and the common ratio is r^2.

Note If the terms of the GP are not given, then the terms are chosen as $a, ar, ar^2, ar^3, \dots$.

Example 11 Find four numbers in GP, whose sum is 85 and product is 4096.

Sol. Let the four numbers in GP be

$$\frac{a}{r^3}, \frac{a}{r}, ar, ar^3 \quad \text{...(i)}$$

Product of four numbers = 4096 [given]

$$\Rightarrow \left(\frac{a}{r^3}\right)\left(\frac{a}{r}\right)(ar)(ar^3) = 4096$$

$$\Rightarrow a^4 = 4096 \Rightarrow a^4 = 8^4$$

On comparing the base of the power 4, we get

$$a = 8$$

and sum of four numbers = 85 [given]

$$\Rightarrow \frac{a}{r^3} + \frac{a}{r} + ar + ar^3 = 85 \Rightarrow a\left[\frac{1}{r^3} + \frac{1}{r} + r + r^3\right] = 85$$

$$\Rightarrow 8\left[r^3 + \frac{1}{r^3}\right] + 8\left[r + \frac{1}{r}\right] = 85 \quad [\because a = 8]$$

$$\Rightarrow 8\left[\left(r + \frac{1}{r}\right)^3 - 3\left(r + \frac{1}{r}\right)\right] + 8\left(r + \frac{1}{r}\right) = 85$$

$$[\because a^3 + b^3 = (a+b)^3 - 3(a+b)]$$

$$\Rightarrow 8\left(r + \frac{1}{r}\right)^3 - 16\left(r + \frac{1}{r}\right) - 85 = 0 \quad \text{...(ii)}$$

On putting $\left(r + \frac{1}{r}\right) = x$ in Eq. (ii), we get

$$8x^3 - 16x - 85 = 0$$

$$\Rightarrow (2x - 5)(4x^2 + 10x + 17) = 0$$

$$\Rightarrow 2x - 5 = 0 \quad [\because 4x^2 + 10x + 17 = 0 \text{ has imaginary roots}]$$

$$\Rightarrow x = \frac{5}{2} \Rightarrow r + \frac{1}{r} = \frac{5}{2} \quad \left[\text{put } x = r + \frac{1}{r}\right]$$

$$\Rightarrow 2r^2 - 5r + 2 = 0$$

$$\Rightarrow (r-2)(2r-1) = 0 \Rightarrow r = 2 \text{ or } r = \frac{1}{2}$$

On putting $a = 8$ and $r = 2$ or $r = \frac{1}{2}$ in Eq. (i), we get

four numbers as $\frac{8}{2^3}, \frac{8}{2}, 8 \times 2, 8 \times 2^3$

$$\text{or } \frac{8}{(1/2)^3}, \frac{8}{(1/2)}, 8 \times \frac{1}{2}, 8 \times \left(\frac{1}{2}\right)^3$$

i.e. 1, 4, 16, 64 or 64, 16, 4, 1.

Example 12 Let S be the sum, P be the product and R be the sum of the reciprocals of 3 terms of a GP. Then, find $P^2R^3 : S^3$.

Sol. Let us take a GP with three terms $\frac{a}{r}, a, ar$.

Then, $$S = \frac{a}{r} + a + ar = \frac{a(r^2 + r + 1)}{r}$$

$$P = \left(\frac{a}{r}\right)(a)(ar) = a^3 \text{ and } R = \frac{r}{a} + \frac{1}{a} + \frac{1}{ar} = \frac{1}{a}\left(\frac{r^2 + r + 1}{r}\right)$$

Now, $$\frac{P^2R^3}{S^3} = \frac{a^6 \cdot \frac{1}{a^3}\left(\frac{r^2 + r + 1}{r}\right)^3}{a^3\left(\frac{r^2 + r + 1}{r}\right)^3} = 1$$

Therefore, the required ratio is 1 : 1.

Properties of a Geometric Progression

(i) If all the terms of a GP are multiplied by the same quantity, then the resulting sequence is also a GP with the same common ratio.

(ii) The reciprocals of the terms of a given GP also form a GP.

(iii) If each term of a GP is raised to same power, then the resulting sequence is also a GP.

(iv) In a finite GP, the product of the terms equidistant from the beginning and from the end is always same and is equal to the product of the first and the last terms.

(v) The resulting sequence formed by taking the product of the corresponding terms of two GP's is also a GP.

(vi) The resulting sequence formed by dividing the terms of a GP by the corresponding terms of another GP is also a GP.

(vii) If the terms of a given GP are chosen at regular intervals, then the new sequence forms a GP.

Example 13 If a, b, c and d are in GP, then show that

$(a^2 + b^2 + c^2)(b^2 + c^2 + d^2) = (ab + bc + cd)^2$. **[NCERT]**

Sol. Given, a, b, c, d are in GP.

$$\therefore \quad \frac{b}{a} = \frac{c}{b} = \frac{d}{c} = r \text{ (say)}$$

$$\Rightarrow b = ar, c = br, d = cr$$

$$\Rightarrow b = ar, c = (ar)r, d = (br)r$$

$$\Rightarrow b = ar, c = ar^2, d = br^2$$

$$\Rightarrow b = ar, c = ar^2, d = (ar)r^2 = ar^3 \quad \text{...(i)}$$

Now, we have to prove that

$$(a^2+b^2+c^2)(b^2+c^2+d^2)=(ab+bc+cd)^2$$

$$\begin{aligned}\text{LHS} &= (a^2+b^2+c^2)(b^2+c^2+d^2)\\ &= (a^2+a^2r^2+a^2r^4)(a^2r^2+a^2r^4+a^2r^6)\\ &= a^2(1+r^2+r^4)a^2r^2(1+r^2+r^4)\\ &= a^4r^2(1+r^2+r^4)^2=[a^2r(1+r^2+r^4)]^2\\ &= [a^2r+a^2r^3+a^2r^5]^2\\ &= [a\cdot ar+ar\cdot ar^2+ar^2\cdot ar^3]^2\\ &= [ab+bc+cd]^2 \qquad \text{[from Eq. (i)]}\\ &= \text{RHS}\end{aligned}$$

Example 14 If a, b, c are respectively the pth, qth and rth terms of a GP, show that

$$(q-r)\log a+(r-p)\log b+(p-q)\log c=0.$$

Sol. Let A be the first term and R the common ratio of the given GP.

Then, $a = p\text{th term} \Rightarrow a = AR^{p-1}$

$\Rightarrow \log a = \log A + (p-1)\log R$ ...(i)

$b = q\text{th term} \Rightarrow b = AR^{q-1}$

$\Rightarrow \log b = \log A + (q-1)\log R$ ...(ii)

$c = r\text{th term} \Rightarrow c = AR^{r-1}$

$\Rightarrow \log c = \log A + (r-1)\log R$ ...(iii)

Now, LHS $=(q-r)\log a+(r-p)\log b+(p-q)\log c$

On substituting the values of log a, log b and log c, we get

$$\begin{aligned}\text{LHS} &= (q-r)\{\log A+(p-1)\log R\}\\ &\quad +(r-p)\{\log A+(q-1)\log R\}\\ &\quad +(p-q)\{\log A+(r-1)\log R\}\\ &= \log A\{(q-r)+(r-p)+(p-q)\}\\ &\quad +\log R\{(p-1)(q-r)+(q-1)(r-p)+(r-1)(p-q)\}\\ &= (\log A)0+\{p(q-r)+q(r-p)\\ &\quad +r(p-q)-(q-r)-(r-p)-(p-q)\}\log R\\ &= (\log A)0+(\log R)0=0=\text{RHS}\end{aligned}$$

Topic Practice 4

Very Short Answer Type Questions

2 Marks

1 Which term of the following sequences

(i) $\sqrt{3}, 3, 3\sqrt{3}, \dots$ is 729 ?

(ii) $\frac{1}{3}, \frac{1}{9}, \frac{1}{27}, \dots$ is $\frac{1}{19683}$?

2 For what value of x are the numbers $(x+9)$, $(x-6)$ and 4 are in GP?

3 Show that the following progressions is a GP. Also, find the common ratio in each case.

(i) $4, -2, 1, -1/2, \dots$ (ii) $a, \frac{3a^2}{4}, \frac{9a^3}{16}, \dots$

4 Find the term of the following GP.

(i) 11th term of the GP 3, 6, 12, 24, ...

(ii) 10th term of the G.P 12, 4, $\frac{4}{3}, \frac{4}{9}, \dots$

(iii) 17th term of the GP $2, 2\sqrt{2}, 4, 8\sqrt{2}, \dots$

(iv) 8th term of the GP 0.3, 0.06, 0.012, ...

(v) 12th term of the GP $\frac{1}{a^3x^3}, ax, a^5x^5, \dots$

5 Find the 10th term of the GP $5+25+125+\dots$. Also, find its nth term.

6 Find 12th term of a GP, whose 8th term is 192 and common ratio is 2.

7 Find the 6th term from the end of the GP $8, 4, 2, \dots, \frac{1}{1024}$.

8 Find the geometric series whose 5th and 8th terms are 80 and 640, respectively.

Short Answer Type Questions

4 Marks

9 If $a, b, c\ d$ are in GP, then prove that $a^2-b^2, b^2-c^2, c^2-d^2$ are also in GP.

10 Find the 20th and nth terms of the GP; $\frac{5}{2}, \frac{5}{4}, \frac{5}{8}, \dots$.

11 Prove that in a finite GP the product of the terms equidistant form the beginning and the end is always same and equal to the product of first and last term.

12 Find a GP for which sum of the first two terms is -4 and fifth term is 4 times the third term.

13 The first term of a GP is 1. the sum of the third term and fifth term is 90. Find the common ratio of the GP.

14 The sum of first three terms of a GP is $\frac{39}{10}$ and their product is 1. Find the common ratio and the terms.

15 The sum of three numbers in GP is 21 and the sum of their squares is 189. Find the numbers.

16 If the pth, qth and rth terms of a GP are a, b and c respectively, then prove that $a^{q-r}\, b^{r-p}\, c^{p-q} = 1$.

17 If the first and nth terms of a GP are a and b respectively and P is the product of n terms, then prove that $p^2 = (ab)^n$.

18 The sum of first three terms of a GP is $\frac{13}{12}$ and their product is -1. Find the terms.

19 Find the three numbers in GP, whose sum is 19 and product is 216.

Hints & Answers

1. (i) Here, $a = \sqrt{3},\ r = \frac{3}{\sqrt{3}} = \sqrt{3},\ T_n = 729$

$\because \quad T_n = ar^{n-1}$ **Ans.** 12

(ii) Here, $a = \frac{1}{3},\ r = \frac{1/9}{1/3} = \frac{3}{9} = \frac{1}{3}$

and $T_n = \frac{1}{19683}$

Now, apply the formula, $T_n = ar^{n-1}$. **Ans.** 9

2. 0 or 16

3. (i) $-\frac{1}{2}$ (ii) $\frac{3a}{4}$

4. (i) 3072 (ii) $\frac{4}{6561}$ (iii) 512

(iv) $(0.3)(0.2)^7$ (v) $(ax)^{41}$

5. $5^{10}, 5^n$

6. Here, $T_8 = 192$ and $r = 2$

$\because \quad T_8 = ar^{8-1} = ar^7$

$\therefore \quad a = \frac{3}{2}$

Now, $\quad T_{12} = 3072$

7. $\frac{1}{32}$

8. $5 + 10 + 20 + 40 + \ldots$

9. Here, $\frac{b}{a} = \frac{c}{b} = \frac{d}{c} = r$

$\Rightarrow \quad b = ar,\ c = br = ar^2,\ d = cr = ar^3$

Now, $\quad a^2 - b^2 = a^2 - a^2r^2 = a^2(1 - r^2)$

$b^2 - c^2 = a^2r^2 - a^2r^4 = a^2r^2\,(1 - r^2)$

and $\quad c^2 - d^2 = a^2r^4 - a^2r^6 = a^2r^4\,(1 - r^2)$

Therefore, $\frac{b^2 - c^2}{a^2 - b^2} = \frac{c^2 - d^2}{b^2 - c^2} = r^2$

10. Here, a = first term $= \frac{5}{2}$ and

common ratio $(r) = \frac{5/4}{5/2} = \frac{2}{4} = \frac{1}{2}$

$T_{20} = \frac{5}{2^{20}}$ and $T_n = \frac{5}{2^n}$

11. a_k = kth term from the begining $= a_1 r^{k-1}$

a_{n-k+1} = kth term from the end $= a_n \left(\frac{1}{r}\right)^{k-1}$

where, $1 < k < n$

$$a_k\, a_{n-k+1} = (a_1 r^{k-1})\, a_n \left(\frac{1}{r}\right)^{k-1} = a_1 a_n$$

for all k satisfying $1 < k < n$.

12. Given, $\quad a + ar = -4$ ...(i)

and $\quad T_5 = 4T_3 \Rightarrow ar^{5-1} = 4ar^{3-1} \Rightarrow r = \pm 2$

If $r = 2$, then from Eq. (i),

$$a + a(2) = -4 \Rightarrow 3a = -4$$

$\therefore \quad a = -\frac{4}{3}$

If $r = -2$, then from Eq. (i),

$$a + a(-2) = -4 \Rightarrow -a = -4$$

$\therefore \quad a = 4$

Hence, GP is $\ldots -\frac{4}{3}, -\frac{8}{3}, -\frac{16}{3}, \ldots$ or $4, -8, 16, \ldots$

13. Let the GP be $a, ar, ar^2, ar^3, \ldots$

Given, $a = 1$ and $T_3 + T_5 = 90$

$\therefore \quad ar^2 + ar^4 = 90 \Rightarrow r^2 + r^4 = 90$

$\Rightarrow \quad r^4 + r^2 - 90 = 0$ [as $a = 1$]

$\Rightarrow \quad (r^2 + 10)(r^2 - 9) = 0$ **Ans.** $r = \pm 3$

14. Here, $\quad \frac{a}{r} + a + ar = \frac{39}{10}$ and $\left(\frac{a}{r}\right) \times (a) \times (ar) = 1$

$\Rightarrow \quad a^3 = 1 \Rightarrow a = 1$

On putting the value of $a = 1$ in Eq. (i) we get

$$\frac{1}{r} + 1 + r = \frac{39}{10} \Rightarrow \frac{1 + r + r^2}{r} = \frac{39}{10}$$

$\Rightarrow \quad 10r^2 - 29r + 10 = 0$

$\Rightarrow \quad (5r - 2)(2r - 5) = 0$

$\therefore \quad r = \frac{2}{5}$ or $r = \frac{5}{2}$

When $a = 1$ and $r = \frac{2}{5}$, then the numbers are $\frac{5}{2}, 1, \frac{2}{5}$.

When $a = 1$ and $r = \frac{5}{2}$, then the numbers are $\frac{2}{5}, 1, \frac{5}{2}$.

15. $a + ar + ar^2 = 21$

$\Rightarrow \quad a^2 + (ar)^2 + (ar^2)^2 = 189$

Ans. (3, 6, 12) or (12, 6, 3)

16. Given, $T_p = a \Rightarrow AR^{p-1} = a$ ...(i)

$T_q = b \Rightarrow AR^{q-1} = b$ ...(ii)

and $T_r = c \Rightarrow AR^{r-1} = c$ ...(iii)

Now, LHS $= a^{q-r} b^{r-p} b^{p-q}$

17. Let the GP be $A, AR, AR^2, AR^3 ...$

Given, first term, $A = a$ ...(i)

and nth term, $AR^{n-1} = b$ ...(ii)

Now, p = Product of n terms

$\Rightarrow p = A \times AR^1 \times AR^2 \times AR^3 \times ... \times n$ terms

$\Rightarrow p = A^{1+1+1+...+n \text{ terms}} R^{1+2+3+...+(n-1)}$

$\Rightarrow p = A^n R^{\frac{n(n-1)}{2}}$

$\Rightarrow p^2 = A^n A^n R^{n(n-1)} = A^n (AR^{n-1})^n$

$\Rightarrow p^2 = a^n b^n$ [using Eqs. (i) and (ii)]

18. Here, sum $= \frac{a}{r} + a + ar = \frac{13}{12}$

$\Rightarrow a(1 + r + r^2) = \frac{13}{12} r$ ...(i)

Their product $= \frac{a}{r} \cdot a\, ar = -1$

$\Rightarrow a^3 = -1$

$\Rightarrow a = -1$ [taking cube root both sides] ...(ii)

On putting the value of a in Eq. (i), we get

$$(-1)[1 + r + r^2] = \frac{13}{12} r$$

$\Rightarrow 12r^2 + 25r + 12 = 0$

$\therefore r = -\frac{4}{3}$ or $r = \frac{-3}{4}$

When $a = -1$ and $r = -\frac{4}{3}$, then the numbers are $\frac{3}{4}, -1, \frac{4}{3}$.

When $a = -1$ and $r = -\frac{3}{4}$, then the numbers are $\frac{4}{3}, -1, \frac{3}{4}$.

19. Product of three numbers $= \frac{a}{r} \cdot a \cdot ar = 216$

$\therefore a = 6$

And sum of three numbers $= \frac{a}{r} + a + ar = 19$

$\Rightarrow 6 + 6r + 6r^2 = 19r \Rightarrow 6r^2 - 13r + 6 = 0$

$\therefore r = \frac{13 \pm \sqrt{(-13)^2 - 4 \cdot 6 \cdot 6}}{2 \cdot 6} = \frac{13 \pm 5}{12} = \frac{3}{2}$ or $\frac{2}{3}$

When $r = \frac{3}{2}$, then the numbers are 4, 6, 9.

When $r = \frac{2}{3}$, then the numbers are 9, 6, 4.

TOPIC 05 Sum of First n Terms of a GP

If a and r are the first term and common ratio of a GP respectively, then sum of n terms of this GP is given by

$$S_n = \frac{a(1 - r^n)}{1 - r}, \text{ where } r < 1$$

or

$$S_n = \frac{a(r^n - 1)}{r - 1}, \text{ where } r > 1\ (r \neq 1)$$

Note

(i) If $r = 1$, then $S_n = a + a + ... n$ terms $= na$

(ii) Suppose a GP contains n terms with first term $= a$, common ratio $= r$ and last term $= l$. The sum of GP

$$S_n = \frac{a - lr}{1 - r}, \text{ where } r < 1$$

or

$$S_n = \frac{lr - a}{r - 1}, \text{ where } r > 1$$

Sum of an Infinite GP

If a is the first term and r is the common ratio of a GP such that $|r| < 1$, then sum of an infinite GP is given by

$$S = \frac{a}{1 - r}$$

Problems Based on Sum of Terms of a GP

There are so many problems which can be solved by using the sum of terms of a finite GP or infinite GP directly or indirectly i.e. we can find the values of other terms related to GP with the help of sum formula.

Some types of these problems are given below

|TYPE I|

Problems Based on Finding the Sum of Given Number of Terms of Finite GP

In this type of problems, a finite GP is given and we have to find sum of given number of terms.

Example 1 Find the sum of the following sequences.

(i) $\frac{1}{2}, \frac{3}{2}, \frac{9}{2}, ...$ upto 10 terms

(ii) $2, -\frac{1}{2}, \frac{1}{8}, ...,$ upto 12 terms

Sol. (i) We have, sequence $\frac{1}{2}, \frac{3}{2}, \frac{9}{2}, \ldots$

Clearly, the successive ratio of the terms is same.

So, the above sequence forms a GP, with first term, $a = \frac{1}{2}$ and common ratio, $r = \frac{3}{2} \div \frac{1}{2} = 3$.

$$\therefore \quad S_{10} = \frac{\frac{1}{2}[3^{10} - 1]}{3 - 1} \quad \left[\because S_n = \frac{a(r^n - 1)}{r - 1} \text{ as } r > 1\right]$$

$$= \frac{1}{2}\frac{(3^{10} - 1)}{2} = \frac{1}{4}[3^{10} - 1] = 14762$$

(ii) We have, sequence $2, -\frac{1}{2}, \frac{1}{8}, \ldots$

Clearly, the successive ratio of the terms is same. So, the above sequence forms a GP with first term, $a = 2$ and common ratio, $r = -\frac{1}{2} \div 2 = \frac{-1}{4}$.

$$\therefore \quad S_{12} = \frac{2\left[1 - \left(\frac{-1}{4}\right)^{12}\right]}{1 - \left(\frac{-1}{4}\right)} \quad \left[\because S_n = \frac{a(1 - r^n)}{1 - r} \text{ as } r < 1\right]$$

$$= \frac{2\left[1 - \frac{1}{(4)^{12}}\right]}{1 + \frac{1}{4}} = \frac{2\left[1 - \left(\frac{1}{4}\right)^{12}\right]}{\left(\frac{5}{4}\right)} = \frac{8}{5}\left[1 - \left(\frac{1}{4}\right)^{12}\right]$$

Example 2 Find the sum of the series

2 + 6 + 18 + 54 + … + 4374.

Sol. Given series is $2 + 6 + 18 + 54 + \ldots + 4374$.

Clearly, the successive ratio of the terms is same. So, the above series forms a GP with first term, $a = 2$, common ratio, $r = \frac{6}{2} = 3 > 1$ and last term, $l = 4374$.

$$\therefore \text{Required sum} = \frac{(lr - a)}{(r - 1)} = \frac{(4374 \times 3 - 2)}{(3 - 1)}$$

$$= \frac{13120}{2} = 6560$$

Hence, the sum of the given series is 6560.

Example 3 Find the sum to n terms of the sequence given by $a_n = 2^n + 3n, n \in N$.

Sol. Let S_n denote the sum to n terms of the given sequence.

Then, $S_n = a_1 + a_2 + a_3 + \ldots + a_n$

$$\Rightarrow \quad S_n = (2^1 + 3 \times 1) + (2^2 + 3 \times 2) + (2^3 + 3 \times 3) + \ldots + (2^n + 3 \times n)$$

$$\Rightarrow \quad S_n = (2^1 + 2^2 + 2^3 + \ldots + 2^n) + (3 \times 1 + 3 \times 2 + 3 \times 3 + \ldots + 3 \times n)$$

$$= (2^1 + 2^2 + 2^3 + \ldots + 2^n) + 3(1 + 2 + 3 + \ldots + n)$$

$$= 2\left(\frac{2^n - 1}{2 - 1}\right) + 3\left\{\frac{n}{2}(1 + n)\right\}$$

[$\because 2 + 2^2 + 2^3 + 2^n$ is a GP and $1 + 2 + 3 + \ldots + n$ is an AP]

$$= 2(2^n - 1) + \frac{3n}{2}(n + 1)$$

Example 4 Find the sum of series

$\frac{3}{5} + \frac{4}{5^2} + \frac{3}{5^3} + \frac{4}{5^4} + \ldots$ to $2n$ terms.

Sol. We have, $S = \frac{3}{5} + \frac{4}{5^2} + \frac{3}{5^3} + \frac{4}{5^4} + \ldots$ to $2n$ terms

$$= \left[\frac{3}{5} + \frac{3}{5^3} + \ldots + \text{to } n \text{ terms}\right] + \left[\frac{4}{5^2} + \frac{4}{5^4} + \ldots + \text{to } n \text{ terms}\right]$$

$$= \frac{\frac{3}{5}\left[1 - \left(\frac{1}{5^2}\right)^n\right]}{\left[1 - \left(\frac{1}{5^2}\right)\right]} + \frac{\frac{4}{5^2}\left[1 - \left(\frac{1}{5^2}\right)^n\right]}{\left[1 - \left(\frac{1}{5^2}\right)\right]}$$

$$\left[\because \text{sum of GP} = \frac{a(1 - r^n)}{1 - r}, |r| < 1\right]$$

$$= \frac{\frac{3}{5}\left[1 - \frac{1}{5^{2n}}\right]}{1 - \frac{1}{25}} + \frac{\frac{4}{25}\left[1 - \frac{1}{5^{2n}}\right]}{1 - \frac{1}{25}}$$

$$= \frac{\frac{3}{5}\left[1 - \frac{1}{5^{2n}}\right]}{\frac{24}{25}} + \frac{\frac{4}{25}\left[1 - \frac{1}{5^{2n}}\right]}{\frac{24}{25}}$$

$$= \frac{5}{8}\left[1 - \frac{1}{5^{2n}}\right] + \frac{1}{6}\left[1 - \frac{1}{5^{2n}}\right]$$

$$= \left[1 - \frac{1}{5^{2n}}\right]\left[\frac{5}{8} + \frac{1}{6}\right] = \left[1 - \frac{1}{5^{2n}}\right]\left[\frac{15 + 4}{24}\right]$$

$$= \frac{19}{24}\left[1 - \frac{1}{5^{2n}}\right]$$

Example 5 A GP consists of an even number of terms. If the sum of all the terms is 5 times the sum of terms occupying odd places, then find its common ratio.

Sol. Let the GP is $a, ar, ar^2, ar^3, ar^4, \ldots, ar^{2n-2}, ar^{2n-1}$, where $a, ar^2, ar^4, ar^6, \ldots$ occupy odd places and $ar, ar^3, ar^5, ar^7 \ldots$ occupy even places.

According to the question,

Sum of all terms

= 5 × Sum of terms occupying odd places

i.e. $a + ar + ar^2 + \ldots + ar^{2n-1}$

$$= 5 \times (a + ar^2 + ar^4 + \ldots + ar^{2n-2})$$

$$\Rightarrow \frac{a(r^{2n}-1)}{r-1}=\frac{5a[(r^2)^n-1]}{r^2-1} \quad \left[\because S_n=\frac{a(r^n-1)}{r-1}, r>1\right]$$

$$\Rightarrow \frac{r^{2n}-1}{r-1}=\frac{5(r^{2n}-1)}{(r-1)(r+1)} \Rightarrow 1=\frac{5}{r+1}$$

$$\Rightarrow r+1=5 \Rightarrow r=4$$

Note Students should remember that if a GP has $2n$ (even terms), then there are n even and n odd terms.

Example 6 Find the sum of the products of the corresponding terms of the sequence 2, 4, 8, 16, 32 and 128, 32, 8, 2, $\frac{1}{2}$.

Sol. Given, sequences are 2, 4, 8, 16, 32 ...(i)

and 128, 32, 8, 2, $\frac{1}{2}$ ...(ii)

Multiplying the corresponding terms of Eqs. (i) and (ii) we get a new sequence, 256, 128, 64, 32, 16

Let $S=256+128+64+32+16$

Clearly, the successive ratio of the terms is same. So, the above obtained series forms a GP, with first term,

$a=256$ and comon ratio, $r=\frac{128}{256}=\frac{1}{2}$.

$$\therefore \text{ Required sum, } S_n=\frac{256\left[1-\left(\frac{1}{2}\right)^5\right]}{1-\frac{1}{2}}=256\times 2\left(1-\frac{1}{2^5}\right)$$

$$\left[\because S_n=\frac{a(1-r^n)}{1-r}, r<1\right]$$

$$=512\times\left(1-\frac{1}{32}\right)$$

$$=512\left(\frac{32-1}{32}\right)=16\times 31=496$$

Example 7 The sum of the first three terms of a GP is 16 and the sum of next three terms is 128. Determine the first term, the common ratio and the sum to n terms of the GP. **[NCERT]**

Sol. Let the GP be $a, ar, ar^2, ar^3, \ldots$

According to the given condition,

Sum of first three terms $=a+ar+ar^2=16$ ...(i)

and sum of next three terms $=ar^3+ar^4+ar^5=128$ ...(ii)

On dividing Eq. (i) by Eq. (ii), we get

$$\frac{a+ar+ar^2}{ar^3+ar^4+ar^5}=\frac{16}{128}$$

$$\Rightarrow \frac{a(1+r+r^2)}{ar^3(1+r+r^2)}=\frac{1}{8} \Rightarrow \left(\frac{1}{r}\right)^3=\left(\frac{1}{2}\right)^3$$

On comparing the base of the power 3 from both sides, we get $\frac{1}{r}=\frac{1}{2} \Rightarrow r=2$

On putting $r=2$ in Eq. (i), we get

$$a+2a+4a=16 \Rightarrow 7a=16 \Rightarrow a=\frac{16}{7}$$

Now, sum of n terms, $S_n=\frac{a(r^n-1)}{r-1}$ $[\because r=2>1]$

$$=\frac{\frac{16}{7}(2^n-1)}{2-1}=\frac{16}{7}(2^n-1)$$

Hence, $a=\frac{16}{7}$, $r=2$ and $S_n=\frac{16}{7}(2^n-1)$

Example 8 If S_1, S_2 and S_3 are respectively the sum of n, $2n$ and $3n$ terms of a GP, then prove that $S_1(S_3-S_2)=(S_2-S_1)^2$.

Sol. Let a be the first term and r be the common ratio of the given GP.

Then,

$$S_1(S_3-S_2)=\frac{a(1-r^n)}{(1-r)}\cdot\left\{\frac{a(1-r^{3n})}{(1-r)}-\frac{a(1-r^{2n})}{(1-r)}\right\}$$

$$=\frac{a(1-r^n)}{(1-r)}\cdot\frac{(a-ar^{3n}-a+ar^{2n})}{(1-r)}$$

$$=\frac{a(1-r^n)}{(1-r)}\cdot\frac{ar^{2n}(1-r^n)}{(1-r)}$$

$$=\frac{a^2r^{2n}(1-r^n)^2}{(1-r)^2} \quad \text{...(i)}$$

$$\text{and } (S_2-S_1)^2=\left\{\frac{a(1-r^{2n})}{(1-r)}-\frac{a(1-r^n)}{(1-r)}\right\}^2$$

$$=\frac{(a-ar^{2n}-a+ar^n)^2}{(1-r)^2}$$

$$=\frac{\{(ar^n(1-r^n)\}^2}{(1-r)^2}=\frac{a^2r^{2n}(1-r^n)^2}{(1-r)^2} \quad \text{...(ii)}$$

Hence, from Eqs. (i) and (ii), we get

$$S_1(S_3-S_2)=(S_2-S_1)^2$$

Example 9 Let S be the sum, P be the product and R be the sum of reciprocals of n terms in a GP. Prove that $P^2R^n=S^n$.

Sol. Let the GP is $a, ar, ar^2, ar^3 \ldots ar^{n-1}$.

Given, $S=$ Sum of n terms

$$=a+ar+ar^2+ar^3+\ldots+ar^{n-1}$$

$$=\frac{a(r^n-1)}{r-1} \quad [\text{let } r>1] \quad \text{...(i)}$$

and R = Sum of the reciprocals of n terms

$$= \frac{1}{a} + \frac{1}{ar} + \frac{1}{ar^2} + \dots + \frac{1}{ar^{n-1}} \left(\frac{1}{r} < 1\right)$$

$$= \frac{\frac{1}{a}\left[1 - \left(\frac{1}{r}\right)^n\right]}{1 - \frac{1}{r}} = \frac{1}{a}\left[\frac{1}{1} - \frac{1}{r^n}\right] \times \frac{1}{\frac{r-1}{r}}$$

$$= \frac{1}{a}\left[\frac{r^n - 1}{r^n}\right] \times \frac{r}{r-1} \Rightarrow R = \frac{(r^n - 1)r}{ar^n(r-1)} \quad \text{...(ii)}$$

and $\quad P$ = Product of n terms

$$= a \times ar \times ar^2 \times ar^3 \times \dots \times ar^{n-1}$$

$$= a^{1+1+1+\dots+n \text{ terms}} \, r^{1+2+3+\dots+(n-1)\text{terms}}$$

$$= a^n r^{\frac{n(n-1)}{2}}$$

[$\because 1 + 2 + 3 + \dots + (n-1)$th terms, is an AP]

$$\Rightarrow \quad P^2 = a^{2n} r^{n(n-1)} \quad \text{...(iii)}$$

Now, we have to prove $P^2 R^n = S^n$

or $\quad P^2 = \frac{S^n}{R^n}$ or $P^2 = \left(\frac{S}{R}\right)^n$

$$\text{RHS} = \left(\frac{S}{R}\right)^n = \left[\frac{a(r^n - 1)}{r - 1} \times \frac{ar^n(r-1)}{(r^n - 1)r}\right]^n$$

[using Eqs. (i) and (ii)]

$$= [a^2 r^n r^{-1}]^n = (a^2 r^{n-1})^n = [a^{2n} r^{n(n-1)}]$$

$$= P^2 = \text{LHS} \quad \text{[from Eq. (iii)]}$$

Hence proved.

Note Students should remembered that if you are taking $r < 1$ in S, then you have to take $r > 1$ in R.

|TYPE III|

Problems Based on Finding the Sum of Terms of an Infinite GP

In this type of problems, an infinite GP is given and we have to find the sum of the infinite GP.

Example 10 Find the sum of an infinite GP

$$1, \frac{1}{3}, \frac{1}{9}, \dots \infty.$$

Sol. Given infinite GP is $1, \frac{1}{3}, \frac{1}{9}, \dots \infty$

Here, $a = 1$ and $r = \frac{1}{3} \div 1 = \frac{1}{3}$

We know that, $S_\infty = \frac{a}{1 - r}$

$$\therefore \quad S_\infty = \frac{1}{1 - \frac{1}{3}} = \frac{1}{\frac{2}{3}} = \frac{3}{2}$$

Example 11 If $b = a + a^2 + a^3 + \dots \infty$, then prove that $a = \frac{b}{1+b}$.

Sol. We have, $b = a + a^2 + a^3 + \dots \infty$

Clearly, RHS is a geometric series with first term 'a' and common ratio 'a'

$$\therefore \quad b = \frac{a}{1-a} \Rightarrow b - ab = a \Rightarrow a = \frac{b}{1+b}$$

Example 12 Find the sum of the series

$$9^{1/3} \cdot 9^{1/9} \cdot 9^{1/27} \dots \infty$$

Sol. Let $E = 9^{\frac{1}{3}} \cdot 9^{1/9} \cdot 9^{1/27} \dots \infty = 9^{\frac{1}{3} + \frac{1}{9} + \frac{1}{27} + \dots \infty}$ ...(i)

Again let $S_\infty = \frac{1}{3} + \frac{1}{9} + \frac{1}{27} + \dots \infty$

Clearly, the successive ratio of the terms is same. So, the abvoe obtained series forms a GP, with first term, $a = \frac{1}{3}$ and common ratio, $\frac{1}{9} \div \frac{1}{3} = \frac{1}{3}$.

Then, $\quad S_\infty = \frac{\frac{1}{3}}{1 - \frac{1}{3}} = \frac{1}{2} \quad \left[\because S_\infty = \frac{a}{1-r}\right]$

Then, from Eq. (i), we get $E = 9^{\frac{1}{2}} = 3$

Example 13 If $|x| < 1$ and $|y| < 1$, find the sum of infinity of the following series:

$$(x + y) + (x^2 + xy + y^2) + (x^3 + x^2y + xy^2 + y^3) + \dots$$

Sol. We have,

$$(x + y) + (x^2 + xy + y^2) + (x^3 + x^2y + xy^2 + y^3) + \dots \infty$$

$$= \frac{1}{x - y}\{(x^2 - y^2) + (x^3 - y^3) + (x^4 - y^4) + \dots \text{to } \infty\}$$

$$\left[\because \frac{x^n - a^n}{x - a} = x^{n-1} \cdot a^0 + x^{n-2} \cdot a + x^{n-3} a^2 + \dots + a^{n-1}, n \in N\right]$$

$$= \frac{1}{x - y}\{(x^2 + x^3 + x^4 + \dots \text{to } \infty) - (y^2 + y^3 + y^4 + \dots \text{to } \infty)\}$$

$$= \frac{1}{x - y}\left\{\frac{x^2}{1 - x} - \frac{y^2}{1 - y}\right\}$$

$$= \frac{1}{x - y} \frac{\{x^2 - x^2y - y^2 + y^2x\}}{(1 - x)(1 - y)}$$

$$= \frac{1}{(x - y)} \frac{\{(x^2 - y^2) - xy(x - y)\}}{(1 - x)(1 - y)} = \frac{x + y - xy}{(1 - x)(1 - y)}$$

Example 14 If $x = \sum_{n=0}^{\infty} \cos^{2n}\theta,\ y = \sum_{n=0}^{\infty} \sin^{2n}\phi,$

$z = \sum_{n=0}^{\infty} \cos^{2n}\theta \sin^{2n}\phi$, where $0 < \theta, \phi < \pi/2$, then prove that $xz + yz - z = xy$.

Sol. We have, $x = \sum_{n=0}^{\infty} \cos^{2n}\theta = 1 + \cos^2\theta + \cos^4\theta + \ldots \infty$

$$\Rightarrow \quad x = \frac{1}{1-\cos^2\theta} \Rightarrow \sin^2\theta = \frac{1}{x}$$

$$y = \sum_{n=0}^{\infty} \sin^{2n}\phi = 1 + \sin^2\phi + \sin^4\phi + \ldots \infty$$

$$\Rightarrow \quad y = \frac{1}{1-\sin^2\phi} \Rightarrow \cos^2\phi = \frac{1}{y}$$

and $\quad z = \sum_{n=0}^{\infty} \cos^{2n}\theta \sin^{2n}\phi$

$$= 1 + \cos^2\theta\sin^2\phi + \cos^4\theta\sin^4\phi + \ldots \infty$$

$$\Rightarrow \quad z = \frac{1}{1-\cos^2\theta\sin^2\phi}$$

$$\Rightarrow \quad z = \frac{1}{1-(1-\sin^2\theta)(1-\cos^2\phi)}$$

$$\Rightarrow \quad z = \frac{1}{1-\left(1-\frac{1}{x}\right)\left(1-\frac{1}{y}\right)} \Rightarrow z = \frac{1}{\frac{1}{x}+\frac{1}{y}-\frac{1}{xy}}$$

$$\Rightarrow \quad z = \frac{xy}{x+y-1} \Rightarrow xz + yz - z = xy$$

|TYPE III|

Problems Based on Finding the Value of Unknown/GP when Sum of *n* Terms of a Finite GP is Given

In this type of problems, a GP and sum is given and we have to find r and n. Sometimes GP is not given and we have to find a, r and then GP with the help of given information related to sum.

Example 15 How many terms of GP $3, \frac{3}{2}, \frac{3}{4}, \ldots$ are needed to give the sum $\frac{3069}{512}$? [NCERT]

Sol. Given, GP is $3, \frac{3}{2}, \frac{3}{4}, \ldots$

Here, $\quad a = 3, r = \frac{3}{2} \div 3 = \frac{1}{2}$

Let n be the number of terms needed.

Then, $\quad S_n = \frac{3069}{512} \Rightarrow \frac{a(1-r^n)}{1-r} = \frac{3069}{512} \quad [\because r < 1]$

$$\Rightarrow \quad \frac{3\left\{1-\frac{1}{2^n}\right\}}{1-\frac{1}{2}} = \frac{3069}{512}$$

$$\Rightarrow \quad 6\left(1-\frac{1}{2^n}\right) = \frac{3069}{512} \Rightarrow 1-\frac{1}{2^n} = \frac{3069}{3072}$$

$$\Rightarrow \quad \frac{1}{2^n} = 1 - \frac{3069}{3072} = \frac{3072-3069}{3072}$$

$$\Rightarrow \quad \frac{1}{2^n} = \frac{3}{3072} = \frac{1}{1024} \Rightarrow 2^n = 1024 \Rightarrow 2^n = 2^{10}$$

On comparing the powers from both sides, we get

$$n = 10$$

Hence, 10 terms are needed to give the sum $\frac{3069}{512}$.

Example 16 Find the least value of n for which the sum $1 + 3 + 3^2 + \ldots$ to n terms is greater than 7000.

Sol. We have, $S_n = 1 + 3 + 3^2 + \ldots$ to n terms

Clearly, the successive ratio of the terms is same. So, the above series forms a GP, with first term, $a = 1$ and common ratio, $\frac{3}{1} = 3 > 1$.

$$\therefore \quad S_n = 1 \times \left(\frac{3^n - 1}{3-1}\right) = \frac{3^n-1}{2} \quad \left[\because S_n = a\left(\frac{r^n-1}{r-1}\right)\right]$$

Now, $\quad S_n > 7000$

$$\Rightarrow \quad \frac{3^n-1}{2} > 7000 \Rightarrow 3^n - 1 > 14000$$

$$\Rightarrow \quad 3^n > 14001 \Rightarrow n\log 3 > \log 14001$$

$$\Rightarrow \quad n > \frac{\log 14001}{\log 3}$$

$$\Rightarrow \quad n > \frac{4.1461}{0.4771} = 8.69$$

Hence, the least value of n is 9.

|TYPE IV|

Problems Based on Finding the Value of Unknown/GP when Sum of an Infinite GP is Given

In this type of problems, sum of an infinite GP is given and we have to find the values of unknown a, r and sometimes we have to find GP.

Example 17 The sum of an infinite GP is 57 and the sum of their cubes is 9747. Find the GP.

Sol. Let a be the first term and r be the common ratio of an infinite GP.

Given, sum = 57

$$\Rightarrow \frac{a}{1-r} = 57 \quad \text{...(i)}$$

and sum of the cubes = 9747

$$\Rightarrow a^3 + a^3r^3 + a^3r^6 + \dots = 9747$$

$$\Rightarrow \frac{a^3}{1-r^3} = 9747 \quad \text{...(ii)}$$

On dividing the cube of Eq. (i) by Eq. (ii), we get

$$\frac{a^3}{(1-r)^3} \cdot \frac{(1-r^3)}{a^3} = \frac{(57)^3}{9747}$$

$$\Rightarrow \frac{1-r^3}{(1-r)^3} = 19$$

$$\Rightarrow \frac{1+r+r^2}{(1-r)^2} = 19$$

$$[\because a^3 - b^3 = (a-b)(a^2+b^2+ab)]$$

$$\Rightarrow 1+r+r^2 = 19(1+r^2-2r)$$

$$[\because (a-b)^2 = a^2+b^2-2ab]$$

$$\Rightarrow 18r^2 - 39r + 18 = 0$$

$$\Rightarrow (3r-2)(6r-9) = 0$$

$$\Rightarrow r = 2/3 \text{ or } r = 3/2$$

$$\Rightarrow r = 2/3$$

$$[\because r \neq 3/2, \text{ because } -1 < r < 1 \text{ for an infinite GP}]$$

On putting $r = 2/3$ in Eq. (i), we get

$$\frac{a}{1-(2/3)} = 57$$

$$\Rightarrow 3a = 57 \Rightarrow a = 19$$

Hence, the required GP is $19, 19 \times \frac{2}{3}, 19 \times \left(\frac{2}{3}\right)^2, \dots$

i.e. 19, 38/3, 76/9, ...

|TYPE V|

Problems Based on Finding a Rational Number whose Decimal Expansion is Given

Sometimes a number in non-terminating repeating decimal expansion form i.e. of the form $0.a\overline{bc}$ is given and we have to write it as rational number. For finding the corresponding rational number, we use the following steps

***Step* I** First, write the given decimal expansion in the form of series.

i.e. write $0.a\overline{bc}$ as

$0.a + 0.0bc + 0.000bc + 0.00000bc + \dots \infty$.

***Step* II** Remove the decimal point from each term by multiply and divide by suitable power of 10.

i.e. $0.a\overline{bc} = \frac{a}{10} + \frac{bc}{10^3} + \frac{bc}{10^5} + \dots \infty$.

***Step* III** Now, find the sum of infinite GP obtained in step II, by suitable formula, to get required rational number.

Example 18 Write the rational number corresponding to the decimal expansion $0.3\overline{56}$.

Sol. Given decimal expansion is $0.3\overline{56}$.

In series form, it can be written as

$$0.3\overline{56} = 0.3 + 0.056 + 0.00056 + 0.0000056 + \dots \infty$$

$$\Rightarrow 0.3\overline{56} = 0.3 \times \frac{10}{10} + 0.056 \times \frac{10^3}{10^3} + 0.00056 \times \frac{10^5}{10^5} + \dots \infty$$

$$= \frac{3}{10} + \frac{56}{10^3} + \frac{56}{10^5} + \dots \infty$$

$$\Rightarrow 0.3\overline{56} = \frac{3}{10} + \left[\frac{56}{10^3} + \frac{56}{10^5} + \dots \infty\right]$$

Here, first term $a = \frac{56}{10^3}$

and common ratio $= \frac{56}{10^5} \div \frac{56}{10^3} = \frac{1}{10^2} < 1$

$$\therefore \quad 0.3\overline{56} = \frac{3}{10} + \frac{\frac{56}{10^3}}{1 - \frac{1}{10^2}} \quad \left[\because S_\infty = \frac{a}{1-r}, \text{ if } r < 1\right]$$

$$= \frac{3}{10} + \frac{56}{10^3} \times \frac{10^2}{99} = \frac{3}{10} + \frac{56}{990}$$

$$\therefore 0.3\overline{56} = \frac{353}{990}$$

|TYPE VI|

Problems Based on Finding the Sum of Special Series by Converting it into GP

In this type of problem a special series is given to find sum then we convert it into GP by suitable method and then find its sum. Let the special series of the type $S = a + aa + aaa + \dots n$ term be given.

The sum of this type of series can be find by using the following steps

***Step* I** First, take common a from each term. i.e. write given series as a $(1 + 11 + 111 + \dots n\text{th term})$.

***Step* II** Multiply and divide each term by 9.

i.e. $\frac{a}{9}(9 + 99 + 999 + \dots n\text{th term})$

Step III Write each term as difference of multiple of 10 and 1.

i.e. $\frac{a}{9}[(10-1)+(100-1)+(1000-1)+\ldots n\text{th term}]$

Step IV Separate the terms i.e.

$\frac{a}{9}[(10+10^2+10^3+\ldots n\text{th term})]-(1+1+\ldots n\text{th term})]$

Step V Find the sum of first series by using formula of GP

i.e. $\frac{a}{9}\left[\frac{10(10^n-1)}{10-1}-n\right]=\frac{a}{9}\left[\frac{10(10^n-1)}{9}-n\right]$

Example 19 Find the sum of the series $4+44+444+\ldots n$ terms.

Sol. Given series is $4+44+444+\ldots n$ terms.

On taking common 4, we get

$$S_n=4(1+11+111+\ldots n\text{ terms})$$

On multiplying and dividing each term of RHS by 9, we get

$$S_n=\frac{4}{9}(9+99+999+\ldots)$$

$$\Rightarrow S_n=\frac{4}{9}[(10-1)+(100-1)+(1000-1)+\ldots n\text{ terms}]$$

$$\Rightarrow S_n=\frac{4}{9}[(10+100+1000+\ldots n\text{ terms})-(1+1+1+\ldots n\text{ terms})\ \ldots\text{(i)}$$

For first series, $10+100+1000+\ldots n$ terms

$$r=\frac{100}{10}=10>1$$

$$\therefore S_n=10(1+10+10^2+\ldots n\text{ terms})$$

$$=10\left(\frac{10^n-1}{10-1}\right)\quad\left[\because \text{sum}=\frac{a(r^n-1)}{r-1}\right]$$

$$=\frac{10}{9}(10^n-1)$$

Now, from Eq. (i), we get

$$S_n=\frac{4}{9}\left[\frac{10}{9}(10^n-1)-n\right]=\frac{40}{81}(10^n-1)-\frac{4}{9}n$$

Applications of GP

Sometimes we can solve the some real life problems by using the concept of GP. Some of them are given below

Example 20 At the end of each year the value of a certain machine has depreciated by 20% of its value at the beginning of that year. If its initial value was ₹ 1250, then find the value at the end of 5 yr. **[NCERT Exemplar]**

Sol. Given, depreciation in value of machine = 20%

After each year the value of the machine is 80% (100 − 20)% of its value of the previous year, so at the end of 5 yr, the machine will depreciate as many times as 5.

Hence, we have to find the 6th terms of the GP whose first term a_1 is 1250 and common ratio r is (0.8).

Hence, value at the end 5 yr

$$=t_6=a_1 r^5$$

$$=1250\,(0.8)^5=409.6$$

Note In depreciation, the cost value decrease every year.

Example 21 The lengths of three unequal edges of a rectangular solid block are in GP. If the volume of the block is 216 cm^3 and the total surface area is 252 cm^2, then find the length of its edges. **[NCERT Exemplar]**

Sol. Let the length, breadth and height of rectangular solid block is $\frac{a}{r}$, a and ar, respectively.

$\therefore$ Volume $=\frac{a}{r}\times a\times ar=216\text{ cm}^3$

$\Rightarrow a^3=216\Rightarrow a^3=6^3$

$\therefore a=6$

Surface area $=2\left(\frac{a^2}{r}+a^2r+a^2\right)=252$

$\Rightarrow 2a^2\left(\frac{1}{r}+r+1\right)=252$

$\Rightarrow 2\times 36\left(\frac{1+r^2+r}{r}\right)=252$

$\Rightarrow \frac{1+r^2+r}{r}=\frac{252}{2\times 36}$

$\Rightarrow 1+r^2+r=\frac{126}{36}r$

$\Rightarrow 1+r^2+r=\frac{21}{6}r$

$\Rightarrow 6+6r^2+6r=21r$

$\Rightarrow 6r^2-15r+6=0$

$\Rightarrow 2r^2-5r+2=0$

$\Rightarrow (2r-1)(r-2)=0\Rightarrow r=\frac{1}{2}$ or 2

For $r=\frac{1}{2}$, length $=\frac{a}{r}=\frac{6\times 2}{1}=12$

Breadth $=a=6$ and height $=ar=6\times\frac{1}{2}=3$

For $r=2$, length $=\frac{a}{r}=\frac{6}{2}=3$

Breadth $=a=6$

and height $=ar=6\times 2=12$

Topic Practice 5

Very Short Answer Type Questions

2 Marks

1 Find the sum of following geometric progressions

(i) (a) $\sqrt{7}, \sqrt{21}, 3\sqrt{7}, \ldots n$ terms

(b) $1, -a, a^2, -a^3, \ldots n$ terms (if $a \neq -1$)

(ii) (a) $1, \sqrt{3}, 3, 3\sqrt{3} \ldots$ upto 10 terms

(b) 0.15, 0.015, 0.0015, ... 20 terms

2 Evaluate $\sum_{k=1}^{11}(2+3^k)$.

3 The sum of some terms of GP is 315, whose first term and common ratio are 5 and 2, respectively. Find the last term and number of terms. **[NCERT]**

4 Find the sum to infinity of the following GP.

(i) 6, 1.2, 0.24, ... ∞ (ii) 10, – 9, 8.1, ... ∞

5 The common ratio of a GP is $-\frac{4}{5}$ and the sum to infinity is $\frac{80}{9}$. Find the first term.

6 A person has 2 parents, 4 grandparents and so on. Find the numbers of his ancestors during the ten generations preceding his own. **[NCERT]**

7 How many terms of the series $1+3+3^2+3^3+\ldots$ must be taken to make 3280?

8 The first term of a GP is 27 and its 8th term is $\frac{1}{81}$. Find the sum of its first 10 terms.

9 The 2nd and 5th terms of a GP are $\frac{-1}{2}$ and $\frac{1}{16}$, respectively. Find the sum of the GP upto 8 terms.

10 In a GP of even number of terms, the sum of all terms is 5 times the sum of the odd terms. Then, common ratio of the GP. **[NCERT Exemplar]**

11 Given a GP with $a = 729$ and 7th term 64, determine S_7. **[NCERT]**

12 Show that the ratio of the sum of the first n terms of a GP to the sum of terms from $(n+1)$th to $(2n)$th term is $\frac{1}{r^n}$. **[NCERT]**

13 The sum of an infinite geometric series is 15 and the sum of the squares of these terms is 45. Find the series.

Short Answer Type Questions

4 Marks

14 Find the sum of the following series

(i) $5 + 55 + 555 + \ldots$ upto n terms.

(ii) $7 + 77 \times 777 + \ldots$ upto n terms. **[NCERT]**

15 Find the sum of the following series

(i) $0.6 + 0.66 + 0.666 + \ldots$ upto n terms

(ii) $0.3 + 0.33 + 0.333 + \ldots$ upto n terms **[NCERT]**

16 Represent the following as rational numbers $0.1\overline{5}$.

17 Find the three numbers in GP, whose sum is 52 and sum of whose product in pairs is 624.

18 In a GP $[a_n]$, if $T_1 = 3$, $T_n = 96$ and $S_n = 189$, then find n.

19 If $x = a + \frac{a}{r} + \frac{a}{r^2} + \ldots \infty$, $y = b - \frac{b}{r} + \frac{b}{r^2} - \ldots \infty$ and $z = c + \frac{c}{r^2} + \frac{c}{r^4} + \ldots \infty$, then prove that $\frac{xy}{z} = \frac{ab}{c}$.

20 Prove that $2^{\frac{1}{2}} \cdot 4^{\frac{1}{8}} \cdot 8^{\frac{1}{24}} \cdot 16^{\frac{1}{64}} \ldots \infty = 2$.

21 The inventor of the chessboard suggested a reward of one grain of wheat for the first square; 2 grains for the second; 4 grains for the third and so on, doubling the number of grains for subsequent squares. How many grains would have to be given to the inventor? (Note that there are 64 squares in the chessboard.)

Long Answer Type Questions

6 Marks

22 The side of a given square is equal to a. The mid-points of its sides are joined to form a new square. Again, the mid-points of the sides of this new square are joined to form another square. This process is continued indefinitely. Find the sum of the areas of the squares and the sum of the perimeters of the squares.

23 Rajeev buys a scooter for ₹22000. He pays ₹ 4000 cash and agrees to pay the balance in annual instalment of ₹ 1000 plus 10% interest on the unpaid amount. How much will scooter cost him?

24 If $S_1, S_2, S_3, \ldots, S_p$ denote the sum of infinite GP whose first terms are 1, 2, 3, ..., p respectively and whose common ratios are $\frac{1}{2}, \frac{1}{3}, \frac{1}{4}, \ldots, \frac{1}{p+1}$, respectively. Show that

$$S_1 + S_2 + S_3 + \ldots + S_p = \frac{p(p+3)}{2}.$$

25 If f is a function satisfying $f(x+y)=f(x)+(y)$ for all $x, y \in N$ such that $f(1)=3$ and $\sum_{x=1}^{n} f(x)=120$, find the value of n.

Hints & Answers

1. (i) (a) Here, $a=\sqrt{7}, r=\frac{\sqrt{21}}{\sqrt{7}}=\frac{\sqrt{7\times 3}}{\sqrt{7}}=\sqrt{3}>1$

$$\Rightarrow \quad S_n=\frac{\sqrt{7}[(\sqrt{3})^n-1]}{\sqrt{3}-1}=\frac{\sqrt{7}}{2}(\sqrt{3}+1)(3^{n/2}-1)$$

(b) Here, $a=1, r=-\frac{a}{1}=-a<1$

$$S_n=\frac{1\{1-(-a)^n\}}{1-(-a)}=\frac{1-(-a)^n}{1+a}$$

(ii) (a) Solve as part (i) (a). **Ans.** $121(\sqrt{3}+1)$

(b) Solve as part (i) (a). **Ans.** $\frac{1}{6}[1-(0.1)^{20}]$

2. $\sum_{k=1}^{11} 2+\sum_{k=1}^{11} 3^k=2\times 11+(3^1+3^2+3^3+\ldots+3^{11})$

$$=22+\frac{3(3^{11}-1)}{3-1}=22+\frac{3(3^{11}-1)}{2}$$

3. Here, $a=5$ and $r=2$

$$\because \quad \frac{a(r^n-1)}{r-1}=315 \Rightarrow \frac{5(2^n-1)}{2-1}=315$$

Ans. Number of terms $=6$ and last term $=160$.

4. (i) Here, $a=6$ and $r=\frac{T_2}{T_1}=\frac{1.2}{6}=0.2$

Since, $|0.2|=0.2<1$ **Ans.** $S_\infty=7.5$

(ii) Here, $a=10$ and $r=\frac{T_2}{T_1}=\frac{-9}{10}=-0.9$

Since, $|-0.9|=0.9<1$ **Ans.** $S_\infty=\frac{100}{19}$

5. We have, $r=-\frac{4}{5}$ and $S=\frac{80}{9}$.

$$\therefore \quad \frac{80}{9}=\frac{a}{1-\left(\frac{-4}{5}\right)}$$ **Ans.** $a=16$

6. Here, $a=2, r=\frac{4}{2}=2$ and $n=10$

$$\because \quad S_{10}=\frac{2(2^{10}-1)}{2-1}=2(2^{10}-1)=2(1024-1)=2046$$

7. Here, $a=1, r=\frac{3}{1}=3$, then $\frac{1\cdot(3^n-1)}{3-1}=3280$ **Ans.** $n=8$

8. $\frac{1}{81}=27(r)^{8-1} \Rightarrow r=\frac{1}{3}$ **Ans.** $\frac{81}{2}\left(1-\frac{1}{3^{10}}\right)$

9. $\frac{85}{128}$

10. We have, $\frac{a(r^{2n}-1)}{r-1}=\frac{5a((r^2)^n-1)}{r^2-1}$

$$\Rightarrow \quad \frac{a(r^{2n}-1)}{r-1}=5\frac{a(r^{2n}-1)}{(r^2-1)} \Rightarrow r=4$$

11. $ar^{7-1}=64 \Rightarrow r^6=\left(\frac{2}{3}\right)^6 \Rightarrow r=\frac{2}{3}$

$$\therefore \quad S_7=\frac{729\left[1-\left(\frac{2}{3}\right)^7\right]}{1-\frac{2}{3}}=2059$$

12. Let the GP is $\underbrace{ar, ar^2, ar^3, ar^4, ar^5, \ldots, ar^{n-1}}_{n \text{ terms}}, \underbrace{ar^n, ar^{n+1}, \ldots, ar^{2n-1}}_{n \text{ terms}}$

$$\text{Now, required ratio}=\frac{\dfrac{a(r^n-1)}{r-1}}{\dfrac{ar^n(r^n-1)}{r-1}}$$

13. $\because$ Sum $=15 \Rightarrow \frac{a}{1-r}=15$

and sum of the squares $=45$

$$\Rightarrow \quad (a^2+a^2r^2+a^2r^2+\ldots\infty)=45$$

$$\Rightarrow \quad \frac{a^2}{1-r^2}=45 \quad \frac{a^2}{(1-r)^2}\times\frac{1-r^2}{a^2}=\frac{(15)^2}{45}$$

Ans. $5+\frac{10}{3}+\frac{20}{9}+\frac{40}{27}+\ldots\infty$.

14. (i) $5+55+555+\ldots$ n terms

$$=\frac{5}{9}(9+99+999+\ldots n \text{ terms})$$

$$=\frac{5}{9}[(10-1)+(10^2-1)+(10^3-1)+\ldots+(10^n-1)]$$

$$=\frac{5}{9}[(10+10^2+10^3+\ldots+10^n)-(1+1+1+\ldots+1)\ n \text{ terms}]$$

$$=\frac{5}{9}\left[10\left(\frac{10^n-1}{10-1}\right)-n\right]$$ **Ans.** $\frac{50}{81}(10^n-1)-\frac{5n}{9}$

(ii) Solve as part (i). **Ans.** $\frac{70}{81}(10^n-1)-\frac{7n}{9}$

15. (i) $6\times 0.1+6\times 0.11+6\times 0.111+\ldots$ n terms

$$=\frac{6}{9}[0.9+0.99+0.999+\ldots n \text{ terms}]$$

$$=\frac{2}{3}\left[\frac{9}{10}+\frac{99}{100}+\frac{999}{1000}+\ldots n \text{ terms}\right]$$

$$=\frac{2}{3}\left[\left(1-\frac{1}{10}\right)+\left(1-\frac{1}{100}\right)+\left(1-\frac{1}{1000}\right)+\ldots n \text{ terms}\right]$$

$$= \frac{2}{3}\left[(1+1+1+\ldots n \text{ terms}) - \left(\frac{1}{10}+\frac{1}{10^2}+\frac{1}{10^3}+\ldots n \text{ terms}\right)\right]$$

Ans. $\frac{2}{3}n - \frac{2}{27}(1-10^{-n})$

(ii) $\frac{1}{3}n - \frac{1}{27}(1-10^{-n})$

16. $0.1\bar{5} = 0.15555\ldots = 0.1 + 0.05 + 0.005 + 0.0005 + \ldots \infty]$

$$= 0.1 + \left[\frac{5}{100}+\frac{5}{1000}+\frac{5}{10000}+\ldots\infty\right] = 0.1 + \frac{\left(\frac{5}{100}\right)}{1-\frac{1}{10}} = \frac{7}{45}$$

17. $\frac{a}{r} + a + ar = 52 \Rightarrow a\left(\frac{1}{r}+1+r\right) = 52$ ...(i)

and $\frac{a}{r}\cdot a + a\cdot ar + \frac{a}{r}\cdot ar = 624 \Rightarrow a^2\left(\frac{1}{r}+r+1\right) = 624$ ...(ii)

On dividing Eq. (ii) by Eq. (i), we get $a = 12$

On putting $a = 12$ in Eq. (i), we get

$$12\left(\frac{1}{r}+r+1\right) = 52 \Rightarrow r = \frac{1}{3} \text{ or } r = 3$$

Ans. When $r = \frac{1}{3}$, then numbers are 36, 12, 4.

When $r = 3$, then numbers are 4, 12, 36.

18. Here, $T_1 = a = 3$, $T_n = 96$ and $S_n = 189$

$$S_n = \frac{a(r^n - 1)}{r-1} = \frac{ar^n - a}{r-1}$$

$$\Rightarrow \quad S_n = \frac{(ar^{n-1})r - a}{r-1} \Rightarrow 189 = \frac{96r - a}{r-1} \Rightarrow r = 2$$

Now, $T_n = ar^{n-1} \Rightarrow 96 = 3 \times 2^{n-1}$

$\Rightarrow \quad 2^5 = 2^{n-1}$

On equating exponential power from both sides, we get

$$n = 6$$

19. Clearly, x, y and z are the sums of infinite geometric progressions.

$$\therefore \quad x = \frac{a}{1-\frac{1}{r}} = \frac{ar}{r-1},\ y = \frac{b}{1-\left(-\frac{1}{r}\right)} = \frac{br}{1+r}$$

and $$z = \frac{c}{1-\frac{1}{r^2}} = \frac{cr^2}{r^2-1}$$

Now, $$xy = \left(\frac{ar}{r-1}\right)\left(\frac{br}{r+1}\right) = \frac{abr^2}{r^2-1}$$

$$\Rightarrow \quad \frac{xy}{z} = \left\{\left(\frac{abr^2}{r^2-1}\right) \div \frac{cr^2}{(r^2-1)}\right\} = \frac{ab}{c}$$

20. $2^{1/2}\cdot 4^{1/8}\cdot 8^{1/24}\cdot 16^{1/64}\ldots\infty$

$$= 2^{\frac{1}{2}}\cdot 2^{\frac{1}{4}}\cdot 2^{\frac{3}{24}}\cdot 2^{\frac{1}{16}}\ldots = 2^{\frac{1}{2}+\frac{1}{4}+\frac{1}{8}+\frac{1}{16}+\ldots\infty}$$

21. Required number of grains $= 1 + 2 + 2^2 + \ldots$ to 64 terms

$$= 1 + (2 + 2^2 + 2^3 + \ldots + 2^{63})$$

$$= \left\{1 + \frac{2(2^{63}-1)}{(2-1)}\right\} = (2^{64} - 1)$$

22. Since the diagonal of a square is $\sqrt{2}$ times the sides of a square, we get the following series as an infinite GP of the areas of the squares.

$$a^2 + \left(\sqrt{2}\times\frac{a}{2}\right)^2 + \left(\sqrt{2}\times\sqrt{2}\times\frac{a}{4}\right)^2 + \left(\sqrt{2}\times\sqrt{2}\times\sqrt{2}\times\frac{a}{8}\right)^2 + \ldots \text{ to } \infty$$

$$= a^2 + \frac{a^2}{2} + \frac{a^2}{4} + \frac{a^2}{8} + \ldots \text{ to } \infty$$

$$\therefore \quad S_\infty = \frac{a^2}{1-\frac{1}{2}} = 2a^2 \text{ sq units.}$$

Ans. $4\sqrt{2}(\sqrt{2}+1)$ sq units

23. ₹ 39100

24. $\because S_1 = \frac{1}{1-\frac{1}{2}} = 2,\ S_2 = \frac{2}{1-\frac{1}{3}} = 3,\ S_3 = \frac{3}{1-\frac{1}{4}} = 4$

....

....

and $$S_p = \frac{p}{1-\frac{1}{p+1}} = p+1$$

25. Given, $f(x+y) = f(x)f(y)$ ...(i)

Putting $x = y = 1$ in Eq. (i), we get

$$f(1+1) = f(1)f(1) \Rightarrow f(2) = 3\times 3 = 9 \quad [\because f(1) = 3]$$

Putting $x = 2$, $y = 1$ in Eq. (i),

$$f(2+1) = f(2)f(1)$$

$$\Rightarrow \quad f(3) = 9\times 3 = 27 \quad [\because f(2) = 9,\ f(1) = 3]$$

Putting $x = 3$, $y = 1$ in Eq. (i), we get

$$f(3+1) = f(3)f(1)$$

$$\Rightarrow \quad f(4) = 27\times 3 = 81 \quad [\because f(3) = 27]$$

Now, $\sum_{x=1}^{n} f(x) = 120$

$$\Rightarrow f(1) + f(2) + f(3) + \ldots + f(n) = 120$$

$$\Rightarrow \quad 3 + 9 + 27 + \ldots n \text{ terms} = 120$$

$$= \frac{3(3^n - 1)}{3-1} = 120 \quad \left[\text{here, } a = 3,\ r = \frac{9}{3} = 3\right]$$

$$\Rightarrow 3(3^n - 1) = 120\times 2 \Rightarrow 3(3^n - 1) = 240$$

$$\Rightarrow \quad 3^n - 1 = \frac{240}{3} \Rightarrow 3^n - 1 = 80 \Rightarrow 3^n = 80 + 1$$

On comparing the power of 3 from both sides, we get

$$3^n = 81 \Rightarrow 3^n = 3^4 \Rightarrow n = 4$$

TOPIC 06 Geometric Mean and Relation between AM & GM

Geometric Mean (GM)

Let a and b be two positive numbers. If we insert a single number G between them, so that a, G, b is a GP, then G is called **geometric mean**.

Thus, a, G and b are in GP.

$$\therefore \quad \frac{G}{a} = \frac{b}{G} \Rightarrow G^2 = ab \Rightarrow \boxed{G = \sqrt{ab}}$$

Inserting Two or More Geometric Means between any Two Numbers

Let a and b be two positive numbers and $G_1, G_2, G_3, \ldots, G_n$ be the n GM's between a and b.

Then, $a, G_1, G_2, G_3, \ldots, G_n, b$ are in GP with common ratio r and number of terms are $n+2$.

Here, b is $(n+2)$th term.

i.e. $$b = T_{n+2} = ar^{n+1} \Rightarrow r = \left(\frac{b}{a}\right)^{\frac{1}{n+1}}$$

Thus, the n geometric means are given below

$$G_1 = ar = a\left(\frac{b}{a}\right)^{\frac{1}{n+1}}$$

$$G_2 = ar^2 = a\left(\frac{b}{a}\right)^{\frac{2}{n+1}}$$

....

....

$$G_n = ar^n = a\left(\frac{b}{a}\right)^{\frac{n}{n+1}}$$

Example 1 Find a geometric mean of 4 and 16.

Sol. Geometric mean between 4 and 16 $= \sqrt{4 \times 16} = \sqrt{64} = 8$

Example 2 Insert two numbers between 3 and 81, so that resulting sequence is GP. **[NCERT]**

Sol. Let the two numbers are a and b, then 3, a, b, 81 are in GP.

$\because$ nth term, $T_n = Ar^{n-1}$

$\therefore$ $T_4 = 81 = 3r^{4-1}$

$\Rightarrow$ $r^3 = \frac{81}{3}$

$\Rightarrow$ $r^3 = 27 \Rightarrow r^3 = 3^3$

On comparing the base of power 3 from both sides, we get $r = 3$,

Hence, $a = Ar = 3 \times 3 = 9$, $b = Ar^2 = 3 \times 3^2 = 27$.

Example 3 Insert 4 GM's between 3 and 96.

Sol. Let G_1, G_2, G_3 and G_4 be the required GM's. Then, 3, G_1, G_2, G_3, G_4, 96 are in GP.

Let r be the common ratio. Here, 96 is the 6th term.

$\therefore$ $96 = ar^{6-1} = 3r^5$

$\Rightarrow$ $32 = r^5 \Rightarrow (2)^5 = r^5 \Rightarrow r = 2$

$\therefore$ $G_1 = ar = 3 \cdot 2 = 6$

$G_2 = ar^2 = 3 \cdot 2^2 = 12$

$G_3 = ar^3 = 3 \cdot 2^3 = 24$

and $G_4 = ar^4 = 3 \cdot 2^4 = 48$

Example 4 If the 4th, 10th and 16th terms of a GP are x, y and z respectively, then prove that x, y and z are in GP.

Sol. Given, $T_4 = x \Rightarrow ar^{4-1} = x \Rightarrow ar^3 = x$ ...(i)

$T_{10} = y \Rightarrow ar^{10-1} = y \Rightarrow ar^9 = y$ ...(ii)

and $T_{16} = z \Rightarrow ar^{16-1} = z \Rightarrow ar^{15} = z$ ...(iii)

On multiplying Eq. (i) by Eq. (iii), we get

$ar^3 \times ar^{15} = x \times z \Rightarrow a^2r^{3+15} = xz$

$\Rightarrow$ $a^2r^{18} = xz \Rightarrow (ar^9)^2 = xz$

$\Rightarrow$ $y^2 = xz$ [from Eq. (ii)]

Therefore, x, y, z are in GP.

Example 5 If a, b, c, d are in GP, then prove that $a+b$, $b+c$, $c+d$ are also in GP.

Sol. Let r be the common ratio of the GP a, b, c, d. Then,

$b = ar$, $c = ar^2$ and $d = ar^3$

$\therefore$ $a + b = a + ar = a(1 + r)$, $b + c = ar + ar^2$

$= ar(1 + r)$ and $c + d = ar^2 + ar^3 = ar^2(1 + r)$

Now, $(b + c)^2 = \{ar(1 + r)\}^2 = a^2r^2(1 + r)^2$

$= \{a(1 + r)\}\{ar^2(1 + r)\} = (a + b)(c + d)$

$[\because a + b = a(1 + r)$ and $c + d = ar^2(1 + r)]$

Here, $a + b$, $b + c$, $c + d$ are in GP.

Example 6 If $a^2 + b^2$, $ab + bc$ and $b^2 + c^2$ are in GP, then prove that a, b, c are also in GP.

Sol. Given that $a^2 + b^2$, $ab + bc$, $b^2 + c^2$ are in GP.

$$\therefore \quad (ab+bc)^2 = (a^2+b^2)(b^2+c^2)$$

$$\Rightarrow a^2b^2 + b^2c^2 + 2ab^2c = a^2b^2 + a^2c^2 + b^2c^2 + b^4$$

$$\Rightarrow \quad b^4 + a^2c^2 - 2ab^2c = 0$$

$$\Rightarrow (b^2 - ac)^2 = 0 \Rightarrow b^2 = ac \Rightarrow a, b, c \text{ are in GP.}$$

Example 7 If a, b, c and d are in GP, then prove that $a^n + b^n$, $b^n + c^n$, $c^n + d^n$ are in GP. **[NCERT]**

Sol. Given a, b, c, d are in GP.

$$\Rightarrow \quad b = ar,\ c = ar^2,\ d = ar^3 \quad \text{...(i)}$$

Now, we have to prove $a^n + b^n$, $b^n + c^n$, $c^n + d^n$ are in GP.

$$\Rightarrow \quad (b^n + c^n)^2 = (a^n + b^n)(c^n + d^n)$$

Now, $\text{RHS} = (a^n + b^n)(c^n + d^n)$

$$= [a^n + a^n r^n] \times [a^n r^{2n} + a^n r^{3n}] \quad \text{[from Eq. (i)]}$$

$$= a^n(1 + r^n)a^n r^{2n}(1 + r^n)$$

$$= a^{2n} r^{2n}(1 + r^n)^2 = [a^n r^n (1 + r^n)]^2$$

$$= [a^n r^n + a^n r^{2n}]^2$$

$$= [(ar)^n + (ar^2)^n]^2 = [b^n + c^n]^2 \quad \text{[from Eq. (i)]}$$

$$= \text{LHS}$$

$\therefore \quad$ LHS = RHS **Hence proved.**

Example 8 The sum of two numbers is 6 times their geometric mean, show that the numbers are in the ratio $(3 + 2\sqrt{2}) : (3 - 2\sqrt{2})$. **[NCERT]**

After taking the given condition, we will use componendo and dividendo,

i.e. $\dfrac{a}{b} = \dfrac{c}{d} \Rightarrow \dfrac{a+b}{a-b} = \dfrac{c+d}{c-d}$.

Sol. Let the numbers are a and b.

According to the question $a + b = 6\sqrt{ab}$

$$\Rightarrow \quad \frac{a+b}{2\sqrt{ab}} = \frac{3}{1}$$

Now, applying componendo and dividendo, we get

$$\frac{a+b+2\sqrt{ab}}{a+b-2\sqrt{ab}} = \frac{3+1}{3-1}$$

$$\Rightarrow \quad \frac{(\sqrt{a})^2 + (\sqrt{b})^2 + 2\sqrt{ab}}{(\sqrt{a})^2 + (\sqrt{b})^2 - 2\sqrt{ab}} = \frac{4}{2}$$

$$\Rightarrow \quad \frac{(\sqrt{a}+\sqrt{b})^2}{(\sqrt{a}-\sqrt{b})^2} = \frac{2}{1}$$

$$\Rightarrow \quad \frac{\sqrt{a}+\sqrt{b}}{\sqrt{a}-\sqrt{b}} = \frac{\sqrt{2}}{1}$$

Again, applying componendo and dividendo, we get

$$\frac{\sqrt{a}+\sqrt{b}+\sqrt{a}-\sqrt{b}}{\sqrt{a}+\sqrt{b}-(\sqrt{a}-\sqrt{b})} = \frac{\sqrt{2}+1}{\sqrt{2}-1}$$

$$\Rightarrow \quad \frac{2\sqrt{a}}{2\sqrt{b}} = \frac{\sqrt{2}+1}{\sqrt{2}-1}$$

$$\Rightarrow \quad \frac{\sqrt{a}}{\sqrt{b}} = \frac{\sqrt{2}+1}{\sqrt{2}-1}$$

Now, on squaring both sides, we get

$$\frac{a}{b} = \frac{(\sqrt{2}+1)^2}{(\sqrt{2}-1)^2}$$

$$\Rightarrow \quad \frac{a}{b} = \frac{2+1+2\sqrt{2}}{2+1-2\sqrt{2}} \quad \left[\begin{array}{l} \because (a+b)^2 = a^2 + b^2 + 2ab \text{ and} \\ (a-b)^2 = a^2 + b^2 - 2ab \end{array}\right]$$

$$\Rightarrow \quad \frac{a}{b} = \frac{3+2\sqrt{2}}{3-2\sqrt{2}}$$

$$\therefore \quad a : b = (3 + 2\sqrt{2}) : (3 - 2\sqrt{2})$$

Example 9 Prove that the product of n GMs between any two positive numbers is equal to nth power of the GM between them.

Sol. Let $G_1, G_2, \ldots, G_n$ be the n GMs between positive numbers a and b. Then, $a, G_1, G_2, G_3, \ldots, G_n, b$ are in GP. Let r be the common ratio of this GP and b is $(n+2)$ th term.

Now, $\quad b = T_{n+2} = ar^{n+1}$

$$\Rightarrow \quad r = \left(\frac{b}{a}\right)^{\frac{1}{n+1}}$$

Product of n GMs between a and b

$$= G_1, G_2, \ldots, G_n = ar \cdot ar^2, \ldots, ar^n$$

$$= a^n\, r^{1+2+\ldots+n} = a^n \cdot r^{\frac{n}{2}[2a+(n-1)d]}$$

$$= a^n \cdot r^{\frac{n(n+1)}{2}} = a^n \left[\left(\frac{b}{a}\right)^{\frac{1}{n+1}}\right]^{\frac{n(n+1)}{2}} \quad \left[\because r = \left(\frac{b}{a}\right)^{1/n+1}\right]$$

$$= a^n \left(\frac{b}{a}\right)^{\frac{n}{2}} = a^{n-\frac{n}{2}} \cdot b^{\frac{n}{2}} = a^{\frac{n}{2}} \cdot b^{\frac{n}{2}} = (\sqrt{ab})^n$$

Hence, product of n GMs between a and b is equal to the nth power of the GM between a and b.

Relation between AM and GM

Let A and G be the AM and GM of two positive real numbers a and b, respectively.

Then, $A=\dfrac{a+b}{2}$ and $G=\sqrt{ab}$

Now, $A-G=\dfrac{a+b}{2}-\sqrt{ab}=\dfrac{a+b-2\sqrt{ab}}{2}$

$\Rightarrow\quad A-G=\dfrac{(\sqrt{a}-\sqrt{b})^2}{2}\geq 0\Rightarrow \boxed{A\geq G}$

Method of Finding Two Numbers when AM and GM are Given

Let A and G be the AM and GM between two positive numbers, then the two positive numbers will be

$$a=A+\sqrt{A^2-G^2}\text{ and }b=A-\sqrt{A^2-G^2}$$

e.g. Suppose arithmetic mean is $A=5$ and geometric mean is $G=3$. Then, the two numbers will be

$$a=A+\sqrt{A^2-G^2}=5+\sqrt{(5)^2-(3)^2}$$
$$=5+\sqrt{25-9}=5+\sqrt{16}=5+4=9$$

and $$b=A-\sqrt{A^2-G^2}=5-\sqrt{(5)^2-(3)^2}$$
$$=5-\sqrt{25-9}=5-\sqrt{16}=5-4=1$$

Example 10 If arithmetic mean and geometric mean between two numbers is 5 and 4 respectively, then find the two numbers.

Sol. Given, arithmetic mean, $A=5$

and geometric mean, $G=4$

Let the two numbers be a and b.

Then, $a=A+\sqrt{A^2-G^2}$ and $b=A-\sqrt{A^2-G^2}$

$\therefore\quad a=5+\sqrt{5^2-4^2}$ and $b=5-\sqrt{5^2-4^2}$

$\Rightarrow\quad a=5+\sqrt{25-16}$ and $b=5-\sqrt{25-16}$

$\Rightarrow\quad a=5+\sqrt{9}$ and $b=5-\sqrt{9}$

$\Rightarrow\quad a=5+3$ and $b=5-3\Rightarrow a=8$ and $b=2$

Hence, the required numbers are 2 and 8.

Example 11 Find two positive numbers whose difference is 12 and whose AM exceeds the GM by 2.

Sol. Let the two numbers be a and b such that $a>b$.

Given, $a-b=12$ ...(i)

and AM − GM = 2

$\Rightarrow\quad \dfrac{a+b}{2}-\sqrt{ab}=2\quad\left[\because \text{AM}=\dfrac{a+b}{2}\text{ and GM}=\sqrt{ab}\right]$

$\Rightarrow\quad a+b-2\sqrt{ab}=4$

$\Rightarrow\quad (\sqrt{a}-\sqrt{b})^2=4$

$\Rightarrow\quad \sqrt{a}-\sqrt{b}=2$ ...(ii)

Now, $a-b=12$

$\Rightarrow\quad (\sqrt{a}+\sqrt{b})(\sqrt{a}-\sqrt{b})=12$

$[\because x^2-y^2=(x-y)(x+y)]$

$\Rightarrow\quad (\sqrt{a}+\sqrt{b})\times(2)=12$ [using Eq. (ii)]

$\Rightarrow\quad \sqrt{a}+\sqrt{b}=6$ ...(iii)

On adding Eqs. (ii) and (iii), we get

$2\sqrt{a}=8\Rightarrow\sqrt{a}=4$

$\Rightarrow\quad a=(4)^2\Rightarrow a=16$

Then, from Eq. (i), we get

$16-b=12$

$\Rightarrow\quad b=16-12=4$

Hence, the required numbers are 16 and 4.

Example 12 Find the minimum value of 4^x+4^{1-x}, $x\in R$. **[NCERT Exemplar]**

Sol. We know that, AM ≥ GM

$\therefore\quad \dfrac{4^x+\dfrac{4}{4^x}}{2}\geq\sqrt{4^x\times\dfrac{4}{4^x}}$

$\Rightarrow\quad 4^x+\dfrac{4}{4^x}\geq 2\sqrt{4}$

$\Rightarrow\quad 4^x+\dfrac{4}{4^x}\geq 4$

Hence, the minimum value of given expression is 4.

Example 13

(i) If a, b, c, d are four distinct positive quantities in AP, then show that $bc>ad$.

(ii) If a, b, c, d are four distinct positive quantities in GP then show that $a+d>b+c$. **[NCERT Exemplar]**

Sol. (i) Given a, b, c, d are in AP and we know that AM > GM, then for the first three terms.

$b>\sqrt{ac}\quad\left[\text{here, }\dfrac{a+c}{2}=b\right]$

On squaring both sides, we get

$b^2>ac$ ...(i)

Similarly, for the last three terms

$c>\sqrt{bd}\quad\left[\text{here, }\dfrac{b+d}{2}=c\right]$

$\Rightarrow\quad c^2>bd$ ...(ii)

On multiplying Eqs. (i) and (ii), we get

$b^2c^2>(ac)(bd)$

$\Rightarrow\quad bc>ad$

(ii) Given, a, b, c, d are in GP and we know that AM > GM then for the first three terms

$$\frac{a+c}{2} > b \qquad [\because \sqrt{ac} = b]$$

$$\Rightarrow \quad a + c > 2b \qquad \text{...(iii)}$$

Similarly, for the last three terms

$$\frac{b+d}{2} > c \qquad [\because \sqrt{bd} = c]$$

$$\Rightarrow \quad b + d > 2c \qquad \text{...(iv)}$$

On adding Eqs. (iii) and (iv), we get

$$(a+c) + (b+d) > 2b + 2c$$

$$\Rightarrow \quad a + d > b + c$$

Example 14 The ratio of the AM and GM of two positive numbers a and b is $m : n$. Show that $a : b = (m + \sqrt{m^2 - n^2}) : (m - \sqrt{m^2 - n^2})$. **[NCERT]**

Sol. Let the AM of the number a and b is A and GM of a and b is G, then $A = \frac{a+b}{2}$ and $G = \sqrt{ab}$

Given, $A : G = m : n$

i.e. $\frac{A}{G} = \frac{m}{n} \Rightarrow \frac{a+b}{2\sqrt{ab}} = \frac{m}{n}$

On applying componendo and dividendo rule, we get

$$\frac{a+b+2\sqrt{ab}}{a+b-2\sqrt{ab}} = \frac{m+n}{m-n}$$

$$\Rightarrow \frac{(\sqrt{a})^2 + (\sqrt{b})^2 + 2\sqrt{ab}}{(\sqrt{a})^2 + (\sqrt{b})^2 - 2\sqrt{ab}} = \frac{m+n}{m-n}$$

$$\Rightarrow \frac{(\sqrt{a}+\sqrt{b})^2}{(\sqrt{a}-\sqrt{b})^2} = \frac{m+n}{m-n} \Rightarrow \frac{\sqrt{a}+\sqrt{b}}{\sqrt{a}-\sqrt{b}} = \frac{\sqrt{m+n}}{\sqrt{m-n}}$$

Again, applying componendo and dividendo rule, we get

$$\frac{(\sqrt{a}+\sqrt{b}) + (\sqrt{a}-\sqrt{b})}{(\sqrt{a}+\sqrt{b}) - (\sqrt{a}-\sqrt{b})} = \frac{\sqrt{m+n}+\sqrt{m-n}}{\sqrt{m+n}-\sqrt{m-n}}$$

$$\Rightarrow \frac{2\sqrt{a}}{2\sqrt{b}} = \frac{\sqrt{m+n}+\sqrt{m-n}}{\sqrt{m+n}-\sqrt{m-n}}$$

$$\Rightarrow \frac{\sqrt{a}}{\sqrt{b}} = \frac{\sqrt{m+n}+\sqrt{m-n}}{\sqrt{m+n}-\sqrt{m-n}}$$

Now, squaring both sides, we get

$$\frac{a}{b} = \frac{(\sqrt{m+n}+\sqrt{m-n})^2}{(\sqrt{m+n}-\sqrt{m-n})^2} \quad \left[\begin{array}{l}\because (a+b)^2 = a^2 + b^2 + 2ab \\ \text{and } (a-b)^2 = a^2 + b^2 - 2ab\end{array}\right]$$

$$\Rightarrow \frac{a}{b} = \frac{m+n+m-n+2\sqrt{m+n}\sqrt{m-n}}{m+n+m-n-2\sqrt{m+n}\sqrt{m-n}}$$

$$\Rightarrow \frac{a}{b} = \frac{2m + 2\sqrt{m^2 - n^2}}{2m - 2\sqrt{m^2 - n^2}} \qquad [\because (a+b)(a-b) = a^2 - b^2]$$

$$\Rightarrow \frac{a}{b} = \frac{m + \sqrt{m^2 - n^2}}{m - \sqrt{m^2 - n^2}}$$

or $a : b = (m + \sqrt{m^2 - n^2}) : (m - \sqrt{m^2 - n^2})$ **Hence proved.**

Problems Based on AP and GP

Sometimes, in given problem we have some terms in AP or in GP and we have to show that other given terms will be in GP or in AP.

To solve these types of problems we use the following conditions and then simplify

(i) a, b and c are in AP iff $b = \frac{a+c}{2}$.

(ii) a, b and c are in GP iff $b^2 = ac$.

Example 15 Three numbers whose sum is 15 are in AP. If 1, 4, 19 be added to them respectively, then they are in GP. Find the numbers.

Sol. Let the three numbers be $a - d, a, a + d$.

Then, sum $= 15 \Rightarrow (a - d) + a + (a + d) = 15 \Rightarrow a = 5$.

So, the numbers are $5 - d, 5, 5 + d$. Adding 1, 4, 19, respectively to these numbers, we get $6 - d, 9, 24 + d$.

These numbers are in GP.

$$\therefore \quad 9^2 = (6-d)(24+d)$$

$$\Rightarrow \quad 81 = 144 + 6d - 24d - d^2$$

$$\Rightarrow \quad d^2 + 18d - 63 = 0$$

$$\Rightarrow \quad (d + 21)(d - 3) = 0$$

$$\Rightarrow \quad d = -21 \text{ or } d = 3.$$

When $d = -21$ then numbers are $5 - (-21), 5, 5 + (-21)$ i.e., $26, 5, -16$ and when $d = 3$, then numbers are $5 - 3, 5, 5 + 3$ i.e., 2, 5, 8.

Hence, the numbers are $26, 5, -16$ or 2, 5, 8.

Example 16 If pth, qth, rth terms of an AP and GP are both a, b and c, respectively, then show that $a^{b-c} \cdot b^{c-a} \cdot c^{a-b} = 1$ **[NCERT Exemplar]**

Sol. Let A and d be the first term and common difference of AP and x, R be the first term and common ratio of GP, respectively.

According to the given condition,

$$A + (p-1)d = a \qquad \text{...(i)}$$

$$A + (q-1)d = b \qquad \text{...(ii)}$$

$$A + (r-1)d = c \qquad \text{...(iii)}$$

$$a = xR^{p-1} \qquad \text{...(iv)}$$

$$b = xR^{q-1} \qquad \text{...(v)}$$

and $$c = xR^{r-1} \qquad \text{...(vi)}$$

On subtracting Eq. (ii) from Eq. (i), we get

$$d(p-1-q+1) = a-b$$

$\Rightarrow \quad a-b = d(p-q)$ ...(vii)

On subtracting Eq. (iii) from Eq. (ii), we get

$$d(q-1-r+1) = b-c$$

$\Rightarrow \quad b-c = d(q-r)$ ...(viii)

On subtracting Eq. (i) from Eq. (iii), we get

$$d(r-1-p+1) = c-a$$

$\Rightarrow \quad c-a = d(r-p)$ ...(ix)

Now, we have to prove $a^{b-c} b^{c-a} c^{a-b} = 1$

LHS $= a^{b-c} b^{c-a} c^{a-b}$

Using Eqs. (iv), (v), (vi), (vii), (viii) and (ix), we get

$$\text{LHS} = (xR^{p-1})^{d(q-r)} (xR^{q-1})^{d(r-p)} (xR^{r-1})^{d(p-q)}$$

$$= x^{d(q-r)+d(r-p)+d(p-q)} R^{(p-1)d(q-r)+(q-1)d(r-p)+(r-1)d(p-q)}$$

$$= x^{d(q-r+r-p+p-q)} R^{d(pq-pr-q+r+qr-pq-r+p+rp-rq-p+q)}$$

$= x^0 \cdot R^0 = 1 = \text{RHS}$ **Hence proved.**

Topic Practice 6

Very Short Answer Type Questions

2 Marks

1 Find the GM between the numbers

(i) 1 and $\frac{9}{16}$ (ii) a^3b and ab^3.

2 Insert three GMs between 1 and 256. **[NCERT]**

3 Insert two numbers between 9 and 243, so that the resulting sequence is an GP.

4 Insert three numbers between $\frac{1}{3}$ and 432, so that the resulting sequence is a GP.

5 Insert four numbers between 6 and 192, so that the resulting sequence is an GP.

6 Find two numbers whose arithmetic mean is 34 and the geometric mean is 16.

7 Find the minimum values of the expression $3^x + 3^{1-x}, x \in R$. **[NCERT Exemplar]**

8 If x, y, z are positive integers, then prove that $(x+y)(y+z)(z+x) > 8xyz$. **[NCERT Exemplar]**

Short Answer Type Questions

4 Marks

9 If a, b and c are in GP, then prove that

(i) $a(b^2+c^2) = c(a^2+b^2)$

(ii) $\frac{1}{a^2-b^2} + \frac{1}{b^2} = \frac{1}{b^2-c^2}$.

10 If a, b, c and d are in GP, then prove that

(i) $\frac{ab-cd}{b^2-c^2} = \frac{a+c}{b}$

(ii) $(b+c)(b+d) = (c+a)(c+d)$.

11 The sum of the three numbers in GP is 56. If we substract the 1, 7, 21 from these numbers in that order, we obtain an arithmetic progression (AP). Find the numbers. **[NCERT]**

12 If x, $2y$ and $3z$ are in AP, where the distinct numbers x, y, z are in GP, then find the common ratio of the GP. **[NCERT Exemplar]**

13 If A is the arithmetic mean and G_1, G_2 be two geometric means between any two numbers, then prove that $\frac{G_1^2}{G_2} + \frac{G_2^2}{G_1} = 2A$.

14 Find all the sequences which are simultaneously arithmetic and geometric progressions.

15 If a, b, c are in AP and b, c, d are in GP and $\frac{1}{c}, \frac{1}{d}, \frac{1}{e}$ are in AP, then prove that a, c, e are in GP. **[NCERT]**

Long Answer Type Questions

6 Marks

16 If a, b and c are in GP, then prove that

$$\frac{a^2+ab+b^2}{bc+ca+ab} = \frac{b+a}{c+a}.$$

17 Find the value of n so that $\frac{a^{n+1}+b^{n+1}}{a^n+b^n}$ may be the geometric mean between a and b. **[NCERT]**

Hints & Answers

1. Use the formula, $G^2 = ab$

Ans. (i) $\frac{3}{4}$ (ii) a^2b^2

2. Let 1, G_1, G_2, G_3, 256 are in GP.

$\therefore \quad T_5 = 256$

$\Rightarrow \quad 1(r)^{5-1} = 256 \Rightarrow r = \pm 4$

If $r = 4$, then $G_1 = 1 \times (4)^1 = 4$;

$G_2 = 1(4)^2 = 16$

$G_3 = 1(4)^3 = 64$

and if $r = -4$, then $G_1 = 1(-4) = -4$;

$G_2 = 1(-4)^2 = 16$;

$G_3 = (-4)^3 = -64$

Ans. Hence, 4, 16, 64 or – 4, 16, – 64 are the three GMs.

3. 27, 81

4. (2, 12, 72) or (– 2, 12, – 72)

5. 12, 24, 48, 96

6. Let the two numbers be a and b such that $a > b$.

Then, $\frac{a+b}{2} = 34$ and $\sqrt{ab} = 16$

Now, $(a-b)^2 = (a+b)^2 - 4ab \Rightarrow a - b = 60$

Ans. 64 and 4.

7. We know that, AM $\geq$ GM

$\Rightarrow \quad \frac{3^x + 3^{1-x}}{2} \geq \sqrt{3^x \cdot 3^{1-x}}$ **Ans.** Minimum $= 2\sqrt{3}$

8. Since, AM > GM

$\frac{x+y}{2} > \sqrt{xy}, \frac{y+z}{2} > \sqrt{yz}$ and $\frac{z+x}{2} > \sqrt{zx}$

On multiplying the above inequalities, we get

$\frac{x+y}{2} \cdot \frac{y+z}{2} \cdot \frac{z+x}{2} > \sqrt{(xy)(yz)(zx)}$

or $(x+y)(y+z)(z+x) > 8xyz$

9. (i) a, b, c are in GP.

Let $a = a, b = ar, c = ar^2$

$\text{LHS} = a(b^2 + c^2) = a(a^2r^2 + a^2r^4)$

$= ar^2(a^2 + (ar)^2)$

$= c(a^2 + b^2)$

(ii) Solve as part (i).

10. (i) a, b, c, d are in GP.

Let $a = a, b = ar, c = ar^2, d = ar^3$

$$\text{LHS} = \frac{ab - cd}{b^2 - c^2}$$

$$= \frac{a \cdot ar - ar^2 \cdot ar^3}{a^2r^2 - a^2r^4}$$

$$= \frac{a^2r(1-r^4)}{a^2r^2(1-r^2)} = \frac{a^2r(1+r^2)}{a^2r^2} = \frac{a + ar^2}{ar} = \frac{a+c}{b}$$

(ii) Solve as part (i).

11. Given, $\quad a + ar + ar^2 = 56$ ...(i)

Again, $a - 1$, $ar - 7$, $ar^2 - 21$ are in AP.

$\Rightarrow \quad 2(ar - 7) = (a - 1) + (ar^2 - 21)$

$\Rightarrow \quad a + ar^2 - 2ar = 8$ ...(ii)

On dividing Eq. (i) by Eq. (ii), we get

$$\frac{a + ar + ar^2}{a + ar^2 - 2ar} = \frac{56}{8}$$

$\Rightarrow \quad 6r^2 - 15r + 6 = 0$

$\Rightarrow \quad r = 2, \frac{1}{2}$

If $r = 2$, then from Eq. (i),

$a + 2a + 4a = 56 \Rightarrow a = 8$

If $r = \frac{1}{2}$, then from Eq. (i),

$\frac{a}{1} + \frac{a}{2} + \frac{a}{4} = 56 \Rightarrow a = 32$

Ans. Required numbers are 8, 16, 32 or 32, 16, 8.

12. Since, x, $2y$ and $3z$ are in AP.

$\therefore \quad 4y = x + 3z$ ...(i)

And x, y, z are in GP.

$\therefore \quad y = rx$ and $z = xr^2$

On putting the value of y and z in Eq. (i), we get

$4xr = x + 3xr^2$

$\Rightarrow \quad 3r^2 - 4r + 1 = 0$

Ans. $\quad r = \frac{1}{3}$ $\quad [\because r = 1$ is not possible$]$

13. $A = \frac{a+b}{2}$ and $G_1 = ar$, $G_2 = ar^2$

where, $r = \left(\frac{b}{a}\right)^{\frac{1}{2+1}} = \left(\frac{b}{a}\right)^{1/3}$ ...(i)

$\therefore \quad \frac{G_1^2}{G_2} + \frac{G_2^2}{G_1} = \frac{a^2r^2}{ar^2} + \frac{a^2r^4}{ar}$

14. Let $T_1, T_2, T_3, \ldots$ be a sequence which is AP as well as GP.

Let $T_n = a + (n-1)d, \forall\, n \in N$

So, the sequence is $a, a + d, a + 2d, \ldots$

This is also a GP.

$\therefore \quad \frac{T_{n+1}}{T_n} = \frac{T_{n+2}}{T_{n+1}}, \forall\, n \in N$

$\Rightarrow \quad \frac{a + nd}{a + (n-1)d} = \frac{a + (n+1)d}{a + nd}$

Ans. $a, a, a \ldots$

15. Since, a, b, c are in AP.

$$\therefore \quad b = \left(\frac{a+c}{2}\right) \quad \text{...(i)}$$

Now, b, c, d are in GP.

$$\Rightarrow \quad c^2 = bd \quad \text{...(ii)}$$

Similarly, $\frac{1}{c}, \frac{1}{d}, \frac{1}{e}$ are in AP.

$$\Rightarrow \quad \frac{2}{d} = \frac{1}{c} + \frac{1}{e}$$

$$\Rightarrow \quad d = \frac{2ce}{c+e} \quad \text{...(iii)}$$

On putting the values of b and d from Eq. (i) and (iii), in Eq. (ii), we get

$$c^2 = \left(\frac{a+c}{2}\right) \times \left(\frac{2ce}{c+e}\right) \Rightarrow c^2 = ae$$

Therefore, a, c, e are in GP.

16. Solve as Question 9 (i).

17. Given, $\frac{a^{n+1} + b^{n+1}}{a^n + b^n} = \frac{a^{\frac{1}{2}} b^{\frac{1}{2}}}{1}$

$$\Rightarrow \quad a^{n+1} + b^{n+1} = a^{n+\frac{1}{2}} b^{\frac{1}{2}} + a^{\frac{1}{2}} b^{n+\frac{1}{2}}$$

$$\Rightarrow \quad (a^{n+1} - a^{n+\frac{1}{2}} b^{\frac{1}{2}}) + (b^{n+1} - a^{\frac{1}{2}} b^{n+\frac{1}{2}}) = 0$$

$$\Rightarrow \quad (a^{n+\frac{1}{2}} - b^{n+\frac{1}{2}})(a^{\frac{1}{2}} - b^{\frac{1}{2}}) = 0$$

$$\Rightarrow \quad a^{n+\frac{1}{2}} - b^{n+\frac{1}{2}} = 0 \quad [\because a^{\frac{1}{2}} - b^{\frac{1}{2}} \neq 0]$$

$$\therefore \quad a^{n+\frac{1}{2}} = b^{n+\frac{1}{2}}$$

$$\Rightarrow \quad \left(\frac{a}{b}\right)^{n+\frac{1}{2}} = 1 = \left(\frac{a}{b}\right)^0$$

$$\Rightarrow \quad n + \frac{1}{2} = 0 \Rightarrow n = -\frac{1}{2}$$

TOPIC 07 Some Special Sum

Sum of *n* Terms of Special Series

Sometimes, we can find the sum of given series directly by using some standard results. If we need to find the sum of special series without using the standard results, then it takes long time to solve it.

So, some standard result relates to sum of n terms of special series such as series of natural numbers, series of squares of natural numbers, series of cubes of natural numbers are given below

Sum of First *n* Natural Numbers

Sum of first n natural numbers 1, 2, 3, ..., n is denoted by Σn and defined as

$$1 + 2 + 3 + \ldots + n = \Sigma n = \frac{n(n+1)}{2}$$

Sum of Squares of First *n* Natural Numbers

We know that first n natural numbers are 1, 2, 3, ..., n. Then, sum of their squares is denoted by Σn^2 and defined as

$$1^2 + 2^2 + 3^2 + \ldots + n^2 = \Sigma n^2 = \frac{n(n+1)(2n+1)}{6}$$

Sum of Cubes of First *n* Natural Numbers

We know that first n natural numbers are 1, 2, 3, ..., n.

Then, sum of their cubes is denoted by Σn^3 and defined as

$$1^3 + 2^3 + 3^3 + \ldots + n^3 = \Sigma n^3 = \left[\frac{n(n+1)}{2}\right]^2$$

Method to Find the Sum of *n* Terms of a Given Series

Sometimes given series is of the form other than AP and GP, then for finding the sum of its n terms, we may use the sum of special series directly.

For solving these types of problems, we use the following steps

***Step* I** First, write the nth term of given series.

***Step* II** Simplify the nth term to write as a polynomial in n, as

$$T_n = an^3 + bn^2 + cn + d.$$

***Step* III** Take the summation from 1 to n on both sides.

***Step* IV** Use the suitable formulae Σn, Σn^2 and Σn^3 and get the required sum.

Example 1 Find the sum of n terms of the series whose nth term is given by $(2n-1)^2$. **[NCERT]**

Sol. Given, nth term $T_n = (2n-1)^2 \Rightarrow T_n = 4n^2 + 1 - 4n$

Now, $S = \Sigma T_n = \Sigma(4n^2 + 1 - 4n)$

$$= 4\Sigma n^2 + \Sigma 1 - 4\Sigma n$$

$$= \frac{4n(n+1)(2n+1)}{6} + n - \frac{4n(n+1)}{2}$$

$$\left[\because \Sigma 1 = n,\ \Sigma n = \frac{n(n+1)}{2} \text{ and } \Sigma n^2 = \frac{n(n+1)(2n+1)}{6}\right]$$

$$= n\left[\frac{2(n+1)(2n+1)}{3} + \frac{1}{1} - \frac{2(n+1)}{1}\right]$$

$$= n\left[\frac{2(2n^2 + n + 2n + 1) + 3 - 6(n+1)}{3}\right]$$

$$= \frac{n[4n^2 + 6n + 2 + 3 - 6n - 6]}{3}$$

$$= \frac{n(4n^2 - 1)}{3} = \frac{n}{3}(2n+1)(2n-1)$$

$$[\because (a^2 - b^2) = (a-b)(a+b)]$$

Example 2 Find the sum of n terms of the series $1\cdot 2 + 2\cdot 3 + 3\cdot 4 + 4\cdot 5 + \ldots$. **[NCERT]**

Sol. Let $S = 1\cdot 2 + 2\cdot 3 + 3\cdot 4 + 4\cdot 5 + \ldots$

Then, nth term, $T_n = n(n+1) = n^2 + n$

On taking summation from 1 to n both sides, we get

$$S_n = \sum_1^n T_n = \sum_1^n n^2 + \sum_1^n n$$

$$= \frac{n(n+1)(2n+1)}{6} + \frac{n(n+1)}{2}$$

$$= \frac{n(n+1)}{6}[2n + 1 + 3]$$

$$= \frac{n(n+1)}{6}[2n + 4] = \frac{n(n+1)(n+2)}{3}$$

Example 3 Find the sum of the n terms of a series $3\times 1^2 + 5\times 2^2 + 7\times 3^2 + \ldots$ **[NCERT]**

Sol. Let given series be

$$S = 3\times 1^2 + 5\times 2^2 + 7\times 3^2 + \ldots$$

First, we will split the given series into two parts which are 3, 5, 7, ... and $1^2, 2^2, 3^2, \ldots$, then find the nth term of each part separately to find the nth term of the given series.

nth term of given series,

$$T_n = (n\text{th term of } 3, 5, 7\ldots) \times (n\text{th term of } 1, 2, 3, \ldots)^2$$

$$= [3 + (n-1)2][1 + (n-1)1]^2$$

$$= (3 + 2n - 2)(n)^2 = (2n+1)n^2 = 2n^3 + n^2$$

Now, taking summation both sides, we get

$$S = \Sigma T_n = 2\Sigma n^3 + \Sigma n^2$$

$$= 2\left[\frac{n(n+1)}{2}\right]^2 + \frac{n(n+1)(2n+1)}{6}$$

$$\left[\because \Sigma n^3 = \left\{\frac{n(n+1)}{2}\right\}^2 \text{ and } \Sigma n^2 = \frac{n(n+1)(2n+1)}{6}\right]$$

$$= \frac{n(n+1)}{2}\left[2\times\frac{n(n+1)}{2} + \frac{2n+1}{3}\right]$$

$$= \frac{n(n+1)}{2}\left[\frac{3n(n+1) + 2n + 1}{3}\right]$$

$$= \frac{n(n+1)}{6}\times(3n^2 + 3n + 2n + 1)$$

$$= \frac{n(n+1)(3n^2 + 5n + 1)}{6}$$

Example 4 Find the sum of the series

$$5^2 + 6^2 + 7^2 + \ldots + 20^2.$$ **[NCERT]**

Sol. Let the given series is

$$S = 5^2 + 6^2 + 7^2 + \ldots + 20^2$$

$$= (1^2 + 2^2 + 3^2 + 4^2 + 5^2 + 6^2 + \ldots + 20^2) - (1^2 + 2^2 + 3^2 + 4^2)$$

$$= \frac{20\times(20+1)\times(2\times 20+1)}{6} - \frac{4(4+1)(2\times 4+1)}{6}$$

$$\left[\because \Sigma n^2 = \frac{n(n+1)(2n+1)}{6}\right]$$

$$= \frac{20\times 21\times 41}{6} - \frac{4\times 5\times 9}{6} = \frac{17220}{6} - \frac{180}{6}$$

$$= \frac{17220 - 180}{6} = \frac{17040}{6} = 2840$$

Example 5 Find the sum of the following series upto n terms.

$$\frac{1^3}{1} + \frac{1^3 + 2^3}{1+3} + \frac{1^3 + 2^3 + 3^3}{1+3+5} + \ldots$$

Sol. Here, nth term of numerator is $1^3 + 2^3 + 3^3 + \ldots + n^3$, so it can be written as Σn^3 and nth term of denominator is $1 + 3 + 5 + \ldots + n$ which is an AP, so write its sum of n terms. Then, nth term

$$T_n = \frac{\Sigma n^3}{\frac{n}{2}[2\times 1 + (n-1)2]} = \frac{\Sigma n^3}{\frac{n}{2}(2n)} = \frac{\Sigma n^3}{n^2}$$

$$T_n = \frac{\Sigma n^3}{n^2} = \frac{\left[\frac{n(n+1)}{2}\right]^2}{n^2} = \frac{(n+1)^2}{4} = \frac{1}{4}(n^2 + 2n + 1)$$

On taking the summation from 1 to n both sides, we get

$$\Sigma T_n = \Sigma\left[\frac{1}{4}(n^2 + 2n + 1)\right]$$

$$\therefore \quad S_n = \Sigma \frac{(n^2 + 1 + 2n)}{4}$$

$$= \frac{1}{4}[\Sigma n^2 + \Sigma 1 + 2\,\Sigma n]$$

$$= \frac{1}{4}\left[\frac{n(n+1)(2n+1)}{6} + n + \frac{2n(n+1)}{2}\right]$$

$$= \frac{n}{4}\left[\frac{2n^2 + n + 2n + 1}{6} + 1 + n + 1\right]$$

$$= \frac{n}{4}\left[\frac{2n^2 + 3n + 1 + 6n + 12}{6}\right]$$

$$= \frac{n}{24}[2n^2 + 9n + 13]$$

Example 6 If S_1, S_2, S_3 are the sum of first n natural numbers, their square and their cubes respectively, show that $9S_2^2 = S_3(1 + 8S_1)$. **[NCERT]**

Sol. Given, S_1 = Sum of first n natural numbers = Σn

$$\Rightarrow \quad S_1 = \frac{n(n+1)}{2} \quad \text{...(i)}$$

and S_2 = Sum of squares of first n natural numbers = Σn^2

$$\Rightarrow S_2 = \frac{n(n+1)(2n+1)}{6} \quad \text{...(ii)}$$

and S_3 = Sum of cubes of first n natural numbers = Σn^3

$$\Rightarrow S_3 = \left[\frac{n(n+1)}{2}\right]^2 \quad \text{...(iii)}$$

Now, we have to prove, $9S_2^2 = S_3(1 + 8S_1)$

Taking RHS $= S_3(1 + 8S_1)$

$$= \left[\frac{n(n+1)}{2}\right]^2 \left[1 + 8 \times \frac{n(n+1)}{2}\right] \quad \text{[using Eqs. (i) and (iii)]}$$

$$= \left[\frac{n(n+1)}{2}\right]^2 [1 + 4n(n+1)] = \left[\frac{n(n+1)}{2}\right]^2 [4n^2 + 4n + 1]$$

$$\left[\because \Sigma n^2 = \frac{n(n+1)(2n+1)}{6},\ \Sigma n = \frac{n(n+1)}{2},\ \Sigma 1 = n\right]$$

$$= \left[\frac{n(n+1)}{2}\right]^2 (2n+1)^2$$

On multiplying and dividing by 9, we get

$$= 9 \times \frac{n^2(n+1)^2}{4} \times \frac{(2n+1)^2}{9}$$

$$= 9\left[\frac{n(n+1)(2n+1)}{6}\right]^2$$

$$= 9 \times S_2^2 = 9S_2^2 \quad \text{[using Eq. (ii)]}$$

= LHS **Hence proved.**

Difference Method of Finding the *n*th Term

Sometimes the *n*th term of given series cannot be determined directly by observing. If the difference between two successive terms of given series

i.e. $(T_2 - T_1), (T_3 - T_2), (T_4 - T_3)$, ... and so on are either in AP or in GP, then we determined its *n*th term by the method of difference and then find the sum of the series by using suitable formula.

This method can be understand with the help of following examples

Example 7 Find the sum to n terms of the series $3 + 15 + 35 + 63 + \ldots$

Sol. Given series is $3 + 15 + 35 + 63 + \ldots$

Here, the difference between two successive terms are $15 - 3 = 12$, $35 - 15 = 20$, $63 - 35 = 28$,...

Clearly, these difference are in AP.

So, we use the difference method to find its *n*th term.

Let T_n be the *n*th term and S_n be the sum to n terms of given series. Then,

$$S_n = 3 + 15 + 35 + 63 + \ldots + T_{n-1} + T_n \quad \text{...(i)}$$

Also, $S_n = 3 + 15 + 35 + \ldots + T_{n-1} + T_n$ ...(ii)

On subtracting Eq. (ii) from Eq. (i), we get

$$0 = 3 + \{12 + 20 + 28 + \ldots + (T_n - T_{n-1})\} - T_n$$

$$\Rightarrow \quad T_n = 3 + 12 + 20 + 28 + \ldots + (T_n - T_{n-1})$$

$$= 3 + \left[\frac{(n-1)}{2}\{2 \times 12 + (n-1-1)8\}\right]$$

[$\because 12 + 20 + 28 + \ldots + (T_n - T_{n-1})$ form an AP with first term 12, common difference 8 and number of terms $(n-1)$]

$$= 3 + (n-1)(12 + 4n - 8)$$

$$= 3 + (n-1)(4n+4)$$

$$= 3 + 4n^2 + 4n - 4n - 4$$

$$\Rightarrow \quad T_n = 4n^2 - 1$$

Now, on taking summation both sides, we get

$$S_n = \Sigma T_n = \Sigma(4n^2 - 1) = 4\Sigma n^2 - \Sigma 1$$

$$= 4\left\{\frac{n(n+1)(2n+1)}{6}\right\} - n$$

$$= \frac{n}{3}\{2(n+1)(2n+1) - 3\}$$

$$= \frac{n}{3}\{4n^2 + 2n + 4n + 2 - 3\}$$

$$= \frac{n}{3}(4n^2 + 6n - 1)$$

Summation of Some Special Series

Sometimes the given series is of the form

$$\frac{1}{a(a+d)}+\frac{1}{(a+d)(a+2d)}+\frac{1}{(a+2d)(a+3d)}+\dots$$

For finding the sum of these types of series we firstly write its each term as the difference of two terms and then add them, to get the required sum.

Example 8 Find the sum of n terms of series

$$\frac{1}{1\times 2}+\frac{1}{2\times 3}+\frac{1}{3\times 4}+\dots$$ **[NCERT]**

Sol. Let the given series be

$$S=\frac{1}{1\times 2}+\frac{1}{2\times 3}+\frac{1}{3\times 4}+\dots$$

Then, nth term $(T_n)=\dfrac{1}{n(n+1)}$

Now, we will split the denominator of the nth term into two parts or we will write T_n as the difference of two terms.

$$\therefore \quad T_n=\frac{1}{n(n+1)}=\frac{(n+1)-n}{n(n+1)}$$

$$=\frac{n+1}{n(n+1)}-\frac{n}{n(n+1)}=\frac{1}{n}-\frac{1}{n+1}$$

On putting $n = 1, 2, 3, 4, \dots$ successively, we get

$$T_1=\frac{1}{1}-\frac{1}{2},\ T_2=\frac{1}{2}-\frac{1}{3},\ T_3=\frac{1}{3}-\frac{1}{4}$$

....

....

$$T_n=\frac{1}{n}-\frac{1}{n+1}$$

On adding all these terms, we get

$$S=T_1+T_2+T_3+\dots+T_n$$

$$=\left(\frac{1}{1}-\frac{1}{2}\right)+\left(\frac{1}{2}-\frac{1}{3}\right)+\dots+\left(\frac{1}{n}+\frac{1}{n+1}\right)$$

$$=1-\frac{1}{n+1}$$

$$=\frac{1}{1}-\frac{1}{n+1}$$

$$=\frac{n+1-1}{n+1}$$

$$\Rightarrow \quad S=\frac{n}{n+1}$$

Note When given series is in the terms of fraction, then we cannot directly use the formula of Σn, Σn^2 and Σn^3,

i.e. if $T_n=\dfrac{(n+1)}{n^2}$, then $\Sigma T_n \neq \dfrac{\Sigma(n+1)}{\Sigma n^2}$.

Topic Practice 7

Very Short Answer Type Questions

(2 Marks)

1 Find the 20th term of the series
$2\times 4+4\times 6+6\times 8+\dots+n$ terms. **[NCERT]**

2 Find the sum of n terms of the series whose nth term is given **[NCERT]**
(i) $n(n+1)(n+4)$ (ii) n^2+2^n (iii) $2n^2-3n+5$

3 Find the sum of the series $3.8+6.11+9.14+\dots$ to n terms. **[NCERT]**

4 If $\sum_{n=1}^{n} n=21$, then find the value of $\sum_{n=1}^{n} n^2$.

5 Find the sum upto n terms of the series
$3+7+13+21+31+\dots$ **[NCERT]**

6 Find the sum of the following series.
$1\cdot n+2\cdot(n-1)+3\cdot(n-2)+\dots+(n-1)\cdot 2+n\cdot 1$

7 If $S_k=\dfrac{1+2+\dots+k}{k}$, then find the value of
$S_1^2+S_2^2+\dots+S_n^2$.

8 Find the sum upto n term of the series
$1^2+(1^2+2^2)+(1^2+2^2+3^2)+\dots$ **[NCERT]**

9 Find the sum to n terms of the following series.
$1+5+12+22+35+\dots$

10 Find the nth term of the series $1+2+4+7+\dots$

Short Answer Type Questions

(4 Marks)

11 Find the sum to infinity
$1^2+2^2x+3^2x^2+4^2x^3+\dots, x<1$ numerically.

12 Show that $3^{1/3}\cdot 9^{1/9}\cdot 27^{1/27}\dots$ upto $\infty = 3^{3/4}$.

13 If T_n denotes the nth term of the series
$2+3+6+11+18+\dots$, then find the value of T_{50}.

14 Let S_n denotes the sum of the cubes of first n natural numbers and s_n denotes the sum of the first n natural numbers, then find the value of $\sum_{n=1}^{n}\dfrac{S_r}{s_r}$.

15 Find the sum to n terms of the following series.

$$\frac{3}{1^2 \cdot 2^2}+\frac{3}{2^2 \cdot 3^2}+\frac{3}{3^2 \cdot 4^2}+\ldots$$

16 Find the sum to n terms of the series

$$\frac{1}{1+1^2+1^4}+\frac{2}{1+2^2+2^4}+\frac{3}{1+3^2+4^4}+\ldots$$

Long Answer Type Questions

6 Marks

17 Find the sum of the following series to n terms.

$$\frac{1}{1 \cdot 2 \cdot 3}+\frac{1}{2 \cdot 3 \cdot 4}+\frac{1}{3 \cdot 4 \cdot 5}+\ldots$$

18 Show that

$$\frac{1 \times 2^2+2 \times 3^2+\ldots+n \times (n+1)^2}{1^2 \times 2+2^2 \times 3+\ldots+n^2 \times (n+1)}=\frac{3n+5}{3n+1}.$$ [NCERT]

Hints & Answers

1. $T_n = (n\text{th term of } 2, 4, 6 \ldots) \times (n\text{th term of } 4, 6, 8, \ldots)$
$= [2+(n-1)2][4+(n-1)2] \quad [\because T_n = a+(n-1)d]$
$= 2n(2n+2)$ **Ans.** $T_{20} = 1680$

2. (i) Let $T_n = n(n^2+4n+n+4) = n^3+5n^2+4n$
Now, $S = \Sigma T_n = \Sigma(n^3+5n^2+4n)$
$= \Sigma n^3 + 5\Sigma n^2 + 4\Sigma n$
Ans. $\dfrac{n(n+1)(3n^3+23n+34)}{12}$

(ii) Let $T_n = n^2+2^n$
$S = \Sigma T_n = \Sigma(n^2+2^n) = \Sigma n^2 + \Sigma 2^n$
$= \dfrac{n(n+1)(2n+1)}{6} + (2^1+2^2+2^3+2^4+\ldots+2^n)$
$\Rightarrow S = \dfrac{n(n+1)(2n+1)}{6} + 2(2^n-1)$

(iii) $S_n = \sum_{k=1}^{n} T_k = \sum_{k=1}^{n}(2k^2-3k+5)$
$= 2\sum_{k=1}^{n} k^2 - 3\sum_{k=1}^{n} k + \sum_{k=1}^{n} 5$
$\Rightarrow S_n = 2\left\{\dfrac{n(n+1)(2n+1)}{6}\right\} - 3\left\{\dfrac{n(n+1)}{2}\right\} + 5n$
Ans. $S_n = \dfrac{n}{6}(4n^2-3n+23)$

3. $T_n = (n\text{th term of } 3, 6, 9, \ldots) \times (n\text{th term of } 8, 11, 14, \ldots)$
$\Rightarrow T_n = [3+(n-1)\times 3][8+(n-1)\times 3] = 9n^2+15n$
$S_n = \sum_{k=1}^{n} T_k = \sum_{k=1}^{n}(9k^2+15k) = 9\sum_{k=1}^{n} k^2 + 15\sum_{k=1}^{n} k$
Ans. $S_n = 3n(n+1)(n+3)$

4. $\sum_{n=1}^{n} n = 21 \Rightarrow \dfrac{n(n+1)}{2} = 21$
$\Rightarrow n^2+n-42 = 0 \Rightarrow n = 6$
$\sum_{n=1}^{n} n^2 = \dfrac{n(n+1)(2n+1)}{6}$
Put $n=6$ **Ans.** 91

5. $S_n = \dfrac{n(n^2+3n+5)}{3}$

6. $T_r = r\{n-(r-1)\} = r(n-r+1)$
$= r\{(n+1)-r\} = (n+1)r - r^2$
$\therefore S_n = \sum_{r=1}^{n} T_r = \sum_{r=1}^{n}\{(n+1)r-r^2\} = (n+1)\left(\sum_{r=1}^{n} r\right) - \left(\sum_{r=1}^{n} r^2\right)$
Ans. $S_n = \dfrac{n(n+1)(n+2)}{6}$

7. $\because S_k = \dfrac{k(k+1)}{2k} = \dfrac{k+1}{2}$
$\therefore \quad S_1^2+S_2^2+\ldots+S_n^2 = \sum_{k=1}^{n} S_k^2 = \sum_{k=1}^{n}\left(\dfrac{k+1}{2}\right)^2$
$= \dfrac{1}{4}\sum_{k=1}^{n}(k+1)^2 = \dfrac{1}{4}\{2^2+3^2+\ldots+(n+1)^2\}$
$= \dfrac{1}{4}\{1^2+2^2+\ldots+(n+1)^2-1^2\}$
$= \dfrac{1}{4}\left\{\dfrac{(n+1)(n+1+1)\{2(n+1)+1\}}{6}-1\right\}$
$= \dfrac{n}{24}(2n^2+9n+13)$

8. Here, $T_n = 1^2+2^2+\ldots+n^2$
$T_n = \Sigma n^2 \Rightarrow T_n = \dfrac{2n^3+3n^2+n}{6}$
$\therefore S = \Sigma T_n = \dfrac{1}{6}(2n^3+3n^2+n) = \dfrac{1}{6}[2\Sigma n^3 + 3\Sigma n^2 + \Sigma n]$
Now, $S_n = \dfrac{n(n+1)^2(n+2)}{12}$

9. $\dfrac{n^2(n+1)}{2}$ 10. $\dfrac{n^2-n+2}{2}$ 11. $S = \dfrac{1+x}{(1-x)^3}$

12. LHS $= 3^{1/3} \times 9^{1/9} \times 27^{1/27} \ldots \infty$
$= 3^{1/3} + 3^{2/2} + 3^{3/3} + \ldots \infty$
$= 3^{1/3}\left(1+2\cdot\dfrac{1}{3}+3\cdot\dfrac{1}{3^2}+\ldots\infty\right) = 3^{1/3}\left[\dfrac{1}{1-1/3}+\dfrac{1/3}{(1-1/3)^2}\right]$
$= 3^{1/3}\left[\dfrac{3}{2}+\dfrac{1/3}{4/9}\right] = 3^{\frac{1}{3}\times\frac{9}{4}} = 3^{\frac{3}{4}}$

13. $T_{50} = 2403$

14. $$\sum_{r=1}^{n}\frac{S_r}{s_r}=\sum_{r=1}^{n}\frac{\frac{r^2(r+1)^2}{4}}{\frac{r(r+1)}{2}}$$

$$=\sum_{r=1}^{n}\frac{r(r+1)}{2}=\frac{1}{2}\sum_{r=1}^{n}(r^2+r)=\frac{1}{2}\left[\sum_{r=1}^{n}r^2+\sum_{r=1}^{n}r\right]$$

Ans. $\dfrac{n(n+1)(n+2)}{6}$

15. $T_r=\dfrac{(2r+1)}{r^2(r+1)^2}, r=1,2,3,\ldots$

$$\Rightarrow T_r=\frac{(r+1)^2-r^2}{r^2(r+1)^2}, r=1,2,3,\ldots$$

$$\Rightarrow T_r=\left\{\frac{1}{r^2}-\frac{1}{(r+1)^2}\right\}$$

$$\therefore S_n=\sum_{r=1}^{n}T_r=\sum_{r=1}^{n}\left\{\frac{1}{r^2}-\frac{1}{(r+1)^2}\right\}=1-\frac{1}{(n+1)^2}$$

Ans. $S_n=\dfrac{2n+n^2}{(n+1)^2}$

16. $T_r=\dfrac{r}{1+r^2+r^4}, r=1,2,3,\ldots,n$

$$\Rightarrow T_r=\frac{r}{(r^2+r+1)(r^2-r+1)}$$

$$=\frac{1}{2}\left\{\frac{2r}{(r^2+r+1)(r^2-r+1)}\right\}$$

$$=\frac{1}{2}\left\{\frac{(r^2+r+1)-(r^2-r+1)}{(r^2+r+1)(r^2-r+1)}\right\}$$

$$T_r=\frac{1}{2}\left\{\frac{1}{r^2-r+1}-\frac{1}{r^2+r+1}\right\}, r=1,2,\ldots,n$$

$$\therefore S_n=\sum_{r=1}^{n}T_r=\frac{1}{2}\left\{\sum_{r=1}^{n}\left(\frac{1}{r^2-r+1}-\frac{1}{r^2+r+1}\right)\right\}$$

$$=\frac{1}{2}\left[\left(1-\frac{1}{3}\right)+\left(\frac{1}{3}-\frac{1}{7}\right)+\left(\frac{1}{7}-\frac{1}{13}\right)+\ldots+\left(\frac{1}{n^2-n+1}-\frac{1}{n^2+n+1}\right)\right]$$

Ans. $\dfrac{n^2+n}{2(n^2+n+1)}$

17. $t_n=\dfrac{1}{n(n+1)(n+2)}$ ...(i)

Let $t_n=\dfrac{A}{n}+\dfrac{B}{n+1}+\dfrac{C}{n+2}$

Put $n=0 \quad \therefore A=\dfrac{1}{(0+1)(0+2)}=\dfrac{1}{2}$

Put $n+1=0$, i.e. $n=-1$

$\therefore \quad B=\dfrac{1}{-1(-1+2)}=-1$

Put $n+2=0$ i.e. $n=-2$

$\therefore \quad C=\dfrac{1}{-2(-2+1)}=\dfrac{1}{2}$

From Eq. (i), $t_n=\dfrac{1}{2n}-\dfrac{1}{n+1}+\dfrac{1}{2(n+2)}$

$$t_1=\frac{1}{2\cdot1}-\frac{1}{2}+\frac{1}{2\cdot3}$$
$$t_2=\frac{1}{2\cdot2}-\frac{1}{3}+\frac{1}{2\cdot4}$$
$$t_3=\frac{1}{2\cdot3}-\frac{1}{4}+\frac{1}{2\cdot5}$$
$$\ldots \quad \ldots \quad \ldots$$
$$\ldots \quad \ldots \quad \ldots$$
$$t_{n-2}=\frac{1}{2(n-2)}-\frac{1}{n-1}+\frac{1}{2n}$$
$$t_{n-1}=\frac{1}{2(n-1)}-\frac{1}{n}+\frac{1}{2(n+1)}$$
$$t_n=\frac{1}{2n}-\frac{1}{n+1}+\frac{1}{2(n+2)}$$

Ans. $S_n=\dfrac{n(n+3)}{4(n+1)(n+2)}$

18. For numerator, $T_n=n(n+1)^2$

$$=n(n^2+1+2n)=n^3+2n^2+n$$

$$\Rightarrow S_n=\Sigma T_n=\Sigma(n^3+2n^2+n)=\Sigma n^3+2\Sigma n^2+\Sigma n$$

$$=\left[\frac{n(n+1)}{2}\right]^2+\frac{2n(n+1)(2n+1)}{6}+\frac{n(n+1)}{2}$$

$$=\frac{n(n+1)(n+2)(3n+5)}{12} \quad \ldots(i)$$

Again, for denominator

Let $T_n'=n^2(n+1)=n^3+n^2$

Now, $S_n'=\Sigma T_n'=\Sigma(n^3+n^2)=\Sigma n^3+\Sigma n^2$

$$=\left[\frac{n(n+1)}{2}\right]^2+\frac{n(n+1)(2n+1)}{6}$$

$$\Rightarrow S_n'=\frac{n(n+1)(3n+1)(n+2)}{12} \quad \ldots(ii)$$

Hence, required sum of the series become

$$\frac{S_n}{S_n'}=\frac{\frac{n(n+1)(n+2)(3n+5)}{12}}{\frac{n(n+1)(3n+1)(n+2)}{12}}$$

Chapter Practice

Multiple Choice Type Questions

1 Mark

1. The third term of GP is 4, the product of the first five term is
(a) 1024 (b) 512
(c) 256 (d) None of these

2. The minimum value of $4^x + 4^{1-x}, x \in R$ is
(a) 2 (b) 8 (c) 4 (d) 0

3. The sum of the GP $\frac{1}{3}, \frac{1}{9}, \frac{1}{27}, \frac{1}{81}, \ldots$ to n terms is
(a) $\frac{2}{3}\left[\left(\frac{1}{3}\right)^n - 1\right]$ (b) $\frac{1}{2}\left[1-\left(\frac{1}{3}\right)^n\right]$
(c) $\frac{1}{2}\left[\left(\frac{1}{3}\right)^n - 1\right]$ (d) None of these

4. The 9th term of the GP $2, 2\sqrt{2}, 4, 8\sqrt{2}, \ldots$ is
(a) 16 (b) 64 (c) 32 (d) 128

5. The product $32, (32)^{1/6}, (32)^{1/36}, \ldots$ upto ∞ is equal to
(a) 64 (b) 16 (c) 32 (d) 0

6. The length of three unequal edges of a rectangular solid block are in GP. The volume of the Hock is 216 cm^3 and the total surface area is 252 cm^2. The length of the longest edges is
(a) 6 cm (b) 14 cm
(c) 10 cm (d) 12 cm

Assertion-Reason Type Questions

1 Mark

Directions (Q. Nos. 7-10) *In the questions given below are two statements labelled as Assertion (A) and Reason (R). In the context of the two statements, which one of the following is correct?*

(a) Both A and R are correct; R is the correct explanation of A
(b) Both A and R are correct; R is not the correct explanation of A
(c) A is correct; R is incorrect
(d) R is correct; A is incorrect

7. **Assertion (A)** 1, 2, 4, 8, ... is a GP 4, 8, 16, 32, ... is a GP and $1+4, 2+8, 4+16, 8+32, \ldots$ is also a GP.
Reason (R) Let general term of a GP with common ratio r be T_{k+1} and general term of another GP with common ratio r be T_{k+1}, then the series whose general term $T_{k+1} = T_{k+1} + T_{k+1}$ is also a GP with common ratio r.

8. **Assertion (A)** The minimum value of $4^{\sin^2 x} + 4^{\cos^2 x}$ is 2.
Reason (R) AM $\geq$ GM.

9. **Assertion (A)** For $x = \pm 1$, the numbers $-\frac{2}{7}, x, \frac{-7}{2}$ are in G.P.
Reason (R) Three numbers a, b, c are in G.P. if $b^2 = ac$.

10. **Assertion (A)** If the sum of n terms of an A.P. in $3n^2 + 5n$ and its mth term is 164, then the value of m is 27.
Reason (R) 20th term of the G.P. $\frac{5}{2}, \frac{5}{4}, \frac{5}{8}, \ldots$ is $\frac{5}{2^{20}}$.

Very Short Answer Type Questions

2 Marks

11. Find the sum of the series $\frac{3}{\sqrt{5}} + \frac{4}{\sqrt{5}} + \sqrt{5} + \ldots + 25$ terms.

12. Which term of the sequence $\frac{1}{3}, \frac{1}{9}, \frac{1}{27}, \ldots$ is $\frac{1}{19683}$?

13. If 5th and 8th terms of a GP be 48 and 384 respectively. Find the GP, if terms of GP are real numbers ?

14. If the pth term of an AP is x and qth term is y, show that the sum of $(p+q)$ terms is $\frac{p+q}{2}\left[x + y + \left(\frac{x-y}{p-q}\right)\right]$.

15. If the number of terms of an AP be $2n+1$, then find the ratio of sum of the odd terms of sum of even terms.

16. If a, b, c are the 1st, 3rd, and nth terms respectively of an AP, then prove that the sum to n terms is $\frac{c+a}{2} + \frac{c^2 - a^2}{b - a}$.

17. Find an inifinite GP whose first term is 1 and each term is the sum of all the terms which follow it.

18. The sum of first two terms of an infinite GP is 5 and each term is three times the sum of the succeeding terms. Find the GP. [NCERT]

19. If a, b, c are in GP, then prove that $\log a, \log b, \log c$ are in AP.

20. If $a^x = b^y = c^z$ and x, y, z are in GP, show that
$$\log_b a = \log_c b.$$

21. Evaluate $\sum_{r=1}^{n}(3^r - 2^r)$.

22. Find the sum of n terms of the series
$$(a+b)+(a^2+2b)+(a^3+3b)+\ldots$$

23. The fourth term of a GP in the square of its second term and the first term is – 3. Determine its 7th term.

Short Answer Type Questions

4 Marks

24. If $ab + bc + ca \neq 0$ and a, b, c are is AP, prove that $a^2(b+c), b^2(c+a), c^2(a+b)$ are also in AP.

25. 150 workers were engaged to finish a job in a certain number of days, 4 workers dropped out on second day, 4 more workers dropped out an third day and so on. It took 8 more days of finish the work. Find the numbers of days in which the work was completed. [NCERT]

26. Find the sum of the AP $a_1, a_2, a_3, \ldots a_{30}$, given that $a_1 + a_7 + a_{10} + a_{21} + a_{24} + a_{30} = 540$.

27. If $\frac{a^n + b^n}{a^{n-1} + b^{n-1}}$ may be the AM between a and b, then show that $n = 1$.

28. If AM between pth and qth terms of an AP is equal to the AM between rth and sth terms, then show that $p + q = r + s$.

Long Answer Type Questions

6 Marks

29. Find the three numbers in GP whose sum is 21 and the sum of their squares is 189.

30. Find the nth term and the sum of n terms of the series
$$\frac{1}{1\times4} + \frac{1}{4\times7} + \frac{1}{7\times10} + \ldots$$

Case-Based Type Question

6 Marks

31. The side of a given square is 10 cm. The mid-points of its sides are joined to form a new square. Again, the mid-point of the sides of this new square are joined to form another square. This process is continued indefinitely.

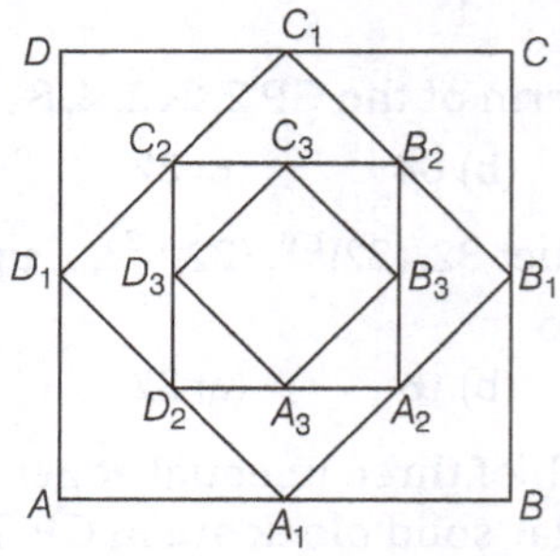

Based on above information. Answer the following.

(i) Find the side of the 5th square.

(ii) Find the sum of all sides of the square.

(iii) Find the sum of areas of squares.

(iv) Find the sum of perimeter of all squares.

(v) Find the sum of diagonal of all square.

Hints & Answers

1. (a) 2. (c) 3. (b) 4. (c) 5. (a)
6. (d) 7. (a) 8. (d) 9. (a) 10. (b)

11. Let $S_n = \frac{3}{\sqrt{5}} + \frac{4}{\sqrt{5}} + \sqrt{5} + \ldots$ 25th terms

$\Rightarrow \quad S_n = \frac{3}{\sqrt{5}} + \frac{4}{\sqrt{5}} + \frac{5}{\sqrt{5}} + \ldots$ 25th terms

Clearly, the successive difference of the terms is same. So, RHS of the above series forms an AP, with first term,

$a = \frac{3}{\sqrt{5}}$ and common difference, $d = \frac{4}{\sqrt{5}} - \frac{3}{\sqrt{5}} = \frac{1}{\sqrt{5}}$

$$\therefore \quad S_{25} = \frac{25}{2}\left[2 \times \frac{3}{\sqrt{5}} + (25-1)\frac{1}{\sqrt{5}}\right]$$

$$= 25\left[\frac{3}{\sqrt{5}} + \frac{12}{\sqrt{5}}\right]$$

$$= 25 \times \frac{15}{5} \times \sqrt{5}$$

$$= 75\sqrt{5}$$

12. Given sequence is $\frac{1}{3}, \frac{1}{9}, \frac{1}{27}, \ldots$

Clearly, the successive ratio of the terms is same. So, the above sequence forms a GP, with first term, $a = \frac{1}{3}$ and common ratio, $r = \frac{1}{9} \div \frac{1}{3} = \frac{1}{3}$.

Let the nth term of given sequence be $\frac{1}{19683}$.

Then, $\quad T_n = \frac{1}{19683}$

Also, $\quad T_n = ar^{n-1}$

$$\Rightarrow \quad \frac{1}{19683} = \frac{1}{3}\left(\frac{1}{3}\right)^{n-1}$$

$$\Rightarrow \quad \left(\frac{1}{3}\right)^9 = \left(\frac{1}{3}\right)^n$$

On equating the exponential power, we get $n = 9$

Hence, 9th term of given GP is $\frac{1}{19683}$.

13. Let a be the first term and r be the common ratio of the given GP.

According to the question,

$$T_5 = 48$$

$$\Rightarrow \quad ar^4 = 48 \qquad \ldots\text{(i)}$$

and

$$T_8 = 384$$

$$\Rightarrow \quad ar^7 = 384 \qquad \ldots\text{(ii)}$$

On dividing Eq. (ii) by Eq. (i), we get

$$\frac{ar^7}{ar^4} = \frac{384}{48}$$

$$\Rightarrow \quad r^3 = 8$$

$$\Rightarrow \quad r = 2$$

On putting $r = 2$ in Eq^n (i), we get $a = 3$

$\therefore \quad$ 3, 6, 12, ... are in GP.

14. Let A be the first term and D be the common difference of the given AP.

Then, $\quad T_p = x \Rightarrow A + (p-1)D = x \qquad \ldots\text{(i)}$

and $\quad T_q = y \Rightarrow A + (q-1)D = y \qquad \ldots\text{(ii)}$

On subtracting Eq. (ii) from Eq. (i) we get

$$(p-q)D = x - y \Rightarrow D = \frac{x-y}{p-q} \qquad \ldots\text{(iii)}$$

On adding Eqs. (i) and (ii), we get

$$2A + (p+q-2)D = x + y$$

$$\Rightarrow \quad 2A + pD + qD - 2D = x + y$$

$$\Rightarrow \quad 2A + pD + qD - D - D = x + y$$

$$\Rightarrow \quad 2A + (p+q-1)D = x + y + D \qquad \ldots\text{(iv)}$$

$$2A + (p+q-1)D = x + y + \left(\frac{x-y}{p-q}\right)$$

Now, $\quad S_{p+q} = \frac{p+q}{2}[2A + (p+q-1)D] \quad$ [from Eq. (iii)]...(iv)

15. $S(\text{odd}) = a + a + 2d + \ldots + a + (2n)d$

$S(\text{even}) = a + d + a + 3d + \ldots + a + (2n-1)d$

$$\frac{S_o}{S_e} = \frac{\frac{n+1}{2}(2a + 2nd)}{\frac{n}{2}(2a + 2nd)} = \frac{n+1}{n}$$

Ans. $(n+1) : n$

16. Let A be the first term and D be the common difference of the given AP.

According to the question,

$$T_1 = A = a \qquad \ldots\text{(i)}$$

$$T_3 = A + 2D = b \qquad \ldots\text{(ii)}$$

and $\quad T_n = A + (n-1)D = c \qquad \ldots\text{(iii)}$

On solving Eqs. (i) and (ii), we get

$$D = \frac{b-a}{2}$$

On putting $A = a$ and $D = \left(\frac{b-a}{2}\right)$ in Eq. (iii), we get

$$a + (n-1)\left(\frac{b-a}{2}\right) = c$$

$$\Rightarrow \quad (n-1) = \frac{2(c-a)}{b-a} \Rightarrow n = \frac{2c - 3a + b}{b-a}$$

Now, $\quad S_n = \frac{n}{2}(A + T_n) = \frac{(2c - 3a + b)}{2(b-a)}(a + c)$

$$= \frac{1}{2(b-a)}[2ac - 3a^2 + ab + 2c^2 - 3ac + bc]$$

$$= \frac{1}{2(b-a)}[bc - ac + ab - a^2 + 2c^2 - 2a^2]$$

$$= \frac{1}{2(b-a)}[c(b-a) + a(b-a) + 2(c^2 - a^2)]$$

$$= \frac{1}{2(b-a)}[(b-a)(c+a) + 2(c^2 - a^2)]$$

17. Let a be the first term and $r(|r|<1)$, the common ratio of the GP.

$\therefore$ The GP is $a, ar, ar^2, \ldots$

According to the question, $a = 1$

and $T_n = T_{n+1} + T_{n+2} + T_{n+3} + \ldots$

$\Rightarrow \quad ar^{n-1} = ar^n + ar^{n+1} + ar^{n+2} + \ldots$

$\Rightarrow \quad \frac{ar^n}{r} = ar^n \; [1 + r + r^2 + \ldots]$

$\Rightarrow \quad 1 = r\left(\frac{1}{1-r}\right)$

$\Rightarrow \quad 1 - r = r$

$\Rightarrow \quad r = \frac{1}{2}$

$\therefore 1, \frac{1}{2}, \frac{1}{4}, \ldots$ is the required GP.

18. Let a be the first term and $r(|r|<1)$, the common ratio of the GP.

$\therefore$ The GP is $a, ar, ar^2, \ldots$

According to the question,

$T_1 + T_2 = 5 \Rightarrow a + ar = 5 \Rightarrow a(1+r) = 5$ ...(i)

and $T_n = 3(T_{n+1} + T_{n+2} + T_{n+3} + \ldots)$

$\Rightarrow \quad ar^{n-1} = 3(ar^n + ar^{n+1} + ar^{n+2} + \ldots)$

$\Rightarrow \quad ar^{n-1} = 3ar^n(1 + r + r^2 + \ldots)$

$\Rightarrow \quad 1 = 3r\left(\frac{1}{1-r}\right)$

$\Rightarrow \quad 1 - r = 3r \Rightarrow r = \frac{1}{4}$

From Eq. (i), we get $a = 4$

$\therefore \; 4, 1, \frac{1}{4}, \ldots$ is the required GP.

19. a, b, c are in G.P.

$\therefore \; b^2 = ac$

Taking log both side, we get $2 \log b = \log a + \log c$

20. Let $a^x = b^y = c^z = k$

$\therefore x = \log_a k, \; y = \log_b k, \; z = \log_c k$

Since, x, y, z are in GP.

$\therefore \quad \frac{\log_b k}{\log_a k} = \frac{\log_c k}{\log_b k}$

$\Rightarrow \quad \frac{\log_k a}{\log_k b} = \frac{\log_k b}{\log_k c}$

21. Let $S_n = \sum_{r=1}^{n} (3^r - 2^r)$

$\Rightarrow S_n = (3^1 + 3^2 + 3^3 + \ldots$ upto n terms)

$+ (2^1 + 2^2 + 2^3 + \ldots$ upto n terms)

$\Rightarrow S_n = \frac{3(3^n - 1)}{3-1} + \frac{2(2^n - 1)}{2-1}$ $\quad \left[\because S_n = \frac{a(r^n - 1)}{r-1}, r > 1\right]$

$$= \frac{3^{n+1} - 3}{2} + \frac{2^{n+1} - 2}{1}$$

$$= \frac{3^{n+1} - 3 + 2^{n+2} - 4}{2}$$

$$= \frac{1}{2}(3^{n+1} + 2^{n+2} - 7)$$

22. Let $S_n = (a+b) + (a^2 + 2b) + (a^3 + 3b) + \ldots$ upto n terms

$= (a + a^2 + a^3 + \ldots$ upto n terms)

$+ (b + 2b + 3b + \ldots$ upto n terms)

$$= a\left(\frac{a^n - 1}{a-1}\right) + \frac{n}{2}[2b + (n-1)b]$$

$$\left[\because S_{n(\text{GP})} = \frac{A(R^n - 1)}{R-1}, R > 1 \text{ and } S_{n(\text{AP})} = \frac{n}{2}\{2A + (n-1)D\}\right]$$

Ans. $\frac{a(1-a^n)}{1-a} + \frac{bn(n+1)}{2}$

23. Let a be the first term and r be the common ratio of the given GP.

According to the question,

$T_4 = (T_2)^2$ and $a = -3$

$\because \quad T_4 = (T_2)^2 \Rightarrow ar^3 = (ar)^2$

$\Rightarrow \quad -3r^3 = (-3)^2 r^2$ $\quad [\because a = -3]$

$\Rightarrow \quad r = -3$

Now, $T_7 = ar^6 = -3(-3)^6 = -3 \times 729 = -2187$

24. $a^2(b+c), \; b^2(c+a), \; c^2(a+b)$ are in AP.

$\Rightarrow a^2b + a^2c, b^2c + b^2a, c^2a + c^2b$ are in AP.

$\Rightarrow a^2b + a^2c + abc, \; b^2c + b^2a + abc, c^2a + c^2b + abc$

are in AP. [adding abc to each term]

$\Rightarrow a(ab + ac + bc), \; b(bc + ba + ac), \; c(ca + cb + ab)$ are in AP.

$\Rightarrow a, b, c$ are in AP. [dividing each term by $(ab + bc + ca)$]

25. Let the number or days in which the work is completed, is n.

Now, according to the question, 4 workers dropped on everyday i.e. the devils of number of workers is 150, 146, 142, 138, ...

Clearly, the work done in both conditions is same.

[had the workers not dropped, then the work would have finished in $(n-8)$ days with 150 workers working on each day. Hence, the total number of workers who would have worked for all the n days is $150(n-8)$]

$\Rightarrow \quad 150(n-8) = \frac{n}{2}[2 \times 150 + (n-1)(-4)]$

$$\left[\because S_n = \frac{n}{2}\{2a + (n-1)d\}\right]$$

$\Rightarrow \quad 150n - 1200 = \frac{n}{2} \times 2(150 - 2n + 2)$

$\Rightarrow \quad 150n - 1200 = \frac{n}{2} \times 2(152 - 2n)$

On dividing each term by 2, we get

$$75n-600=n(76-n) \Rightarrow 75n-600=76n-n^2$$

$$\Rightarrow n^2-76n+75n-600=0 \Rightarrow n^2-n-600=0$$

Now factorising it by splitting the middle term,

$\Rightarrow \quad n^2-(25n-24n)-600=0$

$\Rightarrow \quad n^2-25n+24n-600=0$

$\Rightarrow \quad n(n-25)+24(n-25)=0$

$\Rightarrow \quad (n-25)(n+24)=0$

$\Rightarrow \quad n=25$

and $n \neq -24$, because it is not possible.

Hence, the work will be completed in 25 days.

26. We know that the sum of terms equidistant from the beginning and end of an AP is always same and equals to the sum of the first and last term.

Here, the given AP consists of 30 terms.

$\therefore a_1+a_{30}=a_7+a_{24}=a_{10}+a_{21}$

Given, $a_1+a_7+a_{10}+a_{21}+a_{24}+a_{30}=540$

$\Rightarrow (a_1+a_{30})+(a_7+a_{24})+(a_{10}+a_{21})=540$

$\Rightarrow \quad 3(a_1+a_{30})=540$

$\Rightarrow \quad a_1+a_{30}=180$

$\therefore$ Sum of the given AP $=S_{30}=\frac{30}{2}(a_1+a_{30})$ $\left[\because S_n=\frac{n}{2}(a+l)\right]$

$=15\times 180=2700$

27. $\frac{a^n+b^n}{a^{n-1}+b^{n-1}}=\frac{a+b}{2}$

28. $\frac{a_p+a_q}{2}=\frac{a_r+a_s}{2}$

$\Rightarrow \quad a+(p-1)d+a+(q-1)d=a+(r-1)d+a+(s-1)d$

$=p+q=r+s$

29. 3, 6, 12 or 12, 6, 3

30. $\frac{1}{(3n-2)(3n+1)}$; $\frac{n}{3n+1}$

31. (i) $\frac{5}{2}$

(ii) $(20+10\sqrt{2})$ cm

(iii) 200 cm^2

(iv) $(80+40\sqrt{2})$ cm

(v) $(20+20\sqrt{2})$ cm

CHAPTER

10

Straight Lines

In earlier classes during the study of coordinate geometry, we studied about coordinate axes, coordinate plane, plotting of points in a plane, distance between two points, section formula etc. All these are the basic concept of coordinate geometry. In this chapter, we shall continue the study of coordinate geometry to understand the properties of straight lines.

- Recall of Coordinate Geometry
- Slope (or Gradient) of a Straight Line
- Various Forms of Equation of a Line
- General Equation of a Line and Distance of a Point from a Line
- Family of Lines and Locus of a Point

TOPIC 01 Recall of Coordinate Geometry

Coordinate Axes

Let $X'OX$ and $Y'OY$ be two perpendicular lines intersect at O. Then, point O is called **origin** and the lines $X'OX$ and $Y'OY$ are called **coordinate axes or rectangular axes.**

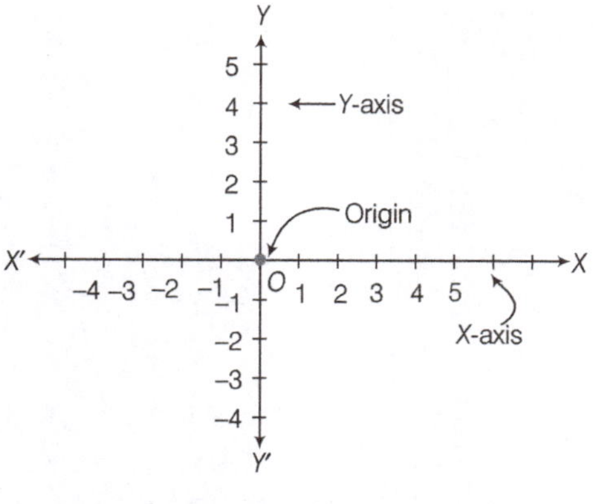

The horizontal line $X'OX$ is called **X-axis** and the vertical line $Y'OY$ is called **Y-axis.**

Coordinate Plane

The intersection of X-axis and Y-axis divide the plane into four parts. These four parts are called **quadrant**, $\left(\frac{1}{4}\text{th part}\right)$ numbered I, II, III and IV anti-clockwise from OX.

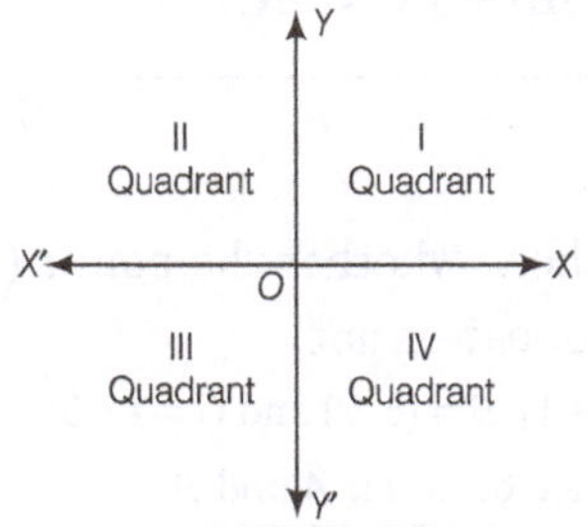

Thus, the plane consists of the axes and four quadrants, is known as XY-plane or **cartesian plane** or **cartesian coordinate system.**

Coordinates of a Point in Cartesian Plane

Let P be any point in a plane. If the distance of point P from Y-axis is x and the distance of point P from X-axis is y. Then, the coordinates of a point P are (x, y) where, x is called **x-coordinate** or **abscissa** and y is called the **y-coordinate** or **ordinate.**

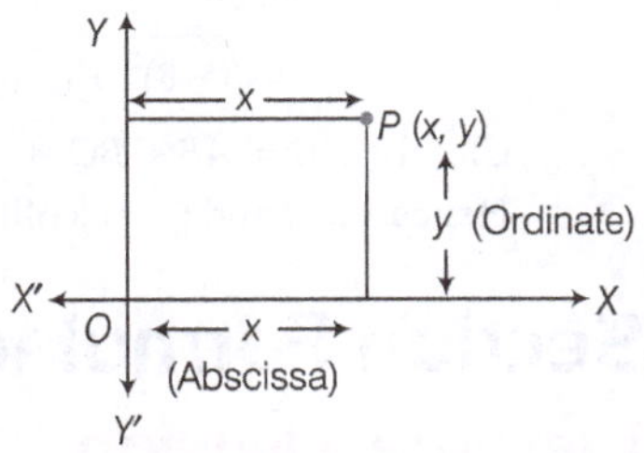

The coordinates of a point on the X-axis are of the form $(x, 0)$ and of a point on the Y-axis are of the form $(0, y)$.

Note (i) The abscissa of any point on Y-axis is zero.
(ii) The ordinate of any point on X-axis is zero.
(iii) The coordinates of the origin are (0, 0).

Sign Convention of Coordinates

The signs of coordinates of points in all the four quadrants are expressed in the table given below

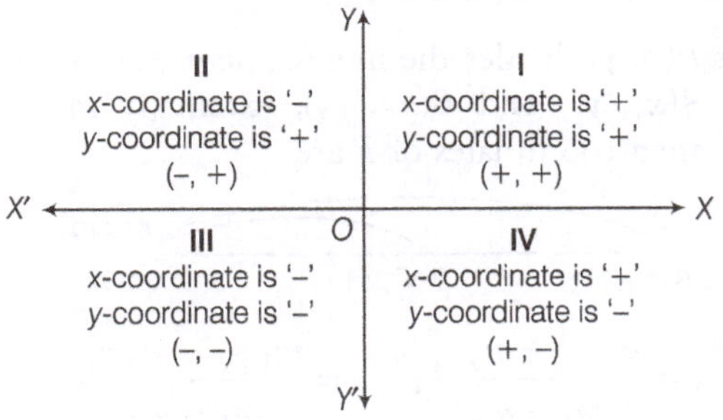

Quadrant	Sign of x-coordinate	Sign of y-coordinate	Point
I	+	+	(+, +)
II	–	+	(–, +)
III	–	–	(–, –)
IV	+	–	(+, –)

Example 1 In which quadrant, the following points lie?

(i) (6, – 3) (ii) (–4, 1) (iii) (–1, – 1) (iv) (5, 4)

Sol. (i) Let $A = (6, -3)$

Since, x-coordinate of A is positive and its y-coordinate is negative, therefore A lies in the fourth quadrant.

(ii) Let $B = (-4, 1)$

Since, x-coordinate of B is negative and its y-coordinate is positive, therefore B lies in the second quadrant.

(iii) Let $C = (-1, -1)$

Since, x-coordinate of C is negative and its y-coordinate is also negative, therefore C lies in the third quadrant.

(iv) Let $D = (5, 4)$

Since, x-coordinate of D is positive and its y-coordinate is also positive, therefore D lies in the first quadrant.

Distance Formula

The distance between two points $A(x_1, y_1)$ and $B(x_2, y_2)$ is given by

$$AB = \sqrt{(x_2 - x_1)^2 + (y_2 - y_1)^2}$$

or $$AB = \sqrt{(x_1 - x_2)^2 + (y_1 - y_2)^2}$$

Example 2 Find the distance between the points $P(a\cos\alpha, a\sin\alpha)$ and $Q(a\cos\beta, a\sin\beta)$.

Sol. The distance between P and Q is

$$PQ = \sqrt{(a\cos\beta - a\cos\alpha)^2 + (a\sin\beta - a\sin\alpha)^2}$$ [by distance formula]

$$= \sqrt{a^2(\cos^2\beta + \cos^2\alpha - 2\cos\alpha\cos\beta) + a^2(\sin^2\beta + \sin^2\alpha - 2\sin\beta\sin\alpha)}$$

$$= a\sqrt{(\cos^2\beta + \sin^2\beta) + (\cos^2\alpha + \sin^2\alpha) - 2(\cos\alpha\cos\beta + \sin\alpha\sin\beta)}$$

$$= a\sqrt{1 + 1 - 2\cos(\alpha - \beta)} = a\sqrt{2[1 - \cos(\alpha - \beta)]}$$

[$\because \cos^2\theta + \sin^2\theta = 1$ and $\cos A\cos B + \sin A\sin B = \cos(A - B)$]

$$= a\sqrt{2\times 2\sin^2\left(\frac{\alpha-\beta}{2}\right)} \quad [\because \cos\theta = 1 - 2\sin^2\theta/2]$$

$$= 2a\sin\left(\frac{\alpha-\beta}{2}\right) \text{ units}$$

Application of Distance Formula

Distance formula is also used to identify that which geometrical figure is represented by the given points. Conditions corresponding to three and four points are given below

1. Three points will represent
   (i) an **equilateral triangle** iff all sides are equal.
   (ii) an **isosceles triangle** iff two sides are equal.
2. Four points will represent
   (i) a **parallelogram** iff opposite sides are equal.
   (ii) a **rectangle** iff opposite sides are equal and diagonals are also equal.
   (iii) a **rhombus** iff all the four sides are equal.
   (iv) a **square** iff all the four sides are equal and diagonals are also equal.

Example 3 Show that four points (0, – 1), (6, 7), (–2, 3) and (8, 3) are the vertices of a rectangle.

Sol. Let, $A(0, -1)$, $B(6, 7)$, $C(-2, 3)$ and $D(8, 3)$ be the given points.

Then, $AD = \sqrt{(8-0)^2 + (3+1)^2}$ [by distance formula]

$= \sqrt{64+16} = \sqrt{80} = 4\sqrt{5}$ units

$CB = \sqrt{(6+2)^2 + (7-3)^2}$

$= \sqrt{64+16} = \sqrt{80} = 4\sqrt{5}$ units

$AC = \sqrt{(-2-0)^2 + (3+1)^2}$

$= \sqrt{4+16} = \sqrt{20} = 2\sqrt{5}$ units

and $BD = \sqrt{(8-6)^2 + (3-7)^2}$

$= \sqrt{4+16} = \sqrt{20} = 2\sqrt{5}$ units

Thus, $AD = CB$ and $AC = BD$

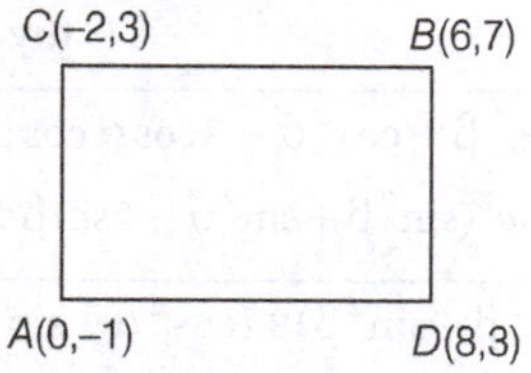

So, $ADBC$ is a parallelogram.

Now, $AB = \sqrt{(6-0)^2 + (7+1)^2}$

$= \sqrt{36+64} = \sqrt{100} = 10$ units

and $CD = \sqrt{(8+2)^2 + (3-3)^2} = \sqrt{100} = 10$ untis

Clearly, $AB = CD$

Hence, $ADBC$ is a rectangle.

Collinearity of Three Points

Three points A, B and C are collinear, if they lie on a same straight line, i.e. $AB + BC = AC$.

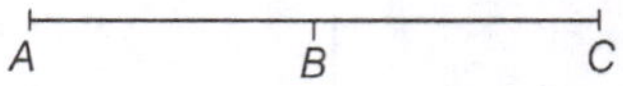

Example 4 Check whether the points (1, – 1), (5, 2) and (9, 5) are collinear or not.

Sol. Let $A = (1, -1)$, $B = (5, 2)$ and $C = (9, 5)$

Now, distance between A and B,

$AB = \sqrt{(5-1)^2 + (2+1)^2}$ [by distance formula]

$= \sqrt{(4)^2 + (3)^2} = \sqrt{16+9} = \sqrt{25} = 5$

Distance between B and C, $BC = \sqrt{(5-9)^2 + (2-5)^2}$

$= \sqrt{(-4)^2 + (-3)^2} = \sqrt{16+9} = \sqrt{25} = 5$

Distance between A and C,

$AC = \sqrt{(1-9)^2 + (-1-5)^2}$

$= \sqrt{(-8)^2 + (-6)^2} = \sqrt{64+36} = 10$

Clearly, $AC = AB + BC$

Hence, A, B and C are collinear points.

Section Formulae

1. Internal Division

If point $P(x, y)$ divides the line segment AB, obtained by joining $A(x_1, y_1)$ and $B(x_2, y_2)$, internally in the ratio $m_1 : m_2$, then coordinates of P are

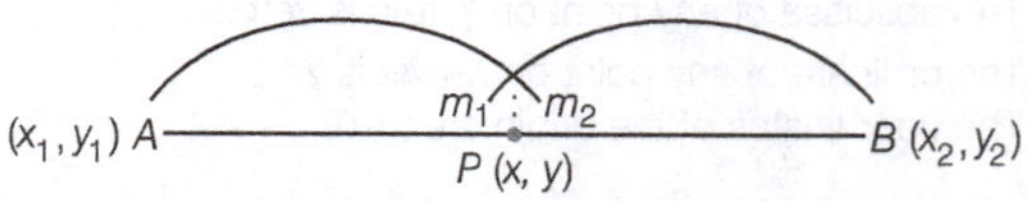

$$x = \frac{m_1x_2 + m_2x_1}{m_1 + m_2}, \; y = \frac{m_1y_2 + m_2y_1}{m_1 + m_2}$$

2. External Division

If point $P(x, y)$ divides the line segment AB, obtained by joining $A(x_1, y_1)$ and $B(x_2, y_2)$, externally in the ratio $m_1 : m_2$, then coordinates of P are

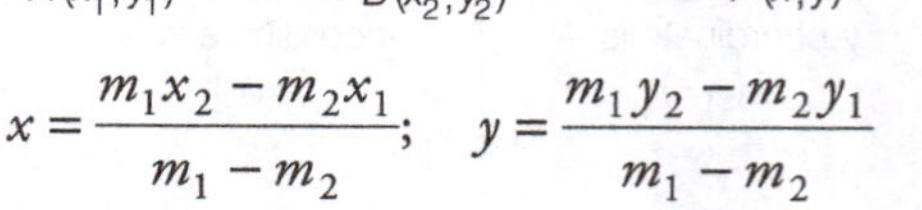

$$x = \frac{m_1x_2 - m_2x_1}{m_1 - m_2}; \quad y = \frac{m_1y_2 - m_2y_1}{m_1 - m_2}$$

Note The coordinates of mid-points of line segment obtained by joining $A(x_1, y_1)$ and $B(x_2, y_2)$ are $\left(\frac{x_1+x_2}{2}, \frac{y_1+y_2}{2}\right)$.

Example 5 Find the coordinates of the point which divides the join of (– 1, 7) and (4, – 3) in the ratio 2 : 3
(i) internally. (ii) externally.

Sol. Let $A(x_1, y_1) \equiv A(-1, 7)$
and $B(x_2, y_2) \equiv B(4, -3)$.
Again, let $P(x, y)$ be the required point.

(i) Here, P divides AB internally in the ratio 2 : 3.

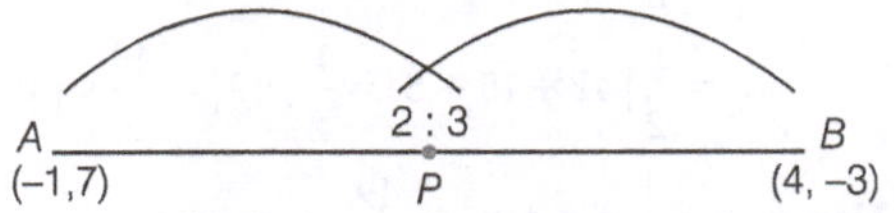

$$\therefore \ P(x, y) \equiv P\left[\frac{2\times 4+3\times(-1)}{2+3}, \frac{2\times(-3)+3\times 7}{2+3}\right]$$
[by internal division formula and $m_1 = 2, m_2 = 3$]
$$\Rightarrow \quad P(x, y) \equiv P\left(\frac{8-3}{5}, \frac{-6+21}{5}\right)$$
$$\Rightarrow \quad P(x, y) \equiv P(1, 3)$$
Thus, (1, 3) is the required point.

(ii) Here, P divides AB externally in the ratio of 2 : 3.

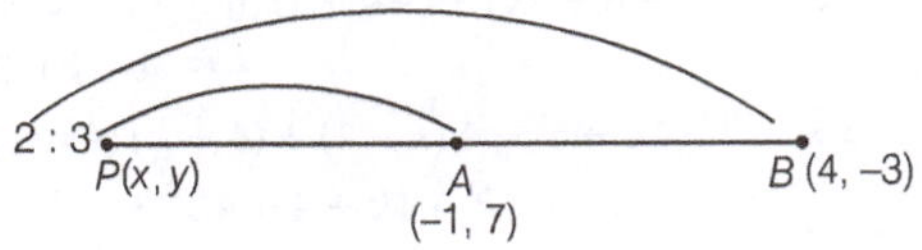

$$\therefore \ P(x, y) = \left(\frac{2\times 4-3\times(-1)}{2-3}, \frac{2\times(-3)-3\times 7}{2-3}\right)$$
[by external division formula and $m_1 = 2, m_2 = 3$]
$$= \left(\frac{8+3}{-1}, \frac{-6-21}{-1}\right)$$
$$\Rightarrow P(x, y) = (-11, 27)$$
Thus, (–11, 27) is the required point.

Example 6 Without using distance formula, show that the points (–2, – 1), (4, 0), (3, 3) and (–3, 2) are the vertices of a parallelogram.

Sol. Let $A(x_1, y_1) \equiv A(-2, -1)$, $B(x_2, y_2) \equiv B(4, 0)$, $C(x_3, y_3) \equiv C(3, 3)$ and $D(x_4, y_4) \equiv (-3, 2)$

Now, mid-point of $AC = \left(\frac{x_1+x_3}{2}, \frac{y_1+y_3}{2}\right)$
$$= \left(\frac{-2+3}{2}, \frac{-1+3}{2}\right) = \left(\frac{1}{2}, 1\right) \quad \text{...(i)}$$

and mid-point of $BD = \left(\frac{x_2+x_4}{2}, \frac{y_2+y_4}{2}\right)$
$$= \left(\frac{4-3}{2}, \frac{0+2}{2}\right) = \left(\frac{1}{2}, 1\right) \quad \text{...(ii)}$$

From Eqs. (i) and (ii), we get
Mid-point of AC = Mid-point of BD
Thus, mid-points of both diagonals are coincide each other.
Hence, the points A, B, C and D are vertices of a parallelogram.

3. Points of Trisection

Trisection means a line is divided into three equal parts.

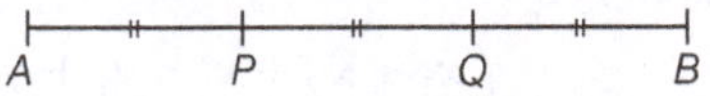

This can be done by finding two points P and Q on the line segments AB, such that $AP = PQ = QB$.

Let $AP = PQ = QB = x$.
Then, $AP = x$ and $PB = PQ + QB = x + x = 2x$
$\therefore \quad AP : PB = x : 2x = 1 : 2$
Also, $AQ = AP + PQ = 2x$ and $QB = x$
$\therefore \quad AQ : QB = 2x : x = 2 : 1$
Hence, to find points of trisection, we find two points P and Q which divides AB in the ratio 1 : 2 and 2 : 1, respectively.

Example 7 Find the coordinates of the points of trisection of the line segments joining (2, – 3) and (4, – 1).

Sol. Let $A(x_1, y_1) \equiv A(2, -3)$ and $B(x_2, y_2) \equiv B(4, -1)$
Again, let P and Q be two points of trisection as shown below

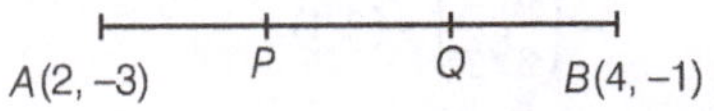

Then, $AP : PB = 1 : 2$ and $AQ : QB = 2 : 1$

(i) Here, P divides AB internally in the ratio of 1 : 2.

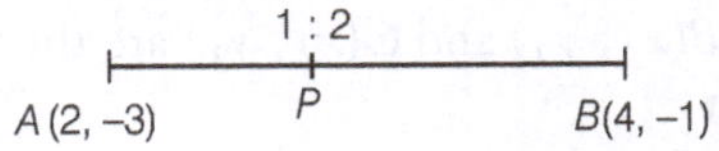

$$\therefore \ P \equiv \left(\frac{1\times 4+2\times 2}{1+2}, \frac{1\times(-1)+2\times(-3)}{1+2}\right)$$
[by internal division formula]
$$\equiv \left(\frac{4+4}{3}, \frac{-1-6}{3}\right) \equiv \left(\frac{8}{3}, \frac{-7}{3}\right)$$

(ii) Here, Q divides AB internally in the ratio of 2 : 1

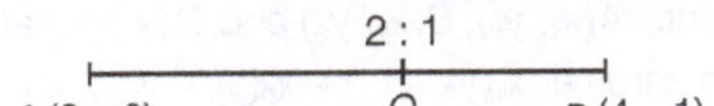

$$\therefore \quad Q \equiv \left(\frac{2\times4+1\times2}{2+1}, \frac{2\times(-1)+1\times(-3)}{2+1}\right)$$

[by internal division formula]

$$\equiv \left(\frac{8+2}{3}, \frac{-2-3}{3}\right)$$

$$\equiv \left(\frac{10}{3}, \frac{-5}{3}\right)$$

Centroid of a Triangle

If G is the centroid of a triangle whose vertices are (x_1, y_1), (x_2, y_2) and (x_3, y_3), then

$$\text{Coordinates of } G = \left(\frac{x_1+x_2+x_3}{3}, \frac{y_1+y_2+y_3}{3}\right)$$

Note The centroid divides each median in the ratio of 2 : 1.

Example 8 If the vertices of a triangle are $P(1, 3)$, $Q(2, 5)$ and $R(3, -5)$, then find the centroid of a ΔPQR.

Sol. We know that, if the vertices of a triangle are (x_1, y_1), (x_2, y_2) and (x_3, y_3), then centroid of a triangle is

$$\left(\frac{x_1+x_2+x_3}{3}, \frac{y_1+y_2+y_3}{3}\right)$$

Here, $P(1, 3) \equiv P(x_1, y_1)$; $Q(2, 5) \equiv Q(x_2, y_2)$ and $R(3, -5) \equiv R(x_3, y_3)$

$\therefore$ Centroid of a triangle

$$= \left(\frac{1+2+3}{3}, \frac{3+5-5}{3}\right)$$

$$= \left(\frac{6}{3}, \frac{3}{3}\right) = (2, 1)$$

Area of a Triangle

If $A(x_1, y_1)$, $B(x_2, y_2)$ and $C(x_3, y_3)$ are the vertices of a ΔABC, then

Area of ΔABC,

$$\Delta = \frac{1}{2}|x_1(y_2-y_3)+x_2(y_3-y_1)+x_3(y_1-y_2)|$$

$$= \frac{1}{2}|x_1y_2+x_2y_3+x_3y_1-(x_1y_3+x_2y_1+x_3y_2)|$$

Note Three points $A(x_1, y_1)$, $B(x_2, y_2)$ and $C(x_3, y_3)$ are collinear, if area of triangle is zero i.e. $x_1(y_2-y_3)+x_2(y_3-y_1)+x_3(y_1-y_2)=0$.

Example 9 Find the area of a ΔABC, whose vertices are $A(6, 3)$, $B(-3, 5)$ and $C(4, -2)$.

Sol. Area of ΔABC

$$= \frac{1}{2}|x_1(y_2-y_3)+x_2(y_3-y_1)+x_3(y_1-y_2)|$$

Here, $(x_1, y_1) \equiv (6, 3)$, $(x_2, y_2) \equiv (-3, 5)$

and $(x_3, y_3) \equiv (4, -2)$

$\therefore$ Area of ΔABC

$$= \frac{1}{2}|6(5+2)+(-3)(-2-3)+4(3-5)|$$

$$= \frac{1}{2}|6(7)-3(-5)+4(-2)|$$

$$= \frac{1}{2}|42+15-8| = \frac{1}{2}|49| = \frac{49}{2} \text{ sq units}$$

Hence, area of ΔABC is $\frac{49}{2}$ sq units.

Example 10 For what value of k, points $(k, 2-2k)$, $(-k+1, 2k)$ and $(-4-k, 6-2k)$ are collinear?

Sol. Let three points be $A(x_1, y_1) \equiv (k, 2-2k)$,

$B(x_2, y_2) \equiv (-k+1, 2k)$

and $C(x_3, y_3) \equiv (-4-k, 6-2k)$

Condition for three points to be collinear is, area of triangle formed by these three points = 0

$$\therefore \quad x_1(y_2-y_3)+x_2(y_3-y_1)+x_3(y_1-y_2)=0$$

$$\Rightarrow k(2k-6+2k)+(-k+1)(6-2k-2+2k)+(-4-k)(2-2k-2k)=0$$

$$\Rightarrow k(4k-6)-4(k-1)+(4+k)(4k-2)=0$$

$$4k^2-6k-4k+4+4k^2+14k-8=0$$

$$\Rightarrow 8k^2+4k-4=0 \Rightarrow 2k^2+k-1=0$$

$$\Rightarrow (2k-1)(k+1)=0 \Rightarrow k=\frac{1}{2} \text{ or } k=-1$$

But for $k=\frac{1}{2}$, A and B are same.

$$\therefore \quad k=-1$$

Hence, the given points are collinear for $k=-1$.

Shifting of Origin

An equation corresponding to a set of points with reference to a system of coordinate axes may be simplified by taking the set of points in some other suitable coordinate system such that all geometric properties remain unchanged. One such transformation is that in which the new axes are transformed parallel to the original axes and origin is shifted to a new point. A **transformation** of this kind is called a **translation of axes.**

Let O be the origin and $X'OX$ and $Y'OY$ be the X-axis and Y-axis, respectively. Again, let O' and P be two points in the plane having coordinates (h, k) and (x, y), respectively referred to $X'OX$ and $Y'OY$ as the coordinate axes.

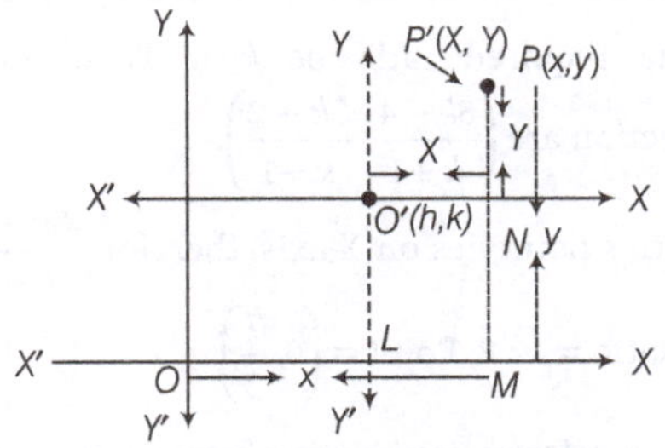

Let the origin be transferred to O' and $X'O'X$ and $Y'O'Y$ be new rectangular axes. Again, let the coordinates of P referred to new axes as the coordinate axes be $P'(X, Y)$.

Then, $O'N = X, PN = Y, OM = x,$

$PM = y, OL = h$ and $O'L = k$

Now, $x = OM = OL + LM = OL + O'N = h + X$

and $y = PM = PN + NM = PN + O'L = Y + k$

$\therefore$ $x = X + h$ and $y = Y + k$

Thus, if (x, y) are coordinates of a point referred to old axes and (X, Y) are the coordinates of the same point referred to new axes, then

$$x = X + h \text{ and } y = Y + k \qquad \ldots(i)$$

i.e. (old x-coordinate) = (new x-coordinate) + h

and (old y-coordinate) = (new y-coordinate) + k

Hence, if the origin is shifted at a point (h, k), we must substitute $X + h$ and $Y + k$ for x and y, respectively.

Method to Solve the Problems Based on Shifting of Origin

There are two types of problems based on shifting of origin, which are given below

Type I If coordinates of a point say P with respect to old axes are given say (x, y) and origin is shifted to (α, β), then coordinates of point P with respect to new axes will be $(x - \alpha, y - \beta)$.

Type II If an equation of a curve in x and y with respect to old axes is given and origin is shifted to (α, β), then new equation of curve with respect to new axes will be obtained by putting $X + \alpha$ in place of x and $Y + \beta$ in place of y in old equation.

Example 11 Find the new coordinates of point $(3, -4)$, if the origin is shifted to $(1, 2)$ by a translation.

Sol. The coordinates of the new origin are $h = 1, k = 2$ and the original coordinates are given point are $x = 3, y = -4$.

The transformation relation between the old coordinates (x, y) and the new coordinates (X, Y) are given by

$$x = X + h, \text{ i.e. } X = x - h \qquad \ldots(i)$$

and $$y = Y + k, \text{ i.e. } Y = y - k \qquad \ldots(ii)$$

On substituting the values $x = 3, y = -4, h = 1$ and $k = 2$ in Eqs. (i) and (ii), we get

$$X = 3 - 1 = 2 \text{ and } Y = -4 - 2 = -6$$

Hence, the coordinates of point $(3, -4)$ in the new system are $(2, -6)$.

Example 12 If the axes are shifted to the point $(-2, 3)$ without rotation, then transform the equation of line $y + 3x = 2$ into new axes.

Sol. Let coordinates of a point P changes from (x, y) to (X, Y) in new coordinate axes whose origin has the coordinates $h = -2, k = 3$.

Then, $x = X - 2$ and $y = Y + 3$

Given equation of line with respect to old axes is

$$y + 3x = 2 \qquad \ldots(i)$$

On putting $x = X - 2$ and $y = Y + 3$ in Eq. (i), we get

$$Y + 3 + 3(X - 2) = 2$$

$$\Rightarrow Y + 3X + 3 - 6 = 2 \Rightarrow Y + 3X = 5$$

Hence, the required equation of line with respect to new axes is $y + 3x = 5$.

Topic Practice 1

Very Short Answer Type Questions

(2 Marks)

1 Find the distance between the points
 (i) $A(2, -3)$ and $B(6, -3)$
 (ii) $A(1, -4)$ and $B(0, -3)$
 (iii) $P(3, 4)$ and $Q(0, 0)$.

2 Find the point on the X-axis which is equidistant from the points (7, 6) and (3, 4).

3 If A is a point on the X-axis with abscissa -5 and B is a point on the Y-axis with ordinate 8. Find the distance AB.

4 Find the transformed equation of $xy - y^2 - x + y = 0$, when the origin is shifted to the point (1, 1), after translation of axes. **[NCERT]**

5 Using the distance formula show that the points $A(3 - 2)$, $B(5, 2)$ and $C(8, 8)$ are collinear.

6 If the points $A(-2, -1)$, $B(1, 0)$, $C(x, 3)$ and $D(1, y)$ are the vertices of a parallelogram, find the values of x and y (without using distance formula).

7 Find the area of ΔABC, the mid-points of whose sides AB, BC and CA are $D(3, -1)$, $E(5, 3)$ and $F(1, -3)$, respectively.

8 In what ratio is the line segment joining the points $A(-4, 2)$ and $B(8, 3)$ divided by the Y-axis? Also, find the point of intersection.

Short Answer Type Questions

4 Marks

9 Find the new coordinates of the points in each of the following cases if the origin is shifted to the point $(-3, -2)$ by a translation of axes.

(i) $(-1, -2)$ (ii) $(1, 1)$
(iii) $(0, 1)$ (iv) $(5, 0)$

10 The base of an equilateral triangle with side $2a$ lies along the Y-axis such that the mid-point of the base is at the origin. Find vertices of the triangle. **[NCERT]**

11 Show that the points $A(7, 10)$, $B(-2, 5)$ and $C(3, -4)$ are the vertices of an isosceles right angled triangle.

12 Draw the quadrilateral in the cartesian plane, whose vertices are $(-4, 5)$, $(0, 7)$, $(5, -5)$ and $(-4, -2)$. Also, find its area. **[NCERT]**

Hints & Answers

1. (i) 4 (ii) $\sqrt{2}$ (iii) 5

2. Let the point be $P(x, 0)$.
Given, $(x-7)^2 + (0-6)^2 = (x-3)^2 + (0-4)^2$
Ans. $\left(\frac{15}{2}, 0\right)$

3. Point $A = (-5, 0)$ and $B = (0, 8)$, then use distance formula.
Ans. $\sqrt{89}$

4. On putting $x = X + 1$ and $y = Y + 1$ in given equation, we get $(X+1)(Y+1) - (Y+1)^2 - (X+1)$
$+ (Y+1) = 0 \Rightarrow XY - Y^2 = 0$
Ans. $xy - y^2 = 0$

5. Show that $AB + BC = AC$

6. Mid-point of AC = Mid-point of BD **Ans.** $x = 4$, $y = 2$

7. Since, D, E and F are the mid-points of sides AB, BC and CA, respectively of a ΔABC.
$\therefore$ ar $(\Delta ABC) = 4 \times$ ar (ΔDEF) **Ans.** 8 sq units

8. Let the required ratio be $k:1$. Then, the point of intersection are $\left(\frac{8k-4}{k+1}, \frac{3k+2}{k+1}\right)$.
Since, this point lies on Y-axis, therefore $\frac{8k-4}{k+1} = 0$
Ans. Ratio = 1 : 2, Point = $\left(0, \frac{7}{3}\right)$

9. (i) The transformation relation between the old coordinate (x, y) and the new coordinate (X, Y) are given by
$x = X + h$ and $y = Y + k$
$\Rightarrow X = x - h$ and $Y = y - k$
$\Rightarrow X = -1 - (-3)$ and $Y = (-2) - (-2)$ **Ans.** $(2, 0)$
(ii) Solve as part (i). **Ans.** $(4, 3)$
(iii) Solve as part (i). **Ans.** $(3, 3)$
(iv) Solve as part (i). **Ans.** $(8, 2)$

10. Let ΔABC be the given equilateral triangle, with base BC on Y-axis. Then, cordinates of B and C are $(0, a)$ and $(0, -a)$ respectively. Let the coordinates of A be (h, k).
Since, ΔABC is an equilateral, therefore $AB = BC = AC$
$\Rightarrow$ $AB = AC \Rightarrow AB^2 = AC^2$
Also, $AB^2 = BC^2$
Ans. $(\sqrt{3}a, 0), (0, a), (0, -a)$ or $(-\sqrt{3}a, 0), (0, a), (0, -a)$

11. First, find out the values of AB, BC, CA by distance formula and prove that ΔABC is an isosceles triangle, then prove that this triangle is also right angled triangle by converse of Pythagoras theorem.

12. Let the given points be $A(-4, 5)$, $B(0, 7)$, $C(5, -5)$ and $D(-4, -2)$. Area of quadrilateral $ABCD$
= Area of ΔADC + Area of ΔABC
Now, area of ΔADC
$= \frac{1}{2}|[-4(-2+5) - 4(-5-5) + 5(5+2)]|$
Area of $\Delta ABC = \frac{1}{2}|[-4(7+5) + 0(-5-5) + 5(5-7)]|$
Ans. $\frac{121}{2}$ sq units

TOPIC 02 Slope (or Gradient) of a Straight Line

A **straight line** is a curve, such that all the points on the line segment joining any two points of it lies on it.

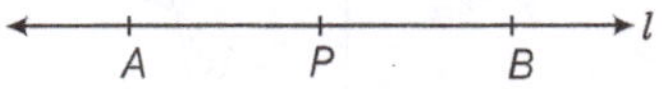

Angle of Inclination of a Line

An angle 'θ' made by the line with positive X-axis in anti-clockwise direction is called the **angle of inclination** (or inclination) of a line. A line in coordinate plane forms two angles with the X-axis, which are supplementary.

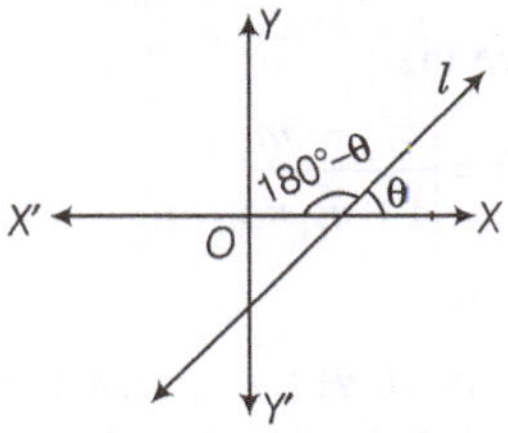

Thus, $\quad 0° \le \theta \le 180°$

Note (i) When $\theta = 0°$, then line is parallel **to X-axis (or horizontal line)**.

(ii) When $\theta = 90°$, then line is perpendicular to X-axis, i.e. parallel to **Y-axis (or vertical line)**.

(iii) A line, which is neither horizontal nor vertical, is called the **oblique line**.

Slope or Gradient of a Line

If θ is the angle of inclination of a line l, then $\tan\theta$ is called the slope or gradient of the line l and it is denoted by m.

i.e. $\quad m = \tan\theta$

Or

The slope of a line is the tangent of the angle made by the line in the anti-clockwise direction with the positive X-axis, i.e. $m = \tan\theta$.

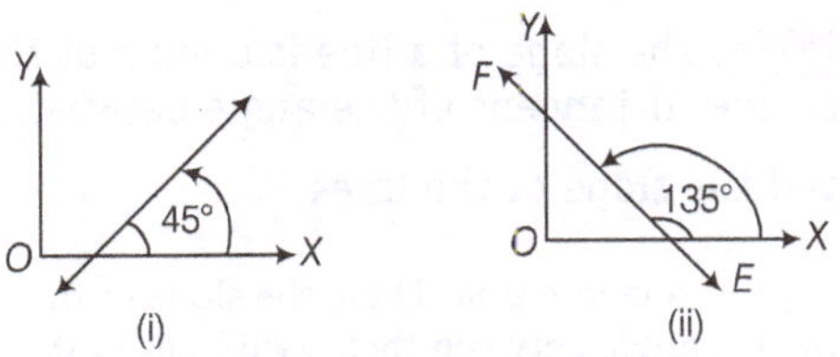

(i) (ii)

e.g. For figure (i), $\quad m = \tan 45° = 1$

and for figure (ii), $m = \tan 135° = -1$

Note (i) The slope of X-axis is $m = \tan 0° = 0$.

(ii) The slope of a line, when $\theta = 90°$ is not defined, i.e. the slope of Y-axis is not defined.

Example 1 Find the slope of line, whose inclination is 60° and 150°.

Sol. Let θ be the inclination of a line, then its slope $= \tan\theta$.

At $\theta = 60°$, $\quad$ slope of a line $= \tan 60° = \sqrt{3}$

At $\theta = 150°$, Slope of a line $= \tan(150°)$

$= \tan(180° - 30°)$

$= -\tan 30° = -\dfrac{1}{\sqrt{3}} \quad [\because \tan(180° - \theta) = -\tan\theta]$

Example 2 Find the slope of a line, which makes an angle of 30° with the positive direction of Y-axis measured anti-clockwise. **[NCERT]**

Sol. Given, $\angle YPQ = 30°$

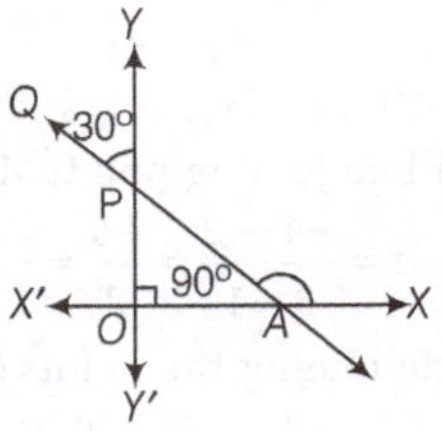

Here, $\angle YPQ = \angle OPA \quad$ [vertically opposite angle]

$\because \quad \angle OPA + \angle POA + \angle PAO = 180°$

[∵ sum of all angles of a triangle is 180°]

$\therefore \quad 30° + 90° + \angle PAO = 180°$

$\Rightarrow \quad \angle PAO = 180° - 120° = 60°$

$\Rightarrow \quad \angle PAX = 180° - 60° = 120° \quad$ [by linear pair axiom]

$\therefore$ Slope of line $AQ = m = \tan 120° \quad [\because m = \tan\theta]$

$= \tan(180° - 60°)$

$[\because \tan(180° - \theta) = -\tan\theta]$

$= -\tan 60° = -\sqrt{3}$

Slope of a Line joining Two Points

Let $A(x_1, y_1)$ and $B(x_2, y_2)$ be two given points and θ be the inclination of the line AB, so that $m = \tan\theta$.

From A and B, draw AM and BN perpendiculars to the axis and draw $AC \perp BN$.

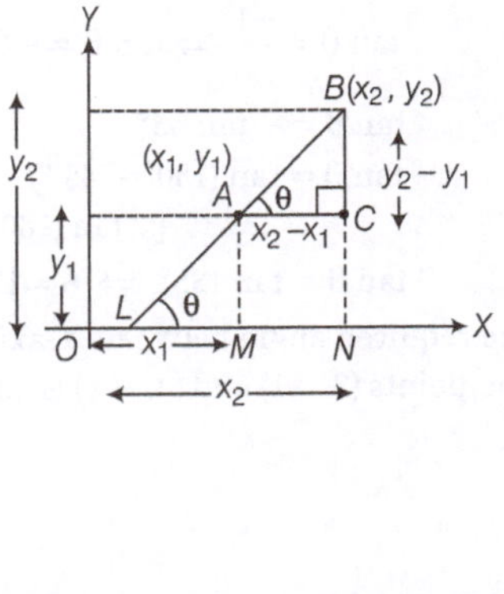

Let BA meets OX at L.

Then, $\angle CAB = \angle XLB = \theta$ [corresponding angles]

$\therefore$ $AC = MN = ON - OM = x_2 - x_1$

and $BC = BN - CN = BN - AM = y_2 - y_1$

In ΔACB, we have $\tan\theta = \dfrac{BC}{AC}$

$$\Rightarrow \quad m = \tan\theta = \frac{y_2 - y_1}{x_2 - x_1} \text{ or } \frac{y_1 - y_2}{x_1 - x_2}$$

This relation is true in both the cases, whether θ is an acute angle or an obtuse angle.

Example 3 Find the slope of a line joining following two points

(i) $A(1, 2)$ and $B(3, -4)$ (ii) $(3,-2)$ and $(7, -2)$.

Sol. We know that, slope of a line joining two points (x_1, y_1) and (x_2, y_2) is $m = \dfrac{y_2 - y_1}{x_2 - x_1}$

(i) Given, $A(1, 2) \equiv (x_1, y_1)$ and $B(3, -4) \equiv (x_2, y_2)$

$\therefore$ Slope of line joining points A and B is

$$m = \frac{-4-2}{3-1} = \frac{-6}{2} = -3$$

(ii) Slope of line joining the points $(3,-2)$ and $(7,-2)$ is

$$m = \frac{-2-(-2)}{7-3} = \frac{0}{4} = 0$$

Example 4 Find the angle between the X-axis and the line joining the points $(3, -1)$ and $(4, -2)$. **[NCERT]**

Sol. Given, $(x_1, y_1) \equiv (3, -1)$ and $(x_2, y_2) \equiv (4, -2)$

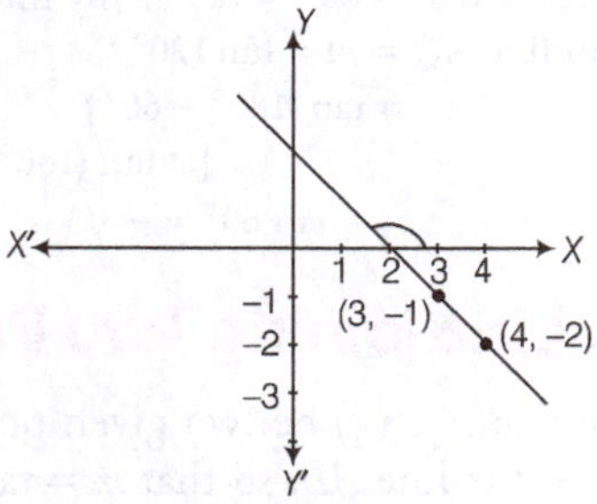

Slope of line, $m = \dfrac{y_2 - y_1}{x_2 - x_1} = \dfrac{-2+1}{4-3}$

$\Rightarrow \quad \tan\theta = \dfrac{-1}{1} \Rightarrow \tan\theta = -1$

$\Rightarrow \quad \tan\theta = -\tan 45°$ [$\because 1 = \tan 45°$]

$\Rightarrow \quad \tan\theta = \tan(180° - 45°)$

[$\because \tan(180° - \theta) = -\tan\theta$]

$\Rightarrow \quad \tan\theta = \tan 135° \Rightarrow \theta = 135°$

Hence, the required angle between X-axis and the line joining the points $(3, -1)$ and $(4, -2)$ is $135°$.

Angle between Two Lines

Let l_1 and l_2 be two lines and their inclination are α_1 and α_2, respectively. Then, their slopes are $m_1 = \tan\alpha_1$ and $m_2 = \tan\alpha_2$.

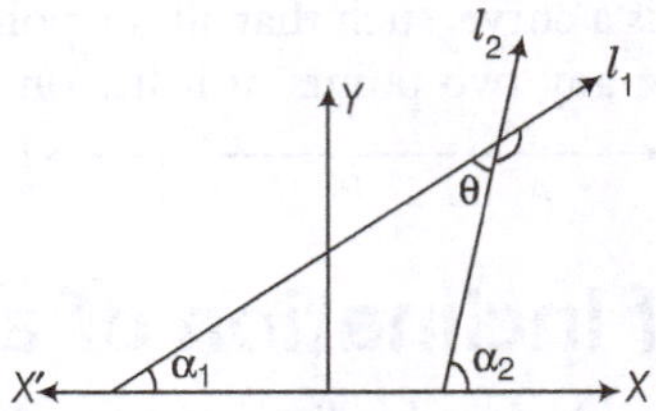

Let θ be the angle between l_1 and l_2, then.

$$\tan\theta = \pm\frac{m_2 - m_1}{1 + m_1 m_2}$$

For acute angle, we take

$$\tan\theta = \left|\frac{m_2 - m_1}{1 + m_1 m_2}\right|$$

Note

(i) If $\tan\theta$ is positive, then θ will be an acute angle.

(ii) If $\tan\theta$ is negative, then θ will be an obtuse angle.

Example 5 Find the tangent of angle between the lines joining the points $(0,0)$, $(2,3)$ and the points $(2, -2)$, $(3, 5)$.

Sol. Let θ be the angle between the given lines.

We have, m_1 = Slope of the line joining $(0, 0)$ and $(2, 3)$

$$= \frac{3-0}{2-0} = \frac{3}{2}$$

and m_2 = Slope of the line joining $(2, -2)$ and $(3, 5)$

$$= \frac{5+2}{3-2} = 7$$

Now, $\tan\theta = \pm\left(\dfrac{m_2 - m_1}{1 + m_1 m_2}\right) = \pm\left(\dfrac{7 - 3/2}{1 + 7(3/2)}\right)$

$$= \pm\left(\frac{11/2}{23/2}\right) = \pm\left(\frac{11}{23}\right)$$

Example 6 The slope of a line is double of the slope of another line. If tangent of the angle between them is $\frac{1}{3}$, then find the slope of the lines. **[NCERT]**

Sol. If slope of one line is m. Then, the slope of the other line is $2m$. Let angle between these two lines be θ.

Then, $\tan\theta = \dfrac{1}{3}$ [given]

$\Rightarrow \quad \left|\dfrac{2m - m}{1 + 2m \cdot m}\right| = \dfrac{1}{3}$ $\left[\because \tan\theta = \left|\dfrac{m_2 - m_1}{1 + m_1 \cdot m_2}\right|\right]$

$$\Rightarrow \quad \frac{m}{1+2m^2} = \pm\frac{1}{3}$$

Here, two cases arise.

Case **I** When $\frac{m}{1+2m^2} = \frac{1}{3}$, then $3m = 1 + 2m^2$

$$\Rightarrow \quad 2m^2 - 3m + 1 = 0$$
$$\Rightarrow \quad 2m^2 - 2m - m + 1 = 0$$
$$\Rightarrow \quad 2m(m-1) - 1(m-1) = 0$$
$$\Rightarrow \quad (m-1)(2m-1) = 0$$
$$\Rightarrow m - 1 = 0 \text{ or } 2m - 1 = 0 \Rightarrow m = 1 \text{ or } m = \frac{1}{2}$$

As the slopes of the lines are m and $2m$, therefore the slopes of the lines are 1 and 2 or $\frac{1}{2}$ and 1.

Case **II** When $\frac{m}{1+2m^2} = \frac{-1}{3}$, then

$$3m = -1 - 2m^2$$
$$\Rightarrow \quad 2m^2 + 3m + 1 = 0$$
$$\Rightarrow \quad 2m^2 + 2m + m + 1 = 0$$
$$\Rightarrow \quad 2m(m+1) + 1(m+1) = 0$$
$$\Rightarrow \quad (2m+1)(m+1) = 0$$
$$\Rightarrow \quad 2m + 1 = 0 \text{ or } m + 1 = 0$$
$$\Rightarrow \quad m = \frac{-1}{2} \text{ or } m = -1$$

As the slopes of the lines are m and $2m$, therefore the slopes of the lines are $\frac{-1}{2}$ and -1 or -1 and -2.

Condition of Parallelism (Parallel Lines)

If two lines of slopes m_1 and m_2 are parallel, then the angle θ between them is 0°.

$$\therefore \quad \tan\theta = \tan 0° = 0 \qquad [\because \tan 0° = 0]$$

$$\Rightarrow \quad \frac{m_2 - m_1}{1 + m_1 m_2} = 0 \Rightarrow m_2 - m_1 = 0 \Rightarrow m_1 = m_2$$

Thus, two lines are parallel, if and only if their slopes are equal i.e. iff $m_1 = m_2$.

Example 7 What is the value of y so that the line through (3, y) and (2, 7) is parallel to the line through (−1, 4) and (0, 6)?

Sol. Let $A(3, y)$, $B(2, 7)$, $C(-1, 4)$ and $D(0, 6)$ be the given points.

Then, m_1 = Slope of the line $AB = \frac{7-y}{2-3} = (y-7)$

and m_2 = Slope of the line $CD = \frac{6-4}{0-(-1)} = 2$

Since, AB and CD are parallel.

$$\therefore \quad m_1 = m_2 \Rightarrow y - 7 = 2 \Rightarrow y = 9$$

Condition of Perpendicularity (Perpendicular Lines)

If two lines of slopes m_1 and m_2 are perpendicular, then the angle θ between them is 90°.

$$\therefore \quad \tan\theta = \tan 90° = \frac{\sin 90°}{\cos 90°} = \frac{1}{0}$$

$$\Rightarrow \quad \frac{m_2 - m_1}{1 + m_1 m_2} = \frac{1}{0} \Rightarrow 1 + m_1 m_2 = 0$$

$$\therefore \quad m_1 m_2 = -1$$

Thus, two lines are perpendicular, if and only if their slopes m_1 and m_2 satisfy the following condition

$$\boxed{m_1 \cdot m_2 = -1} \text{ or } \boxed{m_1 = -\frac{1}{m_2}}$$

Hence, two lines are perpendicular to each other if and only if their slopes are negative reciprocals of each other.

Example 8 Line through the points (−2, 6) and (4, 8) is perpendicular to the line through the (8, 12) and (x, 24). Find the value of x. **[NCERT]**

Sol. Slope of the line through the points (−2, 6) and (4, 8) is

$$m_1 = \frac{8-6}{4-(-2)} = \frac{2}{6} = \frac{1}{3}$$

Slope of the line through the points (8, 12) and (x, 24) is

$$m_2 = \frac{24-12}{x-8} = \frac{12}{x-8}$$

Since, two lines are perpendicular,

$$\therefore \quad m_1 m_2 = -1$$

$$\Rightarrow \quad \frac{1}{3} \times \frac{12}{x-8} = -1$$

$$\Rightarrow \quad 4 = -(x-8) \Rightarrow x = 4$$

Example 9 Using slopes, prove that the points $A(-2, -1)$, $B(4, 0)$, $C(3, 3)$ and $D(-3, 2)$ are the vertices of a parallelogram.

Sol. Given points are $A(-2, -1)$, $B(4, 0)$, $C(3, 3)$ and $D(-3, 2)$.

Now, slope of $AB = \frac{0-(-1)}{4-(-2)} = \frac{1}{6}$

Slope of $DC = \frac{3-2}{3-(-3)} = \frac{1}{6}$

Slope of $BC = \frac{3-0}{3-4} = \frac{3}{-1} = -3$

and slope of $AD = \frac{2-(-1)}{-3-(-2)} = \frac{3}{-1} = -3$

$\because$ Slope of AB = Slope of DC, therefore $AB \parallel DC$

Slope of BC = Slope of AD, therefore $BC \parallel AD$

Thus, $ABCD$ is a parallelogram. **Hence proved.**

Collinearity of Three Points

If A, B and C are three points in XY-plane, then they will be collinear i.e. will lie on a same line if and only if

Slope of AB = Slope of BC

Example 10 Prove that the points A (1, 4), B (3, − 2) and C (4, − 5) are collinear.

Sol. Given points are A (1, 4), B (3, − 2) and C(4, − 5)

From the condition of collinearity of three points A, B and C, we should have

Slope of AB = Slope of BC

i.e. $$\frac{-2-4}{3-1} = \frac{-5+2}{4-3} \quad \left[\because \text{slope} = \frac{y_2 - y_1}{x_2 - x_1}\right]$$

$$\Rightarrow \frac{-6}{2} = \frac{-3}{1} \Rightarrow -3 = -3, \text{ which is true.}$$

Thus, points A, B and C are collinear. **Hence proved.**

Example 11 If three points $(h, 0)$, (a, b) and $(0, k)$ lie on a line, show that $\frac{a}{h} + \frac{b}{k} = 1$. **[NCERT]**

Sol. Let the given points be $A(h, 0)$, $B(a, b)$ and $C(0, k)$.

If A, B and C are collinear, then

Slope of AB = Slope of BC = Slope of CA

$$\Rightarrow \frac{b-0}{a-h} = \frac{k-b}{0-a} = \frac{0-k}{h-0}$$

On taking first two terms, we get

$$\frac{b}{a-h} = \frac{k-b}{-a}$$

$$\Rightarrow -ab = (a-h)(k-b)$$

$$\Rightarrow -ab = ak - ab - hk + bh$$

$$\Rightarrow ak + bh = hk$$

Dividing each term by hk, we get

$$\frac{ak}{hk} + \frac{bh}{hk} = \frac{hk}{hk} \Rightarrow \frac{a}{h} + \frac{b}{k} = 1$$ **Hence proved.**

Topic Practice 2

Very Short Answer Type Questions

(2 Marks)

1 Find the slope of a line whose inclination is
(i) 30° (ii) 135°

2 Find the inclination of a line whose slope is
(i) $\frac{1}{\sqrt{3}}$ (ii) $-\sqrt{3}$

3 Find the slope of a line which passes through the points
(i) (0, − 3) and (2, 1) (ii) (− 2, 3) and (4, − 6)
(iii) $(at_1^2, 2at_1)$ and $(at_2^2, 2at_2)$

4 If the slope of the line joining the points $A(x, 2)$ and $B(6, -8)$ is $-5/4$, then find the value of x.

5 Find the slope and inclination of line through pair of points (1, 2) and (5, 6).

6 Find the slope of a line perpendicular to the line, which passes through (0, 8) and (− 5, 2).

7 What is the value of y, so that the line through (4, y) and (3, 8) is parallel to the line through (− 2, 5) and (1, 8)?

8 State whether the two lines in each of the following are parallel, perpendicular or neither.
(i) Through (5, 6) and (2, 3); through (9, − 2) and (6, − 5).
(ii) Through (6, 3) and (1, 1); through (− 2, 5) and (2, − 5)
(iii) Through (3, 15) and (16, 6); through (− 5, 3) and (8, 2).

9 Find the angle between the lines whose slopes are
(i) $\sqrt{3}$ and $\frac{1}{\sqrt{3}}$ (ii) $(2-\sqrt{3})$ and $(2+\sqrt{3})$

10 Without using Pythagoras theorem, show that $A(12, 8)$, $B(-2, 6)$ and $C(6, 0)$ are the vertices of right angled triangle.

11 Find the coordinate of the orthocentre of the triangle whose vertices are (− 1, 3), (2, − 1) and (0, 0).

12 By using slope method, show that the points $P(4, 8)$, $Q(5, 12)$ and $R(9, 28)$ are collinear.

13 By using slope method, find the value of x for which the points $A(5, 1)$, $B(1, -1)$ and $C(x, 4)$ are collinear.

14 Find the slope of a line, which passes through the origin and mid-point of the line segment joining the points $P(0, -4)$ and $Q(8, 0)$. **[NCERT]**

15 A line passes through the points $A(4, -6)$ and $B(-2, -5)$. Show that the line AB makes an obtuse angle with the X-axis.

16 Determine $\angle B$ of the triangle with vertices $A(-2, 1)$, $B(2, 3)$ and $C(-2, -4)$.

17 A quadrilateral has the vertices at the points $A(-4, 2)$, $B(2, 6)$, $C(8, 5)$ and $D(9, -7)$. Show that the mid-points of the sides of this quadrilateral are the vertices of a parallelogram.

18 Two lines passing through the point (2, 3) make an angle of 45°. If the slope of one of the lines is 2, then find the slope of the other line.

Hints & Answers

1. Use the formula, $m = \tan\theta$ **Ans.** (i) $\frac{1}{\sqrt{3}}$ (ii) -1

2. (i) 30° (ii) 120° **3.** (i) 2 (ii) $-\frac{3}{2}$ (iii) $\frac{2}{t_2 + t_1}$

4. $x = -2$ **5.** 1; 45° **6.** $-\frac{5}{6}$

7. $m_1 = \frac{8-y}{3-4}$, $m_2 = \frac{8-5}{1+2}$

Also, $m_1 = m_2 \Rightarrow \frac{8-y}{-1} = 1 \Rightarrow y = 9$

8. (i) parallel (ii) perpendicular (iii) neither

9. (i) 30° or 150° (ii) 60° or 120°

10. Let $A(12, 8)$, $B(-2, 6)$ and $C(6, 0)$ are vertices of ΔABC

Slope of $AB = \frac{6-8}{-2-12} = \frac{-2}{-14} = \frac{1}{7}$

Slope of $BC = \frac{0-6}{6+2} = \frac{-6}{8} = \frac{-3}{4}$

Slope of $AC = \frac{0-8}{6-12} = \frac{-8}{-6} = \frac{4}{3}$

Now, as slope of $BC \times$ slope of $AC = \frac{-3}{4} \times \frac{4}{3} = -1$,

therefore $\angle C = \frac{\pi}{2}$.

11. The orthocentre is the point of intersection of the altitudes from the vertices to the opposite sides.

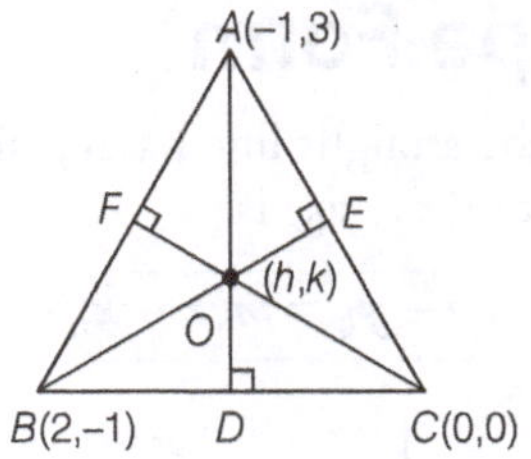

$$h - 3k - 5 = 0 \quad \text{...(ii)}$$

Slope of line $AO \times$ Slope of line $BC = -1$

$$\Rightarrow \frac{k-3}{h+1} \times \left(-\frac{1}{2}\right) = -1 \quad [\because m_1 \times m_2 = -1]$$

$$\Rightarrow \frac{k-3}{h+1} = 2 \Rightarrow 2h - k + 5 = 0$$

Also, $BO \perp AC$ ...(i)

$\therefore$ Slope of line $BO \times$ Slope of line $AC = -1$

$\Rightarrow \frac{k+1}{h-2} \times \frac{3-0}{-1-0} = -1$ **Ans.** $(-4, -3)$

12. Slope of PQ = Slope of QR

13. Slope of AB = Slope of BC **Ans.** $x = 11$

14. Mid-point of $PQ = \left(\frac{0+8}{2}, \frac{-4+0}{2}\right) = (4, -2)$

Ans. Slope of required line $= -\frac{1}{2}$

15. Slope of AB is negative.

16. Slope of line, $AB = \frac{3-1}{2+2} = \frac{2}{4} = \frac{1}{2} = m_1$ (say)

Slope of line, $BC = \frac{-4-3}{-2-2} = \frac{7}{4} = m_2$ (say)

$\therefore \tan B = \left|\frac{m_2 - m_1}{1 + m_1 m_2}\right| = \left|\frac{\frac{7}{4} - \frac{1}{2}}{1 + \frac{1}{2}\cdot\frac{7}{4}}\right|$ **Ans.** $\angle B = \tan^{-1}\left(\frac{2}{3}\right)$

17. Coordinates of E = Mid-point of $A(-4, 2)$ and $B(2, 6)$

$$= \left(\frac{-4+2}{2}, \frac{2+6}{2}\right) = (-1, 4)$$

Coordinates of F = Mid-point of $B(2, 6)$ and $C(8, 5)$

$$= \left(\frac{2+8}{2}, \frac{6+5}{2}\right) = \left(5, \frac{11}{2}\right)$$

Coordinates of G = Mid-point of $C(8, 5)$ and $D(9, -7)$

$$= \left(\frac{8+9}{2}, \frac{5-7}{2}\right) = \left(\frac{17}{2}, -1\right)$$

Coordinates of H = Mid-point of $A(-4, 2)$ and $D(9, -7)$

$$= \left(\frac{9-4}{2}, \frac{-7+2}{2}\right) = \left(\frac{5}{2}, \frac{-5}{2}\right)$$

$$\text{Slope of } EF = \frac{\frac{11}{2} - 4}{5 - (-1)} = \frac{1}{4}$$

$$\text{Slope of } GH = \frac{-\frac{5}{2} - (-1)}{\frac{5}{2} - \frac{17}{2}} = \frac{1}{4}$$

$\therefore$ Slope of EF = Slope of $GH \Rightarrow EF \parallel GH$

Similarly, slope of FG = slope of $EH \Rightarrow FG \parallel EH$

18. Angle between these two lines is 45°.

$\therefore 1 = \left|\frac{2-m}{1+2m}\right| \Rightarrow 1 = \pm\frac{(2-m)}{1+2m}$ **Ans.** $m = \frac{1}{3}$ or -3

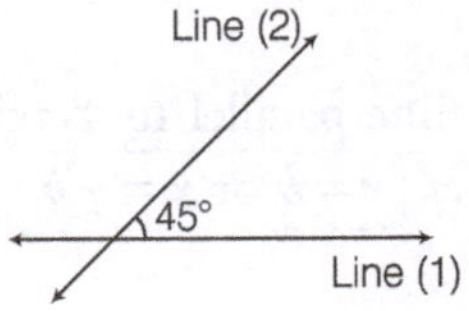

TOPIC 03

Various Forms of Equation of a Line

The equation of a straight line is the relation between x (the abscissa) and y (the ordinate) which is satisfied by the coordinates of each and every point on the line and is not satisfied by the coordinates of any point which does not lie on the line.

The various forms of the equation of a line under different conditions are given below

Equation of Line Parallel to X-axis (or Equation of Horizontal Line)

Let L be a straight line parallel to X-axis at a distance a from it, then the ordinate of every point lying on the line is either a or $-a$. Equation of line parallel to X-axis (i.e. equation of horizontal line) is either $\boxed{y = a \text{ or } y = -a.}$

The choice of sign will depend upon the position of the line according as the line is on the positive or negative side of the Y-axis.

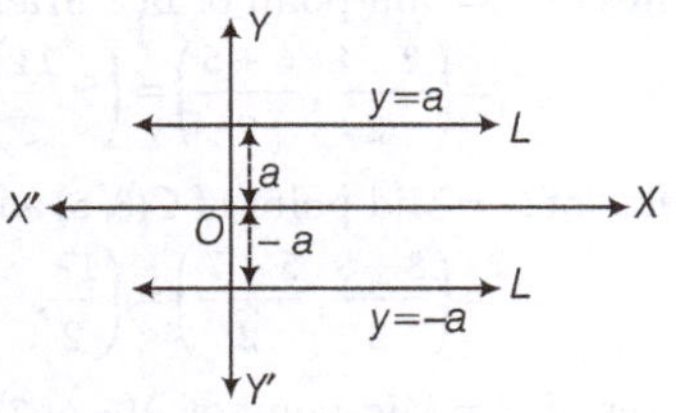

Example 1 Write down the equation of a line parallel to the X-axis

(i) at a distance of 6 units above the X-axis.

(ii) at a distance of 3 units below the X-axis.

Sol. (i) The equation of a line parallel to the X-axis at a distance of 6 units above X-axis is $y = 6$.

(ii) The equation of a line parallel to the X-axis at a distance of 3 units below the X-axis is $y = -3$.

Equation of Line Parallel to Y-axis (or Equation of Vertical Line)

Let L be a straight line parallel to Y-axis at a distance b from it, then the abscissa of every point lying on the line is either b or $-b$.

$\therefore$ Equation of the line parallel to Y-axis (i.e. equation of vertical line) is either $\boxed{x = b \text{ or } x = -b.}$

Here, the choice of sign will depend upon the position of the line according as the line is on the positive or negative side of the X-axis.

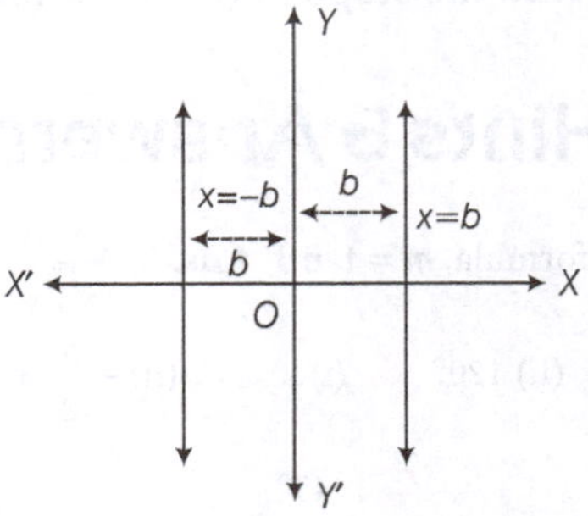

Note (i) Equation of X-axis is $y = 0$.

(ii) Equation of Y-axis is $x = 0$.

Example 2 Write down the equation of a line parallel to the Y-axis

(i) at a distance of 5 units on left hand side of the Y-axis,

(ii) at a distance of 7 units on right hand side of the Y-axis.

Sol. (i) The equation of a line parallel to the Y-axis at a distance of 5 units on its left is $x = -5$.

(ii) The equation of a line parallel to the Y-axis at a distance of 7 units on its right is $x = 7$.

Example 3 Find the equation of the lines parallel to the axes and passing through the point $(-3, 5)$.

Sol. Clearly, the equation of a line parallel to the X-axis and passing through $(-3, 5)$ is $y = 5$.

The equation of a line parallel to the Y-axis and passing through $(-3, 5)$ is $x = -3$.

Point-Slope Form

The equation of the straight line having slope m and passes through the point $Q(x_0, y_0)$ is

$$\boxed{y - y_0 = m(x - x_0)}$$

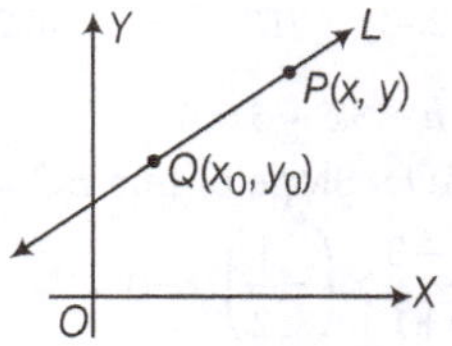

Example 4 Find the equation of the line passing through (–4, 3) and having slope $\frac{1}{2}$.

Sol. Equation of the line passing through the point (x_0, y_0) and having slope m is $y - y_0 = m(x - x_0)$ ...(i)

Given, m = slope of the line $= \frac{1}{2}$ and $x_0 = -4$, $y_0 = 3$

From Eq. (i), required equation of the line is

$$y - 3 = \frac{1}{2}(x + 4)$$

$$\Rightarrow \quad 2y - 6 = x + 4$$

$$\Rightarrow \quad x - 2y + 10 = 0$$

Example 5 Find the equation of line intersecting the Y-axis at a distance of 2 units above the origin and making an angle of 30° with the positive direction of the X-axis. **[NCERT]**

Sol. Given, the line intersect the Y-axis at distance of 2 units above the origin. It shows that the line passes through (0, 2).

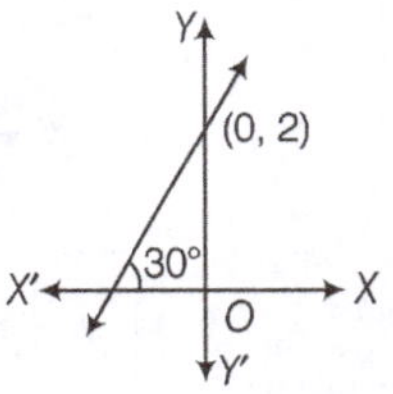

$\because$ It makes an angle 30° with the positive direction of X-axis. So, the slope of the line,

$$m = \tan 30° = \frac{1}{\sqrt{3}} \quad [\because m = \tan\theta]$$

Thus, the equation of straight line is

$$y - 2 = \frac{1}{\sqrt{3}}(x - 0) \quad [\because y - y_0 = m(x - x_0)]$$

$$\Rightarrow \quad \frac{x}{\sqrt{3}} - y + 2 = 0 \Rightarrow x - \sqrt{3}\,y + 2\sqrt{3} = 0$$

Example 6 Find the equation of the perpendicular bisector of the line segment joining the points $A(2, 3)$ and $B(6, -5)$.

Sol. The slope of AB is given by

$$m = \frac{-5 - 3}{6 - 2} = -2 \quad \left[\because m = \frac{y_2 - y_1}{x_2 - x_1}\right]$$

$\therefore$ Slope of a line perpendicular to $AB = -\frac{1}{m} = \frac{1}{2}$

Let P be the mid-point of AB. Then, the coordinates of P are $\left(\frac{2+6}{2}, \frac{3-5}{2}\right)$ i.e. $(4, -1)$.

Thus, the required line passes through $P(4, -1)$ and has slope $\frac{1}{2}$. So, its equation is

$$y + 1 = \frac{1}{2}(x - 4) \quad [\because y - y_0 = m(x - x_0)]$$

$$\Rightarrow \quad x - 2y - 6 = 0$$

Example 7 A line perpendicular to the line segment joining the points (1, 0) and (2, 3) divides it in the ratio $1 : n$. Find the equation of the line. **[NCERT]**

Sol. Let the given points be $A(1, 0)$ and $B(2, 3)$.

Let the line PQ divide AB in the ratio $1 : n$ at R internally.

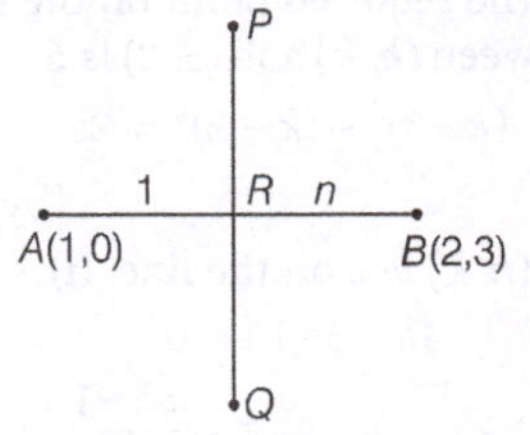

Then, coordinates of R

$$= \left(\frac{1 \times x_2 + n \times x_1}{1 + n}, \frac{1 \times y_2 + n \times y_1}{1 + n}\right)$$

[by internal division formula]

$$= \left(\frac{1 \times 2 + n \times 1}{1 + n}, \frac{1 \times 3 + n \times 0}{1 + n}\right)$$

$[\because x_1 = 1, y_1 = 0, x_2 = 2, y_2 = 3]$

$$= \left(\frac{n + 2}{n + 1}, \frac{3}{1 + n}\right)$$

Let slope of line PQ be m.

$\because \quad PQ \perp AB$

$\therefore$ Slope of line $PQ \times$ Slope of line $AB = -1$

$[\because m_1 m_2 = -1]$

$$\Rightarrow \quad m \times \frac{y_2 - y_1}{x_2 - x_1} = -1 \Rightarrow m \times \frac{3 - 0}{2 - 1} = -1$$

$[\because x_1 = 1, y_1 = 0, x_2 = 2, y_2 = 3]$

$$\Rightarrow \quad m \times 3 = -1 \Rightarrow m = -\frac{1}{3}$$

Now, equation of line PQ by using $y - y_0 = m(x - x_0)$ is

$$y - \frac{3}{1 + n} = \frac{-1}{3}\left(x - \frac{n + 2}{n + 1}\right)$$

$$\left[\because R\left(\frac{n + 2}{n + 1}, \frac{3}{1 + n}\right) = (x_0, y_0)\right]$$

$$\Rightarrow \quad \frac{3(n+1)\,y - 9}{1 + n} = \frac{-x(n+1) + (n + 2)}{n + 1}$$

$$\Rightarrow \quad 3(n+1)\,y - 9 = -x(n+1) + (n + 2)$$

$$\Rightarrow \quad x(n+1) + 3(n+1)\,y = n + 2 + 9$$

$$\Rightarrow \quad x(n+1) + 3(n+1)\,y = n + 11$$

which is the required equation of line.

Example 8 If the slope of a line passing through the point A (3, 2) is $\frac{3}{4}$, then find the points on the line which are 5 units away from the point A. **[NCERT Exemplar]**

Sol. Equation of the line passing through (3, 2) having slope $\frac{3}{4}$ is given by

$$y-2=\frac{3}{4}(x-3) \quad [\because y-y_0=m(x-x_0)]$$

$$\Rightarrow \quad 4y-3x+1=0 \quad \text{...(i)}$$

Let (h, k) be the required point on the line such that distance between (h, k) and (3, 2) is 5

$$\Rightarrow \quad (h-3)^2+(k-2)^2=25 \quad \text{...(ii)}$$

[by distance formula]

Since, point (h, k) lies on the line (i)

$$4k-3h+1=0 \quad \text{...(iii)}$$

$$\Rightarrow \quad k=\frac{3h-1}{4} \quad \text{...(iv)}$$

On putting the value of k in Eq. (ii) and simplifying, we get

$$25h^2-150h-175=0 \Rightarrow h^2-6h-7=0$$

$$\Rightarrow \quad (h+1)(h-7)=0 \Rightarrow h=-1 \text{ or } h=7$$

On putting these values of h in Eq. (iv), we get

$$k=-1 \text{ or } k=5$$

Therefore, the coordinates of the required points are either $(-1, -1)$ or (7, 5).

Example 9 The mid-points of the sides of a triangle are (2, 1), (− 5, 7) and (− 5, − 5). Find the equations of the sides of the triangle.

Sol. Let $D(2, 1)$, $E(-5, 7)$ and $F(-5, -5)$ be the mid-points of sides BC, CA and AB, respectively of ΔABC.

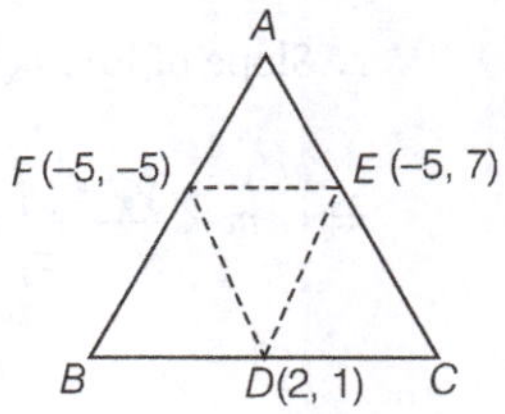

We know that the line joining the mid-points of two sides of a triangle is parallel to the third side.

$\therefore \quad DE \parallel AB$, $EF \parallel BC$ and $DF \parallel AC$

$\therefore$ Slope of AB = Slope of DE,

Slope of BC = Slope of EF and slope of AC = slope of DF

Let m_1, m_2 and m_3 be the slopes of AB, BC and CA, respectively.

Then, m_1 = Slope of AB = Slope of DE $=\frac{7-1}{-5-2}=\frac{-6}{7}$

m_2 = Slope of BC = Slope of EF $=\frac{7+5}{-5+5}$ (undefined)

and m_3 = Slope of CA = Slope of DF $=\frac{1+5}{2+5}=\frac{6}{7}$

Since, the side AB passes through $F(-5, -5)$ and has slope $m_1=\frac{-6}{7}$. So, its equation is

$$y+5=\frac{-6}{7}(x+5) \quad \text{[by using point-slope form]}$$

$$\Rightarrow \quad 6x+7y+65=0$$

Since, slope of side BC not defined, therefore it is parallel to Y-axis. Also, as it is passes through $D(2, 1)$. Therefore, its equation is $x=2$.

Hence, equation of BC is $x=2$.

Since, side CA passes through $E(-5, 7)$ and has slope $m_3=\frac{6}{7}$.

So, its equation is $y-7=\frac{6}{7}(x+5)$

$$\Rightarrow \quad 6x-7y+79=0$$

Two-Point Slope Form

The equation of a line passing through the points (x_1, y_1) and (x_2, y_2) is given by

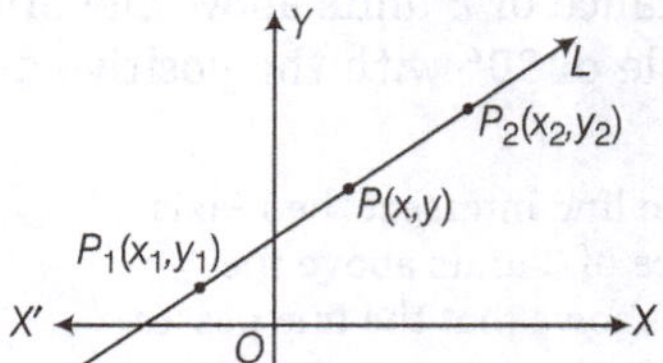

$$y-y_1=\frac{y_2-y_1}{x_2-x_1}(x-x_1)$$

Example 10 Find the equation of line passing through the points (−1, 1) and (2, − 4). **[NCERT]**

Sol. Let the given points be $A(x_1, y_1) \equiv A(-1, 1)$ and $B(x_2, y_2) \equiv B(2, -4)$, then the equation of line AB is

$$y-1=\frac{-4-1}{2+1}(x+1) \quad \left[\because y-y_1=\frac{y_2-y_1}{x_2-x_1}(x-x_1)\right]$$

$$\Rightarrow y-1=\frac{-5}{3}(x+1) \Rightarrow 3y-3=-5x-5$$

$$\Rightarrow \quad 5x+3y+2=0$$

Example 11 Find the equations of the sides of a triangle whose vertices are $A(-1, 8)$, $B(4, -2)$ and $C(-5, -3)$.

Sol. Here, we use two points form to find the equation of sides.

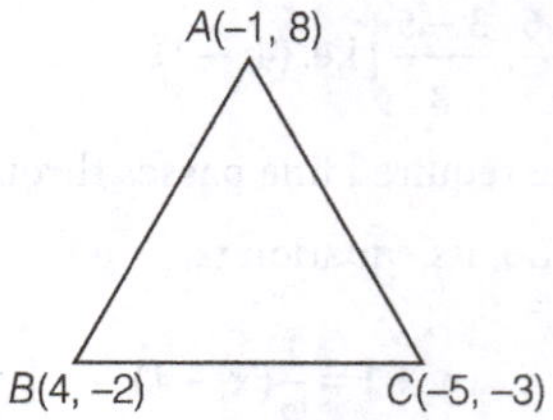

Equation of AB is $y-8=\frac{-2-8}{4+1}(x+1)$

$$\Rightarrow 5(y-8)+10(x+1)=0 \Rightarrow 10x+5y-30=0$$

$$\Rightarrow \quad 2x+y-6=0 \quad \text{[dividing both sides by 5]}$$

Equation of BC is

$$y+2=\frac{-3+2}{-5-4}(x-4)$$

$$\Rightarrow \quad -9(y+2)+(x-4)=0 \Rightarrow x-9y-22=0$$

Equation of AC is $y-8=\dfrac{-3-8}{-5+1}(x+1)$

$$\Rightarrow -4(y-8)+11(x+1)=0 \Rightarrow 11x-4y+43=0$$

Example 12 If $A(2, 1)$, $B(-2, 3)$ and $C(4, 5)$ are the vertices of a ΔABC, then find the equation of

(i) the median through C. (ii) the altitude through B.

(iii) the right bisector of side BC.

Sol. (i) Let F be the mid-point of side AB.

Then, CF is the median through C.

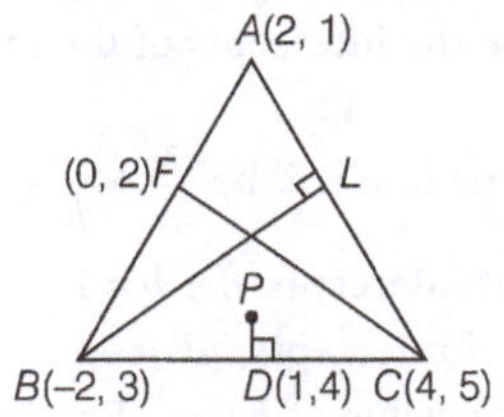

Coordinates of F are $F\left(\dfrac{2+(-2)}{2}, \dfrac{1+3}{2}\right)$, i.e. $F(0, 2)$.

So, the equation of median CF is given by

$$y-5=\frac{2-5}{0-4}(x-4)$$

[by using two points form]

$$\Rightarrow \quad y-5=\frac{3}{4}(x-4)$$

$$\Rightarrow \quad 4(y-5)=3(x-4)$$

$$\Rightarrow \quad 3x-4y+8=0$$

Hence, the equation of median CF is $3x-4y+8=0$.

(ii) Draw $BL \perp AC$. Then, BL is the altitude through B.

Slope of $AC = \dfrac{5-1}{4-2} = 2$

Let the slope BL be m. Since, $BL \perp AC$, So, we have $2m=-1$ and therefore, $m=\dfrac{-1}{2}$.

Thus, the slope of BL is $\dfrac{-1}{2}$.

Now, the equation of BL is given by $y-3=\dfrac{-1}{2}(x+2)$

[by using point slope form]

$$\Rightarrow \quad 2(y-3)=-(x+2) \Rightarrow x+2y-4=0.$$

Hence, the equation of altitude BL is $x+2y-4=0$.

(iii) Let D be the mid-point of BC. Then, the coordinates of D are $D\left(\dfrac{-2+4}{2}, \dfrac{3+5}{2}\right)$, i.e. $D(1, 4)$.

Through D, draw $DP \perp BC$.

Slope of $BC = \dfrac{5-3}{4+2} = \dfrac{2}{6} = \dfrac{1}{3}$

Let the slope of PD be m.

Since, $PD \perp BC$. So, we have $m \times \dfrac{1}{3} = -1 \Rightarrow m=-3$

Thus, the slope of PD is -3.

Now, the equation of PD is

$$y-4=-3(x-1)$$

[by using point slope form]

$$\Rightarrow \quad 3x+y-7=0$$

Hence, the equation of the right bisector of BC is $3x+y-7=0$.

Slope-Intercept Form

Suppose a line L with slope m cuts the Y-axis at a distance c from the origin (distance c is called the y-intercept of the line). Then, the equation of line L is

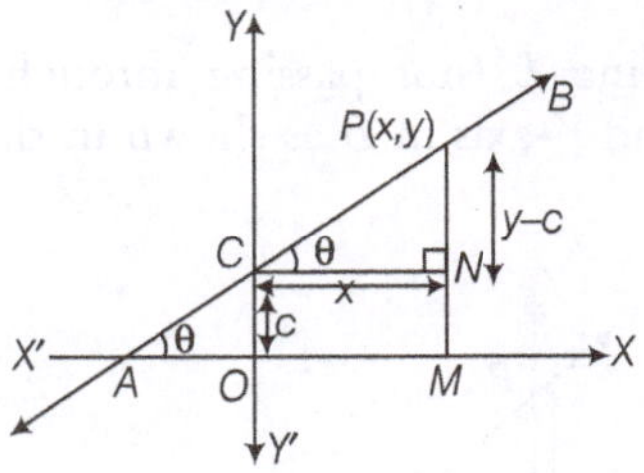

$$\boxed{y=mx+c}$$

Suppose a line L with slope m cuts the X-axis at a distance d from the origin i.e. makes x-intercept, d. Then, the equation of line L is

$$\boxed{y=m(x-d)}$$

Note

(i) The values of c and d will be positive or negative according as the intercept is made on the positive or negative side of the axies, respectively.

(ii) If the line passes through origin, then $0=m(0)+c \Rightarrow c=0$

$\therefore$ Equation of line passing through the origin is $y=mx$, where m is the slope of the line.

(iii) If the line is parallel to X-axis, then $m=0$. Therefore, the equation of a line parallel to X-axis is $y=c$.

Example 13 Find the equations of the line which have slope 1/2 and cuts-off an intercept

(i) –5 on Y-axis. (ii) 4 on X-axis.

Sol. Given, m = Slope of the line $=\dfrac{1}{2}$

(i) Here, c = Intercept of the line on Y-axis $=-5$

Hence, required equation of the line is

$$y=\frac{1}{2}x-5 \qquad [\because y=mx+c]$$

$$\Rightarrow \quad x-2y-10=0$$

(ii) Here, d = Intercept of the line on X-axis = 4.
Hence, required equation of the line is

$$y = \frac{1}{2}(x - 4)$$

$$\Rightarrow \quad x - 2y - 4 = 0 \quad [\because y = m(x - d)]$$

Example 14 Find the equation of the line intersecting the X-axis at a distance of 3 units to the left of origin with slope -2.

Sol. Given, the line intersecting the X-axis to the left of origin. It means it cuts the negative X-axis at a distance of 3 units from the origin.

$\therefore$ x-intercept of line on X-axis $(d) = -3$

Hence, required equation of the line is given by

$$y = -2(x + 3) \quad [y = m(x - d)]$$

$$\Rightarrow \quad y = -2x - 6$$

$$\Rightarrow \quad 2x + y + 6 = 0$$

Intercepts

If a straight line L (not passing through origin) meets X-axis in A and Y-axis in B as shown in the figure below, then

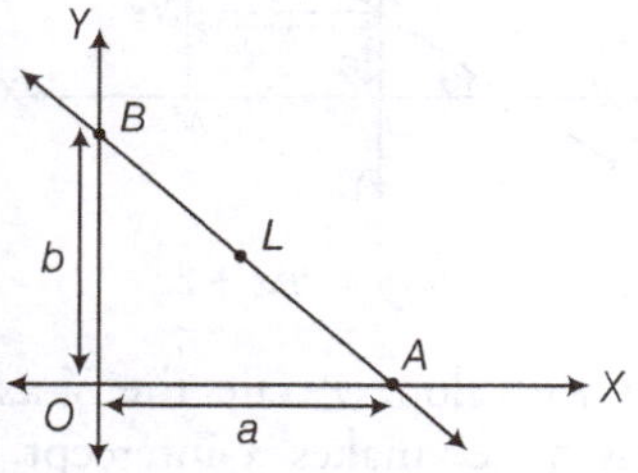

(i) OA is called **x-intercept** or the **intercept** made by the line L on x-axis.

(ii) OB is called **y-intercept** or the **intercept** made by the line L on Y-axis.

(iii) OA and OB taken together in this very order are called the **intercepts** made by the line L on axes.

(iv) AB is called the **portion** of the line intercepted between the axes.

Rules for the Sign of Intercepts

(i) x-intercept is considered positive if it is measured to the right of the origin and negative if measured to the left of the origin.

(ii) y-intercept is considered positive if it is measured above the origin and negative if measured below the origin.

Intercept Form

The equation of a line which cuts-off intercepts a and b on the X-axis and Y-axis respectively, is

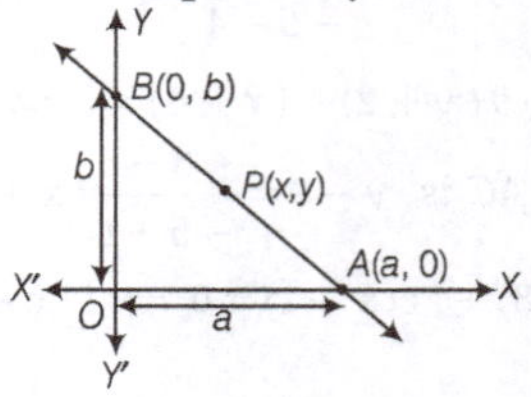

$$\frac{x}{a} + \frac{y}{b} = 1$$

Example 15 Find the equation of the lines which cuts-off intercepts on the axes whose sum and product are 1 and -6, respectively.

Sol. Let a and b be the intercepts of the line on X and Y-axes, respectively.

Equation of the line will be $\frac{x}{a} + \frac{y}{b} = 1$ ...(i)

Given, sum of intercepts, $a + b = 1$ ...(ii)

and product of intercepts, $ab = -6$ ...(iii)

On putting the value of b from Eq. (ii) in Eq. (iii), we get

$$a(1 - a) = -6 \Rightarrow a^2 - a - 6 = 0$$

$$\Rightarrow \quad a^2 - 3a + 2a - 6 = 0 \Rightarrow (a - 3)(a + 2) = 0$$

$$\Rightarrow \quad a = 3 \text{ or } -2$$

From Eq. (ii), when $a = 3$, $b = -2$ and when $a = -2$, $b = 3$.

On putting the values of a and b in Eq. (i), required equation of the lines are

$$\frac{x}{3} + \frac{y}{-2} = 1 \text{ and } \frac{x}{-2} + \frac{y}{3} = 1$$

$$\Rightarrow \quad 2x - 3y - 6 = 0 \text{ and } 3x - 2y + 6 = 0$$

Example 16 Find the equation of the line which passes through the point $(-4, 3)$ and the portion of the line intercepted between the axes is divided internally in the ratio 5 : 3 by this point. **[NCERT Exemplar]**

Sol. Let the line intersects X and Y-axes respectively at $A(x, 0)$ and $B(0, y)$.

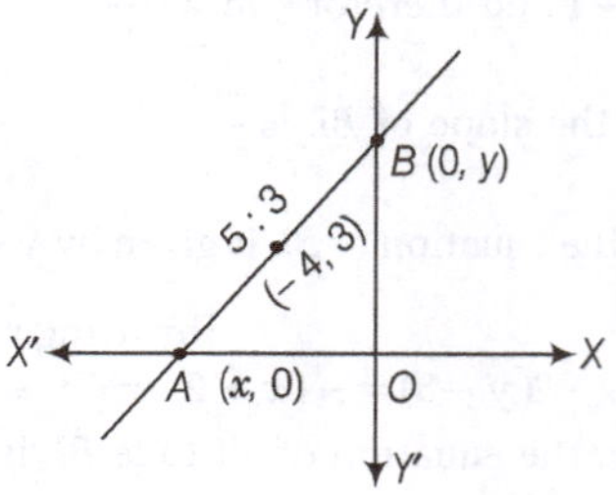

Then, $-4 = \dfrac{5 \times 0 + 3x}{5+3} \Rightarrow -4 = \dfrac{3x}{8} \Rightarrow x = \dfrac{-32}{3}$

and $3 = \dfrac{5 \times y + 3 \times 0}{5+3} \Rightarrow 3 = \dfrac{5y}{8} \Rightarrow y = \dfrac{24}{5}$

Thus, the intercept on the X and Y-axes respectively are $a = \dfrac{-32}{3}$ and $b = \dfrac{24}{5}$.

Hence, the equation of required line is

$$\frac{x}{-32/3} + \frac{y}{24/5} = 1$$

$$\Rightarrow \quad \frac{-3x}{32} + \frac{5y}{24} = 1$$

$$\Rightarrow \quad -9x + 20y = 96$$

$$\Rightarrow \quad 9x - 20y + 96 = 0$$

Example 17 Find the equation of the line which passes through $P(1, -7)$ and meets the axes at A and B respectively so that $4AP - 3BP = 0$.

Sol. Let the equation of the required line be

$$\frac{x}{a} + \frac{y}{b} = 1 \quad \text{...(i)}$$

Since, it passes through $P(1, -7)$.

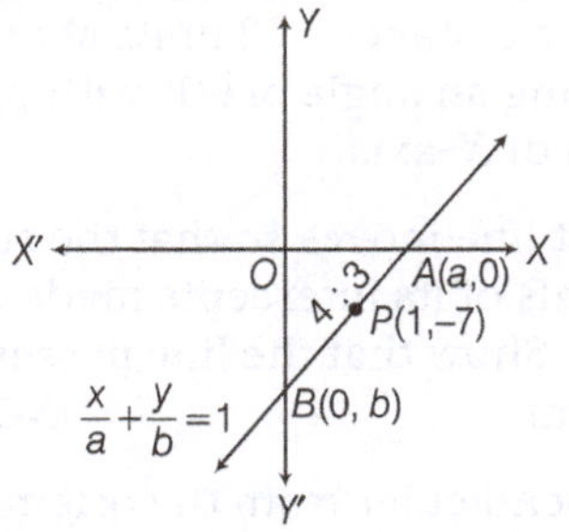

$$\therefore \quad \frac{1}{a} - \frac{7}{b} = 1 \quad \text{...(ii)}$$

It is given that the point $P(1, -7)$ divides segment AB in such a way that

$$4AP - 3BP = 0 \Rightarrow \frac{AP}{BP} = \frac{3}{4} \Rightarrow AP : BP = 3 : 4$$

This means that P divides AB internally in the ratio 3 : 4. So, the coordinates of P are

$$\left(\frac{3 \times 0 + 4 \times a}{3+4}, \frac{3 \times b + 4 \times 0}{3+4}\right) = \left(\frac{4a}{7}, \frac{3b}{7}\right)$$

But, the coordinates of P are given as $(1, -7)$.

$$\therefore \quad \frac{4a}{7} = 1 \text{ and } \frac{3b}{7} = -7 \Rightarrow a = \frac{7}{4} \text{ and } b = -\frac{49}{3}$$

On substituting the values of a and b in Eq. (i), we get $\dfrac{4x}{7} - \dfrac{3y}{49} = 1$ or $28x - 3y = 49$, which is the required equation.

Normal or Perpendicular Form

The equation of the straight line upon which the length of perpendicular (i.e. normal) from the origin is p and this perpendicular (i.e. normal) makes an angle α with the positive direction of X-axis is

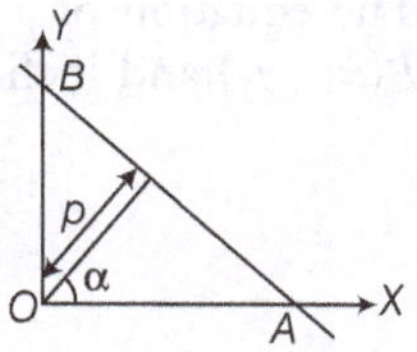

$$\boxed{x \cos \alpha + y \sin \alpha = p}$$

Note Slope of line $= -\dfrac{1}{\tan \alpha} = -\dfrac{\cos \alpha}{\sin \alpha}$

Example 18 Find the equation of the line upon which the length of perpendicular p from origin and the angle α made by this perpendicular with the positive direction of X-axis are $p = 4$, $\alpha = 120°$.

Sol. we know that, equation of the line, having perpendicular distance p from the origin and angle α which the perpendicular makes with the positive direction of X-axis, is $x \cos \alpha + y \sin \alpha = p$

Here, $p = 4$ and $\alpha = 120°$, therefore required equation of the line is $x \cos 120° + y \sin 120° = 4$

$$\Rightarrow \quad x \cos(90° + 30°) + y \sin(90° + 30°) = 4$$

$$\Rightarrow \quad -x \sin 30° + y \cos 30° = 4$$

$$\Rightarrow \quad -x \times \frac{1}{2} + y \times \frac{\sqrt{3}}{2} = 4 \Rightarrow -x + 3\sqrt{y} = 8$$

Example 19 The length of the perpendicular from the origin to a line is 7 and the line makes an angle of 150° with the positive direction of Y-axis. Find the equation of the line.

Sol. It is evident from the figure that the perpendicular OQ from the origin to the line makes an angle of 30° with the positive direction of X-axis. Therefore, $\alpha = 30°$. It is given that $OQ = 7$, therefore $p = 7$.

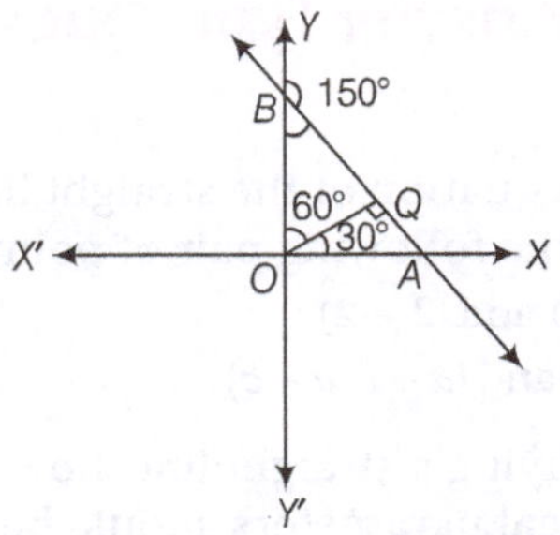

Hence, the equation of the required line is

$$x \cos 30° + y \sin 30° = 7 \quad [\because x \cos \alpha + y \sin \alpha = p]$$

$$\Rightarrow \frac{\sqrt{3}x}{2} + \frac{y}{2} = 7 \Rightarrow \sqrt{3}x + y = 14$$

Symmetrical (or Distance) Form

The equation of a straight line passing through the point $P(x_1, y_1)$ and inclination θ is given by

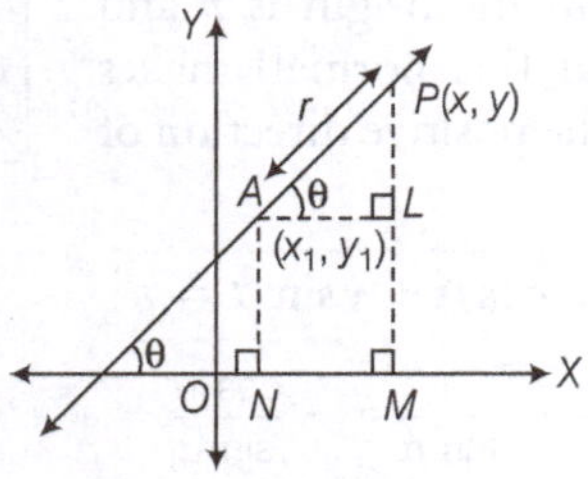

$$\frac{x - x_1}{\cos\theta} = \frac{y - y_1}{\sin\theta} = r$$

where r is the directed distance of any point (x, y) from the point (x_1, y_1).

Note The coordinates of any point on the line are $(x_1 + r\cos\theta, y_1 + r\sin\theta)$.

Example 20 Find the equation of the line through the point (– 1, 3) in symmetrical form when the angle made by the line with positive direction of X-axis is 120°.

Sol. Here, θ = 120° and the line passes through the point (– 1, 3); using symmetrical form, then the equation of required line is

$$\frac{x - (-1)}{\cos 120^\circ} = \frac{y - 3}{\sin 120^\circ} = r$$

$$\Rightarrow \quad \frac{x + 1}{-1/2} = \frac{y - 3}{\sqrt{3}/2} = r$$

Topic Practice 3

Very Short Answer Type Questions

(2 Marks)

1 Find the equation of the straight line passing through the following pair of points.
(i) (0, 0) and (2, – 2)
(ii) (a, b) and $(a + b, a - b)$

2 For specifying a straight line, how many geometrical parameters should be known? **[NCERT Exemplar]**

3 A line cutting off intercept – 3 from the Y-axis and the tangent at angle to the X-axis is $\frac{3}{5}$. Find its equation.

4 Find the equation of a line passing through the point (– 4, 3) with slope –1/2.

5 Find the equation of a line, which passes through the point (2, 3) and makes an angle of 30° with the positive direction of X-axis. **[NCERT Exemplar]**

6 Find the equation of line joining the points (1, 1) and (2, 3).

7 If the line $\frac{x}{a} + \frac{y}{b} = 1$ passes through the points (2, – 3) and (4, – 5), then find (a, b).

8 Find the equation of straight line, which passes through the point (5, 6) and has intercepts on the axes equal in magnitude but opposite in sign.

9 Find the equation of the straight line, which passes through the point (1, – 2) and cuts-off equal intercepts from axes.

10 Find the equation of the line for which $p = 2$, $\sin\alpha = \frac{4}{5}$.

11 Find the equation of line, which intersect the Y-axis at a distance of 2 units above the origin and making an angle of 60° with positive direction of X-axis. **[NCERT]**

12 A straight line moves so that the sum of the reciprocals of its intercepts made on axes is constant. Show that the line passes through a fixed point. **[NCERT Exemplar]**

13 The perpendicular from the origin to a line meets it at the point (– 2, 9). Find the equation of the line.

14 Find the equation of the line passing through the point (5, 2) and perpendicular to the line joining the points (2, 3) and (3, – 1). **[NCERT Exemplar]**

15 Find the equation of line, whose perpendicular distance from the origin is 5 units and the angle made by the perpendicular with the positive X-axis is 30°.

16 Find the equation of line passing through $(2, 2\sqrt{3})$ and inclined with X-axis at an angle of 75°.

17 Find the equation of the passing through the point (– 2, 5) in symmetrical form when the angle made by the line with positive direction of X-axis is 120°.

18 Find the equation of a line, whose inclination with the X-axis is 150° and which passes through the point (3, – 5).

19 The intercept cuts-off by a line from Y-axis is twice than that from X-axis and the line passes through the point (1, 2). Find the equation of the line.

20 If the coordinates of the middle point of the portion of a line intercepted between the coordinate axes is (3, 2), then find the equation of the line. **[NCERT Exemplar]**

21 A line passes through $P(1, 2)$ such that its intercept between the axes is bisected at P. Find the equation of line.

22 Find the equation of the straight line which bisects the distance between the points $A(a, b)$, $B(a', b')$ and also bisects the distance between the points $C(-a, b)$ and $D(a', -b')$.

23 Find the equation of lines passing through (1, 2) and making an angle 30° with positive Y-axis, measured clockwise.

24 $P(a, b)$ is the mid-point of a line segment between axes. Show that the equation of the line is $\frac{x}{a}+\frac{y}{b}=2$.

25 By using the concept of equation of a line, prove that the points $A(3, 0)$, $B(-2, -2)$ and $C(8, 2)$ are collinear. **[NCERT]**

26 Find the equation of a straight line on which length of perpendicular from the origin is four units and the line makes an angle of 120° with the positive direction of X-axis.

27 The vertices of ΔPQR are $P(2, 1)$, $Q(-2, 3)$ and $R(4, 5)$. Find the equation of the median through the vertex Q.

Short Answer Type Questions

4 Marks

28 Find the equations of two straight lines which are at a distance 1/2 from the origin and passes through the point (0, 1).

29 If the intercept of a line between the coordinate axes is divided by the point (– 5, 4) in the ratio 1 : 2, then find the equation of the line.

30 Find equation of the line passing through the point (2, 2) cutting off intercepts on the axes whose sum is 9. **[NCERT]**

31 A line forms a triangle in the first quadrant with the coordinate axes. If the area of the triangle is $54\sqrt{3}$ sq units and perpendicular drawn from the origin to the line makes an angle 60° with X-axis, then find the equation of the line.

32 Show that the perpendicular drawn from the point (4, 1) on the line segment joining (6, 5) and (2, – 1) divides it internally in the ratio 8 : 5.

33 The hypotenuse of a right angled triangle has its ends at the points (1, 3) and (– 4, 1). Find the equation of the legs (perpendicular sides) of the triangle.

34 Show that the points $(at_1^2, 2at_1)$, $(at_2^2, 2at_2)$ and $(a, 0)$ are collinear, if $t_1t_2 = -1$.

Long Answer Type Questions

6 Marks

35 Find the equations of the altitudes of a ΔABC, whose vertices are $A(2, -2)$, $B(1, 1)$ and $C(-1, 0)$.

36 Find the equations of the medians of a ΔABC, whose vertices are $A(2, 5)$, $B(-4, 9)$ and $C(-2, -1)$.

37 A straight line passes through the points $(a, 0)$ and $(0, b)$. The length of the line segment contained between the axes is 13 and the product of the intercepts on the axes is 60. Calculate the values of a and b and find the equation of straight line.

Hints & Answers

1. (i) $y = -x$ (ii) $(a-2b)x - by + b^2 + 2ab - a^2 = 0$
2. For (i) $y = mx + c$, number of parameters = 2

   (ii) $\frac{x}{a}+\frac{y}{b}=1$, number of parameters = 2

   (iii) $y - y_1 = m(x - x_1)$, number of parameters = 2

   (iv) $x\cos\alpha + y\sin\alpha = p$, parameter = 2

   Ans. Two parameter should be known.
3. m = slope of line = $\tan\theta = \frac{3}{5}$.

   Ans. $5y - 3x + 15 = 0$
4. $x + 2y - 2 = 0$
5. $m = \tan 30° = \frac{1}{\sqrt{3}}$

   Ans. $x - \sqrt{3}y + 3\sqrt{3} - 2 = 0$
6. $2x - y - 1 = 0$
7. According to given condition, we have

$$\frac{2}{a}-\frac{3}{b}=1 \text{ and } \frac{4}{a}-\frac{5}{b}=1$$

Let $\frac{1}{a}=u$ and $\frac{1}{b}=v$.

Then, we get $2u-3v=1$ and $4u-5v=1$

Ans. $(a, b)=(-1,-1)$

8. Let the equation of line in intercept form be $\frac{x}{a}+\frac{y}{b}=1$

We have, $a=-b$

Now, equation of line becomes $\frac{x}{-b}+\frac{y}{b}=1$

$\because$ It passes through (5, 6)

$\therefore \quad \frac{5}{-b}+\frac{6}{b}=1 \Rightarrow b=1$

Ans. $x-y+1=0$

9. Let the intercepts along the X and Y-axes be a and a, respectively.

$\therefore$ Equation of the line is

$$\frac{x}{a}+\frac{y}{a}=1 \quad \text{...(i)}$$

Since, the point $(1,-2)$ lies on the line.

$$\therefore \quad \frac{1}{a}-\frac{2}{a}=1 \Rightarrow a=-1$$

Ans. $x+y+1=0$

10. We know, $\cos\alpha=\pm\sqrt{1-\sin^2\alpha}=\pm\sqrt{1-\frac{16}{25}}=\pm\frac{3}{5}$

Equation of line in normal form, when $\cos\alpha=\frac{3}{5}$ is

$$x\cdot\left(\frac{3}{5}\right)+y\cdot\left(\frac{4}{5}\right)=2$$

Equation of line in normal form, when $\cos\alpha=-3/5$ is

$$x\cdot\left(-\frac{3}{5}\right)+y\cdot\left(\frac{4}{5}\right)=2$$

Ans. $3x+4y=10$ and $3x-4y+10=0$

11. Since, the line intersect the Y-axis above the origin. It means that the line intersects the positive Y-axis.

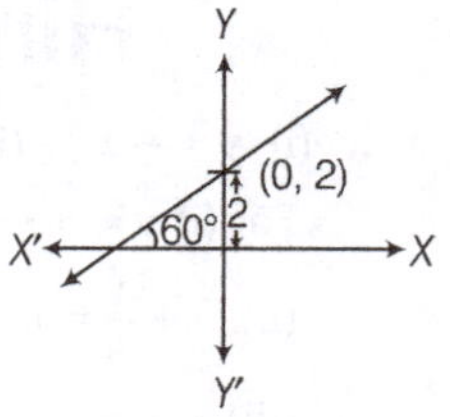

Here, $c=2$

and $m=\tan 60°=\sqrt{3}$

Ans. $\sqrt{3}x-y+2=0$

12. Given that, $\frac{1}{a}+\frac{1}{b}=$ constant $=\frac{1}{k}$ (say)

$$\because \quad \frac{1}{a}+\frac{1}{b}=\frac{1}{k} \Rightarrow \frac{k}{a}+\frac{k}{b}=1$$

So, the point (k, k) lies on $\frac{x}{a}+\frac{y}{b}=1$.

13. Since, $PQ \perp OR$

$\therefore$ Slope of $PQ \times$ Slope of $OR=-1$

$$m\times\left(\frac{9-0}{-2-0}\right)=-1$$

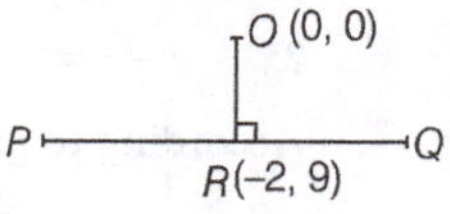

$$\Rightarrow \quad m=\frac{2}{9}$$

Ans. $2x-9y+85=0$

14. Slope of line joining (2, 3) and (3, –1) is

$$m_1=\frac{-1-3}{3-2}=-4$$

Slope of the line perpendicular to it is $m_2=\frac{-1}{-4}=\frac{1}{4}$

Ans. $x-4y+3=0$

15. Here, $p=5$ and $\alpha=45°$

So, equation of line in normal form is

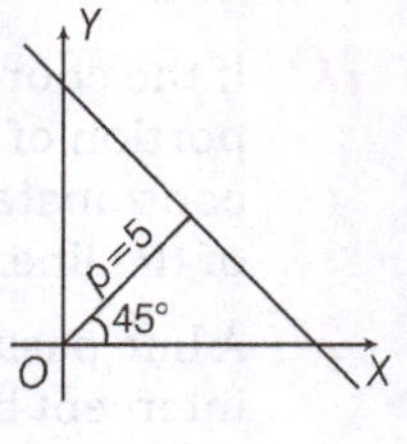

$$x\cos\alpha+y\sin\alpha=p$$

$$\therefore \quad x\cos 30°+y\sin 30°=5$$

$$\Rightarrow \quad \frac{\sqrt{3}}{2}x+\frac{1}{2}y=5$$

$$\Rightarrow \quad \sqrt{3}x+y=10$$

16. $m=\tan 75°=\tan(45°+30°)$;

$\therefore \quad m=2+\sqrt{3}$ **Ans.** $(2+\sqrt{3})x-y-4=0$

17. $\frac{x+2}{-\frac{1}{2}}=\frac{y-5}{\frac{\sqrt{3}}{2}}=r$

18. Here, $m=\tan 150°=\tan(180°-30°)=-\tan 30°=-\frac{1}{\sqrt{3}}$

Ans. $x+\sqrt{3}y+(-3+5\sqrt{3})=0$

19. Here, equation of line is of the form $\frac{x}{a}+\frac{y}{2a}=1$. It passes through (1, 2).

So, we have $\frac{1}{a}+\frac{2}{2a}=1 \Rightarrow a=2$

Ans. $2x+y=4$

20. Let equation of line is $\frac{x}{a}+\frac{y}{b}=1$

Since, the coordinates of the middle point are $P(3, 2)$.

$$\therefore \quad 3=\frac{0+a}{2} \Rightarrow 3=\frac{a}{2} \Rightarrow a=6$$

Similarly, $\quad b=4$ **Ans.** $2x+3y=12$

21. Let equation of line is $\frac{x}{a}+\frac{y}{b}=1$. Here, we have $1=\frac{a+0}{2}$

and $2=\frac{0+b}{2}$ **Ans.** $2x+y-4=0$

22. Let the line MN bisects the line AB at M and CD at N.

$\therefore$ Coordinates of $M=\left(\frac{a+a'}{2},\frac{b+b'}{2}\right)$

and coordinates of $N=\left(\frac{-a+a'}{2},\frac{b-b'}{2}\right)$

Now, equation of line MN is

$$\left(y-\frac{b+b'}{2}\right)=\left(\frac{\frac{b-b'}{2}-\frac{b+b'}{2}}{\frac{-a+a'}{2}-\frac{a+a'}{2}}\right)\left(x-\frac{a+a'}{2}\right)$$

Ans. $2b'x-2ay+ab-a'b'=0$

23. Given that, angle with Y-axis $= 30°$

$\therefore$ Angle with X-axis $= 60°$

$\Rightarrow$ Slope of the line, $m = \tan 60° = \sqrt{3}$

Ans. $y - \sqrt{3}x - 2 + \sqrt{3} = 0$

24. Let the equation of line AB be $\frac{x}{h} + \frac{y}{k} = 1$, which intersect on X and Y-axes at $A(h, 0)$ and $B(0, k)$.

Mid-point of $AB = \left(\frac{h+0}{2}, \frac{0+k}{2}\right)$

$\because P(a, b)$ is the mid-point of AB.

$\therefore \quad \frac{h+0}{2} = a$ and $\frac{0+k}{2} = b$

25. Equation of line joining the points $A(3, 0)$ and $B(-2, -2)$ is $y - 0 = \frac{-2-0}{-2-3}(x-3)$

$\Rightarrow \quad 2x - 5y - 6 = 0 \quad$ ...(i)

On putting the point $C(8, 2)$ in Eq. (i), we get

$2 \times 8 - 5 \times 2 - 6 = 0 \Rightarrow 0 = 0$, which is true.

Thus, point C also lies on the line.

Hence, the points are collinear.

26. Given that, $OC = p = 4$ units

and $\quad \angle BAX = 120°$

Let $\quad \angle COA = \alpha, \angle OCA = 90°$

$\because \quad \angle BAX = \angle COA + \angle OCA$

[by exterior angle property]

$\Rightarrow \quad 120° = \alpha + 90°;$

$\therefore \quad \alpha = 30°$

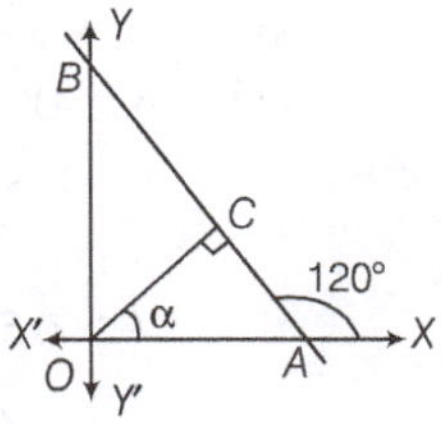

Ans. $\sqrt{3}x + y = 8$

27. Let QS be the median through Q. Since the median bisects the opposite side, i.e. S is the mid-point of PR.

$$S = \left(\frac{2+4}{2}, \frac{1+5}{2}\right) = (3, 3)$$

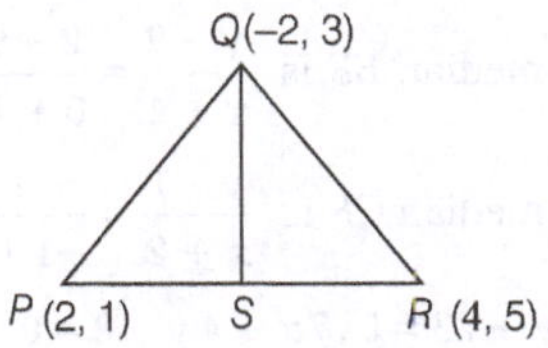

$\therefore$ Equation of line QS is $y - 3 = \frac{3-3}{3+2}(x+2)$

Ans. $y = 3$

28. The equation of any line which is at a distance $\frac{1}{2}$ from origin is $x\cos\alpha + y\sin\alpha = \frac{1}{2}$

$\because$ It passes through the point $(0, 1)$.

$\therefore \quad 0\cdot(\cos\alpha) + 1(\sin\alpha) = \frac{1}{2} \Rightarrow \sin\alpha = \frac{1}{2}$

Now, $\quad \cos\alpha = \pm\sqrt{1 - \sin^2\alpha} = \pm\sqrt{1 - \left(\frac{1}{2}\right)^2} = \pm\frac{\sqrt{3}}{2}$

Ans. $\sqrt{3}x + y - 1 = 0$ and $\sqrt{3}x - y + 1 = 0$

29. Let intercept of a line be (h, k).

The coordinates of A and B, where the line cuts the X-axis and and Y-axis, are $(h, 0)$ and $(0, k)$ respectively.

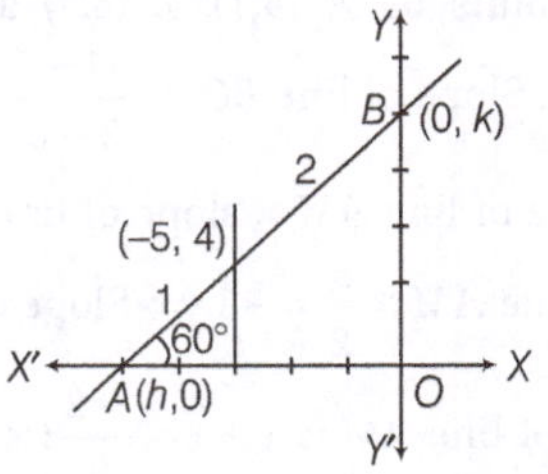

Then, $\quad -5 = \frac{1 \times 0 + 2 \times h}{1+2} \Rightarrow h = -\frac{15}{2}$

and $\quad 4 = \frac{1\cdot k + 0\cdot 2}{1+2} \Rightarrow k = 12$

$\therefore \quad A = \left(-\frac{15}{2}, 0\right)$ and $B = (0, 12) \Rightarrow 5y = 8x + 60$

Ans. $8x - 5y + 60 = 0$

30. Equation of the line in intercept form is

$$\frac{x}{a} + \frac{y}{b} = 1 \quad ...(i)$$

Given, $\quad a + b = 9 \quad$ ...(ii)

and line (i) passes through the point $(2, 2)$.

$\therefore \quad \frac{2}{a} + \frac{2}{b} = 1 \quad$ ...(iii)

$\Rightarrow \quad \frac{2}{a} + \frac{2}{9-a} = 1 \quad$ [from Eq. (ii)]

$\Rightarrow \quad a^2 - 9a + 18 = 0$

$\Rightarrow \quad a = 6$ or $3 \Rightarrow b = 3$ or 6

Hence, Eq. (i) becomes $\frac{x}{6} + \frac{y}{3} = 1$ or $\frac{x}{3} + \frac{y}{6} = 1$

Ans. $x + 2y = 6$ or $2x + y = 6$

31. Let $OM = p$, $OA = a$, $OB = b$

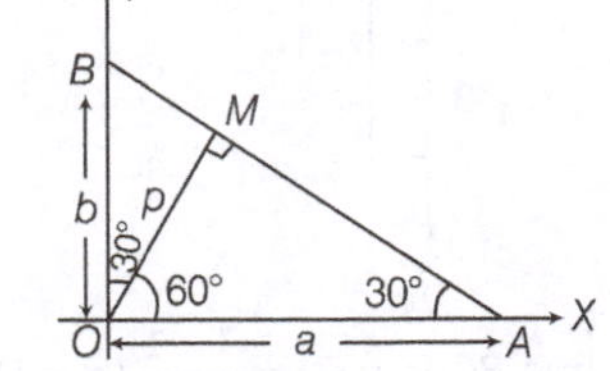

In ΔOMA, $\quad \frac{p}{a} = \cos 60° = \frac{1}{2} \Rightarrow a = 2p$

In ΔOMB, $\quad \frac{p}{b} = \cos 30° = \frac{\sqrt{3}}{2} \Rightarrow b = \frac{2p}{\sqrt{3}}$

Now, Area of $\Delta OAB = \frac{1}{2} \times ab = 54\sqrt{3}$

$\Rightarrow \quad \frac{1}{2}(2p) \times \frac{(2p)}{\sqrt{3}} = 54\sqrt{3}$

$\Rightarrow \quad p = 9$

[∵ distance is always positive, so we take positive sign]

Using normal form equation of line AB is

$x \cos 60° + y \sin 60° = 9$ **Ans.** $x + \sqrt{3}\,y - 18 = 0$

32. Let the points be A (4,1), B (6,5) and C (2, −1). Draw $AM \perp BC$. Slope of line $BC = \frac{-1-5}{2-6} = \frac{3}{2}$

Now, slope of line $AM \times$ slope of line $BC = -1$

Slope of line $AM \times \frac{3}{2} = -1 \Rightarrow$ Slope of line $AM = \frac{-2}{3}$

Equation of line AM is $y - 1 = \frac{-2}{3}(x - 4)$

$\Rightarrow \quad 2x + 3y - 11 = 0$ ...(i)

Let M divides BC in the ratio $k:1$ internally.

Then, Coordinates of M are $\left(\frac{2k+6}{k+1}, \frac{-k+5}{k+1}\right)$.

Since, M is on line AM, therefore the coordinates of M will satisfy the Eq. (i).

$\therefore \quad 2\left(\frac{2k+6}{k+1}\right) + 3\left(\frac{-k+5}{k+1}\right) - 11 = 0$ **Ans.** $8:5$

33. First we plot the points $A(1, 3)$ and $B(-4, 1)$ in the XY-plane. From the point $A(1, 3)$, we draw a line parallel to Y-axis and from the point $B(-4, 1)$, we draw a line parallel to X-axis. The point of intersection of two lines is on C, which is right angled at C.

Clearly, the coordinate of C are (1, 1).

Now, Equation of line passing through $A(1, 3)$ and $C(1, 1)$ is

$$y - 3 = \frac{1-3}{1-1}(x - 1) \Rightarrow x = 1$$

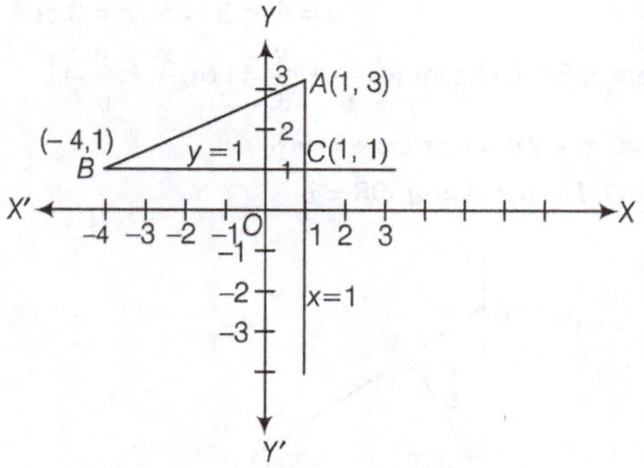

Equation of line BC is $y - 1 = \frac{1-1}{1+4}(x - 1)$

$\Rightarrow \quad y = 1$

Ans. The legs of a triangle are $x = 1$ and $y = 1$.

34. $\because \quad y - 2at_1 = \frac{2at_2 - 2at_1}{at_2^2 - at_1^2}(x - at_1^2)$

$\Rightarrow \quad y - 2at_1 = \frac{2}{(t_2 + t_1)}(x - at_1^2)$

$\Rightarrow (t_1 + t_2)(y - 2at_1) = 2(x - at_1^2)$ ...(i)

Now, given three points are collinear, if $(a, 0)$ lies on Eq. (i). i.e.

$$(t_1 + t_2)(0 - 2at_1) = 2(a - at_1^2)$$

$\Rightarrow \quad t_1 t_2 = -1$

35. Slope of $BC = \frac{1}{2}$, therefore slope of $AD = -2$

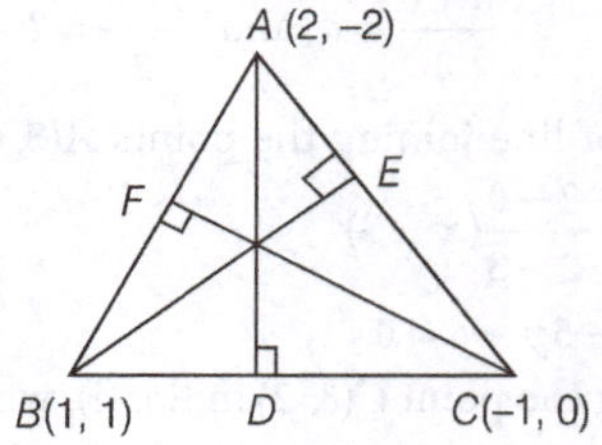

Equation of altitude AD, $y + 2 = -2(x - 2)$

Similarly, we can find the others equations.

Ans. $2x + y - 2 = 0,\ 3x - 2y - 1 = 0$

and $\quad x - 3y + 1 = 0$

36.

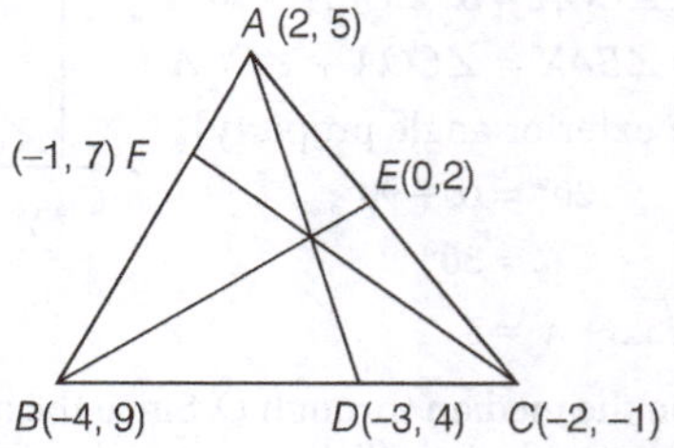

Equation of median AD is $\frac{y-5}{x-2} = \frac{4-5}{-3-2}$

Equation of median BE is $\frac{y-9}{x+4} = \frac{2-9}{0+4}$

Equation of median CF is $\frac{y+1}{x+2} = \frac{7+1}{-1+2}$

Ans. $x - 5y + 23 = 0,\ 7x + 4y - 8 = 0$

and $\quad 8x - y + 15 = 0$

37. Here, $\sqrt{a^2 + b^2} = 13$ and $ab = 60$

Ans. $a = 12,\ b = 5$

$\frac{x}{12} + \frac{y}{5} = 1$ and $a = -12,\ b = -5$

$\frac{x}{12} + \frac{y}{5} = -1$

TOPIC 04 General Equation of a Line and Distance of a Point from a Line

An equation of the form $Ax+By+C=0$, where A, B, C are real constants and atleast one of A and B is non-zero, is called **general linear equation or general equation** of a line.

Different Forms of $Ax+By+C=0$

The general equation of a line can be reduced into various forms of the equation of a line, which are given below

Slope-Intercept Form

If $B \neq 0$, then $Ax+By+C=0$ can be written as

$$\boxed{y=\frac{-A}{B}x-\frac{C}{B}} \quad \text{or} \quad y=mx+c \qquad \text{...(i)}$$

where, $m=\frac{-A}{B}$ and $c=\frac{-C}{B}$.

$\therefore$ Slope of a line $=-\frac{\text{Coefficient of } x}{\text{Coefficient of } y}$

and y-intercept $=-\frac{\text{Constant term}}{\text{Coefficient of } y}$

If $B=0$, then we get $x=-\frac{C}{A}$, which is a vertical line whose slope is not defined and x-intercept is $-\frac{C}{A}$.

Intercept Form

If $C \neq 0$, then $Ax+By+C=0$ can be written as

$$\boxed{\frac{x}{-C/A}+\frac{y}{-C/B}=1} \quad \text{or} \quad \frac{x}{a}+\frac{y}{b}=1$$

where, $a=\frac{-C}{A}$ and $b=\frac{-C}{B}$

Here, x-intercept $=-\frac{\text{Constant term}}{\text{Coefficient of } x}$

and y-intercept $=-\frac{\text{Constant term}}{\text{Coefficient of } y}$.

If $C=0$, then we get $Ax+By=0$, which is a line passing through origin and hence it has zero intercepts on the axes.

Note Equation $Ax+By+C=0$ will represent a horizontal line if $A=0$ i.e. if coefficient of $x=0$.

Normal Form

Let $x\cos\omega + y\sin\omega = p$ be the normal form of the line represented by the equation $Ax+By+C=0$ or $Ax+By=-C$. Thus, both the equations are same and therefore

$$\frac{A}{\cos\omega}=\frac{B}{\sin\omega}=\frac{-C}{p}$$

which gives $\quad \cos\omega=\frac{-Ap}{C}$ and $\sin\omega=\frac{-Bp}{C}$

Now, $\sin^2\omega+\cos^2\omega=\left(-\frac{Ap}{C}\right)^2+\left(\frac{-Bp}{C}\right)^2$

$$\Rightarrow \quad 1=\frac{A^2p^2}{C^2}+\frac{B^2p^2}{C^2}$$

$$\Rightarrow \quad p^2=\frac{C^2}{A^2+B^2}$$

$$\Rightarrow \quad p=\pm\frac{C}{\sqrt{A^2+B^2}}$$

Therefore, $\cos\omega=\pm\frac{A}{\sqrt{A^2+B^2}}$ and $\sin\omega=\pm\frac{B}{\sqrt{A^2+B^2}}$

Thus, the normal form of the equation $Ax+By+C=0$ is

$$\boxed{x\cos\omega+y\sin\omega=p}$$

where, $\cos\omega=\pm\frac{A}{\sqrt{A^2+B^2}}$, $\sin\omega=\pm\frac{B}{\sqrt{A^2+B^2}}$

and $\quad p=\pm\frac{C}{\sqrt{A^2+B^2}}$

Proper choice of signs is mode so that P should be positive

Method to Tranform the General Equation to Normal Form

In order to transform the general equation of a line to the normal form, we use the following steps

(i) Shift the constant term on the RHS and make it positive.

(ii) Divide both sides by $\sqrt{(\text{coeff. of } x)^2+(\text{coeff. of } y)^2}$.

The equation so obtained is in the normal form.

Example 1 Transform the equation of the line $3x + 2y - 7 = 0$ to

(i) slope-intercept form and also find the slope and y-intercept.

(ii) intercept form and also find the intercepts on the coordinate axes.

(iii) normal form and also find the inclination of the perpendicular segment from the origin on the line with the axis and its length.

Sol. (i) Given equation is $3x + 2y - 7 = 0.$

It can be rewritten as

$$2y = -3x + 7 \text{ or } y = -\frac{3}{2}x + \frac{7}{2} \quad \text{...(i)}$$

which is the required slope intercept form of the given line.

On comparing Eq. (i) with $y = mx + c$, we get

Slope, $m = -\frac{3}{2}$ and y-intercept, $c = \frac{7}{2}$

(ii) Given equation can be rewritten as

$$3x + 2y = 7$$

or
$$\frac{x}{7/3} + \frac{y}{7/2} = 1 \quad \text{...(i)}$$

which is the required intercept form of the given line.

On comparing Eq. (i) with $\frac{x}{a} + \frac{y}{b} = 1$, we get

$$a = \frac{7}{3} \text{ and } b = \frac{7}{2}$$

Hence, x-intercept, $a = \frac{7}{3}$ and y-intercept, $b = \frac{7}{2}$

(iii) Given equation is $3x + 2y - 7 = 0.$ ...(i)

On comparing Eq. (i) with $Ax + By + C = 0$, we get

$A = 3$, $B = 2$ and $C = -7$

$\therefore \sqrt{A^2 + B^2} = \sqrt{3^2 + 2^2} = \sqrt{9+4} = \sqrt{13}$

On dividing both sides of Eq. (i) by $\sqrt{13}$, we get

$$\frac{3}{\sqrt{13}}x + \frac{2}{\sqrt{13}}y - \frac{7}{\sqrt{13}} = 0$$

$$\Rightarrow \frac{3}{\sqrt{13}}x + \frac{2}{\sqrt{13}}y = \frac{7}{\sqrt{13}} \quad \text{...(ii)}$$

which is the required normal form of the given line.

On comparing Eq. (ii) with $x \cos \omega + y \sin \omega = p$, we get

$$\cos \omega = \frac{3}{\sqrt{13}}, \ \sin \omega = \frac{2}{\sqrt{13}} \text{ and } p = \frac{7}{\sqrt{13}}$$

Since, cos ω and sin ω both are positive, therefore ω is in the first quadrant and is such that $\tan\omega = \frac{2}{3}$

Hence, for the given line, we have

$$\tan \omega = \frac{2}{3} \text{ and } p = \frac{7}{\sqrt{13}}.$$

Example 2 Reduce the lines $3x - 4y + 4 = 0$ and $4x - 3y + 12 = 0$ to the normal form and hence determine which line is nearer to the origin.

Sol. Given equation to the first line is

$$3x - 4y + 4 = 0$$

$$\Rightarrow -3x + 4y = 4$$

On dividing throughout by $\sqrt{(-3)^2 + 4^2}$, we get

$$-\frac{3x}{\sqrt{(-3)^2 + 4^2}} + \frac{4y}{\sqrt{(-3)^2 + 4^2}} = \frac{4}{\sqrt{(-3)^2 + 4^2}}$$

$$\Rightarrow -\frac{3x}{\sqrt{9+16}} + \frac{4y}{\sqrt{9+16}} = \frac{4}{\sqrt{9+16}}$$

$$\Rightarrow -\frac{3x}{\sqrt{25}} + \frac{4y}{\sqrt{25}} = \frac{4}{\sqrt{25}} \Rightarrow -\frac{3}{5}x + \frac{4}{5}y = \frac{4}{5}$$

This is the normal form of $3x - 4y + 4 = 0$ from which we find that the length of the perpendicular from the origin to it is given by $p_1 = \frac{4}{5}$.

The equation of the second line is

$4x - 3y + 12 = 0$ or $-4x + 3y = 12$

On dividing throughout by $\sqrt{(-4)^2 + 3^2}$, we get

$$-\frac{4x}{\sqrt{(-4)^2 + 3^2}} + \frac{3y}{\sqrt{(-4)^2 + 3^2}} = \frac{12}{\sqrt{(-4)^2 + 3^2}}$$

$$\Rightarrow -\frac{4x}{\sqrt{16+9}} + \frac{3y}{\sqrt{16+9}} = \frac{12}{\sqrt{16+9}}$$

$$\Rightarrow -\frac{4x}{\sqrt{25}} + \frac{3y}{\sqrt{25}} = \frac{12}{\sqrt{25}}$$

$$\Rightarrow -\frac{4}{5}x + \frac{3}{5}y = \frac{12}{5}$$

This is the normal form of $4x - 3y + 12 = 0$ from which we find that the length of the perpendicular from the origin to it is given, by $p_2 = \frac{12}{5}$.

Since, $p_2 > p_1$, therefore the line $3x - 4y + 4 = 0$ is nearer to the origin.

Angle between Two lines

Let general equations of lines be $A_1x + B_1y + C_1 = 0$ and $A_2x + B_2y + C_2 = 0$. Then, the slope of the given lines are $m_1 = -\frac{A_1}{B_1}$ and $m_2 = -\frac{A_2}{B_2}$.

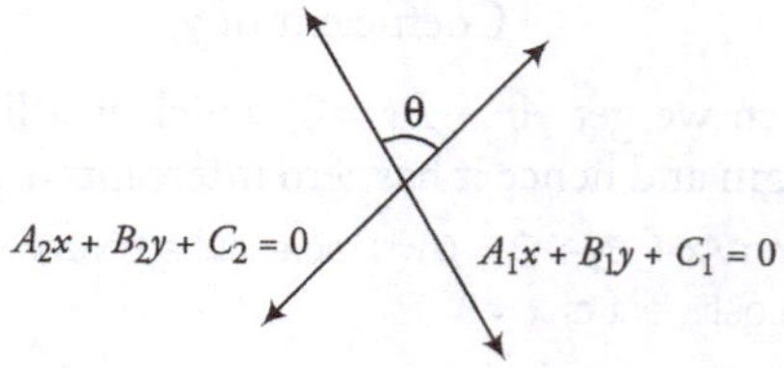

Let θ be the angle between two lines, then

$$\tan\theta = \pm\left(\frac{m_2 - m_1}{1 + m_1 m_2}\right) = \pm\left(\frac{-\frac{A_2}{B_2} + \frac{A_1}{B_1}}{1 + \left(\frac{-A_1}{B_1}\right)\times\left(\frac{-A_2}{B_2}\right)}\right)$$

$$\Rightarrow \quad \tan\theta = \pm\left(\frac{A_1B_2 - A_2B_1}{A_1A_2 + B_1B_2}\right)$$

Note (i) For acute angle, we take $\tan\theta = \left|\frac{A_1B_2 - A_2B_1}{A_1A_2 + B_1B_2}\right|$

(ii) For obtuse angle, we take $\tan\theta = -\left(\frac{A_1B_2 - A_2B_1}{A_1A_2 + B_1B_2}\right)$

(iii) The formula $\tan\theta = \pm\left(\frac{m_2 - m_1}{1 + m_1 m_2}\right)$ is not applied when one of the lines is parallel to the Y-axis i.e. of the form $x = a$, whose slop is ∞. In that cases we use the formula $\tan\theta = \pm\left(\frac{A_1B_2 - A_2B_1}{A_1A_2 + B_1B_2}\right)$.

Example 3 Find the angle between the lines $x - 2y + 3 = 0$ and $3x + y - 1 = 0$.

Sol. Let m_1 and m_2 be the slopes of the straight lines $x - 2y + 3 = 0$ and $3x + y - 1 = 0$.

Then, $m_1 = -\frac{1}{-2} = \frac{1}{2}$ and $m_2 = -\frac{3}{1} = -3$

Let θ be the angle between the given lines.

Then, $\tan\theta = \pm\left(\frac{m_2 - m_1}{1 + m_1 m_2}\right) = \pm\left|\frac{-3 - \frac{1}{2}}{1 - \frac{3}{2}}\right| = \pm 7$

∴ $\tan\theta = \pm 7$

Example 4 Find the equation of one of the sides of an isosceles right angled triangle whose hypotenuse is given by $3x + 4y = 4$ and the opposite vertex of the hypotenuse is (2, 2). **[NCERT Exemplar]**

Sol. Let slope of line AC be m and the angle between line AC and BC be θ.

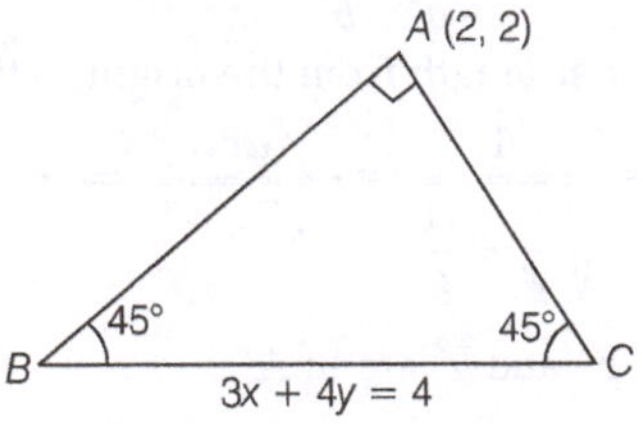

∴ Slope of the line $BC = \frac{-3}{4}$

$\left[\because 3x + 4y = 4 \Rightarrow y = \frac{-3}{4}x + 1\right]$

Then, $\tan\theta = \left|\frac{m + \frac{3}{4}}{1 - \frac{3m}{4}}\right| \Rightarrow \tan 45° = \left|\frac{m + \frac{3}{4}}{1 - \frac{3m}{4}}\right|$ $[\because \theta = 45°]$

$$\Rightarrow \quad \pm 1 = \left(\frac{m + \frac{3}{4}}{1 - \frac{3m}{4}}\right)$$

Taking positive sign, we get

$$1 = \frac{m + \frac{3}{4}}{1 - \frac{3m}{4}} \Rightarrow m + \frac{3}{4} = 1 - \frac{3m}{4}$$

$$\Rightarrow m + \frac{3m}{4} = 1 - \frac{3}{4} \Rightarrow \frac{7m}{4} = \frac{1}{4} \Rightarrow m = \frac{1}{7}$$

Taking negative sign, we get

$$-1 = \left(\frac{m + \frac{3}{4}}{1 - \frac{3m}{4}}\right) \Rightarrow -1 + \frac{3m}{4} = m + \frac{3}{4}$$

$$\Rightarrow m - \frac{3m}{4} = -1 - \frac{3}{4} \Rightarrow \frac{m}{4} = \frac{-7}{4} \Rightarrow m = -7$$

Now, equation of side AC is $y - 2 = \frac{1}{7}(x - 2)$

$\Rightarrow \quad 7y - 14 = x - 2 \Rightarrow x - 7y + 12 = 0$

or $\quad y - 2 = -7(x - 2)$

$\Rightarrow \quad y - 2 = -7x + 14 \Rightarrow 7x + y - 16 = 0$

Condition for Two Lines to be Parallel

If the lines $A_1x + B_1y + C_1 = 0$ and $A_2x + B_2y + C_2 = 0$ are parallel, then their slopes are equal,

i.e. $\quad m_1 = m_2 \Rightarrow -\frac{A_1}{B_1} = -\frac{A_2}{B_2} \Rightarrow \boxed{\frac{A_1}{B_1} = \frac{A_2}{B_2}}$

Condition for Two Lines to be Perpendicular

If the lines $A_1x + B_1y + C_1 = 0$ and $A_2x + B_2y + C_2 = 0$ are perpendicular, then the product of their slopes is equal to negative unity,

i.e. $\quad m_1 m_2 = -1$

$$\Rightarrow \quad -\frac{A_1}{B_1}\times\left(-\frac{A_2}{B_2}\right) = -1 \Rightarrow A_1A_2 + B_1B_2 = 0$$

Example 5 A line passing through the points $(a, 2a)$ and $(-2, 3)$ is perpendicular to the line $4x + 3y + 5 = 0$, find the value of a.

Sol. Let m_1 be the slope of the line joining $A(a, 2a)$ and $B(-2, 3)$.

Then, $\quad m_1 = \frac{2a - 3}{a + 2}$

Let m_2 be the slope of the line $4x+3y+5=0$.

Then, $m_2 = -\frac{4}{3}$ $\left[\because y = \frac{-4}{3}x - \frac{5}{3}\right]$

Since, given lines are perpendicular.

Therefore, $m_1 m_2 = -1$

$\Rightarrow \frac{2a-3}{a+2} \times -\frac{4}{3} = -1$

$\Rightarrow 8a - 12 = 3a + 6 \Rightarrow 5a = 18 \Rightarrow a = \frac{18}{5}$

Distance of a Point from a Line

The distance of a point from a line is the **length of perpendicular** drawn from the point to the line. Let $L: Ax + By + C = 0$ be a line, whose perpendicular distance from the point $P(x_1, y_1)$ is d.

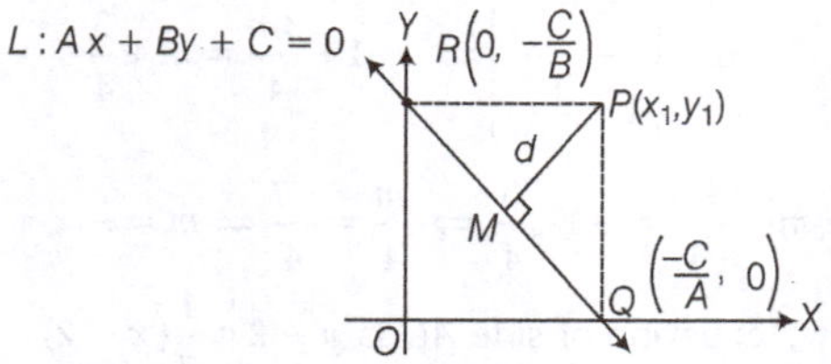

Then, $$d = \frac{|Ax_1 + By_1 + C|}{\sqrt{A^2+B^2}}$$

Note Distance of origin from the line $Ax + By + C = 0$ is $d = \frac{|C|}{\sqrt{A^2+B^2}}$.

Example 6 Find the distance of the point (2, − 3) from the line $2x - 3y + 6 = 0$.

Sol. Given equation of line is

$$2x - 3y + 6 = 0$$

$\therefore$ Required distance of the point from the line
= Perpendicular distance from point to the line

$$= \frac{|2 \times 2 - 3(-3) + 6|}{\sqrt{2^2 + (-3)^2}} = \frac{|4+9+6|}{\sqrt{4+9}} = \frac{19}{\sqrt{13}}$$

Example 7 Find the length of perpendicular from the point (a, b) to the line $\frac{x}{a} + \frac{y}{b} = 1$.

Sol. The given point is $P(a, b)$ and the given line is $bx + ay - ab = 0$.

Let d be the length of perpendicular from $P(a, b)$ to the line $bx + ay - ab = 0$.

Then, $d = \frac{|b \times a + a \times b - ab|}{\sqrt{b^2+a^2}} = \frac{|ab|}{\sqrt{a^2+b^2}}$ units

Example 8 Find the points on X-axis whose perpendicular distance from the line $4x + 3y = 12$ is 4.

Sol. Given points are on X-axis, so let its coordinates be $(\alpha, 0)$.

Then, length of perpendicular from $(\alpha, 0)$ to the line $4x + 3y - 12 = 0$ is 4.

$\therefore \frac{|4\alpha + 3(0) - 12|}{\sqrt{(4)^2+(3)^2}} = 4$

$\Rightarrow \frac{|4\alpha - 12|}{\sqrt{16+9}} = 4$

$\Rightarrow |4\alpha - 12| = 4 \times \sqrt{25} = 4 \times 5$

$\Rightarrow \alpha - 3 = \pm 5 \Rightarrow \alpha = 8$ or -2

Hence, the required points are (8, 0) and (−2, 0).

Example 9 Find the locus of a point which moves in such a way that the square of its distance from the point (3, − 2) is numerically equal to its distance from the line $5x - 12y = 13$. **[NCERT Exemplar]**

Sol. Let $P(h, k)$ be a variable point moving in such a way that the square of its distance from $A(3, -2)$ is numerically equal to its distance from the line $5x - 12y = 13$.

$\therefore (h-3)^2 + (k+2)^2 = \frac{|5h - 12k - 13|}{\sqrt{5^2 + (-12)^2}}$

$\Rightarrow 13\{(h-3)^2 + (k+2)^2\} = \pm(5h - 12k - 13)$

$\Rightarrow 13(h^2 + k^2) - 83h + 64k + 182 = 0$

or $13(h^2 + k^2) - 73h + 40k + 156 = 0$

Hence, the locus of (h, k) is

$13(x^2 + y^2) - 83x + 64y + 182 = 0$

or $13(x^2 + y^2) - 73x + 40y + 156 = 0$

Example 10 If p is the length of perpendicular from the origin on the line $\frac{x}{a} + \frac{y}{b} = 1$ and a^2, p^2 and b^2 are in AP, then show that $a^4 + b^4 = 0$. **[NCERT Exemplar]**

Sol. Given equation of line is

$$\frac{x}{a} + \frac{y}{b} = 1 \quad \text{...(i)}$$

Perpendicular length from the origin to the line (i) is

$$p = \frac{1}{\sqrt{\frac{1}{a^2} + \frac{1}{b^2}}} = \frac{ab}{\sqrt{a^2+b^2}} \Rightarrow p^2 = \frac{a^2b^2}{a^2+b^2}$$

Since, a^2, p^2 and b^2 are in AP.

$\therefore 2p^2 = a^2 + b^2 \Rightarrow \frac{2a^2b^2}{a^2+b^2} = a^2 + b^2$

$\Rightarrow 2a^2b^2 = (a^2+b^2)^2 \Rightarrow 2a^2b^2 = a^4 + b^4 + 2a^2b^2$

$\Rightarrow a^4 + b^4 = 0$ **Hence proved.**

Example 11 Find the perpendicular distance from the origin of the line joining the points $(\cos\theta, \sin\theta)$ and $(\cos\phi, \sin\phi)$. **[NCERT]**

Sol. Let the given points be $A(\cos\theta, \sin\theta)$ and $B(\cos\phi, \sin\phi)$.

Then, equation of line AB is

$$y - \sin\theta = \frac{\sin\phi - \sin\theta}{\cos\phi - \cos\theta}(x - \cos\theta)$$

$$\left[\because y - y_1 = \frac{y_2 - y_1}{x_2 - x_1}(x - x_1)\right]$$

$$\Rightarrow \quad y - \sin\theta = \frac{2\cos\left(\frac{\phi+\theta}{2}\right)\sin\left(\frac{\phi-\theta}{2}\right)}{-2\sin\left(\frac{\phi+\theta}{2}\right)\sin\left(\frac{\phi-\theta}{2}\right)}(x - \cos\theta)$$

$$\left[\because \sin C - \sin D = 2\cos\left(\frac{C+D}{2}\right)\sin\left(\frac{C-D}{2}\right)\right]$$

$$\Rightarrow \quad y\sin\left(\frac{\phi+\theta}{2}\right) - \sin\theta\sin\left(\frac{\phi+\theta}{2}\right) = -x\cos\left(\frac{\phi+\theta}{2}\right) + \cos\theta\cos\left(\frac{\theta+\phi}{2}\right)$$

$$\Rightarrow \quad x\cos\left(\frac{\theta+\phi}{2}\right) + y\sin\left(\frac{\theta+\phi}{2}\right) - \left\{\cos\theta\cos\left(\frac{\theta+\phi}{2}\right) + \sin\theta\sin\left(\frac{\theta+\phi}{2}\right)\right\} = 0$$

$$\Rightarrow \quad x\cos\left(\frac{\theta+\phi}{2}\right) + y\sin\left(\frac{\theta+\phi}{2}\right) - \cos\left(\theta - \frac{\theta+\phi}{2}\right) = 0$$

$$\Rightarrow \quad x\cos\left(\frac{\theta+\phi}{2}\right) + y\sin\left(\frac{\theta+\phi}{2}\right) - \cos\left(\frac{\theta-\phi}{2}\right) = 0$$

Now, perpendicular distance from origin

$$= \frac{\left|0 + 0 - \cos\left(\frac{\theta-\phi}{2}\right)\right|}{\sqrt{\cos^2\left(\frac{\theta+\phi}{2}\right) + \sin^2\left(\frac{\theta+\phi}{2}\right)}}$$

$$\left[\because \text{distance from } (x_1, y_1) \text{ to the line } ax + by + c = 0 \text{ is } \frac{|ax_1 + by_1 + c|}{\sqrt{a^2 + b^2}}\right]$$

$$= \left|\cos\left(\frac{\theta-\phi}{2}\right)\right|$$

Distance between Two Parallel Lines

If two lines are parallel, then they have the same distance between them throughout. Therefore, the distance between two parallel lines can be find by the following method.

The distance between two parallel lines

$$y = mx + c_1 \quad \text{...(i)}$$

and

$$y = mx + c_2 \quad \text{...(ii)}$$

is given by

$$d = \frac{|c_1 - c_2|}{\sqrt{1 + m^2}}$$

If the lines are given in general form, i.e. the given lines are $Ax + By + C_1 = 0$ and $Ax + By + C_2 = 0$, then distance between these lines,

$$d = \frac{|C_1 - C_2|}{\sqrt{A^2 + B^2}}$$

Example 12 Find the distance between following parallel lines.

(i) $3x - 4y + 9 = 0$ and $6x - 8y - 15 = 0$

(ii) $l(x + y) + h = 0$ and $l(x + y) - r = 0$ **[NCERT]**

Sol. (i) Given parallel lines are

$$3x - 4y + 9 = 0 \quad \text{...(i)}$$

and

$$6x - 8y - 15 = 0$$

$$\Rightarrow \quad 3x - 4y - \frac{15}{2} = 0 \quad \text{...(ii)}$$

On comparing Eqs. (i) and (ii) with $Ax + By + C_1 = 0$ and $Ax + By + C_2 = 0$, we get

$$A = 3, B = -4, C_1 = 9 \text{ and } C_2 = \frac{-15}{2}$$

$$\therefore \text{ Required distance} = \frac{|C_1 - C_2|}{\sqrt{A^2 + B^2}} = \frac{\left|9 + \frac{15}{2}\right|}{\sqrt{3^2 + (-4)^2}}$$

$$= \frac{\left|\frac{18 + 15}{2}\right|}{\sqrt{9 + 16}} = \frac{33}{2\sqrt{25}} = \frac{33}{2 \times 5} = \frac{33}{10} \text{ units}$$

Hence, the required distance is $\frac{33}{10}$ units.

(ii) Given parallel lines are

$$lx + ly + h = 0 \text{ and } lx + ly - r = 0$$

On comparing with $Ax + By + C_1 = 0$

and $Ax + By + C_2 = 0$, we get

$$A = l, B = l, C_1 = h, C_2 = -r$$

$$\therefore \text{Required distance} = \frac{|C_1 - C_2|}{\sqrt{A^2 + B^2}} = \left|\frac{h + r}{\sqrt{l^2 + l^2}}\right| = \left|\frac{h + r}{\sqrt{2}\, l}\right|$$

Example 13 Find the equation of the line midway between the parallel lines $9x + 6y - 7 = 0$ and $3x + 2y + 6 = 0$.

Sol. Converting each of the given equations to the form $y = mx + C$, we get

$$9x + 6y - 7 = 0 \Rightarrow y = \frac{-3}{2}x + \frac{7}{6} \quad \text{...(i)}$$

and $\quad 3x + 2y + 6 = 0 \Rightarrow y = \frac{-3}{2}x - 3$ ...(ii)

Clearly, the slope of each one of the given lines is $\frac{-3}{2}$.

Let the given lines be $y = mx + C_1$ and $y = mx + C_2$.

Then, $\quad m = \frac{-3}{2}, C_1 = \frac{7}{6}$ and $C_2 = -3$

Let L be the required line. Then, L is parallel to each one of lines (i) and (ii) and equidistant from each one of them.

$\therefore \quad$ Slope of $L = \frac{-3}{2}$

Let the equation of L be $y = \frac{-3}{2}x + C$ ...(iii)

Then, distance between lines (i) and (iii) must be equal to the distance between lines (ii) and (iii).

$$\therefore \quad \frac{|C_1 - C|}{\sqrt{1+m^2}} = \frac{|C_2 - C|}{\sqrt{1+m^2}} \Rightarrow |C_1 - C| = |C_2 - C|$$

$$\Rightarrow \quad \left|\frac{7}{6} - C\right| = |-3 - C| \Rightarrow \left|\frac{7}{6} - C\right| = |3 + C|$$

$$\Rightarrow \quad \frac{7}{6} - C = \pm(3 + C) \Rightarrow 2C = \frac{-11}{6} \Rightarrow C = \frac{-11}{12}$$

$\therefore$ Equation of L is $y = \frac{-3}{2}x - \frac{11}{12}$, i.e. $18x + 12y + 11 = 0$

Hence, the line $18x + 12y + 11 = 0$ is midway between the parallel lines $9x + 6y - 7 = 0$ and $3x + 2y + 6 = 0$.

Position of Two Points Relative to a Line

Let $P(x_1, y_1)$ and $Q(x_2, y_2)$ be two given points and

$$Ax + By + C = 0 \quad \text{...(i)}$$

be the given line.

Let the line (i) divide the segment PQ in the ratio $k:1$ at the point R, then the coordinates of R are $\left(\frac{kx_2 + x_1}{k+1}, \frac{ky_2 + y_1}{k+1}\right)$.

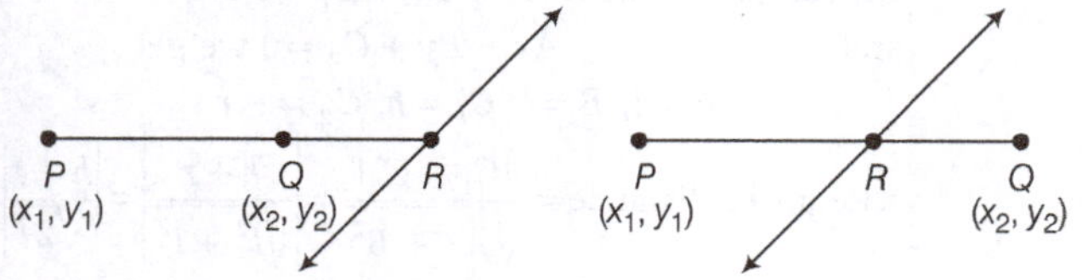

Since, the point R lies on Eq. (i), we get

$$A \cdot \frac{kx_2 + x_1}{k+1} + B \cdot \frac{ky_2 + y_1}{k+1} + C = 0$$

$$\Rightarrow \quad (Ax_2 + By_2 + C)k + (Ax_1 + By_1 + C) = 0$$

$$\Rightarrow \quad k = -\frac{Ax_1 + By_1 + C}{Ax_2 + By_2 + C}$$

From the given figure, clearly the given points $P(x_1, y_1)$ and $Q(x_2, y_2)$ will lie on the same side or on opposite sides of the line (i) according as the division is external or internal i.e. according as k is − ve or + ve i.e. according as $\frac{Ax_1 + By_1 + C}{Ax_2 + By_2 + C}$ is negative or positive i.e. according as $\frac{Ax_1 + By_1 + C}{Ax_2 + By_2 + C}$ is positive or negative.

i.e. according as the expressions $Ax_2 + By_2 + C$ and $Ax_1 + By_1 + C$ have the same sign or opposite signs.

Hence, the given points $P(x_1, y_1)$ and $Q(x_2, y_2)$ lie on the same side or on opposite sides of the line $Ax + By + C = 0$ according as the expressions $Ax_1 + By_1 + C$ and $Ax_2 + By_2 + C$ have same sign or opposite signs.

Example 14 Determine whether the pair of points (− 1, 2) and (3, 4) lie on the same side or on the opposite sides of the line $2x - 3y = 7$.

Sol. The equation of the given line is $2x - 3y = 7$

i.e. $\quad 2x - 3y - 7 = 0$ ...(i)

On substituting (−1, 2) in LHS of Eq. (i), we get

$$-2 - 6 - 7 = -15;$$

and substituting (3, 4) in LHS of Eq. (i), we get

$$6 - 12 - 7 = -13$$

Since, both the expressions have same sign, so the given points lie on the same side.

Equation of Lines Bisecting the Angle between Two Lines (or Angle Bisectors)

An angular bisector of two lines is the locus of a point which is equidistant from the two lines. If the lines are $l_1: A_1x + B_1y + C_1 = 0$, $\quad l_2: A_2x + B_2y + C_2 = 0$ and $P(h, k)$ is any point on the bisector, then $|PM| = |PN|$

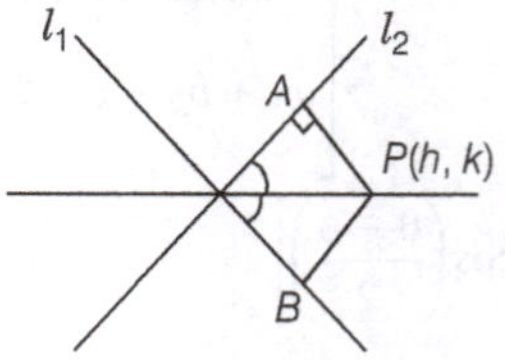

i.e. $$\frac{|A_1h + B_1k + C_1|}{\sqrt{A_1^2 + B_1^2}} = \frac{|A_2h + B_2k + C_2|}{\sqrt{A_2^2 + B_2^2}}$$

$\therefore$ Locus of the point $P(h, k)$ is

$$\frac{|A_1x + B_1y + C_1|}{\sqrt{A_1^2 + B_1^2}} = \frac{|A_2x + B_2y + C_2|}{\sqrt{A_2^2 + B_2^2}}$$

Hence, the **equations of the bisectors of the angles between lines** l_1 **and** l_2 **are given by**

$$\frac{A_1x+B_1y+C_1}{\sqrt{A_1^2+B_1^2}}=\pm\frac{A_2x+B_2y+C_2}{\sqrt{A_2^2+B_2^2}}.$$

Note The two bisectors can be **distinguished** with respect to the origin by working out as follows

(i) Make the constant terms positive in the equations of the given lines (right sides being zero).

(ii) The equation obtained on taking the + ve sign will be the equation of the bisector b_1 that bisects the angle in which the origin lies. The other equation will represent the bisector b_2 that bisects the angle in which the origin does not lie.

Example 15 Find the equations of the bisectors of the angles between the lines $12x+5y-4=0$ and $3x+4y+7=0$. Distinguish (i) the one which bisects the angle in which the origin lies and (ii) the one which bisects the acute angle between the lines.

Sol. Writing the given equations so that the constant terms are positive, we get

$$-12x-5y+4=0 \quad \text{...(i)}$$

and $$3x+4y+7=0 \quad \text{...(ii)}$$

∴ Equations of the angular bisectors of Eqs. (i) and (ii) are

$$\frac{-12x-5y+4}{\sqrt{(-12)^2+(-5)^2}}=\pm\frac{3x+4y+7}{\sqrt{3^2+4^2}}$$

The bisector of the angle in which the origin lies is

$$\frac{-12x-5y+4}{13}=\frac{3x+4y+7}{5}$$

$$\Rightarrow \quad 5(-12x-5y+4)=13(3x+4y+7)$$

$$\Rightarrow \quad 99x+77y+71=0. \quad \text{...(iii)}$$

The equation of the other bisector is

$$\frac{-12x-5y+4}{13}=-\frac{3x+4y+7}{5},$$

$$\Rightarrow \quad 5(-12x-5y+4)=-13(3x+4y+7)$$

$$\Rightarrow \quad 21x-27y-111=0$$

$$\Rightarrow \quad 7x-9y-37=0 \quad \text{...(iv)}$$

Of Eqs. (iii) and (iv), that bisector will be the bisector of the acute angle, which makes an angle $\theta<45^\circ$ with any of the lines (i) or (ii). To find this, we make use of the fact that if $\theta<45^\circ$, $\tan\theta$ is numerically <1.

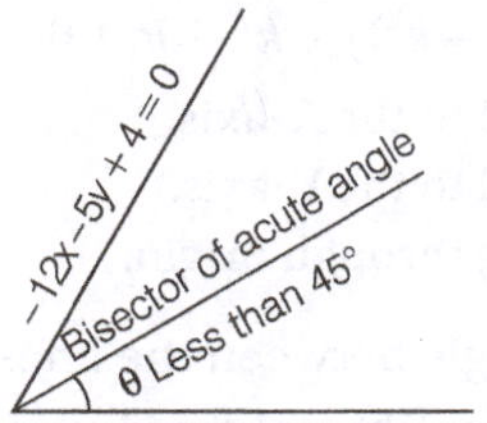

Consider the line (ii) and the bisector (iv). If θ is the angle between them, then

$$\tan\theta=\frac{28+27}{-21+36}=\frac{55}{15}>1\Rightarrow\theta>45^\circ$$

∴ Eq. (iv) is the bisector of the obtuse angle.

Hence, the other bisector, namely, $99x+77y+71=0$ bisects, the acute angle.

Topic Practice 4

Very Short Answer Type Questions

(2 Marks)

1 Reduce the following equations into slope intercept form and find their slopes and the y-intercepts.
(i) $x+7y=0$ (ii) $y=0$ **[NCERT]**

2 Reduce the following equations into intercept form and find their intercepts on the axes.
(i) $6x+y-6=0$ (ii) $2y+5=0$

3 Reduce the equation $\sqrt{3}x+y=4$ into normal form and hence find the values of p and α.

4 Find the angle between the straight lines, whose equations are $3x+y-7=0$ and $x+2y+9=0$.

5 Find the equation of the line perpendicular to the line $x-7y+5=0$ and having x-intercept 3. **[NCERT]**

6 Find the inclination of the line $x-y+3=0$ with the positive direction of X-axis. **[NCERT Exemplar]**

7 Prove that the line through the point (x_1, y_1) and parallel to the line $Ax+By+C=0$ is
$A(x-x_1)+B(y-y_1)=0.$ **[NCERT]**

8 Show that the straight lines given by $x(a+2b)+y(a+3b)=a+b$ for different values of a and b pass through a fixed point.

9 Find the values of θ and p, if the equation $x\cos\theta+y\sin\theta=p$ is the normal form of the line $\sqrt{3}x+y+2=0$. **[NCERT]**

10 In what ratio, the line joining (–1, 1) and (5, 7) is divided by the line $x+y=4$?

11 Find the equation of the line passing through (1, 2) and perpendicular to $x+y+7=0$.

12 Find the coordinates of the foot of perpendicular from the point (–1, 3) to the line $3x - 4y - 16 = 0$.

13 Show that the tangent of an angle between the lines $\frac{x}{a} + \frac{y}{b} = 1$ and $\frac{x}{a} - \frac{y}{b} = 1$ is $\frac{2ab}{a^2 - b^2}$.

14 Find the distance between the following pair of lines.

(i) $3x + 4y = 9$ and $6x + 8y = 15$

(ii) $y = mx + c$ and $y = mx + d$

(iii) $4x + 3y - 11 = 0$ and $8x + 6y = 15$

[NCERT Exemplar]

15 If p is the length of perpendicular from origin to the line whose intercept on the axes are a and b, then show that $\frac{1}{p^2} = \frac{1}{a^2} + \frac{1}{b^2}$.

16 The equation of two sides of a square are $5x - 12y - 65 = 0$ and $5x - 12y + 26 = 0$. Find the area of a square.

17 Find the values of k for which the length of perpendicular from the point (4,1) on the line $3x - 4y + k = 0$ is 2 units.

18 The perpendicular distance of a line from the origin is 5 units and its slope is –1. Find the equation of the line.

19 Determine whether the pair of points (0, – 5) and (– 2, – 1) lie on the same side or on the opposite side of the line $2x - 3y = 7$.

Short Answer Type Questions

4 Marks

20 Find the angle between the lines $\sqrt{3}x + y = 1$ and $x + \sqrt{3}y = 1$.

21 For what values of a and b the intercepts cuts-off on the coordinates axes by the line $ax + by + 8 = 0$ are equal in length but opposite in signs to those cuts-off by the line $2x - 3y + 6 = 0$ on the axes? **[NCERT Exemplar]**

22 If a line passes through (2, 2) and is perpendicular to the line $3x + y = 3$, then find its y-intercept.

23 Reduce the equation $5x - 12y = 60$ to intercept form. Hence, find the length of the portion of the line intercepted between the axes.

24 The perpendicular from the origin to the line $y = mx + c$ meets it at the point (–1, 2). Find the values of m and c. **[NCERT]**

25 If p and q are the lengths of perpendiculars from the origin to the lines $x\cos\theta - y\sin\theta = k\cos 2\theta$ and $x\sec\theta + y\,\text{cosec}\,\theta = k$, respectively. Prove that $p^2 + 4q^2 = k^2$.

26 Find the points on the Y-axis, whose perpendicular distance from the line $4x - 3y - 12 = 0$ is 3.

27 If sum of perpendicular distances of a variable point $P(x, y)$ from the lines $x + y - 5 = 0$ and $3x - 2y + 7 = 0$ is always 10. Show that P must moves on a line. **[NCERT]**

28 Which of the lines $2x - y + 3 = 0$ and $x - 4y - 7 = 0$, is farther from the origin?

29 Find the points on the line $x + y = 4$ which lie at a unit distance from the line $4x + 3y = 10$. **[NCERT Exemplar]**

30 Find a point which is equidistant from the lines $4x + 3y + 10 = 0$, $5x - 12y + 26 = 0$ and $7x + 24y - 50 = 0$. **[NCERT Exemplar]**

31 Find the equation of two straight lines which are parallel to $x + 7y + 2 = 0$ and at unit distance from the point (1, –1).

32 A triangle is formed by the lines whose equations are $3x + 4y - 6 = 0$, $12x - 5y - 3 = 0$ and $4x - 3y + 12 = 0$. Find the internal bisector of the angle opposite to the side $3x + 4y - 6 = 0$.

Long Answer Type Questions

6 Marks

33 Reduce the equation $x - \sqrt{3}y + 8 = 0$ into normal form. Find the perpendicular distance from the origin and angle between perpendicular and the positive X-axis.

34 Find the values of k for which the line $(k - 3)x - (4 - k^2)y + k^2 - 7k + 6 = 0$ is

(i) parallel to the X-axis.

(ii) parallel to the Y-axis.

(iii) passing through origin.

35 Find the angle between the lines $y = (2 - \sqrt{3})(x + 5)$ and $y = (2 + \sqrt{3})(x - 7)$.

36 Find the equation of the lines passing through the point (1,0) and at a distance $\frac{\sqrt{3}}{2}$ from the origin. **[NCERT Exemplar]**

37 Find the ratio in which the line $3x+4y+2=0$ divides the distance between the lines $3x+4y+5=0$ and $3x+4y-5=0$. **[NCERT Exemplar]**

38 The points $A(2,3)$, $B(4,-1)$ and $C(-1,2)$ are the vertices of ΔABC. Find the length of perpendicular from C on AB and hence find the area of ΔABC.

Hints & Answers

1. (i) $y=-\frac{1}{7}x+0, m=-\frac{1}{7}, c=0$

(ii) $y=0x+0, m=0, c=0$

2. (i) $\frac{x}{1}+\frac{y}{6}=1$; x-intercept $=1$ and y-intercept $=6$

(ii) $0\cdot x+\frac{y}{-5/2}=1$; x-intercept $=\infty$ and y-intercept $=-\frac{5}{2}$

3. On dividing both sides of given equation by $\sqrt{(\sqrt{3})^2+(1)^2}$, we get

$$x\cdot\left(\frac{\sqrt{3}}{2}\right)+y\cdot\left(\frac{1}{2}\right)=2$$

Ans. $\alpha=30°$ and $p=2$ units

4. Here, $m_1=-3$ and $m_2=\frac{-1}{2}$ $\Rightarrow$ $\tan\theta=\pm1$

Ans. $\theta=45°$ or $135°$

5. The slope of given line is $m_1=\frac{1}{7}$.

$\therefore$ The slope of perpendicular line is $m=-7$.

It is given that x-intercept $(d)=3$

$\therefore$ The required equation of line is given by

$y=m(x-d)$ [by using slope intercept form]

Ans. $7x+y=21$

6. Here, $m=\tan\theta=1$ **Ans.** $\theta=45°$

7. Equation of line parallel to $Ax+By+C=0$ is $Ax+By+k=0$.

Since, this line passes through the point (x_1, y_1) i.e. it satisfy this line

$\therefore$ $Ax_1+By_1+K=0$

$\Rightarrow$ $K=-(Ax_1+By_1)$

8. Given equation can be written as

$$a(x+y-1)+b(2x+3y-1)=0$$

$\Rightarrow$ $(x+y-1)+\lambda(2x+3y-1)=0$, where $\lambda=\frac{b}{a}$

9. Given equation of line is $\sqrt{3}x+y+2=0$

$\Rightarrow$ $-\sqrt{3}x-y=2$ ...(i)

Divide both sides of Eq. (i) by $\sqrt{(-\sqrt{3})^2+(-1)^2}=2$,

Ans. $\theta=210°$ and $p=1$

10. Let the line $x+y=4$ divides the line joining the points $A(-1,1)$ and $B(5,7)$ in the ratio $k:1$, at point P.

Then, $P=\left[\frac{k\times5+1\times(-1)}{k+1}, \frac{k\times7+1\times1}{k+1}\right]$

$=\left(\frac{5k-1}{k+1}, \frac{7k+1}{k+1}\right)$

$\because$ Point P will satisfy the line $x+y=4$.

$\therefore$ $\frac{5k-1}{k+1}+\frac{7k+1}{k+1}=\frac{4}{1}$

Ans. $k:1=1:2$ (internally)

11. Equation of line perpendicular to $x+y+7=0$ is $y-x+k=0$.

Ans. $y-x-1=0$

12. We have, $y=\frac{3}{4}x-4$ ...(i)

Let m_1 be the slope of this line, then $m_1=\frac{3}{4}$.

If m_2 is the slope of any other line perpendicular to line (i), then $m_2=-\frac{4}{3}$

Equation of perpendicular line passing through $(-1, 3)$ and having slope $m_2=\frac{-4}{3}$, is $y-3=\frac{-4}{3}(x+1)$

$\Rightarrow$ $4x+3y-5=0$ ...(ii)

Now, find the point of intersection of lines (i) and (ii).

Ans. $\left(\frac{68}{25}, \frac{-49}{25}\right)$

13. Here, slope, $m_1=-\frac{b}{a}$ and slope, $m_2=\frac{b}{a}$

14. (i) Given equations can be rewritten as

$3x+4y-9=0$ and $3x+4y-\frac{15}{2}=0$

Since, the slope of these lines are same and hence they are parallel to each other.

Therefore, the distance between them is given by

$$d=\left|\frac{9-(15/2)}{\sqrt{3^2+4^2}}\right|$$

Ans. $\frac{3}{10}$ unit

(ii) Solve as part (i). **Ans.** $\frac{|c-d|}{\sqrt{1+m^2}}$ units

(iii) Solve as part (i). **Ans.** $\frac{7}{10}$ unit

15. Equation of line in intercept form is

$$\frac{x}{a}+\frac{y}{b}=1$$

$$\Rightarrow \quad \frac{x}{a}+\frac{y}{b}-1=0$$

Its distance from origin is $\left|\frac{0+0-1}{\sqrt{\frac{1}{a^2}+\frac{1}{b^2}}}\right|=p$

16. Side of a square, $a=\frac{|26+65|}{\sqrt{5^2+12^2}}=\frac{91}{\sqrt{169}}$ units

Area of square $= a^2$ **Ans.** 49 sq units

17. $\frac{(3\times4-4\times1+k)}{\sqrt{3^2+(-4)^2}}=\pm2$ **Ans.** $k=2$ or $k=-18$

18. Let the required equation be $y=-x+c$.

$$\therefore \quad \frac{|0+0-c|}{\sqrt{1^2+1^2}}=5 \Rightarrow |c|=5\sqrt{2}$$

$$\Rightarrow \quad c=5\sqrt{2} \text{ or } c=-5\sqrt{2}$$

Ans. $x+y+5\sqrt{2}=0$ or $x+y-5\sqrt{2}=0$

19. Opposite side of the line.

20. $m_1=-\sqrt{3}$ and $m_2=-\frac{1}{\sqrt{3}}$

Ans. $\theta=30°$ or $150°$

21. Given, $ax+by+8=0 \Rightarrow \frac{x}{\frac{-8}{a}}+\frac{y}{\frac{-8}{b}}=1$

So, the intercepts are $\frac{-8}{a}$ and $\frac{-8}{b}$.

and $\quad 2x-3y+6=0 \Rightarrow \frac{x}{-3}+\frac{y}{2}=1$

So, the intercepts are −3 and 2.

Ans. $a=-\frac{8}{3}, b=4$

22. Slope of the required perpendicular line $=\frac{1}{3}$

$\therefore$ Equation of the required perpendicular line is

$$y-2=\frac{1}{3}(x-2)$$

For y-intercept, put $x=0$ **Ans.** $y=\frac{4}{3}$

23. Here, x-intercept, $a=12$ and y-intercept, $b=-5$.

Length of the portion $=\sqrt{a^2+b^2}$

Ans. $\frac{x}{12}+\frac{y}{-5}=1$; 13 units

24. Since, $(-1, 2)$ lies on line $y=mx+c$.

$$\therefore \quad 2=m(-1)+c$$

$$\Rightarrow \quad c=m+2 \quad \text{...(i)}$$

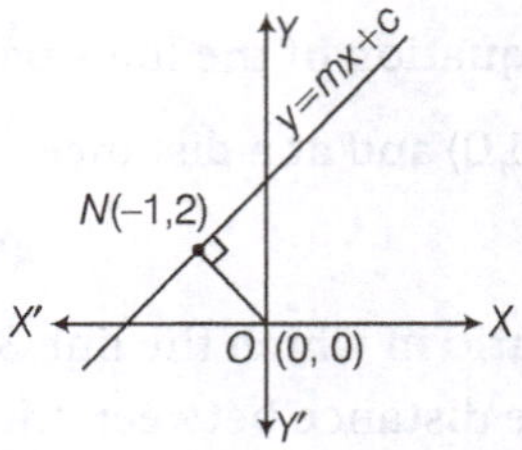

Slope of $ON\,(m_1)=\frac{0-2}{0+1}=-2$

Since, ON perpendicular to line $y=mx+c$

$\therefore \quad m_1 m=-1$ **Ans.** $m=\frac{1}{2}$ and $c=\frac{5}{2}$

25. Here, $\quad p=\frac{|0\cdot\cos\theta-0\cdot(-\sin\theta)-k\cos2\theta|}{\sqrt{\cos^2\theta+\sin^2\theta}}$

$$\Rightarrow \quad p=|k\cos2\theta|$$

and $\quad q=\frac{|0\cdot\sec\theta+0\cdot\text{cosec}\,\theta-k|}{\sqrt{\sec^2\theta+\text{cosec}^2\theta}}$

$$\therefore \quad q=\frac{|k|}{\sqrt{\frac{1}{\cos^2\theta}+\frac{1}{\sin^2\theta}}}=\frac{|k|}{\sqrt{\frac{\sin^2\theta+\cos^2\theta}{\sin^2\theta\cdot\cos^2\theta}}}$$

$$=\frac{|k|\cdot|\sin\theta\cos\theta|}{1}\times\frac{2}{2}=\frac{1}{2}|k(2\sin\theta\cos\theta)|$$

$$\Rightarrow \quad q=\frac{1}{2}|k\sin2\theta| \Rightarrow 2q=|k\sin2\theta|$$

$$\therefore\; p^2+4q^2=k^2\cos^2 2\theta+k^2\sin^2 2\theta$$

26. $\frac{|4(0)-3(y_1)-12|}{\sqrt{4^2+(-3)^2}}=3 \Rightarrow \frac{3y_1+12}{\sqrt{16+9}}=\pm3$

Ans. $(0,1)$ and $(0,-9)$

27. $\frac{|x+y-5|}{\sqrt{(1)^2+(1)^2}}+\frac{|3x-2y+7|}{\sqrt{3^2+(-2)^2}}=10$

$$\Rightarrow \sqrt{13}|x+y-5|+\sqrt{2}|3x-2y+7|-10\sqrt{26}=0$$

$$\Rightarrow x(\sqrt{13}+3\sqrt{2})+y(\sqrt{13}-2\sqrt{2})+7\sqrt{2}-5\sqrt{13}-10\sqrt{26}=0$$

[assuming $(x+y-5)$ and $(3x-2y+7)$ as positive]

Similarly, we can obtain the equation of line for any signs of $(x+y-5)$ and $(3x-2y+7)$.

Thus, point P must move on a line.

28. $P_1=\frac{|0+0+3|}{\sqrt{(-2)^2+(1)^2}}=\frac{3}{\sqrt{5}}$; $P_2=\frac{|0+0-7|}{\sqrt{(1)^2+(-4)^2}}=\frac{7}{\sqrt{17}}$

Again, $\quad P_1=\frac{3}{\sqrt{5}}\times\frac{\sqrt{17}}{\sqrt{17}}=\sqrt{\frac{153}{85}}$

and $\quad P_2=\frac{7}{\sqrt{17}}\times\frac{\sqrt{5}}{\sqrt{5}}=\sqrt{\frac{245}{85}}$

$$\because \quad \sqrt{\frac{245}{85}}>\sqrt{\frac{153}{85}} \Rightarrow P_2>P_1$$

Ans. $x-4y-7=0$ is farther.

29. Let the required point be (h, k).

Since, point (h, k) lies on the line $x+y=4$,

therefore $h+k=4$ ...(i)

Also, the distance of the point (h, k) from the line

$$4x+3y=10 \text{ is } \left|\frac{4h+3k-10}{\sqrt{16+9}}\right|=1$$

$\Rightarrow 4h+3k-10=\pm 5$

Ans. (3,1) and (−7,11)

30. Let the point (h, k) is equidistant from the given lines.

Distance from line (i) $=\dfrac{|4h+3k+10|}{\sqrt{16+9}}$

Distance from line (ii) $=\dfrac{|5h-12k+26|}{\sqrt{25+144}}$

Distance from line (iii) $=\dfrac{|7h+24k-50|}{\sqrt{7^2+24^2}}$

Since, the point (h, k) is equidistant from lines (i), (ii) and (iii).

$$\therefore \frac{|4h+3k+10|}{\sqrt{16+9}}=\frac{|5h-12k+26|}{\sqrt{25+144}}=\frac{|7h+24k-50|}{\sqrt{49+576}}$$

$$\Rightarrow \frac{|4h+3k+10|}{5}=\frac{|5h-12k+26|}{13}=\frac{|7h+24k-50|}{25}$$

Clearly, if $h=0$, $k=0$, then $\dfrac{10}{5}=\dfrac{26}{13}=\dfrac{50}{25}=2$

Ans. (0, 0)

31. Slope of required lines $=\dfrac{-1}{7}$

Now, let the equation of required lines be

$$y=\frac{-1}{7}x+c.$$

Then, $$\frac{\left|-1+\frac{1}{7}-c\right|}{\sqrt{1^2+\left(\frac{1}{7}\right)^2}}=1$$

$$\Rightarrow \quad c=\frac{-6\pm 5\sqrt{2}}{7}$$

Ans. $x+7y+6\pm 5\sqrt{2}=0$

32. $112x-64y+141=0$

33. Given equation of line is $-x+\sqrt{3}y=8$ ...(i)

Divide both sides of Eq. (i) by

$$\sqrt{(-1)^2+(\sqrt{3})^2}=2.$$

Ans. $\alpha=120°$, $p=4$

34. Equation of given line is

$(k-3)x-(4-k^2)y+k^2-7k+6=0$ ...(i)

(i) When line (i) is parallel to X-axis, then slope = 0

i.e. $\dfrac{(k-3)}{(4-k^2)}=0$ **Ans.** $k=3$

(ii) When line (i) is parallel to Y-axis, then slope $=\dfrac{1}{0}$

Ans. $k=\pm 2$

(iii) When line (i) is passing through origin (0, 0), then it will satisfy it.

Ans. $k=1, 6$

35. $y=(2-\sqrt{3})x+5(2-\sqrt{3})$ and $y=(2+\sqrt{3})x-7(2+\sqrt{3})$

Slope of above lines are $m_1=2-\sqrt{3}$ and $m_2=2+\sqrt{3}$

Angle between two lines,

$$\tan\theta=\pm\left(\frac{2+\sqrt{3}-(2-\sqrt{3})}{1+(2+\sqrt{3})(2-\sqrt{3})}\right)$$

Ans. $\theta=\dfrac{\pi}{3}$ or $\dfrac{2\pi}{3}$

36. Here, $y-0=m(x-1) \Rightarrow y-mx+m=0$

Since, the distance from origin is $\dfrac{\sqrt{3}}{2}$.

Then, $$\frac{\sqrt{3}}{2}=\frac{|0-0+m|}{\sqrt{1+m^2}}$$

Ans. $\sqrt{3}x-y-\sqrt{3}=0$ and $\sqrt{3}x+y-\sqrt{3}=0$

37. $3x+4y+5=0$

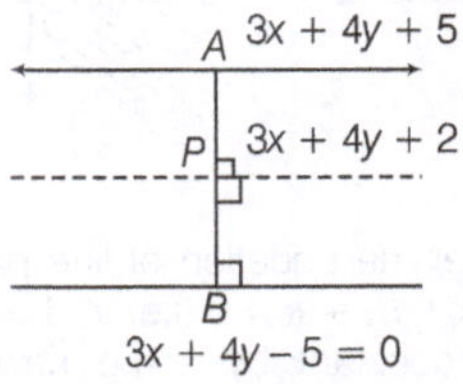

Now, distance between the lines $3x+4y+5=0$ and

$3x+4y+2=0$ is $d_1=\dfrac{|5-2|}{\sqrt{9+16}}=\dfrac{3}{5}$

and distance between the lines $3x+4y+2=0$

and $3x+4y-5=0$ is $d_2=\dfrac{|-5-2|}{\sqrt{9+16}}=\dfrac{7}{5}$ **Ans.** 3 : 7

38. Equation of AB is $\dfrac{y-3}{x-2}=\dfrac{-4}{2} \Rightarrow 2x+y-7=0$

Now, perpendicular distance from C on AB

$$=\frac{|2\times(-1)+2-7|}{\sqrt{2^2+1^2}}=\frac{7}{\sqrt{5}} \text{ units}$$

and ar $(\Delta ABC)=\dfrac{1}{2}\times AB\times\dfrac{7}{\sqrt{5}}$

Ans. $\dfrac{7}{\sqrt{5}}$ units, 7 sq units

TOPIC 05

Family of Lines and Locus of a Point

Family of Lines

If a relation between two arbitrary constants and hence each arbitrary constant determines the other, then the lines which satisfy one condition contain a single arbitrary constant, such a system of the lines is called the **one parameter family of lines** and the unknown arbitrary constant is called the **parameter**.

e.g.

(i) The equation $y = mx + 4$ represents a family of lines with y-intercept 4 units.

(ii) The equation $4x + 5y + k = 0$ represents a family of line with slope $\frac{-4}{5}$.

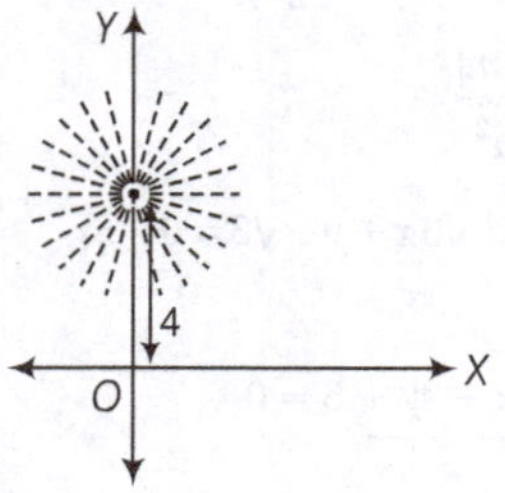

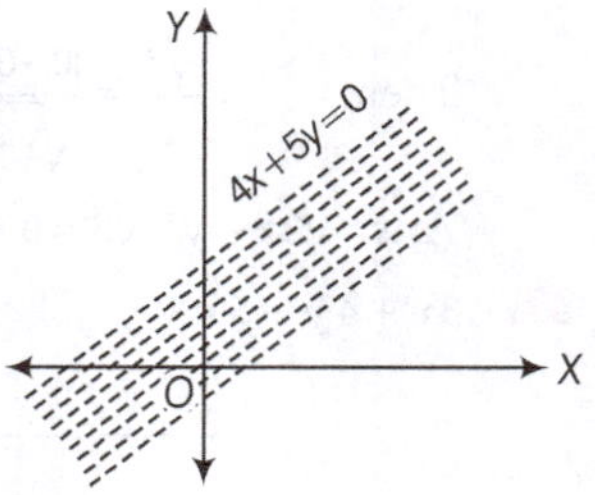

Note

(i) Generally, we consider the equation of line **parallel** to the line $ax + by + c = 0$ as $ax + by + k = 0$ (i.e. in the original equation of line replace the constant by some new constant). This constant k can be determined by putting the given point (x_1, y_1) in $ax + by + k = 0$.

(ii) Generally, we consider the equation of line **perpendicular** to the line $ax + by + c = 0$ as $bx - ay + k = 0$ (i.e. in the original equation of line interchange the coefficients of x and y alongwith their sign and also add some new constant k). This constant k can be determined by putting the given point (x_1, y_1) in $ax - by + k = 0$.

Family of Lines through the Intersection of Two Lines

Let the two given lines be

$$l_1 = a_1x + b_1y + c_1 = 0 \quad \ldots\text{(i)}$$

and $$l_2 = a_2x + b_2y + c_2 = 0 \quad \ldots\text{(ii)}$$

Let $P(x, y)$ be the point of intersection of Eqs. (i) and (ii), then

$$a_1x + b_1y + c_1 = 0 \quad \ldots\text{(iii)}$$

and $$a_2x + b_2y + c_2 = 0 \quad \ldots\text{(iv)}$$

Now, $l_1 + kl_2 = 0$

$$\Rightarrow \quad (a_1x + b_1y + c_1) + k(a_2x + b_2y + c_2) = 0 \quad \ldots\text{(v)}$$

can be written as $(a_1 + ka_2)x + (b_1 + kb_2)\,y + (c_1 + kc_2) = 0$, which being a first degree equation in x and y represents a straight line.

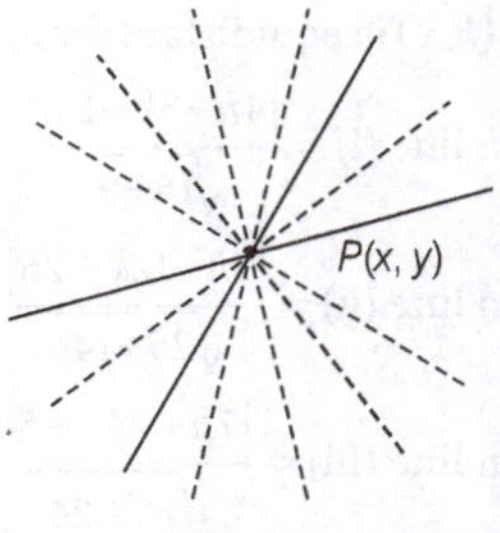

Also, Eq. (v) will pass through the point of intersection of Eqs. (i) and (ii) i.e. the point $P(x, y)$ iff

$$(a_1x + b_1y + c_1) + k(a_2x + b_2y + c_2) = 0 \text{ is true}$$

i.e. iff $0 + k \cdot 0 = 0$ is true [from Eqs. (iii) and (iv)]

i.e. iff $0 = 0$ is true, which is true.

Hence, the equation $l_1 + kl_2 = 0$ for different real values of k, represents a family of lines passing through the point of intersection of the lines l_1 and l_2.

Note The equation $l_1 + kl_2 = 0$ represents all members of the family passing through the intersection of l_1 and l_2 except the line l_2. However, if the line l_2 is needed, take the equation of the family as $l_2 + kl_1 = 0$.

Example 1 Find the equation of line passing through the point $(a\cos^3\theta, a\sin^3\theta)$ and perpendicular to the line $x\sec\theta + y\,\mathrm{cosec}\,\theta = a$. **[NCERT Exemplar]**

Sol. Given point is $(a\cos^3\theta, a\sin^3\theta)$ and the line is

$$x\sec\theta + y\,\mathrm{cosec}\theta = a$$

$\because$ Slope of the given line $= -\frac{\sec\theta}{\mathrm{cosec}\theta} = -\tan\theta$

$$\left[\because y = \frac{-\sec\theta}{\mathrm{cosec}\theta}x + \frac{1}{\mathrm{cosec}\theta}a\right]$$

$\therefore$ Slope of the required line $= \frac{1}{\tan\theta} = \cot\theta$

Now, equation of the required line having slope $\cot\theta$ and passing through $(a\cos^3\theta, a\sin^3\theta)$, is

$$y - a\sin^3\theta = \cot\theta\,(x - a\cos^3\theta)$$

$$\Rightarrow \quad y - a\sin^3\theta = \frac{\cos\theta}{\sin\theta}(x - a\cos^3\theta)$$

$$\Rightarrow \quad y\sin\theta - a\sin^4\theta = x\cos\theta - a\cos^4\theta$$

$$\Rightarrow \quad x\cos\theta - y\sin\theta = a\cos^4\theta - a\sin^4\theta$$

$$\Rightarrow \quad x\cos\theta - y\sin\theta = a[(\cos^2\theta + \sin^2\theta)(\cos^2\theta - \sin^2\theta)]$$

$$\Rightarrow \quad x\cos\theta - y\sin\theta = a\cos 2\theta$$

Example 2 The line through the points $(h, 3)$ and $(4, 1)$ intersects the line $7x - 9y - 19 = 0$ at right angle. Find the value of h. **[NCERT]**

Sol. Equation of line through $(h, 3)$ and $(4, 1)$ is given by

$$y - y_1 = \frac{y_2 - y_1}{x_2 - x_1}(x - x_1)$$

$$\Rightarrow \quad y - 3 = \frac{1-3}{4-h}(x - h)$$

$$[\because x_1 = h, y_1 = 3, x_2 = 4, y_2 = 1]$$

$$\Rightarrow \quad y - 3 = \frac{-2}{4-h}(x - h)$$

$$\Rightarrow \quad y - 3 = -\frac{2x}{4-h} + \frac{2h}{4-h}$$

$$\Rightarrow \quad y = -\frac{2x}{4-h} + \left(3 + \frac{2h}{4-h}\right) \quad \text{...(i)}$$

Given equation of line is

$$7x - 9y - 19 = 0$$

$$\Rightarrow \quad y = \frac{7}{9}x - \frac{19}{9} \quad \text{...(ii)}$$

On comparing Eqs. (i) and (ii) with $y = mx + c$, we get

$$m_1 = -\frac{2}{4-h}$$

and

$$m_2 = \frac{7}{9}$$

$\because$ Lines (i) and (ii) are perpendicular to each other

$\therefore$ Slope of line (i) $\times$ Slope of line (ii) $= -1$

i.e. $m_1 m_2 = -1$

$$\Rightarrow \quad -\frac{2}{4-h} \times \frac{7}{9} = -1$$

$$\Rightarrow \quad 14 = 9(4 - h)$$

$$\Rightarrow \quad 14 = 36 - 9h$$

$$\Rightarrow \quad 9h = 22$$

$$\Rightarrow \quad h = \frac{22}{9}$$

Concurrent Lines

Three or more straight lines are said to be concurrent, if they pass through a common point, i.e. they meet at a point. Thus, if three lines are concurrent, then the point of intersection of two lines lies on the third line.

Method to Show Concurrency of Three Lines

Let three lines be given. Then to show that given lines are concurrent, first we solve any two lines to find the point of intersection of these lines. Now, put this intersection point in third line. If it satisfies the equation, then given lines will be concurrent, otherwise not.

Example 3 Show that the lines $x - y - 6 = 0$, $4x - 3y - 20 = 0$ and $6x + 5y + 8 = 0$ are concurrent.

Sol. Given lines are

$$x - y - 6 = 0 \quad \text{...(i)}$$

$$4x - 3y - 20 = 0 \quad \text{...(ii)}$$

and

$$6x + 5y + 8 = 0 \quad \text{...(iii)}$$

On solving Eqs. (i) and (ii) by cross-multiplication method, we get

$$\frac{x}{20-18} = \frac{y}{-24+20} = \frac{1}{-3+4}$$

$$\Rightarrow \quad \frac{x}{2} = \frac{y}{-4} = \frac{1}{1}$$

$$\Rightarrow \quad x = 2 \text{ and } y = -4$$

Thus, intersection point of first two lines is $(2, -4)$.

Now, if given lines are concurrent, then this point will satisfy the Eq. (iii).

On putting $x = 2$ and $y = -4$ in LHS of Eq. (iii), we get

LHS $= 6(2) + 5(-4) + 8 = 12 - 20 + 8 = 0 =$ RHS

Thus, given three lines are concurrent. **Hence proved.**

Example 4 If the lines $ax + y + 1 = 0$, $x + by + 1 = 0$ and $x + y + c = 0$ are concurrent $c \neq 1$, prove that $\frac{1}{1-a} + \frac{1}{1-b} + \frac{1}{1-c} = 1$.

Sol. The equation of the given lines are

$$ax + y + 1 = 0 \quad \text{...(i)}$$

$$x + by + 1 = 0 \quad \text{...(ii)}$$

$$x + y + c = 0 \quad \text{...(iii)}$$

On solving Eqs. (i) and (ii) by cross-multiplication method, we get

$$\frac{x}{1-b} = \frac{y}{1-a} = \frac{1}{ab-1}$$

$$\Rightarrow \quad x = \frac{1-b}{ab-1} \text{ and } y = \frac{1-a}{ab-1}$$

Thus, the intersection point of first two lines is $\left(\frac{1-b}{ab-1}, \frac{1-a}{ab-1}\right)$

Since, the given lines are concurrent, then this point will satisfy the Eq. (iii).

Thus, we have $\frac{1-b}{ab-1} + \frac{1-a}{ab-1} + c = 0$

$$\Rightarrow \quad (1-b) + (1-a) + c(ab-1) = 0$$

$$\Rightarrow \quad abc = a + b + c - 2 \quad \text{...(i)}$$

Now, $\frac{1}{1-a}+\frac{1}{1-b}+\frac{1}{1-c}$

$$=\frac{(1-b)(1-c)+(1-a)(1-c)+(1-a)(1-b)}{(1-a)(1-b)(1-c)}$$

$$=\frac{1-b-c+bc+1-a-c+ac+1-a-b+ab}{(1-a-b+ab)(1-c)}$$

$$=\frac{3-2(a+b+c)+ab+bc+ca}{1-a-b+ab-c+ac+bc-abc}$$

$$=\frac{3-2(a+b+c)+ab+bc+ca}{1-(a+b+c)+ab+bc+ca-abc}$$

$$=\frac{3-2(a+b+c)+ab+bc+ca}{1-(a+b+c)+(ab+bc+ca)-(a+b+c-2)} \quad \text{[using Eq. (i)]}$$

$$=\frac{3-2(a+b+c)+ab+bc+ca}{3-2(a+b+c)+ab+bc+ca}=1$$

Hence proved.

Intersection of Two Straight Lines

Let the two intersecting lines l_1 and l_2 be given by

$$l_1 \equiv A_1x+B_1y+C_1=0 \quad \ldots\text{(i)}$$

and $$l_2 \equiv A_2x+B_2y+C_2=0 \quad \ldots\text{(ii)}$$

Then, the equation of intersection of the lines (i) and (ii) is

$$A_1x+B_1y+C_1+\lambda(A_2x+B_2y+C_2)=0 \quad \ldots\text{(iii)}$$

where, λ is an arbitrary constant called parameter. Eq. (iii) represents a family of lines and a particular member of this family can be obtained by substituting a value of λ.

Example 5 Find the equation of the straight line which passes through the point (1, – 4) and the point of intersection of the lines $x+y-3=0$ and $2x-y-7=0$

Sol. Clearly, the required line is of the form

$$(x+y-3)+\lambda(2x-y-7)=0 \quad \ldots\text{(i)}$$

where, λ is some constant

Since, it passes through (1, –4).

$\therefore \quad (1-4-3)+\lambda(2+4-7)=0$

$\Rightarrow \quad -6+(-\lambda)=0$

$\Rightarrow \quad \lambda=-6$

On putting $\lambda=-6$ in Eq. (i), we get

$$(x+y-3)-6(2x-y-7)=0$$

$\Rightarrow \quad x+y-3-12x+6y+42=0$

$\Rightarrow \quad -11x+7y+39=0$

$\Rightarrow \quad 11x-7y-39=0$

which is the required equation of line.

Example 6 Find the equation of the line through the intersection of lines $x+2y-3=0$ and $4x-y+7=0$ and which is parallel to $5x+4y-20=0$. [NCERT]

Sol. Let the equation of line passing through the point of intersection of lines $x+2y-3=0$ and $4x-y+7=0$ be $x+2y-3+\lambda(4x-y+7)=0$, where λ is some constant.

$\Rightarrow \quad (1+4\lambda)x+(2-\lambda)y-3+7\lambda=0 \quad \ldots\text{(i)}$

Since, the above line is parallel to

$$5x+4y-20=0.$$

So, their slopes will be equal.

$\therefore \quad m_1=m_2$

$\Rightarrow \quad -\frac{(1+4\lambda)}{(2-\lambda)}=-\frac{5}{4} \quad \left[\because m_1=-\frac{A}{B}\right]$

$\Rightarrow \quad 4+16\lambda=10-5\lambda$

$\Rightarrow \quad 21\lambda=6$

$\Rightarrow \quad \lambda=\frac{2}{7}$

On putting $\lambda=\frac{2}{7}$ in Eq. (i), we get

$$\left(1+\frac{8}{7}\right)x+\left(2-\frac{2}{7}\right)y-3+7\left(\frac{2}{7}\right)=0$$

$\Rightarrow \quad \frac{15}{7}x+\frac{12}{7}y-3+2=0$

$\Rightarrow \quad 15x+12y-7=0$

which is the required equation of line.

Locus of a Point

The curve described by a moving point under given geometrical condition(s), is called the **locus** of that point.

Equation of the Locus of a Point

The equation of the locus of a point is the relation which is satisfied by the coordinates of every point on the locus of the point.

Method to Find the Locus of a Point

For finding the locus of a point, we may use the following steps

***Step* I** First, assume the coordinates of the point, whose locus is to be found, say (h, k).

***Step* II** Write the given condition in mathematical form involving h, k and simplify it.

***Step* III** Eliminate the variable(s), if any.

***Step* IV** Replace h by x and k by y in the result obtained in Step III. The equation so obtained will be the required locus of the point.

Example 7 The sum of the squares of the distances of a moving point from two fixed points $(a, 0)$ and $(-a, 0)$ is equal to a constant quantity $2b^2$. Find the equation to its locus.

Sol. Let $P(h, k)$ be the point whose locus is to be found.

Let given two fixed points be $A(a, 0)$ and $B(-a, 0)$.

According to the given condition, $PA^2 + PB^2 = 2b^2$

$\Rightarrow (h-a)^2 + (k-0)^2 + (h+a)^2 + (k-0)^2 = 2b^2$ [by distance formula]

$\Rightarrow h^2 - 2ah + a^2 + k^2 + h^2 + 2ah + a^2 + k^2 = 2b^2$

$\Rightarrow \quad 2h^2 + 2k^2 + 2a^2 = 2b^2$

$\Rightarrow \quad h^2 + k^2 + a^2 = b^2$ [dividing both sides by 2] ...(i)

Here, in the Eq. (i), there is no other variable(s).

On putting $h = x$ and $k = y$, we get $x^2 + y^2 + a^2 = b^2$ which is the required equation of locus of a given point.

Example 8 A point moves, so that the sum of its distances from $(ae, 0)$ and $(-ae, 0)$ is $2a$, prove that the equation to its locus is $\frac{x^2}{a^2} + \frac{y^2}{b^2} = 1$, where $b^2 = a^2(1-e^2)$.

Sol. Let, $P(h, k)$ be the moving point such that the sum of its distances from $A(ae, 0)$ and $B(-ae, 0)$ is $2a$.

Then, $\quad PA + PB = 2a$

$\Rightarrow \sqrt{(h-ae)^2 + (k-0)^2} + \sqrt{(h+ae)^2 + (k-0)^2} = 2a$ [by distance formula]

$\Rightarrow \quad \sqrt{(h-ae)^2 + k^2} = 2a - \sqrt{(h+ae)^2 + k^2}$

$\Rightarrow \quad (h-ae)^2 + k^2 = 4a^2 + (h+ae)^2 + k^2 - 4a\sqrt{(h+ae)^2 + k^2}$ [squaring both sides]

$h^2 + a^2e^2 - 2hae = 4a^2 + h^2 + a^2e^2 + 2hae - 4a\sqrt{(h+ae)^2 + k^2}$

$\Rightarrow \quad -4aeh - 4a^2 = -4a\sqrt{(h+ae)^2 + k^2}$

$\Rightarrow \quad (eh + a) = \sqrt{(h+ae)^2 + k^2}$

$\Rightarrow \quad (eh+a)^2 = (h+ae)^2 + k^2$ [again, squaring both sides]

$\Rightarrow \quad e^2h^2 + 2aeh + a^2 = h^2 + a^2e^2 + 2aeh + k^2$

$\Rightarrow \quad h^2(1-e^2) + k^2 = a^2(1-e^2)$

$\Rightarrow \quad \frac{h^2}{a^2} + \frac{k^2}{a^2(1-e^2)} = 1$

Hence, locus of point $P(h, k)$ is

$$\frac{x^2}{a^2} + \frac{y^2}{a^2(1-e^2)} = 1$$

or $\quad \frac{x^2}{a^2} + \frac{y^2}{b^2} = 1$

where $b^2 = a^2(1-e^2)$.

Locus of the Point of Intersection of Two Lines whose Equations involve One Parameter

In this method, eliminate the parameter from the equations of the lines and here eliminate is the required locus.

Example 9 Find the locus of the point of intersection of the lines $x + y = 3 + \lambda$ and $5x - y = 7 + 3\lambda$, where λ is a variable.

Sol. Given Equation of the locus will be obtained on eliminating λ between the lines

$$x + y = 3 + \lambda \quad \text{...(i)}$$

and $\quad 5x - y = 7 + 3\lambda$ ...(ii)

From Eq. (i), we get $\lambda = x + y - 3$

On putting the value of λ in Eq. (ii), we get

$$5x - y = 7 + 3(x + y - 3)$$

i.e. $\quad 2x - 4y + 2 = 0$

$\Rightarrow \quad x - 2y + 1 = 0,$

which is the required equation of the locus.

Example 10 Find the locus of the foot of the perpendicular from the origin to the line which always passes through a fixed point (h, k).

Sol. The equation of any line through (h, k) is

$$y - k = m(x - h) \quad \text{...(i)}$$

The equation of the line perpendicular to it from the origin is $y = -\frac{1}{m}x$. ...(ii)

To get the locus of the point of intersection of Eqs. (i) and (ii), we eliminate m from Eqs. (i) and (ii), and then multiplying Eqs. (i) and (ii), we get

$$y(y-k) = -x(x-h)$$

$\Rightarrow \quad x^2 + y^2 - hx - ky = 0,$

which is the required locus.

Topic Practice 5

Very Short Answer Type Questions

(2 Marks)

1 Find the value of p so that the three lines $3x + y - 2 = 0$, $px + 2y - 3 = 0$ and $2x - y - 3 = 0$ may intersect at one point. [NCERT]

2 Prove that the lines $3x + y - 14 = 0$, $x - 2y = 0$ and $3x - 8y + 4 = 0$ are concurrent.

3 Find the equation of the straight line passing through the point of intersection of the lines $5x - 6y - 1 = 0$ and $3x + 2y + 5 = 0$ and perpendicular to the line $3x - 5y + 11 = 0$.

Short Answer Type Questions

(4 Marks)

4 Prove that the following lines are concurrent. $5x - 3y = 1$, $2x + 3y = 23$ and $42x + 21y = 257$

5 Show that the line $3x + 3y + k = 0$, passes through the point of intersection of $3x + 4y + 6 = 0$ and $6x + 5y - 9 = 0$, if $k = -1$.

6 Find the locus of a point such that the sum of its distances from the point $(0, 2)$ and $(0, -2)$ is 6.

7 Find the locus of a point at which the angle subtended by the line segment joining $(1, 2)$ and $(-1, 3)$ is a right angle.

8 If the sum of the distance of a moving point in a plane from the axes is 1, then find the locus of the point. [NCERT Exemplar]

Long Answer Type Questions

(6 Marks)

9 If lines whose equation are $y = m_1x + c_1$, $y = m_2x + c_2$ and $y = m_3x + c_3$, meet at a point, then prove that $m_1(c_2 - c_3) + m_2(c_3 - c_1) + m_3(c_1 - c_2) = 0$. [NCERT]

10 Find the equation of line parallel to Y-axis and drawn through the point of intersection of the lines $x - 7y + 5 = 0$ and $3x + y = 0$. [NCERT]

11 Obtain the equation of the lines passing through the intersection of lines $4x - 3y - 1 = 0$ and $2x - 5y + 3 = 0$ and equally inclined to the axes.

12 If a, b, c are variables such that $3a + 2b + 4c = 0$, then show that the family of lines given by $ax + by + c = 0$ pass through a fixed point. Also, find the point.

13 Find the equation of the lines through the point $(3, 2)$ which make an angle of 45° with the line $x - 2y = 3$. [NCERT]

Hints & Answers

1. Intersection point of lines $3x + y - 2 = 0$ and $2x - y - 3 = 0$ is $(1, -1)$, which satisfy $px + 2y - 3 = 0$.
Ans. $p = 5$

2. If the intersection point of two lines satisfy the third line then the given lines are concurrent.

3. The intersection of lines $5x - 6y - 1 = 0$ and $3x + 2y + 5 = 0$ is $(-1, -1)$. Also, the slope of the line $3x - 5y + 11 = 0$ is $\frac{3}{5}$.
Therefore, the slope of the line perpendicular to this line is $\frac{-5}{3}$.
Ans. $5x + 3y + 8 = 0$

4. Prove that point of intersection of any two lines lies on the third line.

5. We have, $3x + 4y + 6 = 0$ ...(i)
and $6x + 5y - 9 = 0$ ...(ii)
On solving Eqs. (i) and (ii) by, we get
$$x = \frac{22}{3} \text{ and } y = -7$$
The point of intersection of lines (i) and (ii) is $\left(\frac{22}{3}, -7\right)$.
Since, the line $3x + 3y + k = 0$ passes through $\left(\frac{22}{3}, -7\right)$.

6. Let $P(h, k)$ be the moving and $A(0, 2)$ and $B(0, -2)$ be the given points. By the given condition, $PA + PB = 6$
$$\Rightarrow \sqrt{(h-0)^2 + (k-2)^2} + \sqrt{(h-0)^2 + (k+2)^2} = 6$$
$$\Rightarrow (2k + 9) = 3\sqrt{h^2 + (k+2)^2}$$
Ans. $9x^2 + 5y^2 = 45$

7. Let the given points be $A(1, 2)$ and $B(-1, 3)$.

Let $P(h, k)$ be the moving point. Then, $\angle APB = 90°$.

Now, in ΔAPB, $AP^2 + PB^2 = AB^2$

Ans. $x^2 + y^2 - 5y + 5 = 0$

8. $|x| + |y| = 1$

$\Rightarrow \pm x \pm y = 1$, which forms a square.

Ans. The locus of the point is a square.

9. The point of intersection of Eqs. (i) and (ii)

$$= \left(\frac{c_1 - c_2}{m_2 - m_1}, \frac{m_2 c_1 - m_1 c_2}{m_2 - m_1}\right)$$

The three lines will be concurrent, if the point of intersection of Eqs. (i) and (ii) lie on Eq. (iii).

10. Given equation of lines are

$$x - 7y + 5 = 0 \quad \text{...(i)}$$

and $$3x + y = 0 \quad \text{...(ii)}$$

Now, equation of line passing through the intersection of lines (i) and (ii) is given by

$(x - 7y + 5) + \lambda(3x + y) = 0$, where λ is some constant.

$\Rightarrow x(1 + 3\lambda) + y(\lambda - 7) + 5 = 0$

Since, this line is parallel to Y-axis, therefore $\lambda - 7 = 0$

Ans. $22x + 5 = 0$

11. The equation of line passing through the intersection of the given lines is given by

$(4x - 3y - 1) + \lambda(2x - 5y + 3) = 0$, where λ is some constant.

$\Rightarrow \quad x(2\lambda + 4) - y(5\lambda + 3) + 3\lambda - 1 = 0$

Let m be the slope of this line.

Then, $m = \dfrac{2\lambda + 4}{5\lambda + 3}$

As the line is equally inclined with the axes.

$\therefore \quad m = \pm 1$

$\Rightarrow \quad \dfrac{2\lambda + 4}{5\lambda + 3} = \pm 1$

Ans. $x + y - 2 = 0$ and $x = y$

12. Given equation can be rewritten as

$$c = -\frac{3}{4}a - \frac{1}{2}b$$

$\therefore \quad ax + by - \dfrac{3}{4}a - \dfrac{1}{2}b = 0$

$\Rightarrow a\left(x - \dfrac{3}{4}\right) + b\left(y - \dfrac{1}{2}\right) = 0$

$\Rightarrow \left(x - \dfrac{3}{4}\right) + \lambda\left(y - \dfrac{1}{2}\right) = 0$, where $\lambda = \dfrac{b}{a}$

Ans. $\left(\dfrac{3}{4}, \dfrac{1}{2}\right)$

13. Given equation of line is $x - 2y = 3$ ...(i)

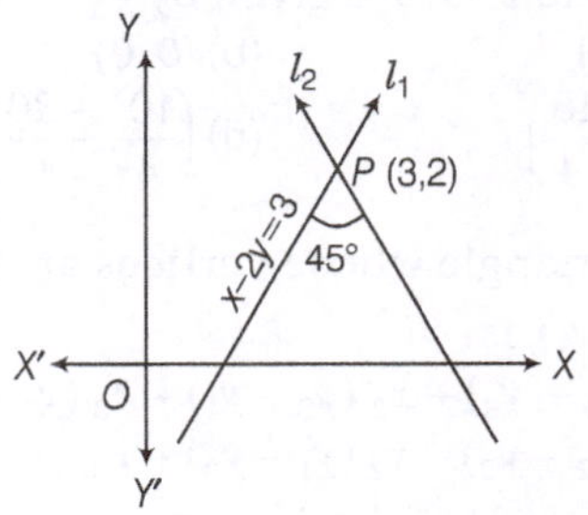

Slope of line (i), $m_1 = -\left(\dfrac{1}{-2}\right) = \dfrac{1}{2}$

Let m be the slope of required line.

$\because$ Angle between two lines is 45°.

$$\therefore \quad \tan 45° = \left|\frac{\frac{1}{2} - m}{1 + \frac{1}{2}m}\right|$$

Ans. $x + 3y - 9 = 0$ and $3x - y - 7 = 0$

Chapter Practice

Multiple Choice Type Questions

1 Mark

1. The distance between the points (6, – 4) and (3, 0) is
(a) 7 units (b) 25 units
(c) $\sqrt[3]{25}$ units (d) 5 units

2. The coordinates of a point which divides the line segment joining A (1, – 3) and B (– 3, 9) internally in the ratio 1 : 3, are given by
(a) (– 2, 6) (b) (0, 0)
(c) $\left(\frac{-6}{4}, \frac{18}{4}\right)$ (d) $\left(\frac{10}{4}, \frac{-30}{4}\right)$

3. Area of triangle whose vertices are (x_1, y_1), (x_2, y_2) and (x_3, y_3), is
(a) $|x_1(y_2 - y_3) + x_2(y_3 - y_1) + x_3(y_1 - y_2)|$
(b) $|x_1(y_2 - y_3) + x_2(y_1 - y_3) + x_3(y_1 - y_2)|$
(c) $\frac{1}{2}|x_1(y_2 - y_3) + x_2(y_3 - y_1) + x_3(y_1 - y_2)|$
(d) $\frac{1}{2}|x_1(y_2 - y_3) + x_2(y_1 - y_3) + x_3(y_1 - y_2)|$

4. The angle between the X-axis and the line joining the points (4, – 2) and (5, – 3) is
(a) 45° (b) 135°
(c) 90° (d) 180°

5. A line passes through (x_1, y_1) and (h, k). If slope of the line is m, then
(a) $y_1 - k = m(h - x_1)$
(b) $k - y_1 = m(h - x_1)$
(c) $h - x_1 = m(y_1 - k)$
(d) $h - x_1 = m(k - y_1)$

6. Suppose a line L make x-intercept a and y-intercept b on the axes. Then, the equation of the line L is
(a) $\frac{x}{a} + \frac{y}{b} = 1$ (b) $\frac{x}{a} - \frac{y}{b} = 1$
(c) $\frac{y}{b} - \frac{x}{a} = 1$ (d) $ax + by = 1$

Assertion-Reason Type Questions

1 Mark

Directions (Q. Nos. 7-10) *In the questions given below are two statements labelled as Assertion (A) and Reason (R). In the context of the two statements, which one of the following is correct?*

(a) Both A and R are correct; R is the correct explanation of A
(b) Both A and R are correct; R is not the correct explanation of A
(c) A is correct; R is incorrect
(d) R is correct; A is incorrect

7. **Assertion** (A) If θ is the inclination of a line l, then the slope or gradient of the line l is $\tan\theta$.
Reason (R) The slope of a line whose inclination is 90°, in not defined.

8. **Assertion** (A) The inclination of the line l may be acute or obtuse.
Reason (R) Slope of X-axis is zero and slope of Y-axis is not defined.

9. **Assertion** (A) The equation of the line making intercepts a and b on X and Y-axes respectively is $\frac{x}{a} + \frac{y}{b} = 1$.
Reason (R) The slope of the line $ax + by + c = 0$ is $\frac{b}{a}$.

10. **Assertion** (A) The distance between the parallel lines $3x - 4y + 9 = 0$ and $6x - 8y - 15 = 0$ is $\frac{33}{10}$.
Reason (R) Distance between the parallel lines $Ax + By + C_1 = 0$ and $Ax + By + C_2 = 0$ is given by $d = \frac{|C_1 - C_2|}{\sqrt{A^2 + B^2}}$.

Very Short Answer Type Questions

2 Marks

11. Without using Pythagoras theorem, show that the points $A(1,2)$, $B(1,5)$ and $C(5,2)$ are the vertices of a right angled triangle.

12. Prove that the line joining the mid-points of the two sides of a triangle is parallel to the third side.

13. If points $(a,0)$, $(0,b)$ and (x,y) are collinear using the concept of slope. Prove that $\frac{x}{a}+\frac{y}{b}=1.$

14. A quadrilateral has the vertices at the points $(4,1)$, $(1,7)$, $(-6,0)$ and $(-1,-9)$. Show that the mid-points of the sides of this quadrilateral are the vertices of a parallelogram.

15. Find the equation of the line which has y-intercept equal to $4/3$ and is perpendicular to $3x-4y+11=0$.

16. Find the equation of angle bisector between the lines $2x+y=4$ and $3x-y+5=0$ in which the origin lies.

17. Are the points (2, 3) and (1, 3) on the same side or on opposite sides of the line $x-2y=-3$.

18. Find the perpendicular distance between the lines $3x+4y-5=0$ and $6x+8y-45=0$.

Short Answer Type Questions

4 Marks

19. Prove that the points $A(2,3)$, $B(6,7)$, $C(6,9)$ and $D(2,5)$ are the vertices of a rectangle.

20. Prove that $A(4,3)$, $B(6,4)$, $C(5,6)$ and $D(3,5)$ are the angular points of a square.

21. Find the equations of the bisectors of the angles between the coordinate axes.

22. Find the equation of a line which divides the join of (1, 0) and (3, 0) in the ratio 2 : 1 and perpendicular to it.

23. Reduce the equation $x^2+4y^2-6x-8y-12=0$ to the form $Ax^2+By^2=k$ by shifting the origin to a suitable point.

24. Find the equation of the line through the point $A(2,3)$ and making an angle of 45° with the X-axis. Also, determine the length of intercept on it between A and the line $x+y+1=0$.

25. Find the distance of the point (2, 5) from the line $3x+y+4=0$ measured parallel to the line $3x-4y+8=0$.

26. Find the equation of the straight line passing through the origin and bisecting the portion of the line $ax+by+c=0$ intercepted between the coordinate axes.

27. Find the equation of a straight line on which the perpendicular from the origin makes an angle 30° with X-axis and which forms a triangle of area $50/\sqrt{3}$ with the axes.

28. Find the value of m for which the lines $mx+(2m+3)y+m+6=0$ and $(2m+1)x+(m-1)y+m-9=0$ intersect at a point on Y-axis.

29. Find the locus of the centroid of the triangle whose vertices are $(a\cos t, a\sin t)$, $(b\sin t, -b\cos t)$ and (1, 0) where t is a parameter.

30. The line $\frac{x}{a}+\frac{y}{b}=1$ moves in such a way that $\frac{1}{a^2}+\frac{1}{b^2}=\frac{1}{c^2}$, where c is a constant. Find the locus of the foot of the perpendicular from the origin on the given line.

Long Answer Type Questions

6 Marks

31. Find the image of the point $(-8,12)$ with respect to the line mirror $4x+7y+13=0$.

32. The vertices of a triangle are $A(10,4)$, $B(-4,9)$ and $C(-2,-1)$. Find the equations of its altitude. Also, find the orthocentre.

33. The sides AB and AC of a ΔABC are $2x+3y=29$ and $x+2y=16$, respectively. If the mid-point of BC is (5, 6), then find the equation of BC.

34. Three sides AB, BC and CA of a ΔABC are $5x-3y+2=0$, $x-3y-2=0$ and $x+y-6=0$, respectively. Find the equation of the altitude through the vertex A.

Case-Based Type Questions

6 Marks

35. Population *vs* Year graph given below.

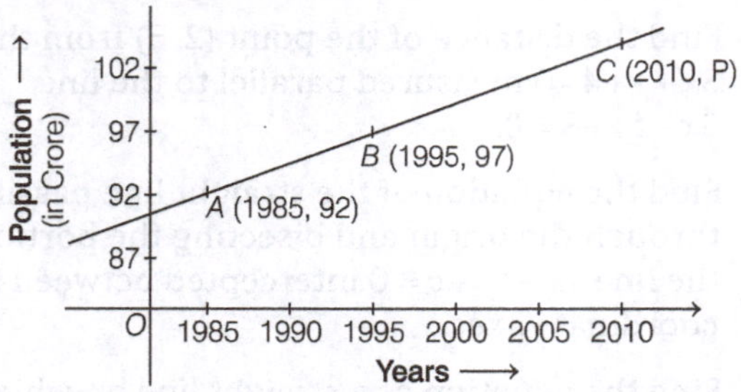

Based on the above information answer the following questions.

(i) Find the slope of line AB.

(ii) Find the equation of line AB.

(iii) Find the population (in crores) in year 2010.

(iv) Find the equation of line perpendicular to line AB and passing through (1995, 97).

(v) Which year the population becomes 110 cr?

36. Consider the ΔABC with vertices $A(1, 4)$, $B(2, -3)$ and $C(-1, -2)$ as shown in the given figure. AD is the median and AM is the altitude through A.

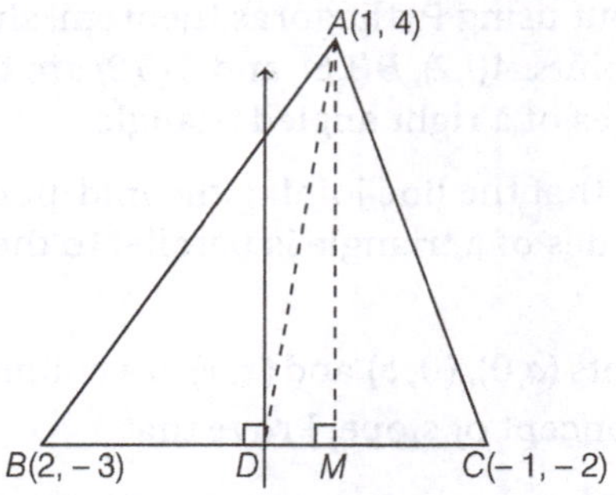

Based on the above information answer the following questions.

(i) Find the distance between A and C.

(ii) Find the slope of BC.

(iii) Find the equation of median through A.

(iv) Find the equation of the altitude through A.

(v) Find the equation of right bisector of side BC.

Hints & Answers

1. (d) **2.** (b) **3.** (c) **4.** (b) **5.** (b)
6. (a) **7.** (b) **8.** (b) **9.** (c) **10.** (a)

11. Slope of AB = Not defined

Slope of $BC = \frac{-3}{4}$ and slope of $AC = 0$

$\because$ AB is parallel to Y-axis and AC is parallel to X-axis.
Thus, $\angle A = 90°$ [$\because$ angle between X-axis and Y-axis is 90°]

12. Let $A(x_1, y_1)$, $B(x_2, y_2)$ and $C(x_3, y_3)$ are the vertices of ΔABC. Also, let D, E and F are the mid-points of sides AB, BC and CA, respectively.

Then, coordinates of

$$D = \left(\frac{x_1 + x_2}{2}, \frac{y_1 + y_2}{2}\right),$$

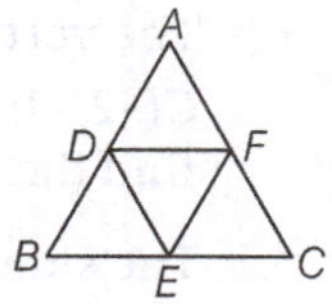

Coordinates of $E = \left(\frac{x_2 + x_3}{2}, \frac{y_2 + y_3}{2}\right)$

and coordinate of $F = \left(\frac{x_1 + x_3}{2}, \frac{y_1 + y_3}{2}\right)$

Now, show that slope of DF = slope of BC,
slope of DE = slope of AC and slope of EF = slope of AB

13. Let the given points are $A(a, 0)$, $B(0, b)$ and $C(x, y)$.

Now, slope of AB = slope of BC

$$\Rightarrow \quad \frac{b}{-a} = \frac{y - b}{x}$$

$$\Rightarrow \quad xb = -ay + ab$$

$$\Rightarrow \quad ay + bx = ab$$

14. Let $ABCD$ be the given quadrilateral.

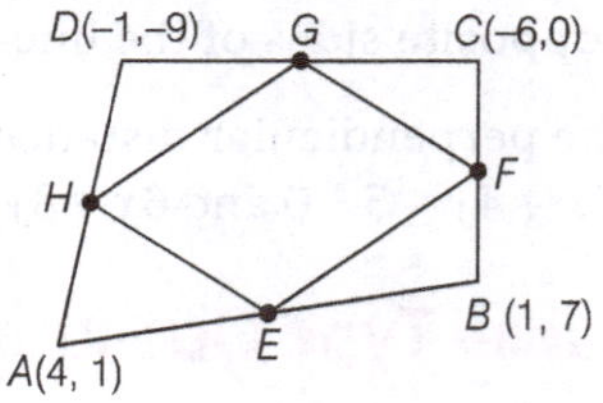

Also, let E, F, G and H are the mid-points of sides AB, BC, CD and DA, respectively.

Now, find the coordinates of E, F, G and H, and then show that slope of EF = slope of GH and slope of FG = slope of EH.

15. $\because$ $3x - 4y + 11 = 0 \Rightarrow 4y = 3x + 11 \Rightarrow y = \frac{3}{4}x + \frac{11}{4}$

Slope of $3x - 4y + 11 = 0$ is $\frac{3}{4}$.

$\therefore$ Slope of perpendicular line is $-\frac{4}{3}$.

$\therefore$ The equation is $y = -\frac{4}{3}x + \frac{4}{3}$ or $4x + 3y = 4$

16. The given lines are $2x + y - 4 = 0$ and $3x - y + 5 = 0$.

Writing the given equations so that the constant terms are positive, we get

$$-2x - y + 4 = 0 \quad \text{...(i)}$$

and

$$3x - y + 5 = 0 \quad \text{...(ii)}$$

∴ The equation of the angle bisector in which the origin lies is

$$\frac{-2x-y+4}{\sqrt{(-2)^2+(-1)^2}}=\frac{3x-y+5}{\sqrt{3^2+(-1)^2}}$$

$$\Rightarrow \quad \frac{-2x-y+4}{\sqrt{5}}=\frac{3x-y+5}{\sqrt{10}}$$

$$\Rightarrow \quad 3x-y+5=\sqrt{2}\,(-2x-y+4)$$

$$\Rightarrow \quad (3+2\sqrt{2})x+(\sqrt{2}-1)y+5-4\sqrt{2}=0$$

17. Given points are on the same side of the line.

18. $\frac{7}{2}$

19.

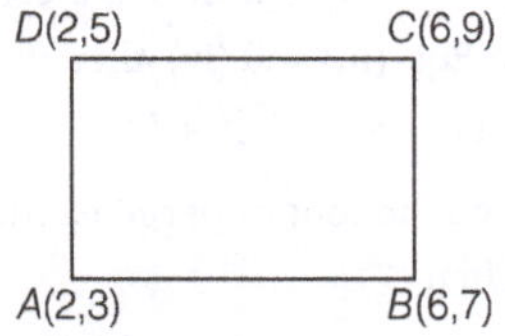

Prove that

(i) Slope of AB = Slope of DC

(ii) Slope of AD = Slope of BC

(iii) Slope of AB × Slope of BC = −1.

20. Prove that

(i) Slope of AB = Slope of DC

(ii) Slope of AD = Slope of BC

(iii) Slope of AC × Slope of BD = −1

(iv) Slope of AB × Slope of BC = −1

21. Bisectors of the angles between the coordinate axes, passes through origin and makes an angle of 45° or 135° with positive direction of X-axis.

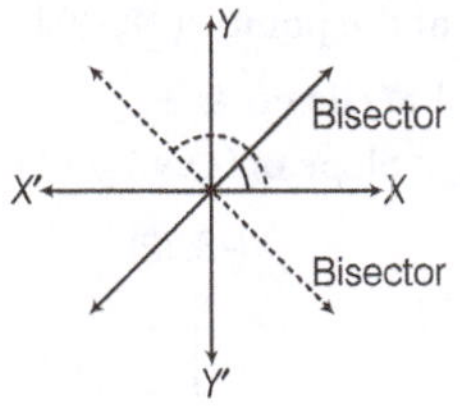

Ans. $x \pm y = 0$

22. Slope of perpendicular line $=\dfrac{-1}{\text{Slope of } AB}$

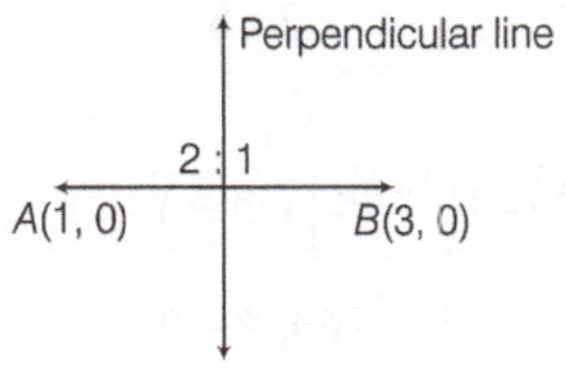

$$=\frac{-1}{0}=\text{Not defined}$$

⇒ Perpendicular line is parallel to Y-axis.

∵ The coordinates of C are $\left(\frac{7}{3}, 0\right)$. **Ans.** $3x-7=0$.

23. Let the origin be shifted to the point (h, k), axes remaining parallel to the original axes. If the coordinates (x, y) of any point on the given curve change to (X, Y), then

$$x = X + h \text{ and } y = Y + k.$$

Substituting for x and y in the given equation, the transformed equation is

$$(X+h)^2+4(Y+k)^2-6(X+h)-8(Y+k)-12=0$$

i.e. $X^2+4Y^2+(2h-6)X+(8k-8)Y+h^2+4k^2$

$$-6h-8k-12=0 \quad \text{...(i)}$$

Since the given equation is to be reduced to the form $AX^2+BY^2=k$, the coefficients of X and Y are zero

$\Rightarrow 2h-6=0$ and $8k-8=0 \Rightarrow h=3, k=1$ and then

$h^2+4k^2-6h-8k-12=9+4.1-6.3-8.1-12=-25.$

Ans. $X^2+4Y^2=25$

24. Equation of line, passing through $A(2, 3)$ and making an angle of 45° with X-axis, is given by

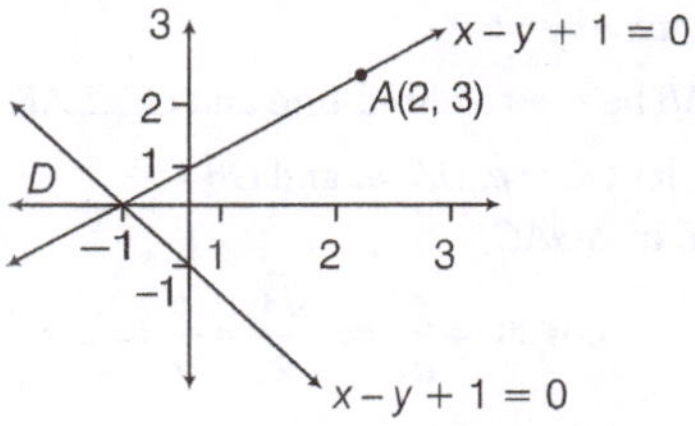

$$y-3=\tan 45°(x-2)$$

Ans. $x-y+1=0;\ 3\sqrt{2}$ units

25. Equation of the line parallel to $3x-4y+8=0$ is given by $3x-4y+k=0$

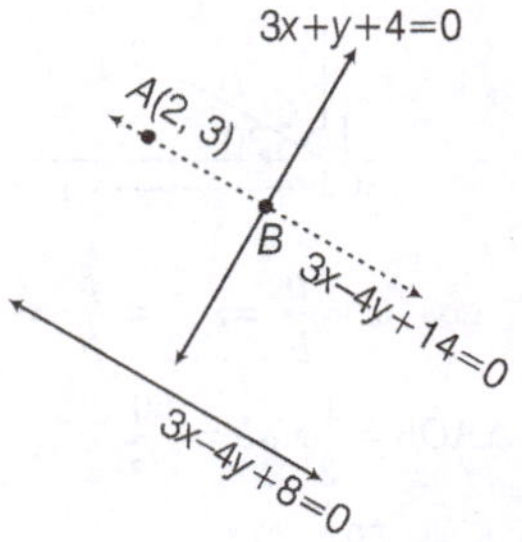

Now, required parallel line should pass through (2, 3). We have,

$$3(2)-4(5)+k=0$$

$$\Rightarrow \quad k=20-6=14$$

Thus, distance of the point (2, 5) from the line $3x+y+4=0$ will be measured along the line

$$3x-4y+14=0.$$

Now, solving $3x+y+4=0$ and $3x-4y+14=0$, we get

$$x=-2 \text{ and } y=2$$

Thus, the coordinates of B are $(-2, 2)$.

Ans. 5 units.

26. Clearly, the line $ax+by+c=0$ intersect X-axis at

$$A\left(\frac{-c}{a},0\right) \text{ and } B\left(0,\frac{-c}{b}\right).$$

Mid-point of AB is $C\left(\frac{-c}{2a},\frac{-c}{2b}\right)$.

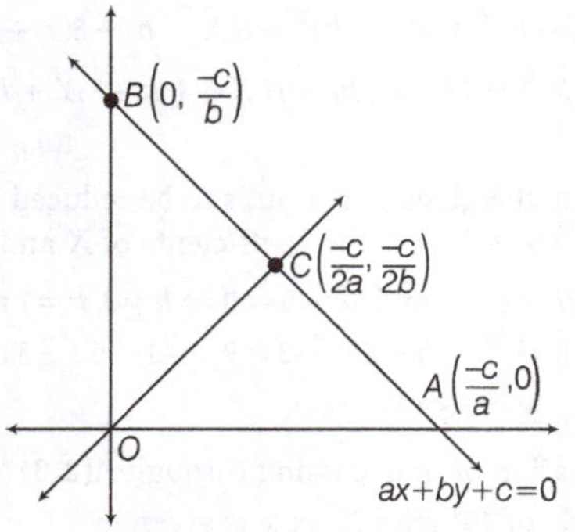

Ans. $ax-by=0$

27. Let AB be the required line and $OC \perp AB$.

Also, let $OC = p$, $OA=a$ and $OB=b$

Then, in ΔOAC,

$$\cos 30° = \frac{p}{a} \Rightarrow \frac{\sqrt{3}}{2} = \frac{p}{a} \Rightarrow a = \frac{2p}{\sqrt{3}}$$

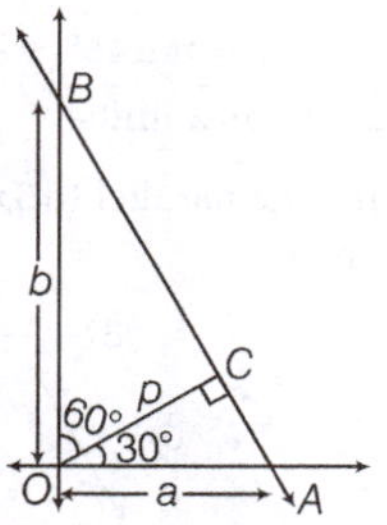

and in ΔOBC, $\cos 60° = \frac{p}{b} \Rightarrow \frac{1}{2} = \frac{p}{b} \Rightarrow b=2p$

Now, area of $\Delta AOB = \frac{1}{2} \times ab = \frac{50}{\sqrt{3}}$

$$\Rightarrow \quad \frac{1}{2}\left(\frac{2p}{\sqrt{3}}\right) \times 2p = \frac{50}{\sqrt{3}}$$

Ans. $x\cos 30° + y \sin 30° = 5$ or $\sqrt{3}x+y=10$.

28. Line (i) intersect Y-axis at $\left(0, \frac{-m+9}{2m+3}\right)$ and line (ii) intersect Y-axis at $\left(0, -\frac{(m-9)}{m-1}\right)$.

Now, for lines to be intersect at a point on Y-axis.

$$-\left(\frac{m+6}{2m+3}\right) = -\left(\frac{m-9}{m-1}\right) \Rightarrow \frac{m+6}{2m+3} = \frac{m-9}{m-1}$$

$$\Rightarrow m^2 - m + 6m - 6 = 2m^2 + 3m - 18m - 27$$

$$\Rightarrow \quad m^2 + 5m - 6 = 2m^2 - 15m - 27$$

Ans. -1, 21

29. The vertices of the triangle are $(a \cos t, a \sin t)$, $(b \sin t, -b \cos t)$ and $(1, 0)$.

Let point $P(x, y)$ be the centroid of the given triangle, then

$$x = \frac{a\cos t + b \sin t + 1}{3} \quad \text{...(i)}$$

and $$y = \frac{a \sin t - b \cos t + 0}{3} \quad \text{...(ii)}$$

For the locus of the centroid $P(x, y)$ of given triangle, we have to eliminate the parameter t.

From the Eqs. (i) and (ii), we get

$$3x - 1 = a \cos t + b \sin t \quad \text{...(iii)}$$

and $$3y = a \sin t - b \cos t \quad \text{...(iv)}$$

On solving Eqs. (iii) and (iv), then we get the required result.

Ans. $(3x-1)^2 + 9y^2 = a^2 + b^2$

30. Let $P(h, k)$ be the foot of perpendicular from the origin to the line. Then,

OP = Distance if origin from the line $\frac{x}{a} + \frac{y}{b} = 1$

$$= \frac{|0+0-1|}{\sqrt{\left(\frac{1}{a}\right)^2 + \left(\frac{1}{b}\right)^2}}$$

$$\Rightarrow \quad \sqrt{(h-0)^2 + (k-0)^2} = \frac{1}{\sqrt{\frac{1}{a^2} + \frac{1}{b^2}}}$$

$$\Rightarrow \quad \sqrt{h^2 + k^2} = \frac{1}{\sqrt{\frac{1}{c^2}}}$$

Ans. $x^2 + k^2 = c^2$.

31. Let the image of the point $P(-8,12)$ be $Q(\alpha, \beta)$. Then,

(a) Mid-point of PQ lie on $4x+7y+13=0$.

(b) Slope of $PQ \times$ Slope of $(4x+7y+13=0) = -1$

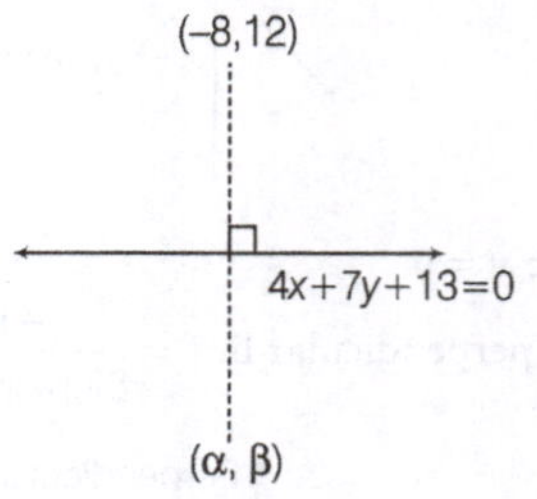

Now,

(a) $$4\left(\frac{-8+\alpha}{2}\right) + 7\left(\frac{12+\beta}{2}\right) + 13 = 0$$

$$\Rightarrow \quad 4\alpha + 7\beta + 78 = 0 \quad \text{...(i)}$$

(b) $$\frac{\beta-12}{\alpha+8} \times \left(\frac{-4}{7}\right) = -1$$

$$\Rightarrow \quad 7\alpha - 4\beta + 104 = 0 \quad \text{...(ii)}$$

Solve Eqs. (i) and (ii)

Ans. $(-16, -2)$

32. Slope of $AD = \dfrac{-1}{\text{Slope of } BC} = \dfrac{-1}{-5} = \dfrac{1}{5}$

Slope of $BE = \dfrac{-1}{\text{Slope of } AC} = \dfrac{-12}{5}$

and slope of $CF = \dfrac{-1}{\text{Slope of } AD} = \dfrac{14}{5}$

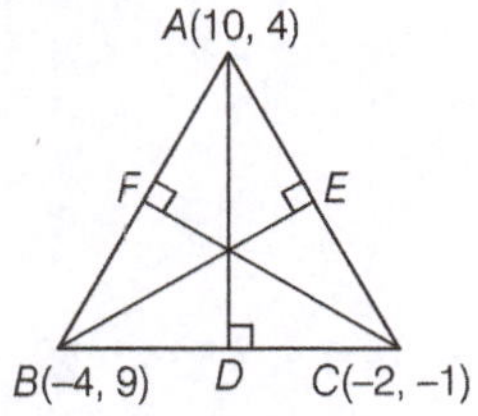

Ans. $x - 5y + 10 = 0$,

$12x + 5y + 3 = 0$,

$14x - 5y + 23 = 0, \left(-1, \dfrac{9}{5}\right)$.

33. Let the coordinates of B and C are (x_1, y_1) and (x_2, y_2), respectively.

Then, we have

$$2x_1 + 3y_1 = 29 \quad \text{...(i)}$$

$$x_2 + 2y_2 = 16 \quad \text{...(ii)}$$

$$\frac{x_1 + x_2}{2} = 5$$

$$\Rightarrow \quad x_1 + x_2 = 10 \quad \text{...(iii)}$$

and $$\frac{y_1 + y_2}{2} = 6$$

$$\Rightarrow \quad y_1 + y_2 = 12 \quad \text{...(iv)}$$

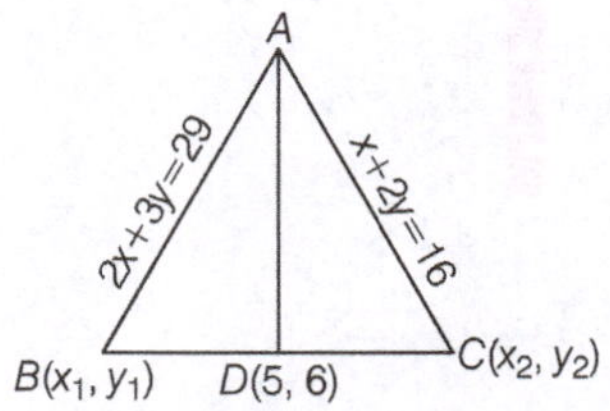

On substituting the values of x_2 and y_2 from Eqs. (iii) and (iv) in Eq. (ii), we get $(10 - x_1) + 2(12 - y_1) = 16$

$$\Rightarrow \quad 10 - x_1 + 24 - 2y_1 = 16 \Rightarrow x_1 + 2y_1 = 18 \quad \text{...(v)}$$

Now, solve Eqs. (i) and (v).

Ans. $x + y - 11 = 0$

34. Let $AD \perp BC$. Then, slope of $AD = \dfrac{-1}{\text{Slope of } BC} = \dfrac{-1}{\left(\frac{1}{3}\right)} = -3$

Now, let the solve the equation of AB and AC, to get the coordinates of vertex A. This will give $A(2, 4)$.

Ans. $3x + y - 10 = 0$

35. (i) $\dfrac{1}{2}$

(ii) $x - 2y = 1801$

(iii) 104.5

(iv) $2x + y = 4087$

(v) 2021

36. (i) $\sqrt{40}$ units

(ii) $-\dfrac{1}{3}$

(iii) $13x - y - 9 = 0$

(iv) $3x - y + 1 = 0$

(v) $3x - y - 4 = 0$

CHAPTER

11

Circles

In this chapter, we will study about the circle. We will learn about the different types of equations of circle such as standard form, general form, parametric form, diametric form. We will also learn about the condition of a line to be tangent and equation of tangent.

- Equations of a Circle in Different Forms
- Diameter Form
- General Form
- Intercept on the Axes

Circle

A circle is the set of all points in a plane that are equidistant from a fixed point in that plane.

Or **A circle** is the locus of a point in a plane which moves in a plane such that its distance from a fixed point in that plane is always constant.

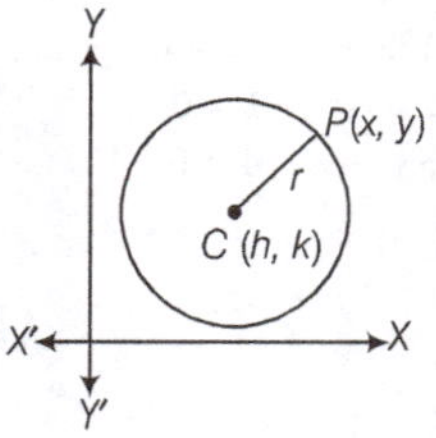

Centre The fixed point C is called the **centre** of the circle.

Radius The constant distance (CP) from the centre (C) to a point on the circle, is **called** the radius (r).

Equations of a Circle in Different Forms

There are various forms of the equations of a circle, which are as follow

Standard (Centre-Radius) Form

In the above figure, let $C(h, k)$ be the centre of the circle, $P(x, y)$ be any point on the circumference of the circle and r be the radius of the circle.

Then, equation of circle in standard form is

$$(x-h)^2+(y-k)^2=r^2 \quad \ldots\text{(i)}$$

This equation is also known as **simplest or central form** of the equation of a circle.

If $h=0$ and $k=0$ i.e. centre of the circle is at origin $(h,k)=(0,0)$, then from Eq. (i), we get

$$\boxed{x^2+y^2=r^2}$$

Example 1 Find the equation of the circle with

(i) centre = (2, 3) and radius = 5

(ii) centre = $(a\cos\theta, a\sin\theta)$ and radius = a

(iii) centre = $(-a, -b)$ and radius = $\sqrt{a^2-b^2}$ **[NCERT]**

(iv) centre = $\left(\frac{1}{2}, \frac{1}{4}\right)$ and radius = $\frac{1}{12}$ units **[NCERT]**

Sol. (i) Given centre is (2, 3).

$\therefore\quad h=2, k=3$ and radius $(r)=5$

On putting these values in equation of the circle $(x-h)^2+(y-k)^2=r^2$, we get

$$(x-2)^2+(y-3)^2=5^2$$

$$\Rightarrow\quad x^2+4-4x+y^2+9-6y=25$$

$[\because (A-B)^2=A^2+B^2-2AB]$

$$\Rightarrow\quad x^2+y^2-4x-6y+13=25$$

$$\Rightarrow\quad x^2+y^2-4x-6y+13-25=0$$

$$\therefore\quad x^2+y^2-4x-6y-12=0$$

which is the required equation of circle.

(ii) Given centre is $(a\cos\theta, a\sin\theta)$.

$\therefore\quad h=a\cos\theta, k=a\sin\theta$ and radius $(r)=a$

On putting these values in equation of the circle $(x-h)^2+(y-k)^2=r^2$, we get

$$(x-a\cos\theta)^2+(y-a\sin\theta)^2=a^2$$

$$\Rightarrow x^2+a^2\cos^2\theta-2ax\cos\theta+y^2+a^2\sin^2\theta-2ay\sin\theta=a^2$$

$$\Rightarrow\quad x^2+y^2-2ax\cos\theta-2ay\sin\theta+a^2(\sin^2\theta+\cos^2\theta)=a^2$$

$$\Rightarrow x^2+y^2-2a(x\cos\theta+y\sin\theta)+a^2=a^2$$

$[\because \sin^2\theta+\cos^2\theta=1]$

$$\therefore\quad x^2+y^2-2a(x\cos\theta+y\sin\theta)=0$$

which is the required equation of circle.

(iii) Given centre is $(-a, -b)$.

$\therefore\quad h=-a, k=-b$ and radius $(r)=\sqrt{a^2-b^2}$

On putting these values in equation of the circle $(x-h)^2+(y-k)^2=r^2$, we get

$$[x-(-a)]^2+[y-(-b)]^2=(\sqrt{a^2-b^2})^2$$

$$\Rightarrow\quad (x+a)^2+(y+b)^2=a^2-b^2$$

$$\Rightarrow x^2+a^2+2ax+y^2+b^2+2by=a^2-b^2$$

$[\because (A+B)^2=A^2+2AB+B^2]$

$$\Rightarrow x^2+y^2+2ax+2by+a^2+b^2=a^2-b^2$$

$$\therefore\quad x^2+y^2+2ax+2by+2b^2=0$$

which is the required equation of circle.

(iv) Given centre is $\left(\frac{1}{2}, \frac{1}{4}\right)$.

$\therefore\ h=\frac{1}{2}, k=\frac{1}{4}$ and radius $(r)=\frac{1}{12}$ unit

On putting these values in equation of circle $(x-h)^2+(y-k)^2=r^2$, we get

$$\left(x-\frac{1}{2}\right)^2+\left(y-\frac{1}{4}\right)^2=\left(\frac{1}{12}\right)^2$$

$$\Rightarrow\quad x^2+\frac{1}{4}-x+y^2+\frac{1}{16}-\frac{y}{2}=\frac{1}{144}$$

$$\Rightarrow\quad x^2+y^2-x-\frac{y}{2}+\frac{1}{4}+\frac{1}{16}-\frac{1}{144}=0$$

$$\Rightarrow\quad x^2+y^2-x-\frac{y}{2}+\frac{11}{36}=0$$

$$\Rightarrow\quad 36x^2+36y^2-36x-18y+11=0$$

[multiplying both sides by 36]

which is the required equation of circle.

Example 2 Find the equation of circle whose centre is (1, 2) and which passes through the point (4, 6).

Sol. Coordinates of centre of given circle is (1, 2) and it passes through the point (4, 6).

Then, radius of the circle is equal to the distance from the centre to a point on a circle.

$\therefore$ Radius of circle $=\sqrt{(1-4)^2+(2-6)^2}=\sqrt{9+16}=5$

[by distance formula]

Hence, the required equation of the circle is

$$(x-1)^2+(y-2)^2=(5)^2$$

$$\Rightarrow\quad x^2+1-2x+y^2+4-4y=25$$

$[\because (A-B)^2=A^2+B^2-2AB]$

$$\Rightarrow\quad x^2+y^2-2x-4y-20=0$$

Equation of Circle in Special Cases

We know that the standard equation of the circle with centre at (h,k) and radius equal to r, is $(x-h)^2+(y-k)^2=r^2$.

It can be change according to the different conditions, which are given below

|TYPE I|

When The Circle Passes Through The Origin

Since, the circle passes through origin (0,0).

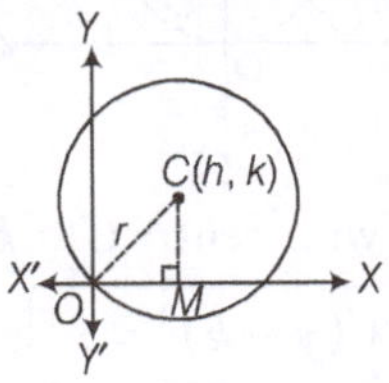

$\therefore$ Radius, r = Distance between the points O and C

$$=\sqrt{h^2+k^2}$$

Hence, the equation of a circle passing through the origin is

$$(x-h)^2+(y-k)^2=h^2+k^2$$

i.e. $\boxed{x^2+y^2-2hx-2ky=0}$

Example 3 Find the equation of the circle whose centre is (a, b) and passes through the origin.

Sol. We know that, circle passes through the origin, so radius of circle will be equal to the distance between point (a, b) and origin.

$\therefore$ Radius of circle = Distance between the points $(0, 0)$ and (a, b)

$= \sqrt{(0-a)^2+(0-b)^2} = \sqrt{a^2+b^2}$ [by distance formula]

$\because$ Centre $= (h, k) = (a, b)$

On putting these values in equation of circle $(x-h)^2+(y-k)^2=r^2$, we get

$$(x-a)^2+(y-b)^2=(\sqrt{a^2+b^2})^2$$

$\Rightarrow x^2+a^2-2ax+y^2+b^2-2by=a^2+b^2$ $[\because (A-B)^2=A^2-2AB+B^2]$

$\Rightarrow \quad x^2+y^2-2ax-2by=0$

which is the required equation of circle.

TYPE II

When the Centre lies on X-Axis or Y-Axis

If the centre lies on X-axis, then $k=0$.

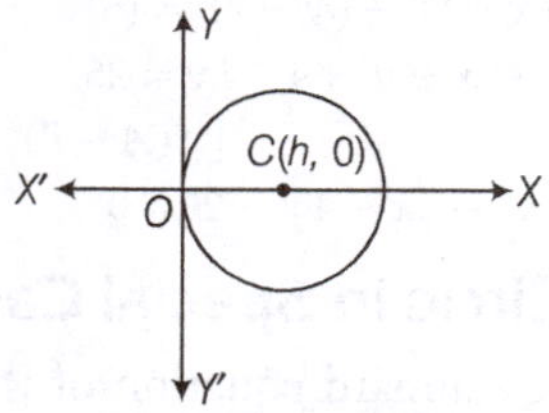

$\therefore$ Equation of circle with centre $C(h, 0)$ is

$$\boxed{(x-h)^2+y^2=r^2}$$

If the centre lies on Y-axis, then $h=0$.

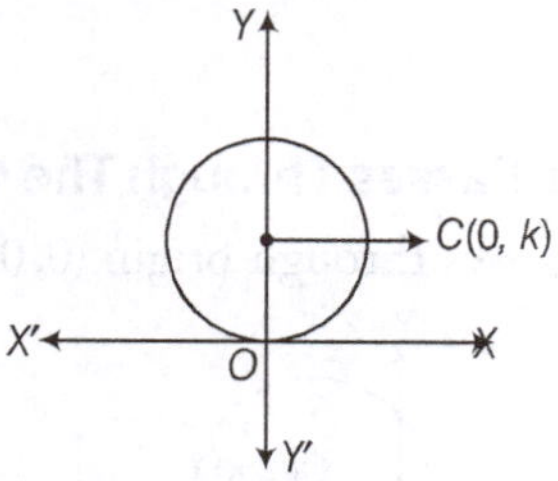

$\therefore$ Equation of circle with centre $C(0,k)$ is

$$\boxed{x^2+(y-k)^2=r^2}.$$

Example 4 If the circle passes through the point (2,3), then find the equation of the circle whose radius is 5 units and centre lies on X-axis.

Sol. Given, radius, $r=5$ units, point lies on circle $=(2, 3)$ and centre of circle is on X-axis.

$\therefore$ Its y-coordinate will be zero.

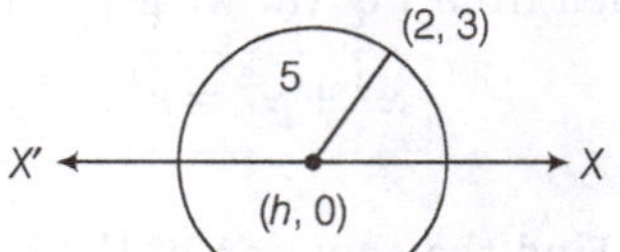

Let centre of circle $=(h, 0)$

Now, distance from the centre to a point on the circle = Radius of circle

$\therefore \quad \sqrt{(h-2)^2+(0-3)^2}=5$ [by distance formula]

$\Rightarrow \quad \sqrt{h^2+4-4h+9}=5$ $[\because (A-B)^2=A^2+B^2-2AB]$

$\Rightarrow \quad h^2+4-4h+9=25$ [squaring both sides]

$\Rightarrow \quad h^2-4h+13-25=0 \Rightarrow h^2-4h-12=0$

$\Rightarrow \quad h^2-6h+2h-12=0 \Rightarrow h(h-6)+2(h-6)=0$

$\Rightarrow \quad (h-6)(h+2)=0$

$\Rightarrow \quad h-6=0$ or $h+2=0 \Rightarrow h=6$ or $h=-2$

So, the centre of circle is $(6, 0)$ or $(-2, 0)$.

When centre $(h, k)=(6, 0)$ and radius $(r)=5$, then the equation of circle is

$(x-6)^2+(y-0)^2=(5)^2$ $[\because (x-h)^2+(y-k)^2=r^2]$

$\Rightarrow \quad x^2+36-12x+y^2=25$ $[\because (a-b)^2=a^2-2ab+b^2]$

$\Rightarrow \quad x^2+y^2-12x+11=0$

When centre $(h, k)=(-2, 0)$ and radius $(r)=5$, then the equation of circle is

$(x+2)^2+(y-0)^2=(5)^2$ $[\because (x-h)^2+(y-k)^2=r^2]$

$\Rightarrow \quad x^2+4+4x+y^2=25$

$\Rightarrow x^2+y^2+4x+4-25=0 \Rightarrow x^2+y^2+4x-21=0$

Hence the required equations of circle are $x^2+y^2-12x+11=0$ and $x^2+y^2+4x-21=0$.

TYPE III

When Circles touches X-Axis

Since, the circles touches X-axis, so $|k|=r$. In this case, circles may lie on upper of X-axis or on the lower of X-axis.

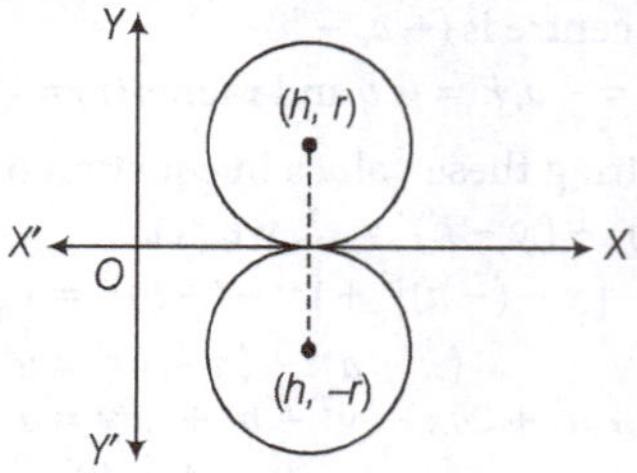

So, if r is the radius of a circle touching X-axis, then its centre is (h, r) or $(h, -r)$. Therefore, the equations of such circles are

$$\boxed{(x-h)^2+(y\mp r)^2=r^2}.$$

Example 5 Find the equation of circle whose centre is (1, 2) and touches X-axis.

Sol. Given, centre $(h, k) = (1, 2)$ and circle touches on X-axis.

$\therefore$ Radius $(r) = y$-coordinate of centre $= 2$

So, equation of circle is

$$(x-1)^2 + (y-2)^2 = 2^2 \qquad [\because (x-h)^2 + (y-k)^2 = r^2]$$

$$\Rightarrow x^2 - 2x + 1 + y^2 - 4y + 4 = 4 \; [\because (a-b)^2 = a^2 + b^2 - 2ab]$$

$$\Rightarrow \; x^2 + y^2 - 2x - 4y + 1 = 0$$

which is the required equation of circle.

|TYPE IV|

When Circles touches Y-Axis

Since, the circles touches Y-axis, so $|h| = r$.

In this case, circles may lie on the right of Y-axis or on the left of Y-axis. So, if r is the radius of a circle touching Y-axis, then its centre is (r, k) or $(-r, k)$. Therefore, the equation of such circles are

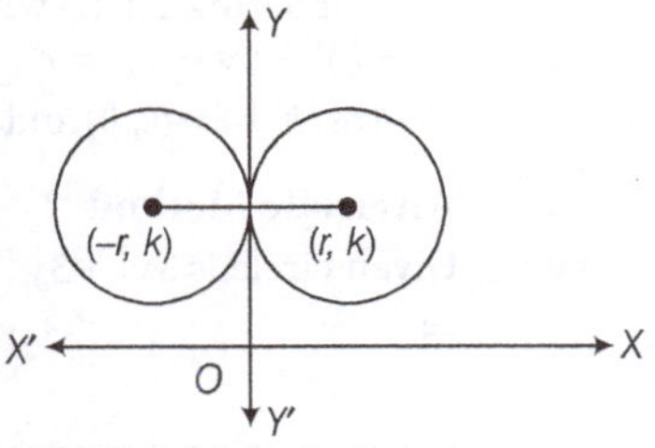

$$\boxed{(x \mp r)^2 + (y-k)^2 = r^2}$$

Example 6 Find the equation of circle whose centre is (2, 0) and touches Y-axis.

Sol. Given, centre $(h, k) = (2, 0)$ and circle touches Y-axis.

$\therefore$ Radius $(r) = x$-coordinate of centre $= 2$

So, the equation of circle is

$$(x-2)^2 + (y-0)^2 = 2^2 \qquad [\because (x-h)^2 + (y-k)^2 = r^2]$$

$$\Rightarrow \quad x^2 + 4 - 4x + y^2 = 4 \quad [\because (A-B)^2 = A^2 + B^2 - 2AB]$$

$$\Rightarrow \quad x^2 + y^2 - 4x + 4 = 4$$

$$\therefore \quad x^2 + y^2 - 4x = 0$$

which is the required equation of circle.

|TYPE V|

When Circles touches Both Coordinate Axes

Since, the circles touches both the coordinate axes, so $|h| = |k| = r$.

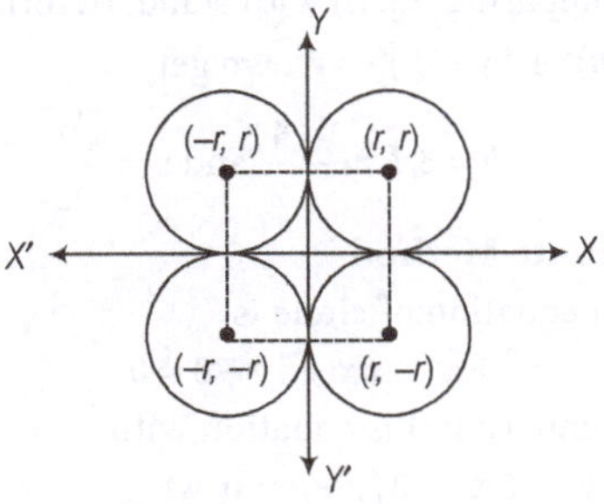

In this case, circles touching both the coordinate axes may lie in any of the four quadrants. If r is the radius of such a circle, then its centre may be $(r, r), (-r, r), (-r, -r)$ and $(r, -r)$. Then, the equations of such circles are

$$\boxed{(x \mp r)^2 + (y \mp r)^2 = r^2}$$

Example 7 Find the equation of the circle which touches both the axes and whose radius is 5.

Sol. Given, radius = 5 and circle touches both the axes.

So, circle may lies in anyone of the four quadrants.

$\therefore$ Centre of circle is $(\pm 5, \pm 5)$.

Hence, the equation of required circle is

$$(x \mp 5)^2 + (y \mp 5)^2 = (5)^2$$

$$\Rightarrow \quad x^2 + 25 \mp 10x + y^2 + 25 \mp 10y = 25$$

$$\Rightarrow \quad x^2 + y^2 \mp 10x \mp 10y + 25 = 0$$

Diameter Form

Let (x_1, y_1) and (x_2, y_2) be the end points of the diameter of a circle. Then, the equation of circle drawn on the diameter is

$$\boxed{(x - x_1)(x - x_2) + (y - y_1)(y - y_2) = 0}.$$

Example 8 Find the equation of the circle, whose end points of a diameter are $A(1, 5)$ and $B(-1, 3)$.

Sol. Given end points of a diameter are $A(1,5)$ and $B(-1,3)$.

We know that the equation of circle, the end points of one of whose diameter are (x_1, y_1) and (x_2, y_2) is given by

$$(x - x_1)(x - x_2) + (y - y_1)(y - y_2) = 0$$

Hence, the required equation of circle is

$$(x-1)(x+1) + (y-5)(y-3) = 0$$

$$\Rightarrow \quad x^2 - 1 + y^2 - 8y + 15 = 0$$

$$\Rightarrow \quad x^2 + y^2 - 8y + 14 = 0$$

Example 9 The abscissa of two points A and B are the roots of the equation $x^2 + 2ax - b^2 = 0$ and their ordinates are the roots of the equation $x^2 + 2px - q^2 = 0$. Find the equation.

Sol. Given equations are

$$x^2 + 2ax - b^2 = 0 \text{ and } x^2 + 2px - q^2 = 0.$$

Let the roots of $x^2 + 2ax - b^2 = 0$ be x_1 and x_2.

We know that, sum of roots $= \dfrac{-\text{Coefficient of } x}{\text{Coefficient of } x^2}$

and product of roots $= \dfrac{\text{Constant term}}{\text{Coefficient of } x^2}$

$\therefore \quad x_1 + x_2 = -2a$ and $x_1x_2 = -b^2$

and the roots of $x^2 + 2px - q^2 = 0$ are y_1 and y_2.

Then, $y_1 + y_2 = -2p$ and $y_1y_2 = -q^2$

Let $A \equiv (x_1, y_1)$ and $B \equiv (x_2, y_2)$

Now, equation of circle whose diameter is AB, will be

$$(x - x_1)(x - x_2) + (y - y_1)(y - y_2) = 0$$

$$\Rightarrow x^2 - (x_1 + x_2)x + x_1x_2 + y^2 - (y_1 + y_2)y + y_1y_2 = 0$$

On substituting the values of $x_1 + x_2$, x_1x_2, $y_1 + y_2$ and y_1y_2, we get

$$x^2 + 2ax - b^2 + y^2 + 2py - q^2 = 0$$

$$\Rightarrow x^2 + y^2 + 2ax + 2py - b^2 - q^2 = 0$$

which is the required equation of circle.

General Form

We know that the equation of the circle having centre (h, k) and radius r is

$$(x - h)^2 + (y - k)^2 = r^2$$

$$\Rightarrow \quad x^2 + y^2 - 2hx - 2ky + h^2 + k^2 - r^2 = 0$$

which is of the form $x^2 + y^2 + 2gx + 2fy + c = 0$

where, $g = -h$, $f = -k$ and $c = h^2 + k^2 - r^2$.

The above equation of a circle is called the general equation of a circle with centre $= (-g, -f)$

and **radius**, $r = \sqrt{h^2 + k^2 - c}$ or $r = \sqrt{g^2 + f^2 - c}$.

Different Types of Questions Based on Circles

|TYPE I|

To Find Centre and Radius When Standard Equation of Circle is Given

Example 10 Find the centre and radius of each of the following circle.

(i) $x^2 + (y + 2)^2 = 9$

(ii) $x^2 + y^2 + 6x - 4y + 4 = 0$

Sol. (i) Given equation of circle is $x^2 + (y + 2)^2 = 9$

$$\Rightarrow \quad (x - 0)^2 + \{y - (-2)\}^2 = 3^2$$

On comparing with $(x - h)^2 + (y - k)^2 = r^2$, we get

$$h = 0, k = -2 \text{ and } r = 3$$

Hence, centre of circle $= (0, -2)$ and radius $= 3$ units.

(ii) Given equation of circle is

$$x^2 + y^2 + 6x - 4y + 4 = 0$$

On comparing this equation with

$x^2 + y^2 + 2gx + 2fy + c = 0$, we get

$$g = \frac{6}{2} = 3, f = \frac{-4}{2} = -2 \text{ and } c = 4$$

$\therefore$ Centre of a circle $= (-3, 2)$

[centre of circle $= (-g, -f)$]

and radius of a circle

$$= \sqrt{(3)^2 + (-2)^2 - 4} = \sqrt{9 + 4 - 4} = \sqrt{9} = 3 \text{ units}$$

[$\because$ radius of circle $= \sqrt{g^2 + f^2 - c}$]

Hence, the required centre of a circle $= (-3, 2)$ and radius $= 3$ units.

Example 11 Find the centre and radius of each of the following circle.

(i) $3x^2 + 3y^2 = 27$ (ii) $x^2 + y^2 - 6x + 5y - 8 = 0$

Sol. (i) Given circle is $3x^2 + 3y^2 = 27$.

or $\quad x^2 + y^2 = 9$ [dividing both sides by 3]

$$\Rightarrow \quad (x - 0)^2 + (y - 0)^2 = 9$$

$$\Rightarrow \quad (x - 0)^2 + (y - 0)^2 = 3^2 \quad \text{...(i)}$$

On comparing Eq. (i) with standard form of circle i.e. $(x - h)^2 + (y - k)^2 = r^2$, we get

Centre $(h, k) = (0, 0)$ and radius $(r) = 3$

Alternate Method

Given circle is $3x^2 + 3y^2 - 27 = 0$

$$\Rightarrow \quad x^2 + y^2 - 9 = 0$$

[dividing both sides by 3]

On comparing this equation with

$x^2 + y^2 + 2gx + 2fy + c = 0$, we get $g = 0$, $f = 0$ and $c = -9$

$\therefore$ Centre of the circle $= (0, 0)$

[$\because$ centre of a circle $(-g, -f)$]

and radius of the circle $= \sqrt{0^2 + 0^2 + 9}$

[$\because$ radius of a circle $= \sqrt{g^2 + f^2 - c}$]

$= 3$ units

Hence, the required centre of the circle $= (0, 0)$ and radius $= 3$ units.

(ii) Given equation of circle is

$$x^2 + y^2 - 6x + 5y - 8 = 0$$

$$\Rightarrow \quad (x^2 - 6x) + (y^2 + 5y) = 8$$

$$\Rightarrow (x^2 - 6x + 3^2) + \left[y^2 + 5y + \left(\frac{5}{2}\right)^2\right] = 3^2 + \left(\frac{5}{2}\right)^2 + 8$$

$$\Rightarrow \quad (x - 3)^2 + \left(y + \frac{5}{2}\right)^2 = \frac{93}{4} \quad \text{...(i)}$$

On comparing Eq. (i) with standard form of circle i.e. $(x - h)^2 + (y - k)^2 = r^2$, we get

$$h = 3, k = -\frac{5}{2} \text{ and } r = \frac{\sqrt{93}}{2}$$

Alternate Method

Given equation of circle is

$$x^2 + y^2 - 6x + 5y - 8 = 0$$

On comparing this equation with

$x^2 + y^2 + 2gx + 2fy + c = 0$, we get

$$g = \frac{-6}{2} = -3, f = \frac{5}{2} \text{ and } c = -8$$

$\therefore$ Centre of the circle $= \left(3, \frac{-5}{2}\right)$

[$\because$ centre of a circle $= (-g, -f)$]

and radius of the circle $= \sqrt{(-3)^2 + \left(\frac{5}{2}\right)^2 + 8}$

[$\because$ radius of a circle $= \sqrt{g^2 + f^2 - c}$]

$$= \sqrt{9 + \frac{25}{4} + 8} = \sqrt{\frac{36 + 25 + 32}{4}} = \frac{\sqrt{93}}{2} \text{ units}$$

Example 12 Find the equation of the circle, if the end points of whose diameter are the centres of the circles $x^2 + y^2 + 6x - 14y - 1 = 0$ and $x^2 + y^2 - 4x + 10y - 2 = 0$.

Sol. Given circles are

$$x^2 + y^2 + 6x - 14y - 1 = 0$$

and $$x^2 + y^2 - 4x + 10y - 2 = 0$$

On comparing the above equation with $x^2 + y^2 + 2gx + 2fy + c = 0$ one-by-one, we get the centres of given circles $(-3, 7)$ and $(2, -5)$, respectively.

Since, the points $(-3, 7)$ and $(2, -5)$ are end points of the diameter of the required circle.

Hence, the equation of circle is

$$(x + 3)(x - 2) + (y - 7)(y + 5) = 0$$

$$\Rightarrow \quad x^2 + y^2 + x - 2y - 41 = 0$$

Intercept on the Axes

For **x-intercept**, put $y = 0$ in the equation of the circle and solve the quadratic equation in x. The x-intercept is equal to the algebraic difference of the two solutions of x, we get from the quadratic equation. Similarly, **for y-intercept**, we put $x = 0$ and do same as x-intercept.

Example 13 Find the lengths of the intercepts of the circle $x^2 + y^2 - 4x - 6y - 5 = 0$ on the both coordinate axes.

Sol. We have, $x^2 + y^2 - 4x - 6y - 5 = 0$

For x-intercept Put $y = 0$ in equation of the circle, we get

$$x^2 - 4x - 5 = 0$$

$$\Rightarrow \quad (x - 5)(x + 1) = 0 \Rightarrow x = 5, -1$$

$\therefore$ Length of x-intercept $= |5 - (-1)| = 6$

For y-intercept Put $x = 0$ in equation of the circle, we get

$$y^2 - 6y - 5 = 0$$

$$\Rightarrow \quad (y - 5)(y - 1) = 0 \Rightarrow y = 5, 1$$

$\therefore$ Length of y-intercept $= |5 - 1| = 4$

Position of a Point w.r.t. Circle

Let $S \equiv x^2 + y^2 + 2gx + 2fy + c = 0$

or $S \equiv (x - h)^2 + (y - k)^2 = r^2$

be the equation of the circle and $P(x_1, y_1)$ be any point in the plane of the circle, then

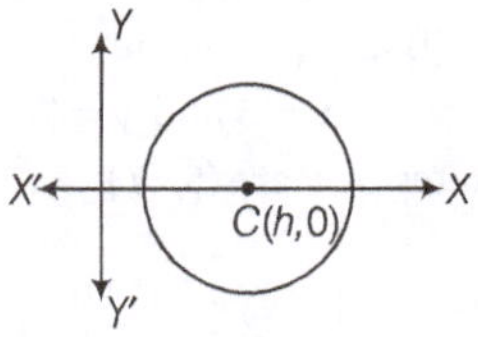

$$S_1 \equiv x_1^2 + y_1^2 + 2gx_1 + 2fy_1 + c = 0$$

or $$S_1 \equiv (x_1 - h)^2 + (y_1 - k)^2 = r^2$$

Case I If $S_1 > 0$, then the point lies **outside** the circle.

Case II If $S_1 = 0$, then the point lies **on** the circle.

Case III If $S_1 < 0$, then the point lies **inside** the circle.

Example 14 Does the point $(-2.5, 3.5)$ lie inside, outside or on the circle $x^2 + y^2 = 25$?

Sol. Given equation of circle is

$$S_1 \equiv x^2 + y^2 = 25 \text{ or } S_1 \equiv x^2 + y^2 - 25 = 0 \quad \ldots(i)$$

Now, put $x = -2.5$ and $y = 3.5$ in Eq. (i), we get

$$S_1 = (-2.5)^2 + (3.5)^2 - 25 = 6.25 + 12.25 - 25$$
$$= 18.5 - 25 = -6.5 < 0$$

Since, $S_1 < 0$, so the given point $(-2.5, 3.5)$ lies inside the circle.

|TYPE II|

To Find the Equation of a Circle satisfying the Given Conditions

Example 15 Find the equation of the circle passing through the point $(2, 4)$ and having its centre at the intersection of the lines $x - y = 4$ and $2x + 3y + 7 = 0$.

Sol. Given equation of lines are $x - y = 4$ and $2x + 3y + 7 = 0$.

On solving these equations, we get $x = 1$ and $y = -3$

Also, the point of intersection of the given lines is centre.

$\therefore$ Coordinates of centre is $(1, -3)$.

Now, the circle passes through the point $(2, 4)$.

$\therefore$ Radius of circle $= \sqrt{(1 - 2)^2 + (-3 - 4)^2} = \sqrt{1 + 49} = \sqrt{50}$

Hence, the required equation of circle whose centre is $(1, -3)$ and radius is $\sqrt{50}$, is

$$(x - 1)^2 + (y + 3)^2 = (\sqrt{50})^2$$

$$\Rightarrow \quad x^2 + 1 - 2x + y^2 + 9 + 6y = 50$$

$$\Rightarrow \quad x^2 + y^2 - 2x + 6y - 40 = 0$$

Example 16 Find the equation of the circle, whose centre is (2, – 3) and passing through the intersection of the lines $3x - 2y = 1$ and $4x + y = 27$.

Sol. Let $P(x, y)$ be the point of intersection of the lines,

$$3x - 2y = 1 \quad \text{...(i)}$$

and $$4x + y = 27 \quad \text{...(ii)}$$

On solving Eqs. (i) and (ii), we get

$$x = 5 \text{ and } y = 7$$

So, the coordinates of P are (5, 7).

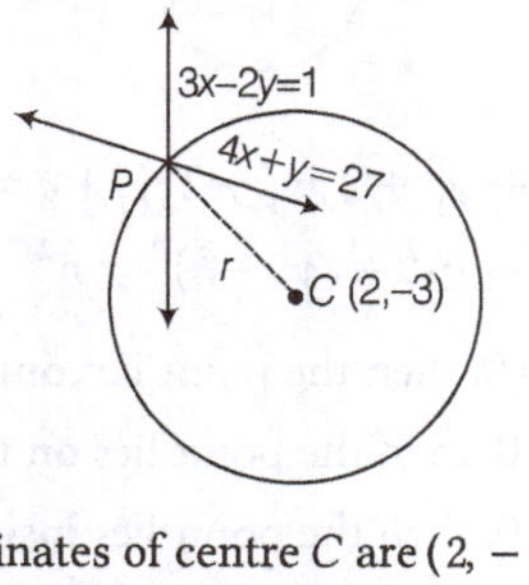

Given, coordinates of centre C are (2, – 3).

$\therefore$ CP = Radius

$\Rightarrow$ $\sqrt{(5-2)^2 + (7+3)^2} = r$

$\Rightarrow$ $\sqrt{9 + 100} = r$

$\Rightarrow$ $r = \sqrt{109}$

Hence, the equation of required circle is

$$(x-2)^2 + (y+3)^2 = (\sqrt{109})^2$$

$\Rightarrow$ $x^2 - 4x + 4 + y^2 + 6y + 9 = 109$

$\Rightarrow$ $x^2 + y^2 - 4x + 6y - 96 = 0$

Example 17 Find the equation of a circle whose diameter are $2x - 3y + 12 = 0$ and $x + 4y - 5 = 0$ and area is 154 sq units.

Sol. Given equations of diameter of circles are

$$2x - 3y + 12 = 0 \text{ and } x + 4y - 5 = 0$$

On solving these equations, we get $x = -3$ and $y = 2$

We know that centre is the point of intersection of diameter.

$\therefore$ Coordinates of centres are (– 3, 2).

Let r be the radius of circle.

Then, area of circle $= 154 = \pi r^2$

$\Rightarrow$ $154 = \frac{22}{7} \times r^2$

$\Rightarrow$ $r^2 = \frac{154 \times 7}{22} = 49$

$\therefore$ $r = 7$ $[\because r > 0]$

Hence, the equation of required circle is

$$(x+3)^2 + (y-2)^2 = (7)^2$$

$\Rightarrow$ $x^2 + 6x + 9 + y^2 - 4y + 4 = 49$

$\Rightarrow$ $x^2 + y^2 + 6x - 4y + 13 - 49 = 0$

$\Rightarrow$ $x^2 + y^2 + 6x - 4y - 36 = 0$

Example 18 Find the equation of the circle passing through two points on Y-axis at distances 3 from the origin and having radius 5.

Sol. Let coordinates of points on Y-axis be $A \equiv (0, 3)$ and $B \equiv (0, -3)$, respectively.

Given circle passes through points A and B, therefore its centre will be on the perpendicular bisector of AB.

Clearly, two such circles are possible.

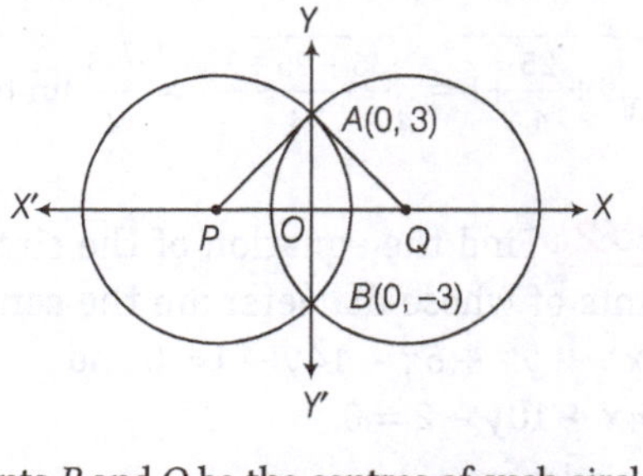

Let points P and Q be the centres of such circles.

Given, $AP = AQ = 5$, $OA = 3$

$\Rightarrow$ $OP = OQ = \sqrt{5^2 - 3^2} = \sqrt{25 - 9} = \sqrt{16} = 4$

Then, centre $P = (-4, 0)$ and centre $Q = (4, 0)$

Thus, centres of the required circles are $P(-4, 0)$ and $Q(4, 0)$ and their radii are 5.

$\therefore$ Equation of the required circles will be

$(x+4)^2 + y^2 = 5^2$ i.e. $x^2 + y^2 + 8x - 9 = 0$

and $(x-4)^2 + y^2 = 5^2$ i.e. $x^2 + y^2 - 8x - 9 = 0$

Example 19 Find the equation of the circle passing through the points (1, – 2) and (4, – 3) and whose centre lies on the line $3x + 4y = 7$.

Sol. Let points $A \equiv (1, -2)$ and $B \equiv (4, -3)$

Given line is $3x + 4y = 7$ ...(i)

Again, let L be the mid-point of AB.

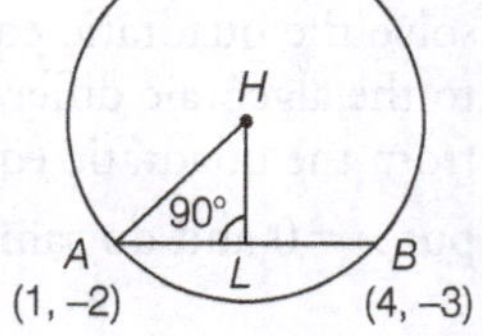

$\therefore$ Mid-point

$$L \equiv \left(\frac{1+4}{2}, \frac{-2+(-3)}{2}\right) = \left(\frac{5}{2}, -\frac{5}{2}\right)$$

Slope of $AB = \frac{y_1 - y_2}{x_1 - x_2} = \frac{-2+3}{1-4} = -\frac{1}{3}$

$\therefore$ Slope of $HL = 3$ $[\because HL \perp AB]$

Then, equation of HL will be

$$y + \frac{5}{2} = 3\left(x - \frac{5}{2}\right)$$

$\Rightarrow$ $2y + 5 = 6x - 15 \Rightarrow 6x - 2y = 20$

$\therefore$ $3x - y = 10$ [dividing both sides by 2] ...(ii)

Centre H of the circle lies on lines (i) and (ii), therefore it is the point of intersection of lines (i) and (ii).

On multiplying Eq. (ii) by 4 and adding it to Eq. (i), we get

$$15x = 47 \Rightarrow x = \frac{47}{15}$$

On subtracting Eq. (ii) from Eq. (i), we get

$$5y = -3 \Rightarrow y = -\frac{3}{5}$$

$$\therefore \quad \text{Centre } H \equiv \left(\frac{47}{15}, -\frac{3}{5}\right)$$

Now, radius of the circle $= HA = \sqrt{\left(\frac{47}{15} - 1\right)^2 + \left(-\frac{3}{5} + 2\right)^2}$

$$= \sqrt{\left(\frac{32}{15}\right)^2 + \left(\frac{7}{5}\right)^2} = \sqrt{\frac{32^2 + 21^2}{15^2}} = \frac{\sqrt{1465}}{15}$$

Hence, the equation of required circle is

$$\left(x - \frac{47}{15}\right)^2 + \left(y + \frac{3}{5}\right)^2 = \frac{1465}{15^2}$$

$$\Rightarrow \quad (15x - 47)^2 + 9(5y + 3)^2 = 1465$$

$$\Rightarrow \quad 225x^2 + 2209 - 1410x + 225y^2 + 81 + 270y = 1465$$

$$\Rightarrow \quad 225x^2 + 225y^2 - 1410x + 270y + 825 = 0$$

$$\Rightarrow \quad 15x^2 + 15y^2 - 94x + 18y + 55 = 0$$

Example 20 Find the equation of a circle passing through the point (7, 3) having radius 3 units and whose centre lies on the line $y = x - 1$.

Sol. Let (h, k) be the centre of circle.

$\therefore$ (h, k) lies on the line $y = x - 1$, then $k = h - 1$

Therefore, the equation of circle is

$$(x - h)^2 + [y - (h - 1)]^2 = (3)^2 \quad \text{...(i)}$$

Since, the circle passes through the point (7, 3).

$$\therefore \quad (7 - h)^2 + (3 - h + 1)^2 = 9$$

$$\Rightarrow \quad (7 - h)^2 + (4 - h)^2 = 9$$

$$\Rightarrow \quad 49 - 14h + h^2 + 16 - 8h + h^2 = 9 \Rightarrow h^2 - 11h + 28 = 0$$

$$\Rightarrow \quad (h - 7)(h - 4) = 0 \Rightarrow h = 7 \text{ or } h = 4$$

When $h = 7$, then $k = 7 - 1 = 6$

and when $h = 4$, then $k = 4 - 1 = 3$

Hence, the required equation of circles are

$$(x - 7)^2 + (y - 6)^2 = 3^2 \text{ or } (x - 4)^2 + (y - 3)^2 = 3^2$$

$$\Rightarrow \quad x^2 + y^2 - 14x - 12y + 76 = 0$$

$$\text{or} \quad x^2 + y^2 - 8x - 6y + 16 = 0$$

Example 21 Find the equation of a circle which touches both the axes and the line $3x - 4y + 8 = 0$ and lies in third quadrant.

Sol. Let a be the radius of the circle, then $(-a, -a)$ will be centre of the circle. [$\because$ circle lies in 3rd quadrant]

Also, the line $3x - 4y + 8 = 0$ touches the circle.

Therefore, the perpendicular distance from centre to the given line is the radius of the circle.

$$\therefore \quad a = \left|\frac{3(-a) - 4(-a) + 8}{\sqrt{3^2 + 4^2}}\right| \Rightarrow a = \left|\frac{-3a + 4a + 8}{5}\right|$$

$$\Rightarrow \quad 5a = a + 8 \Rightarrow a = 2$$

Hence, the equation of the required circle is

$$(x + 2)^2 + (y + 2)^2 = 2^2$$

$$\Rightarrow \quad x^2 + 4x + 4 + y^2 + 4y + 4 = 4$$

$$\Rightarrow \quad x^2 + y^2 + 4x + 4y + 8 - 4 = 0$$

$$\therefore \quad x^2 + y^2 + 4x + 4y + 4 = 0$$

Example 22 Find the equation of circle whose centre is (3, – 1) and which cuts off a chord of length 6 units on the line $2x - 5y + 18 = 0$.

Sol. Given, centre of circle, $O \equiv (3, -1)$.

Let OM be the perpendicular distance from O to the line $2x - 5y + 18 = 0$.

Then, $$OM = \left|\frac{2(3) - 5(-1) + 18}{\sqrt{(2)^2 + (5)^2}}\right| = \left|\frac{29}{\sqrt{29}}\right| = \sqrt{29}$$

In ΔOMP, $OP^2 = OM^2 + PM^2$ [by Pythagoras theorem]

$$\Rightarrow \quad OP^2 = (\sqrt{29})^2 + (3)^2 \quad \left[\because PM = \frac{1}{2}PQ = \frac{1}{2} \times 6 = 3\right]$$

$$\Rightarrow \quad OP^2 = 29 + 9 = 38$$

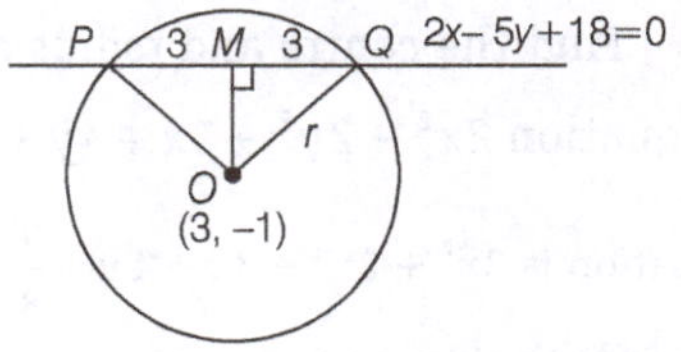

Hence, the equation of required circle is

$$(x - 3)^2 + (y + 1)^2 = 38$$

$$\Rightarrow \quad x^2 - 6x + 9 + y^2 + 2y + 1 = 38$$

$$\Rightarrow \quad x^2 + y^2 - 6x + 2y + 10 - 38 = 0$$

$$\Rightarrow \quad x^2 + y^2 - 6x + 2y - 28 = 0$$

Example 23 A circle of radius 2 lies in the first quadrant and touches both the axes of coordinates. Find the equation of the circle with centre at (6, 5) and touching the above circle externally.

Sol. Given, $AM = AL = AC = 2$ and points $A \equiv (2, 2)$, $B \equiv (6, 5)$

$\therefore$ Distance $AB = \sqrt{(2 - 6)^2 + (2 - 5)^2} = \sqrt{(4)^2 + (3)^2} = 5$

Then, distance $BC = AB - AC = 5 - 2 = 3$

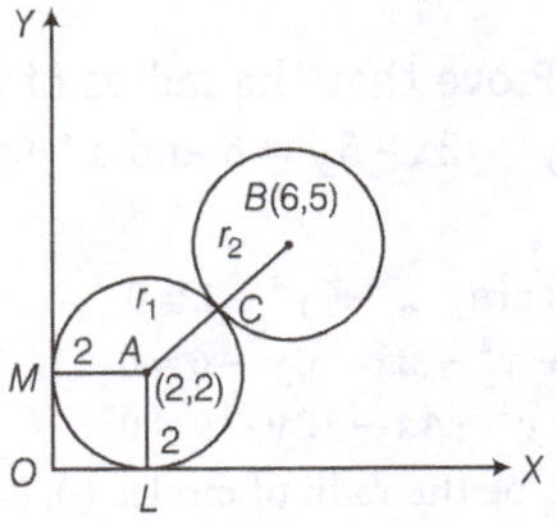

Hence, the equation of required circle whose centre is (6, 5) and radius is 3, will be

$$(x - 6)^2 + (y - 5)^2 = 3^2 \Rightarrow x^2 + y^2 - 12x - 10y + 52 = 0$$

|TYPE III|

To Find Centre and Radius When General Equation of Circle Is Given

To find the centre and radius of a circle, whose general equation is given i.e. $x^2+y^2+2gx+2fy+c=0$, we use the following steps

***Step* I** Make the coefficients of x^2 and y^2 equal to 1.

***Step* II** Find coordinates of centre (α, β),

$$\text{where } \alpha = -\frac{1}{2}(\text{coefficient of } x) = -\frac{1}{2}(2g) = -g$$

$$\text{and } \beta = -\frac{1}{2}(\text{coefficient of } y) = -\frac{1}{2}(2f) = -f$$

***Step* III** Find radius by using the formula,

$$\text{Radius} = \sqrt{\alpha^2 + \beta^2 - \text{Constant term}}$$

$$\text{or} \quad \text{Radius} = \sqrt{g^2+f^2-c}.$$

Example 24 Find the centre and radius of the circle given by the equation $2x^2+2y^2+3x+4y+\frac{9}{8}=0$.

Sol. Given equation is $2x^2+2y^2+3x+4y+\frac{9}{8}=0$.

On dividing both sides by 2, we get

$$x^2+y^2+\frac{3}{2}x+2y+\frac{9}{16}=0 \quad \text{...(i)}$$

From Eq. (i), we get coefficient of $x = \frac{3}{2}$

and coefficient of $y = 2$

$$\therefore \quad \alpha = \frac{-1}{2}\left(\frac{3}{2}\right) = -\frac{3}{4} \text{ and } \beta = \frac{-1}{2}(2) = -1$$

$$\text{Hence, centre} = \left(-\frac{3}{4}, -1\right)$$

From Eq. (i), we get constant term $= \frac{9}{16}$

$$\therefore \text{Radius} = \sqrt{\left(\frac{-3}{4}\right)^2 + (-1)^2 - \frac{9}{16}} = \sqrt{\frac{9}{16}+1-\frac{9}{16}} = 1$$

Example 25 Prove that the radius of the circles $x^2+y^2=1$, $x^2+y^2-2x-6y=6$ and $x^2+y^2-4x-12y=9$ are in AP.

Sol. Given circles are

$$x^2+y^2-1=0 \quad \text{...(i)}$$

$$x^2+y^2-2x-6y-6=0 \quad \text{...(ii)}$$

$$\text{and} \quad x^2+y^2-4x-12y-9=0 \quad \text{...(iii)}$$

Let r_1, r_2 and r_3 be the radii of circles (i), (ii) and (iii), respectively.

We know that the general form of the circle is

$$x^2+y^2+2gx+2fy+c=0 \quad \text{...(iv)}$$

Now, comparing Eq. (i) with Eq. (iv), we get

$$2g=0 \Rightarrow g=0,\ 2f=0 \Rightarrow f=0$$

and $c=-1$

$$\therefore \text{Radius } (r_1) = \sqrt{g^2+f^2-c} = \sqrt{0^2-0^2-(-1)} = 1$$

On comparing Eq. (ii) with Eq. (iv), we get

$$2g=-2 \Rightarrow g=-1,\ 2f=-6 \Rightarrow f=-3$$

and $c=-6$

$$\therefore \text{Radius } (r_2) = \sqrt{g^2+f^2-c} = \sqrt{(-1)^2+(-3)^2+6}$$

$$= \sqrt{1+9+6} = \sqrt{16} = 4$$

Again, comparing Eq. (iii) with Eq. (iv), we get

$$2g=-4 \Rightarrow g=-2$$

$$2f=-12 \Rightarrow f=-6$$

and $c=-9$

$$\therefore \text{Radius } (r_3) = \sqrt{g^2+f^2-c}$$

$$= \sqrt{(-2)^2+(-6)^2-(-9)}$$

$$= \sqrt{4+36+9} = \sqrt{49} = 7$$

Now, $r_2 - r_1 = 4-1 = 3$, $r_3 - r_2 = 7-4 = 3$

So, r_1, r_2 and r_3 are in arithmetic progression. **Hence proved.**

|TYPE IV|

To Find the Equation of a Circle Passing through Three Non-collinear Points

If we have to find the equation of circle passing through three non-collinear points, then for finding this equation of circle, we use the following steps

***Step* I** First, assume the general equation of circle,

i.e. $\quad x^2+y^2+2gx+2fy+c=0 \quad$ ...(i)

***Step* II** Since, circle passes through three points, so each point will satisfy it.

Put each point in Eq. (i) one-by-one and get three equations.

***Step* III** Now, solve these three equations to get the values of g, f, c and put these values in Eq. (i) to get required equation of circle.

Example 26 Find the equation of a circle passing through the points $(2,-6)$, $(6,4)$ and $(-3,1)$.

Sol. Let equation of the circle passing through the given points be $x^2+y^2+2gx+2fy+c=0$ ...(i)

Since, the circle passes through the point $(2,-6)$.

On putting $x=2, y=-6$ in Eq. (i), we get

$$4+36+4g-12f+c=0 \Rightarrow 4g-12f+c=-40 \quad \text{...(ii)}$$

Also, the circle passes through the point $(6,4)$.

On putting $x=6, y=4$ in Eq. (i), we get

$$36+16+12g+8f+c=0$$

$$\Rightarrow \quad 12g+8f+c=-52 \quad \text{...(iii)}$$

Also the circle passes through the point $(-3, 1)$.

On putting $x = -3$ and $y = 1$ in Eq. (i), we get

$$9 + 1 - 6g + 2f + c = 0 \Rightarrow -6g + 2f + c = -10 \quad \text{...(iv)}$$

On subtracting Eq. (iii) from Eq. (ii), we get

$$-8g - 20f = 12 \quad \text{...(v)}$$

On subtracting Eq. (iv) from Eq. (iii), we get

$$18g + 6f = -42 \quad \text{...(vi)}$$

On solving Eqs. (v) and (vi) for g and f, we get

$$g = -\frac{32}{13},\ f = \frac{5}{13}$$

On putting the values of g and f in Eq. (ii), we get

$$c = -\frac{332}{13}$$

Now, putting $g = -\frac{32}{13}$, $f = \frac{5}{13}$

and $c = -\frac{332}{13}$ in Eq. (i), we get

$$x^2 + y^2 - \frac{64}{13}x + \frac{10}{13}y - \frac{332}{13} = 0$$

$$\Rightarrow \quad 13x^2 + 13y^2 - 64x + 10y - 332 = 0$$

which is the required equation of circle.

Example 27 Show that the points (5, 5), (6, 4), (– 2, 4) and (7, 1) are concyclic, i.e. all lie on the same circle. Find the equation, centre and radius of this circle.

Sol. Let the equation of the circle passing through the points (5, 5), (6, 4) and (7, 1) be given by

$$x^2 + y^2 + 2gx + 2fy + c = 0 \quad \text{...(i)}$$

Then, each of these points must satisfy Eq. (i).

$$\therefore \quad 25 + 25 + 10g + 10f + c = 0$$

$$\Rightarrow \quad 10g + 10f + c = -50 \quad \text{...(ii)}$$

$$36 + 16 + 12g + 8f + c = 0$$

$$\Rightarrow \quad 12g + 8f + c = -52 \quad \text{...(iii)}$$

and $\quad 49 + 1 + 14g + 2f + c = 0$

$$\Rightarrow \quad 14g + 2f + c = -50 \quad \text{...(iv)}$$

On solving Eqs. (ii), (iii) and (iv) simultaneously, we get

$$g = -2,\ f = -1 \text{ and } c = -20$$

On putting the values of g, f and c in Eq. (i), we get

$$x^2 + y^2 - 4x - 2y - 20 = 0$$

On putting $x = -2$ and $y = 4$ in the above circle, we get

$$4 + 16 + 8 - 8 - 20 = 0$$

This shows that the point (– 2, 4) also lies on the circle.

Hence, the points (5, 5), (6, 4), (– 2, 4) and (7, 1) are concyclic and equation of this circle is

$$x^2 + y^2 - 4x - 2y - 20 = 0$$

Its centre is $(-g, -f) = (2, 1)$

and radius $= \sqrt{g^2 + f^2 - c} = \sqrt{4 + 1 + 20} = 5$ units

|TYPE V|

Different Problems Based on Circles

Example 28 If the line $y = \sqrt{3}x + k$ touches the circle $x^2 + y^2 = 16$, then find the value of k.

Sol. Given, $y = \sqrt{3}x + k$ touches the circle $x^2 + y^2 = 16$.

So, length of perpendicular distance from the centre of the given circle i.e. (0, 0) on $y = \sqrt{3}x + k$ is equal to radius of circle.

$$\therefore \quad 4 = \left|\frac{0 + 0 + k}{\sqrt{1 + 3}}\right|$$

$$\Rightarrow \quad 4 = \left|\frac{k}{2}\right|$$

$$\Rightarrow \quad \frac{k}{2} = \pm 4$$

$$\Rightarrow \quad k = \pm 8$$

Example 29 Find the equation of the circle passing through the vertices of a triangle whose sides are represented by the equations $x + y = 2$, $3x - 4y = 6$ and $x - y = 0$.

Sol. Let the sides AB, BC and CA of ΔABC be represented by the equations $x + y = 2$, $3x - 4y = 6$ and $x - y = 0$, respectively.

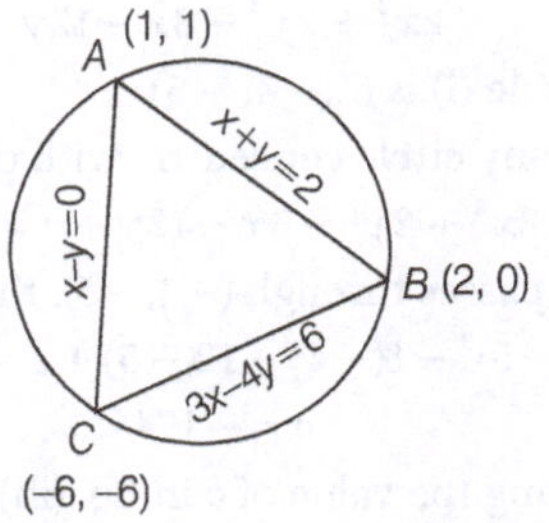

On solving $x + y = 2$ and $3x - 4y = 6$, we get $B(2, 0)$

On solving $3x - 4y = 6$ and $x - y = 0$, we get $C(-6, -6)$

On solving $x + y = 2$ and $x - y = 0$, we get $A(1, 1)$

Let the required equation of the circle be

$$x^2 + y^2 + 2gx + 2fy + c = 0 \quad \text{...(i)}$$

Since, it passes through $A(1, 1)$, $B(2, 0)$ and $C(-6, -6)$, so each of these points satisfy Eq. (i).

$$\therefore \quad 1^2 + 1^2 + 2g + 2f + c = 0$$

$$\Rightarrow \quad 2g + 2f + c = -2 \quad \text{...(ii)}$$

$$2^2 + 0^2 + 4g + c = 0$$

$$\Rightarrow \quad 4g + c + 4 = 0 \quad \text{...(iii)}$$

and $\quad (-6)^2 + (-6)^2 - 12g - 12f + c = 0$

$$\Rightarrow \quad 12g + 12f - c = 72 \quad \text{...(iv)}$$

On subtracting Eqs. (ii) from (iii), we get

$$2g - 2f + 2 = 0$$

$$\Rightarrow \quad g - f = -1 \quad \text{...(v)}$$

On adding Eq. (iv) and Eq. (iii), we get

$$16g + 12f - 68 = 0 \Rightarrow 4g + 3f = 17 \quad \text{...(vi)}$$

On solving Eqs. (v) and (vi), we get $g = 2$ and $f = 3$

On putting $g = 2$ in Eq. (iii), we get $c = -12$

Hence, the required equation of circle is

$$x^2 + y^2 + 4x + 6y - 12 = 0.$$

Concentric Circles

Two circles having the same centre $C\,(h, k)$ but different radii r_1 and r_2, are called **concentric circles**.

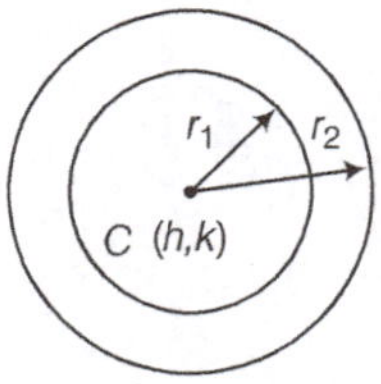

Thus, the circles

$(x-h)^2 + (y-k)^2 = r_1^2$ and

$(x-h)^2 + (y-k)^2 = r_2^2, r_1 \neq r_2$ are

concentric circles.

Note These circles having equals radii are called the **equal circles**.

Example 30 Find the equation of the circle which passes through the centre of circle $x^2 + y^2 + 8x + 10y - 7 = 0$ and is concentric with the circle $2x^2 + 2y^2 - 8x - 12y - 9 = 0$.

Sol. Given, circles are $x^2 + y^2 + 8x + 10y - 7 = 0$ ...(i)

and $2x^2 + 2y^2 - 8x - 12y - 9 = 0$ ...(ii)

Centre of circle (i) is $C_1(-4, -5)$.

Equation of any circle concentric with circle (ii) is

$$2x^2 + 2y^2 - 8x - 12y + c = 0 \quad \text{...(iii)}$$

If this circle passes through $(-4, -5)$, then

$$2(-4)^2 + 2(-5)^2 - 8(-4) - 12(-5) + c = 0$$

$$\Rightarrow \quad c = -174$$

On substituting the value of c in Eq. (iii), we get

$$2x^2 + 2y^2 - 8x - 12y - 174 = 0$$

Hence, the equation of required circle is

$$2x^2 + 2y^2 - 8x - 12y - 174 = 0$$

or $\quad x^2 + y^2 - 4x - 6y - 87 = 0$

Parametric Form

(i) Parametric form of the circle $x^2 + y^2 = a^2$ is given by $x = a\cos\theta,\ y = a\sin\theta$, where $0 \le \theta < 2\pi$, which are known as **parametric equations.**

(ii) Parametric form of the circle $(x-h)^2 + (y-k)^2 = a^2$ is given by $x = h + a\cos\theta,\ y = k + a\sin\theta$, where $0 \le \theta < 2\pi$.

Example 31 Find the parametric equations of the given circles.

(i) $x^2 + y^2 = 16$

(ii) $x^2 + y^2 - 4x + 2y - 4 = 0$

Sol. (i) We have, $x^2 + y^2 = 16$

$$\Rightarrow \quad x^2 + y^2 = 4^2$$

We know that parametric equation of the circle $x^2 + y^2 = a^2$ is $x = a\cos\theta,\ y = a\sin\theta, 0 \le \theta < 2\pi$.

$\therefore$ Parametric equation of the circle $x^2 + y^2 = 4^2$ is $x = 4\cos\theta,\ y = 4\sin\theta, 0 \le \theta < 2\pi$.

(ii) We have,

$$x^2 + y^2 - 4x + 2y - 4 = 0$$

$$\Rightarrow \quad (x-2)^2 + (y+1)^2 = 9$$

$$\Rightarrow \quad (x-2)^2 + (y+1)^2 = 3^2$$

We know that parametric equation of the circle $(x-h)^2 + (y-k)^2 = a^2$ is $x = h + a\cos\theta$, $y = k + a\sin\theta, 0 \le \theta < 2\pi$.

Hence, the parametric equation of the circle $(x-2)^2 + (y+1)^2 = 3^2$ is $x = 2 + 3\cos\theta$ and $y = -1 + 3\sin\theta$, where $0 \le \theta < 2\pi$.

Practice Exercise

Very Short Answer Type Questions

2 Marks

1 Find the centre and radius of the circle of the followings.

(i) $x^2 + y^2 + 8x + 10y - 8 = 0$

(ii) $x^2 + y^2 + 6x - 10y + 16 = 0$

2 Find the equation of the circles whose end points of one of the diameters are

(i) $A(2, -3)$ and $(-3, 5)$

(ii) $P(5, -3)$ and $Q(2, -4)$

3 Find the equation of the circle whose centre is $(2, -5)$ and which passes through the point $(3, 2)$.

4 Find the equation of the circle whose centre is $(2, -3)$ and which passes through the intersection of the lines $3x + 2y = 11$ and $2x + 3y = 4$.

5 Find the equation of a circle concentric with the circle $2x^2 + 2y^2 + 8x + 10y - 39 = 0$ and having its area equal to 16π sq units.

6 If one end of a diameter of circle $x^2 + y^2 - 4x - 6y + 11 = 0$ is (3, 4), then find the coordinate of the other end of the diameter.

7 Find the equation of the circle which touches the both axes in the first quadrant and whose radius is a.

8 Find the equation of the circle having centre (3, – 4) and touching the line $5x + 12y - 19 = 0$.

9 Find the area of the circle having centre at (1, 2) and passing through (4, 6).

10 A circle of radius 5 units touches the coordinate axes in the first quadrant. If the circle makes one complete roll on X-axis along the positive direction of X-axis, then find its equation in the new position.

11 If $lx + my = 1$ touches the circle $x^2 + y^2 = a^2$, then prove that the point (l, m) lies on the circle $x^2 + y^2 = a^{-2}$.

Short Answer Type Questions

4 Marks

12 Find the equation of the circle which passes through the points (2,–2) and (3,4) and whose centre lies on the line $x + y = 2$.

13 Find the equation of the circle passes through the points (2, 3) and (4, 5) and the centre lies on the straight line $y - 4x + 3 = 0$.

14 Find the equation of circle which is circumscribed about the triangle whose vertices are (– 2, 3), (5, 2) and (6, – 1).

15 Find the equation of circle circumscribing the triangle whose sides are the lines $y = x + 2$, $4x - 3y = 0$ and $3x - 2y = 0$.

16 Find the equation of a circle with origin as centre and passing through the vertices of an equilateral triangle whose median of length is $3a$.

17 Show that the points (9, 1), (7, 9), (– 2, 12) and (6, 10) are concyclic.

18 If $y = 2x$ is a chord of the circle $x^2 + y^2 - 10x = 0$, then find the equation of a circle with this chord as diameter.

19 Find the equation of a circle concentric with the circle $x^2 + y^2 - 6x + 12y + 15 = 0$ and has double its area.

20 Show that the points (x, y) given by $x = \frac{2at}{1+t^2}$ and $y = \frac{a(1-t^2)}{1+t^2}$ lies on a circle for all real values of t such that $-1 \le t \le 1$, where a is any given real numbers.

21 Find the equation of the circle concentric with the circle $x^2 + y^2 + 4x + 6y + 11 = 0$ and passing through the point $P(5, 4)$.

Hints & Answers

1. (i) Solve as Example 13. **Ans.** (– 4, – 5), 7

(ii) Solve as Example 13. **Ans.** (– 3, 4), $\sqrt{33}$

2. (i) Required equation of circle is

$$(x-2)(x+3)+(y+3)(y-5)=0.$$

Ans. $x^2 + y^2 + x - 2y - 21 = 0$

(ii) Solve as part (i).

Ans. $x^2 + y^2 - 7x + 7y + 22 = 0$

3. Let the equation of circle be $(x-2)^2 + (y+5)^2 = r^2$

$\Rightarrow \quad x^2 + 4 - 4x + y^2 + 25 + 10y = r^2$

$\Rightarrow \quad x^2 + y^2 - 4x + 10y + 29 - r^2 = 0$

Since, it passes through (3, 2).

$\therefore \quad 9 + 4 - 12 + 20 + 29 - r^2 = 0$

Ans. $x^2 + y^2 - 4x + 10y - 50 = 0$

4. Let the equation of circle be $(x-2)^2 + (y+3)^2 = r^2$

Intersection point is (5, – 2).

Ans. $x^2 + y^2 - 4x + 6y - 10 = 0$

5. Centre of given circle $x^2 + y^2 + 4x + 5y - \frac{39}{2} = 0$ is $\left(-2, -\frac{5}{2}\right)$ and area of circle, $\pi r^2 = 16\pi$

$\Rightarrow \quad r^2 = 16$

Then, the equation of required circle is

$$(x+2)^2 + \left(y + \frac{5}{2}\right)^2 = 16$$

Ans. $4x^2 + 4y^2 + 16x + 20y - 23 = 0$

6. Centre of circle is mid-point of end point of diameter.

Here, centre = (2, 3)

Let the other end be (x, y).

Then, $\frac{x+3}{2} = 2$, $\frac{y+4}{2} = 3$ **Ans.** (1, 2)

7. Required equation of circle is $(x-a)^2+(y-a)^2=a^2$

Ans. $x^2+y^2-2ax-2ay+a^2=0$

8. Centre of circle = $(3, -4)$

Radius of circle = Perpendicular distance of line $5x+12y-19=0$ from $(3, -4)$.

$$=\left|\frac{5(3)+12(-4)-19}{\sqrt{25+144}}\right|=\left|\frac{-52}{13}\right|=4$$

$\therefore$ Required equation of circle is

$$(x-3)^2+(y+4)^2=(4)^2.$$

Ans. $x^2+y^2-6x+8y+9=0$

9. Let equation of circle having centre (1, 2) be

$$(x-1)^2+(y-2)^2=r^2$$

Since, it passes through (4, 6).

$$\therefore \quad (4-1)^2+(6-2)^2=r^2$$

$$\Rightarrow \quad r^2=9+16=25 \Rightarrow r=5$$

Ans. 25π sq units

10. Let C be the centre of the circle in its initial position and D be its centre in the new position.

Then, $C \equiv (5, 5)$ and $D=(5+10\pi, 5)$

Now, centre of the circle in the new position is $(5+10\pi, 5)$ and its radius is 5, therefore its equation will be

$$(x-5-10\pi)^2+(y-5)^2=5^2$$

Ans. $x^2+y^2-10(2\pi+1)x-10y+100\pi^2+100\pi+25=0$

11. Given, $lx+my=1$ touches the circle $x^2+y^2=a^2$.

Then, length of perpendicular distance from the centre of the given circle i.e. (0, 0) on $lx+my+1=0$ is equal to radius.

$$\text{Then, } a=\left|\frac{0-0+1}{\sqrt{l^2+m^2}}\right|$$

12. Let the equation of circle with centre (h, k) and radius r be

$$(x-h)^2+(y-k)^2=r^2 \quad \text{...(i)}$$

Since, circle passes through the points $(2, -2)$ and $(3, 4)$, so the points $(2, -2)$ and $(3, 4)$ will lie on Eq. (i).

$$\therefore \quad (2-h)^2+(-2-k)^2=r^2 \quad \text{...(ii)}$$

$$\text{and} \quad (3-h)^2+(4-k)^2=r^2 \quad \text{...(iii)}$$

Now, from Eqs. (ii) and (iii), we get

$$(2-h)^2+(-2-k)^2=(3-h)^2+(4-k)^2$$

$$\Rightarrow \quad 2h+12k=17 \quad \text{...(iv)}$$

Also, given that centre (h, k) lies on $x+y=2$. So, it will satisfy it.

$$\therefore \quad h+k=2 \quad \text{...(v)}$$

On solving Eqs. (iv) and (v), we get

$$h=0.7, k=1.3$$

Put the values of h and k in Eq. (ii), we get the value of r, then substitute the values of h, k and r in Eq. (i), we get the required result.

Ans. $(x-0.7)^2+(y-1.3)^2=12.58$

13. Solve as Q. 12. **Ans.** $x^2+y^2-4x-10y+25=0$

14. Circle circumscribed about the triangle means the circle passes through the vertices. Let (h, k) be the centre and r be the radius of circle.

$$\text{Then,} \quad (-2-h)^2+(3-k)^2=r^2 \quad \text{...(i)}$$

$$(5-h)^2+(2-k)^2=r^2 \quad \text{...(ii)}$$

$$\text{and} \quad (6-h)^2+(-1-k)^2=r^2 \quad \text{...(iii)}$$

On solving Eqs. (i), (ii) and (iii), we get $h=1$, $k=-1$ and $r=5$. **Ans .** $x^2+y^2-2x+2y-23=0$

15. Solve as Example 29. **Ans.** $x^2+y^2-46x+22y=0$

16. Centroid of the triangle coincides with the centre of circle and the radius of circle is 2/3 of the length of median.

Ans. $x^2+y^2=4a^2$

17. Solve as Example 27.

18. The points of intersection of the given chord and the given circle are obtained by simultaneously solving $y=2x$ and $x^2+y^2-10x=0$.

On putting $y=2x$ in $x^2+y^2-10x=0$, we get

$$x^2+4x^2-10x=0$$

$$\Rightarrow \quad 5x(x-2)=0 \Rightarrow x=0 \text{ or } x=2$$

$$\text{Now,} \quad x=0 \Rightarrow y=0 \text{ and } x=2,\ y=4$$

Put the values of $x_1=0$, $y_1=0$, $x_2=2$ and $y_2=4$ in diametric form of a circle.

Ans. $x^2+y^2-2x-4y=0$

19. Given equation of the circle is

$$x^2+y^2-6x+12y+15=0$$

$\therefore$ Centre of this circle = $(3, -6)$

and radius of this circle = $\sqrt{9+36-15}=\sqrt{30}$

The required circle is concentric to the given circle.

$\therefore$ Its centre is also coincide. So, its centre is $(3, -6)$.

Let r be the radius of the required circle.

Then, according to the question,

$$\pi r^2=2\times\pi(\sqrt{30})^2$$

Ans. $x^2+y^2-6x+12y-15=0$.

20. Given, $x=\dfrac{2at}{1+t^2}$ and $y=\dfrac{a(1-t^2)}{1+t^2}$

On squaring and adding, we get

$$x^2+y^2=\left(\frac{2at}{1+t^2}\right)^2+\left[\frac{a(1-t^2)}{1+t^2}\right]^2$$ **Ans.** $x^2+y^2=a^2$

21. $\because$ Centre of the required circle is $C(-2, -3)$.

$\therefore$ Circle passes through the point $P(5, 4)$.

$$\therefore \quad \text{Radius}=|CP|=\sqrt{(5+2)^2+(4+3)^2}=7\sqrt{2}$$

Ans. $(x+2)^2+(y+3)^2=98$.

Chapter Practice

Multiple Choice Type Questions

1 Mark

1. If the equation of the circle with centre at (h, k) and radius r is $x^2 + y^2 = r^2$. Then, h and k respectively are
   (a) (1, 1) (b) (−1, −1)
   (c) (0, 0) (d) None of these

2. The coordinates of centre of the circle given by the equation $2x^2+2y^2+3x+4y+\frac{9}{8}=0$ are
   (a) $\left(\frac{3}{4},1\right)$ (b) $\left(-1,-\frac{3}{4}\right)$ (c) $\left(-\frac{3}{4},-1\right)$ (d) $\left(\frac{4}{3},1\right)$

3. The equation of circle having centre (2, 2) and rdius $\sqrt{8}$ is
   (a) $(x-2)^2+(y-2)^2=\sqrt{8}$ (b) $(x-2)^2+(y-2)^2=8$
   (c) $(x+2)^2+(y+2)^2=8$ (d) $(x-2)^2+(y-2)^2=-\sqrt{8}$

4. The equation of circle, whose end point of a diameter are $A(1, 5)$ and $B(-1, 3)$ is
   (a) $x^2+y^2-8y-14=0$ (b) $x^2+y^2-8y+14=0$
   (c) $x^2+y^2+8y+14=0$ (d) $x^2+y^2-6y+14=0$

5. The lines $2x-3y=5$ and $3x-4y=7$ are diameters of a circle of area 154 sq units. Then, the equation of circle is
   (a) $x^2+y^2-2x-2y-47=0$
   (b) $x^2+y^2-2x+2y-47=0$
   (c) $x^2+y^2+2x-2y-47=0$
   (d) $x^2+y^2-2x+2y-47=0$

Assertion-Reason Type Questions

1 Mark

Directions (Q. Nos. 6-10) *In the questions given below are two statements labelled as Assertion (A) and Reason (R). In the context of the two statements, which one of the following is correct?*

(a) Both A and R are correct; R is the correct explanation of A
(b) Both A and R are correct; R is not the correct explanation of A
(c) A is correct; R is incorrect
(d) R is correct; A is incorrect

6. **Assertion (A)** The radius of the circle given by the equation $x^2+y^2-6x-4y+4=0$ is 3 units.
   Reason (R) The form of equation $x^2+y^2+2gx+2fy+c=0$ is the general equation of the circle whose radius is $r=\sqrt{g^2+f^2+c}$.

7. **Assertion (A)** If the coordinates of the end points of diameter are (−1, 2) and (4, −3), then the equation of circle is $x^2+y^2-3x+y-10=0$.
   Reason (R) The equation of the circle drawn on the straight line joining two given points (x_1, y_1) and (x_2, y_2) as diameter is $(x-x_1)(x-x_2)+(y-y_1)(y-y_2)=0$.

8. **Assertion (A)** The circles $x^2+y^2-4x-6y-87=0$ and $2x^2+2y^2-8x-12y-9=0$ are concentric circles.
   Reason (R) Two circles having the same centre (h, k) but different radii r_1 and r_2 are called concentric circles.

9. **Assertion (A)** The equation of circle whose end points of a diameter are (−3, 7) and (2, −5) is $x^2+y^2+x-2y-41=0$.
   Reason (R) If (x_1, y_1) and (x_2, y_2) be the end points of the diameter of a circle, then the equation of circle is given by $(x-x_1)(x-x_2)+(y-y_1)(y-y_2)=0$.

10. **Assertion (A)** The point $P\left(-\frac{5}{2},\frac{7}{2}\right)$ lie inside the circle $x^2+y^2=25$.
   Reason (R) A circle $S\equiv x^2+y^2+2gx+2fy+c=0$ at any point (x_1, y_1) is $S_1\equiv x_1^2+y_1^2+2gx_1+2fy_1+c=0$
   If $S_1>0$, then the point P lies inside the circle.

Very Short Answer Type Questions

2 Marks

11. Find the equations of circles which passes through the point (3, 6) and touch both the axes.

12. Find the centre and radius of the circle $x^2+y^2+8x-10y+16=0$.

13. Find the equation of a circle having $(1, -2)$ as its centre and passing through the intersection of the lines $3x + y = 14$ and $2x + 5y = 18$.

14. Find the equation of the circle which passes through the origin and cuts off intercepts -2 and 3 from the coordinate axes.

15. The radius of the circle $x^2 + y^2 - 2x + 3y + k = 0$ is $2\frac{1}{2}$. Find the value of k.

16. Find the centre and radius of the circle $2x^2 + 2y^2 = 3x - 5y + 7$.

17. Find the parametric representation of the circle $x^2 + y^2 - 2x - 4y - 4 = 0$.

18. Find the cartesian equation of the curve $x = 7\cos\theta$, $y = -4 + 7\sin\theta$.

19. Find the lengths of the intercepts of the circle $3x^2 + 3y^2 - 5x + 3y = 0$ on the coordinate axes.

20. Find the length of the chord intercepted by the circle $x^2 + y^2 = 25$ on the line $2x - y + 5 = 0$.

21. One end of a diameter of the circle $x^2 + y^2 - 3x + 5y - 4 = 0$ is $(2, 1)$. Find the coordinates of the other end.

22. Write the equation of the circle whose centre is $(8, -6)$ and which passes through the point $(5, -2)$.

23. Find the equation of the circle which touch both the axes and has radius 3 units.

24. Find the equation of the circle passing through the three points $(5, 7)$, $(6, 6)$ and $(2, -2)$.

25. Find the parametric equation of the circle $x^2 + y^2 + 4x - 6y - 12 = 0$.

Short Answer Type Questions

4 Marks

26. If the equations of the two diameters of a circle are $x + y = 6$ and $x + 2y = 4$ and the radius of the circle is 10. Find the equation of the circle.

27. Find the centre and radius of each of the following circles.

(i) $\left(x - \frac{1}{2}\right)^2 + \left(y + \frac{1}{3}\right)^2 = \frac{1}{4}$

(ii) $x^2 + y^2 - 4x + 6y = 5$

28. Find the equation of the circle which touches the lines $x = 0$, $y = 0$ and $x = 4$ and lies in the first quadrant.

29. Find the equation of the circle concentric with the circle $x^2 + y^2 - 4x - 6y - 3 = 0$ and which touches the Y-axis.

30. If two diameters of a circle lie along the lines $x - y = 9$ and $x - 2y = 7$ and the area of the circle is 38.5 sq cm, then find the equation of the circle.

31. The sides of a rectangle are given by the equations $x = -2$, $x = 4$, $y = -2$ and $y = 5$. Find the equation of the circle drawn on the diagonal of this rectangle as its diameter.

32. Prove that the radii of the circles $x^2 + y^2 = 1$, $x^2 + y^2 - 2x - 6y - 6 = 0$ and $x^2 + y^2 - 4x - 12y - 9 = 0$ are in AP.

33. Find the points of intersection of the circle $3x^2 + 3y^2 - 29x - 19y + 56 = 0$ and the line $y = x + 2$. Also, find the length of the chord intercepts.

34. If $x = 4 + 5\cos\theta$ and $y = 3 + 5\sin\theta$, show that the locus of the point (x, y) as θ varies, is a circle. Find the centre and radius of the circle.

35. Find the equation of the circle circumscribing the triangle formed by the lines $x + y = 6$, $x - y = 4$, $2x - y = 3$.

Case-Based Type Question

6 Marks

36. Mr. Suraj Singh is a sincere citizen of "Laxmi Nikunj Society" in Lucknow. He makes a green garden in his plot which is in the shape of circle, i.e. shown in the below figure.

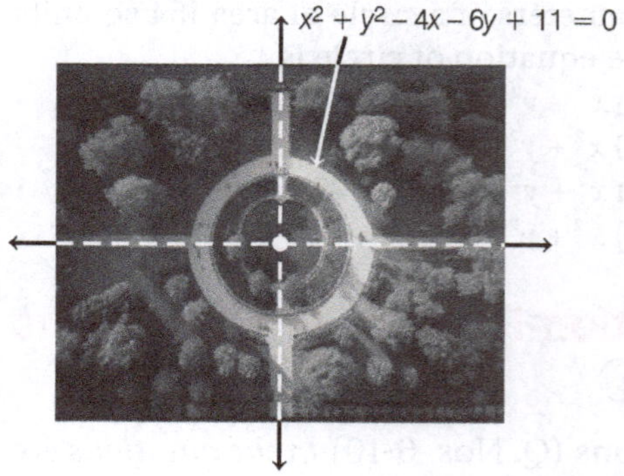

Now, answer the following questions which are based on above garden.

(i) Find the coordinates of centre of the garden.

(ii) What is the diameter of the garden?

(iii) If one end of a diameter of the circle shaped garden is $(3, 4)$, then find the coordinates of the other end of the diameter.

(iv) Write the diameter form of the equation of circle shaped garden.

Hints & Answers

1. (c) 2. (c) 3. (b) 4. (b) 5. (d)
6. (c) 7. (a) 8. (a) 9. (a) 10. (c)

11. Similar as Example 7 of Topic 1.

Ans. $x^2 + y^2 - 6x - 6y + 9 = 0$ and
$x^2 + y^2 - 30x - 30y + 225 = 0$

12. Similar as Example 10. (ii) of Topic 1.

Ans. $(-4, 5)$, 5

13. Similar as Example 14 of Topic 1.

Ans. $x^2 + y^2 - 2x + 4y - 20 = 0$

14.

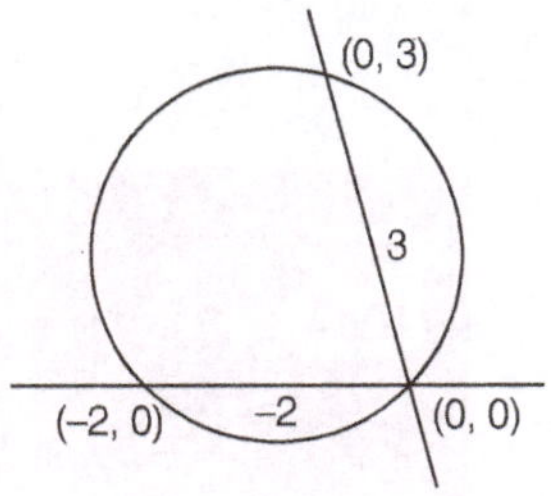

Ans. $x^2 + y^2 + 2x - 3y = 0$

15. $\sqrt{(-1)^2 + \left(-\frac{3}{2}\right)^2 - k} = 2\frac{1}{2}$

Ans. $k = -3$

16. $\left(\frac{3}{4}, \frac{-5}{4}\right); \frac{3}{4}\sqrt{10}$

17. $x = 1 + 3\cos\theta,\ y = 2 + 3\sin\theta$, where θ is a parameter.

18. Here, $x = 7\cos\theta$ and $y = -4 + 7\sin\theta$

$\Rightarrow \quad x^2 = 49\cos\theta, (y+4)^2 = 49\sin^2\theta$

Ans. $x^2 + (y+4)^2 = 49$

19. $\frac{5}{3}, 1$

20. $4\sqrt{5}$ units

21. $(1, -6)$

22. $x^2 + y^2 - 16x + 12y + 75 = 0$

23. $x^2 + y^2 \pm 6x \pm 6y + 9 = 0$

24. $x^2 + y^2 - 4x - 6y - 12 = 0$

25. $x = -2 + 5\cos t,\ y = 3 + 5\sin t,\ 0 \le t < 2\pi$

26. Given, radius, $(r) = 10$

and equations of diameters are

$$x + 2y = 4 \quad \text{...(i)}$$

and

$$x + y = 6 \quad \text{...(ii)}$$

On solving Eqs. (i) and (ii), we get

$$x = 8 \text{ and } y = -2$$

So, centre of the circle is $(8, -2)$.

Ans. $x^2 + y^2 - 16x + 4y - 32 = 0$

27. (i) On comparing the given equation with $(x-h)^2 + (y-k)^2 = r^2$, we get

Ans. $\left(\frac{1}{2}, -\frac{1}{3}\right)$ and $\frac{1}{2}$

(ii) On comparing the given equation with $x^2 + y^2 + 2gx + 2fy + c = 0$, we get

$$g = -2,\ f = 3 \quad \text{and} \quad c = -5$$

Now, centre $\equiv (-g, -f)$

and radius $= \sqrt{g^2 + f^2 - c}$

Ans. $(2, -3)$ and $3\sqrt{2}$

28.

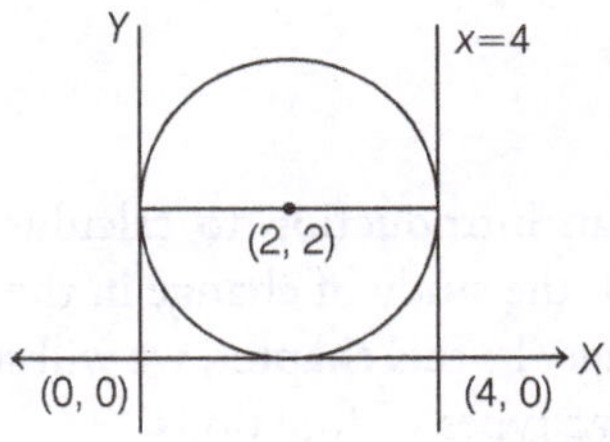

Ans. $(x-2)^2 + (y-2)^2 = 4$

29. Given, $\quad x^2 + y^2 - 4x - 6y - 3 = 0$

$\therefore$ Centre of the required circle is $(2, 3)$.

As it touches Y-axis, so its radius $= x$-coordinate of centre $= 2$.

Ans. $x^2 + y^2 - 4x - 6y + 9 = 0$

30. Given equations of diameters are

$$x - y = 9 \quad \text{...(i)}$$

and

$$x - 2y = 7 \quad \text{...(ii)}$$

On solving Eqs. (i) and (ii), we get

$$x = 11 \text{ and } y = 2$$

$\because$ Area of given circle $= 38.5\ \text{cm}^2$

$\Rightarrow \quad \pi r^2 = 38.5$

Ans. $4x^2 + 4y^2 - 88x - 16y + 451 = 0$

31. $x^2 + y^2 - 2x - 3y - 18 = 0,\ x^2 + y^2 + 4x - 9y + 24 = 0$

32. $x^2 + y^2 = (1)^2$

$\therefore$ Radius $= 1$

$$x^2 + y^2 - 2x - 6y - 6 = 0$$

$\therefore \quad$ Radius $= \sqrt{(1)^2 + (3)^2 + 6} = 4$

$$x^2 + y^2 - 4x - 12y - 9 = 0$$

$\therefore$ Radius $= \sqrt{(2)^2 + (6)^2 + 9} = 7$

33. $(1, 3), (5, 7); 4\sqrt{2}$

34. $x^2 + y^2 - 8x - 6y = 0; (4, 3); 5$

35. $x^2 + y^2 - 2x + 2y - 18 = 0$

36. (i) Centre $= (2, 3)$

(ii) radius $= \sqrt{2}$ units

(iii) $(1, 2)$

(iv) $(x-2)(x-1) + (y-3)(y-2) = 0$

CHAPTER

12

Limits

This chapter is an introduction to calculus, a branch of Mathematics, which mainly deals with the study of change in the value of a function as the points in the domain change. In this chapter, we will study the concept of limit and limits of some particular types of functions.

- Concept of Limit
- Limits of Rational Functions
- Limits of Trigonometric Functions

TOPIC 01 Concept of Limit

Intuitive Idea of Limit

Consider the function $f(x)=\dfrac{x^2-4}{x-2}$. Clearly, this function is defined for all x except at $x=2$ as it assumes the form $\dfrac{0}{0}$ (known as an indeterminate form) at $x=2$. However, if $x\neq 2$, then $f(x)=\dfrac{(x-2)(x+2)}{(x-2)}=(x+2)$ The following table exhibits the values of $f(x)$ at points which are close to 2.

x	$f(x)$
1.4	3.4
1.5	3.5
1.6	3.6
1.7	3.7
1.8	3.8
1.9	3.9
1.99	3.99
2	$\frac{0}{0}$
2.01	4.01
2.1	4.1
2.2	4.2
2.3	4.3
2.4	4.4
2.5	4.5
2.6	4.6

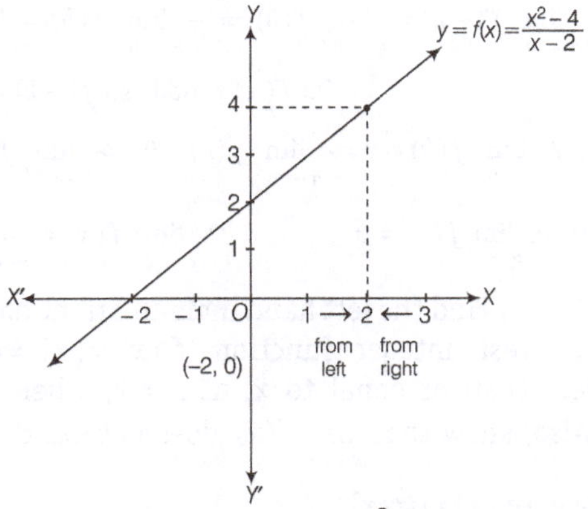

Graph of $f(x) = \dfrac{x^2-4}{x-2}$

It is evident from the above table and the graph of $f(x)$ that as x increases and comes closer to 2 from left hand side of 2, the values of $f(x)$ increase and come closer to 4. This can be restated as,

"When x approaches or tends to 2 from its left hand side, the function $f(x)$ approaches or tends to 4".

We use the notation $\lim_{x\to 2^-} f(x) = 4$ or $\lim_{x\to 2-0} f(x) = 4$ to express the above statement and read as left hand limit of $f(x)$ at $x = 2$ is 4.

Thus, $\lim_{x\to 2^-} f(x) = 4$ means that as x tends to 2 from left hand side, the values of $f(x)$ are tending to 4.

From the above table as well as the graph of $f(x)$, we also observe that as x decreases and comes closer to 2 from right hand side, the values of $f(x)$ decrease and come closer to 4. This can be restated as

"When x approaches or tends to 2 from its right hand side, the function $f(x)$ approaches or tends to 4."

We use the notation

$\lim_{x\to 2^+} f(x) = 4$ or $\lim_{x\to 2+0} f(x) = 4$ to express the above statement and read as right hand limit of $f(x)$ at $x = 2$ is 4.

Thus, $\lim_{x\to 2^+} f(x) = 4$ means that as x tends to 2 from right hand side, the values of $f(x)$ are tending to 4.

It follows from the above discussion that for the function

$$f(x) = \frac{x^2-4}{x-2},$$

(i) $\lim_{x\to 2^-} f(x) = 4$

(ii) $\lim_{x\to 2^+} f(x) = 4$

(iii) $\lim_{x\to 2^-} f(x) = \lim_{x\to 2^+} f(x)$

(iv) $f(2)$ does not exist, i.e. $f(x)$ is not defined at $x = 2$.

Note (i) $x \to a - 0$ or $x \to a^-$ is read as x tends to a from left and it means that x is very close to a but it is always less than a.

(ii) $x \to a + 0$ or $x \to a^+$ is read as x tends to a from right and it means that x is very close to a but it is always greater than a.

(iii) $x \to a$ is read as x tends to a and it means that x is very close to a but it is never equal to a. Here, x can tends or approaches to a from both sides of a.

Definition of Limit

If $f(x)$ approaches to a real number l, when x approaches to a (through lesser or greater values to a) i.e. if $f(x) \to l$ when $x \to a$, then l is called **limit** of the function $f(x)$. In symbolic form, it is written as $\lim_{x\to a} f(x) = l$.

Left Hand Limit (LHL)

A real number l_1 is the left hand limit of function $f(x)$ at $x = a$, if the values of $f(x)$ can be made as close as l_1 at points closed to a and on the left of a. Symbolically, it is written as LHL $= \lim_{x\to a^-} f(x) = l_1$.

Right Hand Limit

A real number l_2 is the right hand limit of function $f(x)$ at $x = a$, if the values of $f(x)$ can be made as close as l_2 at points closed to a and on the right of a.

Symbolically, it is written as

$$\text{RHL} = \lim_{x\to a^+} f(x) = l_2.$$

Existence of Limit

$\lim_{x\to a} f(x)$ exist iff $\lim_{x\to a^-} f(x) = \lim_{x\to a^+} f(x)$.

Note (i) The common value of LHL and RHL will be the limit of $f(x)$.

(ii) $\lim_{x\to a^-}$ (constant) = constant; $\lim_{x\to a^+}$ (constant) = constant and

$\lim_{x\to a}$ (constant) = constant. e.g. $\lim_{x\to 0^+} 2 = 2$

(iii) $\lim_{x\to 0^+} f(-x) = \lim_{x\to 0^-} f(x)$.

Method to Find the Left Hand and Right Hand Limits of a Function

With the help of following steps, we can find the left hand and right hand limits of a function easily

***Step* I** For left hand limit, at $x = a$ consider $\lim_{x\to a^-} f(x)$ and for right hand limit at $x = a$, consider $\lim_{x\to a^+} f(x)$.

***Step* II** For left hand limit, put $x = a - h$ and change the limit $x \to a^-$ by $h \to 0^+$, i.e. write

$$\lim_{h\to 0^-} f(x) = \lim_{h\to 0^+} f(a-h).$$

Similarly, for right hand limit, put $x = a + h$ and change the limit $x \to a^+$ by $h \to 0^+$, i.e. write $\lim_{x \to a^+} f(x) = \lim_{h \to 0^+} f(a+h)$.

Step III Now, simplify the result obtained in step II i.e. $\lim_{h \to 0} f(a-h)$ or $\lim_{h \to 0} f(a+h)$.

Note (i) $\lim_{x \to a^-} f(x) = \lim_{h \to 0^+} f(a-h)$ (ii) $\lim_{x \to a^+} f(x) = \lim_{h \to 0^+} f(a+h)$
(iii) $\lim_{x \to 0} f(x) = \lim_{h \to 0} f(a+h)$

Example 1 Suppose the function is defined by

$$f(x) = \begin{cases} \dfrac{|x-3|}{x-3}, & x \neq 3 \\ 0, & x = 3 \end{cases}$$

(i) Find the left hand limit of $f(x)$ at $x = 3$.
(ii) Find the right hand limit of $f(x)$ at $x = 3$.

Sol. Given, $f(x) = \begin{cases} \dfrac{|x-3|}{x-3}, & x \neq 3 \\ 0, & x = 3 \end{cases}$

(i) Clearly, left hand limit at $x = 3$ is

$$\lim_{x \to 3^-} f(x) = \lim_{x \to 3^-} \frac{|x-3|}{x-3} \quad \text{...(i)}$$

On putting $x = 3 - h$ and changing the limit $x \to 3^-$ by $h \to 0^+$ in Eq. (i), we get

$$\lim_{x \to 3^-} f(x) = \lim_{x \to 3^-} \frac{|x-3|}{x-3} = \lim_{h \to 0^+} \frac{|3-h-3|}{3-h-3}$$

$$= \lim_{h \to 0^+} \frac{|-h|}{-h} = \lim_{h \to 0^+} \frac{|h|}{-h}$$

$$\Rightarrow \lim_{x \to 3^-} f(x) = \lim_{h \to 0^+} \frac{h}{(-h)} \quad [\because |x| = x \text{ if } x > 0]$$

$$= \lim_{h \to 0^+} (-1)$$

(ii) Right hand limit at $x = 3$ is

$$\lim_{x \to 3^+} f(x) = \lim_{x \to 3^+} \frac{|x-3|}{x-3} \quad \text{...(ii)}$$

On putting $x = 3 + h$ and changing the limit $x \to 3^+$ by $h \to 0^+$ in Eq. (ii), we get

$$\lim_{x \to 3^+} f(x) = \lim_{x \to 3^+} \frac{|x-3|}{x-3} = \lim_{h \to 0^+} \frac{|h|}{h}$$

$$= \lim_{h \to 0^+} \frac{h}{h} = 1 \quad [\because |x| = x, \text{ if } x > 0]$$

Example 2 If f is an odd function and $\lim_{x \to 0} f(x)$ exists, then prove that this limit must be zero.

Sol. Since, $\lim_{x \to 0^-} f(x) = \lim_{x \to 0^+} f(x) \quad [\because \lim_{x \to 0} f(x) \text{ exists}]$

$$\Rightarrow \lim_{h \to 0^+} f(0-h) = \lim_{h \to 0^+} f(0+h)$$

$$\Rightarrow \lim_{h \to 0^+} f(-h) = \lim_{h \to 0^+} f(h) \Rightarrow -\lim_{h \to 0^+} f(h) = \lim_{h \to 0^+} f(h)$$

$$[\because f(x) \text{ is odd, so } f(-h) = -f(h)]$$

$$\Rightarrow 2 \lim_{h \to 0^+} f(h) = 0 \Rightarrow \lim_{h \to 0^+} f(h) = 0 \Rightarrow \lim_{x \to 0^+} f(x) = 0$$

Hence, $\lim_{h \to 0} f(x) = 0 \quad [\because \lim_{x \to 0^-} f(x) = \lim_{x \to 0^+} f(x)]$

Example 3 Find the left hand limit and right hand limit of the greatest integer function $f(x) = [x]$ = greatest integer less than or equal to x, at $x = k$, where k is an integer. Also, show that $\lim_{x \to k} f(x)$ does not exist.

Sol. We have, $f(x) = [x]$

LHL of f at $x = k$, $= \lim_{x \to k^-} f(x) = \lim_{h \to 0^+} f(k-h)$

$= \lim_{h \to 0^+} [k-h] = \lim_{h \to 0^+} (k-1)$

$[\because k-1 < k-h < k \Rightarrow [k-h] = k-1]$

$= k-1$

RHL of f at $x = k$, $= \lim_{x \to k^+} f(x)$

$= \lim_{h \to 0^+} f(k+h) = \lim_{h \to 0^+} [k+h]$

$= \lim_{h \to 0^+} k = k \quad [\because k < k+h < k+1 \Rightarrow [k+h] = k]$

Here, LHL $\neq$ RHL

$\therefore \lim_{x \to k} f(x)$ does not exist.

Fundamental Theorems on Limits

Let f and g be two real functions with common domain D, such that $\lim_{x \to a} f(x)$ and $\lim_{x \to a} g(x)$ exists. Then,

(i) Limit of sum of two functions is sum of the limits of the functions,
i.e. $\lim_{x \to a} (f+g)(x) = \lim_{x \to a} f(x) + \lim_{x \to a} g(x)$

(ii) Limit of difference of two functions is difference of the limits of the function,
i.e. $\lim_{x \to a} (f-g)(x) = \lim_{x \to a} f(x) - \lim_{x \to a} g(x)$

(iii) Limit of product of a constant and a function is the product of that constant and limit of a function,
i.e. $\lim_{x \to a} [c \cdot f(x)] = c \lim_{x \to a} f(x)$, where c is a constant.

(iv) Limit of product of two functions is product of the limits of the functions,
i.e. $\lim_{x \to a} [f(x) \cdot g(x)] = \lim_{x \to a} f(x) \cdot \lim_{x \to a} g(x)$

(v) Limit of quotient of two functions is quotient of the limits of the functions,
i.e. $\lim_{x \to a} \dfrac{f(x)}{g(x)} = \dfrac{\lim_{x \to a} f(x)}{\lim_{x \to a} g(x)}$, provided $\lim_{x \to a} g(x) \neq 0$.

(vi) $\lim_{x \to a} [f(x)]^n = [\lim_{x \to 0} f(x)]^n$, where n is a positive integer.

(vii) $\lim_{x \to a} [f(x)]^{g(x)} = [\lim_{x \to a} f(x)]^{\lim_{x \to a} g(x)}$

(viii) $\lim_{x \to a} \log f(x) = \log [\lim_{x \to a} f(x)]$

(ix) If $\lim_{x \to a} f(x) = +\infty$ or $-\infty$, then $\lim_{x \to a} \frac{1}{f(x)} = 0$

Some Useful Expansions

Some of the algebraic trigonometric formulae of immense utility in limits are

(i) $(x + a)^n = x^n + {}^nC_1 x^{n-1} a + {}^nC_2 x^{n-2} a^2 + \dots + a^n$ for all x and $n \in N$. [Binomial theorem for positive integral index]

(ii) $(1 + x)^n = 1 + nx + \frac{n(n-1)}{2!} x^2 + \frac{n(n-1)(n-2)}{3!} x^3 + \dots$ for $|x| < 1$.
[Binomial theorem for any index other than a positive integer]

(iii) $a^x = 1 + x \log_e a + \frac{x^2}{2!} (\log_e a)^2 + \dots \infty$

(iv) $e^x = 1 + x + \frac{x^2}{2!} + \frac{x^3}{3!} + \dots \infty$

(v) $\log_e (1 + x) = x - \frac{x^2}{2} + \frac{x^3}{3} - \frac{x^4}{4} \dots$, for $-1 < x \le 1$

(vi) $\log_e (1 - x) = -x - \frac{x^2}{2} - \frac{x^3}{3} - \frac{x^4}{4} \dots$, for $-1 < x < 1$

(vii) $\sin x = x - \frac{x^3}{3!} + \frac{x^5}{5!} - \frac{x^7}{7!} + \dots \infty$

(viii) $\cos x = 1 - \frac{x^2}{2!} + \frac{x^4}{4!} + \frac{x^6}{6!} + \dots \infty$

(ix) $\tan x = x + \frac{x^3}{3} + \frac{2}{15} x^5 + \dots \infty$

Indeterminate Forms

We know that if $\lim_{x \to a} f(x)$, $\lim_{x \to a} g(x)$ both exist and $\lim_{x \to a} g(x) \neq 0$, then $\lim_{x \to a} \frac{f(x)}{g(x)} = \frac{\lim_{x \to a} f(x)}{\lim_{x \to a} g(x)}$. The question arises, what happens if $\lim_{x \to a} g(x) = 0$?

If $\lim_{x \to a} f(x) = 0 = \lim_{x \to a} g(x)$, then $\frac{f(x)}{g(x)}$ is said to assume indeterminate form $\frac{0}{0}$ when $x \to a$. Besides $\frac{0}{0}$, we also have other indeterminate forms such as $\frac{\infty}{\infty}$, $\infty - \infty$, $0 \times \infty$, 1^∞, $\infty - \infty$ etc.

Limits of Polynomial Function

A function f is said to be a **polynomial function**, if $f(x) = a_0 + a_1 x + a_2 x^2 + \dots + a_n x^n$, where a_i's are real numbers.

Method to Find the Limit of a Polynomial

To find the limit of given polynomial, we use the algebra of limits. It can be understand in the following way

We know that, $\lim_{x \to a} x = a$. Therefore,

$$\lim_{x \to a} x^2 = \lim_{x \to a} (x \cdot x) = \lim_{x \to a} x \cdot \lim_{x \to a} x = a \cdot a = a^2$$

Similarly, $\lim_{x \to a} x^n = a^n$

Now, let $f(x) = a_0 + a_1 x + a_2 x^2 + \dots + a_n x^n$ be a polynomial function.

Then, limit of a polynomial function $f(x)$

$$= \lim_{x \to a} f(x) = \lim_{x \to a} [a_0 + a_1 x + a_2 x^2 + \dots + a_n x^n]$$

$$= \lim_{x \to a} a_0 + \lim_{x \to a} a_1 x + \lim_{x \to a} a_2 x^2 + \dots + \lim_{x \to a} a_n x^n$$

$$= a_0 + a_1 \lim_{x \to a} x + a_2 \lim_{x \to a} x^2 + \dots + a_n \lim_{x \to a} x^n$$

$$= a_0 + a_1 a + a_2 a^2 + \dots + a_n a^n = f(a)$$

Note If $f(x)$ is a polynomial function, then $\lim_{x \to a} f(x) = f(a)$ and so $\lim_{x \to a^-} f(x) = f(a)$ and $\lim_{x \to a^+} f(x) = f(a)$

[$\because \lim_{x \to a} f(a)$ exists iff $\lim_{x \to a^-} f(x) = \lim_{x \to a^+} f(x)$]

Example 4 Evaluate the following limit.

$$\lim_{x \to 3} (4x^3 - 2x^2 - x + 1)$$

Sol. We have, $\lim_{x \to 3} (4x^3 - 2x^2 - x + 1)$

$$= 4 \lim_{x \to 3} x^3 - 2 \lim_{x \to 3} x^2 - \lim_{x \to 3} x + \lim_{x \to 3} 1$$

$$= 4(3)^3 - 2(3)^2 - 3 + 1 = 108 - 18 - 2 = 88$$

Example 5 Let us consider two functions $f(x) = x^2 + 4$ and $g(x) = x - 3$ such that $f(x)$ and $g(x)$ exist at $x = 5$. Find the limit of the following functions at $x = 5$.

(i) $f(x) + g(x)$ (ii) $f(x) - g(x)$

(iii) $f(x) \times g(x)$ (iv) $\frac{f(x)}{g(x)}$

Sol. Given functions are $f(x) = x^2 + 4$ and $g(x) = x - 3$

Clearly, $\lim_{x \to 5} f(x) = \lim_{x \to 5} x^2 + 4$

$= (5)^2 + 4 = 25 + 4 = 29$ ...(i)

and $\lim_{x \to 5} g(x) = \lim_{x \to 5} (x - 3) = (5 - 3) = 2$ ...(ii)

(i) $\lim_{x \to 5} [f(x) + g(x)] = \lim_{x \to 5} f(x) + \lim_{x \to 5} g(x)$

$= 29 + 2$ [from Eqs. (i) and (ii)]

$= 31$

(ii) $\lim_{x \to 5} [f(x) - g(x)] = \lim_{x \to 5} f(x) - \lim_{x \to 5} g(x)$

$= 29 - 2 = 27$ [from Eqs. (i) and (ii)]

(iii) $\lim_{x \to 5} [f(x) \times g(x)] = \lim_{x \to 5} f(x) \times \lim_{x \to 5} g(x)$

$= 29 \times 2 = 58$ [from Eqs. (i) and (ii)]

(iv) $\lim_{x \to 5} \frac{f(x)}{g(x)} = \frac{\lim_{x \to 5} f(x)}{\lim_{x \to 5} g(x)}$ $[\because \lim_{x \to 5} g(x) = 2 \neq 0]$

$= \frac{29}{2} = 14.5$ [from Eqs. (i) and (ii)]

Example 6 Evaluate the left hand and right hand limits of the following function at $x = 2$.

$$f(x) = \begin{cases} 2x + 3, \text{ if } x \leq 2 \\ x + 5, \text{ if } x > 2 \end{cases}$$

Does $\lim_{x \to 2} f(x)$ exist?

Sol. Given, $f(x) = \begin{cases} 2x + 3, \text{ if } x \leq 2 \\ x + 5, \text{ if } x > 2 \end{cases}$

$\text{LHL} = \lim_{x \to 2^-} f(x) = \lim_{x \to 2^-} 2x + 3$

$[\because f(x) = 2x + 3, \text{ if } x \leq 2]$

$= 2(2) + 3 = 4 + 3 = 7$

and $\text{RHL} = \lim_{x \to 2^+} f(x)$

$= \lim_{x \to 2^+} (x + 5)$ $[\because f(x) = x + 5, \text{ if } x > 2]$

$= 2 + 5 = 7$

$\because$ LHL of $f(at\ x = 2) =$ RHL of $f(at\ x = 2)$

$\therefore \lim_{x \to 2} f(x)$ exists and it is equal to 7.

Example 7 Evaluate the left hand and right hand limits of the function defined by

$$f(x) = \begin{cases} 1 + x^2, \text{ if } 0 \leq x \leq 1 \\ 2 - x^2, \text{ if } x > 1 \end{cases} \text{ at } x = 1.$$

Also, show that $\lim_{x \to 1} f(x)$ does not exist.

Sol. We have, $f(x) = \begin{cases} 1 + x^2, \text{ if } 0 \leq x \leq 1 \\ 2 - x^2, \text{ if } x > 1 \end{cases}$

At $x = 1$, $\text{LHL} = \lim_{x \to 1^-} f(x)$

$= \lim_{x \to 1^-} (1 + x^2)$ $[\because f(x) = 1 + x^2, \text{ if } 0 \leq x \leq 1]$

$= 1 + 1^2 = 2$

$\text{RHL} = \lim_{x \to 1^+} f(x)$

$= \lim_{x \to 1^+} (2 - x^2)$ $[\because f(x) = 2 - x^2, \text{ if } x > 1]$

$= 2 - 1^2 = 2 - 1 = 1$

$\because$ LHL $\neq$ RHL

Therefore, $\lim_{x \to 1} f(x)$ does not exist.

Example 8 For what integers m and n does $\lim_{x \to 0} f(x)$ and $\lim_{x \to 1} f(x)$ exist, if $f(x) = \begin{cases} mx^2 + n, & x < 0 \\ nx + m, & 0 \leq x \leq 1 \\ nx^2 + m, & x > 1 \end{cases}$ **[NCERT]**

Sol. Given, $f(x) = \begin{cases} mx^2 + n, & x < 0 \\ nx + m, & 0 \leq x \leq 1 \\ nx^2 + m, & x > 1 \end{cases}$

Limit at $x = 0$

$\text{LHL} = \lim_{x \to 0^-} f(x) = \lim_{x \to 0^-} mx^2 + n = m(0)^2 + n$

$= n$

$\text{RHL} = \lim_{x \to 0^+} f(x) = \lim_{x \to 0^+} nx + m = n(0) + m = m$

Now, for $\lim_{x \to 0} f(x)$ to be exists.

LHL = RHL

$\Rightarrow$ $n = m$

Hence, $\lim_{x \to 0} f(x)$ exist when $m = n$

Limit at $x = 1$

$\text{LHL} = \lim_{x \to 1^-} f(x)$

$= \lim_{x \to 1^-} (nx + m) = n(1) + m = n + m$

$\text{RHL} = \lim_{x \to 1^+} f(x) = \lim_{x \to 1^+} (nx^2 + m)$

$= n(1)^2 + m$

$= n + m$

Now, for $\lim_{x \to 1} f(x)$ to be exists, $\lim_{x \to 1^+} f(x) = \lim_{x \to 1^-} f(x)$

$\Rightarrow h + m = h + m$, which is true for all $n, m \in Z$.

Hence, $\lim_{x \to 1} f(x)$ exists for all $n, m \in Z$.

Example 9 If $f(x) = \begin{cases} |x| + 1, & x < 0 \\ 0, & x = 0 \\ |x| - 1, & x > 0 \end{cases}$, for what value(s) of a does $\lim_{x \to a} f(x)$ exist? **[NCERT]**

Sol. We have, $f(x) = \begin{cases} -x + 1, & x < 0 \\ 0, & x = 0 \\ x - 1, & x > 0 \end{cases}$ $\left[\because |x| = \begin{cases} x, \text{ if } x \geq 0 \\ -x, \text{ if } x < 0 \end{cases}\right]$

Case I. When $a = 0$

In this case, LHL $\lim_{x \to 0^-} f(x) = \lim_{x \to 0^-} f(-x + 1)$

$[\because \text{for } x < 0, f(x) = -x + 1]$

$= -(0) + 1 = 1$

and RHL $= \lim_{x\to 0^+} f(x) = \lim_{x\to 0^+} x-1 = 0-1 = -1$ [$\because$ for $x>0$, $f(x)=x-1$]

$\because$ LHL $\neq$ RHL

$\therefore$ For $a=0$, $\lim_{x\to a} f(x)$ does not exists.

***Case* II. When $a<0$**

In this case, $\lim_{x\to a} f(x) = \lim_{x\to a}(-x+1)$ [$\because$ for $x<0$, $f(x)=-x+1$]

$= -a+1$, which is a fixed real number.

$\therefore$ For $a<0$, $\lim_{x\to a} f(x)$ exists.

***Case* III. When $a>0$**

In this case, $\lim_{x\to a} f(x) = \lim_{x\to a}(x-1)$ [$\because$ for $x>0$, $f(x)=x-1$]

$= a-1$, which is a fixed real number.

$\therefore$ For $a>0$, $\lim_{x\to a} f(x)$ exists.

Hence, from case I, II and III, we conclude that $\lim_{x\to a} f(x)$ exists for all $a\neq 0$.

Topic Practice 1

Very Short Answer Type Questions

2 Marks

1 Evaluate LHL and RHL of the $\lim_{x\to 0}\frac{|x|}{x}$.

2 Show that $\lim_{x\to 4}\frac{|x-4|}{x-4}$ does not exist. **[NCERT Exemplar]**

3 Evaluate $\lim_{x\to 1}[x-1]$, where [·] is greatest integer function.

4 Find the limits (i) $\lim_{x\to 1}[x^2-x-1]$ (ii) $\lim_{x\to 3}[x^2(x+1)]$

5 Find $\lim_{x\to 2^-}(x^2-x+1)$.

6 If $f(x)=\begin{cases} x+2, & x\le -1\\ cx^2, & x>-1\end{cases}$, then find c when $\lim_{x\to -1} f(x)$ exists. **[NCERT Exemplar]**

7 Let $f(x)$ be a function defined by

$$f(x)=\begin{cases} 6x-6, & \text{if } x\le 3\\ 2x-k, & \text{if } x>3\end{cases}.$$

Find the value of k, if $\lim_{x\to 3} f(x)$ exists.

Short Answer Type Questions

4 Marks

8 Evaluate the left hand and right hand limits of the following functions at $x=1$.

$$f(x)=\begin{cases} 5x-4, & \text{if } 0<x\le 1\\ 4x^2-3x, & \text{if } 1<x<2\end{cases}$$

Does $\lim_{x\to 1} f(x)$ exist?

9 Let $f(x)=\begin{cases} 2x+3, & \text{if } x\le 0\\ 3(x+1), & \text{if } x>0\end{cases}$, then

(i) evaluate $\lim_{x\to 0} f(x)$. (ii) evaluate $\lim_{x\to 1} f(x)$.

10 Suppose $f(x)=\begin{cases} a+bx, & x<1\\ 4, & x=1\\ b-ax, & x>1\end{cases}$, and if $\lim_{x\to 1} f(x)=f(1)$, then what are the possible values of a and b? **[NCERT]**

Hints & Answers

1. LHL $= \lim_{x\to 0^-}\frac{|x|}{x} = \frac{-x}{x}$ and RHL $= \lim_{x\to 0^+}\frac{|x|}{x} = \frac{x}{x}$

$\left[\because |x| = \begin{cases} x, & \text{if } x\ge 0\\ -x, & \text{if } x<0\end{cases}\right]$

Ans. LHL $=-1$ and RHL $=1$

2. Given, $\lim_{x\to 4}\frac{|x-4|}{x-4}$

LHL $= \lim_{x\to 4^-}\frac{-(x-4)}{x-4} = -1$ [$\because |x-4| = -(x-4)$, if $x<4$]

RHL $= \lim_{x\to 4^+}\frac{(x-4)}{x-4} = 1$ [$\because |x-4| = (x-4)$, if $x>4$]

3. LHL $= \lim_{x\to 1^-}[x-1] = \lim_{h\to 0^+}[1-h-1] = \lim_{h\to 0^+}[-h] = -1$

and RHL $= \lim_{x\to 1^+}[x-1] = \lim_{h\to 0^+}[1+h-1] = \lim_{h\to 0^+}[h] = 0$

Ans. Does not exist

4. If $f(x)$ is a polynomial function, then $\lim_{x\to a} f(x) = f(a)$

Ans. (i) -1 (ii) 36

5. If $f(x)$ is a polynomial function, then $\lim_{x\to a^-} f(x) = f(a)$.

Ans. 3

6. LHL $= \lim_{x\to -1^-}(x+2) = 1$

RHL $= \lim_{x\to -1^+} f(x) = \lim_{x\to -1^+} cx^2 = c$ **Ans.** $c=1$

7. We have, $f(x)=\begin{cases} 6x-6 & \text{if } x\le 3\\ 2x-k, & \text{if } x>3\end{cases}$

$\therefore$ LHL $= \lim_{x\to 3^-} f(x) = \lim_{x\to 3^-}(6x-6) = 12$

and RHL $= \lim_{x\to 3^+} f(x) = \lim_{x\to 3^+}(2x-k)$

$= 6-k$ **Ans.** $k=-6$

8. LHL $= \lim_{x\to 1^-}(5x-4) = 1$

and RHL $= \lim_{x\to 1^+} f(x) = \lim_{x\to 1^+}(4x^2-3x) = 1$

Ans. $\lim_{x\to 1} f(x)$ exists and it is equal to 1.

9. (i) LHL $= \lim_{x\to 0^-}(2x+3) = 3$, RHL $= \lim_{x\to 0^+} 3(x+1) = 3$ **Ans.** 3

(ii) $\lim_{x\to 1} f(x) = \lim_{x\to 1} 3(x+1)$ **Ans.** 6

10. LHL $= \lim_{x\to 1^-}(a+bx) = a+b$, RHL $= \lim_{x\to 1^+}(b-ax) = b-a$

$\because$ LHL $=$ RHL $= f(1) \Rightarrow a+b = b-a = 4$ **Ans.** $a=0, b=4$

TOPIC 02

Limits of Rational Functions

A function f is said to be a rational function, if $f(x) = \frac{g(x)}{h(x)}$, where $g(x)$ and $h(x)$ are polynomial functions such that $h(x) \neq 0$.

Then, $\lim_{x \to a} f(x) = \lim_{x \to a} \frac{g(x)}{h(x)} = \frac{\lim_{x \to a} g(x)}{\lim_{x \to a} h(x)} = \frac{g(a)}{h(a)}$

However, if $h(a) = 0$, then two cases are arise,
(i) $g(a) \neq 0$ (ii) $g(a) = 0$.

In the first case, we say that the limit does not exist.

In the second case, we can find limit.

Limit of a rational function can be find with the help of following methods

1. Direct Substitution Method

In this method, we substitute the point, to which the variable tends to in the given limit. If it give us a real number, then the number so obtained is the limit of the function and if it does not give us a real number, then use other methods.

Example 1 Find the limits of the following.

(i) $\lim_{x \to 2} \frac{x^2 - 4}{x + 3}$ (ii) $\lim_{x \to -1} \frac{(x-1)^2 + 3x^2}{(x^4 + 1)^2}$

(iii) $\lim_{x \to 0} \frac{\sqrt{2 + x} + \sqrt{2 - x}}{2 + x}$ **[NCERT]**

Sol. (i) $\lim_{x \to 2} \frac{x^2 - 4}{x + 3} = \frac{4 - 4}{2 + 3} = \frac{0}{5} = 0$ [here, $h(a) \neq 0$]

(ii) $\lim_{x \to -1} \frac{(x-1)^2 + 3x^2}{(x^4 + 1)^2} = \frac{(-1-1)^2 + 3(-1)^2}{((-1)^4 + 1)^2} = \frac{(-2)^2 + 3(1)}{(1+1)^2}$

$= \frac{4+3}{2^2} = \frac{7}{4}$

(iii) $\lim_{x \to 0} \frac{\sqrt{2+x} + \sqrt{2-x}}{2+x} = \frac{\sqrt{2+0} + \sqrt{2-0}}{2+0}$

$= \frac{\sqrt{2} + \sqrt{2}}{2} = \frac{2\sqrt{2}}{2} = \sqrt{2}$

Example 2 Evaluate $\lim_{x \to 1} \frac{x - 4}{3 - \sqrt{13 - x}}$.

Sol. $\lim_{x \to 1} \frac{x - 4}{3 - \sqrt{13 - x}} = \frac{-3}{3 - \sqrt{12}}$

$= \frac{-3}{3 - 2\sqrt{3}} = \frac{-3(3 + 2\sqrt{3})}{(3 - 2\sqrt{3})(3 + 2\sqrt{3})} = \frac{-3(3 + 2\sqrt{3})}{9 - 12}$

$= \frac{-3(3 + 2\sqrt{3})}{-3} = 3 + 2\sqrt{3}$

2. Factorisation Method

Let $\lim_{x \to a} \frac{f(x)}{g(x)}$ reduces to the form $\frac{0}{0}$, when we substitute $x = a$.

Then, we factorise $f(x)$ and $g(x)$ and then cancel out the common factor to evaluate the limit.

Working Rule to Determine the Limit by using Factorisation Method

In this method, we use the following steps

***Step* I** Write the given limit, $\lim_{x \to a} \frac{f(x)}{g(x)}$.

If $\lim_{x \to a} f(x) = 0$ and $\lim_{x \to a} g(x) = 0$, then go to next step, otherwise use direct substitution method.

***Step* II** Factorise $f(x)$ and $g(x)$, such that $(x - a)$ is a common factor and write given limit as

$$\lim_{x \to a} \frac{(x - a) f_1(x)}{(x - a) g_1(x)}.$$

***Step* III** Cancel the common factor. The limit obtained in step III becomes $\lim_{x \to a} \frac{f_1(x)}{g_1(x)}$.

***Step* IV** If $\lim_{x \to a} f_1(x) = 0 = \lim_{x \to a} g_1(x)$, then proceed same as in step II. Otherwise use direct substitution method to obtain limit.

Some Important Formulae

(i) $(a^2 - b^2) = (a - b)(a + b)$
(ii) $a^3 - b^3 = (a - b)(a^2 + ab + b^2)$
(iii) $a^3 + b^3 = (a + b)(a^2 - ab + b^2)$
(iv) $a^4 - b^4 = (a^2 - b^2)(a^2 + b^2)$
$= (a - b)(a + b)(a^2 + b^2)$
(v) If $f(\alpha) = 0$, then $x - \alpha$ is a factor of $f(x)$.

Example 3 Evaluate $L = \lim_{x \to 2} \frac{x^3 - 8}{(x - 2)}$.

Sol. We have, $L = \lim_{x \to 2} \frac{x^3 - 8}{x - 2}$.

Let $f(x) = x^3 - 8$ and $g(x) = x - 2$

Here, $\lim_{x \to 2} f(x) = \lim_{x \to 2} x^3 - 8 = 2^3 - 8 = 0$

and $\lim_{x\to 2} g(x) = \lim_{x\to 2} x - 2 = 2 - 2 = 0$

Thus, we get $\frac{0}{0}$ form.

Now, factorise $f(x)$ and $g(x)$ such that $(x-2)$ is a common factor.

Here, $f(x) = x^3 - 8 = (x^3 - 2^3)$

$= (x-2)(x^2 + 4 + 2x)$ and $g(x) = x - 2$

$$\therefore \quad L = \lim_{x\to 2} \frac{(x-2)(x^2+4+2x)}{(x-2)}$$

On cancelling the common factor $(x-2)$, we get

$$L = \lim_{x\to 2} (x^2 + 4 + 2x)$$

$$= (2)^2 + 4 + 2(2) = 4 + 4 + 4 = 12$$

Hence, $\lim_{x\to 2} \frac{x^3-8}{x-2} = 12$

Note We cancelled the term $(x-2)$ in the above calculation, because $x \neq 2$.

Example 4 Evaluate $\lim_{x\to \frac{1}{2}} \frac{4x^2-1}{2x-1}$.

Sol. On putting $x = \frac{1}{2}$, we get the form $\frac{0}{0}$.

So, let us first factorise it.

Consider, $\lim_{x\to \frac{1}{2}} \frac{4x^2-1}{2x-1} = \lim_{x\to \frac{1}{2}} \frac{(2x+1)(2x-1)}{(2x-1)}$

[using factorisation method]

$$= \lim_{x\to \frac{1}{2}} (2x+1) = 2\left(\frac{1}{2}\right) + 1 = 2$$

Example 5 Evaluate $\lim_{x\to 2} \left[\frac{x^2-4}{x^3-4x^2+4x}\right]$.

Sol. On putting $x = 2$, we get the form $\frac{0}{0}$. So, let us first factorise it.

Consider, $\lim_{x\to 2} \frac{x^2-4}{x^3-4x^2+4x} = \lim_{x\to 2} \frac{(x+2)(x-2)}{x(x-2)^2}$

$$= \lim_{x\to 2} \frac{(x+2)}{x(x-2)} = \frac{2+2}{2(2-2)} = \frac{4}{0}$$

which is not defined.

$\therefore \lim_{x\to 2} \left[\frac{x^2-4}{x^3-4x^2+4x}\right]$ does not exist.

Example 6 Evaluate $\lim_{x\to \sqrt{3}} \frac{x^2-3}{x^2+3\sqrt{3}\,x-12}$.

Sol. $\lim_{x\to \sqrt{3}} \frac{x^2-3}{x^2+3\sqrt{3}\,x-12} = \lim_{x\to \sqrt{3}} \frac{(x-\sqrt{3})(x+\sqrt{3})}{x^2+4\sqrt{3}x-\sqrt{3}x-12}$

$$= \lim_{x\to \sqrt{3}} \frac{(x-\sqrt{3})(x+\sqrt{3})}{(x+4\sqrt{3})(x-\sqrt{3})}$$

$$= \lim_{x\to \sqrt{3}} \frac{(x+\sqrt{3})}{(x+4\sqrt{3})} = \frac{\sqrt{3}+\sqrt{3}}{\sqrt{3}+4\sqrt{3}} = \frac{2\sqrt{3}}{5\sqrt{3}} = \frac{2}{5}$$

Example 7 Evaluate $\lim_{x\to 1} \left(\frac{2}{1-x^2} + \frac{1}{x-1}\right)$.

Sol. We have, $\lim_{x\to 1} \left(\frac{2}{1-x^2} + \frac{1}{x-1}\right) = \lim_{x\to 1} \left(\frac{2}{1-x^2} - \frac{1}{1-x}\right)$

[$\infty - \infty$ form]

$$= \lim_{x\to 1} \frac{2-(1+x)}{1-x^2} \quad \left[\frac{0}{0} \text{ form}\right]$$

$$= \lim_{x\to 1} \frac{1-x}{1-x^2} = \lim_{x\to 1} \frac{1}{1+x} = \frac{1}{2}.$$

Example 8 Find the limit

$$\lim_{x\to 1} \left[\frac{x-2}{x^2-x} - \frac{1}{x^3-3x^2+2x}\right].$$

[NCERT]

Sol. Here, $\left[\frac{x-2}{x^2-x} - \frac{1}{x^3-3x^2+2x}\right]$

$$= \left[\frac{x-2}{x(x-1)} - \frac{1}{x(x^2-3x+2)}\right]$$

$$= \left[\frac{x-2}{x(x-1)} - \frac{1}{x(x-1)(x-2)}\right]$$

$$= \frac{(x-2)^2-1}{x(x-1)(x-2)} = \left[\frac{x^2-4x+4-1}{x(x-1)(x-2)}\right]$$

$$= \left[\frac{x^2-4x+3}{x(x-1)(x-2)}\right] = \frac{(x-3)(x-1)}{x(x-1)(x-2)}$$

$$\therefore \quad \lim_{x\to 1} \left[\frac{x^2-2}{x^2-x} - \frac{1}{x^3-3x^2+2x}\right]$$

$$= \lim_{x\to 1} \frac{(x-3)(x-1)}{x(x-1)(x-2)}$$

$$= \lim_{x\to 1} \frac{x-3}{x(x-2)} = \frac{1-3}{1(1-2)} = \frac{-2}{-1} = 2$$

3. Rationalisation Method

If we get $\frac{0}{0}$ form and numerator or denominator or both have radical sign, then we first rationalise the numerator or denominator or both by multiplying their conjugate to remove $\frac{0}{0}$ form and then find limit by direct substitution method.

Example 9 Evaluate $\lim_{x \to 0} \frac{\sqrt{2+x}-\sqrt{2}}{x}$. **[NCERT Exemplar]**

Sol. When $x = 0$, then the expression $\frac{\sqrt{2+x}-\sqrt{2}}{x}$ reduces to $\frac{0}{0}$ form. So,we will rationalise the numerator by multiplying and dividing its conjugate i.e. $\sqrt{2+x}+\sqrt{2}$.

$$\therefore \lim_{x \to 0} \frac{\sqrt{2+x}-\sqrt{2}}{x} = \lim_{x \to 0} \frac{(\sqrt{2+x}-\sqrt{2})(\sqrt{2+x}+\sqrt{2})}{x(\sqrt{2+x}+\sqrt{2})}$$

[multiplying numerator and denominator by $\sqrt{2+x}+\sqrt{2}$]

$$= \lim_{x \to 0} \frac{2+x-2}{x(\sqrt{2+x}+\sqrt{2})} = \lim_{x \to 0} \frac{1}{\sqrt{2+x}+\sqrt{2}} = \frac{1}{2\sqrt{2}}$$

[using direct substitution method]

Example 10 Evaluate $\lim_{x \to a} \frac{\sqrt{a+2x}-\sqrt{3x}}{\sqrt{3a+x}-2\sqrt{x}}$. **[NCERT Exemplar]**

Sol. We have, $\lim_{x \to a} \frac{\sqrt{a+2x}-\sqrt{3x}}{\sqrt{3a+x}-2\sqrt{x}}$

$$= \lim_{x \to a} \frac{\sqrt{a+2x}-\sqrt{3x}}{\sqrt{3a+x}-2\sqrt{x}} \times \frac{\sqrt{a+2x}+\sqrt{3x}}{\sqrt{a+2x}+\sqrt{3x}}$$

[multiplying numerator and denominator by $\sqrt{a+2x}+\sqrt{3x}$]

$$= \lim_{x \to a} \frac{a+2x-3x}{(\sqrt{3a+x}-2\sqrt{x})(\sqrt{a+2x}+\sqrt{3x})}$$

[$\because (A-B)(A+B) = A^2 - B^2$]

$$= \lim_{x \to a} \frac{(a-x)(\sqrt{3a+x}+2\sqrt{x})}{(\sqrt{a+2x}+\sqrt{3x})(\sqrt{3a+x}-2\sqrt{x})(\sqrt{3a+x}+2\sqrt{x})}$$

[multiplying numerator and denominator by $\sqrt{3a+x}+2\sqrt{x}$]

$$= \lim_{x \to a} \frac{(a-x)[\sqrt{3a+x}+2\sqrt{x}]}{(\sqrt{a+2x}+\sqrt{3x})(3a+x-4x)}$$

$$= \lim_{x \to a} \frac{(a-x)(\sqrt{3a+x}+2\sqrt{x})}{(\sqrt{a+2x}+\sqrt{3x})(3a-3x)}$$

$$= \frac{\sqrt{3a+a}+2\sqrt{a}}{3(\sqrt{a+2a}+\sqrt{3a})} = \frac{4\sqrt{a}}{3 \times 2\sqrt{3}\sqrt{a}}$$

$$= \frac{2}{3\sqrt{3}} = \frac{2\sqrt{3}}{9}$$

Example 11 Evaluate $\lim_{x \to 1} \frac{(2x-3)(\sqrt{x}-1)}{2x^2+x-3}$.

Sol. We have, $\lim_{x \to 1} \frac{(2x-3)(\sqrt{x}-1)}{2x^2+x-3}$

$$= \lim_{x \to 1} \frac{(2x-3)(\sqrt{x}-1)(\sqrt{x}+1)}{(\sqrt{x}+1)(2x^2+x-3)}$$

$$= \lim_{x \to 1} \frac{(2x-3)(x-1)}{(\sqrt{x}+1)(2x^2+x-3)} \quad \left[\frac{0}{0}\text{ form}\right]$$

$$= \lim_{x \to 1} \frac{(2x-3)(x-1)}{(\sqrt{x}+1)(2x+3)(x-1)}$$

$$= \lim_{x \to 1} \frac{2x-3}{(\sqrt{x}+1)(2x+3)} = -\frac{1}{10}$$

Some Standard Limits

If the given limit is of the form $\lim_{x \to a} \frac{x^n - a^n}{x-a}$, then we can find the limit directly by using the following theorem

Theorem Let n be any positive integer. Then,

$$\lim_{x \to a} \frac{x^n - a^n}{x-a} = na^{n-1}$$

Proof We know that,

$$x^n - a^n = (x-a)(x^{n-1} + ax^{n-2} + \ldots + a^{n-2}x + a^{n-1})$$

On dividing both sides by $(x-a)$, we get

$$\frac{x^n - a^n}{x-a} = x^{n-1} + ax^{n-2} + \ldots + a^{n-2}x + a^{n-1}$$

Thus, $\lim_{x \to a} \frac{x^n - a^n}{x-a}$

$$= \lim_{x \to a} (x^{n-1} + ax^{n-2} + \ldots + a^{n-2}x + a^{n-1})$$

$$= a^{n-1} + a(a^{n-2}) + \ldots + a^{n-2}\, a + a^{n-1}$$

$$= a^{n-1} + a^{n-1} + \ldots + a^{n-1} + a^{n-1} \quad [n \text{ terms}]$$

$$= na^{n-1}$$

Note The above theorem i.e. $\lim_{x \to a} \frac{x^n - a^n}{x-a} = na^{n-1}$ is also true, if n is any rational number and a is positive.

Example 12 Evaluate $\lim_{x \to 2} \frac{x^{10} - 1024}{x-2}$.

Sol. When $x = 2$, the expression $\frac{x^{10} - 1024}{x-2}$ reduces to $\frac{0}{0}$ form.

Now, $\lim_{x \to 2} \frac{x^{10} - 1024}{x-2} = \lim_{x \to 2} \frac{x^{10} - 2^{10}}{x-2} = 10(2^{10-1}) = 5120$

Example 13 Evaluate $\lim_{x\to 2}\frac{x-2}{\sqrt[3]{x}-\sqrt[3]{2}}$.

Sol. $\lim_{x\to 2}\frac{x-2}{x^{1/3}-2^{1/3}}=\frac{1}{\lim_{x\to 2}\frac{x^{1/3}-2^{1/3}}{x-2}}$

$=\frac{1}{\frac{1}{3}(2^{1/3-1})}=\frac{1}{\frac{1}{3}\times(2^{-2/3})}=3(2^{2/3})$

Example 14 Find all the possible values of a, if $\lim_{x\to a}\frac{x^9-a^9}{x-a}=\lim_{x\to 5}(4+x)$.

Sol. We have, $\lim_{x\to a}\frac{x^9-a^9}{x-a}=\lim_{x\to 5}(4+x)$ ...(i)

Since, $\lim_{x\to a}\frac{x^9-a^9}{x-a}=9(a)^{9-1}=9a^8$ $\left[\because \lim_{x\to a}\frac{x^n-a^n}{x-a}=na^{n-1}\right]$

and $\lim_{x\to 5}(4+x)=4+5=9$

From Eq. (i), $9a^8=9 \Rightarrow a^8=1 \Rightarrow a=\pm 1$

Example 15 If $\lim_{x\to 1}\frac{x^4-1}{x-1}=\lim_{x\to k}\frac{x^3-k^3}{x^2-k^2}$, then find the value of k. **[NCERT Exemplar]**

Sol. Given, $\lim_{x\to 1}\frac{x^4-1}{x-1}=\lim_{x\to k}\frac{x^3-k^3}{x^2-k^2}$

$\Rightarrow 4(1)^{4-1}=\lim_{x\to k}\frac{\frac{x^3-k^3}{x-k}}{\frac{x^2-k^2}{x-k}}$ $\left[\because \lim_{x\to a}\frac{x^n-a^n}{x-a}=na^{n-1}\right]$

$\Rightarrow 4=\frac{\lim_{x\to k}\frac{x^3-k^3}{x-k}}{\lim_{x\to k}\frac{x^2-k^2}{x-k}}$ $\left[\because \lim_{x\to a}\frac{f(x)}{g(x)}=\frac{\lim_{x\to a}f(x)}{\lim_{x\to a}g(x)}\right]$

$\Rightarrow 4=\frac{3k^2}{2k} \Rightarrow 4=\frac{3}{2}k$

$\therefore k=\frac{4\times 2}{3}=\frac{8}{3}$

Example 16 Find the limit $\lim_{x\to 0}\frac{\sqrt{1+x}-1}{x}$. **[NCERT]**

Sol. Put $y=1+x$, then $y\to 1$ as $x\to 0$.

$\therefore \lim_{x\to 0}\frac{\sqrt{1+x}-1}{x}=\lim_{y\to 1}\frac{\sqrt{y}-1}{y-1}$ $[\because x+1=y\Rightarrow x=y-1]$

$=\lim_{y\to 1}\frac{y^{\frac{1}{2}}-1^{\frac{1}{2}}}{y-1}=\frac{1}{2}(1)^{\frac{1}{2}-1}$ $\left[\because \lim_{x\to a}\frac{x^n-a^n}{x-a}=na^{n-1}\right]$

$=\frac{1}{2}$

Example 17 Evaluate $\lim_{x\to a}\frac{(x+2)^{3/2}-(a+2)^{3/2}}{x-a}$.

Sol. Let $x+2=y$, then $y\to a+2$ as $x\to a$

$\therefore \lim_{x\to a}\frac{(x+2)^{3/2}-(a+2)^{3/2}}{x-a}$

$=\lim_{y\to(a+2)}\frac{y^{3/2}-(a+2)^{3/2}}{y-(a+2)}$ $[\because x+2=y\Rightarrow x=y-2]$

$=\frac{3}{2}(a+2)^{\frac{3}{2}-1}=\frac{3}{2}(a+2)^{1/2}$ $\left[\because \lim_{x\to a}\frac{x^n-a^n}{x-a}=na^{n-1}\right]$

Example 18 Evaluate $\lim_{x\to 2}\frac{(2x+4)^{1/3}-2}{x-2}$.

Sol. Put $2x+4=y$, then $y\to 8$, as $x\to 2$

$\therefore \lim_{x\to 2}\frac{(2x+4)^{1/3}-2}{x-2}=\lim_{y\to 8}\frac{y^{1/3}-2}{\frac{y-4}{2}-2}$ $\left[\because 2x+4=y \Rightarrow x=\frac{y-4}{2}\right]$

$=2\lim_{y\to 8}\frac{y^{1/3}-(8)^{1/3}}{y-4-4}$ $[\because 2=(8)^{1/3}]$

$=2\lim_{y\to 8}\frac{y^{1/3}-8^{1/3}}{y-8}$

$=2\cdot\frac{1}{3}(8)^{\frac{1}{3}-1}$ $\left[\because \lim_{x\to a}\frac{x^n-a^n}{x-a}=na^{n-1}\right]$

$=2\cdot\frac{1}{3}(2^3)^{-\frac{2}{3}}=\frac{2}{3}\cdot(2)^{-2}$

$=\frac{2}{3}\times\frac{1}{4}=\frac{1}{6}$

Example 19 Evaluate

$$\lim_{x\to 1}\frac{x^n+x^{n-1}+x^{n-2}+\ldots+x^2+x-n}{x-1}.$$

Sol. $\lim_{x\to 1}\frac{x^n+x^{n-1}+x^{n-2}+\ldots+x^2+x-n}{x-1}$

$=\lim_{x\to 1}\frac{(x^n-1)+(x^{n-1}-1)+\ldots+(x^2-1)+(x-1)}{(x-1)}$

$[\because n=1+1+1+\ldots\text{to } n \text{ terms}]$

$=\lim_{x\to 1}\frac{x^n-1^n}{x-1}+\lim_{x\to 1}\frac{x^{n-1}-1^{n-1}}{x-1}$

$+\ldots+\lim_{x\to 1}\frac{x^2-1^2}{x-1}+\lim_{x\to 1}\frac{x-1}{x-1}$

$=n(1)^{n-1}+(n-1)(1)^{n-2}+\ldots+2(1)^{2-1}+1$ $\left[\because \lim_{x\to a}\frac{x^n-a^n}{x-a}=na^{n-1}\right]$

$=n+(n-1)+\ldots+2+1=\frac{n(n+1)}{2}$ $\left[\because \Sigma n=\frac{n(n+1)}{2}\right]$

Algebraic Limits at Infinity

Consider the functions $f(x)=\frac{1}{x}$ and $g(x)=\frac{1}{x^2}$.

The graphs of these functions are shown in below figure

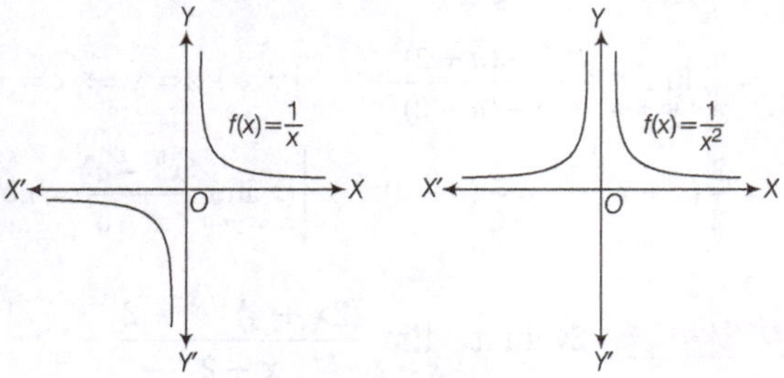

Graph of $f(x)=\frac{1}{x}$ Graph of $f(x)=\frac{1}{x^2}$

We can observe from the graphs that, when x is indefinitely large, then $\frac{1}{x}$ and $\frac{1}{x^2}$ are indefinitely small, i.e. very close to zero. In such cases, we write

$$\lim_{x\to+\infty}\frac{1}{x}=0 \text{ and } \lim_{x\to+\infty}\frac{1}{x^2}=0$$

Similarly, $\lim_{x\to-\infty}\frac{1}{x}=0$ and $\lim_{x\to-\infty}\frac{1}{x^2}=0$

Some More Results from Graphs of Real Functions

(i) $\lim_{x\to+\infty} x\to+\infty$ (ii) $\lim_{x\to-\infty} x\to-\infty$

(iii) $\lim_{x\to+\infty} x^2\to+\infty$ (iv) $\lim_{x\to-\infty} x^2\to+\infty$

To Find $\lim_{x\to\infty} f(x)$

Rule I (i) Firstly divide the numerator and denominator of the fraction by the highest power of x present in the fraction.

(ii) Use the idea of $\frac{1}{x}, \frac{1}{x^2}, \ldots, \to 0$ as $x\to\infty$.

Rule II Put $x=\frac{1}{y}$ and change the limit $x\to\infty$, to $y\to 0$.

Example 20 Evaluate the following limits.

(i) $\lim_{x\to\infty}\frac{(x+1)(2x+3)}{(x+2)(3x+4)}$

(ii) $\lim_{x\to\infty}(\sqrt{x^2+5x+4}-\sqrt{x^2-3x+4})$

Sol. (i) $\lim_{x\to\infty}\frac{(x+1)(2x+3)}{(x+2)(3x+4)}=\lim_{x\to\infty}\frac{2x^2+5x+3}{3x^2+10x+8}$

$$=\lim_{x\to\infty}\frac{2+\frac{5}{x}+\frac{3}{x^2}}{3+\frac{10}{x}+\frac{8}{x^2}}$$

[dividing numerator and denominator by x^2]

$$=\frac{2}{3} \qquad \left[\because \lim_{x\to\infty}\frac{1}{x}=0 \lim_{x\to\infty}\frac{1}{x^2}\right]$$

(ii) $\lim_{x\to\infty}(\sqrt{x^2+5x+4}-\sqrt{x^2-3x+4})$

$$=\lim_{x\to\infty}\frac{\sqrt{x^2+5x+4}-\sqrt{x^2-3x+4}}{1}\cdot\frac{\sqrt{x^2+5x+4}+\sqrt{x^2-3x+4}}{\sqrt{x^2+5x+4}+\sqrt{x^2-3x+4}}$$

[rationalising the numerator]

$$=\lim_{x\to\infty}\frac{(x^2+5x+4)-(x^2-3x+4)}{\sqrt{x^2+5x+4}+\sqrt{x^2-3x+4}}$$

$$=\lim_{x\to\infty}\frac{8x}{\sqrt{x^2+5x+4}+\sqrt{x^2-3x+4}}$$

$$=\lim_{x\to\infty}\frac{8}{\sqrt{1+\frac{5}{x}+\frac{4}{x^2}}+\sqrt{1-\frac{3}{x}+\frac{4}{x^2}}}$$

$$=\frac{8}{\sqrt{1+0+0}+\sqrt{1-0+0}}$$

$$=\frac{8}{\sqrt{1}+\sqrt{1}}=\frac{8}{2}=4$$

Topic Practice 2

Very Short Answer Type Questions

(2 Marks)

1 Find the following limits.

(i) $\lim_{x\to 0}\frac{ax+b}{cx+1}$ (ii) $\lim_{x\to 3}\frac{x^2-9}{x+3}$

2 Evaluate the following limits.

(i) $\lim_{x\to -1}\frac{x^{10}+x^5+1}{x-1}$

(ii) $\lim_{x\to 1}\frac{ax^2+bx+c}{cx^2+bx+a}$, $a+b+c\neq 0$

Directions (Q. Nos. 3-15) *Evaluate the following limits.*

3 $\lim_{x\to -2} \frac{\frac{1}{x}+\frac{1}{2}}{x+2}$.

4 $\lim_{x\to 2} \frac{x^2-3x+2}{x^2+x-6}$

5 $\lim_{x\to 5} \frac{x^2-9x+20}{x^2-6x+5}$

6 $\lim_{x\to 1} \frac{x^3-1}{x-1}$

7 $\lim_{x\to\sqrt{2}} \frac{x^4-4}{x^2+3\sqrt{2}x-8}$

8 $\lim_{x\to 3} \frac{x^4-81}{2x^2-5x-3}$

9 $\lim_{x\to 2} \frac{3x^2-x-10}{x^2-4}$

10 $\lim_{h\to 0} \frac{\sqrt{x+h}-\sqrt{x}}{h}$

11 $\lim_{x\to 0} \frac{\sqrt{a+x}-\sqrt{a}}{x\sqrt{a^2+ax}}$

12 $\lim_{x\to 0} \frac{\sqrt{1+x^3}-\sqrt{1-x^3}}{x^2}$

13 $\lim_{x\to 1} \frac{(\sqrt{3+x}-\sqrt{5-x})}{x^2-1}$

14 $\lim_{x\to 2}\left(\frac{x^2-4}{\sqrt{x+2}-\sqrt{3x-2}}\right)$

15 $\lim_{x\to 0} \frac{(\sqrt{1+x+x^2}-\sqrt{x+1})}{2x^2}$

16 Evaluate the following limits.

(i) $\lim_{x\to 3} \frac{x^4-81}{x-3}$ (ii) $\lim_{x\to b} \frac{\sqrt{x}-\sqrt{b}}{x-b}$

17 Find n, $\lim_{x\to 2} \frac{x^n-2^n}{x-2}=80, n\in N$.

Directions (Q. Nos. 18-22) *Evaluate the following limits.*

18 $\lim_{x\to -1} \frac{x^3+1}{x^5+1}$

19 $\lim_{x\to 1} \frac{x^{15}-1}{x^{10}-1}$

20 $\lim_{x\to 0} \frac{(1+x)^n-1}{x}$

21 $\lim_{x\to 1} \frac{x^m-1}{x^n-1}$

22 $\lim_{x\to b} \frac{(x+3)^{5/2}-(b+3)^{5/2}}{x-b}$

Short Answer Type Questions

4 Marks

Directions (Q. Nos. 23-28) *Evaluate the following limits.*

23 $\lim_{x\to 2} \frac{x^3-7x^2+14x-8}{x^2+2x-8}$

24 $\lim_{x\to 2}\left[\frac{1}{x-2}-\frac{2(2x-3)}{x^3-3x^2+2x}\right]$

25 $\lim_{x\to 0}\left(\frac{\sqrt{1+x^2}-\sqrt{1+x}}{\sqrt{1+x^3}-\sqrt{1+x}}\right)$

26 $\lim_{x\to 1}\left(\frac{x^4-3x^2+2}{x^3-5x^2+3x+1}\right)$

27 $\lim_{x\to 1/2}\left(\frac{8x-3}{2x-1}-\frac{4x^2+1}{4x^2-1}\right)$

28 $\lim_{x\to 1} \frac{x^4-\sqrt{x}}{\sqrt{x}-1}$

29 If $\lim_{x\to(-a)} \frac{x^7+a^7}{x+a}=7$, then find the value of a.

30 Evaluate $\lim_{x\to\infty} 2x(\sqrt{x^2+1}-x)$.

Hints & Answers

1. (i) b (ii) 0 **2.** (i) $-\frac{1}{2}$ (ii) 1

3. $\lim_{x\to -2} \frac{\frac{1}{x}+\frac{1}{2}}{x+2} = \lim_{x\to -2} \frac{(2+x)}{2x(x+2)}$ **Ans.** $-\frac{1}{4}$

4. $\lim_{x\to 2} \frac{x^2-3x+2}{x^2+x-6} = \lim_{x\to 2} \frac{(x-2)(x-1)}{(x-2)(x+3)}$ **Ans.** $\frac{1}{5}$

5. Given limit $= \lim_{x\to 5} \frac{(x-4)(x-5)}{(x-1)(x-5)}$ **Ans.** $\frac{1}{4}$

6. $\lim_{x\to 1} \frac{x^3-1}{x-1} = \lim_{x\to 1} \frac{(x-1)(x^2+x+1)}{(x-1)}$ **Ans.** 3

7. $\lim_{x\to\sqrt{2}} \frac{x^4-4}{x^2+3\sqrt{2}x-8} = \lim_{x\to\sqrt{2}} \frac{(x+\sqrt{2})(x-\sqrt{2})(x^2+2)}{(x-\sqrt{2})(x+4\sqrt{2})}$

Ans. $\frac{8}{5}$

8. $\lim_{x\to 3} \frac{x^4-81}{2x^2-5x-3} = \lim_{x\to 3} \frac{(x-3)(x+3)(x^2+9)}{(x-3)(2x+1)}$ **Ans.** $\frac{108}{7}$

9. $\lim_{x\to 2} \frac{3x^2-x-10}{x^2-4} = \lim_{x\to 2} \frac{(x-2)(3x+5)}{(x-2)(x+2)}$ **Ans.** $\frac{11}{4}$

10. Given limit $= \lim_{h\to 0} \frac{\sqrt{x+h}-\sqrt{x}}{h}\times\frac{\sqrt{x+h}+\sqrt{x}}{\sqrt{x+h}+\sqrt{x}}$ **Ans.** $\frac{1}{2\sqrt{x}}$

11. Given limit $= \lim_{x\to 0} \frac{\sqrt{a+x}-\sqrt{a}}{x\sqrt{a^2+ax}}\times\frac{\sqrt{a+x}+\sqrt{a}}{\sqrt{a+x}+\sqrt{a}}$

$= \lim_{x\to 0} \frac{x}{x(\sqrt{a^2+ax})(\sqrt{a+x}+\sqrt{a})}$ **Ans.** $\frac{1}{2a\sqrt{a}}$

12. Given limit $= \lim_{x\to 0} \frac{\sqrt{1+x^3}-\sqrt{1-x^3}}{x^2}\cdot\frac{\sqrt{1+x^3}+\sqrt{1-x^3}}{\sqrt{1+x^3}+\sqrt{1-x^3}}$

$= \lim_{x\to 0} \frac{(1+x^3)-(1-x^3)}{x^2(\sqrt{1+x^3}+\sqrt{1-x^3})}$

$= \lim_{x\to 0} \frac{2x^3}{x^2(\sqrt{1+x^3}+\sqrt{1-x^3})}$

Ans. 0

13. Given limit $= \lim_{x\to 1}\frac{(\sqrt{3+x}-\sqrt{5-x})}{(x-1)(x+1)}\times\frac{(\sqrt{3+x}+\sqrt{5-x})}{(\sqrt{3+x}+\sqrt{5-x})}$

$= \lim_{x\to 1}\frac{2x-2}{(x-1)(x+1)(\sqrt{3+x}+\sqrt{5-x})}$ **Ans.** $\frac{1}{4}$

14. Given limit

$\lim_{x\to 2}\left(\frac{x^2-4}{\sqrt{x+2}-\sqrt{3x-2}}\right)\times\frac{(\sqrt{x+2}+\sqrt{3x-2})}{(\sqrt{x+2}+\sqrt{3x-2})}$

$= \lim_{x\to 2}\frac{(x-2)(x+2)(\sqrt{x+2}+\sqrt{3x-2})}{-2x+4}$ **Ans.** -8

15. Multiplying numerator and denominator by $\sqrt{1+x+x^2}+\sqrt{x+1}$. **Ans.** $\frac{1}{4}$

16. (i) Given limit $= \lim_{x\to 3}\frac{x^4-3^4}{x-3}$ **Ans.** 108

(ii) $\frac{1}{2\sqrt{b}}$

17. $n2^{n-1}=5\times 2^{5-1}$ **Ans.** 5

18. $\lim_{x\to -1}\frac{x^3+1}{x^5+1}=\lim_{x\to -1}\frac{\frac{x^3+1}{(x+1)}}{\frac{x^5+1}{x+1}}=\lim_{x\to -1}\frac{x^3+1}{x+1}\div\lim_{x\to -1}\frac{x^5+1}{x+1}$

$=\lim_{x\to -1}\frac{x^3-(-1)^3}{x-(-1)}\div\lim_{x\to -1}\frac{x^5-(-1)^5}{x-(-1)}$ **Ans.** $\frac{3}{5}$

19. $\lim_{x\to 1}\frac{x^{15}-1}{x^{10}-1}=\lim_{x\to 1}\frac{\frac{x^{15}-1}{x-1}}{\frac{x^{10}-1}{x-1}}=\lim_{x\to 1}\frac{x^{15}-1}{x-1}\div\lim_{x\to 1}\frac{x^{10}-1}{x-1}$

$=\lim_{x\to 1}\frac{x^{15}-1^{15}}{x-1}\div\lim_{x\to 1}\frac{x^{10}-1^{10}}{x-1}$ **Ans.** $\frac{3}{2}$

20. Put $1+x=y$, then $y\to 1$ as $x\to 0$.

Now, $\lim_{x\to 0}\frac{(1+x)^n-1}{x}=\lim_{y\to 1}\frac{y^n-1}{y-1}=\lim_{y\to 1}\frac{y^n-1^n}{y-1}$ **Ans.** n

21. Given limit $=\lim_{x\to 1}\frac{\frac{x^m-1}{x-1}}{\frac{x^n-1}{x-1}}=\frac{\lim_{x\to 1}\frac{x^m-1^m}{x-1}}{\lim_{x\to 1}\frac{x^n-1^n}{x-1}}$ **Ans.** $\frac{m}{n}$

22. Given limit $=\lim_{y\to(b+3)}=\frac{y^{5/2}-(b+3)^{5/2}}{y-(b+3)}$, where $y=x+3$

Ans. $\frac{5}{2}(b+3)^{3/2}$

23. Given limit $=\lim_{x\to 2}\frac{(x-1)(x-2)(x-4)}{(x-2)(x+4)}$ **Ans.** $-\frac{1}{3}$

24. Given limit $=\lim_{x\to 2}\left[\frac{1}{x-2}-\frac{2(2x-3)}{x(x-1)(x-2)}\right]$

$=\lim_{x\to 2}\left[\frac{x^2-5x+6}{x(x-1)(x-2)}\right]=\lim_{x\to 2}\left[\frac{(x-2)(x-3)}{x(x-1)(x-2)}\right]$ **Ans.** $\frac{-1}{2}$

25. Given limit $=\lim_{x\to 0}\left\{\frac{\sqrt{1+x^2}-\sqrt{1+x}}{(\sqrt{1+x^3}-\sqrt{1+x})}\times\frac{(\sqrt{1+x^3}+\sqrt{1+x})}{(\sqrt{1+x^3}+\sqrt{1+x})}\right\}\times\frac{(\sqrt{1+x^2}+\sqrt{1+x})}{(\sqrt{1+x^2}+\sqrt{1+x})}$

$=\lim_{x\to 0}\frac{\{(1+x^2)-(1+x)\}\times(\sqrt{1+x^3}+\sqrt{1+x})}{\{(1+x^3)-(1+x)\}\times(\sqrt{1+x^2}+\sqrt{1+x})}$

$=\lim_{x\to 0}\frac{x(x-1)(\sqrt{1+x^3}+\sqrt{1+x})}{x(x-1)(x+1)(\sqrt{1+x^2}+\sqrt{1+x})}$ **Ans.** 1

26. Given limit $=\lim_{x\to 1}\frac{(x-1)(x+1)(x^2-2)}{(x-1)(x^2-4x-1)}$ **Ans.** $\frac{1}{2}$

27. $\lim_{x\to 1/2}\left(\frac{8x-3}{2x-1}-\frac{4x^2+1}{4x^2-1}\right)$

$=\lim_{x\to 1/2}\left[\frac{(8x-3)(2x+1)-(4x^2+1)}{(4x^2-1)}\right]=\lim_{x\to 1/2}\left[\frac{12x^2+2x-4}{4x^2-1}\right]$

$=\lim_{x\to 1/2}\frac{2(6x^2+x-2)}{4x^2-1}=\lim_{x\to 1/2}\frac{2[(3x+2)(2x-1)]}{(2x)^2-(1)^2}$

$=\lim_{x\to 1/2}\frac{2(3x+2)(2x-1)}{(2x-1)(2x+1)}$ **Ans.** $\frac{7}{2}$

28. $\lim_{x\to 1}\frac{x^4-\sqrt{x}}{\sqrt{x}-1}=\lim_{x\to 1}\frac{\sqrt{x}[(x)^{7/2}-1]}{\sqrt{x}-1}$

$=\lim_{x\to 1}\frac{(x)^{7/2}-1}{\sqrt{x}-1}\cdot\lim_{x\to 1}\sqrt{x}=\lim_{x\to 1}\frac{\frac{x^{7/2}-1}{x-1}}{\frac{(x)^{1/2}-1}{x-1}}\cdot 1=\frac{\lim_{x\to 1}\frac{x^{7/2}-1}{x-1}}{\lim_{x\to 1}\frac{(x)^{1/2}-1}{x-1}}$

Ans. 7

29. $\lim_{x\to(-a)}\frac{x^7-(-a)^7}{x-(-a)}=7\Rightarrow 7(-a)^{7-1}=7$ **Ans.** $a=\pm 1$

30. $\lim_{x\to\infty}2x(\sqrt{x^2+1}-x)$

$=\lim_{x\to\infty}2x(\sqrt{x^2+1}-x)\cdot\frac{\sqrt{x^2+1}+x}{\sqrt{x^2+1}+x}$

$=\lim_{x\to\infty}\frac{2x[(x^2+1)-x^2]}{\sqrt{x^2+1}+x}$

$=\lim_{x\to\infty}\frac{2x}{\sqrt{x^2+1}+x}=\lim_{x\to\infty}\frac{\frac{2x}{x}}{\sqrt{\frac{x^2}{x^2}+\frac{1}{x^2}}+\frac{x}{x}}$

$=\lim_{x\to\infty}\frac{2}{\sqrt{1+\frac{1}{x^2}}+1}$ **Ans.** 1

TOPIC 03 Limits of Trigonometric Functions

If the angle θ is measured in radians, then

(i) $\lim_{\theta\to 0} \sin\theta = 0$ and $\lim_{\theta\to 0} \cos\theta = 1$

(ii) $\lim_{\theta\to 0} \frac{\sin\theta}{\theta} = 1$ (iii) $\lim_{\theta\to 0} \frac{\tan\theta}{\theta} = 1$

(iv) $\lim_{\theta\to a} \frac{\sin(\theta - a)}{\theta - a} = 1$ (v) $\lim_{\theta\to a} \frac{\tan(\theta - a)}{(\theta - a)} = 1$

Proof

(i) Let ABC be a right angled triangle such that

$\angle C = \frac{\pi}{2}$ and $\angle ABC = \theta$.

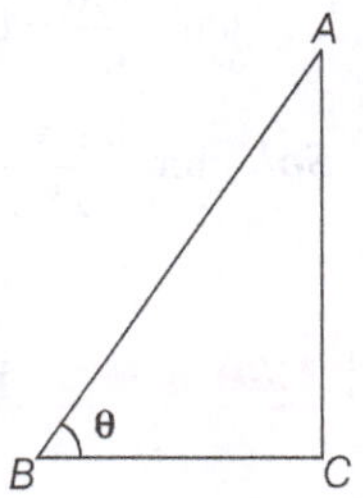

Then, $\sin\theta = \frac{CA}{BA}$ and $\cos\theta = \frac{BC}{BA}$.

Now, if we keep BC fixed and go on decreasing angle θ, then we find that A goes on coming nearer and nearer to C.

$\therefore\ A \to C$ as $\theta \to 0$

This means that $CA \to 0$ and $BA \to BC$, as $\theta \to 0$.

$\Rightarrow \quad \frac{CA}{BA} \to 0$ and $\frac{BC}{BA} \to 1$ [as $\theta \to 0$]

$\Rightarrow \quad \sin\theta \to 0$ and $\cos\theta \to 1$ [as $\theta \to 0$]

(ii) Consider a circle of radius r. Let O be the centre of the circle such that $\angle AOB = \theta$ where θ is measured in radians and it is very small. Suppose the tangent at A meets OB produced at P.

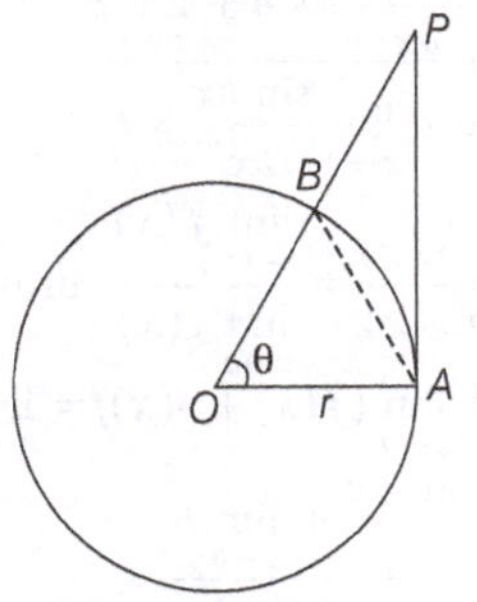

From the above figure, we have

Area of $\Delta OAB <$ Area of sector $OAB <$ Area of ΔOAP

$\Rightarrow \quad \frac{1}{2} OA \cdot OB \sin\theta < \frac{1}{2}(OA)^2\,\theta < \frac{1}{2} OA \cdot AP$

$\Rightarrow \quad \frac{1}{2}r^2 \sin\theta < \frac{1}{2}r^2\theta < \frac{1}{2}r^2 \tan\theta$

[in ΔOAP, $AP = OA\tan\theta$]

$\Rightarrow \quad \sin\theta < \theta < \tan\theta$

$\Rightarrow \quad 1 < \frac{\theta}{\sin\theta} < \frac{1}{\cos\theta}$ [$\because\ \theta$ is small, so $\sin\theta > 0$]

$\Rightarrow \quad 1 > \frac{\sin\theta}{\theta} > \cos\theta$

Now, as $\lim_{\theta\to 0} \cos\theta = 1$, therefore

when $\theta \to 0$, then $\frac{\sin\theta}{\theta} \to 1$

Hence, $\lim_{\theta\to 0} \frac{\sin\theta}{\theta} = 1$

(iii) We have,

$$\lim_{\theta\to 0} \frac{\tan\theta}{\theta} = \lim_{\theta\to 0} \frac{\sin\theta}{\theta} \times \frac{1}{\cos\theta}$$

$$= \lim_{\theta\to 0} \frac{\sin\theta}{\theta} \times \lim_{\theta\to 0} \frac{1}{\cos\theta}$$

$$= 1 \times 1 = 1$$

(iv) We have,

$$\lim_{\theta\to a} \frac{\sin(\theta - a)}{\theta - a} = \lim_{h\to 0} \frac{\sin(a + h - a)}{(a + h - a)}$$

[put $\theta = a + h$, where $h \to 0$ as $\theta \to a$]

$$= \lim_{h\to 0} \frac{\sin h}{h} = 1$$

(v) We have,

$$\lim_{\theta\to a} \frac{\tan(\theta - a)}{\theta - a} = \lim_{h\to 0} \frac{\tan(a + h - a)}{a + h - a}$$

[put $\theta = a + h$, where $h \to 0$ as $\theta \to a$]

$$= \lim_{h\to 0} \frac{\tan h}{h} = 1$$

Note Above results holds when θ is expressed in radians. Whenever degree measure of an angle is given, it should be converted into radian measure by using the relation $1° = \frac{\pi}{180}$ rad.

Method to Determine the Limits of Trigonometric Functions

To evaluate limit of trigonometric function we generally use the following steps

Step I First, check that given variable tends to zero or not. If yes, then go to Step II, otherwise change the limit by suitable substitution, e.g. In $\lim_{x \to a} f(x)$ put $x = a + h$ so that $h \to 0$ when $x \to a$.

Step II Put the limit in given function, if $\frac{0}{0}$ form is obtained, then we go to next step. Otherwise, we may get the required answer.

Step III Simplify the numerator and denominator to eliminate those factors which becomes 0 (zero) on putting the limit.

Step IV Now, convert the result obtained in step III, in the form of $\frac{\sin\theta}{\theta}$ or $\frac{\tan\theta}{\theta}$.

Step V Use the standard limits of trigonometric functions to simplify it.

Example 1 Evaluate $\lim_{\theta \to 0} \theta \operatorname{cosec} \theta$.

Sol. $\lim_{\theta \to 0} \theta \operatorname{cosec}\theta = \lim_{\theta \to 0} \frac{\theta}{\sin\theta} = \lim_{\theta \to 0} \frac{1}{\frac{\sin\theta}{\theta}}$

$$= \frac{1}{\lim_{\theta \to 0}\left(\frac{\sin\theta}{\theta}\right)}$$

$$\left[\because \lim_{\theta \to a} \frac{f(x)}{g(x)} = \frac{\lim_{\theta \to a} f(x)}{\lim_{\theta \to a} g(x)}, \text{ provided } \lim_{\theta \to a} g(x) \neq 0\right]$$

$$= \frac{1}{1} = 1 \qquad \left[\because \lim_{\theta \to 0} \frac{\sin x}{x} = 1\right]$$

Example 2 Evaluate $\lim_{x \to 0} \frac{\sin 3x}{5x}$.

Sol. $\lim_{x \to 0} \frac{\sin 3x}{5x} = \lim_{x \to 0} \frac{\sin 3x}{5x \times \frac{3}{3}}$

$$= \lim_{x \to 0} \frac{3}{5} \cdot \frac{\sin 3x}{3x}$$

$$= \frac{3}{5} \cdot \lim_{3x \to 0} \frac{\sin 3x}{3x} \quad [\text{as } x \to 0, \text{ therefore } 3x \to 0]$$

$$= \frac{3}{5} \times 1 = \frac{3}{5} \qquad \left[\because \lim_{\theta \to 0} \frac{\sin\theta}{\theta} = 1\right]$$

Example 3 Evaluate $\lim_{\theta \to 0} \frac{\sin a\theta}{\sin b\theta}$.

Sol. We have, $\lim_{\theta \to 0} \frac{\sin a\theta}{\sin b\theta} = \lim_{\theta \to 0} \frac{\sin a\theta}{\theta} \div \lim_{\theta \to 0} \frac{\sin b\theta}{\theta}$

$$= a \lim_{a\theta \to 0} \frac{\sin a\theta}{a\theta} \div b \lim_{b\theta \to 0} \frac{\sin b\theta}{b\theta}$$

[as $\theta \to 0$, then $a\theta \to 0$ and $b\theta \to 0$]

$$= a(1) \div b(1) = \frac{a}{b}$$

Example 4 Evaluate $\lim_{x \to 0} \frac{\tan x^\circ}{x^\circ}$.

First, change the angle in radian and then use $\lim_{\theta \to 0} \frac{\tan\theta}{\theta} = 1$.

Sol. $\lim_{x \to 0} \frac{\tan x^\circ}{x^\circ} = \lim_{x \to 0} \frac{\tan \frac{\pi x}{180}}{\frac{\pi x}{180}} = 1 \qquad \left[\because 1^\circ = \frac{\pi}{180} \text{ rad}\right]$

Example 5 Evaluate $\lim_{x \to 0} \frac{\sin 7x}{\tan 5x}$.

Sol. $\lim_{x \to 0} \frac{\sin 7x}{\tan 5x} = \lim_{x \to 0} \frac{7x\left(\frac{\sin 7x}{7x}\right)}{5x\left(\frac{\tan 5x}{5x}\right)} = \frac{7}{5} \frac{\lim_{7x \to 0} \frac{\sin 7x}{7x}}{\lim_{5x \to 0} \frac{\tan 5x}{5x}}$

$$= \frac{7}{5} \times \frac{1}{1} = \frac{7}{5} \qquad \left[\lim_{\theta \to 0} \frac{\sin\theta}{\theta} = 1 \text{ and } \lim_{\theta \to 0} \frac{\tan\theta}{\theta} = 1\right]$$

Example 6 Evaluate $\lim_{x \to 0} \frac{\sin ax + bx}{ax + \sin bx}$; $a, b, a + b \neq 0$. **[NCERT]**

Sol. $\lim_{x \to 0} \frac{\sin ax + bx}{ax + \sin bx} = \lim_{x \to 0} \frac{\frac{\sin ax}{x} + \frac{bx}{x}}{\frac{ax}{x} + \frac{\sin bx}{x}}$

[dividing both numerator and denominator by x]

$$= \frac{\lim_{x \to 0} \frac{\sin(ax)}{ax} \times a + \lim_{x \to 0} b}{\lim_{x \to 0} a + \lim_{x \to 0} \frac{\sin bx}{bx} \times b}$$

$$\left[\because \lim_{x \to a} \frac{f(x)}{g(x)} = \frac{\lim_{x \to a} f(x)}{\lim_{x \to a} g(x)}, \text{ provided } \lim_{x \to a} g(x) \neq 0 \text{ and } \lim_{x \to a} (f(x) + g(x)) = \lim_{x \to a} f(x) + \lim_{x \to a} g(x)\right]$$

$$= \frac{a \lim_{x \to 0} \frac{\sin ax}{ax} + \lim_{x \to 0} b}{\lim_{x \to 0} a + b \lim_{x \to 0} \frac{\sin bx}{bx}}$$

$$= \frac{a(1) + b}{a + b(1)} \qquad \left[\because \lim_{\theta \to 0} \frac{\sin\theta}{\theta} = 1\right]$$

$$= \frac{a + b}{a + b} = 1$$

Example 7 Evaluate $\lim_{x\to 0}\left(\frac{\sin 2x+\sin 6x}{\sin 5x-\sin 3x}\right)$.

Sol. $\lim_{x\to 0}\left(\frac{\sin 2x+\sin 6x}{\sin 5x-\sin 3x}\right)=\lim_{x\to 0}\left(\frac{\frac{\sin 2x+\sin 6x}{x}}{\frac{\sin 5x-\sin 3x}{x}}\right)$

$$=\lim_{x\to 0}\left(\frac{\frac{\sin 2x}{x}+\frac{\sin 6x}{x}}{\frac{\sin 5x}{x}-\frac{\sin 3x}{x}}\right)$$

$$=\lim_{x\to 0}\left(\frac{\frac{2\cdot\sin 2x}{2x}+\frac{6\cdot\sin 6x}{6x}}{\frac{5\cdot\sin 5x}{5x}-\frac{3\cdot\sin 3x}{3x}}\right)$$

$$=\frac{2\cdot\lim_{2x\to 0}\frac{\sin 2x}{2x}+6\cdot\lim_{6x\to 0}\frac{\sin 6x}{6x}}{5\cdot\lim_{5x\to 0}\frac{\sin 5x}{5x}-3\cdot\lim_{3x\to 0}\frac{\sin 3x}{3x}}$$

$$=\frac{2+6}{5-3}\qquad\left[\because \lim_{\theta\to 0}\frac{\sin\theta}{\theta}=1\right]$$

$$=\frac{8}{2}=4$$

Example 8 Evaluate $\lim_{x\to 0}\frac{1-\cos 4x}{x}$.

Sol. $\lim_{x\to 0}\frac{1-\cos 4x}{x}=\lim_{x\to 0}\frac{2\sin^2 2x}{x}\times\frac{x}{x}\qquad[\because 1-\cos 2\theta=2\sin^2\theta]$

$$=\lim_{x\to 0}2\left(\frac{\sin 2x}{2x}\right)^2\times 4x$$

$$=2\left(\lim_{x\to 0}\frac{\sin 2x}{2x}\right)^2\cdot\lim_{x\to 0}4x$$

$$\left[\because \lim_{x\to a}(f(x)\cdot g(x))=\lim_{x\to a}f(x)\cdot\lim_{x\to a}g(x)\quad \text{Also, } \lim_{x\to 0}(f(x))^n=(\lim_{x\to a}f(x))^n,\ n\in N\right]$$

$$=2\times 1\times 0=0\qquad\left[\because \lim_{\theta\to 0}\frac{\sin\theta}{\theta}=1\right]$$

Example 9 Evaluate $\lim_{x\to 0}\frac{\tan 2x-\sin 2x}{x^3}$.

Sol. $\lim_{x\to 0}\frac{\tan 2x-\sin 2x}{x^3}=\lim_{x\to 0}\frac{\frac{\sin 2x}{\cos 2x}-\sin 2x}{x^3}$

$$=\lim_{x\to 0}\frac{\sin 2x-\sin 2x\cdot\cos 2x}{x^3\cdot\cos 2x}$$

$$=\lim_{x\to 0}\frac{\sin 2x\,(1-\cos 2x)}{x^3\cdot\cos 2x}$$

$$=\lim_{x\to 0}\frac{\tan 2x}{x}\cdot\lim_{x\to 0}\frac{2\sin^2 x}{x^2}$$

[by using product of limits and $\cos 2\theta=1-2\sin^2\theta$]

$$=2\cdot\lim_{x\to 0}\frac{\tan 2x}{2x}\times 2\lim_{x\to 0}\left(\frac{\sin x}{x}\right)^2$$

$$=2\,(1)\times 2\,(1)^2\qquad\left[\because \lim_{\theta\to 0}\frac{\sin\theta}{\theta}=\lim_{\theta\to 0}\frac{\tan\theta}{\theta}=1\right]$$

$$=4$$

Example 10 Evaluate $\lim_{x\to 0}\frac{\cos ax-\cos bx}{\cos cx-1}$.

[NCERT Exemplar]

Sol. $\lim_{x\to 0}\frac{\cos ax-\cos bx}{\cos cx-1}$

$$=\lim_{x\to 0}\frac{-2\sin\left[\left(\frac{a+b}{2}\right)x\right]\sin\left(\frac{a-b}{2}\right)x}{-2\sin^2\frac{cx}{2}}$$

$$\left[\because \cos C-\cos D=-2\sin\left(\frac{C+D}{2}\right)\sin\left(\frac{C-D}{2}\right)\ \text{and}\ \cos 2\theta=1-2\sin^2\theta\right]$$

$$=\lim_{x\to 0}\frac{\sin\left(\frac{a+b}{2}\right)x\cdot\sin\left(\frac{a-b}{2}\right)x}{x^2}\cdot\frac{x^2}{\sin^2\frac{cx}{2}}$$

$$=\lim_{x\to 0}\frac{\sin\left(\frac{a+b}{2}\right)x}{\left(\frac{a+b}{2}\right)x\cdot\left(\frac{2}{a+b}\right)}\cdot\frac{\sin\left(\frac{a-b}{2}\right)x}{\left(\frac{a-b}{2}\right)x\cdot\left(\frac{2}{a-b}\right)}\cdot\frac{\left(\frac{cx}{2}\right)^2\times\frac{4}{c^2}}{\sin^2\frac{cx}{2}}$$

$$=\left(\frac{a+b}{2}\times\frac{a-b}{2}\times\frac{4}{c^2}\right)=\frac{a^2-b^2}{c^2}\qquad\left[\because \lim_{\theta\to 0}\frac{\sin\theta}{\theta}=1\right]$$

Example 11 Evaluate

$$\lim_{y\to 0}\frac{(x+y)\sec(x+y)-x\sec x}{y}.$$

[NCERT Exemplar]

Sol. $\lim_{y\to 0}\frac{(x+y)\sec(x+y)-x\sec x}{y}$

$$\lim_{y\to 0}x\frac{x(\sec(x+y)-\sec x)+y\sec(x+y)}{y}$$

$$\Rightarrow \lim_{y\to 0}x\left\{\frac{\sec(x+y)-\sec x}{y}\right\}+\lim_{y\to 0}\frac{y\sec(x+y)}{y}$$

$$=\lim_{y\to 0}\frac{\frac{x}{\cos(x+y)}-\frac{x}{\cos x}}{y}+\lim_{y\to 0}\sec(x+y)$$

$$=\lim_{y\to 0}x\left\{\frac{\cos x-\cos(x+y)}{y\cos x\cos(x+y)}\right\}+\lim_{y\to 0}\sec(x+y)$$

$$=\lim_{y\to 0}\left\{\frac{\cos x-\cos(x+y)}{y}\times\frac{x}{\cos x\cos(x+y)}\right\}$$

$$+\lim_{y\to 0}\sec(x+y)$$

$$= \lim_{y\to 0}\left\{\frac{2\sin\left(x+\frac{y}{2}\right)\sin\left(\frac{y}{2}\right)}{2\left(\frac{y}{2}\right)} \times \frac{x}{\cos x\cos(x+y)}\right\} + \lim_{y\to 0}\sec(x+y)$$

$$\left[\because \cos C - \cos D = 2\sin\left(\frac{C+D}{2}\right)\sin\left(\frac{D-C}{2}\right)\right]$$

$$= \lim_{y\to 0}\sin\left(x+\frac{y}{2}\right) \times \lim_{y\to 0}\frac{\sin\left(\frac{y}{2}\right)}{\frac{y}{2}} \times \lim_{y\to 0}\frac{x}{\cos x\cos(x+y)} + \lim_{y\to 0}\sec(x+y)$$

$$= \sin x \times 1 \times \frac{x}{\cos^2 x} + \sec x = x\tan x\sec x + \sec x$$

Example 12 Evaluate $\lim_{x\to 0}\frac{\sin(2+x)-\sin(2-x)}{x}$. **[NCERT Exemplar]**

Sol. $\lim_{x\to 0}\frac{\sin(2+x)-\sin(2-x)}{x}$

$$= \lim_{x\to 0}\frac{2\cos\left(\frac{2+x+2-x}{2}\right)\sin\left(\frac{2+x-2+x}{2}\right)}{x}$$

$$\left[\because \sin C - \sin D = 2\cos\left(\frac{C+D}{2}\right)\cdot\sin\left(\frac{C-D}{2}\right)\right]$$

$$= \lim_{x\to 0}\frac{2\cos 2\sin x}{x}$$

$$= 2\cos 2\lim_{x\to 0}\frac{\sin x}{x} = 2\cos 2 \quad \left[\because \lim_{\theta\to 0}\frac{\sin\theta}{\theta} = 1\right]$$

Example 13 Evaluate $\lim_{x\to 0}\frac{1-\cos x\sqrt{\cos 2x}}{x^2}$.

Sol. $\lim_{x\to 0}\frac{1-\cos x\sqrt{\cos 2x}}{x^2}$

$$= \lim_{x\to 0}\frac{1-\cos x\sqrt{\cos 2x}}{x^2}\times\frac{1+\cos x\sqrt{\cos 2x}}{1+\cos x\sqrt{\cos 2x}}$$

[rationalising the numerator]

$$= \lim_{x\to 0}\frac{1-\cos^2 x\cos 2x}{x^2(1+\cos x\sqrt{\cos 2x})} = \lim_{x\to 0}\frac{1-\cos^2 x(2\cos^2 x-1)}{x^2(1+\cos x\sqrt{\cos 2x})}$$

$$= \lim_{x\to 0}\frac{1-2\cos^4 x+\cos^2 x}{x^2(1+\cos x\sqrt{\cos 2x})}$$

$$= \lim_{x\to 0}\frac{(1-\cos^2 x)(1+2\cos^2 x)}{x^2(1+\cos x\sqrt{\cos 2x})}$$

$$= \lim_{x\to 0}\frac{\sin^2 x}{x^2}\times\lim_{x\to 0}\frac{1+2\cos^2 x}{\{1+\cos x\sqrt{\cos 2x}\}}$$

$$= 1\times\left(\frac{1+2}{1+1}\right) = \frac{3}{2}$$

Example 14 Evaluate $\lim_{\theta\to 0}\frac{1-\cos 4\theta}{1-\cos 5\theta}$.

Sol. $\lim_{\theta\to 0}\frac{1-\cos 4\theta}{1-\cos 5\theta} = \lim_{\theta\to 0}\frac{2\sin^2(2\theta)}{2\sin^2\left(\frac{5\theta}{2}\right)}$ $[\because 1-\cos 2\theta = 2\sin^2\theta]$

$$= \lim_{\theta\to 0}\frac{\frac{\sin^2(2\theta)}{4\theta^2}\times 4\theta^2}{\frac{\sin^2\frac{5\theta}{2}}{\frac{25\theta^2}{4}}\times\frac{25\theta^2}{4}} = \frac{16}{25}\times\frac{\lim_{2\theta\to 0}\left(\frac{\sin 2\theta}{2\theta}\right)^2}{\lim_{\frac{5\theta}{2}\to 0}\left(\frac{\sin 5\theta/2}{5\theta/2}\right)^2}$$

$$= \frac{16}{25}\times\frac{\left(\lim_{2\theta\to 0}\frac{\sin 2\theta}{2\theta}\right)^2}{\left(\lim_{\frac{5\theta}{2}\to 0}\frac{\sin\frac{5\theta}{2}}{\frac{5\theta}{2}}\right)^2}$$

[as $\theta\to 0$, then $2\theta\to 0$ and $5\theta/2\to 0$]

$$= \frac{16}{25}\times\frac{(1)^2}{(1)^2} = \frac{16}{25} \quad \left[\because \lim_{x\to 0}\frac{\sin x}{x} = 1\right]$$

Example 15 Evaluate

$$\lim_{h\to 0}\frac{(a+h)^2\sin(a+h)-a^2\sin a}{h}.$$ **[NCERT Exemplar]**

Sol. $\lim_{h\to 0}\frac{(a+h)^2\sin(a+h)-a^2\sin a}{h}$

$$= \lim_{h\to 0}\frac{(a^2+h^2+2ah)[\sin a\cos h+\cos a\sin h]-a^2\sin a}{h}$$

$[\because \sin(C+D) = \sin C\cos D+\cos C\sin D]$

$$= \lim_{h\to 0}\left[\frac{a^2\sin a(\cos h-1)}{h}+\frac{a^2\cos a\sin h}{h} + (h+2a)(\sin a\cos h+\cos a\sin h)\right]$$

$$= \lim_{h\to 0}\left[\frac{a^2\sin a\left(-2\sin^2\frac{h}{2}\right)}{\frac{h^2}{4}}\cdot\frac{h}{4}\right] + \lim_{h\to 0}\frac{a^2\cos a\sin h}{h} + \lim_{h\to 0}(h+2a)\sin(a+h)$$

$\left[\because \cos h-1 = -2\sin^2 h/2 \text{ and } \sin a\cos h+\cos a\sin h = \sin(a+h)\right]$

$$= -2a^2\sin a\cdot\lim_{h\to 0}\left(\frac{\sin h/2}{h/2}\right)\cdot\lim_{h\to 0}\frac{h}{4}+a^2\cos a\lim_{h\to 0}\frac{\sin h}{h} + 2a\sin a$$

$$= a^2\sin a\times 0+a^2\cos a(1)+2a\sin a \quad \left[\because \lim_{x\to 0}\frac{\sin x}{x} = 1\right]$$

$$= a^2\cos a+2a\sin a$$

Example 16 Evaluate $\lim_{x\to 0}\dfrac{x\tan 4x}{1-\cos 4x}$.

Sol. $\lim_{x\to 0}\dfrac{x\tan 4x}{1-\cos 4x}=\lim_{x\to 0}\dfrac{x\cdot\dfrac{\sin 4x}{\cos 4x}}{1-\cos 2\cdot(2x)}$

$=\lim_{x\to 0}\dfrac{x\cdot\sin 4x}{\cos 4x\cdot 2\sin^2 2x}$ $\quad[\because 1-\cos 2\theta=2\sin^2\theta]$

$=\lim_{x\to 0}\dfrac{x\cdot\sin 2(2x)}{\cos 4x\,(2\cdot\sin 2x\cdot\sin 2x)}$

$=\lim_{x\to 0}\dfrac{x\,(2\sin 2x\cdot\cos 2x)}{(2\sin 2x\cdot\sin 2x)\cos 4x}$ $\quad[\because \sin 2\theta=2\sin\theta\cos\theta]$

$=\lim_{x\to 0}\dfrac{x\cdot\cos 2x}{(\sin 2x)\cdot\cos 4x}=\lim_{x\to 0}\dfrac{\cos 2x}{\cos 4x}\cdot\left(\dfrac{x}{\sin 2x}\right)$

$=\lim_{x\to 0}\dfrac{1}{\left(\dfrac{\sin 2x}{x}\times\dfrac{2}{2}\right)}\times\lim_{x\to 0}\dfrac{\cos 2x}{\cos 4x}$

$=\dfrac{1}{2}\lim_{x\to 0}\dfrac{1}{\left(\dfrac{\sin 2x}{2x}\right)}\times\lim_{x\to 0}\dfrac{\cos 2x}{\cos 4x}$

$=\dfrac{1}{2}\times\dfrac{1}{1}\times\dfrac{\cos 0}{\cos 0}=\dfrac{1}{2}\times\dfrac{1}{1}\times\dfrac{1}{1}=\dfrac{1}{2}$ $\quad\left[\because \lim_{\theta\to 0}\dfrac{\sin\theta}{\theta}=1\right]$

Example 17 Evaluate $\lim_{x\to 0}\dfrac{\sin x-2\sin 3x+\sin 5x}{x}$.

[NCERT Exemplar]

Sol. $\lim_{x\to 0}\dfrac{\sin x-2\sin 3x+\sin 5x}{x}$

$=\lim_{x\to 0}\dfrac{(\sin 5x+\sin x)-2\sin 3x}{x}$

$=\lim_{x\to 0}\dfrac{2\sin\left(\dfrac{5x+x}{2}\right)\cos\left(\dfrac{5x-x}{2}\right)-2\sin 3x}{x}$

$\left[\because \sin C+\sin D=2\sin\left(\dfrac{C+D}{2}\right)\cos\left(\dfrac{C-D}{2}\right)\right]$

$=\lim_{x\to 0}\dfrac{2\sin 3x\cos 2x-2\sin 3x}{x}=\lim_{x\to 0}\dfrac{2\sin 3x(\cos 2x-1)}{x}$

$=\lim_{x\to 0}2\left(\dfrac{\sin 3x}{3x}\right)\times 3\times\left[\dfrac{-(1-\cos 2x)}{1}\right]$

$=-2\times 1\times 3(1-\cos 0)$ $\quad\left[\because \lim_{\theta\to 0}\dfrac{\sin\theta}{\theta}=1\right]$

$=-6(1-1)=-6\times 0=0$

Example 18 Evaluate $\lim_{x\to 0}\dfrac{\tan x-\sin x}{x^3}$.

Sol. $\lim_{x\to 0}\dfrac{\tan x-\sin x}{x^3}=\lim_{x\to 0}\left(\dfrac{\sin x-\sin x\cos x}{x^3\cos x}\right)$

$=\lim_{x\to 0}\left\{\dfrac{\sin x(1-\cos x)}{x^3\cos x}\right\}=\lim_{x\to 0}\left\{\dfrac{\sin x}{x}\times\dfrac{1-\cos x}{x^2}\times\dfrac{1}{\cos x}\right\}$

$=\left\{\lim_{x\to 0}\dfrac{\sin x}{x}\right\}\times\left\{\lim_{x\to 0}\dfrac{2\sin^2\dfrac{x}{2}}{\left(\dfrac{x}{2}\right)^2\times 4}\right\}\times\lim_{x\to 0}\dfrac{1}{\cos x}$

$=\left\{\lim_{x\to 0}\dfrac{\sin x}{x}\right\}\times\dfrac{1}{2}\times\left\{\lim_{x\to 0}\left(\dfrac{\sin\dfrac{x}{2}}{\dfrac{x}{2}}\right)^2\right\}\times\lim_{x\to 0}\dfrac{1}{\cos x}$

$=1\times\dfrac{1}{2}(1)^2\times\dfrac{1}{1}=\dfrac{1}{2}$

Evaluation of Trigonometric Limits When $x\to a,\ a\neq 0$

If $x\to a\ (a\neq 0)$, then we can proceed by replacing x by $a+h$ or $a-h$ and $x\to a$ by $h\to 0$.

Example 19 Evaluate $\lim_{x\to\pi/4}\left(\dfrac{\sin x-\cos x}{x-(\pi/4)}\right)$.

Sol. Let $L=\lim_{x\to\pi/4}\left(\dfrac{\sin x-\cos x}{x-(\pi/4)}\right)$

Here, given variable is not tending to zero i.e. limit is not of the form $x\to 0$.

So, put $x-\dfrac{\pi}{4}=h\Rightarrow x=\dfrac{\pi}{4}+h$.

Since, $x\to\dfrac{\pi}{4}$, therefore $h\to 0$.

Now, $L=\lim_{h\to 0}\dfrac{\sin\left(\dfrac{\pi}{4}+h\right)-\cos\left(\dfrac{\pi}{4}+h\right)}{h}$ $\quad\left[\dfrac{0}{0}\text{ form}\right]$

$=\lim_{h\to 0}\dfrac{\left[\left(\sin\dfrac{\pi}{4}\cos h+\cos\dfrac{\pi}{4}\sin h\right)-\left(\cos\dfrac{\pi}{4}\cos h-\sin h\sin\dfrac{\pi}{4}\right)\right]}{h}$

$=\lim_{h\to 0}\dfrac{\left[\left(\dfrac{1}{\sqrt 2}\cos h+\dfrac{1}{\sqrt 2}\sin h\right)-\left(\dfrac{1}{\sqrt 2}\cos h-\dfrac{1}{\sqrt 2}\sin h\right)\right]}{h}$

$=\lim_{h\to 0}\dfrac{\dfrac{2}{\sqrt 2}\sin h}{h}=\sqrt 2(1)=\sqrt 2$ $\quad\left[\because \lim_{x\to 0}\dfrac{\sin x}{x}=1\right]$

Example 20 Evaluate $\lim_{x\to\pi/2}\dfrac{1+\cos 2x}{(\pi-2x)^2}$.

Sol. $\lim_{x\to\pi/2}\dfrac{1+\cos 2x}{(\pi-2x)^2}=\lim_{h\to 0}\dfrac{1+\cos 2\left(\dfrac{\pi}{2}+h\right)}{\left[\pi-2\left(\dfrac{\pi}{2}+h\right)\right]^2}$

$\left[\text{putting } x=\dfrac{\pi}{2}+h,\text{ where } h\to 0\text{ as } x\to\dfrac{\pi}{2}\right]$

$$= \lim_{h\to 0} \frac{1+\cos(\pi+2h)}{(\pi-\pi-2h)^2}$$

$$= \lim_{h\to 0} \frac{1-\cos 2h}{4h^2} \quad \left[\frac{0}{0} \text{ form}\right]$$

$$= \lim_{h\to 0} \frac{2\sin^2 h}{4h^2} \quad [\because 1-\cos 2\theta = 2\sin^2\theta]$$

$$= \frac{2}{4}\lim_{h\to 0}\left(\frac{\sin h}{h}\right)^2$$

$$= \frac{2}{4}\times 1 = \frac{1}{2} \quad \left[\because \lim_{\theta\to 0}\frac{\sin\theta}{\theta}=1\right]$$

Example 21 Evaluate $\lim_{x\to\pi} \frac{1+\cos x}{\tan^2 x}$.

Sol. On putting $x=\pi+h$, we get

$$\lim_{x\to\pi}\frac{1+\cos x}{\tan^2 x} = \lim_{h\to 0}\frac{1+\cos(\pi+h)}{\tan^2(\pi+h)}$$

$$[\because \text{ when } x\to\pi, \text{ then } h\to 0]$$

$$= \lim_{h\to 0}\frac{2\cos^2\left(\frac{\pi+h}{2}\right)}{\tan^2 h} \quad \left[\begin{array}{l}\because \tan(\pi+h)=\tan h \\ \text{and } 1+\cos 2\theta = 2\cos^2\theta\end{array}\right]$$

$$= \lim_{h\to 0}\frac{2\cos^2\left(\frac{\pi}{2}+\frac{h}{2}\right)}{\tan^2 h} = \lim_{h\to 0}\frac{2\sin^2\frac{h}{2}}{\tan^2 h}$$

$$\left[\because \cos\left(\frac{\pi}{2}+\theta\right) = -\sin\theta, \text{ therefore } \cos^2\left(\frac{\pi}{2}+\theta\right)=\sin^2\theta\right]$$

$$= \lim_{h\to 0}\frac{2\sin^2\frac{h}{2}}{\sin^2 h}\times\cos^2 h$$

$$= \lim_{h\to 0}\frac{2\sin^2\frac{h}{2}}{\left(2\sin\frac{h}{2}\cdot\cos\frac{h}{2}\right)^2}\cos^2 h \quad \left[\because \sin\theta = 2\sin\frac{\theta}{2}\cdot\cos\frac{\theta}{2}\right]$$

$$= \lim_{h\to 0}\frac{1}{2\cos^2\frac{h}{2}}\times\cos^2 h = \frac{1}{2\times 1}\times(1)^2 = \frac{1}{2} \quad [\because \cos 0 = 1]$$

Example 22 Evaluate $\lim_{x\to\pi/2}(\sec x - \tan x)$. **[NCERT Exemplar]**

Sol. Put $x=\frac{\pi}{2}-y$. Then, as $x\to\frac{\pi}{2}$, therefore $y\to 0$

$$\therefore \lim_{x\to\pi/2}(\sec x-\tan x)$$

$$= \lim_{y\to 0}\left[\sec\left(\frac{\pi}{2}-y\right)-\tan\left(\frac{\pi}{2}-y\right)\right]$$

$$= \lim_{y\to 0}(\operatorname{cosec} y - \cot y)$$

$$\left[\because \sec\left(\frac{\pi}{2}-\theta\right)=\operatorname{cosec}\theta \text{ and } \tan\left(\frac{\pi}{2}-\theta\right)=\cot\theta\right]$$

$$= \lim_{y\to 0}\left(\frac{1}{\sin y}-\frac{\cos y}{\sin y}\right) = \lim_{y\to 0}\left(\frac{1-\cos y}{\sin y}\right)$$

$$= \lim_{y\to 0}\frac{2\sin^2\frac{y}{2}}{2\sin\frac{y}{2}\cos\frac{y}{2}} \quad \left[\begin{array}{l}\because \sin^2\frac{\theta}{2}=\frac{1-\cos\theta}{2} \\ \text{and } \sin\theta = 2\sin\frac{\theta}{2}\cos\frac{\theta}{2}\end{array}\right]$$

$$= \lim_{\frac{y}{2}\to 0}\tan\frac{y}{2}=0 \quad \left[\text{as } y\to 0, \text{ then } \frac{y}{2}\to 0\right]$$

Example 23 Evaluate $\lim_{x\to\pi/6}\frac{\sqrt{3}\sin x-\cos x}{x-\frac{\pi}{6}}$. **[NCERT Exemplar]**

Sol. $$\lim_{x\to\pi/6}\frac{\sqrt{3}\sin x-\cos x}{x-\frac{\pi}{6}} = \lim_{x\to\pi/6}\frac{2\left(\frac{\sqrt{3}}{2}\sin x-\cos x\cdot\frac{1}{2}\right)}{x-\frac{\pi}{6}}$$

$$= \lim_{x\to\pi/6}\frac{2\left(\sin x\cos\frac{\pi}{6}-\cos x\sin\frac{\pi}{6}\right)}{\left(x-\frac{\pi}{6}\right)}$$

$$= 2\lim_{x\to\pi/6}\frac{\sin\left(x-\frac{\pi}{6}\right)}{\left(x-\frac{\pi}{6}\right)}$$

$$[\because \sin A\cos B-\cos A\sin B = \sin(A-B)]$$

$$= 2 \quad \left[\because \lim_{\theta\to a}\frac{\sin(\theta-a)}{(\theta-a)}=1\right]$$

Evaluation of Trigonometric Limits by Factorisation

Sometimes, trigonometric limits can be evaluated by factorisation method.

Example 24 Evaluate $\lim_{x\to\pi/6}\frac{\cot^2 x-3}{\operatorname{cosec} x-2}$. **[NCERT Exemplar]**

Sol. $$\lim_{x\to\pi/6}\frac{\cot^2 x-3}{\operatorname{cosec} x-2}$$

$$= \lim_{x\to\pi/6}\frac{\operatorname{cosec}^2 x-1-3}{\operatorname{cosec} x-2} \quad [\because \operatorname{cosec}^2 x-\cot^2 x = 1]$$

$$= \lim_{x\to\pi/6}\frac{\operatorname{cosec}^2 x-4}{\operatorname{cosec} x-2}$$

$$= \lim_{x\to\pi/6}\frac{(\operatorname{cosec} x-2)(\operatorname{cosec} x+2)}{(\operatorname{cosec} x-2)} \quad [\text{by factorisation}]$$

$$= \lim_{x\to\pi/6}(\operatorname{cosec} x+2) = \operatorname{cosec}\frac{\pi}{6}+2 = 2+2 = 4$$

Example 25 Evaluate $\lim_{x\to\pi/6}\frac{2\sin^2 x+\sin x-1}{2\sin^2 x-3\sin x+1}$ by using factorisation method. **[NCERT Exemplar]**

Sol. $\lim_{x \to \pi/6} \frac{2\sin^2 x + \sin x - 1}{2\sin^2 x - 3\sin x + 1}$

$= \lim_{x \to \pi/6} \frac{(2\sin x - 1)(\sin x + 1)}{(2\sin x - 1)(\sin x - 1)} = \lim_{x \to \pi/6} \frac{\sin x + 1}{\sin x - 1}$

$= \frac{1 + \sin\frac{\pi}{6}}{\sin\frac{\pi}{6} - 1} = \frac{1 + \frac{1}{2}}{\frac{1}{2} - 1} = -3$

Topic Practice 3

Very Short Answer Type Questions

(2 Marks)

Directions (Q. Nos. 1-27) *Evaluate the followings.*

1. $\lim_{x \to 0} x \operatorname{cosec} 3x$
2. $\lim_{x \to 0} x \sin \frac{1}{x}$
3. $\lim_{x \to 0} \frac{\cos x}{\pi - x}$
4. $\lim_{x \to \pi} \frac{\sin x^\circ}{x}$
5. $\lim_{x \to 0} \frac{\tan 2x^\circ}{x^\circ}$
6. $\lim_{x \to \pi} \frac{\sin x}{x - \pi}$
7. $\lim_{x \to \pi} \frac{\sin(\pi - x)}{\pi(\pi - x)}$.
8. $\lim_{x \to 0} \frac{\sin 3x}{\sin 7x}$
9. $\lim_{x \to 0} \frac{\sin^2 5x}{x^2}$
10. $\lim_{x \to 0} \frac{ax + x\cos x}{b \sin x}$
11. $\lim_{x \to 0} \frac{\sin 4x}{\tan 4x}$
12. $\lim_{x \to 0} \frac{\tan x - \sin x}{x}$
13. $\lim_{x \to 0} \frac{\tan 2x - x}{3x - \sin x}$
14. $\lim_{x \to 0} \frac{\sin^2 2x}{\sin^2 4x}$
15. $\lim_{x \to 0} \frac{\sin x}{\sqrt{x+1} - \sqrt{1-x}}$
16. $\lim_{x \to 0} \frac{1 - \cos 2x}{x^2}$
17. $\lim_{x \to 0} \frac{1 - \cos 5x}{x}$
18. $\lim_{x \to 0} \frac{x^2 \cos x}{1 - \cos x}$
19. $\lim_{x \to 0} (\operatorname{cosec} x - \cot x)$
20. $\lim_{x \to 0} \frac{\sin x}{x(1 + \cos x)}$
21. $\lim_{x \to a} \frac{\cos x - \cos a}{x - a}$
22. $\lim_{x \to \pi/2} \frac{\tan 2x}{x - \frac{\pi}{2}}$
23. $\lim_{x \to \pi/2} \left(\frac{\pi}{2} - x\right) \tan x$
24. $\lim_{x \to \pi/2} \frac{1 - \sin x}{\cos x}$
25. $\lim_{x \to \pi/2} \frac{\cos^2 x}{1 - \sin x}$
26. $\lim_{x \to \pi/4} \frac{\sec^2 x - 2}{\tan x - 1}$
27. $\lim_{n \to \infty} \frac{\sin\left(\frac{a}{2^n}\right)}{\sin\left(\frac{b}{2^n}\right)}$

Short Answer Type Questions

(4 Marks)

Directions (Q. Nos. 28-39) *Evaluate the followings.*

28. $\lim_{x \to 0} \frac{\sin 2x + 3x}{2x + \tan 3x}$
29. $\lim_{x \to 0} \frac{1 - \cos mx}{1 - \cos nx}$
30. $\lim_{x \to 0} \frac{\cos 2x - 1}{\cos x - 1}$
31. $\lim_{x \to 0} \frac{\tan x - \sin x}{\sin^3 x}$
32. $\lim_{x \to 0} \frac{2\sin x - \sin 2x}{x^3}$
33. $\lim_{x \to 0} \frac{\sec 4x - \sec 2x}{\sec 3x - \sec x}$
34. $\lim_{x \to 0} \frac{\operatorname{cosec} x - \cot x}{x}$
35. $\lim_{x \to 0} \frac{(\sin 3x + \sin 5x)}{(\sin 6x - \sin 4x)}$
36. $\lim_{x \to a} \frac{\sin\sqrt{x} - \sin\sqrt{a}}{x - a}$
37. $\lim_{x \to a} \frac{\sin x - \sin a}{\sqrt{x} - \sqrt{a}}$
38. $\lim_{x \to \pi/2} \frac{1 - \sin x}{\left(\frac{\pi}{2} - x\right)^2}$
39. $\lim_{x \to \pi/8} \frac{\cot 4x - \cos 4x}{(\pi - 8x)^3}$

Long Answer Type Questions

(6 Marks)

Directions (Q. Nos. 40-44) *Evaluate the followings.*

40. $\lim_{x \to 0} \frac{\tan x + 4\tan 2x - 3\tan 3x}{x^2 \tan x}$
41. $\lim_{x \to \pi/6} \frac{2 - \sqrt{3}\cos x - \sin x}{(6x - \pi)^2}$
42. $\lim_{x \to \pi} \frac{1 - \sin\frac{x}{2}}{\cos\frac{x}{2}\left(\cos\frac{x}{4} - \sin\frac{x}{4}\right)}$
43. $\lim_{x \to \pi} \frac{\sqrt{2 + \cos x} - 1}{(\pi - x)^2}$
44. $\lim_{x \to \pi/2} \frac{\left(\frac{\pi}{2} - x\right)\sin x - 2\cos x}{\left(\frac{\pi}{2} - x\right) + \cot x}$
45. If $f(x) = \begin{cases} \frac{k\cos x}{\pi - 2x}, & \text{when } x \neq \frac{\pi}{2} \\ 3, & \text{when } x = \frac{\pi}{2} \end{cases}$ and $\lim_{x \to \pi/2} f(x) = f\left(\frac{\pi}{2}\right)$, then find the value of k.
46. If $f(x) = \begin{cases} \frac{\sin[x]}{[x]}, & [x] \neq 0 \\ 0, & [x] = 0 \end{cases}$, where [] denotes the greatest integer function, then find $\lim_{x \to 0} f(x)$.

Hints & Answers

1. Given limit $= \lim_{x\to 0} \frac{x}{\sin 3x}$ **Ans.** $\frac{1}{3}$

2. We know, $-1 \le \sin\theta \le 1$, therefore $\lim_{x\to 0} x \sin\frac{1}{x}$

$= \lim_{x\to 0} x \cdot$ (an oscillating number between -1 and 1)

$= 0 \cdot$ (an oscillating number between -1 and 1)

Ans. 0

3. Substitute $x = 0$ **Ans.** $\frac{1}{\pi}$

4. Convert $x°$ in radian measure, i.e. write $x° = \frac{\pi x}{180}$ radian **Ans.** $\pi/180$

5. 2

6. $\lim_{x\to\pi} \frac{\sin x}{x-\pi} = \lim_{x\to\pi} \frac{\sin(\pi - x)}{(x-\pi)} = -\lim_{x\to\pi} \frac{\sin(\pi-x)}{(\pi-x)}$ **Ans.** -1

7. $\frac{1}{\pi}$

8. Given limit $= \frac{3}{7} \cdot \frac{\lim_{x\to 0} \frac{\sin 3x}{3x}}{\lim_{x\to 0} \frac{\sin 7x}{7x}}$ **Ans.** $\frac{3}{7}$

9. Given limit $= \lim_{x\to 0} \left(\frac{\sin 5x}{5x}\right)^2 \times 25$

$= 25 \lim_{5x\to 0} \frac{\sin 5x}{5x} \lim_{5x\to 0} \frac{\sin 5x}{5x}$ **Ans.** 25

10. Divide numerator and denominator by x. **Ans.** $\frac{a+1}{b}$

11. Given limit $= \lim_{x\to 0} \frac{\sin 4x/4x}{\tan 4x/4x}$ **Ans.** 1

12. Given limit $= \lim_{x\to 0} \left[\frac{\tan x}{x} - \frac{\sin x}{x}\right]$ **Ans.** 0

13. $\lim_{x\to 0} \frac{\tan 2x - x}{3x - \sin x} = \lim_{x\to 0} \frac{x\left[\frac{\tan 2x}{x} - 1\right]}{x\left[3 - \frac{\sin x}{x}\right]} = \frac{\lim_{x\to 0} 2 \times \frac{\tan 2x}{2x} - 1}{3 - \lim_{x\to 0} \frac{\sin x}{x}}$

Ans. 1/2

14. $\lim_{x\to 0} \frac{\sin^2 2x}{[\sin 2(2x)]^2} = \lim_{x\to 0} \frac{\sin^2 2x}{(2\sin 2x \cos 2x)^2}$

$= \lim_{x\to 0} \frac{\sin^2 2x}{4\sin^2 2x \cos^2 2x} = \lim_{x\to 0} \frac{1}{4\cos^2 2x}$ **Ans.** $\frac{1}{4}$

15. $\lim_{x\to 0} \frac{\sin x}{\sqrt{x+1} - \sqrt{1-x}} \cdot \frac{\sqrt{x+1} + \sqrt{1-x}}{\sqrt{x+1} + \sqrt{1-x}}$

$= \lim_{x\to 0} \frac{\sin x(\sqrt{x+1} + \sqrt{1-x})}{(x+1) - (1-x)}$

$= \lim_{x\to 0} \frac{\sin x(\sqrt{x+1} + \sqrt{1-x})}{x+1-1+x}$

$= \frac{1}{2} \lim_{x\to 0} \frac{\sin x}{x} \lim_{x\to 0} (\sqrt{x+1} + \sqrt{1-x})$ **Ans.** 1

16. $\lim_{x\to 0} \frac{1 - \cos 2x}{x^2} = \lim_{x\to 0} \frac{2\sin^2 x}{x^2}$

$= \lim_{x\to 0} \frac{2\sin^2 x}{x^2} = 2\lim_{x\to 0} \frac{\sin^2 x}{x^2}$ $2\lim_{x\to 0} \left(\frac{\sin x}{x}\right)^2$ **Ans.** 2

17. Given limit $= \lim_{x\to 0} \frac{2\sin^2 \frac{5x}{2}}{\left(\frac{5x}{2}\right)^2} \times \left(\frac{5}{2}\right)^2 \times x$ **Ans.** 0

18. limit $= \lim_{x\to 0} \frac{x^2 \cos x}{2\sin^2 \frac{x}{2}} = 2\lim_{x\to 0} \frac{\left(\frac{x}{2}\right)^2}{\sin^2 \frac{x}{2}} \cdot \lim_{x\to 0} \cos x$ **Ans.** 2

19. Given limit $= \lim_{x\to 0} \left(\frac{1}{\sin x} - \frac{\cos x}{\sin x}\right)$

$= \lim_{x\to 0} \left(\frac{1 - \cos x}{\sin x}\right) = \lim_{x\to 0} \frac{2\sin^2 \frac{x}{2}}{2\sin\frac{x}{2} \cos\frac{x}{2}}$

$= \lim_{x\to 0} \frac{\sin\frac{x}{2}}{\cos\frac{x}{2}}$ **Ans.** 0

20. $\lim_{x\to 0} \frac{2\sin\frac{x}{2}\cos\frac{x}{2}}{x\left(2\cos^2\frac{x}{2}\right)} = \frac{1}{2} \lim_{x\to 0} \frac{\tan\frac{x}{2}}{\frac{x}{2}}$ **Ans.** $\frac{1}{2}$

21. Given limit $= \lim_{x\to a} \frac{2\sin\left(\frac{x+a}{2}\right)\sin\left(\frac{a-x}{2}\right)}{(x-a)}$

$= 2\lim_{x\to a} \frac{\sin\left(\frac{a-x}{2}\right)}{-\left(\frac{a-x}{2}\right)} \times \frac{1}{2} \times \sin\left(\frac{x+a}{2}\right)$ **Ans.** $-\sin a$

22. Put $x - \frac{\pi}{2} = h$. Then,

Given limit $= \lim_{h\to 0} \frac{\tan 2\left(\frac{\pi}{2} + h\right)}{h} = \lim_{h\to 0} \frac{\tan(\pi + 2h)}{h}$

$= \lim_{h\to 0} \frac{\tan 2h}{h}$ $[\because \tan(\pi + \theta) = \tan\theta]$ **Ans.** 2

23. 1

24. $\lim_{x\to\frac{\pi}{2}} \frac{1 - \sin x}{\cos x} x = \lim_{h\to 0} \left[\frac{1 - \sin\left(\frac{\pi}{2} - h\right)}{\cos\left(\frac{\pi}{2} - h\right)}\right]$

$= \lim_{h\to 0} \frac{1 - \cos h}{\sin h} = \lim_{h\to 0} \frac{2\sin^2 \frac{h}{2}}{2\sin\frac{h}{2}\cos\frac{h}{2}}$ **Ans.** 0

25. Given limit $= \lim_{x\to\pi/2} \dfrac{1-\sin^2 x}{1-\sin x} = \lim_{x\to\pi/2} 1+\sin x$ **Ans.** 2

26. $\lim_{x\to\pi/4} \dfrac{\sec^2 x-2}{\tan x-1} = \lim_{x\to\pi/4} \dfrac{1+\tan^2 x-2}{\tan x-1} = \lim_{x\to\pi/4} \dfrac{\tan^2 x-1}{\tan x-1}$

Ans. 2

27. Put $\dfrac{1}{2^n} = y$, then $y\to 0$ as $n\to\infty$

$\therefore \lim_{x\to\infty} \dfrac{\sin\left(\dfrac{a}{2^n}\right)}{\sin\left(\dfrac{b}{2^n}\right)} = \lim_{y\to\infty} \dfrac{\sin(ay)}{\sin(by)}$ **Ans.** $\dfrac{a}{b}$

28. $\lim_{x\to 0} \dfrac{\sin 2x+3x}{2x+\tan 3x}$

$= \lim_{x\to 0} \dfrac{\left(\dfrac{\sin 2x}{2x}+\dfrac{3x}{2x}\right)2x}{\left(\dfrac{2x}{3x}+\dfrac{\tan 3x}{3x}\right)3x} = \lim_{x\to 0}\left(\dfrac{\dfrac{\sin 2x}{2x}+\dfrac{3}{2}}{\dfrac{2}{3}+\dfrac{\tan 3x}{3x}}\right)\cdot\dfrac{2}{3}$ **Ans.** 1

29. Given, $\lim_{x\to 0} \dfrac{2\sin^2\dfrac{mx}{2}}{2\sin^2\dfrac{nx}{x}} = \left(\dfrac{m}{n}\right)^2 \left[\dfrac{\lim_{\frac{mx}{2}\to 0} \dfrac{\sin\left(\dfrac{mx}{2}\right)}{\dfrac{mx}{2}}}{\lim_{\frac{nx}{2}\to 0} \dfrac{\sin\left(\dfrac{nx}{2}\right)}{\dfrac{nx}{2}}}\right]^2$ **Ans.** $\dfrac{m^2}{n^2}$

30. Given limit $= \lim_{x\to 0} \dfrac{1-\cos 2x}{1-\cos x}$

$= \lim_{x\to 0} \dfrac{2\sin^2 x}{2\sin^2\dfrac{x}{2}} = \lim_{x\to 0}\left(\dfrac{\sin x}{x}\right)^2 \times \left(\dfrac{\dfrac{x}{2}}{\sin\dfrac{x}{2}}\right)^2 \times 4$ **Ans.** 4

31. $\lim_{x\to 0} \dfrac{\tan x-\sin x}{\sin^3 x} = \lim_{x\to 0} \dfrac{1-\cos x}{\cos x\sin^2 x}$

$= \lim_{x\to 0} \dfrac{1-\cos x}{\cos x(1-\cos^2 x)}$ **Ans.** $\dfrac{1}{2}$

32. $\lim_{x\to 0} \dfrac{2\sin x-2\sin x\cos x}{x^3} = 2\lim_{x\to 0} \dfrac{\sin x}{x}\cdot\lim_{x\to 0}\left(\dfrac{1-\cos x}{x^2}\right)$

$= 2\cdot 1\lim_{x\to 0} \dfrac{1-\cos x}{x^2} = 2\lim_{x\to 0} \dfrac{2\sin^2\dfrac{x}{2}}{4\times\dfrac{x^2}{4}}$ **Ans.** 1

33. Given limit $= \lim_{x\to 0}\left(\dfrac{\dfrac{\cos 2x-\cos 4x}{\cos 2x\cos 4x}}{\dfrac{\cos x-\cos 3x}{\cos x\cos 3x}}\right)$

$= \lim_{x\to 0}\left(\dfrac{\cos 2x-\cos 4x}{\cos x-\cos 3x}\times\dfrac{\cos x\cos 3x}{\cos 2x\cos 4x}\right)$

$= \lim_{x\to 0}\left(\dfrac{2\sin 3x\sin x}{2\sin 2x\sin x}\times\dfrac{\cos x\cos 3x}{\cos 2x\cos 4x}\right)$

$= \dfrac{3}{2}\dfrac{\lim_{x\to 0}\dfrac{\sin 3x}{3x}}{\lim_{x\to 0}\dfrac{\sin 2x}{2x}} \times \lim_{x\to 0}\dfrac{\cos x\cos 3x}{\cos 2x\cos 4x}$ **Ans.** $\dfrac{3}{2}$

34. Given limit $= \lim_{x\to 0} \dfrac{\dfrac{1}{\sin x}-\dfrac{\cos x}{\sin x}}{x} = \lim_{x\to 0} \dfrac{1-\cos x}{x\cdot\sin x}$

$= \lim_{x\to 0} \dfrac{2\sin^2\dfrac{x}{2}}{x\cdot 2\sin\dfrac{x}{2}\cos\dfrac{x}{2}} = \lim_{x\to 0} \dfrac{\tan\dfrac{x}{2}}{\dfrac{x}{2}}\cdot\dfrac{1}{2}$ **Ans.** $\dfrac{1}{2}$

35. Given limit $= \lim_{x\to 0} \dfrac{2\sin 4x\cos x}{2\cos 5x\sin x}$

$= \lim_{x\to 0} \dfrac{\sin 4x}{\sin x}\cdot\lim_{x\to 0}\dfrac{\cos x}{\cos 5x}$ **Ans.** 4

36. Given limit $= \lim_{x\to a} \dfrac{2\cos\left(\dfrac{\sqrt{x}+\sqrt{a}}{2}\right)\sin\left(\dfrac{\sqrt{x}-\sqrt{a}}{2}\right)}{(\sqrt{x})^2-(\sqrt{a})^2}$

$= \lim_{x\to a} \dfrac{2\cos\left(\dfrac{\sqrt{x}+\sqrt{a}}{2}\right)}{(\sqrt{x}+\sqrt{a})}\cdot\lim_{x\to a}\dfrac{\sin\left(\dfrac{\sqrt{x}-\sqrt{a}}{2}\right)}{\left(\dfrac{\sqrt{x}-\sqrt{a}}{2}\right)}\times\dfrac{1}{2}$

Ans. $\dfrac{1}{2\sqrt{a}}\cos\sqrt{a}$

37. Given limit $= \lim_{x\to a} \dfrac{\sin x-\sin a}{\sqrt{x}-\sqrt{a}}\times\dfrac{\sqrt{x}+\sqrt{a}}{\sqrt{x}+\sqrt{a}}$

$= \lim_{x\to a} \dfrac{(\sin x-\sin a)(\sqrt{x}+\sqrt{a})}{x-a}$

On putting $x-a=h$, we get

Given limit $= \lim_{h\to 0} \dfrac{[\sin(a+h)-\sin a][\sqrt{a+h}+\sqrt{a}]}{h}$

$[\because x\to a \Rightarrow h\to 0]$

$= \lim_{h\to 0} \dfrac{2\cos\left(\dfrac{a+h+a}{2}\right)\sin\left(\dfrac{a+h-a}{2}\right)(\sqrt{a+h}+\sqrt{a})}{h}$

$= \lim_{h\to 0} \dfrac{2\cos\left(\dfrac{2a+h}{2}\right)\sin\left(\dfrac{h}{2}\right)(\sqrt{a+h}+\sqrt{a})}{2\left(\dfrac{h}{2}\right)}$ **Ans.** $2\sqrt{a}\cos a$

38. Put $x=\dfrac{\pi}{2}+h$. Then, given limit $= \lim_{h\to 0} \dfrac{1-\sin\left(\dfrac{\pi}{2}+h\right)}{\left\{\dfrac{\pi}{2}-\left(\dfrac{\pi}{2}+h\right)\right\}^2}$

$= \lim_{h\to 0} \dfrac{1-\cos h}{h^2} = \lim_{h\to 0} \dfrac{2\sin^2\dfrac{h}{2}}{\left(\dfrac{h}{2}\right)^2}\times\dfrac{1}{4}$ **Ans.** $\dfrac{1}{2}$

39. Given limit $= \lim_{x\to\pi/8} \dfrac{\dfrac{\cos 4x}{\sin 4x} - \cos 4x}{(\pi - 8x)^3}$

$= \lim_{x\to\pi/8} \dfrac{\cos 4x(1-\sin 4x)}{(\pi-8x)^3} \cdot \lim_{x\to\pi/8} \dfrac{1}{\sin 4x}$

$= \lim_{x\to\pi/8} \dfrac{\cos 4x(1-\sin 4x)}{(\pi-8x)^3}$

On putting $x = \dfrac{\pi}{8} + h$, we get

Given limit $= \lim_{h\to 0} \dfrac{\cos 4\left(\dfrac{\pi}{8}+h\right)\left[1-\sin 4\left(\dfrac{\pi}{8}+h\right)\right]}{\left[\pi - 8\left(\dfrac{\pi}{8}+h\right)\right]^3}$

$= \lim_{h\to 0} \dfrac{-\sin 4h(1-\cos 4h)}{(-8h)^3}$ **Ans.** $\dfrac{1}{16}$

40. Given limit $= \lim_{x\to 0} \dfrac{\tan x + 4\tan 2x - 3\tan 3x}{x^2 \tan x}$

$= \lim_{x\to 0} \dfrac{\tan x + 4\cdot\dfrac{2\tan x}{1-\tan^2 x} - 3\cdot\dfrac{3\tan x - \tan^3 x}{1-3\tan^2 x}}{x^2 \tan x}$

$= \lim_{x\to 0} \dfrac{\left(1 + \dfrac{8}{1-\tan^2 x} - \dfrac{9-3\tan^2 x}{1-3\tan^2 x}\right)}{x^2}$

$= \lim_{x\to 0} \left[\dfrac{(1-\tan^2 x)(1-3\tan^2 x) + 8(1-3\tan^2 x) - (9-3\tan^2 x)(1-\tan^2 x)}{x^2(1-\tan^2 x)(1-3\tan^2 x)}\right]$

$= \lim_{x\to 0} \dfrac{-16\tan^2 x}{x^2(1-\tan^2 x)(1-3\tan^2 x)}$

$= -16 \lim_{x\to 0} \left(\dfrac{\tan x}{x}\right)^2 \dfrac{1}{(1-\tan^2 x)(1-3\tan^2 x)}$ **Ans.** -16

41. Given limit $= \lim_{h\to 0} \dfrac{2-\sqrt{3}\cos\left(\dfrac{\pi}{6}+h\right) - \sin\left(\dfrac{\pi}{6}+h\right)}{\left[6\left(\dfrac{\pi}{6}+h\right)-\pi\right]^2}$

$= \lim_{h\to 0} \dfrac{\left[2-\sqrt{3}\left(\cos\dfrac{\pi}{6}\cdot\cos h - \sin\dfrac{\pi}{6}\cdot\sin h\right) - \left(\sin\dfrac{\pi}{6}\cdot\cos h + \cos\dfrac{\pi}{6}\sin h\right)\right]}{(\pi + 6h - \pi)^2}$

$= \lim_{h\to 0} \dfrac{2-\sqrt{3}\cdot\left(\dfrac{\sqrt{3}}{2}\cos h - \dfrac{1}{2}\sin h\right) - \left(\dfrac{1}{2}\cos h + \dfrac{\sqrt{3}}{2}\sin h\right)}{36h^2}$

$= \lim_{h\to 0} \dfrac{1-\cos h}{18h^2} = \lim_{h\to 0} \dfrac{2\sin^2\dfrac{h}{2}}{18h^2}$ **Ans.** $\dfrac{1}{36}$

42. Given limit $= \lim_{x\to\pi} \dfrac{\cos^2\dfrac{x}{4} + \sin^2\dfrac{x}{4} - 2\sin\dfrac{x}{4}\cos\dfrac{x}{4}}{\cos\dfrac{x}{2}\left(\cos\dfrac{x}{4} - \sin\dfrac{x}{4}\right)}$

$= \lim_{x\to\pi} \dfrac{\left(\cos\dfrac{x}{4} - \sin\dfrac{x}{4}\right)^2}{\left(\cos^2\dfrac{x}{4} - \sin^2\dfrac{x}{4}\right)\left(\cos\dfrac{x}{4} - \sin\dfrac{x}{4}\right)}$

Ans. $\dfrac{1}{\sqrt{2}}$

43. Given limit $= \lim_{x\to\pi} \dfrac{(\sqrt{2+\cos x} - 1)}{(\pi - x)^2} \times \dfrac{(\sqrt{2+\cos x}+1)}{(\sqrt{2+\cos x}+1)}$

$= \lim_{x\to\pi} \dfrac{2+\cos x - 1}{(\pi-x)^2(\sqrt{2+\cos x}+1)}$

$= \lim_{x\to\pi} \dfrac{2\cos^2\dfrac{x}{2}}{(\pi-x)^2(\sqrt{2+\cos x}+1)}$

$= \lim_{h\to 0} \dfrac{2\cos^2\left(\dfrac{\pi+h}{2}\right)}{(-h)^2(\sqrt{2+\cos(\pi+h)}+1)}$

$= \lim_{h\to 0} \dfrac{\sin^2\dfrac{h}{2}}{2\left(\dfrac{h}{2}\right)^2(\sqrt{2+\cos(\pi+h)}+1)}$ **Ans.** $\dfrac{1}{4}$

44. Given limit $= \lim_{h\to 0} \dfrac{(-h)\sin\left(\dfrac{\pi}{2}+h\right) - 2\cos\left(\dfrac{\pi}{2}+h\right)}{(-h) + \cot\left(\dfrac{\pi}{2}+h\right)}$

$= \lim_{h\to 0} \dfrac{-h\cos h + 2\sin h}{-h - \tan h}$ **Ans.** $-\dfrac{1}{2}$

45. $\lim_{x\to\pi/2} f(x) = \lim_{x\to\pi/2} \dfrac{k\cos x}{\pi - 2x} = \lim_{h\to 0} \dfrac{k\cos\left(\dfrac{\pi}{2}+h\right)}{\pi - 2\left(\dfrac{\pi}{2}+h\right)}$

$= \lim_{h\to 0} \dfrac{k\sin h}{2h} = \dfrac{k}{2}$

$\because$ It is given that, $\lim_{x\to\pi/2} f(x) = f\left(\dfrac{\pi}{2}\right)$

$\therefore$ $\dfrac{k}{2} = f\left(\dfrac{\pi}{2}\right) = 3$ **Ans.** $k = 6$

46. RHL $= \lim_{x\to 0^+} f(x) = \dfrac{\sin 0}{0}$

Ans. Does not exist

Chapter Practice

Multiple Choice Type Questions

1 Mark

1. Let $f(x)=\begin{cases}\dfrac{k\cos\pi}{\pi-2x}, & x\neq\dfrac{\pi}{2}\\ 3, & x=\dfrac{\pi}{2}\end{cases}$ and if $\lim_{x\to\frac{\pi}{2}} f(x)=f\left(\dfrac{\pi}{2}\right)$, then the value of k is

(a) 3 (b) 4 (c) 5 (d) 6

2. If $f(x)=\begin{cases}x^2-1, & x\leq 1\\ -x^2-1, & x>1\end{cases}$, then

(a) LHL $\neq$ RHL, at $x=1$
(b) LHL = RHL = -2, at $x=1$
(c) LHL = RHL = -1, at $x=1$
(d) None of the above

3. $\lim_{n\to\infty}\dfrac{1+2+3+\ldots\ldots+n}{n^2}$, $n\in N$ is equal to **[NCERT Exemplar]**

(a) 0 (b) 1 (c) $\dfrac{1}{2}$ (d) $\dfrac{1}{4}$

4. $\lim_{x\to 0}\dfrac{\sin x}{\sqrt{x+1}-\sqrt{1-x}}$ is equal to

(a) 2 (b) 0 (c) 1 (d) -1

Assertion-Reason Type Questions

1 Mark

Directions (Q. Nos. 5-8) *In the questions given below are two statements labelled as Assertion (A) and Reason (R). In the context of the two statements, which one of the following is correct?*

(a) Both A and R are correct; R is the correct explanation of A
(b) Both A and R are correct; R is not the correct explanation of A
(c) A is correct; R is incorrect
(d) R is correct; A is incorrect

5. **Assertion (A)** The value of $\lim_{x\to 2^+}\dfrac{x^2-1}{2x+4}$ is $\dfrac{3}{8}$.

Reason (R) $\lim_{x\to a^+} f(x)=\lim_{h\to 0} f(a+h)$.

6. **Assertion (A)** $\lim_{x\to 0}(1+3x)^{1/x}=e^3$

Reason (R) $\lim_{x\to 0}(1+x)^{1/x}=e$

7. **Assertion (A)** Let $a_1, a_2, a_3 \ldots a_n$ be fixed real numbers and define a function $f(x)=(x-a_1)(x-a_2)\ldots(x-a_n)$, then $\lim_{x\to a_1} f(x)=0$.

Reason (R) $\lim_{x\to a} f(x)=(a-a_1)(a-a_2)\ldots(a-a_n)$, for some $a\neq a_1$.

8. **Assertion (A)** $\lim_{x\to 0}\log_e\left(\dfrac{\sin x}{x}\right)=0$

Reason (R) $\lim_{x\to 0} f(g(x))=f(\lim_{x\to 0} g(x))$

Very Short Answer Type Questions

2 Marks

Direction (Q. Nos. 9-14) *Evaluate the following.*

9. $\lim_{x\to 1}\dfrac{x^2+3x+2}{x^2+1}$

10. $\lim_{x\to 4}\dfrac{x^3-2x^2-9x+4}{x^2-2x-8}$

11. $\lim_{x\to 2}\dfrac{x-2}{\sqrt{x^2-4}+\sqrt{x-2}}$

12. $\lim_{x\to 1}\dfrac{x^2-\sqrt{x}}{\sqrt{x}-1}$

13. $\lim_{x\to -3}\dfrac{x^3+27}{x^5+243}$

14. $\lim_{x\to 0}\dfrac{(1+x)^5-1}{3x+5x^2}$

15. Find the positive integer n, so that $\lim_{x\to 3}\dfrac{x^n-3^n}{x-3}=108$.

16. Evaluate

(i) $\lim_{x\to\infty}\dfrac{4x-3}{2x+7}$. (ii) $\lim_{x\to\infty}\dfrac{3x^2+2x-5}{x^2+5x+1}$.

Short Answer Type Questions

(4 Marks)

Directions (Q. Nos. 17-20) *Evaluate the following.*

17. $\lim_{x \to 0} \frac{1 - \cos x \cos 2x \cos 3x}{\sin^2 2x}$

18. $\lim_{x \to 0} \frac{3\sin x - \sin 3x}{x(\cos 2x - \cos 4x)}$

19. $\lim_{x \to 0} \frac{8}{x^8}\left(1 - \cos\frac{x^2}{2} - \cos\frac{x^2}{4} + \cos\frac{x^2}{2}\cos\frac{x^2}{4}\right)$

20. $\lim_{x \to \alpha} \frac{x \sin\alpha - \alpha \sin x}{x - \alpha}$

Long Answer Type Questions

(6 Marks)

21. Find the limit of the function $f(x)$, if it exists and defined as

$$f(x) = \frac{e^{1/x} - 1}{e^{1/x} + 1}, x \neq 0 \text{ as } x \to 0$$

22. Evaluate $\lim_{x \to \pi/4} \frac{4\sqrt{2} - (\cos x + \sin x)^5}{1 - \sin 2x}$.

Case-Based Type Question

(6 Marks)

23. For a function $f(x)$, at $x = a$

I. LHL $= \lim_{x \to a^-} f(x)$

II. RHL $= \lim_{x \to a^+} f(x)$

If at $x = a$, LHL = RHL, then we say that at $x = a$, $\lim_{x \to a} f(x)$ exists.

On the basis of above information, answer the following questions.

(i) Find $\lim_{x \to 0} e^{-1/x}$.

(ii) If $f(x) = \begin{cases} 2x + 3, & x \le 2 \\ x + k, & x > 2 \end{cases}$ and $\lim_{x \to 2} f(x)$ exists, then find the value of k.

(iii) Find $\lim_{x \to 3^+} \frac{x}{[x]}$.

(iv) Find $\lim_{x \to 2^-} \frac{2x}{x + 4}$.

(v) If $f(x) = \begin{cases} x^2 - 1, & x \le 1 \\ -x^2 - 1, & x > 1 \end{cases}$, then find the $\lim_{x \to 1} f(x)$.

Hints & Answers

1. (d)	**2.** (a)	**3.** (c)	**4.** (c)
5. (a)	**6.** (a)	**7.** (b)	**8.** (c)

9. Use direct substitution method. **Ans.** 3

10. $\lim_{x \to 4} \frac{x^3 - 2x^2 - 9x + 4}{x^2 - 2x - 8}$

$= \lim_{x \to 4} \frac{(x-4)(x^2 + 2x - 1)}{(x-4)(x+2)}$ **Ans.** $\frac{23}{6}$

11. $\lim_{x \to 2} \frac{x - 2}{\sqrt{x^2 - 4} + \sqrt{x - 2}}$

$= \lim_{x \to 2} \frac{x - 2}{\sqrt{x - 2}\,[\sqrt{x + 2} + 1]}$

$= \lim_{x \to 2} \frac{\sqrt{x - 2}}{(\sqrt{x + 2} + 1)}$ **Ans.** 0

12. $\lim_{x \to 1} \frac{x^2 - \sqrt{x}}{\sqrt{x} - 1} = \lim_{x \to 1} \frac{(\sqrt{x})^4 - \sqrt{x}}{(\sqrt{x} - 1)}$

$= \lim_{x \to 1} \frac{\sqrt{x}\,[(\sqrt{x})^3 - 1]}{(\sqrt{x} - 1)} = \lim_{x \to 1} \frac{\sqrt{x}\,(\sqrt{x} - 1)(x + 1 + x)}{(\sqrt{x} - 1)}$

$= \lim_{x \to 1} \sqrt{x}\,(2x + 1)$

[as $x \to 1$, so $\sqrt{x} \to \sqrt{1}$ i.e. $\sqrt{x} \to 1$] **Ans.** 3

13. $\lim_{x \to -3} \frac{x^3 + 27}{x^5 + 243} = \lim_{x \to -3} \frac{x^3 - (-3)^3}{x^5 - (-3)^5} = \frac{\lim_{x \to -3} \frac{x^3 - (-3)^3}{(x - 3)}}{\lim_{x \to -3} \frac{x^5 - (-3)^5}{(x - 3)}}$

[multiplying and dividing by $(x - 3)$] **Ans.** $\frac{1}{15}$

14. $\lim_{x \to 0} \frac{(1 + x)^5 - 1}{3x + 5x^2}$ $\left[\frac{0}{0} \text{ form}\right]$

$= \frac{\lim_{x \to 0} \frac{(1 + x)^5 - 1}{x}}{\lim_{x \to 0} \frac{3x + 5x^2}{x}} = \frac{\lim_{(1+x) \to 1} \frac{(1 + x)^5 - 1}{(1 + x) - 1}}{\lim_{x \to 0} (3 + 5x)}$

Ans. $\frac{5}{3}$

15. Given, $\lim_{x \to 3} \frac{x^n - 3^n}{x - 3} = 108$

$\Rightarrow \quad n \cdot 3^{n-1} = 108$ $\left[\because \lim_{x \to a} \frac{x^n - a^n}{x - a} = na^{n-1}\right]$

$\Rightarrow \quad n \cdot 3^{n-1} = 4 \times 3^{4-1}$ **Ans.** $n = 4$

16. (i) 2 (ii) 3

17. Let $\cos x \cos 2x \cos 3x = \frac{1}{2}(2\cos x \cos 3x \cos 2x)$

$$= \frac{1}{2}[(\cos 2x + \cos 4x)\cos 2x]$$

$$= \frac{1}{4}(2\cos^2 2x + 2\cos 2x \cos 4x)$$

$$= \frac{1}{4}(1 + \cos 4x + \cos 2x + \cos 6x)$$

Now, $\lim_{x\to 0} \frac{1 - \cos x \cos 2x \cos 3x}{\sin^2 2x}$

$$= \lim_{x\to 0} \frac{1 - \frac{1}{4}(1 + \cos 4x + \cos 2x + \cos 6x)}{\sin^2 2x}$$

$$= \lim_{x\to 0} \frac{3 - (\cos 4x + \cos 2x + \cos 6x)}{4\sin^2 2x}$$

$$= \lim_{x\to 0} \frac{(1-\cos 2x) + (1-\cos 4x) + (1-\cos 6x)}{4\sin^2 2x}$$

Ans. $\frac{7}{4}$

18. $\lim_{x\to 0} \frac{3\sin x - \sin 3x}{x(\cos 2x - \cos 4x)}$ $\left[\frac{0}{0}\text{ form}\right]$

$$= \lim_{x\to 0} \frac{3\sin x - 3\sin x + 4\sin^3 x}{x\left[2\sin\left(\frac{4x+2x}{2}\right)\sin\left(\frac{4x-2x}{2}\right)\right]}$$

$$= \lim_{x\to 0} \frac{2\sin^3 x}{x\sin 3x \sin x}$$

$$= \frac{2}{3}\lim_{x\to 0} \frac{\left(\frac{\sin x}{x}\right)^2}{\frac{\sin 3x}{3x}}$$

Ans. $\frac{2}{3}$

19. $\lim_{x\to 0} \frac{8}{x^8}\left(1 - \cos\frac{x^2}{2} - \cos\frac{x^2}{4} + \cos\frac{x^2}{2}\cos\frac{x^2}{4}\right)$

$$= \lim_{x\to 0} \frac{8}{x^8}\left[\left(1 - \cos\frac{x^2}{2}\right) - \cos\frac{x^2}{4}\left(1 - \cos\frac{x^2}{2}\right)\right]$$

$$= \lim_{x\to 0} \frac{8}{x^8}\left(1 - \cos\frac{x^2}{2}\right)\left(1 - \cos\frac{x^2}{4}\right)$$

$$= \lim_{x\to 0} \frac{8}{x^8} 2\sin^2\frac{x^2}{4}\cdot 2\sin^2\frac{x^2}{8}$$

$$\lim_{x\to 0} 32\left(\frac{\sin\frac{x^2}{4}}{\frac{x^2}{4}\cdot 4}\right)^2\cdot\left(\frac{\sin\frac{x^2}{8}}{\frac{x^2}{8}\cdot 8}\right)^2$$

Ans. $\frac{1}{32}$

20. Put $x = \alpha + h$.

Then, $\lim_{x\to\alpha} \frac{x\sin\alpha - \alpha\sin x}{x - \alpha}$

$$= \lim_{h\to 0} \frac{(\alpha+h)\sin\alpha - \alpha\sin(\alpha+h)}{\alpha + h - \alpha}$$

$$= \lim_{h\to 0} \frac{\alpha\sin\alpha + h\sin\alpha - \alpha\sin(\alpha+h)}{h}$$

$$= \lim_{h\to 0} \frac{\alpha\cdot 2\cos\left(\frac{2\alpha+h}{2}\right)\sin\left(-\frac{h}{2}\right)}{h} + \frac{h\sin\alpha}{h}$$

$$= \lim_{h\to 0} \frac{\alpha\cdot 2\cos\left(\frac{2\alpha+h}{2}\right)\cdot\frac{\sin\left(\frac{-h}{2}\right)}{\left(\frac{-h}{2}\right)}\cdot\left(\frac{-h}{2}\right)}{h} + \sin\alpha$$

Ans. $\sin\alpha - \alpha\cos\alpha$

21. $\lim_{x\to 0} f(x)$ does not exist.

22. $\lim_{x\to\frac{\pi}{4}} \frac{4\sqrt{2} - (\cos x + \sin x)^5}{1 - \sin 2x} = \lim_{x\to\frac{\pi}{4}} \frac{2^{5/2} - (\cos x + \sin x^2)^{5/2}}{2 - (1 + \sin 2x)}$

$$= \lim_{x\to\frac{\pi}{4}} \frac{2^{5/2} - (1 + \sin 2x)^{5/2}}{2 - (1 + \sin 2x)}$$

Put $1 + \sin 2x = t$, so that when $x \to \frac{\pi}{4}$, then $t \to 2$

$$\therefore \lim_{x\to\frac{\pi}{4}} \frac{4\sqrt{2} - (\cos x + \sin x)^5}{1 - \sin 2x} = \lim_{t\to 2} \frac{2^{5/2} - t^{5/2}}{2 - t}$$

Ans. $5\sqrt{2}$

23. (i) Does not exist

(ii) 5

(iii) 1

(iv) $\frac{2}{3}$

(v) Does not exist

CHAPTER

13

Derivatives

There are several real life situations in which we need to know the rate at which a certain parameter is changing with respect to some other parameter. For example, we may need to find the rate change in the value of a particular share with respect to the time or we may be interested in finding. The rate of change of distance travelled by the car with respect to the time. This can be done with the help of derivatives. Also, derivatives helps in finding the sloped of tangent to the curve.

- Derivative and First Principle of Derivative
- Algebra of Derivative of Functions
- Derivative of Trigonometric Functions

TOPIC 01 Derivative and First Principle of Derivative

Concept of Derivative

Suppose f is a real valued function and a is a point in its domain. Then, **derivative of f at a** is defined by

$$\lim_{h \to 0} \frac{f(a+h)-f(a)}{h} \text{ provided this limit exists.}$$

The derivative of $f(x)$ at a is denoted by $f'(a)$.

Note The process of finding derivative of a function is called differentiation.

Example 1 Find the derivative of $f(x) = 4x + 5$ at $x = 3$.

Sol. Given, $f(x) = 4x + 5$

We know that, at $x = a$,

$$f'(a) = \lim_{h \to 0} \frac{f(a+h)-f(a)}{h}$$

$$\therefore \quad f'(3) = \lim_{h \to 0} \frac{f(3+h)-f(3)}{h} = \lim_{h \to 0} \frac{4(3+h)+5-(4 \times 3+5)}{h}$$

$$= \lim_{h \to 0} \frac{12+4h+5-17}{h} = \lim_{h \to 0} \frac{4h}{h} = 4$$

Example 2 Find the derivative of the function $f(x) = 2x^2 + 3x - 5$ at $x = -1$. Also, prove that $f'(0) + 3f'(-1) = 0$. **[NCERT]**

Sol. Clearly, $f'(-1) = \lim_{h \to 0} \frac{f(-1+h) - f(-1)}{h}$

$$\left[\because f'(a) = \lim_{h \to 0} \frac{f(a+h) - f(a)}{h}\right]$$

$$= \lim_{h \to 0} \frac{[2(-1+h)^2 + 3(-1+h) - 5] - [2(-1)^2 + 3(-1) - 5]}{h}$$

$$= \lim_{h \to 0} \frac{[2(1+h^2 - 2h) - 3 + 3h - 5] - [2 - 3 - 5\}]}{h}$$

$$= \lim_{h \to 0} \frac{2h^2 - h}{h} = \lim_{h \to 0}(2h - 1) = 2(0) - 1 = -1$$

and $f'(0) = \lim_{h \to 0} \frac{f(0+h) - f(0)}{h}$

$$\left[\because f'(a) = \lim_{h \to 0} \frac{f(a+h) - f(a)}{h}\right]$$

$$= \lim_{h \to 0} \frac{[2(0+h)^2 + 3(0+h) - 5] - [2(0)^2 + 3(0) - 5]}{h}$$

$$= \lim_{h \to 0} \frac{2h^2 + 3h}{h} = \lim_{h \to 0}(2h + 3) = 2(0) + 3 = 3$$

Now, $f'(0) + 3f'(-1) = 3 - 3 = 0$ **Hence proved.**

Physical Interpretation of Derivative

Let a particle be moving in a straight line OX starting from point O towards point X as shown in the figure below

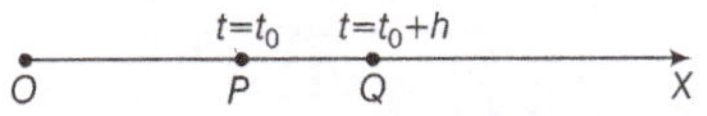

Clearly, the position of the particle at any time t depends upon the time elapsed. In other words the distance of the particle from O depends upon the time i.e. it is a function f of time t taken by the particle.

Let at any time t_0 i.e. at time $t = t_0$, the particle be at P and after a further time h i.e. at time $t = t_0 + h$, is at Q.

$\therefore$ $OP = f(t_0)$ and $OQ = f(t_0 + h)$

Distance travelled in time $h = PQ = OQ - OP$

$$= f(t_0 + h) - f(t_0)$$

Clearly, average speed of the particle during the journey

from P to $Q = \frac{PQ}{h} = \frac{f(t_0 + h) - f(t_0)}{h}$

If $h \to 0$, we observe that $Q \to P$.

$\therefore$ Instantaneous speed at time $t = t_0$

$$= \lim_{h \to 0} \frac{f(t_0 + h) - f(t_0)}{h} = f'(t_0)$$

Thus, if $f(t)$ gives the distance of a moving particle at time t, then $f'(t_0)$, i.e. the derivative of f at $t = t_0$ represents the instantaneous speed of the particle at time $t = t_0$ or rate of change of distance at $t = t_0$.

Geometrical Interpretation of Derivative

Let $y = f(x)$ be a function and let its graph be as shown in the figure below

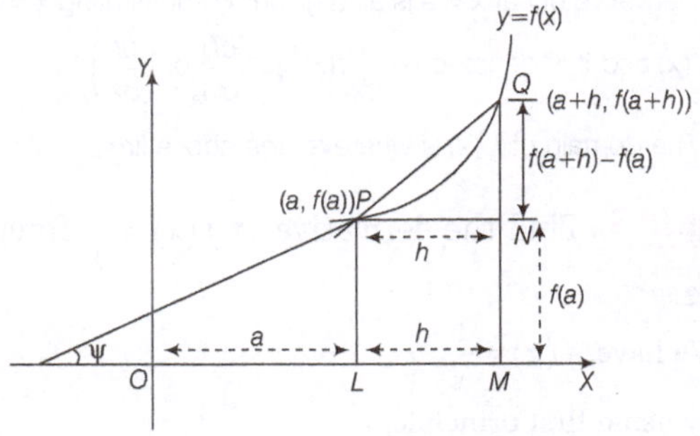

Let P and Q be two points on the curve whose coordinates are $(a, f(a))$ and $(a+h, f(a+h))$, respectively.

From points P and Q draw perpendiculars PL and QM on the X-axis and also draw PN perpendicular on MQ.

From the figure, $\tan(\angle QPN) = \frac{QN}{PN}$

$$= \frac{f(a+h) - f(a)}{h} \quad \text{...(i)}$$

It is obvious that as $h \to 0$, then $Q \to P$. So, in the limiting position the secant PQ becomes that tangent at P and $\angle QPN$ will tend to angle ψ, which the tangent at P makes with the positive direction of the X-axis.

Thus, when $Q \to P$ or $h \to 0$, then Eq. (i) becomes

$$\lim_{h \to 0} \frac{f(a+h) - f(a)}{h} = \lim_{Q \to P} \tan \angle QPN$$

or $\boxed{f'(a) = \textbf{Slope of tangent at } P(x, y)}$

Hence, the derivative of $f(x)$ at any point 'a' is the slope of tangent to the curve at $P(a, f(a))$.

Differentiation using First Principle

We know how to find the derivative of a function at a point. In general, we define derivative of a function as follows. Suppose f is a real valued function, the function defined by $\lim_{h \to 0} \frac{f(x+h) - f(x)}{h}$, wherever the limit exists, is defined to be the derivative of f at x and is denoted by $f'(x)$. This definition of derivative is called the **first principle of derivative.**

Thus, $f'(x) = \lim_{x \to 0} \frac{f(x+h) - f(x)}{h}$

Sometimes $f'(x)$ is denoted by $\frac{d}{dx}[f(x)]$ or if $y = f(x)$, then it is denoted by $\frac{dy}{dx}$ and referred to as derivative of $f(x)$ or y with respect to x. It is also denoted by $D[f(x)]$.

Note (i) Derivative of f at $x = a$ is also given by substituting $x = a$ in $f'(x)$ and it is denoted by $\frac{d}{dx} f(x)\Big|_a$ or $\frac{df}{dx}\Big|_a$ or $\left(\frac{df}{dx}\right)_{x=a}$.

(ii) The domain of $f'(x)$ is wherever the above limit exists.

Example 3 Find the derivative of $f(x) = \frac{1}{x}$ from first principle.

Sol. We have, $f(x) = \frac{1}{x}$

By using first principle,

$$f'(x) = \lim_{h \to 0} \frac{f(x+h) - f(x)}{h}$$

$$\therefore f'(x) = \lim_{h \to 0} \frac{\frac{1}{x+h} - \frac{1}{x}}{h} \quad \left[\because f(x) = \frac{1}{x} \quad \therefore f(x+h) = \frac{1}{x+h}\right]$$

$$= \lim_{h \to 0} \frac{1}{h}\left[\frac{x - (x+h)}{x(x+h)}\right] = \lim_{h \to 0} \frac{1}{h}\left[\frac{-h}{x(x+h)}\right]$$

$$= \lim_{h \to 0} \left[\frac{-1}{x(x+h)}\right] = \frac{-1}{x^2}$$

Example 4 Find the derivative of $f(x) = ax + b$, where a and b are non-zero constants, by first principle.

Sol. We have, $f(x) = ax + b$

By definition of first principle, we have

$$f'(x) = \lim_{h \to 0} \frac{f(x+h) - f(x)}{h}$$

$$= \lim_{h \to 0} \frac{a(x+h) + b - (ax+b)}{h} = \lim_{h \to 0} \frac{ah}{h} = a$$

Example 5 Find the derivative of $f(x) = x^n$, where n is positive integer, by first principle. **[NCERT]**

Sol. By definition of first principle, we have

$$f'(x) = \lim_{h \to 0} \frac{f(x+h) - f(x)}{h} = \lim_{h \to 0} \frac{(x+h)^n - x^n}{h} \quad \text{...(i)}$$

By Binomial theorem, we have

$$(x+h)^n = {}^nC_0 x^n + {}^nC_1 x^{n-1} h + {}^nC_2 x^{n-2} h^2 + \dots + {}^nC_n h^n$$

$$\Rightarrow (x+h)^n = x^n + nhx^{n-1} + \frac{n(n-1)}{2} h^2 x^{n-2} + \dots + h^n$$

$$\Rightarrow (x+h)^n - x^n = nhx^{n-1} + \frac{n(n-1)}{2} h^2 x^{n-2} + \dots + h^n$$

On putting this value in Eq. (i), we get

$$f'(x) = \lim_{h \to 0} \frac{nhx^{n-1} + \frac{n(n-1)}{2} h^2 x^{n-2} + \dots + h^n}{h}$$

$$= \lim_{h \to 0} \frac{h\left(nx^{n-1} + \frac{n(n-1)}{2} hx^{n-2} + \dots + h^{n-1}\right)}{h}$$

$$= \lim_{h \to 0} \left[nx^{n-1} + \frac{n(n-1)}{2} hx^{n-2} + \dots + h^{n-1}\right] = nx^{n-1}$$

Hence, $f'(x)$ or $\frac{d}{dx} f(x) = nx^{n-1}$

Example 6 Find the derivative of $(x-1)(x-2)$ from first principle. **[NCERT]**

Sol. Let $f(x) = (x-1)(x-2) = x^2 - 3x + 2$

By first principle of derivative, we have

$$f'(x) = \lim_{h \to 0} \frac{f(x+h) - f(x)}{h}$$

$$= \lim_{h \to 0} \frac{[(x+h)^2 - 3(x+h) + 2] - [x^2 - 3x + 2]}{h}$$

$$= \lim_{h \to 0} \frac{[x^2 + h^2 + 2xh - 3x - 3h + 2] - [x^2 - 3x + 2]}{h}$$

$$= \lim_{h \to 0} \frac{2hx + h^2 - 3h}{h} = \lim_{h \to 0} \frac{h(2x + h - 3)}{h} = 2x - 3$$

Example 7 Find the derivative of $\left(\frac{x+1}{x-1}\right)$ from the first principle. **[NCERT]**

Sol. Let $f(x) = \frac{x+1}{x-1}$

By first principle of derivative, we have

$$f'(x) = \lim_{h \to 0} \frac{f(x+h) - f(x)}{h} = \lim_{h \to 0} \frac{\left[\frac{(x+h)+1}{(x+h)-1} - \frac{x+1}{x-1}\right]}{h}$$

$$= \lim_{h \to 0} \frac{(x+h+1)(x-1) - (x+1)(x+h-1)}{h(x+h-1)(x-1)}$$

$$= \lim_{h \to 0} \frac{(x^2 - x + xh - h + x - 1) - (x^2 + xh - x + x + h - 1)}{h(x+h-1)(x-1)}$$

$$= \lim_{h \to 0} \frac{-2h}{h(x+h-1)(x-1)} = \lim_{h \to 0} \frac{-2}{(x+h-1)(x-1)} = \frac{-2}{(x-1)^2}$$

Example 8 Find the derivative of e^x, using first principle.

Sol. Let $f(x) = e^x$

By using first principle of derivative, we have

$$f'(x) = \lim_{h \to 0} \frac{f(x+h) - f(x)}{h} = \lim_{h \to 0} \frac{e^{x+h} - e^x}{h}$$

$$= \lim_{h\to 0} \frac{e^x(e^h - 1)}{h} = e^x \lim_{h\to 0} \frac{(e^h - 1)}{h}$$

$$= e^x \lim_{h\to 0} \frac{\left[\left(1 + \frac{h}{1!} + \frac{h^2}{2!} + \frac{h^3}{3!} + \ldots \infty\right) - 1\right]}{h}$$

$$= e^x \lim_{h\to 0} \frac{h\left[1 + \frac{h}{2!} + \frac{h^2}{3!} + \ldots \infty\right]}{h} = e^x \times 1 = e^x$$

Example 9 Find the derivative of a^x from first principle.

Sol. Let $f(x) = a^x$.

By using first principle of derivative, we have

$$\therefore \quad f'(x) = \lim_{h\to 0} \frac{f(x+h) - f(x)}{h}$$

$$\Rightarrow \quad f'(x) = \lim_{h\to 0} \frac{a^{x+h} - a^x}{h} = \lim_{h\to 0} \frac{a^x a^h - a^x}{h}$$

$$\Rightarrow \quad f'(x) = a^x \lim_{h\to 0}\left(\frac{a^h - 1}{h}\right) = a^x \log_e a$$

$$\left[\because \lim_{x\to 0} \frac{a^x - 1}{x} = \log_e a\right]$$

Example 10 Find the derivative of e^{x^2} from first principle.

Sol. Let $f(x) = e^{x^2}$

By using first principle of derivative, we have

$$f'(x) = \lim_{h\to 0} \frac{f(x+h) - f(x)}{h} = \lim_{h\to 0} \frac{e^{(x+h)^2} - e^{x^2}}{h}$$

$$= \lim_{h\to 0} \frac{e^{x^2 + h^2 + 2hx} - e^{x^2}}{h}$$

$$= \lim_{h\to 0} e^{x^2}\left[\frac{e^{h(h+2x)} - 1}{h}\right] \times \frac{(h+2x)}{(h+2x)}$$

$$= e^{x^2} \lim_{h\to 0}\left[\frac{e^{h(h+2x)} - 1}{h(h+2x)}\right] \times \lim_{h\to 0}(h+2x)$$

$$= e^{x^2} \times 1 \times (0 + 2x) = 2x\, e^{x^2} \quad \left[\because \lim_{y\to 0} \frac{e^y - 1}{y} = 1\right]$$

Example 11 Find the derivative of $e^{\sqrt{x}}$ from first principle.

Sol Let $f(x) = e^{\sqrt{x}}$

By using first principle of derivative, we have

$$f'(x) = \lim_{h\to 0} \frac{f(x+h) - f(x)}{h} = \lim_{x\to 0} \frac{e^{\sqrt{x+h}} - e^{\sqrt{x}}}{h}$$

$$= \lim_{h\to 0} \frac{e^{\sqrt{x}}(e^{\sqrt{x+h} - \sqrt{x}} - 1)}{(x+h) - x}$$

$$= \lim_{h\to 0} \frac{e^{\sqrt{x}}(e^{\sqrt{x+h} - \sqrt{x}} - 1)}{(\sqrt{x+h} - \sqrt{x})(\sqrt{x+h} + \sqrt{x})}$$

$$= e^{\sqrt{x}} \lim_{h\to 0} \frac{e^{\sqrt{x+h} - \sqrt{x}} - 1}{(\sqrt{x+h} - \sqrt{x})} \times \lim_{h\to 0} \frac{1}{(\sqrt{x+h} + \sqrt{x})}$$

$$= e^{\sqrt{x}} \times 1 \times \frac{1}{2\sqrt{x}} = \frac{e^{\sqrt{x}}}{2\sqrt{x}} \quad \left[\because \lim_{y\to 0} \frac{e^y - 1}{y} = 1\right]$$

Example 12 Find the derivative of the function $\log x$, by using first principle.

Sol. Let $f(x) = \log x$

By using first principle of derivative, we have

$$f'(x) = \lim_{h\to 0} \frac{f(x+h) - f(x)}{h} = \lim_{h\to 0} \frac{\log(x+h) - \log x}{h}$$

$$= \lim_{h\to 0} \frac{\log\left(\frac{x+h}{x}\right)}{h} = \lim_{h\to 0} \frac{\log\left(1 + \frac{h}{x}\right)}{\frac{h}{x}} \times \frac{1}{x}$$

$$= 1 \times \frac{1}{x} = \frac{1}{x} \quad \left[\because \lim_{y\to 0} \frac{\log(1+y)}{y} = 1\right]$$

Example 13 Find the derivative of $\log_a x$ from first principle.

Sol. Let $f(x) = \log_a x$

By using first principle of derivative, we have

$$f'(x) = \lim_{h\to 0} \frac{f(x+h) - f(x)}{h}$$

$$\Rightarrow f'(x) = \lim_{h\to 0} \frac{\log_a(x+h) - \log_a x}{h} = \lim_{h\to 0} \frac{\log_a\left(\frac{x+h}{x}\right)}{h}$$

$$\Rightarrow f'(x) = \lim_{h\to 0} \frac{\log_a\left(1 + \frac{h}{x}\right)}{h}$$

$$= \lim_{h\to 0} \frac{\log_e\left(1 + \frac{h}{x}\right)}{(\log_e a)\cdot h} \quad \left[\because \log_a \lambda = \frac{\log_e \lambda}{\log_e a}\right]$$

$$\Rightarrow f'(x) = \frac{1}{\log_e a} \lim_{h\to 0} \frac{\log_e\left(1 + \frac{h}{x}\right)}{x\left(\frac{h}{x}\right)}$$

$$= \frac{1}{x \log_e a} \quad \left[\because \lim_{h\to 0} \frac{\log\left(1 + \frac{h}{x}\right)}{\frac{h}{x}} = 1\right]$$

Example 14 Find the derivative of the following function by using first principle.

(i) $\sin x$ (ii) $\sec x$ (iii) $\tan x$ **[NCERT Exemplar]**

Sol. (i) Let $f(x) = \sin x$

By using first principle of derivative, we have

$$f'(x) = \lim_{h\to 0} \frac{f(x+h) - f(x)}{h} = \lim_{h\to 0} \frac{\sin(x+h) - \sin x}{h}$$

$$= \lim_{h\to 0} \frac{2\cos\left(\frac{x+h+x}{2}\right)\cdot \sin\left(\frac{x+h-x}{2}\right)}{h}$$

$$\left[\because \sin C - \sin D = 2\cos\left(\frac{C+D}{2}\right) \times \sin\left(\frac{C-D}{2}\right)\right]$$

$$= \lim_{h\to 0} \frac{2\cos\left(x+\frac{h}{2}\right)\cdot \sin\frac{h}{2}}{h}$$

$$= \lim_{h\to 0} \cos\left(x+\frac{h}{2}\right)\cdot \lim_{\frac{h}{2}\to 0} \frac{\sin\frac{h}{2}}{\frac{h}{2}} \quad \left[\because h\to 0 \Rightarrow \frac{h}{2}\to 0\right]$$

$$= \lim_{h\to 0} \cos\left(x+\frac{h}{2}\right)\times 1 \quad \left[\because \lim_{\theta\to 0} \frac{\sin\theta}{\theta} = 1\right]$$

$$= \cos(x+0) = \cos x \quad \text{[put } h = 0\text{]}$$

$$\therefore \frac{d}{dx}(\sin x) = \cos x$$

(ii) Let $f(x) = \sec x$

By using first principle of derivative, we have

$$f'(x) = \lim_{h\to 0} \frac{f(x+h) - f(x)}{h}$$

$$\therefore f'(x) = \lim_{h\to 0} \frac{\sec(x+h) - \sec x}{h}$$

$$= \lim_{h\to 0} \frac{\frac{1}{\cos(x+h)} - \frac{1}{\cos x}}{h}$$

$$= \lim_{h\to 0} \frac{\cos x - \cos(x+h)}{h \times \cos x \cdot \cos(x+h)}$$

$$= \lim_{h\to 0} \left[\frac{-2\sin\left(\frac{x+x+h}{2}\right)\cdot \sin\frac{(x-x-h)}{2}}{h\cdot \cos x \cdot \cos(x+h)}\right]$$

$$\left[\because \cos C - \cos D = -2\sin\left(\frac{C+D}{2}\right)\sin\left(\frac{C-D}{2}\right)\right]$$

$$= \lim_{h\to 0} \left[\frac{-2\sin\left(x+\frac{h}{2}\right)\cdot\left(-\sin\frac{h}{2}\right)}{h\cdot \cos x \cos(x+h)}\right] \quad [\because \sin(-\theta) = -\sin\theta]$$

$$= \lim_{h\to 0} \frac{\sin\left(x+\frac{h}{2}\right)}{\cos(x+h)\cdot \cos x} \cdot \lim_{h\to 0} \frac{\sin\frac{h}{2}}{\frac{h}{2}}$$

$$= \frac{\sin x}{\cos^2 x} \times 1 \quad \left[\because \lim_{\theta\to 0} \frac{\sin\theta}{\theta} = 1\right]$$

$$= \frac{\sin x}{\cos x} \cdot \frac{1}{\cos x} = \tan x \cdot \sec x$$

(iii) Let $f(x) = \tan x$. Then, by first principle of derivative,

$$f'(x) = \lim_{h\to 0} \frac{f(x+h) - f(x)}{h}$$

$$= \lim_{h\to 0} \frac{\tan(x+h) - \tan x}{h}$$

$$= \lim_{h\to 0} \frac{1}{h}\left[\frac{\sin(x+h)}{\cos(x+h)} - \frac{\sin x}{\cos x}\right]$$

$$= \lim_{h\to 0} \frac{1}{h}\left[\frac{\sin(x+h)\cos x - \sin x \cos(x+h)}{\cos(x+h)\cos x}\right]$$

$$= \lim_{h\to 0} \frac{1}{h}\left[\frac{\sin(x+h-x)}{\cos(x+h)\cos x}\right]$$

$$[\because \sin A \cos B - \cos A \sin B = \sin(A-B)]$$

$$= \lim_{h\to 0} \frac{\sin h}{h} . \lim_{h\to 0} \frac{1}{\cos(x+h)\cos x}$$

$$= 1 \cdot \frac{1}{\cos(x+0)\cos x}$$

$$= \frac{1}{\cos^2 x} = \sec^2 x \quad \left[\because \lim_{\theta\to 0} \frac{\sin\theta}{\theta} = 1\right]$$

Hence, $f'(x)$ or $\frac{d}{dx}(\tan x) = \sec^2 x$

Example 15 Find the derivative of $f(x) = \tan(ax+b)$, by first principle. **[NCERT Exemplar]**

Sol. We have, $f(x) = \tan(ax+b)$

By first principle of derivative, we have

$$f'(x) = \lim_{h\to 0} \frac{f(x+h) - f(x)}{h}$$

$$= \lim_{h\to 0} \frac{\tan[a(x+h)+b] - \tan(ax+b)}{h}$$

$$= \lim_{h\to 0} \frac{\frac{\sin(ax+ah+b)}{\cos(ax+ah+b)} - \frac{\sin(ax+b)}{\cos(ax+b)}}{h}$$

$$= \lim_{h\to 0} \frac{\left[\frac{\sin(ax+ah+b)\cos(ax+b) - \sin(ax+b)\cos(ax+ah+b)}{}\right]}{h\cos(ax+b)\cos(ax+ah+b)}$$

$$= \lim_{h\to 0} \frac{a\sin(ah)}{a\cdot h\cos(ax+b)\cos(ax+ah+b)}$$

$$[\because \sin A \cos B - \cos A \sin B = \sin(A-B)]$$

$$= \lim_{h\to 0} \frac{a}{\cos(ax+b)\cos(ax+ah+b)} \lim_{ah\to 0} \frac{\sin ah}{ah}$$

$$[\because h\to 0, \Rightarrow ah\to 0]$$

$$= \frac{a}{\cos^2(ax+b)} \times 1 \quad \left[\because \lim_{\theta\to 0} \frac{\sin\theta}{\theta} = 1\right]$$

$$= a\sec^2(ax+b)$$

Example 16 Differentiate the function $\cos(x^2+1)$ by the first principle. **[NCERT Exemplar]**

Sol. Let $f(x)=\cos(x^2+1)$. We know by first principle,

$$f'(x)=\lim_{h\to 0}\frac{f(x+h)-f(x)}{h}$$

$$\therefore\ f'(x)=\lim_{h\to 0}\frac{\cos[(x+h)^2+1]-\cos(x^2+1)}{h}$$

$$[\because f(x)=\cos(x^2+1)]$$

$$=\lim_{h\to 0}\frac{-2\sin\frac{(x+h)^2+1+x^2+1}{2}\sin\frac{(x+h)^2+1-(x^2+1)}{2}}{h}$$

$$\left[\because \cos C-\cos D=-2\sin\left(\frac{C+D}{2}\right)\sin\left(\frac{C-D}{2}\right)\right]$$

$$=\lim_{h\to 0}\frac{-2\sin\frac{(x+h)^2+x^2+2}{2}\sin\frac{(x+h)^2-x^2}{2}}{h}$$

$$=\lim_{h\to 0}\frac{-2\sin\frac{(x+h)^2+x^2+2}{2}\left[\dfrac{\sin\frac{(x+h)^2-x^2}{2}}{\frac{(x+h)^2-x^2}{2}}\right]}{h\times\frac{(x+h)^2-x^2}{2}}$$

$$=\lim_{h\to 0}\frac{-2\sin\frac{(x+h)^2+x^2+2}{2}\times\frac{x^2+h^2+2xh-x^2}{2}}{h}$$

$$\left[\because \lim_{h\to 0}\frac{\sin\left(\frac{(x+h)^2-x^2}{2}\right)}{\frac{(x+h)^2-x^2}{2}}=1\right]$$

$$=\lim_{h\to 0}\frac{-2\sin\left[\frac{(x+h)^2+x^2+2}{2}\right](2x+h)\frac{h}{2}}{h}$$

$$=-2\sin\left(\frac{2x^2+2}{2}\right)\times 2x\times\frac{1}{2}=-2x\sin(x^2+1)$$

Example 17 By using first principle, find the derivative of function $f(x)=\sin^2 x$.

Sol. We have, $f(x)=\sin^2 x$

By using first principle of derivative,

$$f'(x)=\lim_{h\to 0}\frac{f(x+h)-f(x)}{h}$$

$$=\lim_{h\to 0}\frac{\sin^2(x+h)-\sin^2 x}{h}$$

$$=\lim_{h\to 0}\frac{[\sin(x+h)-\sin x][\sin(x+h)+\sin x]}{h}$$

$$=\lim_{h\to 0}\frac{\left[2\cos\left(\frac{2x+h}{2}\right)\sin\left(\frac{h}{2}\right)\right]\left[2\sin\left(\frac{2x+h}{2}\right)\cos\left(\frac{h}{2}\right)\right]}{h}$$

$$\left[\begin{array}{l}\because \sin C-\sin D=2\cos\frac{C+D}{2}\sin\frac{C-D}{2}\\ \text{and } \sin C+\sin D=2\sin\frac{C+D}{2}\cos\frac{C-D}{2}\end{array}\right]$$

$$=\lim_{h\to 0}\cos\left(\frac{2x+h}{2}\right)\frac{\sin\frac{h}{2}}{\frac{h}{2}}\times\lim_{h\to 0}2\sin\left(\frac{2x+h}{2}\right)\cos\frac{h}{2}$$

$$=\cos\left(\frac{2x+0}{2}\right)\times 1\times 2\sin\left(\frac{2x+0}{2}\right)\cos 0$$

$$=\cos x\times 2\sin x\times 1=\sin 2x$$

Example 18 Find the derivative of $\sin\sqrt{x}$ functions by using first principle.

Sol. Let $f(x)=\sin\sqrt{x}$. By using first principle of derivative,

$$f'(x)=\lim_{h\to 0}\frac{f(x+h)-f(x)}{h}$$

$$=\lim_{h\to 0}\frac{\sin\sqrt{x+h}-\sin\sqrt{x}}{h}$$

$$=\lim_{h\to 0}\frac{2\cos\left(\frac{\sqrt{x+h}+\sqrt{x}}{2}\right)\sin\left(\frac{\sqrt{x+h}-\sqrt{x}}{2}\right)}{(x+h)-x}$$

$$\left[\because \sin C-\sin D=2\cos\left(\frac{C+D}{2}\right)\sin\left(\frac{C-D}{2}\right)\right]$$

$$=\lim_{h\to 0}\frac{2\cos\left(\frac{\sqrt{x+h}+\sqrt{x}}{2}\right)\sin\left(\frac{\sqrt{x+h}-\sqrt{x}}{2}\right)}{(\sqrt{x+h})^2-(\sqrt{x})^2}$$

$$=\lim_{h\to 0}\frac{\sin\left(\frac{\sqrt{x+h}-\sqrt{x}}{2}\right)}{\frac{\sqrt{x+h}-\sqrt{x}}{2}}\times\lim_{h\to 0}\cos\left(\frac{\sqrt{x+h}+\sqrt{x}}{2}\right)$$

$$\times\lim_{h\to 0}\left(\frac{1}{\sqrt{x+h}+\sqrt{x}}\right)$$

$$=1\times\cos(\sqrt{x})\times\frac{1}{2\sqrt{x}}=\frac{1}{2\sqrt{x}}\cos\sqrt{x}$$

$$\left[\because \lim_{\theta\to 0}\frac{\sin\theta}{\theta}=1\right]$$

Example 19 Find the derivative of $\sqrt{\cos x}$.

Sol. (i) Let $f(x)=\sqrt{\cos x}$

By using first principle of derivative,

$$f'(x)=\lim_{h\to 0}\frac{f(x+h)-f(x)}{h}$$

$$=\lim_{h\to 0}\frac{\sqrt{\cos(x+h)}-\sqrt{\cos x}}{h}$$

$$=\lim_{h\to 0}\frac{\sqrt{\cos(x+h)}-\sqrt{\cos x}}{h}\times\frac{(\sqrt{\cos(x+h)}+\sqrt{\cos x})}{(\sqrt{\cos(x+h)}+\sqrt{\cos x})}$$

$$=\lim_{h\to 0}\frac{\cos(x+h)-\cos x}{h(\sqrt{\cos(x+h)}+\sqrt{\cos x})}$$

$$=\lim_{h\to 0}\frac{-2\sin\left(\frac{2x+h}{2}\right)\sin\left(\frac{h}{2}\right)}{h(\sqrt{\cos(x+h)}+\sqrt{\cos x})}$$

$$\left[\because \cos C-\cos D=-2\sin\left(\frac{C+D}{2}\right)\sin\left(\frac{C-D}{2}\right)\right]$$

$$=-\lim_{h\to 0}\frac{\sin\left(\frac{2x+h}{2}\right)}{(\sqrt{\cos(x+h)}+\sqrt{\cos x})}\times\lim_{h\to 0}\frac{\sin\frac{h}{2}}{\frac{h}{2}}$$

$$=-\frac{\sin\left(\frac{2x}{2}\right)}{\sqrt{\cos(x)}+\sqrt{\cos(x)}}\times 1=-\frac{\sin x}{2\sqrt{\cos x}}$$

Example 20 Find the derivative of $x\sin x$ from first principle. **[NCERT]**

Sol. We have, $f(x)=x\sin x$

By using first principle of derivative,

$$f'(x)=\lim_{h\to 0}\frac{f(x+h)-f(x)}{h}$$

$$\therefore\ f'(x)=\lim_{h\to 0}\frac{(x+h)\sin(x+h)-x\sin x}{h}$$

$$=\lim_{h\to 0}\frac{(x+h)[\sin x\cdot\cos h+\cos x\cdot\sin h]-x\sin x}{h}$$

$$[\because \sin(A+B)=\sin A\cos B+\cos A\sin B]$$

$$=\lim_{h\to 0}\frac{\left[\begin{array}{r}x\sin x\cdot\cos h+x\cdot\cos x\cdot\sin h+h\sin x\cdot\cos h\\ +h\cos x\cdot\sin h-x\sin x\end{array}\right]}{h}$$

$$=\lim_{h\to 0}\frac{\left[\begin{array}{r}x\sin x(\cos h-1)+x\cdot\cos x\cdot\sin h\\ +h(\sin x\cdot\cos h+\cos x\cdot\sin h)\end{array}\right]}{h}$$

$$=\lim_{h\to 0}\frac{x\sin x(\cos h-1)}{h}+\lim_{h\to 0}x\cdot\cos x\cdot\frac{\sin h}{h}+\lim_{h\to 0}\frac{h(\sin x\cdot\cos h+\cos x\cdot\sin h)}{h}$$

$$=x\sin x\lim_{h\to 0}\left[\frac{-(1-\cos h)}{h}\right]+x\cdot\cos x(1)+\sin x$$

$$=-x\sin x\cdot\lim_{\frac{h}{2}\to 0}\frac{2\sin^2\frac{h}{2}}{h\times\frac{h}{4}}\times\frac{h}{4}+x\cos x+\sin x$$

$$=-x\cdot\sin x\cdot\frac{2}{4}\lim_{\frac{h}{2}\to 0}\left(\frac{\sin\frac{h}{2}}{\frac{h}{2}}\right)^2\times h+x\cos x+\sin x$$

$$=-x\sin x\cdot\frac{1}{2}(1)\times 0+x\cdot\cos x+\sin x\qquad\left[\because \lim_{\theta\to 0}\frac{\sin\theta}{\theta}=1\right]$$

$$=x\cos x+\sin x$$

Example 21 Differentiate $e^{\sqrt{\tan x}}$ from first principles.

Sol. Let $f(x)=e^{\sqrt{\tan x}}$

Then, $f(x+h)=e^{\sqrt{\tan(x+h)}}$

$$\because\ \frac{d}{dx}(f(x))=\lim_{h\to 0}\frac{f(x+h)-f(x)}{h}$$

$$\therefore\ \frac{d}{dx}(f(x))=\lim_{h\to 0}\frac{e^{\sqrt{\tan(x+h)}}-e^{\sqrt{\tan x}}}{h}$$

$$\Rightarrow\ \frac{d}{dx}(f(x))=\lim_{h\to 0}e^{\sqrt{\tan x}}\left\{\frac{e^{\sqrt{\tan(x+h)}-\sqrt{\tan x}}-1}{h}\right\}$$

$$\Rightarrow\ \frac{d}{dx}(f(x))=e^{\sqrt{\tan x}}\lim_{h\to 0}\left\{\begin{array}{l}\dfrac{e^{\sqrt{\tan(x+h)}-\sqrt{\tan x}}-1}{\sqrt{\tan(x+h)}-\sqrt{\tan x}}\\ \times\lim\limits_{h\to 0}\dfrac{\sqrt{\tan(x+h)}-\sqrt{\tan x}}{h}\end{array}\right\}$$

$$\Rightarrow\frac{d}{dx}(f(x))=e^{\tan x}\times 1\times\lim_{h\to 0}\frac{\tan(x+h)-\tan x}{h}\times\frac{1}{\sqrt{\tan(x+h)}+\sqrt{\tan x}}$$

$$\Rightarrow\ \frac{d}{dx}(f(x))=e^{\sqrt{\tan x}}\times\lim_{h\to 0}\frac{\sin h}{h\cos(x+h)\cos x}\times\frac{1}{\sqrt{\tan(x+h)}+\sqrt{\tan x}}$$

$$\Rightarrow\ \frac{d}{dx}(f(x))=e^{\sqrt{\tan x}}\times\frac{1}{\cos^2 x}\times\frac{1}{2\sqrt{\tan x}}$$

$$\Rightarrow\ \frac{d}{dx}(f(x))=\frac{e^{\sqrt{\tan x}}}{2\sqrt{\tan x}}\sec^2 x$$

Topic Practice 1

Very Short Answer Type Questions

(2 Marks)

1 Find the derivative of $f(x) = ax^2 + bx + c$, where a, b and c are non-zero constant, by first principle. [NCERT Exemplar]

2 Find the derivative of $x^2 - 2$ at $x = 10$ from first principle.

3 By using first principle, find the derivative of $99x$ at $x = 100$. [NCERT]

Directions (Q. Nos. 4-8) *Find the derivative of the following functions from first principle.*

4 $x^3 - 27$ 5 $\frac{1}{x^3}$ 6 $\sqrt{4-x}$

7 $x^{2/3}$ 8 $(x^2+1)(x-5)$

Short Answer Type Questions

(4 Marks)

Directions (Q. Nos. 9-32) *Evaluate the followings.*

9 $\frac{ax+b}{cx+d}$ 10 e^{2x} 11 a^{2x}

12 $\log x^2$ 13 $\log(x+k)$ 14 $\cos x$

15 $\operatorname{cosec} x$ 16 $\cot x$ 17 $\sin(x+1)$

18 $\cos\left(x - \frac{\pi}{8}\right)$ 19 $\sin(2x-3)$ 20 $\cos\sqrt{x}$

21 $\sec\sqrt{x}$ 22 $\tan\sqrt{x}$ 23 $\sin(x^2+1)$

24 $\tan(x^2+1)$ 25 $\frac{\sin x}{x}$ 26 $\cos^2 x$

27 $x\cos x$ 28 $x\tan x$ 29 $x\sec x$

30 xe^x 31 $e^{\sqrt{\cot x}}$ 32 $e^{\sqrt{\sec x}}$

Hints & Answers

1. $f'(x) = \lim_{h\to 0} \frac{a(x+h)^2 + b(x+h) + c - ax^2 - bx - c}{h}$

Ans. $2ax + b$

2. $f'(10) = \lim_{h\to 0} \frac{[(10+h)^2 - 2] - [(10)^2 - 2]}{h}$ **Ans.** 20

3. $f'(x) = \lim_{h\to 0} \frac{99(x+h) - 99x}{h}$ **Ans.** 99

4. $f'(x) = \lim_{h\to 0} \frac{[(x+h)^3 - 27] - (x^3 - 27)}{h}$ $[\because f(x) = x^3 - 27]$

$= \lim_{h\to 0} \frac{(x+h)^3 - x^3}{h} = \lim_{h\to 0} \frac{h^3 + 3xh(x+h)}{h}$

$= \lim_{h\to 0} \frac{h[h^2 + 3x(x+h)]}{h}$ **Ans.** $3x^2$

5. $f'(x) = \lim_{h\to 0} \frac{\frac{1}{(x+h)^3} - \frac{1}{x^3}}{h} = \lim_{h\to 0} \frac{x^3 - (x+h)^3}{(x+h)^3 x^3 h}$

$= \lim_{h\to 0} \frac{x^3 - [x^3 + h^3 + 3xh(x+h)]}{(x+h)^3 x^3 h}$

$= \lim_{h\to 0} \frac{-h[h^2 + 3x(x+h)]}{(x+h)^3 x^3 h}$ **Ans.** $\frac{-3}{x^4}$

6. $f'(x) = \lim_{h\to 0} \frac{\sqrt{4-(x+h)} - \sqrt{4-x}}{h}$

$\Rightarrow \frac{d}{dx} f(x) = \lim_{h\to 0} \frac{\{\sqrt{4-(x+h)} - \sqrt{4-x}\}\{\sqrt{4-(x+h)} + \sqrt{4-x}\}}{h\{\sqrt{4-(x+h)} + \sqrt{4-x}\}}$

Ans. $\frac{-1}{2\sqrt{4-x}}$

7. $f'(x) = \lim_{h\to 0}\left[\frac{(x+h)^{2/3} - x^{2/3}}{h}\right]$

$= \lim_{(x+h)\to x}\left[\frac{(x+h)^{2/3} - x^{2/3}}{(x+h) - x}\right]$ **Ans.** $\frac{2}{3}x^{-1/3}$

8. $f'(x) = \lim_{h\to 0} \frac{((x+h)^2+1)(x+h-5) - (x^2+1)(x-5)}{h}$

Ans. $3x^2 - 10x + 1$

9. $f'(x) = \lim_{h\to 0} \frac{1}{h}\left[\frac{a(x+h)+b}{c(x+h)+d} - \frac{ax+b}{cx+d}\right]$

$= \lim_{h\to 0} \frac{1}{h}\left[\frac{(ax+ah+b)(cx+d) - (ax+b)(cx+ch+d)}{\{c(x+h)+d\}(cx+d)}\right]$

$= \lim_{h\to 0} \frac{1}{h}\left[\frac{adh - bch}{\{c(x+h)+d\}(cx+d)}\right]$ **Ans.** $\frac{ad-bc}{(cx+d)^2}$

10. $f'(x) = \lim_{h\to 0} \frac{e^{2x+2h} - e^{2x}}{h}$

$= \lim_{h\to 0} \frac{e^{2x}(e^{2h}-1)}{2h} \times 2$ **Ans.** $2e^{2x}$

11. $f'(x) = \lim_{h\to 0} \frac{a^{2(x+h)} - a^{2x}}{h}$

$= \lim_{h\to 0} \frac{a^{2x}(a^{2h}-1)}{2h} \times 2$ **Ans.** $2a^{2x}\log a$

12. $f'(x)=\lim_{h\to 0}\dfrac{\log(x+h)^2-\log x^2}{h}$

$=\lim_{h\to 0}\dfrac{2\log(x+h)-2\log x}{h}$

$=\lim_{h\to 0}\dfrac{2\log\left[1+\dfrac{h}{x}\right]}{\dfrac{h}{x}}\times\dfrac{1}{x}$ **Ans.** $\dfrac{2}{x}$

13. $f'(x)=\lim_{h\to 0}\dfrac{\log(x+k+h)-\log(x+k)}{h}$

$=\lim_{h\to 0}\dfrac{\log\left(1+\dfrac{h}{x+k}\right)}{\dfrac{h}{(x+k)}\cdot(x+k)}$ **Ans.** $\dfrac{1}{x+k}$

14. $f'(x)=\lim_{h\to 0}\dfrac{\cos(x+h)-\cos x}{h}$

$=\lim_{h\to 0}\dfrac{-2\sin\left(\dfrac{x+h+x}{2}\right)\sin\left(\dfrac{x+h-x}{2}\right)}{h}$

$=\lim_{h\to 0}\left\{-\sin\left(\dfrac{2x+h}{2}\right)\right\}\left\{\dfrac{\sin\dfrac{h}{2}}{\dfrac{h}{2}}\right\}$ **Ans.** $-\sin x$

15. $f'(x)=\lim_{h\to 0}\dfrac{\operatorname{cosec}(x+h)-\operatorname{cosec} x}{h}$

$=\lim_{h\to 0}\dfrac{\sin x-\sin(x+h)}{h\sin x\sin(x+h)}$

$=\lim_{h\to 0}\dfrac{2\cos\left(x+\dfrac{h}{2}\right)\sin\left(-\dfrac{h}{2}\right)}{\sin x\sin(x+h)h}$

Ans. $-\operatorname{cosec} x\cot x$

16. $f'(x)=\lim_{h\to 0}\dfrac{\cot(x+h)-\cot x}{h}$

$\Rightarrow\quad f'(x)=\lim_{h\to 0}\dfrac{\sin x\cos(x+h)-\sin(x+h)\cos x}{h\sin(x+h)\sin x}$

$=\lim_{h\to 0}\dfrac{\sin(-h)}{h\sin(x+h)\sin x}$

Ans. $-\operatorname{cosec}^2 x$

17. $f'(x)=\lim_{h\to 0}\dfrac{\sin(x+h+1)-\sin(x+1)}{h}$

$=\lim_{h\to 0}\dfrac{2\cos\left(\dfrac{x+h+1+x+1}{2}\right)\sin\left(\dfrac{x+h+1-x-1}{2}\right)}{h}$

$=\lim_{h\to 0}\dfrac{2\cos\dfrac{2x+h+2}{2}\sin\dfrac{h}{2}}{2\times\dfrac{h}{2}}$

Ans. $\cos(x+1)$

18. $f'(x)=\lim_{h\to 0}\dfrac{\cos\left(x+h-\dfrac{\pi}{8}\right)-\cos\left(x-\dfrac{\pi}{8}\right)}{h}$

$=\lim_{h\to 0}\dfrac{-2\sin\left(\dfrac{x+h-\dfrac{\pi}{8}+x-\dfrac{\pi}{8}}{2}\right)\sin\left(\dfrac{x+h-\dfrac{\pi}{8}-x+\dfrac{\pi}{8}}{2}\right)}{h}$

$=\lim_{h\to 0}\dfrac{-2\sin\left(\dfrac{2x-2\left(\dfrac{\pi}{8}\right)+h}{2}\right)\sin\dfrac{h}{2}}{2\times\dfrac{h}{2}}$

Ans. $-\sin\left(x-\dfrac{\pi}{8}\right)$

19. $f'(x)=\lim_{h\to 0}\dfrac{\sin[2(x+h)-3]-\sin(2x-3)}{h}$

Ans. $2\cos(2x-3)$

20. $f'(x)=\lim_{h\to 0}\dfrac{\cos\sqrt{x+h}-\cos\sqrt{x}}{h}$

$=\lim_{h\to 0}\dfrac{-2\sin\left(\dfrac{\sqrt{x+h}+\sqrt{x}}{2}\right)\sin\left(\dfrac{\sqrt{x+h}-\sqrt{x}}{2}\right)}{(x+h)-x}$

$=\lim_{h\to 0}\dfrac{-2\sin\left(\dfrac{\sqrt{x+h}+\sqrt{x}}{2}\right)}{(\sqrt{x+h}+\sqrt{x})}\times\lim_{h\to 0}\dfrac{\sin\left(\dfrac{\sqrt{x+h}-\sqrt{x}}{2}\right)}{2\left(\dfrac{\sqrt{x+h}-\sqrt{x}}{2}\right)}$

Ans. $-\dfrac{1}{2}\dfrac{\sin\sqrt{x}}{\sqrt{x}}$.

21. $f'(x)=\lim_{h\to 0}\dfrac{\sec\sqrt{x+h}-\sec\sqrt{x}}{h}$

$=\lim_{h\to 0}\dfrac{\cos\sqrt{x}-\cos\sqrt{x+h}}{h\cos\sqrt{x}\cos\sqrt{x+h}}$

$=\lim_{h\to 0}\dfrac{-2\sin\left(\dfrac{\sqrt{x}+\sqrt{x+h}}{2}\right)\sin\left(\dfrac{\sqrt{x}-\sqrt{x+h}}{2}\right)}{\{(x+h)-x\}\cos\sqrt{x}\cos\sqrt{x+h}}$

$=\lim_{h\to 0}\dfrac{-2\sin\left(\dfrac{\sqrt{x}+\sqrt{x+h}}{2}\right)}{(\sqrt{x+h}+\sqrt{x})\cos\sqrt{x}\cos\sqrt{x+h}}$

$\times\lim_{h\to 0}\dfrac{\sin\left(\dfrac{\sqrt{x}-\sqrt{x+h}}{2}\right)}{(\sqrt{x+h}-\sqrt{x})}$

Ans. $\dfrac{\sec\sqrt{x}\tan\sqrt{x}}{2\sqrt{x}}$

22. $f'(x)=\lim_{h\to 0}\dfrac{\dfrac{\sin\sqrt{x+h}}{\cos\sqrt{x+h}}-\dfrac{\sin\sqrt{x}}{\cos\sqrt{x}}}{h}$

$=\lim_{h\to 0}\dfrac{\sin\sqrt{x+h}\cdot\cos\sqrt{x}-\sin\sqrt{x}\cdot\cos\sqrt{x+h}}{h\cdot\cos\sqrt{x+h}\cos\sqrt{x}}$

$=\lim_{h\to 0}\dfrac{\sin(\sqrt{x+h}-\sqrt{x})}{h\cos\sqrt{x}\cdot\cos\sqrt{x+h}}\times\dfrac{\sqrt{x+h}-\sqrt{x}}{\sqrt{x+h}-\sqrt{\sqrt{x}}}$

$=\lim_{h\to 0}\dfrac{1}{\cos\sqrt{x}\cdot\cos\sqrt{x+h}}\times\lim_{h\to 0}\dfrac{\sin(\sqrt{x+h}-\sqrt{x})}{\sqrt{x+h}-\sqrt{x}}$

$\times\lim_{h\to 0}\dfrac{\sqrt{x+h}-\sqrt{x}}{h}$

Ans. $\dfrac{\sec^2\sqrt{x}}{2\sqrt{x}}$

23. $f'(x)=\lim_{h\to 0}\dfrac{\sin[(x+h)^2+1]-\sin(x^2+1)}{h}$

$=\lim_{h\to 0}\dfrac{2\cos\left(\dfrac{(x+h)^2+x^2+2}{2}\right)\sin\left(\dfrac{(x+h)^2-x^2}{2}\right)}{h}$

$=\lim_{h\to 0}2\cos\left(\dfrac{2x^2+h^2+2hx+2}{2}\right)$

$\times\lim_{h\to 0}\dfrac{\sin\left(\dfrac{h(h+2x)}{2}\right)}{h(h+2x)}\times\lim_{h\to 0}(h+2x)$

Ans. $2x\cos(x^2+1)$

24. $f'(x)=\lim_{h\to 0}\dfrac{\tan[(x+h)^2+1]-\tan(x^2+1)}{h}$

$=\lim_{h\to 0}\dfrac{\left[\sin[(x+h)^2+1]\cos(x^2+1)-\cos[(x+h)^2+1]\sin(x^2+1)\right]}{h\cdot\cos[(x+h)^2+1]\cos(x^2+1)}$

$=\lim_{h\to 0}\dfrac{\sin[(x+h)^2+1-x^2-1]}{h\cos[(x+h)^2+1]\cos(x^2+1)}$ **Ans.** $2x\sec^2(x^2+1)$

25. $f'(x)=\lim_{h\to 0}\dfrac{\dfrac{\sin(x+h)}{x+h}-\dfrac{\sin x}{x}}{h}$

$=\lim_{h\to 0}\dfrac{x[\sin(x+h)-\sin x]-h\sin x}{h\cdot x(x+h)}$

$=\lim_{h\to 0}\dfrac{x\left[2\cdot\cos\left(\dfrac{x+h+x}{2}\right)\cdot\sin\left(\dfrac{x+h-x}{2}\right)\right]-h\sin x}{h\cdot x(x+h)}$

$=\lim_{h\to 0}\dfrac{x\left[2\cdot\sin\dfrac{h}{2}\cdot\cos\left(x+\dfrac{h}{2}\right)\right]-h\sin x}{h\cdot x(x+h)}$

$=\lim_{\frac{h}{2}\to 0}\dfrac{\sin\left(\dfrac{h}{2}\right)}{\left(\dfrac{h}{2}\right)}\cdot\lim_{h\to 0}\dfrac{\cos\left(x+\dfrac{h}{2}\right)}{(x+h)}-\lim_{h\to 0}\dfrac{\sin x}{x(x+h)}$

Ans. $\dfrac{\cos x}{x}-\dfrac{\sin x}{x^2}$

26. $f'(x)=\lim_{h\to 0}\dfrac{\cos^2(x+h)-\cos^2 x}{h}$

$=\lim_{h\to 0}[\cos(x+h)+\cos x]\lim_{h\to 0}\dfrac{[\cos(x+h)-\cos x]}{h}$

$=2\cos x\lim_{h\to 0}-\dfrac{2\sin\left(x+\dfrac{h}{2}\right)\sin\left(\dfrac{h}{2}\right)}{h}$ **Ans.** $-\sin 2x$

27. $f'(x)=\lim_{h\to 0}\dfrac{1}{h}[(x+h)\cos(x+h)-x\cos x]$

$=\lim_{h\to 0}\dfrac{1}{h}[x\{\cos(x+h)-\cos x\}+h\cos(x+h)]$

$=\lim_{h\to 0}\dfrac{1}{h}\left[x\left\{-2\sin\left(\dfrac{2x+h}{2}\right)\sin\dfrac{h}{2}\right\}+h\cos(x+h)\right]$

$=\lim_{h\to 0}\left[-2x\sin\left(x+\dfrac{h}{2}\right)\dfrac{\sin\dfrac{h}{2}}{h}+\cos(x+h)\right]$

$=-2x\lim_{h\to 0}\sin\left(x+\dfrac{h}{2}\right)\lim_{h\to 0}\dfrac{\sin\dfrac{h}{2}}{\dfrac{h}{2}}\cdot\dfrac{1}{2}+\lim_{h\to 0}\cos(x+h)$

Ans. $\cos x-x\sin x$

28. $f'(x)=\lim_{h\to 0}\dfrac{[(x+h)\tan(x+h)-x\tan x]}{h}$

$=\lim_{h\to 0}\dfrac{x[\tan(x+h)-\tan x]+h\tan(x+h)}{h}$

$=\lim_{h\to 0}\dfrac{x[\sin(x+h)\cos x-\cos(x+h)\sin x]}{h\cos(x+h)\cos x}$

$+\lim_{h\to 0}\tan(x+h)$

$=x\lim_{h\to 0}\dfrac{1}{\cos(x+h)\cos x}\times\lim_{h\to 0}\dfrac{\sin h}{h}+\tan x$

Ans. $x\sec^2 x+\tan x$

29. $\sec x+x\sec x\tan x$

30. $\lim_{h\to 0}\dfrac{(xe^{x+h}-xe^x)+he^{x+h}}{h}$

$=xe^x\lim_{h\to 0}\left(\dfrac{e^h-1}{h}\right)+\lim_{h\to 0}e^{x+h}$

Ans. $(x+1)e^x$

31. $\dfrac{-e^{\sqrt{\cot x}}}{2\sqrt{\cot x}}\cdot\operatorname{cosec}^2 x$

32. $\dfrac{e^{\sqrt{\sec x}}}{2\sqrt{\sec x}}\cdot\sec x\tan x$

TOPIC 02 Algebra of Derivative of Functions

Let f and g be two functions such that their derivatives are defined in a common domain. Then,

(i) Derivative of sum of two functions is sum of the derivatives of the functions.

$$\frac{d}{dx}[f(x)+g(x)]=\frac{d}{dx}f(x)+\frac{d}{dx}g(x)$$

(ii) Derivative of difference of two functions is difference of the derivatives of the functions.

$$\frac{d}{dx}[f(x)-g(x)]=\frac{d}{dx}f(x)-\frac{d}{dx}g(x)$$

(iii) Derivative of product of two functions is given by the following product rule

$$\frac{d}{dx}[f(x)\cdot g(x)]=f(x)\frac{d}{dx}g(x)+g(x)\frac{d}{dx}f(x)$$

This is also known as **Leibnitz rule** of derivative.

Extension of the product rule If f, g and h are three differentiable functions at x, then

$$\frac{d}{dx}\{f(x)\,g(x)\,h(x)\}=f(x)\,g(x)\frac{d}{dx}\{h(x)\}+f(x)\,h(x)\frac{d}{dx}\{g(x)\}+g(x)\,h(x)\cdot\frac{d}{dx}\{f(x)\}$$

(iv) Derivative of quotient of two functions is given by the following quotient rule.

$$\frac{d}{dx}\left[\frac{f(x)}{g(x)}\right]=\frac{g(x)\frac{d}{dx}f(x)-f(x)\frac{d}{dx}g(x)}{[g(x)]^2},\ g(x)\neq 0$$

Note $\frac{d}{dx}[c\cdot f(x)]=c\frac{d}{dx}f(x)$

Some Important Theorems

Theorem 1 Differentiation of a constant function is zero

i.e. $\frac{d}{dx}(c)=0$, where c is a constant.

Proof Let $f(x)=c$ be a constant function.

Then, $\frac{d}{dx}(f(x))=\lim_{h\to 0}\frac{f(x+h)-f(x)}{h}=\lim_{h\to 0}\frac{c-c}{h}=0$

Hence, $\frac{d}{dx}(c)=0$, where c is a constant.

Theorem 2 An additive constant disappears in differentiation,

i.e. $\frac{d}{dx}[f(x)+c]=\frac{d}{dx}[f(x)]$, where c is a constant.

Theorem 3 Derivative of $f(x)=x^n$ is nx^{n-1} for any positive integer n.

Note The above theorem is true for all rational powers of x i.e. n can be any rational number.

Theorem 4 Derivative of $(ax+b)^n$ is $n\,(ax+b)^{n-1}a$, where n is any positive integer and a, b are fixed real numbers.

***Theorem* 5 Derivative of polynomials**

Let $f(x)=a_nx^n+a_{n-1}x^{n-1}+\ldots+a_1x+a_0$ be a polynomial function, where a_i's are all real numbers. Then, the derivative of this function is given by

$$\frac{d}{dx}[f(x)]=na_nx^{n-1}+(n-1)a_{n-1}x^{n-2}+\ldots+2a_2x+a_1$$

Example 1 Differentiate the following functions w.r.t. x.

(i) $\log_x x$ (ii) $e^{3\log x}$ (iii) $2^{\log_2 x}$

Sol. (i) We know that, $\log_x x=1$

$\therefore\ \frac{d}{dx}(\log_x x)=\frac{d}{dx}(1)=0$

(ii) We know that, $e^{\log k}=k$

$\therefore\ \frac{d}{dx}(e^{3\log x})=\frac{d}{dx}(e^{\log x^3})=\frac{d}{dx}(x^3)=3x^2$

(iii) We know that, $a^{\log_a n}=n$

$\therefore\ \frac{d}{dx}(2^{\log_2 x})=\frac{d}{dx}(x)=1$

Example 2 Differentiate $2x^3-4x^2+6x+8$ w.r.t. x.

Sol. Let $y=2x^3-4x^2+6x+8$

On differentiating both sides w.r.t. x, we get

$$\frac{dy}{dx}=\frac{d}{dx}(2x^3-4x^2+6x+8)$$

$$=2\frac{d}{dx}(x^3)-4\frac{d}{dx}(x^2)+6\frac{d}{dx}(x)+\frac{d}{dx}(8)$$

$$=2(3x^2)-4(2x)+6(1)+0 \quad \left[\because \frac{d}{dx}(x^n)=nx^{n-1}\right]$$

$$=6x^2-8x+6$$

Example 3 Find the derivative of

$$f(x) = 1 + x + x^2 + x^3 + \ldots + x^{50} \text{ at } x = 1. \quad \text{[NCERT]}$$

Sol. Given, $f(x) = 1 + x + x^2 + x^3 + \ldots + x^{50}$

On differentiating both sides w.r.t. x, we get

$$f'(x) = 0 + 1 + 2x + 3x^2 + \ldots + 50x^{49}$$

At $x = 1$,

$$f'(1) = 1 + 2(1) + 3(1)^2 + \ldots + 50(1)^{49}$$

$$= 1 + 2 + 3 + \ldots + 50$$

$$= \frac{(50)(51)}{2} = 1275 \quad \left[\because \Sigma n = \frac{n(n+1)}{2}\right]$$

Example 4 If $u = 7t^4 - 2t^3 - 8t - 5$, then find $\frac{du}{dt}$ at $t = 2$.

Sol. We have, $u = 7t^4 - 2t^3 - 8t - 5$

On differentiating both sides w.r.t. t, we get

$$\frac{du}{dt} = \frac{d}{dt}[7t^4 - 2t^3 - 8t - 5]$$

$$= 7(4t^3) - 2(3t^2) - 8(1) - 0 \quad \left[\because \frac{d}{dx}(x^n) = nx^{n-1}\right]$$

$$= 28t^3 - 6t^2 - 8$$

Now, $\left(\frac{du}{dt}\right)_{t=2} = 28(2)^3 - 6(2)^2 - 8 = 224 - 24 - 8 = 192$

Example 5 For the function

$$f(x) = \frac{x^{100}}{100} + \frac{x^{99}}{99} + \ldots + \frac{x^2}{2} + x + 1.$$

Prove that $f'(1) = 100 f'(0)$. [NCERT]

Sol. Given, $f(x) = \frac{x^{100}}{100} + \frac{x^{99}}{99} + \ldots + \frac{x^2}{2} + x + 1$

$$\Rightarrow \quad f'(x) = \frac{100x^{99}}{100} + \frac{99x^{98}}{99} + \ldots + \frac{2x}{2} + 1 + 0$$

$$[\because \text{if } f(x) = x^n, \text{ then } f'(x) = nx^{n-1}]$$

$$\Rightarrow \quad f'(x) = x^{99} + x^{98} + \ldots + x + 1 \quad \ldots\text{(i)}$$

On putting $x = 1$, we get

$$f'(1) = (1)^{99} + (1)^{98} + \ldots + 1 + 1 = \underbrace{1 + 1 + 1 \ldots + 1 + 1}_{100 \text{ times}}$$

$$\Rightarrow \quad f'(1) = 100 \quad \ldots\text{(ii)}$$

Again, putting $x = 0$, we get

$$f'(0) = 0 + 0 + \ldots + 0 + 1 \Rightarrow f'(0) = 1 \quad \ldots\text{(iii)}$$

From Eqs. (ii) and (iii), $f'(1) = 100 f'(0)$ **Hence proved.**

Example 6 Differentiate the following functions w.r.t. x.

(i) $\left(x + \frac{1}{x}\right)^3$ (ii) $(ax + b)(cx + d)^2$ (iii) $\frac{px^2 + qx + r}{(ax + b)}$ [NCERT]

Sol. (i) Let $y = \left(x + \frac{1}{x}\right)^3 = x^3 + 3x \times \frac{1}{x^2} + 3x^2 \times \frac{1}{x} + \frac{1}{x^3}$

$$[\because (A + B)^3 = A^3 + 3A^2B + 3AB^2 + B^3]$$

$$= x^3 + \frac{3}{x} + 3x + \frac{1}{x^3}$$

On differentiating both sides w.r.t. x, we get

$$\frac{dy}{dx} = \frac{d}{dx}(x^3) + \frac{d}{dx}\left(\frac{3}{x}\right) + \frac{d}{dx}(3x) + \frac{d}{dx}\left(\frac{1}{x^3}\right)$$

$$= 3x^2 + 3\frac{d}{dx}(x^{-1}) + 3 \times 1 + \frac{d}{dx}(x^{-3})$$

$$= 3x^2 + \frac{-3}{x^2} + 3 - \frac{3}{x^4}$$

(ii) Let $y = (ax + b)(cx + d)^2$

On differentiating both sides w.r.t. x, we get

$$\frac{dy}{dx} = (ax + b)\frac{d}{dx}(cx + d)^2 + (cx + d)^2 \frac{d}{dx}(ax + b)$$

[using product rule of derivative]

$$= (ax + b)\frac{d}{dx}(c^2x^2 + d^2 + 2cxd) + (cx + d)^2 (a \times 1 + 0)$$

$$[\because (A + B)^2 = A^2 + 2AB + B^2]$$

$$= (ax + b)(c^2(2x) + 0 + 2c \times 1 \times d) + (cx + d)^2 \times a$$

$$= (ax + b)(2c^2x + 2cd) + a(cx + d)^2$$

$$= (ax + b)\, 2c\,(cx + d) + a(cx + d)^2$$

$$= (cx + d)[2c(ax + b) + a(cx + d)]$$

$$= (cx + d)(2acx + 2bc + acx + ad)$$

$$= (cx + d)(3acx + 2bc + ad)$$

(iii) Let $y = \frac{px^2 + qx + r}{(ax + b)}$

On differentiating both sides w.r.t. x, we get

$$\frac{dy}{dx} = \frac{\left[(ax + b)\frac{d}{dx}(px^2 + qx + r) - (px^2 + qx + r)\frac{d}{dx}(ax + b)\right]}{(ax + b)^2}$$

[by quotient rule]

$$= \frac{(ax + b)(2px + q + 0) - (px^2 + qx + r)(a \times 1 + 0)}{(ax + b)^2}$$

$$= \frac{(ax+b)(2px+q)-(px^2+qx+r)a}{(ax+b)^2}$$

$$= \frac{(2apx^2+aqx+2bpx+bq)-(apx^2+aqx+ra)}{(ax+b)^2}$$

$$= \frac{2apx^2+aqx+2bpx+bq-apx^2-aqx-ra}{(ax+b)^2}$$

$$\frac{dy}{dx} = \frac{apx^2+2bpx+bq-ra}{(ax+b)^2}$$

Example 7 If $y = \dfrac{x}{x+5}$, then prove that

$$x\frac{dy}{dx} = y(1-y).$$

Sol. We have, $y = \dfrac{x}{x+5}$ ...(i)

On differentiating both sides of Eq. (i) w.r.t. x, we get

$$\frac{dy}{dx} = \frac{d}{dx}\left(\frac{x}{x+5}\right)$$

$$= \frac{(x+5)\frac{d}{dx}x - x\frac{d}{dx}(x+5)}{(x+5)^2}$$

$$\left[\because \frac{d}{dx}\left(\frac{u}{v}\right) = \frac{v\frac{du}{dx} - u\frac{dv}{dx}}{v^2}\right]$$

$$= \frac{(x+5)(1) - x(1+0)}{(x+5)^2} = \frac{x+5-x}{(x+5)^2}$$

$$\Rightarrow \frac{dy}{dx} = \frac{5}{(x+5)^2}$$

Now, LHS $= x\dfrac{dy}{dx} = \dfrac{5x}{(x+5)^2}$ ...(ii)

and RHS $= y(1-y) = \dfrac{x}{x+5}\left(1 - \dfrac{x}{x+5}\right)$

$= \dfrac{x}{x+5}\left(\dfrac{x+5-x}{x+5}\right) = \dfrac{5x}{(x+5)^2}$ ...(iii)

From Eqs. (ii) and (iii), we get

$$x\frac{dy}{dx} = y(1-y)$$ **Hence proved.**

Example 8 Differentiate $\dfrac{x^2+3x-9}{x^2-9x+3}$ w.r.t. x.

Sol. Let $y = \dfrac{x^2+3x-9}{x^2-9x+3}$

On differentiating both sides w.r.t. x, we get

$$\frac{dy}{dx} = \frac{d}{dx}\left[\frac{x^2+3x-9}{x^2-9x+3}\right]$$

$$= \frac{\left\{(x^2-9x+3)\left[\frac{d}{dx}(x^2+3x-9)\right] - (x^2+3x-9)\frac{d}{dx}(x^2-9x+3)\right\}}{(x^2-9x+3)^2}$$

[using quotient rule of derivative]

$$= \frac{\left[(x^2-9x+3)(2x+3-0) - (x^2+3x-9) \times (2x-9+0)\right]}{(x^2-9x+3)^2}$$

$$= \frac{[(x^2-9x+3)(2x+3) - (x^2+3x-9)(2x-9)]}{(x^2-9x+3)^2}$$

$$= \frac{\left[2x(x^2-9x+3) + 3(x^2-9x+3) - 2x(x^2+3x-9) + 9(x^2+3x-9)\right]}{(x^2-9x+3)^2}$$

$$= \frac{\left[2x(x^2-9x+3-x^2-3x+9) + (3x^2-27x+9 + 9x^2+27x-81)\right]}{(x^2-9x+3)^2}$$

$$= \frac{2x(-12x+12)+(12x^2-72)}{(x^2-9x+3)^2} = \frac{-24x^2+24x+12x^2-72}{(x^2-9x+3)^2}$$

$$= \frac{-12x^2+24x-72}{(x^2-9x+3)^2} = \frac{-12(x^2-2x+6)}{(x^2-9x+3)^2}$$

Topic Practice 2

Very Short Answer Type Questions

2 Marks

1. Find $f'(x)$, if $f(x)=(x-2)^2(2x-3)$.
2. For some constants a and b, find the derivative of the following functions. (Each part carries 2 marks)
   (i) $(x-a)(x-b)$ (ii) $(ax^2+b)^2$
   (iii) $\dfrac{x-a}{x-b}$ (iv) $\dfrac{1}{ax^2+bx+c}$
3. Find the derivative of the functions w.r.t. x.
   (i) $5(2^{3\log_2 x})$ (ii) $5e^x$ (iii) $9(3^x)$
4. If $y=\sqrt{x}+\dfrac{1}{\sqrt{x}}$, then find $\dfrac{dy}{dx}$ at $x=1$. **[NCERT Exemplar]**
5. Find the derivative of $x^n+ax^{n-1}+a^2x^{n-2}+\ldots+a^{n-1}x+a^n$ for some fixed real number a. **[NCERT]**

Short Answer Type Questions

4 Marks

6 Find the derivative of the following functions. (Each part carries 4 marks)

(i) $\frac{x^4+x^3+x^2+1}{x}$ (ii) $\frac{x^2+x+1}{\sqrt{x}}$

(iii) $(5x^3+3x-1)(x-1)$ (iv) $\frac{2}{x+1}-\frac{x^2}{3x-1}$ **[NCERT]**

(v) $\frac{3x+4}{5x^2-7x+9}$ **[NCERT Exemplar]**

7 Find the derivative of $\frac{(x-1)(x-2)}{(x-3)(x-4)}$.

8 If $f(x)=1-x+x^2-x^3+\ldots-x^{99}+x^{100}$, then find $f'(1)$.

9 If $f(x)=x^{100}+x^{99}+\ldots+x+1$, then find $f'(1)$. **[NCERT Exemplar]**

Hints & Answers

1. $f(x)=2x^3-11x^2+20x-12$ **Ans.** $6x^2-22x+20$

2. (i) Let $f(x)=(x-a)(x-b)=x^2-(a+b)x+ab$

Ans. $2x-a-b$

(ii) Let $f(x)=(ax^2+b)^2=a^2x^4+b^2+2abx^2$

Ans. $4ax(ax^2+b)$

(iii) $\frac{a-b}{(x-b)^2}$ (iv) $\frac{-(2ax+b)}{(ax^2+bx+c)^2}$

3. (i) $15x^2$ (ii) $5e^x$ (iii) $3^{x+2}\log_e 3$

4. $\frac{dy}{dx}=\frac{1}{2\sqrt{x}}-\frac{1}{2x^{3/2}}$ **Ans.** 0

5. Let $f(x)=x^n+ax^{n-1}+a^2x^{n-2}+\ldots+a^{n-1}x+a^n$

Then, $f'(x)=\frac{d}{dx}(x^n)+\frac{d}{dx}(ax^{n-1})+\frac{d}{dx}(a^2x^{n-2})+\ldots+\frac{d}{dx}(a^{n-1}x)+\frac{d}{dx}(a^n)$

Ans. $nx^{n-1}+a(n-1)x^{n-2}+a^2(n-2)x^{n-3}+\ldots+a^{n-1}$

6. (i) $\frac{d}{dx}\left(\frac{x^4+x^3+x^2+1}{x}\right)=\frac{d}{dx}\left(x^3+x^2+x+\frac{1}{x}\right)$

Ans. $\frac{3x^4+2x^3+x^2-1}{x^2}$

(ii) $\frac{d}{dx}\left(\frac{x^2+x+1}{\sqrt{x}}\right)=\frac{d}{dx}(x^{3/2}+x^{1/2}+x^{-1/2})$

Ans. $\frac{3}{2}x^{\frac{1}{2}}+\frac{1}{2}x^{-\frac{1}{2}}-\frac{1}{2}x^{-\frac{3}{2}}$

(iii) $20x^3-15x^2+6x-4$ (iv) $\frac{-2}{(x+1)^2}-\frac{x(3x-2)}{(3x-1)^2}$

(v) Let $y=\frac{3x+4}{5x^2-7x+9}$

$$\frac{dy}{dx}=\frac{(5x^2-7x+9)\frac{d}{dx}(3x+4)-(3x+4)\frac{d}{dx}(5x^2-7x+9)}{(5x^2-7x+9)^2}$$

Ans. $\frac{55-15x^2-40x}{(5x^2-7x+9)^2}$

7. Let $y=\frac{(x-1)(x-2)}{(x-3)(x-4)}=\frac{x^2-3x+2}{x^2-7x+12}$

On differentiating both sides w.r.t. x, we get

$$\frac{dy}{dx}=\frac{\left[(x^2-7x+12)\frac{d}{dx}(x^2-3x+2)-(x^2-3x+2)\frac{d}{dx}(x^2-7x+12)\right]}{(x^2-7x+12)^2}$$

Ans. $\frac{-4x^2+20x-22}{(x-3)^2(x-4)^2}$

8. $f'(x)=0-1+2x-3x^2+\ldots-99x^{98}+100x^{99}$

$=-1+2x-3x^2+\ldots-99x^{98}+100x^{99}$

$\therefore$ $f'(1)=-1+2-3+\ldots-99+100$

$=(-1-3-5-\ldots-99)+(2+4+\ldots+100)$

$=-\frac{50}{2}[2\times1+(50-1)2]+\frac{50}{2}[2\times2+(50-1)2]$ **Ans.** 50

9. $f'(x)=100x^{99}+99x^{98}+\ldots+1+0=100x^{99}+99x^{98}+\ldots+1$

Now, $f'(1)=100+99+\ldots+1$

Ans. 5050

TOPIC 03 Derivative of Trigonometric Functions

To find the derivative of trigonometric functions, we use the algebra of derivative and the following formulae

1. The differentiation of $\sin x$ w.r.t. x is $\cos x$,
   i.e. $\frac{d}{dx}(\sin x) = \cos x$.
2. The differentiation of $\cos x$ w.r.t. x is $-\sin x$,
   i.e. $\frac{d}{dx}(\cos x) = -\sin x$.
3. The differentiation of $\tan x$ w.r.t. x is $\sec^2 x$,
   i.e. $\frac{d}{dx}(\tan x) = \sec^2 x$.
4. The differentiation of $\cot x$ w.r.t. x is $-\text{cosec}^2 x$, i.e. $\frac{d}{dx}(\cot x) = -\text{cosec}^2 x$
5. The differentiation of $\sec x$ w.r.t. x is $\sec x \tan x$,
   i.e. $\frac{d}{dx}(\sec x) = \sec x \tan x$.
6. The differentiation of $\text{cosec}\, x$ w.r.t. x is $-\text{cosec}\, x \cot x$, i.e. $\frac{d}{dx}(\text{cosec}\, x) = -\text{cosec}\, x \cot x$.

Note We can prove these results by using first principle of derivative.

Example 1 Differentiate the following functions w.r.t. x.

(i) $\cos(x+a)$

(ii) $\frac{\sin(x+a)}{\cos x}$

Sol. (i) Let $y = \cos(x+a)$

$$y = \cos x \cos a - \sin x \sin a$$

$[\because \cos(A+B) = \cos A \cos B - \sin A \sin B]$

On differentiating both sides w.r.t. x, we get

$$\frac{dy}{dx} = \cos a \frac{d}{dx}(\cos x) - \sin a \frac{d}{dx}(\sin x)$$

$$= \cos a(-\sin x) - \sin a(\cos x)$$

$$= -\cos a \sin x - \sin a \cos x = -\sin(x+a)$$

$[\because \sin A \cos B + \cos A \sin B = \sin(A+B)]$

(ii) Let $y = \frac{\sin(x+a)}{\cos x} = \frac{\sin x \cos a + \cos x \sin a}{\cos x}$

$[\because \sin(A+B) = \sin A \cos B + \cos A \sin B]$

$$= \frac{\sin x \cos a}{\cos x} + \frac{\cos x \sin a}{\cos x}$$

$$= \cos a \tan x + \sin a$$

On differentiating both sides w.r.t. x, we get

$$\frac{dy}{dx} = \cos a \frac{d}{dx}(\tan x) + \frac{d}{dx}(\sin a)$$

$$= \cos a \sec^2 x + 0 \qquad \left[\because \frac{d}{dx}(\text{constant}) = 0\right]$$

$$= \frac{\cos a}{\cos^2 x} \qquad \left[\because \sec x = \frac{1}{\cos x}\right]$$

Example 2 Find the derivative of the following functions. **[NCERT]**

(i) $f(x) = \sin^2 x$

(ii) $f(x) = \sin 2x$

(iii) $f(x) = (\cos^2 x - \sin^2 x)$

Sol. (i) We have,

$$f(x) = \sin^2 x$$

On differentiating both sides w.r.t. x, we get

$$f'(x) = \frac{d}{dx}(\sin x \sin x)$$

$$= (\sin x)\frac{d}{dx}(\sin x) + (\sin x)\frac{d}{dx}(\sin x)$$

[using product rule of derivative]

$$= (\cos x)\sin x + \sin x(\cos x)$$

$$= 2\sin x \cos x = \sin 2x$$

(ii) We have,

$$f(x) = \sin 2x$$

$$f(x) = 2\sin x \cos x$$

On differentiating both sides w.r.t. x, we get

$$f'(x) = 2\left[\sin x \frac{d}{dx}(\cos x) + \cos x \frac{d}{dx}(\sin x)\right]$$

[using product rule of derivative]

$$= 2[\sin x \cdot (-\sin x) + \cos x \cdot \cos x]$$

$$= 2(-\sin^2 x + \cos^2 x)$$

$$= 2(\cos^2 x - \sin^2 x) = 2\cos 2x$$

(iii) We have, $f(x)=(\cos^2 x-\sin^2 x)$

$f(x)=(\cos x-\sin x)(\cos x+\sin x)$

On differentiating both sides w.r.t. x, we get

$$f'(x)=(\cos x-\sin x)\frac{d}{dx}(\cos x+\sin x)+(\cos x+\sin x)\frac{d}{dx}(\cos x-\sin x)$$

[using product rule of derivative]

$$=(\cos x-\sin x)(-\sin x+\cos x)+(\cos x+\sin x)(-\sin x-\cos x)$$

$$=(\cos x-\sin x)(\cos x-\sin x)-(\cos x+\sin x)(\cos x+\sin x)$$

$$=(\cos x-\sin x)^2-(\cos x+\sin x)^2$$

$$=(\cos^2 x+\sin^2 x-2\sin x\cos x)-(\cos^2 x+\sin^2 x+2\sin x\cos x)$$

$$=-2\sin x\cos x-2\sin x\cos x$$

$$=-\sin 2x-\sin 2x=-2\sin 2x$$

Example 3 Find the derivative of following functions.

(i) $x^2 \cos x$ (ii) $x^2 \sec x$

(iii) $x^2 \tan x$

Sol. (i) Let $y=x^2\cos x$

On differentiating both sides w.r.t. x, we get

$$\frac{dy}{dx}=\frac{d}{dx}(x^2\cos x)$$

$$=x^2\frac{d}{dx}(\cos x)+\cos x\frac{d}{dx}(x^2)$$

[using product rule of derivative]

$$=x^2(-\sin x)+\cos x(2x)$$

$$=2x\cos x-x^2\sin x$$

(ii) Let $y=x^2\sec x$

On differentiating both sides w.r.t. x, we get

$$\frac{dy}{dx}=x^2\frac{d}{dx}(\sec x)+\sec x\frac{d}{dx}(x^2)$$

[using product rule of derivative]

$$=x^2\cdot\sec x\tan x+\sec x(2x)$$

$$=x^2\sec x\tan x+2x\sec x$$

$$=x\sec x(x\tan x+2)$$

(iii) Let $y=x^2\tan x$

On differentiating both sides w.r.t. x, we get

$$\frac{dy}{dx}=x^2\frac{d}{dx}(\tan x)+\tan x\frac{d}{dx}(x^2)$$

[using product rule of derivative]

$$=x^2\sec^2 x+\tan x\,(2x)$$

$$=x^2\sec^2 x+2x\tan x$$

Example 4 Find the derivative of $\dfrac{4x+5\sin x}{3x+7\cos x}$. [NCERT]

Sol. Let $f(x)=\dfrac{4x+5\sin x}{3x+7\cos x}$

On differentiating both sides w.r.t. x, we get

$$f'(x)=\frac{\left[(3x+7\cos x)\frac{d}{dx}(4x+5\sin x)-(4x+5\sin x)\times\frac{d}{dx}(3x+7\cos x)\right]}{(3x+7\cos x)^2}$$

$$\left[\because \frac{d}{dx}\left(\frac{f(x)}{g(x)}\right)=\frac{g(x)\frac{d}{dx}f(x)-f(x)\frac{d}{dx}g(x)}{[g(x)]^2}\right]$$

$$=\frac{(3x+7\cos x)(4+5\cos x)-(4x+5\sin x)[3+7(-\sin x)]}{(3x+7\cos x)^2}$$

$$=\frac{\left[(12x+15x\cdot\cos x+28\cdot\cos x+35\cos^2 x)-(12x-28x\cdot\sin x+15\sin x-35\sin^2 x)\right]}{(3x+7\cos x)^2}$$

$$=\frac{\left[35(\sin^2 x+\cos^2 x)+28x\cdot\sin x+15x\cdot\cos x+28\cos x-15\sin x\right]}{(3x+7\cos x)^2}$$

$$=\frac{35+28x\sin x+15x\cdot\cos x-15\sin x+28\cos x}{(3x+\cos x)^2}$$

Example 5 Differentiate $(x+\sec x)\cdot(x-\tan x)$ w.r.t. x. [NCERT]

Sol. We have, $y=(x+\sec x)(x-\tan x)$

On differentiating both sides w.r.t. x, we get

$$\frac{dy}{dx}=\frac{d}{dx}[(x+\sec x)(x-\tan x)]$$

$$=(x+\sec x)\cdot\frac{d}{dx}(x-\tan x)+(x-\tan x)\frac{d}{dx}(x+\sec x)$$

[using product rule of derivative]

$$=(x+\sec x)(1-\sec^2 x)+(x-\tan x)(1+\sec x\cdot\tan x)$$

Example 6 Differentiate the following functions w.r.t. x.

(i) $1-2\sin^2\dfrac{x}{2}$ (ii) $2\cos^2\dfrac{x}{2}-1$

(ii) $3\sin\dfrac{x}{3}-4\sin^3\dfrac{x}{3}$ (iv) $e^{\log_e \sin x}$

(v) $\log_e e^{\cos x}$

Sol. (i) Let $y = 1 - 2\sin^2\frac{x}{2}$

$\Rightarrow \quad y = \cos x \quad [\because \cos 2\theta = 1 - 2\sin^2\theta]$

On differentiating both sides w.r.t. x, we get

$$\frac{dy}{dx} = \frac{d}{dx}(\cos x) = -\sin x$$

(ii) Let $y = 2\cos^2\frac{x}{2} - 1$

$\Rightarrow \quad y = \cos x \quad [\because \cos 2\theta = 2\cos^2\theta - 1]$

On differentiating both sides w.r.t. x, we get

$$\frac{dy}{dx} = \frac{d}{dx}(\cos x) = -\sin x$$

(iii) Let $y = 3\sin\frac{x}{3} - 4\sin^3\frac{x}{3} = \sin 3\left(\frac{x}{3}\right)$

$[\because \sin 3\theta = 3\sin\theta - 4\sin^3\theta]$

$\Rightarrow \quad y = \sin x$

On differentiating both sides w.r.t. x, we get

$$\frac{dy}{dx} = \frac{d}{dx}(\sin x) = \cos x$$

(iv) Let $y = e^{\log_e \sin x}$

$\Rightarrow \quad y = \sin x \quad [\because e^{\log_e f(x)} = f(x)]$

On differentiating both sides w.r.t. x, we get

$$\frac{dy}{dx} = \frac{d}{dx}(\sin x) = \cos x$$

(v) Let $y = \log_e e^{\cos x}$

$\Rightarrow \quad y = \cos x \quad \left[\begin{array}{l}\because \log m^n = n\log m \text{ and } \log_e e = 1 \\ \because \log_e e^{\cos x} = \cos x \log_e e = \cos x\end{array}\right]$

On differentiating both sides w.r.t. x, we get

$$\frac{dy}{dx} = \frac{d}{dx}(\cos x) = -\sin x$$

Example 7 Differentiate $(ax^2 + \sin x)(p + q\cos x)$ w.r.t. x.

Sol. Let $y = (ax^2 + \sin x)(p + q\cos x)$

On differentiating both sides w.r.t. x, we get

$$\frac{dy}{dx} = (ax^2 + \sin x)\frac{d}{dx}(p + q\cos x) + (p + q\cos x)\frac{d}{dx}(ax^2 + \sin x)$$

[using product rule of derivative]

$$= (ax^2 + \sin x)(0 - q\sin x) + (p + q\cos x)(2ax + \cos x)$$

$$= -q\sin x(ax^2 + \sin x) + (p + q\cos x)(2ax + \cos x)$$

Example 8 Find the derivative of the following functions.

(i) $\dfrac{\sin x + \cos x}{\sin x - \cos x}$ (ii) $\dfrac{\sec x + \tan x}{\sec x - \tan x}$

[NCERT; NCERT Exemplar]

Sol. Let $f(x) = \dfrac{\sin x + \cos x}{\sin x - \cos x}$

On differentiating both sides w.r.t. x, we get

$$f'(x) = \frac{\left[\begin{array}{l}(\sin x - \cos x)\frac{d}{dx}(\sin x + \cos x) \\ -(\sin x + \cos x)\frac{d}{dx}(\sin x - \cos x)\end{array}\right]}{(\sin x - \cos x)^2}$$

$$\left[\because \frac{d}{dx}\left(\frac{f(x)}{g(x)}\right) = \frac{g(x)\frac{d}{dx}f(x) - f(x)\frac{d}{dx}g(x)}{[g(x)]^2}\right]$$

$$= \frac{\left[\begin{array}{l}(\sin x - \cos x)\left[\frac{d}{dx}(\sin x) + \frac{d}{dx}(\cos x)\right] \\ -(\sin x + \cos x)\left[\frac{d}{dx}(\sin x) - \frac{d}{dx}(\cos x)\right]\end{array}\right]}{(\sin x - \cos x)^2}$$

$$= \frac{(\sin x - \cos x)(\cos x - \sin x) - (\sin x + \cos x)(\cos x + \sin x)}{(\sin x - \cos x)^2}$$

$$\left[\because \frac{d}{dx}(\sin x) = \cos x \text{ and } \frac{d}{dx}(\cos x) = -\sin x\right]$$

$$= \frac{-(\sin x - \cos x)^2 - (\sin x + \cos x)^2}{(\sin x - \cos x)^2}$$

$$= -\left[\frac{(\sin x - \cos x)^2 + (\sin x + \cos x)^2}{(\sin x - \cos x)^2}\right]$$

$$= \frac{\left[\begin{array}{l}-(\sin^2 x + \cos^2 x - 2\sin x\cos x + \sin^2 x \\ + \cos^2 x + 2\sin x\cos x)\end{array}\right]}{(\sin x - \cos x)^2}$$

$$= \frac{-2(\sin^2 x + \cos^2 x)}{(\sin x - \cos x)^2} = \frac{-2}{(\sin x - \cos x)^2}$$

$[\because \sin^2\theta + \cos^2\theta = 1]$

(ii) Let $y = \dfrac{\sec x + \tan x}{\sec x - \tan x} = \dfrac{\frac{1}{\cos x} + \frac{\sin x}{\cos x}}{\frac{1}{\cos x} - \frac{\sin x}{\cos x}} \Rightarrow y = \dfrac{1 + \sin x}{1 - \sin x}$

On differentiating both sides w.r.t. x, we get

$$\frac{dy}{dx} = \frac{d}{dx}\left(\frac{\sec x + \tan x}{\sec x - \tan x}\right) = \frac{d}{dx}\left(\frac{1 + \sin x}{1 - \sin x}\right)$$

$$= \frac{(1 - \sin x)\frac{d}{dx}(1 + \sin x) - (1 + \sin x)\frac{d}{dx}(1 - \sin x)}{(1 - \sin x)^2}$$

[using quotient rule of derivative]

$$= \frac{(1 - \sin x)(0 + \cos x) - (1 + \sin x)(0 - \cos x)}{(1 - \sin x)^2}$$

$$= \frac{2\cos x}{(1 - \sin x)^2}$$

Topic Practice 3

Very Short Answer Type Question

2 Marks

1 Find the derivative of the following functions. (Each part carries 2 Marks)

(i) $\sin x \cos x$ (ii) $5\sec x + 4\cos x$
(iii) $3\cot x + 5 \operatorname{cosec} x$ (iv) $5\sin x + 6\cos x + 7$
(v) $2\tan x - 7\sec x$ **[NCERT]**

2 Find the derivative of the following functions. (Each part carries 2 Marks)

(i) $\operatorname{cosec} x \cot x$ (ii) $(\sec x - 1)(\sec x + 1)$
(iii) $(ax^2 + \cot x)(p + q\cos x)$ **[NCERT Exemplar]**
(iv) $(x^2 + 1)\cos x$ (v) $\sin(x + a)$

Directions (Q. Nos. 3-13) *Find the derivative of the following functions.*

3 $(x + \cos x)(x - \tan x)$

4 $x^4(5\sin x - 3\cos x)$

5 $\dfrac{\sec x - 1}{\sec x + 1}$

6 $\dfrac{x^2\cos\left(\frac{\pi}{4}\right)}{\sin x}$

7 $\dfrac{x}{1+\tan x}$

8 $(3x+5)(1+\tan x)$

9 $\dfrac{x^5 - \cos x}{\sin x}$

10 $\dfrac{a+b\sin x}{c+d\cos x}$

11 $\dfrac{a}{x^4} - \dfrac{b}{x^2} + \cos x$

12 $\dfrac{\cos x}{1+\sin x}$

13 $\dfrac{\cos(x-a)}{\cos x}$

14 If $y = \dfrac{\sin(x+9)}{\cos x}$, then find $\dfrac{dy}{dx}$ at $x=0$.

15 Find the derivative of $\dfrac{1-\cos x}{1+\cos x}$.

Short Answer Type Questions

4 Marks

16 If $y = \dfrac{\sin x + \cos x}{\sin x - \cos x}$, then find $\dfrac{dy}{dx}$ at $x=0$. **[NCERT Exemplar]**

17 Find the derivative of $x^2\sin x + \cos 2x$.

18 Find the derivative of the following functions.

(i) $\dfrac{x\tan x}{(\sec x + \tan x)}$ (ii) $\dfrac{\sin x - x\cos x}{x\sin x + \cos x}$

Hints & Answers

1. (i) $\cos 2x$

(ii) $5\sec x\tan x - 4\sin x$

(iii) $-3\operatorname{cosec}^2 x - 5\operatorname{cosec} x\cot x$

(iv) $5\cos x - 6\sin x$

(v) $2\sec^2 x - 7\sec x\tan x$

2. (i) $-\operatorname{cosec}^3 x - \cot^2 x\operatorname{cosec} x$

(ii) $(\sec x - 1)(\sec x + 1) = \sec^2 x - 1 = \tan^2 x$

$= \tan x \cdot \tan x$ **Ans.** $2\tan x\sec^2 x$

(iii) Let $y = (ax^2 + \cot x)(p + q\cos x)$.

Then, $\dfrac{dy}{dx} = (ax^2 + \cot x)\dfrac{d}{dx}(p + q\cos x) + (p + q\cos x)\dfrac{d}{dx}(ax^2 + \cot x)$

Ans. $-q\sin x(ax^2 + \cot x) + (p + q\cos x)(2ax - \operatorname{cosec}^2 x)$

(iv) $-x^2\sin x - \sin x + 2x\cos x$

(v) $\sin(x + a) = \sin x\cos a + \cos x\sin a$ **Ans.** $\cos(x+a)$

3. $\dfrac{d}{dx}\{(x + \cos x)(x - \tan x)\}$

$= (x + \cos x)\cdot\dfrac{d}{dx}(x - \tan x) + (x - \tan x)\cdot\dfrac{d}{dx}(x + \cos x)$

Ans. $(x + \cos x)(-\tan^2 x) + (x - \tan x)(1 - \sin x)$

4. $x^3[5x\cos x + 3x\sin x + 20\sin x - 12\cos x]$

5. Let $y = \dfrac{\sec x - 1}{\sec x + 1}$

On differentiating w.r.t. x, we get

$$\frac{dy}{dx} = \frac{(\sec x + 1)\frac{d}{dx}(\sec x - 1) - (\sec x - 1)\frac{d}{dx}(\sec x + 1)}{(\sec x + 1)^2}$$

$$= \frac{(\sec x + 1)(\sec x\tan x - 0) - (\sec x - 1)(\sec x\tan x + 0)}{(\sec x + 1)^2}$$

$$= \frac{(\sec x + 1)(\sec x\tan x) - (\sec x - 1)(\sec x\tan x)}{(\sec x + 1)^2}$$

Ans. $\dfrac{2\sec x\tan x}{(\sec x + 1)^2}$

6. Let $y = \left(\cos\dfrac{\pi}{4}\right) \times \dfrac{x^2}{\sin x}$

Then, $\dfrac{dy}{dx} = \cos\dfrac{\pi}{4} \times \dfrac{d}{dx}\left(\dfrac{x^2}{\sin x}\right)$ $\left[\because \cos\dfrac{\pi}{4} \text{ is constant}\right]$

Ans. $\dfrac{x\cos\frac{\pi}{4}[2\sin x - x\cos x]}{\sin^2 x}$

7. Let $y=\dfrac{x}{1+\tan x}$

On differentiating w.r.t.x, we get

$$\frac{dy}{dx}=\frac{(1+\tan x)\frac{d}{dx}(x)-x\frac{d}{dx}(1+\tan x)}{(1+\tan x)^2}$$

Ans. $\dfrac{1+\tan x-x\sec^2 x}{(1+\tan x)^2}$

8. Let $y=(3x+5)(1+\tan x)$.

Then, $\dfrac{dy}{dx}=\dfrac{d}{dx}[(3x+5)(1+\tan x)]$

$$=(3x+5)\frac{d}{dx}(1+\tan x)+(1+\tan x)\frac{d}{dx}(3x+5)$$

Ans. $3x\sec^2 x+5\sec^2 x+3\tan x+3$

9. $\dfrac{d}{dx}\left(\dfrac{x^5-\cos x}{\sin x}\right)$

$$=\frac{\sin x\frac{d}{dx}(x^5-\cos x)-(x^5-\cos x)\frac{d}{dx}\sin x}{(\sin x)^2}$$

$$=\frac{\sin x(5x^4+\sin x)-(x^5-\cos x)\cos x}{\sin^2 x}$$

Ans. $\dfrac{5x^4\sin x-x^5\cos x+1}{\sin^2 x}$

10. Let $y=\dfrac{a+b\sin x}{c+d\cos x}$. Then,

$$\frac{dy}{dx}=\frac{\left[(c+d\cos x)\frac{d}{dx}(a+b\sin x)-(a+b\sin x)\frac{d}{dx}(c+d\cos x)\right]}{(c+d\cos x)^2}$$

$$=\frac{(c+d\cos x)(b\cos x)-(a+b\sin x)(-d\sin x)}{(c+d\cos x)^2}$$

Ans. $\dfrac{bc\cos x+ad\sin x+bd}{(c+d\cos x)^2}$

11. $-\dfrac{4a}{x^5}+\dfrac{2b}{x^3}-\sin x$

12. $\dfrac{-1}{1+\sin x}$

13. $y=\dfrac{\cos x\cos a+\sin x\sin a}{\cos x}=\cos a+\tan x\sin a$

Ans. $\sec^2 x\cdot\sin a$

14. Given, $y=\dfrac{\sin(x+9)}{\cos x}=\dfrac{\sin x\cos 9+\cos x\sin 9}{\cos x}$

$=\tan x\cos 9+\sin 9$

$\therefore\ \dfrac{dy}{dx}=\sec^2 x\cos 9$

Ans. $\cos 9$

15. Use the quotient rule of derivative.

Ans. $\dfrac{2\sin x}{(1+\cos x)^2}$

16. Similar as Example 8 (i).

Ans. -2

17. $\dfrac{d}{dx}(x^2\sin x+\cos 2x)$

$$=\frac{d}{dx}(x^2\sin x)+\frac{d}{dx}(\cos 2x)$$

$$=\frac{d}{dx}(x^2\sin x)+\frac{d}{dx}(2\cos^2 x-1)$$

$$=\frac{d}{dx}(x^2\sin x)+\frac{d}{dx}(2\cos x\cos x-1)$$

$$=x^2\cdot\cos x+\sin x\,2x$$

$$+\left[2\left(\cos x\frac{d}{dx}(\cos x)+\cos x\frac{d}{dx}(\cos x)\right)-\frac{d}{dx}(1)\right]$$

Ans. $x^2\cos x+2x\sin x-2\sin 2x$

18. (i) $\dfrac{x\sec x(\sec x-\tan x)+\tan x}{(\sec x+\tan x)}$

(ii) $\dfrac{x^2}{(x\sin x+\cos x)^2}$

Chapter Practice

Multiple Choice Type Questions

1 Mark

1. The derivative of the function $f(x) = 3x$ at $x = 2$ is
(a) 0 (b) 1 (c) 2 (d) 3

2. If $\frac{d}{dx}\left\{\frac{1}{f(x)}\right\} = \frac{p}{q}$, where p and q respectively are
(a) $f'(x), \{f(x)\}^2$ (b) $-f'(x), \{f(x)\}^2$
(c) $-f'(x), f(x)$ (d) $f(x), f'(x)$

3. If $y = \frac{1+\frac{1}{x^2}}{1-\frac{1}{x^2}}$, then $\frac{dy}{dx}$ is **[NCERT Exemplar]**
(a) $\frac{-4x}{(x^2-1)^2}$ (b) $\frac{-4x}{x^2-1}$
(c) $\frac{1-x^2}{4x}$ (d) $\frac{4x}{x^2-1}$

4. Which of the following is/are true?
I. The derivative of $f(x) = \sin 2x$ is $2(\cos^2 x - \sin^2 x)$.
II. The derivative of $g(x) = \cot x$ is $-\operatorname{cosec}^2 x$.
(a) Both I and II are true
(b) Only I is true
(c) Only II is true
(d) Both I and II are false

5. If $y = \left\{\frac{1-\tan x}{1+\tan x}\right\}$ and $\frac{dy}{dx} = \frac{k}{1+\sin 2x}$, then the value of k is
(a) 1 (b) 2 (c) -1 (d) -2

Assertion-Reason Type Questions

1 Mark

Directions (Q. Nos. 6-9) *In the questions given below are two statements labelled as Assertion (A) and Reason (R). In the context of the two statements, which one of the following is correct?*

(a) Both A and R are correct; R is the correct explanation of A
(b) Both A and R are correct; R is not the correct explanation of A
(c) A is correct; R is incorrect
(d) R is correct; A is incorrect

6. **Assertion (A)** The derivative of $f(x) = \cos x$ at $x = 0$ is 0.

Reason (R) For a function $f(x)$,
$$f'(a) = \lim_{h \to 0} \frac{f(a+h)-f(a)}{h}.$$

7. **Assertion (A)** For a function
$f(x) = \begin{cases} \frac{\sin x}{x}, & x \neq 0 \\ 2, & x = 0 \end{cases}$, $\lim_{x\to 0} f(x)$ does not exist.

Reason (R) For a function $f(x)$, at $x = a$, limit will exists if LHL (at $x = a$) = RHL (at $x = a$).

8. **Assertion (A)** Derivative of $f(x) = x|x|$ is $2|x|$.

Reason (R) For function u and v, $(uv)' = uv' + vu'$.

9. **Assertion (A)** Derivative of $f(x) = 2$ is zero.

Reason (R) Differentiation of constant function is zero.

Very Short Answer Type Questions

2 Marks

Directions (Q. Nos. 10-14) *Find the derivatives of the following functions.*

10. $\frac{x}{5} + \frac{5}{x}, x \neq 0$

11. $(ax)^m + b^m$

12. $(px+q)\left(\frac{r}{x} + s\right)$

13. If $f(x) = \frac{7}{4}x^2$, then find $f'\left(\frac{1}{7}\right)$.

14. If $y = \frac{2-3\cos x}{\sin x}$, then find $\left.\frac{dy}{dx}\right|_{\text{at } x = \frac{\pi}{4}}$.

Short Answer Type Questions

(4 Marks)

15. Differentiate $\sin^3 x$ w.r.t. x from first principle.

16. For the function f, given by $f(x) = x^2 - 6x + 8$, prove that $f'(5) - 3f'(2) = f'(8)$.

17. If $y = 1 + x + \frac{x^2}{2!} + \frac{x^3}{3!} + \frac{x^4}{4!} + \ldots \infty$, then show that $\frac{dy}{dx} = y$.

18. Differentiate $s = t^2(t+1)^{-1}$ w.r.t. t.

Long Answer Type Questions

(6 Marks)

19. Find the derivative of $\sin(x+a)$ from first principle. Hence find the derivative of $\frac{\sin(x+a)}{\cos x}$.

20. Differentiate $\log \sin x$ using first principle.

21. Find the coordinates of the points on the curve $y = \frac{x}{1-x^2}$ for which $\frac{dy}{dx} = 1$.

Case-Based Type Question

(6 Marks)

22. Let u and v are two functions of x. Then,

I. $\frac{d}{dx}(u \pm v) = \frac{du}{dx} \pm \frac{dv}{dx}$

II. $\frac{d}{dx}(u \cdot v) = u\frac{dv}{dx} + v\frac{du}{dx}$

III. $\frac{d}{dx}\left(\frac{u}{v}\right) = \frac{v\frac{du}{dx} - u\frac{dv}{dx}}{v^2}$

On the basis of above information, answer the following questions.

(i) Evaluate $\frac{d}{dx}(x \sin x)$.

(ii) Evaluate $\frac{d}{dx}(\cos(x+a))$.

(iii) Evaluate $\frac{d}{dx}\left(\frac{1+\log x}{1-\log x}\right)$.

(iv) If $f(x) = \frac{x^n - a^n}{x - a}$, then find the value of $f'(a)$.

Hints & Answers

1. (d) **2.** (b) **3.** (a) **4.** (a) **5.** (d)

6. (a) **7.** (d) **8.** (a) **9.** (a)

10. $\frac{1}{5} - \frac{5}{x^2}, x \neq 0$

11. $ma^m x^{m-1}$

12. $ps - \frac{qr}{x^2}$

13. $f'(x) = \frac{7}{2}x$

Ans. $\frac{1}{2}$

14. $f'(x) = \frac{3 - 2\cos x}{\sin^2 x}$

Ans. $2(3 - \sqrt{2})$

15. Let $f(x) = \sin^3 x$ ...(i)

By definition of first principle of derivative, we get

$$f'(x) = \lim_{h \to 0} \frac{f(x+h) - f(x)}{h}$$

$$= \lim_{h \to 0} \frac{\sin^3(x+h) - \sin^3 x}{h} \quad \text{[from Eq. (i)]}$$

$$= \lim_{h \to 0} \frac{[\{\sin(x+h) - \sin x\}\{\sin^2(x+h) + \sin^2 x + \sin(x+h)\sin x\}]}{h}$$

$$= \lim_{h \to 0} \frac{\left[2\sin\frac{h}{2}\cos\left(x+\frac{h}{2}\right)(\sin^2(x+h) + \sin^2 x + \sin(x+h)\sin x)\right]}{h}$$

$$= \lim_{h \to 0} \frac{\sin h/2}{h/2} \cdot \lim_{h \to 0} \cos\left(x + \frac{h}{2}\right) \cdot \lim_{h \to 0} [\sin^2(x+h) + \sin^2 x + \sin(x+h)\sin x]$$

Ans. $3\sin^2 x \cos x$

16. Given, $f(x) = x^2 - 6x + 8$

On differentiating both sides w.r.t., x, we get

$$f'(x) = 2x - 6 \quad \text{...(i)}$$

Now, $f'(5) - 3f'(2) = (2 \times 5 - 6) - 3(2 \times 2 - 6)$ [from Eq. (i)]

$= 10 - 6 - 12 + 18 = 10$ ...(ii)

and $f'(8) = 2 \times 8 - 6$ [from Eq. (ii)]

$= 10$ ...(iii)

From Eqs. (ii) and (iii), we get the result.

17. We have, $y = 1 + x + \frac{x^2}{2!} + \frac{x^3}{3!} + \frac{x^4}{4!} + \ldots \infty,$

$$\Rightarrow \quad \frac{dy}{dx} = \frac{d}{dx}(1) + \frac{d}{dx}(x) + \frac{1}{2!}\cdot\frac{d}{dx}(x^2) + \frac{1}{3!}\cdot\frac{d}{dx}(x^3) + \frac{1}{4!}\cdot\frac{d}{dx}(x^4) + \ldots\infty$$

$$= 0 + 1 + \frac{2x}{2!} + \frac{3x^2}{3!} + \frac{4x^3}{4!} + \ldots$$

$$= 1 + x + \frac{x^2}{2!} + \frac{x^3}{3!} + \frac{x^4}{4!} + \ldots$$

$$= y$$

18. To find $\frac{ds}{dt}$ and for this use quotient rule of derivative.

Ans. $\frac{ds}{dt} = \frac{t^2 + 2t}{(t+1)^2}$

19. Let $f(x) = \sin(x + a)$.

Then, $f'(x) = \lim_{h \to 0} \frac{f(x+h) - f(x)}{h}$

$$= \lim_{h \to 0} \frac{\sin(x + h + a) - \sin(x + a)}{h}$$

$$\Rightarrow \quad f'(x) = \cos(x + a)$$

Now, let $g(x) = \frac{\sin(x+a)}{\cos x}$, then

$$g'(x) = \frac{\cos x \cdot \frac{d}{dx}(\sin(x + a)) - \sin(x + a) \cdot \frac{d}{dx}(\cos x)}{\cos^2 x}$$

Ans. $\cos(x + a)$; $\cos a \cdot \sec^2 x$.

20. Let $f(x) = \log \sin x$.

Then, $f'(x) = \lim_{h \to 0} \frac{f(x+h) - f(x)}{h}$

$$= \lim_{h \to 0} \frac{\log \sin(x+h) - \log \sin x}{h}$$

$$= \lim_{h \to 0} \frac{\log\left(\frac{\sin(x+h)}{\sin x}\right)}{h}$$

$$= \lim_{h \to 0} \frac{\log\left(1 + \frac{\sin(x+h)}{\sin x} - 1\right)}{h}$$

$$= \lim_{h \to 0} \frac{\log\left(1 + \frac{\sin(x+h) - \sin x}{\sin x}\right)}{h}$$

$$= \lim_{h \to 0} \frac{\log\left(1 + \frac{\sin(x+h) - \sin x}{\sin x}\right)}{h \times \left\{\frac{\sin(x+h) - \sin x}{\sin x}\right\}} \times \left\{\frac{\sin(x+h) - \sin x}{\sin x}\right\}$$

Ans. $\cot x$

21. Given, $\frac{dy}{dx} = 1$

$$\Rightarrow \quad \frac{d}{dx}\left(\frac{x}{1 - x^2}\right) = 1$$

$$\Rightarrow \quad \frac{(1 - x^2)\cdot 1 - x(-2x)}{(1 - x^2)^2} = 1$$

$$\Rightarrow \quad 1 - x^2 + 2x^2 = (1 - x^2)^2$$

$$\Rightarrow \quad 1 + x^2 = 1 + x^4 - 2x^2$$

$$\Rightarrow \quad x^2 - 3x^2 = 0$$

$$\Rightarrow \quad x^2(x^2 - 3) = 0$$

$$\Rightarrow \quad x = 0$$

or $\quad x = \pm\sqrt{3}$

Now, substitute the values of x in the given equation of curve.

Ans. $(0, 0)$, $\left(\sqrt{3}, -\frac{\sqrt{3}}{2}\right)$, $\left(-\sqrt{3}, \frac{\sqrt{3}}{2}\right)$.

22. (i) $x \cos x + \sin x$

(ii) $-\sin(x + a)$

(iii) $\frac{2}{x(1 - \log x)^2}$

(iv) Does not exist

CHAPTER

14

Statistics

Statistics is the study of collection, organisation, analysis, interpretation and presentation of data. The word 'statistics' has different meanings in different contexts. Some people regards statistics as data, facts or measurements, while other belive it to be the study of figures. Statistics deals with data collected for specific purposes. We can make decisions about the data by analysing and interpreting it.

- Measures of Central Tendency
- Measures of Dispersion
- Variance and Standard Deviation

TOPIC 01 Measures of Central Tendency

A certain value that represent the whole data and signifying its characteristics is called measure of **central tendency**. **Mean or average**, **median** and **mode** are the measures of central tendency.

Mean (Arithmetic Mean)

The arithmetic mean (or simple mean) of a set of observations is obtained by dividing the sum of the values of observations by the number of observations.

Mean of Ungrouped Data

The mean of n observations $x_1, x_2, x_3, \dots, x_n$ is given by

$$\text{Mean } (\bar{x}) = \frac{x_1 + x_2 + x_3 + \dots + x_n}{n} = \frac{\sum_{i=1}^{n} x_i}{n}$$

Mean of Grouped Data

(i) **Direct Method** Let $x_1, x_2, \dots, x_n$ be n observations with respective frequencies $f_1, f_2, \dots, f_n$.

Then, mean $(\bar{x}) = \dfrac{\sum_{i=1}^{n} f_i x_i}{\sum_{i=1}^{n} f_i}$

(ii) **Assumed Mean Method** (Shortcut Method) Mean $= a + \dfrac{\Sigma f_i d_i}{\Sigma f_i}$

where, a = assumed mean, $d_i = x_i - a$ = deviation from assumed mean.

(iii) **Step-deviation Method** Mean $(\bar{x}) = a + \dfrac{\Sigma f_i u_i}{\Sigma f_i} \times h$

where, a = assumed mean, $u_i = \dfrac{x_i - a}{h}$

and h = width of the class interval.

Note (i) Algebraic sum of the deviations of a set of values from their arithmetic mean is zero.

(ii) The sum of the squares of the deviations of a set values is minimum when taken about the mean.

Median

Median is defined as the middle most or the central value of the observations, when the observations are arranged either in ascending or descending order of their magnitudes.

Median of Ungrouped Data

Let n be the number of observations. First, arrange the data in ascending or descending order.

(i) If n is odd, then

$$\text{Median} = \text{Value of the} \left(\frac{n+1}{2}\right)\text{th observation}$$

(ii) If n is even, then

$$\text{Median} = \frac{\text{Sum of values of the} \left(\frac{n}{2}\right)\text{th and} \left(\frac{n}{2}+1\right)\text{th observations}}{2}$$

Median of Grouped Data

I. For Discrete Data First, arrange the data in ascending or descending order and find cumulative frequency. Now, find $\dfrac{N}{2}$, where $N = \Sigma f_i$.

After that, find the median by using the following formula.

(i) If $\Sigma f_i = N$ is even, then

$$\text{Median} = \frac{\text{Value of} \left(\frac{N}{2}\right)\text{th observation} + \text{Value of} \left(\frac{N}{2}+1\right)\text{th observation}}{2}$$

(ii) If $\Sigma f_i = N$ is odd, then

$$\text{Median} = \text{Value of} \left(\frac{N+1}{2}\right)\text{th observation.}$$

II. **For Continuous Data** First arrange the data in ascending or descending order and find the cumulative frequencies of all the classes.

Now, find $\dfrac{N}{2}$, where $N = \Sigma f_i$

Further, find the class interval, whose cumulative frequency is just greater than or equal to $\dfrac{N}{2}$.

Then, median $= l + \dfrac{\left(\frac{N}{2} - cf\right)}{f} \times h$

where, l = lower limit of median class

N = number of observations

cf = cumulative frequency of class preceding the median class

f = frequency of the median class

and h = class width (assuming class size to be equal)

Note The intersection point of less than ogive and more than ogive is the median.

Example 1 If $\bar{x}$ is the mean of $x_1, x_2, \ldots, x_n$ show the the mean of $x_1 + a, x_2 + a, \ldots, x_n + a$ is $\bar{x} + a$, where a is any number positive or negative.

Sol. $\because \bar{x} = \dfrac{x_1 + x_2 + x_3 + \ldots + x_n}{n}$ ...(i)

Let $\bar{X}$ be the mean of the number $x_1 + a, x_2 + a, \ldots, x_n + a$, then

$$\bar{X} = \frac{(x_1 + a) + (x_2 + a) + (x_3 + a) + \ldots + (x_n + a)}{n}$$

$$= \frac{(x_1 + x_2 + \ldots + x_n) + na}{n}$$

$$= \frac{x_1 + x_2 + \ldots + x_n}{n} + \frac{na}{n} = \bar{x} + a$$

Example 2 Find the mean for the following distribution.

x	73	72	71	70	69	68	67	66	65
f	2	4	6	10	11	7	5	4	1

Sol. Let the assumed mean be $a = 69$

x	f	$d = x - a = x - 69$	fd	fx
73	2	4	8	146
72	4	3	12	288
71	6	2	12	426
70	10	1	10	700
69	11	0	0	759
68	7	−1	−7	476
67	5	−2	−10	335
66	4	−3	−12	264
65	1	−4	−4	65
Total	$\Sigma f = 50$		$\Sigma fd = 9$	$\Sigma fx = 3459$

By using direct method,

$$\text{Mean } (\bar{x}) = \frac{\Sigma fx}{\Sigma f} = \frac{3459}{50} = \frac{6918}{100} = 69.18$$

By using shortcut method,

$$\text{Mean } (\bar{x}) = a + \frac{\Sigma fd}{\Sigma d} = 69 + \frac{9}{50} = 69 + \frac{18}{100}$$

$$= 69 + 0.18 = 69.18$$

Example 3 Find the median of the following numbers.

(i) 3, 5, 0, 4, 9, 7, 6, 2, 8

(ii) 3, 5, 1, 2, 4, 6, 0, 2, 2, 3

Sol. (i) On arranging the given numbers in ascending order, we get 0, 2, 3, 4, 5, 6, 7, 8, 9

Here number of observation, $n = 9$ which is odd.

$$\therefore \text{ Median} = \frac{n+1}{2} \text{ th observation} = \frac{9+1}{2}$$

i.e. 5th observation = 5

(ii) On arranging the given numbers in ascending order, we get 0, 1, 2, 2, 2, 3, 3, 4, 5, 6

Here, number of observation $n = 10$, which is even.

$$\therefore \text{ Median} = \frac{\frac{n}{2}\text{th observation} + \left(\frac{n}{2}+1\right)\text{th observation}}{2}$$

$$= \frac{\text{5th observation} + \text{6th observation}}{2}$$

$$= \frac{2+3}{2} = \frac{5}{2} = 2.5$$

Example 4 In a unit test, the marks obtained by 100 students (out of 50) are given below

Marks obtained	20	29	28	33	42	38	43	25
Number of students	6	28	24	15	2	4	1	20

Calculate the median marks.

Sol. On arranging marks in ascending order and construct the commulative frequency table as given below

Marks obtained	20	25	28	29	33	38	42	43
Number of students	6	20	24	28	15	4	2	1
commulative frequency	6	26	50	78	93	97	99	100

Here, $N = 100$, which is even.

$$\therefore \text{ Median} = \frac{\frac{n}{2}\text{th observation} + \left(\frac{n}{2}+1\right)\text{th observation}}{2}$$

$$= \frac{\text{50th observation} + \text{51th observation}}{2}$$

$$= \frac{28+29}{2} = \frac{57}{2} = 28.5$$

Example 5 The weights of 40 eggs were recorded as given below

Weight (in gram)	85-89	90-94	95-99	100-104	105-109
Number of eggs	10	12	12	4	2

Calculate the median weight, correct upto 2 decimal places.

Sol. From the given data, we note that the classes are of equal width 5 but discontinuous. Hence, using the adjustment factor $= \frac{90-89}{2} = 0.5$, we get continuous distribution and then find cumulative frequency distribution as under

Weight (in gram)	84.5-89.5	89.5-94.5	94.5-99.5	99.5-104.5	104.5-109.5
Frequency	10	12	12	4	2
Cumulative frequency	10	22	34	38	40

Here, $N = 40$. $\frac{N}{2}$th i.e. 20th observation lies in class 89.5-94.5, which is the median class.

$\therefore l = 89.5, h = 5, f = 12, cf = 10$

$$\therefore \text{ Median} = l + \frac{\left(\frac{N}{2} - cf\right)}{f} \times h = 89.5 + \frac{20-10}{12} \times 5$$

$$= 89.5 + \frac{50}{12} = 89.5 + 4.17 = 93.67 \text{ gm}$$

Mode

Mode of a statistical data is the variate which occurs most frequently. In other words, mode of a statistical data is the variate which has maximum frequency.

Mode for Grouped Data When Frequency Distribution is Given in the Form of Classes

In a grouped frequency distribution, it is not possible to determine the mode just by looking at the frequencies of the classes.

Modal Class

The class with maximum frequency is called the modal class. The mode is the value which lies inside the modal class and is given by the formula

$$\text{Mode} = l + \frac{f_m - f_{m-1}}{2f_m - f_{m-1} - f_{m+1}} \times c$$

where,

l = lower limit of the modal class

c = size of class (assuming that all classes have equal size)

f_m = frequency of the modal class

f_{m-1} = frequency of the class preceding the modal class

and f_{m+1} = frequency of the class succeeding the modal class

Relation between Mean, Median and Mode

The empirical relation between mean, median and mode is

$$\text{Mode} = 3\ \text{Median} - 2\ \text{Mean}$$

Example 6 Find the mode of the following data.

5, 3, 0, 1, 7, 3, 2, 4, 6, 2, 3

Sol. Arrange the given data in ascending order, we get

0, 1, 2, 2, 3, 3, 3, 4, 5, 6, 7.

Since, 3 occurs most frequently, i.e. three times, so mode is 3.

Example 7 Find the mode of the following distribution.

Marks obtained	10-24	25-39	40-54	55-69	70-84	85-99
Number of students	25	29	23	19	14	10

Sol. From the given data, we note that the classes are of equal width 15 but discontinuous.

Hence, using the adjustment factor $= \frac{25-24}{2} = 0.5$, we get the continuous distribution, which are as follow

Marks obtained	9.5-24.5	24.5-39.5	39.5-54.5	54.5-69.5	69.5-84.5	84.5-99.5
Number of students	25	29	23	19	14	10

The class 24.5-39.5 has maximum frequency 29, therefore 24.5-39.5 is the modal class.

Here, $l = 24.5, f_m = 29, f_{m-1} = 25, f_{m+1} = 23$ and $c = 15$.

Using the formula, $\text{Mode} = l + \frac{f_m - f_{m-1}}{2f_m - f_{m-1} - f_{m+1}} \times c$,

$$\text{Mode} = 24.5 + \frac{29-25}{2\times 29 - 25 - 23} \times 15$$

$$= 24.5 + \frac{4}{10} \times 15 = 24.5 + 6 = 30.6$$

Hence, mode = 30.6 marks.

Topic Practice 1

Very Short Answer Type Questions

2 Marks

1 Find the median of the following set of numbers

10, 75, 3, 81, 18, 27, 4, 48, 12, 47, 9, 15

2 If the mean of the following distribution is 6, find the value of P.

x	2	4	6	10	$P+5$
f	3	2	3	1	2

3 Calculate the median from the following distribution.

Class	5-10	10-15	15-20	20-25	25-30	30-35	35-40	40-45
Frequency	5	6	15	10	5	4	2	2

4 Compute the mode for the following distribution.

Size of items	0-4	4-8	8-12	12-16	16-20	20-24	24-28	28-32	32-36	36-40
Frequency	5	7	9	17	12	10	6	3	1	0

5 Find the mean wage from the following data.

Wages (in ₹)	800	820	860	900	920	980	1000
No. of workers	7	14	19	25	20	10	5

6 Find the median from the following data.

Mid value	115	125	135	145	155	175	185	195
Frequency	6	25	48	72	116	38	22	3

Short Answer Type Questions

4 Marks

7 If the median of the distribution given below is 28.5, find the value of x and y.

Class interval	0-10	10-20	20-30	30-40	40-50	50-60
No. of students	5	x	20	15	y	5

8 The following table shows the age distribution of cases of a certain disease admitted during a year in a particular hospital.

Age (in years)	5-14	15-24	25-34	35-44	45-54	55-64
No. of cases	6	11	21	23	14	5

Find the average age for which maximum cases occurred.

9 The mean of the following frequency table is 50. But the frequencies f_1 and f_2 in class 20-40 and 60-80 are missing. Find the missing frequencies.

Class interval	0-20	20-40	40-60	60-80	80-100	Total
Frequency	17	f_1	32	f_2	19	120

Hints & Answers

1. Arranging the given numbers in ascending order, we have

3, 4, 9, 10, 12, 15, 18, 27, 47, 48, 75, 81

$\because \; n = 12$

$$\therefore \text{Median} = \frac{\text{Value of}\left(\frac{12}{2}\right)\text{th observation} + \text{Value of}\left(\frac{12}{2}+1\right)\text{th observation}}{2}$$

$$= \frac{15+18}{2} = \frac{33}{2} = 16.5$$

2. Solve as Example 2. **Ans.** $P = 7$

3. First we prepare the following cumulative table to compute the median.

Class	Frequency	Cumulative frequency
5-10	5	5
10-15	6	11
15-20	15	26
20-25	10	36
25-30	5	41
30-35	4	45
35-40	2	47
40-45	2	49
	$N = 49$	

Here, $N = 49$

$\therefore \; \frac{N}{2} = \frac{49}{2} = 24.5$ **Ans.** 19.5

4. Solve as Example 7. **Ans.** 32.66

5. **Ans.** Mean wage = ₹ 891.2

6. **Ans.** 153.80

7. We have, median = 28.5

Class interval	Frequency (f)	Cumulative frequency (cf)
0-10	5	5
10-20	x	$5+x$
20-30	20	$25+x$
30-40	15	$40+x$
40-50	y	$40+x+y$
50-60	5	$45+x+y$
	$\Sigma_{fi} = 60$	

Clearly, it lies in the class interval 20-30. So, 20-30 is the median class.

$\therefore \; l = 20, h = 10, f = 20, cf = 5 + x$ and $N = 60$

Ans. $x = 8$ and $y = 7$

8. **Ans.** Mode = 36.31

9. **Ans.** $f_1 = 28$ and $f_2 = 24$

TOPIC 02 Measures of Dispersion

The measures of central tendency are not sufficient to give complete information about given data. Variability is another factor which is required to be studied under statistics. The single number that describe variability is called **measure of dispersion.**

In other words, **dispersion** (or variation) of the data indicates the extent to which the individual measures differ from an average. It is the measure of spreading (scatter) of the data about some central tendency.

The dispersion or scatter in a data is measured on the basis of the observations and the types of measure of central tendency used.

There are following measures of dispersion

1. Range
2. Quartile deviation
3. Mean deviation
4. Standard deviation.

Range

Range is the difference of maximum and minimum values of data.

Range = Maximum value − Minimum value

The range of data gives us a rough idea of variability or scatter but does not tell about the dispersion of the data from a measure of central tendency.

Mean Deviation

Mean deviation is an important measure of dispersion, which depend upon the deviations of the observations from a central tendency. Mean deviation is defined as the arithmetic mean of the absolute deviations of all the values taken from a central value or a fixed number 'a' and the mean devation from 'a' is denoted as MD (a). Thus, mean deviation from 'a',

$$\text{MD}(a) = \frac{\left[\begin{array}{r}\text{Sum of absolute values of} \\ \text{deviations from } a\end{array}\right]}{\text{Number of observations}}$$

Note Mean deviation may be obtained from any measure of central tendency. But in this chapter, we study deviation from mean and median.

Mean Deviation for Ungrouped Data

Let $x_1, x_2, \ldots, x_n$ be n observations. Then, mean deviation about mean or median can be determined by using following steps

***Step* I** Find the mean or median of given observations using the suitable formula.

***Step* II** Find the deviation of each observation x_i from $\bar{x}$ (mean) or M (median) and then take their absolute values i.e. $|x_i - \bar{x}|$ or $|x_i - M|$.

***Step* III** Find the sum of absolute values of deviations obtained in step III, i.e. $\sum_{i=1}^{n}|x_i - \bar{x}|$ or $\sum_{i=1}^{n}|x_i - M|$.

***Step* IV** Now, find the mean deviation about mean or median by using the formula $\frac{\sum_{i=1}^{n}|x_i - \bar{x}|}{n}$ or $\frac{\sum_{i=1}^{n}|x_i - M|}{n}$, where n is the number of observations.

Example 1 Find the range and mean deviation about the mean for the following data. **[NCERT]**

38, 70, 48, 40, 42, 55, 63, 46, 54, 44.

Sol. Given observations are 38, 70, 48, 40, 42, 55, 63, 46, 54 and 44.

Arrange the given data in ascending order, we get

38, 40, 42, 44, 46, 48, 55, 63, 70

$\therefore$ Range = Maximum value − Minimum value
$= 70 - 38 = 32$

Here, number of observations, $n = 10$

$$\therefore \text{Mean}, \bar{x} = \frac{(38+70+48+40+42+55+63+46+54+44)}{10}$$

$$= \frac{500}{10} = 50$$

Let us make the table for deviation and absolute deviation

x_i	$x_i - \bar{x}$	$\lvert x_i - \bar{x}\rvert$
38	38 − 50 = − 12	12
70	70 − 50 = 20	20
48	48 − 50 = − 2	2
40	40 − 50 = − 10	10
42	42 − 50 = − 8	8
55	55 − 50 = 5	5
63	63 − 50 = 13	13
46	46 − 50 = − 4	4
54	54 − 50 = 4	4
44	44 − 50 = − 6	6
Total		$\sum_{i=1}^{10}\lvert x_i - \bar{x}\rvert = 84$

$$\therefore \text{MD} = \frac{\sum_{i=1}^{10}|x_i - \bar{x}|}{10} = \frac{84}{10} = 8.4$$

Example 2 Find the mean deviation from the mean for the following data.

6.5, 5, 5.25, 5.5, 4.75, 4.5, 6.25, 7.75, 8.5

Sol. Given observations are 6.5, 5, 5.25, 5.5, 4.75, 4.5, 6.25, 7.75 and 8.5.

Here, number of observations, $n = 9$

Let $\bar{x}$ be the mean of given data.

Then, $\bar{x} = \dfrac{6.5 + 5 + 5.25 + 5.5 + 4.75 + 4.5 + 6.25 + 7.75 + 8.5}{9}$

$= \dfrac{54}{9} = 6$

Let us make the table for deviation and absolute deviation.

x_i	$x_i - \bar{x}$	$\lvert x_i - \bar{x}\rvert$
6.5	0.5	0.50
5.0	−1	1.00
5.25	−0.75	0.75
5.5	−0.5	0.50
4.75	−1.25	1.25
4.5	−1.50	1.50
6.25	0.25	0.25
7.75	1.75	1.75
8.5	2.5	2.50
Total		$\sum_{i=1}^{9} \lvert x_i - \bar{x}\rvert = 10.00$

$\therefore$ Mean deviation about mean,

$$\text{MD}(\bar{x}) = \frac{\sum_{i=1}^{9} |x_i - \bar{x}|}{9} = \frac{10}{9} = 1.1$$

Hence, the mean deviation about mean is 1.1.

Example 3 Find the mean deviation about the median for the data 34, 66, 30, 38, 44, 50, 40, 60, 42, 51.

Sol. The given data can be arranged in ascending order as 30, 34, 38, 40, 42, 44, 50, 51, 60, 66.

Here, total number of observations are 10, i.e. $n = 10$, which is even.

$\therefore$ Median (M)

$$= \frac{\left(\frac{n}{2}\right)\text{th observation} + \left(\frac{n}{2}+1\right)\text{th observation}}{2}$$

$$= \frac{\left(\frac{10}{2}\right)\text{th observation} + \left(\frac{10}{2}+1\right)\text{th observation}}{2}$$

$$= \frac{\text{5th observation} + \text{6th observation}}{2}$$

$$= \frac{42 + 44}{2} = \frac{86}{2} = 43$$

Let us make the table for absolute deviation

x_i	$\lvert x_i - M\rvert$
30	$\lvert 30 - 43\rvert = 13$
34	$\lvert 34 - 43\rvert = 9$
38	$\lvert 38 - 43\rvert = 5$
40	$\lvert 40 - 43\rvert = 3$
42	$\lvert 42 - 43\rvert = 1$
44	$\lvert 44 - 43\rvert = 1$
50	$\lvert 50 - 43\rvert = 7$
51	$\lvert 51 - 43\rvert = 8$
60	$\lvert 60 - 43\rvert = 17$
66	$\lvert 66 - 43\rvert = 23$
Total	$\sum_{i=1}^{10} \lvert x_i - M\rvert = 87$

Now, mean deviation about median,

$$\text{MD} = \frac{\sum_{i=1}^{10} |x_i - M|}{10} = \frac{87}{10} = 8.7$$

Example 4 The mean of 6, 8, 5, 7, a and 4 is 7. Find the mean deviation about median of these observation.

Sol. Here, number of observations, $n = 6$

By the given condition, $\dfrac{6 + 8 + 5 + 7 + a + 4}{6} = 7$

$\Rightarrow \quad 30 + a = 6 \times 7 \Rightarrow a = 42 - 30 = 12$

Now, on arranging the observations in ascending order, we have 4, 5, 6, 7, 8, 12.

$$\therefore \text{Medain, } M = \frac{\left(\frac{6}{2}\right)\text{th observation} + \left(\frac{6}{2}+1\right)\text{th observation}}{2}$$

$$= \frac{\text{3rd observation} + \text{4th observation}}{2}$$

$$= \frac{6+7}{2} = \frac{13}{2} = 6.5$$

Let us make the table for deviation and absolute deviation.

x_i	$x_i - M$	$\lvert x_i - M\rvert$
4	−2.5	2.5
5	−1.5	1.5
6	−0.5	0.5
7	0.5	0.5
8	1.5	1.5
12	5.5	5.5
Total		$\sum_{i=1}^{6} \lvert x_i - M\rvert = 12$

$$\therefore \text{Mean deviation about median} = \frac{\sum_{i=1}^{6} |x_i - M|}{6} = \frac{12}{6} = 2$$

Example 5 Calculate the mean deviation about the mean of the set of first n natural numbers, when n is an odd number. **[NCERT Exemplar]**

Sol. Consider first n natural number when n is an odd, i.e. 1, 2, 3, 4, ..., n (odd).

Clearly, mean $(\bar{x}) = \dfrac{1+2+3+\ldots+n}{n} = \dfrac{n(n+1)}{2n} = \dfrac{n+1}{2}$

$$\left[\because \text{sum of first } N \text{ Natural number} = \frac{N(N+1)}{2}\right]$$

Now, $$\text{MD} = \frac{\left|1-\frac{n+1}{2}\right| + \left|2-\frac{n+1}{2}\right| + \left|3-\frac{n+1}{2}\right| + \ldots + \left|n-\frac{n+1}{2}\right|}{n} \quad \left[\because \text{MD} = \frac{\sum_{i=1}^{n}|x_i-\bar{x}|}{n}\right]$$

$$= \frac{\left|1-\frac{n+1}{2}\right| + \left|2-\frac{n+1}{2}\right| + \ldots + \left|\frac{n-1}{2}-\frac{n+1}{2}\right| + \left|\frac{n+1}{2}-\frac{n+1}{2}\right| + \left|\frac{n+3}{2}-\frac{n+1}{2}\right| + \ldots + \left|\frac{2n-2}{2}-\frac{n+1}{2}\right| + \left|n-\frac{n+1}{2}\right|}{n}$$

$$= \frac{\left|\frac{1-n}{2}\right| + \left|\frac{3-n}{2}\right| + \ldots + |-1| + 0 + |1| + |2| + \ldots + \left|\frac{n-3}{2}\right| + \left|\frac{n-1}{2}\right|}{n}$$

$$= \frac{2}{n}\left[\underbrace{1+2+\ldots+\frac{n-3}{2}+\frac{n-1}{2}}_{\left(\frac{n-1}{2}\right)\text{ terms}}\right] = \frac{2}{n}\left[\frac{\left(\frac{n-1}{2}\right)\left(\frac{n-1}{2}+1\right)}{2}\right]$$

$$\left[\because \text{sum of first } N \text{ natural numbers} = \frac{N(N+1)}{2}\right]$$

$$= \frac{2}{n}\cdot\frac{1}{2}\left[\left(\frac{n-1}{2}\right)\left(\frac{n+1}{2}\right)\right]$$

$$= \frac{1}{n}\left(\frac{n^2-1}{4}\right) = \frac{n^2-1}{4n}$$

Example 6 Calculate the mean deviation about the mean of the set of first n natural numbers when n is an even number. **[NCERT Exemplar]**

Sol. Consider first n natural number, when n is even i.e. 1, 2, 3, 4, ..., n (even).

Clearly, Mean $(\bar{x}) = \dfrac{1+2+3+\ldots+n}{n} = \dfrac{n(n+1)}{2n} = \dfrac{n+1}{2}$

$$\text{Now, MD} = \frac{1}{n}\left[\left|1-\frac{n+1}{2}\right| + \left|2-\frac{n+1}{2}\right| + \left|3-\frac{n+1}{2}\right| + \ldots + \left|\frac{n-2}{2}-\frac{n+1}{2}\right| + \left|\frac{n}{2}-\frac{n+1}{2}\right| + \left|\frac{n+2}{2}-\frac{n+1}{2}\right| + \ldots + \left|n-\frac{n+1}{2}\right|\right]$$

$$= \frac{1}{n}\left[\left|\frac{1-n}{2}\right| + \left|\frac{3-n}{2}\right| + \left|\frac{5-n}{2}\right| + \ldots + \left|\frac{-3}{2}\right| + \left|\frac{1}{2}\right| + \ldots + \left|\frac{n-1}{2}\right|\right]$$

$$= \frac{1}{n}\left[\underbrace{\frac{1}{2}+\frac{3}{2}+\ldots+\frac{n-1}{2}}_{\left(\frac{n}{2}\right)\text{ terms}}\right] = \frac{1}{n}\cdot\left(\frac{n}{2}\right)^2$$

$$[\because \text{sum of first } N \text{ odd natural numbers} = N^2]$$

$$= \frac{1}{n}\cdot\frac{n^2}{4} = \frac{n}{4}$$

Example 7 If $\bar{x}$ is the mean and MD$(\bar{x})$ is mean deviation from mean then find the number of observations lying between $\bar{x}$ − MD$(\bar{x})$ and $\bar{x}$ + MD$(\bar{x})$. Use the data 22, 24, 30, 27, 29, 31, 25, 28, 41, 42.

Sol. Arrange the given data in ascending order, we get

22, 24, 25, 27, 28, 29, 30, 31, 41, 42

$$\therefore \text{Mean } (\bar{x}) = \frac{22+24+25+27+28+29+30+31+41+42}{10}$$

$$= \frac{299}{10} = 29.9$$

and mean deviation from the mean, $\text{MD}(\bar{x}) = \dfrac{\sum_{i=1}^{n}|x_i-\bar{x}|}{n}$

$$= \frac{\left[\begin{array}{r}|22-29.9|+|24-29.9|+|25-29.9|+|27-29.9|\\ +|28-29.9|+|29-29.9|+|30-29.9|\\ +|31-29.9|+|41-29.9|+|42-29.9|\end{array}\right]}{10}$$

$$= \frac{7.9+5.9+4.9+2.9+1.9+0.9+0.1+1.1+11.1+12.1}{10}$$

$$= \frac{48.8}{10} = 4.88 = 4.9 \text{ (approx.)}$$

$\therefore \quad \bar{x} - \text{MD}(\bar{x}) = 29.9 - 4.9 = 25$

and $\quad \bar{x} + \text{MD}(\bar{x}) = 29.9 + 4.9 = 34.8$

On examining the arranged data, we find that observations between 25 and 34.8 are 27, 28, 29, 30, 31. Hence, there are 5 observations lying between $\bar{x}$ − MD$(\bar{x})$ and $\bar{x}$ + MD$(\bar{x})$.

Mean Deviation for Grouped Data

1. For Discrete Frequency Distribution

Let the given data have n distinct values $x_1, x_2, \ldots, x_n$ and their corresponding frequencies are $f_1, f_2, \ldots, f_n$, respectively. Then, this data can be represented in the tabular form as

x_i	x_1	x_2	x_3	...	x_n
f_i	f_1	f_2	f_3	...	f_n

and is called discrete frequency distribution.

Here, mean deviation about mean or median is given by

$$= \frac{\sum_{i=1}^{n} f_i |x_i - A|}{N}, \text{ where } N = \sum_{i=1}^{n} f_i = \text{total frequency and}$$

A = mean or median.

Working Rule for Finding the Mean Deviation about Mean

For finding the mean deviation about mean, we use the following steps

***Step* I** Find the mean of given observations using the formula $\bar{x} = \dfrac{\Sigma f_i x_i}{\Sigma f_i}$.

***Step* II** Find the deviation of each observation x_i from $\bar{x}$ and take their absolute values i.e. $|x_i - \bar{x}|$ and then find $f_i|x_i - \bar{x}|$.

***Step* III** Find the sum of absolute values of deviations obtained in step II i.e. $\Sigma f_i |x_i - \bar{x}|$.

***Step* IV** Now, find the mean deviation about mean by using the formula, $\dfrac{\Sigma f_i |x_i - \bar{x}|}{\Sigma f_i}$,

Example 8 Find the mean deviation about the mean for the following data.

x_i	2	5	6	8	10	12
f_i	2	8	10	7	8	5

Sol. Let us make the following table from the given data.

x_i	f_i	$f_i x_i$	$\lvert x_i - \bar{x}\rvert$	$f_i\lvert x_i - \bar{x}\rvert$
2	2	4	5.5	11
5	8	40	2.5	20
6	10	60	1.5	15
8	7	56	0.5	3.5
10	8	80	2.5	20
12	5	60	4.5	22.5
Total	40	300		92

Here, $N = \Sigma f_i = 40$ and $\Sigma f_i x_i = 300$

Now, mean $(\bar{x}) = \dfrac{1}{N} \Sigma f_i x_i = \dfrac{1}{40} \times 300 = 7.5$

$\therefore$ Mean deviation about the mean,

$$\text{MD}(\bar{x}) = \frac{1}{N} \Sigma f_i |x_i - \bar{x}| = \frac{1}{40} \times 92 = 2.3$$

Hence, the mean deviation about mean is 2.3.

Working Rule for Finding the Mean Deviation about Median

For finding the mean deviation about median, we use the following steps

***Step* I** Arrange the given data either in ascending order or descending order.

***Step* II** Make a cumulative frequency table.

***Step* III** Find the median by using the formula,

(i) If $\Sigma f_i = N$ is even, then

$$\text{Median} = \frac{\text{Value of}\left(\dfrac{N}{2}\right)\text{th observation} + \text{Value of}\left(\dfrac{N}{2}+1\right)\text{th observation}}{2}$$

(ii) If $\Sigma f_i = N$ is odd, then

$$\text{Median} = \text{Value of}\left(\frac{N+1}{2}\right)\text{th observation}$$

***Step* IV** Find the absolute values of deviations of observations x_i from M.

***Step* V** Find the product of frequency with absolute deviations, i.e. $f_i |x_i - M|$.

***Step* VI** Find the mean deviation from median by using the formula, $\text{MD} = \dfrac{\Sigma f_i |x_i - M|}{\Sigma f_i}$.

Coefficient of Mean Deviation

For the purpose of comparing variation of two different series which are expressed in the same or different units, a relative mean deviation is required. The relative mean deviation is obtained by dividing the means deviation by the average and it is called coefficient of mean deviation or the coefficient of dispersion.

$\therefore$ Coefficient of mean deviation

$$= \frac{\text{Mean deviation}}{\text{Average used as (Mean or Median or Mode)}}$$

If the result is desired in percentage, then .

$$\text{Coefficient of mean deviation} = \frac{\text{Mean deviation}}{\text{Average speed}} \times 100$$

Example 9 Find the mean deviation and coefficient of mean deviation from the median of the following frequency distribution.

Age (in years)	10	12	15	18	21	23
Frequency	3	5	4	10	8	4

Sol. The given observations are already in ascending order. Now, let us make the cumulative frequency.

Age (x_i)	Frequency (f_i)	cf
10	3	3
12	5	8
15	4	12
18	10	22
21	8	30
23	4	34
Total	$N = 34$	

Here, $\Sigma f_i = N = 34$, which is even.

$\therefore$ Median

$$= \frac{\left[\text{Value of} \left(\frac{34}{2}\right)\text{th observation} + \text{Value of} \left(\frac{34}{2}+1\right)\text{th observation}\right]}{2}$$

$$= \frac{\text{Value of 17th observation} + \text{Value of 18th observation}}{2}$$

$$= \frac{18+18}{2} = 18$$

[$\because$ both of these observation lies in the cumulative frequency 22 and its corresponding observation is 18]

Now, let us make the following table from the given data.

$\|x_i - 18\|$	8	6	3	0	3	5	Total
$f_i\|x_i - 18\|$	24	30	12	0	24	20	110

$$= \frac{\Sigma f_i |x_i - M|}{\Sigma f_i} = \frac{110}{34} = 3.24 \text{ years}$$

Now, coefficient of mean deviation

$$= \frac{\text{Mean deviation}}{\text{Median}} = \frac{3.24}{18} = 0.18$$

Example 10 Find the mean deviation from the median for the following data. **[NCERT]**

x_i	15	21	27	30	35
f_i	3	5	6	7	8

Sol. The given observations are already in ascending order. Now, let us make the following table from the given data.

x_i	f_i	cf	$\|x_i - M\|$	$f_i\|x_i - M\|$
15	3	3	15	45
21	5	8	9	45
27	6	14	3	18
30	7	21	0	0
35	8	29	5	40
Total	29		32	148

Here, $N = \Sigma f_i = 29$, which is odd.

So, the median $= \left(\frac{N+1}{2}\right)$th observation

i.e. $\frac{29+1}{2} = 15$th observation, which is equal to 30.

[$\because$ 15th observation lie in the cumulative frequency 21 and its corresponding observation is 30]

Thus, the median $(M) = 30$.

Hence, mean deviation from the median

$$= \frac{\Sigma f_i |x_i - 30|}{\Sigma f_i} = \frac{148}{29} = 5.1$$

Example 11 Find the mean deviation from the median of the following frequency distribution.

Age (in years)	10	11	12	13	14	15	16
Frequency	3	8	14	19	7	6	3

Sol. The given observations are already in ascending order. Now, let us make the following table from the given data.

Age (x_i)	Frequency (f_i)	cf	$\|x_i - M\| = \|x_i - 13\|$	$f_i\|x_i - M\|$
10	3	3	3	9
11	8	11	2	16
12	14	25	1	14
13	19	44	0	0
14	7	51	1	7
15	6	57	2	12
16	3	60	3	9
Total	$N = 60$			67

Here, $N = \Sigma f_i = 60$, which is even.

$\therefore$ Median (M)

$$= \frac{\left(\frac{N}{2}\right)\text{th observation} + \left(\frac{N}{2}+1\right)\text{th observation}}{2}$$

$$= \frac{\left(\frac{60}{2}\right)\text{th observation} + \left(\frac{60}{2}+1\right)\text{observation}}{2}$$

$$= \frac{\text{30th observation} + \text{31st observation}}{2} = \frac{13+13}{2} = 13$$

[$\because$ both of these observations lie in the cumulative frequency 44 and its corresponding observation is 13]

$\therefore$ Mean deviation from the median

$$= \frac{\Sigma f_i |x_i - M|}{N} = \frac{67}{60} = 1.12 \text{ yr}$$

2. For Continuous Frequency Distribution

A continuous frequency distribution is a series in which the data is classified into different class intervals without gaps alongwith their respective frequencies.

Mean Deviation about Mean For calculating mean deviation from mean of a continuous frequency distribution, the procedure is same as for a discrete frequency distribution. The only difference is that here we have to obtain the mid-points of the various classes and take the deviations of the these mid-points from the mean.

Example 12 Find the mean deviation and coefficient mean deviation about the mean for the following data.

Marks obtained	10-20	20-30	30-40	40-50	50-60	60-70	70-80
Number of students	2	3	8	14	8	3	2

Sol. Let us make the following table from the given data.

Marks obtained	Number of students (f_i)	Mid-points (x_i)	f_ix_i	$\|x_i - \bar{x}\|$	$f_i\|x_i - \bar{x}\|$
10-20	2	15	30	30	60
20-30	3	25	75	20	60
30-40	8	35	280	10	80
40-50	14	45	630	0	0
50-60	8	55	440	10	80
60-70	3	65	195	20	60
70-80	2	75	150	30	60
Total	40		1800		400

Here, $N = \sum_{i=1}^{7} f_i = 40$ and $\sum_{i=1}^{7} f_i x_i = 1800$

Therefore, mean $(\bar{x}) = \frac{1}{N}\sum_{i=1}^{7} f_i x_i$

$= \frac{1800}{40} = 45$

Now, mean deviation,

$$\text{MD}(\bar{x}) = \frac{1}{N}\sum_{i=1}^{7} f_i|x_i - \bar{x}| \quad \left[\because \sum_{i=1}^{7} f_i|x_i - \bar{x}| = 400\right]$$

$$= \frac{1}{40} \times 400 = 10$$

Coefficient mean deviation $= \frac{\text{MD}}{\text{Mean}}$

$= \frac{10}{45} = 0.22$

Hence, the mean deviation and the coefficient of mean deviation about mean are 10 and 0.22, respectively.

Mean Deviation about Median For calculating mean deviation from median of a continuous frequency distribution, the procedure is same as about mean. The only difference is that, here we replace mean by median and median is calculated by the following formula,

$$\text{Median } (M) = l + \frac{\frac{N}{2} - cf}{f} \times h$$

l, f, h and cf are respectively the lower limit, the frequency, the width of median class (assuming class size to be equal) and cumulative frequency of class just preceding the median class.

Example 13 Find the mean deviation about the median of the following frequency distribution.

Class	0-6	6-12	12-18	18-24	24-30
Frequency	8	10	12	9	5

Sol. Let us make the following table from the given data.

Class	Mid value (x_i)	Frequency (f_i)	Cumulative frequency (cf)	$\|x_i - 14\|$	$f_i\|x_i - 14\|$
0-6	3	8	8	11	88
6-12	9	10	18	5	50
12-18	15	12	30	1	12
18-24	21	9	39	7	63
24-30	27	5	44	13	65
Total		$N = \Sigma f_i = 44$			$\Sigma f_i\|x_i - 14\| = 278$

Here, $N = 44$, so $\frac{N}{2} = 22$ and the cumulative frequency just greater than $\frac{N}{2}$ is 30. Therefore, 12-18 is the median class.

Now, median $= l + \frac{\frac{N}{2} - cf}{f} \times h$

where, $l = 12$, $f = 12$, $cf = 18$ and $h = 6$

$\therefore \quad \text{Median} = 12 + \frac{22 - 18}{12} \times 6$

$= 12 + \frac{4 \times 6}{12} = 14$

Mean deviation about median $= \frac{1}{N}\Sigma f_i|x_i - 14|$

$= \frac{278}{44} = 6.318$

Example 14 Calculate the mean deviation about median for the following data. **[NCERT]**

Class	0-10	10-20	20-30	30-40	40-50	50-60
Frequency	6	7	15	16	4	2

Sol. Let us make the following table from the given data.

Class	f_i	cf	Mid-point (x_i)	$\lvert x_i - M\rvert$	$f_i \lvert x_i - M\rvert$
0-10	6	6	5	23	138
10-20	7	13	15	13	91
20-30	15	28	25	3	45
30-40	16	44	35	7	112
40-50	4	48	45	17	68
50-60	2	50	55	27	54
Total	50				508

Here, $\frac{N}{2} = \frac{50}{2} = 25$

which item lies in the cumulative frequency 28.
Therefore, 20-30 is the median class.

So, we have $l = 20$, $cf = 13$, $f = 15$, $h = 10$ and $N = 50$

Now, Median, $M = l + \frac{\frac{N}{2} - cf}{f} \times h = 20 + \frac{25 - 13}{15} \times 10$

$= 20 + 8 = 28$

Hence, the mean deviation about median is given by

$$\text{MD}(M) = \frac{1}{N}\sum_{i=1}^{6} f_i\lvert x_i - M\rvert = \frac{1}{50} \times 508 = 10.16$$

Hence, the mean deviation about median is 10.16.

Example 15 Calculate the mean deviation about median for the age distribution of 100 persons given below. **[NCERT]**

Age	16-20	21-25	26-30	31-35	36-40	41-45	46-50	51-55
Number	5	6	12	14	26	12	16	9

Sol. Let us make the following table from the given data.

Class	f_i	cf	Mid value (x_i)	$\lvert x_i - M\rvert$	$f_i\lvert x_i - M\rvert$
15.5-20.5	5	5	18	$\lvert 18 - 38\rvert = 20$	100
20.5-25.5	6	11	23	$\lvert 23 - 38\rvert = 15$	90
25.5-30.5	12	23	28	$\lvert 28 - 38\rvert = 10$	120
30.5-35.5	14	37	33	$\lvert 33 - 38\rvert = 5$	70
35.5-40.5	26	63	38	$\lvert 38 - 38\rvert = 0$	0
40.5-45.5	12	75	43	$\lvert 43 - 38\rvert = 5$	60
45.5-50.5	16	91	48	$\lvert 48 - 38\rvert = 10$	160
50.5-55.5	9	100	53	$\lvert 53 - 38\rvert = 15$	135
Total	$N = 100$				735

Here, $\frac{N}{2} = 50$

So, the median class is 35.5-40.5.

$\therefore$ $l = 35.5$, $cf = 37$, $f = 26$ and $h = 5$

Now, Median $(M) = l + \frac{\frac{N}{2} - cf}{f} \times h$

$= 35.5 + \frac{50 - 37}{26} \times 5 = 35.5 + \frac{13}{26} \times 5$

$= 35.5 + 2.5 = 38$

and Mean deviation about the median

$= \frac{\Sigma f_i \lvert x_i - M\rvert}{\Sigma f_i}$

$= \frac{735}{100} = 7.35$

Hence, the mean deviation about median is 7.35.

Shortcut Method for Calculating the Mean Deviation about Mean

Sometimes, the data is too large and then the calculation by the previous method is tedious. So, we apply the step deviation method. In this method, we take an assumed mean, which is in the middle or just close to it, in the data. The process of taking step deviation is the change of scale on the number line as shown in the figure below

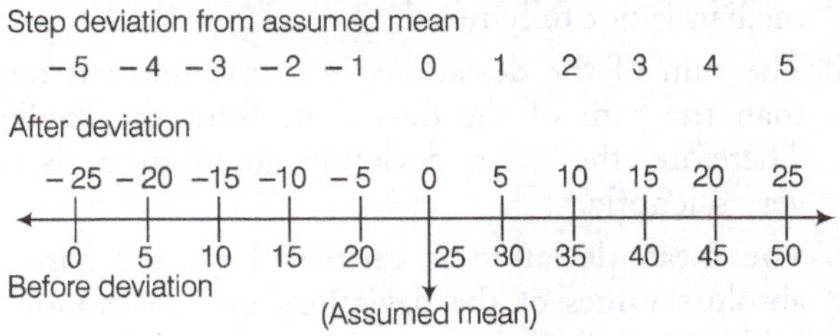

For step deviation method, we denote the new variable by u_i and it is defined as $u_i = \frac{x_i - a}{h}$, where a is the assumed mean and h is the common factor or length of the class interval. The mean $\bar{x}$ by step deviation method is given by

$$\bar{x} = a + \frac{\sum_{i=1}^{n} f_i u_i}{N} \times h$$

Example 16 Find the mean deviation from the mean of the following data by shortcut or step deviation method.

Class	0-100	100-200	200-300	300-400	400-500	500-600	600-700	700-800
Frequency	4	8	9	10	7	5	4	3

Sol. Let us make the following table for step deviation and product of frequency with absolute deviation.

Class	f_i	Mid-points (x_i)	$u_i = \frac{x_i - 450}{100}$ $(a = 450, h = 100)$	$f_i u_i$	$\lvert x_i - \bar{x}\rvert = \lvert x_i - 358\rvert$	$f_i\lvert x_i - \bar{x}\rvert$
0-100	4	50	−4	−16	308	1232
100-200	8	150	−3	−24	208	1664
200-300	9	250	−2	−18	108	972
300-400	10	350	−1	−10	8	80
400-500	7	450	0	0	92	644
500-600	5	550	1	5	192	960
600 – 700	4	650	2	8	292	1168
700 – 800	3	750	3	9	392	1176
Total	$N = \Sigma f_i = 50$			−46		7896

Here, $a = 450, \Sigma f_i u_i = -46$ and $h = 100$.

$$\therefore \quad \bar{x} = a + h\left(\frac{1}{N}\Sigma f_i u_i\right) = 450 + 100 \times \left(-\frac{46}{50}\right) = 358$$

Now, mean deviation $= \frac{1}{N}\Sigma f_i\lvert x_i - \bar{x}\rvert = \frac{7896}{50} = 157.92$

Limitations of Mean Deviation

The limitations of mean deviations are given below

(i) If the data is more scattered or the degree of variability is very high, then the median is not a valid representative. Thus, the mean deviation about the median is not fully relied.

(ii) The sum of the deviations from the mean is more than the sum of the deviations from the median. Therefore, the mean deviation about mean is not very scientific.

(iii) The mean deviation is calculated on the basis of absolute values of the deviations and so cannot be subjected to further algebraic treatment. Sometime, it gives unsatisfactory results.

Topic Practice 2

Short Answer Type Questions

4 Marks

1 Find the range and mean deviation from the mean for the following data.

6, 5, 5.25, 5.5, 4.75, 4.5, 6.25, 7.75, 9

2 Find the range and mean deviation of the data 3, 10, 10, 4, 7, 10, 5 from the mean.

3 The scores of a batsman in 10 innings are 48, 80, 58, 44, 52, 65, 73, 56, 64, 54. Find the mean deviation from the median.

4 Find the mean deviation from the median for the given data 3, 9, 5, 3, 12, 10, 18, 4, 7, 19, 21 **[NCERT]**

5 Find the mean deviation about the median for the following data.

x_i	3	6	9	12	13	15	21	22
f_i	3	4	5	2	4	5	4	3

6 Find the mean deviation from the median for the following data. **[NCERT]**

x_i	15	21	27	30	35
f_i	3	5	6	7	8

7 Calculate the mean deviation and coefficient of mean deviation from the mean of the following distribution.

Marks	0-10	10-20	20-30	30-40	40-50
Number of students	5	8	15	16	6

8 Find the mean deviation from the mean for the following data.

Class	0-10	10-20	20-30	30-40	40-50	50-60
Frequency	6	8	14	16	4	2

9 Calculate the mean deviation from the mean of the following distribution.

Marks	0-10	10-20	20-30	30-40	40-50
Number of students	5	8	15	16	6

Long Answer Type Questions

6 Marks

10 Find the mean deviation from the median for the following data.

x_i	74	89	42	54	91	94	35
f_i	20	12	2	4	5	3	4

11 Calculate the mean deviation from the median for the following data.

Wages per day	Number of workers
20-30	3
30-40	8
40-50	12
50-60	9
60-70	8

12 Find the mean deviation about the mean for the following data. **[NCERT]**

Marks obtained	10-20	20-30	30-40	40-50	50-60	60-70	70-80
Number of students	2	3	8	14	8	3	2

13 Find the mean deviation from the mean for the following data by shortcut method.

Class	10-20	20-30	30-40	40-50	50-60	60-70	70-80	80-90
Frequency	8	10	15	25	20	18	9	5

Hints & Answers

1. Given observations can be arrange in ascending order as 4.5, 4.75, 5, 5.25, 5.5, 6, 6.25, 7.75, 9

$\therefore$ Range = 9 − 4.5 = 4.5

Let $\bar{x}$ be the mean of given data.

Here, $\bar{x} = \dfrac{\sum_{i=1}^{n} xi}{n} = \dfrac{54}{9} = 6$

We make the table from the given data.

x_i	$x_i - \bar{x} = x_i - 6$	$\lvert x_i - \bar{x} \rvert$
6	0	0
5.0	− 1	1.00
5.25	− 0.75	0.75
5.5	− 0.5	0.50
4.75	− 1.25	1.25
4.5	− 1.50	1.50
6.25	0.25	0.25
7.75	1.75	1.75
9	3	3
Total		10.00

$\therefore$ Mean deviation from mean,

$$\text{MD}(\bar{x}) = \frac{\Sigma \lvert x_i - \bar{x} \rvert}{n} = \frac{10}{9}$$

Ans The mean deviation from the mean is 1.1.

2. Solve as Q.1 **Ans.** 7 and 2.57

3. Here, $n = 10$. So, median is the mean of 5th and 6th terms.

$\therefore$ $$\text{Median } (M) = \left(\frac{56+58}{2}\right) = 57$$

We make the table from the given data.

Scores (x_i)	Deviation from median ($x_i - M$)	$\lvert x_i - M \rvert$
44	44 − 57 = − 13	13
48	48 − 57 = − 9	9
52	52 − 57 = − 5	5
54	54 − 57 = − 3	3
56	56 − 57 = − 1	1
58	58 − 57 = 1	1
64	64 − 57 = 7	7
65	65 − 57 = 8	8
73	73 − 57 = 16	16
80	80 − 57 = 23	23
Total		86

$$\therefore \text{ Mean deviation} = \frac{\Sigma \lvert x_i - M \rvert}{n} = \frac{86}{10}$$

Ans. The mean deviation from the median is 8.6.

4. Solve as Q. 3. **Ans.** 5.27

5. Find the median and then calculate the mean deviation about the median by using the formula $\dfrac{\Sigma f_i \lvert x_i - M \rvert}{\Sigma f_i}$.

Here, $N = 30$, which is even.

So, median is the mean of the 15th and 16th.

We make the table from the given data.

x_i	f_i	cf	$\lvert x_i - M \rvert$	$f_i \lvert x_i - M \rvert$
3	3	3	10	30
6	4	7	7	28
9	5	12	4	20
12	2	14	1	2
13	4	18	0	0
15	5	23	2	10
21	4	27	8	32
22	3	30	9	27

$$\therefore \text{ Median } (M) = \frac{15\text{th observation} + 16\text{th observation}}{2}$$

$$= \frac{13+13}{2} = 13$$

We have, $\Sigma f_i = 30$ and $\Sigma f_i \lvert x_i - M \rvert = 149$

$$\text{MD}(M) = \frac{1}{N} \Sigma f_i \lvert x_i - M \rvert = \frac{1}{30} \times 149$$

Ans. 4.97

6. Find the median and then calculate the mean deviation about the median by using the formula $\frac{\Sigma f_i|x_i - M|}{\Sigma f_i}$.

Here, $N = \Sigma f_i = 29$, which is odd. So, the median is the $\left(\frac{n+1}{2}\right)$th observation, i.e. $\frac{29+1}{2} = 15$th observation, which is equal to 30. Thus, median is 30.

We make the table from the given data.

x_i	f_i	cf	$\|x_i - M\|$	$f_i\|x_i - M\|$
15	3	3	15	45
21	5	8	9	45
27	6	14	3	18
30	7	21	0	0
35	8	29	5	40
Total	29			148

$$\therefore \text{MD}(M) = \frac{\Sigma f_i|x_i - 30|}{\Sigma f_i} = \frac{148}{29}$$

Ans. 5.1

7. We make the table from the given data.

Class	Mid value (x_i)	f_i	$u_i = \frac{x_i - 25}{10}$	f_iu_i	$\|x_i - \bar{x}\| = \|x_i - 27\|$	$f_i\|x_i - \bar{x}\|$
0-10	5	5	−2	−10	22	110
10-20	15	8	−1	−8	12	96
20-30	25	15	0	0	2	30
30-40	35	16	1	16	8	128
40-50	45	6	2	12	18	108
Total		50		10		472

$$\therefore \quad \text{Mean, } \bar{x} = a + \frac{\Sigma f_iu_i}{\Sigma f_i} \times h$$

$$= 25 + \frac{10}{50} \times 10 = 27$$

$$\therefore \text{Mean deviation from mean} = \frac{\Sigma f_i|x_i - \bar{x}|}{\Sigma f_i}$$

$$[\because \Sigma f_i|x_i - \bar{x}| = 472]$$

$$= \frac{472}{50}$$

$$\text{Coefficient of mean deviation} = \frac{9.44}{27}$$

Ans. 9.44, 0.34

8. Solve as Q. 7. **Ans.** 10.576

9. Solve as Q. 7. **Ans.** 9.44

10. Solve as Q. 5. **Ans.** 12.5

11. Let us make the following table from the given data.

Wages per day (in ₹)	Mid value (x_i)	f_i	cf	$\|x_i - M\| = \|x_i - 47.5\|$	$f_i\|x_i - M\|$
20-30	25	3	3	22.5	67.5
30-40	35	8	11	12.5	100.0
40-50	45	12	23	2.5	30.0
50-60	55	9	32	7.5	67.5
60-70	65	8	40	17.5	140.0
Total		40			405.0

Here, $\frac{N}{2} = \frac{40}{2} = 20$. The cumulative frequency just greater than 20 is 23, so the median class is 40-50.

$$\text{Now, median } (M) = l + \frac{\frac{N}{2} - cf}{f} \times h$$

$$= 40 + \frac{20 - 11}{12} \times 10 = 47.5$$

and mean deviation from the median

$$= \frac{\Sigma f_i|x_i - M|}{N} = \frac{405}{40}$$

Ans. 10.125

12. Take the assumed mean $a = 45$ and $h = 10$.

Make the table for step deviation and product of frequency with absolute deviation

Marks obtained	Number of students (f_i)	Mid-points(x_i)	$u_i = \frac{x_i - 45}{10}$	f_iu_i	$\|x_i - \bar{x}\|$	$f_i\|x_i - \bar{x}\|$
10-20	2	15	− 3	− 6	30	60
20-30	3	25	− 2	− 6	20	60
30-40	8	35	− 1	− 8	10	80
40-50	14	45	0	0	0	0
50-60	8	55	1	8	10	80
60-70	3	65	2	6	20	60
70-80	2	75	3	6	30	60
Total	40			0		400

$$\text{Now,} \quad \bar{x} = a + \frac{\sum_{i=1}^{7} f_iu_i}{\sum_{i=1}^{7} f_i} \times h = 45 + \frac{0}{40} \times 10 = 45$$

$\therefore$ Mean deviation about mean

$$= \frac{1}{\sum_{i=1}^{7} f_i} \sum_{i=1}^{7} f_i|x_i - \bar{x}| = \frac{400}{40}$$

Ans. 10

13. Solve as Q. 12. **Ans.** 14.95

TOPIC 03 Variance and Standard Deviation

Due to the limitations of mean deviation, some other method is required for measure of dispersion. Standard deviation is such a measure of dispersion.

Variance

The absolute values are considered in calculating the mean deviation about mean or median, otherwise the deviation being negative or positive and may cancel among themselves.

To overcome this difficulty of the signs of the deviations, we take the squares of all the deviations, so that all deviations become non-negative.

Let $x_1, x_2, \ldots, x_n$ be n observations and $\bar{x}$ be their mean.

Then, $(x_1 - \bar{x})^2 + (x_2 - \bar{x})^2 + \ldots + (x_n - \bar{x})^2$

$$= \sum_{i=1}^{n} (x_i - \bar{x})^2$$

An illustration to explain the variance

Let us consider two sets of observations. Set '*A*' contains eight observations 4, 8, 12, 16, 20, 24, 28, 32 and set '*B*' contains 16 observations 2, 4, 6, 8, 10, 12, 14, 16, 18, 20, 24, 26, 28, 31, 33, 36.

Here, the mean obtained by both set of observations have same mean, i.e.18.

Now, we determine the sum of squares of deviation from mean.

For set *A*

$$\sum_{i=1}^{8} (x_i - \bar{x})^2 = (4 - 18)^2 + \ldots + (32 - 18)^2 = 672$$

For set *B*

$$\sum_{i=1}^{16} (y_i - \bar{y})^2 = (2 - 18)^2 + \ldots + (36 - 18)^2 = 1738$$

If $\sum_{i=1}^{n} (x_i - \bar{x})^2$ is simply our measure of dispersion or scatter about mean, then from the above we can say that set *A* has lesser dispersion than set *B*, even though the observations in set *A* are more scattered about mean, which is clear from the following diagrams.

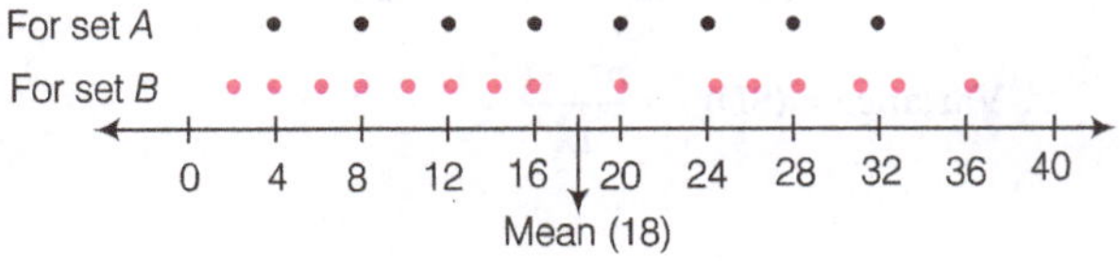

Thus, we can say that the sum of squares of deviations about mean is not a proper measure of dispersion.

To overcome this difficulty, we take the mean of the squares of the deviations i.e. $\frac{1}{n}\Sigma(x_i - \bar{x})^2$.

Definition The mean of the squares of the deviations from mean is called the **variance** and it is denoted by the symbol σ^2.

Significance of Deviation

(i) If the deviation is zero, it means there is no deviation at all and all observations are equal to mean.

(ii) If deviation is small, this indicates that the observation are close to the mean.

(iii) If the deviation is large, there is a high degree of dispersion of the observation from the mean.

Standard Deviation

Standard deviation is the square root of the arithmetic mean of the squares of deviations from mean and it is denoted by the symbol σ.

Or The square root of variance, is called **standard deviation** (or root mean squared deviation). i.e. $\sqrt{\sigma^2}$ or σ. It is also known as **root mean square deviation.**

Variance and Standard Deviation of Ungrouped Data

Variance of n observations $x_1, x_2, x_3, \ldots x_n$ is given by

$$\text{var}(x) \text{ or } \sigma^2 = \frac{\sum_{i=1}^{n} (x_i - \bar{x})^2}{n} \text{ or } \frac{\sum_{i=1}^{n} x_i^2}{n} - \left(\frac{\sum_{i=1}^{n} x_i}{n}\right)^2$$

We know that, Standard deviation $= \sqrt{\text{Variance}}$

$$\therefore \quad \sigma = \sqrt{\frac{\sum_{i=1}^{n} (x_i - \bar{x})^2}{n}} \text{ or } \sqrt{\frac{\sum_{i=1}^{n} x_i^2}{n} - \left(\frac{\sum_{i=1}^{n} x_i}{n}\right)^2}$$

$$\text{or} \quad \frac{1}{n}\sqrt{n\sum_{i=1}^{n} x_i^2 - \left(\sum_{i=1}^{n} x_i\right)^2}$$

Working Rule to Finding the Variance and Standard Deviation

To find the standard deviation or variance when deviations are taken from actual mean, we use the following steps

Step I Calculate the mean $\bar{x}$ of the given observation $x_1, x_2, \ldots, x_n$.

Step II Take the deviations of the observations from their mean i.e. find $x_i - \bar{x}$; $i = 1, 2, \ldots, n$.

Step III Square the deviations obtained in step II and then find the sum i.e. $\sum_{i=1}^{n}(x_i - \bar{x})^2$.

Step IV Find the variance and standard deviation by using the formula, variance, $\sigma^2 = \frac{\sum_{i=1}^{n}(x_i - \bar{x})^2}{n}$

and standard deviation $= \sqrt{\sigma}$.

Example 1 Find the variance and standard deviation for the data 6, 7, 10, 12, 13, 4, 8, 12.

Sol. Given observations are 6, 7, 10, 12, 13, 4, 8, 12.

$\because$ Number of observations = 8

$\therefore$ Mean $(\bar{x}) = \frac{6+7+10+12+13+4+8+12}{8} = \frac{72}{8} = 9$

Now, let us make the following table for deviation.

x_i	$x_i - \bar{x}$	$(x_i - \bar{x})^2$	x_i	$x_i - \bar{x}$	$(x_i - \bar{x})^2$
6	− 3	9	13	4	16
7	− 2	4	4	− 5	25
10	1	1	8	− 1	1
12	3	9	12	3	9
Total		74	Total		74

$\therefore$ Sum of squares of deviations $= \sum_{i=1}^{8}(x_i - \bar{x})^2 = 74$

Hence, variance, $\sigma^2 = \frac{\sum_{i=1}^{8}(x_i - \bar{x})^2}{n} = \frac{74}{8} = 9.25$

and standard deviation $= \sqrt{\sigma} = \sqrt{9.25} = 3.04$

Example 2 Find the variance and standard deviation for the following data.

45, 60, 62, 60, 50, 65, 58, 68, 44, 48

Sol. Let $\bar{x}$ be the mean of the given set of observations.

$\because$ Number of observations = 10

$\therefore \quad \bar{x} = \frac{\left[\begin{array}{r}45+60+62+60+50+65+58\\+68+44+48\end{array}\right]}{10} = \frac{560}{10} = 56$

Make a table from the given data.

x_i	$x_i - \bar{x}$	$(x_i - \bar{x})^2$
45	45 − 56 = − 11	121
60	60 − 56 = 4	16
62	62 − 56 = 6	36
60	60 − 56 = 4	16
50	50 − 56 = − 6	36
65	65 − 56 = 9	81
58	58 − 56 = 2	4
68	68 − 56 = 12	144
44	44 − 56 = − 12	144
48	48 − 56 = − 8	64
Total		662

We have, $n = 10$ and $\Sigma(x_i - \bar{x})^2 = 662$

$\therefore$ Variance, $\sigma^2 = \frac{1}{n}\Sigma(x_i - \bar{x})^2 = \frac{662}{10} = 66.2$

and standard deviation $= \sqrt{\sigma} = \sqrt{66.2} = 8.136$

Example 3 Find the standard deviation and the variance of first n natural numbers.

Sol. We know that first n natural numbers are $1, 2, 3, \ldots, n$.

$\because$ Standard deviation,

$$SD = \sqrt{\frac{\sum_{i=1}^{n} x_i^2}{n} - \left(\frac{\sum_{i=1}^{n} x_i}{n}\right)^2}$$

$$\therefore \quad SD = \sqrt{\frac{n(n+1)(2n+1)}{6n} - \left(\frac{n(n+1)}{2n}\right)^2}$$

$$\left[\because \sum_{i=1}^{n} x_i^2 = \frac{n(n+1)(2n+1)}{6} \text{ and } \sum_{i=1}^{n} x_i = \frac{n(n+1)}{2}\right]$$

$$= \sqrt{(n+1)\left(\frac{2n+1}{6} - \frac{n+1}{4}\right)}$$

$$= \sqrt{(n+1)\left(\frac{4n+2-3n-3}{12}\right)}$$

$$= \sqrt{\frac{(n+1)(n-1)}{12}} = \sqrt{\frac{n^2-1}{12}}$$

$$\therefore \text{Variance} = (SD)^2 = \frac{n^2-1}{12}$$

Variance and Standard Deviation of a Discrete Frequency Distribution

Let the discrete frequency distribution be
$x : x_1, x_2, x_3, \ldots, x_n$ and $f : f_1, f_2, f_3, \ldots, f_n$. Then, by

Direct Method

Variance $(\sigma^2) = \frac{1}{N}\sum_{i=1}^{n} f_i(x_i - \bar{x})^2$, where $\bar{x} = \frac{\Sigma f_i x_i}{\Sigma f_i}$

or $\sigma^2 = \frac{1}{N}\Sigma f_i x_i^2 - \left(\frac{\Sigma f_i x_i}{N}\right)^2$

and standard deviation,

$$\sigma = \sqrt{\frac{1}{N}\sum_{i=1}^{n} f_i(x_i - \bar{x})^2}$$

or $\sigma = \frac{1}{N}\sqrt{N\Sigma f_i x_i^2 - (\Sigma f_i x_i)^2}$ where, $N = \sum_{i=1}^{n} f_i$

Shortcut Method

Variance, $\sigma^2 = \frac{1}{N}\sum_{i=1}^{n} f_i d_i^2 - \left(\frac{\Sigma f_i d_i}{N}\right)^2$

and standard deviation, $\sigma = \sqrt{\frac{1}{N}\sum_{i=1}^{n} f_i d_i^2 - \left(\frac{\Sigma f_i d_i}{N}\right)^2}$

where, $d_i = x_i - a$, deviation from assumed mean and a = assumed mean.

Example 4 Find the variance and standard deviation of the following data. [NCERT]

x_i	4	8	11	17	20	24	32
f_i	3	5	9	5	4	3	1

Sol. Let us make the following table from the given data.

x_i	f_i	$f_i x_i$	$x_i - \bar{x} = x_i - 14$	$(x_i - \bar{x})^2$	$f_i(x_i - \bar{x})^2$
4	3	12	−10	100	300
8	5	40	−6	36	180
11	9	99	−3	9	81
17	5	85	3	9	45
20	4	80	6	36	144
24	3	72	10	100	300
32	1	32	18	324	324
Total	30	420			1374

Here, we have, $N = \Sigma f_i = 30, \Sigma f_i x_i = 420$

$$\therefore \quad \bar{x} = \frac{\sum_{i=1}^{7} f_i x_i}{N} = \frac{420}{30} = 14$$

Hence, variance $(\sigma^2) = \frac{1}{N}\sum_{i=1}^{7} f_i (x_i - \bar{x})^2$

$$\left[\because \sigma^2 = \frac{1}{N}\left\{\sum_{i=1}^{n} f_i(x_i - \bar{x})^2\right\}\right]$$

$$= \frac{1}{30} \times 1374 = 45.8$$

and standard deviation, $\sigma = \sqrt{\sigma^2} = \sqrt{45.8} = 6.77$

Example 5 For the frequency distribution

x	A	2A	3A	4A	5A	6A
f	2	1	1	1	1	1

where, A is a positive integer, has a variance of 160. Determine the value of A.

Sol. Taking assumed mean as $3A$, we construct the table

x_i	f_i	$d_i = x_i - 3A$	d_i^2	$f_i d_i$	$f_i d_i^2$
A	2	−2A	$4A^2$	−4A	$8A^2$
2A	1	−A	A^2	−A	A^2
3A	1	0	0	0	0
4A	1	A	A^2	A	A^2
5A	1	2A	$4A^2$	2A	$4A^2$
6A	1	3A	$9A^2$	3A	$9A^2$
Total	7			A	$23A^2$

$$\therefore \quad \text{Variance} = \frac{\Sigma f_i d_i^2}{N} - \left(\frac{\Sigma f_i d_i}{N}\right)^2 = 160 \quad \text{[given]}$$

$$\Rightarrow \quad \frac{23A^2}{7} - \left(\frac{A}{7}\right)^2 = 160$$

$$\Rightarrow \quad \left(\frac{23}{7} - \frac{1}{49}\right)A^2 = 160$$

$$\Rightarrow \quad \frac{160}{49}A^2 = 160$$

$$\Rightarrow \quad A^2 = 49$$

$$\Rightarrow \quad A = 7 \quad [\because A \text{ is +ve integer}]$$

Example 6 Find the mean, variance and standard deviation of the following data. [NCERT]

x_i	92	93	97	98	102	104	109
f_i	3	2	3	2	6	3	3

Sol. Let the assumed mean be $a = 98$.

Now, let us make the following table from the given data.

x_i	f_i	$d_i = x_i - 98$	d_i^2	$f_i d_i$	$f_i d_i^2$
92	3	−6	36	−18	108
93	2	−5	25	−10	50
97	3	−1	1	−3	3
98	2	0	0	0	0
102	6	4	16	24	96
104	3	6	36	18	108
109	3	11	121	33	363
Total	22			44	728

Here, $N = \Sigma f_i = 22$, $\Sigma f_i d_i = 44$ and $\Sigma f_i d_i^2 = 728$

Now, $\bar{x} = a + \dfrac{\Sigma f_i d_i}{\Sigma f_i} = 98 + \dfrac{44}{22} = 98 + 2 = 100$

$$\text{Variance, } \sigma^2 = \frac{1}{N}(\Sigma f_i d_i^2) - \left(\frac{\Sigma f_i d_i}{N}\right)^2$$

$$= \frac{1}{22}(728) - \left(\frac{1}{22} \times 44\right)^2$$

$$= \frac{1}{22}(728) - (2)^2$$

$$= \frac{1}{22}(728 - 22 \times 2^2) = \frac{1}{22}(728 - 88)$$

$$= \frac{1}{22} \times 640 = \frac{320}{11} = 29.09$$

and standard deviation, $\sigma = \sqrt{29.09} = 5.394$

Variance and Standard Deviation for Grouped Data

In this method, we first replace each class by its mid-point, then this method becomes similar to the discrete frequency distribution.

If there is a frequency distribution of n classes and each class defined by its mid-point x_i with corresponding frequency f_i, then variance and standard deviation are respectively

$$\sigma^2 = \frac{1}{N}\sum_{i=1}^{n} f_i (x_i - \bar{x})^2$$

and $$\sigma = \sqrt{\frac{1}{N}\sum_{i=1}^{n} f_i (x_i - \bar{x})^2}$$

or $$\sigma^2 = \frac{1}{N^2}[N \Sigma f_i x_i^2 - (\Sigma f_i x_i)^2]$$

and $$\sigma = \frac{1}{N}\sqrt{N \Sigma f_i x_i^2 - (\Sigma f_i x_i)^2}$$

Example 7 Calculate the variance and standard deviation for the following distribution.

Class	30-40	40-50	50-60	60-70	70-80	80-90	90-100
Frequency	3	7	12	15	8	3	2

Sol. Let us construct the following table.

Class	Frequency (f_i)	Mid-point (x_i)	$f_i x_i$	$(x_i - \bar{x})$	$(x_i - \bar{x})^2$	$f_i(x_i - \bar{x})^2$
30-40	3	35	105	−27	729	2187
40-50	7	45	315	−17	289	2023
50-60	12	55	660	−7	49	588
60-70	15	65	975	3	9	135
70-80	8	75	600	13	169	1352
80-90	3	85	255	23	529	1587
90-100	2	95	190	33	1089	2178
Total	50		3100			10050

Here, $N = 50$ and $\Sigma f_i x_i = 3100$

$\therefore$ Mean, $\bar{x} = \dfrac{1}{N}\Sigma f_i x_i = \dfrac{3100}{50} = 62$

Now, variance, $\sigma^2 = \dfrac{1}{N}\Sigma f_i (x_i - \bar{x})^2 = \dfrac{1}{50} \times 10050 = 201$

and standard deviation, $\sigma = \sqrt{201} = 14.18$

Shortcut (or Step Deviation) Method

Sometimes the values of mid-points x_i of different classes in a continuous distribution are large and so the calculation of mean and variance becomes tedious and time consuming. For this, we use the **step deviation method** to find mean and variance.

$$\text{Variance, } \sigma^2 = h^2\left[\frac{1}{N}\sum_{i=1}^{n} f_i u_i^2 - \left(\frac{\sum_{i=1}^{n} f_i u_i}{N}\right)^2\right]$$

and standard deviation,

$$\sigma = h\sqrt{\frac{1}{N}\sum_{i=1}^{n} f_i u_i^2 - \left(\frac{\sum_{i=1}^{n} f_i u_i}{N}\right)^2}$$

where, $u_i = \dfrac{x_i - a}{h}$, a = assumed mean and h = width of class-interval.

Working Rule to Finding the Variance and Standard Deviation by Shortcut Method

To find variance and standard deviation, use the following steps

Step I Select an assumed mean, say a and then calculate $u_i = \frac{x_i - a}{h}$, where h = width of class interval or common factor.

Step II Multiply the frequency of each class with the corresponding u_i and obtain $\Sigma f_i u_i$.

Step III Square the values of u_i and multiply them with the corresponding frequencies and obtain $\Sigma f_i u_i^2$.

Step IV Substitute the values of $\Sigma f_i u_i$, $\Sigma f_i u_i^2$ and $\Sigma f_i = N$ in the formula,

$$\text{Variance } (\sigma^2) = h^2\left[\frac{1}{N}\Sigma f_i u_i^2 - \left(\frac{1}{N}\Sigma f_i u_i\right)^2\right]$$

and standard deviation = $\sqrt{\sigma}$

to get the required values.

Example 8 The diameter of circles (in mm) drawn in a design are given below

Diameter (in mm)	33-36	37-40	41-44	45-48	49-52
Number of circles	15	17	21	22	25

Calculate the standard deviation and mean diameter of circles. **[NCERT]**

Sol. Let us first make the data continuous by making classes as 32.5-36.5, 36.5-40.5, 40.5-44.5, 44.5-48.5, 48.5-52.5.

Let assumed mean is 42.5 and $h = 4$.

Then, $u_i = \frac{x_i - a}{h} = \frac{x_i - 42.5}{4}$

Now, let us make the following table from the given data.

Class interval	Mid value (x_i)	f_i	$u_i = \frac{x_i - 42.5}{4}$	$f_i u_i$	u_i^2	$f_i u_i^2$
32.5-36.5	34.5	15	−2	−30	4	60
36.5-40.5	38.5	17	−1	−17	1	17
40.5-44.5	42.5	21	0	0	0	0
44.5-48.5	46.5	22	1	22	1	22
48.5-52.5	50.5	25	2	50	4	100
Total		100		25		199

Now, Mean $(\bar{x}) = a + \frac{\Sigma f_i u_i}{\Sigma f_i} \times h = 42.5 + 4 \times \frac{25}{100}$

[∵ by using step deviation method]

$= 42.5 + 1 = 43.5$

Standard deviation, $(\sigma) = \sqrt{h^2\left[\frac{1}{N}\Sigma f_i u_i^2 - \left(\frac{1}{N}\Sigma f_i u_i\right)^2\right]}$

[by shortcut method]

$$= \sqrt{(4)^2\left[\frac{1}{100} \times 199 - \left(\frac{1}{100} \times 25\right)^2\right]}$$

$$= \sqrt{16\left(1.99 - \frac{1}{16}\right)} = \sqrt{16\left(\frac{31.84 - 1}{16}\right)}$$

$$= \sqrt{30.84} = 5.55$$

Hence, standard deviation and mean diameter of circles are 5.55 and 43.5.

Example 9 Calculate the mean and standard deviation of the following cumulative data.

Wages (in ₹)	0-15	15-30	30-45	45-60	60-75	75-90	90-105	105-120
Number of workers	12	30	65	107	157	202	222	230

Sol. We have given the cumulative frequency distribution. So, first we will prepare the frequency distribution as given below

Class interval	cf	Mid value (x_i)	f_i	$u_i = \frac{x_i - 67.5}{15}$	$f_i u_i$	$f_i u_i^2$
0-15	12	7.5	12	−4	−48	192
15-30	30	22.5	18	−3	−54	162
30-45	65	37.5	35	−2	−70	140
45-60	107	52.5	42	−1	−42	42
60-75	157	67.5	50	0	0	0
75-90	202	82.5	45	1	45	45
90-105	222	97.5	20	2	40	80
105-120	230	112.5	8	3	24	72
Total			230		−105	733

Here, $a = 67.5$, $h = 15$, $N = \Sigma f_i = 230$, $\Sigma f_i u_i = -105$ and $\Sigma f_i u_i^2 = 733$

Now, Mean $= a + h\left(\frac{1}{N}\Sigma f_i u_i\right) = 67.5 + 15\left(\frac{-105}{230}\right)$

$= 67.5 - 6.85 = 60.65$

Standard deviation,

$$(\sigma) = \sqrt{h^2\left[\frac{1}{N}\Sigma f_i u_i^2 - \left(\frac{1}{N}\Sigma f_i u_i\right)^2\right]}$$

$$= \sqrt{225\left[\frac{733}{230} - \left(-\frac{105}{230}\right)^2\right]} = \sqrt{225\,[3.187 - (0.46)^2]}$$

$$= \sqrt{225\,(3.1870 - 0.2116)} = \sqrt{669.465} = 25.87$$

Topic Practice 3

Very Short Answer Type Questions

(2 Marks)

1 The marks obtained by 7 students are 8, 9, 11, 13, 14, 15, 21. Find the variance and standard deviation of these marks.

2 Find the variance of the data 6, 5, 9, 13, 12, 8 and 10.

3 Find the standard deviation of first 10 natural numbers.

Short Answer Type Questions

(4 Marks)

4 Find the standard deviation and variance of the following data.

x_i	140	145	150	155	160	165	170	175
f_i	4	6	15	30	36	24	8	2

5 Find the mean, variance and standard deviation for the following.

x_i	4	8	11	17	20	24	32
f_i	3	5	9	5	4	3	1

[NCERT]

6 Calculate mean and variance of the given data.

x_i	2	4	6	8	10	12	14	16
f_i	4	4	5	15	8	5	4	5

7 The mean and the standard deviation of 25 observations are 60 and 3. Later on it was decided to omit an observation which was incorrectly recorded as 50. Find the mean and the standard deviation of the remaining 24 observations.

8. Calculate the mean and variance for the following data.

Class	0-30	30-60	60-90	90-120	120-150	150-180	180-210
Frequency (f)	2	3	5	10	3	5	2

9 Calculate the mean, variance and standard deviation for the following distribution.

Class	0-5	5-10	10-15	15-20	20-25	25-30	30-35	35-40	40-45
Frequency	20	24	32	28	20	11	26	15	24

Hints & Answers

1. Solve as Example 1.
Ans. variance is 16.29 and standard deviation is 4.04

2. Solve as Example 1 **Ans.** 52/7

3. Solve as Example 3. **Ans.** 2.87

4. Let us take assumed mean, $a = 155$

We make the table from the given data.

x_i	f_i	$u_i = \frac{x_i - 155}{5}$	u_i^2	$f_i u_i$	$f_i u_i^2$
140	4	−3	9	−12	36
145	6	−2	4	−12	24
150	15	−1	1	−15	15
155	30	0	0	0	0
160	36	1	1	36	36
165	24	2	4	48	96
170	8	3	9	24	72
175	2	4	16	8	32
Total	125			77	311

$$\therefore \text{ Variance, } \sigma^2 = \left[\frac{\sum f_i u_i^2}{N} - \left(\frac{\sum f_i u_i}{N}\right)^2\right] \times h^2$$

$$= \left[\frac{311}{125} - \left(\frac{77}{125}\right)^2\right] \times 25$$

$$= 25 \times \frac{311}{125} - 25 \times \frac{77 \times 77}{125 \times 125}$$

$$= \frac{7775}{125} - \frac{148225}{15625}$$

$$= 62.200 - 9.4864$$

$$= 52.7136$$

$$\therefore \text{Standard deviation} = \sqrt{\text{Variance}}$$

$$= \sqrt{52.7136} = 7.26 \text{ (approx.)}$$

5. Solve as Example 6.
Ans. 14, 45.85, 6.77

6. Solve as Example 6.
Ans. 9, 15.08

7. Let the 25 observations be $x_1, x_3, x_3, ..., x_{23}, x_{24}, x_{25}$

Then, $\dfrac{x_1 + x_2 + x_3 + ... + x_{23} + x_{24} + x_{25}}{25} = 60$

If $x_{25} = 50$, then $\dfrac{x_1 + x_2 + x_3 + ... + x_{23} + x_{24} + 50}{25} = 60$

or $x_1 + x_2 + x_3 + ... + x_{23} + x_{24} = 60 \times 25 - 50 = 1450$

The mean of the remaining 24 observations

$$= \frac{x_1 + x_2 + x_3 + ... + x_{23} + x_{24}}{24}$$

$$= \frac{1450}{24} = 60\frac{5}{12}$$

Now, $\sigma^2 = \dfrac{\Sigma x^2}{n} - \bar{x}^2$

$$\Rightarrow \quad 3^2 = \frac{x_1^2 + x_2^2 + x_3^2 + ... + x_{25}^2}{25} - 60^2$$

$$\Rightarrow \quad 9 = \frac{x_1^2 + x_2^2 + x_3^2 + ... + x_{24}^2}{25} + \frac{50^2}{25} - 60^2 \text{ [let } x_{25} = 50]$$

$$\Rightarrow \quad \frac{x_1^2 + x_2^2 + x_3^2 + ... + x_{24}^2}{25} = 9 + 3600 - 100 = 3509$$

$$\Rightarrow \quad x_1^2 + x_2^2 + x_3^2 + ... + x_{24}^2 = 25 \times 3509$$

If σ_1 is the standard deviation of the remaining 24 observations, then

$$\sigma_1^2 = \frac{x_1^2 + x_2^2 + x_3^2 + ... + x_{24}^2}{24} - \left(\frac{1450}{24}\right)^2$$

$$= \frac{25 \times 3509}{24} - \frac{(1450)^2}{24 \times 24} = \frac{24 \times 25 \times 3509 - (1450)^2}{24 \times 24}$$

$$= \frac{2105400 - 2102500}{24 \times 24} = \frac{29 \times 100}{24 \times 24}$$

$$\Rightarrow \quad \sigma_1 = \frac{10}{24} \times \sqrt{29} = \frac{10}{24} \times 5.385 = 2.24$$

8. Here, $h = 30$ and $a = 105$

We make the table from the given data.

Class interval	Frequency (f_i)	Mid value (x_i)	$u_i = \dfrac{x_i - 105}{30}$	$f_i u_i$	u_i^2	$f_i u_i^2$
0-30	2	15	– 3	– 6	9	18
30-60	3	45	– 2	– 6	4	12
60-90	5	75	– 1	– 5	1	5
90-120	10	105	0	0	0	0
120-150	3	135	1	3	1	3
150-180	5	165	2	10	4	20
180-210	2	195	3	6	9	18
Total	**30**			**2**		**76**

Here, $N = 30$, $\Sigma f_i u_i = 2$, $\Sigma f_i u_i^2 = 76$ and $h = 30$

$$\therefore \text{ Mean } (\bar{x}) = a + \left(\frac{1}{N} \Sigma f_i u_i\right) \times h$$

$$= 105 + \left(\frac{1}{30} \times 2\right) \times 30$$

$$= 105 + 2 = 107$$

$$\text{Variance, } \sigma^2 = h^2 \left[\frac{1}{N} \Sigma f_i u_i^2 \, \Sigma - \left(\frac{1}{N} \Sigma f_i u_i\right)^2\right]$$

$$= (30)^2 \left[\frac{1}{30} \times 76 - \left(\frac{1}{30} \times 2\right)^2\right]$$

$$= (30)^2 \left[\frac{76}{30} - \frac{1}{225}\right]$$

$$= 30 \left[76 - \frac{30}{225}\right]$$

$$= 30\,[76 - 013]$$

$$= 30 \times 75.87 = 2276.1$$

Hence, the mean is 107 and variance is 2276.1.

9. Solve as Q. 8. **Ans.** 21.5, 164.75, 12.835

Chapter Practice

Multiple Choice Type Questions

1 Mark

1. Which of the following is/are used as the measures of dispersion?
(a) Range
(b) Quartile deviation
(c) Standard deviation
(d) All of the above

2. Mean deviation about median for continuous frequency distribution is calculated by using the formula

(a) $MD(M) = \frac{1}{N}\sum_{i=1}^{n} f_i|x_i + M|$

(b) $MD(M) = \frac{1}{N}\sum_{i=1}^{n} f_i|x_i - M|$

(c) $MD(M) = \frac{1}{N}\sum_{i=1}^{n} \frac{f_i}{|x_i - M|}$

(d) $MD(M) = \frac{1}{N}\sum_{i=1}^{n} \frac{|x_i - M|}{f_i}$

3. The mean deviation about the mean of the set of first n natural numbers when n is an even number, is
(a) $\frac{n}{2}$ (b) $\frac{n}{4}$ (c) $\frac{n}{6}$ (d) $\frac{n}{8}$

4. If x_1, x_2, x_3, x_4 and x_5 be the observations with mean m and standard deviation s, then the standard deviation of the observations kx_1, kx_2, kx_3, kx_4 and kx_5 is
(a) $k + s$ (b) $\frac{s}{k}$ (c) ks (d) s

5. The standard deviation for the following data is

x_i	3	8	13	18	23
f_i	7	10	15	10	6

(a) 6.21 (b) 6.31 (c) 6.12 (d) 6.13

6. If the mean deviation of numbers, $1, 1+d, 1+2d, \dots, 1+100d$ from their mean is 255, then d is equal to
(a) 10.0 (b) 20.0 (c) 10.1 (d) 20.2

Assertion-Reason Type Questions

1 Mark

Directions (Q. Nos. 7-10) *In the questions given below are two statements labelled as Assertion (A) and Reason (R). In the context of the two statements, which one of the following is correct?*

(a) Both A and R are correct; R is the correct explanation of A
(b) Both A and R are correct; R is not the correct explanation of A
(c) A is correct; R is incorrect
(d) R is correct; A is incorrect

7. **Assertion (A)** If $y_i = -2x_i + 3$ and $\sigma_x = 4$, then $\sigma_y = 8$.
Reason (R) If $y_i = ax_i + b$, then $\sigma_y = |a|\sigma_x$.

8. **Assertion (A)** The variance of first 10 natural number is $\frac{33}{4}$.
Reason (R) The variance of first n natural number is $\frac{n^2-1}{12}$.

9. **Assertion (A)** The mean deviation about the mean for the following data 38, 70, 48, 40, 42, 55, 63, 46, 54, 44 is 9.4.
Reason (R) Mean deviation $= \frac{\sum_{i=1}^{n} |x_i - \bar{x}|}{n}$

10. **Assertion (A)** The variance of first n natural numbers is $\frac{n^2-1}{12}$.
Reason (R) (Standard deviation)^2 = Variance.

Very Short Answer Type Questions

2 Marks

11. The mean of 100 observations is 50 and their standard deviation is 5. Find the sum of all squares of all the observations. **[NCERT Exemplar]**

12. The following relates to sample of size 60, $\Sigma x^2 = 18000$ and $\Sigma x = 960$, find the variance.

Short Answer Type Questions

(4 Marks)

13. Find the Range mean deviation about the mean and coefficient of mean deviation for the following data

12, 3, 18, 17, 4, 9, 17, 19, 20, 15, 8, 17, 2, 3, 16, 11, 3, 1, 0, 5

14. Find the mean deviation for the following distribution.

Class interval	0-10	10-20	20-30	30-40	40-50
Frequency	7	3	5	2	8

15. Find the mean and standard deviation for the following data.

Class interval	0-10	10-20	20-30	30-40	40-50	50-60	60-70	70-80	80-90	90-100
Frequency	3	2	4	6	5	5	5	2	8	5

16. Calculate mean deviation (from median) for the following data.

Marks	0-10	10-20	20-30	30-40	40-50
Number of students	5	8	15	16	6

17. Find the mean and standard deviation of the following frequency distribution. **[NCERT]**

x_i	6	10	14	18	24	28	30
f_i	2	4	7	12	8	4	3

18. Find the standard deviation for the following data.

x_i	3	8	13	18	23
f_i	7	10	15	10	6

19. Find the mean and standard deviation for the following data.

Age (in years)	Number of teachers
25-30	30
30-35	23
35-40	20
40-45	14
45-50	10
50-55	3

20. Find the variance and standard deviation for the following distribution.

x_i	4.5	14.5	24.5	34.5	44.5	54.5	64.5
f_i	1	5	12	22	17	9	4

Long Answer Type Questions

(6 Marks)

21. An original frequency table with mean 11 and variance 9.9 was lost but the following table derived from it was found. Construct the original table.

Value of deviation (d)	−2	−1	0	1	2
Frequency (f)	1	6	7	4	2

22. The runs of two players for 10 innings each are as follows.

A	58	59	60	54	65	66	52	75	69	52
B	94	26	92	65	96	78	14	34	98	13

Whom may be regarded as more consistent player?

23. The mean and variance of eight observations are 9 and 9.25, respectively. If six of the observations are 6, 7, 10, 12, 12 and 13, then find the remaining two observations. **[NCERT]**

Case-Based Type Questions

(6 Marks)

24. The marks of students of class XI in Maths test (out of 20) are given below:

Marks (x_i)	5	7	9	11	13	15	17
Number of students (f_i)	2	4	6	8	10	12	8

On the basis of above information, answer the following questions.

(i) Find the total number of students in the class.

(ii) What is the cumulative frequency corresponding to mark 11.

(iii) Find the median (M) of given data.

(iv) Find the value of $\sum_{i=1}^{n} f_i \mid x_i - M \mid$.

(v) What is the value of mean deviation from median of given data?

25. Let x_i and y_i are two data such that $y_i = ax_i + b$. If $\bar{x}, \bar{y}$ are mean and σ_x, σ_y are standard deviation of the given data x_i and y_i respectively. Then, we have $\bar{y} = a\bar{x} + b$ and $\sigma_y = |a|\sigma_x$.

On the basis of above information, answer the following question.

(i) If $y_i = 4x_i - 3$ and $\bar{x}$ is 10, then find the value of $\bar{y}$.

(ii) If $y_i = \dfrac{ax_i + b}{c}$, then find the value of σ_y.

(iii) If $y_i = x_i + 10$, then find the value of σ_y.

(iv) If $y_i = ax_i + b$, then find the value of var(Y).

Hints & Answers

1. (d) **2.** (b) **3.** (b) **4.** (c) **5.** (c)
6. (c) **7.** (a) **8.** (a) **9.** (d) **10.** (a)

11. Given, $\bar{x} = 50$, $n = 100$ and $\sigma = 5$

We know that,

$$\sigma^2 = \frac{\Sigma x_i^2}{n} - (\bar{x})^2 \Rightarrow \frac{\Sigma x_i^2}{n} = \sigma^2 + (\bar{x})^2$$

$$\Rightarrow \Sigma x_i^2 = n[\sigma^2 + (\bar{x})^2] = 100[5^2 + (50)^2]$$ **Ans.** 252500

12. Use, $\sigma^2 = \frac{\Sigma x_i^2}{n} - \left(\frac{\Sigma x_i}{n}\right)^2$ **Ans.** 44

13. The data values in the ascending order are

0, 1, 2, 3, 3, 3, 4, 5, 8, 9, 11, 12, 15, 16, 17, 17, 17, 18, 19, 20

Range = Maximum value − Minimum value = 20 − 0 = 20

Here, the total number of observation = 20,

$$\text{Mean} = \frac{\left[\begin{array}{c}0+1+2+3+3+3+4+5+8+9+11+12+15\\+16+17+17+17+18+19+20\end{array}\right]}{20} = \frac{200}{20}$$

The absolute values of the deviations from the mean, i.e. $|x_i - 10|$ are 10, 9, 8, 7, 7, 7, 6, 5, 2, 1, 1, 2, 5, 6, 7, 7, 7, 8, 9, 10.

$\therefore$ Mean deviation about the mean $= \frac{\Sigma|x_i - 10|}{n} = \frac{124}{20}$

And coefficient of mean deviation $= \frac{\text{Mean deviation}}{\text{Mean}} = \frac{6.2}{10}$

Ans. 20, 6.2, 0.62

14. 14.08

15. Here, $h = 10$ and $a = 55$

Let us make the following table from the given data.

Class interval	f_i	Mid value (x_i)	$u_i = \frac{x_i - 55}{10}$	$f_i u_i$	u_i^2	$f_i u_i^2$
0-10	3	5	−5	−15	25	75
10-20	2	15	−4	−8	16	32
20-30	4	25	−3	−12	9	36
30-40	6	35	−2	−12	4	24
40-50	5	45	−1	−5	1	5
50-60	5	55	0	0	0	0
60-70	5	65	1	5	1	5
70-80	2	75	2	4	4	8
80-90	8	85	3	24	9	72
90-100	5	95	4	20	16	80
Total	$N = \Sigma f_i = 45$			$\Sigma f_i u_i = 1$,		$\Sigma f_i u_i^2 = 337$

Here, $N = \Sigma f_i = 45$, $\Sigma f_i u_i = 1$ and $\Sigma f_i u_i^2 = 337$

$\therefore$ Mean $(\bar{x}) = a + \left(\frac{1}{N}\Sigma f_i u_i\right) \times h$

and standard deviation,

$$\sigma = h\sqrt{\left\{\frac{1}{N}\Sigma f_i u_i^2 - \left(\frac{1}{N}\Sigma f_i u_i\right)^2\right\}}$$

Ans. 55.22, 27.36

16. Let us make the following table from the given data.

Marks (Class interval)	Number of students (f_i)	cf	x_i	$\lvert x_i - M\rvert = \lvert x_i - 28\rvert$	$f_i\lvert x_i - 28\rvert$
0-10	5	5	5	23	115
10-20	8	13	15	13	104
20-30	15	28	25	3	45
30-40	16	44	35	7	112
40-50	6	50	45	17	102
Total	$N = \Sigma f_i = 50$				$\Sigma f_i\lvert x_i - 28\rvert = 478$

Now, median $(M) = \frac{l + \frac{N}{2} - cf}{f} \times h = 20 + \frac{25 - 13}{15} \times 10 = 28$

$\therefore$ Mean deviation about median $= \frac{1}{N}(\Sigma f_i|x_i - M|)$ **Ans.** 9.56

17. Let us make the following table from the given data.

x_i	f_i	$f_i x_i$	$(x_i - \bar{x}) = (x_i - 19)$	$(x_i - \bar{x})^2$	$f_i(x_i - \bar{x})^2$
6	2	12	−13	169	338
10	4	40	−9	81	324
14	7	98	−5	25	175
18	12	216	−1	1	12
24	8	192	5	25	200
28	4	112	9	81	324
30	3	90	11	121	363
Total	$\Sigma f_i = 40$	$\Sigma f_i x_i = 760$			$\Sigma f_i(x_i - \bar{x})^2 = 1736$

$\therefore$ Mean $(\bar{x}) = \frac{\Sigma f_i x_i}{N}$

and standard deviation $= \sqrt{\frac{1}{N}[\Sigma f_i(x_i - \bar{x})^2]}$ **Ans.** 19; 6.59

18. Let us make the table from the given data.

x_i	f_i	$f_i x_i$	x_i^2	$f_i x_i^2$
3	7	21	9	63
8	10	80	64	640
13	15	195	169	2535
18	10	180	324	3240
23	6	138	529	3174
Total	$\Sigma f_i = 48$	$\Sigma f_i x_i = 614$		$\Sigma f_i x_i^2 = 9652$

$\therefore$ Standard deviation, $\sigma = \frac{1}{N}\sqrt{N\Sigma f_i x_i^2 - (\Sigma f_i x_i)^2}$ **Ans.** 6.12

19. Let assume mean, $a = 42.5$

Let us make the table from the given data.

Class	Mid value (x_i)	f_i	$u_i = \frac{x_i - A}{5}$	u_i^2	$f_i u_i$	$f_i u_i^2$
25-30	27.5	30	−3	9	−90	270
30-35	32.5	23	−2	4	−46	92
35-40	37.5	20	−1	1	−20	20

Class	Mid value (x_i)	f_i	$u_i = \frac{x_i - A}{5}$	u_i^2	f_iu_i	$f_iu_i^2$
40-45	42.5	14	0	0	0	0
45-50	47.5	10	1	1	10	10
50-55	52.5	3	2	4	6	12
Total		Σf_i =100			Σf_iu_i = −140	$\Sigma f_iu_i^2$ = 404

$\therefore$ Mean, $\bar{x} = a + \frac{1}{N}\Sigma f_iu_i \times h$

Standard deviation $= \left[\sqrt{\frac{1}{N}\Sigma f_iu_i^2 - \left(\frac{1}{N}\Sigma f_iu_i\right)^2}\right] \times h$

Ans. 35.5 yr, 7.21 yr

20. Let us make the table from the given data.

x_i	f_i	$d_i = x_i - 34.5$	$u_i = \frac{x_i - 34.5}{10}$	u_i^2	f_iu_i	$f_iu_i^2$
4.5	1	−30	−3	9	−3	9
14.5	5	−20	−2	4	−10	20
24.5	12	−10	−1	1	−12	12
34.5	22	0	0	0	0	0
44.5	17	10	1	1	17	17
54.5	9	20	2	4	18	36
64.5	4	30	3	9	12	36
Total	Σf_i =70				Σf_iu_i = 22	$\Sigma f_iu_i^2$ = 130

Variance, $\sigma^2 = \left[\frac{1}{N}\Sigma f_iu_i^2 - \left(\frac{1}{N}\Sigma f_iu_i\right)^2\right] \times h^2$

and standard deviation $= \sqrt{\text{Variance}}$ **Ans.** 175.8; 13.259

21. Let us make the table from the given data.

d	f	d^2	fd	fd^2
−2	1	4	−2	4
−1	6	1	−6	6
0	7	0	0	0
1	4	1	4	4
2	2	4	4	8
Total	Σf = 20		Σfd = 0	Σfd^2 = 22

We know that, $\bar{x} = a + h\frac{\Sigma fd}{\Sigma f} \Rightarrow a = 11$

Also, variance, $\sigma^2 = h^2\left[\frac{\Sigma fd^2}{\Sigma f} - \left(\frac{\Sigma fd}{\Sigma f}\right)^2\right]$

$\Rightarrow h = 3$

Deviation, $(d) = \frac{x-a}{h}$

$\Rightarrow x = a + dh$

$\therefore$ Different values of x for different values of d, we have

$11 - 2 \times 3, 11 - 1 \times 3, 11 - 0 \times 3, 11 + 1 \times 3, 11 + 2 \times 3$

i.e. 5, 8, 11, 14, 17.

Ans The original frequency table is as follows

Class	3.5-6.5	6.5-9.5	9.5-12.5	12.5-15.5	15.5-18.5
Frequency	1	6	7	4	2

22. Let us make the table from the given data

Player A			Player B		
x_i	$x_i - 61$	$(x_i - 61)^2$	y_i	$y_i - 61$	$(y_i - 61)^2$
58	−3	9	94	33	1089
59	−2	4	26	−35	1225
60	−1	1	92	31	961
54	−7	49	65	4	16
65	4	16	96	35	1225
66	5	25	78	17	289
52	−9	81	14	−47	2209
75	14	196	34	−27	729
69	8	64	98	37	1369
52	−9	81	13	−48	2304
Σx_i = 610		$\Sigma (x_i - 61)^2$ = 526	Σy_i = 610		$\Sigma (y_i - 61)^2$ 11416

For player A

Mean $= \frac{\Sigma x_i}{n} = \frac{610}{10} = 61$

and SD $= \sqrt{\frac{\Sigma(x_i - 61)^2}{N}} = \sqrt{\frac{526}{10}} = 7.25$

For player B Mean $= \frac{\Sigma y_i}{n} = \frac{610}{10} = 61$

and SD $= \sqrt{\frac{\Sigma(y_i - 61)^2}{N}} = \sqrt{\frac{11416}{10}} = 33.79$

Since, SD for player A is 7.25 < SD for player B is 33.79.

Ans. Player A is more consistent player.

23. Let the remaining two observations be a and b.

Given, $\bar{x} = 9$ and $\sigma^2 = 9.25 \Rightarrow \bar{x} = 9$

$\Rightarrow \frac{\text{Sum of all observations}}{\text{Number of observations}} = 9$

$\Rightarrow$ Sum of all observations $= 9 \times 8$

$\Rightarrow 6 + 7 + 10 + 12 + 12 + 13 + a + b = 72$

$\Rightarrow a + b = 12$ ...(i)

Again, $\sigma^2 = \frac{\Sigma x_i^2}{n} - \left(\frac{\Sigma x_i}{n}\right)^2 \Rightarrow \sigma^2 = \frac{\Sigma x_i^2}{n} - (\bar{x})^2$

$\Rightarrow 9.25 = \frac{36 + 49 + 100 + 144 + 144 + 169 + a^2 + b^2}{8} - (9)^2$

$\Rightarrow a^2 + b^2 = 80$ ...(ii)

Now, from Eq. (i), put $b = (12 - a)$ in Eq. (ii), we get

$a = 4$ or 8

On putting $a = 4$ or $a = 8$ Eq. (i), we get $b = 8$ or $b = 4$

Ans. 4 and 8

24. (i) 50 (ii) 20 (iii) 13 (iv) 136 (v) 2.72

25. (i) 37 (ii) $\left|\frac{a}{c}\right|\sigma_x$ (iii) σ_x (iv) a^2 var(X)

CHAPTER

15

Probability

In earlier classes, we have study the statistical and classical approach of probability, but both the theories have some serious difficulties and limitations. To overcome these difficulties, modern probability theory has been developed axiomatically. This theory of probability was developed by Russian Mathematician A.N. Kolmogorov in 1933. In his book "Foundation of probability", he laid down some axioms to interpret probability. To understand this approach, we must know about some basic terms, *viz*. experiment, random experiment, sample space, events, etc.

TOPIC 01 Random Experiment and Events

Experiment

An operation which can produce some well-defined outcomes, is known as experiment. There are two types of experiments, *viz.*

(i) **Deterministic Experiments** An experiment which gives the same result every time, when it is repeated under identical conditions, is called the deterministic experiments.

(ii) **Random Experiments** In our daily life, we perform many experimental activities, where the result may not be same, when they are repeated under identical conditions. e.g. when a fair coin is tossed it may turn up a head or a tail, but we are not sure which one of these results will be actually obtained. Such experiments are called the random experiments. Thus, rolling an unbiased die, drawing a card from a well-shuffled pack of cards are all examples of random experiments.

Or

An experiment is called random experiment, if it satisfies the following two conditions

(i) It has more than one possible outcomes.

(ii) It is not possible to predict the outcomes in advance.

Outcomes and Sample Space

A possible result of a random experiment is called its outcome. The set of all possible outcomes of a random experiment is called the sample space of the random experiment and it is generally denoted by S, i.e.Sample space (S) = {All possible outcomes}.

Each element of a sample space is called a **sample point** or an **event point.**

e.g. (i) On tossing a fair coin, there are two possible outcomes, namely head (H) and tail (T).

$\therefore$ The sample space S is

$$\{H, T\} \text{i.e. } S = \{H, T\}.$$

(ii) When we throw a die, then possible outcomes of this experiment are 1, 2, 3, 4, 5 or 6.

$\therefore$ The sample space S is $\{1, 2, 3, 4, 5, 6\}$

i.e. $S = \{1, 2, 3, 4, 5, 6\}$

Note A sample space S is called a **discrete sample space**, if S is a finite set.

Example 1 A bag contains 4 identical red balls and 3 identical black balls. The experiment consists of drawing one ball, then putting it into the bag and again drawing a ball. What are the possible outcomes of the experiment?

Sol. Let R denotes a red ball and B denotes a black ball. Then, possible outcomes of the experiment are RR, RB, BR and BB.

Example 2 An experiment consists of recording boy-girl composition of families with 2 children.

(i) What is the sample space, if we are interested in knowing whether it is a boy or girl in the order of their births?

(ii) What is the sample space, if we are interested in the number of girls in the family? **[NCERT]**

Sol. Let B denotes a boy and G denotes a girl. Then,

(i) Required sample space = $\{BB, BG, GB, GG\}$

(ii) There can be no girl, 1 girl or 2 girls.

$\therefore$ Required sample space = $\{0, 1, 2\}$

Example 3 Describe the sample space for the experiment of tossing a coin four times. **[NCERT]**

Sol. Let us denote head by H and tail by T, then the possibilities are

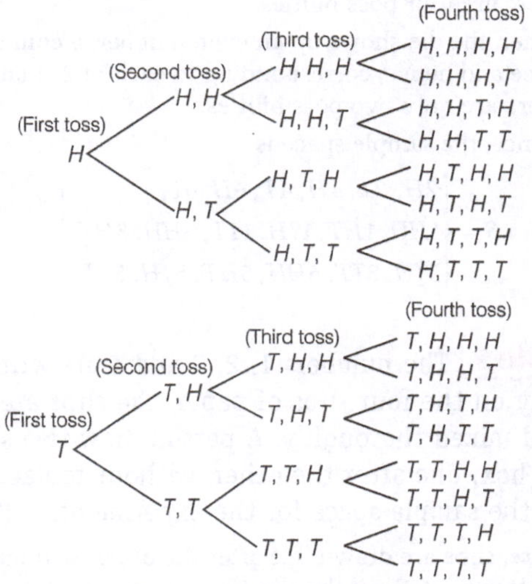

Thus, the sample space for this experiment is given by {$HHHH$, $HHHT$, $HHTH$, $HHTT$, $HTHH$, $HTHT$, $HTTH$, $HTTT$, $THHH$, $THHT$, $THTH$, $THTT$, $TTHH$, $TTHT$, $TTTH$, $TTTT$}

Example 4 An experiment consists of rolling a die and then tossing a coin once, if the number on the die is even. If the number on the die is odd, then coin is tossed twice. Write the sample space for this experiment. **[NCERT]**

Sol. It is a two stage experiment. When a die is rolled, then it may show up any one of the six numbers 1, 2, 3, 4, 5, 6.

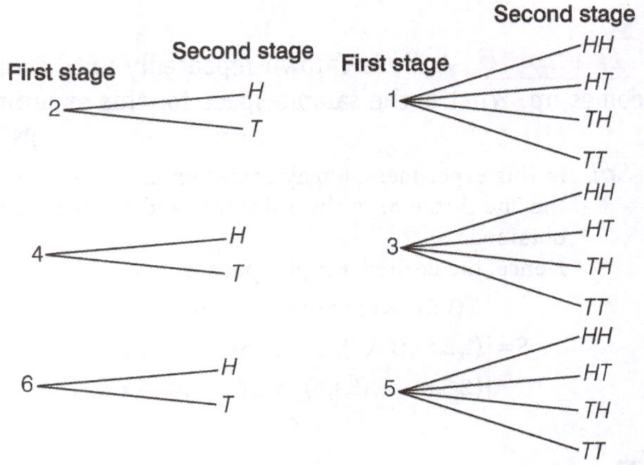

When the die shows up an odd number, a coin is tossed twice and hence, corresponding to each of 1, 3 and 5, there are four possibilities.

When the die shows up an even number, a coin is tossed once and hence, corresponding to each of 2, 4 and 6, there are only two possibilities.

Hence, the sample space is

$$S=\begin{Bmatrix} 2H, 2T, 4H, 4T, 6H, 6T, \\ 1HH, 1HT, 1TH, 1TT, 3HH, 3HT, \\ 3TH, 3TT, 5HH, 5HT, 5TH, 5TT \end{Bmatrix}$$

Example 5 The numbers 1, 2, 3 and 4 are written separately on the four slips of paper, the slips are put in a box and mixed thoroughly. A person draw two slips from the box, one after the other, without replacement. Describe the sample space for the experiment. **[NCERT]**

Sol. Here, slips are drawn one after the other, without replacement. So, if the slip 1 is drawn in first draw, then the slip drawn in second draw may be the numbers 2, 3 and 4.

Thus, in this case, possible outcomes are (1, 2), (1, 3) and (1, 4). If the slip 2 is drawn in first draw, then the slip drawn in second draw may be the numbers 1, 3 and 4.Thus, in this case, possible outcomes are (2, 1), (2, 3) and (2, 4).

Similarly, the possible outcomes when the slip 3 and 4 are drawn in first draw are

(3, 1), (3, 2), (3, 4) and (4, 1), (4, 2), (4, 3) respectively.

Hence, sample space of the experiment is

$$S=\begin{Bmatrix} (1,2),(1,3),(1,4),(2,1),(2,3),(2,4), \\ (3,1),(3,2),(3,4),(4,1),(4,2),(4,3) \end{Bmatrix}$$

Example 6 A die is thrown repeatedly until a six comes up. What is the sample space for this experiment? **[NCERT]**

Sol. In this experiment, 6 may comes up in 1st throw or in the 2nd throw or in the 3rd throw and so on, till 6 is obtained.

Hence, the desired sample space is

$$S=\begin{Bmatrix} 6,(1,6),(2,6),(3,6),(4,6),(5,6),(1,1,6), \\ (1,2,6),(1,3,6),\ldots,(1,5,6),(2,1,6),\ldots, \\ (2,5,6),\ldots,(5,1,6),(5,2,6),\ldots,(5,5,6),\ldots \end{Bmatrix}.$$

Event

A subset E of a sample space S associated with a random experiment is called an event.

e.g. On throwing a die, we have the sample space

$$S=\{1,2,3,4,5,6\}$$

Then, $E=\{2, 3, 4\}$ is an event. $[\because E\subseteq S]$

Note We can define as many events as there are subsets of a sample space. Thus, number of events of a sample space $S=n(P(S))$, where $P(s)$ is the power set of S.

Example 7 List all events associated with the random experiment of tossing of two coins.

Sol. On tossing of two coins, we have the sample space

$$S=\{HH, HT, TH, TT\}$$

Here, $n(P(S))=2^4=16$

So, there are 16 events, which are defined as follows.

[if a set have n elements, then its power set have 2^n elements]

$\{\phi, \{HH\}, \{HT\}, \{TH\}, \{TT\}, \{HH,HT\}, \{HH, TH\}, \{HH, TT\}, \{HT, TH\}, \{HT, TT\}, \{TH, TT\}, \{HH, HT, TH\}, \{HH, HT, TT\}, \{HH, TH, TT\}, \{HT, TH, TT\}, \{HH, HT, TH, TT\}\}$

Example 8 An ordinary deck of cards contains 52 cards divided into four suits. The red suits are diamonds and hearts and black suits are clubs and spades. The cards Jack (J), Queen (Q), King (K) are called face cards. Suppose we pick one card from the deck at random.

(i) What is the sample space of the experiment?

(ii) Describe the event that the chosen card is a black face card. **[NCERT Exemplar]**

Sol. We have the following flowchart.

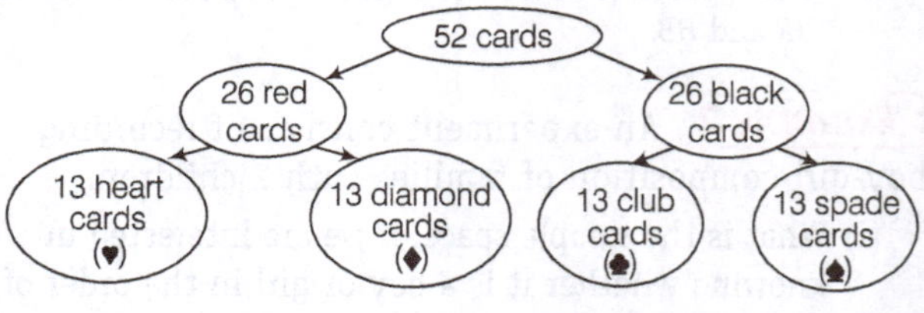

(i) Since, a card is drawn at random, therefore the outcomes in the sample space S are all 52 cards in the deck.

(ii) Let E be the event that the chosen card is a black face card. Then, the outcomes in E are Jack, Queen, King of spade and club cards. Symbolically.

$$E=\{J♣, Q♣, K♣, J♠, Q♠, K♠\}$$

Occurrence of an Event

An event associated with a random experiment is said to occur, if any one of the elementary events associated to it is an outcome of the experiment.

e.g. Suppose a die is thrown and let A be an event of getting an odd number. Then, $A=\{1, 3, 5\}$.

Now, if the outcome of experiment is 3. Then, we can say that event A has occurred. Suppose, in another trial, outcome is 4, then we can say that event A has not occurred.

Types of Events

Events can be classified into various types on the basis of their elements, which are as follow

(i) **Simple Event** If an event has only one sample point of a sample space, then it is called a **simple** or **elementary** or **indecomposible event.**

e.g. Let a die is thrown, then sample space

$$S = \{1, 2, 3, 4, 5, 6\}$$

Again, let A = Event of getting $4 = \{4\}$

B = Event of getting $1 = \{1\}$

Here, A and B are simple events.

(ii) **Compound Event** If an event has more than one sample point, then it is called a **compound** or **composite event** or **decomposible.**

e.g. On rolling a die, we have sample space

$$S = \{1, 2, 3, 4, 5, 6\}$$

Then, the events

E : Getting an even number

F : Getting an odd number

G : Getting a multiple of 3

are all compound events. The subsets of S associated with these events are

$$E = \{2, 4, 6\},$$
$$F = \{1, 3, 5\}, G = \{3, 6\}$$

Each of the above subsets contain more than one sample point, therefore they are all compound events.

Note All events other than elementary events and impossible events associated with a random experiment are compound events.

(iii) **Sure Event** The whole sample space S is also a subset of S, so it represents an event. Since, every outcome of an experiment carried out a member of S, therefore the event represented by S is called a sure or a certain event.

e.g.

(a) Sun rises in the East, is a sure event.

(b) On tossing a coin, either head or tail will occur, is a sure event.

(iv) **Impossible Event** The empty set ϕ is also a subset of the sample space (S) so it represents an event. Since, there is no element in the empty set, therefore it can not occurs.

e.g. On throwing a die, then we have the sample space

$$S = \{1, 2, 3, 4, 5, 6\}$$

Let E = Event of getting a number less than 1.

Then, $E = \phi$. So, E is called an impossible event.

(v) **Equally Likely Outcomes** The outcomes of a random experiment are said to be **equally likely**, if none of them are expected to occur in preference to the other. e.g.

In drawing a card from well shuffled pack, all 52 possible outcomes are equally likely. Getting a spade is as likely as getting a heart; getting a king is as likely as getting a queen.

Example 9 Identify that following events are sure/impossible events.

(i) Event of getting a number multiple of 7 in a single toss of a die.

(ii) Event of getting five kings in a pack of cards.

(iii) Event of getting a number less than 7 on throwing a die.

Sol. (i) We know that in a single toss of a die only 1 to 6 number exist. So, multiple of 7 does not exist. Hence, it is an impossible event.

(ii) We know that in a pack of cards only four kings exist. So five kings does not exist. Hence, it is an impossible event.

(iii) On throwing a die, we have sample space

$$S = \{1, 2, 3, 4, 5, 6\}.$$

Let E = Event of getting a number less than 7.

Then, $E = \{1, 2, 3, 4, 5, 6\}$.

So, E is a sure event.

Example 10 Two dice are rolled. Let A, B, C be the events of getting a sum of 2, a sum of 3 and a sum of 4 respectively.

(i) Which events are elementary events?

(ii) Which events are compound events?

Sol. On throwing of two dice, we get the sample space

$$S = \begin{Bmatrix} (1,1), (1,2), (1,3), (1,4), (1,5), (1,6), \\ (2,1), (2,2), (2,3), (2,4), (2,5), (2,6), \\ (3,1), (3,2), (3,3), (3,4), (3,5), (3,6), \\ (4,1), (4,2), (4,3), (4,4), (4,5), (4,6), \\ (5,1), (5,2), (5,3), (5,4), (5,5), (5,6), \\ (6,1), (6,2), (6,3), (6,4), (6,5), (6,6) \end{Bmatrix}$$

Now, as A is the event of getting a sum of 2.

$\therefore \quad A=\{(1,1)\}$

Similarly, $\quad B=\{(1,2),(2,1)\}$

and $\quad C=\{(1,3),(3,1),(2,2)\}$

(i) Since, A consists a single sample point, therefore it is an elementary or simple event.

(ii) Since, both B and C contain more than one sample points, therefore each of them is compound event.

Algebra of Events

We know that how to combine two or more sets by using the operations on sets union ($\cup$), intersection ($\cap$)and difference (−). Like-wise we, can combine two or more events by using the analogous set notations. Let A and B are two events associated with a sample space S, then

1. Complementary Event

For every event E, there corresponds another event E' called the complementary event of E, which consist of those outcomes that do not correspond to the occurrence of E. E' is also called the event 'not E'.

e.g. In tossing three coins, the sample space is

$$S=\{HHH, HHT, HTH, THH, HTT, THT, TTH, TTT\}$$

Let $E=\{THT, TTH, HTT\}$

= event of getting only one head.

Clearly, for outcome HHT, event E has not occurred

$\therefore \quad HHT \in E'$

Similarly, for the outcomes HTH, THH, TTT and HHH, event E has not occurred.

$\therefore \quad E' = \{HHT, HTH, THH, TTT, HHH\}$

It can be seen that E' contains only those outcomes which are not in E.

Example 11 Two dice are thrown once. The events A, B, E are as follows

A : Getting an even number on first die.

B : Getting an odd number on first die.

E : Getting the sum of numbers on the dice ≥ 10.

Describe the events

(i) A' (ii) B' (iii) E' [NCERT]

Sol. On throwing of two dice, we have sample space

$$S=\begin{Bmatrix}(1,1),(1,2),(1,3),(1,4),(1,5),(1,6),\\(2,1),(2,2),(2,3),(2,4),(2,5),(2,6),\\(3,1),(3,2),(3,3),(3,4),(3,5),(3,6),\\(4,1),(4,2),(4,3),(4,4),(4,5),(4,6),\\(5,1),(5,2),(5,3),(5,4),(5,5),(5,6),\\(6,1),(6,2),(6,3),(6,4),(6,5),(6,6)\end{Bmatrix}$$

(i) A : Getting an even number on first die.

$\Rightarrow A'$: Getting an odd number on first die.

$$=\begin{Bmatrix}(1,1),(1,2),(1,3),(1,4),(1,5),(1,6),\\(3,1),(3,2),(3,3),(3,4),(3,5),(3,6),\\(5,1),(5,2),(5,3),(5,4),(5,5),(5,6)\end{Bmatrix}$$

(ii) B : Getting an odd number on first die.

$\Rightarrow B'$: Getting an even number on first die.

$$=\begin{Bmatrix}(2,1),(2,2),(2,3),(2,4),(2,5),(2,6),\\(4,1),(4,2),(4,3),(4,4),(4,5),(4,6),\\(6,1),(6,2),(6,3),(6,4),(6,5),(6,6)\end{Bmatrix}$$

(iii) E : Getting the sum of the numbers on the dice ≥ 10.

$\Rightarrow E'$: Getting the sum of the numbers on the dice < 10.

$$=\begin{Bmatrix}(1,1),(1,2),(1,3),(1,4),(1,5),(1,6),(2,1),(2,2),\\(2,3),(2,4),(2,5),(2,6),(3,1),(3,2),(3,3),\\(3,4),(3,5),(3,6),(4,1),(4,2),(4,3),(4,4),(4,5),\\(5,1),(5,2),(5,3),(5,4),(6,1),(6,2),(6,3)\end{Bmatrix}$$

2. Event '*A* or *B*'

The event 'A or B' is same as the event $A \cup B$ and it contains all those elements which are either in event A or in events B or in both.

Thus, A or $B = A \cup B = \{\omega : \omega \in A \text{ or } \omega \in B\}$

3. Event '*A* and *B*'

The event 'A and B' is same as the event '$A \cap B$' and it contains all those elements which are common to both A and B. Thus, A and $B = A \cap B = \{\omega : \omega \in A \text{ and } \omega \in B\}$

4. Event '*A* but not *B*'

The events 'A but not B' is same as the event $A - B = (A \cap B')$ and it contains all those elements which are in A but not in B.

Thus, A but not $B = A - B = \{\omega : \omega \in A \text{ and } \omega \notin B\}$

Note For any event E, associated with a sample space S, $E' = \text{not } E = S - E = \{\omega : \omega \in S \text{ and } \omega \notin E\}$.

In the following table, we give verbal description of some events and their equivalent set alongwith the Venn diagram.

Events	Verbal Description	Equivalent Set	Venn Diagram
(i) Neither A nor B	It is the intersection of sets $\bar{A}$ and $\bar{B}$, which contains the common elements of $\bar{A}$ and $\bar{B}$.	$\bar{A} \cap \bar{B}$ or $U - (A \cup B)$	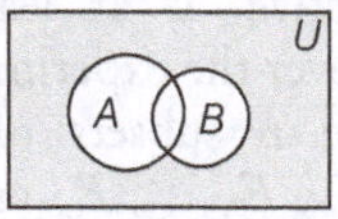
(ii) Exactly one of A and B	It is the union of one event and complement of other events. or It is the difference of union and intersection of both events.	$(A \cap \bar{B}) \cup (\bar{A} \cap B)$ or $(A \cup B) - (A \cap B)$	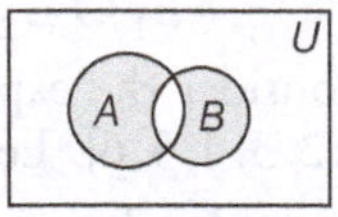
(iii) Atleast one of A, B or C	It is a union of all three sets, which contains either A or B or C etc.	$A \cup B \cup C$	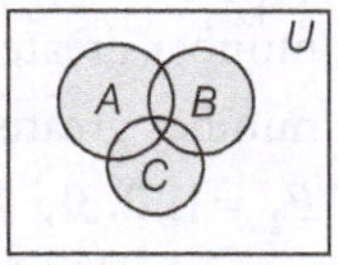
(iv) All three of A, B and C	It is an intersection of all three sets, which contains common elements of A, B and C.	$A \cap B \cap C$	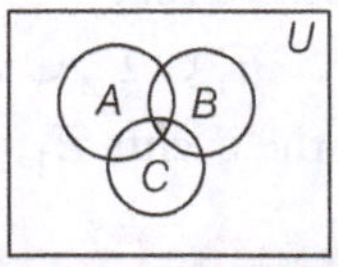
(v) Exactly two of A, B and C	It is the union of three conditions, where in each condition we take intersection of any two events and complement of remaining third event.	$(A \cap B \cap \bar{C}) \cup (A \cap \bar{B} \cap C) \cup (\bar{A} \cap B \cap C)$	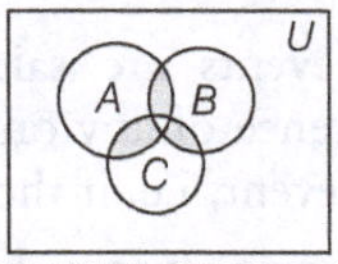

Example 12 A die is thrown. Describe the following events

(i) A : a number less than 7.
(ii) B : a number greater than 7.
(iii) C : a multiple of 3.
(iv) D : a number less than 4.
(v) E : an even number greater than 4.
(vi) F : a number not less than 3.

Also, find $A \cup B, A \cap B, B \cup C, E \cap F, D \cap E, A - C, D - E, F'$ and $E \cap F'$. [NCERT]

Sol. When a die is thrown, then sample space

$S = \{1, 2, 3, 4, 5, 6\}$

(i) A : a number less than 7 $= \{1, 2, 3, 4, 5, 6\}$
(ii) B : a number greater than 7 $= \{\ \} = \phi$
(iii) C: a multiple of 3 $= \{3, 6\}$
(iv) D: a number less than 4 $= \{1, 2, 3\}$
(v) E : an even number greater than 4 $= \{6\}$
(vi) F : a number not less than 3 $= \{3, 4, 5, 6\}$

Now, $A \cup B$ = The elements which are in A or in B or in both

$= \{1, 2, 3, 4, 5, 6\} \cup \phi$
$= \{1, 2, 3, 4, 5, 6\}$

$A \cap B$ = The elements which are common in both A and B

$= \{1, 2, 3, 4, 5, 6\} \cap \phi = \phi$

$B \cup C$ = The elements which are in B or C or both

$= \{\ \} \cup \{3, 6\} = \{3, 6\}$

$E \cap F$ = The elements which are common in both E and F

$= \{6\} \cap \{3, 4, 5, 6\} = \{6\}$

$D \cap E$ = The elements which are common in both D and E

$= \{1, 2, 3\} \cap \{6\} = \phi$

$A - C$ = The elements which are in A but not in C

$= \{1, 2, 3, 4, 5, 6\} - \{3, 6\}$
$= \{1, 2, 4, 5\}$

$D - E$ = The elements which are in D but not in E

$= \{1, 2, 3\} - \{6\} = \{1, 2, 3\}$

F' = The elements which are not in F

$= (S - F)$
$= \{1, 2, 3, 4, 5, 6\} - \{3, 4, 5, 6\} = \{1, 2\}$

and $E \cap F' = E \cap (S - F)$

$= E \cap (\{1, 2, 3, 4, 5, 6\} - \{3, 4, 5, 6\})$
$= \{6\} \cap \{1, 2\} = \phi$

Exhaustive Events

For a random experiment, a set of events is said to be exhaustive, if at least one of them necessarily occurs whenever the experiment is performed. Let $E_1, E_2, E_3, \ldots, E_n$ be n subsets of a sample space S. Then, events $E_1, E_2, E_3, \ldots, E_n$ are called exhaustive events, if

$$E_1 \cup E_2 \cup E_3 \cup \ldots \cup E_n = S.$$

e.g. Consider the experiment of throwing a die. We have, $S = \{1, 2, 3, 4, 5, 6\}$. Let us define the following events

E_1 : a number less than 4 appears.

E_2 : a number greater than 2 but less than 5 appears.

E_3 : a number greater than 4 appears.

Then, $E_1 = \{1,2,3\}$, $E_2 = \{3,4\}$, $E_3 = \{5,6\}$.

We observe that

$$E_1 \cup E_2 \cup E_3 = \{1, 2, 3\} \cup \{3, 4\} \cup \{5, 6\} = S.$$

Thus, the events E_1, E_2 and E_3 are exhaustive events.

Mutually Exclusive Events

Two events are said to be mutually exclusive, if the occurrence of any one of them excludes the occurrence of other event, i.e. if they cannot occur simultaneously.

Thus, two events E_1 and E_2 are said to be mutually exclusive, if $E_1 \cap E_2 = \phi$.

e.g. In throwing a die, we have sample space

$$S = \{1, 2, 3, 4, 5, 6\}$$

Let E_1 = Event of getting even numbers = $\{2, 4, 6\}$

and E_2 = Event of getting odd numbers = $\{1, 3, 5\}$

Here, $E_1 \cap E_2 = \phi$.

So, E_1 and E_2 are mutually exclusive events.

In general, events $E_1, E_2, \ldots, E_n$ are said to be mutually exclusive, if they are pair-wise disjoint, i.e. if $E_i \cap E_j = \phi$ for all $i \neq j$.

Note Simple events of a sample space are always mutually exclusive.

Mutually Exclusive and Exhaustive Events

If $E_i \cap E_j = \phi$ for $i \neq j$, i.e. events E_i and E_j are pairwise disjoint and $\bigcup_{i=1}^{n} E_i = S$, then events $E_1, E_2, \ldots, E_n$ are called **mutually exclusive** and **exhaustive events.**

Exhaustive Number of Cases

Exhaustive number of cases is the total number of possible outcomes of an experiment such that when a coin is thrown, then the exhaustive number of cases is 2 as we may get either head or tail. When a die is thrown, then the exhaustive number of cases is 6. When three dice are thrown simultaneously, then the exhaustive number of cases is 6^3 i.e. 216. When 3 cards are drawn simultaneously from a pack of playing cards, then the exhaustive number of cases is ${}^{52}C_3$, and so on.

Favourable Number of Cases

The number of cases favourable to an event is known as the favourable number of cases. Such that, if the experiment is simultaneous throw of three coins, then the number of cases favourable to the event 'getting atleast two heads' is 4 as the cases HHH, HHT, HTH, THH are favourable to it.

Not Mutually Exclusive as Partially Overlapping Events

Two or more events are considered partially overlapping (also called not mutually exclusive), if some part of one event and some part of another event can occur together.

e.g. The events comprising spade and face cards are not mutually exclusive.

Example 13 An experiment involves rolling a pair of dice and recording the numbers that comes up. Describe the following events.

A : the sum is greater than 8.

B : 2 occurs on either die.

C : the sum is at least 7 and multiple of 3.

Which pairs of these events are mutually exclusive? **[NCERT]**

Sol. There are 36 elements in the sample space

$$S = \{(x, y) : x, y = 1, 2, 3, 4, 5, 6\}$$

Given, A = events of getting the sum greater than 8, i.e. events of getting the sum 9, 10, 11 and 12.

$$\therefore \quad A = \{(6,3), (3,6), (4,5), (5,4), (6,4), (4,6), (5,5), (6,5), (5,6), (6,6)\}$$

and B = event of getting 2 on either die.

$$\therefore \quad B = \{(2,1), (2,2), (2,3), (2,4), (2,5), (2,6), (1,2), (3,2), (4,2), (5,2), (6,2)\}$$

and C = event of getting the sum atleast 7 and a multiple of 3, i.e. event of getting the sum 9 and 12.

$$= \{(4,5), (5,4), (6,3), (3,6), (6,6)\}$$

Here, $A \cap B = \phi$, $B \cap C = \phi$

and $A \cap C \neq \phi$

Thus, we can say that, the pairs A and B; B and C are mutually exclusive events.

Example 14 Three coins are tossed once. Let A denotes the event "three heads show", B denotes the event "two heads and one tail show", C denotes the event "three tails show" and D denotes the event "a head shows on the first coin". Which pair of events are **[NCERT]**

(i) mutually exclusive events. (ii) simple events.

(iii) compound events.

Sol. When three coins are tossed, then the sample space is

$S = \{HHH, HHT, HTH, THH, HTT, THT, TTH, TTT\}$

Given, A = event of getting three heads

$\therefore \quad A = \{HHH\}$

B = event of getting two heads and one tail

$\therefore \quad B = \{HHT, HTH, THH\}$

C = event of getting three tails

$\therefore \quad C = \{TTT\}$

and $\quad D$ = event of getting a head on first coin.

$\therefore \quad D = \{HHH, HTT, HHT, HTH\}$

(i) Clearly, $A \cap B = \phi$, $A \cap C = \phi$,

$A \cap D = \{HHH\}$, $B \cap C = \phi$,

$B \cap D = \{HHT, HTH\}$ and $C \cap D = \phi$

$\therefore$ We can say. A and B; A and C; B and C; C and D are mutually exclusive events.

(ii) A and C are simple events, since both have only one sample point.

(iii) B and D are compound event, since they have more than one sample point.

Example 15 A coin is tossed three times, consider the following events?

A : No head appears.

B : Exactly one head appears.

and C : Atleast two heads appears.

Do they form a set of mutually exclusive and exhaustive events? **[NCERT]**

Sol. When a coin is tossed three times, then the sample space is

$S = \{HHH, HHT, HTH, THH, THT, TTH, HTT, TTT\}$

Given, A = event of getting no head

$\therefore \quad A = \{TTT\}$

B = event of getting exactly one head

$\therefore \quad B = \{TTH, HTT, THT\}$

and $\quad C$ = event of getting atleast two heads

$\therefore \quad C = \{HHT, HTH, THH, HHH\}$

Clearly, $A \cap B = \phi$, $A \cap C = \phi$ and $B \cap C = \phi$

So, we can say that A, B and C are mutually exclusive events. [$\because$ A, B and C are pairwise disjoint]

Also, $\quad A \cup B \cup C = \{TTT, TTH, HTT, THT, HHT, HTH, THH, HHH\} = S$

$\therefore$ A, B and C are exhaustive events.

Hence, A, B and C form a set of mutually exclusive and exhaustive events.

Topic Practice 1

Very Short Answer Type Questions

2 Marks

1 A coin is tossed. If it shows tail, we draw a ball from a box which contains 2 red and 3 black balls. If it shows head, we throw a die. Find the sample space for this experiment. **[NCERT]**

2 A coin is tossed twice. If the second throw results in a tail, a die is thrown. Describe the sample space for this experiment.

3 From a group of 2 boys and 2 girls, we select two persons to form a committee. What will be the sample space for this experiment?

4 A box contains 1 red and 3 black balls. Two balls are drawn at random in succession without replacement. Write the sample space for this experiment.

5 A coin is tossed repeatedly until a head comes up. Describe the sample space. **[NCERT]**

6 The numbers 4, 5, 6 and 7 are written separately on the form slips of the paper. The slips are put in a box and mixed thoroughly. A person draw two slips from the box, one after the other without replacement. Describe the sample space for the experiment.

7 One ticket is drawn at random from a box containing 30 tickets numbered 1 to 30. Represent the sample space and also write the sample space of drawing a ticket containing number which is a multiple of 4.

8 Two coloured dice Black (B) and Pink (P) are placed in a bag. One die is drawn at random from the bag and its colour and the number appearing on its top face is noted. Describe the sample space for this experiment.

9 Consider the experiment of rolling a die. Let A be the event 'getting a prime number' and B be the event 'getting an odd number'. Write the sets representing events **[NCERT]**

(i) A and B. (ii) A or B.
(iii) A but not B. (iv) not A.

10 Two dice are rolled. Let E_1, E_2 and E_3 be the events of getting a sum of 4, 5 and 6 respectively.

(i) Which events are elementary events?
(ii) Which events are compound events?

11 An experiment involves tossing of two coins and recording them in the following events

A: No tail B: exactly one tail
C: at least one tail.

Write the sets representing events
(i) A and C. (ii) A not B.

12 A die is tossed. Let E denotes the event of getting a number multiple of 2 and F denotes the event of getting a number less than 7. Simplify the following event

(i) $E \cup F$ (ii) $F - E$ (iii) E' (iv) $E \cap F$

Short Answer Type Questionss

4 Marks

13 A coin is tossed two times, consider the following events?

E_1: No head appears.
E_2: Exactly one head appears.
and E_3: At least one head appears.
Do, they form a set of mutually exclusive and exhaustive events?

14 Two dice are rolled, A is the event that the sum of the numbers shown on the two dice is 5 and B is the event that atleast one of the dice shown up a 3. Are the two events A and B

(i) mutually exclusive?
(ii) exhaustive?

Long Answer Type Questions

6 Marks

15 Two dice are thrown and the sum of the numbers which come up on the dice is noted. Let us consider the following events associated with this experiment.

A: 'the sum is even'.
B: 'the sum is a multiple of 3'.
C: 'the sum is less than 4'.
D: 'the sum is greater than 11'.
Which pairs of these events are mutually exclusive? **[NCERT]**

16 Three coins are tossed once. Let A denotes the event "three tails show", B denotes the event "one tail and two head show", C denotes the event "tail on the first coin".

Which pair of events are
(i) mutually exclusive? (ii) simple events?
(iii) compound events?

17 Two dice are thrown. The events A, B and C are as follows:

A: getting an even number on the first die.
B: getting an odd number on the first die.
C: getting the sum of the numbers on the dice ≤ 5.

Decribe the events

(i) A' (ii) not B
(iii) A or B (iv) A and B
(v) A but not C (vi) B or C
(vii) B and C (viii) $A \cap B' \cap C'$

Hints & Answers

1. Let the balls in the box be represented by R_1, R_2 and B_1, B_2, B_3.
Ans. $\{TR_1\ TR_2, TB_1, TB_2, TB_3, H1, H2, H3, H4, H5, H6\}$
2. $\{HH, TH, (HT1), (HT2), (HT3), (HT4), (HT5), (HT6), (TT1), (TT2), (TT3), (TT4), (TT5), (TT6)\}$
3. $\{(B_1, B_2), (B_1, G_1), (B_1, G_2), (B_2, G_1), (B_2, G_2), (G_1, G_2)\}$
4. Let us represent the red ball by R and 3 black balls by B_1, B_2, B_3.
Ans. $\{(R, B_1), (R, B_2), (R, B_3), (B_1, R), (B_1, B_2), (B_1, B_3), (B_2, R), (B_2, B_1), (B_2, B_3), (B_3, R), (B_3, B_1), (B_3, B_2)\}$
5. Solve as Example 6. **Ans.** $\{H, TH, TTH, TTTH, TTTTH, \dots\}$
6. Solve as Example 5.
Ans. $\{(4, 5), (4, 6), (4, 7), (5, 4), (5, 6), (5, 7), (6, 4), (6, 5), (6, 7), (7, 4), (7, 5), (7, 6)\}$
7. Let S be the sample space of containing the number on ticket from 1 to 30. And E be the event of getting a number which is a multiple of 4.
Ans. $S = \{1, 2, \dots, 30\}$ and $E = \{4, 8, 12, 16, 20, 24, 28\}$.
8. If a die of black colour is selected, the possible outcomes are $(B, 1)(B, 2)(B, 3)(B, 4)(B, 5)(B, 6)$, similarly for die of pink colour.
Ans. $\{(B, 1), (B, 2), (B, 3), (B, 4), (B, 5), (B, 6), (P, 1), (P, 2), (P, 3), (P, 4), (P, 5), (P, 6)\}$
9. Here, $A = \{2, 3, 5\}$ and $B = \{1, 3, 5\}$
Ans. (i) $\{3, 5\}$ (ii) $\{1, 2, 3, 5\}$ (iii) $\{2\}$ (iv) $\{1, 4, 6\}$

10. Here, $E_1 = \{(1, 3), (2, 2), (3, 1)\}$,
$E_2 = \{(1, 4), (2, 3), (3, 2), (4, 1)\}$
and $E_3 = \{(1, 5), (2, 4), (3, 3), (5, 1), (4, 2)\}$
Similar as Example 10.
Ans. (i) No event. (ii) E_1, E_2 and E_3

11. $A = \{(H, H)\}$, $B = \{(H, T), (T, H)\}$
and $C = \{(H, T), (T, H), (T, T)\}$
(i) A and $C = A \cap C = \phi$
(ii) A not $B = A - B = \{(H, H)\}$

12. Here, $E = \{2, 4, 6\}$ and $F = \{1, 2, 3, 4, 5, 6\}$
Ans. (i) $\{1, 2, 3, 4, 5, 6\}$ (ii) $\{1, 3, 5\}$
(iii) $\{1, 3, 5\}$ (iv) $\{2, 4, 6\}$

13. Here, $E_1 = \{(T, T)\}$, $E_2 = \{(H, T), (T, H)\}$
and $E_3 = \{(H, T), (T, H), (H, H)\}$
Here, $E_1 \cap E_2 = \phi$, $E_1 \cap E_3 = \phi$ and $E_2 \cap E_3 \neq \phi$
Also, $E_1 \cup E_2 \cup E_3 = \{(H, T), (T, H), (T, T), (H, H)\} = S$
Ans. E_1, E_2 and E_3 are not mutually exclusive but they are exhaustive events.

14. (i) $A = \{(1, 4), (4, 1), (3, 2), (2, 3)\}$
and $B = \{(3, 1), (3, 2), (3, 3), (3, 4), (3, 5), (3, 6), (1, 3), (2, 3), (4, 3), (5, 3), (6, 3)\}$
$\therefore \; A \cap B = \{(3, 2), (2, 3)\} \neq \phi$
(ii) $A \cup B \neq S$ **Ans.** (i) No (ii) No

15. Solve as Example 13. **Ans.** C and D

16. Solve as Example 14.
Ans. (i) A and B, B and C (ii) A (iii) B and C.

17. (i) $A = \left\{\begin{matrix}(2,1),(2,2),\ldots,(2,6),\\(4,1),(4,2),\ldots,(4,6),\\(6,1),(6,2),\ldots,(6,6)\end{matrix}\right\}$, $B = \left\{\begin{matrix}(1,1),(1,2),\ldots,(1,6),\\(3,1),(3,2),\ldots,(3,6),\\(5,1),(5,2),\ldots,(5,6)\end{matrix}\right\}$

and $C = \{(1,1),(1,2),(2,1),(1,3),(3,1),(2,2),(2,3),(3,2),(1,4),(4,1)\}$

Ans. (i) $A' = \left\{\begin{matrix}(1,1),(1,2),\ldots,(1,6),\\(3,1),(3,2),\ldots,(3,6),\\(5,1),(5,2),\ldots,(5,6)\end{matrix}\right\} = B$

(ii) $B' = \{(2,1),(2,2),(2,3),(2,4),(2,5),(2,6),(4,1),(4,2),(4,3),(4,4),(4,5),(4,6),(6,1),(6,2),(6,3),(6,4),(6,5),(6,6)\} = A$

(iii) $A \cup B = \{(1,1),(1,2),(1,3),(1,4),(1,5),(1,6),(3,1),(3,2),(3,3),(3,4),(3,5),(3,6),(5,1),(5,2),(5,3),(5,4),(5,5),(5,6),(2,1),(2,2),(2,3),(2,4),(2,5),(2,6),(4,1),(4,2),(4,3),(4,4),(4,5),(4,6),(6,1),(6,2),(6,3),(6,4),(6,5),(6,6)\} = S$

(iv) $A \cap B = \phi$

(v) $A - C = \{(2,4),(2,5),(2,6),(4,2),(4,3),(4,4),(4,5),(4,6),(6,1),(6,2),(6,3),(6,4),(6,5),(6,6)\}$

(vi) $B \cup C = \{(1,1),(1,2),(1,3),(1,4),(1,5),(1,6),(2,1),(2,2),(2,3),(3,1),(3,2),(3,3),(3,4),(3,5),(3,6),(4,1),(5,1),(5,2),(5,3),(5,4),(5,5),(5,6)\}$

(vii) $B \cap C = \{(1,1),(1,2),(1,3),(1,4),(3,1),(3,2)\}$

(viii) $A \cap B' \cap C' = \{(2,4),(2,5),(2,6),(4,2),(4,3),(4,4),(4,5),(4,6),(6,1),(6,2),(6,3),(6,4),(6,5),(6,6)$

TOPIC 02 Axiomatic Approach to Probability

Probability of Occurrence of an Event

A numerical value that conveys the chance of occurrence of an event, when we perform an experiment, is called the probability of that event.

1. Axiomatic Approach to Probability

Let S be the sample space of a random experiment. The probability P is a real valued function whose domain is the power set of S and range is the interval [0, 1] satisfying the following **axioms**

(i) For any event E, $P(E) \geq 0$

(ii) $P(S) = 1$

(iii) If E and F are mutually exclusive events, then
$$P(E \cup F) = P(E) + P(F).$$

Now, let S be a sample space containing outcomes
$$E_1, E_2, \ldots, E_n$$
i.e. $$S = \{E_1, E_2, \ldots, E_n\}.$$

Then, from the axiomatic definition of probability, we have

(i) $0 \leq P(E_i) \leq 1, \forall \, E_i \in S$

(ii) $P(E_1) + P(E_2) + \ldots + P(E_n) = 1$

(iii) For any event A, $P(A) = \sum_{i=1}^{n} P(E_i), E_i \in A$

Note (i) $P(\phi) = 0$.
(ii) For notational convenience, we write $P(E_i)$ for $P(\{E_i\})$.

Example 1 Which of the following cannot be valid assignments of probabilities for outcomes of sample space. $S = \{W_1, W_2, W_3, W_4, W_5, W_6, W_7\}$?

Assignment	W_1	W_2	W_3	W_4	W_5	W_6	W_7
(i)	0.1	0.01	0.05	0.03	0.01	0.2	0.6
(ii)	$\frac{1}{7}$	$\frac{1}{7}$	$\frac{1}{7}$	$\frac{1}{7}$	$\frac{1}{7}$	$\frac{1}{7}$	$\frac{1}{7}$
(iii)	0.1	0.2	0.3	0.4	0.5	0.6	0.7
(iv)	−0.1	0.2	0.3	0.4	−0.2	0.1	0.3
(v)	$\frac{1}{14}$	$\frac{2}{14}$	$\frac{3}{14}$	$\frac{4}{14}$	$\frac{5}{14}$	$\frac{6}{14}$	$\frac{15}{14}$

Sol. (i) Here, each of $P(W_i)$, where $i = 1$ to 7 is positive and less than 1.

Also, sum of probabilities

$= 0.1 + 0.01 + 0.05 + 0.03 + 0.01 + 0.2 + 0.6 = 1$

$\therefore$ This assignment is valid.

(ii) Here, each of $P(W_i)$, where $i = 1$ to 7 is positive and less than 1. Also, sum of probabilities $= 7 \times \frac{1}{7} = 1$

$\therefore$ This assignment is also valid.

(iii) Here, each of $P(W_i)$, where $i = 1$ to 7 is positive and less than 1.

But sum of probabilities

$= 0.1 + 0.2 + 0.3 + 0.4 + 0.5 + 0.6 + 0.7$

$= 2.8 \neq 1$

$\therefore$ This assignment is not valid.

(iv) Here, $P(W_1)$ and $P(W_5)$ are negative.

$\therefore$ This assignment is not valid.

$[\because 0 \le P(W_i) \le 1 \ \forall \ W_i \in S]$

(v) Here, $P(W_7) > 1$.

$\therefore$ This assignment is not valid.

$[\because 0 \le P(W_i) \le 1 \ \forall \ W_i \in S]$

Hence, assignments (iii), (iv) and (v) are not valid.

2. Statistical Approach to Probability

In statistical approach, probability of an event 'A' is defined as

$$P(A) = \frac{\text{Number of trials in which the event } A \text{ happened}}{\text{Total number of trials}}$$

Example 2 A die is thrown 500 times with frequencies for the outcomes 1, 2, 3, 4, 5 and 6 as given in the following table

Outcome	1	2	3	4	5	6
Frequency	110	115	100	50	45	80

Find the probability of getting outcome 3?

Sol. Here, total frequency = Total number of times a die is thrown = 500

and number of observed frequency, A

= Number of times the outcome 3 is thrown = 100

$\therefore$ Probability of getting outcome 3,

$$P(A) = \frac{\text{Number of observed frequency}}{\text{Total frequency}} = \frac{100}{500} = \frac{1}{5}$$

3. Classical Approach to Probability

To obtain the probability of an event, we find the ratio of the number of outcomes favourable to the event, to the total number of equally likely outcomes. This theory is known as classical theory of probability,

i.e. $$P(A) = \frac{\text{Number of favourable outcomes}}{\text{Total number of possible outcomes}}$$

This is also known as **theoretical probability.**

Example 3 Suppose we throw a die once. Find the probability of getting a number greater than 4.

Sol. Let A be the event of getting a number greater than 4

Here, total number of possible outcomes

= Total number of outcomes on throwing a die = 6

and number of favourable outcomes

= Number of outcomes which are favourable to event A

$= \{5, 6\} = 2$

$\therefore$ Probability of getting a number greater than 4,

$$P(A) = \frac{2}{6} = \frac{1}{3}$$

Probability of Equally Likely Outcomes

The outcomes of a random experiment are said to be **equally likely,** if the chance of occurrence of each outcome is same, i.e. chances of each outcome is same.

Let the sample space of an experiment be

$$S = \{s_1, s_2, \dots, s_n\}$$

Also, let all the outcomes are equally likely.

i.e. $P(s_i) = p$, for all $s_i \in S$, where $0 \le p \le 1$

Since, by axiomatic approach to probability, $\sum_{i=1}^{n} P(s_i) = 1$

$$\therefore \quad \underbrace{p + p + \dots + p}_{(n \text{ times})} = 1$$

$$\Rightarrow \quad np = 1 \Rightarrow p = \frac{1}{n}$$

Thus, $P(s_i) = \frac{1}{n}, \forall \ i = 1, 2, \dots, n.$

Note Let E be an event associated with a sample space S, such that $n(S) = n$ and $n(E) = m$, then by axiomatic approach

$$P(E) = \underbrace{\frac{1}{n} + \frac{1}{n} + \frac{1}{n} + \dots + \frac{1}{n}}_{m \text{ times}} = m \times \frac{1}{n} = \frac{m}{n}$$

and by classical approach,

$$P(E) = \frac{\text{Number of favourable outcomes to } E}{\text{Total number of possible outcomes}} = \frac{m}{n}$$

Thus, in case of equally likely outcomes axiomatic approach coincide with the classical approach.

Example 4 One urn contains two black balls (labelled B_1 and B_2) and one white (W) ball. A second urn contains one black (B) ball and two white balls (labelled W_1 and W_2). Suppose the following experiment is performed. One of the two urns is chosen at random. Next, a ball is randomly chosen from the urn. Then, a second ball is chosen at random from the same urn without replacing the first ball. What is the probability that two balls of opposite colour are chosen? **[NCERT Exemplar]**

Sol. Clearly, the sample space of the experiment is

$$S = \{B_1B_2, B_1W, B_2B_1, B_2W, WB_1, WB_2, BW_1, BW_2, W_1B, W_1W_2, W_2B, W_2W_1\}$$

Let E be the event that balls of opposite colour are chosen, then

$$E = \{B_1W, WB_1, B_2W, WB_2, BW_1, BW_2, W_1B, W_2B\}$$

$$\therefore P(E) = \frac{8}{12} = \frac{2}{3}$$

Note In one-by-one selection, order of things is considered.

Example 5 What is the probability that in a leap year chosen at random will contain 53 Sunday or 53 Monday?

Sol. Since, a leap year has 366 days, so there are 52 weeks and 2 days. These 2 days can be {Sun-Mon, Mon-Tues, Tues-Wed, Wed-Thurs, Thurs-Fri, Fri-Sat, Sat-Sun}.

$\therefore$ P(53 Sunday or 52 Monday)

$$= P(\text{ getting Sun-Mon, Mon-Tue, Sat-Sun}) = \frac{3}{7}.$$

Odds in Favour of an Event and Odds Against an Event

Let S be the sample space of a random experiment and all the outcomes are equally likely.

If an event A occur in 'm' ways and not occurs in 'n' ways, then odds in favour of A are $m:n$, odds against A are $n:m$, and probability of A is

$$P(A) = \frac{m}{m+n}$$

If the probability of event A is given to be P, then odds in favour of event $(A) = \dfrac{P}{1-P}$

and odds against event $(A) = \dfrac{1-P}{P}$

Example 6 The odds in favour of an event are 2 : 4. Find the probability of the occurrence of his event.

Sol. We know that, if odds in favour of an event are $m:n$, then probability of occurrence of this event is $\dfrac{m}{m+n}$

$\therefore$ Required probability $= \dfrac{2}{2+4} = \dfrac{2}{6} = \dfrac{1}{3}$

Example 7 The chance of one event happening is the square of the chance of second event. But the odds against the first are cube of the odds against to the second. Then, find the chance of each event.

Sol. Let the probabilities of two events happening are P_1 and P_2.

$$\therefore \quad P_1 = P_2^2 \text{ and } \frac{1-P_1}{P_1} = \left(\frac{1-P_2}{P_2}\right)^3$$

By putting $P_1 = P_2^2$ in second equation, we get

$$\frac{1-P_2^2}{P_2^2} = \frac{(1-P_2)^3}{P_2^3} \Rightarrow P_2(1+P_2) = (1-P_2)^2$$

$$\Rightarrow \quad P_2 + P_2^2 = 1 + P_2^2 - 2P_2 \Rightarrow 3P_2 = 1 \Rightarrow P_2 = \frac{1}{3}$$

$$\therefore \quad P_1 = P_2^2 = \left(\frac{1}{3}\right)^2 = \frac{1}{9}$$

Hence, P_1 and P_2 are $\frac{1}{9}$ and $\frac{1}{3}$, respectively.

Different Problems Based on Probability

TYPE I

Problems Based on Coins

Example 8 A fair coin with 1 marked on one face and 6 marked on the other and a fair die are both tossed. Find the probability that the sum of numbers that turn up is (i) 3 (ii) 12.

Sol. Let S be a sample space associated with the given experiment.

Then, $S = \{(1,1), (1,2), (1,3), (1,4), (1,5), (1,6), (6,1), (6,2), (6,3), (6,4), (6,5), (6,6)\}$

$\Rightarrow \quad n(S) = 12$

(i) Let A be the event of getting the sum of numbers 3.

Then, $\quad A = \{(1,2)\} \Rightarrow n(A) = 1$

$\therefore \quad P(A)=\dfrac{n(A)}{n(S)}=\dfrac{1}{12}$

(ii) Let B be the event of getting the sum of numbers 12.

Then, $\quad B=\{(6,6)\} \Rightarrow n(B)=1$

$\therefore \quad P(B)=\dfrac{n(B)}{n(S)}=\dfrac{1}{12}$

Example 9 Three coins are tossed once. Find the probability of getting

(i) 3 heads. (ii) atleast 2 heads.

(iii) atmost 2 heads. [NCERT]

Sol. In random experiment of tossing three coins, the sample space is

$S=\{HHH, HHT, HTH, THH, HTT, THT, TTH, TTT\}$

$\Rightarrow \quad n(S)=8$

(i) Let E_1 be the event of getting 3 heads. Then, outcomes favourable to E_1 is $\{HHH\}$.

Thus, $n(E_1)=1$,

$\therefore \quad P(E_1)=\dfrac{n(E_1)}{n(S)}=\dfrac{1}{8}$

(ii) Let E_2 be the event of getting atleast 2 heads. Then, outcomes favourable to E_2 are $\{HHT, HTH, THH$ and $HHH\}$.

Thus, $\quad n(E_2)=4$

$\therefore \quad P(E_2)=\dfrac{n(E_2)}{n(S)}=\dfrac{4}{8}=\dfrac{1}{2}$

(iii) Let E_3 be the event of getting atmost 2 heads. Then, outcomes favourable to E_3 are $\{HHT, HTH, THH, TTH, THT, HTT, TTT\}$.

Thus, $\quad n(E_3)=7$

$\therefore \quad P(E_3)=\dfrac{n(E_3)}{n(S)}=\dfrac{7}{8}$

|TYPE II|

Problems Based on Dice

Example 10 A die is thrown. Find

(i) P (a prime number) (ii) P(a number ≥ 3)

(iii) P(a number more than 6) [NCERT]

Sol. In throwing a die, the sample space will be

$S=\{1, 2, 3, 4, 5, 6\}$

$\therefore \quad n(S)=6$

(i) Let E_1 be the event of getting a prime number.

Then, $E_1=\{2, 3, 5\}$

$\therefore \quad n(E_1)=3$

Now, probability of getting a prime number,

$P(E_1)=\dfrac{n(E_1)}{n(S)}=\dfrac{3}{6}=\dfrac{1}{2}$

(ii) Let E_2 be the event of getting a number ≥ 3.

Then, $\quad E_2=\{3, 4, 5, 6\}$

$\therefore \quad n(E_2)=4$

Now, probability of getting a number ≥ 3,

$P(E_2)=\dfrac{n(E_2)}{n(S)}=\dfrac{4}{6}=\dfrac{2}{3}$

(iii) Let E_4 be the event of getting a number more than 6.

Then, $\quad E_4=\{\}=\phi$

$\Rightarrow E_4$ is an impossible event.

$\therefore \quad n(E_4)=0$

Now, probability of getting a number more than 6,

$P(E_4)=\dfrac{n(E_4)}{n(S)}=\dfrac{0}{6}=0$

Example 11 Three dice are rolling simultaneously. Find the probability of getting same numbers on all dice.

Sol. In rolling of three dice, the number of possible outcomes are $n(S)=6\times6\times6=216$.

Let E be the event of getting same numbers on all dice.

Then, the outcomes favourable to E are (1, 1, 1), (2, 2, 2), (3, 3, 3), (4, 4, 4), (5, 5, 5) and (6, 6, 6).

$\Rightarrow \quad n(E)=6$

Now, required probability, $P(E)=\dfrac{n(E)}{n(S)}=\dfrac{6}{216}=\dfrac{1}{36}$.

|TYPE III|

Problems Based on Playing Cards

Example 12 A card is drawn from a pack of 100 cards numbered 1 to 100. Find the probability of drawing a number which is a square.

Sol. Here, a card is drawn at random from a pack of 100 cards numbered 1 to 100.

$\therefore$ Total number of possible outcomes $n(S)=100$

Now, let A be the event of getting a number which is a square. Then, the outcomes favourable of A are 1, 4, 9, 16, 25, 36, 49, 64, 81, 100.

$\Rightarrow \quad A=\{1, 4, 9, 16, 25, 36, 49, 64, 81, 100\}$

$\Rightarrow \quad n(A)=10$

Hence, required probability, $P(A)=\dfrac{n(A)}{n(S)}=\dfrac{10}{100}=\dfrac{1}{10}$

Example 13 A card is selected from a pack of 52 cards.

(i) How many points are there in the sample space?

(ii) Calculate the probability that the card is an ace of spades.

(iii) Calculate the probability that the card is

(a) an ace (b) black card. **[NCERT]**

Sol. (i) A card is drawn at random from a pack of 52 cards, therefore there are 52 sample points in the sample space.

(ii) There is only one ace of spades, therefore number of favourable outcomes is 1.

Hence, required probability is $\frac{1}{52}$.

(iii) (a) Since, there are four ace in a pack of 52 cards, therefore number of favourable outcomes are 4.

Hence, required probability is $\frac{4}{52}$ or $\frac{1}{13}$.

(b) Since, there are 26 black cards in a pack of 52 cards, therefore number of favourable outcomes are 26.

Hence, required probability is $\frac{26}{52}$ or $\frac{1}{2}$.

|TYPE IV|

Problems Based on Letters/Numbers

Example 14 A single letter is selected at random from the word 'PROBABILITY', then find the probability that letter is a vowel. **[NCERT Exemplar]**

Sol. There are 11 letters in the word PROBABILITY.

Since, a letter is selected randomly, therefore the possible outcomes are P, R, O, B, A, I, L, T, Y.

But here, outcomes are not equally likely

as $P(\text{letter P}) = \frac{1}{11}$; $P(\text{letter } R) = \frac{1}{11}$

$P(\text{letter O}) = \frac{1}{11}$; $P(\text{letter B}) = \frac{2}{11}$

[$\because$ *B* repeated twice in the word]

$P(\text{letter A}) = \frac{1}{11}$; $P(\text{letter I}) = \frac{2}{11}$

$P(\text{letter L}) = \frac{1}{11}$; $P(\text{letter T}) = \frac{1}{11}$

and $P(\text{letter Y}) = 1/11$

Now, let *E* be event of getting a vowel. Then outcomes favourable to *E* are A, I and O.

$\Rightarrow$ $E = \{\text{A, I, O}\}$

Now, $P(E) = P(\text{A}) + P(\text{I}) + P(\text{O})$

[by axiomatic approach to probability]

$$= \frac{1}{11} + \frac{2}{11} + \frac{1}{11} = \frac{4}{11}$$

Example 15 What is the probability that a number selected from the number 1, 2,..., 25 is a prime number? You may assume that each of the 25 numbers is equally likely to be selected.

Sol. Here, a number is selected at random from the numbers 1, 2, 3,..., 25

$\therefore$ Total number of possible outcomes, $n(S) = 25$

Now, let *A* be event of getting a prime number.

Then, the outcomes favourable to *A* are 2, 3, 5, 7, 11, 13, 17, 19, 23

$\Rightarrow A = \{2, 3, 5, 7, 11, 13, 17, 19, 23\} \Rightarrow n(A) = 9$

Hence, required probability, $P(A) = \frac{n(A)}{n(S)} = \frac{9}{25}$

|TYPE V|

Problems Based on Combinations

When two or more things are selected, then to find the total outcomes or outcomes favourable to an event, we use the combination. Number of combinations out of *n* things taken *r* at a time is denoted by ^nC_r and it is defined as

$$^nC_r = \frac{n!}{r!(n-r)!}$$

Note $^nC_r = {^nC_{n-r}}$

Example 16 An urn contains 7 white, 5 black and 3 red balls. Two balls are drawn at random. Find the probability that

(i) both the balls are red.

(ii) one ball is red, other is black.

(iii) one ball is white.

Sol. Given, number of white balls = 7, number of black balls = 5 and number of red balls = 3

Total number of balls = 7 + 5 + 3 = 15

Total number of ways of drawing 2 balls out of 15 balls

$= {^{15}C_2}$

$\Rightarrow$ Total number of possible outcomes $= {^{15}C_2}$

(i) If both balls are red, then number of favourable outcomes $= {^3C_2}$

Hence, *P* (drawing both balls are red)

$$= \frac{^3C_2}{^{15}C_2} = \frac{3}{\frac{15 \times 14}{2 \times 1}} = \frac{1}{35}$$

(ii) If one ball is red and other is black, then number of favourable outcomes $= {^3C_1} \times {^5C_1} = 3 \times 5 = 15$

Hence, *P* (drawing one red ball and one black ball)

$$= \frac{^3C_1 \times {^5C_1}}{^{15}C_2} = \frac{15}{\frac{15 \times 14}{2 \times 1}} = \frac{1}{7}$$

(iii) If one ball is white, then other ball can be red or black.

So, number of favourable outcomes $= {^7C_1} \times {^8C_1}$

$= 7 \times 8 = 56$

Hence, *P*(drawing one white ball)

$$= \frac{56}{^{15}C_2} = \frac{56}{\frac{15 \times 14}{2 \times 1}} = \frac{8}{15}$$

Example 17 While shuffling a pack of 52 playing cards, 2 are accidentally dropped. Find the probability that the missing cards to be of different colours. **[NCERT Exemplar]**

Sol. Probability that the missing cards to be different colours

$$= \frac{{}^{26}C_1 \times {}^{26}C_1}{{}^{52}C_2}$$

[∵ in a pack of cards, there are two colours, each of them contain 26 cards]

$$= \frac{26 \times 26}{\frac{52 \times 51}{2 \times 1}} = \frac{26}{51}$$

Example 18 Four cards are drawn at random from pack of 52 playing cards. Find the probability of getting

(i) all face cards.
(ii) two red cards and two black cards.
(iii) one card from each suit.

Sol. Total number of possible outcomes $= {}^{52}C_4$

(i) We know that, there are 12 face cards.

∴ Number of favourable outcomes $= {}^{12}C_4$

Hence, P (getting all face cards) $= \frac{{}^{12}C_4}{{}^{52}C_4}$

(ii) We know that, there are 26 red cards and 26 black cards.

∴ Number of favourable outcomes $= {}^{26}C_2 \times {}^{26}C_2$

Hence, P (getting 2 red and 2 black cards) $= \frac{({}^{26}C_2)^2}{{}^{52}C_4}$

(iii) We know that, there are 4 suits each having 13 cards.

∴ Number of favourable outcomes

$= {}^{13}C_1 \times {}^{13}C_1 \times {}^{13}C_1 \times {}^{13}C_1 = (13)^4$

Hence, P (getting one card from each suit) $= \frac{(13)^4}{{}^{52}C_4}$.

Example 19 In a lottery, a person chooses six different natural numbers at random from 1 to 20 and if these six numbers match with the six numbers already fixed by the lottery committee, he wins the prize. What is the probability of winning the prize in the game?

Sol. Total number of ways of selecting six different natural numbers out of first 20 natural numbers $= {}^{20}C_6$.

⇒ Total number of possible outcomes $= {}^{20}C_6$

Note that, number of favourable outcomes = 1

[∵ it is given that a persons win the prize if six selected numbers match with the six numbers already fixed by the lottery committee]

Hence, required probability $= \frac{1}{{}^{20}C_6} = \frac{1}{38760}$

Example 20 Three of six vertices of a regular hexagon are chosen at random, what is the probability that the triangle with these vertices is equilateral? **[NCERT Exemplar]**

Sol. Let $ABCDEF$ be a regular hexagon.

Clearly, out of 6 vertices, 3 vertices can be chosen in ${}^6C_3$ ways = 20 ways.

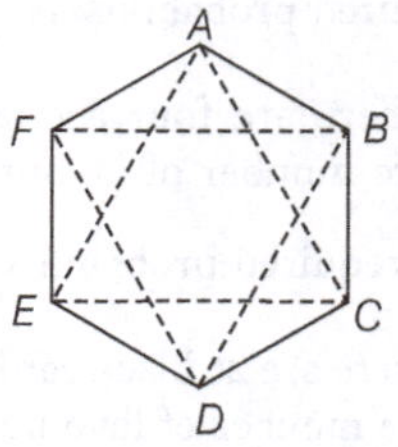

Thus, total number of triangles so formed = 20

[∵ no three points are collinear]

Note that, out of these 20 triangles only ΔACE and ΔBDF are equilateral triangles

∴ Required probability $= \frac{2}{20} = \frac{1}{10}$

TYPE VII

Problems Based on Permutation or Arrangements

Example 21 If the letters of the word ALGORITHM are arranged at random in a row, what is the probability the letters GOR must remain together as a unit? **[NCERT Exemplar]**

Sol. There are 9 letters in the word 'ALGORITHM'.

These 9 letters can be arranged in a row in 9! ways.

∴ Total number of possible outcomes = 9!

Now, if the letters GOR remain together, then we have 7 letters (considering GOR as 1 letter i.e. ALITHMGOR) which can be arranged in 7!.

Number of favourable outcomes = 7!

Hence, required probability $= \frac{7!}{9!} = \frac{1}{9 \times 8} = \frac{1}{72}$

Example 22 Three letters are dictated to three persons and an envelope is addressed to each of them. The letters are inserted into the envelopes at random so that each envelope contains exactly one letter. Find the probability that atleast one letter is in its proper envelope. **[NCERT]**

Sol. Let L_1, L_2, L_3 be three letters and E_1, E_2, E_3 be their corresponding envelopes.

Clearly, 3 letters can be inserted into 3 addressed envelopes in ${}^3P_3 = 3! = 6$ ways, which are shown as follows

$\{(L_1, E_1), (L_2, E_3), (L_3, E_2); (L_1, E_2), (L_2, E_1), (L_3, E_3);$
$(L_1, E_3), (L_2, E_2), (L_3, E_1); (L_1, E_1), (L_2, E_2), (L_3, E_3);$
$(L_1, E_2), (L_2, E_3), (L_3, E_1); (L_1, E_3), (L_2, E_1), (L_3, E_2)\}$

Note that, there are 4 ways in which atleast one letter is in its proper envelope.

$\therefore$ Required probability $= \frac{4}{6} = \frac{2}{3}$

Example 23 The letters of the word 'FORTUNATES' are arranged at random in a row. What is the chance that the two 'T' come together.

Sol. There are 10 letters in the word 'FORTUNATES' out of which 2 are T's.

$\therefore$ Total number of arrangements $= \frac{10!}{2!}$

$\Rightarrow$ Total number of possible outcomes $= \frac{10!}{2!}$

Now, if two 'T' come together, then we have 9 distinct letter (considering two 'T' as one letter) which can be arranged in 9! ways.

$\Rightarrow$ Number of favourable outcomes = 9!

Hence, required probability $= \frac{9!}{\left(\frac{10!}{2!}\right)} = \frac{9! \times 2}{10!} = \frac{2}{10} = \frac{1}{5}$

Example 24 6 boys and 6 girls sit in a row randomly. Find the probability that all 6 girls sit together. **[NCERT Exemplar]**

Sol. Total number of persons = 12, which can be arranged in a row in 12! ways.

Now, if 6 girls sit together, then we have 7 persons (considering 6 girls as one person), which can be in a row in 7! ways. But 6 girls can be arrange in 6! ways.

$\therefore$ Required probability $= \frac{7! \times 6!}{12!} = \frac{1}{132}$

Example 25 The number lock of a suitcase has four wheels, each labelled with 10 digits i.e., from 0 to 9. The lock opens with a sequence of four digits with no repeats. What is the probability of a person getting the right sequence to open the suitcase? **[NCERT]**

Sol. When the digits are not repeated, then first place may have one of 10 digits, the second 9, third 8 and fourth 7.

Number of 4-digit numbers, $n(S) = 10 \times 9 \times 8 \times 7 = 5040$

Now, lock can be opened only in 1 way.

$\therefore \quad n(E) = 1$

Hence, probability of opening the lock $= \frac{n(E)}{n(S)} = \frac{1}{5040}$

Example 26 Without repetition of the number, four digit numbers are formed with the numbers 0, 2, 3, 5. Find the probability of such a numbers is divisible by 5. **[NCERT Exemplar]**

Sol. In a four digit number, 0 cannot put in thousand's place. So, the number of ways of filling up the thousand's place = 3.

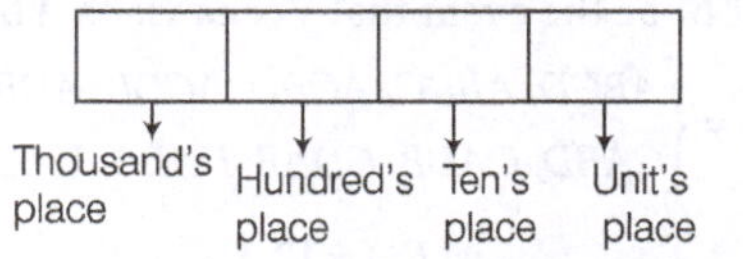

Now, we left with three digits (including 0) and 3 places.

Note that, hundred's place can be filled up in 3 ways.

ten's place can be filled up in 2 ways and unit's place can be filled up in 1 ways

So, the number of 4-digits numbers $= 3 \times 3 \times 2 \times 1 = 18$

$\Rightarrow$ Total number of possible outcomes = 18

Now, if the number is divisible by 5, then its unit's place is filled by either 5 or 0.

Case **I** When units place filled by 0.

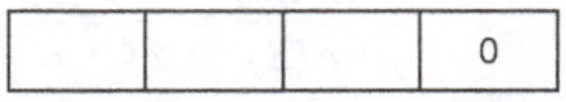

In this case, thousand's place can be filled up in 3 ways, hundred's place can be filled up in 2 ways and ten's place can be filled up in 1 ways.

Thus, in this case, number of four digits number divisible by $5 = 3 \times 2 \times 1 = 6$

Case **II** When unit's place is filled by 5.

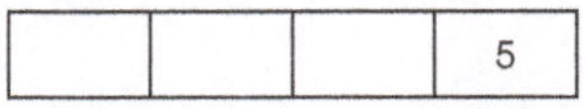

In this case, thousand's place can be filled up in 2 ways.

hundred's place can be filled up in 2 ways and ten's place can be filled up in 1 ways

Thus, in this case, number of four digits number divisible by $5 = 2 \times 2 \times 1 = 4$. From cases I and II,

Total number of 4-digits numbers divisible by 5

$= 6 + 4 = 10$

$\Rightarrow$ Number of favourable outcome = 10

Hence, required probability $= \frac{10}{18} = \frac{5}{9}$

Example 27 On her vacations, Veena visits four cities (*A*, *B*, *C* and *D*) in a random order. What is the probability that she visits

(i) *A* before *B*?

(ii) *A* before *B* and *B* before *C*?

(iii) *A* first and *B* last? **[NCERT]**

Sol. Number of ways, in which Veena can visit four cities *A*, *B*, *C* and *D*, is 4! i.e. 24.

$\therefore \quad n(S) = 24$

Clearly, sample space for this experiment is

$$S = \left\{\begin{matrix} ABCD, ABDC, ACBD, ACDB, ADBC, ADCB, \\ BACD, BADC, BCAD, BCDA, BDAC, BDCA, \\ CABD, CADB, CBAD, CBDA, CDAB, CDBA, \\ DABC, DACB, DCAB, DCBA, DBAC, DBCA \end{matrix}\right\}$$

(i) Let E_1 be the event that Veena visits A before B. Then

$$E_1 = \left\{\begin{matrix} ABCD, ABDC, ACBD, ACDB, ADBC, ADCB, \\ CABD, CADB, CDAB, DABC, DACB, DCAB \end{matrix}\right\}$$

$$\Rightarrow \quad n(E_1) = 12$$

$$\therefore P(\text{she visits } A \text{ before } B) = P(E_1) = \frac{n(E_1)}{n(S)} = \frac{12}{24} = \frac{1}{2}$$

(ii) Let E_2 be the event that she visits A before B and B before C.

Then $E_2 = \{ABCD, ABDC, ADBC, DABC\}$

$$\Rightarrow \quad n(E_2) = 4$$

$$\therefore P(\text{she visits } A \text{ before } B \text{ and } B \text{ before } C) = P(E_2) = \frac{n(E_2)}{n(S)} = \frac{4}{24} = \frac{1}{6}$$

(iii) Let E_3 be the event that she visits A first and B last.

Then, $E_3 = \{ACDB, ADCB\} \Rightarrow n(E_3) = 2$

$$\therefore P(\text{she visits } A \text{ first and } B \text{ last}) = P(E_3) = \frac{n(E_3)}{n(S)} = \frac{2}{24} = \frac{1}{12}$$

|TYPE VIII|

Miscellaneous Problems

Example 28 There are four men and six women on the city council. If one council member is selected for a committee at random, how likely is it that it is a woman?

Sol. Total number of person = 4 (men) + 6 (women) = 10

Since, a person is selected at random, therefore total number of possible outcomes = 10

Now, let A be the event of selecting a woman. Then number of outcomes favourable to A are 6.

Hence, probability of selecting a woman, $P(A) = \frac{6}{10} = \frac{3}{5}$

Example 29 A bag contains 9 red, 7 white and 4 black balls. A ball is drawn at random. Find the probability that the ball drawn is

(i) red (ii) white

(iii) not black

Sol. Total number of balls = 9 red + 7 white + 4 black = 20

$\Rightarrow$ Total number of possible outcomes, $n(S) = 20$

(i) Let E_1 be the event of getting a red ball.

Then, $n(E_1) = 9$

Now, $P(\text{getting a red ball}) = P(E_1) = \frac{n(E_1)}{n(S)} = \frac{9}{20}$

(ii) Let E_2 be the event of getting a white ball.

Then, $n(E_2) = 7$

Now, $P(\text{getting a white ball}) = P(E_2) = \frac{n(E_2)}{n(S)} = \frac{7}{20}$

(iii) Let E_3 be the event of getting a non-black ball. Then, $n(E_3) = 9 + 7 = 16$

Now, P (getting a non-black ball)

$$= P(E_3) = \frac{n(E_3)}{n(S)} = \frac{16}{20} = \frac{4}{5}$$

Example 30 One mapping (function) is selected at random from all the mappings of the set $A = \{1, 2, 3, \ldots, n\}$ into itself. Find the probability that the mapping selected is one to one.

Sol. We know that, total number of mappings from a set A having n elements into itself is n^n.

and the total number of one to one mapping is $n!$.

$\therefore$ Required probability $= \frac{n!}{n^n}$

Topic Practice 2

Very Short Answer Type Questions

2 Marks

1 A coin is tossed twice, what is the probability that at least one head occurs?

2 In a simultaneous toss of two coins, find the probability of

(i) exactly 1 tail (ii) no tail.

3 A bag contains 6 red, 4 white and 8 blue balls. If three balls are drawn at random, find the probability that the drawn balls are of different colours.

4 What is the probability of drawing a 'King' from a well-shuffled deck of 52 cards?

5 A bag contains 5 green and 7 red balls. Two balls are drawn. What is the probability that one is green and other is red?

6 Two cards are drawn at random from a pack of 52 cards. What is the probability that both the drawn cards are aces?

7 4 cards are drawn from a well-shuffled deck of 52 cards. What is the probability of obtaining 3 diamonds and one spade? **[NCERT]**

8 A die is rolled. If the outcome is an odd number, then what is the probability that it is a prime number?

9 Find the probability that in a random arrangement of the letters of the word 'SOCIAL' vowels come together.

10 What is the probability that in a leap year chosen at random will contain 53 Tuesday or 53 Wednesday?

11 Two cards are drawn without replacement from a well-shuffled pack of 52 cards. What is the probability that one is red queen and the other is a king of black colour?

12 The letters of the word 'CLIFTON' are arranged at random in a row. What is the chance that two vowels come together?

13 What is the probability that a number selected from the number 1, 2, 3, ..., 35 is a prime number?

14 Find the probability that in a random arrangement of the letters of the word 'UNIVERSITY' the two I's come together.

15 There are 4 letters and 4 addressed envelopes. Find the probability that all the letters are not dispatched in right envelopes.

16 One mapping is selected at random from all the mappings of the set $B = \{1, 2, 3, \ldots, 6\}$ into itself. Find the probability that the mapping selected is one-to-one.

17 In a lottery, a person choose 4 different natural numbers at random from 1 to 30 and if there four numbers match with the six numbers already fixed by the lottery committee, he wins the prize. What is the probability of winning the prize in the game?

18 Three-digit numbers are formed using the digits 0, 2, 4, 6, 8. A number is chosen at random out of these numbers. What is the probability that this number has the same digits? **[NCERT Exemplar]**

19 If letters of the word PENCIL are arranged in random order, then what is the probability that N is always next to E?

20 There are three events E_1, E_2 and E_3 one of which must only one can happen. The odds are 7 to 5 against E_1 and 5 to 3 against E_2. Find the odds against E_3.

21 Let a sample space be $S = \{\omega_1, \omega_2, \ldots, \omega_6\}$. Which of the following assignments of probabilities to each outcome are valid?

Outcomes	ω_1	ω_2	ω_3	ω_4	ω_5	ω_6
(i)	$\frac{1}{6}$	$\frac{1}{6}$	$\frac{1}{6}$	$\frac{1}{6}$	$\frac{1}{6}$	$\frac{1}{6}$
(ii)	1	0	0	0	0	0
(iii)	$\frac{1}{8}$	$\frac{2}{3}$	$\frac{1}{3}$	$\frac{1}{3}$	$-\frac{1}{4}$	$-\frac{1}{3}$
(iv)	$\frac{1}{12}$	$\frac{1}{12}$	$\frac{1}{6}$	$\frac{1}{6}$	$\frac{1}{6}$	$\frac{3}{2}$
(v)	0.1	0.2	0.3	0.4	0.5	0.6

Short Answer Type Questions

4 Marks

22 A card is selected from a pack of 52 cards.
(i) How many points are there in the sample space.
(ii) Find the probability that the card is an ace of club.
(iii) Find the probability that the card is
(a) a king
(b) red card

23 Three coins are tossed once. Find the probability of getting
(i) 2 heads.
(ii) no head.
(iii) 3 tails.
(iv) atmost two tails.

24 A die is thrown, find the probability of getting
(i) an even number.
(ii) a number less than or equal to 4.
(iii) a number less than or equal to 6.

25 Two dice are thrown simultaneously. Find the probability of getting

(i) an even number as the sum.
(ii) a doublet.
(iii) a doublet of even number.
(iv) a multiple of 3 as the sum.

26 From a well-shuffled deck of 52 cards, a card is drawn at random. Find the probability of getting

(i) a heart (ii) a red card
(iii) a face card (iv) an eight of hearts

27 A letter is chosen at random from the word 'ASSASSINATION'. Find the probability that letter is **[NCERT]**

(i) a vowel. (ii) a consonant.

28 A single letter is selected at random from the word 'ASSESSMENT', then find the probability that letter is a vowel.

29 20 cards are numbered from 1 to 20. In those of them, one card is drawn at random. What is the probability that the number on the card drawn is

(i) a prime number? (ii) an odd number?
(iii) a multiple of 5? (iv) not divisible by 3?

30 A bag contains 8 red and 5 white balls. Three balls are drawn at random. Find the probability that

(i) all the three balls are white.
(ii) all the three balls are red.
(iii) one ball is red and two balls are white.

31 A box contains 10 bulbs, of which just three are defective. If a random sample of five bulbs is drawn, find the probability that the sample contains

(i) all defective bulbs. (ii) good bulbs.
(iii) exactly 2 defective bulbs.

32 A committee of two persons is selected from two men and two women. What is the probability that the committee will have

(i) no man? (ii) one man? (iii) two men?

33 A box contains 150 bulbs, 40 of which are defective. 20 bulbs are selected for inspection. Find the probability that

(i) no bulb is defective.
(ii) exactly one bulb is defective.
(iii) exactly two bulbs are defective.

34 A five digit number is formed by the digits 1,2,3,4,5 without repetition. Find the probability that the number is divisible by 4.

35 A combination lock on a suitcase has 3 wheels, each labelled with nine digits from 1 to 9. If an opening combination is a particular sequence of three digits with no repeats, what is the probability of a person guessing the right combination?

36 Three squares of chess board are selected at random. Find the probability of getting 2 squares of one colour and other of a different colour. **[NCERT Exemplar]**

37 In a relay race, there are five teams *A*, *B*, *C*, *D* and *E*.

(i) What is the probability that *A*, *B* and *C* finish first, second and third, respectively.
(ii) What is the probability that *A*, *B* and *C* are first three to finish (in any order), assume that all finishing orders are equally likely. **[NCERT]**

38 A typical PIN (personal identification number) is a sequence of any four symbols chosen from the 26 letters in the alphabet and the ten digits. If all PINs are equally likely, what is the probability that a randomly chosen PIN contains a repeated symbol? **[NCERT Exemplar]**

39 What is the probability that in a group of 2 people, both will have the same birthday, assuming that there are 365 days in a year and no one has his/her birthday on 29th February.

40 Two balls are drawn at random from a bag containing 3 white, 3 red, 4 green and 4 black balls, one-by-one without replacement. Find the probability that both the balls are of different colour.

Long Answer Type Questions

6 Marks

41 A bag contains 8 red, 3 white and 9 blackballs. If three balls are drawn at random, determine the probability that

(i) all the three balls are of blue colour.
(ii) all the balls are of different colours.
(iii) one is red and two are white.

42 A group consist of 3 men, 2 women and 4 children. If four persons are selected at random, find the probability of selecting

(i) 1 man, 1 woman and 2 children.

(ii) exactly 2 children.

(iii) 2 women.

43 A die is rolled in such a way that each odd number is twice as likely to occur as each even number. Find $P(G)$, where G is the event that a number greater than 3 occurs on a single roll of the die. **[NCERT Exemplar]**

44 In a lottery of 50 tickets numbered 1 to 50, two tickets are drawn simultaneously. Find the probability that

(i) both the tickets drawn have prime number.

(ii) none of the tickets drawn have prime number.

(iii) one ticket has prime number.

45 If 4-digit numbers greater than 5000 are randomly formed from the digits 0, 1, 3, 5 and 7. What is the probability of forming a number divisible by 5 when,

(i) the digits are repeated?

(ii) the repetition of digits are not allowed? **[NCERT]**

Hints & Answers

1. $S = \{HH, HT, TH, TT\}$

$\therefore n(S) = 4$

n (at least one head occur) $= 3$

Ans. $\frac{3}{4}$

2. (i) Favourable outcomes $= \{HT, TH\}$

(ii) Favourable outcome $= \{HH\}$

Ans. (i) $\frac{1}{2}$ (ii) $\frac{1}{4}$

3. Let E_2 be the event of getting all balls of different colours. then $n(E_2) = {}^6C_1 \times {}^4C_1 \times {}^8C_1 = 192$

Required probability $= \frac{192}{{}^{18}C_3}$ **Ans.** $\frac{4}{17}$

4. Probability $= \frac{{}^4C_1}{{}^{52}C_1}$ **Ans.** $\frac{1}{13}$

5. Solve as Example 16 part (ii). **Ans.** $\frac{35}{66}$

6. Number of favourable outcomes ${}^4C_2$. **Ans.** $\frac{1}{221}$

7. Total number of possible outcomes $= {}^{52}C_4$

Number of favourable outcomes $= {}^{13}C_3 \times {}^{13}C_1$.

Ans. $\frac{{}^{13}C_3 \cdot {}^{13}C_1}{{}^{52}C_4}$

8. On rolling a die, we get outcomes as odd number. So, sample space, $S = \{1, 3, 5\} \Rightarrow n(S) = 3$

Let E be the event of getting a prime number then, $E = \{3, 5\} \Rightarrow n(E) = 2$

Ans. $\frac{2}{3}$

9. Total number of outcomes $= 6!$

Favourable outcomes $= 4! \times 3!$ **Ans.** $\frac{1}{5}$

10. Solve as Example 5. **Ans.** $\frac{3}{7}$

11. Number of ways of selecting 2 cards out of 52 cards $= {}^{52}C_2 = 26 \times 51$

$\Rightarrow$ Total number of possible outcomes $= 26 \times 51$

We know that, there are 2 red queen and 2 kings of black colour in a pack of 52 cards

$\therefore$ Number of favourable outcomes $= {}^2C_1 \times {}^2C_1 = 2 \times 2 = 4$

Ans. $\frac{2}{663}$

12. There are 7 letters in the word 'CLIFTON'.

These 7 letters can be arranged in a row in 7! ways.

$\Rightarrow$ Total number of possible outcomes $= 7!$

Now, if vowels (I, O) come together, then we have 6 letters (considering vowel as one letter i.e. CLFTN IO) which can be arranged in 6! ways.

But two vowels can be put together in 2! ways.

$\therefore$ The total number of arrangements in which two vowels come together is $6! \times 2!$

$\Rightarrow$ Number of favourable outcomes $= 6! \times 2!$ **Ans.** $\frac{2}{7}$

13. Prime numbers are $\{2, 3, 5, 7, 11, 13, 17, 19, 23, 29, 31\}$

Ans. $\frac{11}{35}$

14. Solve as Example 23. **Ans.** $\frac{1}{5}$

15. Clearly, 4 letters can be inserted into 4 addressed envelope in ${}^4P_4 = 4! = 24$ ways.

$\Rightarrow$ Total number of possible ways is 24.

$\therefore$ P (all letters are not dispatched in right envelopes)

$= 1 - P$ (all letters are dispatched in right envelope)

$= 1 - \frac{1}{24}$ [$\because$ there is exactly one way in which all letters are dispatched in right envelope]

Ans. $\frac{23}{24}$

16. Solve as Example 30. **Ans.** $\frac{6!}{6^6}$

17. Solve as Example 19. **Ans.** $\frac{1}{^{30}C_4}$

18. Since, a 3-digit number cannot start with 0, therefore hundredth place can be filled up in 4 ways.

Now, as repetition of digits is allowed, therefore each of ten's and unit's place can be filled in 5 ways.

Thus, the total number of possible 3-digit number

$= 4 \times 5 \times 5 = 100$

Note that, there are three digits numbers, which has the same digits, *viz.* 222, 444, 666 and 888.

$\Rightarrow$ Number of favourable outcomes = 4 **Ans.** $\frac{1}{25}$

19. There are 6 letters in the word 'PENCIL', which can be arranged in 6! ways.

$\Rightarrow$ Total number of possible outcomes = 6!

Now, if letter N is always next to E, then we have 5 letters (considering EN as one letter i.e. PCIL EN) which can be arranged in 5! ways

$\Rightarrow$ Number of favourable outcomes = 5! **Ans.** $\frac{1}{6}$

20. Since, one and only one of the three events E_1, E_2 and E_3 can happen i.e. they are mutually exclusive, therefore $P_1 + P_2 + P_3 = 1$ where $P_1 = P(E_1)$, $P_2 = P(E_2)$, $P_3 = P(E_3)$ ... (i)

Odds against E_1 are 7 : 5

$\Rightarrow \quad P_1 = \frac{5}{7+5} = \frac{5}{12}$ ...(ii)

Odds against E_2 are 5 : 3

$\Rightarrow \quad P_2 = \frac{3}{5+3} = \frac{3}{8}$ ...(iii)

$\therefore \quad \frac{5}{12} + \frac{3}{8} + P_3 = 1 \Rightarrow P_3 = \frac{20}{96}$

Hence, the odds against E_3 are $\frac{1-P_3}{P_3}$ **Ans.** $\frac{19}{5}$

21. Solve as Example 1. **Ans.** (i) and (ii)

22. Solve as Example 13.

Ans. (i) 52 (ii) $\frac{1}{52}$ (iii) (a) $\frac{1}{13}$ (b) $\frac{1}{2}$

23. Solve as Example 9.

Ans. (i) $\frac{3}{8}$ (ii) $\frac{1}{8}$ (iii) $\frac{1}{8}$ (iv) $\frac{7}{8}$

24. Solve as Example 10.

Ans. (i) $\frac{1}{2}$ (ii) $\frac{2}{3}$ (iii) 1

25. Total number of outcomes = 36 $\Rightarrow n(s) = 36$

(i) Possible outcomes are (1, 1) (1, 3) (3, 1), (2, 2), (1, 5), (5, 1), (2, 4), (4, 2), (3, 3), (3, 5), (5, 3), (4, 4), (4, 6), (2, 6), (6, 2), (6, 4), (5, 5), (6, 6) $\therefore n(E) = 18$

(ii) Possible outcomes are (1, 1), (2, 2), (3, 3), (4, 4), (5, 5), (6, 6)

(iii) Possible outcomes are (2, 2), (4, 4), (6, 6).

(iv) Possible outcomes are (1, 2), (2, 1), (1, 5), (2, 4), (3, 3), (4, 2), (5, 1), (3, 6), (6, 3), (4, 5), (5, 4), (6, 6).

Ans. (i) $\frac{1}{2}$ (ii) $\frac{1}{6}$ (iii) $\frac{1}{12}$ (iv) $\frac{1}{3}$

26. (i) Required probability $= \frac{13}{52}$

(ii) Required probability $= \frac{26}{52}$

(iii) Required probability $= \frac{12}{52}$

(iv) Required probability $= \frac{1}{52}$

Ans. (i) $\frac{1}{4}$ (ii) $\frac{1}{2}$ (iii) $\frac{3}{13}$ (iv) $\frac{1}{52}$

27. In word ASSASSINATION, number of constant = 7 and number of vowel = 6

Ans. (i) $\frac{6}{13}$ (ii) $\frac{7}{13}$

28. Solve as Example 14. **Ans.** $\frac{3}{10}$

29. (i) Favourable outcomes are 2, 3, 5, 7, 11, 13, 17 and 19.

Ans. $\frac{2}{5}$

(ii) Favourable outcomes are 1, 3, 5, 7, 9, 11, 13, 15, 17 and 19.

Ans. $\frac{1}{2}$

(iii) Favourable outcomes are 5, 10, 15 and 20.

Ans. $\frac{1}{5}$

(iv) Favourable outcomes are 1, 2, 4, 5, 7, 8, 10, 11, 13, 14, 16, 17, 19, 20. **Ans.** $\frac{7}{10}$

30. (i) Number of favourable outcomes $= {}^5C_3$

Total number of possible outcomes $= {}^{13}C_3$

Ans. $\frac{5}{143}$

(ii) Number of favourable outcomes $= {}^8C_3$

Ans. $\frac{28}{143}$

(iii) Number of favourable outcomes $= {}^8C_1 \times {}^5C_2$

Ans. $\frac{40}{143}$

31. Total outcomes $= {}^{10}C_5$, defective bulbs = 3

Non-defective bulbs = 7

Ans. (i) $\frac{{}^3C_3 \times {}^7C_2}{{}^{10}C_5}$ (ii) $\frac{{}^7C_5}{{}^{10}C_5}$ (iii) $\frac{{}^3C_2 \times {}^7C_3}{{}^{10}C_5}$

32. Total number of possible outcomes = $^4C_2$

(i) Number of favourable outcomes = $^2C_2$

Ans. $\frac{1}{6}$

(ii) Number of favourable outcomes = $^2C_1 \times {^2C_1}$

Ans. $\frac{2}{3}$

(iii) Number of favourable outcomes = $^2C_2$

Ans. $\frac{1}{6}$

33. Total outcomes = $^{150}C_{20}$

Number of defective bulbs = 40

Number of non-defective bulbs = 110

Ans. (i) $\frac{^{110}C_{20}}{^{150}C_{20}}$ (ii) $\frac{^{40}C_1 \times {^{110}C_{19}}}{^{150}C_{20}}$ (iii) $\frac{^{40}C_2 \times {^{110}C_{18}}}{^{150}C_{20}}$

34. For a number to be divisible by 4, last two digits should be divisible by 4. (i.e. 12, 24, 32, 52).

Favourable cases = $3! \times 4$ **Ans.** $\frac{1}{5}$

35. Solve as Example 25. **Ans.** $\frac{1}{504}$

36. We know that, in a chess board, there are 64 squares of which 32 are white and 32 are black.

Clearly, 3 squares can be selected in $^{64}C_3$ ways.

Let E be the event of getting 2 squares of one colour and other of a different colour.

Then, $n(E) = {^{32}C_2} \times {^{32}C_1} + {^{32}C_1} \times {^{32}C_2}$

[$\because$ 2 squares of one colour and 1 of other can be $2W, 1B$ or $1W, 2B$]

$= 2 \times {^{32}C_2} \times {^{32}C_1}$ **Ans.** $\frac{16}{21}$

37. The sample space consisting of all finishing orders in the first three places, will have

$^5P_3$, i.e. $\frac{5!}{(5-3)!} = 5 \times 4 \times 3 = 60$ sample points, each with a probability of $\frac{1}{60}$.

(i) If A, B and C finish first, second and third respectively, then there is only one finishing order for this, i.e. ABC.

Ans. $\frac{1}{60}$

(ii) If A, B and C are the first three finishers, then there will be 3! arrangements for A, B and C. Thus, the sample points corresponding to this event will be 3! in number.

Hence, $P(A, B$ and C are first three to finish)

$= \frac{3!}{60}$ **Ans.** $= \frac{1}{10}$

38. Total number of symbols = 36

There are $36 \times 36 \times 36 \times 36 = (36)^4 = 1679616$ PINs in all.

[by fundamental principle of counting]

Note that, when repetition of symbols is not allowed, then there are $36 \times 35 \times 34 \times 33 = 1413720$ different PINs.

Now, the number of PINs that contain atleast one repeated symbol = 1679616 – 1413720 = 265896

Ans. 0.1583

39. Clearly, the total number of ways in which two persons may have their birthday

$= 365 \times 365 = (365)^2$

[$\because$ first person may have birthday in anyone of 365 days. Similarly, second person may have birthday in anyone of 365 days]

Note that, the number of ways in which two persons have the same birthday = 365

Ans. $\frac{1}{365}$

40. Total number of balls = 3 + 3 + 4 + 4 = 14

Since, two balls are to be drawn one-by-one without replacement. Then, there will be 4 cases arise

	First ball	Second ball	Probability
Case I	1 White (3)	1 Non-white (11)	$\frac{^3C_1}{^{14}C_1} \times \frac{^{11}C_1}{^{13}C_1} = \frac{3}{14} \times \frac{11}{13}$
Case II	1 Red (3)	1 Non-red (11)	$\frac{^3C_1}{^{14}C_1} \times \frac{^{11}C_1}{^{13}C_1} = \frac{3}{14} \times \frac{11}{13}$
Case III	1 Green (4)	1 Non-green (10)	$\frac{^4C_1}{^{14}C_1} \times \frac{^{10}C_1}{^{13}C_1} = \frac{4}{14} \times \frac{10}{13}$
Case IV	1 Black (4)	1 Non-black (10)	$\frac{^4C_1}{^{14}C_1} \times \frac{^{10}C_1}{^{13}C_1} = \frac{4}{14} \times \frac{10}{13}$

$\therefore$ Required probability

$$= \frac{3}{14} \times \frac{11}{13} + \frac{3}{14} \times \frac{11}{13} + \frac{4}{14} \times \frac{10}{13} + \frac{4}{14} \times \frac{10}{13}$$

Ans. $\frac{73}{91}$

41. Total number of balls = 8 + 3 + 9 = 20

Number of ways of selecting 3 balls out of 20 balls = $^{20}C_3$

(i) Let E_1 be the event of getting all balls of blue colour.

Then, $n(E_1) = {^9C_3}$

Hence, required probability = $\frac{^9C_3}{^{20}C_3}$

Ans. $\frac{7}{95}$

(ii) Let E_2 be the event of getting all balls of different colours. Then,

$$n(E_2) = {}^8C_1 \times {}^3C_1 \times {}^9C_1$$
$$= 8 \times 3 \times 9$$

Hence, required probability $= \dfrac{8 \times 3 \times 9}{{}^{20}C_3}$

Ans. $\dfrac{18}{95}$

(iii) Let E_3 be the event of getting one red and two white balls. Then,

$$n(E_3) = {}^8C_1 \times {}^3C_2 = 8 \times 3$$

Hence, required probability $= \dfrac{8 \times 3}{{}^{20}C_3}$

Ans. $\dfrac{2}{95}$

42. Total number of persons in the group $= 3 + 2 + 4 = 9$
Clearly, out of 9 persons 4 persons can be selected in ${}^9C_4$ ways.

Total number of possible ways $= {}^9C_4 = 126$

(i) Let E_1 be the event of getting 1 man, 1 woman and 2 children.

Then, $n(E_1) = {}^3C_1 \times {}^2C_1 \times {}^4C_2 = 3 \times 2 \times 6$

Ans. $\dfrac{2}{7}$

(ii) Let E_2 be the event of getting exactly 2 children.

Then, $n(E_2) = {}^4C_2 \times {}^5C_2 = 6 \times 10$

[$\because$ remaining two persons will be selected from 3 men and 2 women]

Ans. $\dfrac{10}{21}$

(iii) Let E_3 be the event of getting 2 women.

Then $\quad n(E_3) = {}^2C_2 \times {}^7C_2 = 1 \times 21 = 21$

Ans. $\dfrac{1}{6}$

43. When a die is rolled, then we get 1 or 2 or 3 or 4 or 5 or 6.

$\therefore \quad S = \{1, 2, 3, 4, 5, 6\}$

It is given that

$$P(\text{each odd number}) = 2 \times P(\text{each even number})$$

Let P (each even number) $= x$. Then, we get

$P(1) = 2x, P(2) = x, P(3) = 2x, P(4) = x,$
$P(5) = 2x$ and $P(6) = x$

$\therefore P(1) + P(2) + P(3) + P(4) + P(5) + P(6) = 1$

$\Rightarrow \quad 2x + x + 2x + x + 2x + x = 1$

$\Rightarrow \quad 9x = 1 \Rightarrow x = \dfrac{1}{9}$

Thus, $\quad P(1) = P(3) = P(5) = \dfrac{2}{9}$

and $\quad P(2) = P(4) = P(6) = \dfrac{1}{9}$

Now, $\quad P(G) = P$ (getting 4 or 5 or 6)
$= P(4) + P(5) + P(6)$

Ans. $\dfrac{4}{9}$

44. Total number of ways of drawing two number $= {}^{50}C_2$

Prime numbers are 1, 3, 5, 7, 11, 13, 17, 19, 23, 29, 31, 37, 41, 43, 47.

(i) Probability $= \dfrac{{}^{15}C_2}{{}^{50}C_2}$

(ii) Probability $= \dfrac{{}^{35}C_2}{{}^{50}C_2}$

(iii) Probability $= \dfrac{{}^{15}C_1 \times {}^{35}C_1}{{}^{50}C_2}$

Ans. (i) $\dfrac{21}{245}$ (ii) $\dfrac{17}{35}$ (iii) $\dfrac{3}{7}$

45. (i) (a) Thousand's place can be filled in 2 ways (5 or 7).

(b) The remaining 3 places can be filled by any of the digits 0, 1, 3, 5 and 7, as repetition of digits is allowed.

$\Rightarrow$ Number of 4-digits numbers
$= (2 \times 5 \times 5 \times 5) - 1 \quad$ [$\because$ 5000 cannot be counted]

(c) If the number is divisible by 5, then its units place is filled by 0 or 5.

$\Rightarrow$ Number of 4-digits numbers divisible by
$5 = (2 \times 5 \times 5 \times 2) - 1$

[here, repetition of digits is allowed]

Ans. $\dfrac{33}{83}$

(ii) (a) Thousand's place can be filled in 2 ways (5 or 7).

(b) The remaining 3 places can be filled in $4 \times 3 \times 2$ ways.

$\therefore$ Number of 4-digits numbers $= 2 \times 4 \times 3 \times 2$

(c) If the number is divisible by 5, then its units place is either 0 or 5.

(d) If units place is 0, then thousands, place can be filled in 2 ways and other two places can be filled in 3×2 ways.

(e) If units place is 5, then thousands's place can be filled in 1 way and other two places can be filled in 3×2 ways.

$\therefore$ Number of 4-digits numbers divisible by 5
$= 2 \times 3 \times 2 + 1 \times 3 \times 2$

Ans. $\dfrac{3}{8}$

TOPIC 03 Laws of Probability

Theorem 1. If A and B are two events associated with a random experiment having sample space S and if $A \subset B$, then

(i) $P(A) \le P(B)$ (ii) $P(B - A) = P(B) - P(A)$

Proof

(i) Let any arbitrary elementary event $E_i \in A$, then $E_i \in B$ [$\because A \subset B$, given that]

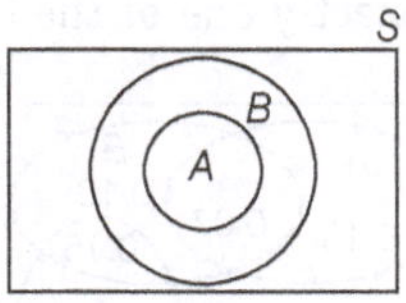

$\Rightarrow \quad \Sigma P(E_i) \,\forall\, E_i \in A \le \Sigma P(E_j) \,\forall\, E_j \in B$

$\Rightarrow \quad P(A) \le P(B)$

(ii) From the above Venn diagram, we have

$$B = A \cup (B - A) \quad \ldots \text{(i)}$$

Since, A and $(B - A)$ are mutually exclusive, we have

$$P(A \cup (B - A)) = P(A) + P(B - A)$$

$\Rightarrow \quad P(B) = P(A) + P(B - A)$ [using Eq. (i)]

$\Rightarrow \quad P(B - A) = P(B) - P(A)$

Corollary.

(i) If A and B are mutually exclusive events associated with a random experiment having sample space S, then $P(A \cup B) = P(A) + P(B)$.

(ii) If $A_1, A_2, \ldots, A_n$ are mutually exclusive events associated with a random experiment, then

$$P(A_1 \cup A_2 \ldots \cup A_n) = P(A_1) + P(A_2) + \ldots + P(A_n).$$

Theorem 2. If A and B are mutually exclusive and exhaustive events associated with a random experiment having sample space S, then $P(A) + P(B) = 1$.

Proof Since, A and B are mutually exclusive, then

$$P(A \cup B) = P(A) + P(B) \quad \ldots \text{(i)}$$

Also, A and B are exhaustive, so $A \cup B = S$

$\Rightarrow \quad P(A \cup B) = P(S) = 1$

$\Rightarrow \quad P(A) + P(B) = 1$ [using Eq. (i)]

Generalised form of the above theorem is

If $A_1, A_2, \ldots A_n$ are mutually exclusive and exhaustive events associated with a random experiment having sample space S, then

$$P(A_1) + P(A_2) + \ldots + P(A_n) = 1.$$

Addition Theorem of Probability

Theorem 3. If A and B are two events associated with a random experiment, then

$$P(A \cup B) = P(A) + P(B) - P(A \cap B)$$

Proof Let S be the sample space associated with the given random experiment. Suppose the random experiment results in n mutually exclusive ways. Then S contain n elementary events.

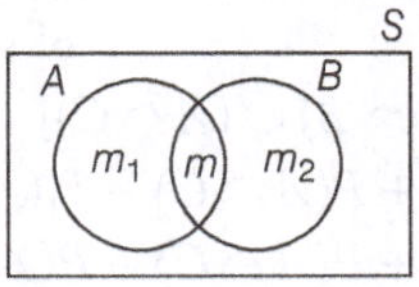

Let m_1, m_2 and m be the number of elementary events favourable to A, B and $A \cap B$ respectively, then

$$P(A) = \frac{m_1}{n}, \; P(B) = \frac{m_2}{n} \text{ and } P(A \cap B) = \frac{m}{n}$$

The number of elementary events favourable to A only is $m_1 - m$. Similarly, the number of elementary events favourable to B only is $m_2 - m$. Since, m elementary events are favourable to both A and B.

Therefore, the number of elementary events favourable to A or B or both i.e. $A \cup B$ is

$$m_1 - m + m_2 - m + m = m_1 + m_2 - m$$

So, $P(A \cup B) = \dfrac{m_1 + m_2 - m}{n} = \dfrac{m_1}{n} + \dfrac{m_2}{n} - \dfrac{m}{n}$

$\Rightarrow \quad P(A \cup B) = P(A) + P(B) - P(A \cap B)$

Corollary. If A and B are mutually exclusive events, then

$$P(A \cap B) = 0$$

$\therefore \quad P(A \cup B) = P(A) + P(B)$

This is the **addition theorem for mutually exclusive events.**

Theorem 4. If A and B are any two events associated with a random experiment, then

(i) $P(A \cup B) = P(A - B) + P(B - A) + P(A \cap B)$

(ii) $P(A \cup B) = P(A) + P(B - A) = P(B) + P(A - B)$

(iii) $P(A) = P(A - B) + P(A \cap B)$

(iv) $P(B) = P(B - A) + P(A \cap B)$

(v) $P(A - B) = P(A \cap \overline{B})$

(vi) $P(B - A) = P(\overline{A} \cap B)$

(vii) $P(A) + P(B) = P(A - B) + P(B - A) + 2P(A \cap B)$

(viii) $P(A \cap B) \le P(A)$ and $P(A \cap B) \le P(B)$

[if these conditions hold true, then events are said to be consistently defined]

Note
(i) If $A \subset A \cup B, B \subset A \cup B$ then $P(A) \le P(A \cup B), P(B) \le P(A \cup B)$
(ii) If $A \cap B \subset A, A \cap B \subset B$ then $P(A \cap B) \le P(A), P(A \cap B) \le P(B)$

Theorem 5. If A, B and C are three events associated with a random experiment, then

$$P(A \cup B \cup C) = P(A) + P(B) + P(C) - P(A \cap B) - P(B \cap C) - P(A \cap C) + P(A \cap B \cap C)$$

[addition theorem for three events]

Proof Let $D = B \cup C$. Then, $P(A \cup B \cup C) = P(A \cup D)$

$$= P(A) + P(D) - P(A \cap D) \quad \text{...(i)}$$

But, $A \cap D = A \cap (B \cup C) = (A \cap B) \cup (A \cap C)$

[by using distribution property of intersection of sets over the union]

$$\therefore\ P(A \cap D) = P[(A \cap B) \cup (A \cap C)]$$
$$= P(A \cap B) + P(A \cap C) - P[(A \cap B) \cap (A \cap C)]$$
$$= P(A \cap B) + P(A \cap C) - P(A \cap B \cap C) \quad \text{...(ii)}$$

and $P(D) = P(B \cup C) = P(B) + P(C) - P(B \cap C)$ ...(iii)

From Eqs. (i), (ii) and (iii), we get

$$P(A \cup B \cup C) = P(A) + P(B) + P(C) - P(B \cap C) - [P(A \cap B) + P(A \cap C) - P(A \cap B \cap C)]$$

$$\Rightarrow P(A \cup B \cup C) = P(A) + P(B) + P(C) - P(A \cap B) - P(A \cap C) - P(B \cap C) + P(A \cap B \cap C)$$

Corollary. If A, B and C are mutually exclusive events, then

$$P(A \cap B) = P(B \cap C) = P(A \cap C) = P(A \cap B \cap C) = 0$$
$$\therefore P(A \cup B \cup C) = P(A) + P(B) + P(C)$$

Theorem 6. Let E be any event and $\bar{E}$ (or E') be its complementary event. Then,

$$P(\bar{E}) = 1 - P(E) \text{ or } P(\text{not } E) = 1 - P(E)$$

Note The odds in favour of occurrence of the event E are defined by $P(E) : P(\bar{E})$ and the odds against the occurrence of event E are defined by $P(\bar{E}) : P(E)$.

Problems Based on Addition Theorem of Probability

|TYPE I|

Problems Directly Based on Formula

Example 1 If A and B are two events such that

$$P(A) = \frac{1}{4}, P(B) = \frac{1}{2} \text{ and } P(A \cap B) = \frac{1}{8}.$$

Then, find P (not A and not B).

Sol. P (not A and not B) $= P(\bar{A} \cap \bar{B})$

$$= P(\overline{A \cup B}) = 1 - P(A \cup B)$$
$$= 1 - [P(A) + P(B) - P(A \cap B)]$$
$$= 1 - \left[\frac{1}{4} + \frac{1}{2} - \frac{1}{8}\right] = 1 - \left[\frac{2 + 4 - 1}{8}\right]$$
$$= 1 - \frac{5}{8} = \frac{3}{8}$$

Example 2 The accompanying Venn diagram shows three events A, B and C and also the probabilities of the various intersections [for instance $P(A \cap B) = 0.07$]. Determine [NCERT Exemplar]

(i) $P(A)$ (ii) $P(B \cap \bar{C})$
(iii) $P(A \cup B)$ (iv) $P(A \cap \bar{B})$
(v) $P(B \cap C)$
(vi) Probability of exactly one of the three event occurs.

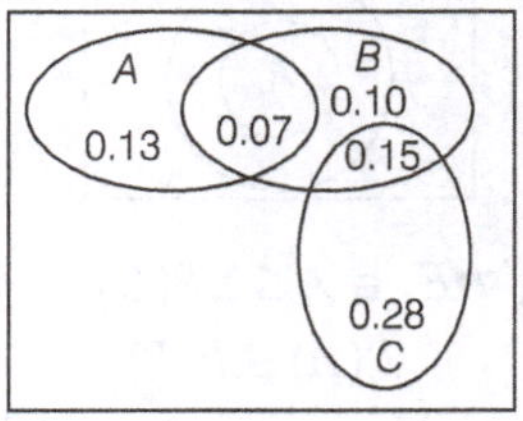

Sol. (i) $P(A) = 0.13 + 0.07 = 0.20$

(ii) $P(B \cap \bar{C}) = P(B) - P(B \cap C)$
$= (0.07 + 0.10 + 0.15) - (0.15) = 0.17$

(iii) $P(A \cup B) = P(A) + P(B) - P(A \cap B)$
$= 0.20 + (0.07 + 0.10 + 0.15) - 0.07$
$= 0.20 + 0.25 = 0.45$

(iv) $P(A \cap \bar{B}) = P(A) - P(A \cap B) = 0.20 - 0.07 = 0.13$

(v) $P(B \cap C) = 0.15$

(vi) P (exactly one of the three events occurs)
$= P(A \text{ only}) + P(B \text{ only}) + P(C \text{ only})$
$= 0.13 + 0.10 + 0.28 = 0.51$

Example 3 A and B are two events that $P(A) = 0.54$, $P(B) = 0.69$ and $P(A \cap B) = 0.35$. Find

(i) $P(A \cup B)$ (ii) $P(A' \cap B')$ [NCERT]

Sol. We have, $P(A) = 0.54$, $P(B) = 0.69$ and $P(A \cap B) = 0.35$

(i) $P(A \cup B) = P(A) + P(B) - P(A \cap B)$
$= 0.54 + 0.69 - 0.35 = 0.88$

(ii) $P(A' \cap B') = P((A \cup B)') = 1 - P(A \cup B)$ [$\because P(E') = 1 - P(E)$]
$= 1 - 0.88 = 0.12$

Example 4 The probability that at least one of the events A and B occurs is 0.6. If A and B occurs simultaneously with probability 0.2, then find $P(\bar{A}) + P(\bar{B})$. [NCERT Exemplar]

Sol. We have, $P(A \cup B) = 0.6$ and $P(A \cap B) = 0.2$

We know, $P(A \cup B) = P(A) + P(B) - P(A \cap B)$

$\therefore \quad 0.6 = P(A) + P(B) - 0.2$

$\Rightarrow \quad P(A) + P(B) = 0.6 + 0.2 = 0.8$ ...(i)

Now, $P(\overline{A}) + P(\overline{B}) = 1 - P(A) + 1 - P(B)$

$= 2 - (P(A) + P(B))$

$= 2 - 0.8$ [using Eq. (i)]

$= 1.2$

Example 5 If A and B are any two events having $P(A \cup B) = \frac{1}{2}$ and $P(\overline{A}) = \frac{2}{3}$, then find $P(\overline{A} \cap B)$. **[NCERT Exemplar]**

Sol. We have, $P(A \cup B) = \frac{1}{2}$ and $P(\overline{A}) = \frac{2}{3}$

$\Rightarrow \quad 1 - P(A) = \frac{2}{3}$

$\Rightarrow \quad P(A) = 1 - \frac{2}{3} = \frac{1}{3}$

Also, we have

$P(A \cup B) = P(A) + P(B) - P(A \cap B)$

$\Rightarrow \quad \frac{1}{2} = \frac{1}{3} + P(B \cap \overline{A})$

$\Rightarrow \quad P(B \cap \overline{A}) = \frac{1}{2} - \frac{1}{3} = \frac{1}{6}$

$[\because P(\overline{A} \cap B) = P(B \cap \overline{A}) = P(B) - P(A \cap B)]$

Example 6 Events E and F are such that P(not E or not F) = 0.25. State whether E and F are mutually exclusive. **[NCERT]**

Sol. We have, $P(\overline{E} \cup \overline{F}) = 0.25$

$\Rightarrow \quad P(\overline{E \cap F}) = 0.25 \quad [\because \overline{E \cap F} = \overline{E} \cup \overline{F}]$

$\Rightarrow \quad 1 - P(E \cap F) = 0.25$

$\Rightarrow \quad P(E \cap F) = 1 - 0.25 = 0.75 \neq 0$

$\therefore$ E and F are not mutually exclusive events.

Example 7 If A, B and C are three mutually exclusive and exhaustive events of an experiment such that $3P(A) = 2P(B) = P(C)$, then find $P(A)$.

Sol. Let $3P(A) = 2P(B) = P(C) = p$.

Then, $P(A) = \frac{p}{3}$, $P(B) = \frac{p}{2}$ and $P(C) = p$

Since, A, B and C are mutually exclusive and exhaustive.

$\therefore \quad P(A) + P(B) + P(C) = 1$

$\Rightarrow \quad \frac{p}{3} + \frac{p}{2} + p = 1 \Rightarrow \frac{2p + 3p + 6p}{6} = 1$

$\Rightarrow \quad 11p = 6 \Rightarrow p = \frac{6}{11}$

Hence, $P(A) = \frac{p}{3} = \frac{6}{11} \times \frac{1}{3} = \frac{2}{11}$

Example 8 Check whether the following probabilities $P(A)$ and $P(B)$ are consistently defined

(i) $P(A) = 0.5$, $P(B) = 0.7$, $P(A \cap B) = 0.6$

(ii) $P(A) = 0.5$, $P(B) = 0.4$, $P(A \cup B) = 0.8$ **[NCERT]**

Sol. (i) We have, $P(A) = 0.5$, $P(B) = 0.7$ and $P(A \cap B) = 0.6$.

We know that,

$A \cap B \subseteq A$ and $A \cap B \subseteq B$

$\therefore P(A \cap B) \leq P(A)$ and $P(A \cap B) \leq P(B)$

But for the given probabilities $P(A \cap B) \not\leq P(B)$.

So given probabilities are not consistently defined.

(ii) We have, $P(A) = 0.5$, $P(B) = 0.4$ and $P(A \cup B) = 0.8$

Clearly, $P(A \cap B) = P(A) + P(B) - P(A \cup B)$

$= 0.5 + 0.4 - 0.8 = 01$

Here, $P(A \cap B) \leq P(A)$

and $P(A \cap B) \leq P(B)$.

So, given probabilities are consistently defined.

Example 9 Let A, B and C be three events such that $P(A) = 0.3$, $P(B) = 0.4$, $P(C) = 0.8$, $P(A \cap B) = 0.08$, $P(B \cap C) = 0.28$ and $P(A \cap B \cap C) = 0.09$. If $P(A \cup B \cup C) \geq 0.8$, then show that $P(A \cap C)$ lies in the interval $[0.23, 0.43]$.

Sol. We have, $P(A \cup B \cup C) \geq 0.8$

$\therefore \quad 0.8 \leq P(A \cup B \cup C) \leq 1$

[$\because$ probability of occurrence of an event is always less than or equal to 1]

$\Rightarrow \quad 0.8 \leq P(A) + P(B) + P(C) - P(A \cap B) - P(B \cap C) - P(A \cap C) + P(A \cap B \cap C) \leq 1$

$\Rightarrow \quad 0.8 \leq 0.3 + 0.4 + 0.8 - 0.08 - 0.28 - P(A \cap C) + 0.09 \leq 1$

$\Rightarrow \quad 0.8 \leq 1.23 - P(A \cap C) \leq 1$

$\Rightarrow \quad 0.8 - 1.23 \leq -P(A \cap C) \leq 1 - 1.23$

[subtracting 1.23 from each terms]

$\Rightarrow \quad -0.43 \leq -P(A \cap C) \leq -0.23$

$\Rightarrow \quad 0.23 \leq P(A \cap C) \leq 0.43$

[multiplying each term by (-1)]

Hence, $P(A \cap C)$ lies in the interval [0.23, 0.43].

Hence proved.

|TYPE II|

Problems Based on Coins

Example 10 Find the probability of getting atmost two tails or atleast two heads in a toss of three coins.

Sol. Clearly, the sample space

$S = \{HHH, HHT, HTH, THH, TTH, THT, HTT, TTT\}$

Let A be the event of getting atmost two tails and B be the event of getting atleast two heads.

Then, $A=\{HHH, HHT, HTH, THH, TTH, THT, HTT\}$
and $B=\{HHT, HTH, THH, HHH\}$

$P(A)=\frac{7}{8}$; $P(B)=\frac{4}{8}$ and $P(A\cap B)=\frac{4}{8}$

Now, required probability $= P(A\cup B)$

$$=P(A)+P(B)-P(A\cap B)=\frac{7}{8}+\frac{4}{8}-\frac{4}{8}=\frac{7}{8}$$

|TYPE III|

Problems Based on Dice

Example 11 A coin is tossed and a die is thrown. Find the probability that the outcome will be a head or a number greater than 4.

Sol. When a coin and a die are thrown, then sample space is
$S=\{H1, H2, H3, H4, H5, H6, T1, T2, T3, T4, T5, T6\}$

$\therefore \quad n(S)=12$

Let A : Event of getting a head.

$\Rightarrow \quad A=\{H1, H2, H3, H4, H5, H6\}$

$\therefore \quad n(A)=6$

Then, $P(A)=\frac{n(A)}{n(S)}=\frac{6}{12}$

B : Event of getting a number greater than 4.

$\Rightarrow \quad B=\{H5, H6, T5, T6\}$

$\therefore \quad n(B)=4$

Then, $P(B)=\frac{n(B)}{n(S)}=\frac{4}{12}$

Also, $A\cap B$ = event of getting a head and a number greater than 4 $=\{H5, H6\}$

$\therefore \quad n(A\cap B)=2$

Then, $P(A\cap B)=\frac{2}{12}$

Now, required probability,

$$P(A\cup B)=P(A)+P(B)-P(A\cap B)$$
$$=\frac{6}{12}+\frac{4}{12}-\frac{2}{12}=\frac{8}{12}=\frac{2}{3}$$

Example 12 Two dice are tossed together. Find the probability of getting a doublet or a total of 6.

Sol. Let S be the sample space. Then, $n(S)=36$.

Also, let A be the event of getting a doublet and B be the event of getting a total of 6.

Then, $A=\{(1,1),(2,2),(3,3),(4,4),(5,5),(6,6)\}$
and $B=\{(1,5),(5,1),(2,4),(4,2),(3,3)\}$

$\Rightarrow \quad n(A)=6, n(B)=5$ and $n(A\cap B)=1$

Then, $P(A)=\frac{6}{36}$; $P(B)=\frac{5}{36}$ and $P(A\cap B)=\frac{1}{36}$

Now, required probability $= P(A\cup B)$

$$=P(A)+P(B)-P(A\cap B)=\frac{6}{36}+\frac{5}{36}-\frac{1}{36}=\frac{10}{36}=\frac{5}{18}$$

Example 13 Find the probability of getting an even number on the first die or a total of 8 in a single throw of two dice.

Sol. Let S be the sample space. Then, $n(S)=36$.

Also, let A be the event of getting an even number on the first die and B be the event of getting a total of 8.

$$\text{Then, } A=\left\{\begin{array}{l}(2,1),(2,2),(2,3),(2,4),(2,5),(2,6),\\(4,1),(4,2),(4,3),(4,4),(4,5),(4,6),\\(6,1),(6,2),(6,3),(6,4),(6,5),(6,6)\end{array}\right\}$$

$B=\{(2,6),(6,2),(4,4),(3,5),(5,3)\}$

and $A\cap B=\{(2,6),(6,2),(4,4)\}$

$\Rightarrow \quad n(A)=18, n(B)=5$

and $n(A\cap B)=3$

$\therefore \quad P(A)=\frac{18}{36}$

$P(B)=\frac{5}{36}$

and $P(A\cap B)=\frac{3}{36}$

Now, required probability $= P(A\cup B)$

$$=P(A)+P(B)-P(A\cap B)$$
$$=\frac{18}{36}+\frac{5}{36}-\frac{3}{36}=\frac{20}{36}=\frac{5}{9}$$

Example 14 Two dice are thrown together. What is the probability that sum of the numbers on the two faces is neither divisible by 3 nor by 4?

Sol. Let S be the sample space. Then, $n(S)=36$.

Also, let A be the event that sum of numbers of two faces is divisible by 3 and B be the event that sum of numbers is divisible by 4, i.e. A be the event of getting the sum 3, 6, 9, 12 and B be the event of getting the sum 4, 8, 12.

Then, $A=\{(1,2),(2,1),(2,4),(4,2),(3,3),(1,5),(5,1),(4,5),(5,4),(6,3),(3,6),(6,6)\}$

$B=\{(2,2),(1,3),(3,1),(2,6),(6,2),(5,3),(3,5),(4,4),(6,6)\}$

and $A\cap B=\{(6,6)\}$

$\Rightarrow \quad n(A)=12; n(B)=9$ and $n(A\cap B)=1$

$\therefore \quad P(A)=\frac{12}{36}, P(B)=\frac{9}{36}$ and $P(A\cap B)=\frac{1}{36}$

Now, $P(A\cup B)=P(A)+P(B)-P(A\cap B)$

$$=\frac{12}{36}+\frac{9}{36}-\frac{1}{36}=\frac{20}{36}=\frac{5}{9}$$

Now, required probability $= P(\overline{A}\cap\overline{B})$

$$=P(\overline{A\cup B})$$
$$=1-P(A\cup B)$$
$$=1-\frac{5}{9}=\frac{4}{9}$$

|TYPE IV|

Problem Based on Playing Cards

Example 15 A card is drawn at random from a well-shuffled pack of 52 cards. Find the probability that it is either a king or a spade.

Sol. Let S be the sample space associated with the given random experiment, then $n(S) = 52$.

Also, let A be the event that the drawn card is a king and B be the event that the drawn card is a spade.

Then, $n(A) = 4; n(B) = 13$ and $n(A \cap B) = 1$

[$\because A \cap B$ denotes the event that the drawn card is a king of spade.]

$$\therefore \quad P(A) = \frac{4}{52}; P(B) = \frac{13}{52} \text{ and } P(A \cap B) = \frac{1}{52}$$

Now, required probability $= P(A \cup B)$

$$= P(A) + P(B) - P(A \cap B)$$

$$= \frac{4}{52} + \frac{13}{52} - \frac{1}{52} = \frac{16}{52} = \frac{4}{13}$$

Example 16 A card is drawn from a deck of 52 cards. Find the probability of getting a king or a heart or a red card. **[NCERT Exemplar]**

Sol. Let S be the sample space. Then, $n(S) = 52$

Let A, B and C be the events of getting a king, a heart and a red card, respectively.

Then, $n(A) = 4, n(B) = 13, n(C) = 26$

$$\therefore \quad P(A) = \frac{n(A)}{n(S)} = \frac{4}{52} = \frac{1}{13}$$

$$P(B) = \frac{n(B)}{n(S)} = \frac{13}{52} = \frac{1}{4}$$

$$P(C) = \frac{n(C)}{n(S)} = \frac{26}{52} = \frac{1}{2}$$

Clearly, $(A \cap B)$ is the event of getting a king among hearts.
$(B \cap C)$ is the event of getting a heart among red cards.
$(A \cap C)$ is the event of getting a king among red cards.
$(A \cap B \cap C)$ is the event of getting a king among heart and the red cards.

$$\Rightarrow \quad n(A \cap B) = 1, n(B \cap C) = 13, n(A \cap C) = 2$$

and $n(A \cap B \cap C) = 1$

$$\therefore \quad P(A \cap B) = \frac{n(A \cap B)}{n(S)} = \frac{1}{52},$$

$$P(B \cap C) = \frac{n(B \cap C)}{n(S)} = \frac{13}{52} = \frac{1}{4}$$

$$P(A \cap C) = \frac{n(A \cap C)}{n(S)} = \frac{2}{52} = \frac{1}{26}$$

$$\text{and} \quad P(A \cap B \cap C) = \frac{n(A \cap B \cap C)}{n(S)} = \frac{1}{52}$$

Now, P (getting a king or heart or red card)

$$= P(A \text{ or } B \text{ or } C) = P(A \cup B \cup C)$$

$$= P(A) + P(B) + P(C) - P(A \cap B) - P(A \cap C) - P(B \cap C) + P(A \cap B \cap C)$$

$$= \frac{1}{13} + \frac{1}{4} + \frac{1}{2} - \frac{1}{52} - \frac{1}{26} - \frac{1}{4} + \frac{1}{52} = \frac{28}{52} = \frac{7}{13}$$

Example 17 Four cards are drawn at a time from a pack of 52 playing cards. Find the probability of getting all the four cards of the same unit.

Sol. Let S be the sample space associated with the given random experiment. Then, $n(S) = {}^{52}C_4$.

Now, let A be the event of getting all spade cards,
B be the event getting all club cards,
C be the event getting all heart cards and
D be the event of getting all diamond cards.

Then, $n(A) = {}^{13}C_4; n(B) = {}^{13}C_4; n(C) = {}^{13}C_4$

and $n(D) = {}^{13}C_4$

$$\Rightarrow \quad P(A) = \frac{{}^{13}C_4}{{}^{52}C_4}; P(B) = \frac{{}^{13}C_4}{{}^{52}C_4}; P(C) = \frac{{}^{13}C_4}{{}^{52}C_4}$$

$$\text{and} \quad P(D) = \frac{{}^{13}C_4}{{}^{52}C_4}.$$

Now, required probability $= P(A \cup B \cup C \cup D)$

[$\because$ A, B, C and D are mutually exclusive events]

$$= 4 \times \frac{{}^{13}C_4}{{}^{52}C_4} = \frac{44}{4165}$$

Example 18 Find the probability that, when a hand of 7 cards is drawn from a well-shuffled deck of 52 cards, it contains

(i) all kings. (ii) 3 kings. (iii) at least 3 kings. **[NCERT]**

Sol. Let S be the sample space associated with the given random experiment. Then, $n(S) = {}^{52}C_7$

(i) Let A be the event that it contains all kings.

Then, $n(A) = {}^4C_4 \times {}^{48}C_3$

$$\Rightarrow \quad P(A) = \frac{{}^{48}C_3}{{}^{52}C_7} = \frac{\dfrac{48 \times 47 \times 46}{3 \times 2 \times 1}}{\dfrac{52 \times 51 \times 50 \times 49 \times 48 \times 47 \times 46}{7 \times 6 \times 5 \times 4 \times 3 \times 2 \times 1}}$$

$$= \frac{1}{7735} \qquad [\because {}^4C_4 = 1]$$

(ii) Let B be the event that it contains 3 kings.

Then, $n(B) = {}^4C_3 \times {}^{48}C_4$

$$\Rightarrow P(B) = \frac{4 \times {}^{48}C_4}{{}^{52}C_7} = \frac{\dfrac{48 \times 47 \times 46 \times 45}{4 \times 3 \times 2 \times 1}}{\dfrac{52 \times 51 \times 50 \times 49 \times 48 \times 47 \times 46}{7 \times 6 \times 5 \times 4 \times 3 \times 2 \times 1}}$$

$$= \frac{9}{1547} \qquad [\because {}^4C_3 = {}^4C_1 = 4]$$

(iii) Let C be the event that it contains at least 3 kings.
Then, $P(C) = P(A \cup B)$
$= P(A) + P(B)$ [$\because A$ and B are mutually exclusive]
$= \frac{1}{7735} + \frac{9}{1547} = \frac{46}{7735}$

Example 19 A card is drawn from an ordinary pack and a gambler bets that it is spade or an ace. What are the odds against the winning his bet?

Sol. Let S be the sample space associated with the given random experiment. Then, $n(S)=52$.
Now, let A be the event of getting a spade and B be the event of getting an ace. $A \cap B$ denote the event of getting an ace of spade.

Then, $n(A) = 13$ and $n(B) = 4$
$n(A \cap B) = 1$

Thus, we have $P(A) = \frac{13}{52}$; $P(B) = \frac{4}{52}$ and $P(A \cap B) = \frac{1}{52}$

Now, P (winning the bet) $= P$ (getting a spade or an ace)
$= P(A \cup B) = P(A) + P(B) - P(A \cap B)$
$= \frac{13}{52} + \frac{4}{52} - \frac{1}{52} = \frac{16}{52} = \frac{4}{13}$

$\Rightarrow P$ (not winning the bet) $= 1 - \frac{4}{13} = \frac{9}{13}$

Hence, odds against the winning his bet
$$= \frac{P(\text{not winning the bet})}{P(\text{winning the bet})} = \frac{9/13}{4/13} = \frac{9}{4} = 9:4$$

|TYPE V|
Problems Based on Selecting Numbers

Example 20 An integer is chosen at random from first two hundred natural numbers. What is the probability that the integer chosen is divisible by 6 or 8?

Sol. Let S be the sample space associated with the given random experiment.
Then, $n(S)=200$
Now, let A be the event that the chosen number is divisible by 6 and B be the event that the chosen number is divisible by 8.

Then, $A = \{6, 12, 18, \ldots, 198\}$
and $B = \{8, 16, 24, \ldots, 192\}$
$\Rightarrow n(A) = 33$ and $n(B) = 24$
[to find $n(A)$ and $n(B)$, divide 198 by 6 and 192 by 8]

Also, $A \cap B = \{24, 48, 72, \ldots, 192\}$
[$\because A \cap B$ denotes the event that the chosen number is divisible by LCM (6,8)]

Now, $P(A) = \frac{33}{200}$; $P(B) = \frac{24}{200}$ and $P(A \cap B) = \frac{8}{200}$

$\therefore P$ (chosen integer is divisible by 6 or 8)
$= P(A \cup B) = P(A) + P(B) - P(A \cap B)$
$= \frac{33}{200} + \frac{24}{200} - \frac{8}{200} = \frac{49}{200}$

Example 21 Tickets numbered 1 to 20 are mixed up together and then a ticket is drawn at random. What is the probability that the ticket has a number which is a multiple of 3 or 7?

Sol. Let S be the sample space associated with the given random experiment. Then, $n(S)=20$.
Now, let A be the event of getting a ticket bearing number which is a multiple of 3 and B be the event of getting a ticket bearing a number which is a multiple of 7.

Then, $A = \{3, 6, 9, 12, 15, 18\}$ and $B = \{7, 14\}$
$\Rightarrow n(A) = 6$, $n(B) = 2$ and $n(A \cap B) = 0$
$\therefore P(A) = \frac{6}{20}$ and $P(B) = \frac{2}{20}$

Now, required probability $= P(A \cup B) = P(A) + P(B)$
[$\because A$ and B are mutually exclusive events]
$= \frac{6}{20} + \frac{2}{20} = \frac{8}{20} = \frac{2}{5}$

Example 22 Three numbers are chosen from 1 to 20. Find the probability that they are not consecutive. **[NCERT Exemplar]**

Sol. Let S be the sample space associated with the given experiment. Then,
$$n(S) = {}^{20}C_3 = 1140$$
Now, let E be the event that the chosen numbers are consecutive.
Then, $\bar{E}$ be the event that the chosen numbers are not consecutive.

Thus, $E = \{(1,2,3), (2,3,4), (3,4,5), \ldots, (18,19,20)\}$
$\Rightarrow n(E) = 18 \Rightarrow P(E) = \frac{18}{1140} = \frac{3}{190}$

Now, $P(\bar{E}) = 1 - P(E) = 1 - \frac{3}{190} = \frac{187}{190}$

Hence, the required probability is $\frac{187}{190}$.

Example 23 A number is chosen at random from the numbers ranging from 1 to 50. What is the probability that the number chosen is a multiple of 2 or 3 or 10?

Sol. Let S be the sample space associated with the given random experiment. Then, $n(S)=50$.
Now, let A be the event that the chosen number is a multiple of 2, B be the event that the chosen number is a multiple of 3 and C be the event that the chosen number is a multiple of 10.

Then, $A = \{2, 4, 6, \ldots, 48, 50\}$, $B = \{3, 6, 9 \ldots, 48\}$
and $C = \{10, 20, \ldots, 50\}$
$A \cap B$ denotes the event that chosen number is multiple of $6 = \text{LCM}(2, 3)$
$B \cap C$ denotes the event that chosen number is a multiple of $30 = \text{LCM}(3, 10)$
$A \cap C$ denotes the event that chosen number is a multiple of $10 = \text{LCM}(2, 10)$
and $A \cap B \cap C$ denotes the event that chosen number is a multiple of $30 = \text{LCM}(2, 3, 10)$

$\therefore \quad A \cap B = \{6, 12, \ldots, 48\}, n(B) = 16,$
$B \cap C = \{30\}, A \cap C = \{10, 20 \ldots, 50\}$
and $\quad A \cap B \cap C = \{30\}$
$\Rightarrow n(A) = 25; n(B) = 16; n(C) = 5; n(A \cap B) = 8,$
$n(B \cap C) = 1, n(A \cap C) = 5$ and $n(A \cap B \cap C) = 1$

$$\therefore \quad P(A) = \frac{n(A)}{n(S)} = \frac{25}{50}$$

$$P(B) = \frac{n(B)}{n(S)} = \frac{16}{50}$$

$$P(C) = \frac{n(C)}{n(S)} = \frac{5}{50}$$

$$P(A \cap B) = \frac{n(A \cap B)}{n(S)} = \frac{8}{50},$$

$$P(B \cap C) = \frac{n(B \cap C)}{n(S)} = \frac{1}{50},$$

$$P(A \cap C) = \frac{n(A \cap C)}{n(S)} = \frac{5}{50}$$

and $P(A \cap B \cap C) = \dfrac{n(A \cap B \cap C)}{n(S)} = \dfrac{1}{50}$

Now, required probability $= P(A \cup B \cup C)$
$= P(A) + P(B) + P(C) - P(A \cap B)$
$- P(B \cap C) - P(A \cap C) + P(A \cap B \cap C)$

$$= \frac{25}{50} + \frac{16}{50} + \frac{5}{50} - \frac{8}{50} - \frac{1}{50} - \frac{5}{50} + \frac{1}{50} = \frac{25+8}{50} = \frac{33}{50}$$

Hence, the required probability is $\dfrac{33}{50}$.

|TYPE VII|

Problems Based on Selecting Things from a Bag/Box Containing Different Types of Things

Example 24 A basket contains 20 apples and 10 oranges out of which 5 apples and 3 oranges are defective. If a person takes out 2 at random, then what is the probability that either both are apples or both are good?

Sol. Let S be the sample space associated with the given experiment. Then, $n(S) = {}^{30}C_2$.

[$\because$ total number of fruits $= 20 + 10 = 30$]

Now, let A be the event that both are apples and B be the event that both are good fruits. $A \cap B$ denotes the event that both are good apples.

Then, $n(A) = {}^{20}C_2$ and $n(B) = {}^{22}C_2$.

[$\because$ number of good fruits $= 15 + 7 = 22$]

$n(A \cap B) = {}^{15}C_2$ [$\because$ number of good apples $= 15$]

$$\therefore \quad P(A) = \frac{{}^{20}C_2}{{}^{30}C_2}, P(B) = \frac{{}^{22}C_2}{{}^{30}C_2} \text{ and } P(A \cap B) = \frac{{}^{15}C_2}{{}^{30}C_2}$$

Now, required probability,

$$P(A \cup B) = P(A) + P(B) - P(A \cap B)$$

$$= \frac{{}^{20}C_2}{{}^{30}C_2} + \frac{{}^{22}C_2}{{}^{30}C_2} - \frac{{}^{15}C_2}{{}^{30}C_2}$$

$$= \frac{190 + 231 - 105}{{}^{30}C_2} = \frac{316}{435}$$

Example 25 A box contains 6 red, 4 white and 5 black balls. A person draws 4 balls from the box at random. Find the probability that among the balls drawn, there is atleast one ball of each colour.

Sol. Given, total number of red balls = 6
Total number of white balls = 4
and total number of black balls = 5
$\therefore$ Total number of balls = 15

Let S be the sample space associated with the random experiment. Then, $n(S) = {}^{15}C_4 = 1365$

Here, atleast one ball of each colour can be drawn in one of the following ways :

(i) 1 red, 1 white and 2 black balls
(ii) 2 red, 1 white and 1 black balls
(iii) 1 red, 2 white and 1 black balls

Now, let A be the event of getting 1 red, 1 white and 2 black balls; B be the event of getting 2 red, 1 white and 1 black balls and C be the event of getting 1 red, 2 white and 1 black balls.

Then, $\quad n(A) = {}^6C_1 \times {}^4C_1 \times {}^5C_2 = 6 \times 4 \times 10 = 240$
$n(B) = {}^6C_2 \times {}^4C_1 \times {}^5C_1 = 15 \times 4 \times 5 = 300$
and $\quad n(C) = {}^6C_1 \times {}^4C_2 \times {}^5C_1 = 6 \times 6 \times 5 = 180$

$$\therefore \quad P(A) = \frac{240}{1365}; P(B) = \frac{300}{1365} \text{ and } P(C) = \frac{180}{1365}$$

Now, required probability

$= P(A \cup B \cup C)$
$= P(A) + P(B) + P(C)$

[$\because$ A, B and C are mutually exclusive events]

$$= \frac{240}{1365} + \frac{300}{1365} + \frac{180}{1365}$$

$$= \frac{720}{1365} = \frac{48}{91}$$

|TYPE VIII|
Miscelleneous Problems

Example 26 Probability that Ram passed in Mathematics is $\frac{2}{3}$ and the probability that he passed in English is $\frac{4}{9}$. If the probability of passing in both subjects is $\frac{1}{4}$, then what is the probability that Ram will pass in atleast one of these subjects?

Sol. Let M be the event that Ram passed in Mathematics, E be the event that Ram passed in English and $M \cap E$ be the event that Ram passed in both subjects

Now, P (Ram pass in atleast one subject) $= P(M \cup E)$

$$= P(M) + P(E) - P(M \cap E) = \frac{2}{3} + \frac{4}{9} - \frac{1}{4} = \frac{24 + 16 - 9}{36} = \frac{31}{36}$$

Example 27 In class XI of a school, 40% of the students study Mathematics and 30% study Biology. 10% of the class study both Mathematics and Biology. If a student is selected at random from the class, then find the probability that he will be studying Mathematics or Biology. **[NCERT]**

Sol. Let M be the event that selected student studies Mathematics and B be the event that selected student studies Biology. Then, $P(M) = 40\% = 0.4$

$P(B) = 30\% = 0.3$ and $P(M \cap B) = 10\% = 0.1$

Now, P (he will study Mathematics or Biology)

$= P(M \cup B) = P(M) + P(B) - P(M \cap B) = 0.4 + 0.3 - 0.1 = 0.6$

Hence, the required probability is 0.6.

Example 28 Probability that a truck stopped at a roadblock will have faulty brakes or badly worn tires are 0.23 and 0.24, respectively. Also, the probability is 0.38 that a truck stopped at the roadblock will have faulty brakes and/or badly working tires. What is the probability that a truck stopped at this roadblock will have faulty breaks as well as badly worn tires?

Sol. Let B be the event that a truck stopped at the roadblock will have faulty breaks and T be the event that it will have badly worn tires. Then, we have

$$P(B) = 0.23,\ P(T) = 0.24 \text{ and } P(B \cup T) = 0.38$$

Now, consider, $P(B \cup T) = P(B) + P(T) - P(B \cap T)$

$\Rightarrow \quad 0.38 = 0.23 + 0.24 - P(B \cap T)$

$\Rightarrow \quad P(B \cap T) = 0.23 + 0.24 - 0.38 = 0.09$

Hence, the probability that a truck stopped at the roadblock will have faulty breaks as well as badly worn tires is 0.09.

Example 29 The probability that a student will pass the final examination in both English and Hindi is 0.5 and the probability of passing neither is 0.1. If the probability of passing the English examination is 0.75, then what is the probability of passing the Hindi examination? **[NCERT]**

Sol. Let events H and E denote the students that, passing Hindi and English examination, respectively.

Given, probability of passing both examinations

$$= P(H \cap E) = 0.5$$

and probability of passing neither examinations

$$= P(H' \cap E') = P(H \cup E)' = 0.1$$

Then, $P(H \cup E) = 1 - P(H \cup E)' = 1 - 0.1 = 0.9$

Also, it is given, that probability of passing English examination,

$$P(E) = 0.75$$

Now, consider $P(H \cup E) = P(H) + P(E) - P(H \cap E)$

$\Rightarrow \quad 0.9 = P(H) + 0.75 - 0.5$

$\Rightarrow \quad 0.9 = P(H) + 0.25$

$\Rightarrow \quad P(H) = 0.9 - 0.25 = 0.65$

Hence, probability of passing Hindi examination is 0.65.

Example 30 In an interview for a job in call center, 5 boys and 3 girls appeared. If 4 persons are to be selected at random from this group, then find the probability that 3 boys and 1 girl or 1 boy and 3 girls are selected.

Sol. Given, number of boys = 5 and number of girls = 3

Let A : Selection of 3 boys and 1 girl

B : Selection of 1 boy and 3 girls

$$\therefore \quad P(A) = \frac{{}^5C_3 \times {}^3C_1}{{}^8C_4} = \frac{\frac{5 \times 4}{2 \times 1} \times 3}{\frac{8 \times 7 \times 6 \times 5}{4 \times 3 \times 2 \times 1}} = \frac{30}{70} = \frac{3}{7}$$

and
$$P(B) = \frac{{}^5C_1 \times {}^3C_3}{{}^8C_4} = \frac{5 \times 1}{\frac{8 \times 7 \times 6 \times 5}{4 \times 3 \times 2 \times 1}} = \frac{5}{70} = \frac{1}{14}$$

Hence, the required probability,

$$P(A \cup B) = P(A) + P(B) - P(A \cap B)$$
$$= P(A) + P(B) - 0 = \frac{3}{7} + \frac{1}{14} = \frac{7}{14} = \frac{1}{2}$$

Example 31 The probability that a student will receive A, B, C or D grade are 0.40, 0.35, 0.15 and 0.10, respectively. Find the probability that a student will receive

(i) B or C grade (ii) atleast C grade.

Sol. Let E_1, E_2, E_3 and E_4 denote respectively the events that a student will receive A, B, C and D grades. Then, we have

$$P(E_1) = 0.40,\ P(E_2) = 0.35,\ P(E_3) = 0.15 \text{ and } P(E_4) = 0.10$$

(i) P(getting B or C grade) $= P(E_2 \cup E_3) = P(E_2) + P(E_3)$
$= 0.35 + 0.15 = 0.5$

[$\because E_2$ and E_3 are mutually exclusive events]

(ii) P(getting atleast C grade) $= P$(getting C or D grade)
$= P(E_3 \cup E_4) = P(E_3) + P(E_4) = 0.15 + 0.10 = 0.25$

Example 32 Four candidates A, B, C, D have applied for the assignment to coach a school cricket team. If A is twice as likely to be selected as B, and B and C are given about the same chance of being selected, while C is twice as likely to be selected as D, what are the probabilities that

(i) C will be selected? (ii) A will not be selected?

Sol. Let E_1, E_2, E_3 and E_4 denote respectively the events that the person A, B, C and D is selected.

Also, let the probability of D selected be p, i.e. $P(E_4) = p$.

Then, according to given condition we have

$P(E_1) = 2P(E_2)$ and $P(E_2) = P(E_3) = 2P(E_4)$

$\Rightarrow \quad P(E_1) = 2 \times 2p,\ P(E_2) = 2p$ and $P(E_3) = 2p$

$\Rightarrow \quad P(E_1) = 4p,\ P(E_2) = 2p$ and $P(E_3) = 2p$

Since, E_1, E_2, E_3 and E_4 are mutually exclusive and exhaustive events, therefore we have

$$P(E_1) + P(E_2) + P(E_3) + P(E_4) = 1$$

$$\Rightarrow \quad 4p + 2p + 2p + p = 1$$

$$\Rightarrow \quad 9p = 1 \Rightarrow p = \frac{1}{9}$$

(i) $P(C \text{ selected}) = P(E_3) = 2p = \frac{2}{9}$

(ii) Now, $P(A \text{ selected}) = P(E_1) = 4p = \frac{4}{9}$

$\therefore \quad P(A \text{ is not selected}) = 1 - P(A \text{ selected})$

$$= 1 - \frac{4}{9} = \frac{5}{9}$$

Example 33 A box contains 100 bolts and 50 nuts. It is given that 50% bolts and 50% nuts are rusted. Two objects are selected from the box at random. Find the probability that either both are bolts or both are rusted.

Sol. Given, total number of bolts = 100

and total number of nuts = 50

Now, total number of rusted objects

$= 50\%$ of $100 + 50\%$ of 50

$$= \frac{1}{2} \times 100 + \frac{1}{2} \times 50 = 50 + 25 = 75$$

Clearly, total number of objects = 100 + 50 = 150

Let S be the sample space associated with the given experiment. Then, $n(S) = {}^{150}C_2$

Now, let A be the event that both objects are bolts and B be the event that both objects are rusted.

Then, $n(A) = {}^{100}C_2$ and $n(B) = {}^{75}C_2$

$A \cap B$ denotes the event that both objects are rusted bolts.

$\therefore \quad n(A \cap B) = {}^{50}C_2$

[$\because$ number of rusted bolts = 50% of 100 = 50]

Now, $P(A) = \frac{n(A)}{n(S)} = \frac{{}^{100}C_2}{{}^{150}C_2};\ P(B) = \frac{n(B)}{n(S)} = \frac{{}^{75}C_2}{{}^{150}C_2}$

and $P(A \cap B) = \frac{n(A \cap B)}{n(S)} = \frac{{}^{50}C_2}{{}^{150}C_2}$

$\therefore$ Required probability $= P(A \cup B)$

$$= P(A) + P(B) - P(A \cap B) = \frac{{}^{100}C_2 + {}^{75}C_2 - {}^{50}C_2}{{}^{150}C_2}$$

$$= \frac{4950 + 2775 - 1225}{11175} = \frac{6500}{11175} = 0.58$$

Hence, the required probability is 0.58.

Example 34 Out of 100 students, two sections of 40 and 60 are formed. If you and your friend are among the 100 students, then what is the probability that

(i) you both enter the same section?

(ii) you both enter the different sections?

Sol. Let there be two sections A and B of 40 and 60 students, respectively.

(i) Let both students enter the section A.

So, 38 students are to selected out of 98, since two particular students are already in section A.

$\therefore$ Number of ways of selecting 38 students out of 98 = ${}^{98}C_{38}$ ways

Number of exhaustive cases of selecting 40 students out of 100 = ${}^{100}C_{40}$ ways

$\therefore$ P (both students enter section A)

$$= \frac{{}^{98}C_{38}}{{}^{100}C_{40}} = \frac{98!}{38!\,60!} \div \frac{100!}{40!\,60!}$$

$$= \frac{98!}{38!\,60!} \times \frac{40!\,60!}{100!} = \frac{40 \times 39}{100 \times 99} = \frac{26}{165}$$

If both students enter the section B. Then, the number of ways of selecting 58 students out of 98 = ${}^{98}C_{58}$ ways.

Total number of ways of selecting 60 students out of 100 = ${}^{100}C_{60}$ ways.

$\therefore$ Probability that two students enter section B

$$= \frac{{}^{98}C_{58}}{{}^{100}C_{60}} = \frac{98!}{58!\,40!} \div \frac{100!}{60!\,40!} \quad \left[\because {}^nC_r = \frac{n!}{r!(n-r)!}\right]$$

$$= \frac{98!}{58!\,40!} \times \frac{60!\,40!}{100!} = \frac{60 \times 59}{100 \times 99} = \frac{59}{165}$$

$\therefore$ P (that two particular students enter either section A or B)

$$= \frac{26}{165} + \frac{59}{165} = \frac{85}{165} = \frac{17}{33}$$

(ii) The probability that they enter in different sections

$= 1 - P$ (that two particular students enter either section A or B)

$$= 1 - \frac{17}{33} = \frac{16}{33}$$

Topic Practice 3

Very Short Answer Type Questions

(2 Marks)

1 A and B are two events, such that $P(A) = 0.42$, $P(B) = 0.48$ and $P(A \text{ and } B) = 0.16$. Determine

(i) $P(\text{not } A)$ (ii) $P(\text{not } B)$ (iii) $P(A \text{ or } B)$ [NCERT]

2 If E and F are events such that $P(E) = \frac{1}{4}, P(F) = \frac{1}{2}$ and $P(E \text{ and } F) = \frac{1}{8}$, then find

(i) $P(E \text{ or } F)$ (ii) P (not E and not F)

3 If A and B are mutually exclusive events, such that $P(A) = 0.28$ and $P(B) = 0.38$, then find

(i) $P(A \cup B)$ (ii) $P(A \cap B)$
(iii) $P(A \cap B')$ (iv) $P(A' \cap B')$

4 If E_1, E_2 and E_3 are three mutually exclusive and exhaustive events of an experiment such that $2P(E_1) = 3\,P(E_2) = P(E_3)$, then find $P(E_1)$.

5 Check whether the following probabilities $P(A) = 0.3$, $P(B) = 0.65$ and $P(A \cup B) = 7$ are consistently defined.

6 The probabilities of happening of two events A and B are 0.25 and 0.50, respectively. If the probablity of happening of A and B together is 0.14, then find the probability that neither A nor B occurs.

7 The probability of an event A occurring is 0.5 and that of B is 0.3. If A and B are mutually exclusive events, then find the probability that neither A nor B occurs.

8 A and B are mutually exclusive events of an experiment. If $P(\text{not } A) = 0.65$, $P(A \cup B) = 0.65$ and $P(B) = p$, then find the value of p.

9 In an entrance test that is graded on the basis of two examinations, the probability of a randomly chosen student passing the first examination is 0.8 and the probability of passing the second examination is 0.7. The probability of passing atleast one of them is 0.95. What is the probability of passing both? [NCERT]

10 The probability that atleast one of the events A and B occurs is 0.7. If A and B occurs simultaneously with probability 0.35, then find $P(\overline{A}) + P(\overline{B})$.

11 Events E_1 and E_2 are such that $P(\text{not } E_1 \text{ or not } E_2) = 0.35$. State whether E_1 and E_2 are mutually exclusive.

12 In any school examination, probability that Mohan passed in Chemistry is $\frac{1}{3}$ and the probability that he passed in Physics is $\frac{2}{5}$. If the probability of passing in both subjects is $\frac{1}{6}$, then what is the probability that Mohan will pass in atleast one of these subjects?

13 If A, B are events associated with a random experiment and $P(A \cup B) = P(A \cap B)$, then show that $P(A) = P(B)$.

14 In a given race, the odds in favour of four horses A, B, C and D are $1:3, 1:4, 1:5$ and $1:6$, respectively. Assuming that a dead heat is impossible, find the chance that one of them wins the race.

Short Answer Type Questions

(4 Marks)

15 The probabilities of three events shown in the Venn diagram is shown below

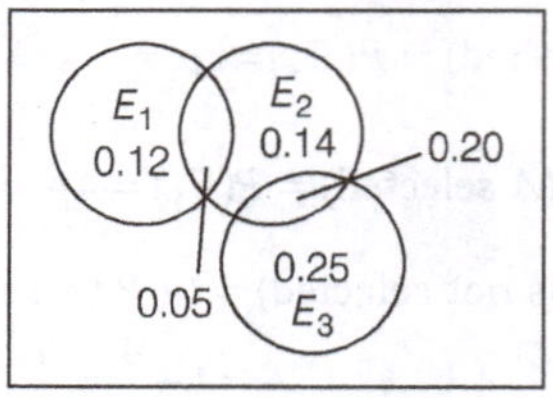

Determine

(i) $P(E_2)$ (ii) $P(E_2 \cap \overline{E}_3)$
(iii) $P(E_1 \cup E_2)$ (iv) $P(E_1 \cap \overline{E}_2)$

16. Let A, B and C are three events, such that $P(A) = 0.4$, $P(B) = 0.42$, $P(C) = 0.7$, $P(A \cap B) = 0.2$, $P(A \cap C) = 0.32$ and $P(A \cap B \cap C) = 0.07$. If $P(A \cup B \cup C) \geq 0.7$, then show that $P(B \cap C)$ lies in the interval [0.07, 0.37].

17 Find the probability of getting atmost two heads or atleast two tails in a toss of three coins.

18 The probability that a person will get an electric contract is $\frac{2}{5}$ and the probability that he will not get plumbing contract is $\frac{4}{7}$. If the probability of getting atleast one contract is $\frac{2}{3}$, then what is the probability that he will get both?

19 In a large metropolitan area, the probabilities are 0.87, 0.36, 0.30 that a family (randomly chosen for a sample survey) owns a colour television set, a black and white television set, or both kinds of sets. What is the probability that a family owns either anyone or both kinds of sets? **[NCERT Exemplar]**

20 Two unbiased dice are thrown. Find the probability that neither a doublet nor a total of 10 will appear.

21 Two dice are thrown together. What is the probability that sum of the numbers on the two faces is divisible by 3 or 4?

22 If $\frac{5}{14}$ is the probability of occurrence of an event, find

(i) the odds in favour of its occurrence.
(ii) the odds against its occurrence.

23 In a drawing competition, the odds in favour of competitors A, B, C and D are 1:2, 1:3, 1:4 and 1:5, respectively. Find the probability that one of them wins the competition.

24 From a well-shuffled pack of 52 cards, a card is drawn at random. Find the probability that it is either a heart or a queen.

25 One number is chosen from numbers 1 to 200. Find the probability that it is divisible by 4 or 6.

26 A coin is tossed and a die is thrown. Find the probability that the outcomes will be a tail or a number greater than 3.

27 Find the probability of getting an odd number of the first die or a total of 7 in a single throw of two dice.

28 Two dice are thrown together. What is the probability that sum of the numbers on the two faces is neither divisible by 3 nor by 5?

29 Two dice are thrown. Find

(i) odds in favour of getting the sum 5.
(ii) the odd against getting the sum 6.

30 If a person visits his dentist, suppose the probability that he will have his teeth cleaned is 0.48, the probability that he will have a cavity filled is 0.25, the probability that he will have a tooth extracted is 0.20, the probability that he will have a teeth cleaned and a cavity filled is 0.09, the probability that he will have his teeth cleaned and a tooth extracted is 0.12, the probability that he will have a cavity filled and a tooth extracted is 0.07, and the probability that he will have his teeth cleaned, a cavity filled, and a tooth extracted is 0.03. What is the probability that a person visiting his dentist will have atleast one of these things done to him? **[NCERT Exemplar]**

31 Find the probability that, when a hand of 5 cards is drawn from a well-shuffled deck of 52 cards, it contains

(i) all queens. (ii) 3 queens.
(iii) at least 3 queens.

32 Tickets numbered 1 to 30 are mixed up together and then a ticket is drawn at random. What is the probability that the ticket has a number which is a multiple of 2 or 5?

33 Let A, B and C be three events. If the probability of occuring exactly one event out of A and B is $1-x$, out of B and C is $1-2x$, out of C and A is $1-x$, and that of occuring three events simultaneously is x^2, then prove that the probability that at least one out of A, B, C will occur is greater than 1/2.

34 Suppose an integer from 1 through 1000 is chosen at random. Find the probability that the integer is a multiple of 2 or a multiple of 9. **[NCERT Exemplar]**

35 In a race, the odds in favour of horses P, Q, R and S are $1:2$, $1:3$, $1:4$ and $1:5$, respectively. Find the probability that one of them wins the race.

36. A basket contains 15 guava and 12 banana, out of which 5 guava and 7 banana are defective. If a person takes out 3 at random, then what is the probability that either all are guava or all are good?

37 A card is drawn from an ordinary pack and a gambler bets that it is a diamond or a jack. What are the odds favour in the winning his bet?

38. In higher secondary school, 30% students study Economics and 40% study Accounts. 20% of the class study both Economics and Accounts. If a student is selected at random from the class, then find the probability that he will be studying Economics or Accounts.

39. The probability that a student will receive A, B, C and D grades are 0.50, 0.40, 0.20 and 0.15, respectively. Find the probability that a student will receive

(i) B or C grade. (ii) atleast C grade.

40 A box contains 4 red, 5 white and 6 black balls. A person draws 4 balls from the box at random. Find the probability of selecting atleast one ball of each colour.

41 A die has two faces each with number '1', three faces each with number '2' and one faces with number '3'. If die is rolled once, determine

(i) $P(2)$ (ii) $P(1 \text{ or } 3)$ (iii) $P(\text{not } 3)$.

42 A bag contains 5 white and 7 black balls and a man draw 4 balls at random. What are the odds against these being all black?

Long Answer Type Questions

6 Marks

43 A number is chosen at random from the numbers ranging from 20 to 50. What is the probability that the number chosen is a multiple of 3 or 5 or 7?

44 A card is drawn from a well-shuffled deck of 52 cards. Find

(i) the odds in favour of getting a face card.
(ii) the odds against getting a spade.

45 A box contains 200 bolts and 70 nuts. It is given that 60% bolts and 40% nuts are rusted. Two objects are selected at random from the box. Find the probability that either both are bolts or both are rusted.

46 If A and B are mutually exclusive events, such that $P(A) = 0.35$ and $P(B) = 0.45$, then find

(i) $P(A')$ (ii) $P(B')$
(iii) $P(A \cup B)$ (iv) $P(A \cap B)$
(v) $P(A \cap B')$ (vi) $P(A' \cap B')$

[NCERT Exemplar]

Hints & Answers

1. (i) $P(\text{not } A) = 1 - P(A)$ **Ans.** 0.58

(ii) $P(\text{not } B) = 1 - P(B)$ **Ans.** 0.52

(iii) $P(A \text{ or } B) = P(A) + P(B) - P(A \cap B)$ **Ans.** 0.74

2. (i) $P(E \text{ or } F) = P(E) + P(F) - P(E \text{ and } F)$

(ii) $P(\bar{E} \cap \bar{F}) = P(\overline{E \cup F}) = 1 - P(E \cup F)$

Ans. (i) $\frac{5}{8}$ (ii) $\frac{3}{8}$

3. (i) $P(A \cup B) = P(A) + P(B)$

(ii) $P(A \cap B) = 0$

(iii) $P(A \cap B') = P(A) - P(A \cap B)$

(iv) $P(A' \cap B') = P(A \cup B)' = 1 - P(A \cup B)$

Ans. (i) 0.66 (ii) 0
(iii) 0.28 (iv) 0.34

4. Solve as Example 7 **Ans.** $\frac{3}{11}$

5. Solve as Example 8 part (ii). **Ans.** Yes.

6. $P(A \cup B) = 0.25 + 0.50 - 0.14 = 0.61$

$\therefore P(\text{neither } A \text{ nor } B) = P(\bar{A} \cap \bar{B})] = 1 - P(A \cup B)$

Ans. 0.39

7. $P(\bar{A} \cap \bar{B}) = P(\overline{A \cup B})$

$= 1 - P(A \cup B) = 1 - [P(A) + P(B)]$ **Ans.** 0.2

8. Use $P(A \cup B) = P(A) + P(B)$, for mutually exclusive events.

Ans. 0.3

9. Let E and F denote the events that, students passing the first and second examination, respectively.

Then, $P(E) = 0.8$, $P(F) = 0.7$ and $P(E \cup F) = 0.95$

Ans. 0.55

10. Solve as Example 4. **Ans.** 1.05

11. Solve as Example 6.

Ans. Not mutually exclusive events.

12. Solve as Example 26. **Ans.** $\frac{17}{30}$

13. We know that, $P(A) \le P(A \cup B)$ but

$P(A \cup B) = P(A \cap B) \Rightarrow P(A) \le P(A \cap B)$ ...(i)

Also, we know that $P(A \cap B) < P(A)$ ...(ii)

From Eqs. (i) and (ii), we get $P(A) = P(A \cap B)$.

Similarly, $P(B) = P(A \cap B)$.

Thus, $P(A) = P(A \cap B) = P(B)$.

Hence, $P(A) = P(B)$.

14. Let p_1, p_2, p_3, and p_4 be the probabilities of winning of the horses A, B, C, D respectively. Since a dead heat (in which all the four horses win i.e. they cover same distance in same time) is not possible, the events are mutually exclusive. Odds in favour of A are 1 : 3.

$\therefore p_1 = \frac{1}{1+3} = \frac{1}{4}$. Similarly, $p_2 = \frac{1}{5}$, $p_3 = \frac{1}{6}$, $p_4 = \frac{1}{7}$

If P is the chance that one of them wins, then we have, $P = p_1 + p_2 + p_3 + p_4$

$$= \frac{1}{4} + \frac{1}{5} + \frac{1}{6} + \frac{1}{7}$$

Ans. $\frac{319}{420}$.

15. Solve as Example 2.

Ans. (i) 0.39 (ii) 0.19
(iii) 0.31 (iv) 0.12

16. Solve as Example 9.

17. Solve as Example 10. **Ans.** $\frac{7}{8}$

18. Let A be the event that the person get an electric contract. and B be the event that the person get an plumbing contract.

Then, $P(A)=\frac{2}{5}, P(\bar{B})=\frac{4}{7}$ and $P(A\cup B)=\frac{2}{3}$ **Ans.** $\frac{32}{105}$

19. Let A be the event that the family owns a colour television set and B be the event that the family owns a black and white television. Then, we have

$P(A)=0.87, P(B)=0.36, P(A\cap B)=0.30$ **Ans.** 0.93

20. Solve as Example 12.

P (getting neither a doublet nor a total of 10)

$=1-P$ (getting a doublet or a total of 10) **Ans.** $\frac{7}{9}$

21. Solve as Example 14. **Ans.** $\frac{5}{9}$

22. Let $P(E)=\frac{5}{14}$. Then, $P(\bar{E})=1-P(E)=1-\frac{5}{14}=\frac{9}{14}$

Now,

(i) Odds in favour of occurrence of event $E=\frac{P(E)}{P(\bar{E})}$

Ans. 5 : 9

(ii) Odds against the occurrence of event $E=\frac{P(\bar{E})}{P(E)}$

Ans. $\frac{9}{5}$

23. Let E_1, E_2, E_3 and E_4 be the events that the competitors A, B, C and D respectively win the competition.

Then, $P(E_1)=\frac{1}{3}; P(E_2)=\frac{1}{4}; P(E_3)=\frac{1}{5}$ and $P(E_4)=\frac{1}{6}$

Now, required probability

$=P(E_1\cup E_2\cup E_3\cup E_4)=P(E_1)+P(E_2)+P(E_3)+P(E_4)$

(Since, events are mutually exclusive). **Ans.** $\frac{19}{20}$

24. Solve as Example 19. **Ans.** $\frac{4}{13}$

25. Solve as Example 20. **Ans.** $\frac{67}{200}$

26. Solve as Example 11. **Ans.** $\frac{3}{4}$

27. Solve as Example 13. **Ans.** $\frac{1}{4}$

28. Let A and B be the events that sum of numbers of two faces is divisible by 3 and 5 respective.

$\therefore A=\{(1, 2), (2, 1), (2, 4), (4, 2), (3, 3), (1, 5), (5, 1), (4, 5), (5, 4), (6, 3), (3, 6), (6, 6)\}$

and $B=\{(1, 4), (4, 1), (2, 3), (3, 2), (4, 6), (6, 4), (5, 5)\}$

and $A\cap B=\{\}$. Now, solve as Example 14. **Ans.** $\frac{17}{36}$

29. Let S be the sample space associated with the given random experiment. Then, $n(S)=36$.

(i) Let E be the event of getting the sum 5.

Then, $E=\{(1,4),(4,1),(2,3),(3,2)\}$

$\Rightarrow \quad n(E)=4$

$\therefore \quad P(E)=\frac{n(E)}{n(S)}=\frac{4}{36}=\frac{1}{9} \Rightarrow P(\bar{E})=1-\frac{1}{9}=\frac{8}{9}$

Hence, odds in favour of getting the sum 5 = $\frac{P(E)}{P(\bar{E})}$

Ans. 1:8

(ii) Let F be the event of getting the sum 6.

Then, $F=\{(1,5),(5,1),(2,4),(4,2),(3,3)\}\Rightarrow n(F)=5$

$\therefore \quad P(F)=\frac{n(F)}{n(S)}=\frac{5}{36} \Rightarrow P(\bar{F})=1-\frac{5}{36}=\frac{31}{36}$

Hence, odds against getting the sum 6 = $\frac{P(\bar{F})}{P(F)}$

Ans. 31:5

30. Let C be the event that the person will have his teeth cleaned. F be the event that the person will have a cavity filled. and E be the event that the person will have a tooth extracted.

Then, $P(C)=0.48, P(F)=0.25, P(E)=0.20$,

$P(C\cap F)=0.09, P(C\cap E)=0.12, P(E\cap F)=0.07$

and $P(C\cap F\cap E)=0.03$

Now, P (that a person will have at least one of these things)

$=P(C\cup F\cup E)=P(C)+P(F)+P(E)-P(C\cap F)-P(F\cap E)-P(C\cap E)+P(C\cap F\cap E)$

Ans. 0.68

31. Solve as Example 18.

Ans. (i) $\frac{1081}{812175}$ (ii) $\frac{47}{10829}$ (iii) $\frac{4606}{812175}$

32. Solve as Example 21. **Ans.** $\frac{3}{5}$

33. P (Exactly one event out of A and B occurs)

$=P[(A\cap B')\cup(A'\cap B)]$

$=P(A)+P(B)-2P(A\cap B)$

$\therefore \quad P(A)+P(B)-2P(A\cap B)=1-x$ ...(i)

Similarly, $P(B)+P(C)-2P(B\cap C)=1-2x$ ...(ii)

$P(C)+P(A)-2P(C\cap A)=1-x$ ...(iii)

and $P(A\cap B\cap C)=x^2$

Now, $P(A\cup B\cup C)=P(A)+P(B)+P(C)-P(A\cap B)-P(B\cap C)-P(C\cap A)+P(A\cap B\cap C)$

$=\frac{1}{2}[P(A)+P(B)-2P(A\cap B)+P(B)+P(C)-2P(B\cap C)+P(C)+P(A)-2P(C\cap A)]+P(A\cap B\cap C)$

$=\frac{1}{2}[1-x+1-2x+1-x]+x^2$ [using Eqs. (i), (ii) and (iii)]

$=\frac{3}{2}-2x+x^2$

$=\frac{1}{2}+(x-1)^2>\frac{1}{2}$

34. Solve as Example 23. **Ans.** 0.556

35. Let A, B, C and D be the events that the horses P, Q, R and S respectively win the race.

Then, $P(A)=\frac{1}{3}$, $P(B)=\frac{1}{4}$, $P(C)=\frac{1}{5}$ and $P(D)=\frac{1}{6}$.

Since, there can be only one winner.

$\therefore$ A, B, C and D are mutually exclusive event.

Required probability $= P(A \cup B \cup C \cup D)$ **Ans.** $\frac{19}{20}$

36. Solve as Example 24. **Ans.** 0.27

37. Solve as Example 19. **Ans.** $\frac{4}{9}$

38. Solve as Example 27. **Ans.** 0.5

39. Solve as Example 31. **Ans.** (i) 0.60 (ii) 0.35

40. Let A = event that 1 red, 1 white and 2 black balls are drawn,

B = event that 1 red, 2 white and 1 black balls are drawn and

C = event that 2 red, 1 white and 1 black balls are drawn.

Here A, B and C are mutually exclusive events.

Hence, required probability

$$= P(A \cup B \cup C) = P(A) + P(B) + P(C) \quad \textbf{Ans. } \frac{48}{91}$$

41. (i) Number of faces with number '2' = 3

$\therefore \quad P(2)=\frac{3}{6}$

(ii) $P(1 \text{ or } 3) = (P \text{ not } 2) = 1 - P(2)$

(iii) Number of faces with number '3' = 1

$\therefore \quad P(3)=\frac{1}{6}$

$\Rightarrow P(\text{not } 3) = 1 - P(3)$

Ans. (i) $\frac{1}{2}$ (ii) $\frac{1}{2}$ (iii) $\frac{5}{6}$

42. Given, total number of white balls = 5

and total number of black balls = 7

$\therefore$ Total number of balls = 12

Let S be the sample space associated with the given experiment. Then, $n(S)={}^{12}C_4$.

Now, let E be the event of getting black balls only.

Then, $n(E)={}^{7}C_4$

$$\Rightarrow \quad P(E)=\frac{{}^{7}C_4}{{}^{12}C_4}=\frac{7}{99}$$

$$\Rightarrow \quad P(\bar{E})=1-P(E)=\frac{92}{99}$$

Hence, odds against getting black balls

$$=\frac{P(\bar{E})}{P(E)}$$

Ans. 92 : 7

43. $A = \{21, 24, 27, 30, 33, 36, 39, 42, 45, 48\}$

$B = \{20, 25, 30, 35, 40, 45, 50\}$, $C = \{7, 14, 21, 28, 35, 42, 49\}$

Now, solve as Example 23. **Ans.** $\frac{19}{30}$

44. Let S be the sample space associated with the given random experiment.

Then, $n(S)=52$.

(i) Let E be the event of getting of face card.

Then, $n(E)=12$

$$\therefore \quad P(E)=\frac{n(E)}{n(S)}=\frac{3}{13}$$

$$\Rightarrow \quad P(\bar{E})=1-P(E)=\frac{10}{13}$$

Hence, odds in favour of getting a face card

$$=\frac{P(E)}{P(\bar{E})}$$

(ii) Let F be the event of getting a spade. Then $n(F)=13$.

$$\therefore \quad P(F)=\frac{n(F)}{n(S)}=\frac{13}{52}=\frac{1}{4}$$

$$\Rightarrow \quad P(\bar{F})=1-P(F)=1-\frac{1}{4}=\frac{3}{4}$$

Hence, odds against of getting a spade

$$=\frac{P(\bar{F})}{P(F)}=\frac{3/4}{1/4}=\frac{3}{1}=3:1$$

Ans. (i) 3 : 10 (ii) 3 : 1

45. Solve as Example 33.

Ans. $\frac{28363}{36315}$

46. We have, A and B are mutually exclusive events.

Also, it is given that $P(A) = 0.35$ and $P(B) = 0.45$

(i) $P(A') = 1 - P(A)$

(ii) $P(B') = 1 - P(B)$

(iii) $P(A \cup B) = P(A) + P(B)$

[$\because$ A and B are mutually exclusive]

(iv) $P(A \cap B)$

[$\because$ A and B are mutually exclusive, therefore $A \cap B = \phi$]

(v) $P(A \cap B') = P(A) - P(A \cap B)$

$= P(A) - 0$

[$\because$ A and B are mutual exclusive $\therefore P(A \cap B) = 0$]

(vi) $P(A' \cap B') = P((A \cup B)')$

$= 1 - P(A \cup B)$

Ans. (i) 0.65 (ii) 0.55 (iii) 0.8 (iv) 0 (v) 0.35 (vi) 0.2

Chapter Practice

Multiple Choice Type Questions

1 Mark

1. A coin is tossed twice. If the second throw results in a tail, a die is thrown. The number of possible events of this experiment are
(a) 12 (b) 14 (c) 16 (d) 18

2. Which of the following is true?
I. The empty set ϕ is called an impossible event.
II. The whole sample space S is called the sure event.
(a) Only I is true
(b) Only II is true
(c) Both I and II are true
(d) Both I and II are false

3. Consider the experiment of rolling a die. Let A be the event 'getting a prime number' and B be the event 'getting an odd number'.
Then, which of the following is true?
I. A or $B = A \cup B = \{1, 2, 3\}$
II. A and $B = A \cap B = \{3, 5\}$
III. A but not $B = A - B = \{2\}$
IV. Not $A = A' = \{1, 5, 6\}$
(a) Only I is true
(b) Only II is true
(c) II and III are true
(d) Only IV is true

4. A die is rolled. Let E be the event "die shows 4" and F be the event "die shows even number". Then, E and F are
(a) mutually exclusive
(b) exhaustive
(c) mutually exclusive and exhaustive
(d) None of the above

5. Seven persons are to be seated in a row. The probability that two particular persons sit next to each other, is
(a) $\frac{1}{3}$ (b) $\frac{1}{6}$
(c) $\frac{2}{7}$ (d) $\frac{1}{2}$

6. P and Q are two condidates seeking admission in NEET. The probability that P is selected is 0.5 and the probability that both P and Q are selected is at most 0.3. Then, the probability of Q being selected is
(a) ≤ 0.8 (b) ≥ 0.8
(c) $= 0.8$ (d) None of these

Assertion-Reason Type Questions

1 Mark

Directions (Q. Nos. 7-10) *In the questions given below are two statements labelled as Assertion (A) and Reason (R). In the context of the two statements, which one of the following is correct?*
(a) Both A and R are correct; R is the correct explanation of A
(b) Both A and R are correct; R is not the correct explanation of A
(c) A is correct; R is incorrect
(d) R is correct; A is incorrect

7. **Assertion (A)** If probability of winning a prize is $\frac{3}{4}$, then probability of not winning the prize is $\frac{1}{4}$.
Reason (R) For any event A, $P(A) + P(\bar{A}) = 1$.

8. **Assertion (A)** If A, B and C are three mutually exclusive and exhaustive events such that $P(B) = \frac{3}{2}P(A)$ and $P(C) = \frac{1}{2}P(B)$, then $P(A) = \frac{4}{13}$.
Reason (R) If A, B and C are mutually exclusive and exhaustive events, then $A \cup B \cup C = S$.

9. **Assertion (A)** The probability of an event can be $\frac{3}{2}$.
Reason (R) For any event A, $0 \le P(A) \le 1$.

10. **Assertion (A)** If the odds against the occurence of an event are 4 : 9, then the probability of occurence of the event is $\frac{9}{14}$.
Reason (R) If odds against of an event are $n : m$, then the probability of occurence of this event is $\frac{m}{m+n}$.

Very Short Answer Type Questions

(2 Marks)

11. In each of the following experiments, specify appropriate sample space.

(i) A boy has a 1 rupee coin, a 2 rupee coin and a 5 rupee coin in his pocket. He takes out two coins out of his pocket, one after the other.

(ii) A person is noting down the number of accidents along a busy highway during a year. [NCERT]

12. From a group of 3 boys and 3 girls, we select 2 children. What would be the sample space for this experiment?

13. A box contains 1 red and 3 identical white balls. Two balls are drawn at random in succession without replacement. Write the sample space for this experiment. [NCERT]

14. A bag contains one white and one red balls. A ball is drawn from the bag. If the ball drawn is white, it is replaced in the bag and again a ball is drawn. Otherwise, a die is tossed. Write the sample space for this experiment.

15. A pair of dice is rolled. If the outcome is a doublet, a coin is tossed. Determine the total number of elementary events associated to this experiment.

16. If the odds in favour of an event are 4 to 5, then find the probability that it will occur.

17. An experiment has four possible outcomes A, B, C and D, that are mutually exclusive. Explain why the following assignments of probabilities are not permissible?

(i) $P(A) = 0.12$, $P(B) = 0.63$, $P(C) = 0.45$, $P(D) = -0.20$

(ii) $P(A) = \frac{9}{120}$, $P(B) = \frac{45}{120}$, $P(C) = \frac{27}{120}$, $P(D) = \frac{46}{120}$

18. A bag contains 9 red and 12 white balls. One ball is drawn at random. Find the probability that the ball drawn is red.

19. In a lottery, there are 10 prizes and 25 blanks. Find the probability of getting a prize.

20. (i) How many two-digit positive integers are multiple of 3?

(ii) What is the probability that a randomly chosen two-digit positive integer is a multiple of 3?

21. What is the probability that a leap year selected at random will contain 53 Sunday?

22. Five marbles are drawn from a bag which contains 7 blue marbles and 4 black marbles. What is the probability that

(i) all will be blue?

(ii) 3 will be blue and 2 black?

23. If A and B are two events associated with a random experiment such that $P(A) = 0.3$, $P(B) = 0.2$ and $P(A \cap B) = 0.1$, then find the value of $P(A \cap \overline{B})$.

Short Answer Type Questions

(4 Marks)

24. There are four events E_1, E_2, E_3 and E_4 one of which must and only one can happen. The odds are $2:5$ in favour of E_1, $3:4$ in favour of E_2 and $1:3$ in favour at E_3. Then find the odds against E_4.

25. A bag contains 6 discs of which 4 are red, 3 are blue and 2 are yellow. The discs are similar in shape and size. A disc is drawn at random from the bag. Calculate the probability that it will be

(i) red (ii) yellow

(iii) blue (iv) not blue

(v) either red or blue. [NCERT]

26. One card is drawn from a well-shuffled deck of 52 cards. Calculate the probability that the card will be

(i) a diamond (ii) an ace

(iii) a black card (iv) not a diamond

(v) not an ace (vi) not a black card

(vii) a red card. [NCERT Exemplar]

27. Two students Anil and Ashima appeared in an examination. The probability that Anil will qualify the examination is 0.05 and that Ashima will qualify the examination is 0.10. The probability that both will qualify the examination is 0.02. Find the probability that [NCERT]

(i) both Anil and Ashima will not qualify the examination.

(ii) atleast one of them will not qualify the examination.

(iii) only one of them will qualify the examination.

28. In a single throw of three dice, find the probability of getting a total of 17 or 18.

Long Answer Type Questions

(6 Marks)

29. Let there be a word 'REGULATIONS'. If the letters of the given word be arranged at random, what is the chance that there will be exactly 4 letters between R and E?

30. What is the probability that a non-leap year selected at random will contain 53 Tuesday or 53 Wednesday?

31. A team of medical students doing their internship have to assist during surgeries at a city hospital. The probabilities of surgeries rated as very complex, routine, simple rated as very complex, complex, complex, routine, simple or very simple respectively 0.15, 0.20, 0.31, 0.26 and 0.08.

Find the probabilities that a particular surgery will be rated

(i) complex or very complex.

(ii) neither very complex nor very simple.

(iii) routine or complex.

(iv) routine or simple. **[NCERT Exemplar]**

32. When two dice are thrown, calculate the probability of throwing a total of (i) 7 or 11 (ii) a doublet or a total of 6.

Case-Based Type Questions

(6 Marks)

33. Two friends are playing with two dice. They throw them simultaneously and note the results on both dice.

On the basis of above information, answer the following questions.

(i) Find the probability (an even number as the sum).

(ii) Find the probability (a total of at least 10).

(iii) Find the probability (same number on both dice).

(iv) Find the probability (a multiple of 3 as the sum).

(v) Find the probability (the sum as a prime number).

34. Sonia ask Priya, "Please draw four cards from this pack of 52 playing cards." Priya draw four cards and shows to Sonia.

On the basis of above information, answer the following questions.

(i) Find the probability (all face cards).

(ii) Find the probability (one card of each suit).

(iii) Find the probability (all are of same colour).

(iv) Find the probability (all the four cards of the same number).

(v) Find the probability (two red and two black cards).

Hints & Answers

1. (b) **2.** (c) **3.** (c) **4.** (d) **5.** (c)

6. (a) **7.** (a) **8.** (a) **9.** (d) **10.** (d)

11. (i) $\{QH, QR, HQ, HR, RH, RQ\}$, where Q denotes a 1 rupee coin, H denotes a 2 rupee coin and R denotes a 5 rupee coin.

(ii) $\{0, 1, 2, 3 \ldots\ldots\}$

12. Let B_1, B_2 and B_3 denotes the 3 boys and G_1, G_2 and G_3 denotes the 3 girls.

Ans. $\{(B_1, B_2), (B_1, B_3)\ (B_1, G_1), (B_1, G_2), (B_1, G_3), (B_2, B_3), (B_2, G_1), (B_2, G_2), (B_2, G_3), (B_3, G_1), (B_3, G_2), (B_3, G_3), (G_1, G_2), (G_2, G_3), (G_1, G_3)\}$

13. $\{RW, WR, WW\}$

14. $\{(W, W), (W, R), (R, 1), (R, 2), (R, 3), (R, 4), (R, 5), (R, 6)\}$

15. 42 **16.** $\frac{4}{9}$

17. Probability of any event cannot be negative or cannot greater than unity.

Ans. (i) $P(D)$ is not possible (ii) $P(S) \neq 1$

18. $\frac{3}{7}$ **19.** $\frac{2}{7}$ **20.** (i) 30 (ii) $\frac{1}{3}$

21. $\frac{2}{7}$ **22.** (i) $\frac{1}{22}$ (ii) $\frac{5}{11}$

23. 0.2 **24.** 27 : 1

25. (i) $\frac{4}{9}$ (ii) $\frac{2}{9}$ (iii) $\frac{1}{3}$ (iv) $\frac{2}{3}$ (v) $\frac{7}{9}$

26. (i) $\frac{1}{4}$ (ii) $\frac{1}{13}$ (iii) $\frac{1}{2}$ (iv) $\frac{3}{4}$ (v) $\frac{12}{13}$ (vi) $\frac{1}{2}$ (vii) $\frac{1}{2}$

27. Let E and F denote the events that Anil and Ashima will qualify the examination,

$P(E) = 0.05$, $P(F) = 0.10$ and $P(E \cap F) = 0.02$

(i) The event both Anil and Ashima will not qualify of examination

$\therefore P(E' \cap F') = P(\overline{E \cup F}) = 1 - P(E \cup F)$

(ii) P (at least one of them will not qualify)

$= 1 - P$ (both of them will qualify)

(iii) P (only one of them will qualify)

$= P(E \cap F') \cup (E' \cap F)$

$= P(E) + P(F) - 2P(E \cap F)$

Ans. (i) 0.87 (ii) 0.98 (iii) 0.11

28. $\frac{1}{54}$ **29.** $\frac{6}{55}$ **30.** $\frac{2}{7}$

31. (i) 0.35 (ii) 0.77 (iii) 0.51 (iv) 0.57

32. $n(S) = 36$

Let A be the event of getting 7.

Then, $A = \{(1, 6), (6, 1), (2, 5), (5, 2), (3, 4), (4, 3)\}$

$n(A) = 6$

$\therefore P(A) = \frac{6}{36} = \frac{1}{6}$ and B be the event of getting 11.

Then, $B = \{(5, 6), (6, 5)\}$

$n(B) = 2$, $P(B) = \frac{2}{36} = \frac{1}{18}$

Ans. (i) $\frac{2}{9}$ (ii) $\frac{5}{18}$

33. (i) $\frac{1}{2}$ (ii) $\frac{1}{6}$ (iii) $\frac{1}{6}$ (iv) $\frac{1}{3}$ (v) $\frac{5}{12}$

34. (i) $\frac{99}{54145}$ (ii) $\frac{2197}{20825}$ (iii) $\frac{2({}^{26}C_4)}{{}^{52}C_4}$

(iv) $\frac{13}{270725}$ (v) $\frac{{}^{26}C_2 \times {}^{26}C_2}{{}^{52}C_4}$

CHAPTER

16

Conic Sections

In this chapter, we will study about some curves such as ellipse, parabola and hyperbola. These curves are known as **conic sections** or **conics**, because they can be obtained as intersections of a plane with a double napped right circular cone.

- Parabola
- Ellipse
- Hyperbola

Sections of a Cone

The sections of a cone are the curves obtained by intersecting a cone by a plane. The shape of section depends upon the position of the cutting plane.

Right Circular Cone

The locus of a line passing through a fixed point say A and making a constant angle θ with a fixed line AB passing through the fixed point A is called **right circular cone.**

Here, the fixed point A is called **vertex**, the fixed line AB is called the **axis** and the constant angle θ is called the **semi-vertical angle** of the cone. Also, the moving line is called the **generator** of the cone.

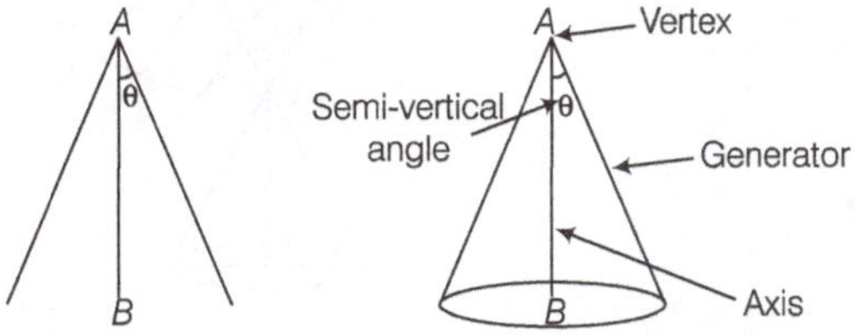

Double Napped Right Circular Cone

Let AB be a fixed line and l be another line intersecting AB at V and making an angle θ with AB. Suppose line l rotates around the line AB, such that it always makes an angle θ with AB. Then, the surface generated is a **double napped right circular hollow cone.** This surface is usually referred as cone only and extending indefinitely in both directions.

Here, the fixed line AB is called **axis**, fixed point V is called **vertex** of the cone and the constant angle θ is called the **semi-vertical angle** of the cone. The rotated line l in all its positions is called a **generator** of the cone. The two parts of the generated surface separated by vertex V are called **nappes.**

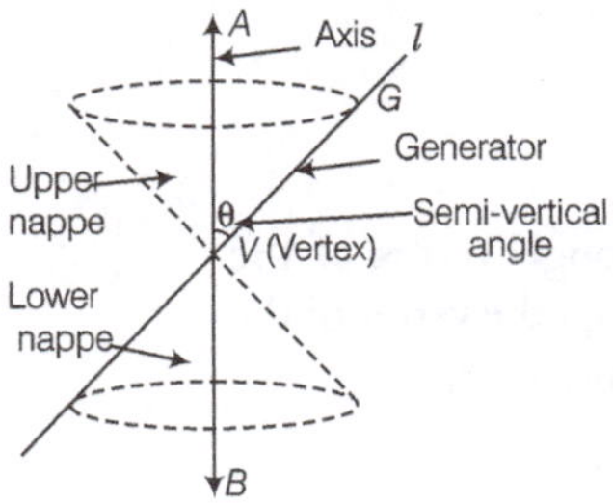

Section of a Doubled Napped Right Circular Cone by a Plane

Consider a double napped right circular cone, having semi-vertical angle θ. Let α be the angle between the plane and the axis of cone. Then, we will get different sections (curves) as follows

Case I **When the plane passes through vertex of the cone**
If the plane passes through the vertex of the cone, then it cuts both nappes. According to the value of α, we get the following sections

(i) When $\theta < \alpha \leq 90°$, then the section is a **point**.

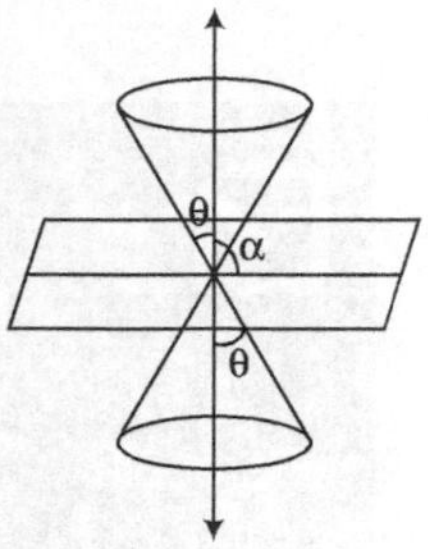

(ii) When $\theta = \alpha$, then the plane contains the generator of cone and the section is a **straight line.**

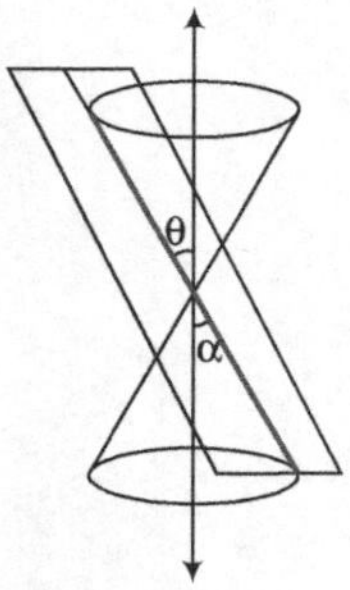

(iii) When $0 \leq \alpha < \theta$, then section is a pair of intersecting lines.

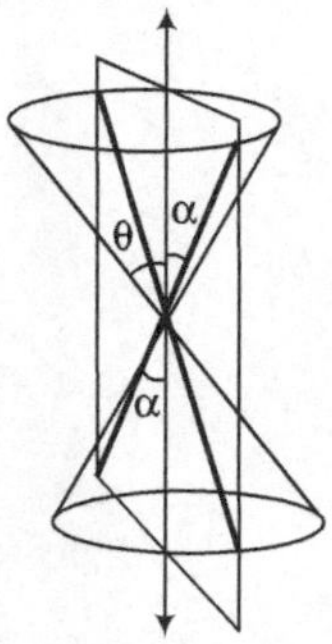

Case II **When the plane does not pass through vertex of the cone** If the plane does not pass through the vertex of the cone, then according to different values of α, we get the following sections

(i) When $\alpha = 90°$, then cutting plane section is a **circle.**

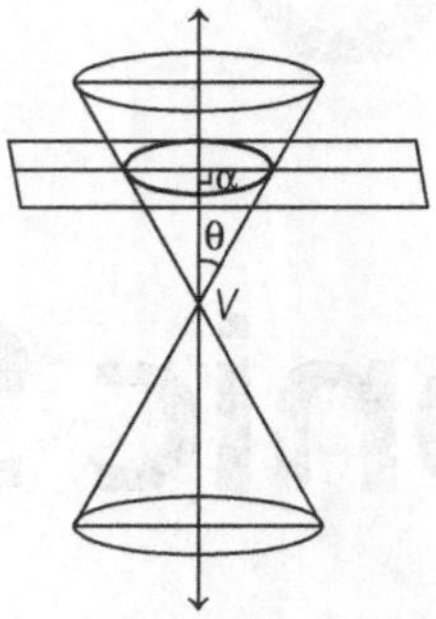

(ii) When $\theta < \alpha < 90°$, then cutting plane section is an **ellipse.**

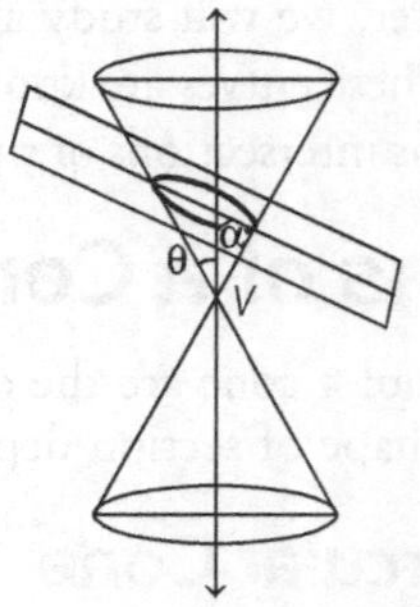

(iii) When $\alpha = \theta$ i.e. plane is parallel to a generator, then cutting plane is **parabola.**

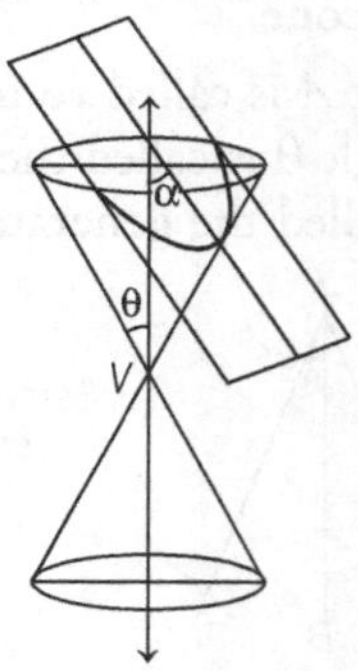

(iv) When $0 \leq \alpha < \theta$, then the plane intersects both the nappes and section is a **hyperbola.**

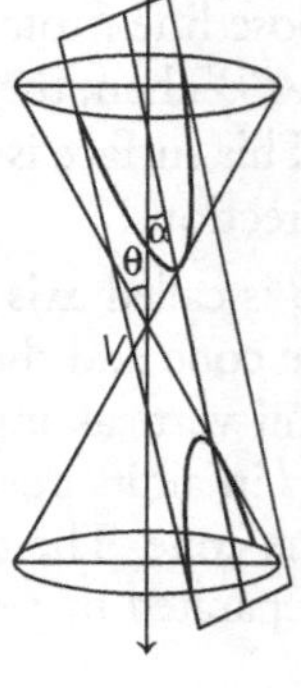

Note (i) When the plane intersect the vertex of the cone, then the resulting conic is called a **degenerate conic**. Its include a point a line and two intersecting lines.

(ii) When the plane does not intersect the vertex, then the resulting conic is called a **non-degenerate conic**.

Conic Sections as a Locus of a Point

A conic is the locus of a point which moves in a plane in such a way that the ratio of its distance from a fixed point to its distance from a fixed straight line is a constant. Then,

(i) the fixed point is called **focus** and is denoted by S.

(ii) the fixed straight line LM is called **directrix**.

(iii) the constant ratio is called **eccentricity** and is denoted by e.

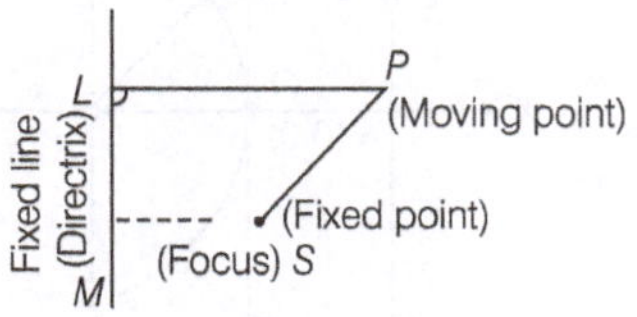

In the given figure, $\frac{PS}{PL} = e = \text{constant}$

On the basis of the value of e, we get the following cases

(a) **Parabola** If eccentricity, $e = 1$, then the conic is called parabola.

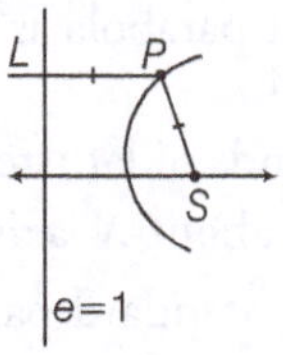

(b) **Ellipse** If eccentricity, $e < 1$, then the conic is called ellipse.

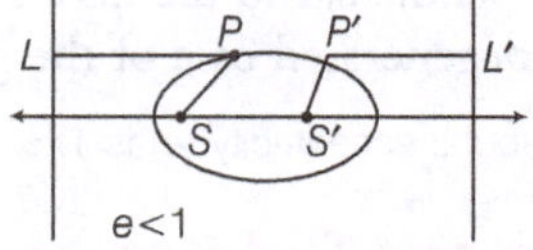

(c) **Hyperbola** If eccentricity, $e > 1$, then the conic is called hyperbola.

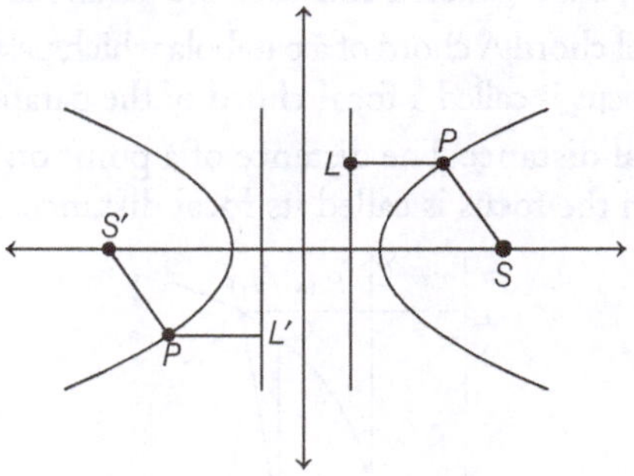

(iv) The straight line passing through the focus and perpendicular to the directrix, is called the **axis** of the conic.

(v) The point of intersection of the conic and its axis, is called **vertex** of the conic.

(vi) A chord perpendicular to the axis of the conic and passing through its focus is called **latusrectum**.

(vii) The point which bisects every chord of the conic passing through it, is called the **centre** of the conic.

TOPIC 01 Parabola

A parabola is the locus of a point which moves in a plane such that its distance from a fixed point is always equal to its distance from a fixed straight line in the same plane.

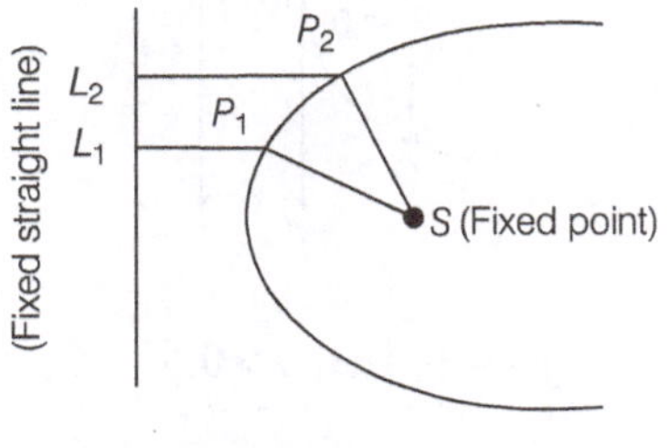

From the figure, $P_1S = P_1L_1$ and $P_2S = P_2L_2$

Here, the fixed line is called the **directrix** and the fixed point is called **focus** of the parabola. A line through the focus and perpendicular to the directix is called the **axis** of the parabola and point of intersection of parabola with the axis is called the **vertex** of the parabola.

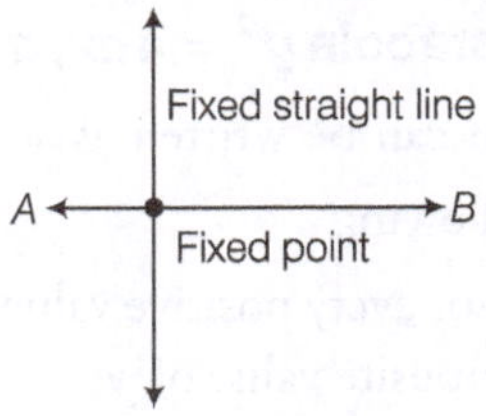

If the fixed point lies on the fixed line, then the set of points in the plane, which are equidistant from the fixed point and the fixed line is the straight line through the fixed point and perpendicular to the fixed line. The straight line AB is called a **degenerated case of the parabola.**

Note In case of parabola, eccentricity (e) is 1.

Important Terms Related to a Parabola

(i) **Chord** A line segment joining any two points on the parabola is called a **chord** of the parabola.

(ii) **Focal chord** A chord of a parabola which passes through its focus is called a **focal chord** of the parabola.

(iii) **Focal distance** The distance of a point on a parabola from the focus is called its **focal distance.**

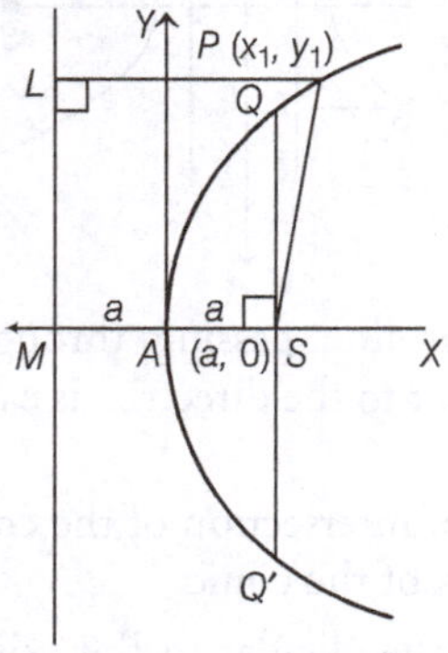

(iv) **Latusrectum** A chord passing through the focus and perpendicular to the axis of the parabola is called the latusrectum.

In the above figure, QQ' is the latusrectum.

Standard Forms of a Parabola

If a parabola have vertex at origin and the axis of symmetry along either X-axis or Y-axis, then the parabola is said to be in the standard form.

Right Handed Parabola

If parabola opens towards right side, then it is called right handed parabola. The equation of right handed parabola is of the form $\boxed{y^2 = 4ax, a > 0}$

Sketching the Parabola $y^2 = 4ax, a > 0$

The given equation can be written as $y = \pm 2\sqrt{ax}$

We observe the following

(i) **Symmetry** For every positive value of x, there are two equal and opposite value of y.

(ii) **Region** For every negative value of x, the value of y is imaginary. Therefore, no part of the curve lies to the left of Y-axis.

(iii) **Intersection with the axes** The curve meets the coordinate axes only at the origin.

(iv) **Space occupied** As $x \to \infty$, $y \to \infty$. Therefore, the curve extends to infinity to the right of Y-axis.

With the help of the above facts and by joining some convenient points on the parabola the general shape of the parabola $y^2 = 4ax$ can be obtained shown below.

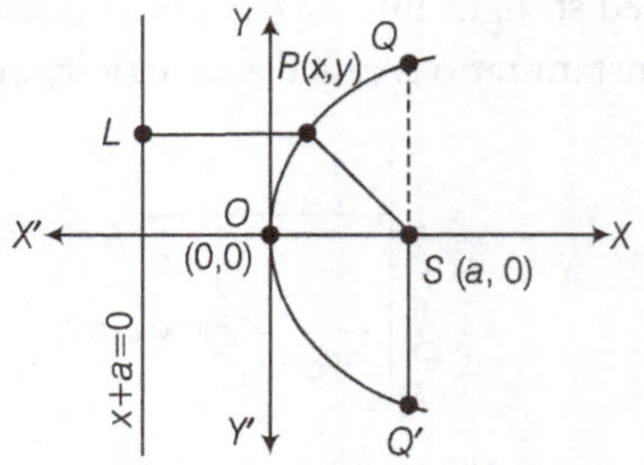

Some important terms related to this parabola are

(i) Vertex is O (0, 0). (ii) Axis is the line $y = 0$.

(iii) Focus is S $(a, 0)$.

(iv) Directrix is the line $x + a = 0$.

(v) Latusrectum of a parabola is the line segment QQ' and its length $= 4a$.

(vi) Coordinates of ends of latusrectum are $(a, \pm 2a)$

(vii) It is symmetrical about X-axis.

There are another three standard parabola which are given below.

Left Handed Parabola

If parabola opens towards left side, then it is called left handed parabola. The equation of the left handed parabola is of the form

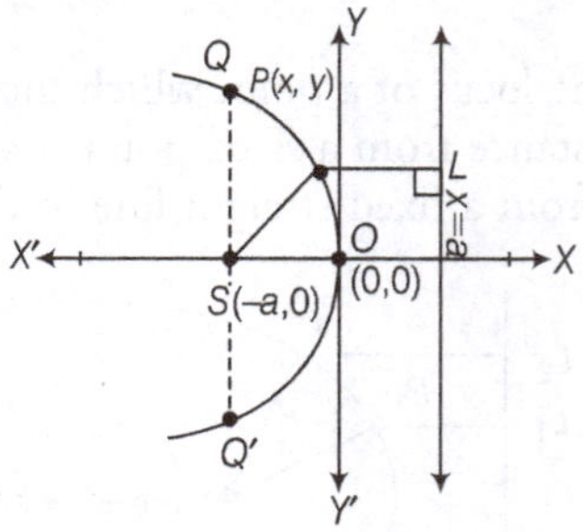

$\boxed{y^2 = -4ax, a > 0}$

Some important terms related to this parabola are

(i) Vertex is $O\,(0, 0)$.
(ii) Axis is the line $y = 0$.
(iii) Focus is $S(-a, 0)$.
(iv) Directrix is the line $x - a = 0$.
(v) Length of the latusrectum is $4a$.
(vi) Coordinates of ends of latusrectum are $(-a, \pm 2a)$
(vii) It is symmetrical about X-axis.

Upward Parabola

If parabola opens upward, then it is called upward parabola. The equation of the upward parabola is of the form

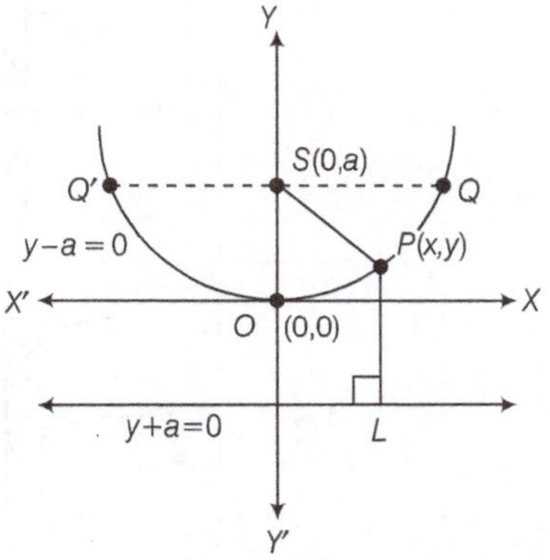

$$x^2 = 4ay,\ a > 0$$

Some important terms related to this parabola are

(i) Focus is $S(0, a)$.
(ii) Vertex is $O(0, 0)$.
(iii) Directrix is the line $y + a = 0$.
(iv) Axis is the line $x = 0$.
(v) Length of latusrectum is $4a$.
(vi) Coordinates of ends of latusrectum are $(\pm 2a, a)$
(vii) It is symmetrical about Y-axis.

Downward Parabola

If parabola opens downwards, it is called downward parabola. The equation of downward parabola is of the form

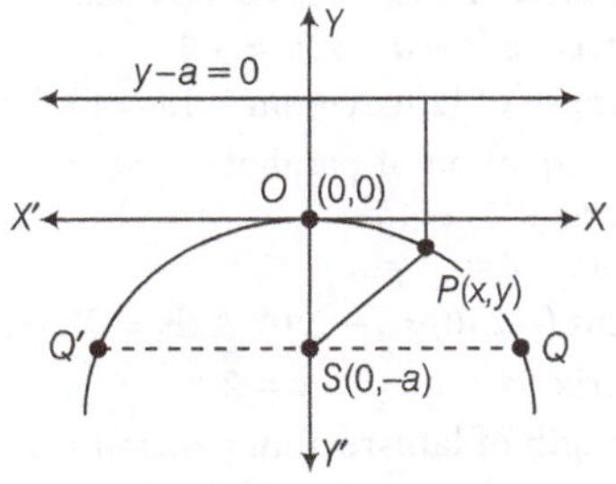

$$x^2 = -4ay,\ a > 0$$

Some important terms related to this parabola are

(i) Focus is $S(0, -a)$.
(ii) Vertex is $O(0, 0)$.
(iii) Directrix is the line $y - a = 0$.
(iv) Axis is the line $x = 0$.
(v) Length of latusrectum is $4a$.
(vi) Coordinates of ends of latusrectum are $(\pm 2a, (-a))$
(vii) It is symmetrical about Y-axis.

Observations from Standard Equation

We observe the following points from the four standard parabolas.

(i) Vertex of each parabola is at the origin $(0, 0)$.
(ii) Focus of each parabola lies on one of the coordinate axes and the directrix is parallel to the other coordinate axis. Thus, directrix is perpendicular to the line segment joining the vertex and the focus.
(iii) Each parabola is symmetrical about its axis.
(iv) (a) If the standard equation of a parabola contains y^2, then its axis is $y = 0$, i.e. the X-axis.
(b) If the standard equation of a parabola contains x^2, then its axis is $x = 0$, i.e. the Y-axis.
(v) If the axis of parabola is along the X-axis, then it is horizontal parabola and its equation is $y^2 = 4ax$ or $y^2 = -4ax$ $(a > 0)$.
(a) If the coefficient of x is positive, the parabola opens to the right, i.e. its concavity is in the direction of positive X-axis.

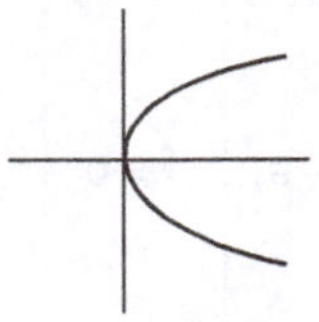

$y^2 = 4ax\ (a>0)$

(b) If the coefficient of x is negative, the parabola opens to the left, i.e. its concavity is in the negative direction of X-axis.

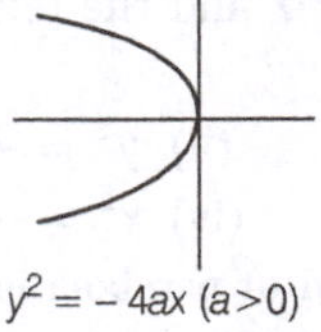

$y^2 = -4ax\ (a>0)$

(vi) If the axis of the parabola is along the Y-axis, then it is a vertical parabola. The equation of the parabola is $x^2 = 4ay$ or $x^2 = -4ay$ $(a > 0)$.

(a) If the coefficient of y is positive, then the parabola opens upwards, i.e. its concavity is in the positive direction of Y-axis.

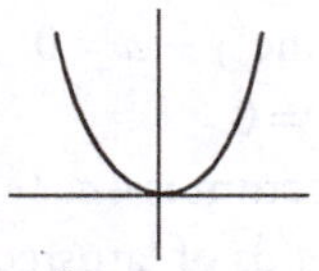

$x^2 = 4ay\ (a>0)$

(b) If the coefficient of y is negative, then the parabola opens downwards, i.e. its concavity is in the negative direction of Y-axis.

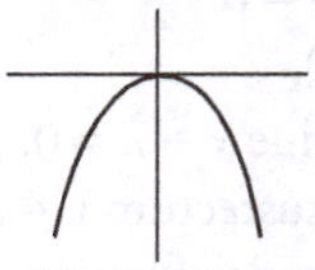

$x^2 = -4ay\ (a>0)$

Table for Different Types of Parabola

Parabola	Vertex	Focus	Axis	Equation of Directrix	Length of Latusrectum	Coordinates of ends of latusrectum	Eccentricity	Figure
$y^2 = 4ax$	(0, 0)	(a, 0)	y = 0	x + a = 0	4a	(a, ± 2a)	1	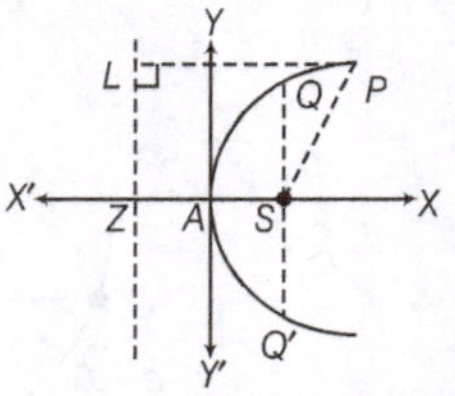
$y^2 = -4ax$	(0, 0)	(− a, 0)	y = 0	x − a = 0	4a	(− a, ± 2a)	1	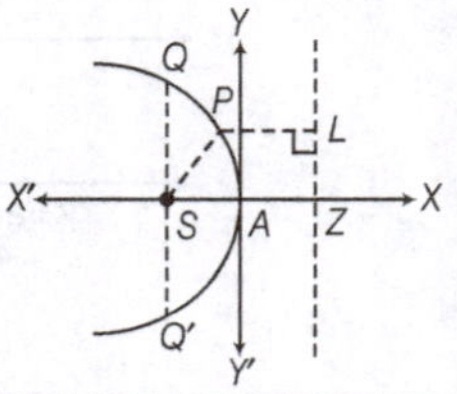
$x^2 = 4ay$	(0, 0)	(0, a)	x = 0	y + a = 0	4a	(± 2a, a)	1	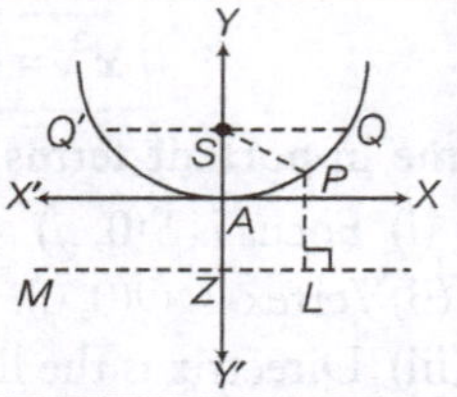
$x^2 = -4ay$	(0, 0)	(0, − a)	x = 0	y − a = 0	4a	(±2a, −a)	1	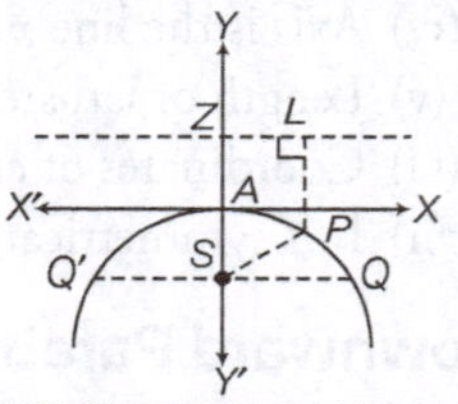

Example 1 In each of the following questions, find the coordinates of the focus, axis of the parabola, the equation of the directrix and the length of the latusrectum.

(i) $y^2 = 12x$ (ii) $y^2 = -8x$

(iii) $x^2 = 10y$ (iv) $x^2 = -9y$

Sol. (i) Given equation of parabola is $y^2 = 12x$ which is of the form, $y^2 = 4ax$.

Here, $4a = 12 \Rightarrow a = 3$

$\therefore$ Focus $(a, 0) = (3, 0)$; Axis $= X$-axis

Directrix, $x = -a \Rightarrow x = -3$

and length of latusrectum $= 4a = 4 \times 3 = 12$

(ii) Given, equation of parabola is $y^2 = -8x$ which is of the form $y^2 = -4ax$.

Here, $4a = 8 \Rightarrow a = 2$

$\therefore$ Focus $(-a, 0) = (-2, 0)$; Axis $= X$-axis

Directrix, $x = a \Rightarrow x = 2$

and length of latusrectum $= 4a = 4 \times 2 = 8$

(iii) Given, equation of parabola is $x^2 = 10y$, which is of the form $x^2 = 4ay$.

Here, $4a = 10 \Rightarrow a = \frac{5}{2}$

$\therefore$ Focus $(0, a) = \left(0, \frac{5}{2}\right)$; Axis $= Y$-axis

Directrix, $y = -a \Rightarrow y = -\frac{5}{2}$

and length of latusrectum $= 4a = 4 \times \frac{5}{2} = 10$

(iv) Given, equation of parabola is $x^2 = -9y$, which is of the form $x^2 = -4ay$.

Here, $4a = 9 \Rightarrow a = \frac{9}{4}$

$\therefore$ Focus $(0, -a) = \left(0, -\frac{9}{4}\right)$; Axis $= Y$-axis

Directrix, $y = a \Rightarrow y = \frac{9}{4}$

and length of latusrectum $= 4a = 9$

Equation of Parabola When Vertex (0, 0) is Shifted to Another Point say α, β

If the vertex is shifted to $A(\alpha, \beta)$, while its axes remains parallel to X-axis or Y-axis, then the equation of parabolas are

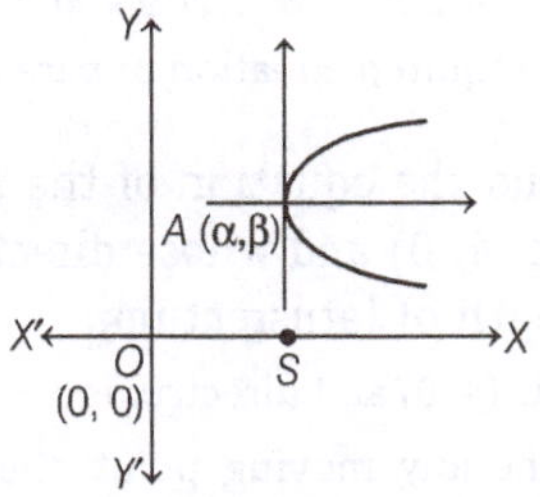

(i) $(y - \beta)^2 = 4a(x - \alpha)$

(ii) $(y - \beta)^2 = -4a(x - \alpha)$

(iii) $(x - \alpha)^2 = 4a(y - \beta)$

(iv) $(x - \alpha)^2 = -4a(y - \beta)$

Some Important Observations

(i) Length of latus rectum in each case is $4a$.

(ii) The focus, directrix, axis, etc, can be found by expressing the above equations in standard form. This can be done by shifting the origin to (α, β) with the help of following substitutions.

$$x - \alpha = X \text{ and } y - \beta = Y$$

(iii) The equation $(y - \beta)^2 = 4a(x - \alpha)$ can be rewritten as $y^2 - 2\beta y + \beta^2 = 4ax - 4a\alpha$

$\Rightarrow 4ax = y^2 - 2\beta y + \beta^2 + 4a\alpha$

$\Rightarrow x = \frac{1}{4a}y^2 + \frac{(-2\beta)}{4a}y + \frac{\beta^2 + 4a\alpha}{4a}$

$\Rightarrow x = Ay^2 + By + C$, where A, B, C are constants.

Thus, the equation of the parabola whose is parallel to X-axis can be taken as $x = ay^2 + by + c$, where a, b, c are constants.

Similarly, the equation of the parabola whose axis is parallel to the Y-axis can be taken as $y = ax^2 + bx + c$, where a, b, c are constants.

Example 2 Find the vertex, axis, focus, directrix and length of latusrectum of parabola $y^2 - 8y - x + 19 = 0$.

Sol. Given equation is $y^2 - 8y - x + 19 = 0$

$\Rightarrow \quad y^2 - 8y + 16 = x - 19 + 16$

$\Rightarrow \quad (y - 4)^2 = x - 3 \quad$ ...(i)

Let $y - 4 = Y$ and $x - 3 = X \quad$ ...(ii)

Then, Eq. (i) becomes $Y^2 = X \quad$ ...(iii)

Now, from Eq. (iii), coordinates of vertex are given by

$X = 0$ and $Y = 0$

$\Rightarrow \quad x - 3 = 0$ and $y - 4 = 0$

[put the values from Eq. (ii)]

$\Rightarrow \quad x = 3$ and $y = 4$

The equation of axis of parabola (iii) is $Y = 0$.

$\Rightarrow \quad y - 4 = 0 \Rightarrow y = 4$

On comparing Eq. (iii) with $Y^2 = 4aX$, we get

$4a = 1 \Rightarrow a = \frac{1}{4}$

Coordinates of focus of parabola (iii) are given by

$X = a, Y = 0$

$\Rightarrow \quad x - 3 = \frac{1}{4}, \; y - 4 = 0$

$\Rightarrow \quad x = \frac{1}{4} + 3, \; y = 4$

$\Rightarrow \quad x = \frac{13}{4}, \; y = 4$

Equation of directrix of parabola (iii) is

$X = -a$

$\Rightarrow \quad x - 3 = -\frac{1}{4}$

$\Rightarrow \quad x = -\frac{1}{4} + 3$

$\Rightarrow \quad x = \frac{11}{4}$

Length of latusrectum $= 4a = 4 \cdot \frac{1}{4} = 1$

Hence, for given parabola vertex $\equiv (3, 4)$, axis $\equiv y = 4$, focus $\equiv \left(\frac{13}{4}, 4\right)$, directrix $\equiv x = \frac{11}{4}$ and length of latusrectum $= 1$.

General Equation of a Parabola

So far we have found the equations of standard parabolas where the directrix is parallel to either of the axes We will now obtain the equation of a parabola when the focus is any point, the vertex is any point, and the directrix is any line.

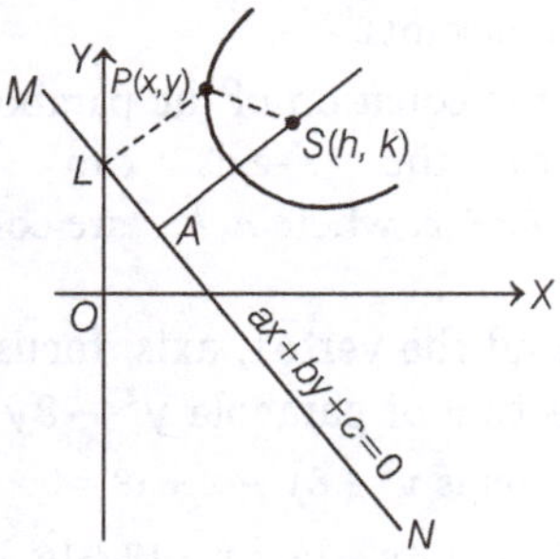

Let (h, k) be the focus S and $ax+by+c=0$ be the equation of the directrix MN of a parabola. Again, let $P(x, y)$ be any point on the parabola.

Then, by definition, $|PS| = PL$

$$\sqrt{(x-h)^2+(y-k)^2} = \frac{|ax+by+c|}{\sqrt{a^2+b^2}}$$

$$\Rightarrow \quad (x-h)^2+(y-k)^2 = \frac{(ax+by+c)^2}{a^2+b^2}$$

$$\Rightarrow \quad (a^2+b^2)(x-h)^2+(a^2+b^2)(y-k)^2 = a^2x^2+b^2y^2+c^2+2abxy+2acx+2bcy$$

$$\Rightarrow \quad (a^2+b^2)x^2+(a^2+b^2)y^2-a^2x^2-b^2y^2-2abxy + x \text{ term} + y \text{ term} + \text{constant} = 0$$

$$\Rightarrow \quad (b^2x^2+a^2y^2-2abxy) + x \text{ term} + y \text{ term} + \text{constant} = 0$$

which is of the form $(bx-ay)^2+2gx+2fy+d=0$.

This equation is known as **general equation of a parabola of second degree.**

Some Particular Types of Problems Based on Parabola

| TYPE I |

Finding the Equation of Parabola When Focus and Directrix are Given

If focus S and directrix of a parabola are given, then we can find the equation of parabola with the help of following steps

***Step* I** Take any point $P(x, y)$ on the parabola.

***Step* II** Find the distance between the point P and the focus S by distance formula.

***Step* III** Also, find the distance of the point from the directrix by distance formula.

***Step* IV** Equate the distances calculated in step II and step III (by definition of parabola).

The expression so obtained is the required equation of parabola.

Example 3 Find the equation of the parabola having focus at $(3, -4)$ and directrix as $x+y=2$. **[ISC 2007]**

Sol. Let $P(x, y)$ be any point on the parabola.

Given, focus $= (3, -4)$ and directrix equation is $x+y=2$.

$\because$ Distance of P from focus = Perpendicular distance of P from the directrix [by definition of parabola]

$$\therefore \quad \sqrt{(x-3)^2+(y+4)^2} = \left|\frac{x+y-2}{\sqrt{1+1}}\right|$$

On squaring both sides, we get

$$(x-3)^2+(y+4)^2 = \frac{(x+y-2)^2}{2}$$

$$\Rightarrow \quad 2(x^2-6x+9+y^2+8y+16) = x^2+y^2+4+2xy-4y-4x$$

$$\Rightarrow \quad 2x^2-12x+50+2y^2+16y = x^2+y^2+4+2xy-4y-4x$$

$$\Rightarrow \quad x^2+y^2-2xy-8x+20y+46=0$$

which is the required equation of parabola.

Example 4 Find the equation of the parabola, whose focus is the point $(4, 0)$ and whose directrix is $x=-4$. Also, find the length of latusrectum.

Sol. Here, focus is $(4, 0)$ and directrix is $x+4=0$.

Let $P(x, y)$ be any moving point, then draw $PL \perp ZZ'$ from P to the directrix.

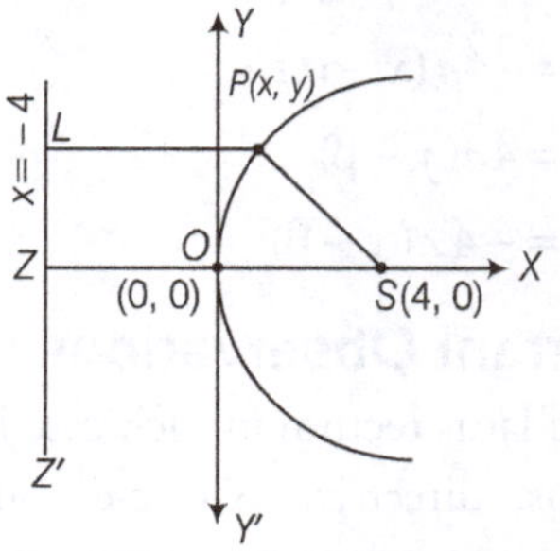

Now, $\quad PS = PL$ [by definition of parabola]

$$\Rightarrow \quad PS^2 = PL^2$$

$$\Rightarrow \quad (x-4)^2+(y-0)^2 = \frac{(x+4)^2}{(\sqrt{1})^2}$$

$$\Rightarrow \quad x^2-8x+16+y^2 = x^2+8x+16$$

$$\Rightarrow \quad y^2 = 16x$$

which is the required equation of parabola.

Hence, length of latusrectum is 16.

Alternate Method

Since the focus (4, 0) lies on X-axis, therefore X-axis is the axis of the parabola.

Also, the equation of directrix is $x=-4$, i.e. $x+4=0$, therefore the parabola is of form $y^2=4ax$.

Here, $a=4$

[$\because$ focus of $y^2=4ax$ is $(a, 0)$ and here focus $=(4, 0)$]

$\therefore$ The required equation of the parabola is

$$y^2=4\times 4x=16x.$$

Length of latusrectum $=4a=16$.

Example 5 Find the equation of the following parabolas.

(i) Directrix $x=0$, focus at (6, 0)

(ii) Focus at (2, 3) directrix $x-4y+3=0$. Also, find the equation of the axis.

Sol. (i) Let $P(x, y)$ be any point on the parabola. Then, by definition of parabola.

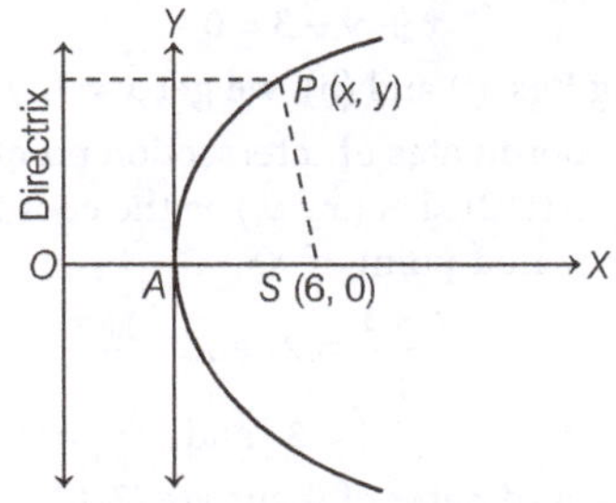

Distance of P from the focus

= Distance of P from the directrix.

$$\therefore \quad \sqrt{(x-6)^2+(y-0)^2}=|x|$$

$$\Rightarrow \quad x^2-12x+36+y^2=x^2 \Rightarrow y^2=12x-36$$

which is the required equation.

(ii) Let $P(x, y)$ be any point on the parabola. By definition, the distance of P from (2, 3) is equal to the perpendicular distance of P from $x-4y+3=0$.

Therefore, $\sqrt{(x-2)^2+(y-3)^2}=\dfrac{|x-4y+3|}{\sqrt{1^2+(-4)^2}}$

$$\Rightarrow \quad (x-2)^2+(y-3)^2=\frac{(x-4y+3)^2}{17}$$

$$\Rightarrow 17(x^2-4x+4+y^2-6y+9)$$
$$=x^2+16y^2+9-8xy+6x-24y$$

which simplifies to

$$16x^2+8xy+y^2-74x-78y+212=0$$

which is the required equation.

We know the axis of the parabola is the line passing through the focus (2, 3) and perpendicular to the directrix $x-4y+3=0$.

Equation of any line perpendicular to the line

$$x-4y+3=0 \text{ is } 4x+y+k=0 \quad \text{...(i)}$$

where, k is any arbitrary constant.

If it passes through the point (2, 3), then

$$4\times 2+3+k=0$$

$$\Rightarrow \quad k=-11 \quad \text{...(ii)}$$

Hence, from Eqs. (i) and (ii) we get the equation of the axis which is $4x+y-11=0$.

| TYPE II |

Finding the Equation of Parabola When Vertex and Focus are Given

If vertex V and focus S of a parabola are given, then we use the following steps for finding the equation of parabola.

***Step* I** Find the point of intersection of axis and directrix by using the mid-point formula.

***Step* II** Find the slope of the line formed by joining focus and vertex, i.e. Slope of axis, by the formula $m_1=\dfrac{y_2-y_1}{x_2-x_1}$.

***Step* III** Find the slope of the directrix by the formula $m_1\cdot m_2=-1$, as axis is perpendicular to directrix, where m_1 is the slope of axis of the parabola and m_2 is the slope of directrix.

***Step* IV** Write down the equation of directrix by using slope point form $(y-y_1)=m(x-x_1)$.

***Step* V** Now, focus and directrix are known, so find the equation of parabola by using the definition of parabola, $FP=PN$.

Example 6 Find out the equation of parabola, if the focus is at $(-6,-6)$ and the vertex is at $(-2, 2)$.

Sol. Given, focus is at $S(-6,-6)$ and vertex is at $A(-2, 2)$.

Let $B(x_1, y_1)$ be the coordinates of the point of intersection of axis and directrix. Then, $A(-2, 2)$ is the mid-point of line segment joining $S(-6,-6)$ and $B(x_1, y_1)$.

$$\therefore \quad -2=\frac{x_1-6}{2}\Rightarrow x_1=2 \text{ and } 2=\frac{y_1-6}{2}\Rightarrow y_1=10$$

So, the point of intersection of axis and directrix is $B(2, 10)$.

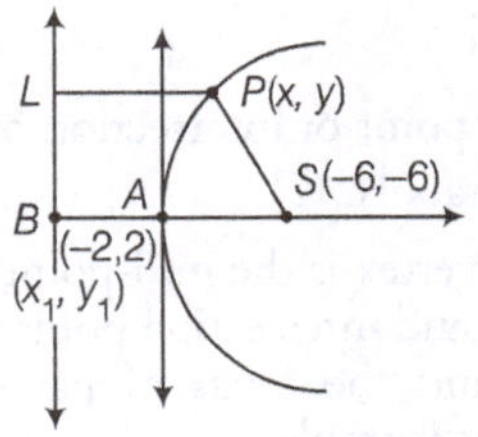

Now, slope of line joining vertex and focus is

$$m_1=\frac{-6-2}{-6+2}=\frac{-8}{-4}=2$$

$\therefore$ Slope of directrix, $m_2 = \frac{-1}{2}$

$$\left[\because AB \perp LB, \text{ so } m_1 m_2 = -1 \Rightarrow m_2 = \frac{-1}{m_1}\right]$$

Now, the equation of directrix is $y - 10 = \frac{-1}{2}(x-2)$

$\Rightarrow \quad 2y - 20 = -x + 2$

$\Rightarrow \quad x + 2y = 22$

Let $P(x, y)$ be any point on parabola and PL be the length of perpendicular from P on directrix and PS be the distance between focus S and point P.

So, $\quad PS = PL \Rightarrow (PS)^2 = (PL)^2$

$$\Rightarrow (x+6)^2 + (y+6)^2 = \left(\frac{x + 2y - 22}{\sqrt{1+4}}\right)^2$$

$$\Rightarrow x^2 + 36 + 12x + y^2 + 36 + 12y = \frac{x^2 + 4y^2 + 484 + 4xy - 44x - 88y}{5}$$

$$\Rightarrow 5x^2 + 180 + 60x + 5y^2 + 60y + 180 = x^2 + 4y^2 + 484 + 4xy - 44x - 88y$$

$$\Rightarrow 4x^2 + y^2 - 4xy + 104x + 148y - 124 = 0$$

which is the required equation of parabola.

Example 7 Find the equation of parabola when the vertex is at (0, 0) and focus is at (0, – 4).

Sol. Here, the vertex is at (0, 0) and focus is at (0, −4) which lies on Y-axis. So, Y-axis is the axis of the parabola. Also, focus lies below the X-axis, therefore equation of parabola is of the form

$$x^2 = -4ay \Rightarrow x^2 = -4(4)y \quad [\because a = 4]$$

$$\therefore \quad x^2 = -16y$$

| TYPE III |

Finding the Equation of Parabola When Vertex and Directrix are Given

If vertex V and equation of directrix of parabola are given, then we use the following steps for finding the equation of parabola.

Step I Find the equation of axis of parabola which is perpendicular to the directrix and passing through the vertex.

Step II Find the point of intersection of axis and directrix of the parabola.

Step III Now, as vertex is the mid-point of the line joining the focus and intersection point obtained from step II. So, find the focus of parabola by using the mid-point formula.

Step IV Thus, focus and directrix are known. Now, find the equation of parabola by using the definition of parabola i.e. $PF = PM$.

Example 8 Find the equation of the parabola whose vertex is at (2, 1) and the directrix is $x - y + 1 = 0$.

Sol. Let $V(2, 1)$ be the vertex and given equation of directrix is $\quad x - y + 1 = 0 \quad$ ...(i)

Then, equation of axis, which is perpendicular to directrix, is $\quad x + y + \lambda = 0$

Since, this will passes through vertex (2, 1).

$\therefore \quad 2 + 1 + \lambda = 0 \Rightarrow \lambda = -3$

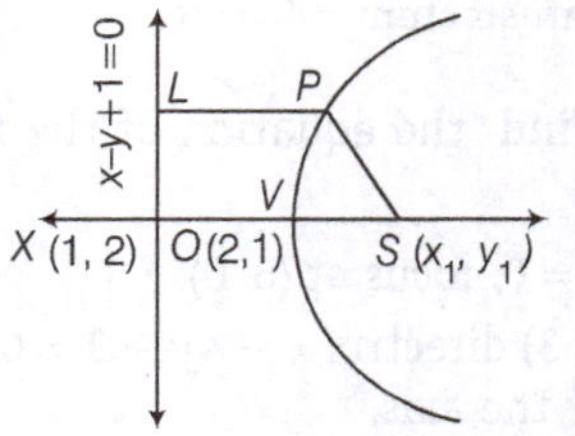

So, the equation of line perpendicular to directrix, i.e. equation of axis of parabola is

$$x + y - 3 = 0 \quad \text{...(ii)}$$

On solving Eqs. (i) and (ii), we get $x = 1, y = 2$

Thus, the coordinates of intersection point of directrix and axis is $X(1, 2)$. Let (x_1, y_1) be the coordinates of S, then V is the mid-point of XS.

$$\therefore \quad \frac{x_1 + 1}{2} = 2 \text{ and } \frac{y_1 + 2}{2} = 1$$

$$\Rightarrow \quad x_1 = 3 \text{ and } y_1 = 0$$

Thus, the coordinates of focus are (3, 0).

Now let $P(x, y)$ be any point on the parabola.

Then by definition, $PS = PL \Rightarrow PS^2 = PL^2$

$$\Rightarrow \quad (x-3)^2 + y^2 = \frac{(x - y + 1)^2}{2}$$

$$\Rightarrow 2(x^2 - 6x + 9 + y^2) = x^2 + y^2 + 1 - 2xy + 2x - 2y$$

$$\Rightarrow \quad x^2 + y^2 + 2xy - 14x + 2y + 17 = 0$$

which is the required equation of parabola.

| TYPE IV |

Miscellaneous Problems Based on Parabola

Example 9 Find the coordinates of a point on the parabola $y^2 = 8x$, whose focal distance is 4.

Sol. Given equation of parabola is $y^2 = 8x$.

Here, $a = 2$

$\therefore$ Focus $(S) \equiv (2, 0)$

$\therefore \quad PS =$ Focal distance

$$\Rightarrow \quad PS = \sqrt{(x-a)^2 + y^2} \quad \text{[by distance formula]}$$

$$\Rightarrow \quad 4 = \sqrt{(x-2)^2 + 8x} \quad [\because a = 2]$$

$$\Rightarrow \quad 16 = x^2 - 4x + 4 + 8x \quad \text{[squaring both sides]}$$

$$\Rightarrow \quad 16 = (x+2)^2$$

$\Rightarrow \quad x + 2 = 4$

[taking positive square root on both sides, as x can not be negative]

$\Rightarrow \quad x = 2$

Now, $\quad y^2 = 8 \times 2 \Rightarrow y^2 = 16 \Rightarrow y = \pm 4$

Hence, the coordinates of a point are (2, 4) or (2, – 4).

Note The distance of a point P on the parabola from the focus is called focal distance of the point P.

Example 10 Find the length of the line segment joining the vertex of the parabola $y^2 = 4ax$ and a point on the parabola, where the line segment makes an angle θ to the X-axis.

Sol. Given equation of parabola is $y^2 = 4ax$ ...(i)

Clearly, its vertex is (0, 0).

Again, let any point on the parabola be $P(h, k)$.

On putting the values $x = h$ and $y = k$ in Eq. (i), we get

$$k^2 = 4ah \quad \text{...(ii)}$$

Let $OP(=l)$ be the line segment joining the vertex and point P. Also, let it makes an angle θ with the X-axis.

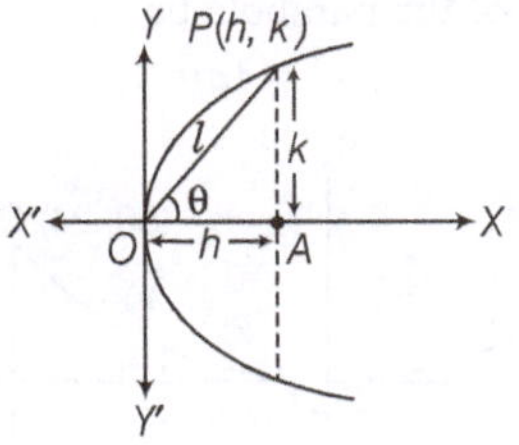

In right angled ΔOAP,

$$\sin\theta = \frac{PA}{OP} \Rightarrow \sin\theta = \frac{k}{l} \Rightarrow k = l\sin\theta$$

and $\quad \cos\theta = \frac{OA}{OP} \Rightarrow \cos\theta = \frac{h}{l} \Rightarrow h = l\cos\theta$

On substituting the values of h and k in Eq. (ii), we get

$$l^2\sin^2\theta = 4al\cos\theta \Rightarrow l = \frac{4a\cos\theta}{\sin^2\theta}$$

which is the required length.

Example 11 A straight line $2x + y + p = 0$ is a focal chord of the parabola $y^2 = -8x$. Then, find the value of p. **[ISC 2006]**

Sol. Given equation of parabola is $y^2 = -8x$.

On comparing with $y^2 = -4ax$, we get $a = 2$

$\therefore$ Focus = (– 2, 0)

Given, line $2x + y + p = 0$ is a focal chord, so it will pass through (– 2, 0).

$\therefore \quad 2(-2) + 0 + p = 0$

$\Rightarrow \quad -4 + p = 0$

$\Rightarrow \quad p = 4$

Example 12 An equilateral triangle is inscribed in the parabola $y^2 = 4ax$, where one vertex is at the vertex of the parabola. Find the length of the side of the triangle.

Sol. Let us first draw the parabola in the positive side of X-axis and inside that, draw an equilateral ΔOAB.

Let $OB = OA = AB = l$

Clearly, $\angle BOA = 60° \Rightarrow \angle BOP = 30°$

In ΔBOP,

$$\sin 30° = \frac{PB}{OB} \Rightarrow \frac{1}{2} = \frac{PB}{\;} \Rightarrow PB = \frac{\;}{2}$$

and $\quad \cos 30° = \frac{OP}{OB} \Rightarrow \frac{\sqrt{3}}{2} = \frac{OP}{\;} \Rightarrow OP = \frac{\sqrt{3}}{2}$

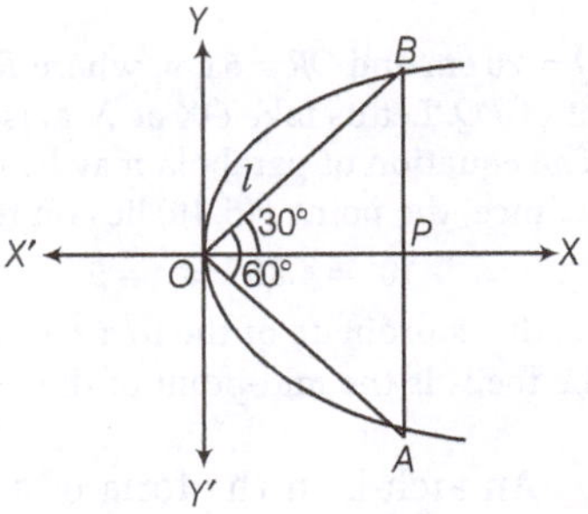

Thus, coordinates of $B = (OP, PB) = \left(\frac{\sqrt{3}}{2}, \frac{\;}{2}\right)$, which will satisfy $y^2 = 4ax$.

$$\therefore \quad \left(\frac{\;}{2}\right)^2 = \frac{4a \times \sqrt{3}}{2}$$

$$\Rightarrow \quad \frac{^2}{4} = \frac{4a\sqrt{3}}{2} \Rightarrow \; = 8\sqrt{3}a$$

Hence, the length of side of the triangle is $8\sqrt{3}a$.

Example 13 Find the area of the triangle formed by the lines joining the vertex of the parabola $x^2 = 12y$ to the ends of its latusrectum. **[NCERT]**

Sol. Given, $x^2 = 12y$, which is of the form $x^2 = 4ay$

$\therefore \; 4a = 12 =$ Length of latusrectum ACB

$\Rightarrow$ Focus $C = (0, 3)$

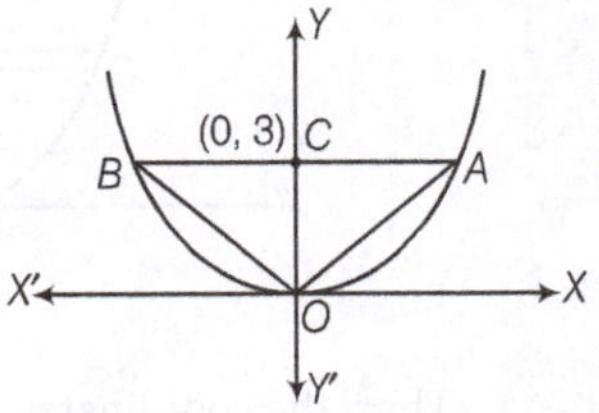

$\therefore$ Area of ΔOAB

$$= \frac{1}{2} \times AB \times OC$$

$$= \frac{1}{2} \times 12 \times 3$$

$$= 6 \times 3 = 18 \text{ sq units}$$

| TYPE V |

Problems Based on Applications of Parabola

Example 14 If a parabolic reflector is 20 cm in diameter and 5 cm deep. Find the focus.

Sol. Let POQ be the parabolic reflector which is 20 cm in diameter and 5 cm deep.

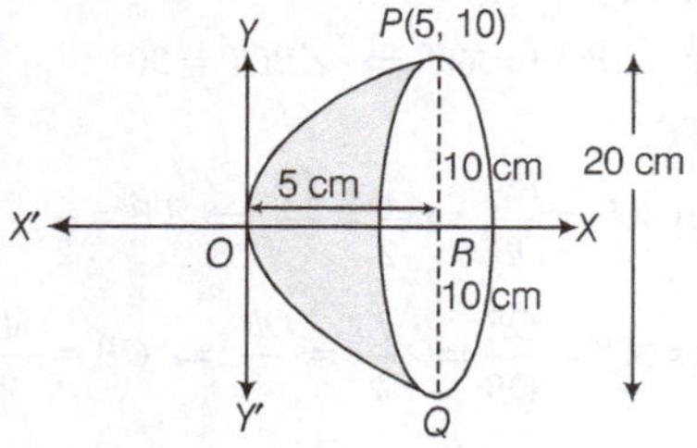

Then, $PQ = 20$ cm and $OR = 5$ cm, where R is the mid-point of PQ. Let us take OX as X-axis and OY as Y-axis. The equation of parabola may be taken as $y^2 = 4ax$. Since, the point $P(5, 10)$ lies on the parabola.

$\therefore \quad 10^2 = 4a(5) \Rightarrow a = 5$

Therefore, the coordinate of the focus are $(a, 0)$ i.e. $(5, 0)$.
Hence, the focus is the mid-point of the given diameter.

Example 15 An arch is in the form of a parabola with its axis vertical. The arch is 10 m high and 5 m wide at the base. How wide it is 2 m from the vertex of the parabola?

Sol. Here, axis is vertical, so let the arch is in the form of

$$x^2 = 4ay \quad \text{...(i)}$$

Given, $OB = 10$ m

and $\quad AC = 5$ m $\Rightarrow AB = \dfrac{5}{2}$ m $\quad \left[\because AB = BC = \dfrac{BC}{2}\right]$

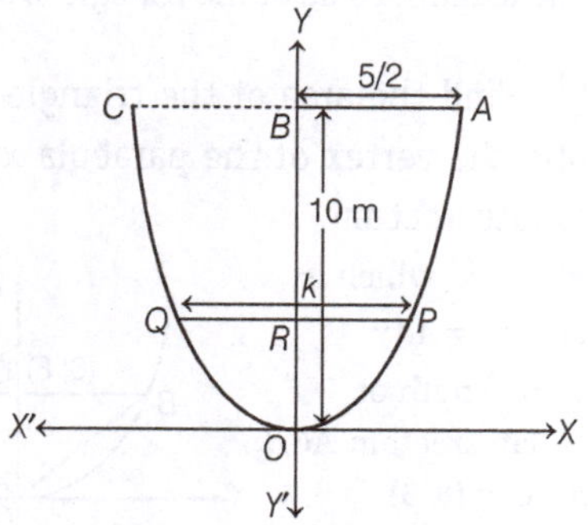

Thus, the coordinates of $A = \left(\dfrac{5}{2}, 10\right)$, which will satisfy Eq. (i).

$$\therefore \quad \left(\frac{5}{2}\right)^2 = 4a \times 10$$

$$\Rightarrow \quad \frac{25}{4} = 40a \Rightarrow a = \frac{5}{32}$$

From Eq. (i), $x^2 = 4 \times \dfrac{5}{32} y \Rightarrow x^2 = \dfrac{5}{8} y$

Now, let $OR = 2$ and $PQ = k \Rightarrow RP = \dfrac{k}{2}$

Therefore, $P = \left(\dfrac{k}{2}, 2\right)$ will lie on parabola.

$$\therefore \quad \left(\frac{k}{2}\right)^2 = \frac{5}{8} \times 2 \Rightarrow \frac{k^2}{4} = \frac{5}{4}$$

$$\Rightarrow \quad k = \sqrt{5} = 2.23 \text{ m (approx.)}$$

Example 16 The cable of a uniformly loaded suspension bridge hangs in the form of a parabola. The roadway which is horizontal and 100 m long is supported by vertical wires attached to the cable, the longest wire being 30 m and the shortest being 6 m. Find the length of a supporting wire attached to the roadway 18 m from the middle.

Sol. Here, wires are vertical.

Let equation of the parabola be

$$x^2 = 4ay \quad \text{...(i)}$$

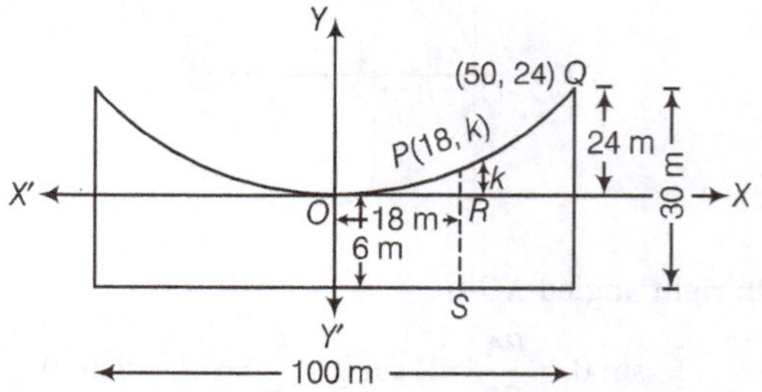

Since, the shortest and longest vertical supports are 6 m and 30 m respectively and roadway is 100 m long.

$\therefore$ The coordinates of Q will be $(50, 24)$ and it will satisfy Eq. (i).

Now, we have $(50)^2 = 4a \times 24 \Rightarrow 2500 = 96a$

$$\Rightarrow \quad a = \frac{2500}{96}$$

Hence, from Eq. (i), we get

$$x^2 = 4 \times \frac{2500}{96} y \Rightarrow x^2 = \frac{2500}{24} y$$

Let $\quad PR = k$ m

Then, point $P(18, k)$ will satisfy the equation of parabola.

$\therefore$ From Eq. (i), we get $(18)^2 = \dfrac{2500}{24} \times k$

$$\Rightarrow 324 = \frac{2500}{24} k \Rightarrow k = \frac{324 \times 24}{2500} = \frac{324 \times 6}{625} = \frac{1944}{625}$$

$$\Rightarrow \quad k = 3.11$$

Hence, required length $= 6 + k = 6 + 3.11 = 9.11$ m (approx.)

Topic Practice 1

Very Short Answer Type Questions

2 Marks

1 In each of the following questions, find the coordinates of the focus, axis of the parabola, the equation of the directrix and length of the latusrectum.
(i) $x^2 = -6y$ (ii) $x^2 = 16y$
(iii) $y^2 = 8x$

2 Find the equation of the parabola whose focus is (0, – 3) and directrix is $y = 3$.

3 Find the equation of the parabola with vertex at the origin and focus at (– 2, 0).

4 Find the equation of the parabola with focus (4, 0) and directrix is $x + 4 = 0$.

5 Find the equation of the parabola which is symmetric about the Y-axis, having vertex at (0, 0) and passes through the point (2, – 3).

6 Find the equation of the parabola with vertex at the origin, the axis along the X-axis and passing through the point (2, 3).

7 If the parabola $y^2 = 4ax$ passes through the point (3, 2), find the length of its latusrectum.

8 Find the vertex and the directrix of the parabola $y^2 - 3x - 2y + 7 = 0$.

9 The focal distance of a point on the parabola $y^2 = 12x$ is 4. Find the abscissa of this point.

Short Answer Type Questions

4 Marks

10 Find the vertex, focus, directrix and length of the latusrectum of the parabola $y^2 - 4y - 2x - 8 = 0$.

11 Find the vertex, focus, directrix and length of latusrectum of the parabola $2y^2 + 3y - 4x - 3 = 0$.

12 Find the equation of the parabola whose focus is (1, – 1) and vertex is (2, 1).

13 Find the equation of the parabola whose vertex is (6, – 3) and directrix is $3x - 5y + 1 = 0$.

14 Find the area of the triangle formed by the lines joining the vertex of the parabola $x^2 = -36y$ to the ends of the latusrectum.

15 Find the equation of parabola with latusrectum joining points (4, 6) and (4, – 2). **[ISC 2014]**

Hints & Answers

1. (i) $\left(0, \frac{-3}{2}\right)$, $x = 0$, $y = \frac{3}{2}$, 6
(ii) (0, 4), $x = 0$, $y + 4 = 0$, 16
(iii) (2, 0), $y = 0$, $x = -2$, 8

2. Required equation of parabola is $x^2 + (y+3)^2 = \frac{(y-3)^2}{(\sqrt{1})^2}$
Ans. $x^2 = -12y$

3. Equation of parabola is $y^2 = -4ax = -4(2)x$.
Ans. $y^2 = -8x$

4. Equation of parabola is $(x-4)^2 + (y-0)^2 = \frac{(x+4)^2}{(\sqrt{1})^2}$.
Ans. $y^2 = 16x$

5. Parabola is symmetrical about Y-axis and has its vertex at (0, 0).
So, equation of parabola is of the form $x^2 = 4ay$. or $x^2 = -4ay$, where the sign depends on whether the parabola opens upwards or downwards. But parabola passes through (2, – 3) which lies in IVth quadrant, therefore equation will be $x^2 = -4ay$.
On putting $x = 2$, $y = -3$, we get
$$4 = -4a(-3) \Rightarrow a = \frac{1}{3}$$
Ans. $3x^2 = -4y$

6. Equation of parabola, whose axis is X-axis, vertex at (0, 0) and passing through the point (2, 3), will be of the form $y^2 = 4ax$.
On putting $x = 2$ and $y = 3$, we get
$$9 = 4a(2) \Rightarrow a = \frac{9}{8}$$
Ans. $2y^2 = 9x$

7. Parabola $y^2 = 4ax$ passes through the point (3, 2).

$\therefore \quad (2)^2 = 4a(3)$

$\Rightarrow \quad a = \frac{1}{3}$

Then, length of latusrectum = $4a$

Ans. 4/3

8. Given parabola is $y^2 - 3x - 2y + 7 = 0$

$\Rightarrow \quad y^2 - 2y + 1 - 1 = 3x - 7$

$\Rightarrow \quad (y-1)^2 = 3(x-2)$

which is of the form $Y^2 = 4aX$, where $Y = y - 1$ and $X = x - 2$

Ans. $(2, 1)$, $4x - 5 = 0$

9. Solve as Example 9. **Ans.** 1

10. Solve as Example 2.

Ans. $(-6, 2), \left(-\frac{11}{2}, 2\right), 2x + 13 = 0, 2$

11. Given equation of parabola is $2y^2 + 3y - 4x - 3 = 0$.

$\therefore \quad 2\left[y^2 + 2 \cdot y \cdot \frac{3}{4} + \left(\frac{3}{4}\right)^2 - \left(\frac{3}{4}\right)^2\right] = 4x + 3$

$\Rightarrow \quad 2\left(y + \frac{3}{4}\right)^2 = 4x + 3 + \frac{9}{8}$

$\Rightarrow \quad \left(y + \frac{3}{4}\right)^2 = 2\left(x + \frac{33}{32}\right)$

This is of the form $Y^2 = 4aX$, where

$Y = y + \frac{3}{4}$ and $X = x + \frac{33}{32}$

Ans. $\left(\frac{-33}{32}, \frac{-3}{4}\right), \left(\frac{-17}{32}, \frac{-3}{4}\right), x = \frac{-49}{32}, 2$

12. Solve as Example 6.

Ans. $4x^2 + y^2 - 4xy + 8x + 46y - 71 = 0$

13. Solve to Example 8.

Ans. $25x^2 + 9y^2 - 618x + 554y + 30xy + 4929 = 0$

14. Given equation of parabola is

$x^2 = -36y$

$\Rightarrow \quad x^2 = -4(9y)$

Here, $a = 9$

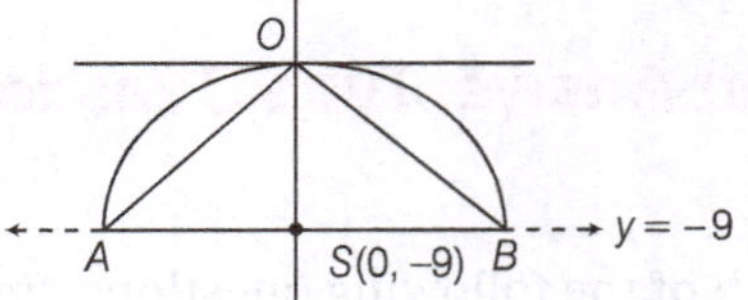

Focus $\equiv (0, -a) = (0, -9)$

Let AB be the latusrectum.

On putting $y = -9$, in the given equation, we get

$x^2 = -36(-9)$

$\Rightarrow \quad x = \pm 18$

So, the coordinates of A and B are $(-18, -9)$ and $(18, 9)$, respectively.

Area of $\Delta AOB = 2 \times$ Area of ΔOSB

$= 2 \times \left(\frac{1}{2} \times 18 \times 9\right)$

Ans. 162 sq units

15. Since, the line joining the points (4, 6) and (4, − 2) is parallel to Y-axis, so the axis will be parallel to the X-axis, the equation of two possible parabolas will be of the form

$(y - \beta)^2 = \pm 4a(x - \alpha)$.

Since, the length of latusrectum is 8, therefore

$a = 2$

Now, the equation of parabola is

$(y - \beta)^2 = \pm 8(x - \alpha)$ ...(i)

Since, (4, 6) and (4, − 2) lie on Eq. (i), therefore

$(6 - \beta)^2 = \pm 8(4 - \alpha)$ ...(ii)

and $(-2 - \beta)^2 = \pm 8(4 - \alpha)$ ...(iii)

On solving Eqs. (ii) and (iii), we get

$(6 - \beta)^2 - (-2 - \beta)^2 = 0$

$\Rightarrow \quad \beta = 2$

On putting $\beta = 2$ in Eq. (ii), we get

$(6 - 2)^2 = \pm 8(4 - \alpha)$

$\therefore \quad \alpha = 2$ or $\alpha = 6$

So, (α, β) may be (2, 2) or (6, 2).

Ans. $(y - 2)^2 = 8(x - 2)$ and $(y - 2)^2 = -8(x - 6)$

TOPIC 02 Ellipse

An ellipse is the locus of a point in a plane which moves in the plane in such a way that the ratio of its distance from a fixed point (called **focus**) in the same plane to its distance from a fixed straight line (called **directrix**) is always constant, which is always less than unity. The constant ratio is denoted by e and is called the **eccentricity of the ellipse.**

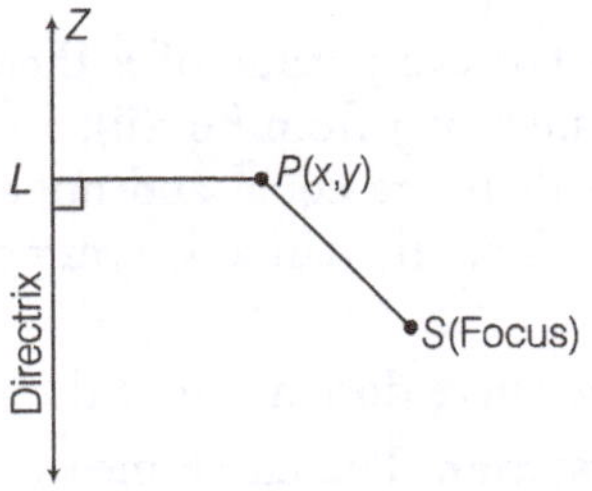

In the given figure, S is the focus, ZL is the directrix and P is any point on ellipse. Then by definition,

$$\frac{PS}{PL} = e,\ 0 < e < 1 \Rightarrow PS = e \cdot PL$$

Note The ellipse has a second focus S' and a second directrix $Z'L'$, because we get same curve if we start with S' as focus and $Z'L'$ as directrix.

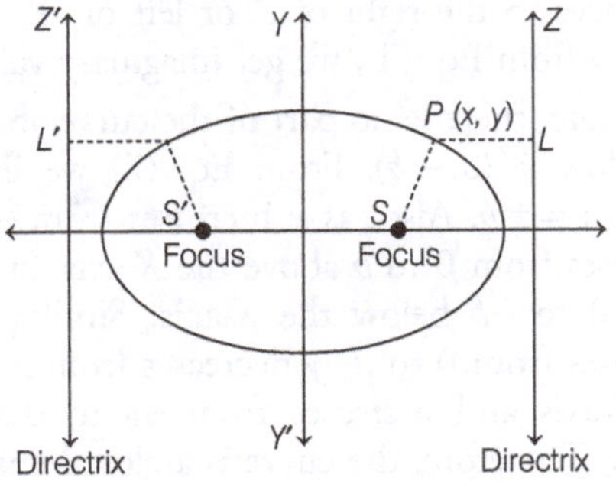

In other words, we can say that, an ellipse is the set of all points in a plane, the sum of whose distance from two fixed points in the plane is a constant.

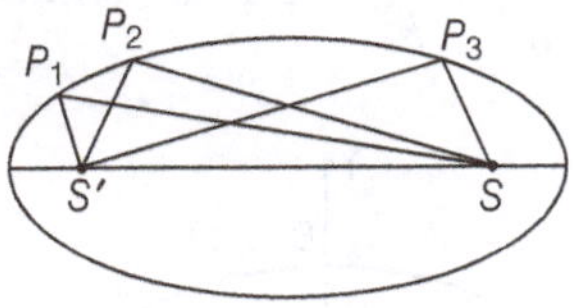

$\therefore\ P_1S' + P_1S = P_2S' + P_2S = P_3S' + P_3S =$ Constant

We can say that an ellipse is the locus of a point in a plane, which moves in such a way that the sum of its distance from two fixed point in the plane is a constant and this constant is greater than the distance between two fixed points.

Important Terms Related to an Ellipse

(i) **Focus** Two fixed points are called the **foci** (plural of focus) of the ellipse and denoted by S and S'. The distance between two foci S and S' is denoted by $2c$.

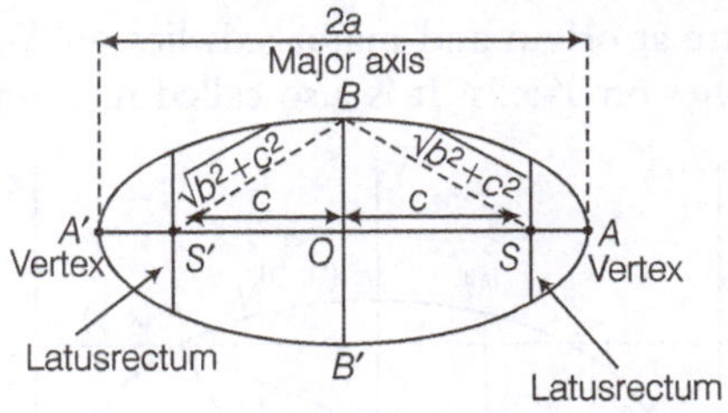

(ii) **Centre** The mid-point of the line segment joining the foci, is called centre of **ellipse.**

(iii) **Major Axis** The line segment through the foci of the ellipse, is called the **major axis.** The length of major axis is denoted by $2a$.

(iv) **Minor Axis** The line segment through the centre and perpendicular to the major axis is called **minor axis.** The length of minor axis is denoted by $2b$.

(v) **Vertices** The end points of the major axis, are called **vertices** of the ellipse.

(vi) **Latusrectum** of an ellipse is a line segment perpendicular to the major axis through any of the foci and whose end points lie on the ellipse.

Relation among Semi-major, Semi-minor Axes and Distance of Focus from the Centre

Let a and b be the length of semi-major and semi-minor axes, respectively. Again, let c be the distance of the focus from the centre.

Then, relation among a, b and c is given by

$$AS + AS' = BS + BS' \qquad \text{[by definition]}$$

$$\Rightarrow \quad a - c + a + c = 2\sqrt{b^2 + c^2} \Rightarrow a = \sqrt{b^2 + c^2}$$

$$\Rightarrow \quad c = \sqrt{a^2 - b^2}$$

Special Cases of an Ellipse

In the equation $c^2 = a^2 - b^2$, if we keep a fixed and vary c from 0 to a, the resulting ellipse will vary in shape.

Case I If $c = 0$, then $a = b$. Thus, ellipse becomes a circle.

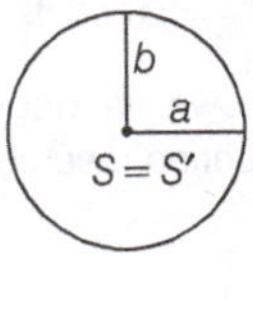

Case II If $c = a$, then $b = 0$. Thus, ellipse reduce to line segment SS'.

Standard Equation of an Ellipse

The standard equation of ellipse is $\frac{x^2}{a^2}+\frac{y^2}{b^2}=1$, $a>b$, having centre at origin and major axis lies on X-axis and minor axis lies on Y-axis. It is also called horizontal ellipse.

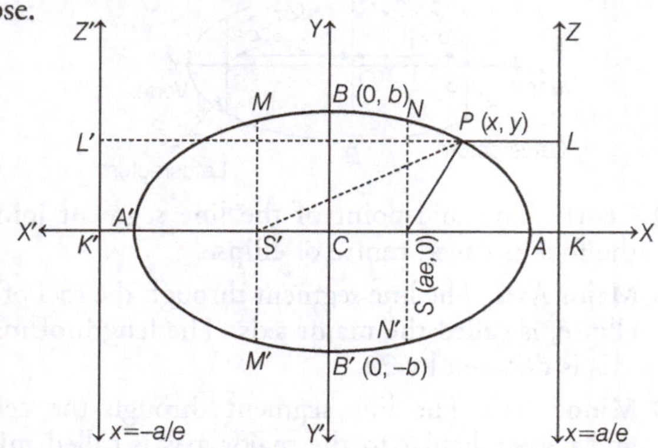

Some important terms related to horizontal ellipse are

(i) Centre is $O(0, 0)$. (ii) Vertices are $(\pm a, 0)$.

(iii) Foci are $S'(-c, 0)$ and $S(c, 0)$, where $c=\sqrt{a^2-b^2}$.

(iv) Length of the major axis, $AA' = 2a$

(v) Length of the minor axis, $BB' = 2b$

(vi) Eccentricity, $e=\frac{c}{a}=\frac{\sqrt{a^2-b^2}}{a}$

(vii) Equation of major axis, $y = 0$

(viii) Equation of minor axis, $x = 0$

(ix) Length of latusrectum $=\frac{2b^2}{a}$

(x) Coordinates of ends of latusrectum $=\left(\pm c, \pm\frac{b^2}{a}\right)$

(xi) Equation of directrices, $x=\pm\frac{a}{e}$

Note (i) $e=\frac{\sqrt{a^2-b^2}}{a} \Rightarrow b^2=a^2(1-e^2)$

(ii) The equation $\frac{x^2}{a^2}+\frac{y^2}{b^2}=0$ has its locus only the point (0, 0).

Such a locus is known as **degenerate ellipse** or **point ellipse**, since its equation resembles that of an ellipse.

Sketching the Ellipse $\frac{x^2}{a^2}+\frac{y^2}{b^2}=1$, $a>b$

We have, $\frac{x^2}{a^2}+\frac{y^2}{b^2}=1$, where $a>b$ ...(i)

$\therefore$ $y=\pm\frac{b}{a}\sqrt{a^2-x^2}$ ...(ii)

and $x=\pm\frac{a}{b}\sqrt{b^2-y^2}$ ...(iii)

In order to sketch the ellipse (i), we observe following points.

(i) **Symmetry** For every value of x there are equal and opposite values of y from Eq. (ii). Similarly, for every value of y there are equal and opposite values of x [Eq. (iii)]. Thus, the curve is symmetric about both the axes.

(ii) **Origin** The curve does not pass through the origin.

(iii) **Axes intersection** The curve meets X-axis at $y = 0$, Putting $y = 0$ in Eq. (iii), we get $x=\pm a$. So, the curve meets X-axis at $A(a, 0)$ and $A'(-a, 0)$.

Putting $x = 0$ in Eq. (ii), we get $y=\pm b$. So, the curve meets Y-axis at $B(0, b)$ and $B'(0, -b)$.

(iv) **Region** If $x>a$ or $x<-a$, from Eq. (ii), we get imaginary values of y. Therefore, there is no part of the curve to the right of A or left of A'. If $y>b$ or $y<-b$ from Eq. (ii), we get imaginary values of x. Therefore, there is no part of the curve above $B(0, b)$ or below $B'(0, -b)$. From Eq. (ii) we find that at $x = 0$, $y=\pm b$. Also, as x increases from $-a$ to 0, y increases from 0 to b above the X-axis and decreases from 0 to $-b$ below the X-axis. Similarly, when x increases from 0 to a, y decreases from b to 0 above the X-axis and increases from $-b$ to 0 below the X-axis. Therefore, the curve is a closed curve.

With the help of the above facts and by joining some convenient points on the ellipse, the general shape of the ellipse $\frac{x^2}{a^2}+\frac{y^2}{b^2}=1$ is as shown in the figure below.

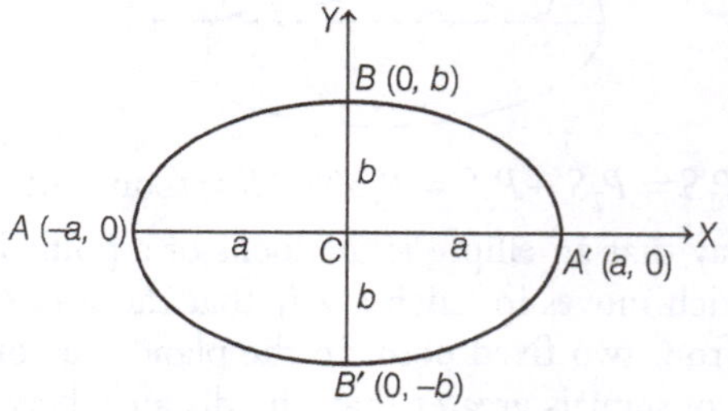

Another Standard Form of an Ellipse

The another form of the equation of an ellipse is $\frac{x^2}{b^2}+\frac{y^2}{a^2}=1$, $a>b$, having centre at origin, major axis lies on Y-axis and minor axis lies on X-axis. It is also called vertical ellipse.

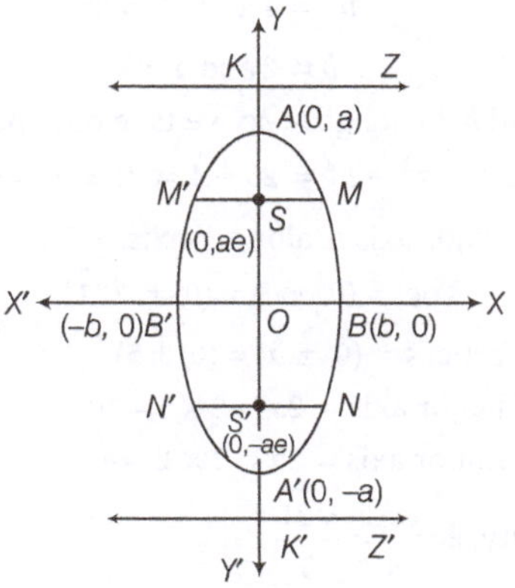

Some important terms related to vertical ellipse are

(i) Centre is $O(0, 0)$.

(ii) Vertices are $A(0, a)$ and $A'(0, -a)$.

(iii) Foci are $S(0, c)$ and $S'(0, -c)$.

(iv) Length of the major axis, $AA' = 2a$

(v) Length of the minor axis, $BB' = 2b$

(vi) Eccentricity, $e=\frac{c}{a}=\frac{\sqrt{a^2-b^2}}{a}$

(vii) Equation of major axis, $x=0$

(viii) Equation of minor axis, $y=0$

(ix) Length of latusrectum $=\frac{2b^2}{a}$

(x) Coordinates of latusrectum $=\left(\pm\frac{b^2}{a}, \pm c\right)$

(xi) Equation of directrices, $y=\pm\frac{a}{e}$

Note From the above equation of an ellipse, it follows that for every point $P(x, y)$ on the ellipse,

we have $\frac{x^2}{a^2}=1-\frac{y^2}{b^2}\le 1$ i.e. $x^2\le a^2 \Rightarrow -a\le x\le a$

Therefore, the ellipse lie between the lines $x=-a$ and $x=a$ and touches these lines. Similarly, the ellipse lie between the lines $y=-b$ and $y=b$ and touches these lines.

Observations from Standard Equation

From the standard equations of the ellipses, we observed the following points.

(i) If we replace (x, y) either by $(x, -y)$ or $(-x, y)$ or $(-x, -y)$, then the equation of ellipse does not change. It means, it is symmetric with respect to both the coordinate axes.

(ii) Foci are always lie on the major axis of an ellipse.

(iii) If the coefficient of x^2 has the larger denominator, then major axis is along X-axis.

(iv) If the coefficient of y^2 has the larger denominator, then major axis is along Y-axis.

Comparison between Two Standard Ellipse

S.No.	Terms	Horizontal ellipse $\frac{x^2}{a^2}+\frac{y^2}{b^2}=1$, $a>b>0$	Vertical ellipse $\frac{x^2}{b^2}+\frac{y^2}{a^2}=1$, $a>b>0$
1.	Shape	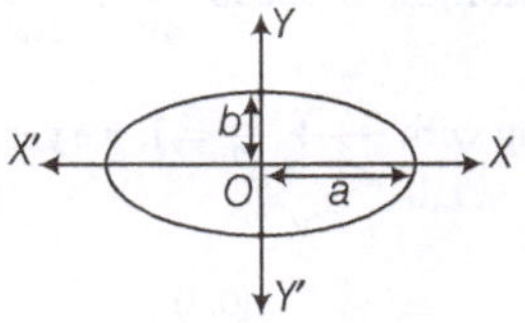	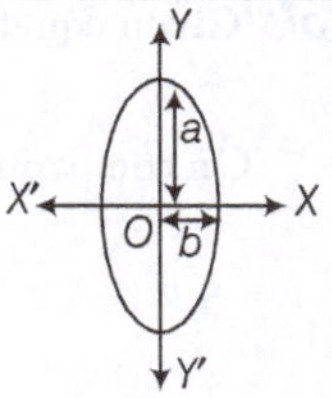
2.	Centre	$O(0, 0)$	$O(0, 0)$
3.	Vertices	$(\pm a, 0)$	$(0, \pm a)$
4.	Major axis	$2a$	$2a$
5.	Minor axis	$2b$	$2b$
6.	Value of c	$c=\sqrt{a^2-b^2}$	$c=\sqrt{a^2-b^2}$
7.	Equation of major axis	$y=0$	$x=0$
8.	Equation of minor axis	$x=0$	$y=0$
9.	Directrices	$x=\pm\frac{a}{e}$	$y=\pm\frac{a}{e}$
10.	Foci	$(\pm c, 0)$	$(0, \pm c)$
11.	Eccentricity	$e=\frac{c}{a}=\sqrt{1-\frac{b^2}{a^2}}$	$e=\frac{c}{a}=\sqrt{1-\frac{b^2}{a^2}}$
12.	Length of latusrectum	$\frac{2b^2}{a}$	$\frac{2b^2}{a}$
13.	Coordinates of latusrectum	$\left(\pm c, \pm\frac{b^2}{a}\right)$	$\left(\pm\frac{b^2}{a}, \pm c\right)$

Some Particular Types of Problems Based on Ellipse

| TYPE I |

To Find the Different Terms of Ellipse When Equation of Ellipse is Given

For finding the values of different terms, first we identify the equation of ellipse i.e. it is horizontal or vertical ellipse. Then, find the values of terms by using the formulae from the above chart.

Example 1 Draw the shape of ellipse $\frac{x^2}{49}+\frac{y^2}{16}=1$ and find the

(i) length of major axis (ii) length of minor axis
(iii) value of c (iv) vertices
(v) eccentricity (vi) directrices
(vii) foci (viii) length of latusrectum

Sol. Given equation of ellipse is $\frac{x^2}{49}+\frac{y^2}{16}=1$.

On comparing with $\frac{x^2}{a^2}+\frac{y^2}{b^2}=1$, we get $a=7, b=4$

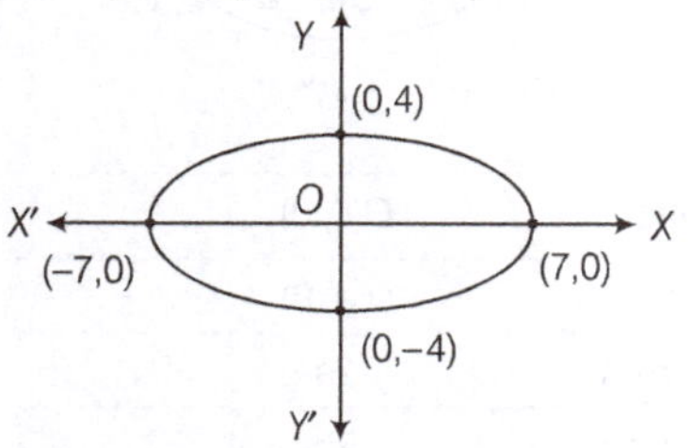

Here, $a>b$, so major axis is along X-axis.

(i) Major axis, $2a=2\times 7=14$

(ii) Minor axis, $2b=2\times 4=8$

(iii) $c=\sqrt{a^2-b^2}=\sqrt{(7)^2-(4)^2}=\sqrt{49-16}=\sqrt{33}$

(iv) Vertices, $(\pm a, 0)=(\pm 7, 0)$

(v) Eccentricity, $e=\frac{c}{a}=\frac{\sqrt{33}}{7}$

(vi) Directrices, $x=\pm\frac{a}{e}=\pm\frac{49}{\sqrt{33}}$

(vii) Foci, $(\pm c, 0)=(\pm\sqrt{33}, 0)$

(viii) Length of latusrectum, $\frac{2b^2}{a}=\frac{2\times 16}{7}=\frac{32}{7}$

Example 2 Find the coordinates of the foci, the vertices, the length of major and minor axis, the eccentricity and the length of the latusrectum of the ellipse $\frac{x^2}{4}+\frac{y^2}{25}=1$. [NCERT]

Sol. Given equation of ellipse is $\frac{x^2}{4}+\frac{y^2}{25}=1$.

Since, the denominator of x^2 is smaller than the denominator of y^2.

So, the major axis is along Y-axis.

On comparing the given equation with $\frac{x^2}{b^2}+\frac{y^2}{a^2}=1$, we get

$$b^2=4 \text{ and } a^2=25$$

$$\Rightarrow \quad b=2 \text{ and } a=5$$

Here, a and b are lengths, so we take only positive sign.

$$\because \quad c^2=a^2-b^2=25-4=21\Rightarrow c=\sqrt{21}$$

Here, the major axis is along Y-axis.

$$\therefore \quad \text{Foci}=(0,\pm c)=(0,\pm\sqrt{21})$$

$$\text{Vertices}=(0,\pm a)=(0,\pm 5)$$

Length of major axis $=2a=2\times 5=10$

Length of minor axis $=2b=2\times 2=4$

Eccentricity, $e=\frac{c}{a}=\frac{\sqrt{21}}{5}$

Length of latusrectum $=\frac{2b^2}{a}=\frac{2\times 4}{5}=\frac{8}{5}$

| TYPE II |

Finding the Equation of Ellipse in Different Cases

***Case* I When Vertices and Foci are Given**

If the x-coordinate of vertices is zero, then required ellipse will be of vertical, otherwise horizontal ellipse. Now, compare the vertices and foci with standard values and simplify to get the values of a, e and b and put these values in required standard equation.

Example 3 Find the equation of the ellipse whose axes are along the coordinate axes, vertices are $(\pm 5, 0)$ and foci at $(\pm 4, 0)$. [NCERT]

Sol. Given, vertices $\equiv(\pm 5, 0)$ and foci $\equiv(\pm 4, 0)$.

$\because$ y-coordinate of vertices are zero. So, let equation of ellipse be $\frac{x^2}{a^2}+\frac{y^2}{b^2}=1, a>b$

Now, $\quad$ vertices $\equiv(\pm a, 0)=(\pm 5, 0)$

$$\Rightarrow \quad a=5$$

and $\quad$ foci $\equiv(\pm ae, 0)=(\pm 4, 0)$

$$\Rightarrow \quad ae=4 \Rightarrow e=\frac{4}{a}=\frac{4}{5} \quad [\because a=5]$$

Now, $b^2=a^2(1-e^2)=25\left(1-\frac{16}{25}\right)=25\,\frac{(25-16)}{25}=9$

Hence, the required equation of ellipse is $\frac{x^2}{25}+\frac{y^2}{9}=1$.

Case II When Major (or Minor) axis and Foci are Given

If major (minor) axis and foci are given, then find the values of a (or b) and c. After this, find the value of b (or a) with the help of $c^2 = a^2 - b^2$. Then, put the values of a and b to get the required equation of an ellipse.

Example 4 Find the equation of the ellipse, if foci are $(\pm 3, 0)$ and $a = 4$. [NCERT]

Sol. Given foci are on X-axis. So, the major axis will be along the X-axis. So, the equation of ellipse is of the form

$$\frac{x^2}{a^2} + \frac{y^2}{b^2} = 1, \; a > b$$

Also, we have $a = 4$ and $c = 3$

$\because \; b^2 = a^2 - c^2 \Rightarrow b = \sqrt{a^2 - c^2} = \sqrt{16 - 9} = \sqrt{7}$

Hence, the equation of an ellipse is $\frac{x^2}{16} + \frac{y^2}{7} = 1.$

Example 5 Find the equation of the ellipse, if length of major axis is 26 and foci $(\pm 5, 0)$. [NCERT]

Sol. We have, foci $(\pm 5, 0)$ which are on X-axis, so the equation of ellipse is of the form

$$\frac{x^2}{a^2} + \frac{y^2}{b^2} = 1, a > b$$

Since, foci $\equiv (\pm c, 0) = (\pm 5, 0) \Rightarrow c = 5$

Length of major axis $= 2a = 26 \Rightarrow a = 13$

We know that, $c^2 = a^2 - b^2$

$\Rightarrow \quad b = \sqrt{a^2 - c^2} = \sqrt{169 - 25} = \sqrt{144}$

$\therefore \quad b = 12$

Hence, the equation of an ellipse is

$$\frac{x^2}{a^2} + \frac{y^2}{b^2} = 1 \text{ i.e. } \frac{x^2}{169} + \frac{y^2}{144} = 1.$$

Example 6 Find the equation of the ellipse having length of minor axis = 16 and foci $(0, \pm 6)$. [NCERT]

Sol. Length of minor axis, $2b = 16 \Rightarrow b = 8$

Foci are $(0, \pm 6) \Rightarrow c = 6$

$\therefore \; a^2 = b^2 + c^2 = (8)^2 + (6)^2 = 64 + 36 \Rightarrow a^2 = 100$

Here, x-coordinate of foci is zero. So, major axis is on Y-axis. Therefore, equation of ellipse is

$$\frac{x^2}{64} + \frac{y^2}{100} = 1$$

Case III When Major and Minor Axes both are Given

If major and minor both axis are given, then find the value of a, b then put the value in the standard equation of ellipse.

Example 7 Find the equation of the ellipse, if the ends of major axis are $(\pm 3, 0)$ and ends of minor axis are $(0, \pm 2)$. [NCERT]

Sol. Since, ends of the vertices are on X-axis and therefore the equation is of the form $\frac{x^2}{a^2} + \frac{y^2}{b^2} = 1, a > b$

Since, major and minor axes are $(\pm 3, 0)$ and $(0, \pm 2)$, respectively.

$\therefore \quad a = 3$ and $b = 2$

Hence, the equation of an ellipse is $\frac{x^2}{9} + \frac{y^2}{4} = 1.$

Case IV When Latusrectum and Eccentricity are Given

Example 8 Find the equation of ellipse, whose axes are along the axes of coordinates and centre at the origin and axes whose latusrectum = 8 and $e = \frac{1}{\sqrt{2}}$.

Sol. Let the equation of an ellipse be $\frac{x^2}{a^2} + \frac{y^2}{b^2} = 1$, where $a > b$

Given, latusrectum $= \frac{2b^2}{a} = 8$

$\therefore \quad b^2 = 4a \quad$ ...(i)

Also, $\quad e = \frac{1}{\sqrt{2}}; \; b^2 = a^2(1 - e^2)$

$\therefore \quad 4a = a^2\left(1 - \frac{1}{2}\right) \quad \left[\text{put } e = \frac{1}{\sqrt{2}}\right]$

$\Rightarrow \quad 4 = \frac{1}{2}a \Rightarrow a = 8$ and $b^2 = 4a = 4 \times 8 = 32$

Hence, the equation of ellipse is

$$\frac{x^2}{64} + \frac{y^2}{32} = 1 \quad [\text{put } a^2 = 64 \text{ and } b^2 = 32]$$

Note In this question, major or minor axis is not clear, so we consider by default major axis as X-axis.

Example 9 Find the equation of the ellipse whose centre lies at origin, major axis lies on the X-axis, the eccentricity is $\frac{2}{3}$ and the length of the latusrectum is 5 units.

Sol. We have, major axis of ellipse lies on the X-axis, so the equation of ellipse is

$$\frac{x^2}{a^2} + \frac{y^2}{b^2} = 1, \; a > b$$

Length of latusrectum $= \frac{2b^2}{a} = 5$

$\Rightarrow \quad \frac{2a^2(1 - e^2)}{a} = 5 \quad [\because b^2 = a^2(1 - e^2)]$

$$\Rightarrow \quad 2a\left(1-\frac{4}{9}\right)=5 \quad [\because e=2/3, \text{ given}]$$

$$\Rightarrow \quad a=\frac{9}{2} \text{ and } b^2=\frac{5}{2}a=\frac{5}{2}\times\frac{9}{2}=\frac{45}{4}$$

Thus, $a^2=\left(\frac{9}{2}\right)^2=\frac{81}{4}$ and $b^2=\frac{45}{4}$

Hence, the required equation of an ellipse is

$$\frac{4x^2}{81}+\frac{4y^2}{45}=1,$$

i.e. $20x^2+36y^2=405.$

Case V When Other Parts of an Ellipse are Given

If some other parts of an ellipse are given, then find the values of a and b by using these parts or conditions and find the required equation of an ellipse.

Example 10 Find the equation of ellipse, if it satisfies the condition $b=3, c=4$, centre at origin, foci on the X-axis.

Sol. Given, foci lies on X-axis and cantre is at origin. So, the equation of ellipse will be of the form $\frac{x^2}{a^2}+\frac{y^2}{b^2}=1$,

$a>b$ ...(i)

Also given that, $b=3$ and $c=4$

$$\therefore \quad c^2=a^2-3^2 \Rightarrow (4)^2=a^2-9 \Rightarrow 16=a^2-9$$

$$\Rightarrow \quad a^2=16+9 \quad\Rightarrow\quad a^2=25$$

On putting the values of $a^2=25$ and $b^2=9$ in Eq. (i), we get

$$\frac{x^2}{25}+\frac{y^2}{9}=1$$

Example 11 Find the equation of the ellipse, whose distance between directrices is 5 and distance between foci is 4.

Sol. Let the equation of ellipse be $\frac{x^2}{a^2}+\frac{y^2}{b^2}=1, a>b.$

Then, the equation of directrices are

$$x=\frac{a}{e} \text{ and } x=-\frac{a}{e}$$

$\therefore$ Distance between directrices $=\frac{2a}{e}=5$

$$\therefore \quad e=\frac{2a}{5}$$

Also, its foci are $(\pm c, 0)$ or $(\pm ae, 0)$.

$\therefore$ Distance between foci $=2ae=4 \Rightarrow ae=2$

$$\Rightarrow \quad a\left(\frac{2a}{5}\right)=2 \Rightarrow a^2=5 \quad \left[\text{put } e=\frac{2a}{5}\right]$$

$$\therefore \quad e=\frac{2\sqrt{5}}{5}=\frac{2}{\sqrt{5}} \text{ and } b^2=a^2(1-e^2)$$

$$\Rightarrow \quad b^2=5\left(1-\frac{4}{5}\right)=5\times\frac{1}{5} \quad [\text{put } a^2=5]$$

Thus, $b^2=1$

Hence, the equation of ellipse is

$$\frac{x^2}{5}+\frac{y^2}{1}=1 \quad [\text{put } a^2=5 \text{ and } b^2=1]$$

$$\Rightarrow \quad x^2+5y^2=5$$

Example 12 Find the equation of the ellipse, whose foci are (± 3, 0) and passing through (4, 1).

Sol. We have, foci of ellipse at (±3, 0) which are on X-axis.

Therefore, equation of the ellipse is of the form

$$\frac{x^2}{a^2}+\frac{y^2}{b^2}=1, a>b \quad \text{...(i)}$$

Its foci are $(\pm c, 0)=(\pm 3, 0)$

$$\therefore \quad c=3$$

Now, $c^2=a^2-b^2 \Rightarrow 9=a^2-b^2$ $[\because ae=3]$ ...(ii)

Since, Eq. (i) passes through (4, 1).

$$\therefore \quad \frac{16}{a^2}+\frac{1}{b^2}=1 \Rightarrow \frac{16}{9+b^2}+\frac{1}{b^2}=1 \quad [\text{from Eq. (ii)}]$$

$$\Rightarrow \quad 16b^2+9+b^2=b^2(9+b^2)$$

$$\Rightarrow \quad 17b^2+9=9b^2+b^4$$

$$\Rightarrow \quad b^4-8b^2-9=0$$

$$\Rightarrow \quad (b^2-9)(b^2+1)=0 \Rightarrow b^2=9 \text{ or } -1$$

But $b^2\neq -1 \Rightarrow b^2=9$

From Eq. (ii), we get $a^2=9+b^2 \Rightarrow a^2=9+9$

$$\Rightarrow \quad a^2=18$$

On putting the values of a^2 and b^2 in Eq. (i), we get

$$\frac{x^2}{18}+\frac{y^2}{9}=1 \Rightarrow x^2+2y^2=18$$

Example 13 Find the equation of the ellipse whose eccentricity is $\frac{1}{2}$ and whose foci are (±2, 0). **[ISC 2006]**

Sol. Let the equation of ellipse be $\frac{x^2}{a^2}+\frac{y^2}{b^2}=1$ ...(i)

Clearly, distance between foci = 4 $[\because \text{foci}=(\pm 2, 0)]$

$$\therefore \quad 2ae=4$$

$$\Rightarrow \quad 2a\times\frac{1}{2}=4 \quad \left[\text{given, } e=\frac{1}{2}\right]$$

$$\Rightarrow \quad a=4 \quad \text{...(ii)}$$

Now, $b^2=a^2(1-e^2)$

$$\Rightarrow \quad b^2=16\left(1-\frac{1}{4}\right) \Rightarrow b^2=4\times 3=12 \quad \text{...(iii)}$$

Hence, the required equation of ellipse becomes

$$\frac{x^2}{16}+\frac{y^2}{12}=1 \quad [\text{from Eqs. (i), (ii) and (iii)}]$$

Example 14 Find the equation of the ellipse, whose centre is at origin and major axis is on X-axis and passes through (4, 3) and (6, 2). **[NCERT]**

Sol. Since, the centre is at (0, 0) and the major axis be along X-axis, then the equation of ellipse is

$$\frac{x^2}{a^2}+\frac{y^2}{b^2}=1,\ a>b \quad \text{...(i)}$$

Since, the ellipse is passing through the points (4, 3) and (6, 2). So, the point (4, 3) lies on it.

$$\therefore \quad \frac{16}{a^2}+\frac{9}{b^2}=1 \quad \text{...(ii)}$$

Also, the point (6, 2) lies on it.

$$\therefore \quad \frac{36}{a^2}+\frac{4}{b^2}=1 \quad \text{...(iii)}$$

On multiplying Eq. (ii) by 4 and Eq. (iii) by 9 and then subtracting Eq. (ii) from Eq. (iii), we get

$$\frac{324}{a^2}-\frac{64}{a^2}=9-4$$

$$\Rightarrow \quad \frac{260}{a^2}=5 \Rightarrow a^2=\frac{260}{5}=52 \Rightarrow a^2=52$$

On putting the value of a^2 in Eq. (ii), we get

$$\frac{16}{52}+\frac{9}{b^2}=1 \Rightarrow \frac{9}{b^2}=1-\frac{16}{52}=\frac{36}{52} \Rightarrow b^2=13$$

Hence, the equation of ellipse is

$$\frac{x^2}{52}+\frac{y^2}{13}=1 \quad [\text{put } a^2=52 \text{ and } b^2=13 \text{ in Eq. (i)}]$$

Example 15 Find the equation of the ellipse, if the centre is at (0, 0), major axis on the Y-axis and passing through the points (3, 2) and (1, 6). **[NCERT]**

Sol. Since, the centre is at (0, 0) and major axis is along Y-axis, so equation of ellipse is $\frac{x^2}{b^2}+\frac{y^2}{a^2}=1,\ a>b$ ...(i)

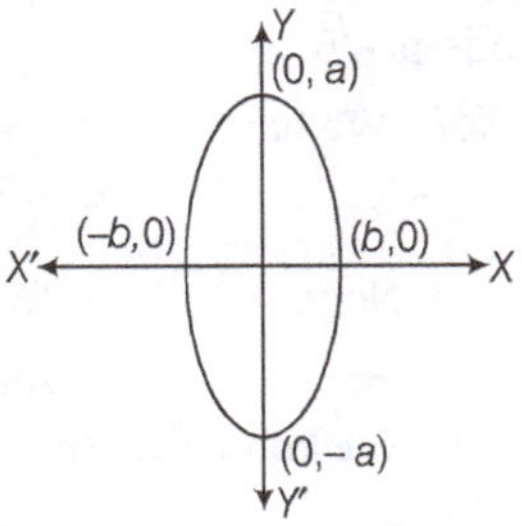

Now, as the ellipse is passing through the points (3, 2) and (1, 6). So, the point (3, 2) lies on Eq. (i), which gives

$$\frac{9}{b^2}+\frac{4}{a^2}=1 \quad \text{...(ii)}$$

Also, the point (1, 6) lies on Eq. (i).

$$\therefore \quad \frac{1}{b^2}+\frac{36}{a^2}=1 \Rightarrow \frac{9}{b^2}+\frac{324}{a^2}=9 \quad \text{...(iii)}$$

On subtracting Eq. (ii) from Eq. (iii), we get

$$\frac{320}{a^2}=8 \Rightarrow a^2=\frac{320}{8}=40$$

On putting the value of a^2 in Eq. (ii), we get

$$\frac{9}{b^2}+\frac{4}{40}=1 \Rightarrow \frac{9}{b^2}=1-\frac{1}{10}=\frac{9}{10} \Rightarrow b^2=10$$

On putting the values of a and b in Eq. (i), we get

$$\frac{x^2}{10}+\frac{y^2}{40}=1$$

|TYPE III|

Problems Based on Finding the Eccentricity in Different Conditions

Example 16 If the latusrectum of an ellipse is equal to half of minor axis, then find its eccentricity. **[NCERT Exemplar]**

Sol. Given, latusrectum of an ellipse is equal to the half of minor axis.

We know, length of latusrectum $=\frac{2b^2}{a}$

and length of minor axis $=2b$

According to the condition, $\frac{2b^2}{a}=\frac{1}{2}(2b) \Rightarrow \frac{b}{a}=\frac{1}{2}$

We know that, $e=\sqrt{1-\frac{b^2}{a^2}} \Rightarrow e=\sqrt{1-\frac{1}{4}}=\frac{\sqrt{3}}{2}$

Hence, the eccentricity of ellipse is $\frac{\sqrt{3}}{2}$.

Example 17 If a latusrectum of an ellipse subtends a right angle at the centre of the ellipse, then write the eccentricity of the ellipse.

Sol. Let the equation of ellipse be $\frac{x^2}{a^2}+\frac{y^2}{b^2}=1,\ a>b$

Since, latusrectun LL' subtends an angle of 90° to the centre.

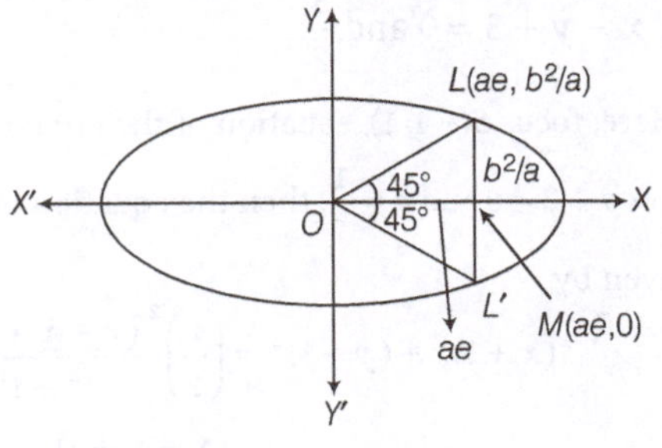

$$\therefore \quad \angle LOL'=90^\circ$$

Since, OM is the median of $\Delta OLL'$.

$$\therefore \quad \angle LOM=\angle L'OM=45^\circ$$

In right angled ΔOML,

$$\tan 45^\circ=\frac{b^2/a}{ae} \Rightarrow b^2=a^2e \quad [\because \tan 45^\circ=1]$$

Now, $e^2 = 1 - \dfrac{b^2}{a^2}$

$\Rightarrow \quad e^2 = 1 - \dfrac{a^2 e}{a^2} \Rightarrow e^2 + e - 1 = 0$

$\Rightarrow \quad e = \dfrac{-1 \pm \sqrt{1^2 + 4 \times 1}}{2 \times 1} = \dfrac{-1 \pm \sqrt{5}}{2}$

$\therefore \quad e = \dfrac{-1 + \sqrt{5}}{2} \qquad [\because 0 < e < 1]$

General Equation of an Ellipse

(Finding the Equation of Ellipse when Focus and Directrix are Given)

Here, we will find the equation of an ellipse when the focus is any point, directrix is any line and eccentricity is 'e'.

Let the focus S be (α, β) and the equation of the corresponding directrix be $lx + my + n = 0$ and eccentricity be 'e'. Let $P(x, y)$ be any point on the ellipse. Then, by definition of the ellipse,

Distance of any point P on the ellipse from focus
$= e \times$ (Distance of P from the directrix)

$$\Rightarrow \quad \sqrt{(x-\alpha)^2 + (y-\beta)^2} = e \times \frac{|lx + my + n|}{\sqrt{l^2 + m^2}} \qquad [\because l^2 + m^2 \neq 0]$$

or $\quad [(x-\alpha)^2 + (y-\beta)^2] = e^2 \dfrac{(lx + my + n)^2}{(l^2 + m^2)}$

The equation, when simplified, reduces to the form $ax^2 + 2hxy + by^2 + 2gx + 2fy + c = 0$, which is the general equation of an ellipse.

Example 18 Find the equation of the ellipse, whose focus, directrix and eccentricity are respectively $(-1, 1)$, $x - y + 3 = 0$ and $\dfrac{1}{2}$.

Sol. Here, focus $S(-1, 1)$, equation of the directrix is $x - y + 3 = 0$ and $e = \dfrac{1}{2}$, then the equation of ellipse is given by

$$(x+1)^2 + (y-1)^2 = \left(\frac{1}{2}\right)^2 \frac{(x-y+3)^2}{1^2 + 1^2}$$

$\Rightarrow \quad (x+1)^2 + (y-1)^2 = \dfrac{(x-y+3)^2}{8}$

$\Rightarrow \quad 8[(x+1)^2 + (y-1)^2] = (x-y+3)^2$

$\Rightarrow \quad 8(x^2 + 2x + 1 + y^2 - 2y + 1)$
$= x^2 + y^2 + 9 - 2xy + 6x - 6y$

$\Rightarrow \quad 7x^2 + 7y^2 + 2xy + 10x - 10y + 7 = 0$

Focal Property of Ellipse

Let $P(x, y)$ be any point on the ellipse $\dfrac{x^2}{a^2} + \dfrac{y^2}{b^2} = 1$

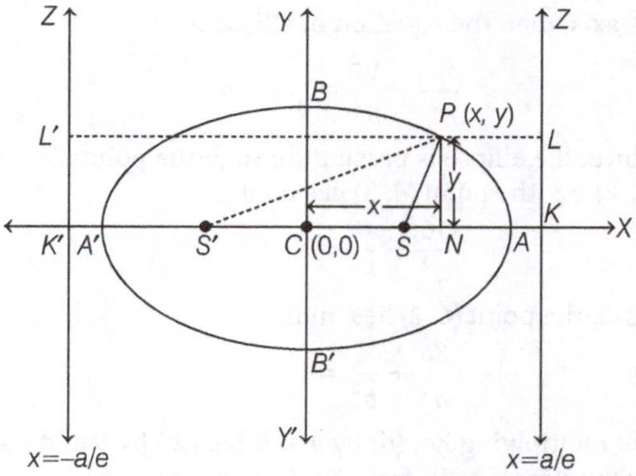

Then, $\quad SP = ePL = e(NK) = e(CK - CN)$

$= e\left(\dfrac{a}{e} - x\right) = a - ex$

and $\quad S'P = ePL' = e(NK') = e(CK' + CN)$

$= e\left(\dfrac{a}{e} + x\right) = a + ex$

Now, $\quad SP + S'P = a - ex + a + ex = 2a$

$=$ Major axis $=$ (constant)

Hence, the **sum of the focal distance of a point on the ellipse is constant and is equal to the length of the major axis of the ellipse.**

Example 19 Find the equation of the ellipse whose foci are $(2, 3)$, $(-2, 3)$ and whose length of semi-minor axis is $\sqrt{5}$.

Sol. We have, $\quad S \equiv (2, 3)$,

$S' \equiv (-2, 3)$ and $b = \sqrt{5}$

Now, $\quad SS' = \sqrt{(-2-2)^2 + (3-3)^2} = \sqrt{4^2} = 2$

$\Rightarrow \quad 2ae = 4 \Rightarrow ae = 2$

We know that, $(ae)^2 = a^2 - b^2$

$\Rightarrow \quad 4 = a^2 - 5 \Rightarrow a^2 = 9 \Rightarrow a = 3$

Let $P(x, y)$ be any point on the ellipse, then by another definition of ellipse,

$PS + PS' = 2a$

$\Rightarrow \quad \sqrt{(x-2)^2 + (y-3)^2} + \sqrt{(x+2)^2 + (y-3)^2} = 6$

$\Rightarrow \quad \sqrt{(x-2)^2 + (y-3)^2} = 6 - \sqrt{(x+2)^2 + (y-3)^2}$

On squaring both sides, we get

$(x-2)^2 + (y-3)^2 = 36 + (x+2)^2 + (y-3)^2$
$- 12\sqrt{(x+2)^2 + (y-3)^2}$

$$\Rightarrow (x+2)^2-(x-2)^2+36=12\sqrt{(x+2)^2+(y-3)^2}$$

$$\Rightarrow x^2+4x+4-(x^2-4x+4)+36=12\sqrt{(x+2)^2+(y-3)^2}$$

$$\Rightarrow \quad 8x+36=12\sqrt{(x+2)^2+(y-3)^2}$$

$$\Rightarrow \quad 2x+9=3\sqrt{(x+2)^2+(y-3)^2}$$

[divide both sides by 4]

$$\Rightarrow (2x+9)^2=9[(x+2)^2+(y-3)^2] \text{ [squaring both sides]}$$

$$\Rightarrow \quad 4x^2+36x+81=9[x^2+4x+4+y^2-6y+9]$$

$$\Rightarrow \quad 5x^2+9y^2-54y+36=0$$

Some Applications of Ellipse

Example 20 A rod of length 12 cm moves with its ends always touching the coordinate axes. Determine the equation of the locus of a point P on the rod, which is 3 cm from the end in contact with the X-axis. **[NCERT]**

Sol. Let AB be the rod of length 12 cm.

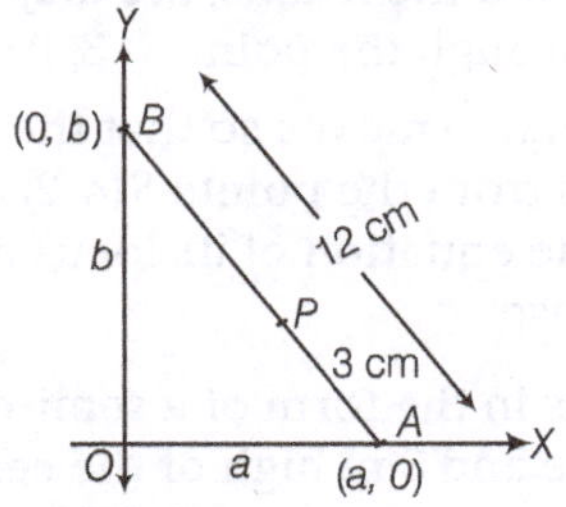

Let $\quad OA=a$ and $OB=b$

Using Pythagoras theorem in ΔOAB,

$$a^2+b^2=(12)^2 \Rightarrow a^2+b^2=144 \quad \ldots\text{(i)}$$

Let $AP=3$ cm, then $PB=AB-AP=12-3=9$ cm

$\therefore \quad AP:PB=3:9=1:3$

Let the coordinates of P be (h, k). If $P\ (h, k)$ divides the points A and B internally in the ratio $m:n$, then

$$h=\frac{mx_2+nx_1}{m+n} \quad \text{and} \quad k=\frac{my_2+ny_1}{m+n}$$

$$\therefore \quad h=\frac{1\times 0+3\times a}{1+3} \Rightarrow h=\frac{3a}{4}$$

$$\Rightarrow \quad a=\frac{4h}{3} \quad \text{and} \quad k=\frac{1\times b+3\times 0}{1+3}$$

$$\Rightarrow \quad k=\frac{b}{4} \Rightarrow b=4k$$

Putting the values of $a=\dfrac{4h}{3}$ and $b=4k$ in Eq. (i), we get

$$\left(\frac{4h}{3}\right)^2+(4k)^2=144 \Rightarrow \frac{16h^2}{9}+16k^2=144$$

$$\Rightarrow \quad \frac{h^2}{9}+k^2=9 \Rightarrow \frac{h^2}{81}+\frac{k^2}{9}=1$$

Hence, the locus of a point $P(h, k)$ is $\dfrac{x^2}{81}+\dfrac{y^2}{9}=1$, which respresent an ellipse.

Example 21 An arch is the form of a semi-ellipse. It is 8 m wide and 2 m high of the centre. Find the height of the arch at a point 1.5 m from one end. **[NCERT]**

Sol. Clearly, equation of ellipse takes the form

$$\frac{x^2}{a^2}+\frac{y^2}{b^2}=1 \quad \ldots\text{(i)}$$

Here, it is given that $2a=8$ and $b=2$

$$\Rightarrow \quad a=4 \text{ and } b=2$$

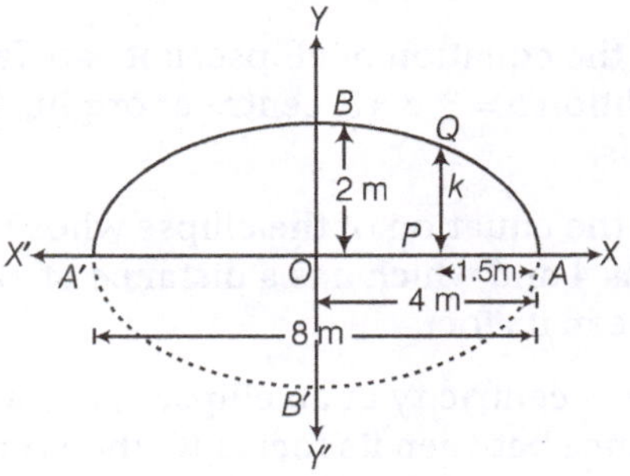

Put the values of a and b in Eq. (i), we get

$$\frac{x^2}{16}+\frac{y^2}{4}=1$$

Given, $\quad AP=1.5$ m

$\Rightarrow \quad OP=OA-AP=4-1.5 \Rightarrow OP=2.5$ m

Let $PQ=k$.

Then, the coordinate $Q\ (2.5, k)$ will satisfy the equation of ellipse.

i.e. $$\frac{(2.5)^2}{16}+\frac{k^2}{4}=1$$

$$\Rightarrow \quad \frac{6.25}{16}+\frac{k^2}{4}=1 \Rightarrow \frac{k^2}{4}=\frac{1}{1}-\frac{6.25}{16}=\frac{16-6.25}{16}$$

$$\Rightarrow \quad \frac{k^2}{4}=\frac{9.75}{16} \Rightarrow k^2=\frac{9.75}{4} \Rightarrow k^2=2.4375$$

$\therefore \quad k=1.56$ m (approx.)

Topic Practice 2

Very Short Answer Type Questions

2 Marks

1 Draw the shape of the following ellipse.

(i) $5x^2+12y^2=60$ (ii) $16x^2+5y^2=80$

(iii) $9x^2+4y^2=36$

2 Find the equation of the ellipse, whose foci $(0, \pm 5)$ and vertices $(0, \pm 13)$. **[NCERT]**

3 Find the equation of the ellipse, if foci are $(\pm 5, 0)$ and $a=6$.

4 Find the equation of the ellipse, if length of major axis is 22 and foci $(\pm 3, 0)$.

5 Find the equation of the ellipse having foci $(0, \pm 1)$ and length of whose minor axis is unity.

6 Find the equation of the ellipse, if the ends of major axis are $(\pm 2, 0)$ and ends of minor axis are $(0, \pm 7)$.

7 Find the equation of ellipse, if it satisfies the condition $b = 4$, $c = 9$, centre at origin , foci on the X-axis.

8 Find the equation of ellipse, if it satisfies the condition $b = 3$, $c = 8$, centre at origin, foci an the Y-axis.

9 Find the equation of the ellipse whose minor axis is 4 and which has a distance of 6 units between its foci. **[ISC 2007]**

10 If the eccentricity of an ellipse is 5/8 and distance between its foci is 10, then find latusrectum of the ellipse. **[NCERT Exemplar]**

11 Find the equation of the ellipse with foci at $(\pm 5, 0)$ and $x = \frac{36}{5}$ as one of the directrices. **[NCERT Exemplar]**

12 Find the equation of the ellipse with vertices at $(0, \pm 10)$ and $e = \frac{4}{5}$.

13 If the latusrectum of an ellipse is equal to the half of its major axis, then find its eccentricity.

14 Find the distance between the directrices of the ellipse $\frac{x^2}{36} + \frac{y^2}{20} = 1$.

15 If P is a point on the ellipse $\frac{x^2}{16} + \frac{y^2}{25} = 1$ whose foci are S and S', then find the value of $PS + PS'$.

Short Answer Type Questions

4 Marks

16 Draw the shape of $\frac{x^2}{64} + \frac{y^2}{25} = 1$ and find their vertices, length of major and minor axis, eccentricity, foci and length of latusrectum.

17 Draw the shape of $\frac{x^2}{100} + \frac{y^2}{400} = 1$ and find their vertices length of major and minor axis, eccentricity foci, and length of latusrectum.

18 Find the coordinates of the foci, the vertices, the length of major and minor axis, the eccentricity and the length of the latusrectum of ellipse $3x^2 + 2y^2 - 6 = 0$.

19 Find the equation of the ellipse passing through (6, 4), foci is on Y-axis, centres at the origin having eccentricity $\frac{3}{4}$.

20 Find the equation of the ellipse, whose distance between directices is 8 and distance between foci is 2.

21 Findthe equation of the ellipse referred to its axes as the axes of coordinates with latusrectum of length 8 and distane between foci $6\sqrt{3}$.

22 Find the equation of the ellipse, whose foci are $(\pm 4, 0)$ and passing through (3, 2).

23 Find the equation of the ellipse, whose axes along coordinates axes, passing through (4, 3) and (− 1, 4). **[NCERT]**

24 Find the equation of the ellipse whose centre is at origin and the X-axis, the major axis, which passes through the points (−3, 1) and (2,−2).

25 A point $P(x, y)$ moves so that the sum of its distances from the points $S(4, 2)$ and $S'(-2, 2)$ is 8. Find the equation of its locus and show that it is an ellipse.

26 An arch is in the form of a semi-ellipse. It is 10 m wide and 3 m high of the centre. Find the height of the arch at a point 2 m from one end.

Hints & Answers

1. (i) Given, $5x^2 + 12y^2 = 60$

$\Rightarrow \frac{x^2}{12} + \frac{y^2}{5} = 1$ [dividing both sides by 60]

Ans.

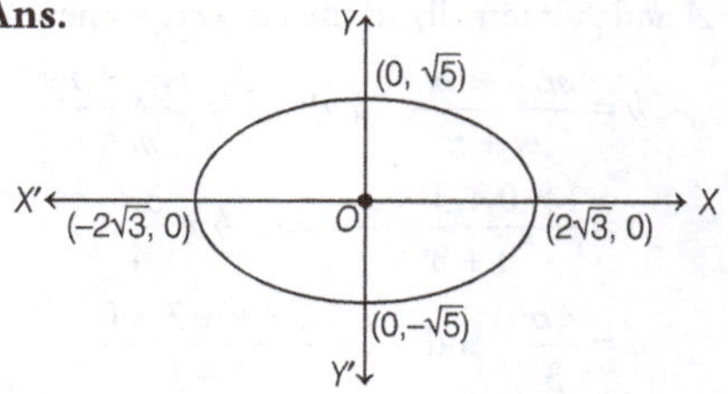

(ii) Solve as part (i).

Ans.

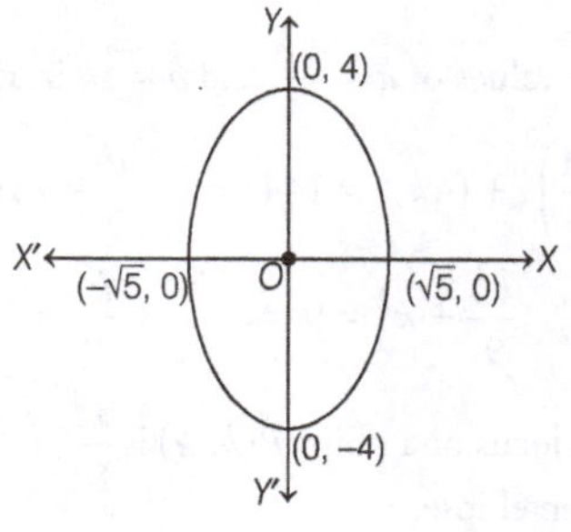

(iii) Solve as part (i).

Ans.

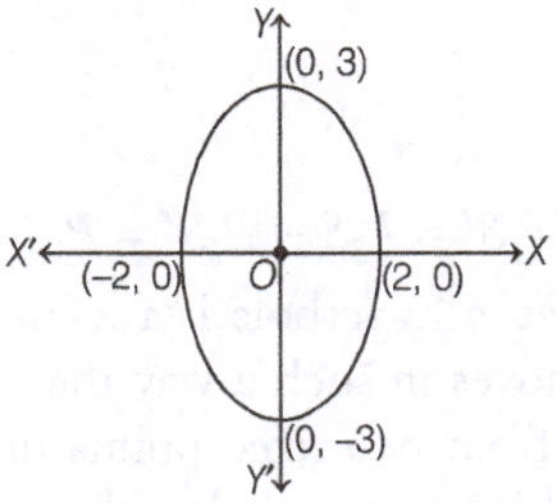

2. $(0,\pm c) = (0,\pm 5),\ (0,\pm a) = (0,\pm 13) \Rightarrow c = 5 \text{ and } a = 13$

$\because\ b^2 = a^2 - c^2 = 169 - 25 \Rightarrow b^2 = 144$

Ans. $\dfrac{x^2}{144} + \dfrac{y^2}{169} = 1$

3. $\dfrac{x^2}{36} + \dfrac{y^2}{11} = 1$

4. Solve as Example 5. **Ans.** $\dfrac{x^2}{121} + \dfrac{y^2}{112} = 1$

5. Solve as Example 6. **Ans.** $20x^2 + 4y^2 = 5$

6. Solve as Example 7. **Ans.** $\dfrac{x^2}{4} + \dfrac{y^2}{49} = 1$

7. Solve as Example 10. **Ans.** $\dfrac{x^2}{97} + \dfrac{y^2}{16} = 1$

8. Let the equation of an ellipse be $\dfrac{y^2}{a^2} + \dfrac{x^2}{b^2} = 1.$

$\because\ c^2 = a^2 - b^2$ **Ans.** $\dfrac{y^2}{73} + \dfrac{x^2}{9} = 1$

9. Given, length of minor axis = 4

and distance between its foci = 6

$\because\ b^2 = a^2(1 - e^2)$

The equation of ellipse is $\dfrac{x^2}{a^2} + \dfrac{y^2}{b^2} = 1.$

Ans. $\dfrac{x^2}{13} + \dfrac{y^2}{4} = 1$

10. $e = \dfrac{5}{8},\ 2ae = 10 \Rightarrow a = \dfrac{5}{5/8} = 8$

$\because\ e = \sqrt{1 - \dfrac{b^2}{a^2}} \Rightarrow \dfrac{25}{64} = \dfrac{64 - b^2}{64} \Rightarrow b^2 = 39$

Latusrectum $= \dfrac{2b^2}{a}$ **Ans.** $\dfrac{39}{4}$

11. $\dfrac{x^2}{36} + \dfrac{y^2}{11} = 1$

12. Here, $(0, \pm a) = (0, \pm 10)$ and $e = \dfrac{4}{5}$

$\because\quad e^2 = 1 - \dfrac{b^2}{a^2} \Rightarrow \dfrac{16}{25} = 1 - \dfrac{b^2}{100}$

$\Rightarrow\quad \dfrac{b^2}{100} = \dfrac{9}{25} \Rightarrow b^2 = 36$

Ans. $25x^2 + 9y^2 = 900$

13. $\dfrac{2b^2}{a} = \dfrac{1}{2}(2 \times a) \Rightarrow b^2 = \dfrac{a^2}{2}$

Now, $e = \sqrt{1 - \dfrac{b^2}{a^2}} = \sqrt{1 - \dfrac{a^2/2}{a^2}}$ **Ans.** $\dfrac{1}{\sqrt{2}}$

14. Distance between directrices $= \dfrac{2a}{e}$

Now, $e = \sqrt{1 - \dfrac{20}{36}} = \dfrac{4}{6}$ **Ans.** 18

15. $PS + PS' = 2a$ **Ans.** 10

16. Vertices $= (\pm 8, 0)$, Major axis = 16,

Minor axis = 10, Eccentricity $= \dfrac{\sqrt{39}}{8}$

Foci $= (\pm\sqrt{39}, 0)$, Latusrectum $= \dfrac{25}{4}$

17. Vertices $= (0, \pm 20)$

Major axis = 40, Minor axis = 20, $e = \dfrac{\sqrt{3}}{2}$

Foci $= (0, \pm 10\sqrt{3})$, Latusrectum = 10

18. $(0, \pm 1), (0, \pm\sqrt{3}), 2\sqrt{3}, 2\sqrt{2}, \dfrac{1}{\sqrt{3}}, \dfrac{4}{\sqrt{3}}$

19. $16x^2 + 7y^2 = 688$

20. Solve as Example 11. **Ans.** $\dfrac{x^2}{4} + \dfrac{y^2}{3} = 1$

21. Solve as Example 8. **Ans.** $\dfrac{x^2}{35 + 4\sqrt{31}} + \dfrac{y^2}{8 + 4\sqrt{31}} = 1$

22. Solve as Example 12. **Ans.** $\dfrac{x^2}{\dfrac{29 + \sqrt{265}}{2}} + \dfrac{y^2}{\dfrac{-3 + \sqrt{265}}{2}} = 1$

23. Let equation of ellipse be $\dfrac{x^2}{a^2} + \dfrac{y^2}{b^2} = 1, a > b$

$\therefore\quad \dfrac{16}{a^2} + \dfrac{9}{b^2} = 1$ and $\dfrac{1}{a^2} + \dfrac{16}{b^2} = 1$

$\Rightarrow\quad b^2 = \dfrac{247}{15}$ and $a^2 = \dfrac{247}{7}$

Ans. $7x^2 + 15y^2 = 247$

24. Solve as Example 14. **Ans.** $3x^2 + 5y^2 = 32$

25. Given, $PS + PS' = 8$

$\Rightarrow\quad \sqrt{(4-x)^2 + (2-y)^2} + \sqrt{(-2-x)^2 + (2-y)^2} = 8$

$\Rightarrow\quad \sqrt{(4-x)^2 + (2-y)^2} = 8 - \sqrt{(2+x)^2 + (2-y)^2}$

$\Rightarrow\quad (4-x)^2 + (2-y)^2 = 64 + (2+x)^2 + (2-y)^2 - 16\sqrt{(2+x)^2 + (2-y)^2}$

$\Rightarrow 4\sqrt{(2+x)^2 + (2-y)^2} = 13 + 3x$

$\Rightarrow\quad 7(x^2 - 2x + 1) + 16(y^2 - 4y + 4) = 112$

Ans. $\dfrac{(x-1)^2}{16} + \dfrac{(y-2)^2}{7} = 1$

26. Solve as Example 21. **Ans.** 2.4 m

TOPIC 03 Hyperbola

A **hyperbola** is the locus of a point in a plane which moves in the plane in such a way that the ratio of its distance from a fixed point (called **focus**) in the same plane to its distance from a fixed straight line (called **directrix**) is always constant, which is always greater than unity. The constant ratio is denoted by e and is called the eccentricity of the hyperbola.

In the given figure, S is the focus, AA' is the directrix and P is any point on hyperbola.

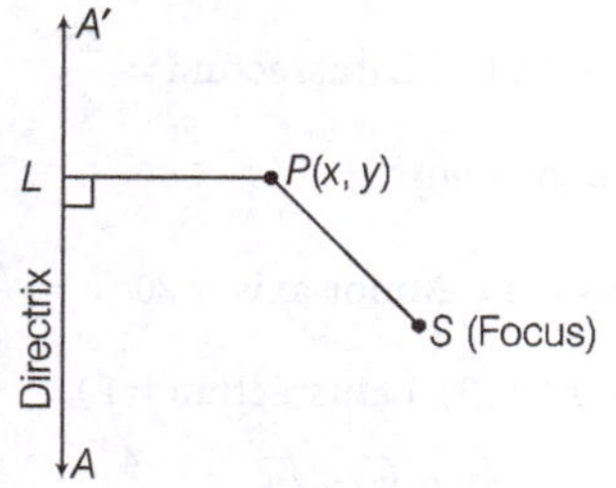

Then by definition,

$$\frac{PS}{PL} = e, \text{ where } e > 1 \Rightarrow PS = e \cdot PL$$

Note A hyperbola has a second focus S' and second directrix $Z'L'$, because if we start with focus S' and directrix $Z'L'$, then we get the same curve.

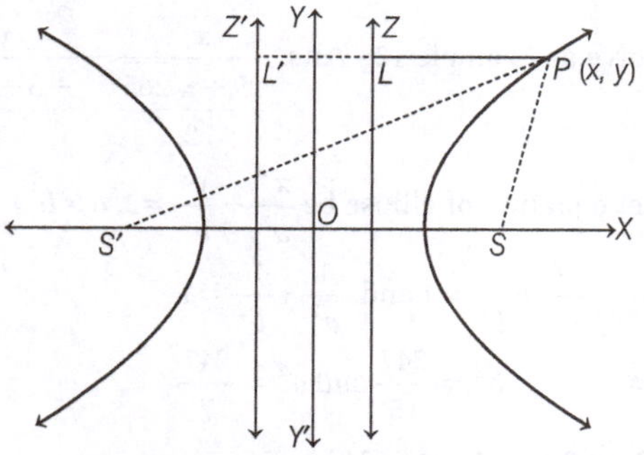

In other words, we can say that, a hyperbola is the set of all points in a plane, the difference of whose distances from two fixed points in the plane is a constant.

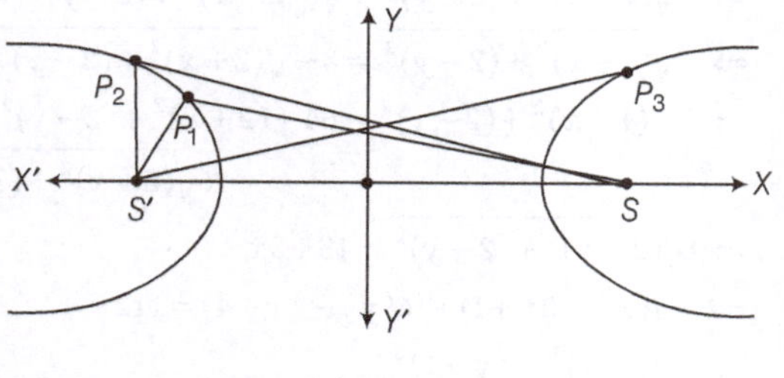

$$\therefore \quad P_1S - P_1S' = P_2S - P_2S' = P_3S' - P_3S$$

We can say that, a hyperbola is a locus of a point in a plane which moves in such a way that the difference of its distance from two fixed points in the plane is constant and this constant is less than the distance between two fixed points.

Note Here, the term difference used in the definition means the distance to the farther point minus the distance to the closer point.

Important Terms Related to a Hyperbola

(i) **Focus** The two fixed points are called the foci of the hyperbola and denoted by S and S'. The distance between two foci S and S' is denoted by $2c$.

(ii) **Centre** The mid-point of the line segment joining the foci, is called centre of hyberbola.

(iii) **Vertices** The points, where the line passing through foci intersect the hyperbola, are called the vertices of the hyperbola. The distance between two vertices is denoted by $2a$.

(iv) **Transverse axis** The line segment joining the vertices, is called the transverse axis.

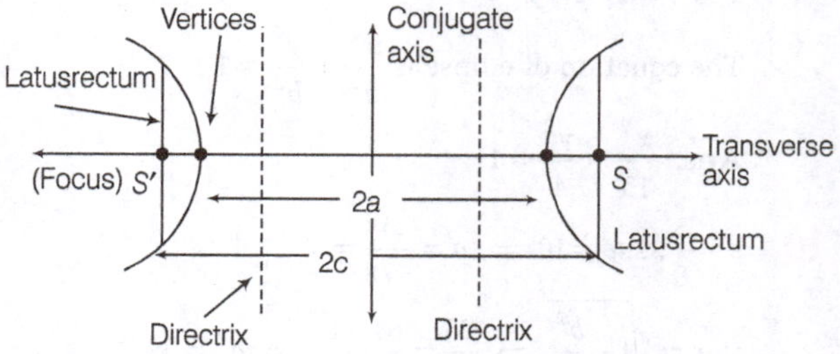

(v) **Conjugate axis** The line segment through the centre and perpendicular to the transverse axis, is called the conjugate axis.

(vi) **Latusrectum** of a hyperbola is a line segment perpendicular to the transverse axis through any of the foci and whose end points lie on the hyperbola.

Standard Equation of a Hyperbola

Standard equation of hyperbola is the form of $\frac{x^2}{a^2} - \frac{y^2}{b^2} = 1$, whose transverse axis is along X-axis and conjugate axis is along Y-axis.

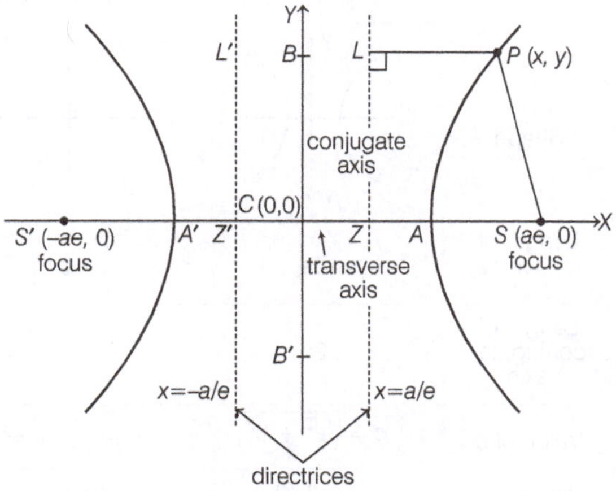

Some important terms related to standard hyperbola are

(i) Vertices are $A(a, 0)$ and $A'(-a, 0)$.
(ii) Centre is $O(0, 0)$.
(iii) Length of transverse axis is $2a$.
(iv) Length of conjugate axis is $2b$.
(v) Foci are $S(c, 0)$ and $S'(-c, 0)$.
(vi) Directrices are $x = \frac{a^2}{c}$ or $\frac{a}{e}$ and $x = -\frac{a^2}{c}$ or $-\frac{a}{e}$
(vii) Eccentricity, $e = \frac{c}{a} = \sqrt{\frac{a^2 + b^2}{a^2}}$ or $b^2 = a^2(e^2 - 1)$
(viii) Length of latusrectum $= \frac{2b^2}{a}$
(ix) Coordinates of latusrectum $= \left(\pm ae, \pm \frac{b^2}{a}\right)$
(x) Focal length $= 2ae$

Sketching the Hyperbola $\frac{x^2}{a^2} - \frac{y^2}{b^2} = 1$

The equation of hyperbola is

$$\frac{x^2}{a^2} - \frac{y^2}{b^2} = 1 \quad \ldots\text{(i)}$$

$$\therefore \quad y = \pm \frac{b}{a}\sqrt{x^2 - a^2} \quad \ldots\text{(ii)}$$

and

$$x = \pm \frac{a}{b}\sqrt{y^2 + b^2} \quad \ldots\text{(iii)}$$

In order to sketch the graph of the hyperbola (i), we observe the following points

(i) **Symmetry** For every value of x there are equal and opposite values of y [Eq. (ii)]. Similarly, for every value of y there are equal and opposite values of x [Eq. (iii)]. So, the curve is symmetric about both the axes.

(ii) **Origin** The curve does not pass through the origin.

(iii) **Axes intersections** The curve meets X-axis at $y = 0$, Putting $y = 0$ in Eq. (iii), we get $x = \pm a$ putting $x = 0$ in Eq. (ii), we get imaginary values of y. So, the curve does not meet Y-axis.

(iv) **Region** From Eq. (ii), we find that for $-a < x < a$, the values of y are imaginary. So, the curve does not exist between the lines $x = -a$ and $x = a$.

From Eq. (ii), we find that $y = 0$ at $x = \pm a$ and also if x increases from a to ∞, the values of y increases from a to ∞ above the X-axis and decreases 0 to $-\infty$ below the X-axis. Similarly, if x decreases from $-a$ to $-\infty$, y increases from 0 to ∞ above the X-axis and decreases from 0 to $-\infty$ below the X-axis.

With the help of the above facts and by joining some convenient points the general shape of the hyperbola $\frac{x^2}{a^2} - \frac{y^2}{b^2} = 1$ can be obtained.

Another Standard Form of a Hyperbola

The equation of another form of hyperbola is $\frac{y^2}{a^2} - \frac{x^2}{b^2} = 1$

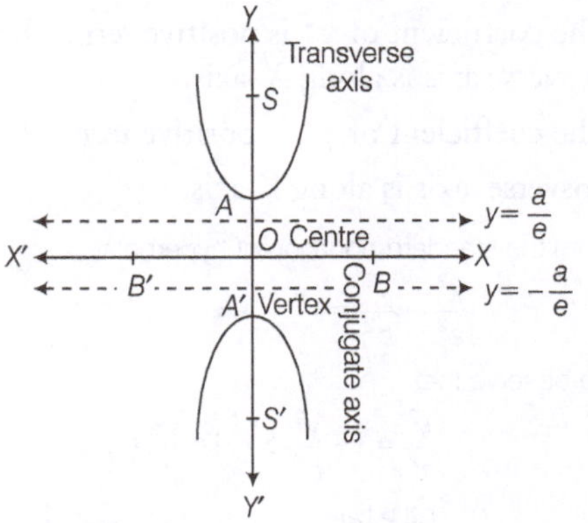

whose conjugate axis is along X-axis and transverse axis is along Y-axis.

Some important terms related to conjugate hyperbola are

(i) Vertices are $A(0, a)$ and $A'(0, -a)$.

(ii) Centre is $O(0, 0)$.

(iii) Length of transverse axis is $2a$.

(iv) Length of conjugate axis is $2b$.

(v) Foci are $(0, \pm c)$.

(vi) Directrices are $y = \frac{a^2}{c}$ or $\frac{a}{e}$ and $y = \frac{-a^2}{c}$ or $-\frac{a}{e}$

(vii) Eccentricity, $e = \frac{c}{a} = \sqrt{1 + \frac{b^2}{a^2}}$ or $b^2 = a^2(e^2 - 1)$

(viii) Length of latusrectum $= \frac{2b^2}{a}$

(ix) Coordinate of latusrectum $= \left(\pm \frac{b^2}{a}, \pm ae\right)$

(x) Focal length $= 2ae$

Note **Conjugate hyperbola** The hyperbola whose transverse and conjugate axis are respectively the conjugate and transverse axis of a given hyperbola is called the conjugate hyperbola of the given hyperbola. So, if $\frac{x^2}{a^2} - \frac{y^2}{b^2} = 1$ is the given hyperbola, then $\frac{y^2}{b^2} - \frac{x^2}{a^2} = 1$ is its conjugate hyperbola.

Observations from Standard Equation

From the standard equations of the hyperbola, we observed the following points.

(i) If we replace (x, y) either by $(x, -y)$ or $(-x, y)$ or $(-x, -y)$, then the equation of hyperbola does not change. It means, it is symmetrical with respect to both the coordinate axes.

(ii) Foci are always lie on the transverse axis of the hyperbola.

(iii) If the coefficient of x^2 is positive term, then transverse axis is along X-axis.

(iv) If the coefficient of y^2 is positive term, then transverse axis is along Y-axis.

Note From the standard equation of hyperbola,

$$\frac{x^2}{a^2} - \frac{y^2}{b^2} = 1$$

We observe that

$$\frac{x^2}{a^2} = 1 + \frac{y^2}{b^2} \geq 1, \text{ i.e. } \left|\frac{x}{a}\right| \geq 1$$

$$\Rightarrow \quad |x| \geq |a|$$

$$\Rightarrow \quad x \leq -a \text{ and } x \geq a$$

Hence, no portion of the curve lies between the lines $x = a$ and $x = -a$ (i.e. no real intercepts on the conjugate axis).

Comparison between Two Standard Hyperbola

S. No.	Terms	Horizontal hyperbola	Vertical hyperbola
	Equation of hyperbola	$\frac{x^2}{a^2} - \frac{y^2}{b^2} = 1$ (when coefficient of y^2 is – ve)	$\frac{y^2}{a^2} - \frac{x^2}{b^2} = 1$ (when coefficient of x^2 is – ve)
1.	Shape	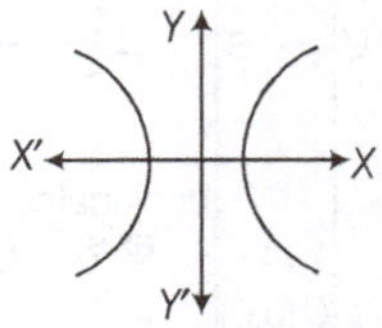	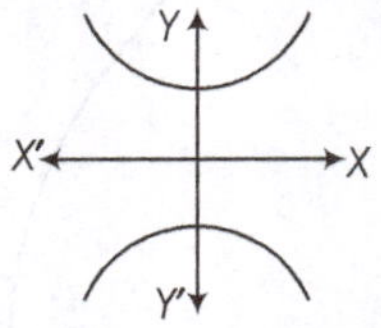
2.	Length of transverse axis	$2a$	$2a$
3.	Length of conjugate axis	$2b$	$2b$
4.	Value of c	$c = \sqrt{a^2 + b^2}$	$c = \sqrt{a^2 + b^2}$
5.	Vertices	$(\pm a, 0)$	$(0, \pm a)$
6.	Directrices	$x = \pm \frac{a^2}{c}$ or $\pm \frac{a}{e}$	$y = \pm \frac{a^2}{c}$ or $\pm \frac{a}{e}$
7.	Foci	$(\pm ae, 0)$ or $(\pm c, 0)$	$(0, \pm ae)$ or $(0, \pm c)$
8.	Eccentricity	$e = \sqrt{1 + \frac{b^2}{a^2}}$ or $\frac{c}{a}$	$e = \sqrt{1 + \frac{b^2}{a^2}}$ or $\frac{c}{a}$
9.	Length of latusrectum	$\frac{2b^2}{a}$	$\frac{2b^2}{a}$

Some Particular Types of Problems Based on Hyperbola

| TYPE I |

To Find the Different Terms of Hyperbola When Equation of Hyperbola is Given

For finding the different terms of a given hyperbola, first we check that given hyperbola is of the form

$$\frac{x^2}{a^2} - \frac{y^2}{b^2} = 1 \text{ or } \frac{y^2}{a^2} - \frac{x^2}{b^2} = 1.$$

Then, we find the terms of hyperbola by using the formulae from the given chart.

Example 1 Draw the shape of the hyperbola $\frac{x^2}{49} - \frac{y^2}{9} = 1$ and find their shape, centre, length of transverse and conjugate axis, value of c, vertices, directrices and foci.

Sol. Given equation of hyperbola is $\frac{x^2}{49} - \frac{y^2}{9} = 1$

On comparing it with $\frac{x^2}{a^2} - \frac{y^2}{b^2} = 1$, we get $a = 7, b = 3$

(i) Since, coefficient of y^2 is negative, therefore transverse axis of hyperbola is along X-axis and hence shape of hyperbola is as shown below.

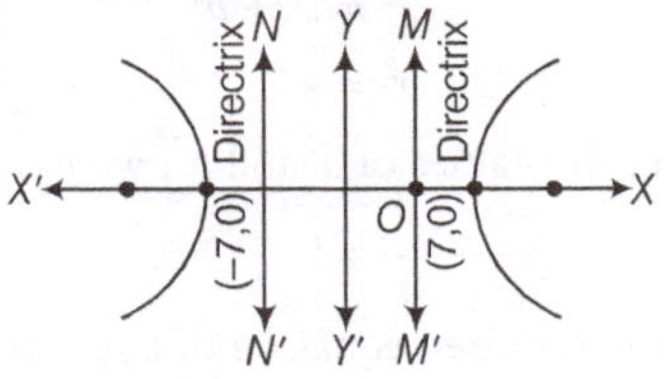

(ii) Centre (0, 0)

(iii) Length of transverse axis, $2a = 2 \times 7 = 14$

(iv) Length of conjugate axis, $2b = 2 \times 3 = 6$

(v) Value of $c = \sqrt{a^2 + b^2} = \sqrt{49 + 9} = \sqrt{58}$

(vi) Vertices $= (\pm a, 0) = (\pm 7, 0)$

(vii) Directrices, $x = \pm \frac{a^2}{c} = \pm \frac{49}{\sqrt{58}}$

(viii) Foci $= (\pm c, 0) = (\pm \sqrt{58}, 0)$

Example 2 Draw the shape of the hyperbola $\frac{y^2}{9} - \frac{x^2}{27} = 1$ and find their centre, length of transverse and conjugate axis, value of c, vertices, directrices, foci, eccentricity and latusrectum. **[NCERT]**

Sol. Given equation of hyperbola is $\frac{y^2}{9} - \frac{x^2}{27} = 1$

On comparing with $\frac{y^2}{a^2} - \frac{x^2}{b^2} = 1$, we get

$$a^2 = 9, b^2 = 27 \text{ or } a = 3, b = 3\sqrt{3}$$

(i) Since coefficient of x^2 is negative, therefore the transverse axis of hyperbola is along Y-axis and hence shape of hyperbola is as shown below.

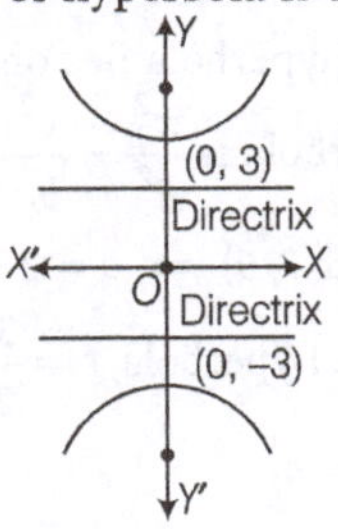

(ii) Centre = (0, 0)

(iii) Length of transverse axis, $2a = 2 \times 3 = 6$

(iv) Length of conjugate axis, $2b = 2 \times 3\sqrt{3} = 6\sqrt{3}$

(v) Value of $c = \sqrt{a^2 + b^2} = \sqrt{9 + 27} = \sqrt{36} = 6$

(vi) Vertices $= (0, \pm a) = (0, \pm 3)$

(vii) Directrices, $y = \pm \frac{a^2}{c} = \pm \frac{9}{6} = \pm \frac{3}{2}$

(viii) Foci $= (0, \pm c) = (0, \pm 6)$

(ix) Eccentricity, $e = \frac{c}{a} = \frac{6}{3} = 2$

(x) Length of latusrectum $= \frac{2b^2}{a} = \frac{2 \times 27}{3} = 18$

Example 3 Draw the shape of the hyperbola $5y^2 - 9x^2 = 36$ and find its centre, length of transverse and conjugate axis, value of c, vertices, directrices, foci, eccentricity and length of latusrectum.

Sol. Given, equation of hyperbola is $5y^2 - 9x^2 = 36$

It can be written as $\frac{y^2}{\left(\frac{6}{\sqrt{5}}\right)^2} - \frac{x^2}{(2)^2} = 1$

On comparing with $\frac{y^2}{a^2} - \frac{x^2}{b^2} = 1$, we get

$$a^2 = \left(\frac{6}{\sqrt{5}}\right)^2 \text{ and } b^2 = 2^2 \Rightarrow a = \frac{6}{\sqrt{5}} \text{ and } b = 2$$

(i) Since, coefficient of x^2 is negative, therefore transverse axis is along Y-axis and hence shape of hyperbola is as shown below.

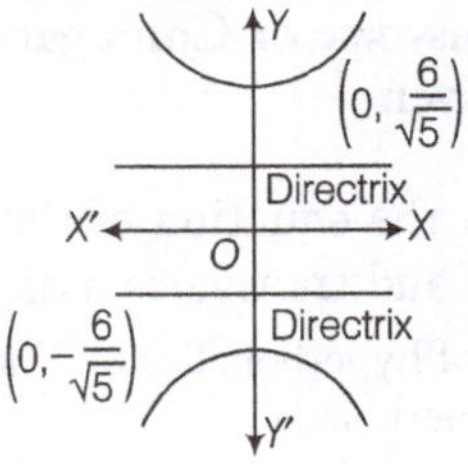

(ii) Centre (0, 0)

(iii) Length of transverse axis, $2a = 2 \times \frac{6}{\sqrt{5}} = \frac{12}{\sqrt{5}}$

(iv) Length of conjugate axis, $2b = 2 \times 2 = 4$

(v) Value of $c = \sqrt{a^2 + b^2} = \sqrt{\frac{36}{5} + 4} = \sqrt{\frac{56}{5}} = \frac{2\sqrt{14}}{\sqrt{5}}$

(vi) Vertices $= (0, \pm a) = \left(0, \pm \frac{6}{\sqrt{5}}\right)$

(vii) Directrices, $y = \pm \frac{a^2}{c} = \pm \frac{36 \times \sqrt{5}}{5 \times 2\sqrt{14}} = \pm \frac{18}{\sqrt{70}}$

(viii) Foci $= (0, \pm c) = \left(0, \pm \frac{2\sqrt{14}}{\sqrt{5}}\right)$

(ix) Eccentricity, $e = \frac{c}{a} = \frac{2\sqrt{\frac{14}{5}}}{\frac{6}{\sqrt{5}}} = \frac{\sqrt{14}}{3}$

(x) Length of latusrectum, $\frac{2b^2}{a} = \frac{2 \times 4}{\frac{6}{\sqrt{5}}} = \frac{4\sqrt{5}}{3}$

| TYPE II |

To Find the Equation of Hyperbola in Different Cases

When some parts of a hyperbola are given, then for finding the equation of hyperbola, we find the values of a and b with the help of given parts and then put these values in standard equation of hyperbola.

Case I When Foci and Vertices are Given

Example 4 Find the equation of the hyperbola, whose vertices are (0, ± 5) and foci (0, ± 8). **[NCERT]**

Sol. Here, the foci and vertices lie on Y-axis, therefore the equation of hyperbola is of the form $\frac{y^2}{a^2}-\frac{x^2}{b^2}=1$ ...(i)

Since, vertices $(0, \pm a)=(0, \pm 5)$, $a=5$

and foci $(0, \pm c)=(0, \pm 8)$, $c=8$

We know that, $c^2=a^2+b^2 \Rightarrow 64=25+b^2$

$\Rightarrow b^2=64-25 \Rightarrow b^2=39$

Hence, the equation of hyperbola is

$$\frac{y^2}{25}-\frac{x^2}{39}=1 \quad \text{[from Eq. (i)]}$$

Case II When Transverse or Conjugate Axis and Foci are Given

Example 5 Find the equation of the hyperbola having foci (0, ± 4) and transverse axis of length 6.

Sol. Here, the foci of hyperbola lies on Y-axis. So, the equation of hyperbola is

$$\frac{y^2}{a^2}-\frac{x^2}{b^2}=1$$

Length of its transverse axis $=2a$

$\therefore \quad 2a=6 \Rightarrow a=3$

Foci $\equiv(0, \pm c)=(0, \pm 4) \Rightarrow c=4$

We know that, $c^2=a^2+b^2$

$\Rightarrow 16=9+b^2 \Rightarrow b^2=7$

Thus, $a^2=9, b^2=7$

Hence, the equation of hyperbola is $\frac{y^2}{9}-\frac{x^2}{7}=1$

Example 6 Find the equation of hyperbola, when foci are at (±5, 0) and transverse axis is of length 8. **[NCERT]**

Sol. Since, the foci lie on X-axis, therefore the equation of hyperbola is of the form

$$\frac{x^2}{a^2}-\frac{y^2}{b^2}=1 \quad \text{...(i)}$$

Here, foci are at (± 5, 0).

$\therefore \quad (\pm c, 0)=(\pm 5, 0) \Rightarrow c=5$

and length of transverse axis $=2a=8 \Rightarrow a=4$

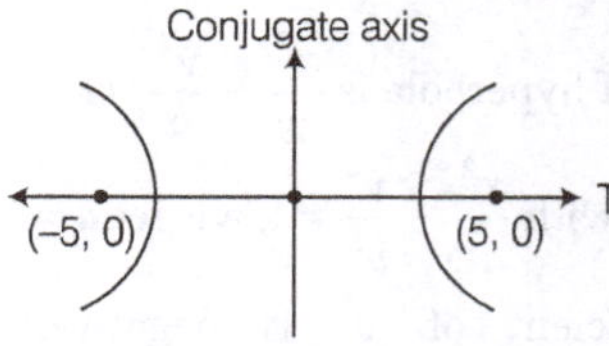

Also, we know that, $c^2=a^2+b^2$

$\Rightarrow 25=16+b^2 \quad [\because a=4, c=5]$

$\Rightarrow b^2=9$

On putting the values of a^2 and b^2, we get

$$\frac{x^2}{16}-\frac{y^2}{9}=1 \quad \text{[from Eq. (i)]}$$

which is the required equation of hyperbola.

Example 7 Find the equation of the hyperbola whose foci are at (0, ± 6) and length of whose conjugate axis is $2\sqrt{11}$.

Sol. Here, foci of the hyperbola lies on Y-axis.

So, the equation of hyperbola is $\frac{y^2}{a^2}-\frac{x^2}{b^2}=1$

Now, foci $\equiv(0, \pm c)=(0, \pm 6) \Rightarrow c=6$

and length of its conjugate axis $=2b$

$\therefore \quad 2b=2\sqrt{11} \Rightarrow b=\sqrt{11}$

We know that, $c^2=a^2+b^2 \quad [\because c=6 \text{ and } b=\sqrt{11}]$

$\therefore \quad 6^2=a^2+(\sqrt{11})^2 \Rightarrow a^2=36-11=25$

Thus, $a^2=25, b^2=11$

Hence, the equation of hyperbola is $\frac{y^2}{25}-\frac{x^2}{11}=1$

Case III When Vertices or Foci and Eccentricity are Given

Example 8 Find the equation of the hyperbola whose eccentricity is $\frac{3}{2}$ and foci are (± 2, 0). **[NCERT Exemplar]**

Sol. Here, foci of the hyperbola lies on X-axis. So, the equation of hyperbola is $\frac{x^2}{a^2}-\frac{y^2}{b^2}=1$ ...(i)

Foci $\equiv(\pm c, 0)=(\pm 2, 0) \Rightarrow c=2$

Eccentricity of the hyperbola, $e=\frac{3}{2}$

We know that, $c=ae$

$\therefore \quad 2=a\left(\frac{3}{2}\right) \Rightarrow a=\frac{4}{3}$

Also, we know that, $c^2=a^2+b^2$

$\Rightarrow (2)^2=\left(\frac{4}{3}\right)^2+b^2$

$\Rightarrow b^2=\frac{20}{9}$

Thus, $a^2 = \frac{16}{9}$, $b^2 = \frac{20}{9}$

Hence, equation of hyperbola is

$$\frac{9x^2}{16} - \frac{9y^2}{20} = 1 \quad \text{[from Eq. (i)]}$$

$$\Rightarrow \quad 45x^2 - 36y^2 = 80$$

Example 9 Find the equation of hyperbola, if vertices are at (± 7, 0) and $e = \frac{4}{3}$. **[NCERT]**

Sol. Here, vertices of hyperbola lies on X-axis. So, the equation of hyperbola is $\frac{x^2}{a^2} - \frac{y^2}{b^2} = 1$ ...(i)

Vertices ≡ $(\pm a, 0) = (\pm 7, 0) \Rightarrow a = 7$

$$\because \quad e = \sqrt{1 + \frac{b^2}{a^2}}, \text{ therefore } e^2 = 1 + \frac{b^2}{a^2}$$

$$\Rightarrow \quad \left(\frac{4}{3}\right)^2 = 1 + \frac{b^2}{7^2} \quad [\because e = 4/3 \text{ and } a = 7]$$

$$\Rightarrow \quad \frac{b^2}{49} = \frac{16}{9} - 1 \Rightarrow b^2 = \frac{343}{9}$$

Thus, $a^2 = 49, b^2 = \frac{343}{9}$

Hence, the equation of hyperbola is

$$\frac{x^2}{49} - \frac{9y^2}{343} = 1 \Rightarrow 7x^2 - 9y^2 = 343 \quad \text{[from Eq. (i)]}$$

Case IV When Foci and Length of Latusrectum are Given

Example 10 Find the equation of hyperbola whose foci are (0, ± 12) and the length of latusrectum is 36.

Sol. Here, foci of the hyperbola lies on Y-axis. So, the equation of hyperbola is

$$\frac{y^2}{a^2} - \frac{x^2}{b^2} = 1 \quad \text{...(i)}$$

Foci ≡ $(0, \pm c) = (0, \pm 12) \Rightarrow c = 12$

Length of its latusrectum $= \frac{2b^2}{a}$

$$\Rightarrow \quad \frac{2b^2}{a} = 36 \Rightarrow b^2 = 18a$$

Now, $c^2 = a^2 + b^2 \Rightarrow (12)^2 = a^2 + 18a$

$$\Rightarrow \quad a^2 + 18a - 144 = 0 \Rightarrow (a + 24)(a - 6) = 0$$

$$\Rightarrow \quad a = 6 \quad [\because a \neq -24]$$

Thus, $a^2 = 36$ and $b^2 = 18a = 18 \times 6 = 108$

Hence, the equation of hyperbola is

$$\frac{y^2}{36} - \frac{x^2}{108} = 1$$

$$\Rightarrow \quad 3y^2 - x^2 = 108 \quad \text{[from Eq. (i)]}$$

Case V When Vertices and Directrix are Given

Example 11 Find the equation of hyperbola whose vertices are (± 6, 0) and one of the directrices is $x = 4$.

Sol. Here, vertices of hyperbola lies on X-axis.

So, the equation of hyperbola is

$$\frac{x^2}{a^2} - \frac{y^2}{b^2} = 1 \quad \text{...(i)}$$

Vertices of hyperbola ≡ $(\pm a, 0) = (\pm 6, 0) \Rightarrow a = 6$

Equation of directrix is $x = \frac{a}{e} \Rightarrow \frac{a}{e} = 4$

$$\Rightarrow \quad \frac{6}{e} = 4 \Rightarrow e = \frac{3}{2}$$

Now, $e = \sqrt{1 + \frac{b^2}{a^2}}$

$$\Rightarrow \quad a^2e^2 = a^2 + b^2$$

$$\Rightarrow \quad \left(6 \times \frac{3}{2}\right)^2 = 6^2 + b^2$$

$$\Rightarrow \quad b^2 = 9^2 - 6^2 = 45$$

Thus, $a^2 = 36, \; b^2 = 45$

Hence, the equation of hyperbola is $\frac{x^2}{36} - \frac{y^2}{45} = 1$. [from Eq. (i)]

Case VI When Other Parts of Hyperbola are Given

Example 12 Find the equation of hyperbola, the length of whose latusrectum is 8, eccentricity is $\frac{3}{\sqrt{5}}$ and whose transverse and conjugate axes are along the X and Y-axes respectively.

Sol. Since, transverse axis is along the X-axis. So, the equation of hyperbola is

$$\frac{x^2}{a^2} - \frac{y^2}{b^2} = 1 \quad \text{...(i)}$$

Length of its latusrectum $= \frac{2b^2}{a}$

$$\Rightarrow \quad \frac{2b^2}{a} = 8 \Rightarrow b^2 = 4a$$

Now, $e = \sqrt{1 + \frac{b^2}{a^2}} \Rightarrow \frac{3}{\sqrt{5}} = \sqrt{1 + \frac{4a}{a^2}}$

$$[\because e = 3/\sqrt{5} \text{ and } b^2 = 4a]$$

$$\Rightarrow \quad \frac{9}{5} = 1 + \frac{4}{a} \Rightarrow \frac{4}{a} = \frac{4}{5} \Rightarrow a = 5$$

Thus, $a^2 = 25$ and $b^2 = 4a = 4(5) = 20$

Hence, the equation of hyperbola is $\frac{x^2}{25} - \frac{y^2}{20} = 1$.

[from Eq. (i)]

| TYPE III |

Problems Based on Finding the Eccentricity in Different Conditions

Example 13 Find the eccentricity of the hyperbola whose length of latusrectum is 8 and conjugate axis is equal to the half of its distance between the foci. **[NCERT Exemplar]**

Sol. Since, conjugate axis is half of distance between foci.

$\therefore \quad 2b = \frac{1}{2} 2c \Rightarrow 2b = c \Rightarrow 4b^2 = c^2$

$\Rightarrow \quad 4b^2 = a^2 + b^2 \Rightarrow \frac{b^2}{a^2} = \frac{1}{3}$

Now, $\quad e = \sqrt{1 + \frac{b^2}{a^2}} \Rightarrow e = \sqrt{1 + \frac{1}{3}} \Rightarrow e = \frac{2}{\sqrt{3}}$

Example 14 If e and e' are the eccentricities of the hyperbola $\frac{x^2}{a^2} - \frac{y^2}{b^2} = 1$ and its conjugate hyperbola, then prove that $\frac{1}{e^2} + \frac{1}{e'^2} = 1$.

Sol. Given hyperbola is $\frac{x^2}{a^2} - \frac{y^2}{b^2} = 1$.

The eccentricity e of this hyperbola is

$$e^2 = 1 + \frac{b^2}{a^2}$$

$$\Rightarrow \quad e^2 = \frac{a^2 + b^2}{a^2}$$

$$\Rightarrow \quad \frac{1}{e^2} = \frac{a^2}{a^2 + b^2} \quad \text{...(i)}$$

The equation of the conjugate hyperbola is

$$\frac{y^2}{b^2} - \frac{x^2}{a^2} = 1$$

The eccentricity e' of this hyperbola is

$$e'^2 = 1 + \frac{a^2}{b^2}$$

$$\Rightarrow \quad e'^2 = \frac{b^2 + a^2}{b^2}$$

$$\Rightarrow \quad \frac{1}{e'^2} = \frac{b^2}{a^2 + b^2} \quad \text{...(ii)}$$

On adding Eqs. (i) and (ii), we get

$$\frac{1}{e^2} + \frac{1}{e'^2} = \frac{a^2 + b^2}{a^2 + b^2} = 1$$

$$\therefore \quad \frac{1}{e^2} + \frac{1}{e'^2} = 1$$ **Hence proved.**

Note Equation of vertical hyperbola is $\frac{y^2}{a^2} - \frac{x^2}{b^2} = 1$, which is different from $\frac{y^2}{b^2} - \frac{x^2}{a^2} = 1$.

General Equations of a Hyperbola

Here, we will obtain the equation of hyperbola when focus is any point directrix is any line and eccentricity is (e).

By definition, we have

Distance of point P on hyperbola from the focus
$= e \times$ (distance of P from the directrix)

Let the focus S be (α, β) and the equation of the corresponding directrix be $lx + my + n = 0$ and eccentricity be 'e'.

Let $P(x, y)$ be any point on the hyperbola.

Then by definition,

$$\sqrt{(x-\alpha)^2 + (y-\beta)^2} = e \times \frac{|lx + my + n|}{\sqrt{l^2 + m^2}}$$

or $$[(x-\alpha)^2 + (y-\beta)^2] = e^2 \frac{(lx + my + n)^2}{(l^2 + m^2)}$$

This equation, when simplified reduces to the form.

$$ax^2 + 2hxy + by^2 + 2gx + 2fy + c = 0$$

which is the general equation of the hyperbola.

Example 15 Find the equation of the hyperbola whose focus is (1,1), directrix is $2x + y - 1 = 0$ and eccentricity is $\sqrt{3}$.

Sol. Here, focus S is (1, 1), equation of directrix is $2x + y - 1 = 0$ and $e = \sqrt{3}$.

Let $P(x, y)$ be any point on the hyperbola, then equation of hyperbola is

$$(x-1)^2 + (y-1)^2 = (\sqrt{3})^2 \cdot \frac{(2x + y - 1)^2}{2^2 + 1^2}$$

$$\Rightarrow \quad 5[(x-1)^2 + (y-1)^2] = 3(2x + y - 1)^2$$

$$\Rightarrow \quad 5(x^2 + y^2 - 2x - 2y + 2) = 3(4x^2 + y^2 + 1 + 4xy - 4x - 2y)$$

$$\Rightarrow \quad 7x^2 - 2y^2 + 12xy - 2x + 4y - 7 = 0$$

$$\Rightarrow \quad 7x^2 + 12xy - 2y^2 - 2x + 4y - 7 = 0$$

Focal Property of Hyperbola

The difference of the focal distance of any point on a hyperbola is constant and equal to the length of the transverse axis of the hyperbola.

Proof Let $P(x, y)$ be any point on the hyperbola

$\frac{x^2}{a^2} - \frac{y^2}{b^2} = 1$. Then by definition,

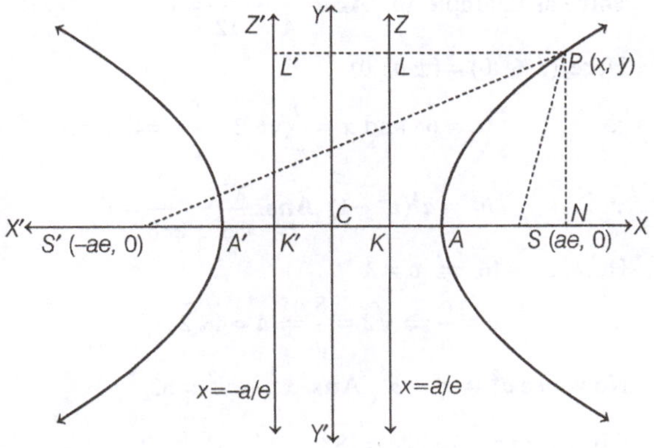

$$SP = ePL \text{ and } S'P = ePL'$$

Now, $SP = ePL$

$\Rightarrow$ $SP = e(NK) = e(CN - CK)$

$$= e\left(x - \frac{a}{e}\right) = ex - a$$

and $S'P = ePL'$

$\Rightarrow$ $S'P = e(NK') = e(CN + CK')$

$$= e\left(x + \frac{a}{e}\right) = ex + a$$

$\Rightarrow$ $S'P - SP = (ex + a - en + a) = 2a$

= Length of transverse axis

Hence, the difference of the focal distances of a point on the hyperbola is constant and is equal to the length of the transverse axis of the hyperbola.

Example 16 Find the equation of the locus of all points such that difference of their distance from (4, 0) and (– 4, 0) is always to 2.

Sol. Clearly, the locus will be hyperbola, whose foci are (4, 0) and (–4, 0).

Since, foci of the hyperbola lies on X-axis and mid-point of line joining the foci is (0, 0), therefore the equation of hyperbola is

$$\frac{x^2}{a^2} - \frac{y^2}{b^2} = 1 \quad \text{...(i)}$$

Let the given points be S (4, 0) and S'(– 4, 0).

Now, $SS' = \sqrt{(4+4)^2 + (0-0)^2} = 8$

We know that,

$$SS' = 2c$$

$\therefore$ $2c = 8 \Rightarrow c = 4$

Let $P(x, y)$ be any point on the hyperbola.

According to question,

$$|PS - PS'| = 2$$

Also,we know

$$|PS - PS'| = 2a$$

$\therefore$ $2a = 2 \Rightarrow a = 1$

$\because$ $c^2 = a^2 + b^2$

$\therefore$ $16 = 1 + b^2$

$\Rightarrow$ $b^2 = 15$ $\quad [\because c = 4 \text{ and } a = 1]$

On putting the values of $a^2 = 1$ and $b^2 = 15$ in Eq. (i), we get

$$\frac{x^2}{1} - \frac{y^2}{15} = 1$$

i.e. $15x^2 - y^2 = 15$

which is the required equation of hyperbola.

Topic Practice 3

Very Short Answer Type Questions

2 Marks

1. Find the distance between the directrices of the hyperbola $x^2 - y^2 = 8$.
2. Find the latusrectum of the hyperbola $16x^2 - 9y^2 = 144$.
3. Find the eccentricity and the coordinates of foci of the hyperbola $25x^2 - 9y^2 = 225$. **[ISC 2014]**
4. Find the equation of hyperbola having vertices (± 5, 0) and foci at (± 7, 0).
5. Find the equation of hyperbola, having foci (± 4, 0) and length of latusrectum is 12. **[NCERT]**
6. Find the equation of the hyperbola whose vertices are (±6, 0) and one of the directrix is $x = 2$.
7. If the distance between the foci of a hyperbola is 16 and its eccentricity is $\sqrt{2}$, then find the equation of the hyperbola. **[NCERT Exemplar]**
8. Find the equation of the hyperbola whose conjugate axis is 5 and the distance between the foci is 13. **[ISC 2012]**
9. Find the eccentricity of the hyperbola, the length of whose conjugate axis is 3/4 of the length of transverse axis.

Short Answer Type Questions

4 Marks

10 Draw the shape of hyperbola and find the length of the axes, coordinate of the vertices, coordinate of the foci, eccentricity and length of the latusrectum of each of the following hyperbola.

(i) $\frac{x^2}{25}-\frac{y^2}{4}=1$ (ii) $\frac{x^2}{9}-\frac{y^2}{16}=1$

11 Find the lengths of transverse and conjugate axes, eccentricity and coordinate of foci and vertices, length of latusrectum, equation of the directrix of the hyperbola $25x^2-36y^2=225$.

12 Find the eccentricity of the hyperbola $\frac{x^2}{a^2}-\frac{y^2}{b^2}=1$, when passes through the points $(3, 0)$ and $(3\sqrt{2}, 2)$. **[NCERT Exemplar]**

13 Find the equation of the hyperbola whose one directrix is $x+y=9$, the corresponding focus is $(2, 2)$ and eccentricity is 2.

Hints & Answers

1. Distance between directrices $=\frac{2a}{e}$

Here, $a=b=2\sqrt{2}$ and $e=\sqrt{1+\frac{b^2}{a^2}}=\sqrt{2}$ **Ans.** 4

2. Given equation is $\frac{x^2}{9}-\frac{y^2}{16}=1$

Here, $a^2=9$, $b^2=16$ and length of latusrectum $=\frac{2b^2}{a}$

Ans. $\frac{32}{3}$

3. Given equation of hyperbola is

$$25x^2-9y^2=225$$

$$\Rightarrow \frac{x^2}{9}-\frac{y^2}{25}=1$$

On comparing above equation with hyperbola $\frac{x^2}{a^2}-\frac{y^2}{b^2}=1$, we get

$$a=3 \text{ and } b=5$$

Now, $e=\sqrt{1+\frac{b^2}{a^2}}$ and Foci $\equiv(\pm ae, 0)$

Ans. $\frac{\sqrt{34}}{3}$ and $(\pm\sqrt{34}, 0)$

4. Here, $(\pm a, 0)=(\pm 5, 0) \Rightarrow a=5$

and $(\pm c, 0)=(\pm 7, 0) \Rightarrow c=7$

$\because c^2=a^2+b^2 \Rightarrow 49=25+b^2 \Rightarrow b^2=24$

Ans. $\frac{x^2}{25}-\frac{y^2}{24}=1$

5. Solve as Example 10. **Ans.** $\frac{x^2}{4}-\frac{y^2}{12}=1$

6. Here, $(\pm 6, 0)=(\pm a, 0)$

$\therefore$ $a=6$ and $x=\frac{a}{e} \Rightarrow 2=\frac{6}{e} \Rightarrow e=3$

$\because$ $b^2=a^2(e^2-1)$ **Ans.** $\frac{x^2}{36}-\frac{y^2}{288}=1$

7. Here, $2c=16 \Rightarrow c=8$

$\because$ $e=\frac{c}{a} \Rightarrow \sqrt{2}=\frac{8}{a} \Rightarrow a=4\sqrt{2}$

Now, use $c^2=a^2+b^2$ **Ans.** $x^2-y^2=32$

8. Given, $2b=5$ and $2c=13$

$\Rightarrow$ $b=\frac{5}{2}$ and $c=\frac{13}{2}$

Now, use $c^2=a^2+b^2$ **Ans.** $\frac{x^2}{144}-\frac{y^2}{25}=\frac{1}{4}$

9. $\because$ $2b=\frac{3}{4}(2a) \Rightarrow b=\frac{3}{4}a.$

Now, $e=\sqrt{1+\frac{b^2}{a^2}}$ **Ans.** $\frac{5}{4}$

10. (i) Solve as Example 1.

Ans. 10, 4, $(\pm 5, 0)$, $(\pm\sqrt{29}, 0)$, $\frac{\sqrt{29}}{5}$, $\frac{8}{5}$

(ii) Solve as Example 1. **Ans.** 6, 8, $(\pm 3, 0)$, $(\pm 5, 0)$, $\frac{5}{3}$, $\frac{32}{3}$

11. $\frac{x^2}{9}-\frac{y^2}{\frac{225}{36}}=1$

Here, $a^2=9$, $b^2=\frac{225}{36}$

and $c^2=\sqrt{a^2+b^2}$

$$=\sqrt{9+\frac{225}{36}}=\sqrt{\frac{549}{36}}=\frac{\sqrt{549}}{6}=\frac{3\sqrt{61}}{6}=\frac{\sqrt{61}}{2}$$

Ans. 6, 5, $\frac{\sqrt{61}}{6}$, $\left(\pm\frac{\sqrt{61}}{2}, 0\right)$, $(\pm 3, 0)$, $\frac{25}{6}$, $x=\pm\frac{18}{\sqrt{61}}$

12. Since, the hyperbola passes through $(3, 0)$ and $(3\sqrt{2}, 2)$.

$\therefore$ $\frac{9}{a^2}-0=1$ and $\frac{18}{a^2}-\frac{4}{b^2}=1$

$\Rightarrow$ $a^2=9$ and $b^2=4$

Now, $e=\sqrt{1+\frac{b^2}{a^2}}$ **Ans.** $e=\frac{\sqrt{13}}{3}$

13. Solve as Example 15.

Ans. $x^2+4xy+y^2-32x-32y+154=0$

Chapter Practice

Multiple Choice Type Questions

1 Mark

1. The vertex separates the double napped right circular cone into ...*M*... parts called ...*N*... . Here, *M* and *N* respectively stand for
(a) three, nappes
(b) two, shapes
(c) two, nappes
(d) three, cones

2. Different kinds of conic sections are obtained depending on
(a) the position of the intersecting plane with respect to the cone
(b) angle made by intersecting plane with the vertical axis of the cone
(c) Both (a) and (b)
(d) Neither (a) nor (b)

3. Vertex of the parabola $9x^2 - 6x + 36y + 9 = 0$, is
(a) $\left(\frac{1}{3}, -\frac{2}{9}\right)$ (b) $\left(-\frac{1}{3}, -\frac{1}{2}\right)$
(c) $\left(-\frac{1}{3}, \frac{1}{2}\right)$ (d) $\left(\frac{1}{3}, \frac{1}{2}\right)$

4. The length of the latusrectum of the parabola $9x^2 - 6x + 36y + 19 = 0$, is
(a) 36 (b) 9
(c) 6 (d) 4

5. Latusrectum of an ellipse is a line segment ...*A*... to the major axis through any of the ...*B*... and whose end points lie on the ellipse. Here, *A* and *B* respectively are
(a) perpendicular, foci
(b) parallel, vertices
(c) parallel, foci
(d) perpendicular, vertices

6. The number of possible orientations of hyperbola is/are
(a) one (b) two
(c) three (d) four

Assertion-Reason Type Questions

1 Mark

Directions (Q. Nos. 7-10) *In the questions given below are two statements labelled as Assertion (A) and Reason (R). In the context of the two statements, which one of the following is correct?*
(a) Both A and R are correct; R is the correct explanation of A
(b) Both A and R are correct; R is not the correct explanation of A
(c) A is correct; R is incorrect
(d) R is correct; A is incorrect

7. **Assertion (A)** The distance between the directrices of the ellipse $\frac{x^2}{25} + \frac{y^2}{16} = 1$ is $\frac{2}{3}$.
Reason (R) The distance between the directrices of the ellipse $\frac{x^2}{a^2} + \frac{y^2}{b^2} = 1$ is $\frac{2a}{e}$.

8. **Assertion (A)** If the line $2x + 3y + k = 0$ touches the parabola $y^2 = 16x$, the value of k is 18.
Reason (R) If the line $lx + my + n = 0$ touches the parabola $y^2 = 4ax$, then $ln = am^2$.

9. **Assertion (A)** Slope of tangents drawn from (4, 10) to parabola $y^2 = 9x$ are $\frac{1}{4}, \frac{9}{4}$.
Reason (R) Every parabola is symmetric about its directrix.

10. **Assertion (A)** The slope of the common tangent between the hyperbola $\frac{x^2}{a^2} - \frac{y^2}{b^2} = 1$ and $\frac{-x^2}{b^2} + \frac{y^2}{a^2} = 1$ may be 1 or –1.
Reason (R) The locus of the point of intersection of lines $\frac{x}{a} - \frac{y}{b} = m$ and $\frac{x}{a} + \frac{y}{b} = \frac{1}{m}$ is a hyperbola (where m is variable and $ab \neq 0$).

Very Short Answer Type Questions

(2 Marks)

11. Find the equation of the parabola whose focus is (2, 0) and directrix is $x = -2$.

12. Find the equation of the parabola with vertex at the origin, the axis along the X-axis and passing through the point (2, 3).

13. Find the equation of the parabola whose vertex and focus lie on the Y-axis at distance b and b' respectively from the origin.

14. Find the equation of the parabola whose focus is (–1, 2) and directrix is $x - 2y - 15 = 0$.

15. Find the equation of the parabola whose focus is (a, b) and directrix $\frac{x}{a} + \frac{y}{b} = 1$

16. Find the equation of parabola whose vertex is at (–2, 3) and the focus at (1, 3).

17. Find the focus and directrix of the parabola $3x^2 + 12x + 8y = 0$.

18. The points (0, 4) and (0, 2) are respectively the vertex and focus of a parabola. Find the equation of the parabola. **[ISC 2005]**

19. Find the equation of ellipse having ends of major and minor axes are $(0, \pm\sqrt{5})$ and $(\pm 1, 0)$. **[NCERT]**

20. Find the equation of the ellipse, having eccentricity $\frac{1}{2}$ and semi-major axis is 4.

21. Find the equation of the hyperbola, having foci $(\pm 3\sqrt{5}, 0)$ and length of latusrectum is 8.

22. Find the equation of the hyperbola whose vertices are $(\pm 2, 0)$ and the eccentricity is 2.

23. Find the equation of the hyperbola with vertices at $(0, \pm 6)$ and $e = \frac{5}{3}$. Find its foci. **[NCERT Exemplar]**

24. Find the equation of hyperbola, if length of transverse axis is 10 and conjugate axis is 8.

25. Identify the curve represented by the equation $x^2 + 4xy + y^2 - 2x + 2y - 6 = 0$.

Short Answer Type Questions

(4 Marks)

26. Find the coordinates of the focus and the vertex, the equation of directrix and the axis of the following. (i) $x^2 = 10y$ (ii) $3x^2 = 8y$

27. Find the coordinates of the focus and the vertex, equation of directrix and length of latusrectum of the following.
   (i) $y^2 = 10x$ (ii) $5y^2 = -16x$

28. Find the axis, vertex, directrix and length of latusrectum of parabola $9y^2 - 16x - 12y - 57 = 0$.

29. The focus of a parabolic mirror as shown in figure is at a distance 6 cm from its vertex. If the mirror is 20 cm deep, then find the distance LM.

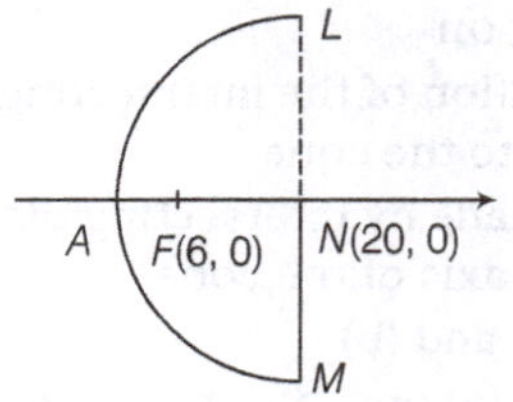

30. If the latusrectum of an ellipse with axis along X-axis and centre at origin is 10, distance between foci is equal to length of minor axis, then find the equation of ellipse. **[NCERT]**

31. Find the equation of the ellipse which passes through the point (–3, 1) and has eccentricity $\frac{\sqrt{2}}{5}$, with X-axis as its major axis and centre at the origin. **[NCERT Exemplar]**

32. Find the equation of the ellipse, whose focus is (1, – 2), the directrix $3x - 2y + 5 = 0$ and eccentricity equal to $\frac{1}{2}$.

33. Find the coordinates of the foci, vertices, eccentricity and length of latusrectum of the following hyperbola.
   (i) $49y^2 - 16x^2 = 784$ (ii) $16x^2 - 9y^2 = 576$

34. Find the length of the axes, vertices, foci, eccentricity and length of the latusrectum of the following hyperbola.
   (i) $9x^2 - 16y^2 = 144$ (ii) $9y^2 - 4x^2 = 36$

35. Find the equation of the hyperbola, whose foci are $(0, \pm 13)$ and the length of the conjugate axis is 20. **[ISC 2011]**

36. Find the equation of the hyperbola whose foci are at $(0, \pm\sqrt{10})$ and which passes through the point (2, 3).

37. Find the equation of hyperbola, having directrix $x - y + 3 = 0$, focus $(-1, 1)$ and eccentricity 3.

38. From the following information, find the equation of the hyperbola and the equation of its transverse axis.

Focus $= (-2, 1)$, directrix, $2x - 3y + 1 = 0$ and $e = \dfrac{2}{\sqrt{3}}$

[ISC 2013]

Case-Based Type Questions

6 Marks

39. Salim made a flower-bed in his garden. Surprisingly which is in the shape of a parabola whose equation is $y^2 = 8x$, the flower-bed is shown as in below figure.

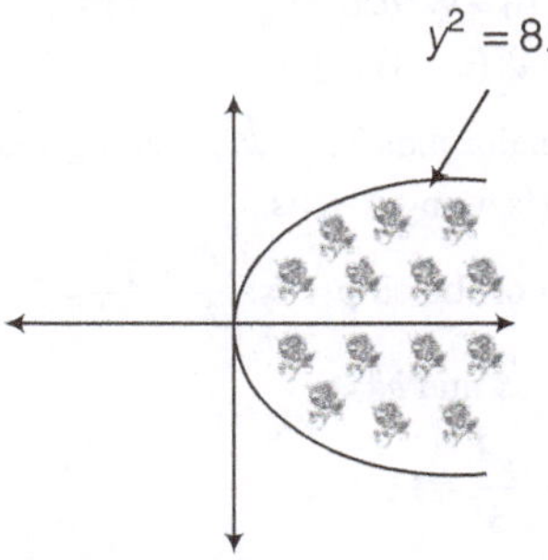

Then, answer the following questions which are based on above figure.

(i) Find the focus of given parabola.
(ii) Find the axis of the parabola.
(iii) Find the equation of the directrix of the parabola.
(iv) Find the length of the latusrectum of the parabola.
(v) If the focal distance of a point on the parabola is 3, then find abscissa of the point.

Hints & Answers

1. (c) **2.** (c) **3.** (a) **4.** (d) **5.** (a)
6. (b) **7.** (d) **8.** (a) **9.** (c) **10.** (b)

11. $\because$ Directrix is $x = -2$ and the focus is (2, 0).

$\therefore$ Required equation of parabola is $y^2 = 4ax$, where $a = 2$.

Ans. $y^2 = 8x$

12. Equation of the parabola with vertex at the origin, the axis along the X-axis is

$$y^2 = 4ax \quad ...(i)$$

Since, parabola (i) passes through the point (2, 3).

$\therefore \quad 9 = 4 \times a \times 2$ [from Eq. (i)]

$\Rightarrow \quad 9 = 8a$

$\Rightarrow \quad a = \dfrac{9}{8}$

Ans. $y^2 = \dfrac{9}{2}x.$

13. $x^2 = 4(b' - b)y - 4b(b' - b)$

14. Let $P(x, y)$ be any point on the parabola. Distance of $P(x, y)$ from the focus $(-1, 2) =$ Distance of $P(x, y)$ from the directrix $x - 2y - 15 = 0$ [by definition of parabola]

$\therefore$ Required equation of the parabola is given by

$$(x+1)^2 + (y-2)^2 = \left|\frac{x - 2y - 15}{\sqrt{1^2 + (-2)^2}}\right|^2$$

Ans. $4x^2 + 4xy + y^2 + 40x - 80y - 200 = 0$

15. Let $P(x, y)$ be any point on the hyperbola.

Then, distance of P from the focus

$=$ Its distance from the directrix.

$$\therefore \quad \sqrt{(x-a)^2 + (y-b)^2} = \frac{|bx + ay - ab|}{\sqrt{a^2 + b^2}}$$

Ans. $a^2x^2 - 2abxy + b^2y^2 - 2a^3x - 2b^3y + (a^4 + a^2b^2 + b^4) = 0$

16. $y^2 - 6y - 12x - 15 = 0$

17. Given, $3x^2 + 12x + 8y = 0$

$\Rightarrow \quad x^2 + 4x + \dfrac{8}{3}y = 0$ [dividing both sides]

$\Rightarrow \quad x^2 + 4x + 4 = -\dfrac{8}{3}y + 4$

$\Rightarrow \quad (x+2)^2 = -4\left(\dfrac{2}{3}y - 1\right)$

Let $\quad X = x + 2$

and $\quad Y = \left(\dfrac{2}{3}y - 1\right) \quad ...(i)$

$\therefore \quad X^2 = -4Y \quad ...(ii)$

Ans. Focus $\equiv (-2, 0)$ and directrix, $y = 3$

18. Given, vertex $= (0, 4)$ and focus $= (0, 2)$

It implies, axis of parabola is Y-axis.

Also, distance between vertex and focus $= 4 - 2 = 2$

i.e. $\quad a = 2$

Let the equation of parabola be

$$(x-\alpha)^2 = -4a(y-\beta)$$

where, $(\alpha, \beta) \equiv$ vertex.

Ans. $x^2 = -8(y-4)$

19. Since, the major axis $(0, \pm\sqrt{5})$ is along Y-axis and minor axis $(\pm 1, 0)$ is along X-axis.

$\therefore$ Equation of the ellipse is $\frac{x^2}{b^2} + \frac{y^2}{a^2} = 1$

where, $a = \sqrt{5}$ and $b = 1$

Ans. $\frac{x^2}{1} + \frac{y^2}{5} = 1$

20. Given, $e = \frac{1}{2}$ and $a = 4$

$$\therefore \quad e^2 = \frac{a^2 - b^2}{a^2} \Rightarrow \frac{1}{4} = \frac{16 - b^2}{16} \Rightarrow b^2 = 12$$

Ans. $3x^2 + 4y^2 = 48$

21. Let foci $(\pm c, 0) \equiv (\pm 3\sqrt{5}, 0) \Rightarrow c = 3\sqrt{5}$

and length of latusrectum $= \frac{2b^2}{a} = 8 \Rightarrow b^2 = 4a$

On putting $c = 3\sqrt{5}$ and $b^2 = 4a$ in $c^2 = a^2 + b^2$, we get

$$45 = a^2 + 4a \Rightarrow a^2 + 4a - 45 = 0$$

$$\Rightarrow \quad a = -9 \text{ or } a = 5$$

But $\quad a \neq -9 \Rightarrow a = 5$

On putting $a = 5$ in $b^2 = 4a$, we get $b^2 = 20$

Ans. $\frac{x^2}{25} - \frac{y^2}{20} = 1.$

22. Let vertices $(\pm a, 0) \equiv (\pm 2, 0)$

$\Rightarrow a = 2$ and eccentricity, $e = 2$

On putting $a = 2$ and $e = 2$ in $e^2 = \frac{a^2 + b^2}{a^2}$, we get

$$4 = \frac{4 + b^2}{4} \Rightarrow b^2 = 12$$

Ans. $\frac{x^2}{4} - \frac{y^2}{12} = 0.$

23. Let vertices $\equiv (0, \pm b) = (0, \pm 6)$

$$b = 6 \text{ and } e = \frac{5}{3}$$

$$\therefore \quad e^2 = \frac{a^2 + b^2}{b^2}$$

$$\Rightarrow \quad \frac{25}{9} = \frac{36 + a^2}{36} \Rightarrow a^2 = 64$$

$\therefore \quad$ Foci $= (0, \pm be)$

Ans. $\frac{y^2}{36} - \frac{x^2}{64} = 1, (0, \pm 10)$

24. $\because$ We have length of transverse axis $= 2a = 10 \Rightarrow a = 5$

and length of conjugate axis $= 2b = 8 \Rightarrow b = 4$

Ans. $\frac{x^2}{25} - \frac{y^2}{16} = 1$

25. The given equation is $x^2 + 4xy + y^2 - 2x + 2y - 6 = 0$

Comparing it with the equation

$ax^2 + 2hxy + by^2 + 2gx + 2fy + c = 0$, we get

$$a = 1, h = 2, b = 1, g = -1, f = 1, c = -6$$

Here, $\quad \Delta = abc + 2fgh - af^2 - bg^2 - ch^2 \neq 0$

and $\quad h^2 > ab$ **Ans.** Hyperbola.

26. (i) $F\left(0, \frac{5}{2}\right)$; $O(0, 0)$; $2y + 5 = 0$; $x = 0$

(ii) $F\left(0, \frac{2}{3}\right)$, $O(0, 0)$; $3y + 2 = 0$; $x = 0$

27. (i) $F\left(\frac{5}{2}, 0\right)$; $O(0, 0)$; $2x + 5 = 0$; 10 units

(ii) $F\left(-\frac{4}{5}, 0\right)$; $O(0, 0)$; $5x - 4 = 0$; $\frac{16}{5}$ units

28. Given equation of parabola is $9y^2 - 16x - 12y - 57 = 0$

$$\Rightarrow (3y)^2 - 2 \times 2 \times 3y + 2^2 = 2^2 + 57 + 16x$$

$$\Rightarrow (3y-2)^2 = 61 + 16x \Rightarrow 9\left(y - \frac{2}{3}\right)^2 = 16\left(x + \frac{61}{16}\right)$$

$$\Rightarrow \quad \left(y - \frac{2}{3}\right)^2 = \frac{16}{9}\left(x + \frac{61}{16}\right) \quad \text{...(i)}$$

Let $\quad Y = y - \frac{2}{3}$ and $X = x + \frac{61}{16}$ ...(ii)

$\therefore \quad Y^2 = \frac{16}{9}X^2$ [from Eqs. (i) and ii)] ...(iii)

Ans. $y = \frac{2}{3}; \left(\frac{-61}{16}, \frac{2}{3}\right), x = \frac{-613}{144}, \frac{16}{9}$

29. $8\sqrt{30}$ cm

30. Given, $\frac{2b^2}{a} = 10$

and $\quad 2ae = 2b \Rightarrow b = ae \because b^2 = a^2(1 - e^2)$

$\Rightarrow \quad e = \frac{1}{\sqrt{2}}$ [using $b = ae$]

Thus, $\quad a = b\sqrt{2}$

Again, $\quad \frac{2b^2}{a} = 10 \Rightarrow b = 5\sqrt{10}$ [$\because a = 10$]

Ans. $\frac{x^2}{100} + \frac{y^2}{50} = 1.$

31. Let $\frac{x^2}{a^2} + \frac{y^2}{b^2} = 1$ be the equation of the ellipse passing through the point $(-3, 1)$.

$$\therefore \quad \frac{9}{a^2} + \frac{1}{b^2} = 1 \Rightarrow 9b^2 + a^2 = a^2b^2$$

$$\Rightarrow 9a^2(a^2 - e^2) + a^2 = a^2a^2(1 - e^2) \quad [\because b^2 = a^2(1 - e^2)]$$

$$\Rightarrow \quad a^2 = \frac{32}{3}$$

Again, $b^2 = a^2(1 - e^2) = \frac{32}{3}\left(1 - \frac{2}{5}\right) = \frac{32}{5}$

Ans. $3x^2 + 5y^2 = 32$

32. Given, focus (1, – 2) and equation of directrix

$3x - 2y + 5 = 0$ and eccentricity, $e = \frac{1}{2}$.

$\therefore$ The equation of ellipse is given by

$$(x-1)^2 + (y+2)^2 = \left(\frac{1}{2}\right)^2 \frac{(3x-2y+5)^2}{3^2 + (-2)^2}$$

Ans. $43x^2 + 48y^2 + 12xy - 134x + 228y + 235 = 0$

33. (i) Given, $49y^2 - 16x^2 = 784$

$\Rightarrow \quad \frac{y^2}{16} - \frac{x^2}{49} = 1$ [dividing both sides by 784]

On comparing it with $\frac{y^2}{a^2} - \frac{x^2}{b^2} = 1$, we get

$a = 4$ and $b = 7$

Ans. $(0, \pm\sqrt{65}), (0 \pm 4), \frac{\sqrt{65}}{4}, \frac{49}{2}$

(ii) $(\pm 10, 0), (\pm 6, 0), \frac{5}{3}, \frac{64}{3}$

34. (i) Given, $9x^2 - 16y^2 = 144$

$\Rightarrow \quad \frac{x^2}{16} - \frac{y^2}{9} = 1$ [dividing both sides by 144]

On comparing it with $\frac{x^2}{a^2} - \frac{y^2}{b^2} = 1$, we get

$a = 4$ and $b = 3$

Ans. 8, 6, $(\pm 4, 0), (\pm 5, 0), \frac{5}{4}, \frac{9}{2}$

(ii) 8, 6, $(0, \pm 2), \left(0, \pm\frac{\sqrt{13}}{2}\right), \frac{\sqrt{13}}{2}, 9$

35. The given hyperbola has foci on Y-axis.

$\therefore$ Length of conjugate axis $= 2a = 20$ [given]

$\Rightarrow \quad a = 10$

$\because \quad be = 13$ [given, foci $= (0, \pm 13)$]

We know that, $a^2 = b^2(e^2 - 1)$

$\Rightarrow \quad 100 = b^2e^2 - b^2$

$\Rightarrow \quad b^2 = b^2e^2 - 100$

$= 13^2 - 100 = 169 - 100 = 69$

Ans. $\frac{y^2}{69} - \frac{x^2}{100} = 1$

36. Given, foci $= (0, \pm\sqrt{10}) \equiv (0, \pm c)$ (say)

$\Rightarrow \quad c = \sqrt{10}$

$\because \quad c^2 = a^2 + b^2 \Rightarrow 10 = a^2 + b^2 \Rightarrow a^2 = 10 - b^2$ ...(i)

Let the required equation of hyperbola is

$$\frac{y^2}{a^2} - \frac{x^2}{b^2} = 1 \quad \text{...(ii)}$$

According to the question, this hyperbola passes through (2, 3).

$\therefore \quad \frac{9}{a^2} - \frac{4}{b^2} = 1$ [from Eq. (ii)]

$\Rightarrow \quad \frac{9}{10 - b^2} - \frac{4}{b^2} = 1$ [from Eq. (i)]

$\Rightarrow \quad \frac{9b^2 - 40 + 4b^2}{(10 - b^2)b^2} = 1$

$\Rightarrow \quad 13b^2 - 40 = 10b^2 - b^4$

$\Rightarrow \quad b^4 + 3b^2 - 40 = 0 \Rightarrow b^2 = 5$ or -8

But $\quad b^2 > 0 \Rightarrow b^2 = 5$

On substituting $b^2 = 5$ in Eq. (i), we get

$a^2 = 10 - 5 = 5$

Ans. $y^2 - x^2 = 5$

37. Given, focus $= (-1, 1)$, equation of directrix is

$x - y + 3 = 0$

and Eccentricity, $e = 3$

$\because \quad (x - x_1)^2 + (y - y_1)^2 = \frac{e^2(ax + by + c)^2}{a^2 + b^2}$

$\therefore \quad (x+1)^2 + (y-1)^2 = \frac{9(x - y + 3)^2}{1^2 + (-1)^2}$

Ans. $7(x^2 + y^2) - 18xy + 50x - 50y + 77 = 0$

38. Given, focus $(-2, 1)$, directrix, $2x - 3y + 1 = 0$

and eccentricity $(e) = \frac{2}{\sqrt{3}}$

Let $P(x, y)$ be any point on the hyperbola.

Then, distance of point P from focus

= e (Perpendicular distance of P from the directrix) [definition of hyperbola]

$\Rightarrow \quad \sqrt{(x+2)^2 + (y-1)^2} = \frac{2}{\sqrt{3}}\left(\frac{2x - 3y + 1}{\sqrt{2^2 + 3^2}}\right)$

$\Rightarrow \quad \sqrt{(x+2)^2 + (y-1)^2} = \frac{2(2x - 3y + 1)}{\sqrt{3}\sqrt{13}}$

On squaring both sides, we get

$(x+2)^2 + (y-1)^2 = \frac{4}{39}(2x - 3y + 1)^2$

$\Rightarrow \quad 23x^2 + 3y^2 + 140x - 54y + 48xy + 191 = 0$

We know that transverse axis is perpendicular to the directrix $2x - 3y + 1 = 0$

Now, slope of transverse axis

$= \frac{-1}{\text{Slope of directrix}} = \frac{-1}{-\left(\frac{2}{-3}\right)} = \frac{-3}{2}$

Then, equation of transverse axis is

$y = \frac{-3x}{2} + c \Rightarrow 2y = -3x + 2c$

$\Rightarrow \quad 3x + 2y - 2c = 0$

As, transverse axis passes through focus $(-2, 1)$.

$\therefore \quad 3(-2) + 2 \times 1 - 2c = 0$

$\Rightarrow \quad 2c = -6 + 2 \Rightarrow c = \frac{-4}{2} = -2$

Ans. $23x^2 + 3y^2 + 140x - 54y + 48xy + 191 = 0$;
$3x + 2y + 4 = 0$.

39. (i) (2, 0) (ii) $y = 0$ (iii) $x + 2 = 0$
(iv) 8 (v) 4

CHAPTER

17

Introduction to Three Dimensional Geometry

We know that the position of a point in a plane can be determined, if the coordinates of the point with reference to two mutually perpendicular lines called X and Y-**axes**, are known. In order to locate a point in space, two coordinate axes are insufficient. So, we need three coordinate axes called X, Y and Z-**axes**. In fact three dimensional coordinate system is extension of two dimensional coordinate system.

The three numbers representing the three distances are called the coordinates of the point with reference to the three coordinate axes. So, a point in space has three coordinates. In this chapter, we shall study the basic concepts of geometry in three dimensional space.

- Coordinate Axex and Coordinate Planes in Three Dimensions
- Distance Formula and Section Formulae

TOPIC 01 Coordinate Axes and Coordinate Planes of Three Dimensions

Coordinate Axes

Let XOX', YOY' and ZOZ' be the three mutually perpendicular lines, intersecting at O. The point O (0, 0, 0) is called the **origin** and the lines (XOX', YOY' and ZOZ') are called **rectangular coordinate axes**, say X, Y and Z, respectively.

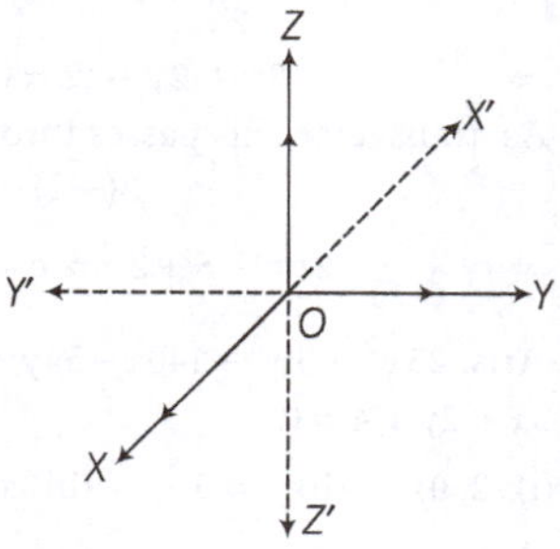

In the above figure, $X'OX$ is called the X-**axis**, $Y'OY$ is called the Y-**axis** and $Z'OZ$ is called the Z-**axis**.

Coordinate Planes

The three coordinate axes define three mutually perpendicular planes XOY, YOZ and ZOX (or XY, YZ and ZX) called **coordinate planes** which divide the space into eight parts called **octants**.

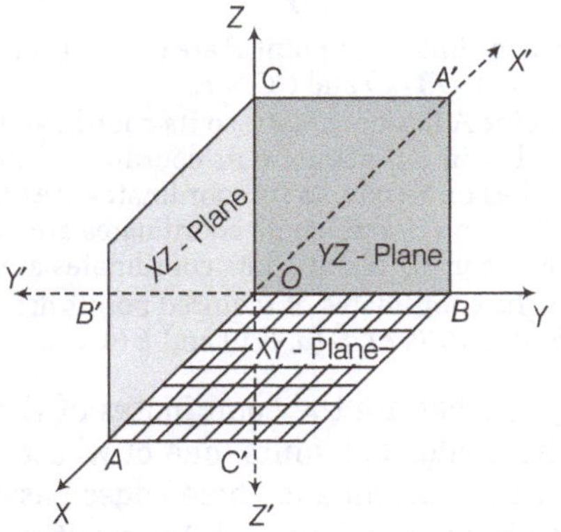

Thus, in the figure, XOY is called the XY**-plane**, YOZ is called the YZ**-plane**, ZOX is called the ZX**-plane**, $XOYZ, X'OYZ, XOY'Z, X'OY'Z, XOYZ', X'OYZ', XOY'Z'$ and $X'OY'Z'$ are called **octants**.

Coordinates of a Point in Space

Let P be a point in space. Through P, draw three planes parallel to the coordinate axes to meet the axes in A, B and C, respectively. Let $OA = x$, $OB = y$ and $OC = z$. These three numbers taken in order are called **coordinates** of a point P and written as $P(x, y, z)$.

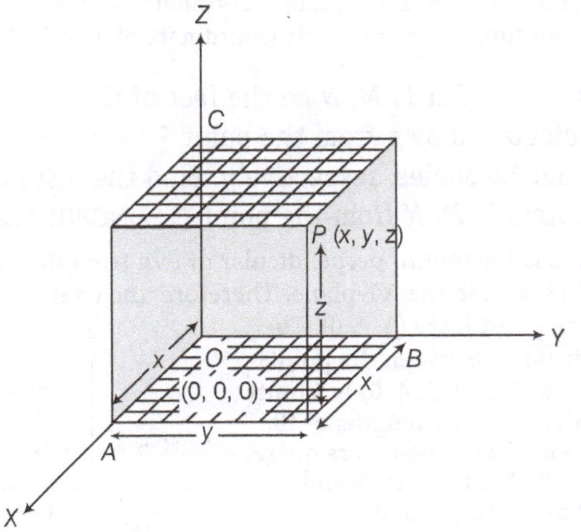

Thus, x**-coordinate of a point** P = length of perpendicular from P to YZ-plane with proper sign.

y**-coordinate of a point** P = length of perpendicular from P to ZX-plane with proper sign.

z**-coordinate of a point** P = length of perpendicular from P to XY-plane with proper sign.

Sign of Coordinates

As we know that, three mutually perpendicular lines $X'OX, Y'OY$ and $Z'OZ$ divide the space into eight parts known as **octants.** Here, OX is the positive direction and OX' is the negative direction of X-axis. Similarly, OY is the positive and OY' is the negative direction of Y-axis and OZ is the positive and OZ' is the negative direction of Z-axis.

The sign of coordinates of the points in the octants in which the space is divided are given in the following table

Octant / Coordinate	I	II	III	IV	V	VI	VII	VIII
	$OXYZ$	$OX'YZ$	$OX'Y'Z$	$OXY'Z$	$OXYZ'$	$OX'YZ'$	$OX'Y'Z'$	$OXY'Z'$
x	+	−	−	+	+	−	−	+
y	+	+	−	−	+	+	−	−
z	+	+	+	+	−	−	−	−

Example 1 Name the octants in which the following points lie.

$(1, 2, 3), (4, -2, 3), (4, -2, -5), (4, 2, -5), (-4, 2, -5),$
$(-4, 2, 5), (-3, -1, 6), (2, -4, -7)$ **[NCERT]**

Sol. The name of octants in which given points lie, are given in the following table

Point	Octant	Name
(1, 2, 3)	I (all the coordinates are positive)	$XOYZ$
(4, −2, 3)	IV (y-coordinate is negative)	$XOY'Z$
(4, −2, − 5)	VIII (y and z-coordinates are negative)	$XOY'Z'$
(4, 2, − 5)	V (z-coordinate is negative)	$XOYZ'$
(−4, 2, − 5)	VI (x and z-coordinates are negative)	$X'OYZ'$
(−4, 2, 5)	II (x-coordinate is negative)	$X'OYZ$
(−3, − 1, 6)	III (x and y-coordinates are negative)	$X'OY'Z$
(2, − 4, −7)	VIII (y and z-coordinates are negative)	$XOY'Z'$

Example 2 Find the octant in which the points $(-3, 4, 2)$ and $(-3, 1, -4)$ lie.

Sol. The point $(-3, 4, 2)$ lies in II octant and the point $(-3, 1, -4)$ lies in VI octant.

Coordinates of a Point on Coordinate Axes

Let $P(x, y, z)$ be any point on a space and we draw three perpendicular lines from P to the coodinate axes meet at points A, B and C. The coordinates of a point P on X-axis will be of the form $(x, 0, 0)$. Here, x is the distance of foot of perpendicular from P to X-axis from the origin with suitable sign.

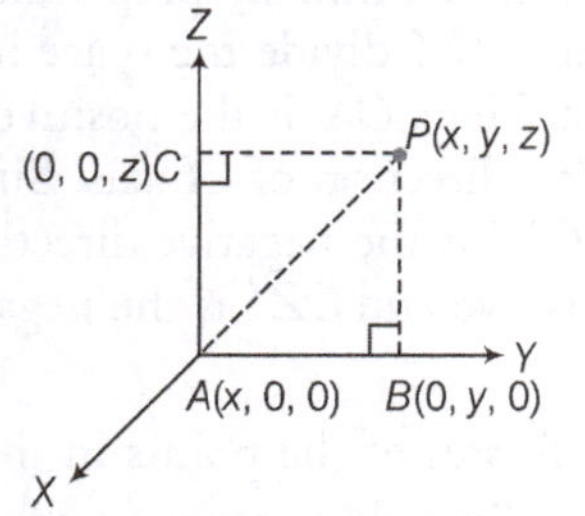

The sign of x is positive or negative, according as the foot of perpendicular lies on positive or negative direction of X-axis. Thus, the coordinates of a point on

(i) X axis will be of the form $(x, 0, 0)$.
(ii) Y-axis will be of the form $(0, y, 0)$.
(iii) Z-axis will be of the form $(0, 0, z)$.

Example 3 A point is on the X-axis. What are its y and z-coordinates?

Sol. Coordinates of any point on the X-axis is $(x, 0, 0)$.
Because at X-axis, both y and z-coordinates are zero.
So, y and z-coordinates of point are zero.

Coordinates of a Point in Coordinate Planes

Let $P(x, y, z)$ be any point on a space and we draw three perpendicular lines from P to the coordinate planes XY, YZ and ZX, respectively.

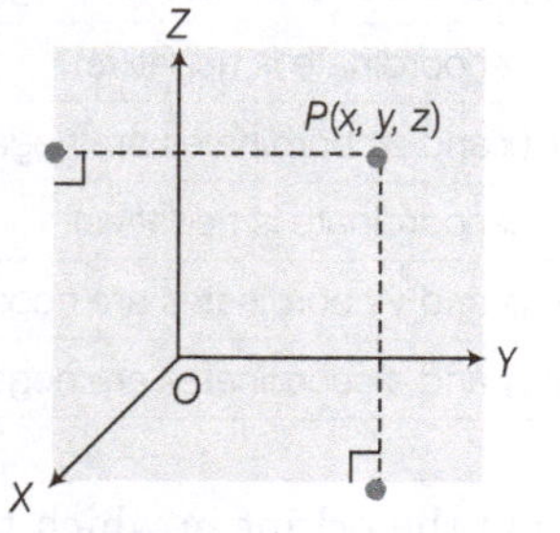

Then, coordinates of a point in

(i) XY-plane will be of the form $(x, y, 0)$.
[$\because$ In XY-plane, the z-coordinate of a point is zero]
(ii) YZ-plane will be of the form $(0, y, z)$ and
(iii) ZX-plane will be of the form $(x, 0, z)$.

Example 4 In the given figure, if the coordinates of point P are (a, b, c), then write the coordinates of A, D, B, C and E.

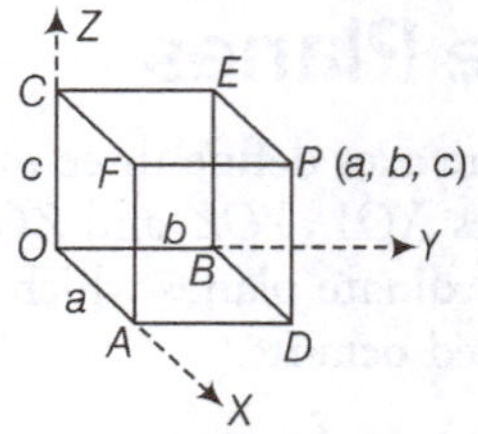

Sol. Given, coordinates of point P are (a, b, c), which shows that $OA = a$, $OB = b$ and $OC = c$.
Now, point A lies on X-axis, so its coordinates are $(a, 0, 0)$.
Point D lies in XY-plane, so its coordinates are $(a, b, 0)$.
Point B lies on Y-axis, so its coordinates are $(0, b, 0)$.
Point C lies on Z-axis, so its coordinates are $(0, 0, c)$ and point E lies in YZ-plane, so its coordinates are $(0, b, c)$.
Hence, the coordinates of required points are $A(a, 0, 0)$, $B(0, b, 0)$, $C(0, 0, c)$, $D(a, b, 0)$ and $E(0, b, c)$.

Example 5 What are the coordinates of the vertices of a cube whose edge is 5 units, one of whose vertices coincides with the origin and three edges passing through the origin coincides with the positive direction of the axes through the origin?

Sol. Given, edge of a cube is 5 units.

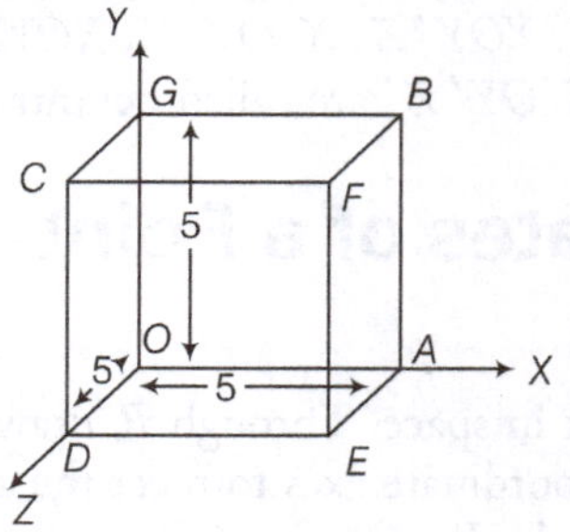

It is clear that
Coordinate of $O = (0, 0, 0)$; Coordinate of $A = (5, 0, 0)$
Coordinate of $G = (0, 5, 0)$; Coordinate of $D = (0, 0, 5)$
Coordinate of $B = (5, 5, 0)$; Coordinate of $F = (5, 5, 5)$
Coordinate of $E = (5, 0, 5)$; Coordinate of $C = (0, 5, 5)$

Example 6 Let L, M, N be the feet of the perpendiculars drawn from the point $P(3, 4, 5)$ on the XY, YZ and ZX-planes, respectively. Find the distance of these points L, M, N from the point P. **[NCERT Exemplar]**

Sol. $\because L$ is the foot of perpendicular drawn from the point $P(3, 4, 5)$ to the XY-plane. Therefore, the coordinates of the point L are $(3, 4, 0)$. The distance between the points $(3, 4, 5)$ and $(3, 4, 0)$ is 5 units. Similarly, the lengths of the foot of perpendiculars on YZ and ZX-planes are 3 and 4 units, respectively.

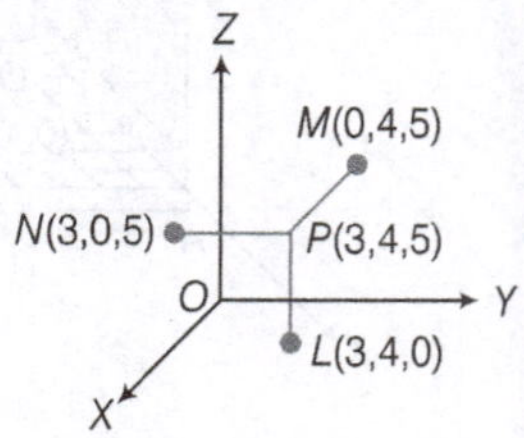

Example 7 L is the foot of the perpendicular drawn from a point P (5, 4, 6) on the XY-plane. Find the coordinates of point L.

Sol. Since, in XY-plane, z-coordinate will be zero. Hence, the coordinates of the foot of the perpendicular L (5, 4, 0).

Method to Locate a Point $P(x, y, z)$ in Space

To locate a point $P(x, y, z)$ in space, we use the following steps

Step I First, take a point A in suitable direction of X-axis (i.e. positive or negative) at a distance $|x|$ from origin O.

Step II Now, from point A, draw a line perpendicular to X-axis which will be parallel to Y-axis. Then, take point B at this line at a distance $|y|$ from A.

Step III Through point B, draw a line perpendicular to XY-plane which will be parallel to Z-axis. Then, take point C at this line at a distance $|z|$ from B.

Thus, point C will represent the given point in space.

Example 8 Locate the point (2, 3, 4) in space.

Sol. Given point is (2, 3, 4). Here, x-coordinate i.e. 2 is positive. So, we take a point A in positive direction of X-axis at a distance 2 from O. Thus, point A be (2, 0, 0). From point A, we draw a line perpendicular to X-axis which will be parallel to Y-axis and take point B at a distance 3 from A in positive direction.

Thus, point B be (2, 3, 0). Draw a line parallel to Z-axis from point B, which is perpendicular to XY-plane and take point C at this line in positive direction at a distance 4 units from B. Thus, point C (2, 3, 4) is the required location of given point in space, which is shown in the figure.

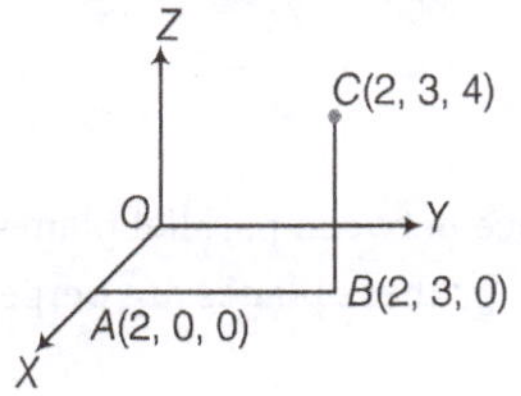

Topic Practice 1

Very Short Answer Type Questions

(2 Marks)

1 Name the octant in which each of the following points lies. **[NCERT Exemplar]**

(i) (4, –2, 3) (ii) (4, –2, – 5)

(iii) (4, 2, – 5) (iv) (– 3, –1, 6)

2 L is the foot of the perpendicular drawn from a point P(6, 7, 8) on the XY-plane. What are the coordinates of point L? **[NCERT Exemplar]**

3 Let L, M, N be the feet of the perpendiculars drawn from a point P(3, 4, 5) on the X, Y and Z-axes respectively. Find the coordinates of L, M and N. **[NCERT Exemplar]**

4 If A, B, C are the feet of perpendiculars from a point P on the XY, YZ and ZX-planes respectively, then find the distance of A, B and C in each of the following, where the point P is

(i) (3, 4, 2) (ii) (– 5, 3, 7)

5 If A, B and C are the feet of perpendiculars from a point on XY, YZ and ZX-planes respectively, then find the coordinates of A, B and C in each of the following, where the point P is

(i) (–5, 3, 7) (ii) (4, – 3, – 5)

6 In the given figure, if the coordinates of the point P are (3, 4, 6), then write the coordinates of A, D, B, C and E.

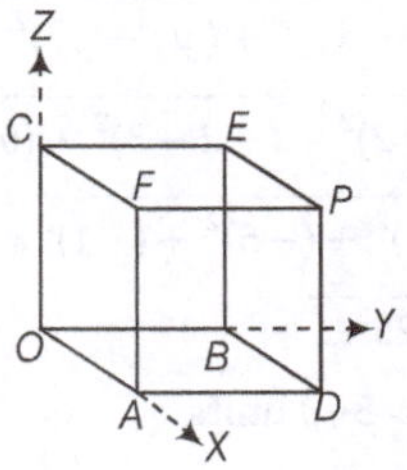

7 Locate the point (– 2, – 3, 4) in space.

Hints & Answers

1. (i) Fourth octant (ii) Eighth octant
(iii) Fifth octant (iv) Third octant

2. (6, 7, 0)

3. L (3, 0, 0), M (0, 4, 0) and N (0, 0, 5)

4. (i) 2 units, 3units, 4 units (ii) 7units, 5 units, 3 units

5. (i) A(–5, 3, 0), B(0, 3, 7), C(–5, 0, 7)
(ii) A(4, – 3, 0), B(0, – 3, – 5), C(4, 0, – 5)

6. (3, 0, 0), (3, 4, 0), (0, 4, 0), (0, 0, 6), (0, 4, 6)

7.

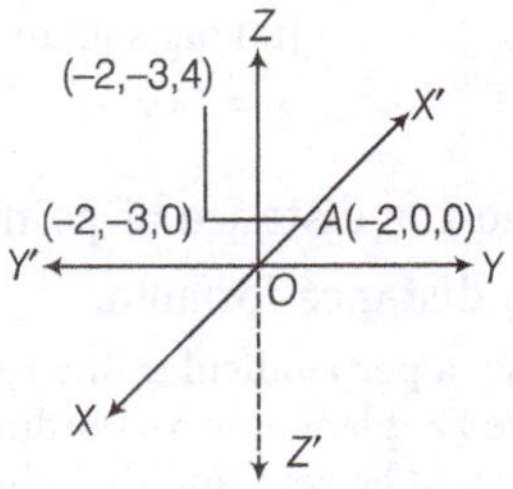

TOPIC 02

Distance Formula and Section Formulae

Distance between Two Points

The distance between two points $P(x_1, y_1, z_1)$ and $Q(x_2, y_2, z_2)$ is given by

$$PQ = \sqrt{(x_2 - x_1)^2 + (y_2 - y_1)^2 + (z_2 - z_1)^2}$$

or $$PQ = \sqrt{(x_1 - x_2)^2 + (y_1 - y_2)^2 + (z_1 - z_2)^2}$$

Note If O is the origin and $P(x_1, y_1, z_1)$ is a point in space, then
$$OP = \sqrt{(x_1 - 0)^2 + (y_1 - 0)^2 + (z_1 - 0)^2} = \sqrt{x_1^2 + y_1^2 + z_1^2}.$$

Example 1 Find the distance between the points $A(2, 3, 1)$ and $B(1, -2, 0)$.

Sol. Given points are $A(2, 3, 1)$ and $B(1, -2, 0)$.

Here, $x_1 = 2, y_1 = 3, z_1 = 1$ and $x_2 = 1, y_2 = -2, z_2 = 0$

$\therefore$ Distance between the points A and B

$$= \sqrt{(x_2 - x_1)^2 + (y_2 - y_1)^2 + (z_2 - z_1)^2}$$
$$= \sqrt{(1-2)^2 + (-2-3)^2 + (0-1)^2}$$
$$= \sqrt{(-1)^2 + (-5)^2 + (-1)^2}$$
$$= \sqrt{1 + 25 + 1}$$
$$= \sqrt{27} = 3\sqrt{3} \text{ units}$$

Example 2 Find the values of x, if the distance between two points $(x, -8, 4)$ and $(3, -5, 4)$ is 5 units.

Sol. Given points are $(x, -8, 4)$ and $(3, -5, 4)$.

and distance between these points = 5 units

$$\therefore \sqrt{(x-3)^2 + (-8+5)^2 + (4-4)^2} = 5$$
$$\Rightarrow \sqrt{(x-3)^2 + (-3)^2 + 0} = 5$$
$$\Rightarrow (x-3)^2 + 9 + 0 = 25$$
[on squaring both sides]
$$\Rightarrow (x-3)^2 = 16$$
$$\Rightarrow (x-3)^2 = (4)^2$$
$$\Rightarrow x - 3 = \pm 4$$
[taking square root on both sides]
$$\therefore x = 7 \text{ or } -1$$

Example 3 Find the distance of point $P(3, 6, 9)$ from the YZ-plane using distance formula.

Sol. When we draw a perpendicular line from the point $P(3, 6, 9)$ on the YZ-plane, the x-coordinate of foot of perpendicular will be zero and the other coordinates (y and z) will be 6 and 9, i.e. coordinates of a point on YZ-plane (which is the foot of perpendicular drawn from P to YZ plane) be $Q(0, 6, 9)$.

$\therefore$ Distance between P and Q,

$$QP = \sqrt{(3-0)^2 + (6-6)^2 + (9-9)^2}$$
$$\left[\because \text{distance} = \sqrt{(x_2 - x_1)^2 + (y_2 - y_1)^2 + (z_2 - z_1)^2}\right]$$
$$= \sqrt{3^2 + 0^2 + 0^2} = 3 \text{ units}$$

Example 4 If a parallelopiped is formed by planes drawn through the points (5, 8, 10) and (3, 6, 8) parallel to the coordinate planes, then find the length of edges and diagonal of the parallelopiped by using distance formula.

Sol. Let $P \equiv (3, 6, 8)$ and $Q \equiv (5, 8, 10)$

$\therefore PE$ = Distance between parallel planes $ABCP$ and $FQDE$
$= |10 - 8|$ [$\because$ these planes are perpendicular to Z-axis]
$= 2$ units

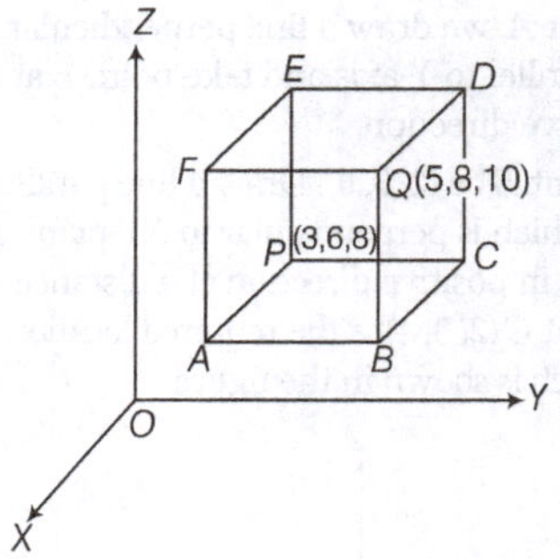

PA = Distance between parallel planes $ABQF$ and $PCDE$
$= |5 - 3|$ [$\because$ these planes are perpendicular to X-axis]
$= 2$ units

PC = Distance between parallel planes $APEF$ and $BCDQ$
$= |8 - 6|$ [$\because$ these planes are perpendicular to Y-axis]
$= 2$ units

$\therefore$ Length of diagonal = Distance between P and Q

$$= \sqrt{(5-3)^2 + (8-6)^2 + (10-8)^2}$$
[using the distance formula]
$$= \sqrt{2^2 + 2^2 + 2^2}$$
$$= \sqrt{4 + 4 + 4} = \sqrt{12}$$
$$= 2\sqrt{3} \text{ units}$$

Hence, the length of each edge of parallelopiped is 2 units and the length of its diagonal is $2\sqrt{3}$ units.

Example 5 Find the equation of the curve formed by the set of all points whose distances from the points (3, 4, – 5) and (–2, 1, 4) are equal.

Sol. Let $P(x, y, z)$ be any point on the given curve and let $A(3, 4, -5)$ and $B(-2, 1, 4)$ be the given points.

Then, $PA = PB \Rightarrow PA^2 = PB^2$

$$\Rightarrow (x-3)^2 + (y-4)^2 + (z+5)^2 = (x+2)^2 + (y-1)^2 + (z-4)^2$$

$$\Rightarrow x^2 + 9 - 6x + y^2 + 16 - 8y + z^2 + 25 + 10z = x^2 + 4 + 4x + y^2 + 1 - 2y + z^2 + 16 - 8z$$

$$\Rightarrow 10x + 6y - 18z - 29 = 0$$

Hence, the required curve is

$$10x + 6y - 18z - 29 = 0$$

Example 6 Find the equation of set of point P such that $PA^2 + PB^2 = 2k^2$, where A and B are the points (3, 4, 5) and (–1, 3, – 7), respectively. **[NCERT]**

Sol. Given points are $A(3,4,5)$ and $B(-1,3,-7)$.

Let the coordinates of point P be (x, y, z).

Then, $PA^2 = (x-3)^2 + (y-4)^2 + (z-5)^2$

$$\left[\because \text{distance} = \sqrt{(x_2-x_1)^2 + (y_2-y_1)^2 + (z_2-z_1)^2}\right]$$

and $PB^2 = (x+1)^2 + (y-3)^2 + (z+7)^2$

By the given condition $PA^2 + PB^2 = 2k^2$,

$$(x-3)^2 + (y-4)^2 + (z-5)^2 + (x+1)^2 + (y-3)^2 + (z+7)^2 = 2k^2$$

$$\Rightarrow x^2 + 9 - 6x + y^2 + 16 - 8y + z^2 + 25 - 10z + x^2 + 2x + 1 + y^2 + 9 - 6y + z^2 + 49 + 14z = 2k^2$$

$$\Rightarrow 2x^2 + 2y^2 + 2z^2 - 4x - 14y + 4z = 2k^2 - 109$$

which is the required equation.

Example 7 Find the coordinates of a point equidistant from the four points $O(0, 0, 0)$, $A(l, 0, 0)$, $B(0, m, 0)$ and $C(0, 0, n)$. **[NCERT Exemplar]**

Sol. Let $P(x, y, z)$ be required point.

Then, $OP = PA = PB = PC$

Now, $OP = PA \Rightarrow OP^2 = PA^2$

$$\Rightarrow (0-x)^2 + (0-y)^2 + (0-z)^2 = (x-l)^2 + (y-0)^2 + (z-0)^2$$

$$\Rightarrow x^2 + y^2 + z^2 = x^2 - 2lx + l^2 + y^2 + z^2$$

$$\Rightarrow 2lx = l^2 \Rightarrow x = \frac{l}{2}$$

Similarly, $OP = PB \Rightarrow y = \frac{m}{2}$

and $OP = PC \Rightarrow z = \frac{n}{2}$

Hence, the coordinates of the required point are $\left(\frac{l}{2}, \frac{m}{2}, \frac{n}{2}\right)$.

Condition for Collinearity

Three points A, B and C are said to be collinear, if

$$AB + BC = AC.$$

Example 8 Verify that the points (3, – 2, 4), (1, 0, – 2) and (–1, 2, – 8) are collinear.

Sol. Let $A(3, -2, 4)$, $B(1, 0, -2)$ and $C(-1, 2, -8)$ be the given points.

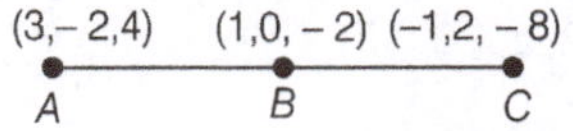

Then, $AB = \sqrt{(1-3)^2 + (0+2)^2 + (-2-4)^2}$ [using distance formula]

$$= \sqrt{4+4+36} = \sqrt{44} = 2\sqrt{11} \text{ units}$$

$BC = \sqrt{(-1-1)^2 + (2-0)^2 + (-8+2)^2}$ [using distance formula]

$$= \sqrt{4+4+36} = \sqrt{44} = 2\sqrt{11} \text{ units}$$

and $CA = \sqrt{(3+1)^2 + (-2-2)^2 + (4+8)^2}$ [using distance formula]

$$= \sqrt{16+16+144} = \sqrt{176} = 4\sqrt{11} \text{ units}$$

We observe that,

$$AB + BC = 2\sqrt{11} + 2\sqrt{11} = 4\sqrt{11} = CA$$

Hence, A, B and C are collinear.

Section Formulae

Let $A(x_1, y_1, z_1)$ and $B(x_2, y_2, z_2)$ be the end points of a line segment AB and C be any point on AB which divide AB in the ratio $m_1 : m_2$.

I. For Internal Ratio

If C divides AB internally in the ratio $m_1 : m_2$, then

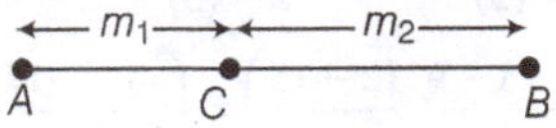

Coordinates of C

$$= \left(\frac{m_1x_2 + m_2x_1}{m_1 + m_2}, \frac{m_1y_2 + m_2y_1}{m_1 + m_2}, \frac{m_1z_2 + m_2z_1}{m_1 + m_2}\right)$$

II. For External Ratio

If C divides AB externally in the ratio $m_1 : m_2$, then Coordinates of C

$$= \left(\frac{m_1x_2 + (-m_2)x_1}{m_1 + (-m_2)}, \frac{m_1y_2 + (-m_2)y_1}{m_1 + (-m_2)}, \frac{m_1z_2 + (-m_2)z_1}{m_1 + (-m_2)}\right)$$

$$= \left(\frac{m_1x_2 - m_2x_1}{m_1 - m_2}, \frac{m_1y_2 - m_2y_1}{m_1 - m_2}, \frac{m_1z_2 - m_2z_1}{m_1 - m_2}\right)$$

Example 9 Find the coordinates of the point which divides the line segment joining the points (–2, 3, 5) and (1, – 4, 6) in the ratio

(i) 2 : 3 internally (ii) 2 : 3 externally **[NCERT]**

Sol. (i) Let $P(x, y, z)$ be any point which divides the line segment joining points $A(-2, 3, 5)$ and $B(1, -4, 6)$ in the ratio 2 : 3 internally.

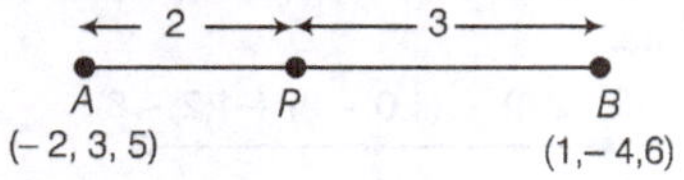

Here, the ratio is 2 : 3.

$\therefore \quad m_1 = 2, m_2 = 3$

Then, coordinates of point P

$$= \left[\frac{m_1x_2 + m_2x_1}{m_1 + m_2}, \frac{m_1y_2 + m_2y_1}{m_1 + m_2}, \frac{m_1z_2 + m_2z_1}{m_1 + m_2}\right]$$

$$= \left[\frac{2 \times 1 + 3 \times (-2)}{2 + 3}, \frac{2(-4) + 3(3)}{2 + 3}, \frac{2(6) + 3(5)}{2 + 3}\right]$$

$$= \left(\frac{2 - 6}{5}, \frac{-8 + 9}{5}, \frac{12 + 15}{5}\right) = \left(\frac{-4}{5}, \frac{1}{5}, \frac{27}{5}\right)$$

(ii) Let $P(x, y, z)$ be any point which divides the line segment joining points $A(-2, 3, 5)$ and $B(1, -4, 6)$ in the ratio 2 : 3 externally.

Here, the ratio is 2 : 3.

$\therefore \quad m_1 = 2, m_2 = 3$

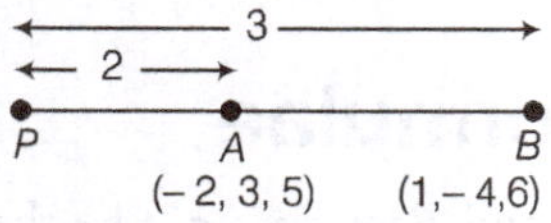

Then, coordinates of point P

$$= \left[\left(\frac{m_1x_2 - m_2x_1}{m_1 - m_2}, \frac{m_1y_2 - m_2y_1}{m_1 - m_2}, \frac{m_1z_2 - m_2z_1}{m_1 - m_2}\right)\right]$$

$$= \left[\frac{2(1) - (3)(-2)}{2 - (3)}, \frac{2(-4) - (3) \times 3}{2 - (3)}, \frac{2(6) - (3)(5)}{2 - (3)}\right]$$

$$= \left(\frac{2 + 6}{2 - 3}, \frac{-8 - 9}{2 - 3}, \frac{12 - 15}{2 - 3}\right) = \left(\frac{8}{-1}, \frac{-17}{-1}, \frac{-3}{-1}\right) = (-8, 17, 3)$$

Coordinates of Mid-point (or Mid-point Formula)

If C is the mid-point of AB, then $m_1 : m_2 = 1 : 1$ so that

$$x = \frac{x_1 + x_2}{2}, \; y = \frac{y_1 + y_2}{2} \text{ and } z = \frac{z_1 + z_2}{2}$$

These are the coordinates of the mid-point of the line segment joining $A(x_1, y_1, z_1)$ and $B(x_2, y_2, z_2)$.

Note The coordinates of the point C which divides AB in the ratio $k : 1$, i.e. $\frac{m_1}{m_2} = \frac{k}{1}$ are $\left(\frac{kx_2 + x_1}{k + 1}, \frac{ky_2 + y_1}{k + 1}, \frac{kz_2 + z_1}{k + 1}\right)$.

Example 10 Three consecutive vertices of a parallelogram $ABCD$ are $A(6, -2, 4)$, $B(2, 4, -8)$ and $C(-2, 2, 4)$. Find the coordinates of the fourth vertex. **[NCERT Exemplar]**

Sol. Let the coordinates of the fourth vertex of a parallelogram be $D(x, y, z)$.

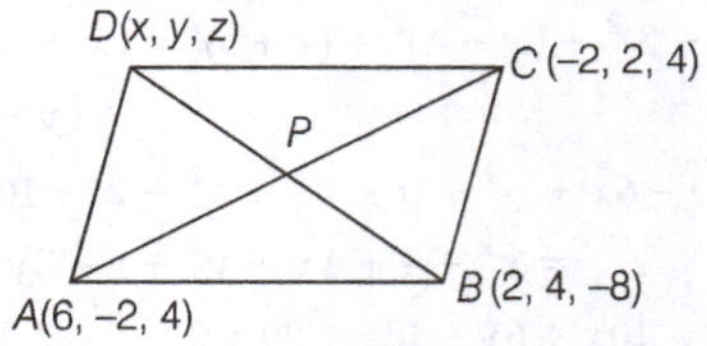

We know that the diagonals of a parallelogram bisect each other.

$\therefore$ Mid-point of AC = Mid-point of BD

$$\Rightarrow \left(\frac{6 - 2}{2}, \frac{-2 + 2}{2}, \frac{4 + 4}{2}\right) = \left(\frac{x + 2}{2}, \frac{y + 4}{2}, \frac{z - 8}{2}\right)$$

$$\Rightarrow \quad (2, 0, 4) = \left(\frac{x + 2}{2}, \frac{y + 4}{2}, \frac{z - 8}{2}\right)$$

On comparing the coordinates both sides, we get

$$\frac{x + 2}{2} = 2, \frac{y + 4}{2} = 0 \text{ and } \frac{z - 8}{2} = 4$$

$\Rightarrow x + 2 = 4, \; y + 4 = 0$ and $z - 8 = 8$

$\Rightarrow \quad x = 2, \; y = -4$ and $z = 16$

Hence, the coordinates of fourth vertex D of a parallelogram are $(2, -4, 16)$.

Example 11 The mid-points of the sides of a triangle are (5, 7, 11), (0, 8, 5) and (2, 3, – 1). Find its vertices. **[NCERT Exemplar]**

Sol. Let vertices of the ΔABC be $A(x_1, y_1, z_1)$, $B(x_2, y_2, z_2)$ and $C(x_3, y_3, z_3)$ and mid-points of the sides BC, CA and AB are $D(5, 7, 11)$, $E(0, 8, 5)$ and $F(2, 3, -1)$, respectively.

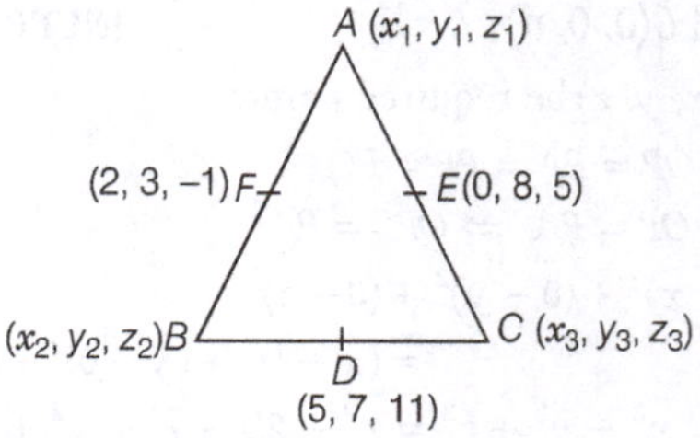

Now, D is the mid-point of BC.

$$\therefore \quad 5 = \frac{x_2 + x_3}{2} \Rightarrow x_2 + x_3 = 10, \quad \text{...(i)}$$

$$7 = \frac{y_2 + y_3}{2} \Rightarrow y_2 + y_3 = 14 \quad \text{...(ii)}$$

$$\text{and} \quad 11 = \frac{z_2 + z_3}{2} \Rightarrow z_2 + z_3 = 22 \quad \text{...(iii)}$$

Similarly, for the sides AB and AC,

$$2=\frac{x_1+x_2}{2} \Rightarrow x_1+x_2=4 \quad \text{...(iv)}$$

$$3=\frac{y_1+y_2}{2} \Rightarrow y_1+y_2=6 \quad \text{...(v)}$$

$$-1=\frac{z_1+z_2}{2} \Rightarrow z_1+z_2=-2 \quad \text{...(vi)}$$

$$0=\frac{x_1+x_3}{2} \Rightarrow x_1+x_3=0 \quad \text{...(vii)}$$

$$8=\frac{y_1+y_3}{2} \Rightarrow y_1+y_3=16 \quad \text{...(viii)}$$

and $$5=\frac{z_1+z_3}{2} \Rightarrow z_1+z_3=10 \quad \text{...(ix)}$$

On adding Eqs. (i) and (iv), we get

$$x_1+2x_2+x_3=14$$

$$\Rightarrow \quad 2x_2+0=14 \quad \text{[from Eq. (vii)]}$$

$$\Rightarrow \quad x_2=7$$

On putting $x_2=7$ in Eqs. (i) and (iv), we get

$$x_3=3 \text{ and } x_1=-3$$

Thus, $x_1=-3$, $x_2=7$ and $x_3=3$

On adding Eqs. (ii) and (v), we get

$$y_1+2y_2+y_3=20$$

$$\Rightarrow \quad 2y_2+16=20 \quad \text{[from Eq. (viii)]}$$

$$\Rightarrow \quad 2y_2=4 \Rightarrow y_2=2$$

On putting $y_2=2$ in Eqs. (ii) and (v), we get

$$y_3=12 \text{ and } y_1=4$$

Thus, $y_1=4$, $y_2=2$ and $y_3=12$

On adding Eqs. (iii) and (vi), we get

$$z_1+2z_2+z_3=20$$

$$\Rightarrow \quad 2z_2+10=20 \quad \text{[from Eq. (ix)]}$$

$$\Rightarrow \quad 2z_2=10 \Rightarrow z_2=5$$

On putting $z_2=5$ in Eqs. (iii) and (vi), we get

$$z_3=17 \text{ and } z_1=-7$$

Thus, $z_1=-7$, $z_2=5$ and $z_3=17$

Hence, the vertices are $A(-3, 4, -7)$, $B(7, 2, 5)$ and $C(3, 12, 17)$.

Example 12 Verify that (–1, 2, 1), (1, –2, 5), (4, –7, 8) and (2, –3, 4) are the vertices of a parallelogram.

Sol. Let $A(-1, 2, 1)$, $B(1, -2, 5)$, $C(4, -7, 8)$ and $D(2, -3, 4)$ be the vertices of a quadrilateral $ABCD$.

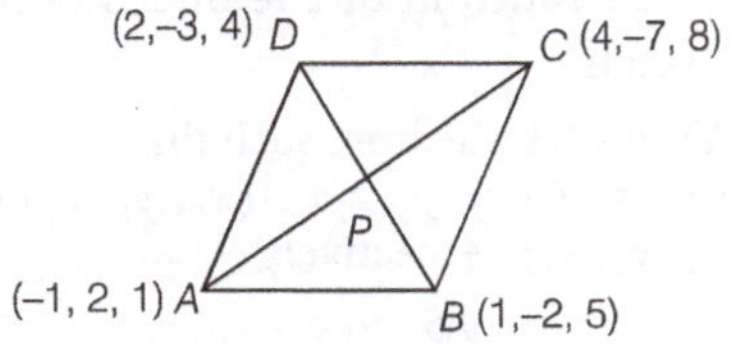

Then, mid-point of AC

$$=\left(\frac{-1+4}{2}, \frac{2-7}{2}, \frac{1+8}{2}\right)=\left(\frac{3}{2}, \frac{-5}{2}, \frac{9}{2}\right)$$

$$\left[\because \text{coordinates of mid-point}=\left(\frac{x_1+x_2}{2}, \frac{y_1+y_2}{2}, \frac{z_1+z_2}{2}\right)\right]$$

and mid-point of $BD=\left(\frac{1+2}{2}, \frac{-2-3}{2}, \frac{5+4}{2}\right)$

$$=\left(\frac{3}{2}, \frac{-5}{2}, \frac{9}{2}\right)$$

Here, mid-points of both the diagonals are same i.e. they bisect each other. Hence, $ABCD$ is a parallelogram.

Example 13 Find the ratio in which the line segment joining the points (4, 8, 10) and (6, 10, –8) is divided by the YZ-plane. **[NCERT]**

Sol. Let YZ-plane divides the line segment joining the points $A(4, 8, 10)$ and $B(6, 10, -8)$ at $P(x, y, z)$ in the ratio $k:1$.

Then, coordinates of $P=\left(\frac{4+6k}{k+1}, \frac{8+10k}{k+1}, \frac{10-8k}{k+1}\right)$

$$\left[\because \text{coordinates of internal ratio} =\left(\frac{m_2x_1+m_1x_2}{m_1+m_2}, \frac{m_2y_1+m_1y_2}{m_1+m_2}, \frac{m_2z_1+m_1z_2}{m_1+m_2}\right)\right]$$

Since, P lies on the YZ-plane, so its x-coordinate is zero,

$$\therefore \quad \frac{4+6k}{k+1}=0 \Rightarrow k=-\frac{2}{3}$$

Therefore, YZ-plane divides AB externally in the ratio 2 : 3.

Note If k is negative, then the given points are divided externally in the ratio $k:1$.

Example 14 A point R with x-coordinate 4 lies on the line segment joining the points $P(2, -3, 4)$ and $Q(8, 0, 10)$. Find the coordinates of the point R. **[NCERT]**

Sol. Let the point $R(x, y, z)$ divides PQ in the ratio $k:1$.

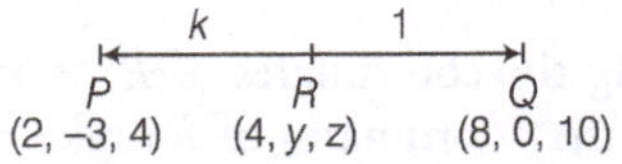

Given, x-coordinate of $R=4$.

$$\therefore \quad \frac{k\times 8+1\times 2}{k+1}=4 \Rightarrow \frac{8k+2}{k+1}=4$$

$$\Rightarrow \quad 8k+2=4k+4$$

$$\Rightarrow \quad 8k-4k=4-2$$

$$\Rightarrow \quad 4k=2 \Rightarrow k=\frac{2}{4}=\frac{1}{2}$$

So, $k:1=\frac{1}{2}:1$ or 1 : 2.

Hence, the point R divides PQ internally in the ratio 1 : 2.

Therefore, y-coordinate of R

$$=\left(\frac{1\times 0+2\times(-3)}{1+2}\right)=\left(\frac{-6}{3}\right)=-2$$

and z-coordinate of R

$$=\left(\frac{1\times 10+2\times 4}{1+2}\right)=\left(\frac{10+8}{3}\right)=\frac{18}{3}=6$$

Hence, the coordiantes of point R are $(4, -2, 6)$.

Example 15 Find the ratio in which the join of the points $P(2, -1, 3)$ and $Q(4, 3, 1)$ is divided by the point $R\left(\frac{20}{7}, \frac{5}{7}, \frac{15}{7}\right)$.

Sol. Given points are $P(2, -1, 3)$ and $Q(4, 3, 1)$.

Let the required ratio be $\lambda : 1$. Then, the coordinates of R are $\left(\frac{4\lambda+2}{\lambda+1}, \frac{3\lambda-1}{\lambda+1}, \frac{\lambda+3}{\lambda+1}\right)$

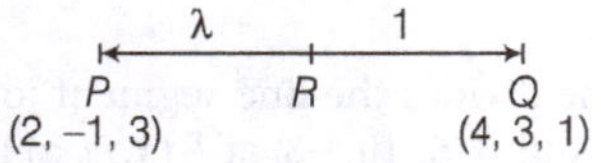

But, the coordinates of R are $\left(\frac{20}{7}, \frac{5}{7}, \frac{15}{7}\right)$. [given]

$$\therefore \quad \frac{4\lambda+2}{\lambda+1} = \frac{20}{7} \quad [\because x\text{-coordinate of } R]$$

$$\Rightarrow \quad 28\lambda + 14 = 20\lambda + 20 \Rightarrow 8\lambda = 6 \Rightarrow \lambda = \frac{3}{4}$$

So, the required ratio is $\frac{3}{4} : 1$, i.e. $3 : 4$.

Note Here, we can also find the ratio $\lambda : 1$ by taking y-coordinate or z-coordinate.

Coordinates of the Point which Trisect the Line Segment

If R_1 and R_2 trisect the line segment AB, then

$$AR_1 = R_1R_2 = R_2B$$

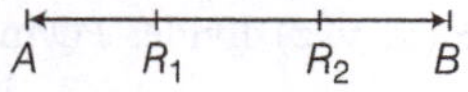

Thus, for finding the coordinates of R_1, take ratio $1:2$ and for finding the coordinates of R_2 take ratio $2:1$.

Centroid of a Triangle

If the vertices of a ΔABC are $A(x_1, y_1, z_1)$, $B(x_2, y_2, z_2)$ and $C(x_3, y_3, z_3)$, then

Centroid of ΔABC

$$= G\left(\frac{x_1+x_2+x_3}{3}, \frac{y_1+y_2+y_3}{3}, \frac{z_1+z_2+z_3}{3}\right)$$

Example 16 Find the coordinates of the points which trisect the line segment joining the points $P(4, 2, -6)$ and $Q(10, -16, 6)$. **[NCERT]**

Sol. Let R_1 and R_2 be two points which trisect the joining of P and Q. Then, $PR_1 = R_1R_2 = R_2Q$

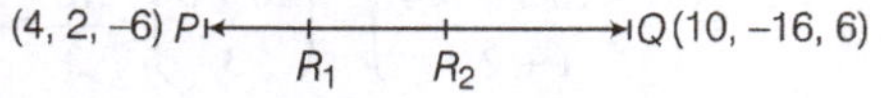

$\because$ Point R_1 divides the join of PQ in the ratio $1:2$.

$\therefore$ Coordinates of R_1

$$= \left(\frac{1\times10+2\times4}{1+2}, \frac{1\times(-16)+2\times2}{1+2}, \frac{1\times6+2\times(-6)}{1+2}\right)$$

$$= \left(\frac{10+8}{3}, \frac{-16+4}{3}, \frac{6-12}{3}\right) = \left(\frac{18}{3}, \frac{-12}{3}, \frac{-6}{3}\right)$$

$$= (6, -4, -2)$$

Also, point R_2 divides the join of PQ in the ratio $2:1$.

$\therefore$ Coordinates of R_2

$$= \left(\frac{2\times10+1\times4}{2+1}, \frac{2\times(-16)+1\times2}{2+1}, \frac{2\times6+1\times(-6)}{1+2}\right)$$

$$= \left(\frac{20+4}{3}, \frac{-32+2}{3}, \frac{12-6}{3}\right) = \left(\frac{24}{3}, \frac{-30}{3}, \frac{6}{3}\right) = (8, -10, 2)$$

Hence, required points are $(6, -4, -2)$ and $(8, -10, 2)$.

Example 17 If the origin is the centroid of the ΔPQR with vertices $P(2a, 2, 6)$, $Q(-4, 3b, -10)$ and $R(8, 14, 2c)$, then find the values of a, b and c.

Sol. Given vertices of ΔPQR are $P(2a, 2, 6)$, $Q(-4, 3b, -10)$ and $R(8, 14, 2c)$.

$\therefore$ Centroid of ΔPQR

$$= \left(\frac{x_1+x_2+x_3}{3}, \frac{y_1+y_2+y_3}{3}, \frac{z_1+z_2+z_3}{3}\right)$$

$$= \left(\frac{2a-4+8}{3}, \frac{2+3b+14}{3}, \frac{6-10+2c}{3}\right)$$

$$= \left(\frac{2a+4}{3}, \frac{3b+16}{3}, \frac{2c-4}{3}\right)$$

Also, given that centroid of triangle is origin i.e. $(0, 0, 0)$.

$$\therefore \quad \frac{2a+4}{3} = 0 \Rightarrow 2a+4 = 0 \Rightarrow a = -2$$

$$\frac{3b+16}{3} = 0 \Rightarrow 3b+16 = 0 \Rightarrow b = \frac{-16}{3}$$

$$\text{and} \quad \frac{2c-4}{3} = 0 \Rightarrow 2c-4 = 0 \Rightarrow c = 2$$

Hence, $a = -2$, $b = \frac{-16}{3}$ and $c = 2$.

Example 18 Prove that the coordinates of the points which divide the lines joining the vertices of a tetrahedron to the centroid of the opposite faces in the ratio 3 : 1 are same. **[HOTS]**

Sol. Let $ABCD$ be a tetrahedron, such that the coordinates of its vertices are $A(x_1, y_1, z_1)$, $B(x_2, y_2, z_2)$, $C(x_3, y_3, z_3)$ and $D(x_4, y_4, z_4)$, respectively.

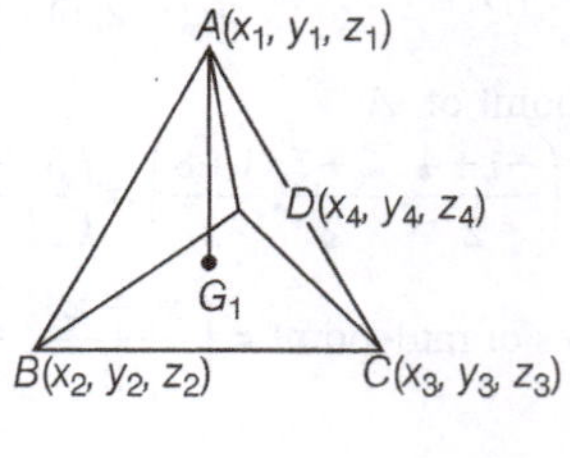

Let the centroid of the faces BCD, ACD, ABD, ABC be G_1, G_2, G_3 and G_4 respectively.
Then, centroid G_1 of face BCD

$$= \left(\frac{x_2 + x_3 + x_4}{3}, \frac{y_2 + y_3 + y_4}{3}, \frac{z_2 + z_3 + z_4}{3}\right)$$

Now, coordinates of point G dividing AG_1 in the ratio 3 : 1

$$= \left[\frac{1 \cdot x_1 + 3\left(\frac{x_2 + x_3 + x_4}{3}\right)}{1+3}, \frac{1 \cdot y_1 + 3\left(\frac{y_2 + y_3 + y_4}{3}\right)}{1+3}, \frac{1 \cdot z_1 + 3\left(\frac{z_2 + z_3 + z_4}{3}\right)}{1+3}\right]$$

$$= \left(\frac{x_1 + x_2 + x_3 + x_4}{4}, \frac{y_1 + y_2 + y_3 + y_4}{4}, \frac{z_1 + z_2 + z_3 + z_4}{4}\right)$$

Similarly, the point dividing BG_2, CG_3 and DG_4 in the ratio 3 : 1 has same coordinates. Thus, the point

$$G\left(\frac{x_1 + x_2 + x_3 + x_4}{4}, \frac{y_1 + y_2 + y_3 + y_4}{4}, \frac{z_1 + z_2 + z_3 + z_4}{4}\right)$$

is common to AG_1, BG_2 CG_3 and DG_4.

Method to Show Collinearity by using Section Formulae

To show that three points say A, B and C are collinear by using section formula, we use the following steps

***Step* I** First, assume that one point, say C divide the line segment, say AB obtained by joining the other two points A and B in the ratio $k:1$ internally.

***Step* II** Write the coordinates of point C in terms of k.

***Step* III** Now, find the value of k by comparing the x-coordinate, y-coordinate and z-coordinate separately of given point C with respective coordinates obtained in step II of C.

***Step* IV** If value of k obtained by comparing each coordinate separately is same, then given points will be collinear otherwise not.

Example 19 Using section formula, show that the points $(2, -3, 4)$, $(-1, 2, 1)$ and $\left(0, \frac{1}{3}, 2\right)$ are collinear. **[NCERT]**

Sol. Let $C\left(0, \frac{1}{3}, 2\right)$ divides the join of $A(2, -3, 4)$ and $B(-1, 2, 1)$ in the ratio $k:1$.
Then, the coordinates of C are

$$\left(\frac{-k+2}{k+1}, \frac{2k-3}{k+1}, \frac{k+4}{k+1}\right) \quad \text{...(i)}$$

[using internal ratio formula]

But coordinates of C are $\left(0, \frac{1}{3}, 2\right)$. [given] ...(ii)

On comparing Eqs. (i) and (ii), we get

$$\frac{-k+2}{k+1} = 0 \Rightarrow -k+2 = 0 \Rightarrow k = 2$$

$$\frac{2k-3}{k+1} = \frac{1}{3} \Rightarrow 6k - 9 = k + 1$$

$$\Rightarrow \quad 5k = 10 \Rightarrow k = 2$$

and $$\frac{k+4}{k+1} = 2$$

$$\Rightarrow \quad k + 4 = 2k + 2 \Rightarrow k = 2$$

From each of these equations, we get $k = 2$
Since, from each equations, we get same value of k.
Therefore, the given points are collinear and C divides AB internally in the ratio 2 : 1. **Hence proved.**

Example 20 Given that $P(3, 2, -4)$, $Q(5, 4, -6)$ and $R(9, 8, -10)$ are collinear. Find the ratio in which Q divides PR. **[NCERT]**

Sol. Let Q divides PR in the ratio $k:1$.

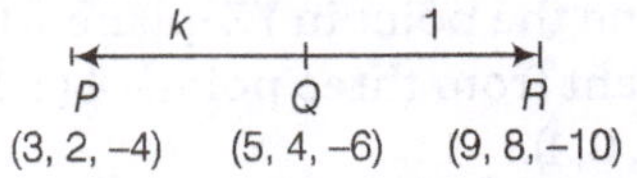

Here, point Q divides the line PR internally in the ratio $k:1$. Coordinates

$$= \left(\frac{k \times 9 + 1 \times 3}{k+1}, \frac{k \times 8 + 1 \times 2}{k+1}, \frac{k(-10) + 1 \times (-4)}{k+1}\right)$$

[using internal ratio formula]

$$= \left(\frac{9k+3}{k+1}, \frac{8k+2}{k+1}, \frac{-10k-4}{k+1}\right)$$

But given that $Q = (5, 4, -6)$
On comparing the corresponding coordinates, we get

$$\frac{9k+3}{k+1} = 5, \quad \frac{8k+2}{k+1} = 4 \text{ and } \frac{-10k-4}{k+1} = -6$$

$$\Rightarrow \quad 9k + 3 = 5k + 5, \; 8k + 2 = 4k + 4$$

and $-10k - 4 = -6k - 6$

$$\Rightarrow \quad 4k = 2 \Rightarrow k = \frac{1}{2}$$

Hence, the point Q divides PR internally in the ratio 1 : 2.

Topic Practice 2

Very Short Answer Type Questions

(2 Marks)

1 Find the distance from the origin to (6, 6, 7). **[NCERT Exemplar]**

2 Find the point on Y-axis which is at a distance $\sqrt{10}$ from the point (1, 2, 3). **[NCERT Exemplar]**

3 Find the distance of a point $P(3, 4, 5)$ from XY- plane.

4 Show that, if $x^2 + y^2 = 1$, then the point $(x, y, \sqrt{1 - x^2 - y^2})$ is at a distance 1 unit from the origin.

5 What is the length of foot of perpendicular drawn from the point $P(3, 4, 5)$ on Y-axis by using distance formula?

6 Find the point on X-axis which is equidistant from the points $A(3, 2, 2)$ and $B(5, 5, 4)$. **[NCERT Exemplar]**

7 If the distance between the points $(a, 0, 1)$ and $(0, 1, 2)$ is $\sqrt{27}$, then find the value of a.

8 Determine the point in YZ-plane which is equidistant from three points $A(2,0,3)$, $B(0, 3, 2)$ and $C(0, 0, 1)$.

9 Find the equation of the set of the point P, the sum of whose distance from $A(4, 0, 0)$ and $B(-4, 0, 0)$ is equal to 10.

10 Find the equation of the set of points which are equidistance from the points (1, 2, 3) and (3, 2, –1). **[NCERT]**

11 Using distance formula, show that the following points are collinear.

(i) Points $P(2, 4, 6)$, $Q(-2, -2, -2)$ and $R(6, 10, 14)$

(ii) Points $A(1, -1, 3)$, $B(2, -4, 5)$ and $C(5, -13, 11)$

12 Find the coordinates of the point which divides the join of $P(2, -1, 4)$ and $Q(4, 3, 2)$ in the ratio 2 : 3 (i) internally (ii) externally.

13 Find the coordinates of the point P which is five-sixth of the way from $A(-2, 0, 6)$ to $B(10, -6, -12)$. **[NCERT Exemplar]**

14 Find the ratio in which the line segment joining the points (2, 4, 5) and (3, 5, – 4) is divided by the XZ-plane.

15 Find the centroid of a triangle, the mid-point of whose sides are $D(1, 2, -3)$, $E(3, 0, 1)$ and $F(-1, 1, -4)$. **[NCERT Exemplar]**

16 Find the third vertex of triangle whose centroid is origin and two vertices are (2, 4, 6) and (0, – 2, 5).

17 Show that the three points $A(2, 3, 4)$, $B(-1, 2, -3)$ and $C(-4, 1, -10)$ are collinear and find the ratio in which C divides AB. **[NCERT Exemplar]**

18 Verify that $A(-1, 2, 1)$, $B(1, -2, 5)$, $C(4, -7, 8)$ and $D(2, -3, 4)$ are the vertices of a parallelogram.

Short Answer Type Questions

(4 Marks)

19 Find the coordinate of the points which trisect the line segment joining the points $A(2, 1, -3)$ and $B(5, -8, 3)$. **[NCERT Exemplar]**

20 The vertices of the triangles are $A(5, 4, 6)$, $B(1, -1, 3)$ and $C(4, 3, 2)$. The internal bisector of $\angle A$ meets BC at D. Find the coordinates of D and the length AD.

21 The mid-point of the sides of a triangle are (1, 5, – 1), (0, 4, – 2) and (2, 3, 4). Find its vertices and also find the centroid of the triangle. **[NCERT Exemplar]**

Hints & Answers

1. $\because$ Origin = (0, 0, 0) **Ans.** 11 units

2. $\sqrt{(1-0)^2 + (2-y)^2 + (3-0)^2} = \sqrt{10}$
$\Rightarrow (y-2)^2 = 0 \Rightarrow y = 2$ **Ans.** (0, 2, 0)

3. $\because$ Point in XY-plane is (3, 4, 0). **Ans.** 5 units

4. Distance of the point $(x, y, \sqrt{1-x^2-y^2})$ from origin is given as $d = |\sqrt{x^2 + y^2 + (\sqrt{1-x^2-y^2})^2}|$

5. $\because$ Point on Y-axis is (0, 4, 0). **Ans.** $\sqrt{34}$ units

6. Let the point on X-axis be $P(x, 0, 0)$.
Then, $(x-3)^2 + (0-2)^2 + (0-2)^2$
$= (x-5)^2 + (0-5)^2 + (0-4)^2$
Ans. $\left(\frac{49}{4}, 0, 0\right)$

7. $\because \quad AB = \sqrt{(a-0)^2 + (0-1)^2 + (1-2)^2}$

$\Rightarrow \quad \sqrt{27} = \sqrt{a^2 + 1 + 1}$

Ans. $a = \pm 5$

8. Let $P(0, y, z)$ be a point on the YZ-plane such that $PA = PB = PC$.

Now, $\quad PA = PB$

$(0-2)^2 + (y-0)^2 + (z-3)^2 = (0-0)^2 + (y-3)^2 + (z-2)^2$

$\Rightarrow \quad z - 3y = 0 \quad \ldots\text{(i)}$

and $\quad PB = PC$

$\Rightarrow \quad (0-0)^2 + (y-3)^3 + (z-2)^2 = (0-0)^2 + (y-0)^2 + (z-1)^2$

$\Rightarrow \quad 3y + z = 6 \quad \ldots\text{(ii)}$

Now, solve Eqs. (i) and (ii). **Ans.** (0, 1, 3)

9. $PA + PB = 10$ **Ans.** $9x^2 + 25y^2 + 25z^2 - 225 = 0$

10. $x - 2z = 0$

11. Similar as Example 8.

(i) Show that $PQ + PR = QR$.

(ii) Show that $AB + BC = CA$.

12. Similar as Example 9.

(i) $\left(\frac{14}{5}, \frac{3}{5}, \frac{16}{5}\right)$ (ii) $(-2, -9, 8)$

13. Let $P(x, y, z)$ be the required point which is $\frac{5}{6}$ of AB i.e.

$AP = \frac{5}{6} AB$

$\Rightarrow \quad \frac{AP}{AB} = \frac{5}{6} \Rightarrow \frac{AP}{AP + PB} = \frac{5}{5+1}$

$\therefore \quad AP : PB = 5:1$ **Ans.** $(8, -5, -9)$

14. Let the joint of $P(2, 4, 5)$ and $Q(3, 5, -4)$ be divided by XZ-plane in the ratio $k:1$ at the point $R(x, y, z)$.

Therefore, $x = \frac{3k+2}{k+1}$, $y = \frac{5k+4}{k+1}$, $z = \frac{-4k+5}{k+1}$

Since, the point $R(x, y, z)$ lies on the XZ-plane, so the y-coordinate should be zero, i.e. $\frac{5k+4}{k+1} = 0$.

Ans. 4 : 5 externally

15. The centroid of a triangle is equal to the centroid of the triangle formed by mid-points of its sides.

Ans. $(1, 1, -2)$

16. Here, $0 = \frac{x+2+0}{3} \Rightarrow x = -2$,

$0 = \frac{y+4-2}{3} \Rightarrow y = -2$

and $\quad 0 = \frac{z+6+5}{2} \Rightarrow z = -11$

Ans. $(-2, -2, -11)$

17. Let C divides the join of A and B in the ratio $k:1$.

$\therefore$ Coordinates of $C = \left(\frac{-k+2}{k+1}, \frac{2k+3}{k+1}, \frac{-3k+4}{k+1}\right)$

Equate $\left(\frac{-k+2}{k+1}, \frac{2k+3}{k+1}, \frac{-3k+4}{k+1}\right) = (-4, 1, -10)$ to find ratio.

Ans. 2:1 externally

18. Show that the mid-point of AC is equal to the mid-point of BD.

19. Let the $P(x_1, y_1, z_1)$ and $Q(x_2, y_2, z_2)$ trisect line segment AB.

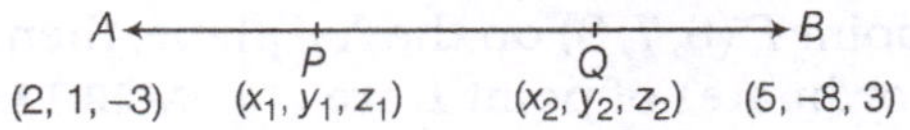

Then, the point P divides line AB in 1 : 2 internally and divides line AB in 2:1.

Ans. $(3, -2, -1)$ and $(4, -5, 1)$

20.

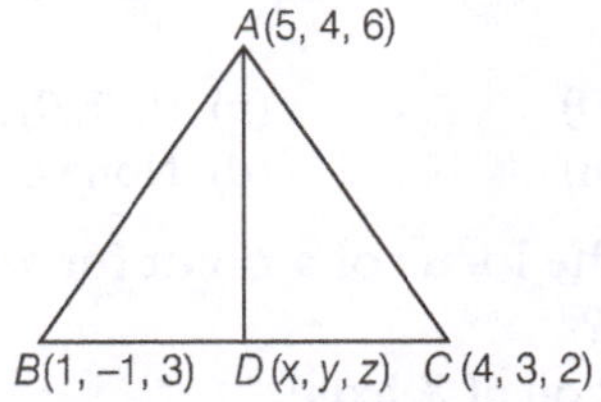

AD is angle bisector of $\angle BAC$

$\therefore \quad \frac{AB}{AC} = \frac{BD}{DC}$

$\Rightarrow \quad \frac{5\sqrt{2}}{3\sqrt{2}} = \frac{BD}{DC}$

$\Rightarrow \quad BD : DC = 5:3$

$\therefore$ Coordinate of $D = \left(\frac{20+3}{8}, \frac{15-3}{8}, \frac{10+9}{8}\right)$

Ans. $\left(\frac{23}{8}, \frac{3}{2}, \frac{19}{8}\right), \frac{\sqrt{1530}}{8}$

21. The vertices of the triangle are A (1, 2, 3), B (3, 4, 5) and C (–1, 6, –7). Also, centroid of the triangles is G (1, 4, 1/3).

Chapter Practice

Multiple Choice Type Questions

1 Mark

1. Which of the following statements is correct?
   (a) The coordinates of the origin O are $(0, 0, 0)$
   (b) The coordinates of any point on the X-axis will be as $(0, y, z)$
   (c) The coordinates of any point in the YZ-plane will be $(x, 0, 0)$
   (d) All of the above are correct

2. L is the foot of the perpendicular drawn from a point $P(6, 7, 8)$ on the XY-plane, then the coordinates of point L are **[NCERT Exemplar]**
   (a) $(6, 0, 0)$ (b) $(6, 7, 0)$
   (c) $(6, 0, 8)$ (d) None of these

3. L is the foot of the perpendicular drawn from a point $(6, 7, 8)$ on X-axis. The coordinates of L are
   (a) $(6, 0, 0)$ (b) $(0, 7, 0)$
   (c) $(0, 0, 8)$ (d) None of these

4. What is the locus of a point for which $y = 0$ and $z = 0$?
   (a) Equation of X-axis
   (b) Equation of Y-axis
   (c) Equation of Z-axis
   (d) None of the above

5. Which of the following statements is correct?
   (a) The X-axis and Y-axis taken together determine a plane known as XY-plane
   (b) The coordinates of a point in the XY-plane are of the form $(0, 0, z)$
   (c) Coordinate planes divide the space into six octants
   (d) All the above are correct

6. The distance between the points $(1, 4, 5)$ and $(2, 2, 3)$ is
   (a) 5 (b) 4 (c) 3 (d) 2

Assertion-Reason Type Questions

1 Mark

Directions (Q. Nos. 7-10) *In the questions given below are two statements labelled as Assertion (A) and Reason (R). In the context of the two statements, which one of the following is correct?*

(a) Both A and R are correct; R is the correct explanation of A
(b) Both A and R are correct; R is not the correct explanation of A
(c) A is correct; R is incorrect
(d) R is correct; A is incorrect

7. **Assertion (A)** Three points $P(1, 2, 3)$, $Q(-1, -1, -1)$ and $R(3, 5, 7)$ are collinear.

   Reason (R) Three points A, B and C are said to be collinear, if $AB + BC = AC$.

8. **Assertion (A)** Points $A(1, 2, 3)$, $B(-1, -2, -1)$, $C(2, 3, 2)$ and $D(4, 7, 6)$ are the vertices of a parallelogram $ABCD$.

   Reason (R) In a parallelogram, opposite sides are equal and diagonals are unequal. Also, diagonal bisect each other.

9. **Assertion (A)** The points $(0, 7, 10)$, $(-1, 6, 6)$ and $(-4, 9, 6)$ are the vertices of a right angled isosceles.

   Reason (R) The square of hypotenuse is equal to the sum of squares of other two sides.

10. **Assertion (A)** If the distance between two points $(x, -8, 4)$ and $(3, -5, 4)$, then the value of x is 5 units.

    Reason (R) The distance between two points

$$= \sqrt{(x_2 - x_1)^2 + (y_2 - y_1)^2 + (z_2 - z_1)^2}$$

Very Short Answer Type Questions

2 Marks

11. Describe the vertices and edges of the rectangular parallelopiped with vertex (3, 5, 6) placed in the first octant with one vertex at origin and edges of parallelopiped lie along X, Y and Z-axes. **[NCERT Exemplar]**

12. Find the locus of a point which moves such that the sum of its distance from points $A(0, 0, -\alpha)$ and $B(0, 0, \alpha)$ is constant.

13. Show that the points (0, 4, 1), (2, 3, −1), (4, 5, 0) and (2, 6, 2) are the vertices of a square.

14. Prove that the points (5, 3, 2), (3, 2, 5) and (2, 5, 3) are the vertices of an equilateral triangle.

15. By using section formula, show that the points (1, 0, 2), (2, 2, 3) and (−1, −1, 2) are collinear.

16. By using distance formula, show that the points (2, −1, 0), (−2, 3, −2) and (0, 3, 0) are collinear.

17. If origin is the centroid of a ΔABC with vertices $A(\alpha, 1, 3)$, $B(-2, \beta, -5)$ and $C(4, 7, \gamma)$, then find the values of α, β and γ.

18. Show that the points (a, b, c), (b, c, a) and (c, a, b) are the vertices of an equilateral triangle.

Short Answer Type Questions

4 Marks

19. If a parallelopiped is formed by the planes drawn through the points (2, 3, 5) and (5, 9, 7) parallel to the coordinate planes, then write the lengths of edges of the parallelopiped and length of the diagonal.

20. Three points $A(1, 2, 3)$, $B(0, 4, 1)$ and $C(-1, -1, -3)$ are the vertices of ΔABC. Find the point in which the bisector of $\angle BAC$ meets BC.

21. If $A(2, 2, -3)$, $B(5, 6, 9)$, $C(2, 7, 9)$ are the vertices of a triangle. The internal bisector of $\angle A$ meets BC at the point D, then find the coordinates of D. **[NCERT Exemplar]**

22. Show that the points (−1, −6, 10), (1, −3, 4), (−5, −1, 1) and (−7, −4, 7) are the vertices of a rhombus.

23. Two vertices of a triangle are $A(3, 4, 2)$ and $B(1, 3, 2)$. The medians of the triangle intersect at (2, 4, 3). Find the remaining vertex C of the triangle.

24. The mid-points of the sides of a triangle are (1, 5, −1), (0, 4, −2) and (2, 3, 4). Find its vertices.

25. Find the coordinates of centroid of ΔABC, where vertices are $A(x_1, y_1, z_1)$, $B(x_2, y_2, z_2)$ and $C(x_3, y_3, z_3)$.

Case-Based Type Questions

6 Marks

26. Three friends Arvind, Lokesh and Pradeep are studying in class XI of Rawat Public School, Jaipur. After completing the study, they relocated to different states which are shown in figure.

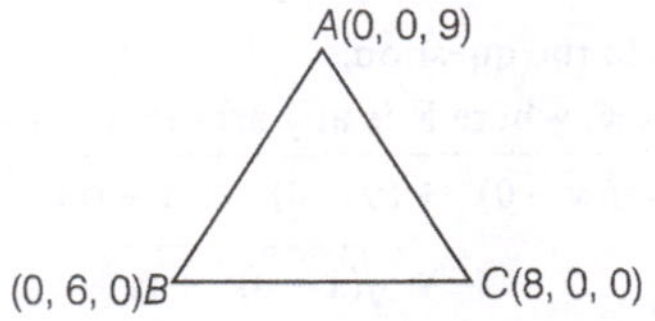

Here, points A, B and C show the positions of Pradeep, Arvind and Lokesh respectively, then answer the following questions which are based on it.

(i) What is the formula to find the distance between two points?

(ii) What is the distance between Pradeep and Arvind?

(iii) What is the distance between Arvind and Lokesh?

(iv) What is the distance between Lokesh and Pradeep?

27. Mr. Mahendra Kumar is a Mathematics teacher of class XI in Delhi Public School, Pawta. One day, he writes some points on the board to check the knowledge about the basic concepts of three dimensional geometry.

(i) (8, 3, 5) (ii) (−7, 5, 3)

(iii) (5, −2, 7) (iv) (9, 5, −6)

(v) (−7, −6, 8) (vi) (−2, 3, 4)

(vii) (−4, 0, 0) (viii) (−5, 0, 3)

Then, answer the following questions which are based on it.

(i) In which octant the point (8, 3, 5) lies?

(ii) Find the image of (–2, 3, 4) in YZ-plane.

(iii) In which octant the point (–7, – 6, 8) lies?

(iv) Find the image of (–5, 0, 3) in XZ-plane.

(v) In which octant the point (5, –2, 7) lies?

Hints & Answers

1. (a) **2.** (b) **3.** (a) **4.** (a) **5.** (a)
6. (c) **7.** (a) **8.** (a) **9.** (b) **10.** (a)

11.

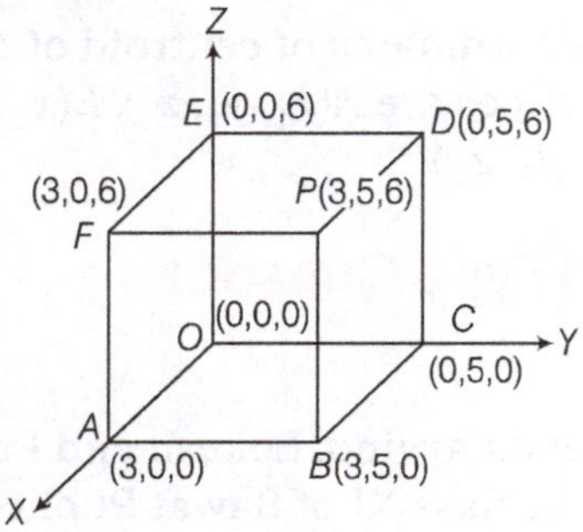

Ans. (0, 0, 0), (9, 0, 0), (0, 5, 0), (0, 0, 6), (9, 5, 0), (9, 0, 6), (0, 5, 6), (3, 5, 6); 6, 5, 9

12. Let $P(x, y, z)$ be the required point.

According to the question,

$AP + BP = K$, where K is any arbitrary constant.

$$\Rightarrow \sqrt{(x-0)^2+(y-0)^2+(z+\alpha)^2} + \sqrt{(x-0)^2+(y-0)^2+(z-\alpha)^2} = K$$

Ans. $4k^2x^2 + 4k^2y^2 + 4z^2(K^2 - 4\alpha^2) + K^2(4\alpha^2 - K^2) = 0$

13. Show that $AB = BC = CD = DA$ and $AC = BD$.

14. Show that $AB = BC = CA$.

15. Let $A(1, 0, 2)$, $B(2, 2, 3)$ and $C(-1, -1, 2)$ be three points.

Again, let B divides the line joining the points A and B in the ratio of $k:1$.

Now, show that value of k obtained by each coordinate is same.

16. To prove collinear, $AB + BC = AC$.

17. $\because$ Coordinates of centroid of a $\Delta ABC = (0, 0, 0)$

$$\Rightarrow \left(\frac{\alpha - 2 + 4}{3}, \frac{1 + \beta + 7}{3}, \frac{3 - 5 + \gamma}{3}\right) = (0, 0, 0)$$

Ans. $\alpha = -2, \beta = -8, \gamma = 2$

18. Show that $AB = BC = CA$.

19. Let $P \equiv (2, 3, 5)$ and $Q \equiv (5, 9, 7)$

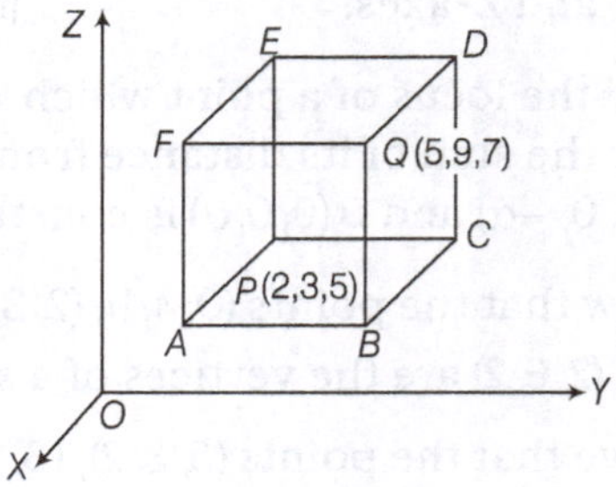

Now,

PE = Distance between parallel planes $ABCP$ and $FQDE$

PA = Distance between parallel planes $ABQF$ and $PCDE$

PC = Distance between parallel planes $APEF$ and $BCDQ$ and length of diagonal = distance between P and Q.

Ans. 3 units, 6 units, 2 units, and 7 units.

20. $\left(\frac{-3}{10}, \frac{5}{2}, \frac{-1}{5}\right)$

21. $\left(\frac{7}{2}, \frac{13}{2}, 9\right)$

22. Show that $AB = BC = CD = DA$ and $AC \neq BD$.

23. Let third vertex of ΔABC be $C(x, y, z)$.

We know that intersection of medians of triangle is known as centroid of a triangle.

$$\therefore \left(\frac{3+1+x}{3}, \frac{4+3+y}{3}, \frac{2+2+z}{3}\right) = (2, 4, 3)$$

Ans. $C(2, 5, 5)$

24. Similar as Example 12 of Topic 2.

Ans. (1, 2, 3), (3, 4, 5) and (–1, 6, –7)

25. Let D be the mid-point of BC and E be the centroid of ΔABC, which divides AD in the ratio of 2 : 1.

Ans. $\left(\frac{x_1 + x_2 + x_3}{3}, \frac{y_1 + y_2 + y_3}{2}, \frac{z_1 + z_2 + z_3}{2}\right)$

26. (i) $\sqrt{(x_2 - x_1)^2 + (y_2 - y_1)^2 + (z_2 - z_1)^2}$
(ii) $\sqrt{117}$ units (iii) 10 units (iv) $\sqrt{145}$ units

27. (i) $XOYZ$ (ii) (0, 3, 4) (iii) $X'OY'Z$
(iv) (– 5, 0, 3) (v) $XOY'Z$

CHAPTER

18

Mathematical Reasoning

In this chapter, we will learn about some basics of mathematical reasoning. In mathematical language, there are two kinds of reasoning; one is inductive reasoning and another is deductive reasoning. Inductive reasoning is already studied in principle of mathematical induction.

In this chapter, we will discuss some basics of deductive reasoning.

- Statements and Negation of Statement
- Basic Logical Connectives and Quantifiers
- Implications
- Validating Statements

TOPIC 01 Statements and Negation of Statement

The basic unit involved in mathematical reasoning is a mathematical statement.

A sentence (or proposition) is called a mathematically acceptable statement, if it is either true or false but not both and it is represented by the lower case letters like $p, q, r, s, \ldots$, etc.

e.g. (i) p : A triangle has four sides.

(ii) q : Patna is capital of Bihar.

Here, e.g. (i) is a false statement and e.g. (ii) is a true statement.

The working nature of a statement in logic is same as nature of a switch in circuit, i.e.

Switch < ON (1) / OFF (0) and Statement < True (T) / False (F)

Consider the following sentences

(i) The set of prime integers is infinite.

(ii) The sum of two positive numbers is positive.

(iii) Two plus two equals five.

(iv) All prime numbers are odd numbers.

(v) The sum of x and y is greater than zero.
(vi) The number x is negative integer.
(vii) How beautiful! (viii) Open the door.
(ix) May god bless you! (x) Who are you?

Clearly, out of these sentences. (i), (ii) are true and (iii), (iv) are false. Therefore, they are statements. Sentences (v), (vi) are not in position to determine whether they are true or false, unless we know what x and y are as sentence (v) is false when $x=3$, $y=-5$ and true when $x=-2$, $y=3$. Therefore, these sentences are not statement.

Now, consider the sentences (vii), (viii), (ix) and (x). Sentence (vii) is an exclamation, (viii) an imperative, (ix) an optative, (x) a question. So, in these sentence, we cannot assign true or false to them. Hence, these sentences are not statement.

Note

(i) **Paradox** A sentence which is both true and false simultaneously, is not a statement rather it is a paradox. It may be true or false. **e.g.** 'I am always a lier'.
(ii) A true statement is known as a **valid statement.**
(iii) A false statement is known as an **invalid statement.**
(iv) Imperative, exclamatory, interrogative, optative sentence are not statements.

Which of the following sentences are statements? Give reasons for your answer.

(i) The square of a number is an even number.
(ii) The sides of a quadrilateral have equal lengths.
(iii) The product of (–1) and 8 is 8.
(iv) The sum of all interior angles of a triangle is 180°.
(v) Today is a windy day.
(vi) The Sun is a star.
(vii) 6 has three prime factors.
(viii) Mathematics is fun.
(ix) The product of x and y is positive integer.
(x) There are 31 days in a month.
(xi) Have you ever seen Taj Mahal?
(xii) $x+3=17$
(xiii) $6+1=7$

Sol. (i) The square of a number may be even or it may be odd. Square of an odd number is always odd and square of an even number is always even.
e.g. $4^2=16$ (even) and $5^2=25$ (odd)
Hence, it is not a statement.

(ii) A quadrilateral may have equal lengths as it may be a rhombus or a square or the quadrilateral may have unequal sides. Hence, it is not a statement.

(iii) It is false because product of (-1) and 8 is not 8. It is –8. Hence, it is a statement.

(iv) It is true that sum of all interior angles of a triangle is 180°. Hence, it is a statement.

(v) It is not clear from the context which day is referred. Thus, it cannot be concluded whether it is true or false. Hence, it is not a statement.

(vi) It is a scientific fact that Sun is a star and therefore this sentence is always true. Hence, it is a statement.

(vii) It is false because 6 has two prime factors, i.e. 2 and 3. Hence, it is a statement.

(viii) Mathematics is a fun, is true for those who like Mathematics. But, for others, it may not be true. So, the given sentence may or may not be true. Hence, it is not a statement.

(ix) The sentence "product of x and y is positive integer" is not a statement because we cannot determine it is true or false unless we know what x and y are.

(x) The sentence, "There are 31 days in a month" is not a statement because different month have different days. e.g. April has 30 days while May has 31 days.

(xi) We cannot assign true or false to the sentence "Have you ever seen Taj Mahal", therefore it is not a statement. Infact it is an interrogative.

(xii) We cannot assign true or false to the given sentence, unless we know what x is, so it is not a statement.

(xiii) The sentence, '$6+1=7$' is true, therefore it is a statement.

Example 2 Give two examples of sentence which are not statements. Give reason for your answer.

Sol. The two examples can be
(i) May God bless you! (ii) May you live long!
Each of these sentences is an optative. So, we cannot assign true or false to them and hence none of them is a statement.

Types of Statements

There are three types of statements as follows

1. Simple Statement

A statement which cannot be broken into two or more statements is called a simple statement. Generally, simple statements are denoted by small letters $p, q, s, \ldots$

e.g. (i) $p: \sqrt{2}$ is a real number. [true]
(ii) q : Sun sets in the East. [false]

2. Compound Statement

A statement that can be broken into two or more simple statements is called a compound statement or compound proposition. In this case, each statement is called **component statement** or **sub-statement.** The compound statements are formed by using the connecting words/phrases like 'and', 'or', 'if then', 'if and only if' etc.

e.g.
(i) Roses are red and violets are blue.
(ii) The school is open or a holiday is declared.
(iii) If it rains, then the school may be closed.
(iv) A quadrilateral is a rhombus if and only if its diagonals are at right angles.

Note
(i) The truth value of the simple statement does not depend on any other statement.
(ii) The truth value of the compound statement is completely depend on the truth values of the component statements together with the way in which they are connected.

3. Open Statement

A sentence, which contains one or more variables such that when certain values are given to the variable it becomes a statement, is called an **open statement**.

e.g. 'He is a great man' is an open sentence because in this sentence, 'He' can be replaced by any person.

Example 3 Which of the following statements are compound statements?
(i) 2 is both an even and a prime number.
(ii) 9 is neither an even number nor a prime number.
(iii) Ram and Rahim are friends **[NCERT Exemplar]**

Sol. (i) The given statement can be broken into two simple statements.
p : 2 is an even number.
q : 2 is a prime number.
$\therefore$ It is a compound statement.

(ii) The given statement can be broken into two simple statements.
p : 9 is not an even number.
q : 9 is not a prime number.
$\therefore$ It is a compound statement.

(iii) The given statement cannot be broken into two simple sentences because here the word 'and' refers to two persons Ram and Rahim.
$\therefore$ It is not a compound statement.

Example 4 Identify the component statements and the connecting word in the following compound statements.
(i) It is raining or the Sun is shining.
(ii) All primes are either even or odd.
(iii) Two lines intersect at a point or they are parallel.

Sol. (i) The component statements are
p : It is raining $\quad q$: The Sun is shining.
The connecting word is 'or'.

(ii) The component statements are
p : All primes are even.
q : All primes are odd.
The connecting word is 'or'.

(iii) The component statements are
p : Two lines intersect at a point.
q : Two lines are parallel.
The connecting word is 'or'.

Truth and Falsity of Statement (or Truth Value of a Statement)

The truth or falsity of a statement is called its truth value. If a statement is true, then its truth value is TRUE, denoted by T.

If it is false, then its truth value is FALSE, denoted by F.

e.g. (i) 'Delhi is capital of India'. Its truth value is T.
(ii) 'London is capital of India'. Its truth value is F.

Example 5 Write down the truth value of each of the following statements.
(i) Delhi is in India.
(ii) Chennai is in Pakistan.
(iii) $5+6=11$

Sol. (i) T, because statement 'Delhi is in India' is true.
(ii) F, because statement 'Chennai is in Pakistan' is false.
(iii) T, because statement '$5+6=11$' is true.

Example 6 Find the component statements of the following and check whether they are true or not.
(i) $\sqrt{2}$ is a rational number or an irrational number.
(ii) All integers are positive or negative.
(iii) All primes are either even or odd.
(iv) A square is a quadrilateral and its four sides equal.
(v) 100 is divisible by 3, 11 and 5.

Sol. (i) The component statements are
$p : \sqrt{2}$ is a rational number.
$q : \sqrt{2}$ is an irrational number.
Clearly, p is false and q is true.

(ii) The component statements are
p : All integers are positive.
q : All integers are negative.
Clearly, p and q both are false.

(iii) The component statements are
p : All primes are even.
q : All primes are odd.
Clearly, p and q both are false.

(iv) The component statements are
p : A square is a quadrilateral.
q : A square has all its sides equal.
Clearly, p and q both are true.

(v) The component statements are
p : 100 is divisible by 3
q : 100 is divisible by 11
r : 100 is divisible by 5
Clearly, p, q are false and r is true.

Negation of a Statement

If p is any statement, then the denial of statement p is called the **negation of statement** p and is written as $\sim p$ or p' or $\bar{p}$. As the symbol $\sim$ applies to a single statement, it is called a **modifier** rather than **connective**.

The negation of statement p is formed by writing, 'It is not the case that' or 'It is false that', before p or if possible by inserting the word 'not' in p.

Let us consider the statement

p : I went to my class yesterday.

The negation of this statement is

$\sim p$: I did not go to my class yesterday.

This can also be written as

$\sim p$: I was absent from my class yesterday.

This can also be written as

$\sim p$: It is false that I went to my class yesterday.

This can also be expressed as

$\sim p$: It is not the case that I went to my class yesterday.

Example 7 Write the negation of the following statements and check whether the resulting statement are true.

(i) The sum of 2 and 3 is 4. (ii) $\sqrt{3}$ is rational.
(iii) New Delhi is a city.
(iv) Every natural number is greater than 0.

Sol. (i) The negation of the given statement is
It is false that sum of 2 and 3 is 4.
Or
The sum of 2 and 3 is not equal to 4.
This statement is true because $2+3=5\neq 4$.

(ii) The negation of the given statement is
It is false that $\sqrt{3}$ is rational.
Or
$\sqrt{3}$ is not rational.
This statement is true because $\sqrt{3}$ is irrational.

(iii) The negation of the given statement is
It is false that New Delhi is a city.
Or
New Delhi is not a city.
This statement is false.

(iv) The negation of the given statement is
It is false that every natural number is greater than 0.
This is a false statement.

Note The negation of a statement that contain the words like "for all" "there exists", "Same" or "for every" can be tricky.
e.g. The negation of "All Doctors are Men" is not
"All Doctors are not men"
In fact, the negation of the given statement is
"Not all Doctors are men"
as "There exists a Doctors who is not a man".
as "It is false that all Doctors are men".

Topic Practice 1

Very Short Answer Type Questions

2 Marks

1 Which of the following sentences are statement? Give reason for your answer.
(i) 8 is less than 6.
(ii) The Earth is star.
(iii) Today is a rainy day.
(iv) Shut the door.
(v) Sum of two even number is always even.
(vi) She is a Mathematics graduate.
(vii) Tomorrow is holiday.
(viii) How are you?
(ix) He is Prime Minister of India.
(x) Give me a glass of water.

2 Give three examples of sentence which are not statements. Give reason for your answers. **[NCERT]**

3 Which of the statements are compound statement?
(i) The Earth is round or the Sun is hot.
(ii) 3 is both an odd and a prime number.
(iii) 84 is divisible by 4 and 7.
(iv) Ravi opened the door and run away.

4 Find the component statement of the following and check whether they are true or not.
(i) 5 is a rational number or an irrational number.
(ii) Number 3 is prime or it is odd.
(iii) 200 is divisible by 3, 11 and 5.
(iv) 24 is a multiple of 2, 4 and 8.

5 Find the component statement of the following compound statements. Clearly mention the connecting word.
(i) Jack and Jill went up the hill.
(ii) The sky is blue or the grass is green.
(iii) 7 is both odd and prime number.

6 Write the negation of the following statements and check whether the resulting statements are true.
(i) Australia is continent.
(ii) The number 17 is prime.
(iii) $\sqrt{5}$ is a rational number.
(iv) A leap year has 366 days.

7 Find the component statements of the following compound statements.
(i) There is something wrong with the bulb or with wiring.
(ii) It is raining and it is cold.
(iii) The roof is red and the wall is white.
(iv) The Sun shines or it rains.

8 Write the negation of "All men are Martial".
(i) Using "There exists atleast ... ".
(ii) Without using "There exists ... ".

Hints & Answers

1. (i), (ii) and (v) are statements.

2. (i) Everyone in this room is bold. This is not a statements because from the context it is not clear which room is referred here and the term bold is not precisely defined.
(ii) She is an engineering student. This is also not a statement because who 'she' is.
(iii) $\cos^2\theta$ is always greater than 1/2. Unless, we know what θ is, we cannot say whether the sentence is true or not.

3. (i) p : The Earth is round.
q : The Sun is hot.
$\therefore$ It is a compound statement.
(ii) p : 3 is an odd number.
q : 3 is an prime number.
$\therefore$ It is a compound statement.
(iii) p : 84 is divisible by 4.
q : 84 is divisible by 7.
$\therefore$ It is a compound statement.
(iv) Given statement can not be broken into two simple sentence. So, it is not compound statement.

4. (i) p : 5 is a rational number.
q : 5 is an irrational number.
p is true and q is false.
(ii) p : Number 3 is prime.
q : Number 3 is odd.
p and q both are true.
(iii) p : 200 is divisible by 3.
q : 200 is divisible by 11.
r : 200 is divisible by 5.
p and q are false and r is true.
(iv) p : 24 is a multiple is 2.
q : 24 is a multiple of 4.
r : 24 is a multiple of 8.
All component statements are true.

5. (i) p : Jack went up the hill.
q : Jill went up the hill.
Here the connecting word is "and".
(ii) p : The sky is blue.
q : The grass is green.
Here the connecting word is "or".
(iii) p : 7 is odd number.
q : 7 is prime number.
Here the connecting word is "and".

6. (i) Australia is not continent.
(ii) The number 17 is not prime.
(iii) $\sqrt{5}$ is not a rational number.
(iv) It is false that a leap year has 366 days.

7. (i) p : There is something wrong with the bulb.
q : There is something wrong with the wiring.
(ii) p : It is raining. q : It is cold.
(iii) p : The roof is red. q : The wall is white.
(iv) p : The Sun shines. q : It rains.

8. (i) There exists atleast are man who is not Martial.
(ii) Not all men as Martial.

TOPIC 02

Basic Logical Connectives and Quantifiers

There are many ways of combining simple statements to form new statements. The words which combine to change simple statements to compound statement are called logical connectives. The basic connectives are the word 'and' and the word 'or'.

The Word 'and'

If any two simple statements combined by the word 'and', then it forms a compound statement. This connective word is also called **conjunction** and is denoted by the symbol '$\wedge$'.

e.g. It is cold today and it is raining.
This statement is a compound statement. It can be denoted by 'p and q' or '$p \wedge q$', whose component statements are

p : It is cold today.
q : It is raining.

Note A statement with 'and' is not always a compound statement. e.g. A mixture of alcohol and water can be separated by chemical method. Here, the word 'and' is not used as a connective.

Rules for Connective 'and'

The rules for the connective 'and' are given below

Rule 1. *The compound statement with 'and' as connective is true, if all its component statements are true.*

Logically, the statement $p \wedge q$ has the truth value T (true) whenever both p and q have the truth value T. e.g. 'Valmiki wrote Ramayana and Vedvyas wrote Mahabharata'.

The component statements are

p : Valmiki wrote Ramayana. [true]
q : Vedvyas wrote Mahabharata. [true]

Here, we see that both the component statements are true. Therefore, compound statement $(p \wedge q)$ is a true statement i.e. it has truth value T.

Rule 2. *The compound statement with 'and' as connective is false, if any of its component statements is false.*

Logically, the statement $p \wedge q$ has the truth value F (false) whenever either p or q (or both) have the truth value F.

e.g. Sun is hot and Earth moves around the Moon.

The component statements of '$p \wedge q$' are

p : Sun is hot. [true]
q : Earth moves around the Moon. [false]

Here, we see that the component statement 'Sun is hot' is true, i.e. its truth value is T. 'Earth moves around the Moon' is false ($\because$ Earth moves around the Sun not Moon.) i.e. its truth value is F.

So, statement $p \wedge q$ is false, i.e. it has truth value F because one of its component statement is false.

Above rules can be explained through the truth table, which is easy to remember.

Truth Table for Connective 'and'

If p and q are two statements, then we have the following truth table for 'p and q'.

p	q	p and q (or '$p \wedge q$')
T	T	T
T	F	F
F	T	F
F	F	F

Note A table that shows the relationship between the truth value of compound statement and the truth value of its sub-statements is called the **truth table**. Such a table typically consists of rows and columns with top row representing sub-statements and compound statements.

Example 1 Form the compound statement by using 'and' of the following simple statements.

p : Dinesh is a boy.
q : Nagma is a girl.

Sol. Given simple statements are

p : Dinesh is a boy.
q : Nagma is a girl.

Now, the compound statement is 'Dinesh is a boy and Nagma is a girl'.

Example 2 Write the component statements of the following compound statements and check whether the compound statement is true or false.

(i) 50 is a multiple of both 2 and 5.
(ii) A line is straight and extends indefinitely in both directions.
(iii) All living things have two legs and two eyes.
(iv) 0 is less than every positive integer and every negative integer.

Sol. (i) The component statements of the given statement are

p : 50 is multiple of 2.

q : 50 is a multiple of 5.

We observe that both p and q are true statements. Therefore, the compound statement is true.

(ii) The component statements of the given statement are

p : A line is straight.

q : A line extends indefinitely in both directions.

We observe that both p and q are true. Therefore, the compound statement is true.

(iii) The component statements of the given statement are

p : All living things have two legs.

q : All living things have two eyes.

We observe that both p and q are false statements. Therefore, the compound statement is false.

(iv) The compound statements of the given statement are

p : 0 is less than every positive integer.

q : 0 is less than every negative integer.

We observe that p is true and q is false. Therefore, the compound statement is false.

The Word 'or'

If any two simple statements are combined by the word 'or', then it form a compound statement. This connective word is called **disjunction** and it is denoted by the symbol '$\vee$'.

e.g. Let p represents the statement 'Ravi teaches Computer' and q represents the statement 'Ravi teaches English'.

Then, p or q represents the statement 'Ravi teaches Computer or English'. There are two types of 'or' connective.

Type I **Exclusive 'or'** In a statement p or q, if exactly one of the two simple statements occurs, then the connecting word 'or' is exclusive.

e.g. Consider the statement 'p or q' : An ice-cream or pepsi is available with a thali in a restaurant. This means that a person who does not want ice-cream can have a pepsi with thali or a person who does not want pepsi can have a ice-cream with thali. This means that a person cannot have both ice-cream and pepsi. In such cases, the word 'or' is called **exclusive 'or'**.

Type II **Inclusive 'or'** In a statement 'p or q', if atleast one of the two **simple statements occurs, then the connecting word 'or' is inclusive.**

e.g. Consider the statement 'p or q' : a student who has taken Physics or Mathematics can apply for M.Tech. programme. **This means that the students who have taken Physics or Mathematics or both can apply for M.Tech programme. In such cases, the word 'or' is called inclusive 'or'.**

Note (i) Throughout this chapter, we will use the word 'or' as an 'inclusive or' unless stated otherwise.

(ii) The use of the word "or" in English language is ambiguous.

Rules for Connective 'or'

The rules for the connective 'or' are given below

Rule **1.** *A compound statement with 'or' as connective is true when one of the component statement is true or both the component statements are true.*

e.g. 35 is a multiple of 5 or 7.

The component statements are

p : 35 is a multiple of 5. [true]

q : 35 is a multiple of 7. [true]

Here, we see that both the component statements are true. So, the compound statement $p \vee q$ will also be true and it will have a truth value T.

Rule **2.** *A compound statement with 'or' as connective is false when both the component statements are false.*

e.g. 64 is a multiple of 6 or 7.

The component statements are

p : 64 is a multiple of 6. [false]

q : 64 is a multiple of 7. [false]

Here, we see that both the component statements are false. So, the compound statement $p \vee q$ will also be false and it will have truth value F.

Above rules can be explained through the truth table, which is easy to remember.

Truth Table for Connective 'or'

If p and q are two statements, then we have following truth table for "p or q".

p	q	p or q (or $p \vee q$)
T	T	T
T	F	T
F	T	T
F	F	F

Example 3 For each of the following statement, determine whether an inclusive 'OR' or exclusive 'OR' is used. Give reasons for your answers.

(i) The school is closed if it is holiday or Sunday.

(ii) Sun rises or Moon sets.

(iii) To apply for a driving licence, you should have a ration card or passport.

(iv) A lady gives birth to a baby boy or a baby girl.
(v) All integers are positive or negative.

Sol. (i) Here, 'or' is inclusive, because school is closed in holiday as well as Sunday.
(ii) Here, 'or' is exclusive, because Sun rises and Moon sets during day time.
(iii) Here, 'or' is inclusive, because a person can have both a ration card and a passport to apply for a driving licence.
(iv) Here, 'or' is exclusive, because a lady cannot gave birth to a baby who is both boy and a girl.
(v) Here 'or' is exclusive, because an integer cannot be both positive as well as negative.

Example 4 Form the compound statement by using 'or' of the following simple statements.

p : Two lines intersect at a point.
q : Two lines are parallel.

Sol. The compound statement of given simple statements is 'Two lines intersect at a point or they are parallel'.

Example 5 Write down the truth value of the statement "Patna is in Bihar or $5+6=111$."

Sol. The truth value of given statement is T i.e. true, because first sub-statement 'Patna is in Bihar' is true and '$5+6=111$' is false.

Example 6 Write down the compound statements by using 'and', 'or' of the following statements.

(i) p : It is cold. q : It is raining.
(ii) p : Mohan is honest. q : Mohan is qualified.

Sol. (i) The conjunction of the statements p and q is given by
$p \wedge q$: It is cold and it is raining.
The disjunction of the statements p and q is given by
$p \vee q$: It is cold or it is raining.
(ii) The conjunction of the statements p and q is given by
$p \wedge q$: Mohan is honest and qualified.
The disjunction of the statements p and q is given by
$p \vee q$: Mohan is honest or qualified.

Example 7 Write the component statements of the following compound statements and check whether the compound statement is true or false.

(i) 125 is a multiple of 7 or 8.
(ii) Mumbai is the capital of Gujarat or Maharashtra.
(iii) The school is closed, if there is a holiday or Sunday.

Sol. (i) The component statements of the given statement are
p : 125 is a multiple of 7. q : 125 is a multiple of 8.
We observe that both p and q are false statements. Therefore, the compound statement is also false.
(ii) The component statements of the given statement are
p : Mumbai is the capital of Gujarat.
q : Mumbai is the capital of Maharashtra.
We find that p is false and q is true. Therefore, the compound statement is true.
(iii) The component statements are
p : The school is closed, if there is a holiday.
q : The school is closed, if there is a Sunday.
Both p and q are true statements. Therefore, the compound statement is true.

Quantifiers

In Mathematics, we come across many mathematical statements containing phrases 'there exists' or 'for all' or 'for every'. These phrases are called **quantifiers**.

Depending upon the context, the phrase 'there exists' can be replaced by the equivalent words/phrases 'there is' or 'There is atleast one' or 'It is possible to find' or 'some'.

e.g. Consider the statement
p : There exists a rectangle, whose all sides are equal.
This means that there is atleast one rectangle, whose all sides are equal.
Similarly, depending upon the context, the phrases 'for all' or 'For every' can be replaced by the equivalent word 'all' or 'every'.

The quantifier 'for all' or 'for every' can be interpreted as saying that all members of the given set S, where the property applies, must satisfy that property.

e.g. Consider the statement
p : For every prime number p, $\sqrt{p}$ is an irrational number.
This means that, if S denotes the set of all prime numbers, then for all the members p of the set S, $\sqrt{p}$ is an irrational number.

Note (i) Phrase 'for every' or 'for all' is denoted by the symbol '$\forall$' called the **universal quantifier** and the phrase 'there exists' is denoted by the symbol '$\exists$', known as **existential quantifier**.
(ii) A statement is said to be a **quantified statement**, if it contain quantifier(s).

Example 8 Identify the quantifier in the following questions.

(i) There exists a number which is equal to its cube.
(ii) For every real number x, x is less than $x+5$.

Sol. (i) The quantifier in the given statement is 'There exists'.
(ii) The quantifier in the given statement is 'For every.'

Negation of a Quantified Statement

(i) If the statement contains the phrase 'there exists', then the negation of statement is given by writing 'There does not exist' in place of 'there exists'.

e.g. Negation of the statement

'there exists a number which is equal to its square'

is

'there does not exist a number which is equal to its square'.

(ii) If the statement contains the phrase 'for all' or 'for every', then the negation of statement is given by writing 'there exists or some or there exist atleast one' in place of 'for all', together with negation of the given property.

e.g. Negation of the statement

'For every real number x, x is less than $x+1$' is

'There exists a real number x, x is not less than $x+1$'.

Example 9 Write the negation of the following statements.

(i) Everyone in Germany speaks German.

(ii) All primes are odd.

(iii) All mathematicians are man.

Sol. (i) The negation of the given statement is

There exists a person in Germany who does not speak German.

Or

Atleast one person in Germany does not speak German.

Or

Some person in Germany does not speak German.

(ii) The negation of the given statement is

There exists a prime which is not odd.

Or

Some primes are not odd.

Or

Atleast one prime is not odd.

(iii) The negation of the given statement is

Some mathematicians are not man.

Or

There exists a mathematician who is not man.

Or

Atleast one mathematician is not man.

Topic Practice 2

Very Short Answer Type Questions

(2 Marks)

1 Form the compound statement by using 'and' of the following simple statements.

(i) p : John went up the hill.
q : Jill went up the hill.

(ii) p : The sky is blue.
q : The grass is green.

(iii) p : 25 is a multiple of 5.
q : 25 is a multiple of 8.

(iv) p : Rekha is studying in class eleven.
q : Rekha has to offer 5 subjects.

2 Form the compound statement by using 'or' of the following simple statements.

(i) p : The Sun shines.
q : It rains.

(ii) p : The Earth is round.
q : The Sun is cold.

(iii) p : $\sqrt{2}$ is a rational number.
q : $\sqrt{2}$ is an irrational number.

(iv) p : Square of an integer is positive.
q : Square of an integer is negative.

3 Considers the two statements.

p : Rajkumar is alive.

q : Rajkumar lives in Delhi.

Write the following statements in symbolic form.

(i) Rajkumar is alive and he lives in Delhi.

(ii) Eithers Rajkumar is alive or he lives in Delhi.

(iii) Raj Kumar is neither alive, nor does he live in Delhi.

(iv) It is not true that Rajkumar is alive and he lives in Delhi.

4 Identify the quantifier in the following statement

(i) For every prime number x, $\sqrt{x}$ is an irrational number.

(ii) $x+4>3$ for all $x \in N$.

5 Write the negation of the following statements.

(i) Every natural number is an integer.

(ii) Both the diagonals of a rectangle have the same length.

(iii) I will not go to school.

(iv) Some even integers are prime.

6 Check whether the following pair of statements are negation of each other. Give reason for your answer.

(i) $x + y = y + x$ is true for every real numbers x and y.

(ii) There exist real numbers x and y for which $x + y = y + x$

7 For each of the following statements, determine whether an inclusive 'OR' or exclusive 'OR' is used. Give reasons for your answers.

(i) Students can take Hindi or Sanskrit as their third language.

(ii) $\sqrt{7}$ is a rational or an irrational number.

8 Write the negation of the following statements.

(i) For all positive integers x, we have $x + 2 > 8$.

(ii) Every natural number is an integer.

9 Identify the quantifier(s) in the following statement and write the negation of the statement.

'There exists a capital for every state in India.' **[NCERT]**

Short Answer Type Questions

4 Marks

10 Write the component statements of the following compound statement and check whether the compound statement is true or false.

(i) $2 + 4 = 6$ or $2 + 4 = 7$.

(ii) A rectangle is a quadrilateral or a 5-sided polygon.

(iii) Every rectangle is a square and every square is a rectangle.

(iv) The Sun is a star or Sun is planet.

11 Identify the quantifiers and write the negation of the following statements.

(i) For all even integers x, x^2 is also even.

(ii) There exists a number which is a multiple of 6 and 9. **[NCERT Exemplar]**

Hints & Answers

1. (i) John and Jill went up the hill.

(ii) The sky is blue and the grass is green.

(iii) 25 is a multiple of 5 and 8.

(iv) Rekha is studying in class eleven and she has to offer 5 subjects.

2. (i) The Sun shines or it rains.

(ii) The Earth is round or the Sun is cold.

(iii) $\sqrt{2}$ is a rational or an irrational number.

(iv) Square of an integer is positive or negative.

3. (i) $p \wedge q$ (ii) $p \vee q$

(iii) $\sim p \wedge \sim q$ (iv) $\sim (p \wedge q)$

4. (i) For every (ii) For all

5. (i) There exists natural number which is not an integer.

(ii) It is false that both the diagonals of a rectangle have the same length.

(iii) I will go to school.

(iv) No even integer is prime.

6. The negation of first statement is 'There exist numbers x and y for which $x + y \neq x + y$'.

Ans. No

7. (i) Exclusive 'OR' because students cannot take both Hindi and Sanskrit as their third language.

(ii) Exclusive 'OR' because we know that $\sqrt{7}$ is an irrational number.

8. (i) There exists a positive integer x such that $x + 2 \leq 8$.

(ii) Some natural numbers are not integer.

Or

Atleast one natural number is not an integer.

9. 'There exists' and 'For every'.

'There exists a state in India, which does not have a capital.'

10. (i) True,

$$p : 2 + 4 = 6; q : 2 + 4 = 7$$

(ii) True,

p : A rectangle is a quadrilateral.

q : A rectangle is a 5-sided polygon.

(iii) False,

p : Every rectangle is a square.

q : Every square is a rectangle.

(iv) True,

p : The Sun is a star.

q : The Sun is a planet.

11. (i) 'for all',

"There exists an even integer x such that x^2 is not even."

(ii) 'there exists',

There does not exist a number which is a multiple of both 6 and 9.

TOPIC 03 Implications

If any two simple statements are combined by the phrase 'if-then', then it form a compound statement. This compound statement is called an **implication** or a **conditional statement.**

The conditional statement 'if p then q' can be expressed in several different ways as follow

(i) p implies q, denoted by $p \Rightarrow q$ or $p \rightarrow q$. Here, the symbol '$\Rightarrow$' or '$\rightarrow$' stands for implies.

(ii) p is sufficient for q.

(iii) p only if q

(iv) q is necessary condition for p.

(v) $\sim q$ implies $\sim p$ or $\sim q \Rightarrow \sim p$

e.g. Let p : Train reaches in time.

and q : I can attend the meeting.

Then, $p \Rightarrow q \equiv$ If train reaches in time, then I can attend the meeting. Here, p is called **antecedent** or **hypothesis** or **premise** and q is called **consequent** or **conclusion.**

Rules for 'If ... then' Implication

The conditional statement $p \Rightarrow q$ is false, only if p is true and q is false and it is true in all other cases. These rules can be explained through the truth table, which is easy to remember.

Truth Table for Implication

If p and q are two statements, then we have the following truth table for implication $p \Rightarrow q$

p	q	$p \Rightarrow q$
T	T	T
T	F	F
F	T	T
F	F	T

Note It is important to note that '$\Rightarrow$' is not commutative. Thus, $p \Rightarrow q$ is different from $q \Rightarrow p$. Also note that "P only if q" means "$p \rightarrow q$" whereas "p if q" means $q \rightarrow p$.

Example 1 Find the conditional statement of 'You will get a sweet dish after the dinner'.

Sol. The conditional statement of given statement is 'If you take the dinner, then you will get a sweet dish.'

Example 2 For the given statement, identify the necessary and sufficient condition.

t : If you drive over 80 km/h, then you will get a fine.

[NCERT]

Sol. Let p : You drive over 80 km/h and q : You will get a fine.

The implication $p \Rightarrow q$ indicates that p is sufficient for q i.e. driving over 80 km/h is sufficient to get fine.

Here, the sufficient condition is 'driving over 80 km/h'.

Similarly, if p then q also indicates that q is necessary for p i.e. when you drive over 80 km/h, you will necessarily get a fine. Here, the necessary condition is 'getting a fine'.

Example 3 Rewrite the following statement with 'if-then' in five different ways conveying the same meaning 'If a natural number is odd, then its square is also odd'.

Sol. The component statements of the given statement are

p : A natural number is odd.

q : Square of a natural number is odd.

The given statement is 'if p then q'.

It can be expressed in five different ways as follows

(i) $p \Rightarrow q$ i.e. x is an odd natural number $\Rightarrow x^2$ is an odd natural number.

(ii) p is a sufficient condition for q i.e. knowing that a natural number is odd is sufficient to conclude that its square is odd.

(iii) p only if q i.e. a natural number is odd only if its square is odd.

(iv) q is necessary condition for p i.e. when a natural number is odd, its square is necessarily odd.

(v) $\sim q \Rightarrow \sim p$ i.e. if the square of a natural number is not odd, then the natural number is not odd.

Example 4 Rewrite each of the following statements in the form of conditional statements

(i) Mohan will be a good student if he studies hard.

(ii) Ramesh will get dessert only if he eats his dinner.

(iii) When you sing, my ears hurt.

(iv) A necessary condition for Indian team to win a cricket match is that the selection committee selects an all-rounder.

(v) A sufficient condition for Tara to visit New Delhi is that she goes to the Rashtrapati Bhawan.

[NCERT Exemplar]

Sol. (i) The given statement is of the form "q if p", where

p : Mohan studies hard.

q : He will be a good student.

It is an equivalent form of the statement " if p then q". So the equivalent formulation of the given statement is

"If Mohan studies hard, then he will be a good student".

(Here, note that in p, he is replaced by Mohan and in q, Mohan is replaced by he.)

(ii) The given statement is of the form

"p only if q" which is an equivalent form of the statement "if p then q". So, the equivalent formulation of the given statement is

"If Ramesh eats his dinner, then he will get dessert".

(iii) Here 'when' means the same as 'if' and so the equivalent formulation of the given statement is

"If you sing, then my ears hurt"

(iv) The given statement is of the form "q is necessary for p" where

p : Indian team wins a cricket match

q : The selection committee selects an all-rounder

which is an equivalent form of "if p then q". So the equivalent formulation of the given statement is

"If the teams wins a cricket match then selection committee selects an all rounder."

(v) The given statement is of the form "p" is sufficient for "q" where

p : Tara goes to Rashtrapati Bhawan

q : She visit New Delhi

which is an equivalent form of "if p, then q", so the equivalent formulation of the given statement is

"If Tara goes to Rashtrapati Bhawan, then she visits New Delhi".

Contrapositive of Implication

The statement "$(\sim q) \Rightarrow (\sim p)$" is called the **contrapositive** of the statement $p \Rightarrow q$.

Example 5 Write the contrapositive of the following statements.

(i) If a triangle is equilateral, then it is isosceles.

(ii) If you are born in India, then you are a citizen of India.

(iii) If a number is divisible by 9, then it is divisible by 3. **[NCERT]**

Sol. The contrapositive of these statements are

(i) If a triangle is not isosceles, then it is not equilateral.

(ii) If you are not a citizen of India, then you are not born in India.

(iii) If a number is not divisible by 3, then it is not divisible by 9.

Converse of Implication

If p and q are two statements, then the converse of the implication 'if p, then q' is 'if q, then p' i.e. $q \Rightarrow p$.

Example 6 Write the converse of the following statements.

(i) If $x < y$, then $x + 5 < y + 5$.

(ii) If ABC is an equilateral triangle, then ABC is an isosceles triangle. **[NCERT Exemplar]**

Sol. (i) Let $p : x < y$ and $q : x + 5 < y + 5$.

Then, converse of $p \Rightarrow q$ is $q \Rightarrow p$ i.e.

'If $x + 5 < y + 5$, then $x < y$'.

(ii) The converse of the given statement is 'if ABC is an isosceles triangle, then ABC is an equilateral triangle'.

Inverse of Implication

If p and q are two statements, then the inverse of 'if p, then q' is 'if $\sim p$, then $\sim q$' i.e. $\sim p \Rightarrow \sim q$.

Example 7 Write the inverse of the following statements.

(i) If 2 + 2 = 4, then Jawahar Lal Nehru is the first Prime Minister of India.

(ii) If you get a job, then your credentials are good.

Sol. (i) The inverse of the given statement is

'If $2 + 2 \neq 4$, then Jawahar Lal Nehru is not the first Prime Minister of India'.

(ii) The inverse of the given statement is 'If you do not get a job, then your credentials are not good'.

'If and only if' Implication (or Biconditional Statement or Equivalence)

If any two simple statements are combined with the phrase 'If and only if', then it form a compound statement. This compound statement is called **biconditional.**

The equivalent forms of biconditional statement 'p if and only if q' are

(i) $p \Leftrightarrow q$ or $p \leftrightarrow q$, where the symbol $\leftrightarrow$ or $\Leftrightarrow$ stands for if and only if.

(ii) q if and only if p.

(iii) p is necessary and sufficient condition for q and *vice-versa*.

e.g. Let $p : ABC$ is an isosceles triangle.

and q : Two sides of a triangle are equal.

Then, $p \Leftrightarrow q \equiv ABC$ is an isosceles triangle if and only if two sides of a triangle are equal.

Note *$p \Rightarrow q$ together with its converse, gives p if and only if q.*

Rules for 'If and only if' Implication

(i) The biconditional statement $p \Leftrightarrow q$ is true, if either both the statements are true or both are false.

(ii) The statement $p \Leftrightarrow q$ is false, if exactly one of the statement is false.

These rules can be explained through the truth table, which is easy to remember.

Truth Table for 'If and only if' Implication

If p and q are two statements, then we have the following truth table for implication $p \Leftrightarrow q$

p	q	$p \Leftrightarrow q$
T	T	T
T	F	F
F	T	F
F	F	T

Example 8 Given below are two pairs of statements. Combine these two statements using 'if and only if'.

(i) p : If a rectangle is a square, then all its four sides are equal.

q : If all four sides of a rectangle are equal, then the rectangle is square.

(ii) p : If the sum of digits is divisible by 3, then the number is divisible by 3.

q : If a number is divisible by 3, then the sum of its digits is divisible by 3. [NCERT]

Sol. (i) A rectangle is a square if and only if its four sides are equal.

(ii) A number is divisible by 3 if and only if the sum of its digits is divisible by 3.

Example 9 Write the truth value of the following compound statements.

(i) If the number $R = 57423$ is divisible by 3, then the sum of digits forming R is divisible by 3.

(ii) $4 \times 5 = 20$, if and only if $5 \times 4 = 10$.

Sol. (i) The connective 'If-then' is used in the given compound statement.

Let p : The number $R = 57423$ is divisible by 3.

and q : The sum of digits forming R is divisible by 3.

Here, both the statements p and q are true.

Therefore, the compound statement is true and its truth value is T.

(ii) The connective 'If and only if' is used in the given compound statement.

Let $p : 4 \times 5 = 20$

and $q : 5 \times 4 = 10$

Here, the statement p is true and the statement q is false.

Therefore, the compound statement is false and its truth value is F.

Example 10 Write the truth value of each of the following biconditional statements.

(i) $3 < 2$ if and only if $2 < 1$.

(ii) $3 + 5 > 7$ if and only if $4 + 6 < 10$.

Sol. (i) Let $p : 3 < 2$ and $q : 2 < 1$.

Here, both p and q are false and therefore $p \Leftrightarrow q$ is true.

Hence, the truth value of the given statement is T.

(ii) Let $p : 3 + 5 > 7$ and $q : 4 + 6 < 10$.

Here, p is true and q is false, therefore $p \Leftrightarrow q$ is false.

Hence, the truth value of the given statement is F.

Negation of a Compound Statement

The negation of compound statements according to connectives/implication are given below

1. **Negation of p and q** (Conjunction) The negation of p and q i.e. conjunction $p \wedge q$ is the disjunction of the negation of p and the negation of q.

   Symbolically, we write $\sim (p \wedge q) \equiv \sim p \vee \sim q$.

   i.e. the negation of the conjunction would mean the negation of atleast one of the two component statements.

2. **Negation of p or q** (Disjunction) The negation of p or q i.e. disjunction $p \vee q$ is the conjunction of the negation of p and negation of q.

   Symbolically, we write $\sim (p \vee q) \equiv \sim p \wedge \sim q$.

   i.e. negation of the disjunction would mean the negation of both p and q simultaneously.

3. **Negation of negation** Negation of negation of a statement is the statement itself.
Symbolically, we write $\sim(\sim p) \equiv p$.

4. **Negation of conditional statement 'if p then q'** The truth table for negation of implication 'if p then q' is given below

p	q	$p \Rightarrow q$	$\sim(p \Rightarrow q)$	$\sim q$	$p \wedge \sim q$
T	T	T	F	F	F
T	F	F	T	T	T
F	T	T	F	F	F
F	F	T	F	T	F

Thus, the negation of an implication or conditional statement is $p \wedge \sim q$, i.e. $\sim(p \Rightarrow q) \equiv p \wedge \sim q$.

5. **Negation of a biconditional statement 'p if and only if q'** The truth table for negation of the biconditional 'p if and only if q' is given below

p	q	$p \Leftrightarrow q$	$\sim p$	$\sim q$	$p \wedge \sim q$	$\sim p \wedge q$	$(p \wedge \sim q) \vee (\sim p \wedge q)$	$\sim(p \Leftrightarrow q)$
T	T	T	F	F	F	F	F	F
T	F	F	F	T	T	F	T	T
F	T	F	T	F	F	T	T	T
F	F	T	T	T	F	F	F	F

Thus, the negation of biconditional statement is
$(p \wedge \sim q) \vee (\sim p \wedge q)$
i.e. $\sim(p \Leftrightarrow q) \equiv (p \wedge \sim q) \vee (\sim p \wedge q)$.

Table for Negation of Compound Statement

Connective	Symbol	Symbolic form of compound statement	Negation
and	$\wedge$	$p \wedge q$	$\sim p \vee \sim q$
or	$\vee$	$p \vee q$	$\sim p \wedge \sim q$
not	$\sim$	$\sim p$	$\sim(\sim p) \equiv p$
if ... then	$\rightarrow$ or $\Rightarrow$	$p \rightarrow q$ or $p \Rightarrow q$	$p \wedge \sim q$
if and only if	$\leftrightarrow$ or $\Leftrightarrow$	$p \leftrightarrow q$ or $p \Leftrightarrow q$	$(p \wedge \sim q) \vee (q \wedge \sim p)$

Example 11 Write down the negation of the following statements.

(i) It is raining and it is cool.
(ii) Ramesh is cruel or he is strict.
(iii) If ΔABC is isosceles, then the base angles A and B are equal.
(iv) India will be prosperous, if and only if its citizens are industrious.

Sol. (i) In a given compound statement, the connective word 'and' is used.
Let p : It is raining.
and q : It is cool.
Then, $p \wedge q$: It is raining and it is cool.
Now, $\sim p$: It is not raining.
$\sim q$: It is not cool.
$\therefore$ The negation of the given statement is 'It is not raining or it is not cool'.
$[\because \sim(p \wedge q) \equiv \sim p \vee \sim q]$

(ii) In a given compound statement, the connective word 'or' is used.
Let p : Ramesh is cruel.
and q : Ramesh is strict.
Then, $p \vee q$: Ramesh is cruel or he is strict.
Now, $\sim p$: Ramesh is not cruel.
$\sim q$: Ramesh is not strict.
$\therefore$ The negation of the given statement is 'Ramesh is not cruel and he is not strict'.
$[\because \sim(p \vee q) \equiv \sim p \wedge \sim q]$

(iii) In a given compound statement, the connective 'If ... then' is used.
Let p : ΔABC is isosceles.
and q : The base angles A and B of ΔABC are equal.
Then, $p \Rightarrow q$: If ΔABC is isosceles, then the base angles A and B are equal.
Now, $\sim q$: The base angles A and B of ΔABC are not equal.
$\therefore$ The negation of the given statement is 'ΔABC is isosceles and the base angles A and B are not equal'. $[\because \sim(p \Rightarrow q) \equiv (p \wedge \sim q)]$

(iv) In a given compound statement, the connective 'If and only if' is used.
Let p : India will be prosperous.
and q : The citizens of India are industrious.
Then, $p \Leftrightarrow q$: India will be prosperous, if and only if its citizens are industrious.
Now, $\sim p$: India will not be prosperous.
$\sim q$: The citizens of India are not industrious.
$\therefore$ The negation of the given statement is 'Either India will be prosperous and its citizens are not industrious or the citizens of India are industrious and India will not be prosperous.'
$[\because p \Leftrightarrow q \equiv (p \wedge \sim q) \vee (q \wedge \sim p)]$

Example 12 Write the negation of the following statments.

(i) Paris is in France and London is in England.
(ii) $2 + 3 = 5$ and $8 < 10$. **[NCERT Exemplar]**

Sol. (i) Let p : Paris is in France
and q : London is in England.

Now, $\sim p$: Paris is not in France.
and $\sim q$: London is not in England.
So, negation of $p \wedge q$ is
Paris is not in France or London is not in England.
$[\because \sim(p \wedge q) = \sim p \vee \sim q]$

(ii) Let $p : 2+3=5$ and $q : 8<10$
Now, $\sim p : 2+3 \neq 5$ and $\sim q : 8 \not< 10$
Then, the negation of $p \wedge q$ is
$\sim(p \wedge q) \equiv \sim p \vee \sim q : 2+3 \neq 5$ or $8 \geq 10$

Example 13 Write the negation of the following statement 'Amit is smart and healthy'.

Sol. Let p : Amit is smart and q : Amit is healthy.
Then $p \wedge q$: Amit is smart and healthy.
$\sim p$: Amit is not smart.
$\sim q$: Amit is not healthy.
The negation of the given statement is given by
$\sim(p \wedge q) \equiv \sim p \vee \sim q$: Amit is either not smart or not healthy.

Example 14 Write the negation of the statement "7 is greater than 4 or 6 is less than 7".

Sol. Let p : 7 is greater than 4.
and q : 6 is less than 7.
Then, the given statement is disjunction $p \vee q$.
Now $\sim p$: 7 is not greater than 4.
and $\sim q$: 6 is not less than 7.
So, negation of $p \vee q$ is given by
$\sim(p \vee q) \equiv \sim p \wedge \sim q$: 7 is either not greater than 4 and 6 or not less than 7.

Truth Table

A truth table is a mathematical table used to determine if a compound statement is true or false. In a truth table, each statement is typically represented by a letter or variable, like p, q or r and each statement also has its own corresponding column in the truth table that lists all of the possible truth values.

Let $S(p, q, r, \ldots)$ be a compound statement having $p, q, r, \ldots$ as component statements. The truth table shows the truth value of component statements $p, q, r, \ldots$ and the truth value all of the compound statement S is known as truth table for the statement S.

In the truth table, last column shows the truth value of the compound statement S and the initial columns shows the truth values of the component statements.

Example 15 Construct the truth tables for the following statements.

(i) $p \wedge (\sim p)$ (ii) $\sim(p \vee q)$

Sol. (i) The truth table for $p \wedge (\sim p)$

p	$\sim p$	$p \wedge (\sim p)$
T	F	F
F	T	F

(ii) The truth table for $\sim(p \vee q)$

p	q	$p \vee q$	$\sim(p \vee q)$
T	T	T	F
T	F	T	F
F	T	T	F
F	F	F	T

Example 16 Construct the truth tables for the following compound statements.

(i) $(\sim p \wedge \sim q) \vee (p \wedge \sim q)$
(ii) $(p \wedge q) \vee r$

Sol. (i) The truth table for $(\sim p \wedge \sim q) \vee (p \wedge \sim q)$

p	q	$\sim p$	$\sim q$	$\sim p \wedge \sim q$	$p \wedge \sim q$	$(\sim p \wedge \sim q) \vee (p \wedge \sim q)$
T	T	F	F	F	F	F
T	F	F	T	F	T	T
F	T	T	F	F	F	F
F	F	T	T	T	F	T

(ii) The truth table for $(p \wedge q) \vee r$

p	q	r	$p \wedge q$	$(p \wedge q) \vee r$
T	T	T	T	T
T	T	F	T	T
T	F	T	F	T
T	F	F	F	F
F	T	T	F	T
F	T	F	F	F
F	F	T	F	T
F	F	F	F	F

Tautology and Contradiction

A statement pattern is called a **tautology**, if it is always true, what ever, may be truth values of constitute statements. e.g. Let p be any statement. The truth table for the compound statement $p \vee \sim p$ is

p	$\sim p$	$p \vee \sim p$
T	F	T
F	T	T

Therefore, $p \vee \sim p$ is a tautology.

A statement pattern is called a **contradiction** if it is always false, whatever may be true values of its constitute statements. A contradiction is also called a **fallacy** e.g. Let p be any statement. The truth table for the compound statement $p \wedge \sim p$ is

p	$\sim p$	$p \wedge (\sim p)$
T	F	F
F	T	F

Therefore, $p \wedge \sim p$ is a contradiction.

Logical Equivalence

Two compound statements $S_1(p, q, r, ...)$ are called **logically equivalent** or **simply equivalent** if their truth values are same for all possible truth values of their component statements. It is written as $S_1 \cong S_2$.

e.g. Let p be any statement. Then, $p \cong \sim(\sim p)$

p	$\sim p$	$\sim(\sim p)$
T	F	T
F	T	F

Note that the truth values in column 1 and column 3 are same.

Note Negation of tautology is a contradiction and negation of a contradiction is a tautology.

Example 17 If p and q are two statements, prove that

(i) $\sim(p \wedge q) \cong \sim p \vee \sim q$ (ii) $\sim(p \vee q) \cong \sim p \wedge \sim q$

Sol. (i) The truth table for $\sim(p \wedge q)$ and $\sim p \vee \sim q$

p	q	$\sim p$	$\sim q$	$p \wedge q$	$\sim(p \wedge q)$	$\sim p \vee \sim q$
T	T	F	F	T	F	F
T	F	F	T	F	T	T
F	T	T	F	F	T	T
F	F	T	T	F	T	T

From columns 6 and 7, we find that the truth values of $\sim(p \wedge q)$ and $\sim p \vee \sim q$ are same, therefore $\sim(p \wedge q) \cong \sim p \vee \sim q$

(ii) The truth tables for $\sim(p \vee q)$ and $\sim p \wedge \sim q$

p	q	$\sim p$	$\sim q$	$p \vee q$	$\sim(p \vee q)$	$\sim p \wedge \sim q$
T	T	F	F	T	F	F
T	F	F	T	T	F	F
F	T	T	F	T	F	F
F	F	T	T	F	T	T

From columns 6 and 7, we find that the truth values of $\sim(p \vee q)$ and $\sim p \wedge \sim q$ are same, therefore $\sim(p \vee q) \cong \sim p \wedge \sim q$.

Example 18 For any three statements p, q and r, show that $p \wedge (q \vee r) \cong (p \wedge q) \vee (p \wedge r)$.

Sol. Truth table for $p \wedge (q \vee r)$ and $(p \wedge q) \vee (p \wedge r)$

p	q	r	$q \vee r$	$p \wedge (q \vee r)$	$p \wedge q$	$p \wedge r$	$(p \wedge q) \vee (p \wedge r)$
T	T	T	T	T	T	T	T
T	T	F	T	T	T	F	T
T	F	T	T	T	F	T	T
T	F	F	F	F	F	F	F
F	T	T	T	F	F	F	F
F	T	F	T	F	F	F	F
F	F	T	T	F	F	F	F
F	F	F	F	F	F	F	F

From columns 5 and 8, we find that the truth values of $p \wedge (q \vee r)$ and $(p \wedge q) \vee (p \wedge r)$ are the same.

$\therefore p \wedge (q \vee r) \cong (p \wedge q) \vee (p \wedge r)$.

Topic Practice 3

Very Short Answer Type Questions

(2 Marks)

Directions (Q. Nos. 1-3) *Rewrite each of the following statements in the form of conditional statement.*

1 The square of an odd number is odd.

2 The unit digit of an integer is 0 or 5, if it is divisible by 5.

3 The square of a prime number is not prime. **[NCERT Exemplar]**

Directions (Q. Nos. 4-6) *Write down the contrapositive of the following statements.*

4 If n is a natural number, then n is an integer.

5 If x and y are negative integers, then xy is positive.

6 If natural number n is divisible by 6, then n is divisible by 2 and 3. **[NCERT Exemplar]**

Directions (Q. Nos. 7-9) *Write down the converse of the following statements.*

7 If today is Monday, then tomorrow is Tuesday.

8 If the sum of squares of two sides of a triangle is equal to the square of third side of a triangle, then the triangle is right angled. **[NCERT Exemplar]**

9 If S is a cyclic quadrilateral, then the opposite angles of S are supplementary.

10 Write down the converse of the following statements.

(i) If a rectangle R is a square, then R is a rhombus.

(ii) If you go to Agra, then you must visit Taj Mahal. **[NCERT Exemplar]**

(iii) If $x : y = 3:2$, then $2x = 3y$

(iv) If x is zero, then x is neither positive nor negative.

11 Write down the contrapositive of the following statements.

(i) If $x = y$ and $y = 3$, then $x = 3$.

(ii) If all three sides of a triangle are equal, then the triangle is equilateral. **[NCERT Exemplar]**

12 Write down the negation of each of the following statements.

(i) 2 is even and −2 is negative.

(ii) 5 is prime or 15 is even.

(iii) If 7< 5, then 7 is not a prime number.

(iv) The payment will be made, if and only if the work is finished in time.

Short Answer Type Questions

4 Marks

13 Write the negation of the following statements.

(i) If I become a doctor, then I will open a hospital.

(ii) If $2 + 3 = 5$, then 5 is an odd number.

14 Write the negation of the following statements.

(i) A triangle is equilateral if and only if it is equiangular.

(ii) Sets A and B are equal if and only if $A \subseteq B$ and $B \subseteq A$.

15 Construct the truth tables for the following compound statements.

(i) $\sim(\sim p \vee \sim q)$ (ii) $(p \wedge q) \wedge \sim p$

16 For any statements p and q show that

(i) $(\sim p \vee q) \vee (p \wedge \sim q)$ is a tautology.

(ii) $(p \wedge q) \wedge (\sim q)$ is a contradiction.

17 For any two statements, prove that the implication and its contrapositive are logically equivalent statements.

Hints & Answers

1. If the number is odd, then its square is odd number.
2. If an integer is divisible by 5, then its unit digit's are 0 or 5.
3. If the number is prime, then its square is not prime.
4. If n is not an integer, then it is not a natural number.
5. If xy is non-positive integer, then either x or y is non-negative integer.
6. If natural number n is not divisible by 2 and 3, then n is not divisible by 6.
7. If tomorrow is Tuesday, then today is Monday.
8. If the triangle is right angled, then the sum of squares of two sides of a triangle is equal to the square of third side.
9. If the opposite angles of a quadrilateral are supplementary, then S is cyclic.
10. (i) If the rectangle R is rhombus, then R is a square.
    (ii) If you must visit Taj Mahal, then you go to Agra.
    (iii) If $2x = 3y$, then $x : y = 3 : 2$
    (iv) If x is neither positive nor negative, then x is zero.
11. (i) If $x \neq 3$, then $x \neq y$ or $y \neq 3$.
    (ii) If the triangle is not equilateral, then all three sides of the triangle are not equal.
12. (i) 2 is odd or −2 is non-negative.
    (ii) 5 is not prime and 15 is odd.
    (iii) $7 < 5$ and 7 is a prime number.
    (iv) Either the work is finished in time and the payment is not made or the payment is made and the work is not finished in time.
13. (i) Let p : I become a doctor.
    and q : I will open a hospital.
    Ans. 'I will become a doctor and I will not open a hospital.'
    (ii) Let $p : 2 + 3 = 5$
    and q : 5 is an odd number.
    Ans. $2 + 3 = 5$ and 5 is an even number.

14. (i) Let p : A triangle is equilateral.
and q : The triangle is equiangular.
Ans. 'There exists either an equilateral triangle which is not equiangular or an equiangular triangle which is not equilateral.'

(ii) Let p : Sets A and B are equal.
and $q : A \subseteq B$ and $B \subseteq A$.
Then, the given statement is $p \Leftrightarrow q$.
Ans. 'Either $A = B$ and ($A \not\subseteq B$ or $B \not\subseteq A$) or ($A \subseteq B$ and $B \subseteq A$) and $A \neq B$.'

15. (i)

p	q	$\sim p$	$\sim q$	$\sim p \vee \sim q$	$\sim(p \vee \sim q)$
T	T	F	F	F	T
T	F	F	T	T	F
F	T	T	F	T	F
F	F	T	T	T	F

(ii)

p	q	$\sim p$	$p \wedge q$	$(p \wedge q) \wedge \sim p$
T	T	F	T	F
T	F	F	F	F
F	T	T	F	F
F	F	T	F	F

16. (i)

p	q	$\sim p$	$\sim q$	$\sim p \vee q$	$p \wedge \sim q$	$(\sim p \vee q) \vee (p \wedge \sim q)$
T	T	F	F	T	F	T
T	F	F	T	F	T	T
F	T	T	F	T	F	T
F	F	T	T	T	F	T

(ii)

p	q	$\sim q$	$p \wedge q$	$(p \wedge q) \wedge (\sim q)$
T	T	F	T	F
T	F	T	F	F
F	T	F	F	F
F	F	T	F	F

17. For any two statement p, q the truth tables for the implication $p \rightarrow q$ and its contrapositive is

p	q	$\sim p$	$\sim q$	$p \rightarrow q$	$\sim q \rightarrow \sim p$
T	T	F	F	T	T
T	F	F	T	F	F
F	T	T	F	T	T
F	F	T	T	T	T

TOPIC 04 Validating Statements

Validating statement means checking when the statement is true and when it is not true. This depends upon which of the connectives and quantifiers used in the statement.
To check the validity of the statements, we use following methods.

Direct Method

In this method, we use following rules to check whether a statement is true or not.

|RULE I|
Validity of Statements with 'and'

If p and q are two mathematical statements, then in order to show that the statement '$p \wedge q$' is true, we proceed as follows

Step I Show that the statement p is true.

Step II Show that the statement q is true.

Example 1 Consider the statement,
S : 80 is a multiple of 5 and 4. Check its validity.

Sol. The given compound statement is
S : 80 is a multiple of 5 and 4.
The component statements of the given compound statement are
p : 80 is a multiple of 5.
and q : 80 is a multiple of 4.
Then, $S \equiv p \wedge q$
We know that, 80 is multiple of 5 as well as 4.
Therefore, the statements p and q are true.
Hence, the compound statement $S \equiv p \wedge q$ is also true
i.e. $S \equiv p \wedge q$ is a valid statement.

Example 2 If p and q are two statements given by

p : 25 is a multiple of 5.

q : 25 is a multiple of 8.

Write the compound statement by using the connective 'and' and check its validity.

Sol. The compound statement is '25 is a multiple of 5 and 8'. Since, 25 is a multiple of 5 but it is not a multiple of 8. Therefore, p is true but q is not true. Hence, the compound statement is not true i.e. the statement 'p and q' is not a valid statement.

|RULE II|

Validity of Statements with 'or'

If p and q are two mathematical statements, then in order to show that the compound statement 'p or q' is true, we proceed as follows

Case I Assume that p is false, show that q must be true.

Or

Case II Assume that q is false, show that p must be true.

Example 3 Check the validating of the statement.
'Square of an integer is positive or negative'

Sol. The given statement is a compound statement with 'OR' whose component statements are

p : Square of an integer is positive.

and q : Square of an integer is negative.

Assume that p is false, i.e. square of an integer is not positive.

Then, for any integer x, $x^2 \ngeq 0$

$\Rightarrow \quad x^2 < 0$

Since, the square of an integer is negative.

$\therefore$ q is true.

Thus, if we assume that p is false, then q is true.

Hence, '$p \vee q$' is a valid statement as the given statement is true.

|RULE III|

Validating of Statements with 'If...then'

If p and q are two mathematical statements, then in order to show that the compound statement, 'if p then q' is true, we proceed as follows

Step I Assume that p is true.

Step II Prove that q must be true, i.e. $p \Rightarrow q$.

Example 4 Check the validity of the statement 'If x and y are odd integers, then xy is an odd integer'.

Sol. Let p and q be the statements given by

$p : x$ and y are odd integers.

and $q : xy$ is an odd integer.

Then, the given statement is 'if p then q'.

Now, let p be true.

$\Rightarrow$ x and y are odd integers.

$\Rightarrow \quad x = 2m + 1$

and $\quad y = 2n + 1$ for some integers m and n.

$\Rightarrow \quad xy = (2m + 1)(2n + 1)$

$\Rightarrow \quad xy = 2(2mn + m + n) + 1$

Since, xy is an odd integer.

$\therefore$ q is true.

Thus, p is true.

$\Rightarrow$ q is true.

Hence, 'if p then q' is a valid statement as the given statement is true.

|RULE IV|

Validity of the Statements with 'If and only if'

In order to prove the validity of the statement 'p if and only if q', we proceed as follows

Step I Show that, if p is true, then q is true.

Step II Show that, if q is true, then p is true.

Example 5 Using the words 'The necessary and sufficient', rewrite following statement.
'The integer n is odd, if and only if n^2 is odd'.
Also, check the validity of the given statement.

Sol. The given statement can be rewritten as 'The necessary and sufficient condition that the integer n is odd, is n^2 must be odd'.

Let p and q be statements given by

p : The integer n is odd.

and q : The integer n^2 is odd.

Then, the given statement is 'p if and only if q'.

In order to check its validity, we have to check the validity of the following statements

(i) 'If p, then q'.

(ii) 'If q, then p'.

(i) **Validity of 'If** p, **then** q'

The statement 'if p, then q' is given by
'If the integer n is odd, then n^2 is odd'.

Let n be odd. Then,

$n = 2m + 1$ [where, m is an integer]

$\Rightarrow n^2 = (2m+1)^2 \Rightarrow n^2 = 4m(m+1)+1$

$\Rightarrow n^2$ is odd integer. Thus, n is odd $\Rightarrow n^2$ is odd integer.

Hence, 'If p, then q' is true.

(ii) **Validity of 'If q, then p'**

The statement 'if q, then p' is given by 'If n is an integer and n^2 is odd, then n is odd'.

So, let n be an even integer.

Then, $n = 2k$, for some integer k.

$\Rightarrow n^2 = 4k^2$

$\Rightarrow n^2$ is an even integer.

$\Rightarrow n^2$ is not an odd integer.

Thus, n is not odd.

$\Rightarrow n^2$ is not odd.

$\therefore$ 'If q, then p' is true.

Hence, 'p if and only if q' is true.

So, the given statement is valid.

Contrapositive Method

In this method to check the validity of $p \Rightarrow q$, we proceed as follows

***Step* I** Assume that q is false.

***Step* II** Prove that p is false, i.e. $\sim q \Rightarrow \sim p$.

Example 6 Show that the statement p : 'If x is a real number such that $x^3 + 4x = 0$, then x is 0' is true by

(i) direct method. **[NCERT]**

(ii) method of contrapositive.

Sol. Let p be the given statement

i.e. p : 'If x is a real number such that $x^3 + 4x = 0$, then $x = 0$'.

(i) **Direct method**

Let $x^3 + 4x = 0, x \in R \Rightarrow x(x^2 + 4) = 0, x \in R$

$\Rightarrow x = 0$ [if $x \in R$, then $x^2 + 4 \geq 4$]

(ii) **Method of contrapositive**

Let $q : x \in R$ and $x^3 + 4x = 0$

r : '$x = 0$'

Given statement p is $q \Rightarrow r$

Its contrapositive is $\sim r \Rightarrow \sim q$

i.e. 'If x is a non-zero real number, then $x^3 + 4x$ is also non-zero'.

Now we have $x \neq 0, x \in R \Rightarrow x^2 > 0$

$\Rightarrow x^2 + 4 > 4 \Rightarrow x^2 + 4 \neq 0$

$\Rightarrow x(x^2 + 4) \neq 0 \Rightarrow x^3 + 4x \neq 0$ i.e. $\sim r \Rightarrow \sim q$

Thus, the statement $\sim r \Rightarrow \sim q$ is always true.

Hence, $q \Rightarrow r$ is always true.

Note If the product of two numbers is zero, then atleast one of them is surely zero.

Contradiction Method

In this method to check whether a statement p is true, it is assumed that p is not true, i.e. $\sim p$ is true. Then, a result is obtained which contradicts the assumption. Therefore, it is concluded that p is true.

To examine the validity of statement with 'if then' using the contradiction method, we use the following steps

***Step* I** Assume that p is true and q is false.

***Step* II** Obtain a contradiction from assumption.

Example 7 Check the validity of the statement given below by contradiction method.

"p : The sum of an irrational number and a rational number is irrational".

Sol. If possible, let p be not true. Then, p is false.

$\Rightarrow$ The sum of an irrational number and a rational number is not irrational.

$\Rightarrow$ There exists an irrational number x (say) and a rational number y (say) such that $x + y$ is not irrational.

$\Rightarrow x + y$ is not irrational.

$\therefore x + y$ is rational, say z.

$\Rightarrow x + y = z$

$\Rightarrow x = z - y$

$\Rightarrow x$ is rational [$\because z - y$ is rational]

But, x is irrational. So, we arrive at a contradiction.

Thus, our supposition is wrong.

Hence, p is true.

Invalidity of Statements by Counter Examples

In Mathematics, counter examples are used to disprove the statement. However, generating examples in favour of a statement do not provide validity of the statement. To prove that given statement is false, we give a counter example.

Example 8 By giving a counter example, show that the following statement is false.

'If n is an odd integer, then n is prime'. **[NCERT]**

Sol. Let p and q be two statements given by

$p : n$ is an odd integer.

and $q : n$ is prime.

Then, the given statement is 'if p, then q'.

We have to show that this is false.

For this purpose, we need to show that 'if p, then $\sim q$.

Thus, we have to find an integer n, such that n is odd but n is not prime. So, take $n = 9$

Then, n is odd but n is not prime.

Thus, we conclude that the given statement is false.

Topic Practice 4

Very Short Answer Type Questions

2 Marks

1 Given below are two statements
p : 100 is a multiple of 5.
q : 100 is a multiple of 4.
Write the compound statement connecting these two statements with 'and' and check its validity.

2 If p and q are two statements given by
p : 30 is a multiple of 5.
q : 30 is a multiple of 8.
Write the compound statement by using the connective 'and' check its validity.

3 Check the validity of the following statements
(i) p : 20 is a multiple of 4 and 5.
(ii) r : 60 is a multiple of 3 or 5.

4 By giving a counter example, show that the following statement is false. If x is even integer, then x is a prime.

5 Using contrapositive method, prove that if n^2 is an even integer, then n is also an even integer. **[NCERT Exemplar]**

6 Which of the following statements are true and which are false? In each case, give a valid reason for saying so.
(i) Each chord of a circle is its diameter.
(ii) The centre of a circle bisects each chord of the circle.

Short Answer Type Questions

4 Marks

7 Show that the following statement is true.
p : For any real numbers x, y if $x = y$, then $2x + a = 2y + a$ when $a \in Z$. **[NCERT Exemplar]**

8 Show that the statement p : 'If x is a real number such that $x^3 + x = 0$, then 'x is 0' is true by
(i) direct method.
(ii) method of contrapositive.

9 Verify by method of contradiction $p: \sqrt{11}$ is irrational. **[NCERT]**

10 By giving a counter example, show that the following statement is not true.
p : If all the angles of a triangle are equal, then the triangle is an obtuse angled triangle.

Hints & Answers

1. '100 is multiple of 5 and 4'.
'p and q' is a valid statement.

2. '30 is a multiple of 5 and 8'.
The statement 'p and q' is not a valid statement.

3. (i) Valid (ii) Valid

4. For this, we have to give an example.
Now, take a number greater than x which is even, but not a prime. So, $x = 10$ is counter example.

5. Let $p : n^2$ is an even integer
and $q : n$ is also an even integer.

6. (i) False
(ii) False

7. **Direct method**
For any real number $x,\ y$ given
$$x = y$$
$$\Rightarrow \quad 2x = 2y$$
$$\Rightarrow \quad 2x + a = 2y + a \text{ for some } a \in z$$
Contrapositive method
For any real number $x,\ y$ if
$2x + a \neq 2y + a$, where $a \in z$, then $x \neq y$
Given, $2x + a \neq 2y + a$
$$\Rightarrow \quad 2x \neq 2y \quad \Rightarrow \quad x \neq y$$

8. Solve as Example 6.

9. In this method, we assume that the given statement is false, i.e. we assume that $\sqrt{11}$ is rational.
Now, prove that our assumption is wrong.

10. Solve as Example 8.

Chapter Practice

Multiple Choice Type Questions

1 Mark

1. The negation of the statement "Rahul or Anshika lived in Lucknow" is
   (a) Rahul did not live in Lucknow or Anshika lives in Lucknow.
   (b) Rahul lives in Lucknow and Anshika did not live in Lucknow.
   (c) Rahul did not live in Lucknow or Anshika did not live in Lucknow.
   (d) Rahul did not live in Lucknow or Anshika did not live in Lucknow.

2. The converse of the statement 'If Sun is not shining, then sky is filled with clouds' is
   (a) If Sun is shining, then sky is filled with clouds
   (b) If sky is filled with clouds, then the sun is not shining
   (c) If Sun is not shining, then sky is not filled with clouds
   (d) If sky is clear, then sun is shining

3. If truth values of P be F and q be T, then truth value of $\sim(\sim p \vee q)$ is
   (a) T (b) F
   (c) either T or F (d) Neither T nor F

4. The statement $p \to (q \to p)$ is equivalent to
   (a) $p \to (p \wedge q)$ (b) $p \to (p \leftrightarrow q)$
   (c) $p \to (p \vee q)$ (d) $p \to (p \to q)$

5. The contrapositive of the statement "If p, then q", is
   (a) If $\sim p$, then $\sim q$
   (b) If $\sim q$, then $\sim p$
   (c) If p, then $\sim q$
   (d) If q, then p

Assertion-Reason Type Questions

1 Mark

Directions (Q. Nos. 6-9) *In the questions given below are two statements labelled as Assertion (A) and Reason (R). In the context of the two statements, which one of the following is correct?*

(a) Both A and R are correct; R is the correct explanation of A
(b) Both A and R are correct; R is not the correct explanation of A
(c) A is correct; R is incorrect
(d) R is correct; A is incorrect

6. **Assertion (A)** The sentence "69 is less than 79" is a statement.
   Reason (R) A sentence is called a statement, if it is either true or false but not both.

7. **Assertion (A)** $\sim(p \leftrightarrow \sim q)$ is equivalent to $p \leftrightarrow q$.
   Reason (R) $\sim(p \leftrightarrow \sim q)$ is a tautology.

8. **Assertion (A)** Contrapositive of statement "If a number is divisible by 9, then it is divisible by 3' is 'If a number is not divisible by 3, then it is not divisible by 9.
   Reason (R) The statement "$(\sim q) \Rightarrow (\sim p)$" is contrapositive of the statement $p \Rightarrow q$.

9. **Assertion (A)** Statement $\sim p \wedge p$ is a contradiction.
   Reason (R) A compound statement is called contradiction, if its truth value is F.

Very Short Answer Type Questions

2 Marks

Directions (Q. Nos. 10-14) *Find out which of the following sentences are statements and which are not? Justify your answer.*

10. Switch on the fan.
11. Have you ever seen 'AYODHYA'?
12. Wish you all the best.
13. Hurrah! We have won the match.
14. Good evening to all.

Directions (Q. Nos. 15-17) *Determine the truth value of each of the following statements.*

15. Kolkata is in India and $2+2=4$.

16. Write the negation of the following statements.
  (i) Chennai is the capital of Tamil Nadu.
  (ii) $\sqrt{2}$ is not a complex number.
  (iii) All triangles are not equilateral triangle.
  (iv) The number 2 is greater than 7.

17. Form the biconditional statements $p \leftrightarrow q$, where
  (i) p: The unit digit of an integer is zero.
      q: It is divisible by 5.
  (ii) p: A natural number n is odd.
      q: Natural number n is not divisible by 2.
  (iii) p: A triangle is an equilateral triangle.
      q: All three sides of a triangle are equal.

Directions (Q. Nos. 18-19) *Find the component statements of the following compound statements and check whether they are true or false.*

18. Number 3 is prime or it is odd. **[NCERT]**

19. 100 is divisible by 3, 11 and 5. **[NCERT]**

Directions (Q. Nos. 20-22) *Write negation of each of the following statements.*

20. Ramesh is smart and healthy.

21. Mridul is cruel or he is strict.

22. All triangles are squares.

Directions (Q. Nos. 23-25) *For each of the following compound statements, first identify the connecting words and then break into component statements.*

23. The sand heats up quickly in the Sun and does not cool down fast at night. **[NCERT]**

24. $x = 2$ and $x = 3$ are the roots of the equation $3x^2 - x - 10 = 0$. **[NCERT]**

25. Write the contrapositive and converse of the statement 'Something is cold implies that it has low temperature'.

Directions (Q. Nos. 26-29) *Write down the contrapositive of the following statements.*

26. If Lara Dutta is Miss Universe, then she is beautiful.

27. If PT Usha stands first in 200 m race, then she will be awarded.

28. If x is a prime number, then x is odd.

29. If two lines are parallel, then they do not intersect in the same plane.

Short Answer Type Questions

4 Marks

30. Construct the truth table for $(p \wedge q) \vee (\sim (p \wedge q))$.

31. If x and y are positive real numbers, then prove that $x < y \Leftrightarrow x^2 < y^2$ is a true statement.

32. Write the following statement in five different ways, conveying the same meaning.
  p: If a triangle is equiangular, then it is an obtuse angled triangle. **[NCERT]**

33. Write down the negation of each of the following
  (i) $2+4>5$ or $3+4<6$
  (ii) $x=2 \Rightarrow x^2=4$
  (iii) ΔABC is isosceles, if and only if $\angle B = \angle C$

34. Construct the truth tables for the following compound statements.
  (i) $\sim p \vee q$
  (ii) $\sim p \wedge \sim q$
  (iii) $\sim (p \vee \sim q)$

35. Prove that for any statements p, q, r the implication $(p \vee q) \rightarrow r$ and its contrapositive $\sim r \rightarrow (\sim p \wedge \sim q)$ are equivalent.

Hints & Answers

1. (d) 2. (b) 3. (b) 4. (c) 5. (b)
6. (a) 7. (c) 8. (a) 9. (a)

10. The sentence, 'Switch on the fan' cannot be assigned true or false and so it is not a statement as it is an imperative sentence. Infact, it is a command.

11. The sentence, 'Have you ever seen AYODHYA' cannot be assigned true or false and so it is not a statement as it is an sentence. Infact, it is a question.

12. The sentence, 'Wish you all the best' cannot be assigned true or false, so it is not a statement as it is an optative sentence. Infact it is a wish.

13. The sentence, 'Hurrah! We have won the match' cannot be assigned true or false and so it is not a statement as it is an exclamatory sentence. Infact it is exclamatory.

14. The sentence 'Good evening to all' cannot be assigned true or false and so it is not a statement as it is an optative sentence. Infact, it is a wish.

15. Let p : kolkata is in India.
and $q: 2+2=4$
Ans. T (True)

16. (i) Chennai is not the capital of Tamil Nadu.
(ii) $\sqrt{2}$ is a complex number.
(iii) There exists a triangle which is equilateral.
(iv) The number 2 is not greater than 7.

17. (i) The unit digit of an integer is zero, if and only if it is divisible by 5.
(ii) A natural number n is odd, if and only if it is not divisible by 2.
(iii) A triangle is an equilateral triangle, if and only if all the three sides of triangle are equal.

18. The component statements are
p : Number 3 is prime
q : Number 3 is odd

19. The component statements are
p : 100 is divisible by 3
q : 100 is divisible by 11
r : 100 is divisible by 5
So, $p \wedge q \wedge r$ is false

20. Ramesh is either not smart or not healthy.

21. Mridul is neither cruel nor strict.

22. There exists a triangle which is not a square.

23. "And".
p : The sand heats up quickly in the Sun.
q : The sand does not cool down fast at night.

24. "And".
$p: x=2$ is a root of the equation $3x^2 - x - 10 = 0$.
$q: x=3$ is a root of the equation $3x^2 - x - 10 = 0$.

25. **Contrapositive statement** If the temperature of something is not low, then it is not cold.
Converse statement If something has low temperature, then it is cold.

26. If Lara Dutta is not beautiful, then she is not Miss Universe.

27. If PT Usha is not awarded, then she does not stand first in 200 m race.

28. It x is not odd, then x is not a prime number.

29. If two lines intersect in the same plane, then they are not parallel.

30.

p	q	$p \wedge q$	$\sim(p \wedge q)$	$(p \wedge q) \vee (\sim(p \wedge q))$
T	T	T	F	T
T	F	F	T	T
F	T	F	T	T
F	F	F	T	T

31. Let $p: x < y$; $q: x^2 < y^2$
First, we prove that $p \Rightarrow q$
Let p be true $\Rightarrow x < y$
$\Rightarrow y - x$ is a positive real.
$\Rightarrow$ $(y - x)(y + x)$ is a positive real.
[$\because$ x, y are positive real so, $x + y$ is also positive and product of two positive reals is positive]

Next, we prove that $q \Rightarrow p$
Let q be true $\Rightarrow x^2 < y^2 \Rightarrow y^2 - x^2$ is positive real.
$\Rightarrow$ $(y - x)(y + x)$ is a positive real.
$\Rightarrow$ $y - x$ is positive real.

32. (i) A triangle is equiangular implies that it is an obtuse angled triangle.
(ii) A triangle is equiangular only, if it is an obtuse angled triangle.
(iii) For a triangle to be equiangular, it is necessary that it is an obtuse angled triangle.
(iv) For a triangle to be obtuse angled triangle, it is sufficient that it is equiangular.
(v) If a triangle is not obtuse angled triangle, then it is not an equiangular triangle.

33. (i) $2 + 4 \leq 5$ and $3 + 4 \geq 6$ (ii) $x = 2$ and $x^2 \neq 4$
(iii) Either ΔABC is isosceles and $\angle B \neq \angle C$ or ΔABC is not isosceles and $\angle B = \angle C$.

34. (i)

p	q	$\sim p$	$\sim p \vee q$
T	T	F	T
T	F	F	F
F	T	T	T
F	F	T	T

(ii)

p	q	$\sim p$	$\sim q$	$\sim p \wedge \sim q$
T	T	F	F	F
T	F	F	T	F
F	T	T	F	F
F	F	T	T	T

(iii) Do same as (ii).

35.

p	q	r	$\sim p$	$\sim q$	$\sim r$	$p \vee q$	$\sim p \wedge \sim q$	$(p \vee q) \to r$	$\sim r \to (\sim p \wedge \sim q)$
T	T	T	F	F	F	T	F	T	T
T	T	F	F	F	T	T	F	F	F
T	F	T	F	T	F	T	F	T	T
T	F	F	F	T	T	T	F	F	F
F	T	T	T	F	F	T	F	T	T
F	T	F	T	F	T	T	F	F	F
F	F	T	T	T	F	F	T	T	T
F	F	F	T	T	T	F	T	T	T

CHAPTER 19

Statistics (Continued)

In this chapter, we will discuss about combined mean and standard deviation. We will also studied about quartile, decile, percentile, mode. We will also learn about median by formula as well as using graphs.

- Combined Mean
- Standard Deviation
- Median
- Quartiles
- Mode
- Cumulative Frequency Curve or an Ogive Curve

Combined Mean

If $n_1, \bar{x}$ are number of observations and mean of first set and $n_2, \bar{x}_2$ are number of observation and mean of second set, then combined mean $\bar{x}$ of two sets is given by

$$\bar{x} = \frac{n_1\bar{x}_1 + n_2\bar{x}_2}{n_1 + n_2}$$

Note This formula can be extended to any number of distributions thus the combined mean for r distribution with observations $n_1, n_2, \ldots, n_r$ and their corresponding means are $\bar{x}_1, \bar{x}_2, \ldots, \bar{x}_r$

$$\bar{x} = \frac{n_1\bar{x}_1 + n_2\bar{x}_2 + \ldots + n_r\bar{x}_r}{n_1 + n_2 + \ldots + n_r}$$

Example 1 There are 600 students in school of which 250 are girls. The average weight of 250 girls is 40 kg and that of 350 boys is 53 kg. Find the mean weight in kg of the entire class.

Sol. Let $\bar{x}_1, \bar{x}_2$ are the average weight of girls and boys respectively and n_1, n_2 are number of girls and boys, respectively.

Here, $\bar{x}_1 = 40$, $\bar{x}_2 = 53$, $n_1 = 250$, and $n_2 = 350$

$\therefore$ Mean weight of class, $\bar{x} = \dfrac{n_1\bar{x}_1 + n_2\bar{x}_2}{n_1 + n_2}$

$$= \frac{250 \times 40 + 350 \times 53}{250 + 350} = 47.583 \text{ kg}$$

Example 2 The mean monthly salary paid to all employees of a company is ₹ 8300. The mean monthly salary paid to male and female employees was ₹ 8000 and ₹ 9000, respectively. Determine the percentage of males and females employed by the company.

Sol. Let the total number of employees be 100 and the number of male employees be n, then number of female employees $= (100 - n)$.

Here, $\bar{x} = 8300$, $\bar{x}_1 = 8000$, $\bar{x}_2 = 9000$, $n_1 = n$ and $n_2 = (100 - n)$

Now, $\bar{x} = \dfrac{n_1\bar{x}_1 + n_2\bar{x}_2}{n_1 + n_2}$

$\Rightarrow \quad 8300 = \dfrac{n \times 8000 + (100 - n) \times 9000}{100}$

$\Rightarrow \quad 830000 = 8000n + 900000 - 9000n$

$\Rightarrow \quad n = 70$

$\therefore$ Number of male employees= 70 and number of female employees=30

Hence, the number of males and females in the company are 70% and 30% respectively.

Standard Deviation

Let the standard deviation, mean and number of observations of two series are $\sigma_1, \bar{x}_1, n_1$ and $\sigma_2, \bar{x}_2, n_2$ respectively. Then their standard deviation σ or σ is given by

$$\sigma \quad \sigma = \sqrt{\frac{n_1\sigma_1^2 + n_2\sigma_2^2 + n_1d_1^2 + n_2d_2^2}{n_1 + n_2}}$$

or

$$= \sqrt{\frac{n_1(\sigma_1^2 + d_1^2) + n_2(\sigma_1^2 + d_2^2)}{n_1 + n_2}}$$

where, $d_1 = (\bar{x}_1 - \bar{x})$ and $d_2 = (\bar{x}_2 - \bar{x})$ and $\bar{x}$ is combined mean of both series.

Example 3 The means of two samples of size 400 and 600 were respectively 180 and 170. The corresponding standard deviations were respectively 9 and 10. Calculate combined mean and standard deviation.

Sol. We have, $n_1 = 400, \bar{x}_1 = 180, \sigma_1 = 9$

and $n_2 = 600, \bar{x}_2 = 170, \sigma_2 = 10$

$\therefore$ Combined mean, $\bar{x} = \dfrac{n_1\bar{x}_1 + n_2\bar{x}_2}{n_1 + n_2}$

$$= \frac{400 \times 180 + 600 \times 170}{400 + 600}$$

$$= \frac{72000 + 102000}{1000} = 174$$

$\therefore \quad d_1 = \bar{x}_1 - \bar{x} = 180 - 174 = 6$

and $\quad d_2 = \bar{x}_2 - \bar{x} = 170 - 174 = -4$

$\therefore$ Standard deviation,

$$\sigma_{12} = \sqrt{\frac{n_1(\sigma_1^2 + d_1^2) + n_2(\sigma_2^2 + d_2^2)}{n_1 + n_2}}$$

$$= \sqrt{\frac{400 \times (9^2 + 6^2) + 600\,[10^2 + (-4)]^2}{400 + 600}}$$

$$= \sqrt{\frac{400 \times 117 + 600 \times 116}{1000}}$$

$$= \sqrt{\frac{46800 + 69600}{1000}} = \sqrt{\frac{116400}{1000}}$$

$$= \sqrt{116.4} = 10.7889$$

Median

Median is defined as the middle-most or the central observation, when the observations are arranged either in ascending or descending order of their magnitudes.

Median divides the arranged series into two equal parts, i.e. 50% of the observations lie below the median and the remaining are above the median.

Let n be the total number of observations and let they are arranged in ascending or descending order.

Median of the data depends on the number of observations (n).

(i) If n is odd, then

$$\text{Median} = \text{Value of} \left(\frac{n+1}{2}\right)\text{th observation}$$

(ii) If n is even, then

$$\text{Median} = \text{Mean of value of} \left(\frac{n}{2}\right)\text{th and} \left(\frac{n}{2} + 1\right)\text{th observations}$$

$$= \frac{1}{2} \times \text{Value of} \left[\left(\frac{n}{2}\right)\text{th} + \left(\frac{n}{2} + 1\right)\text{th}\right] \text{observations}$$

Example 4 Find the median of the first ten prime numbers.

Sol. We know that first ten prime numbers in ascending order are 2, 3, 5, 7, 11, 13, 17, 19, 23 and 29.

Here, $n = 10$ [even]

$\therefore$ Median

$$= \frac{1}{2} \times \text{Value of} \left[\left(\frac{n}{2}\right)\text{th} \quad \left(\frac{n}{2} + 1\right)\text{th}\right] \text{observations}$$

$$= \frac{1}{2} \times \text{Value of} \left[\left(\frac{10}{2}\right)\text{th} \quad \left(\frac{10}{2} + 1\right)\text{th}\right] \text{observations}$$

$$= \frac{1}{2}[\text{Value of 5th observation + Value of 6th observation}]$$

$$= \frac{1}{2}(11 + 13) = \frac{24}{2} = 12$$

Median for Discrete Series

A series having observations $x_1, x_2, x_3, \ldots, x_n$ with respective frequencies $f_1, f_2, f_3 \ldots, f_n$ is known as **discrete** series.

Method to Find the Median of Discrete Series

First, we arrange the data in the ascending or descending order of x_i, then we find the cumulative frequencies of all the observations.

Let n be the total number of observations (sum of frequencies), then median of the data depends on the number of observations (n).

If n is odd, then Median = Value of $\left(\frac{n+1}{2}\right)$th observation.

If n is even, then

Median = Mean of $\left(\frac{n}{2}\right)$th and $\left(\frac{n}{2}+1\right)$th observations

$$= \frac{1}{2} \times \text{Value of} \left[\left(\frac{n}{2}\right)\text{th} + \left(\frac{n}{2}+1\right)\text{th}\right] \text{observations}$$

Here, for the value of observation, first look at the cumulative frequency which is equal to or just greater than (and nearest to) the position of required observations. Then, determine the corresponding value of the observation.

Example 5 Find the median of the following data.

Marks obtained	20	29	28	42	19	35	51
Number of students	3	4	5	7	9	2	3

Sol. Let us arrange the data in ascending order of x_i and make a cumulative frequency table.

Marks obtained (x_i)	Number of students (f_i)	cf
19	9	9
20	3	9 + 3 = 12
28	5	12 + 5 = 17
29	4	17 + 4 = 21
35	2	21 + 2 = 23
42	7	23 + 7 = 30
51	3	30 + 3 = 33

Here, $n = 33$ (odd)

$\therefore$ Median = Value of $\left(\frac{n+1}{2}\right)$th observation

= Value of $\left(\frac{33+1}{2}\right)$th observation

= Value of 17th observation

$\because$ Corresponding value of 17th observation of cumulative frequency in x_i is 28.

Hence, the required median is 28.

Example 6 Obtain the median for the following frequency distribution.

x	1	2	3	4	5	6	7	8	9
f_i	8	10	11	16	20	25	15	9	6

Sol. Here, the given data is in ascending order of x_i.

Cumulative frequency table for the given data is

x_i	f_i	cf
1	8	8
2	10	18
3	11	29
4	16	45
5	20	65
6	25	90
7	15	105
8	9	114
9	6	120

Here, $n = 120$ (even)

$$\therefore \text{Median} = \frac{1}{2}\left[\text{Value of} \left\{\left(\frac{n}{2}\right)\text{th} + \left(\frac{n}{2}+1\right)\text{th}\right\}\right] \text{observations}$$

$$= \frac{1}{2}\left[\text{Value of} \left\{\left(\frac{120}{2}\right)\text{th} + \left(\frac{120}{2}+1\right)\text{th}\right\}\right] \text{observations}$$

$$= \frac{1}{2} [\text{Value of 60th observation} + \text{Value of 61th observation}]$$

Both 60th and 61th observations lie in the cumulative frequency 65 and its corresponding value in x_i is 5.

$\therefore$ Median $= \frac{1}{2}(5+5) = 5$

Median for Grouped Data

In a grouped data, we may not find the middle observation by looking at the cumulative frequencies, since the middle observation will be some value in a class interval, so it is necessary to find the value inside a class that divides the whole distribution into two halves.

For this, we find the cumulative frequencies of all the classes and $\frac{n}{2}$, where n = number of observations. Now, locate the class whose cumulative frequency is greater than (and nearest to) $\frac{n}{2}$ and this class is called **median class**.

After finding the median class, use the following formula for calculating the median.

$$\text{Median} = l + \left\{ \frac{\frac{n}{2} - cf}{f} \right\} \times h$$

where, l = lower limit of median class
n = number of observations
cf = cumulative frequency of the class preceding the median class
f = frequency of the median class
and h = class width (assuming class sizes to be equal)

Note The median of grouped data with unequal class sizes can also be calculated. However, we shall not discuss it here.

Example 7 200 surnames were randomly picked up from a local telephone directory and the frequency distribution of the number of letters in English alphabets in the surnames was obtained as follows

Number of letters	0-5	5-10	10-15	15-20	20-25
Number of surnames	20	60	80	32	8

Find the median of the above data.

Sol. The cumulative frequency table of given data is

Number of letters	Number of surnames (f_i)	Cumulative frequency (cf)
0-5	20	20
5-10	60	20 + 60 = 80 (cf)
10-15	80 = f	80 + 80 = 160
15-20	32	160 + 32 = 192
20-25	8	192 + 8 = 200
Total	$n = 200$	

Here, $n = 200$

$\therefore \quad \frac{n}{2} = \frac{200}{2} = 100$

Since, the cumulative frequency just greater than 100 is 160 and the corresponding class interval is 10-15.

$\therefore$ Median class = 10-15, $l = 10$, $cf = 80$, $h = 5$ and $f = 80$

Now, median $= l + \left\{ \frac{\frac{n}{2} - cf}{f} \right\} \times h = 10 + \left\{ \frac{100 - 80}{80} \right\} \times 5$

$= 10 + \left(\frac{20}{80} \right) \times 5$

$= 10 + 1.25 = 11.25$

Example 8 A survey regarding the heights (in cm) of 51 boys of class X of a school was conducted and the given data was obtained

Heights (in cm)	Number of boys
Less than 140	4
Less than 145	11
Less than 150	29
Less than 155	40
Less than 160	46
Less than 165	51

Find the median height.

Sol. To calculate the median height, we need to convert the given data in the continuous grouped frequency distribution.

Given distribution is of less than type and 140, 145, 150, ..., 165 gives the upper limits of the corresponding class intervals. So, the classes should be below 140, 140-145, 145-150, ..., 160-165.

Clearly, the frequency of class interval below 140 is 4, since there are 4 boys with height less than 140. For the frequency of class interval 140-145 subtract the number of boys having height less than 140 from the number of boys having height less than 145.

Thus, the frequency of class interval 140-145 is $11 - 4 = 7$. Similarly, we can calculate the frequencies of other class intervals and get the following table

Class interval	Frequency	Cumulative frequency (cf)
Below 140	4	4
140-145	$11 - 4 = 7$	11 (cf)
145-150	$29 - 11 = 18 = f$	29
150-155	$40 - 29 = 11$	40
155-160	$46 - 40 = 6$	46
160-165	$51 - 46 = 5$	51

Here, $n = 51 \Rightarrow \frac{n}{2} = \frac{51}{2} = 25.5$

Since, the cumulative frequency just greater than 25.5 is 29 and the corresponding class interval is 145-150.

$\therefore$ Median class = 145-150

Now, $l = 145$, $f = 18$, $cf = 11$ and $h = 5$

$\therefore \quad \text{Median} = l + \left\{ \frac{\frac{n}{2} - cf}{f} \right\} \times h = 145 + \left\{ \frac{25.5 - 11}{18} \right\} \times 5$

$= 145 + \frac{72.5}{18} = 145 + 4.03 = 149.03$

Hence, the required median height is 149.03 cm.

Example 9 Find the missing frequencies in the following frequency distribution table, if $n = 100$ and median is 32.

Marks obtained	0-10	10-20	20-30	30-40	40-50	50-60	Total
Number of students	10	?	25	30	?	10	100

Sol. Given, median = 32 and $n = \Sigma f = 100$

Let f_1 and f_2 be the frequencies of the class interval 10-20 and 40-50, respectively.

Since, sum of frequencies = 100

$\therefore \quad 10 + f_1 + 25 + 30 + f_2 + 10 = 100$

$\Rightarrow \quad f_1 + f_2 = 100 - 75$

$\Rightarrow \quad f_1 + f_2 = 25$

$\Rightarrow \quad f_2 = 25 - f_1 \quad$ ...(i)

Now, the cumulative frequency table for given distribution is

Class interval	Frequency (f)	Cumulative frequency (cf)
0-10	10	10
10-20	f_1	$10 + f_1$
20-30	25	$35 + f_1$ (cf)
30-40	$30 = f$	$65 + f_1$
40-50	f_2	$65 + f_1 + f_2$
50-60	10	$75 + f_1 + f_2$
Total	$n = f_1 + f_2 + 75$	

Here, $n = 100 \Rightarrow \frac{n}{2} = 50$

Given, median = 32, which belongs to the class 30-40.

So, the median class is 30 -40.

Then, $l = 30, h = 10, f = 30$ and $cf = 35 + f_1$

$$\because \quad \text{Median} = l + \left\{\frac{\frac{n}{2} - cf}{f}\right\} \times h$$

$$\therefore \quad 32 = 30 + \left\{\frac{50 - 35 - f_1}{30}\right\} \times 10$$

$$\Rightarrow \quad 32 - 30 = \frac{15 - f_1}{3}$$

$$\Rightarrow \quad 2 \times 3 = 15 - f_1$$

$$\Rightarrow \quad f_1 = 15 - 6 = 9$$

On putting the value of f_1 in Eq. (i), we get

$$f_2 = 25 - 9 = 16$$

Hence, the missing frequencies are 9 and 16.

Quartiles

If the given data is arranged in ascending order of magnitude, then **Quartiles** are the value which divide the data set into four equal parts called **quarters**. Therefore, there are three quartiles and corresponding four quarters.

(i) Q_1 is the **lower or first quartile.**

(ii) Q_2 is the middle or second quartile and same as median.

(iii) Q_3 is the **upper or third quartile.**

Note $Q_3 - Q_1$ is known as the **inter quartile range**.

The above stated values are called **partition values.** The values are given as below

1. For Discrete Data

First, the values are arranged in ascending order of magnitude.

Then, $Q_1 = \frac{n+1}{4}$th value,

Median $Q_2 = \frac{n+1}{2}$th value, $Q_3 = \frac{3(n+1)}{4}$th value,

In general, $Q_r = \frac{r(n+1)}{4}$ th value, where $r = 1, 2, 3.$

2. For Grouped Frequency Distribution (In the Form of Classes)

We use n instead of $n + 1$.

Lower quartile $(Q_1) = l + \dfrac{\frac{n}{4} - C}{f} \times c$, where l = lower boundary of class where Q_1 lies i.e. $\frac{n}{4}$th value lies;

C = cumulative frequency of class previous to this class

f = frequency of class in which $\frac{n}{4}$th value lies,

c = width of class in which $\frac{n}{4}$th value lies.

Similarly, $Q_2(\text{median}) = l + \dfrac{\frac{n}{2} - C}{f} \times c, Q_3 = l + \dfrac{\frac{3n}{4} - C}{f} \times c,$

In general, $Q_r = l + \dfrac{\frac{rn}{4} - C}{f} \times c;\ r = 1, 2, 3$

[where, the value refer to class in which $\frac{rn}{100}$th value lies]

Example 10 Calculate median and quartiles from the following data of the marks obtained by 10 students in an examination.

22, 26, 14, 30, 18, 11, 35, 41, 12, 32

Sol. Arrange the given data in ascending order, we have

11, 12, 14, 18, 22, 26, 30, 32, 35, 41

Here, $n = 10 \Rightarrow \frac{n+1}{2} = \frac{10+1}{2} = 5.5$

$\therefore$ Median = Size of 5.5th item

$= \frac{1}{2}$(5th item + 6th item)

$= \frac{22+26}{2} = \frac{48}{2} = 24$ marks

Now, $\frac{n+1}{4} = \frac{10+1}{4} = 2.75$ and $\frac{3(n+1)}{4} = 3 \times 2.75 = 8.25$

$\therefore$ Q_1 = Size of 2.75th item

= 2nd item + 0.75 (3rd item − 2nd item)

$= 12 + 0.75\,(14 - 12) = 12 + 1.5 = 13.5$ marks

and Q_3 = Size of 8.25th item

= 8th item + 0.25 (9th item − 8th item)

$= 32 + 0.25\,(35 - 32) = 32 + 0.25 \times 3$

$= 32 + 0.75 = 32.75$ marks

Example 11 For the following data compute the values of upper and lower quartiles and median.

Marks	Number of students	Marks	Number of students
Below 10	5	40-50	90
10-20	25	50-60	40
20-30	40	60-70	20
30-40	70	Above 70	10

Sol. First, construct the table, which are as follow

Marks	f	cf
Below-10	5	5
10-20	25	30
20-30	40	70
30-40	70	140
40-50	90	230
50-60	40	270
60-70	20	290
Above-70	10	300
	$n = 300$	

Here, $\frac{n}{4} = \frac{300}{4} = 75$, and $\frac{3n}{4} = 3 \times 75 = 225$

$\because$ Q_1 lies in the class 30-40.

$$\therefore \quad Q_1 = L + \frac{i}{f}\left(\frac{n}{4} - c\right)$$

[where, i = width of class in which $\frac{n}{4}$th value lies]

$$= 30 + \frac{10}{70}(75 - 70)$$

$= 30 + 0.714 = 30.714$ or 31 approx.

This means that there are 25% students (i.e. 75) whose marks are below 31 and 75% students (i.e. 225) whose marks are above 31.

$\because$ Q_3 lies in the class 40-50.

$$\therefore \quad Q_3 = L + \frac{i}{f}\left(\frac{3n}{4} - c\right) = 40 + \frac{10}{90}(225 - 140)$$

$$= 40 + \frac{85}{9} = 40 + 9.44 = 49.44 \text{ or } 49 \text{ (approx.)}$$

This means that there are 75% students (i.e. 225) whose marks are below 49 and 25% students (i.e. 75) whose marks are above 49.

$$\frac{n}{2} = \frac{300}{2} = 150$$

$\because$ M_d lies in the class 40-50.

$$\therefore \quad M_d = L + \frac{i}{f}\left(\frac{n}{2} - c\right)$$

$$= 40 + \frac{10}{90}(150 - 140)$$

$$= 40 + \frac{10}{9} = 40 + 1.11 = 41.11 \text{ or } 41 \text{ (approx.)}$$

This means that there are 50% students (i.e. 150) whose marks are below 41 and 50% students whose marks are above 41.

Mode

The observation, which occurs most frequently among the given observations, i.e. the value of the observation having maximum frequency is called **mode**. e.g. Mode of the numbers 2, 3, 4, 4, 6, 6, 6, 6, 7 and 9 is 6 because it is repeated maximum number of times, i.e. 4 times.

Sometimes, it is possible that more than one value may have the same maximum frequency. Thus, in this situation, the data is said to be **multimodal**. Here, we will discuss the problems having single mode only. Thus, in case of ungrouped data, the mode is the observation with maximum frequency.

Example 12 In a class of 72 students, marks obtained by the students in a class test (out of 10) are given below

Marks obtained (Out of 10)	1	2	3	4	6	7	9	10
Number of students	3	5	12	18	23	8	2	1

Find the mode of the data.

Sol. The mode of the given data is 6 as it has the maximum frequency, i.e. 23 among all the observations.

Modal Class

In a grouped frequency distribution, it is not possible to determine the mode by looking at the frequencies. So, here we first locate a class with the maximum frequency. This class is called modal class. e.g.

Class interval	0-10	10-20	20-30	30-40	40-50	50-60
Number of students	2	9	14	20	22	8

Here, the highest frequency is of the class 40-50, which is 22. Hence, the modal class is 40-50.

Mode of Grouped Data

In grouped data, mode is a value that lies in the modal class and it is given by the formula,

$$\text{Mode} = l + \left\{\frac{f_1 - f_0}{2f_1 - f_0 - f_2}\right\} \times h$$

where, l = lower limit of the modal class

h = size of the class intervals (assuming all class sizes to be equal)

f_1 = frequency of the modal class

f_0 = frequency of the class preceding the modal class

and f_2 = frequency of the class succeeding the modal class

Note

(i) Mode can also be calculated for a grouped data with unequal class sizes.

(ii) Mode can be less, equal or more than the mean of the data.

Example 13 An NGO working for welfare of cancer patients, maintained its records as follows

Age of patients (in years)	0-20	20-40	40-60	60-80
Number of patients	35	315	120	50

Find the mode.

Sol. Here, maximum frequency is 315 and the class corresponding to this frequency is 20-40. So, the modal class is 20-40.

Age of patients (in years)	0-20	20-40	40-60	60-80
Number of patients	$35 = f_0$	$315 = f_1$	$120 = f_2$	50

$\therefore\ l = 20,\ f_1 = 315,\ f_0 = 35,\ f_2 = 120$ and $h = 20$

Now, $\text{Mode} = l + \left(\frac{f_1 - f_0}{2f_1 - f_0 - f_2}\right) \times h$

$$= 20 + \left(\frac{315 - 35}{2 \times 315 - 35 - 120}\right) \times 20$$

$$= 20 + \frac{280}{475} \times 20$$

$$= 20 + 11.79$$

$$= 31.79$$

Hence, the average age of maximum number of patients is 31.79.

Example 14 If mode of the following series is 54, then find the value of f.

Class interval	0-15	15-30	30-45	45-60	60-75	75-90
Frequency	3	5	f	16	12	7

Sol. Here, the given mode is 54, which lies between 45-60. Therefore, the modal class is 45-60.

$\therefore\ l = 45,\ f_1 = 16,\ f_0 = f,\ f_2 = 12$ and $h = 15$

$\because\quad \text{Mode} = l + \left(\frac{f_1 - f_0}{2f_1 - f_0 - f_2}\right) \times h$

$\therefore\quad 54 = 45 + \left(\frac{16 - f}{2 \times 16 - f - 12}\right) \times 15$

$\Rightarrow\quad 9 = \frac{16 - f}{20 - f} \times 15$

$\Rightarrow\quad 9(20 - f) = 15(16 - f)$

$\Rightarrow\quad 180 - 9f = 240 - 15f$

$\Rightarrow\quad 6f = 240 - 180$

$= 60$

$\Rightarrow\quad f = 10$

Hence, the required value of f is 10.

Relationship between Mean, Median and Mode

There is an empirical relationship between the three measures of central tendency, which is given by

$$\text{Mode} = 3(\text{Median}) - 2(\text{Mean})$$

or $$\text{Mean} = \frac{3\,(\text{Median}) - \text{Mode}}{2}$$

or $$\text{Median} = \frac{\text{Mode} + 2\,(\text{Mean})}{3}$$

Example 15 If median = 137 units and mean = 137.05 units, then find the mode.

Sol. Given, median = 137 units and mean = 137.05 units.

We know that,

$\text{Mode} = 3\,(\text{Median}) - 2\,(\text{Mean})$

$= 3(137) - 2(137.05)$

$= 411 - 274.10$

$= 136.90$

Hence, the value of mode is 136.90 units.

Procedure for Graphing the Location of Mode

In this procedure, we use the following steps

Step I Draw a histogram of the data, for convenience only three rectangles may be drawn, i.e. rectangles for the modal, pre-modal and post-modal classes.

Step II Draw two lines diagonally inside the modal class rectangle, starting from each upper corner of the modal rectangle to the upper corner of the adjacent rectangle.

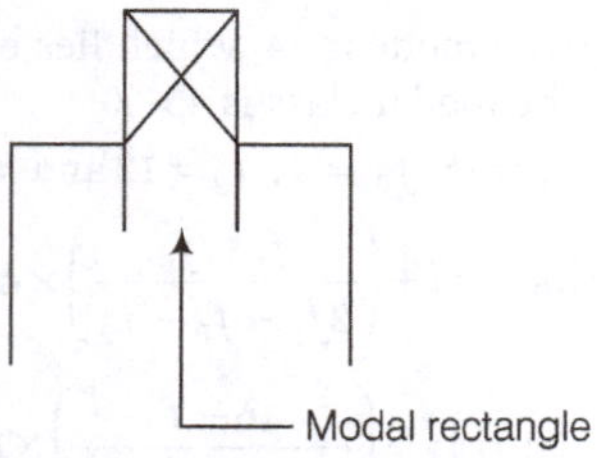

Step III From the point of intersection of both these lines draw a perpendicular to the X-axis, the point where this perpendicular meets the X-axis is the value of the mode.

Mode can also be determined by drawing a frequency polygon. In such a case, a perpendicular is drawn from the apex of the frequency polygon and the point where the perpendicular touches the X-axes, gives the modal value.

Mode cannot be determined graphically if two or more classes have the same highest frequency. e.g. For the data given below, mode cannot be determined graphically.

Size of shop	3-6	6-9	9-12	12-15	15-18	18-21
Number of persons	8	13	15	18	18	8

Example 16 Find the mode of the distribution given below, by drawing a histogram.

Class interval	0-20	20-40	40-60	60-80
Frequency	15	6	18	10

Sol. We draw the histogram by taking 1 cm = 20 units on horizontal axis and 1 cm = 5 units on vertical axis. Now, inside the highest rectangle, we join A to D and B to C. AD and BC meet at M.

From M we draw the perpendicular MN to the horizontal axis meeting it at N. We estimate ON approximately equal to 52 units.

Hence, the required mode = 52.

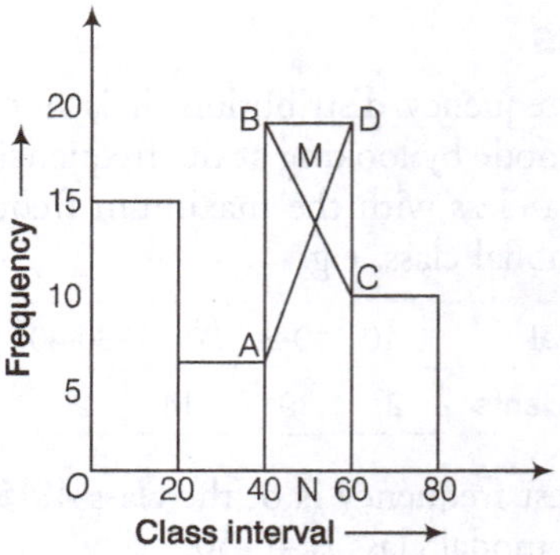

Cumulative Frequency Curve or an Ogive Curve

The term 'ogive' is pronounced as 'ojeev' and is derived from the word ogee. An ogive is a shape consisting of a concave arc flowing into a convex arcs. So, forming an S-shaped curve with vertical ends. Graphical representation of cumulative frequency distribution is of two types, less than type ogive and more than type ogive. The process of graphical representation of less than type or more than type cumulative frequency distribution are given below

1. Less than Type Ogive

It is the graph drawn between the upper limits and cumulative frequencies of a distribution. Here, we mark the points with upper limit as x-coordinate and corresponding cumulative frequency as y-coordinate and join them by a free hand smooth curve. This type of graph is cumulated upward.

Example 17 From the following frequency distribution, prepare the 'less than' ogive.

Rainfall (in cm)	5-15	15-25	25-35	35-45	45-55	55-65
Number of days	22	10	8	15	5	6

Sol. Let us first prepare the less than cumulative frequency distribution as given below.

Rainfall (in cm)	Number of days	Rainfall (in cm)	Cumulative frequency
5-15	22	less than 15	22
15-25	10	less than 25	22 + 10 = 32
25-35	8	less than 35	32 + 8 = 40
35-45	15	less than 45	40 + 15 = 55
45-55	5	less than 55	55 + 5 = 60
55-65	6	less than 65	60 + 6 = 66

Now, mark the upper limits of class intervals on X-axis and cumulative frequencies on Y-axis, by choosing a convenient scale. Then, plot the points (15, 22), (25, 32), (35, 40), (45, 55), (55, 60) and (65, 66), and join them by a freehand smooth curve.

Thus, we get 'less than type' ogive as shown in the figure.

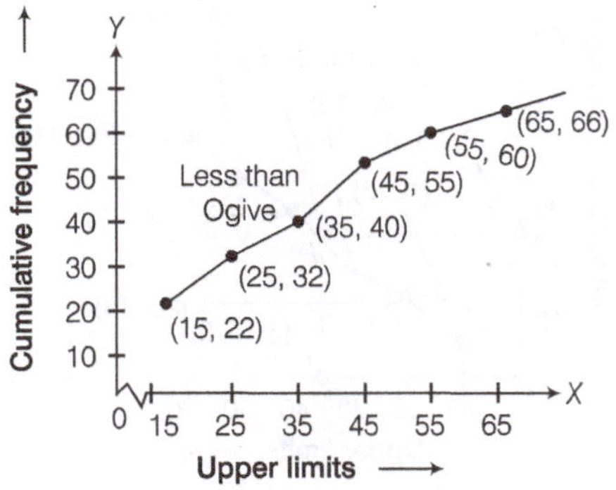

2. More than Type Ogive

It is the graph drawn between lower limits and cumulative frequencies of a distribution. Here, we mark the points with lower limit as x-cordinate and corresponding cumulative frequency as y-coordinate and join them by freehand smooth curve. This type of graph is cumulated downward.

Example 18 Change the given distribution to 'more than type' distribution and draw its ogive.

Marks obtained	20-25	25-30	30-35	35-40	40-45	45-50
Number of candidates	3	6	12	9	6	4

Sol. Let us first prepare the more than type cumulative frequency distribution as given below.

Class interval	Cumulative frequency (*cf*)
20 or more than 20	40
25 or more than 25	40 − 3 = 37
30 or more than 30	37 − 6 = 31
35 or more than 35	31 − 12 = 19
40 or more than 40	19 − 9 = 10
45 or more than 45	10 − 6 = 4

Now, mark the lower limits of the class intervals along the X-axis and cumulative frequencies along Y-axis, on the graph paper by choosing a convenient scale. Then, plots the points (20, 40), (25, 37), (30, 31), (35,19), (40, 10) and (45, 4), and join them by a freehand smooth curve.

Thus, we get 'more than type' ogive as shown in the figure.

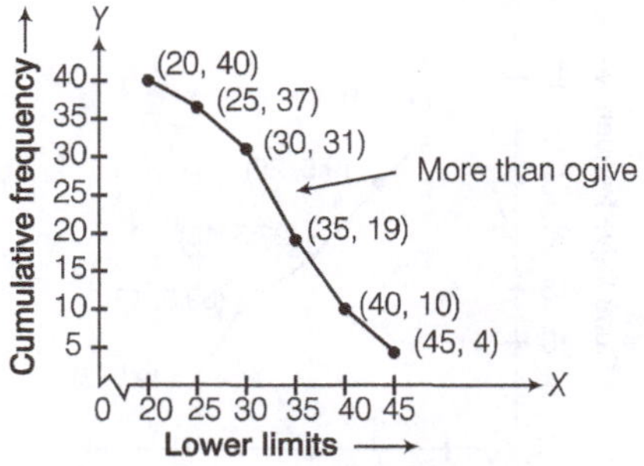

This curve is called cumulative frequency curve of more than type.

Example 19 Draw a 'more than type' ogive from the following distribution.

Marks obtained	10-19	20-29	30-39	40-49	50-59
Number of candidates	6	7	5	10	3

Sol. Here, the data is not in continuous form, so we convert it into continuous classes for finding the 'more than type' ogive. For this subtract 0.5 from lower limit of each class interval and add 0.5 to upper limit of each class interval.

Marks obtained	9.5-19.5	19.5-29.5	29.5-39.5	39.5-49.5	49.5-59.5
Number of candidates	6	7	5	10	3

For 'more than type' ogive, we form cumulative frequency distribution of more than type as given below

Marks obtained	Number of candidates
9.5 or more than 9.5	31
19.5 or more than 19.5	31 − 6 = 25
29.5 or more than 29.5	25 − 7 = 18
39.5 or more than 39.5	18 − 5 =13
49.5 or more than 49.5	13 − 10 = 3

Now, mark the lower limits along the X-axis and cumulative frequencies along Y-axis, on the graph paper by choosing a suitable scale. Then, plot the points (9.5, 31), (19.5, 25), (29.5, 18), (39.5, 13) and (49.5, 3) on a graph paper and join them by a freehand smooth curve.

Thus, we get 'more than type' ogive as shown in the figure.

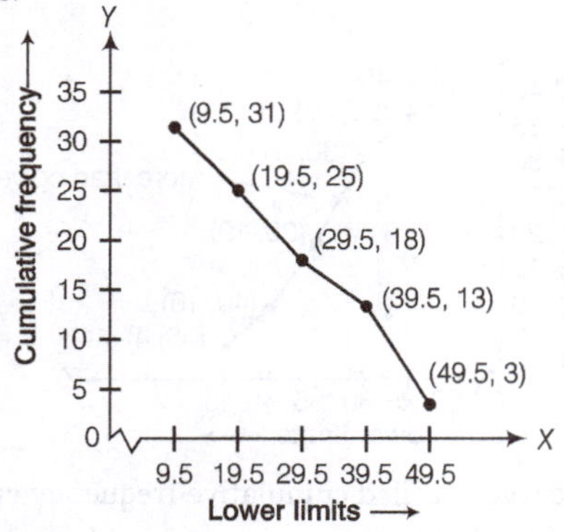

Median from Cumulative Frequency Curve

For finding the median from cumulative frequency curve either less than ogive or more than ogive, locate $n/2$ on the Y-axis, where n is the total number of observations. From this point, draw a line parallel to the X-axis cutting the curve at a point. From this point, draw a perpendicular to the X-axis. The abscissa of point of intersection of this perpendicular with the X-axis is the median of the data.

Also, if we have both ogives (i.e. less than type and more than type), then these two ogives intersect each other at a point. From this point, draw a perpendicular on X-axis, the point at which it cuts the X-axis gives the median, i.e. the x-coordinate of intersection point gives the median.

Example 20 Draw a 'less than type' ogive for the following frequency distribution.

Marks	0-10	10-20	20-30	30-40	40-50	50-60
Number of students	5	8	6	10	6	6

Find the median from the graph and also verify the result.

Sol. For the given distribution 'less than type' cumulative frequency distribution is as follows:

Marks	Number of students	Marks	Cumulative frequency
0-10	5	Less than 10	5
10-20	8	Less than 20	5 + 8 = 13
20-30	6	Less than 30	13 + 6 = 19
30-40	10	Less than 40	19 + 10 = 29
40-50	6	Less than 50	29 + 6 = 35
50-60	6	Less than 60	35 + 6 = 41

Now, mark the upper limits on the X-axis and cumulative frequencies along Y-axis and then plot the points (10, 5), (20, 13), (30, 19), (40, 29), (50, 35) and (60, 41). Join these points by a freehand smooth curve to obtain the 'less than type' ogive as shown in the figure

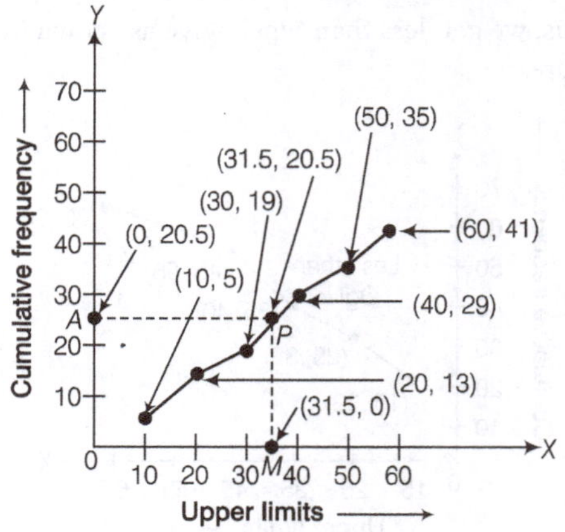

Now, $\dfrac{n}{2} = \dfrac{41}{2} = 20.5$

Take a point A on Y-axis representing 20.5. Through A, draw a line AP parallel to X-axis which meet the ogive at P. Draw PM, perpendicular to X-axis, meeting X-axis at point M.

The abscissa of M is 31.5 which is the required median.

Verification

Here, $n = 41$

$\therefore \quad \dfrac{n}{2} = \dfrac{41}{2} = 20.5$

Since, the cumulative frequency just greater than 20.5 is 29 and the corresponding class interval is 30-40.

$\therefore\ l = 30, h = 10, cf = 19$ and $f = 10$

Now, median $= l + \left\{ \dfrac{\dfrac{n}{2} - cf}{f} \right\} \times h$

$= 30 + \left\{ \dfrac{20.5 - 19}{10} \right\} \times 10$

$= 30 + 1.5 = 31.5$ **Hence verified.**

Example 21 The following table gives the height of trees

Height (Less than)	7	14	21	28	35	42	49	56
Number of trees	26	57	92	134	216	287	341	360

Draw 'less than ogive' and 'more than ogive'. Also, find the median.

Sol. Given distribution is cumulative frequency distribution of less than type.

Now, we mark the upper limits along X-axis and cumulative frequencies along Y-axis, on the graph paper. Then, plot the points (7, 26), (14, 57), (21, 92), (28, 134), (35, 216), (42, 287), (49, 341) and (56, 360). Join all these points by a freehand smooth curve to obtain an ogive of less than type.

Now, let us form the cumulative frequency distribution of more than type, as shown below

Height	Frequency	Height (More than or equal to)	Cumulative frequency
0-7	26	0	360
7-14	57 – 26 = 31	7	360 – 26 = 334
14-21	92 – 57 = 35	14	334 – 31 = 303
21-28	134 – 92 = 42	21	303 – 35 = 268
28-35	216 – 134 = 82	28	268 – 42 = 226
35-42	287 – 216 = 71	35	226 – 82 = 144
42-49	341 – 287 = 54	42	144 – 71 = 73
49-56	360 – 341 = 19	49	73 – 54 = 19

Now, we plot the points (0, 360), (7, 334), (14, 303), (21, 268), (28, 226), (35,144), (42,73) and (49, 19) on the same graph paper by choosing a sutable scale. Join all these points by a free hand smooth curve to obtain an ogive of more than type.

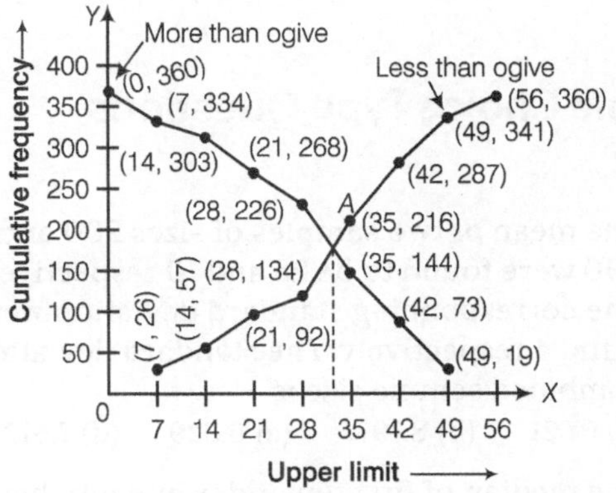

The two ogives intersect at point A. Now, we draw a perpendicular line from A to the X-axis, the intersection point on X-axis is 31.9. Thus, the required median is 31.9.

Chapter Practice

Multiple Choice Type Questions

1 Mark

1. The mean of two samples of sizes 200 and 300 were found to be 25 and 10 respectively. The corresponding standard deviation were 3 and 4 respectively. The standard deviation of combined sample size is
(a) 67.21 (b) 8.197 (c) 6.329 (d) 7.572

2. The median of first ten odd prime numbers is
(a) 10 (b) 12 (c) 15 (d) 18

3. The mode of the following series is 55.

Class interval	0-15	15-30	30-45	45-60	60-75	75-90
Frequency	10	7	f	15	10	12

Then, the missing frequency f is
(a) 9 (b) 11 (c) 5 (d) 15

4. The mode of the following data is

Class Interval	0-20	20-40	40-60	60-80
Frequency	35	315	120	50

(a) 21.79 (b) 32 (c) 41.79 (d) 31.79

5. If mean and mode of a data are 137.05 units and 136.9 units respectively, then the median of the data is
(a) 135 units (b) 136 units
(c) 137 units (d) 139 units

Assertion-Reason Type Questions

1 Mark

Directions (Q. Nos. 6-9) *In the questions given below are two statements labelled as Assertion (A) and Reason (R). In the context of the two statements, which one of the following is correct?*

(a) Both A and R are correct; R is the correct explanation of A
(b) Both A and R are correct; R is not the correct explanation of A
(c) A is correct; R is incorrect
(d) R is correct; A is incorrect

6. **Assertion (A)** The median of the following data is 24.

x_i	0-10	10-20	20-30	30-40	40-50
f_i	13	22	25	16	14

Reason (R) The median of the data depends on the number of observations.

7. **Assertion (A)** The mode of the following data is 36 years.

Age in years	5-15	15-25	25-35	35-45	45-55	55-65
Number of Patients	6	11	21	23	14	5

Reason (R) In grouped data, mode is a value that lie in the modal class.

8. **Assertion (A)** The mode of the following data is 52.

Class interval	0-20	20-40	40-60	60-80
Frequency	15	6	18	10

Reason (R) For a grouped data, mode is given by the formula,

$$\text{Mode} = l + \left\{\frac{f_1 + f_0}{2f_1 + f_0 - f_2}\right\} \times h$$

9. **Assertion (A)** If mode and median of a data are 131.35 units and 135.25 units respectively, then the mean of the data is 137.2.

Reason (R) The relationship between mean, median and mode is given by

$$\text{Median} = 3\,(\text{Mode}) - 2\,(\text{Mean})$$

Short Answer Type Questions

4 Marks

10. There are two branches of a company employing 100 and 80 persons respectively. The arithmetic means of the monthly salaries paid by the two branches are ₹ 1570 and ₹ 1750 respectively. Find the combined mean of the salaries of the employees.

11. A school has 4 sections in class XI having 45, 42, 35 and 40 students. The mean marks obtained by the students of the four sections in a Mathematics test were 55, 45, 60 and 50 respectively. What was the overall average of the marks per student?

12. Find the mean and SD or wages of all casual labourers in the two firms taken together standard deviation 4. A test was given to 400 students of whom 150 were boys and the rest were girls. The boys had an average score of 72 with SD 7, while the girls had an average score of 73 with SD 6.4. Find the mean and SD of the class as a whole.

13. Marks obtained by 36 students are given below

Marks	35	45	50	64	70	72
Number of students	3	5	8	10	5	5

Calculate the median marks.

14. Marks obtained by 70 students are given below

Marks	20	70	50	60	75	90	40
Number of students	8	12	18	6	9	5	12

Calculate the median marks.

15. Calculate the median marks for the following data.

Height (in cm)	Number of boys
135-140	4
140-145	9
145-150	18
150-155	28
155-160	24
160-165	10
165-175	7

16. The measurements (in mm) of the diameters of the heads of 107 screws gave the following frequency distribution

Diameter	33-35	36-38	39-41	42-44	45-47
Frequency	17	19	23	21	27

Estimate the median head diameter per screw.

17. Find the values of a and b from the following data.

Variable	10-20	20-30	30-40	40-50	50-60	60-70
Frequency	4	28	a	20	b	16

Given that median is 41.5 and total frequency is 100.

18. The average monthly pocket money of 10 children is ₹ 38 and median is ₹ 40.
   (i) What is the total amount of pocket money?
   (ii) If the child getting highest pocket money starts receiving an additional ₹ 20 per month, what would be the new mean? the new median?

19. Find Q_1 and Q_3 for the following data.

x_i	18	19	20	21	22	23	24	25	26	27
f_i	15	18	25	27	40	25	19	16	8	7

20. For the following data, compute lower and upper quartiles.

Marks	Below 10	10-20	20-40	40-60	60-80	Above 80
Number of students	8	10	22	25	10	5

21. Calculate the mean and median for the following frequency distribution.

Wages (in ₹)	Number of workers
15-19	31
20-24	47
25-29	59
30-34	78
35-39	104
40-44	113
45-49	81
50-54	60
55-59	52
60-64	25

Also, calculate Q_1 and Q_3.

Hint Reconstruct table with continuous classes as 14.5-19.5, 19.5-24.5, ...

22. From the following data, calculate the percentage of workers who earn more than ₹ 840 per week.

Weekly wages (in ₹)	Number of workers
500-600	12
600-700	17
700-800	22
800-900	29
900-1000	12
1000-1100	6

23. Given below is the distribution of daily earnings of 60 workers in a factory

More than (in ₹)	240	210	180	150	120	90	60
Number of workers	0	4	27	39	50	57	60

If 55% of the workers fulfil their requirements, find the minimum daily earnings to meet the requirements of a worker.

24. Find out first quartile and third quartile.

Size of item	*f*	Size of item	*f*
0-10	2	40-50	35
10-20	18	50-60	20
20-30	30	60-70	6
30-40	45	70-80	3

25. Following are the different sizes and number of shoes in a shoe shop. Calculate median, first quartile and third quartile.

Size of shoes	Number of shoes	Size of shoes	Number of shoes
4.5	4	8	40
5	8	8.5	20
5.5	12	9	15
6	15	9.5	24
6.5	20	10	12
7	35	10.5	5
7.5	50	11	3

26. Calculate the median.

x	0-5	5-10	10-15	15-20	20-25
f	7	18	25	30	20

27. Find the interquartile range, quartile deviation for the following data.

Age (in yr)	20	30	40	50	60	70	80
Number of members	3	61	132	153	140	51	3

28. The daily wages (in ₹) of 30 employees in an establishment are distributed as follows

Daily wages	0-10	10-20	20-30	30-40	40-50	50-60
Number of employees	1	8	10	5	4	2

Estimate the modal daily wages for this distribution.

29. Consider the following distribution

Weight (in kg)	40-44	45-49	50-54	55-59	60-64	65-69
Number of students	2	8	12	10	6	4

Hence, estimate the modal weight.

30. Find the mode of the following distribution.

Mid value	12	18	24	30	36	42	48
Frequency	20	12	8	24	16	8	12

Also, state the modal class.

31. The following table shown the distribution of the heights of a group of workers in a factory

Height (in cm)	Number of workers
150-155	6
155-160	12
160-165	18
165-170	20
170-175	13
175-180	8
180-185	6

Convert the distribution to more than cumulative frequency distribution and draw its ogive. Hence obtain the median from the graph.

32. 100 students in a school have heights as tabulated below

Height (in cm)	Number of pupils
121-130	12
131-140	16
141-150	30
151-160	20
161-170	14
171-180	8

Draw the ogive for the above data and from its determine the median (use graph paper).

Case-Based Type Question

(6 Marks)

33. A competition was organised in a school having 500 students. 400 students participated the competition.

The marks out of 100, scored by 400 students in the examination are as follows

Marks	Number of students
0-10	10
10-20	20
20-30	22
30-40	40
40-50	55
50-60	75
60-70	80
70-80	58
80-90	28
90-100	12

Answer the following questions, based on above informations.

(i) Find the median mark.

(ii) Find the pass marks if 80% of the students pass the examination.

(iii) Write the modal class of the given data.

Hints & Answers

1. (b) **2.** (c) **3.** (c) **4.** (d) **5.** (c)

6. (b) **7.** (c) **8.** (c) **9.** (c)

10. Solve as Example 1. **Ans.** ₹ 1650

11. Solve as Example 1. **Ans.** 52.25

12. Solve as Example 3. **Ans.** 72.6525, 6.65

13. Solve as Example 6. **Ans.** 64

14. Solve as Example 6. **Ans.** 50

15. Solve as Example 7. **Ans.** 153.4

16. Solve as Example 7.
Ans. 40.78 mm

17. Solve as Example 9.
Ans. $a = 15$, $b = 17$

18. (i) ₹ 380 (ii) ₹ 40, ₹ 40

19. Solve as Example 11.
Ans. $Q_1 = 20$, $Q_3 = 24$

20. Solve as Example 11.
Ans. $Q = 21.82$, $Q_3 = 56$

21. Reconstruct table with continuous classes as 14.5-19.5, 19. 5-24.5, ...
Solve as Example 11.
Ans. [39.52, 39.77; 31.13, 47.93]

22. 36.12%

23. ₹ 165

24. 26.58, 46.93

25. 7.5, 7, 8.5

26. 15

27. Quartile deviation $= \dfrac{Q_3 - Q_1}{2}$ **Ans.** 20, 10

28. Solve as Example 13. **Ans.** ₹ 22.9

29. Solve as Example 13. **Ans.** 53 kg

30. Solve as Example 13. **Ans.** 31, 27-33

31. Solve as Example 19. **Ans.** 166.5 cm

32. Solve as Example 20. **Ans.** 148 cm

33. (i) 57 (ii) 37 (iii) Modal Class = 60-70

CHAPTER

20

Correlation Analysis

- Definition
- Scatter Diagram
- Karl Pearson's Coefficient of Correlation

In this chapter, we will learn about correlation between two variable. For this, we will discuss two methods, i.e. Karl Pearson's method and Spearman's method.

Definition

When the values of two variables vary in such a way that fluctuations in one are accompanied by the fluctuations in the other, these variables are said to be **correlated.** e.g.

(i) Increase in the price of a commodity results in a decrease of its demand.

(ii) Increase in the intensity of hotness result in demand of coolers.

(iii) Increase in the weights of children accompanied by an increase in their heights.

Positive and Negative Correlation

If change in two variables are in same direction i.e increase (or decrease) in one variable is associated with the corresponding increase (or decrease) in other variable, then correlation is same to be positive or direct. e.g. Increase in price and increase in supply.

If variations or fluctuations in two variables are in opposite direction or in other words the increase in one variable is associated with the corresponding decrease in other, or vice versa, then correlation is said to be **negative** or **inverse**.

e.g. Increase in price associated with the decrease in demand.

Positive Correlation

Increase in two variables		Decrease in two variables	
Price (in ₹)	**Supply** (in units)	**Age of husband**	**Age of wife**
7	1375	70	65
8	2000	60	55
9	2500	50	45
10	3000	40	35
11	3500	30	25
12	4000	20	15

Negative Correlation

Increase in one and decrease in other		Decrease in one and increase in other	
Price (in ₹)	Demand (in units)	Marks in Economics	Marks in Statistics
7	1750	70	34
8	1650	60	45
9	1500	50	60
10	1350	40	69
11	1200	30	480
12	1100	20	90

Degree of Correlation

When the changes in the corresponding values of two variables are proportional, directly or inversely, the correlation between them is said to be **perfect.**

If the changes in one variable are not generally proportional to the changes in the other, the correlation between them is said to be **imperfect.**

Scatter Diagram

Scatter diagram is a graphical method or device to find correlation between two variables. In such graphs, independent variable or predicting variable is plotted on horizontal axis while dependent variable or predicted variable is plotted on vertical axis.

On the basis of the movements of the pairs of these variables we can easily find their correlation.

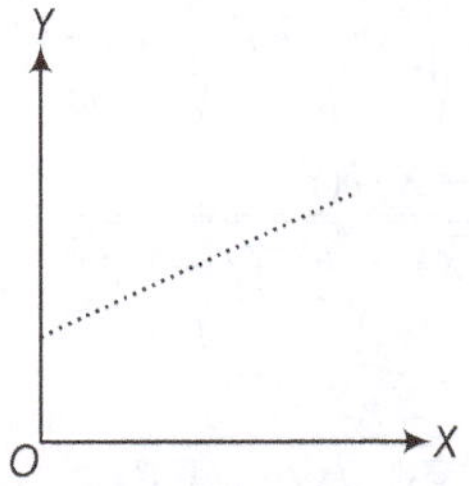
(i) Perfect positive correlation

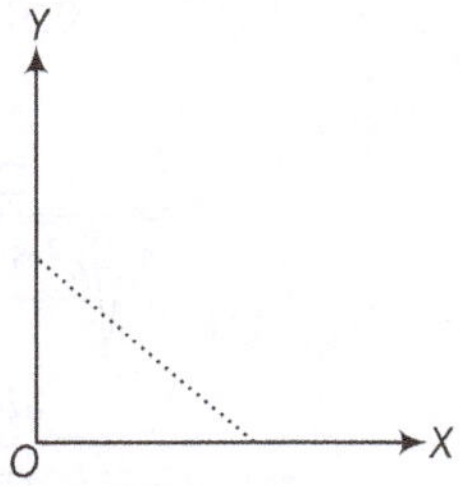
(ii) Perfect negative correlation

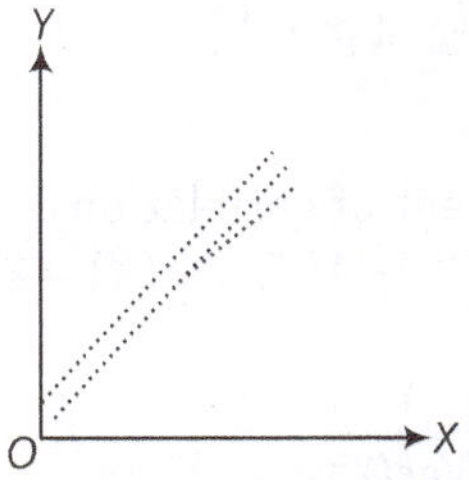
(iii) High degree positive correlation

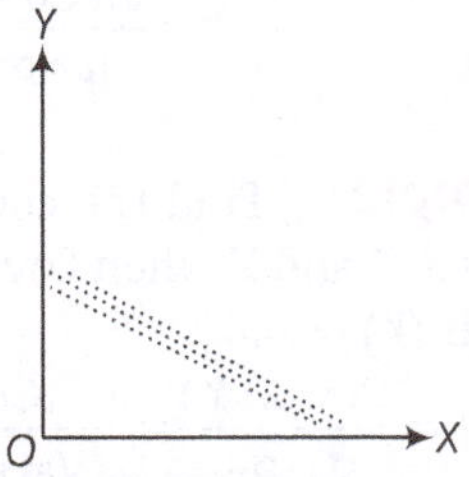
(iv) High degree negative correlation

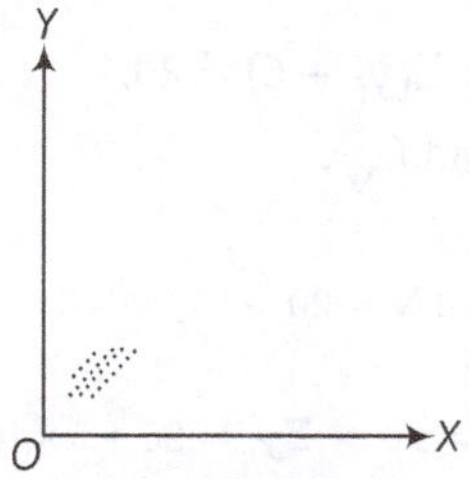
(v) Low degree positive correlation

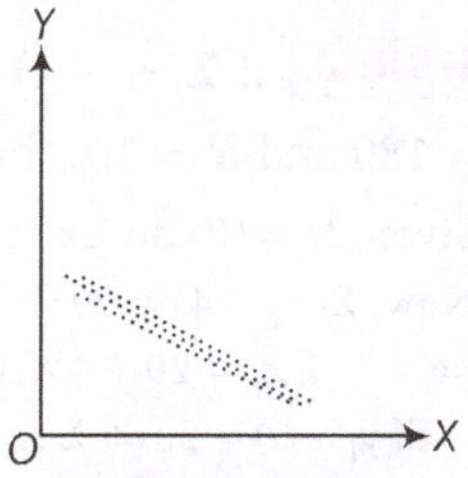
(vi) Low degree negative correlation

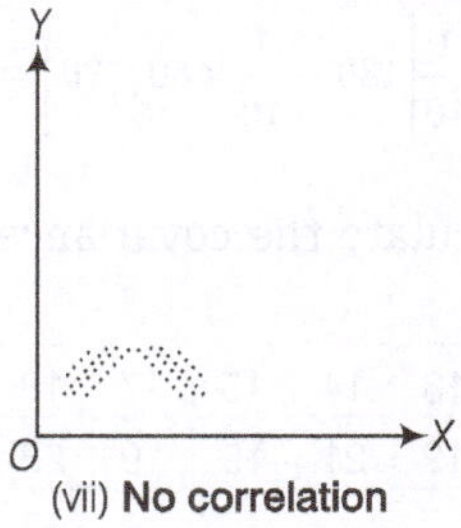
(vii) No correlation

The Line of Best Fit

A line that is drawn to pass as close as possible to all the dotted points on a scatter graph is called **the line of best fit.**

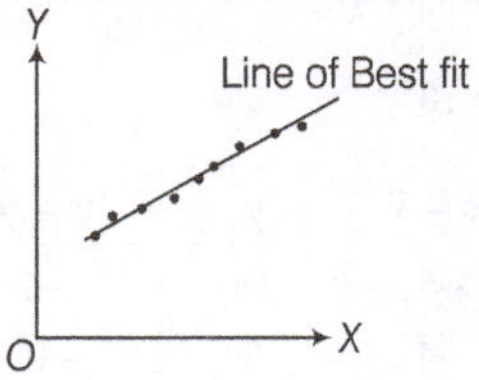

Covariance

The mean of the product of deviation scores $(x_i - \bar{x})$ and $(y_i - \bar{y})$ is called the **covariance** of x and y, respectively. It is denoted by Cov (x, y) or C_{xy}. It is given as Cov (x, y)

or $$C_{xy} = \frac{\Sigma(x-\bar{x})(y-\bar{y})}{N} = \frac{1}{N}\left[\Sigma xy - \frac{1}{N}\Sigma x\, \Sigma y\right]$$

If we take $dx = x_i - \bar{x}$ and $dy = y_i - \bar{y}$, then

$$\text{Cov}(x, y) \text{ or } C_{xy} = \frac{\Sigma dxdy}{N}.$$

Example 1 Find the covariance between x and y if $\Sigma x = 40$, $\Sigma y = -20$, $\Sigma xy = 110$ and $N = 20$.

Sol. Given, $\Sigma x = 40$, $\Sigma y = -20$, $\Sigma xy = 110$ and $N = 20$

$$\therefore \text{Cov}(x, y) = \frac{1}{N}\left[\Sigma xy - \frac{1}{N}\Sigma x\, \Sigma y\right]$$

$$= \frac{1}{20}\left[110 - \frac{1}{20}(40)(-20)\right]$$

$$= \frac{1}{20}[110 + 40] = \frac{150}{20} = 7.5$$

Example 2 If $\Sigma(x_i - 4) = 20$, $\Sigma(y_i - 5) = 20$, $\Sigma x_i y_i = 180$ and $N = 10$, then find C_{xy}.

Sol. Given, $N = 10$ and $\Sigma x_i y_i = 180$

Now, $\Sigma(x_i - 4) = 20 \Rightarrow \Sigma x_i - 4N = 20$

$\Rightarrow \quad \Sigma x_i = 20 + 4 \times 10 = 60$

$\Sigma(y_i - 5) = 20 \Rightarrow \Sigma y_i - 5N = 20 \Rightarrow \Sigma y_i = 20 + 5 \times 10 = 70$

$$\therefore \quad C_{xy} = \frac{1}{N}\left[\Sigma x_i y_i - \frac{1}{N}\Sigma x_i \Sigma y_i\right]$$

$$= \frac{1}{10}\left[180 - \frac{1}{10} \times 60 \times 70\right] = -24$$

Example 3 Calculate the covariance of the following data.

x	11	12	13	14	15	17	18	19	20	21
y	14	8	12	21	19	19	23	22	17	25

Sol. Here, $\bar{x} = \dfrac{11 + 12 + 13 + 14 + 15 + 17 + 18 + 19 + 20 + 21}{10}$

$= \dfrac{160}{10} = 16$

and $\bar{y} = \dfrac{14 + 8 + 12 + 21 + 19 + 19 + 23 + 22 + 17 + 25}{10}$

$= \dfrac{180}{10} = 18$

x	$x - \bar{x}$	y	$y - \bar{y}$	$(x - \bar{x})(y - \bar{y})$
11	–5	14	–4	20
12	–4	8	–10	40
13	–3	12	–6	18
14	–2	21	3	–6
15	–1	19	1	–1
17	1	19	1	1
18	2	23	5	10
19	3	22	4	12
20	4	17	–1	–4
21	5	25	7	35
Total				125

$$\text{Cov}(x, y) = \frac{1}{N}[\Sigma(x - \bar{x})(y - \bar{y})] = \frac{125}{10} = 12.5$$

Karl Pearson's Coefficient of Correlation

According to Karl Pearson, the quotient obtained when we divide the covariance by the product of the individual standard deviation is called the correlation coefficient. Correlation coefficient is denoted by $\rho(x, y)$ or r.

$$\therefore \quad r \text{ or } \rho(x, y) = \frac{\text{Cov}(x, y)}{\sqrt{\text{Var}(x)}\sqrt{\text{Var}(y)}} = \frac{\text{Cov}(x, y)}{\sigma_x \sigma_y}$$

Formula Used for Calculating Coefficient of Correlation by Karl Pearson

According to Karl Pearson,

1. If $x - \bar{x}$ and $y - \bar{y}$ are small fractionless numbers, then we use

$$r = \frac{\Sigma(x - \bar{x})(y - \bar{y})}{\sqrt{\Sigma(x - \bar{x})^2}\sqrt{\Sigma(y - \bar{y})^2}} \text{ or } \frac{\Sigma dxdy}{\sqrt{(\Sigma dx^2)(\Sigma dy^2)}}$$

where, $dx = x_i - \bar{x}$, $dy = y_i - \bar{y}$ are deviations taken from the actual mean.

2. If x and y are small numbers, we use

$$r = \frac{\Sigma xy - \frac{1}{N}\Sigma x \,\Sigma y}{\sqrt{\Sigma x^2 - \frac{1}{N}(\Sigma x)^2}\sqrt{\Sigma y^2 - \frac{1}{N}(\Sigma y)^2}}$$

3. If we assume means A and B and $u = X - A$ and $v = Y - B$. Then,

$$r = \frac{\Sigma uv - \frac{1}{N}\Sigma u \;\Sigma v}{\sqrt{\Sigma u^2 - \frac{1}{N}(\Sigma u)^2}\sqrt{\Sigma v^2 - \frac{1}{N}(\Sigma v)^2}}$$

Example 4 Show that coefficient of correlation is independent of choice of origin and scale.

Sol. Let $u = aX + b$ and $v = cY + d$.

$$\text{Then,} \quad \rho(u, v) = \frac{\text{Cov}(u, v)}{\sigma_u \sigma_v} = \frac{\Sigma(u - \bar{u})(v - \bar{v})}{\sqrt{\frac{\Sigma(u - \bar{u})^2}{N}}\sqrt{\frac{\Sigma(v - \bar{v})^2}{N}}}$$

$$= \frac{\Sigma[a(X - \bar{X})\, b(Y - \bar{Y})]}{\sqrt{\frac{a^2\,\Sigma(X - \bar{X})^2}{N}}\sqrt{\frac{b^2\Sigma(Y - \bar{Y})^2}{N}}}$$

$$= \frac{ab\Sigma[(X - \bar{X})(Y - \bar{Y})]}{|ab|\sqrt{\frac{\Sigma(X - \bar{X})^2}{N}}\sqrt{\frac{\Sigma(Y - \bar{Y})^2}{N}}}$$

$$= \frac{ab\,\text{Cov}(X, Y)}{|ab|\sigma_X \sigma_Y} = \pm\rho(X, Y)$$

Example 5 Find the coefficient of correlation between X and Y when $\text{Cov}(X, Y) = -16.5$, $\text{Var}(X) = 2.25$ and $\text{Var}(Y) = 144$.

Sol. $$r = \frac{\text{Cov}(X, Y)}{\sigma_X \sigma_Y} = \frac{\text{Cov}(X, Y)}{\sqrt{\text{Var}(X)}\sqrt{\text{Var}(Y)}}$$

$$= \frac{-16.5}{\sqrt{2.25}\sqrt{144}} = \frac{-16.5}{1.5 \times 12} = -0.9166$$

Example 6 Find out Karl Pearson's coefficient of correlation between X and Y variables.

X	10	12	15	18	25	35	45	50	55	65
Y	5	7	13	15	20	21	29	30	36	44

Sol.

X	Y	$X-\bar{X}=dX$	dX^2	$Y-\bar{Y}=dY$	dY^2	$dX\,dY$
10	5	–23	529	–17	289	391
12	7	–21	441	–15	225	315
15	13	–18	324	–9	81	162
18	15	–15	225	–7	49	105
25	20	–8	64	–2	4	16
35	21	2	4	–1	1	2
45	29	12	144	7	49	84
50	30	17	289	8	64	136
55	36	22	484	14	196	308
65	44	32	1024	22	484	704
$\Sigma X = 330$	$\Sigma Y = 220$		$\Sigma dX^2 = 3528$		$\Sigma dY^2 = 1442$	$\Sigma dXdY = 2223$

$$\bar{X} = \frac{\Sigma X}{N} = \frac{330}{10} = 33, \bar{Y} = \frac{\Sigma Y}{N} = \frac{220}{10} = 22$$

$$r = \frac{\Sigma dXdY}{\sqrt{\Sigma dX^2 \times \Sigma dY^2}} = \frac{2223}{\sqrt{3528 \times 1442}}$$

$$= \frac{2219}{\sqrt{5087376}} = \frac{2223}{2255.48} = 0.98$$

Example 7 Find Karl Pearson's coefficient of correlation between X and Y for the following data.

X	5	4	3	2	1
Y	4	2	10	8	6

Sol.

X	X^2	Y	Y^2	XY
5	25	4	16	20
4	16	2	4	8
3	9	10	100	30
2	4	8	64	16
1	1	6	36	6
$\Sigma X = 15$	$\Sigma X^2 = 55$	$\Sigma Y = 30$	$\Sigma Y^2 = 220$	$\Sigma XY = 80$

$$\therefore \quad r = \frac{\Sigma XY - \frac{1}{N}\Sigma X\, \Sigma Y}{\sqrt{\Sigma X^2 - \frac{(\Sigma X)^2}{N}}\sqrt{\Sigma Y^2 - \frac{(\Sigma Y)^2}{N}}}$$

$$= \frac{80 - \frac{1}{5}(15)(30)}{\sqrt{55 - \frac{1}{5}(15)^2}\sqrt{220 - \frac{1}{5}(30)^2}}$$

$$= \frac{-10}{\sqrt{10}\sqrt{40}} = \frac{-10}{20} = -0.5$$

Example 8 For the data given below, calculate Karl Pearson's coefficient of correlation.

Husband's Age	21	23	26	29	33	34	35	39	45	50
Wife's Age	17	19	22	25	30	31	31	35	40	45

Sol.

Husband's age (X)			Wife's age (Y)			
Age (yr)	Deviation from Assumed Mean A = 33	Deviation Squared	Age (yr)	Deviation from Assumed Mean B = 31	Deviation Squared	Product of Deviations
X	(X – A) = u	u^2	Y	(Y – B) = v	v^2	uv
21	–12	144	17	–14	196	168
23	–10	100	19	–12	144	120
26	–7	49	22	–9	81	63
29	–4	16	25	–6	36	24
33	0	0	30	–1	1	0
34	+1	1	31	0	0	0
35	+2	4	31	0	0	0
39	+6	36	35	+4	16	24
45	+12	144	40	+9	81	108
50	+17	289	45	+14	196	238
$\Sigma X = 335$	$\Sigma u = +5$	$\Sigma u^2 = 783$	$\Sigma Y = 295$	$\Sigma v = -15$	$\Sigma v^2 = 751$	$\Sigma uv = 745$

Here, assumed mean of X, $A = 33$
and assumed mean of Y, $B = 31$

$$\therefore \quad r = \frac{\Sigma uv - \frac{1}{N}\Sigma u\, \Sigma v}{\sqrt{\Sigma u^2 - \frac{1}{N}(\Sigma u)^2}\sqrt{\Sigma v^2 - \frac{1}{N}(\Sigma v)^2}}$$

$$= \frac{745 - \frac{1}{10}\times(5)(-15)}{\sqrt{783 - \frac{1}{10}(5)^2}\sqrt{751 - \frac{1}{10}(-15)^2}}$$

$$= \frac{745 + 7.5}{\sqrt{783 - 2.5}\sqrt{751 - 22.5}}$$

$$= \frac{752.5}{\sqrt{780.5}\sqrt{728.5}} = +0.998$$

Example 9 (i) Calculate the value of the correlation coefficient for the following data

(1, 13), (2, 23), (3, 33), (4, 43), (5, 53), (6, 63), (7, 73), (8, 83), (9, 93), (10, 103), (11, 10.5), (12, 11), (13, 11.5), (14, 12), (15, 12.5), (16, 13), (17, 13.5), (18, 14), (19, 14.5), (20, 15)

(ii) Draw the scatter diagram.

(iii) Comment on the result.

Sol. (i) Let the assumed mean for the first variate X be 10 and that for the second variate be 13.

Here, $n = 20$

X	Y	$u = X-10$	$v = Y-13$	u^2	v^2	uv
1	13	−9	0	81	0	0
2	23	−8	10	64	100	−80
3	33	−7	20	49	400	−140
4	43	−6	30	36	900	−180
5	53	−5	40	25	1600	−200
6	63	−4	50	16	2500	−200
7	73	−3	60	9	3600	−180
8	83	−2	70	4	4900	−140
9	93	−1	80	1	6400	−80
10	103	0	90	0	8100	0
11	10.5	1	−2.5	1	6.25	−2.5
12	11	2	−2	4	4.00	−4
13	11.5	3	−1.5	6	2.25	−4.5
14	12	4	−1	16	1.00	−4
15	12.5	5	−0.5	25	0.25	−2.5
16	13	6	0	36	0.00	0
17	13.5	7	0.5	49	0.25	3.5
18	14	8	1	64	1.00	8
19	14.5	9	1.5	81	2.25	13.5
20	15	10	2	100	4.0	20
Total		$\Sigma u = 10$	$\Sigma v = 447.5$	$\Sigma u^2 = 670$	$\Sigma v^2 = 28521.25$	$\Sigma vu = -1172.5$

$$\rho(X, Y) = \frac{\Sigma uv - \frac{1}{n}(\Sigma u)(\Sigma v)}{\sqrt{\left(\Sigma u^2 - \frac{(\Sigma u)^2}{n}\right)} \cdot \sqrt{\left(\Sigma v^2 - \frac{(\Sigma v)^2}{n}\right)}}$$

$$= \frac{-1172.5 - \frac{1}{20}(10)(447.5)}{\sqrt{\left(670 - \frac{(10)^2}{20}\right)}\sqrt{\left(28521.25 - \frac{(447.5)^2}{20}\right)}}$$

$$= -\frac{1396.25}{\sqrt{665}\sqrt{18508.438}}$$

$$= \frac{1396.25}{25.788 \times 136.046}$$

$$= \frac{1396.25}{3508.3542} = -0.39798$$

(ii) Plotting the points (1, 13), (2, 23), ..., (20, 15), we obtain the scatter diagram as shown in given figure.

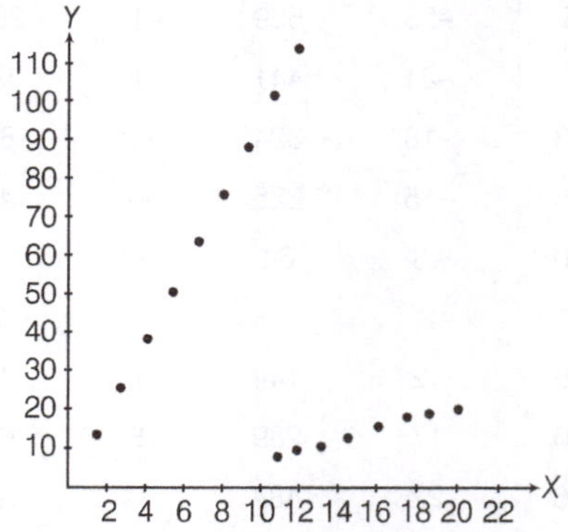

Clearly, the scatter diagram consists of two straight lines.

(iii) With the scatter diagram we would conclude that there is no relationship between the two variables.

Example 10 Coefficient of correlation between x and y for 50 observations is 0.3, $\bar{x} = 10$, $\bar{y} = 6$, $\sigma_x = 3$ and $\sigma_y = 2$. Later on, it was discovered that one pair of values (10,6) was inaccurate and hence weeded out. Calculate the coefficient of correlation between the remaning 49 pairs of values.

Sol. Given, $n = 50$, $\bar{x} = 10$ and $\bar{y} = 6$

$$\Rightarrow \quad \frac{\Sigma x}{n} = 10 \text{ and } \frac{\Sigma y}{n} = 6$$

$$\Rightarrow \quad \Sigma x = 10n \text{ and } \Sigma y = 6n$$

$$\Rightarrow \quad \Sigma x = 10 \times 50 = 500 \text{ and } \Sigma y = 6 \times 50 = 300$$

Using the formula $r = \frac{\text{Cov}(x, y)}{\sigma_x \sigma_y}$, we get

$$0.3 = \frac{\frac{1}{n}\Sigma xy - \frac{\Sigma x}{n} \cdot \frac{\Sigma y}{n}}{3 \times 2} \quad [\because \sigma_x = 3, \sigma_y = 2]$$

$$\Rightarrow \quad 1.8 = \frac{1}{50}\Sigma xy - 10 \times 6$$

$$\Rightarrow \quad 61.8 = \frac{1}{50}\Sigma xy$$

$$\Rightarrow \quad \Sigma xy = 50 \times 61.8 = 3090$$

$$\sigma_x = 3$$

$$\Rightarrow \quad \frac{1}{n}\Sigma x^2 - (\bar{x})^2 = 3^2$$

$$\Rightarrow \quad \frac{1}{50}\Sigma x^2 - 10^2 = 9$$

$$\Rightarrow \quad \Sigma x^2 = 109 \times 50 = 5450; \sigma_y = 2$$

$$\Rightarrow \quad \frac{1}{n}\Sigma y^2 - (\bar{y})^2 = 2^2$$

$$\Rightarrow \quad \frac{1}{50}\Sigma y^2 - 6^2 = 4$$

$$\Rightarrow \quad \Sigma y^2 = 40 \times 50$$

$$= 2000$$

When the inaccurate observation (10,6) is weeded out, remaining observations $n = 49$.

New $\Sigma x = 500 - 10 = 490$, $\Sigma y = 300 - 6 = 294$

$\Sigma x^2 = 5450 - 10^2 = 5350$, $\Sigma y^2 = 2000 - 6^2 = 1964$

and $\Sigma xy = 3090 - 10 \times 6 = 3030.$

Using the formula,

$$r = \frac{\Sigma xy - \frac{1}{n}\Sigma x\, \Sigma y}{\sqrt{\Sigma x^2 - \frac{1}{n}(\Sigma x)^2}\sqrt{\Sigma y^2 - \frac{1}{n}(\Sigma y)^2}}, \text{ we get}$$

$$\text{New } r = \frac{3030 - \frac{1}{49} \times 490 \times 294}{\sqrt{5350 - \frac{1}{49} \times (490)^2}\sqrt{1964 - \frac{1}{49} \times (294)^2}}$$

$$= \frac{3030 - 2940}{\sqrt{5350 - 4900}\sqrt{1964 - 1764}}$$

$$= \frac{90}{\sqrt{450}\sqrt{200}} = \frac{90}{\sqrt{90000}}$$

$$= \frac{90}{300} = \frac{3}{10} = 0.3$$

Interpretation Related to Correlation Coefficient

(i) The coefficient of correlation always lies between −1 and 1, i.e. $-1 \le r \le 1$.

(ii) When $r = 1$, then there is perfect positive correlation between the variables and when $r = -1$, there is perfect negative correlation between the variables.

(iii) The correlation is positive if sign of r is (+) and negative if sign of r is (–).

(iv) When r is zero, then there is no correlation.

(v) When $0.7 < r < 0.999$, then there is a high degree of correlation.

(vi) When $0.5 < r < 0.699$, then there is a modulate degree of correlation.

(vii) When $r < 0.5$, then there is a low degree of correlation.

Chapter Practice

Multiple Choice Type Questions

1 Mark

1. If the values of two variables move in the opposite direction, ...
   (a) The correlation is said to be linear
   (b) The correlation is said to be non linear
   (c) The correlation is said to be positive
   (d) The correlation is said to be negative
2. Correlation coefficient is denoted by ......
   (a) Z (b) P (c) r (d) σ
3. Find the covariance between x and y if $\Sigma x = 30$, $\Sigma y = -35$, $\Sigma xy = 55$ and $N = 30$
   (a) 1 (b) 2.5 (c) 3 (d) 5
4. If the values of two variables move in the same direction ......
   (a) The correlation is said to be non linear
   (b) The correlation is said to be linear
   (c) The correlation is said to be negtive
   (d) The correlation is said to be positive
5. The value of the coefficient of correlation r lies between
   (a) 0 and 1 (b) −1 and 0
   (c) − 1 and + 1 (d) − 0.5 and + 0.5

Assertion-Reason Type Questions

1 Mark

Directions (Q. Nos. 6-8) *In the questions given below are two statements labelled as Assertion (A) and Reason (R). In the context of the two statements, which one of the following is correct?*

(a) Both A and R are correct; R is the correct explanation of A
(b) Both A and R are correct; R is not the correct explanation of A
(c) A is correct; R is incorrect
(d) R is correct; A is incorrect

6. **Assertion (A)** The value of correlation coefficient is in the range of −1 to +1.
   Reason (R) Correlation between two variable does not help in predicting the value of *a* variable even if we know the value of another variable.
7. **Assertion (A)** The value of reliability coefficient of a test varies from 0 to +1 but cannot be negative.
   Reason (R) The correlation of a set of scores with itself or a set of parallel scores can not be negative.
8. **Assertion (A)** When correlation coefficient (r) is between 0.75 and 1, there is a high degree of positive correlation, when it is between − 0.75 and −1, there is a high degree of negative correlation.
   Reason (R) The value of correlation lies between 1 and −1.

Very Short Answer Type Questions

2 Marks

9. Find Cov (x, y) between x and y when $\Sigma x_i = 50$, $\Sigma y_i = 30$, $\Sigma x_i y_i = -115$ and $N = 10$.
10. Calculate covariance for the following data.

X	1	2	3	4	6	7	8	9
Y	16	9	4	1	1	4	9	16

11. Find the coefficient of correlation between X and Y when Cov $(X, Y) = -2.17$, Var$(X) = 6.25$ and Var$(Y) = 20.25$
12. The coefficient of correlation between two variables X and Y is 0.64. Their covariance is 16. The variance of X is 9. Find the standard deviation of Y.
13. Given $r = 0.5$, $\Sigma xy = 120$, $\sigma_y = 8$ and $\Sigma x^2 = 90$, then find the number of items.

Short Answer Type Questions

(4 Marks)

14. Find the correlation coefficient between x and y when $\Sigma x = 125$, $\Sigma y = 100$, $\Sigma x^2 = 650$, $\Sigma y^2 = 464$, $\Sigma xy = 508$ and $n = 25$.

15. Calculate the coefficient of correlation from the following data.

X	12	13	14	15	16	17	18
Y	14	17	18	19	20	24	28

16. Compute Karl Pearson's coefficient of correlation between sales and and expenditures of a firm for given six months.

Sales (in ₹ lakh)	18	20	27	20	21	29
Expenditure (in ₹ lakh)	23	27	28	28	29	30

17. The weights of brothers and sisters (in kg) are given below

Weight of brother	65	66	67	67	68	69	70	72
Weight of sister	67	68	65	68	72	72	69	71

Find the coefficient of correlation.

18. Calculate Karl Pearson's coefficient of correlation between x and y for the following data.

(1, 6), (2, 5), (3, 7), (4, 9), (5, 8), (6, 10), (7, 1), (8, 13), (9, 12).

19. Show that the coefficient of correlation ρ between two variables x and y is given by

$$\rho = \frac{\sigma_x^2 + \sigma_y^2 - \sigma_{x-y}^2}{2\sigma_x \sigma_y},$$ where σ_x^2, σ_y^2 and σ_{x-y}^2 are the variances of x, y and $(x - y)$ respectively.

Directions (Q. Nos. 20-21) *Calculate the coefficient of correlation for following data using assumed mean method.*

20.

X	16	18	21	20	22	26	27	15
Y	22	25	24	26	25	30	33	14

21.

X	1	2	4	5	7	8	10
Y	2	6	8	10	14	16	20

Long Answer Type Questions

(6 Marks)

22. Find the correlation coefficient between the heights of husbands and wives based on the following data.

Couple	Height of husband	Height of wife
1	76	71
2	75	70
3	75	70
4	72	67
5	72	71
6	71	65
7	71	65
8	70	67
9	68	64
10	68	65
11	68	65
12	68	66
13	67	63
14	67	65
15	62	61

Case-Based Type Question

(6 Marks)

23. The following table shows the percentage of cats killed while falling from various storeys from skyscrapers in New York.

Fallen from number of storeys	1	2	3	4	5	6	7	8	9
Percentage killed	3	9	12	15	18	15	12	9	3

Based on given information solve these questions.

(i) Calculate the correlation coefficient.

(ii) Draw the scatter diagram.

Hints & Answers

1. (d) 2. (c) 3. (c) 4. (d) 5. (c)
6. (b) 7. (a) 8. (b)
9. Solve as Example 1. **Ans.** – 26.5
10. Solve as Example 3. **Ans.** 0
11. Solve as Example 5. **Ans.** – 2.444
12. $\because r = \frac{(X, Y)}{\sigma_X \cdot \sigma_Y} \Rightarrow 0.64 = \frac{16}{\sqrt{9} \times \sigma_Y} \Rightarrow \sigma_Y = \frac{16}{3 \times 0.64} = 8.33$
13. $\because r = \frac{\Sigma xy}{n\sigma_x \sigma_y} \Rightarrow r^2 = \frac{(\Sigma xy)^2}{n^2 \sigma_x^2 \sigma_y^2}$

$$\Rightarrow \quad 0.25 = \frac{(120)^2}{n^2 \times \left(\frac{90}{n}\right) \times 64} \quad \left[\because \sigma_x^2 = \frac{\Sigma x^2}{N} = \frac{90}{n}\right]$$

$$\Rightarrow \quad n = 10$$

14. Use the formula,

$$r = \frac{\Sigma xy - \frac{1}{n}\Sigma x \Sigma y}{\sqrt{\Sigma x^2 - \frac{1}{n}(\Sigma x)^2}\sqrt{\Sigma y^2 - \frac{1}{n}(\Sigma y)^2}}$$ **Ans.** 0.2

15. Solve as Example 6. **Ans.** 0.961
16. Solve as Example 8. **Ans.** 0.68
17. Solve as Example 8. **Ans.** 0.603
18. 0.95
19. $\sigma_{x-y}^2 = \frac{1}{n}\Sigma[(x - y) - (\bar{x} - \bar{y})]^2$
20. Solve as Example 8. **Ans.** 0.89
21. Solve as Example 8. **Ans.** 1
22. 0.89
23. (i) 0
(ii)

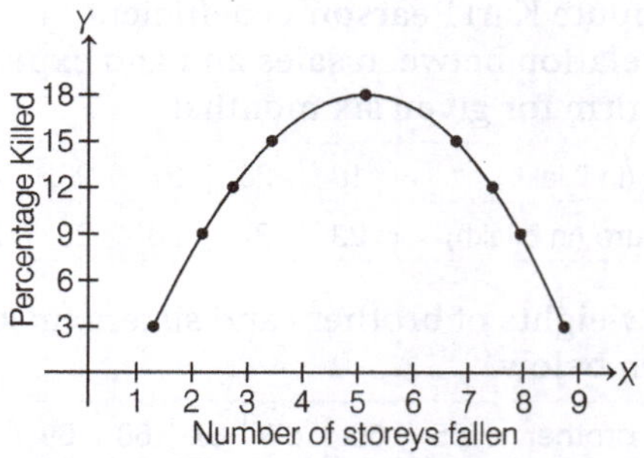

CHAPTER

21

Index Numbers and Moving Averages

- Index Numbers
- Moving Averages
- Variation
- Calculation of Moving Average

Index number are meant to study changes in the effects of factors which cannot be measured directly. According to Bawley, 'Index number are used to measure the changes in some quantity which we cannot observe directly'. e.g. Changes in business activity in a country are not capable of direct measurement, but it is possible to study relative changes in business activity by studying the variations in the values of some such factors which affect business activity, and which are capable and direct measurement.

Index Numbers

Index number is a specialised average designed to measure the change in the level of an activity or item, either with respect to time or geographic location or some other characteristic.

Wholesale Price Index (WPI) and **Consumer Price Index** (CPI) are widely used terms. Consumer price index measures the changes in price level of a market of consumer goods and services purchased by households.

It is based on prices of five sets and items—food, housing (rent), household goods, fuel and light, and miscellaneous. Each item is based on study of a numbers of items. e.g. Food includes rice, wheat, dal, milk and so on.

Characteristic of Index Numbers

The main characteristic of index numbers are as follows

(i) They are specialised averages.

(ii) They are expressed as ratio or percentage.

(iii) They measure the change in the level of a phenomenon.

(iv) They measure the effect of change over a period of time.

Uses of Index Numbers

Index numbers are important tools of business and economic activity. The main uses of index numbers are as follow

(i) It is used to measure the changes in the wholesale price level of a country over a period of time.

(ii) They help in framing suitable policies and take decisions relating to wages, prices, consumption etc.

(iii) It is used to measure the changes in the cost of living of a certain section and the people living in a certain locality.

(iv) They help in forecasting future economic activity.

Types of Index Numbers

There are three types of index numbers which are as follow

(i) **Price Index** or **Price Relative** measure changes in price over a specified period of time. It is basically the ratio of the price of a certain number of commodities at the present year as against base year. e.g. consumer price index, Whole sale price index.

(ii) **Quantity Index** measure changes in volumes of commodities like goods produced or goods consumed e.g. Index of Industrial production, Index of scooter sold etc.

(iii) **Value Index** measure changes in the monetary value of imports exports production or consumption of commodities.

Problems in Construction of Index Numbers

(i) **Purpose or Object** The purpose for which an index number is constructed must be clearly defined. No index number can serve for all purposes.

(ii) **Selection of Base Year** (or Based Period) The period against which relative change is to be measured should be chosen carefully. It should not be too distant in the past. It should be normal period-free of abnormalities like wars, floods, epidemics etc.

(iii) **Selecting of Items** As every item cannot be included, only the relavent and representative items should be chosen. Also, items should be standardised, so that after a time lapse they can be easily identified.

(iv) **Choice of an Average** Since index numbers are specialised averages, a decision has to be made as to which particular average (arithmetic mean, median, mode, geometric mean as harmonic mean) is to be used while constructing the index. Though geometric mean gives best results, usually arithmetic mean is used to save calculation work.

(v) **Quotations** Once the items and their numbers has been decided, the locations (markets, shops) should be selected carefully, so that representative sample of price quotations can be obtained.

(vi) **Weightage** Since different items are consumed in different quantities, suitable weights may be used to reflect the relative importance of different items.

Methods of Construction of Index Numbers

The various method of constructing index numbers can be arranged in two heading

(i) Unweighted indices

(ii) Weighted indices

Different methods are depicted in the following diagram

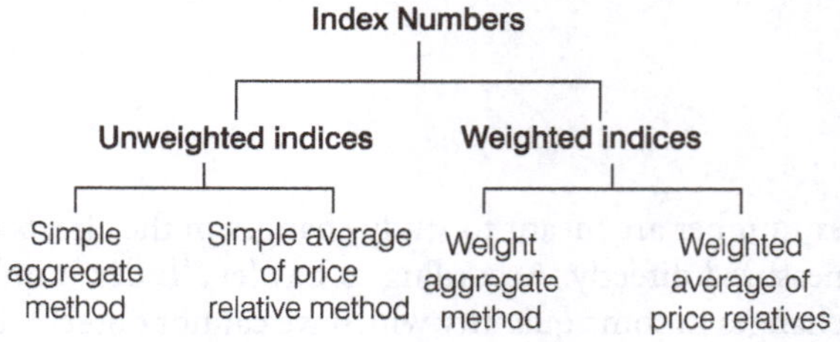

1. Simple Aggregate Method

In this method, the total of current year prices for various commodities under consideration is divided by the corresponding total of base year price and multiplying it by 100, i.e.

$$\text{Simple aggregate price index } (P_{01}) = \frac{\Sigma P_1}{\Sigma P_0} \times 100$$

where, P_{01} = Current price index number,

P_0 = The total of commodity price in the base year

and P_1 = The total of commodity price in the current year

2. Simple Average of Price Relative Method

It is the ratio of a certain commodity's price in a given period to its price in an earlier period (fixed) called base period/year represented in percentage,

i.e. $$\text{Price relative} = \frac{\text{Current price}}{\text{Base price}} \times 100$$

or $$\text{Price relative} = \frac{P_1}{P_0} \times 100$$

In this method the price relative for all commodities is calculated and then their average is taken to calculate the index number, i.e. $$P_{01} = \frac{\Sigma\left(\frac{P_1}{P_0} \times 100\right)}{N}$$

[for AM as average mean]

where, P_{01} is the price index, N is number of items, P_0 is the price of the base year and P_1 is the price of corresponding commodity in the present year.

3. Weighted Aggregate Method

In this method, if the base prices and current prices of a number of items is given as together and the weights/quantities of each are available, then we called it weighted aggregate to find index numbers

$$P_{01} = \frac{\Sigma P_1 w}{\Sigma P_0 w} \times 100$$

where, P_1 = Current year price

w = Weight of each items

and P_0 = Base year price

4. Weighted Average of Price Relative

In this method the price relative for the current year are calculated on the basis of the base year price and these price relatives are multiplied by the respective weights of items. These products are added up and divided by the sum of weights

$$P_{01} = \frac{\Sigma\left(\frac{P_1}{P_0} \times 100\right) \times w}{\Sigma w} \quad \text{or} \quad P_{01} = \frac{\Sigma I w}{\Sigma w}$$

where, $I = \frac{P_1}{P_0} \times 100.$

Cost of living index is a theoretical price index that measures relative cost of living over time on regions. It is an index that measures difference in the price of goods and services.

Example 1 Find the index number for the following data by simple aggregate method.

Commodity	Base price (₹)	Current price (₹)
Rice	30	35
Wheat	22	25
Fish	54	64
Potato	20	25
Coal	15	18

Sol. We construct the following table

Commodity	Base price (₹) (P_0)	Current price (₹) (P_1)
Rice	30	35
Wheat	22	25
Fish	54	64
Potato	20	25
Coal	15	18
Total	$\Sigma P_0 = 141$	$\Sigma P_1 = 167$

∴ Required index number by simple aggregate method,

$$P_{01} = \frac{\Sigma P_1}{\Sigma P_0} \times 100 = \frac{167}{141} \times 100 = 118.44$$

Thus, we see that there is an average increase of about 18.44% in the price of commodities.

Example 2 The price of six different commodities for years 2009 and year 2011 are as follows

Commodities	A	B	C	D	E	F
Price in 2009 (in ₹)	35	80	25	30	80	x
Price in 2011 (in ₹)	50	y	45	70	120	105

The index number for the year 2011 taking 2009 as the base year for the above data was calculated to be 125. Find the values of x and y, if the total price in 2009 is ₹ 360. **[ISC 2014]**

Sol. According to the question,

Commodities	Price in 2009 (P_0)	Price in 2011 (P_1)
A	35	50
B	80	y
C	25	45
D	30	70
E	80	120
F	x	105
Total	$250 + x$	$390 + y$

Given that, the total price in 2009 is ₹ 360.

$\Rightarrow \quad 250 + x = 360 \Rightarrow x = 360 - 250 = 110$

Also, index number = 125

$$\Rightarrow \quad \frac{y + 390}{360} \times 100 = 125 \left[\because \text{price index } (P_{01}) = \frac{\Sigma P_1}{\Sigma P_0} \times 100\right]$$

$$\Rightarrow \quad \frac{y + 390}{36} \times 10 = 125$$

$\Rightarrow \quad 10y + 3900 = 125 \times 36$

$\Rightarrow \quad 10y = 4500 - 3900$

$\Rightarrow \quad 10y = 600 \Rightarrow y = 60$

Hence, $x = 110$ and $y = 60$.

Example 3 A small industrial concern used three raw materials A, B and C in its manufacturing process. The prices of the materials was as shown below

Commodity	Price (in ₹) in the year 1995	Price (in ₹) in the year 2005
A	4	5
B	60	57
C	36	42

Using 1995 as the base year, calculate a simple aggregate price index for 2005. **[ISC 2008]**

Sol. Given table as shown below

Commodity	Price in 1995 (₹ per unit) P_0	Price in 2005 (₹ per unit) P_1
A	4	5
B	60	57
C	36	42
Total	$\Sigma P_0 = 100$	$\Sigma P_1 = 104$

We know that,

Simple aggregate price index

$$(P_{01}) = \frac{\Sigma P_1}{\Sigma P_0} \times 100 = \frac{104}{100} \times 100 = 104$$

Example 4 Taking 2012 as base year, the index numbers for the prices of a commodity in 2013 and 2014 are 120 and 125, respectively. Calculate the index numbers for 2012 and 2014, if 2013 is taken as the base year.

Sol. Let p_0, p_1 and p_2 be the prices of the commodity in 2012, 2013 and 2014, respectively.

According to the given condition,

$$\frac{P_1}{P_0} \times 100 = 120 \quad \text{...(i)}$$

and $$\frac{P_2}{P_0} \times 100 = 125 \quad \text{...(ii)}$$

We need to compute index number of 2012 taking 2013 as base year, i.e. $\frac{P_0}{P_1} \times 100$ and index number for 2014 taking 2013 as base year, i.e. $\frac{P_2}{P_1} \times 100$.

From Eq. (i), we get $\frac{P_0}{P_1} = \frac{100}{120}$

$$\therefore \quad \frac{P_0}{P_1} \times 100 = \frac{100}{120} \times 100 = 83.33$$

On dividing Eq. (ii) by Eq. (i), we get

$$\frac{\frac{P_2}{P_0} \times 100}{\frac{P_1}{P_0} \times 100} = \frac{125}{120} \Rightarrow \frac{P_2}{P_1} = \frac{25}{24}$$

$$\therefore \quad \frac{P_2}{P_1} \times 100 = \frac{25}{24} \times 100 = 104.17$$

Hence, the index number of 2012 taking 2013 as base year is 83.33 and the index number for 2014 taking 2013 as base year = 104.17.

Example 5 From the following data, compute price index by using simple average of price relatives.

Commodity and unit	Prince in 1989 (in ₹)	Price in 1990 (in ₹)
Butter (kg)	20.00	21.00
Cheese (kg)	15.00	14.00
Milk (lt)	3.00	3.00
Bread (1)	2.80	2.80
Eggs (doz)	6.00	8.00
Ghee (1 tin)	250.00	260.00

[ISC 2004]

Sol. First, we tabulate the given data in the following form

Commodity and unit	Prince in 1989 (in ₹) (P_0)	Prince in 1990 (in ₹) (P_1)	Price relatives $\frac{P_1}{P_0} \times 100$
Butter (kg)	20.00	21.00	$\frac{21}{20} \times 100 = 105$
Cheese (kg)	15.00	14.00	$\frac{14}{15} \times 100 = 93.33$
Milk (lt)	3.00	3.00	$\frac{3}{3} \times 100 = 100$
Bread (1)	2.80	2.80	$\frac{2.80}{2.80} \times 100 = 100$
Eggs (doz)	6.00	8.00	$\frac{8}{6} \times 100 = 133.33$
Ghee (1 tin)	250.00	260.00	$\frac{260}{250} \times 100 = 104$
			$\Sigma\left(\frac{P_1}{P_0} \times 100\right) = 635.66$

$$\therefore \quad P_0 = \frac{\Sigma\left(\frac{P_1}{P_0} \times 100\right)}{N} = \frac{635.66}{6} = 105.94$$

Hence, the price index of 1990 taking 1989 as the base year in 105.94.

Example 6 Taking 1975 as the base year, with an index number 100, calculate an index number for 1979, based on weighted average weighted aggregate method from the table given below.

Commodity	A	B	C	D
Weight	30	15	25	30
Price per unit in 1975	20	10	5	40
Price per unit in 1979	24	20	30	40

Sol. To make a table for product of price and weight

Commodity	Price in 1975 (₹ per unit) P_0	Price in 1979 (₹ per unit) P_1	Weight (in kg) (W)	P_0w	P_1w
A	20	24	30	600	720
B	10	20	15	150	300
C	5	30	25	125	750
D	40	40	30	1200	1200
Total				$\Sigma P_0w = 2075$	$\Sigma P_1w = 2970$

We know that, price index number $= \dfrac{\Sigma P_1 w}{\Sigma P_0 w} \times 100$

$[\because \Sigma P_0 w = 2075, \Sigma P_1 w = 2970]$

$$= \frac{2970}{2075} \times 100 = 1.431325 \times 100$$

$$= 143.1325 \approx 143$$

Example 7 The price quotations of four different commodities for 2001 and 2009 are as given below. Calculate the index number for 2009 with 2001 as the base year by using weighted average of price relative method. **[ISC 2011]**

Commodity	Weight	Price (in ₹)	
		2009	2001
A	10	9.00	4.00
B	49	4.40	5.00
C	36	9.00	6.00
D	4	3.60	2.00

Sol. To make a table for product of price relative and weight.

Commodity	Price in 2001 (₹ per unit) P_0	Price in 2009 (₹ per unit) P_1	Price relative $x = \frac{P_1}{P_0} \times 100$	Weight (w)	wx
A	4	9	$\frac{9}{4} \times 100 = 225$	10	2250
B	5	4.40	$\frac{4.40}{5} \times 100 = 88$	49	4312
C	6	9	$\frac{9}{6} \times 100 = 150$	36	5400
D	2	3.60	$\frac{3.60}{2} \times 100 = 180$	4	720
Total				$\Sigma w = 99$	$\Sigma wx = 12682$

We know that, index number $= \dfrac{\Sigma wx}{\Sigma w} = \dfrac{12682}{99} = 128.10$

Moving Averages

A moving average is commonly used with time series data to smooth out short term fluctuation and highlight longer term trends or cycle.

A time series is a sequence of observations which are ordered in time (space). If observations are made on some phenomenon throughout time it is most sensible to display the data in the order in which they arose, particularly, since successive observations will properly be dependent.

Long term trend, called secular trend is calculated by finding regression line, i.e. $y - \bar{y} = b_{yx}(x - \bar{x})$.

Variation

The extent or degree to which something varies, like a variation of ten pound in weights.

Types of Variations

Variation can be divided into following three types

1. **Seasonal Variation** This type of variation depends on weather and other natural **forces** or social conditions. Like sale of ice-creams increase in summer season.
2. **Cyclical Variation** Many industrial or financial sectors face ups and down (booms or slumps) over regular period of time. It is very short period variation and they do not affect the trend such periodic variations are known as cyclical variation.
3. **Irregular Variation**
   (i) Irregular/random variation constitute one of four components of a time series.
   (ii) Irregular variation do not follow a particular model and are not predictable.

Purpose of Moving Averages

The following points are main purpose of moving average

(i) It helps in technical traders like tract the trend of financial assets by smoothing out the day-to-day price fluctuations.

(ii) By identifying trend, moving averages allow traders, to make these trends works in their favour and increases the number of wining trades. It is helps in trading strategies.

Period of Cycles

The time interval covering the number of years is called the period of the cycles.

Note Cycles always found in series.

Calculation of Moving Average

Procedure for calculating the moving average in following two cases

|CASE I|

Period of moving average is an odd number i.e. 3, 5, 7,....

For 3 yearly moving average,

Year	Value	3 yearly moving average
1st	x_1	
2nd	x_2	$\frac{x_1 + x_2 + x_3}{3} = m_1$
3rd	x_3	$\frac{x_2 + x_3 + x_4}{3} = m_2$
4th	x_4	$\frac{x_3 + x_4 + x_5}{3} = m_3$
5th	x_5	$\frac{x_4 + x_5 + x_6}{3} = m_4$
6th	x_6	$\frac{x_5 + x_6 + x_7}{3} = m_5$
7th	x_7	

Note $m_1, m_2, \ldots, m_5$ are moving average points (mean point).

|CASE II|

Period of moving average is an even number, i.e. 4, 6, 8,...

For 4 yearly moving average,

Year	Value	4 yearly moving average	4 yearly moving average centered
1st	x_1		
2nd	x_2	$\frac{x_1 + x_2 + x_3 + x_4}{4} = m_1$	
3rd	x_3	$\frac{x_2 + x_3 + x_4 + x_5}{4} = m_2$	$\frac{m_1 + m_2}{2} = A$
4th	x_4	$\frac{x_3 + x_4 + x_5 + x_6}{4} = m_3$	$\frac{m_2 + m_3}{2} = B$
5th	x_5	$\frac{x_4 + x_5 + x_6 + x_7}{4} = m_4$	$\frac{m_3 + m_4}{2} = C$
6th	x_6		
7th	x_7		

Note A, B and C are centered points m_1, m_2 and m_3 are moving average points.

Example 8 Calculate the 5 yearly moving average of the number of students in a college from the following data and plot them on a graph paper. **[ISC 2012]**

Year	1981	1982	1983	1984	1985	1986	1987	1988	1989	1990
Students	332	317	357	392	402	405	510	427	405	438

Sol. Let the moving average for five years be m.

$$\therefore\ m_1 = \frac{332 + 317 + 357 + 392 + 402}{5} = \frac{1800}{5} = 360 \text{ (say } A)$$

$$m_2 = \frac{317 + 357 + 392 + 402 + 405}{5} = \frac{1873}{5} = 374.6 \text{ (say } B)$$

$$m_3 = \frac{357 + 392 + 402 + 405 + 510}{5} = \frac{2066}{5} = 413.2 \text{ (say } D)$$

$$m_4 = \frac{392 + 402 + 405 + 510 + 427}{5} = \frac{2136}{5} = 427.2 \text{ (say } E)$$

$$m_5 = \frac{402 + 405 + 510 + 427 + 405}{5} = \frac{2149}{5} = 429.8 \text{ (say } F)$$

$$m_6 = \frac{405 + 510 + 427 + 405 + 438}{5} = \frac{2185}{5} = 437 \text{ (say } G)$$

On the basis of above data, we can draw the following moving graph

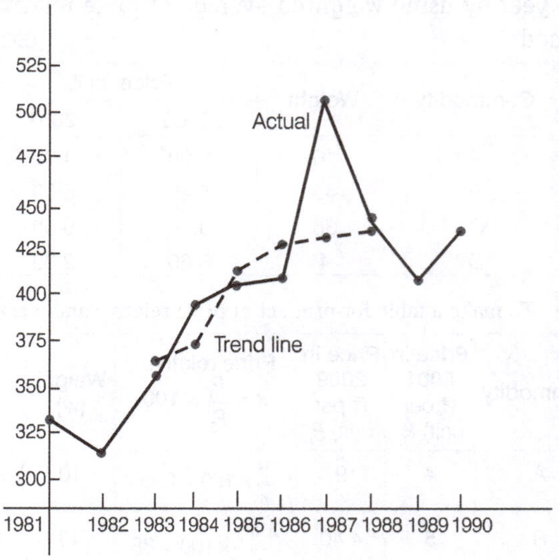

Example 9 The profits of a paper bag manufacturing company (in ₹ lakh) during each month of a year are

Months	Jan	Feb	Mar	Apr	May	Jun	Jul	Aug	Sep	Oct	Nov	Dec
Profit	1.2	0.8	1.4	1.6	2.0	2.4	3.6	4.8	3.4	1.8	0.8	1.2

Plot the given data on a graph sheet. Calculate the four monthly moving averages and plot these on the same graph sheet. **[ISC 2013]**

Sol. Let the moving average for four days be m, then

$$m_1 = \frac{1.2 + 0.8 + 1.4 + 1.6}{4} = \frac{5}{4} = 1.25,$$

$$m_2 = \frac{0.8 + 1.4 + 1.6 + 2.0}{4} = \frac{5.8}{4} = 1.45$$

$$m_3 = \frac{1.4 + 1.6 + 2.0 + 2.4}{4} = \frac{7.4}{4} = 1.85,$$

$$m_4 = \frac{1.6 + 2.0 + 2.4 + 3.6}{4} = \frac{9.6}{4} = 2.4,$$

$$m_5 = \frac{2.0 + 2.4 + 3.6 + 4.8}{4} = \frac{12.8}{4} = 3.2,$$

$$m_6 = \frac{2.4 + 3.6 + 4.8 + 3.4}{4} = \frac{14.2}{4} = 3.55,$$

$$m_7 = \frac{3.6 + 4.8 + 3.4 + 1.8}{4} = \frac{13.6}{4} = 3.4,$$

$$m_8 = \frac{4.8 + 3.4 + 1.8 + 0.8}{4} = \frac{10.8}{4} = 2.7$$

and $$m_9 = \frac{3.4 + 1.8 + 0.8 + 1.2}{4} = \frac{7.2}{4} = 1.8$$

On the basis of above data, we can draw the following moving graph

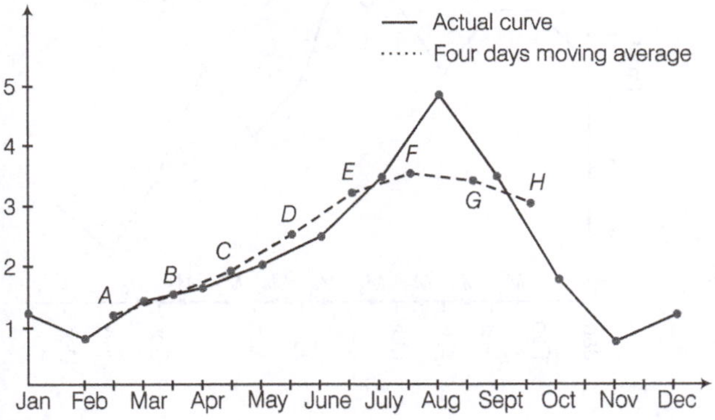

Example 10 The number of road accidents in the city due to rash driving, over a period of 3 yr, is given in the following table.

Year	Jan-Mar	April-June	July-Sept	Oct-Dec
2010	70	60	45	72
2011	79	56	46	84
2012	90	64	45	82

Calculate four quarterly moving average and illustrate them with original figures on one graph using the same for both. **[ISC 2014]**

Sol. Let the moving average for four years be m.

Then, $$m_1 = \frac{70 + 60 + 45 + 72}{4} = \frac{247}{4} = 61.75$$

$$m_2 = \frac{60 + 45 + 72 + 79}{4} = \frac{256}{4} = 64$$

$$m_3 = \frac{45 + 72 + 79 + 56}{4} = \frac{252}{4} = 63$$

$$m_4 = \frac{72 + 79 + 56 + 46}{4} = \frac{253}{4} = 63.25$$

$$m_5 = \frac{79 + 56 + 46 + 84}{4} = \frac{265}{4} = 66.25$$

$$m_6 = \frac{56 + 46 + 84 + 90}{4} = \frac{276}{4} = 69$$

$$m_7 = \frac{46 + 84 + 90 + 64}{4} = \frac{284}{4} = 71$$

$$m_8 = \frac{84 + 90 + 64 + 45}{4} = \frac{283}{4} = 70.75$$

and $$m_9 = \frac{90 + 64 + 45 + 82}{4} = \frac{281}{4} = 70.25$$

Now, the central moving average are

$$\frac{m_1 + m_2}{2} = \frac{61.75 + 64}{2} = 62.875 \text{ (say } A)$$

$$\frac{m_2 + m_3}{2} = \frac{64 + 63}{2} = 63.500 \text{ (say } B)$$

$$\frac{m_3 + m_4}{2} = \frac{63 + 63.25}{2} = 63.125 \text{ (say } C)$$

$$\frac{m_4 + m_5}{2} = \frac{63.25 + 66.25}{2} = 64.750 \text{ (say } D)$$

$$\frac{m_5 + m_6}{2} = \frac{66.25 + 69}{2} = 67.625 \text{ (say } E)$$

$$\frac{m_6 + m_7}{2} = \frac{69 + 71}{2} = 70.000 \text{ (say } F)$$

$$\frac{m_7 + m_8}{2} = \frac{71 + 70.75}{2} = 70.875 \text{ (say } G)$$

and $$\frac{m_8 + m_9}{2} = \frac{70.75 + 70.25}{2} = 70.50 \text{ (say } H)$$

On the basis of above data, we can draw the following moving average

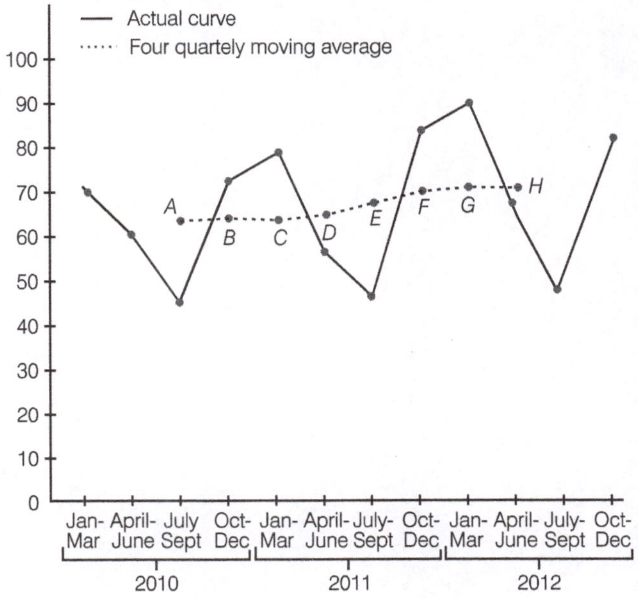

Example 11 The profit of a soft drink firm (in ₹ thousand) during each month of the year is given below

Months	Jan	Feb	Mar	Apr	May	Jun	Jul	Aug	Sep	Oct	Nov	Dec
Profit (in ₹ thousands)	3.6	4.3	4.3	3.4	4.4	5.4	3.4	2.4	3.4	1.8	0.8	1.2

Calculate the four monthly moving averages and plot these and the original data on a graph sheet. **[ISC 2011]**

Sol. Let the moving average for four months be m.

Then, $m_1 = \dfrac{3.6 + 4.3 + 4.3 + 3.4}{4} = \dfrac{15.6}{4} = 3.9$

$m_2 = \dfrac{4.3 + 4.3 + 3.4 + 4.4}{4} = \dfrac{16.4}{4} = 4.1$

$m_3 = \dfrac{4.3 + 3.4 + 4.4 + 5.4}{4} = \dfrac{17.5}{4} = 4.375$

$m_4 = \dfrac{3.4 + 4.4 + 5.4 + 3.4}{4} = \dfrac{16.6}{4} = 4.15$

$m_5 = \dfrac{4.4 + 5.4 + 3.4 + 2.4}{4} = \dfrac{15.6}{4} = 3.9$

$m_6 = \dfrac{5.4 + 3.4 + 2.4 + 3.4}{4} = \dfrac{14.6}{4} = 3.65$

$m_7 = \dfrac{3.4 + 2.4 + 3.4 + 1.8}{4} = \dfrac{11}{4} = 2.75$

$m_8 = \dfrac{2.4 + 3.4 + 1.8 + 0.8}{4} = \dfrac{8.4}{4} = 2.1$

and $m_9 = \dfrac{3.4 + 1.8 + .8 + 1.2}{4} = \dfrac{7.2}{4} = 1.8$

Now, the central moving average are

$\dfrac{m_1 + m_2}{2} = \dfrac{3.9 + 4.1}{2} = \dfrac{8}{2} = 4$ (say A)

$\dfrac{m_2 + m_3}{2} = \dfrac{4.1 + 4.375}{2} = \dfrac{8.475}{2} = 4.237$ (say B)

$\dfrac{m_3 + m_4}{2} = \dfrac{4.375 + 4.15}{2} = \dfrac{8.525}{2} = 4.262$ (say C)

$\dfrac{m_4 + m_5}{2} = \dfrac{4.15 + 3.9}{2} = \dfrac{8.05}{2} = 4.025$ (say D)

$\dfrac{m_5 + m_6}{2} = \dfrac{3.9 + 3.65}{2} = \dfrac{7.55}{2} = 3.775$ (say E)

$\dfrac{m_6 + m_7}{2} = \dfrac{3.65 + 2.75}{2} = \dfrac{6.4}{2} = 3.2$ (say F)

$\dfrac{m_7 + m_8}{2} = \dfrac{2.75 + 2.1}{2} = \dfrac{4.85}{2} = 2.425$ (say G)

and $\dfrac{m_8 + m_9}{2} = \dfrac{2.1 + 1.8}{2} = \dfrac{3.9}{2} = 1.95$ (say H)

On the basis of data, we can draw the moving graph

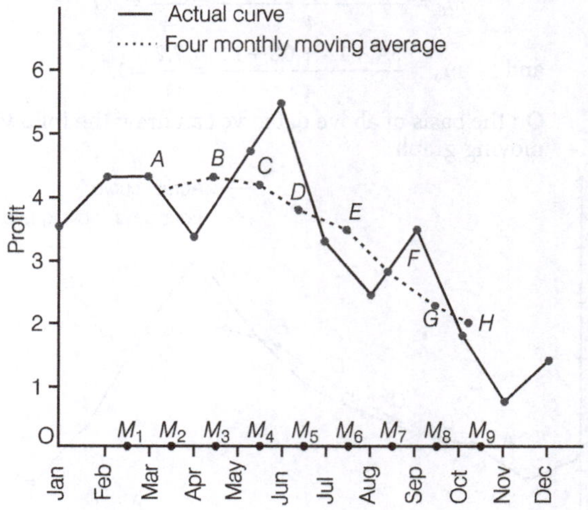

Chapter Practice

Multiple Choice Type Questions

1 Mark

1. Which of the following are the major characteristics of index numbers?
   (a) It is expressed in percentages
   (b) It measures the net or relative changes in variables
   (c) It measures changes over a period of time
   (d) All of the above

2. Index number used to measure the change in the number of goods is known as ....
   (a) Quantity index number
   (b) Simple 1 No.
   (c) Aggregate 1. No.
   (d) Appropriate

3. Index number is a type of
   (a) Dispersion (b) Correlation
   (c) Averages (d) None of these

4. Which of the following statement(s) is/are correct about average prices if the price index is 110?
   (a) The price have increased by 10 percent
   (b) The price have increased by 110 percent
   (c) The price have decreased by 10 percent
   (d) None of the above

Assertion-Reason Type Questions

1 Mark

Directions (Q. Nos. 5-7) *In the questions given below are two statements labelled as Assertion (A) and Reason (R). In the context of the two statements, which one of the following is correct?*

(a) Both A and R are correct; R is the correct explanation of A
(b) Both A and R are correct; R is not the correct explanation of A
(c) A is correct; R is incorrect
(d) R is correct; A is incorrect

5. **Assertion (A)** The index numbers measure the effect of change over a period of time.

   Reason (R) The index number used to measure the change in the cost in the cost of living of a certain section and the people living in a certain locality.

6. **Assertion (A)** Price relative is the ratio of a certain commodity's price in a given period to its price in an earlier period (fixed) called base period represented in percentage.

   Reason (R) Price relative for all commodities is given by

   $$\text{Price relative} = \frac{\text{Current Price}}{\text{Base Price}} \times 100$$

7. **Assertion (A)** The time series forecasting method that gives equal weightage to each of the most recent observations is moving average method.

   Reason (R) Moving averages allow traders, to make these trends work in their favour and increases the number of winning trades.

Short Answer Type Questions

4 Marks

8. The index number of the following data, for the year 2008, taking 2004 as base year was found to be 116. The simple aggregate method was used for calculation. Find the numerical values of x and y, if the sum of the prices in the year 2008 is ₹ 203.

Commodity	Price (in ₹) in the year 2004	Price (in ₹) in the year 2008
A	20	25
B	10	30
C	30	15
D	25	45
E	x	35
F	50	y

9. Calculate the index number for 2015 taking 2014 as the base year by simple average of price relatives method

Commodity	A	B	C	D	E
Price in 2014 (₹)	100	80	160	220	40
Price in 2015 (₹)	140	120	180	240	40

10. Construct the consumer price index number for 1990, taking 1989 as the base year and using simple average of price relative method for the following data.

Commodities	Price in 1989	Price in 1990
Butter	20	21
Cheese	16	12
Milk	3	3
Egg	2.80	2.80

11. The price index for the following data for the year 2011 taking 2001 as the base year was 127. The simple average of price relatives methods was used. Find the value of x.

Items	A	B	C	D	E	F
Price (₹ per unit) in year 2001	80	70	50	20	18	25
Price (₹ per unit) in year 2011	100	87.50	61	22	x	32.50

12. Calculate the index number for the year 2006 with 1996 as the base year by the weighted average of price relatives method from the following data.

Commodity	A	B	C	D	E
Weight	40	25	5	20	10
Price (₹ per unit) year 1996	32.00	80.00	1.00	10.24	4.00
Price (₹ per unit) year 2006	40.00	120.00	1.00	15.36	3.00

13. Find the consumer price index number for the year 2010 using year 2000 as the base year by using method of weighted aggregates.

Commodity	A	B	C	D	E
Year 2000 price (in ₹ per unit)	16	40	0.50	5.12	2
Year 2010 price (in ₹ per unit)	20	60	0.50	6.25	1.50
Weights	40	25	5	20	10

14. The given table shows the prices per unit in 1980 and 1984 with weights of the commodities A, B, C and D

Commodity	Weights	Price per unit in 1980	Price per unit in 1984
A	20	25	30
B	25	20	30
C	15	50	70
D	40	5	10

Taking 1980 as base year with an index number 100, calculate the index number of 1984 based on weighted average of price relatives.

15. The quotations for four different commodities for the years 2000 and 2005 are given below. Calculate the index number for 2005 with 2000 as the base year by using the weighted average of price relatives methods.

Commodity	Weight	Price (in ₹) in the year 2000	Price (in ₹) in the year 2005
A	5	2.00	4.50
B	7	2.50	3.20
C	6	3.00	4.50
D	2	1.00	1.80

16. Calculate the index number for 2005 with 2000 as the base year by the weighted aggregate method.

Commodity	Price (in ₹) in the year 2000	Price (in ₹) in the year 2005	Weight
A	140	180	10
B	400	550	7
C	100	250	6
D	125	150	8
E	200	300	4

17. Taking 2005 as the base year and with index number 100, the index number in 2012 using weighted average prince relative is 182 for the following data

Commodity	A	B	C	D
Price per unit in 2005	20	10	5	40
Price per unit in 2012	24	20	30	40
Weight	40	x	10	y

If the sum of weights is 100, find the values of x and y.

18. Calculate the index number for the year 1979 with 1970 as base from the following data using weighted average of price relatives.

Commodity	Weights	Price (in ₹)	
		1970	1979
A	22	2.50	6.20
B	48	3.30	4.40
C	17	6.25	12.75
D	13	0.65	0.90

19. An index of retail prices is the mean of the five other price index numbers which are weighted as follows

A	*B*	*C*	*D*	*E*
Food	Rent	Household goods	Fuel and lights	Miscellane ous
348	88	106	65	393

The original index of retail prices are established at 100. If the following percentage increases in the various indices have occurred since that time, find the index of retail prices now.

$A = 55\%; B = 180\%; C = 60\%; D = 45\%; E = 90\%$

Long Answer Type Questions

6 Marks

20. Consider the following data

Dates in the month of April	12	13	14	15	16	17	18	19	20	21	22	23	24	25
Number of units sold	2	5	0	12	13	25	45	13	31	18	11	2	3	1

Calculate three days moving average and display these and original figures on same graph.

21. The table below gives details of the electricity generated in million kilowatt hours in each quarter for the years

Year	Quarter			
	1st	2nd	3rd	4th
2002	8	7	6	9
2003	10	7	7	10
2004	11	7	8	10

Calculate the four quarterly moving averages and show these moving averages on a graph.

22. The average number (in lakh) of working days lost in strikes during each year of the period 1981-90 was

1981	1982	1983	1984	1985	1986	1987	1988	1989	1990
1.5	1.8	1.9	2.2	2.6	3.7	2.2	6.4	3.6	5.4

Calculate the three yearly moving averages and draw the moving averages graph. **[ISC 2005]**

23. Coded monthly sales figures of a particular brand of TV for 18 months commencing January 2005 are as follows

Year	Jan	Feb	Mar	Apr	May	Jun	Jul	Aug	Sep	Oct	Nov	Dec
2005	18	16	23	27	28	19	31	29	35	27	28	24
2006	24	28	29	30	29	22						

Calculate six monthly moving averages and display these and the original figures on the same graph using the same axis for both.

24. The production of a soft drink company in thousand of litres during each month of a year is as

Jan	Feb	Mar	Apr	May	Jun	Jul	Aug	Sep	Oct	Nov	Dec
1.2	0.8	1.4	1.6	1.8	2.4	2.6	3.0	3.6	2.8	1.9	3.4

Calculate the five monthly moving average and show these moving averages on a graph.

Case-Based Type Question

6 Marks

25. The table shows the average prices (in ₹) of coffee, sugar and milk in 2022 and 2023 and weights used to calculate the cost of making a cup of coffee.

	Cost in 2022 (Per kg)	Cost in 2010 (Per kg)	Weights
Sugar	3	7	3
Milk	3	3.50	4
Coffee	90	120	2

Answer the following questions, based on the above informations.

(i) Calculate the index number for the cost of a cup of coffee in 2023 using weighted price relations.

(ii) Calculate the index number for the cost of a cup of coffee in 2023 using weighted aggregates taking the index number for 2022 be 100 in each case.

Hints & Answers

1. (d) 2. (a) 3. (c) 4. (a) 5. (b)
6. (a) 7. (b)
8. Solve as Example 2. **Ans.** $x = 40$, $y = 53$
9. Solve as Example 5. **Ans.** 122.32
10. Solve as Example 5. **Ans.** 95
11. Solve as Example 5. **Ans.** 27
12. Solve as Example 5. **Ans.** 130
13. Solve as Example 6. **Ans.** 138.4
14. Solve as Example 7. **Ans.** 162.50
15. Solve as Example 7. **Ans.** 164.05
16. Solve as Example 6. **Ans.** 144.7
17. Solve as Example 7. **Ans.** $x = 24$, $y = 26$
18. Solve as Example 6. **Ans.** 171.24
19. Solve as Example 7. **Ans.** 179.635
20. Solve as Example 8. **Ans.** 3-day moving average are 2.33, 5.66, 8.33, 16.66, 27.66, 27. 66, 29.66, 20.66, 20, 10.33, 5.33, 2.

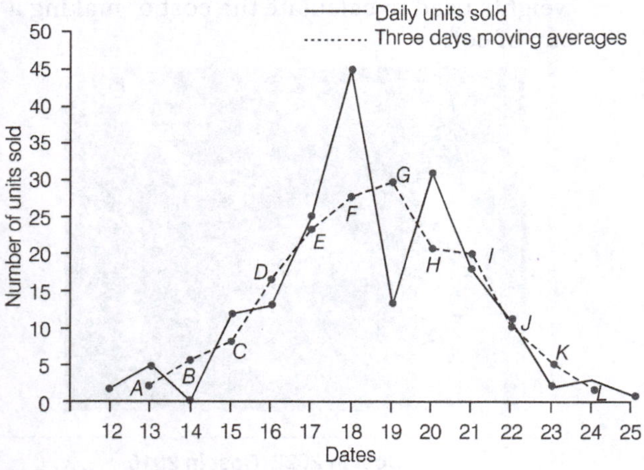

21. Solve as Example 9.
Ans. Four-quarterly moving average centred are 7.75, 8, 8.125, 8.375, 8.625, 8.75, 8.875, 9.

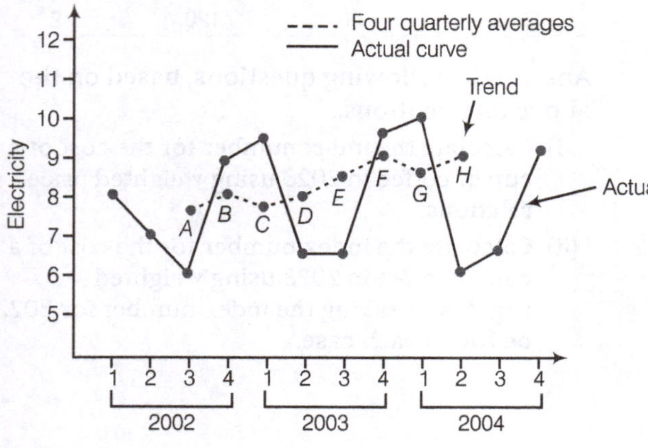

22. Solve as Example 8.
Ans. 3-yearly moving average are 1.7, 2, 2.2, 2.8, 4.1, 4.1, 5.1.

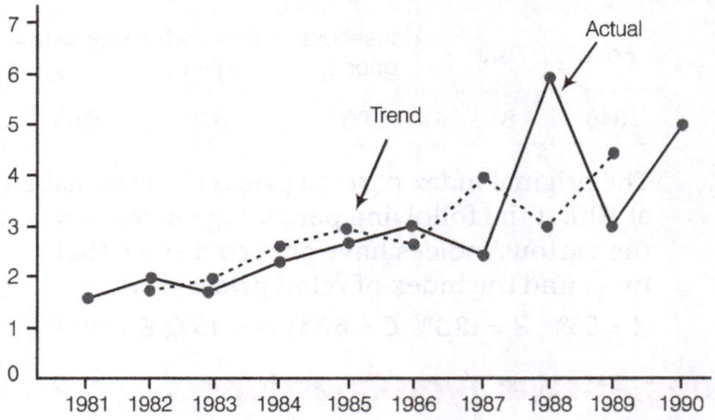

23. Solve as Example 11.
Ans. 6-monthly of centred moving average are 22.91, 25.1, 27.2, 28.2, 28.2, 28.6, 28.415, 27.745, 27.16, 26.91, 27.245, 27.165.

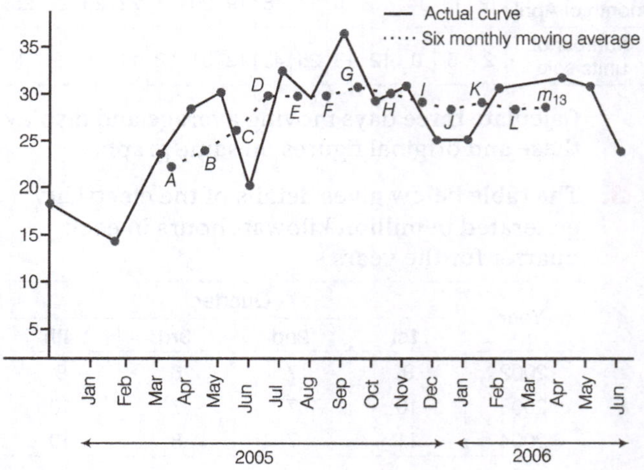

24. Solve as Example 8.
Ans. Mar →1.36, Apr 1.6, May 1.96, June 2.28, July 2.68, Aug 2.88, Sept 2.78, Oct 2.94.

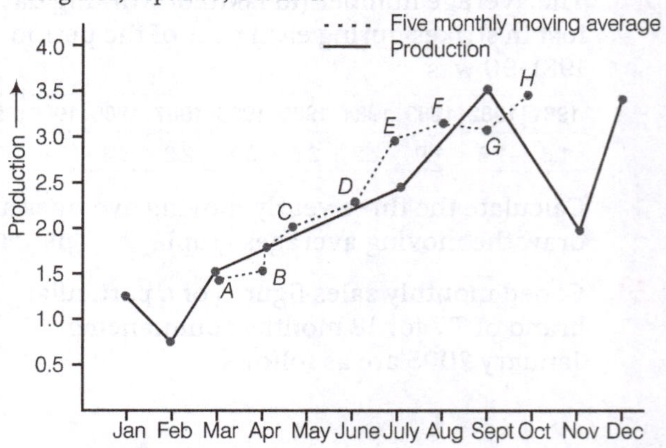

25. (i) 159.3 (ii) 136.8

SAMPLE QUESTION PAPER 1

A Highly Simulated Sample Question Paper for ISC Class XI

MATHEMATICS (Unsolved)

GENERAL INSTRUCTIONS

1. The Question Paper is divided into three sections and has 22 questions in all.
2. **Section A** is compulsory and has fourteen questions.
3. You are required to attempt all questions either from **Section B** or **Section C**.
4. **Section B** and **Section C** has four questions each.
5. Internal choices has been provided in two questions of 2 marks, two questions of 4 marks and two questions of 6 marks in Section A.
6. Internal choices has been provided in one question of 2 marks and one question of 4 marks each in Section and Section C.
7. While attempting Multiple Choice Questions in Section A, B and C, you are required to write only ONE option as the answer.
8. The intended marks for questions or parts of questions are given in brackets [ ].

Time : 3 Hours *Max. Marks : 80*

Section A (65 Marks)

1. In sub-parts (i) to (xi) choose the correct option and in sub-parts (xii) to (xv), answer the questions as instructed.

(i) The number of elements in the power set $P(S)$ of the set $S = \{2, 4, 6, 8\}$ is • ***Analysis* [1]**

(a) 4 (b) 16

(c) 64 (d) 8

(ii) How many two-digit positive integers are multiple of 3? • ***Evaluation* [1]**

(a) 30 (b) 35

(c) 27 (d) 29

(iii) **Statement 1** If $x^2 + 1 = 0$ then the value of x are i and -i.

Statement 2 The value of $(-\sqrt{-1})^{4x+3}$ is i.

(a) Statement 1 is true and Statement 2 is false.

(b) Statement 2 is true and Statement 1 is false.

(c) Both the Statements are true.

(d) Both the Statements are false. • ***Analysis* [1]**

(iv) If two sets A and B are having 99 elements in common, then the number of elements common to each of the sets $A \times B$ and $B \times A$ are • ***Application* [1]**

(a) 2^{99} (b) 99^2

(c) 100 (d) 18

(v) **Assertion (A)** : If A is the arithmetic mean of the numbers a and b then a, A, b, are in A.P.

Reason (R) The arithmetic means of the numbers a and b is $\frac{a+b}{2}$.

(a) Both Assertion and Reason are true and Reason is the correct explanation for Assertion.
(b) Both Assertion and Reason are true but Reason is not the correct explanation for Assertion.
(c) Assertion is true and Reason is false.
(d) Assertion is false and Reason is true. • *Analysis* [1]

(vi) In an experiment, a solution of hydrochloric acid is to be kept between 30°C and 35°C. The range of temperature in degree Fahrenheit, if conversion formula is given by $C = \frac{5}{9}(F-32)$, where C and F represent temperature in degree Celsius and degree Fahrenheit respectively, is between • *Application* [1]

(a) 86°F and 95°F (b) 54°F and 63°F (c) 54°F and 95° F (d) 63°F and 86°F

(vii) A line passes through (x_1, y_1) and (h, k). If slope of the line is m, then • *Analysis* [1]

(a) $y_1 - k = m(h - x_1)$ (b) $k - y_1 = m(h - x)$
(c) $h - x_1 = m(y_1 - k)$ (d) $h - x_1 = m(k - y_1)$

(viii) The angle between the X-axis and the line joining the points $(4, -2)$ and $(5, -3)$ is • *Application* [1]

(a) 45° (b) 135° (c) 90° (d) 180°

(ix) **Statement 1** If $y = \left\{\frac{1-\tan x}{1+\tan x}\right\}$ and $\frac{dy}{dx} = \frac{k}{1+\sin 2x}$ then the value of k is -2. • *Understanding & Evaluation* [1]

Statement 2 If $y = x^2 \cos x$ then the value of $\frac{dy}{dx}$ is $2x\cos x + x^2 \sin x$.

(a) Statement 1 is true and Statement 2 is false.
(b) Statement 2 is true and Statement 1 is false.
(c) Both the Statements are true.
(d) Both the statements are false. [1]

(x) Find the value of $\cos\theta$, if $\sin\theta = -\frac{3}{5}$ and $\pi < \theta < \frac{3\pi}{2}$ • *Application* [1]

(a) $-\frac{5}{3}$ (b) $-\frac{4}{5}$ (c) $\frac{3}{4}$ (d) $-\frac{3}{4}$

(xi) **Assertion (A)** If $A = \{9, 10, 11, 12, 13\}$ and $f: A \to N$ be defined by $f(n) =$ the highest prime factor of n, then the range of f is {3, 5, 11, 12}.

Reason (R) If $R: A \to B$ then the set of second elements of all the ordered pairs present in R is called range of the relation.

(a) Both Assertion and Reason are true and Reason is the correct explanation for Assertion.
(b) Both Assertion and Reason are true but Reason is not the correct explanation for Assertion.
(c) Assertion is true and Reason is false.
(d) Assertion is false and Reason is true. • *Analysis & Evaluation* [1]

(xii) Insert the three numbers between 3 and 19 such that the resulting sequence is an AP. • *Application* [1]

(xiii) Find the number of terms in the expansion of the expression $(z+3a)^{13} - (z-3a)^{13}$ • *Understanding* [1]

(xiv) From a group of 3 boys and 3 girls, we select 2 children. What would be the sample space for this experiment? • *Evaluation* [1]

(xv) Find the number of terms in the expansions of the expression $(x^2 + 1 - 2x)^8$. • *Evaluation* [1]

2. If $\frac{\sin(x+y)}{\sin(x-y)} = \frac{a+b}{a-b}$, then show that $\frac{\tan x}{\tan y} = \frac{a}{b}$. • *Evaluation* [2]

3. Prove that $\cot x \cot 2x - \cot 2x \cot 3x - \cot 3x \cot x = 1$. • *Evaluation* [2]

4. (i) Write all the possible subsets of set $A = \{1, 2, 3\}$. • *Analysis* [2]

Or

(ii) Let $f = \{(1, 1), (2, 3), (0, -1), (-1, -3)\}$ be a function from Z to Z defined by $f(x) = ax + b$, for some integers a, b. Determine (a, b). • *Understanding* [2]

5. An urn contains 7 white, 5 black and 3 red balls. Two balls are drown at random. Find the probability that • *Understanding & Analysis* [2]

(i) both the balls are red.

(ii) one ball is red, other is black.

6. (i) Find the real value of x and y, if $(1+i)(x+iy) = 2 - 5i$. • *Analysis* [2]

Or

(ii) For what value of k will the equation $x^2 - kx - 21 = 0$ and $x^2 - 3kx + 35 = 0$ have one common root. • *Evaluation* [2]

7. Draw the graph of function $y = |x - 2| + |x - 3|$. • *Evaluation* [4]

8. (i) Find the sum of n term of the series $\frac{1}{1.2} + \frac{1}{2.3} + \frac{1}{3.4} + \ldots + \frac{1}{n.(n+1)}$ • *Understanding* [4]

Or

(ii) Find the sum of the following to n terms $\frac{1}{1.2.3} + \frac{1}{2.3.4} + \frac{1}{3.4.5} + \ldots$ • *Understanding* [4]

9. (i) Find the angle between the lines $\sqrt{3}x + y = 1$ and $x + \sqrt{3}y = 1$ • *Analysis* [4]

Or

(ii) Find the values of k for which the line $(k-3)x - (4-k^2)y + k^2 - 7k + 6 = 0$

(a) parallel to the x- axis [1]

(b) passing through the origin [2]

(c) parallel to the y - axis • *Evaluation* [1]

10. Find the number of ways in which 5 boys and 5 girls be seated in a row, so that

(i) no two girls sit together. [2]

(ii) boys and girls sit alternatively. • *Application & Evaluation* [2]

11. Prove that $\cot 4x(\sin 5x + \sin 3x) = \cot x(\sin 5x - \sin 3x)$ • *Analysis* [6]

Or

If $\cos(\alpha - \beta) + \cos(\beta - \gamma) + \cos(\gamma - \alpha) = -\frac{3}{2}$, then prove that

$$\cos\alpha + \cos\beta + \cos\gamma = \sin\alpha + \sin\beta + \sin\gamma = 0$$ • *Evaluation* [6]

12. (i) If x is real, then prove that the value of the expression $\frac{(x-1)(x+3)}{(x-2)(x+4)}$ cannot lie between $\frac{4}{9}$ and 1.

• *Analysis* [6]

Or

(ii) A man wants to go on a country tour on a cycle to promote eco-friendly atmosphere. He wants to tour on a cycle and for that he wants to decorate his cycle with three green piece of cloth. He has cloth of length 91 cm. He wants second length to be 3 cm larger than the shortest and the third length to be twice as long as the shortest. What are the possible length of the shortest cloth, if the third piece is to be atleast 5 cm larger than the second? • *Application & Analysis* [6]

13. The side of a given square is 10 cm. The mid-points of its sides are joined to form a new square. Again, the mid-point of the sides of this new square are joined to form another square. This process is continued indefinitely. • *Understanding & Evaluation*

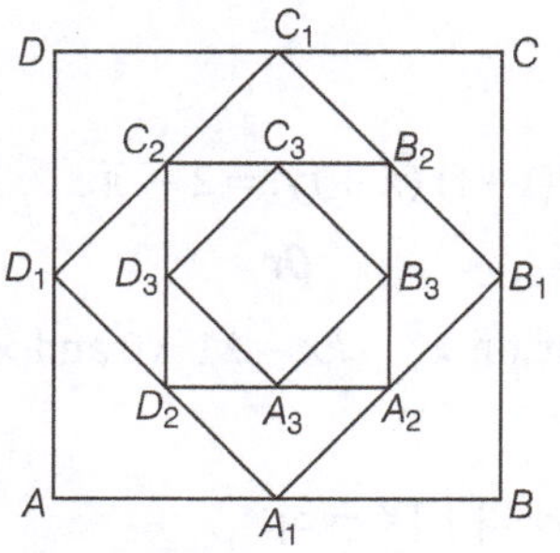

Based on above information. Answer the following.

(i) Find the side of the 5th square. [1]

(ii) Find the sum of all sides of the square. [1]

(iii) Find the sum of areas of squares. [2]

(iv) Find the sum of perimeter of all squares. [2]

14. Find the mean and variance of first n natural numbers. • *Application* [6]

Section B (15 Marks)

15. In sub-parts (i) and (ii) choose the correct option and in sub-parts (iii) to (v), answer the questions as instructed.

(i) **Assertion (A)** The distance of the point (3,4,5) from the point (0,0,0) is $\sqrt{50}$.

Reason (R) The distance between two points $A(x_1, y_1)$ and $B(x_2, y_2)$ is given by

$AB = \sqrt{(x_2 - x_1)^2 + (y_2 - y_1)^2}$

(a) Both Assertion and Reason are true and Reason is the correct explanation for Assertion.
(b) Both Assertion and Reason are true but Reason is not the correct explanation for Assertion.
(c) Assertion is true and Reason is false.
(d) Assertion is false and Reason is true. • *Application & Evaluation* [1]

(ii) The length of the foot of perpendicular drawn from the point $P(3, 4, 5)$ on Y-axis is • *Analysis* [1]

(a) 10 units (b) $\sqrt{34}$ units (c) $\sqrt{113}$ units (d) $5\sqrt{2}$ units

(iii) Find the equation of the ellipse, if the ends of major axis are $(\pm 2, 0)$ and ends of minor axis are $(0, \pm 7)$.

• *Application* [1]

(iv) Write the negation of the following statements.

(a) I will not go to school **[1]**

(b) Every natural number is an integer • *Application* **[1]**

16. (i) Write the converse and inverse of the given conditional statement. If you are born in India, then you are a citizen of India. • *Evaluation* **[2]**

Or

(ii) Prove that $\sim (p \Leftrightarrow \sim q) = (p \Leftrightarrow q)$. • *Evaluation* **[2]**

17. Transform the equation of the line $3x + 2y - 7 = 0$ to

(i) slope- intercept form and also find the slope and y- intercept. **[1]**

(ii) intercept form and also find the intercepts on the coordinate axes. **[1]**

(iii) normal form and also find the inclination of the perpendicular segment from the origin on the line with the axis and its length. • *Understanding & Evaluation* **[2]**

18. (i) Salim made a flower - bed in his garden surprisingly which is in the shape of a parabola whose equation is $y^2 = 8x$, the flower - bed is shown as in below figure

Then answer the following questions which are based on above figure.

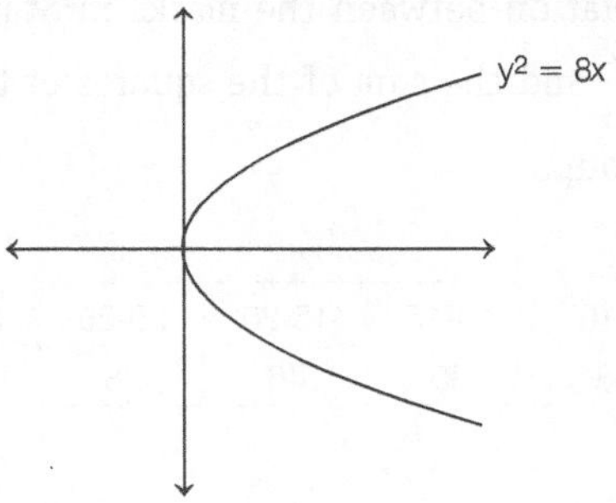

(a) Find the focus of given parabola.

(b) Find the equation of the directrix of the parabola.

(c) Find the length of the latusrectum of the parabola. • *Understanding & Evaluation*

Or

(ii) Find the equation of the hyperbola having foci $(\pm 3\sqrt{5}, 0)$ and the length of lalus rectum is 8. • *Evaluation*

Section C (15 Marks)

19. In sub-parts (i) and (ii) choose the correct option and in sub-parts (iii) to (v), answer the questions as instructed.

(i) Which of the following are the major characteristics of index numbers? • *Understanding & Evaluation*

(a) It measures changes over a period of time

(b) It is expressed in percentages

(c) It measures the net or relative changes in variables

(d) All of the above **[1]**

(ii) Consider the experiment of rolling a die. Let A be the event ' getting a prime number ' and B be the event getting an odd number. Then, which of the following is true ?

I. A or $B = A \cup B = \{1, 2, 3\}$ II. A and $B = A \cap B \neq \{3, 5\}$

III. A but not $B = A - B = \{2\}$ IV. Not $A = A' = \{1, 4, 6\}$

(a) Only (IV) is correct (b) Only (I) and (II) are correct

(c) Only (I) and (IV) are correct (d) Only (III) and (IV) are correct

• *Analysis & Evaluation* [1]

(iii) For the frequency distribution

x_i	3	8	13	18	23
f_i	7	10	15	10	6

(a) Find the mean of given data. [1]

(b) Find the variance. [1]

(c) Calculate the value of standard deviation of the following data. • *Understanding & Evaluation* [1]

20. (i) Two sample sizes of 50 and 100 are given. The mean of these samples respectively are 56 and 50. Find the mean of size 150 by combining the two samples. • *Analysis* [2]

Or

(ii) The coefficient of rank correlation between the marks in Statistics and Mathematics obtained by a certain group of students is $\frac{2}{3}$ and the sum of the squares of the differences in ranks is 55. Find the number of students in the group. • *Analysis* [2]

21. (i) The following distribution

Mark	5-10	10-15	15-20	20-25	25-30	30-35	35-40
Number of students	18	30	46	28	20	12	6

Find

(a) Mean [1]

(b) Variance [1]

(c) Standard deviation • *Evaluation* [2]

(ii) The distribution of a data is given

Size	0-5	5-10	10-15	15-20	20-25	25-30	30-35
Frequency	1	2	5	14	10	9	2

Find

(a) Mean [2]

(b) Mode • *Evaluation* [2]

22. Construct the consumer price index number for 1990, taking 1989 as the base year and using simple average of price relative method for the following data. • *Evaluation* [4]

Commodities	Price in 1989	Price in 1990
Butter	20	21
Cheese	16	12
Milk	3	3
Egg	2.80	2.80

Answers

1. (i) (*b*) (ii) (*a*) (iii) (*c*)
(iv) (*b*) (v) (*a*) (vi) (*a*)
(vii) (*b*) (viii) (*b*) (ix) (*a*)
(x) (*b*) (xi) (d)
(xii) 7,11,15 (xiii) 7
(xiv) $\{(B_1, B_2), (B_1, B_3), (B_1, G_1), (B_1, G_2), (B_1, G_3), (B_2, B_3), (B_2, G_1), (B_2, G_2), (B_2, G_3), (B_3, G_1), (B_3, G_2), (B_3, G_3), (G_1, G_2), (G_2, G_3), (G_1, G_3)\}$
(xv) 17

4. (i) $\{1\}, \{2\}, \{3\}, \{1, 2\}, \{2, 3\}, \{1, 3\}, \{1, 2, 3\}, \phi$

Or

(ii) $a = 2, b = -1$

5. (i) $\frac{1}{35}$ (ii) $\frac{1}{7}$

6. (i) $x = -\frac{3}{2}, y = -\frac{7}{2}$ *Or* (ii) $k = 4$

7.

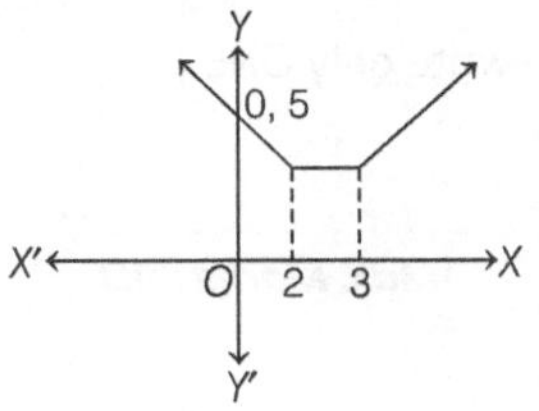

8. (i) $S_n = \frac{n}{n+1}$ *Or* (ii) $S_n = \frac{n(n+3)}{4(n+1)(n+2)}$

9. (i) $\theta = 30°$ or $150°$ *Or*
(ii) (a) $k = 3$ (b) $k = 1, 6$ (c) $k = \pm 2$

10. (i) 86400 (ii) 28800

12. *Or* (ii) greater than or equal to 8, less than or equal to 22.

13. (i) $\frac{5}{2}$ (ii) $(20 + 10\sqrt{2})$ cm (iii) 200 cm^2
(iv) $(80 + 40\sqrt{2})$ cm

14. Mean $= \frac{n+1}{2}$ and Variance $= \frac{n^2 - 1}{12}$.

15. (i) (*a*) (ii) (*b*)
(iii) $\frac{x^2}{4} + \frac{y^2}{49} = 1$
(iv) (a) I will go to school.
(b) There exists natural number which is not an integer.

16. **Converse** If you are a citizen of India then you are born in India.
Inverse If you are not born in India then you are not citizen of India.

17. (i) $m = \frac{3}{2}$ and y–intercept $c = \frac{7}{2}$
(ii) $a = \frac{7}{3}$ and y-intercept $b = \frac{7}{2}$
(iii) $\tan\theta = \frac{2}{3}$ and $p = \frac{7}{\sqrt{13}}$

18. (i) (a) (2, 0) (b) $x + 2 = 0$ (c) 8
(ii) $\frac{x^2}{25} - \frac{y^2}{20} = 1$

19. (i) (*d*) (ii) (*d*)
(iii) (a) 12.79 (b) 39.43 (c) 6.28

20. (i) 52 *Or* (ii) 10

21. (i) (a) 19.43 (b) 68.06 (c) 8.25
Or (ii) (a) 19.98 (b) 18.46

22. 95

SAMPLE QUESTION PAPER 2

A Highly Simulated Sample Question Paper for ISC Class XI

MATHEMATICS (Unsolved)

GENERAL INSTRUCTIONS

1. The Question Paper is divided into three sections and has 22 questions in all.
2. **Section A** is compulsory and has fourteen questions.
3. You are required to attempt all questions either from **Section B** or **Section C**.
4. **Section B** and **Section C** has four questions each.
5. Internal choices has been provided in two questions of 2 marks, two questions of 4 marks and two questions of 6 marks in Section A.
6. Internal choices has been provided in one question of 2 marks and one question of 4 marks each in Section and Section C.
7. While attempting Multiple Choice Questions in Section A, B and C, you are required to write only ONE option as the answer.
8. The intended marks for questions or parts of questions are given in brackets [ ].

Time : 3 Hours ***Max. Marks : 80***

Section A (65 Marks)

1. In sub-parts (i) to (x) choose the correct option and in sub-parts (xi) to (xv), answer the questions as instructed.

(i) The number of combinations of 4 different objects A, B, C, D taken 2 at a time is • ***Analysis*** **[1]**

(a) 4 (b) 6 (c) 7 (d) 8

(ii) the income of a person is ₹ 300000 in the first year and he receives of ₹ 10000 to his income per year for the next 19 yr. Then, the total amount he received in 20 yr, is • ***Evaluation*** **[1]**

(a) ₹ 7900000 (b) ₹ 6000000

(c) ₹ 8000000 (d) ₹ 6900000

(iii) The equation of the line which have slope -2 and cuts-off an intercepts -6 on X-axis is • ***Analysis*** **[1]**

(a) $2x - y + 12 = 0$ (b) $2x + y + 12 = 0$

(c) $-2x + y + 12 = 0$ (d) $2x + y - 12 = 0$

(iv) If $f(x) = \begin{cases} x^2 - 1, & x \le 1 \\ -x^2 - 1, & x > 1 \end{cases}$, then • ***Understanding*** **[1]**

(a) LHL $\neq$ RHL, at $x = 1$

(b) LHL = RHL = -2, at $x = 1$

(c) LHL = RHL = -1, at $x = 1$

(d) None of the above

(v) **Assertion (A)** If the foci and vertices of an ellipse be $(\pm 1, 0)$ and $(\pm 2, 0)$ respectively then the minor axis of the ellipse is $2\sqrt{3}$.

Reason (R) If the foci and vertices of an ellipse be $(\pm c, 0)$ and $(\pm a, 0)$ respectively then its standard form is $\frac{x^2}{a^2}+\frac{y^2}{b^2}=1, a>b$ which $c=\sqrt{a^2-b^2}$

(a) Both Assertion and Reason are true and Reason is the correct explanation for Assertion.
(b) Both Assertion and Reason are true but Reason is not the correct explanation for Assertion.
(c) Assertion is true and Reason is false.
(d) Assertion is false and Reason is true. • ***Understanding & Evaluation*** **[1]**

(vi) If $f(x)=\frac{1+x}{1-x}$, then $\frac{f(x)\cdot f(x^2)}{1+[f(x)]^2}$ is equal to • ***Analysis*** **[1]**

(a) $\frac{1}{4}$ (b) $\frac{1}{6}$ (c) $\frac{1}{8}$ (d) $\frac{1}{2}$

(vii) **Statement-1** The perpendicular distance of the point (6,5,8) from y-axis is 6.

Statement-2 The slop of line, whose inclination is 150°, is $-\frac{1}{\sqrt{3}}$.

(a) Statement 1 is true and Statement 2 is false.
(b) Statement 2 is true Statement 1 is false.
(c) Both the Statements are true.
(d) Both the Statements are false. • ***Understanding & Evaluation*** **[1]**

(viii) Which of the following is an example of quantifiers?
(a) p : There exists a rectangle whose all sides are equal
(b) q : For every prime number P, $\sqrt{P}$ is an irrational number
(c) Both (a) and (b)
(d) None of the above • ***Analysis*** **[1]**

(ix) **Assertion (A)** The sum of 11 terms of an AP $-9, -6, -3, ...$ is 66.

Reason (R) If a be the first terms and l be the last term then the sum of the AP is $S_n=\frac{n}{2}(a+l)$

(a) Both Assertion and Reason are true and Reason is the correct explanation for Assertion.
(b) Both Assertion and Reason are true but Reason is not the correct explanation for Assertion.
(c) Assertion is true and Reason is false.
(d) Assertion is false and Reason is true. • ***Understading & Evaluation*** **[1]**

(x) **Statement-1** If A and B are two sets, $A \cap (A \cup B)$ equal to A.

Statement-2 If A and B are two sets, if $B \subset A$ the $(A-B) \cup B = A$

(a) Statement 1 is true and Statement 2 is false.
(b) Statement 2 is true Statement 1 is false.
(c) Both the Statements are true.
(d) Both the Statements are false. • ***Understanding & Analysis*** **[1]**

(xi) $\frac{(\sin 7x+\sin 5x)+(\sin 9x+3x)}{(\cos 7x+\cos 5x)+(\cos 9x+\cos 3x)}$ is equal to • ***Application*** **[1]**

(a) $\tan 3x$ (b) $\cot 3x$ (c) $\tan 6x$ (d) $\cot 6x$

(xii) If the latusrectum of an ellipse is equal to the half of its major axis, then find its eccentricity.
• *Analysis & Evaluation* [1]

(xiii) Find the number of terms in the expansions of the expression $(4+x^2+4x)^3$. • *Application* [1]

(xiv) Find the positive integer n so that $\lim\limits_{x \to 3} \dfrac{x^n - 3^n}{x-3} = 108$.
• *Analysis & Application* [1]

(xv) If $A \times B = \{(a, 1), (a, 5), (a, 2), (b, 2), (b, 5), (b, 1)\}$, then find A, B and $B \times A$.
• *Understanding & Evaluation* [1]

2. Evaluate $\sin 75°$. • *Application* [2]

3. Prove that $\dfrac{\sin 5x - 2\sin 3x + \sin x}{\cos 5x - \cos x} = \tan x$.
• *Application* [2]

4. (i) If $U = \{1, 2, 3, 4, 5, 6, 7, 8, 9, 10\}$, $A = \{1, 3, 4\}$ and $B = \{5, 6\}$, then verify that $A - B = A \cap B' = B' - A'$.
• *Analysis* [2]

Or

(ii) Find the domain of the function $f(x) = \dfrac{x}{x^2 + 3x + 2}$.
• *Analysis* [1]

5. If $x_1, x_2 \ldots\ldots x_n$ are values in a variable x such that $\sum\limits_{i=1}^{x} (x_i - 2) = 110$ and $\sum\limits_{i=1}^{x} (x_i - 5) = 20$, then

(i) find the value of n. (ii) find its mean. • *Analysis & Understanding* [2]

6. (i) If $\left(\dfrac{1-i}{1+i}\right)^{100} = a + ib$, then find (a, b).
• *Application* [2]

Or

(ii) If α and β be the roots of equation $ax^2 + bx + c = 0$, then find the value of $\left(\dfrac{1}{a\alpha + b} + \dfrac{1}{a\beta + b}\right)$.
• *Analysis & Understanding* [2]

7. If f is a real function defined by $f(x) = \dfrac{x-1}{x+1}$, then prove that $f(2x) = \dfrac{3f(x)+1}{f(x)+3}$.
• *Analysis & Understanding* [4]

8. (i) If the integers $r\,(r > 1), n (> 2)$ and coefficient of (3r)th and $(r+2)$nd term in the expansion of $(1+x)^{2n}$ are equal then prove that $n = 2r$. • *Application* [4]

Or

(ii) For what value of m, the coefficients of the $(2m+1)$th and $(4m+5)$th terms in the expansion of $(1+x)^{10}$ are equal. • *Application* [4]

9. (i) Prove that $4\cos 12° \cos 48° \cos 72° = \cos 36°$. • *Evaluation* [4]

Or

(ii) If A+B $= \dfrac{\pi}{4}$ then prove that

(a) $(1+\tan A)(1+\tan B) = 2$ (b) $(\cot A - 1)(\cot B - 1) = 2$ • *Evaluation* [4]

10. Find the equation of circle which passes through (3, – 2), (–2, 0) and has its centre on the line $2x - y = 3$.

• *Evaluation* [4]

11. (i) If α and β are the solutions of the equation $a\tan\theta + b\sec\theta = c$, then show that

$$\tan(\alpha+\beta) = \frac{2ac}{a^2 - c^2}$$

• *Analysis* [6]

Or

(ii) If α and β are distinict roots of $a\cos\theta + b\sin\theta = c$ then show that $\sin(\alpha+\beta) = \frac{2ab}{a^2+b^2}$.

• *Evaluation* [6]

12. (i) If x is real, then find the maximum and minimum value of $y = \frac{x^2 - 3x + 4}{x^2 + 3x + 4}$.

• *Evaluation* [6]

Or

(ii) If the roots of the equation $ax^2 + bx + c = 0$ of the form $\frac{k+1}{k}$ and $\frac{k+2}{k+1}$, then find $(a+b+c)^2$.

• *Application* [6]

13. Sonia ask Priya, "Please draw four cards from this deck of 52 playing cards". Priya draw four cards and shows to Sonia.

On the basis of above information, answer the following question.

(i) Find the probability (all face cards) [1]

(ii) Find the probability (one cards on each suit) [1]

(iii) Find the probability (all the four cards of the same number) [2]

(iv) Find the probability (two red and two black cards) • *Application* [2]

14. An original frequency table with mean 11 and variance 9.9 was lost but the following table derived from it was found. Construct the original table.

Value of deviation (d)	–2	–1	0	1	2
Frequency (f)	1	6	7	4	2

• *Application* [6]

Section B (15 Marks)

15. In sub-parts (i) and (ii) choose the correct option and in sub-parts (iii) to (v), answer the questions as instructed.

(i) **Assertion (A)** If the lines $x + q = 0$, $y - 2 = 0$ and $3x + 2y + 5 = 0$ are concurrent, then the value of q will be 3.

Reason (R) If three or more separate lines pass through the same location then are said to be concurrent.

(a) Both Assertion and Reason are true and Reason is the correct explanation for Assertion.

(b) Both Assertion and Reason are true but Reason is not the correct explanation for Assertion.

(c) Assertion is true and Reason is false.

(d) Assertion is false and Reason is true.

• *Understanding & Analysis* [1]

(ii) Person wishes to make up as many different parties as he can out of his 20 friends such that each party consists of the same number of persons. The number of friends he should invite are ...*A*... . Here, *A* refers to

(a) 8 (b) 9 (c) 10 (d) None of these

• ***Understanding & Application*** [1]

(iii) Solve for $x : -5 \le \frac{2-3x}{4} \le 9$.

• ***Evaluation*** [1]

(iv) If the 4th and 9th term of a GP are 54 and 13122 respectively then

(a) find the first term and common ration of GP series. [1]

(b) find the GP series.

• ***Application & Evaluation*** [1]

16. (i) A fair coin with 1 marked on one face and 6 on the other and a fair die are both tossed. Find the probability that the sum of numbers that turn up is (a) 3 (b) 12. • ***Application & Evaluation*** [2]

Or (ii) If $y = \frac{1+\frac{1}{x^2}}{1-\frac{1}{x^2}}$, then find $\frac{dy}{dx}$.

• ***Application & Analysis*** [2]

17. Three friend Arvind, Lokesh and Pradeep are Studying in class XI of Rawat Public school, Jaipur. After completing the study, they relocated to different states which are shown in figure.

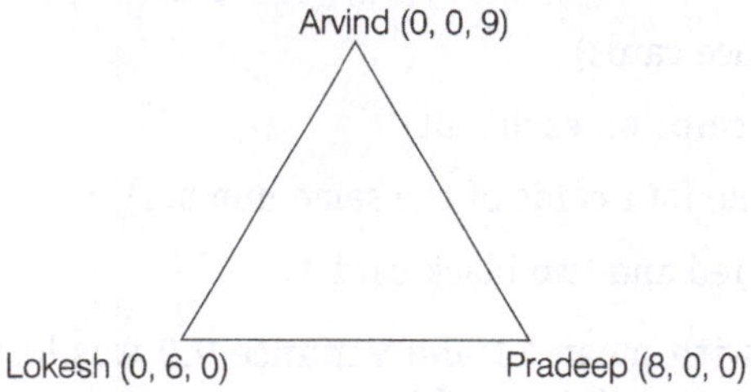

(i) What is the distance between Arivind and lokesh [1]

(ii) What is the distance between lokesh and Pradeep? [1]

(iii) What is the distance between Pradeep and Arvind? Are they at equal distance? • ***Evaluation*** [2]

18. (i) Mr. Suraj Singh is a sincere citizen of "Laxmi Nikunj Society" in Lucknow. He makes a green garden in his plot which is in the shape of circle, i.e. shown in the below figure.

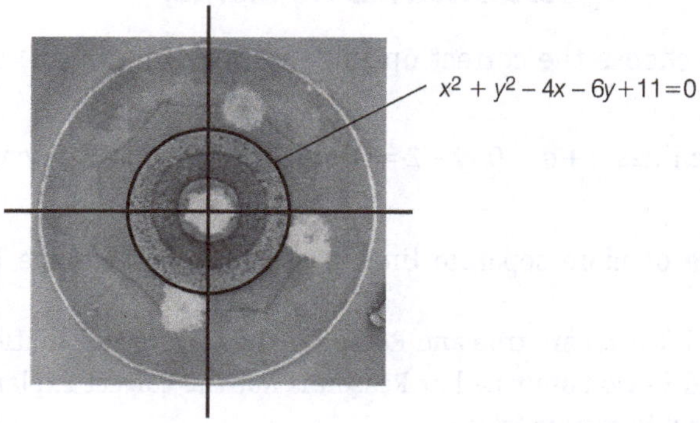

Now, answer the following questions which are based on above garden.

(a) Find the coordinates of centre of the garden. [1]

(b) If one end of a diameter of the circle shaped garden is (3, 4) then find the coordinates of the other end of the diameter. **[2]**

(c) What is the diameter of the garden. • *Application & Analysis* **[1]**

(ii) Find the value of α for which the coefficients of the middle terms in the expansions of $(1+\alpha x)^4$ and $(1-\alpha x)^6$ are equal. • *Analysis* **[4]**

Section C (15 Marks)

19. In sub-parts (i) and (ii) choose the correct option and in sub-parts (iii) to (v), answer the questions as instructed.

(i) $\lim\limits_{\theta \to 0} \dfrac{\sin c\theta}{\sin d\theta}$ is equal to

(a) 0 (b) 1 (c) $\dfrac{c}{d}$ (d) $\dfrac{d}{c}$ • *Analysis* **[1]**

(ii) **Statement-I** If $-3x+12<0$, then $x \in (5, \infty)$

Statement-II If $|4-x|+1<3$, then $x \in (2,6)$

Statement-III If $2x-7>5-x$ and $11-5x \le 1$, then $x \in (4, \infty)$

Statement-IV If $3x+8<2$ then $x \in \{-1, 0, 1, 2 \ldots\}$ when x is an integer

(a) Only I is true (b) Only II is true

(c) Both I and II are true (d) Both I and II are false • *Application* **[1]**

(iii) Consider the triangle ABC with vertices $A(1,4), B(2,-3)$ and $C(-1,-2)$ as shown in the given figure. AD is the median and AM is the altitude through A.

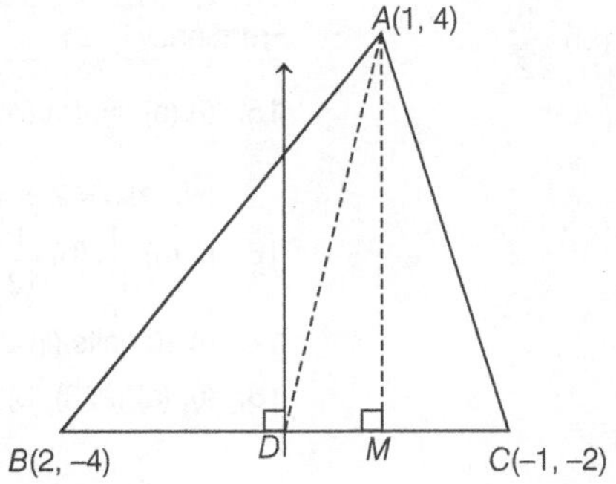

(a) Find the slope of BC. **[1]**

(b) Find the equation of median through A. **[1]**

(c) Find the equation of right bisector of side BC. • *Application* **[1]**

20. (i) Evaluate $\lim\limits_{x \to 1}\left(\dfrac{2}{1-x^2}+\dfrac{1}{x-1}\right)$. • *Evaluation* **[2]**

Or

(ii) In how many ways can 4 red, 3 yellow and 2 green discs be arranged in a row, if the discs of the same colour are indistinguishable? • *Evaluation & Analysis* **[2]**

21. (i) The marks of students of class XI in maths test (out of 20) are given below.

Marks (x_i)	5	7	9	11	13	15	17
Number of students	2	4	6	8	10	12	8

On the basis of above information answer the following question.

(a) What is the comutative frequency corresponding to mark 11. **[1]**

(b) Find the median (m) of given data. **[1]**

(c) What is the value of mean deviation from median of given data. • ***Evaluation*** **[2]**

(ii) Rahul and Ramdas are very close friends. Both the families decide to go to Ayodhya by their own cars. Rahul's car travels at a speed of x km/h while Ramdas's car travels 5 km/h faster than Rahul's car. Rahul took 4 h more than Ramdas to complete the journey of 400 km.

(a) What will be the distance covered by Ramdas's car in 3 h? **[1]**

(b) Find the quadratic equation that describes the speed of Rahul's car. **[1]**

(c) What is the speed of Rahul's car? **[1]**

(d) How much time Ramdas took to travel half distance of total journey? • ***Application & Analysis*** **[1]**

22. (i) If mode of the following series is 54, then find the value of f.

Class interval	0-15	15-30	30-45	45-60	60-75	75-90
Frequency	3	5	f	16	12	7

• ***Application & Analysis*** **[4]**

Answers

1. (i) (b) (ii) (a) (iii) (b) (iv) (a) (v) (a) (vi) (d) (vii) (b) (viii) (c) (ix) (b) (x) (a) (xi) (c) (xii) $\frac{1}{\sqrt{2}}$

(xiii) 7

(xiv) 4

(xv) $\{(1,a),(1,b),(5,a),(5,b),(2,a),(2,b)\}$

2. $\frac{\sqrt{3}+1}{2\sqrt{2}}$

4. (ii) Domain $(f) = R - \{-1, -2\}$

5. (i). 30 (ii) 5.67

6. (i) (1, 0) ***Or*** (ii) $\frac{b}{ac}$

8. or (ii) $m = 1$

10. $x^2 + y^2 + 3x + 12y + 2 = 0$

12. (i) maximum value = 7 and minimum value = $\frac{1}{7}$

Or

(ii) $b^2 - 4ac$

13. (i) $\frac{99}{54145}$ (ii) $\frac{2197}{20825}$

(iii) $\frac{13}{270725}$ (iv) $\frac{^{26}C_2 \times {}^{26}C_2}{^{52}C_4}$

14.

Class	3.5-6.5	6.5-9.5	9.5-12.5	12.5-15.5	15.5-18.5
Frequency	1	6	7	7	2

15. (i) (a) (ii). (c) (iii) $\left[\frac{-34}{3}, \frac{22}{3}\right]$

(iv) (a) $a = 2, r = 2$ (b) 2, 6, 18, 54...

16. (i) (a) $\frac{1}{12}$ (b) $\frac{1}{12}$ Or (ii) $\frac{-4x}{(x^2-1)^2}$

17. (i) 10 units (ii) $\sqrt{145}$ units (iii) $\sqrt{117}$ units, No.

18. (i). (a) (2, 3) (b) (1, 2) (c) $2\sqrt{2}$ units

Or

(ii) $\frac{-3}{10}$

19. (i). (c). (ii). (c)

(iii) (a). $\left(\frac{-1}{3}\right)$ (b) $13x - y - 9 = 0$ (c) $3x - y - 4 = 0$

20. (i) $\frac{1}{2}$ or (ii) 1260

21. (i) (a) 20 (b) 13 (c) 2.72

Or

(ii) (a) $3(x+5)$ km (b) $x^2 + 5x - 500 = 0$

(c) 20 km/h (d) 8h

22. 10

SAMPLE QUESTION PAPER 3

A Highly Simulated Sample Question Paper for ISC Class XI

MATHEMATICS (Unsolved)

GENERAL INSTRUCTIONS

1. The Question Paper is divided into three sections and has 22 questions in all.
2. **Section A** is compulsory and has fourteen questions.
3. You are required to attempt all questions either from **Section B** or **Section C**.
4. **Section B** and **Section C** has four questions each.
5. Internal choices has been provided in two questions of 2 marks, two questions of 4 marks and two questions of 6 marks in Section A.
6. Internal choices has been provided in one question of 2 marks and one question of 4 marks each in Section and Section C.
7. While attempting Multiple Choice Questions in Section A, B and C, you are required to write only ONE option as the answer.
8. The intended marks for questions or parts of questions are given in brackets [ ].

Time : 3 Hours *Max. Marks : 80*

Section A (65 Marks)

1. In sub-parts (i) to (xi) choose the correct option and in sub-parts (xii) to (xv), answer the questions as instructed.

(i) The intersection of all the intervals having the form $\left[1+\frac{1}{n}, 6-\frac{2}{n}\right]$, where n is a positive integer, is • *Understanding* [1]

(a) [1, 6] (b) (1, 6) (c) [2, 4] (d) $\left[\frac{3}{2}, 5\right]$

(ii) The derivative of the function $f(x) = 3x$ at $x = 2$ is • *Analysis* [1]

(a) 0 (b) 1 (c) 2 (d) 3

(iii) **Statement 1** The empty set Q is called an impossible event.

Statement 2 The whole sample space S is called the sure event.

(a) Statement 1 is true and Statement 2 is false.
(b) Statement 2 is true and Statement 1 is false.
(c) Both the Statements are true.
(d) Both the Statements are false. • *Analysis* [1]

(iv) A solution is to be kept between 68°F and 77°F. The range in temperature in degree Celsius (C), if the Celsius/Fahrenheit (F) conversion formula is given by $F = \frac{9}{5}C + 32$, is • *Application* [1]

(a) between 20°C and 22°C
(b) between 20°C and 25°C
(c) between 36°C and 45°C
(d) between 4°C and 5°C

(v) **Assertion (A)** When A = Q, then number of elements in $P(A)$ is 1.

Reason (R) If set A has n elements, then the total number of elements in its power set is 2^n.

(a) Both Assertion and Reason are true and Reason is the correct explanation for Assertion.
(b) Both Assertion and Reason are true but Reson is not the correct explanation for Assertion.
(c) Assertion is true and Reason is false.
(d) Assertion is false and Reason is true. • *Analysis* [1]

(vi) If $\tan\theta = \frac{1}{\sqrt{7}}$, then $\left(\frac{\text{cosec}^2\theta - \sec^2\theta}{\text{cosec}^2\theta + \sec^2\theta}\right)$ is equal to • *Understanding* [1]

(a) $\frac{1}{2}$ (b) $\frac{3}{4}$ (c) $\frac{5}{4}$ (d) (2)

(vii) A die is rolled. Let E be the event "die shows 4" and F be the event "die shows even number". Then, E and F are • *Understanding* [1]

(a) mutually exclusive (b) exhaustive
(c) mutually exclusive and exhaustive (d) None of these

(viii) The graph of the inequality $40x + 20y \le 120$, $x \ge 0$, $y \ge 0$ is • *Evaluation* [1]

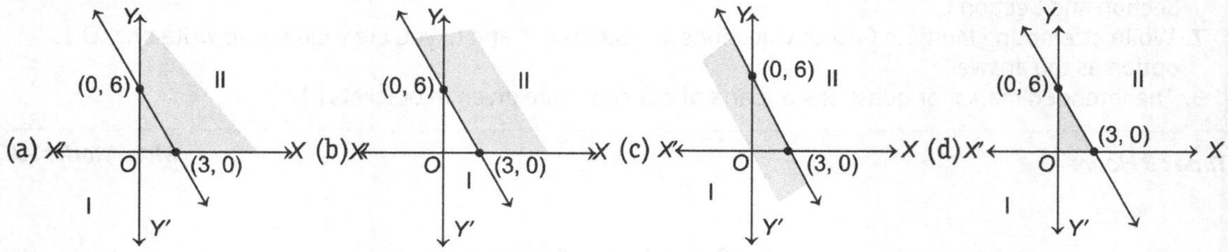

(ix) **Assertion (A)** The arithmetic mean between $(a-b)$ and $(a+b)$ is a.

Reason (R) Arithmetic mean between two given numbers is equal to half of their sum i.e. $AM = \frac{a+b}{2}$.

(a) Both Assertion and Reason are true and Reason is the correct explanation for Assertion.
(b) Both Assertion and Reason are true but Reason is not the correct explanation for Assertion.
(c) Assertion is true and Reason is false.
(d) Assertion is false and Reason is true. • *Understanding* [1]

(x) Suppose you have a suitcase with a number lock. The number lock has 4 wheels each labelled with 10 digits from 0 to 9. The lock can be opened, if 4 specific digits are arranged in a particular sequence with no repetition. Some how, you have forgotten this specific sequence of digits. You remember only the first digit which is 7. In order to open the lock, how many sequences of 3 digits you may have to check with? • *Application* [1]

(a) 720 (b) 504 (c) 500 (d) None of these

(xi) **Statement 1** If A is finite set having n elements then the numbers of relations which can be defined in A in 2^{n^2}.

Statement 2 If $A = \{a, b\}$, $B = \{c, d\}$ and $C = \{d, c, e\}$ then the value of $A \times (B \cup C)$ is $\{(a, c), (a, d), (a, e), (b, c), (b, d), (b, e)\}$.

(a) Statement 1 is true and Statement 2 is false.
(b) Statement 2 is true Statement 1 is false.
(c) Both the Statements are true.
(d) Both the Statements are false. • *Application* [1]

(xii) Find the distance between the points $(6, -4)$ and $(3, 0)$. • *Understanding* [1]

(xiii) Find the value of x, when $1 + 6 + 11 + \ldots + x = 148$. • *Evaluation* [1]

(xiv) Anshu obtained 73, 67 and 72 marks in the Mathematics test. How many marks should he get in his fourth test, so as to have an average of atleast 75? • *Application* [1]

(xv) If $Z = 5i\left(-\frac{3}{5}i\right)$, then find the value of Z. • *Evaluation* [1]

2. The angles A, B and C of a ΔABC are in arithmetic progression. If $2b^2 = 3c^2$, then determine the $\angle A$. • *Evaluation* [2]

3. Prove that $\cot x \cot 2x - \cot 2x \cot 3x - \cot 3x \cot x = 1$. • *Evaluation* [2]

4. (i) If A, B are two mutually exclusive events of a random experiment and $P(A \cup B) = 0.75$, $P(\bar{A}) = 0.6$, then find $P(B)$. • *Analysis & Evaluation* [2]

Or (ii) If $f'(1+x) = x^2 + 1$, then find $f(2-h)$. • *Evaluation* [2]

5. If E and F are events such that $P(E) = \frac{1}{4}$, $P(F) = \frac{1}{2}$ and $P(E \text{ and } F) = \frac{1}{8}$, then find

(i) $P(E \text{ or } F)$ (ii) $P(\text{not } E \text{ and not } F)$. • *Analysis* [2]

6. (i) Find the argument of the complex number $\frac{1+3i}{1-2i}$. • *Evaluation* [2]

Or (ii) Find the least value of $|a|$, for which $\tan\theta$ and $\cot\theta$ are roots of the equation $ax^2 + bx + c = 0$. • *Analysis* [2]

7. Find the domain of the function f defined by $f(x) = \sqrt{4-x} + \frac{1}{\sqrt{x^2-1}}$. • *Evaluation* [4]

8. (i) If the coeffficient of second, third and fourth term in the expansion of $(1+x)^{2n}$ are in AP then show that $2n^2 - 9n = -7$. • *Application* [4]

Or (ii) Show that the middle term in the expansion of $(1+x)^{2n}$ is $\frac{1.3.5.\ldots(2n-1)}{n!} 2^n \cdot x^n$, where n is a positive integer. • *Application* [4]

9. (i) Prove that $\sin 10^\circ \sin 30^\circ \sin 50^\circ \sin 70^\circ = \frac{1}{16}$. • *Evaluation* [4]

Or (ii) If $A - B = \frac{\pi}{4}$ then prove that

(a) $\tan A - \tan B - \tan A \cdot \tan B = 1$ [1]

(b) $(1+\tan A)(1-\tan B) = 2$ [2]

(c) $(1+\cot B)(1-\cot A) = 2$ • *Evaluation* [1]

10. What is the number of ways of choosing 4 cards from a pack of 52 cards? In how many of these

(i) four cards are of the same suit? [2]

(ii) two are red cards and two are black cards? • *Application* [2]

11. If x and y are acute angles such that $\cos x = \frac{13}{14}$ and $\cos y = \frac{1}{7}$ then prove that $x - y = -\frac{\pi}{3}$. • *Evaluation* [6]

Or Find the value of $\tan(\alpha+\beta)$, if $\cot\alpha = \frac{1}{2}, \alpha \in \left(\pi, \frac{3\pi}{2}\right)$ and $\sec\beta = \frac{-5}{3}$, $\beta \in \left(\frac{\pi}{2}, \pi\right)$. • *Evaluation* [6]

12. (i) If α and β are the roots of the equation $ax^2 + bx + c = 0$, find the equation whose roots are $\alpha + \frac{1}{\beta}$ and $\beta + \frac{1}{\alpha}$.

• *Analysis* [6]

Or (ii) If the roots of the equation $\frac{1}{x+p} + \frac{1}{x+q} = \frac{1}{r}$ are equal in magnitude but opposite in sign, find the product of the roots.

• *Evaluation* [6]

13. If the sum of p terms of an AP is q and the sum of q terms is p then find

(i) first term.
(ii) common difference.
(iii) sum of $(p+q)$ terms.
(iv) sum of first $(p-q)$ terms.

• *Evaluation* [6]

14. Calculate the mean, variance and standard deviation for the following distribution.

Class	0-5	5-10	10-15	15-20	20-25	25-30	30-35	35-40	40-45
Frequency	20	24	32	28	20	11	26	15	24

• *Evaluation* [6]

Section B (15 Marks)

15. In sub-parts (i) and (ii) choose the correct option and in sub-parts (iii) to (v), answer the questions as instructed.

(i) **Assertion (A)** If L is the foot of the perpendicular drawn from a point $P(6,7,8)$ on the x-axis then the coordinates of L is $(0, 6, 0)$.

Reason (R) Any point on the x-axis has coordinates of the form $(x,0,0)$.

(a) Both Assertion and Reason are true and Reason is the correct explanation for Assertion.
(b) Both Assertion and Reason are true but Reason is not the correct explanation for Assertion.
(c) Assertion is true and Reason is false.
(d) Assertion is false and Reason is true.

• *Evaluation* [1]

(ii) Area of triangle whose vertices are (x_1, y_1), (x_2, y_2) and (x_3, y_3), is

(a) $|x_1(y_2 - y_3) + x_2(y_3 - y_1) + x_3(y_1 - y_2)|$
(b) $|x_1(y_2 - y_3) + x_2(y_1 - y_3) + x_3(y_1 - y_2)|$
(c) $\frac{1}{2}|x_1(y_2 - y_3) + x_2(y_3 - y_1) + x_3(y_1 - y_2)|$
(d) $\frac{1}{2}|x_1(y_2 - y_3) + x_2(y_1 - y_3) + x_3(y_1 - y_2)|$

• *Application* [1]

(iii) Write the conditional statement of the statement "The square of an odd number is odd".

• *Evaluation* [1]

(iv) If P is a point on the ellipse $\frac{x^2}{16} + \frac{y^2}{25} = 1$, whose foci are S and S' then find

(a) the sum of $PS + PS'$.
(b) vertex.

• *Analysis* [2]

16. (i) Find the equation of the hyperbola having foci $(\pm 3\sqrt{5}, 0)$ and the length of latusrectum is 8. [2]

Or

(ii) If p and q are two statements, then prove that $\sim (p \wedge q) = (\sim p) \vee (\sim q)$.

• *Understanding* [2]

17. Mr. Mahendra Kumar is a Mathematics teacher of class XI in Delhi Public School, Pawta. One day, he writes some points on the board to check the knowledge about the basic concepts of three dimensional geometry.

(I) (8,3,5) (II) (-7, 5, 3) (III) (5,-2, 7) (IV) (9,5,-6)
(V) (-7,-6,8) (VI) (-2, 3, 4) (VII) (-4, 0, 0) (VIII) (-5, 0, 3)

Then, answer the following questions which are based on it.

(i) In which octant the point (–7,–6,8) lies? (ii) Find the image of (–5,0,3) in XZ-plane.

(iii) In which octant the point (5,–2,7) lies? • *Evaluation* **[4]**

18. (i) The equation of parabola $y^2 - 8y - x + 19 = 0$ then find

(a) vertex. (b) axis and focus. (c) length of latusrectum. • ***Understanding*** **[4]**

(ii) An arch is in the form of a semi-ellipse. It is 10 m wide and 3m high of the centre, find the height of the arch at a point 2 m from one end. • ***Analysis*** **[4]**

Section C (15 Marks)

19. In sub-parts (i) and (ii) choose the correct option and in sub-parts (iii) to (v), answer the questions as instructed. **[5]**

(i) Mean deviation about median for continuous frequency distribution is calculated by using the formula

(a) $\text{MD}(M) = \frac{1}{N}\sum_{i=1}^{n} f_i |x_i + M|$ (b) $\text{MD}(M) = \frac{1}{N}\sum_{i=1}^{n} f_i |x_i - M|$

(c) $\text{MD}(M) = \frac{1}{N}\sum_{i=1}^{n} \frac{f_i}{|x_i - M|}$ (d) $\text{MD}(M) = \frac{1}{N}\sum_{i=1}^{n} \frac{|x_i - M|}{f_i}$ • *Evaluation* **[1]**

(ii) Read the following statement and choose the correct option.

(I) The equation of the plane $z = 6$ represents a plane perpendicular to the *XY* plane having *a* z-intercept of 6 units.

(II) The equation of the plane $x = 0$ represents the *XZ*- plane.

(III) The point on the *x*-axis with x-coordiante equal to x_0 is written as $(x, 0, 0)$.

(IV) $x = x_0$ represents a plane parallel to the YZ- plane.

(a) Only (IV) is correct (b) Only (I) and (II) are correct

(c) Only (I) and (IV) are correct (d) Only (III) and (IV) are correct • ***Understanding*** **[1]**

(iii) If $(x + iy)^{1/3} = a + ib$, where $x, y, a, b \in R$ then

(a) find the value of $\frac{x}{a}$ (b) find the value of $\frac{y}{b}$.

(c) find the difference between $\frac{x}{a}$ and $\frac{y}{b}$. • *Evaluation* **[3]**

20. (i) Coefficient of variation of two distributions are 60 and 70 and their standard deviations are 21 and 16, respectively. What are their arithmetic means. **[2]**

Or (ii) Find out rank correlation from the following data • ***Understanding*** **[2]**

S.No.	1	2	3	4	5	6	7	8	9	10
Rank differences	–2	–4	–1	3	2	0	–2	3	3	–2

21. (i) The following distribution

x_i	92	93	97	98	102	104	109
f_i	3	2	3	2	6	3	3

then, find

(a) Mean (b) Variance (c) Standard deviation • *Evaluation* [4]

Or (ii) Let x_i and y_i are two data such that $y_i = ax_i + b$. If $\bar{x}$ and $\bar{y}$ are mean and σ_x and σ are standard deviation of the given data x_i and y_i respectively. Then, we have $\bar{y} = a\bar{x} + b$ and $\sigma_y = |a|\sigma_x$.

On the basis of above information, answer the following question.

(a) If $y_i = 4x_i - 3$ and $\bar{x}$ is 10 then find the value of $\bar{y}$. [1]

(b) If $y_i = \frac{ax_i + b}{c}$ then find find the value of σ_y. [1]

(c) If $y_i = x_i + 10$ then find the value of σ_y. [1]

(d) If $y_i = ax_i + b$ then find the value of var(Y). • *Evaluation* [1]

22. The index number for the year 2005 taking 2000 as base year for the following data was found to be 125. Find the missing entries x and y in the data, if $\Sigma p_0 = 360$.

Commodities	Prices in 2000 (in ₹)	Prices in 2005 (in ₹)
A	40	55
B	60	70
C	20	40
D	50	y
E	x	100
F	110	115

• *Analysis* [4]

Answers

1. (i) (c) (ii) (d) (iii) (c) (iv) (b) (v) (a) (vi) (b) (vii) (d) (viii) (d) (ix) (a) (x) (b) (xi) (c) (xii) 5 units (xiii) $x = 36$ (xiv) 88 marks (xv) $3 + 0i$

2. 75°

4. (i) 0.35 *Or* (ii) $h^2 - 2h + 2$

5. (i) $\frac{5}{8}$ (ii) $\frac{3}{8}$

6. (i) $\frac{3\pi}{4}$ *Or* (ii) 2

7. Domain $= (-\infty, -1) \cup (1, 4]$

10. 270725 (i) 2860 (ii) 105625

11. $\frac{2}{11}$

12. (i) $acx^2 + (a+c)bx + (a+c)^2 = 0$ *Or* (ii) $\frac{-(p^2+q^2)}{2}$

13. (i) $\left[\frac{q}{p} + \frac{(p+q)(p-1)}{pq}\right]$ (ii) $\frac{-2(p+q)}{pq}$ (iii) $-(p+q)$ (iv) $(p-q)\frac{(p+2q)}{p}$

14. Mean = 21.5, Variance = 164.75, Standard deviation = 12.835

15. (i) (d) (ii) (c) (iii) If the number is odd then its square is odd number. (iv) (a) 10 (b) $(0, \pm 5)$

16. (i) $\frac{x^2}{25} - \frac{y^2}{20} = 1$

17. (i) $X'OY'Z$ (ii) $(-5, 0, 3)$ (iii) $XOY'Z$

18. (i) (a) (3, 4) (b) $y = 4$ and $\left(\frac{13}{4}, 4\right)$ (c) 1 (ii) 0.27 m

19. (i) (b) (ii) (d) (iii) (a) $a^2 - 3b^2$ (b) $3a^2 - b^2$ (c) $-2(a^2 + b^2)$

20. (i) 35, 22.86 *Or* (ii) 0.64

21. (i) (a) 100 (b) 29.09 (c) 5.394

Or

(ii) (a) 37 (b) $\left|\frac{a}{c}\right| \sigma x$ (c) σx (d) a^2 var (x)

22. $x = 80$, $y = 70$